LOUISIANA ALMANAC

1988-89

MILBURN CALHOUN, Publisher

Editor: Milburn Calhoun

Assistant Editor: Susan Cole Doré

PELICAN PUBLISHING COMPANY
GRETNA 1988

Manufactured in the United States of America

Published by Pelican Publishing Company, Inc.
1101 Monroe St., P.O. Box 189, Gretna, La. 70053

FOREWORD

This is the twelfth edition of the *Louisiana Almanac*. It continues to be widely recognized as the authoritative source of information on Louisiana. As such it is widely used by students, businessmen, tourists, and ordinary citizens who need ready information at their fingertips. Educators have long recognized its value for students. The *Almanac* is an adopted textbook for the Louisiana unit in social studies, and also widely used as a reference book in Louisiana classrooms.

Statistics and information included in this edition are taken from a wide number of sources. We have attempted to include the source of all information. Since many state agencies issue reports biennially, some of the statistics are necessarily three years old.

The *Louisiana Almanac* in its thirty-nine years has been the work of many hands. It was founded by Stuart Landry in 1949, and we are all indebted to him for his foresight and the strong foundation he laid. Revised in 1969, two editions were edited by Lucy Core. From 1973 until 1984, it was under the general editorship of James Calhoun, Senior Editor of Pelican. Two editions have been greatly improved by the magnificent and arduous research of Helen Kerr Kempe. This edition was researched by Susan Cole Doré. Any omissions or errors are my responsibility.

Finally, many heads and officials of state, city, and private agencies have been most cooperative in furnishing information for the *Almanac*. I am indebted to them for helping to make the *Almanac* a more valuable reference book with each edition.

MILBURN CALHOUN
Editor and Publisher

1988

JANUARY
S	M	T	W	T	F	S
					1	2
3	4	5	6	7	8	9
10	11	12	13	14	15	16
17	18	19	20	21	22	23
24	25	26	27	28	29	30
31						

FEBRUARY
S	M	T	W	T	F	S
	1	2	3	4	5	6
7	8	9	10	11	12	13
14	15	16	17	18	19	20
21	22	23	24	25	26	27
28	29					

MARCH
S	M	T	W	T	F	S
		1	2	3	4	5
6	7	8	9	10	11	12
13	14	15	16	17	18	19
20	21	22	23	24	25	26
27	28	29	30	31		

APRIL
S	M	T	W	T	F	S
					1	2
3	4	5	6	7	8	9
10	11	12	13	14	15	16
17	18	19	20	21	22	23
24	25	26	27	28	29	30

MAY
S	M	T	W	T	F	S
1	2	3	4	5	6	7
8	9	10	11	12	13	14
15	16	17	18	19	20	21
22	23	24	25	26	27	28
29	30	31				

JUNE
S	M	T	W	T	F	S
			1	2	3	4
5	6	7	8	9	10	11
12	13	14	15	16	17	18
19	20	21	22	23	24	25
26	27	28	29	30		

JULY
S	M	T	W	T	F	S
					1	2
3	4	5	6	7	8	9
10	11	12	13	14	15	16
17	18	19	20	21	22	23
24	25	26	27	28	29	30
31						

AUGUST
S	M	T	W	T	F	S
	1	2	3	4	5	6
7	8	9	10	11	12	13
14	15	16	17	18	19	20
21	22	23	24	25	26	27
28	29	30	31			

SEPTEMBER
S	M	T	W	T	F	S
				1	2	3
4	5	6	7	8	9	10
11	12	13	14	15	16	17
18	19	20	21	22	23	24
25	26	27	28	29	30	

OCTOBER
S	M	T	W	T	F	S
						1
2	3	4	5	6	7	8
9	10	11	12	13	14	15
16	17	18	19	20	21	22
23	24	25	26	27	28	29
30	31					

NOVEMBER
S	M	T	W	T	F	S
		1	2	3	4	5
6	7	8	9	10	11	12
13	14	15	16	17	18	19
20	21	22	23	24	25	26
27	28	29	30			

DECEMBER
S	M	T	W	T	F	S
				1	2	3
4	5	6	7	8	9	10
11	12	13	14	15	16	17
18	19	20	21	22	23	24
25	26	27	28	29	30	31

1989

JANUARY
S	M	T	W	T	F	S
1	2	3	4	5	6	7
8	9	10	11	12	13	14
15	16	17	18	19	20	21
22	23	24	25	26	27	28
29	30	31				

FEBRUARY
S	M	T	W	T	F	S
			1	2	3	4
5	6	7	8	9	10	11
12	13	14	15	16	17	18
19	20	21	22	23	24	25
26	27	28				

MARCH
S	M	T	W	T	F	S
			1	2	3	4
5	6	7	8	9	10	11
12	13	14	15	16	17	18
19	20	21	22	23	24	25
26	27	28	29	30	31	

APRIL
S	M	T	W	T	F	S
						1
2	3	4	5	6	7	8
9	10	11	12	13	14	15
16	17	18	19	20	21	22
23	24	25	26	27	28	29
30						

MAY
S	M	T	W	T	F	S
	1	2	3	4	5	6
7	8	9	10	11	12	13
14	15	16	17	18	19	20
21	22	23	24	25	26	27
28	29	30	31			

JUNE
S	M	T	W	T	F	S
				1	2	3
4	5	6	7	8	9	10
11	12	13	14	15	16	17
18	19	20	21	22	23	24
25	26	27	28	29	30	

JULY
S	M	T	W	T	F	S
						1
2	3	4	5	6	7	8
9	10	11	12	13	14	15
16	17	18	19	20	21	22
23	24	25	26	27	28	29
30	31					

AUGUST
S	M	T	W	T	F	S
		1	2	3	4	5
6	7	8	9	10	11	12
13	14	15	16	17	18	19
20	21	22	23	24	25	26
27	28	29	30	31		

SEPTEMBER
S	M	T	W	T	F	S
					1	2
3	4	5	6	7	8	9
10	11	12	13	14	15	16
17	18	19	20	21	22	23
24	25	26	27	28	29	30

OCTOBER
S	M	T	W	T	F	S
1	2	3	4	5	6	7
8	9	10	11	12	13	14
15	16	17	18	19	20	21
22	23	24	25	26	27	28
29	30	31				

NOVEMBER
S	M	T	W	T	F	S
			1	2	3	4
5	6	7	8	9	10	11
12	13	14	15	16	17	18
19	20	21	22	23	24	25
26	27	28	29	30		

DECEMBER
S	M	T	W	T	F	S
					1	2
3	4	5	6	7	8	9
10	11	12	13	14	15	16
17	18	19	20	21	22	23
24	25	26	27	28	29	30
31						

249-YEAR CALENDAR, 1752-2000, A.D., INCLUSIVE

By this calendar one may ascertain the day of week for any day of month and year for the period 1752-2000, inclusive. The calendar covers the period beginning with †1752, the year of the adoption by England of the New Style, or Gregorian calendar.

To ascertain any day of the week, first look in the table for the year required, and under the months are figures which refer to the corresponding figures at the head of the columns of days below. For example: To know on what day of the week Aug. 4 fell in the year 1914, in the table of years look for 1914, and in a parallel line under Aug., is Fig. 6, which directs to Col. 6, in which it will be seen that Aug. 4 fell on Tuesday.

COMMON YEARS, 1753 TO 1999

Years												Jan.	Feb.	Mar.	Apr.	May.	June.	July.	Aug.	Sept.	Oct.	Nov.	Dec.
1761 1801 1903	1767 1807 1914	1778 1818 1925	1789 1829 1931	1795 1835 1942	.... 1846 1953	.... 1857 1959	.... 1863 1970	.... 1874 1981	.... 1885 1987	.... 1891 1998	4	7	7	3	5	1	3	6	2	4	7	2
1762 1802 1909	1773 1813 1915	1779 1819 1926	1790 1830 1937	.... 1841 1943	.... 1847 1954	.... 1858 1965	.... 1869 1971	.... 1875 1982	.... 1886 1993	.... 1897 1999	5	1	1	4	6	2	4	7	3	5	1	3
1757 1803 1910	1763 1814 1921	1774 1825 1927	1785 1831 1938	1791 1842 1949	.... 1853 1955	.... 1859 1966	.... 1870 1977	.... 1881 1983	.... 1887 1994	1898	6	2	2	5	7	3	5	1	4	6	2	4
1754 1805 1901	1765 1811 1907	1771 1822 1918	1782 1833 1929	1793 1839 1935	1799 1850 1946	.... 1861 1957	.... 1867 1963	.... 1878 1974	.... 1889 1985	1895 1991	2	5	5	1	3	6	1	4	7	2	5	7
1755 1806 1902	1766 1817 1913	1777 1823 1919	1783 1834 1930	1794 1845 1941	1800 1851 1947	.... 1862 1958	.... 1873 1969	.... 1879 1975	.... 1890 1986	 1997	3	6	6	2	4	7	2	5	1	3	6	1
1758 1809 1905	1769 1815 1911	1775 1826 1922	1786 1837 1933	1797 1843 1939	.... 1854 1950	.... 1865 1961	.... 1871 1967	.... 1882 1978	.... 1893 1989	1899 1995	7	3	3	6	1	4	6	2	5	7	3	5
1753 1810 1906	1759 1821 1917	1770 1827 1923	1781 1838 1934	1787 1849 1945	1798 1855 1951	.... 1866 1962	.... 1877 1973	.... 1883 1979	.... 1894 1990	1900	1	4	4	7	2	5	7	3	6	1	4	6

LEAP YEARS, 1756 TO 2000

Years										Jan.	Feb.	Mar.	Apr.	May.	June.	July.	Aug.	Sept.	Oct.	Nov.	Dec.
											29										
1764	1792	1804	1832	1860	1888	....	1928	1956	1984	7	3	4	7	2	5	7	3	6	1	4	6
1768	1796	1808	1836	1864	1892	1904	1932	1960	1988	5	1	2	5	7	3	5	1	4	6	2	4
1772	....	1812	1840	1868	1896	1908	1936	1964	1992	3	6	7	3	5	1	3	6	2	4	7	2
1776	....	1816	1844	1872	....	1912	1940	1968	1996	1	4	5	1	3	6	1	4	7	2	5	7
1780	....	1820	1848	1876	....	1916	1944	1972	2000	6	2	3	6	1	4	6	2	3	5	7	3
1756	1784	1824	1852	1880	....	1920	1948	1976	....	4	7	1	4	6	2	4	7	3	5	1	3
1760	1788	1828	1856	1884	....	1924	1952	1980	....	2	5	6	2	4	7	2	5	1	3	6	1

1	2	3	4	5	6	7
Mon. 1	Tues. 1	Wed. 1	Thurs. 1	Fri. 1	Sat. 1	SUN. 1
Tues. 2	Wed. 2	Thurs. 2	Fri. 2	Sat. 2	SUN. 2	Mon. 2
Wed. 3	Thurs. 3	Fri. 3	Sat. 3	SUN. 3	Mon. 3	Tues. 3
Thurs. 4	Fri. 4	Sat. 4	SUN. 4	Mon. 4	Tues. 4	Wed. 4
Fri. 5	Sat. 5	SUN. 5	Mon. 5	Tues. 5	Wed. 5	Thurs. 5
Sat. 6	SUN. 6	Mon. 6	Tues. 6	Wed. 6	Thurs. .. 6	Fri. 6
SUN. 7	Mon. 7	Tues 7	Wed. 7	Thurs. .. 7	Fri. ..., 7	Sat. 7
Mon. 8	Tues. 8	Wed. 8	Thurs. 8	Fri. 8	Sat. 8	SUN. 8
Tues. 9	Wed. 9	Thurs. 9	Fri. 9	Sat. 9	SUN. 9	Mon. 9
Wed. ...10	Thurs. ...10	Fri. ...10	Sat. ...10	SUN. ...10	Mon. ...10	Tues. 10
Thurs. ...11	Fri. ...11	Sat. ...11	SUN. ...11	Mon. ...11	Tues. ...11	Wed. 11
Fri. ...12	Sat. ...12	SUN. ...12	Mon. ...12	Tues. ...12	Wed. ...12	Thurs. 12
Sat. ...13	SUN. ...13	Mon. ...13	Tues. ...13	Wed. ...13	Thurs. ...13	Fri. 13
SUN. ...14	Mon. ...14	Tues. ...14	Wed. ...14	Thurs. ...14	Fri. ...14	Sat. 14
Mon. ...15	Tues. ...15	Wed. ...15	Thurs. ...15	Fri. ...15	Sat. ...15	SUN. 15
Tues. ...16	Wed. ...16	Thurs. ...16	Fri. ...16	Sat. ...16	SUN. ...16	Mon. 16
Wed. ...17	Thurs. ...17	Fri. ...17	Sat. ...17	SUN. ...17	Mon. ...17	Tues. 17
Thurs. ...18	Fri. ...18	Sat. ...18	SUN. ...18	Mon. ...18	Tues. ...18	Wed. 18
Fri. ...19	Sat. ...19	SUN. ...19	Mon. ...19	Tues. ...19	Wed. ...19	Thurs. 19
Sat. ...20	SUN. ...20	Mon. ...20	Tues. ...20	Wed. ...20	Thurs. ...20	Fri. 20
SUN. ...21	Mon. ...21	Tues. ...21	Wed. ...21	Thurs. ...21	Fri. ...21	Sat. 21
Mon. ...22	Tues. ...22	Wed. ...22	Thurs. ...22	Fri. ...22	Sat. ...22	SUN. 22
Tues. ...23	Wed. ...23	Thurs. ...23	Fri. ...23	Sat. ...23	SUN. ...23	Mon. 23
Wed. ...24	Thurs. ...24	Fri. ...24	Sat. ...24	SUN. ...24	Mon. ...24	Tues. 24
Thurs. ...25	Fri. ...25	Sat. ...25	SUN. ...25	Mon. ...25	Tues. ...25	Wed. 25
Fri. ...26	Sat. ...26	SUN. ...26	Mon. ...26	Tues. ...26	Wed. ...26	Thurs. 26
Sat. ...27	SUN. ...27	Mon. ...27	Tues. ...27	Wed. ...27	Thurs. ...27	Fri. 27
SUN. ...28	Mon. ...28	Tues. ...28	Wed. ...28	Thurs. ...28	Fri. ...28	Sat. 28
Mon. ...29	Tues. ...29	Wed. ...29	Thur. ...29	Fri. ...29	Sat. ...29	SUN. 29
Tues. ...30	Wed. ...30	Thurs. ...30	Fri. ...30	Sat. ...30	SUN. ...30	Mon. 30
Wed. ...31	Thurs. ...31	Fri. ...31	Sat. ...31	SUN. ...31	Mon. ...31	Tues. 31

†Days of the week can be calculated for 1752 as follows: 1752 is the same as 1772 from Jan. 1 to Sept. 2, inclusive. It is the same as 1780 from Sept. 14 to Dec. 31. (Note that 1752, 1772 and 1780 are leap years.) Sept. 3 to 13, inclusive, were omitted in the change from Old Style to New Style (Julian to Gregorian) calendar.

CALENDAR, 1988

CHRONOLOGICAL CYCLES AND ERAS

Dominical Letter ... ... CB	Julian Period (year of) 6701
Epact 11	Roman Indiction 11
Golden Number (Lunar Cycle) ... XIII	Solar Cycle· 9

All dates are given in terms of the Gregorian calendar in which
1988 January 14 corresponds to 1988 January 1 of the Julian calendar.

ERA	YEAR	BEGINS	ERA	YEAR	BEGINS
Byzantine	7497	Sept. 14	Japanese	2648	Jan. 1
Jewish (A.M.)*	5749	Sept. 11	Grecian (Seleucidæ) ...	2300	Sept. 14
Chinese	(4625)	Feb. 17			(or Oct. 14)
Roman (A.U.C.)	2741	Jan. 14	Indian (Saka)	1910	Mar. 21
Nabonassar	2737	Apr. 26	Diocletian	1705	Sept. 11
			Islamic (Hegira)* ...	1409	Aug. 13

*Year begins at sunset.

RELIGIOUS CALENDARS

Epiphany ... ... Jan. 6	Ascension Day ... ... May 12
Ash Wednesday ... ... Feb. 17	Whit Sunday—Pentecost ... ... May 22
Palm Sunday ... ... Mar. 27	Trinity Sunday ... ... May 29
Good Friday ... ... Apr. 1	First Sunday in Advent ... ... Nov. 27
Easter Day ... ... Apr. 3	Christmas Day (Sunday) ... ... Dec. 25
First Day of Passover (Pesach) ... Apr. 2	Day of Atonement
Feast of Weeks (Shavuot) ... ... May 22	(Yom Kippur) ... ... Sept. 21
Jewish New Year (tabular)	First Day of Tabernacles
(Rosh Hashanah) ... ... Sept. 12	(Succoth) ... ... Sept. 26
Islamic New Year ... ... Aug. 14	First day of Ramadân ... ... Apr. 18
(tabular)	(tabular)

The Jewish and Islamic dates above are tabular dates, which begin at sunset on the previous
evening and end at sunset on the date tabulated. In practice, the dates of Islamic fasts and festivals
are determined by an actual sighting of the appropriate new moon.

CIVIL CALENDAR—UNITED STATES OF AMERICA

New Year's Day ... ... Jan. 1	Labor Day ... ... Sept. 5
Martin Luther King's Birthday ... Jan. 18	Columbus Day ... ... Oct. 10
Lincoln's Birthday ... ... Feb. 12	General Election Day ... ... Nov. 8
Washington's Birthday ... ... Feb. 15	Veterans Day ... ... Nov. 11
Memorial Day ... ... May 30	Thanksgiving Day ... ... Nov. 24
Independence Day ... ... July 4	

CALENDAR, 1989

CHRONOLOGICAL CYCLES AND ERAS

Dominical Letter	... ...	A	Julian Period (year of)	... ...	6702
Epact ...	... ...	22	Roman Indiction	... ...	12
Golden Number (Lunar Cycle)	...	XIV	Solar Cycle ...	... ...	10

All dates are given in terms of the Gregorian calendar in which
1989 January 14 corresponds to 1989 January 1 of the Julian calendar.

ERA		YEAR	BEGINS	ERA		YEAR	BEGINS
Byzantine ...	... ...	7498	Sept. 14	Japanese ...	...	2649	Jan. 1
Jewish (A.M.)*	... ...	5750	Sept. 29	Grecian (Seleucidæ)	...	2301	Sept. 14
Chinese	... ...	(4626)	Feb. 6				(or Oct. 14)
Roman (A.U.C.)	...	2742	Jan. 14	Indian (Saka)	...	1911	Mar. 22
Nabonassar	...	2738	Apr. 26	Diocletian ...	...	1706	Sept. 11
				Islamic (Hegira)*	...	1410	Aug. 3

*Year begins at sunset.

RELIGIOUS CALENDARS

Epiphany ...	... ...	... Jan. 6		Ascension Day	... ...	... May 4
Ash Wednesday	... ...	... Feb. 8		Whit Sunday — Pentecost ...		... May 14
Palm Sunday	... ...	... Mar. 19		Trinity Sunday	... ...	... May 21
Good Friday	... ...	... Mar. 24		First Sunday in Advent	...	... Dec. 3
Easter Day ...	... ...	... Mar. 26		Christmas Day (Monday) ...		... Dec. 25

First Day of Passover (Pesach)	... Apr. 20		Day of Atonement	
Feast of Weeks (Shavuot) ...	... June 9		(Yom Kippur)	... Oct. 9
Jewish New Year (tabular)			First Day of Tabernacles	
(Rosh Hashanah) ...	... Sept. 30		(Succoth)	... Oct. 14
Islamic New Year	... Aug. 4		First day of Ramadân ...	... Apr. 7
(tabular)			(tabular)	

The Jewish and Islamic dates above are tabular dates, which begin at sunset on the previous
evening and end at sunset on the date tabulated. In practice, the dates of Islamic fasts and festivals
are determined by an actual sighting of the appropriate new moon.

CIVIL CALENDAR—UNITED STATES OF AMERICA

New Year's Day	... ...	... Jan. 1	Labor Day	... Sept. 4
Martin Luther King's Birthday		... Jan. 16	Columbus Day	... Oct. 9
Lincoln's Birthday ...	...	... Feb. 12	Election Day (in certain States)	... Nov. 7
Washington's Birthday	...	... Feb. 20	Veterans Day	... Nov. 11
Memorial Day	... ...	... May 29	Thanksgiving Day	... Nov. 23
Independence Day ...	...	... July 4		

HOLIDAYS IN LOUISIANA	1988	1989	MARDI GRAS DATES
*New Year's Day	January 1	January 1	1969 .. Feb. 18
*Battle of New Orleans	January 8	January 8	1970 .. Feb. 10
*Robert E. Lee's Birthday	January 19	January 19	1971 .. Feb. 23
*Martin Luther King's Birthday	January 18	January 16	1972 .. Feb. 15
Abraham Lincoln's Birthday	February 12	February 12	1973 .. Mar. 6
St. Valentine's Day	February 14	February 14	1974 .. Feb. 26
*George Washington's Birthday	February 20	February 18	1975 .. Feb. 11
**Mardi Gras	February 16	February 7	1976 .. Mar. 2
St. Patrick's Day	March 17	March 17	1977 .. Feb. 22
*Good Friday	April 1	March 24	1978 .. Feb. 7
Easter	April 3	March 26	1979 .. Feb. 27
Mother's Day	May 13	May 12	1980 .. Feb. 19
*Memorial Day	May 28	May 27	1981 .. Mar. 3
*Confederate Memorial Day	June 3	June 3	1982 .. Feb. 23
*Jefferson Davis's Birthday	June 3	June 3	1983 .. Feb. 15
Flag Day	June 14	June 14	1984 .. Mar. 6
Father's Day	June 17	June 16	1985 .. Feb. 19
*Independence Day	July 4	July 4	1986 .. Feb. 11
*Huey P. Long's Birthday	August 30	August 30	1987 .. Mar. 3
*Labor Day	September 3	September 2	1988 .. Feb. 16
*Columbus Day	October 8	October 14	1989 .. Feb. 7
Halloween	October 31	October 31	1990 .. Feb. 27
*All Saint's Day	November 1	November 1	1991 .. Feb. 12
General Election Day	November 6		1992 .. Mar. 3
*Veteran's Day	October 22	October 28	1993 .. Feb. 23
*Thanksgiving Day	November 24	November 23	1994 .. Feb. 15
*Christmas Day	December 25	December 25	1995 .. Feb. 28
			1996 .. Feb. 20
			1997 .. Feb. 11
*Denotes legal holiday in Louisiana.			1998 .. Feb. 24
**Denotes legal holiday in Orleans, Jefferson, St.			1999 .. Feb. 16
Bernard, St. Charles & East Baton Rouge Parishes.			2000 .. Mar. 7

*Denotes legal holiday in Louisiana.
**Denotes legal holiday in Orleans, Jefferson, St. Bernard, St. Charles & East Baton Rouge Parishes. For list of fairs & festivals of Louisiana refer to TOURING & RECREATION Section.

EASTER SUNDAY DATES

1969.... Apr. 6	1977.... Apr. 10	1985.... Apr. 7	1993.... Apr. 11
1970.... Mar. 29	1978.... Mar. 26	1986.... Mar. 30	1994.... Apr. 3
1971.... Apr. 11	1979.... Apr. 15	1987.... Apr. 19	1995.... Apr. 16
1972.... Apr. 2	1980.... Apr. 6	1988.... Apr. 3	1996.... Apr. 7
1973.... Apr. 22	1981.... Apr. 19	1989.... Mar. 26	1997.... Mar. 30
1974.... Apr. 14	1982.... Apr. 11	1990.... Apr. 15	1998.... Apr. 12
1975.... Mar. 30	1983.... Apr. 3	1991.... Mar. 31	1999.... Apr. 4
1976.... Apr. 18	1984.... Apr. 22	1992.... Apr. 19	2000.... Apr. 23

WORLD HOLIDAYS

Christmas and New Year's are observed the world over.

In Episcopal countries, such as England, the only church days which are regular legal holidays, aside from Christmas, are Good Friday, Easter Monday, and Whit-Monday.

In Roman Catholic countries, the church days other than Christmas, which are usually legal holidays are Epiphany, Ascension, Assumption, All Saints', and Immaculate Conception. Throughout the Latin-American countries it is usual to observe Good Friday and Corpus Christi.

In Lutheran countries Epiphany, Annunciation, Good Friday, Easter Monday, Ascension Day, Whit-Monday, Ash Wednesday, and Corpus Christi are holidays.

CENTURY'S END

The 19th century ended with Dec. 31, 1900. All the year 1900 was included in the 19th century, and the 20th century began with Jan. 1, 1901.

In 46 B.C. Julius Caesar revised the calendar by decreeing that the first of January 45 B.C. should commence on the first day of the new moon following the winter solstice. Every fourth year was to be known as leap year.

The Julian calendar was fairly accurate, but in 129 years there was an error of one day. By 1582 this error plus other minor differences amounted to ten days. Pope Gregory XIII reformed the calendar. He did this by dropping ten days on October 5, 1582.

The calendar before this time is known as **Old Style,** and since then as **New Style.** The Gregorian calendar was not adopted officially in England until 1752; in Russia until 1918 and finally in Greece until May, 1923.

To change from the Julian calendar to the Gregorian, add 10 days for the year 1592 to 1700; 11 days from 1700 to 1800; 12 days from 1800 to 1900; 13 days since 1900. Allowing every four years as a leap year less three for each 400 years, the average year is only .00026 of a day in excess of the mean solar year—such a slight difference that it will not be until 5428 A.D. that the error will amount to one day.

THE EARLIEST DATE

4236 B.C. is the earliest fixed date in history states Dr. James H. Breasted, the noted Egyptologist. In that year some unknown ruler of prehistoric Egypt introduced a calendar of 365 days. It began on the 19th of July with the heliacal rising of the star, Sirius. It divided the year into three periods containing the old peasant agricultural seasons—the inundation, the cultivation and the harvest. There were twelve months of thirty days each with five days at the end of the year. It became the earliest known and practically convenient calendar. Because the stellar year is about six hours longer than 365 days, Sirius rose a day late every four years, and his rising as beginning of the year had to be dropped.

THE NAMES OF THE MONTHS

January: named after Janus, protector of the gateway to heaven.

February: named after Februalia, a time period when sacrifices were made to atone for sins.

March: named after Mars, the god of war, presumably signifying that the campaigns interrupted by the winter could be resumed.

April: from **aperire** Latin for "to open" (buds).

May: named after Maia, the goddess of growth of plants.

June: from **juvenis,** Latin for "youth."

July: named after Julius Caesar.

August: named after Augustus, the first Roman Emperor.

September: from **septem,** Latin for "seven."

October: from **octo,** Latin for "eight."

November: from **novem,** Latin for "nine."

December: from **decem,** Latin for "ten."

NOTE: The earliest Latin calendar was a 10-month one: thus September was the seventh month, October, the eighth, etc. July was originally called Quintillis, as the fifth month; August was originally called Sextilis, as the sixth month.

THE NAMES OF THE DAYS

Latin	Saxon	English	Spanish	German
Dies Solis	Sun's Day	Sunday	domingo	Sonntag
Dies Lunae	Moon's Day	Monday	lunes	Montag
Dies Martis	Tiw's Day	Tuesday	martes	Dienstag
Dies Mercurii	Woden's Day	Wednesday	mièrcoles	Mittwoch
Dies Jovis	Thor's Day	Thursday	jueves	Donnerstag
Dies Veneris	Frigg's Day	Friday	viernes	Freitag
Dies Saturni	Seterne's Day	Saturday	sábado	Sonnabend

NOTE: The Romans gave one day of the week to each planet known, the sun and the moon being considered planets in this connection. The Saxon names are a kind of translation of the Roman names. Tiw was substituted for Mars, Woden (Wotan) for Mercury, Thor for Jupiter (Jove), Frigga for Venus, and Seterne for Saturn. The English names are adapted Saxon. The Spanish names which are normally not capitalized, are adapted Latin. The German names follow the Saxon pattern with two exceptions: Wednesday is Mittwoch (Middle of the Week), and Saturday is Sonnabend (Sunday's Eve).

AN INTERESTING FACT!

Each of the seven days of the week is designated as the Sabbath by various nationalities and religions. Monday is the Greek Sabbath, Tuesday the Persian, Wednesday the Assyrian, Thursday the Egyptian, Friday the Turkish, Saturday the Jewish and Sunday the Christian.

Houma is Indian for red rising sun.

HOLIDAY SNAFU!

The "Monday Holiday" law took effect in 1971. Washington's Birthday, Memorial Day, Columbus Day and Veteran's Day are specific in the legislation.

The law says that Washington's Birthday shall be observed on the third Monday of the month. Memorial Day falls on the last Monday in May. Columbus Day will become a national holiday for the first time and is pegged for the second Monday in October. Veteran's Day, which used to be Armistice Day and used to mark the end of World War I, has for some strange reason been earmarked for the fourth Monday in October instead of November 11 when the event actually occurred.

ANCIENT MYTHOLOGICAL GODS

Jupiter ....God of Heaven and Earth
Apollo ......God of Sun, Music, and Medicine
Venus ....Goddess of Love and Beauty
Neptune ....God of the Sea
Mercury.....................God of Commerce
Mars ....God of War

UNUSUAL EASTER DATES

In the year 1940 Easter fell on March 24th. Since the introduction of the Gregorian Calendar in 1582 Easter fell on March 24th just once before—in 1799. There will be no Easter on March 24th until the year 2391. March the 24th as an Easter date is more unusual in the Gregorian Calendar than the earliest possible Easter date of March 22nd. Since the introduction of the Gregorian Calendar Easter has fallen on March 22nd just four times— in 1589, 1693, 1761 and 1818. It will not fall on March 22nd again until the year 2285.

STANDARD TIME DIFFERENCES BETWEEN NEW ORLEANS AND OTHER AMERICAN CITIES

All of Louisiana is in the Central Time Zone. When it is 12 o'clock noon at New Orleans the hands of the clocks in these cities point to:

Atlanta .... 1 P.M.
Baltimore .... 1 P.M.
Birmingham ....12 Noon
Boston .... 1 P.M.
Buffalo .... 1 P.M.
Charleston, S. C. .... 1 P.M.
Chicago ....12 Noon
Cleveland ....12 Noon
Dallas ....12 Noon
Denver ....11 A.M.
El Paso ....11 A.M.
Hartford, Conn. .... 1 P.M.
Houston ....12 Noon
Kansas City ....12 Noon
Los Angeles ....10 A.M.
Minneapolis ....12 Noon
New York .... 1 P.M.
Omaha, Nebr. ....12 Noon
Portland, Ore. ....10 A.M.
Providence, R. I. .... 1 P.M.
Salt Lake City ....11 A.M.
San Francisco ....10 A.M.
Seattle ....10 A.M.
Washington, D. C. .... 1 P.M.

STANDARD TIME DIFFERENCES BETWEEN NEW ORLEANS AND FOREIGN CITIES

At 12 o'clock noon Central Standard Time in New Orleans the standard time in these foreign cities is as follows:

Alexandria, Egypt. ...... 8:00 P.M.
Amsterdam .... 7:00 P.M.
Athens .... 8:00 P.M.
Baghdad .... 9:00 P.M.

Bangkok .... 1:00 A.M.*
Batavia .... 1:30 A.M.*
Belfast .... 6:00 P.M.
Berlin .... 7:00 P.M.
Bombay ....11:30 P.M.
Bremen .... 7:00 P.M.
Brussels .... 6:00 P.M.
Bucharest .... 8:00 P.M.
Budapest .... 7:00 P.M.
Buenos Aires .... 2:00 P.M.
Calcutta ....11:53 P.M.
Capetown .... 8:00 P.M.
Caracas .... 1:30 P.M.
Copenhagen .... 7:00 P.M.
Delhi ....11:30 P.M.
Dublin .... 6:00 P.M.
Freetown (S.L.) .... 5:00 P.M.
Geneva .... 7:00 P.M.
Halifax .... 2:00 P.M.
Havana .... 1:00 P.M.
Havre .... 6:00 P.M.
Honolulu .... 7:30 A.M.
Hong Kong .... 2:00 A.M.*
Istanbul .... 8:00 P.M.
Leningrad .... 8:00 P.M.
Lisbon .... 6:00 P.M.
Liverpool .... 6:00 P.M.
London .... 6:00 P.M.
Manila .... 2:00 A.M.*
Mexico City .... Noon
Moscow .... 8:00 P.M.
Paris .... 6:00 P.M.
Perth .... 2:00 A.M.*
Rio de Janeiro .... 3:00 P.M.
Rome .... 7:00 P.M.
Shanghai .... 2:00 A.M.*
Sydney .... 4:00 A.M.*
Terehan .... 9:00 P.M.
Tokyo .... 3:00 A.M.*
Vancouver ....10:00 A.M.
Vienna .... 7:00 P.M.
Wellington (N. Z.) ...... 5:30 A.M.*
Yokahama .... 3:00 A.M.*

DAYLIGHT SAVING TIME

In 1967, Louisiana began the use of Daylight Saving Time. In 1987 DST was extended and is in effect from 2 a.m. the first Sunday in April to 2 a.m. the last Sunday in October.

To use the tables in this almanac add one hour to the given time during the affected months.

THE STANDARD TIME SYSTEM

Railroad time tables 75 years ago were indeed complicated. There was great confusion in the United States with regard to time. Each locality set its own time by the sun. The clocks were set at 12 noon when the sun was exactly at the meridian. The fact that the solar noon was changing with the seasons was not taken into consideration.

Dr. Charles Dowd, a school teacher of Saratoga, New York, worked out a system in his spare time which divided the United States into four different zones— Eastern, Central Mountain and Pacific.

* *This time is in the morning of the following day.*

There was a fifth which was known as the Atlantic. Each zone represents 15 degrees of longitude, each division registering one hour on the clock. Thus, beginning with the Greenwich meridian, which is at zero degrees longitude, Atlantic time is set by the meridian 60 degrees west of Greenwich, Eastern Time at 75 degrees and so on.

After Dr. Dowd worked for twelve years to persuade the railroad trunk lines to adopt his time plan, although scientific bodies approved it, the plan was put into operation, November 18, 1883 and has been in effect ever since. Dr. Dowd, after spending half his life to standardize the time for railroads without remuneration, ironically was killed by a train at a grade crossing in 1904. The system of time standardization used in the United States has now spread to most countries of the world.

BELL TIME ON SHIP BOARD

A.M.			P.M.	
1 Bell	.....12:30	1 Bell	.....12:30
2 Bells	..... 1:00	2 Bells	..... 1:00
3 "	..... 1:30	3 "	..... 1:30
4 "	..... 2:00	4 "	..... 2:00
5 "	..... 2:30	5 "	..... 2:30
6 "	..... 3:00	6 "	..... 3:00
7 "	..... 3:30	7 "	..... 3:30
8 "	..... 4:00	8 "	..... 4:00
1 Bell	..... 4:30	1 Bell	..... 4:00
2 Bells	..... 5:00	2 Bells	..... 5:00
3 "	..... 5:30	3 "	..... 5:30
4 "	..... 6:00	4 "	..... 6:00
5 "	..... 6:30	5 "	..... 6:30
6 "	..... 7:00	6 "	..... 7:00
7 "	..... 7:30	7 "	..... 7:30
8 "	..... 8:00	8 "	..... 8:00
1 Bell	..... 8:30	1 Bell	..... 8:30
2 Bells	..... 9:00	2 Bells	..... 9:00
3 "	..... 9:30	3 "	..... 9:30
4 "	.....10:00	4 "	.....10:00
5 "	.....10:30	5 "	.....10:30
6 "	.....11:00	6 "	.....11:00
7 "	.....11:30	7 "	.....11:30
8 "	.....Noon	8 "	..Midnight

WATCH AND COMPASS

All watches are compasses. Point the hour hand to the sun and south is exactly half way between the hour hand and the XII on the watch, counting forward up to noon, but backward after the sun has passed the meridian. For instance: Suppose that it is 8 o'clock, point the hand indicating 8 to the sun, and the figure X on the watch is due south. Suppose that it is 4 o'clock, point the hand indicating 4 to the sun and II on the watch is exactly south.

THE 24-HOUR ROUND THE CLOCK TIME SYSTEM

In the English system of keeping time by the army and navy the day begins at midnight, and the hours are numbered around the clock. This system has been in effect in our navy for quite a while. On July 1, 1942 the U. S. Army adopted the 24-hour clock system.

The system works as follows: 6 a.m. is written 0600, and 6:55 a.m. is written 0655. 3 p.m. is 1500 and 7:53 p.m. is 1953 or 19 hours and 53 minutes past midnight. 10:05 p.m. becomes 2205.

NOTED CLOCKS

The most reliable conventional timepiece in the world is the master clock of the Paris Observatory. To insure uniformity of temperature and air pressure, it is kept 90 feet below the surface of the ground in a hermetically sealed receptacle, and is wound by electricity, no one being permitted to approach it for fear of affecting the temperature.

For the past year it has kept absolutely correct time within one four-hundredths of a second, and while it is running a trifle fast, if its rate is taken into consideration, the error is less than one two-hundred-thousandth of a second a day. In other words, for a whole year it should not vary more than one five-hundredth of a second.

Cesium Atomic Clock:
The most accurate clock until 1970 was the cesium atomic clock. Using cesium atoms, the clock's tuning is so precise that the maximum error within one thousand years is only one second. The atomic clock is considered twice as accurate as the most reliable conventional clock.

Maser Clock:
The world's most accurate clock, the Maser (for microwave amplification by simulated emission of radiation) weighs only 30 pounds and is accurate to within one second in 3000 years, or three times as accurate as the Cesium Clock. This is a spectacular improvement over the world's first accurate timekeeper, the 365-day calendar which lost one day every four years.

HOW THE ANCIENTS TOLD THE TIME

Sun Dials:
The use of the Sun Dials to tell the time is very old. It is mentioned in Isaiah 700 years B.C. Most ancient cities had a Town Sun Dial.

Time was measured by the position of a shadow cast by the sun on a graduated plate or surface.

Water Clocks:
The Water Clock dates back 2,000 years. Greek and Roman cities usually possessed one. It was attended by a guard whose duty was to supply the great clock with water at intervals and to sound a trumpet to signal the passage of the hour.

The earliest clock, the water clock measured time by determining the flow of water in or out of a pierced vessel.

Another form of this clock was called the Clepsydra.

Hour Glasses:
The Hour Glass resembles the figure "8". Sand flows from the upper bowl to the lower in exactly one hour. The Greeks often carried hour glasses with them as they strolled in the streets and market places. In the later centuries the hour glass became a standard equipment in church pulpits.

SUNRISE AND SUNSET AT NEW ORLEANS

DAY	JAN. Rise A.M.	JAN. Set P.M.	FEB. Rise A.M.	FEB. Set P.M.	MAR. Rise A.M.	MAR. Set P.M.	APR. Rise A.M.	APR. Set P.M.	MAY Rise A.M.	MAY Set P.M.	JUNE Rise A.M.	JUNE Set P.M.
1	6 56	5 12	6 51	5 37	6 27	5 59	5 50	6 19	5 18	6 37	5 00	6 56
2	6 56	5 12	6 50	5 38	6 25	6 00	5 49	6 19	5 17	6 38	5 00	6 57
3	6 57	5 13	6 50	5 39	6 24	6 01	5 48	6 20	5 16	6 39	4 59	6 57
4	6 57	5 14	6 49	5 40	6 23	6 01	5 47	6 21	5 15	6 39	4 59	6 58
5	6 57	5 15	6 48	5 41	6 22	6 02	5 45	6 21	5 14	6 40	4 59	6 58
6	6 57	5 15	6 48	5 42	6 21	6 03	5 44	6 22	5 14	6 41	4 59	6 59
7	6 57	5 16	6 47	5 42	6 20	6 03	5 43	6 22	5 13	6 41	4 59	6 59
8	6 57	5 17	6 46	5 43	6 19	6 04	5 42	6 23	5 12	6 42	4 59	7 00
9	6 57	5 18	6 45	5 44	6 18	6 05	5 41	6 24	5 11	6 42	4 59	7 00
10	6 57	5 19	6 45	5 45	6 16	6 05	5 39	6 24	5 10	6 43	4 59	7 01
11	6 57	5 19	6 44	5 46	6 15	6 06	5 38	6 25	5 10	6 44	4 59	7 01
12	6 57	5 20	6 43	5 47	6 14	6 07	5 37	6 25	5 09	6 44	4 59	7 01
13	6 57	5 21	6 42	5 47	6 13	6 07	5 36	6 26	5 08	6 45	4 59	7 02
14	6 57	5 22	6 41	5 48	6 12	6 08	5 35	6 27	5 08	6 46	4 59	7 02
15	6 57	5 23	6 40	5 49	6 11	6 08	5 34	6 27	5 07	6 46	4 59	7 03
16	6 57	5 24	6 40	5 50	6 09	6 09	5 33	6 28	5 06	6 47	4 59	7 03
17	6 57	5 24	6 39	5 50	6 08	6 10	5 32	6 28	5 06	6 48	4 59	7 03
18	6 56	5 25	6 38	5 51	6 07	6 10	5 31	6 29	5 05	6 48	4 59	7 03
19	6 56	5 26	6 37	5 52	6 06	6 11	5 30	6 30	5 05	6 49	4 59	7 04
20	6 56	5 27	6 36	5 53	6 05	6 12	5 28	6 30	5 04	6 49	4 59	7 04
21	6 56	5 28	6 35	5 53	6 03	6 12	5 27	6 31	5 04	6 50	5 00	7 04
22	6 55	5 29	6 34	5 54	6 02	6 13	5 26	6 32	5 03	6 51	5 00	7 04
23	6 55	5 30	6 33	5 55	6 01	6 13	5 25	6 32	5 03	6 51	5 00	7 05
24	6 55	5 31	6 32	5 56	6 00	6 14	5 24	6 33	5 02	6 52	5 00	7 05
25	6 54	5 31	6 31	5 56	5 59	6 15	5 23	6 33	5 02	6 53	5 01	7 05
26	6 54	5 32	6 30	5 57	5 57	6 15	5 22	6 34	5 02	6 53	5 01	7 05
27	6 53	5 33	6 29	5 58	5 56	6 16	5 21	6 35	5 01	6 54	5 01	7 05
28	6 53	5 34	6 28	5 59	5 55	6 16	5 21	6 35	5 01	6 54	5 02	7 05
29	6 52	5 35	6 28	5 59	5 54	6 17	5 20	6 36	5 01	6 55	5 02	7 05
30	6 52	5 36			5 52	6 18	5 19	6 37	5 00	6 55	5 02	7 05
31	6 51	5 37			5 51	6 18			5 00	6 56		

Add one hour for Daylight Saving Time if and when in use.

Sunrise corrections to above table for other major Louisiana cities:

Sunrise
Minutes added to New Orleans time

	J	F	M	A	M	J	J	A	S	O	N	D
Baton Rouge	6	4	4	3	3	3	4	4	4	5	6	5
Lake Charles	13	12	13	12	10	12	12	13	12	13	13	13
Lafayette	10	9	9	9	8	8	8	9	9	9	9	10
Shreveport	20	16	14	11	9	9	11	13	15	18	21	21
Alexandria	13	12	10	9	6	6	6	7	9	10	12	13
Monroe	14	11	8	5	2	2	2	5	7	11	13	14

LOUISIANA — CENTRAL STANDARD TIME

JULY Rise A.M.	JULY Set P.M.	AUG. Rise A.M.	AUG. Set P.M.	SEPT. Rise A.M.	SEPT. Set P.M.	OCT. Rise A.M.	OCT. Set P.M.	NOV. Rise A.M.	NOV. Set P.M.	DEC. Rise A.M.	DEC. Set P.M.
5 03	7 05	5 19	6 54	5 37	6 23	5 53	5 46	6 14	5 14	6 38	5 00
5 03	7 05	5 20	6 53	5 38	6 22	5 54	5 45	6 15	5 13	6 39	5 00
5 03	7 05	5 20	6 52	5 38	6 21	5 55	5 44	6 15	5 12	6 40	5 00
5 04	7 05	5 21	6 51	5 39	6 19	5 55	5 42	6 16	5 11	6 41	5 00
5 04	7 05	5 21	6 51	5 39	6 18	5 56	5 41	6 17	5 10	6 41	5 00
5 05	7 05	5 22	6 50	5 40	6 17	5 56	5 40	6 18	5 10	6 42	5 00
5 05	7 05	5 23	6 49	5 40	6 16	5 57	5 39	6 19	5 09	6 43	5 00
5 06	7 05	5 23	6 48	5 41	6 15	5 58	5 38	6 19	5 08	6 44	5 01
5 06	7 04	5 24	6 47	5 41	6 13	5 58	5 37	6 20	5 08	6 44	5 01
5 07	7 04	5 24	6 46	5 42	6 12	5 59	5 35	6 21	5 07	6 45	5 01
5 07	7 04	5 25	6 45	5 42	6 11	5 59	5 34	6 22	5 07	6 46	5 01
5 08	7 04	5 26	6 44	5 43	6 10	6 00	5 33	6 23	5 06	6 46	5 01
5 08	7 03	5 26	6 43	5 44	6 08	6 01	5 32	6 23	5 05	6 47	5 02
5 09	7 03	5 27	6 43	5 44	6 07	6 01	5 31	6 24	5 05	6 48	5 02
5 09	7 03	5 27	6 42	5 45	6 06	6 02	5 30	6 25	5 04	6 48	5 02
5 10	7 02	5 28	6 41	5 45	6 05	6 03	5 29	6 26	5 04	6 49	5 03
5 10	7 02	5 29	6 40	5 46	6 03	6 03	5 28	6 27	5 04	6 50	5 03
5 11	7 02	5 29	6 39	5 46	6 02	6 04	5 27	6 28	5 03	6 50	5 04
5 11	7 01	5 30	6 38	5 47	6 01	6 05	5 26	6 28	5 03	6 51	5 04
5 12	7 01	5 30	6 36	5 47	6 00	6 05	5 25	6 29	5 02	6 51	5 04
5 13	7 00	5 31	6 35	5 48	5 58	6 06	5 24	6 30	5 02	6 52	5 05
5 13	7 00	5 31	6 34	5 48	5 57	6 07	5 23	6 31	5 02	6 52	5 05
5 14	6 59	5 32	6 33	5 49	5 56	6 07	5 22	6 32	5 01	6 53	5 06
5 14	6 59	5 33	6 32	5 49	5 55	6 08	5 21	6 33	5 01	6 53	5 06
5 15	6 58	5 33	6 31	5 50	5 53	6 09	5 20	6 33	5 01	6 54	5 07
5 15	6 58	5 34	6 30	5 51	5 52	6 09	5 19	6 34	5 01	6 54	5 08
5 16	6 57	5 34	6 29	5 51	5 51	6 10	5 18	6 35	5 01	6 54	5 08
5 17	6 56	5 35	6 28	5 52	5 50	6 11	5 17	6 36	5 00	6 55	5 09
5 17	6 56	5 35	6 27	5 52	5 49	6 12	5 16	6 37	5 00	6 55	5 10
5 18	6 55	5 36	6 25	5 53	5 47	6 12	5 15	6 37	5 00	6 56	5 10
5 18	6 54	5 36	6 24			6 13	5 14			6 56	5 11

Sunset corrections to above table for other major Louisiana cities:

Sunset
Minutes added to New Orleans time

	J	F	M	A	M	J	J	A	S	O	N	D
Baton Rouge	3	5	5	5	6	6	5	5	5	5	4	4
Lake Charles	13	13	13	12	13	13	13	13	13	15	12	13
Lafayette	8	9	9	9	9	10	10	10	9	9	9	8
Shreveport	8	11	13	16	19	21	22	19	17	14	10	9
Alexandria	6	8	9	10	12	14	14	12	11	9	7	7
Monroe	3	5	8	10	13	15	14	11	9	7	4	3

ASTRONOMICAL DATA

This information is expressed in universal time (UT) or Greenwich mean time (GMT), the standard time at the Greenwich meridian (0° longitude). A time in UT can be converted to local time by adding for east longitude or subtracting for west longitude at a rate of one hour for every 15°; therefore, New Orleans, at 90° west, is UT minus six hours. (Remember to include Daylight Savings Time where it is applicable.)

PRINCIPAL PHENOMENA OF SUN AND MOON, 1988

THE SUN

		d	h				d	h	m			d	h	m
Perigee	...Jan.	4	00		Equinoxes	...Mar.	20	09	39...	...Sept.	22	19	29
Apogee	...July	6	00		Solstices	...June	21	03	57...	...Dec.	21	15	28

PHASES OF THE MOON

Lunation	New Moon			First Quarter			Full Moon			Last Quarter		
	d	h	m	d	h	m	d	h	m	d	h	m
804							Jan.	4	01	40	Jan.	12	07	04
805	Jan.	19	05	26	Jan.	25	21	53	Feb.	2	20	51	Feb.	10	23	01
806	Feb.	17	15	54	Feb.	24	12	15	Mar.	3	16	01	Mar.	11	10	56
807	Mar.	18	02	02	Mar.	25	04	41	Apr.	2	09	21	Apr.	9	19	21
808	Apr.	16	12	00	Apr.	23	22	32	May	1	23	41	May	9	01	23
809	May	15	22	11	May	23	16	49	May	31	10	53	June	7	06	21
810	June	14	09	14	June	22	10	23	June	29	19	46	July	6	11	36
811	July	13	21	53	July	22	02	14	July	29	03	25	Aug.	4	18	22
812	Aug.	12	12	31	Aug.	20	15	51	Aug.	27	10	56	Sept	3	03	50
813	Sept	11	04	49	Sept	19	03	18	Sept	25	19	07	Oct.	2	16	58
814	Oct.	10	21	49	Oct.	18	13	01	Oct.	25	04	35	Nov.	1	10	11
815	Nov.	9	14	20	Nov.	16	21	35	Nov.	23	15	53	Dec.	1	06	49
816	Dec.	9	05	36	Dec.	16	05	40	Dec.	23	05	29	Dec.	31	04	57

ECLIPSES

Penumbral Moon eclipse	Mar. 3	Alaska, arctic regions, Pacific Ocean, Australasia, Asia, E. Africa, N.E. Europe
Total eclipse of the Sun	Mar. 17-18	E. Asia, Indonesia, N.W. Australia, New Guinea, Micronesia, extreme N.W. of N. America, W. Hawaiian Islands
Partial eclipse of the Moon	Aug. 27	N. America except E., Central America, W. of S. America, Antarctica, Pacific Ocean, Australasia, E. Asia
Annular eclipse of the Sun	Sept. 11	Extreme E. Africa, S. Asia, Indonesia, Australia except extreme N.E., New Zealand, part of Antarctica

PRINCIPAL PHENOMENA OF SUN AND MOON, 1989

THE SUN

		d	h				d	h	m			d	h	m
Perigee	...Jan.	1	22		Equinoxes	...Mar.	20	15	28...	...Sept.	23	01	20
Apogee	...July	4	12		Solstices	...June	21	09	53...	...Dec.	21	21	22

PHASES OF THE MOON

Lunation	New Moon			First Quarter			Full Moon			Last Quarter		
	d	h	m	d	h	m	d	h	m	d	h	m
817	Jan.	7	19	22	Jan.	14	13	58	Jan.	21	21	33	Jan.	30	02	02
818	Feb.	6	07	37	Feb.	12	23	15	Feb.	20	15	32	Feb.	28	20	08
819	Mar.	7	18	19	Mar.	14	10	11	Mar.	22	09	58	Mar.	30	10	21
820	Apr.	6	03	33	Apr.	12	23	13	Apr.	21	03	13	Apr.	28	20	46
821	May	5	11	46	May	12	14	19	May	20	18	16	May	28	04	01
822	June	3	19	53	June	11	06	59	June	19	06	57	June	26	09	09
823	July	3	04	59	July	11	00	19	July	18	17	42	July	25	13	31
824	Aug.	1	16	06	Aug.	9	17	28	Aug.	17	03	07	Aug.	23	18	40
825	Aug.	31	05	44	Sept	8	09	49	Sept	15	11	51	Sept	22	02	10
826	Sept	29	21	47	Oct.	8	00	52	Oct.	14	20	32	Oct.	21	13	19
827	Oct.	29	15	27	Nov.	6	14	11	Nov.	13	05	51	Nov.	20	04	44
828	Nov.	28	09	41	Dec.	6	01	26	Dec.	12	16	30	Dec.	19	23	54
829	Dec.	28	03	20											

ECLIPSES

Total eclipse of the Moon	Feb. 20	N.W. of N. America, arctic regions, Australasia, Asia, extreme E. Africa, N.E. Europe
Partial eclipse of the Sun	Mar. 7	Hawaiian Islands, N.W. of N. America, Greenland, extreme N.E. Asia, arctic regions
Total eclipse of the Moon	Aug. 17	Extreme W. Asia, Europe except N.E., Africa, Iceland, S. of Greenland, The Americas except N.W., Antarctica
Partial eclipse of the Sun	Aug. 31	Extreme S.E. Africa, Madagascar, part of Antarctica

Source: Louisiana Department of Labor, Office of Employment Security

SEED PLANTING TABLES
Southern States

Kind of Crop	Date of Planting	Best Soil	Amount of Seed per Acre	Wks. to Mature
Cotton	Feb. to May 15	Sandy loam	1 to 3 bush	20-30
Corn	Feb. to June	Rich loam	8 qts.	18-20
Wheat	Sept. to Nov.	Clay loam	2 bush	43
Oats	Feb., May, Sept.	Clay loam	2½ bush	17
Barley	April to May	Clay loam	2½ bush	17
Rye	Sept. to Oct.	Clay loam	1½ bush	43
White Beans	March to May	Light loam	1 to 2 bush	7-8
Cabbage	Oct., Mar. to May	Light loam	4 to 8 oz.	14
Watermelons	Mar. 1 to May 10	Rich, light loam	2 to 7 lbs.	16-20
Onions	Feb. 1 to Apr. 10	Loam or muck		16-24
Potatoes	Jan., Feb. to April	Light, loose loam	8 to 10 bush	11-15
Sweet Potatoes	May to June	Sandy loam	10 to 12 bush	12-15
Pumpkins	April 1 to May 1	Rich, light loam	4 to 7 lbs.	17-20
Tomatoes	Jan. 1 to Feb. 9	Rich, sandy loam	4 to 9 oz.	14-20
Turnips	Feb., Aug., April	Rich, light loam	2 to 6 lbs.	8-12
Tobacco	Seed bed March	Sandy loam	Oz. to 6 sq. rd.	18-20
Cow Peas	May 1 to July 15	Sandy loam	2 to 5 pecks	6-8

BREEDING TABLE
Incubation

Canaries	14 days
Chickens	21 Days
Ducks	30 Days
Guineas	28 Days
Geese	30 Days
Ostriches	41 Days
Pheasants	25 Days
Pigeons	21 Days
Parrots	40 Days
Swan	42 Days
Turkeys	28 Days

Gestation

Ass	12 Months
Bear	6 Months
Bitch	9 Weeks
Camel	11-12 Months
Cow	9 Months
Cat	8 Weeks
Deer	8 Months
Dromedary	12 Months
Dormouse	31 Days
Elephant	21 Months
Goat	5 Months
Guinea Pig	21 Days
Giraffe	14 Months
Lion	108 Days
Mare	11 Months
Monkey	7 Months
Opossum	26 Days
Rabbit	30 Days
Sheep	5 Months
Sow	16 Weeks
Squirrels and Rats	28 Days
Wolf and Fox	62 Days

MEASURES
Mariner's Measure

6 feet	1 fathom
120 fathoms	1 cable length
7½ cable lengths	1 mile
5,280 feet	1 statute mile
6,085 feet	1 nautical mile

Paper Measure

24 sheets	1 quire
20 quires	1 ream (480 sheets)
2 reams	1 bundle
5 bundles	1 bale

Square Measure

144 sq. inches	1 sq. ft.
9 sq. ft.	1 sq. yd.
30¼ sq. yds.	1 sq. rod
40 sq. rods	1 rood
4 roods	1 acre
640 acres	1 sq. mile

TEMPERATURES

Milk	Freezes 30° above Zero
Water	Freezes 32° above Zero
Olive Oil	Freezes 36° above Zero
Wine	Freezes 20° above Zero
Vinegar	Freezes 28° above Zero
Alcohol	Boils at 173° above Zero
Water	Boils at 212° above Zero
Petroleum (average)	Boils at 306° above Zero
Blood Heat	98.4° above Zero
Eggs Hatch	104° above Zero

Parish means county, a French word.

KITCHEN WEIGHTS, MEASURES, ETC.

4 large tablespoonsful	½ gill
1 teacup	1 gill
1 common sized tumbler	½ pint
2 cups	1 pint
2 pints	1 quart
1 tablespoonful	½ ounce
1 large wine glass	2 ounces
8 quarts	1 peck
4 cups flour	1 pound
2 cups solid butter	1 pound
4 quarts	1 gallon
2 cups granulated sugar	1 pound
3 cups cornmeal	1 pound
2 cups brown sugar	1 pound
2 cups solid meat	1 pound
2 cups powdered sugar	1 pound
16 ounces	1 pound
2 tablespoons butter, sugar, salt	1 ounce
4 tablespoons flour	1 ounce
16 tablespoonsful	1 cupful
60 drops	1 teaspoonful
8 saltpoonsful	1 teaspoonful
3 teaspoonsful	1 tablespoonful
4 tablespoonsful	¼ cupful
1 cup shelled almonds	¼ pound
¼ pound cornstarch	1 cupful

Cup Measures

1 cup granulated sugar	½ pound
1 cup butter	½ pound
1 cup lard	½ pound
1 cup flour	¼ pound
1 cup rice	½ pound
1 cup cornmeal	5 ounces
1 cup raisins (stemmed)	6 ounces
1 cup currants (cleaned)	6 ounces
1 cup bread crumbs (stale)	2 ounces
1 cup chopped meat	½ pound

Equivalents of Capacity

3 teaspoons	1 tablespoon
½ fluid ounce	1 tablespoon
16 tablespoons	1 cup
2 gills	1 cup
½ liquid pint	1 cup
8 fluid ounces	1 cup
1 liquid pint	2 cups
16 fluid ounces	2 cups

WEIGHTS AND MEASURES

Length

12 inches	1 foot
3 feet	1 yard
5½ yds.	1 rod
40 rods	1 furlong
8 furlongs	1 mile
(A mile is 1760 yds. or 5,280 feet)	
3 miles	1 league
6076.12 ft.	1 nautical mile

* * *

Surface

144 sq. in.	1 sq. ft.
9 sq. ft.	1 sq. yd.
30¼ sq. yds.	1 sq. rod
160 sq. rods	1 acre
640 Acres	1 sq. mile
36 sq. miles	1 township
Arpent	5/6 acre (aprox.)

Circular

60 seconds	1 Minute
60 seconds	1 degree
360 degrees	a circumference

(Since the earth is not a perfect circle, the degree varies slightly as it applies to longitude and various latitude measurements. The average is 69 miles to a degree or 1.15 miles to a minute.)

* * *

Volume

1728 cubic inches	1 cubic foot
27 cubic ft.	1 cubic yard
128 cubic ft.	1 cord of wood (4 ft. x 8)
23-¾ cubic ft.	1 perch (16½ ft. x 1½ x 1)

* * *

Weight
Avoirdupois

27-11/32 grams	1 dram
16 drams	1 ounce
16 oz.	1 pound (7,000 grains)
2,000 lbs.	1 ton
(A long ton is 2240 pounds)	

Troy
(used by jewelers)

24 grains	1 pennyweight
20 pennyweights	1 ounce
12 ounces	1 pound
1 carat	3.168 grains

Apothecaries

20 grains	1 scruple
3 scruples	1 dram

* * *

Dry Measure

2 pints	1 quart
8 quarts	1 peck
4 pecks	1 bushel
(1.2445 cubic feet)	

Liquid Measure

4 gills	1 pint
2 pints	1 quart
4 quarts	1 gallon
31½ gals.	1 barrel
2 barrels	1 hogshead

Lagniappe, meaning small gift, is French and Spanish.

METRIC MEASUREMENTS AND U. S. EQUIVALENTS
Length Measure
Metric To U. S.

1 millimeter	0.03937 inch
1 centimeter	0.03937 inch
1 meter	39.37 inches
1 meter	3.2808 feet
1 kilometer	0.6214 mile

* * *

U.S. to Metric

1 inch	25.4 millimeters
1 inch	2.54 centimeters
1 inch	0.254 meter
1 foot	0.3048 meter
1 mile	1.609 kilometers

* * *

SURFACE MEASURE
Metric to U.S.

1 sq. millimeter	0.0155 sq. inch
1 sq. centimeter	0.155 sq. inch
1 sq. meter	10.764 sq. feet
1 sq. meter	1.196 sq. yards
1 hectare	0.00386 sq. mile
1 sq. kilometer	0.3861 sq. mile

* * *

U.S. to Metric

1 sq. inch	645.2 sq. millimeters
1 sq. inch	6,452 sq. centimeters
1 sq. foot	0.0929 sq. meter
1 sq. yard	0.8361 sq. meter
1 acre	0.4047 hectare
1 sq. mile	258.99 hectare
1 sq. mile	2.59 sq. kilometers

* * * *

LIQUID MEASURE
Metric to U.S.

1 liter	1.0567 quarts
1 liter	0.2642 gallon
1 cubic meter	264.17 gallons

* * * *

U.S. to Metric

1 quart	0.9463 liter
1 gallon	3.7854 liters
1 gallon	0.0038 cubic meter

* * * *

DRY MEASURE
Metric to U.S.

1 liter	0.908 quart
1 hectoliter	2.8375 bushels

* * * *

U.S. to Metric

1 quart	1.1013 liters
1 bushel	0.3524 hectoliter

WEIGHTS
Metric to U.S.

1 milligram	0.0154 grain
1 gram	15.432 grains
1 kilogram	2,2046 pounds
1 metric ton	1.11023 ton (2000 lb.)
1 metric ton	0.9842 long ton (2240 lb.)

1 grain	64.80 milligrams
1 grain	0.0648 gram
1 pound (Avoir.)	0.4536 kilogram
1 ton	0.9072 metric ton
1 long ton	1.0161 metric tons

EQUIVALENTS OF CENTIGRADE AND FAHRENHEIT
Readings on the Thermometer
Degrees

37	98.6	41	105.8
38	100.4	42	107.6
39	102.2	43	109.4
40	104		

LENGTH EQUIVALENTS

1 Light Year = 5,879,000,000,000 miles; (light travels 186,300 miles per second).

1 Angstrom—a minute unit of length = 1/10,000 of a micron or one hundredth million of a centimeter.

1 Micron = 1/1000 of a millimeter, 1 millionth of a meter, .000,039 37 of an inch.

1 Millimicron = .001 of a Micron, .000,-000 0039 37 of an inch.

1 Centimeter = 0.393 7 inch.

1 Chain (Gunther's or Surveyors) = 66 feet, 20.1168 meters (exactly).

1 Fathom = 6 feet; 1,8288 meters (exactly).

1 Foot = 0.348 meters (exactly).

1 Furlong. = 10 chains (surveyors); 660 feet, 220 yards, ½ statute mile, 201.168 meters.

1 Inch = 2.54 centimeters (exactly).

1 League (land) = 3 statute miles, 4.828 kilometers.

LOUISIANA LAND MEASUREMENTS

Arpent	192 ft.
Vara	33 inches
Toise	6.39 ft.
French Foot	1.06575 Am. Ft.

Arpents were used during the French domination, and **Varas** during the Spanish domination, to measure lands in Louisiana.

A "vara" is 33-inches in length. It is found in the old land titles along the Sabine river, in West Calcasieu and West Cameron parishes.

An "arpent", in a decision of the Louisiana Supreme Court of May 25, 1903, was defined as 192 feet to be used as a lineal measure.

According to Edwin Hudley Jordan (engineer with the Sewerage and Water Board, now deceased) "an arpent is a lineal measure comprising 30 toises of six feet each, or 180 feet French measure. The variation of the arpent is from 191 feet 9 3/4 inches to 191 feet 10-3-64 inches or practically 192 feet. An arpent is 0.845 acres. One acre is calculated to be 1.1834 superficial arpents." An arpent is approximately five-sixths of an acre.

Much of the land of Louisiana facing streams was measured in arpents for the frontage and the depths would vary.

TOURING AND RECREATION
Louisiana State Parks and Recreational Areas

INTRODUCTION AND FACILITY CLASSIFICATION

We welcome you to Louisiana's State Parks and invite you to explore and enjoy the "Pelican State." Found throughout the state, our park facilities offer a wide variety of scenic, recreational and educational experiences. If you join us for a week, a day or only a moment, we want to share with you the natural beauty and rich culture and history of Louisiana — you can do all this and more at our State Parks (SP), State Commemorative Areas (SCA), and State Preservation Areas (SPA).

STATE PARKS

State Parks are selected specifically for their natural setting and scenic environment. Emphasis at these sites is placed on outdoor recreational activities such as boating, fishing, sailing, swimming, hiking and picnicking. Modern cabins, group camps and overnight camping are available and every State Park is situated along a body of water.

STATE COMMEMORATIVE AREAS

State Commemorative Areas are historic sites with statewide significance. Through individual interpretive programs at these areas, visitors can learn about and experience the Civil War, colonial French and Spanish occupations, Cajun culture, Louisiana country music, ancient Indian cultures, old forts, a river lock system, 19th century plantation living and much more.

STATE PRESERVATION AREAS

State Preservation Areas are unique natural sites preserved for future generations because of their exceptional scenic, ecological and biological values. Natural history education is the purpose of such areas and is accomplished through active interpretive programs, visitor centers, museums and trail systems. Preservation areas may include a barrier island, beach-marsh-cheniers, coastal prairie, cypress-tupelo swamp and upland mixed hardwoods.

PARKS OPERATING SCHEDULE

STATE PARKS

Summer Schedule (April 1 - September 30)
Hours: 7 a.m. - 10 p.m. daily (Exceptions: Chicot SP, South Landing, 5 a.m. - 10 p.m.; Grand Isle SP and Lake Bistineau SP, 6 a.m. - 10 p.m.)

Winter Schedule (October 1 - March 31)
Hours: 8 a.m. - 7 p.m. daily (Exceptions: Chicot SP, South Landing and Lake Bistineau SP, 7 a.m. - 7 p.m.; Chicot State Park, North Landing gate is open from 3 p.m. Friday until 7 p.m. Sunday).
(Note: Attendant on duty until 10 p.m. on Fridays and Saturdays for camper registration.)

STATE COMMEMORATIVE AREAS

MUSEUMS

Year Round Schedule
Hours: 9 a.m. - 5 p.m. daily (Exceptions: Old Arsenal SCA, 10 a.m. - 4:30 p.m., Wednesday - Monday, year round; closed on Tuesday; See Temporary Operating Schedule)
Closed: New Year's Day, Thanksgiving Day and Christmas.

DAY-USE FACILITIES AND GROUNDS

Summer Schedule (April 1 - September 30)
Hours: Open 9 a.m. - 7 p.m. daily

Winter Schedule (October 1 - March 31)
Hours: Open 9 a.m. - 5 p.m. daily

STATE PRESERVATION AREAS

Year-round Schedule
Hours: 9 a.m. - 5 p.m. Monday-Saturday; 1 p.m. - 5 p.m. Sunday
Closed: New Year's Day, Thanksgiving Day and Christmas Day.

TEMPORARY OPERATING SCHEDULES

Some areas are not fully operational, pending completion of programs or facilities. Please contact the site manager for information regarding special group tours and part-time operating hours at the following park facilities:

Bayou Segnette SP
Centenary SCA
Fort St. Jean Baptiste SCA
Los Adaes SCA
Plaquemine Locks SCA
Port Hudson SCA

DAY-USE ENTRANCE FEE

A day-use fee is charged at all state parks and at Longfellow-Evangeline State Commemorative Area (fee does not include a museum visit at Longfellow-Evangeline SCA; see museum fees). Non-commercial vehicles with up to four people are charged $2.00 per day and each additional person is charged $.50. Buses used as public conveyances are charged $20.00 per day except at Audubon and Longfellow-Evangeline SCAs where buses are charged $40.00 per day. Walk-in visitors are charged $.50 per person for the day. All prices include state and local taxes.

FEES AND FACILITIES

In any cases where entrance fees are charged, there is no additional charge for the use of picnicking (except group shelters when reserved for exclusive use), boat launching or swimming facilities. (See the section on swimming pools and enclosed beach areas for exception.)

DAY-USE EXEMPTIONS

Senior Citizens: All persons age 62 or older are admitted free upon proof of age. All persons accompanying a visitor 62 or older in a private, non-commercial vehicle are exempt from the entrance fees only at those sites which collect such fees through a vehicle permit. Where individual fees are charged only those persons 62 or older are exempt. Senior citizens on bus tours may apply for exemption of the bus entrance fee. To be eligible for this exemption, at least 50 percent of the bus passengers must be 62 or older. To obtain this exemption, the tour organizer must submit a list of passenger names and their ages to the assistant secretary and receive from him written approval for the senior citizen discount and exemption of the bus entrance fee.

Disabled Veterans: A special "Veteran Entrance Permit" allows any disabled U.S. Veteran and any person(s) accompanying him in a single, private, non-commercial vehicle free entrance to all day-use areas and museums. Applications for a veteran permit may be made to the Louisiana Department of Veterans' Affairs Service Office serving the parish in which the applicant resides. After certification of eligibility has been established by the Department of Veterans' Affairs, the Assistant Secretary of the Office of State Parks will issue a permit directly to the applicant.

School Groups: Any school child who is on a field trip conducted as part of the curriculum of the school and any classroom teacher, parent, bus driver and any other person accompanying a school child on such a field trip are exempt from paying the general admission charge to any state park, museum or related state facility in Louisiana. This exemption is valid from Monday through Friday during the school year.

ANNUAL DAY-USE PERMITS

These allow a single, private, non-commercial vehicle and its occupants entry to all state parks at any time during normal operating hours, year-round, at a cost of $25.00 per year. The permit, to be permanently affixed to the vehicle, may be obtained by application and payment to the Office of State Parks, P.O. Drawer 1111, Baton Rouge, LA, 70821. Permit applications are available at all State Park areas. The permit is valid for a period of one year beginning January 1 and ending December 31.

The annual day-use permits are valid for exemption from the general admission day-use charge only.

CAMPING

Reservations for campsites are not accepted.

Improved campsites rent for **$9.00** per night.

Unimproved campsites rent for **$7.00** per night.

Each campsite is restricted to use by one camping unit.

Improved sites are equipped with picnic table, grill, electricity, and water hookups.

Overnight Exemption

Senior Citizen Discount: All persons 62 years of age or older and anyone accompanying such persons in the same vehicle are entitled to a $2.00 per night discount on the use of camping facilities. Proof of age is required.

Primitive Camping

Specific primitive areas accommodating organized groups (Boy Scouts, Girl Scouts, etc.) are located at the following State Park areas:

Chemin-A-Haut SP	Lake Bistineau SP
Chicot SP	Lake Claiborne SP
Fontainebleau SP	Sam Houston Jones SP

Reservations for these areas are made directly with the park manager. The group charge is $10.00 per night. Capacity level is set by the park manager.

Backpacking

Backpacking is available only at Chicot State Park at the present time. A permit is required for all overnight backpacking use and may be obtained at the park entrance station. For group outings this permit must be obtained two (2) weeks in advance and may be obtained by writing to Chicot State Park.

Each person is assessed a fee of $.25 per night. A copy of the backpacking regulations can be obtained by the park entrance station.

RESERVATION POLICY

A primary function of the business office at each state park is to take reservations which must be made at the park where the facilities are to be used. Business offices operate 8 a.m. to 5 p.m., Monday through Friday, and are closed New Year's Day, Thanksgiving Day and Christmas Day.

Reservations are accepted from persons 18 years of age or older and adults must accompany all minors at reserved facilities.

To confirm an advanced reservation the appropriate deposit must be received at the park site within 10 days of the request. If a person is not in compliance with this procedure, their reservation will be cancelled.

A reservation may be cancelled with full refund if requested at least 14 days prior to the reservation date. If a person is not in compliance with this procedure, nor follows the refund guidelines (see Refunds), their advanced deposit will be forfeited.

Overnight Reservations

Overnight reservations may be made for cabins, lodges, group camps and rally campgrounds.

Reservations for overnight use between October 1 and March 31 are accepted beginning July 1 annually. Reservations placed for this period between July 1 and July 10 are accepted by telephone ONLY and are on a first come, first served basis. Reservations for this period are accepted after July 10 annually by either phoning or writing the individual park at which accommodations are desired.

Reservations for overnight use between April 1 and September 30 are accepted beginning January 2 annually. Reservations placed for this period between January 2 and January 10 are accepted by telephone ONLY and are on a first come, first served basis. Reservations for this period are accepted after January 10 annually by either phoning or writing the individual park at which accommodations are desired.

For cabins, lodges, group camps and rally campgrounds the minimum reservation period for a weekend is from 4 p.m. Friday through 4 p.m. Sunday.

An advance deposit equal to the appropriate one night fee is required to reserve any overnight facility. This deposit will be applied to the first night's use.

Day-Use Reservations

Day-use reservations may be made for group camps, rally campgrounds, assembly rooms and group shelters (where available).

Reservations for day-use between October 1 and March 31 are accepted after July 10 annually by either phoning or writing the individual park at which accommodations are desired.

Reservations for assembly rooms, group shelters (where available), group camps and rally campgrounds between April 1 and September 30 are accepted after February 1 annually by either phoning or writing the individual park at which accommodations are desired. Such reservations can be made for a single day period.

An advance deposit is not required to reserve an assembly room. An advance deposit equal to the appropriate day-use rate is required to reserve a group camp, group shelter or rally campground. This deposit will be applied to the first day's use.

CABINS

Cabin Classification & Park Location	Overnight Rate & Required Deposit	Bedding Accommodations	Maximum Capacity
Type I Lake Bistineau SP Bayou Segnette SP Lake Fausse Pointe SP North Toledo Bend SP	$50	6 persons-Deluxe	8
Type II Lake Bistineau SP Chicot SP Sam Houston Jones SP	$45	6 persons-Standard	8
Type III Chemin-A-Haut SP	$40	4 persons-Deluxe	6
Type IV Chemin-A-Haut SP Chicot SP	$35	4 persons-Standard	6

In each case where the bedding accommodations are specified, the maximum overnight occupancy of the cabin cannot be more than two people over the lodging accommodation number. Bedding accommodations will vary and may include a combination of double beds, single beds, bunk beds or sofa sleepers. Visitors must contact the park for information regarding specific bedding arrangements and accommodations.

See the Reservation Policy regarding cabins.

LODGES

These are large overnight structures equipped with kitchen, bath and sleeping facilities and can accommodate a large family or several family groups. The Chicot State Park lodge contains sleeping facilities for twelve (12) persons with a maximum of sixteen (16) persons. The Fontainebleau State Park lodge sleeps nine (9) persons with a maximum of thirteen (13) persons. Both lodges are available at a rate of $75.00 per night. See the Reservation Policy regarding lodges.

GROUP CAMPS

These are available at certain parks for organized group use. The capacity, type of facility, rate and locations are as follows:

Park Location	Type of Facility	Capacity (No. of Persons)	Minimum Rate and Deposit Overnight	Day-Use Rate
Bayou Segnette	20 Cabins	120	$ 180	$ 150
Chemin-A-Haut	1 Dormitory	40	75	50
Chicot Area No. 1	5 Cabins	160	250	150
	1 Dormitory			
Chicot Area No. 2	6 Cabins	48	75	50
Fontainebleau No. 1 (West end large)	1 Dormitory	150	225	150
Fontainebleau No. 2 (West end small)	1 Dormitory	30	50	50
Fontainebleau No. 3 (East end)	2 Dormitories	65	100	50
Lake Bistineau Area No. 1	20 Cabins	160	250	150
Lake Bistineau Area No. 2	6 Cabins	48	75	50
Longfellow-Evangeline	1 Dormitory	60	100	50
North Toledo Bend	10 Cabins	150	225	150

Minimum overnight rate is based on 50% capacity of the facility. Rate is $3.00 per person per night for each person over the 50% capacity.

Group camps may be reserved for day-use only at a basic rate (see chart above). In addition, the normal day-use entrance fee will be assessed each vehicle entering the group camp area.

Beds, kitchen and necessary cooking ware are furnished. User must furnish his own tableware (silver, dishes, glasses, etc.), bed linens, pillows, towels, and toilet necessities.

See the Reservation Policy regarding group camps.

RALLY CAMPGROUNDS

These are areas at some of Louisiana's state parks designated and reserved for use by organized groups of overnight campers. These areas differ from the normal campgrounds since they are available for group use and may be reserved in advance. Sites offering rally campgrounds are Lake Bistineau and Chemin-A-Haut State Parks.

Reservations are obtained through the park's business office on a first-come-first-served basis. A $30.00 advance deposit is required to confirm reservation which will be applied to the first night's use.

A lump sum fee of $30.00 per night is assessed to the group for the exclusive use of the area, plus an additional $7.00 per unit per night for each individual camper rig occupying the area.

The day-use fee for a rally campground is $30 per day for the group, and in addition the standard day-use entrance fee is charged per vehicle.

A maximum carrying capacity for improved and unimproved sites is established by individual parks and information concerning these capacities is available through the individual park offices.

See the Reservation Policy regarding rally campgrounds.

ASSEMBLY ROOMS

Any meeting room or enclosed facility of a park used to accommodate meetings and functions of private groups, clubs and other organizations is available at a rate of $50.00 per day (a normal day is the period between 9:30 a.m. and 3:30 p.m.) or $10.00 per hour for day use, whichever is lower. All use after 3:30 p.m. until normal closing hours of the park is charged at a rate of $15.00 per hour or at a flat rate of $75.00, whichever is lower. Kitchen facilities may be used if available.

Assembly rooms are available at Fort Jesup SCA and Chemin-A-Haut SP.

All use after regular closing hours requires written approval from the Assistant Secretary and is available at a flat rate of $50.00 plus $25.00 per hour.

See the Reservation Policy regarding assembly rooms.

GROUP RENTAL SHELTERS

Group rental shelters are available at Lake Bistineau SP, Cypremort Point SP and Chemin-A-Haut SP for a daily rental fee of $30. Such shelters, when rented, are reserved exclusively for the use of the group or individual who is permitted for such use.

Reserved shelters will be posted, indicating the name of the party and date of use. When such shelters are not so posted or reserved, they are available to the park user on a first come, first served basis as any other non-reserved park shelter. Group rental shelters are not available for reservation on Memorial Day, July 4th or Labor Day.

Exclusive use of such a shelter can only be made by a rental permit and payment of a rental fee. These group shelters can be reserved in advance with a deposit to confirm the reservation.

In addition to the rental fee, users of the reserved group shelters will also be charged the normal day-use entrance fee to the park.

See the Reservation Policy regarding group rental shelters.

MUSEUMS

An admission of $2.00 per adult and $1.00 per child (between the ages of six and twelve) is charged for all state commemorative area museums. This fee includes the museum tour at Longfellow-Evangeline SCA and considers the grounds at Audubon SCA as part of the site tour and program.

All children under six years of age, accompanied by an adult 18 years or older, are admitted free.

Organized groups of 10 or more are requested to notify the park manager in advance of their arrival.

BOATING

Rental boats range in length from 12 feet to 14 feet and are available in most parks. The use of motors on these boats is limited to the manufacturer's recommended horsepower capacity.

Boats with three life jackets and two paddles are available at a rental rate of $8 per boat per day. Additional life jackets are available at a rental rate of $1 each per day.

A refundable deposit of $10 per boat is required at the time of rental. This deposit will be forfeited if the boat and its accessories are not returned in the same condition as rented.

Boat Keys

Certain parks maintain a boat system utilizing a central fee collection and a boat lock system. The boat keys are issued upon renting a boat and must be returned when rental period expires. A refundable deposit of $2.00 is required for the use of the key.

Marina Facilities

Thirty-seven (37) covered boat slips located at Fort Macomb SCA in Orleans Parish are available for rent on an annual basis. The rental rate is $80.00 per month. These slips are approximately 47 feet long by 18 feet wide. For more information contact Fort Pike SCA at (504) 662-5703.

SWIMMING POOLS & ENCLOSED BEACH AREAS

Pools and enclosed beach areas are usually operated from Memorial Day through Labor Day, subject to an operating schedule per individual park. All pools and enclosed beach areas are closed on Mondays, except holidays.

There is a $1.00 per person per day swimming pool fee at St. Bernard State Park.

FISHING PIER

A fishing pier extending into the Gulf of Mexico is located at Grand Isle East State Park. This structure is leased to a concessionaire and a fee is charged for day or night fishing on the pier in addition to the regular day-use or overnight-use fees.

Fishing License Information

Resident freshwater fishing.....................$2.50
Resident saltwater fishing
($5.50 + cost of freshwater license, $2.50) 8.00
Non-resident from Alabama, Arkansas,
Florida, Mississippi and Texas -
reciprocal agreement .... cost varies with state
Non-resident, all other states
Trip fishing 7 days 3.50
Season 6.50

For additional information, contact the Louisiana Department of Wildlife and Fisheries at (504) 925-3617.

SPECIAL USE

Any function requiring special or restricted use of any facility or area within a state park holding must be approved by the Assistant Secretary and the fee for such use will be computed on the same basis as the use for Assembly Rooms. Written request for special use of a facility must be received at the Office of State Parks, P.O. Drawer 1111, Baton Rouge, LA 70821, at least thirty (30) days prior to the scheduled event. No telephone requests are accepted.

POLITICAL ACTIVITIES

Political events involving the use of state park areas are discouraged; however, each event is considered on an individual request basis and, if approved, will be authorized by the Assistant Secretary. Such activities will be considered only, when in the judgment of the Assistant Secretary, the function will not adversely affect the normal programmed use of the area by the general public.

Requests for such events must be submitted in writing to the Assistant Secretary at least thirty (30) days in advance of the proposed use. Such events will be considered "Special Use Events" and fees and permits will be regulated by the special use provisions above. No political candidates·or organizations will be granted or shall expect to receive special consideration for use or fee waivers.

REFUNDS

Refunds will not be issued to visitors evicted for enforcement or disciplinary reasons.

Refunds may be made at the park upon approval of the park manager or a designated representative for those fees paid at the park (except advance payment) for the following reasons:

A. In emergency situations where the park must be closed due to natural or man-made emergencies (water shortage, fire, weather, and equipment failure).

B. When a user chooses to leave a park before use of any facilities.

C. When the user chooses to leave a park before utilizing facilities for the total reservation period, the unused reservation period amount will be refunded unless the refund amount includes all or part of a pre-paid advance reservation payment.

All park-issued refunds will require that the visitor present a valid paid receipt for the amount of the requested refund.

All advance reservation refunds must be issued through the administrative office; however, the refund procedure will be initiated at the individual park. The visitor must remit to the park attendant his original receipt which the park attendant will certify and submit with the appropriate form to the administrative office. The refund decision will be based upon the visitor's explanation and the park attendant's verification of the refund need.

Visitors are encouraged to request a temporary visitor pass for the purpose of inspecting the park facilities prior to an anticipated visit.

Refunds are not granted when a visitor, by his own choosing, leaves the park as a result of inclement weather.

RULES & REGULATIONS

These Rules and Regulations were enacted by the Office of State Parks to govern all State Parks, State Commemorative Areas, State Preservation Areas, and all other holdings under its jurisdiction, pursuant to the authority given in Title 56, Chapter 6 of the Louisiana Revised Statutes of 1950. Park rules and regulations are designed to provide the proper atmosphere for the enjoyment and protection of park facilities and the safety of visitors. We look to our visitors to be responsible for their own actions and to familiarize themselves with these rules.

The Office of State Parks programs and activities are open to all qualified persons regardless of race, color, national origin, age or handicap. If anyone believes he or she has been discriminated against in any Office of State Parks program, activity or facility, he or she may file a complaint alleging discrimination with either the Office of State Parks or the Office for Equal Opportunity, U.S. Department of the Interior, Washington, D.C. 20240.

PARK PROPERTY & ENVIRONMENT

It is strictly forbidden to destroy, deface, remove, or in any other manner, damage any natural feature or plant within a park. The word "Park" is defined for these Rules and Regulations to mean any holding of the Office of State Parks.

It is strictly forbidden to deface, destroy, remove, alter, damage or disturb any building, sign, marker structure or other park property.

No timber may be cut, destroyed or damaged except as necessary to meet established park management criteria including insect control, public safety, and approved park construction. No timber cutting or removal may occur without the written permission of the State Parks Assistant Secretary or his authorized agent.

No building, structure, or other park feature may be altered, erected, or constructed without written consent of the assistant secretary or his authorized agent.

A park manager or his agent may close the park to incoming visitors when the maximum use capacity of the park has been reached or when it is determined that additional users may cause damage to the park.

No food, beverage, or smoking is permitted in structures or areas containing historical furnishings or displays except for designated meeting rooms and assembly locations.

The use of metal detectors or other devices for the purpose of locating surface or subsurface artifacts or relics is prohibited. It's strictly forbidden to dig for or otherwise remove any historical feature, relic or artifact. Excavation and removal of historical features by professional archaeological means may be considered by a special permit for historical or scientific research purposes. All such requests will be reviewed by the Louisiana State Archaeological Survey and Antiquities Commission. Application for such permits must be made to the Assistant Secretary, Office of State Parks.

No plant material may be planted or otherwise introduced on any state park area without the written approval of the Assistant Secretary.

Visitors are prohibited from leaving designated interpretive trails and from walking on historic earthworks, fortifications, mounds or like structures except when such features are on established trails.

CONDUCT OF VISITORS

Disorderly or boisterous conduct is forbidden.

The manager and/or his agent is authorized to control the use and consumption of alcoholic beverages in a park. The consumption of alcoholic beverages may be allowed to the extent that such activity does not adversely affect the use and enjoyment of the park by a majority of the park users.

VEHICLE USE

Automobiles, trucks, motorcycles, bicycles, recreation vehicles or any other wheeled vehicles must be operated only on those roads, lanes or byways designated for vehicular park traffic unless otherwise authorized by the park manager.

Vehicles, including recreation vehicles and boat trailers, must be parked only in designated parking areas unless otherwise authorized by the park manager.

The vehicular speed limit in parks is fifteen (15) miles per hour unless otherwise posted.

The operation of motorcycles, trailbikes, minibikes, motorscooters or other two-wheel motor vehicles is prohibited from 6:30 p.m. to 6:30 a.m., except for traveling into or out of the park. The operation of any vehicle on public roads in state parks must meet all licensing requirements and be properly licensed for operation on public roads as specified by the Louisiana Department of Public Safety or other regulatory agencies.

The operation of all wheeled vehicles on state parks' property must be done in a careful and reasonable manner. The Motor Vehicle and Traffic Regulations of the Louisiana State Digest pursuant to Title 32 are applicable to and enforced on all state parks' holdings.

The cleaning, servicing and/or repairing of any vehicle on state parks' property is prohibited except in emergency situations and in designated areas.

Vehicles will be considered abandoned when left unattended for more than seven consecutive days unless the proper permit or advanced written approval is granted by the park manager.

No two-wheel motor vehicles are allowed beyond the entrance to Grand Isle State Park. All such vehicles must be parked in the designated area, locked and registered with the gate attendant.

The removal of any barrier to gain access to a restricted area is prohibited.

BOATING USE

The operation of all water craft in and on all waters or streams, on or adjacent to Park property, must be done in a careful and reasonable manner, subject to the rules of safety imposed by the laws of Louisiana and by the United State Coast Guard.

It is strictly forbidden to operate or be a passenger in or on any boat, vessel, conveyance or other water craft on any waters owned by or subject to the supervision of the Office of State Parks without a life jacket, ring, belt or other device approved by the United States Coast Guard.

Boats must be launched only from designated boat ramps or launching areas within a park.

Any power boat underway at night must display a white stern light higher than the forward red and green port and starboard running lights. Canoes, pirogues and other similar craft must carry a white light that can be flashed at intervals to prevent collisions.

When at anchor at night all power boats must display a white light that can be seen by any boat approaching from any direction.

Persons renting boats must return the boat to the original docking location after use.

No boat may be operated in a designated swimming area or any other area designated by signs or any area restricted from boat operation or docking.

Boats left docked and unattended must be properly secured in designated areas only. The Office of State Parks will not be responsible for theft or damage to boats, equipment or supplies left unattended. Boats will be considered abandoned when left unattended for more than seven (7) consecutive days unless the proper permit or advanced written approval is granted by the park manager.

Commercial boats, including, but not limited to, tugboats, push boats, barges, crew boats and all similar craft are prohibited from using any state parks' facility without the written consent of the assistant secretary. Loading or unloading of materials, boarding of persons, operating power equipment and non-emergency repair work are prohibited.

SWIMMING

Swimming is permitted only at designated places, and persons are not permitted to swim unaccompanied.

All children under 12 years of age must be accompanied by an adult at any swimming area not under the supervision of a certified lifeguard.

The capacity of all pools and beach areas is determined, regulated and enforced by the park manager.

Glass containers of any kind are prohibited within any perimeter boundaries of pools, enclosed swimming areas, enclosed beach areas, and beach parks. No food or drinks are allowed within enclosed pool and enclosed beach areas.

DAY-USE

Day-Use facilities such as shelters, barbecue pits, tables, etc., which do not require prior reservations, shall not be reserved by placing personal articles at these facilities prior to their immediate use. This includes firewood, ice chests or any other personal property. The use of all such facilities is on a first come, first served basis.

The use of any facility in a park area is subject to certain conditions or policies set down on an individual facility basis by the park manager. These conditions or policies must be approved in writing by the assistant secretary.

OVERNIGHT USE

Any overnight use of a park requires a written permit or cash receipt from the park. Overnight facilities are reserved for the exclusive use of persons properly permitted for the use of overnight facilities and their guests.

Any permit may be terminated by the Assistant Secretary of the Office of State Parks and may be immediately terminated by the park manager upon the violation of any established park rule, regulation or any condition of the permit.

The park manager has the authority to require registration of every person occupying a campsite or overnight facility. Overnight camping and group camp, lodge and cabin use are limited to a fourteen (14) day period within thirty (30) days. No one occupying an overnight facility will be allowed to re-register for the use of that facility for a period of more than fourteen (14) days within a thirty (30) day period.

No campsite may be vacated for longer than a 24-hour continuous period under any permit agreement.

ALL OVERNIGHT FACILITIES HAVE A CHECK-IN TIME OF 4 p.m. AND A CHECK-OUT TIME OF 2 p.m. (EXCEPT SUNDAYS, WHEN THE CHECK-OUT TIME IS 4 p.m.)

In no case will public residency be allowed in a state park.

State Parks campgrounds are intended for tents and recreational vehicles only, and in no case will mobile homes be allowed.

Campsite occupancy is limited to one family unit per night or a non-family unit not to exceed six persons. A family unit is composed of members of an immediate family group (husband, wife and/or children). This is not applicable to areas set aside for special group camping activities (i.e., scouts, etc.).

Only one camping rig will be allowed in each campsite. A camping rig is defined as the maximum combination of camping equipment that will be allowed to occupy one campsite. These allowable combinations are:

A. One passenger vehicle and two tents (family unit only).
B. One passenger vehicle and one camping trailer.
C. One van-type camping vehicle and one tent.
D. One van-type camping vehicle and one camping trailer.
E. One pickup truck camper and one tent.
F. One pickup truck camper and one camping trailer.
G. One motorized camper (or bus) and one passenger vehicle.

In no case may a campsite be reserved by payment or other means prior to actual physical occupancy by the permittee.

Permittee may not transfer or assign any use permit nor sublet any facility or part thereof.

Upon termination of any use permit, the facility must be delivered up in good repair and in the same condition in which it was found. Where applicable, all doors and windows will be closed, all water taps shut and fires extinguished. Permittee is responsible for any and all damages resulting from his use of the facility.

Established time schedules (check-in and check-out) are strictly enforced. Failure to comply without advanced approval of the park manager may result in additional charges and denial of any future use of the facility.

No permittee may repair or install any park equipment or furnishings unless authorized and supervised by the park manager.

Permittee waives and releases all claims against the State of Louisiana for any damage to person or property arising from the privileges granted by any use permit.

No camper may erect or display unsightly or inappropriate structures or features which, in the opinion of the park manager, may create a disturbing or otherwise unpleasant condition detrimental to the general park use.

Tents and/or camping vehicles must be erected or parked only on designated campsites provided for such purposes.

Campers must maintain a reasonable quiet camp between the hours of 10:00 p.m. and 6:00 a.m.

Beds are arranged under Health Service recommendations and cannot be changed without the permission of the park manager.

The park manager will furnish or post in each overnight structure an inventory of moveable equipment and furnishings which is available in the unit. The user should check the inventory immediately upon occupancy and report to the manager any deviation between the actual inventory and the printed inventory. The user may be required to reimburse the Office of State Parks for the cost of any equipment or furnishings which, if not reported upon occupancy, is missing or damaged when the unit is vacated.

Certain parks maintain a system of pass keys or lock combinations which are made available only to properly registered overnight visitors. Keys or lock combinations are issued for the personal use of the permittee, who is prohibited from allowing others to use the key or lock combinations, otherwise making the facilities open so that others not covered by the permit may enter or leave the facility or area. Gate keys are available at some parks for the use of overnight visitors at a refundable deposit rate of $2 each. The key must be surrendered when the visitor completes his stay.

SANITATION AND HEALTH

Visitors using parks must dispose of all paper, garbage, litter and other refuse by placing such materials in receptacles provided for the purpose.

Draining or dumping refuse waste from any trailer or other vehicle except in places or receptacles provided for such uses is prohibited.

Cleaning fish or food, or washing clothing or articles of household use at hydrants or at water faucets located in restrooms is prohibited.

Polluting or contaminating water supplies or water used for human consumption or swimming is prohibited.

Disposing, except into receptacles provided for that purpose, any body waste in or on any portion of any comfort station or any public structure, or depositing any bottles, cans, cloth, rags, metal, wood, stone, or other damaging substance in any of the fixtures in such stations or structures is prohibited.

Using refuse containers or other refuse facilities for dumping household or commercial garbage or trash brought to a park as such is prohibited.

FIRES

Fires shall be built only in places specifically designated for that purpose.

AMPLIFIED SOUND EQUIPMENT

There will be no playing of amplified musical instruments within park areas except when approved by the assistant secretary in conjunction with special events. The playing of non-amplified musical instruments, radios, televisions, tape players and similar equipment in such a way as to disturb other visitors in any park is prohibited. A decibel meter will be used to determine sound loudness and a level above 60 decibels has been established as unacceptable.

The operation or use of any public address systems, whether fixed, portable or vehicle mounted, without prior approval of the park manager is prohibited.

Remote public broadcast activities involving the use of amplified sound equipment are prohibited on all state parks' holdings.

FISHING, HUNTING, TRAPPING & THE USE OF FIREARMS OR FIREWORKS

The wildlife (domestic and natural) in state parks' areas is under strict protection and must not be hunted, molested, disturbed, destroyed, or removed, except for scientific or management purposes when approved by the Assistant Secretary.

Bringing or keeping any hunting dogs on park property for the purpose of hunting inside or adjacent to a park area is prohibited.

The display or discharge of any weapon, including but not limited to shotguns, rifles, pistols, and bow and arrows within a park area is prohibited.

The taking and hunting of frogs on any park property is prohibited.

No fireworks of any type are allowed in a park area.

Anyone fishing on state parks' property must adhere to all state and federal laws and criteria regarding fresh and/or salt water fishing. The taking of fish by nets, traps or any means other than hook or line is prohibited on any state park area except for management purposes authorized by special permit. Taking of flounder by gigs is permitted.

LIVESTOCK, ANIMALS AND PETS

Horseback riding is allowed only on those parks with specifically developed areas and/or trails for their use. Under no circumstances may horses be ridden in parks unless authorized by the park manager.

Dogs or pets are not allowed to run at liberty in the parks. Any dog or pet brought within the park area must be leashed, caged or crated, and under no circumstances, be permitted within buildings or other enclosed structures of the park. The leash is not to exceed five (5) feet in length. Only Seeing Eye dogs will be permitted near developed swimming areas. Owners of pets causing any injury or damage will be fully responsible.

Under no circumstances will livestock be allowed to run or graze on park property.

No pets are allowed on state preservation areas or at the Louisiana State Arboretum.

In the event that a park visitor or employee is attacked, bitten or scratched by an animal on a park area, a report must be made immediately to the park manager. When applicable, the manager will take steps necessary and feasible to ensure that law enforcement and/or animal control agents are properly advised of the incident. Such animals, at the option of the park manager or other enforcement agents, may be seized or impounded for observation. All costs associated with such action will be the responsibility of the animal owner.

No animal may be brought on a park area by a visitor unless he bears a current rabies inoculation tag indicating that he has been properly and currently inoculated against the disease.

Release or final disposition of an impounded animal is the responsibility of parish health officer or a registered veterinarian.

BUSINESS ACTIVITIES

No one may sell or offer for sale any merchandise or service in a park area without the written consent of the Assistant Secretary.

No one may distribute, post, place or erect any advertising device in a park area without the written consent of the Assistant Secretary.

FEES, FINES & RULES ENFORCEMENT

The use of certain parks and/or facilities is subject to charges which will be imposed by the manager according to the schedule of fees approved by the Office of State Parks. The manager or his agents is responsible for the collection and enforcement of these fees.

Persons violating the Rules and Regulations of the respective parks are subject to fines for each violation of not less than $15.00 nor more than $250.00 (L.R.S. 56:1689).

Park managers and the other park agents, including rangers, watchmen, and guards, if certified as Park Wardens, are fully authorized to administer and enforce the Rules and Regulations applicable to the park areas and are empowered to issue citations and make arrests for violation of these Rules and Regulations. The manager and his agents, if certified as "Park Wardens," are permitted to carry concealed weapons (L.R.S. 56:1689).

The Assistant Secretary or his authorized agent may direct the closing of a park to public use when or if any natural or man-made occurrence has affected or is expected to affect the operation and management of the park to a degree that normal public use and enjoyment are altered or when such use may impair the health, safety and well-being of the public or employees of the agency.

Entering a park when closed or entering a park without proper registration or any effort to avoid payment of user fees is prohibited. Anyone entering a park without proper registration will be subject to a fine of not less than $25.00.

LOUISIANA'S STATE PARKS,
STATE PRESERVATION AREAS & STATE COMMEMORATIVE AREAS

○ **STATE PARKS**
□ **STATE COMMEMORATIVE AREAS**
△ **STATE PRESERVATION AREAS**

NOTE: Detailed location maps and site descriptions are available on individual park brochures. These may be obtained by calling or writing the Office of State Parks, P. O. Drawer 1111, Baton Rouge, LA, 70821, 504-925-3830.

1. Audubon State Commemorative Area (P.O. Box 546, St. Francisville, LA 70775, 504-635-3739) is located in West Feliciana Parish, near St. Francisville on LA 956. Oakley Plantation House; 19th century plantation living; site where artist-naturalist John James Audubon created many of his famous bird paintings.

2. Bayou Segnette State Park (1201 Bayou Segnette State Park, Westwego, LA 70094, 504-436-1107) is located in Westwego just off the Westbank Expressway (U.S. 90) at the intersection with Drake Avenue in Jefferson Parish, just across the Mississippi River from New Orleans.

3. Camp Moore State Commemorative Area (P.O. Box 15, Tangipahoa, LA 70465, 504-229-8200) is located in Tangipahoa Parish in the community of Tangipahoa on U.S. 51. Civil War cemetery and training camp.

4. Centenary State Commemorative Area (P.O. Box 574, Jackson, LA 70748, 504-634-7925) is located on East College Street in Jackson in East Feliciana Parish. Historic Centenary College and history of education in Louisiana.

5. Chemin-A-Haut State Park (Route 5, Box 617, Bastrop, LA 71220, 318-281-5805) is located east of LA 139, ten miles north of Bastrop.

6. Chicot State Park (Route 3, Box 494, Ville Platte, La 70586, 318-363-2503) is located in north Evangeline Parish, six miles north of Ville Platte on LA 3042.

7. Cypremort Point State Park (Star Route B, Box 428AA, Franklin, LA 70538, 318-867-4510) is located 24 miles south of Jeanerette off LA 319 in Iberia and St. Mary Parishes.

8. Earl K. Long State Commemorative Area (Route 2, Many, LA 71449, 318-256-5480) is located in the city of Winnfield. Memorial to three-term Governor.

9. Edward Douglas White State Commemorative Area (2311 Highway 1, Thibodaux, LA 70301, 504-447-3473) is located five miles north of Thibodaux in Lafourche Parish on LA 1. Homestead of the Chief Justice of the U.S. Supreme Court.

10. Fairview-Riverside State Park (P.O. Box 97, Madisonville, LA 70447, 504-845-3318) is located two miles east of Madisonville in St. Tammany Parish on LA 22.

11. Fontainebleau State Park (P.O. Box 152, Mandeville, LA 70448, 504-626-8052) is located southeast of Mandeville in St. Tammany Parish on U.S. 190.

12. Fort Jesup State Commemorative Area (Route 2, Many, LA 71449, 318-256-5480) is located on LA 6. formerly the original El Camino Real. Site of fort commanded by Zachary Taylor in mid 1800's.

13. Fort Pike State Commemorative Area (Route 6, Box 194, New Orleans, LA 70129, 504-662-5703) is located adjacent to the Old Spanish Trail (U.S. 90) in eastern New Orleans. Fort constructed after War of 1812 to defend navigational channels leading into New Orleans.

14. Fort St. Jean Baptiste State Commemorative Area (P.O. Box 1127, Natchitoches, LA 71458, 318-357-0001) is located in downtown Natchitoches, oldest town in the Louisiana Purchase. Reconstructed fort as it existed in 1730's during French occupation.

15. Grand Island East State Park (P.O. Box 741, Grand Isle, LA 70358, 504-787-2559) is located on the east end of Grand Isle on LA 1 in Jefferson Parish.

16. Jackson Confederate State Commemorative Area (P.O. Box 574, Jackson, LA 70748, 504-634-7925) is located adjacent to Centenary SCA in the Town of Jackson in East Feliciana Parish. Civil War cemetery.

17. Lake Bistineau State Park (P.O. Box 7, Doyline, LA 71023, 318-745-3503) is located east of LA 163 in Webster Parish, near Doyline.

18. Lake Bruin State Park (Route 1, Box 183, St. Joseph, LA 71366, 318-766-3530) is located east of U.S. 65 near St. Joseph in Tensas Parish.

19. Lake Claiborne State Park (P.O. Box 246, Homer, LA 71040, 318-927-2976) is located in Claiborne Parish on LA 146, just seven miles southeast of Homer.

20. Locust Grove State Commemorative Area (P.O. Box 546, St. Francisville, LA 70775, 504-635-3739) is located northeast of St. Francisville in West Feliciana Parish off U.S. 61. Memorial cemetery.

21. Longfellow-Evangeline State Commemorative Area (1200 N. Main Street, St. Martinville, LA 70582, 318-394-3754) is located in St. Martinville along the banks of Bayou Teche. Cajun culture; 19th century French plantation house.

22. Los Adaes State Commemorative Area (P.O. Box 248, Robeline, LA 71469, 318-472-9449) is located on LA 6, east of Robeline in Natchitoches Parish. Archaeological site; location of Spanish fort originally built in 1721.

23. Louisiana State Arboretum (Route 3, Box 489, Ville Platte, LA 70586, 318-363-6287) is a State Preservation Area located on LA 3042, approximately eight miles north of Ville Platte and a mile and a half from the main entrance to Chicot State Park in Evangeline Parish. Natural history education, nature trails on 600 acre preserve.

24. Mansfield State Commemorative Area (Route 2, Box 459, Mansfield, LA 71052, 318-872-1474) is located four miles south of the town of Mansfield on LA Hwy. 175. Site of significant Civil War battle.

25. Marksville State Commemorative Area (700 Allen Street, Marksville, LA 71351, 318-253-9546) is located adjacent to the town of Marksville, east of LA 1 and LA 452. Archaeological site; location of Indian culture and mounds dating from 1 A.D. to 400 A.D.

26. Old Arsenal State Commemorative Area (P.O. Box 44121, Baton Rouge, LA 70804, 504-342-5097) is located on the new State Capitol grounds in Baton Rouge. Military arsenal built in 1830's; history of Louisiana under ten flags.

27. Plaquemine Locks State Commemorative Area (P.O. Box 107, 208 Main Street, Plaquemine, LA 70764, 504-687-8159) is located in downtown Plaquemine about 15 miles south of Baton Rouge. Lock structure and lockhouse built in 1909; interprets history of the Mississippi River and its boat traffic.

28. Port Hudson State Commemorative Area (Route 1, Box 196, Zachary, LA 70791, 504-654-3775) is located on U.S. Highway 61, 14 miles north of Baton Rouge. Site of significant Civil War battle.

29. Poverty Point State Commemorative Area (HC 60, Box 208A, Epps, LA 71237, 318-926-5492) is located on LA 577, north of Epps in West Carroll Parish. Archaeological site; location of Indian culture and mounds dating from 1700 B.C. to 700 B.C.

30. Rebel State Commemorative Area (P.O. Box 127, Marthaville, LA 71450, 318-472-6255) is located in Natchitoches Parish, three miles north of Marthaville off LA 1221. Louisiana country music museum.

31. St. Bernard State Park (P.O. Box 534, Violet, LA 70092, 504-682-2101) is located 18 miles southeast of New Orleans on LA 39 in St. Bernard Parish.

32. Sam Houston Jones State Park (Route 4, Box 294, Lake Charles, LA 70601, 318-855-2665) is located 12 miles north of Lake Charles on LA 378 in Calcasieu Parish.

33. Winter Quarters State Commemorative Area (Route 1, Box 91, Newellton, LA 71357, 318-467-5439) is located three miles southeast of Newellton on LA 608 in Tensas Parish. 19th century plantation house used as headquarters by General Grant during siege of Vicksburg.

34. Lake Fausse Pointe State Park (Route 5, Box 5648, St. Martinville, LA 70582, 318-229-4764) is located off the West Atchafalaya protection levee road approximately 25 miles east of New Iberia.

35. North Toledo Bend State Park (P.O. Box 56, Zwolle, LA 71486, 318-645-4715) is located approximately 5 miles southwest of Zwolle off LA 3229.

Jean Lafitte National Historical Park

The Jean Lafitte National Historical Park was established by Congress in 1978 as a new kind of "cluster park" for the 23-parish area of the Mississippi River delta. It is part of the National Park Service, financed entirely by the federal government. The park was established to preserve and develop the extraordinary history and terrain of the delta region.

The park includes both historical sites and sites of natural or archeological importance.

Chalmette Battlefield (La. 46 east of New Orleans) is the site of the Battle of New Orleans. The installation includes the Chalmette National Cemetery and a visitor center. The Beauregard Plantation house is being refurbished to serve as an exhibition hall.

Islenos Museum, located in St. Bernard Parish, is housed in an antebellum cottage. The exhibits tell the story of Spanish immigrants from the Canary Islands who came to Louisiana in the eighteenth century.

The French Quarter of New Orleans is a part of Lafitte National Historical Park. Park rangers conduct four different walking tours daily. A visitor center in the French Market features a folklife exhibit. Live concerts in the French Quarter and a series of brass band concerts in Armstrong Park take place on Sunday afternoons.

Barataria Unit (La. 45 south of New Orleans) includes 8,600 acres of wetlands with many kinds of wildlife. Hiking trails, both guided and self-guided, help visitors see the Louisiana swamp.

CAMPING

LEGEND:
Swimming:
P – Pool Available
B – Beach
● – Other Facilities Available

Boating:
R – Rental Boats Available
B – Boat Ramp Available
● – Boating Facility Nearby

Picnicking:
S – Picnic Shelter Available
B – Bar-B-Q Pits & Tables Available
● – No Facility, But Picnicking Is Allowed

Other Categories:
● – Facilities Available

	Trailer Sites	Tent Sites	Cabins or Lodge	Drinking Water	Electric Hookups	Sewer Hookups	Water Hookups	Showers	Dump Station	Swimming	Fishing	Hunting	Boating	Picnicking	Trails
Lake Claiborne State Park	●	●		●	●		●	●	●	B	●		RB	SB	
Lake Bistineau State Park	●	●	●	●	●		●	●	●	B	●		RB	B	●
Caney Lakes Recreation Area	●	●		●			●	●	B	●	●		B	B	●
Corney Lake Recreation Area	●	●		●						●	●		B	B	
Bayou Bodcau Dam Recreation Area	●		●						●	●	B		B	SB	
Chemin-A-Haut State Park	●	●	●	●	●		●	●	●	P	●		R	SB	●
Lake Bruin State Park	●	●		●	●		●	●	●	B	●		RB	SB	
Bucktail Camp Recreation Area	●	●									●				
Turkey Trot Camp	●	●									●				
Chicot State Park	●	●	●	●	●		●	●	●	P	●		RB	SB	●
Stuart Lake Recreation Area	●	●		●				B	●	●	●		B	●	
Valentine Lake Recreation Area	●	●		●				B	●	●	●		SB	●	
Red Bluff Camp Recreation Area	●	●		●					●	●	●		●		
Kisatchie Bayou Recreation Area	●	●		●					●	●	●		●		
Gum Springs Recreation Area	●	●		●					●	●	●		B		
Evangeline Camp Recreation Area	●	●		●					●	●	●		●	●	
Dogwood Recreation Area	●	●		●					●	●	●		B		
Cloud Crossing Recreation Area	●	●		●					●	●	B		B		
Lotus Camp Recreation Area	●	●		●					●	●	●				
Fullerton Lake Recreation Area	●	●		●					●	●	●		B	B	●
Indian Creek Recreation Area	●	●		●			●	●	B	●	●		B	SB	
Sam Houston Jones State Park	●	●	●	●	●		●	●		●	●		RB	SB	●
Fairview Riverside State Park	●	●		●	●		●	●		●	●		●	SB	
St. Bernard State Park	●	●		●	●		●	●	P		●		●	SB	
Fontainebleau State Park	●	●	●	●	●		●	●	BP	●	●		●	SB	●
Grand Isle State Park	●	●		●			●	B	●	●	●		B	S	
Kincaid Recreation Area	●	●		●	●				●	●	●		B	B	●
Crooked Creek Recreation Area*	●	●		●	●		●	●		B	●		B	●	●
Cypress-Black Bayou Recreation Area*	●	●		●	●		●	●		B	●		B	●	●
Cottie Recreation Area*	●	●		●	●		●	●		B	●		B	●	
Acadiana Park*	●	●		●	●		●	●			●			●	●
Grand Bois Park*	●	●		●	●		●	●			●			●	●
Earl Williamson Park*	●	●		●	●		●	●			●		●	●	

*Denotes parish and municipal campgrounds; all other campground listings are state and federal areas.

MILEAGE TABLE

To find the distance between two towns, find the smaller number of the two towns followed by the larger number. The third figure is the distance in miles. Example: From Baton Rouge (No. 3) to New Orleans (No. 27) is 80 miles; in the table 3-27 — 80.

1. ALEXANDRIA	9. FERRIDAY	17. JACKSON, MISS.	25. NATCHITOCHES
2. BASTROP	10. GRAND ISLE	18. LAFAYETTE	26. NEW IBERIA
3. BATON ROUGE	11. GULFPORT, MISS.	19. LAKE CHARLES	27. NEW ORLEANS
4. BOGALUSA	12. HAMMOND	20. LEESVILLE	28. NEW ROADS
5. BUNKIE	13. HATTIESBURG, MISS.	21. LITTLE ROCK, ARK.	29. OAKDALE
6. COUSHATTA	14. HOMER	22. MINDEN	30. OPELOUSAS
7. DALLAS, TEX.	15. HOUMA	23. MONROE	31. RUSTON
8. DE RIDDER	16. HOUSTON, TEX.	24. MORGAN CITY	32. SHREVEPORT
			33. TALLULAH
			34. TEXARKANA, ARK.
			35. THIBODAUX
			36. WINNFIELD
			37. WINNSBORO

1-2 — 118	3-7 — 432	5-16 — 235	7-29 — 331	10-19 — 246	13-18 — 230	16-26 — 243	20-26 — 141	25-30 — 122
1-3 — 113	3-8 — 144	5-17 — 198	7-30 — 379	10-20 — 295	13-19 — 285	16-27 — 358	20-27 — 237	25-31 — 81
1-4 — 206	3-9 — 101	5-18 — 58	7-31 — 262	10-21 — 505	13-20 — 271	16-28 — 265	20-28 — 134	25-32 — 71
1-5 — 33	3-10 — 149	5-19 — 92	7-32 — 195	10-22 — 384	13-21 — 348	16-29 — 199	20-29 — 50	25-33 — 151
1-6 — 82	3-11 — 137	5-20 — 77	7-33 — 352	10-23 — 331	13-22 — 278	16-30 — 219	20-30 — 98	25-34 — 141
1-7 — 319	3-12 — 43	5-21 — 301	7-34 — 184	10-24 — 106	13-23 — 207	16-31 — 297	20-31 — 134	25-35 — 230
1-8 — 75	3-13 — 150	5-22 — 159	7-35 — 484	10-25 — 311	13-24 — 207	16-32 — 231	20-32 — 114	25-36 — 33
1-9 — 63	3-14 — 236	5-23 — 128	7-36 — 281	10-26 — 154	13-25 — 262	16-33 — 362	20-33 — 183	25-37 — 105
1-10 — 258	3-15 — 85	5-24 — 127	7-37 — 331	10-27 — 109	13-26 — 250	16-34 — 291	20-34 — 184	26-27 — 140
1-11 — 248	3-16 — 280	5-25 — 86	8-9 — 138	10-28 — 181	13-27 — 115	16-35 — 321	20-35 — 219	26-28 — 89
1-12 — 154	3-17 — 167	5-26 — 79	8-10 — 284	10-29 — 245	13-28 — 167	16-36 — 265	20-36 — 86	26-29 — 91
1-13 — 214	3-18 — 81	5-27 — 158	8-11 — 283	10-30 — 197	13-29 — 251	16-37 — 329	20-37 — 150	26-30 — 43
1-14 — 122	3-19 — 137	5-28 — 57	8-12 — 185	10-31 — 355	13-30 — 209	17-18 — 237	21-22 — 182	26-31 — 209
1-15 — 194	3-20 — 159	5-29 — 36	8-13 — 295	10-32 — 382	13-31 — 238	17-19 — 270	21-23 — 181	26-32 — 236
1-16 — 236	3-21 — 356	5-30 — 36	8-14 — 164	10-33 — 314	13-32 — 305	17-20 — 234	21-24 — 428	26-33 — 306
1-17 — 177	3-22 — 239	5-31 — 130	8-15 — 215	10-34 — 452	13-33 — 148	17-21 — 260	21-25 — 252	26-34 — 306
1-18 — 91	3-23 — 182	5-32 — 157	8-16 — 167	10-35 — 81	13-34 — 365	17-22 — 193	21-26 — 380	26-35 — 78
1-19 — 93	3-24 — 98	5-33 — 147	8-17 — 252	10-36 — 307	13-35 — 173	17-23 — 122	21-27 — 434	26-36 — 161
1-20 — 57	3-25 — 166	5-34 — 227	8-18 — 109	10-37 — 293	13-36 — 229	17-24 — 239	21-28 — 334	26-37 — 205
1-21 — 268	3-26 — 102	5-35 — 143	8-19 — 46	11-12 — 94	13-37 — 194	17-25 — 217	21-29 — 305	27-28 — 115
1-22 — 126	3-27 — 80	5-36 — 82	8-20 — 21	11-13 — 69	14-15 — 316	17-26 — 258	21-30 — 337	27-29 — 188
1-23 — 95	3-28 — 37	5-37 — 127	8-21 — 326	11-14 — 341	14-16 — 281	17-27 — 190	21-31 — 171	27-30 — 139
1-24 — 160	3-29 — 109	6-7 — 241	8-22 — 178	11-15 — 126	14-17 — 187	17-28 — 169	21-32 — 210	27-31 — 285
1-25 — 53	3-30 — 101	6-8 — 100	8-23 — 74	11-16 — 415	14-18 — 213	17-29 — 214	21-33 — 231	27-32 — 315
1-26 — 112	3-31 — 211	6-9 — 128	8-24 — 130	11-17 — 157	14-19 — 210	17-30 — 215	21-34 — 151	27-33 — 242
1-27 — 188	3-32 — 237	6-10 — 340	8-25 — 222	11-18 — 216	14-20 — 143	17-31 — 153	21-35 — 424	27-34 — 390
1-28 — 83	3-33 — 164	6-11 — 330	8-26 — 130	11-19 — 286	14-21 — 162	17-32 — 219	21-36 — 219	27-35 — 58
1-29 — 37	3-34 — 307	6-12 — 236	8-27 — 133	11-20 — 294	14-22 — 20	17-33 — 63	21-37 — 212	27-36 — 241
1-30 — 69	3-35 — 68	6-13 — 279	8-28 — 133	11-21 — 417	14-23 — 65	17-34 — 276	22-23 — 71	27-37 — 222
1-31 — 97	3-36 — 163	6-14 — 64	8-29 — 41	11-22 — 347	14-24 — 282	17-35 — 209	22-24 — 286	28-29 — 96
1-32 — 124	3-37 — 144	6-15 — 276	8-30 — 67	11-23 — 276	14-25 — 94	17-36 — 181	22-25 — 74	28-30 — 46
1-33 — 126	4-5 — 168	6-16 — 248	8-31 — 155	11-24 — 163	14-26 — 234	17-37 — 110	22-26 — 238	28-31 — 180
1-34 — 194	4-6 — 271	6-17 — 217	8-32 — 135	11-25 — 304	14-27 — 314	18-19 — 71	22-27 — 317	28-32 — 207
1-35 — 177	4-7 — 512	6-18 — 173	8-33 — 201	11-26 — 211	14-28 — 205	18-20 — 120	22-28 — 209	28-33 — 142
1-36 — 49	4-8 — 239	6-19 — 146	8-34 — 205	11-27 — 71	14-29 — 159	18-21 — 359	22-29 — 163	28-34 — 277
1-37 — 93	4-9 — 143	6-20 — 79	8-35 — 208	11-28 — 172	14-30 — 191	18-22 — 217	22-30 — 195	28-35 — 100
2-3 — 201	4-10 — 166	6-21 — 226	8-36 — 107	11-29 — 244	14-31 — 34	18-23 — 186	22-31 — 40	28-36 — 132
2-4 — 243	4-11 — 71	6-22 — 44	8-37 — 168	11-30 — 196	14-32 — 50	18-24 — 40	22-32 — 30	28-37 — 232
2-5 — 148	4-12 — 51	6-23 — 95	9-10 — 250	11-31 — 307	14-33 — 124	18-25 — 144	22-33 — 130	29-30 — 48
2-6 — 195	4-13 — 56	6-24 — 242	9-11 — 211	11-32 — 372	14-34 — 91	18-26 — 21	22-34 — 97	29-31 — 134
2-7 — 318	4-14 — 288	6-25 — 30	9-12 — 137	11-33 — 217	14-35 — 299	18-27 — 159	22-35 — 303	29-32 — 161
2-8 — 195	4-15 — 112	6-26 — 194	9-13 — 151	11-34 — 432	14-36 — 73	18-28 — 68	22-36 — 76	29-33 — 163
2-9 — 100	4-16 — 373	6-27 — 270	9-14 — 145	11-35 — 129	14-37 — 103	18-29 — 70	22-37 — 109	29-34 — 231
2-10 — 350	4-17 — 116	6-28 — 165	9-15 — 186	11-36 — 298	15-16 — 327	18-30 — 22	23-24 — 255	29-35 — 169
2-11 — 283	4-18 — 228	6-29 — 119	9-16 — 299	11-37 — 254	15-17 — 213	18-31 — 188	23-25 — 95	29-36 — 86
2-12 — 237	4-19 — 228	6-30 — 151	9-17 — 114	12-13 — 107	15-18 — 106	18-32 — 217	23-26 — 207	29-37 — 130
2-13 — 212	4-20 — 250	6-31 — 73	9-18 — 141	12-14 — 276	15-19 — 177	18-33 — 217	23-27 — 260	30-31 — 166
2-14 — 78	4-21 — 375	6-32 — 46	9-19 — 138	12-15 — 80	15-20 — 226	18-34 — 291	23-28 — 160	30-32 — 193
2-15 — 286	4-22 — 297	6-33 — 154	9-20 — 120	12-16 — 311	15-21 — 441	18-35 — 99	23-29 — 132	30-33 — 195
2-16 — 357	4-23 — 224	6-34 — 116	9-21 — 255	12-17 — 133	15-22 — 320	18-36 — 184	23-30 — 164	30-34 — 264
2-17 — 129	4-24 — 145	6-35 — 259	9-22 — 152	12-18 — 122	15-23 — 267	18-37 — 184	23-31 — 31	30-35 — 121
2-18 — 206	4-25 — 254	6-36 — 50	9-23 — 61	12-19 — 178	15-24 — 37	19-20 — 69	23-32 — 98	30-36 — 118
2-19 — 211	4-26 — 197	6-37 — 122	9-24 — 199	12-20 — 200	15-25 — 247	19-21 — 361	23-33 — 59	30-37 — 162
2-20 — 174	4-27 — 73	7-8 — 280	9-25 — 111	12-21 — 393	15-26 — 85	19-22 — 190	23-34 — 156	31-32 — 66
2-21 — 155	4-28 — 111	7-9 — 369	9-26 — 162	12-22 — 280	15-27 — 55	19-23 — 188	23-35 — 250	31-33 — 90
2-22 — 97	4-29 — 200	7-10 — 560	9-27 — 177	12-23 — 218	15-28 — 117	19-24 — 140	23-36 — 62	31-34 — 274
2-23 — 26	4-30 — 152	7-11 — 569	9-28 — 79	12-24 — 106	15-29 — 173	19-25 — 120	23-37 — 38	31-35 — 69
2-24 — 195	4-31 — 255	7-12 — 473	9-29 — 119	12-25 — 208	15-30 — 128	19-26 — 92	24-25 — 213	31-36 — 48
2-25 — 121	4-32 — 317	7-13 — 500	9-30 — 119	12-26 — 143	15-31 — 291	19-27 — 215	24-26 — 48	31-37 — 69
2-26 — 227	4-33 — 180	7-14 — 245	9-31 — 72	12-27 — 62	15-32 — 332	19-28 — 122	24-27 — 92	32-33 — 156
2-27 — 279	4-34 — 379	7-15 — 491	9-32 — 174	12-28 — 78	15-33 — 249	19-29 — 56	24-28 — 130	32-34 — 70
2-28 — 179	4-35 — 115	7-16 — 240	9-33 — 112	12-29 — 150	15-34 — 388	19-30 — 75	24-29 — 139	32-35 — 311
2-29 — 155	4-36 — 221	7-17 — 414	9-34 — 236	12-30 — 102	15-35 — 17	19-31 — 190	24-30 — 91	32-36 — 86
2-30 — 187	4-37 — 186	7-18 — 385	9-35 — 169	12-31 — 249	15-36 — 247	19-32 — 181	24-31 — 257	32-37 — 181
2-31 — 57	5-6 — 115	7-19 — 314	9-36 — 78	12-32 — 279	15-37 — 229	19-33 — 219	24-32 — 284	33-34 — 215
2-32 — 123	5-7 — 352	7-20 — 281	9-37 — 41	12-33 — 200	16-17 — 413	19-34 — 262	24-33 — 262	33-35 — 232
2-33 — 66	5-8 — 77	7-21 — 335	10-11 — 180	12-34 — 349	16-18 — 222	19-35 — 170	24-34 — 354	33-36 — 118
2-34 — 169	5-9 — 84	7-22 — 225	10-12 — 134	12-35 — 76	16-19 — 171	19-36 — 142	24-35 — 30	33-37 — 47
2-35 — 269	5-10 — 224	7-23 — 293	10-13 — 224	12-36 — 204	16-20 — 184	19-37 — 186	24-36 — 209	34-35 — 371
2-36 — 84	5-11 — 215	7-24 — 454	10-14 — 380	12-37 — 180	16-21 — 441	20-21 — 305	24-37 — 242	34-36 — 156
2-37 — 57	5-12 — 121	7-25 — 263	10-15 — 69	13-14 — 272	16-22 — 261	20-22 — 123	25-26 — 165	34-37 — 194
3-4 — 95	5-13 — 223	7-26 — 406	10-16 — 397	13-15 — 170	16-23 — 289	20-23 — 305	25-27 — 244	35-36 — 210
3-5 — 80	5-14 — 155	7-27 — 510	10-17 — 267	13-16 — 429	16-24 — 291	20-24 — 189	25-28 — 136	35-37 — 212
3-6 — 195	5-15 — 160	7-28 — 402	10-18 — 175	13-17 — 88	16-25 — 232	20-25 — 53	25-29 — 91	36-37 — 72

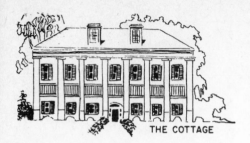

THE COTTAGE

LOUISIANA PURCHASE GARDENS AND ZOO

The Louisiana Purchase Gardens and Zoo, commemorating the fifteen states of the original Louisiana Purchase Territory, is located in Monroe's Bernstein Park.

Features of the gardens area include: a man-made canal serving as a replica of the Mississippi River, with flags and exhibits from territorial states positioned geographically along the waterway; two flat-bottomed boats that ply the canal carrying passengers for amusement rides; an oldtime coal-burning steam engine and four railroad cars to carry visitors; an exact replica of an old stagecoach for amusement rides; an old-fashioned western wagon drawn by Belgian horses for passenger rides; a well-landscaped garden containing varieties of flowers and shrubs from all over the Louisiana Purchase Territory region; and a complete modern zoo.

Future plans call for a small replica of an old paddlewheeler on which tourists will cruise the river replica.

HISTORY FOR RENT

The National Trust for Historic Preservation, which operates ten historic sites across the nation, including one in Louisiana, will now rent one of its famous mansions or estates for a luncheon, tea or similar affair. Among the Trust's properties are: Shadows-on-the-Teche, an old Southern mansion in New Iberia, Louisiana; Lyndhurst, a 130-year-old Gothic castle on New York's Hudson River; Decatur House and President Wilson's town house in Washington, D.C.; and the Belle Grove estate in Middletown, Virginia. Fees vary with the property and the services requested.

Information may be obtained from the National Trust For Historic Preservation, Public Affairs Department, 740 Jackson Place, N.W., Washington, D.C. 20006.

Louisiana Words and Sayings

Andouille and Boudin (ahn-<u>doo</u>-ee and <u>boo</u>-dan) — two types of Cajun sausage. Andouille is made with pork, boudin with pork and rice. Sociologists recognize two major categories of Cajuns — the "River (or andouille) Cajuns" and the "Bayou (or boudin) Cajuns."

Bayou (<u>by</u>-you, bia or <u>by</u>-yo) — a sluggish stream, bigger than a creek and smaller than a river.

Beignet (bin-<u>yay</u>) — a fritter, or a strangely shaped doughnut without a hole. A New Orleans favorite.

Bourré (<u>boo</u>-ray) — popular Cajun card game, sometimes called "Cajun bridge."

Café noir and **café-au-lait** (café-o-lay) — black coffee and coffee with milk or cream.

C'est la vie (say la vee) — "That's life."

Comme ci, comme ca (come-<u>see</u>, come-<u>sah</u>) — so-so

* **Fais-do-do** (fay-doh-doh) — a type of street dance derived from European religious festivals. Originally "fête de Dieu," festival of God.

Gumbo — thick, savory soup with chicken, seafood, sausage or wild game.

Joie de vivre (zhwah duh viv-re) — "The joy of living," the attitude of our citizens which permeates our lifestyle.

Laissez les bons temps rouler (lay-zay lay bawn tawn roulay) — "Let the good times roll," the motto of most Louisianians.

Pirogue (<u>pee</u>-rogue) — Cajun canoe, originally made from a dug-out cypress log.

Poo-yie! — indicates surprised dismay, like "Oh, no!"

Roux (roo) — basic ingredient of many Louisiana recipes. Essentially, seasoned flour browned in a skillet.

* **Veiller** (vay-yay) — to sit up and visit at night.

* **Zydeco** (zod-e-coh) — lively variant of Cajun music, derived from the word haricot, French for string bean.

* * **Il n'y a pas de sauce qui égale l'appétit** — There is no sauce like appetite.

* * **La vie est à moitié finie avant que l'on sache en quoi elle consiste** — Life is half spent before one knows what life is.

* * **Mieux vaut un bon dîner qu'un beau manteau** — Better a good dinner than a fine coat.

* * **Mots doux n'égratignent pas la langue** — Soft words don't scratch the tongue.

* * **Une bonne conscience fait un bon oreiller** — A clear conscience is a good pillow.

  * From *THE LOUISIANA EXPERIENCE* by Mary Alice Fontenot and Julie Landry.
  * * From *LOUISIANA KEEPSAKE*, 1986, by Lillie Petit Gallagher.

Source: State Parks Commission & Other Tourist Attractions

Cheverette comes from French crevette, meaning shrimp.

LOUISIANA PLANTATIONS

(open to the public)

ASHLAND-BELLE HELENE Near Darrow. Classic temple of square columns, eight to a side, this home was built in 1841 with James Gallier as its distinguished architect. On River Road, La. 75 between Geismar and Darrow. Open 9-4 daily.*

ASPHODEL Near Jackson. Called "Jewel of Louisiana" by author Lyle Saxon, this restored Greek Revival mansion was used in filming "The Long Hot Summer." La. 68, north off U.S. 61, 25 mi. north of Baton Rouge. Asphodel Mansion open 10-4 Mon.-Fri.; closed holidays.* Inn, guesthouse and giftshop. Meals at Inn served every day except Christmas. Call (504) 654-5820 for reservations.

BEAUREGARD HOUSE New Orleans. Built 1827, this was the birthplace of famous chess champion Paul Morphy in 1837, and home of CSA Gen. P.G.T. Beauregard during and after Civil War. Later home of Louisiana writer Frances P. Keyes. 113 Chartres St. 10-4 daily.*

BEAUREGARD HOUSE MUSEUM Chalmette. This home is located in the Chalmette National Historical Park, the site of the Battle of New Orleans. The house with Doric columns and wide galleries contains exhibits and an audio-visual presentation on the battle. On La. 46 east of New Orleans. Open 8-5 Sept.-May and 8-6 June-Aug. Closed Christmas and Mardi Gras.

CATALPA Near St. Francisville. Victorian cottage, constructed on one of Louisiana's earliest homesites, remains in the family of the original owners. U.S. 61, five mi. north of St. Francisville. Open daily 9-5; 30-acre gardens. By appointment Dec.-Jan.*

THE COTTAGE Near St. Francisville. This home, actually a series of buildings, was erected from 1795 to 1859. Original furniture and 15 interesting plantation outbuildings. U.S. 61, five mi. north of St. Francisville. Giftshop. Open daily 9-5 except Christmas. Overnight guests are served plantation breakfasts. Call (504) 635-3674 for reservations.*

DESTREHAN MANOR Near St. Rose. Built 1787-90, this plantation home features huge live oaks and fine antiques. Giftshop. On La. 48, five mi. north of St. Rose. Open 10-4 daily.

EDWARD DOUGLASS WHITE MEMORIAL Near Thibodaux. Built 1790, this splendid example of Louisiana's earliest houses—the raised cottage—was home of Chief Justice White. La. 1, six mi. north of Thibodaux. Children under 12 free. Museum open weekdays 9-5, Sun. 1-5, closed Mon. Open holidays except Christmas and New Year's Day.*

THE 1850 HOUSE New Orleans. This townhouse is located in the historic Pontalba Apartments built on Jackson Square in 1849. Contains two stories of fine period furniture. 525 St. Ann St. Tues.-Sun. 10-6.*

GALLIER HOUSE New Orleans. This complex of three buildings, constructed 1857, was home of renowned architect James Gallier. Italianate structures bear the original colors Gallier used and furnishings match items the family owned. One building is an exhibition hall with Gallier's architectural drawings. 1118-32 Royal St. Open 10-4:30 Tues.-Sat.*

GARDEN DISTRICT New Orleans. Greek Revival and mid-Victorian architectural styles of the 1800's are a feature of this residential area built by wealthy Anglo-Saxon citizens. Many homes feature beautiful gardens and superb landscaping. The area stretches from Jackson Ave. to Louisiana Ave. and from Prytania St. to Magazine St. Though these homes are private, they are a superb tour.

HERMANN-GRIMA HOUSE New Orleans. Facade of this house, built 1831, resembles an Eastern seaboard home rather than its French-Spanish counterparts in the area. The complex includes a three-story mansion, garconniere, open-hearth kitchen, two patios and a stable. 820 St. Louis St. Open 10-4 Mon.-Sat.*

HERMITAGE Near Darrow. Built 1812 by Michel Doradou Bringier and named after Andrew Jackson's house in Tennessee. Jackson once visited here in early 19th century. La. 942, one-and-a-half mi. below Darrow. Open by appointment. Call (504) 891-8493.*

HOUMAS HOUSE Near Burnside. Built by John Smith Preston in 1840. In 1857 it was sold to John Burnside who became America's prime sugar planter. Inside are furnishings and antiques of early Louisiana craftsmanship. On La. 942 off La. 44, two mi. below Burnside. Open 10-5 daily Feb.-Oct. and 10-4 Nov.-Jan. Closed Christmas. Call (504) 473-7841 for group tours.*

LEJEUNE New Roads. Built circa 1820, LeJeune features columned galleries and a large collection of antiques. 507 E. Main St. Open by appointment. Call (504)638-9173.*

(Note: For more information, refer to the **Pelican Guide to Plantation Homes of Louisiana**)

*Nominal Entrance Fee.

MADEWOOD Near Napoleonville. More than 600,000 bricks went into the building of this classic, restored Greek Revival home. The house, grounds, carriage house and family cemetery are now on tour. La. 308 south of Napoleonville. Open daily 10-5. Closed Thanksgiving, Christmas.*

MAGNOLIA LANE Near New Orleans. Of West Indies design, this home was built in 1784. Originally known as Fortier Plantation, it raised the South's first strawberries and was first major nursery and fruit cultivation farm in New Orleans area. West Bank, River Road, La. 18 one mi. north of Huey Long Bridge. Open by appointment daily 9-5, closed Mon. and Tues. Call (504) 347-1323.*

MAGNOLIA MOUND Baton Rouge. Built in 1700s. Eighty-foot gallery, outstanding interior woodwork and period furniture. Giftshop. 2161 Nicholson Dr. Open Tues.-Sat. 10-4, Sun. 1-4.*

MERIEULT HOUSE New Orleans. After New Orleans' great fire of 1794, this was one of the city's few surviving principal buildings. Inside is a historic collection of paintings, prints and artifacts. 533 Royal St. Open Tues.-Sat. 10-4:30.*

MIL BANK Jackson. This classic Greek structure, with its imposing Doric columns on front and rear galleries, has served alternately as hotel, bank and private home. Built 1825-37. Open 10-4 Fri. and Sat., 11-4 Sun. Closed Dec. and Jan. On Bank St., one block off La. 10.*

THE MYRTLES St. Francisville. Built circa 1795, this home has 110-foot gallery with iron grillwork, many rare antiques and intricate interior plasterwork. On U.S. 61. Overnight accommodations. Open daily 9-5.*

OAK ALLEY Near Vacheri. Started in 1830, completed 1839 to crown an older double row of magnificent live oaks, this mansion is graced by 28 Doric Columns each 8 ft. in circumference. Trees are 15 to 29 ft. in circumference and branches interlace to form a canopy from road to house. La. 18, three miles west of Vacherie. Open for tours 9-5:30 Mar.-Oct.; 9-5 Nov.-Feb. Closed New Year's, Thanksgiving, Christmas.*

OAKLEY Near St. Francisville. Built 1799, where John James Audubon first became acquainted with Feliciana Country wildlife. Home and grounds are the site of Audubon Memorial State Park. La. 965 off U.S. 61 south of St. Francisville. Giftshop. Open Mon.-Sat. 9-4:45. Sun. 1-4:45 except Christmas and New Year's Day. Children under 12 free.*

PARLANGE Near New Roads. One of the loveliest homes along False River. Built 1750 by Marquis de Ternant and now designated an historic building by the U.S. Dept. of Interior. Parlange is a classic example of raised construction. Present owners are descendants of original builder. La. 1 southwest of New Roads. Daily 9-5; no children under 12.*

POTTS HOUSE Baton Rouge. Built in 1850 as an example of his work by master brickmason Nelson Potts, who built many of the city's homes and buildings of that era. 831 North St. (get tickets at Frame Shop, 801 North St.). Call (504)344-2174 for group tours. Open 10-3, Tues.-Sat.*

ROSEDOWN Near St. Francisville. A magnificent restoration makes this one of America's most distinguished showplaces. The 30-acre garden, inspired by Versailles, contains many old rare Oriental plants and statuary. La. 10 at St. Francisville. Open March-Oct. 9-5, Nov.-Feb. 10-4. House and Garden Tour $4. Children under 12, $2.

SAN FRANCISCO Near Reserve. Gem of the Steamboat Gothic era, this River Road masterpiece was built in 1849. There are 22 rooms furnished with 18th century antiques. The house teems with scrolls, fluted pillars, carved grillwork. La. 44, west of Reserve. Open daily 10-4.*

TEZCUCO Near Burnside. Built 1855, this raised cottage has ironlace side galleries and circular driveway beneath century-old live oaks and magnolias. Elegant late antebellum interior furnishings include collections of four family generations. Giftshop. La. 44, two mi. below Burnside. 10-5 Mar.-Oct., 10-4 Nov.-Feb. Closed New Year's, Thanksgiving, Christmas. Call (504) 473-4250 for group tours.*

TCHOUPITOULAS PLANTATION RESTAURANT Near New Orleans. This 19th century plantation, now a restaurant, features Creole cooking for luncheon and dinner. La. 18, three mi. west of Huey P. Long Bridge. Open weekdays 11:30-3 and 5:30-9:30; Sat. 5:30-9:30; Sun. noon-9. Call (504) 776-1277 for reservations.

*Nominal Entrance Fee

ACADIAN HOUSE MUSEUM   St. Martinville. The unique charm of Louisiana's Acadiana culture is beautifully expressed in this 1765 home on the grounds of Longfellow-Evangeline State Park. La. 31 north of St. Martinville. Open daily 9-5. Closed Christmas, New Year's, Thanksgiving.*

ACADIAN VILLAGE   Lafayette. Tropical gardens and many antebellum Cajun buildings are features of this attraction. Ridge Road, west of U.S. 167. 10-5 daily.*

ALBANIA MANSION   Near Jeanerette. Begun 1837, completed 1842, this immense home includes an incredible unsupported spiral stairway. Its unique Doll Room contains a renowned collection. Overnight lodging available. La. 182, one-half mi. east of Jeanerette. Weekdays 9:30-4:30. Sun. 1:30-4:30. Call (318)276-4816.*

ARLINGTON   Near Washington. Built 1829 by Major Amos Webb, this large restored home of red brick boasts three stories and an interesting underground cellar. La. 103 east of Washington. Open daily 10-5.*

BAYOU FOLK MUSEUM   Cloutierville. This charming home, built in the early 1800's, is a privately owned museum. Long the residence of the avant-garde 19th century writer, Kate Chopin, it contains an extensive collection of period pieces, artifacts and memorabilia of the area. Off La. 1. 13 five mi. southwest of Crowley. Open weekdays; by appointment on weekends. Closed Jan., Feb., and holidays. Call (318) 783-3096.*

BLUE ROSE MUSEUM   Near Crowley. More than 100 years old, this Acadian cottage was moved from Youngsville. Built of cypress, it has original pegged construction, cypress paneling, handmade bricks, and mud-and-moss walls. Collections of fine china, cut glass, silver and antique furniture are on display. Also on the property and open for tours is the antebellum Wright-Andreus Home. Off La. 13 five mi. southwest of Crowley. Open weekdays; by appointment on weekends. Closed Jan., Feb., and holidays. Call (318) 783-3096.*

CHRETIEN POINT   Near Sunset. Built in early 1800's by Hypolite Chretien. Reputedly a hangout for smugglers, including Lafitte and his lieutenants. Located approx. three mi. southwest of Sunset. Drive west on La. 182, south on La. 754 for 200 yds., then left on parish road for approximately two mi. Call (318) 662-3246 for information.*

DULCITO   Near New Iberia. Built in architectural style typical of Spanish period, this home dates to 1788. Used as field hospital during the Civil War. Off U.S. 90, on La. 182. six mi. west of New Iberia. Open by appointment only. Call (318) 369-3368.

FRANCES   Near Franklin. This home is over 160 years old. Antique, gift and interior design shop. U.S. 90, four mi. east of Franklin. Tues.-Sat. 9-5. Call (318) 828-5472.*

FRENCH HOUSE   Lafayette. This "Maison Acadienne Francaise" is open for tours by appointment. Call (318) 234-5424. 1511 Johnston St.

GREVEMBERG HOUSE   Franklin. Built in 1853, this home contains the St. Mary Parish Museum. Sterling Rd. Open 4:30-6:30 Tues. and Fri.; 2-6 Sat. and Sun.

HOMEPLACE   Beggs. This Louisiana country home built 1826 is constructed of cypress. Set in an oak grove near Wikoff Landing, one of the last steamboat landings in the state. At La. 182 and 10. Open 9-5 Mon.-Sat. For group tours call (318) 826-7558.*

JUSTINE   Near New Iberia. Now located 50 miles from its original site, this quaint cottage appears exactly as it did before it was shipped by barge on Bayou Teche from Centerville. Its oldest section was built in 1822. On La. 86, two mi. east of New Iberia. Open by appointment only. Call (318) 364-0973.*

KENT HOUSE   Alexandria. This raised cottage, constructed of plaster-covered mud-and-moss walls, was built about 1795. Newly restored. On La. 496 (Bayou Rapides Rd.), 1 block off McArthur Dr. Mon.-Sat. 9-5, Sun. 1-5.*

LAFAYETTE MUSEUM   Lafayette. Former home of Gov. Alexandre Mouton. Two famous Southern shrubs, sweet olive and magnolia fuscata, flank entrance walk. 1122 Lafayette St., across from Mt. Carmel School. Open Tues.-Sat. 9-5; Sun. 3-5. Closed Mon. and holidays.*

LAND'S END   Near Shreveport. Completed 1847, this two-and-a-half story Greek Revival home was built by a Confederate congressman and has many original furnishings. On Red Bluff Road, 17 mi. south of Shreveport, via Linwood Rd. and Linwood Extension. Open by appointment. Call (318) 925-0266.*

*Nominal Entrance Fee

LEMEE HOUSE Natchitoches. Built about 1830, this one-and-a-half story, brick home has a cradled roof mortised with wooden pegs in hand-hewn cypress logs. Its cellar is rare for this period. At 310 Jefferson St. Open by appointment. Call (318) 352-6472.

MAGNOLIA RIDGE Near Washington. Completed 1830, this superb mansion was originally known as Old Prescott House and, later, as Oakland Plantation. During Civil War it was headquarters for both Confederate and Federal forces. Six mi. north of Opelousas on La. 10 and just off La. 103, northwest of Washington. Open daily by appointment 9-5. Call (318) 826-3967.*

MELROSE Near Natchitoches. This is a complex of antebellum plantation structures including Yucca House (1796), Melrose (1830), the African House (18th century) and others. On Cane River (La. 494) south of Natchitoches. Noon-4 daily, closed Wed. (Mar.-Dec.), and Noon-3:30, Sat.-Sun. (Jan.-Feb.).*

OAKLAWN MANOR Near Franklin. Named for its magnificent live oaks said to have been growing when Columbus discovered America, this restored manor house is a white-pillared prototype of the Southern plantation. On Irish Bend Road, three mi. off U.S. 90 near Franklin. Open daily 10-4.*

ROQUE HOUSE Natchitoches. This house, more than a century old, is an example of pioneer Louisiana construction. It is built of cypress beams with bousillage, a mud-and-moss wall-filling. Now houses Cane River Art Gallery. On Cane River-Lake below Front St., near foot of Lafayette St. Open 9-4 Mon.-Fri.

SHADOWS-ON-THE-TECHE New Iberia. This house-museum is property of the National Trust for Historic Preservation. Erected 1831-1834, it contains accumulated treasures from four generations of a distinguished planter family. The gardens have been restored to new magnificence. At La. 182 and 14. Open daily 9-4:30. Closed New Year's, Thanksgiving, Christmas.*

WINTER QUARTERS Near Newellton. This 19-room house was built on one of the last Spanish land grants in Louisiana. A gallery with five large square columns fronts the house. Originally a three-room hunting cottage used as "winter quarters," it was taken over by Grant's troops during Civil War. La. 604, three mi. southwest of Newellton. Open daily 9-5.*

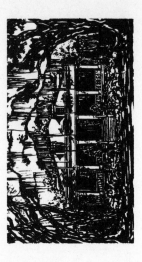

MAJOR LOUISIANA TOURIST SITES

Greater New Orleans

That never-ending festival feeling comes to life in romantic New Orleans. From the Old World charm of the Vieux Carré to the cosmopolitan air of New Orleans nightlife, from jazz bands and riverboat cruises down the Mississippi to candlelight dinners in world-famous restaurants, the Mardi Gras revelry lasts all year long in the "City That Care Forgot."

Attractions

Audubon Park, New Orleans, main entrance from St. Charles Avenue. Oak groves, winding lagoons, fountains and statues. The zoo features exotic wildlife including many rare and endangered species. The landscaped, 40-acre "batture" area (land between the levee and the river) offers a fine view of the Mississippi. The park also has an 18-hole golf course, tennis courts, picnic facilities, horseback riding, swimming pool, bike and roller skate rentals and miniature train. Admission to zoo only. (504) 861-2537.

Audubon Zoo, 6500 Magazine St., New Orleans, at Audubon Park. Features a Children's Village, the Mombasa Railway and the Louisiana Swamp Exhibit. Can be reached by riding the St. Charles Streetcar or taking special "Zoo Cruise" aboard the Cotton Blossom, as well as by bus or car. Open 9:30 a.m.-5 p.m. Mon-Fri, 9:30 a.m.-6 p.m. Sat-Sun and holidays (DST), 9:30 a.m. -5 p.m. Sat-Sun and holidays (CST). Admission. (504) 861-2537.

Bayou and Swamp Tours, in Greater New Orleans area. Tours vary greatly in content and length, and you are advised to inquire fully.

Bayou Cruise aboard the Lafitte Skiffs, Metairie. (504) 888-4882.
Cajun Bayou Cruise, New Orleans. (504) 891-0676.
Cypress Swamp Tours, New Orleans. (504) 899-2027.

Honey Island Swamp Tours, Inc., Slidell. Swamp trips, guided duck hunting and fishing trips, nature photography, environmental studies, birding trips, wildlife observation. (504) 641-1769.

Swamp Parade, New Orleans. (504) 568-0141.

Bon Voyage Tours, La. 1, Grand Isle. Daily tours departing from Bon Voyage Marina through Caminada Bay, Barataria Bay, Gulf of Mexico, and returns through Bayou Rigaud. Admission. (504) 787-3744 or (504) 787-3179.

Bucktown, on Lakeshore Dr. just off Old Hammond Hwy. This old lakefront village offers a cluster of excellent seafood restaurants and retailers, featuring seafood straight from Lake Pontchartrain and the Gulf. (504) 556-5014

City Park, bounded by City Park Ave, Wisner Blvd., Robert E. Lee Blvd., and Marconi Dr. New Orleans Picnic tables, lagoons for boating, golf courses, bike rentals, tennis courts, miniature train, horses, carnival rides, bandstand and Children's Storyland (featuring giant storybook characters in papier mache), across from tennis courts on Victory Drive. Open daily and most holidays. Free, but admission for activities. Also in the park are the famous old Duelling Oaks, where many an Orleanian died by the rules of the Code of Honor, "under the oaks at sunrise." (504) 482-4888.

Country Market and Mail Car Art Gallery, downtown Ponchatoula. Historic train depot in Ponchatoula originally built in 1895, remodeled in 1920. Handmade crafts, foods, antiques sold in depot. Art gallery has paintings in all media by local artists. Open 10 a.m.-5 p.m. Tues, Thurs, Sat. Closed Jan and Sep. (504) 386-9580.

Fair Grounds Racetrack, on Gentilly Blvd. (take Canal St. north toward Lake Pontchartrain and turn right on North Broad). Founded in 1872, this is the third-oldest track in America. Home of the Louisiana Derby. Admission. Thoroughbred racing and parimutuel wagering. For exact season (ordinarily mid-Nov through Apr) and post times, or to inquire about group rates or other special arrangements, call (504) 944-5515.

Jackson Barracks, 6400 St. Claude Avenue (La. 46), New Orleans. This series of fine old brick, columned structures was built in the 1830s to house troops, and it is now headquarters for the Louisiana National Guard. The old powder magazine now contains a museum of military history. Open 7:30 a.m.-3:30 p.m. Mon-Fri, closed state and federal holidays. Appointment. (504) 271-6262.

Jefferson Downs., take I-10 to Williams Blvd. Turn right toward Lake Pontchartrain, then left on Sunset Blvd. to Jefferson Downs, New Orleans. Thoroughbred racing and parimutuel wagering. Post time 7:15 p.m. Tue -Sat. (Apr through mid-Nov). Minors under 12 not admitted. 12-17 must be accompanied by adult. For exact season and other information, call (504) 466-8521.

Kliebert's Turtle and Alligator Tours, Inc., West Yellow Water Road near Hammond. Thousands of alligators and turtles are grown and marketed through this unique operation. All phases of production are explained, and the animals are seen in an extremely natural environment. Terrific bird-watching opportunities. Open noon-dark daily. Closed Nov.-March. Admission. (504) 345-3617.

The Lakefront, along Lakeshore Dr. Picnic tables, shelters, benches, swimming areas and the seawall are located along the shore of Lake Pontchartrain for picnicking and relaxation.

Lake Pontchartrain Causeway Bridge, Causeway Blvd., foot of Lake Pontchartrain. Connects Causeway Blvd. in Metairie with I-12 near Mandeville. Spanning 24 miles, the causeway is the longest over-water highway bridge in the world. Toll.

Longue Vue House and Gardens, 7 Bamboo Rd., New Orleans. The Greek Revival mansion is decorated with authentic furnishings and fine collections. Eight acres of picturesque gardens and fountains focus on the magnificent Spanish Court. There are changing exhibitions in the galleries of Longue Vue House and seasonal horticultural displays in the Gardens. Designated an Historic Landmark. Open 10 a.m.-4:30 p.m. Tue -Fri (last house tour 3:45 p.m.), and 1-5 p.m. Sat-Sun (last house tour 4:15 p.m.). Closed Mon and major holidays. Admission. (504) 488-5488.

Louisiana Nature and Science Center, parking in Joe Brown Park on Lake Forest Blvd.,

New Orleans. This nature center features multi-media programs, exhibits and nature trails through 80 wooded acres. Programs for all ages. A research library and an "environmental theater" are available. Open 9 a.m.-5 p.m. Tue-Fri, noon-5 p.m. Sat-Sun. Closed Mon Admission. Gift shop. (504) 246-9381.

Louisiana Superdome, Sugar Bowl Dr., New Orleans. Walk into tomorrow. Take a guided tour of the world's most magnificent public assembly facility. See the main arena, press box, ballrooms and private suites. Enjoy lunch in the beautiful Stadium Club. Hourly tours from 9 a.m.-4 p.m. daily. Enter from Poydras St. at Gate A, Mezzanine level. Admission. (504) 587-3810.

Mardi Gras World, 233 Newton St., Algiers, across Mississippi River from New Orleans. Artists work on Mardi Gras floats or props, depending on the work scheduled that particular day. Learn how floats and props are created. Gift shop. Group tours of at least 20 people only, call for reservations. Open 10 a.m.-6 p.m. Mon-Fri. Admission. (504) 362-8211.

St. Charles Avenue Streetcar Line, board a streetcar on Canal St. at Carondelet, on Carrollton Ave. at Claiborne, or anywhere along St. Charles Ave., for a memorable ride past the antebellum homes of the famous New Orleans Garden District. This is one of the last functional streetcar lines in the U.S. and it is listed on the National Register of Historic Places. Fare is 60 cents (correct change only). (504) 569-2700.

Sweetwater Riding Stables, Cooper Rd., Loranger. Horseback riding, scenic rides, overnight campouts, horses boarded, surrey and buggy rides, trail rides, hayrides, swimming pool, dining halls with antiques. Pavilion and dance hall. Open 9 a.m.-5 p.m. daily. Reservations. (504) 878-6853.

Tchoupitoulas Plantation Restaurant, 6535 River Rd., Waggaman. Built in 1812, restaurant is a fascinating mixture of Creole New Orleans history and a colorful river setting. Fine menu selections of seafood, fowl, veal, and steaks. Open 11:30 a.m.-3 p.m. and 5:30-9:30 p.m. Mon-Fri, 5:30-9:30 p.m. Sat and noon-9 p.m. Sun. Reservations. (504) 436-1277.

Top of the Mart, No. 2 Canal St., New Orleans, atop the International Trade Mart Building. On the 33rd floor, an incomparable revolving cocktail lounge orbits above "America's Most

Interesting City." Entertainment nightly. Free. One-drink minimum. (504) 522-9795.

Zemurray Gardens, near Hammond, from I-55 drive east on La. 442-40. From I-12 drive north on La. 445. Rustic pathways lead around a lake and through the 150 acres of these gardens, which feature azaleas, camellias, dogwoods and many other flowers. Picnic facilities. Open daylight hours daily Mar and Apr. Admission. (504) 878-9777 or (504) 878-6731.

Tourist Information Centers

State Tourist Center, I-10 Westbound near Slidell. Open 8:30 a.m.-5 p.m. daily. (504) 641-8775.

State Tourist Center, I-55 Southbound near Kentwood. Open 8:30 a.m.-5 p.m. daily. (504) 229-8338.

State Tourist Center, I-59 Southbound near Pearl River. Open 8:30 a.m.-5 p.m. daily. (504) 643-4646.

State Tourist Center, 529 St. Ann St., New Orleans French Quarter facing Jackson Square. Open 10 a.m.-6 p.m. daily. (504) 568-5661

Grand Isle Tourist Commission, on La. 1 in Grand Isle. Open 8 a.m.-5 p.m. Mon-Fri. (504) 787-3700.

Jefferson Parish Tourist Information Center, I-10 at Loyola Drive, Kenner, located in a manufactured house. Open 8 a.m.-7 p.m. daily. (504) 468-8227.

New Orleans Tourist and Convention Commission, 1520 Sugar Bowl Dr. Open 8:30 a.m.-5 p.m. Mon-Fri. (504) 566-5014, or (information only) (504) 566-5031.

St. Tammany Parish Tourist and Convention Commission, 2020 First St., Slidell. Open 8:30 a.m.-4:30 p.m. Mon-Fri. (504) 649-0730.

FRENCH QUARTER

The French Quarter is bounded by Iberville St., Esplanade Ave., Rampart St. and the Mississippi River. The famous French Quarter or Vieux Carré (Old Square) was laid out in a grid pattern in 1721 and remains one of the nation's greatest clusters of colonial and antebellum structures.

1. Archbishop Antoine Blanc Memorial, corner of Chartres and Ursuline streets. This convent building, construction of which began in 1745, was occupied by Ursuline nuns until 1824 and is the oldest building on record in the entire Mississippi Valley. It was later a boys' school, temporary home of the State Legislature, the Archbishop's palace and a presbytere. The old structure has recently been flawlessly restored. Archives (church records from 1730-1900) occupy the second floor. Tours at 2 p.m. Wed only. Donations. (504) 529-2001. Arrangements for large groups Mon-Fri can be made through Memorial Tours, (504) 561-0008.

2. Bank of Louisiana Building, 334 Royal St. Engaged Doric columns support a heavy entablature above the portico entrance of this old building, built in 1826.

3. Beauregard-Keyes House, 1113 Chartres St., Romantic, fascinating Louisiana raised cottage. Greek Revival style, built in 1826 by Joseph LeCarpentier. Listed on the National Register of Historic Places. Courtyard and restored French formal garden. Once the home of Confederate Gen. P.G.T. Beauregard and also the residence of famous novelist Frances Parkinson Keyes. Costumed docents, guided tours daily. Open 10 a.m.-3 p.m. daily. Closed Sun. Gift shop. Admission. (504) 523-7257.

4. The Cabildo, 700 block of Chartres St., facing Jackson Square. Built 1795-99 to replace an older cabildo, this handsome colonial building has been the seat of Louisiana territorial government for France, Spain, the Confederacy and the United States. It was in a second-floor room of this building that France and the U.S. concluded the Louisiana Purchase transaction in 1803. Now a property of the Louisiana State Museum, the Cabildo serves as a museum of artifacts from Louisiana, New Orleans and

Mississippi River history, as well as of such special items as the death mask of Napoleon Bonaparte. Gift shop. Open 10 a.m.-6 p.m. Tue-Sun. Admission. (504) 568-6968.

5. Cathedral of St. Louis King of France,
on Chartres St. facing Jackson Square. Built in 1794 and remodeled in 1850, St. Louis Cathedral (a minor basilica) is the oldest active cathedral in the United States. Free guided tours (donations accepted) are offered 9 a.m.-5 p.m. Mon-Sat, and 1-5 p.m. Sun. Sunday Masses are at 6:30, 8, 9, 10 and 11 a.m., noon and 6 p.m. (504) 525-9585.

6. Contemporary Arts Center, 900 Camp.
Three exhibition galleries and two theaters. Open noon-5 p.m. Tue-Sun. Admission. (504) 523-1216.

7. Customs House (U.S.), 423 Canal St.
Construction of the Customs House began in 1848, and the young Army engineer in charge of construction was P.G.T. Beauregard. The handsome old building still contains some Customs Service offices and other federal offices, and it was used as headquarters by Gen. Butler during Union occupation after 1862. Free. Open 9 a.m.-5 p.m. Mon-Fri.

8. Fortier House and Gallery, 835 Chartres
St. Built in 1803 for Francisco Bouligny (who founded the Louisiana city of New Iberia, and fought with Spanish Governor Galvez in the Revolutionary War battles of Manchac and Baton Rouge in 1779), this home earned its most recent fame for serving as the home of detective James Longstreet in the recent pilot film and series called "Longstreet," which starred James Franciscus. Visit the art gallery (free) or tour the home (nominal admission) to see fine antiques, courtyard, old kitchen and slave dwellings. Open 11 a.m.-5 p.m. Tue-Sat. Art gallery open 11 a.m.-5 p.m. Tours of house by appointment. Closed Jun-Sep. When entering, ring the bell at the iron gate. (504) 523-6791.

9. French Market, Cafe du Monde to Flea
Market, 1008 N. Peters. Five blocks of shopping, dining and entertainment housed in reno-vated historic market buildings. The home of Cafe du Monde's cafe au lait and beignets, pralines, gifts. Sidewalk cafes offer cool drinks, Creole favorites, jazz and ragtime piano. Also fine, elegant riverside dining, flea market and traditional open air Farmer's Market, historic display and sculpture. Shops open 10 a.m.-6 p.m. daily, restaurants vary. Cafe du Monde and Farmer's Market open 24 hours. (504) 522-2624.

10. Gallier House, 1118-1132 Royal St.
This 1860s home of New Orleans architect James Gallier, Jr., has been restored in architectural detail and period furnishings to re-create the period of his residence in the French Quarter. House is now an educational complex that features the detailed historic restoration of the residence and courtyard of the Gallier family. Gift shop. National Historic Landmark. Open 10 a.m.-4:30 p.m. Mon-Sat. Tours every half hour from 10:30 a.m.-4 p.m. Admission. (504) 523-6722.

11. Hermann-Grima Historic House,
820 Rue St. Louis . Tours are a blend of lifestyle and the decorative arts. Period covers 1831 through 1860. The only 1830s functioning Creole kitchen and the last 19th century stable left in the French Quarter. Seasonal cooking demonstrations. Museum open 10 a.m.-4 p.m. Mon-Sat. Tours on the hour and half hour 10 a.m.-3:30 p.m. Admission. (504) 525-5661.

12. Historic New Orleans Collection, 533
Royal St. The complex of buildings is a historic site, museum and research center for state and local history. The main entrance is in the 1792 Merieult House. Free public gallery on first floor. Two separate guided tours. One is the Williams residence, furnished in antique and modern pieces. Second tour is of history galleries with original maps, paintings, documents and photographs. Open 10 a.m.- 3:15 p.m. Tue-Sat. Admission for tours. (504) 523-4664.

13. The 1850 House, located in a portion of
the Pontalba Apartments at 525 St. Ann Street, facing Jackson Square. The two Pontalba Apartment Buildings, said to be the oldest apartments in the U.S. , were constructed 1848-50 for Baroness Pontalba by architect James Gallier, Sr., and notable tenants have included Jenny Lind and William Faulkner. The 1850 House is furnished to present a typical New Orleans dwelling of the 1850s. The furnishings are by Seignouret and Mallard, the city's two most famous 19th century furniture makers. Open 10 a.m.-6 p.m. Tue-Sun. Admission. (504) 568-6968.

14. Jackson Brewery, Jackson Square
at the river. Visit the 1891 landmark Jackson Brewery, once the home of Jax Beer, now a spectacular riverfront marketplace with over 60 unique shopping, dining and entertainment experiences, including Jax fest, a year-round food festival. Open 10 a.m.-10 p.m. daily. (504) 529-1211.

15. Jackson Square, The old "Place d'Armes" (military parade ground) has served as the center of New Orleans life since the city was first laid out in 1721. The statue of Andrew Jackson was erected in 1856, when the Square received its present name. Saturday jazz concerts are held from 2-6 p.m. during Oct-Nov and Apr-Aug.

16. Jean Lafitte National Historical Park, (French Quarter Visitor and Folklife Center), 916 N. Peters St. Park rangers offer tours of historical areas of the French Quarter, Garden District and St. Louis Cemetery. Tours at 9:30, 10:30 and 11:30 a.m., 1, 2 and 3 p.m. daily. Closed New Year's, Mardi Gras, Christmas. Free. (504) 589-2636.

17. Lafitte's Blacksmith Shop, 941 Bourbon St. Built prior to 1772, this "briquette-entre-poteau" building became the blacksmith shop that served as a front for smuggling operations of the pirate Jean Lafitte. The old building now houses a picturesque saloon. Open noon- 2 a.m. daily. (504) 523-0066.

18. Louisiana State Museum, 751 Chartres St., New Orleans. Louisiana history comes alive in the heart of the French Quarter. See the Jazz and Carnival exhibits, costumes, furniture, decorative arts, photographs and more. Special exhibitions planned. As one of the largest historical museum complexes in the country, the museum offers the Presbytere, 1850 House, Cabildo, Madame John's Legacy, and the old U.S. Mint. Open 10 a.m.-6 p.m. Tue-Sun (Mint open 9 a.m.-5 p.m. Tue-Sun). Admission. (504) 568-6968.

19. Lulu White's Mahogany Hall, originally established in 1897 on Basin Street, has been moved to the site of the first Bourbon Street jazz nightclub at 309 Rue Bourbon. This turn-of-the-century French Quarter nightclub, restored with brick walls, tin ceilings and mahogany bar and floor, is home of New Orleans Jazz and the world-famous Dukes of Dixieland. Noon-1 a.m. daily. Admission. Reservations recommended. (504) 525-5595.

20. Madame John's Legacy, 632 Dumaine Street. Now a property of the Louisiana State Museum, this home was built in 1788 and is a classic example of colonial Creole architecture. George Washington Cable (a well-known writer of his day and a friend and speaking-tour companion of Mark Twain) used this home as the setting for "Tite Poulette," from his 1879 book of short stories entitled *Old Creole Days*, and the name "Madame John's Legacy," derived from the home's role in that story, stuck. The house now

serves as a Museum of Folk Art. Open 10 a.m. -6 p.m. Tue-Sun. Admission. (504) 568-6968.

21. The Moon Walk, this section of the Mississippi River Levee adjacent to Jackson Square has always served New Orleans as a "promenade." The area was recently renamed the "Moon Walk," and attractive walkways, steps and fountains have been added. This is a fine spot for watching the cruise ships, cargo ships and steamboats on the Mississippi. The Toulouse Street Wharf at the Moon Walk, as well as the Canal and Poydras Street Wharves a bit upriver, serve as docking places for several excursion steamboats. Visit the Tourist Information Center at 529 St. Ann St. for schedules.

22. Musee Conti Wax Museum, 917 Conti St. Fabulous costumed wax figures tell the history and legends of New Orleans in 31 period settings — accurate in every detail. Also "The Haunted Dungeon," with chilling scenes from Poe, Hugo and other masters of the macabre. Open 10 a.m.-5:30 p.m. daily. Closed Mardi Gras, Christmas. Admission. (504) 525-2605.

23. New Orleans Jazz Clubs:

Preservation Hall, 726 St. Peter. This is the city's most famous jazz club, where pioneers of jazz still perform several "sets" from 8:30 p.m.-12:30 a.m. each night. Admission.
Maison Bourbon, 641 Bourbon St. (504) 522-8818.
Bayard's Jazz Alley, 701 Bourbon St. (504) 524-9200.

24. New Orleans School of Cooking and Louisiana General Store, 620 Decatur St. (Jackson Brewery). Learn the secrets of authentic Creole cooking. Joe Cahn, seen on the Disney Channel and other national and local television shows, founded the school in 1980. He and other New Orleans cooks share their favorite cooking tips. Classes 10 a.m.-1 p.m. Mon-Sat Reservations. General Store open 9:30 a.m.-9:30 p.m. daily. (504) 525-2665.

25. Old Pharmacy Museum, 514 Chartres St. This shop was first used as a pharmacy in 1823, and it is now a museum of old apothecary items, medical instruments, hand-blown pharmacy bottles and "show globes." Visitors will also see a collection of voodoo potions and a botanical garden with herbs and medicinal plants of the 19th century. Open 10 a.m.-5 p.m. Tue-Sat. Admission. (504) 524-9077.

26. Old U.S. Mint, 400 block of Esplanade. This old mint in operation 1838-1862 and

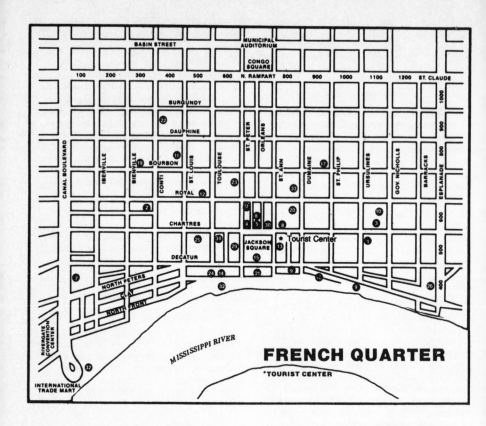

FRENCH QUARTER
*TOURIST CENTER

1879-1920, produced at its peak $5 million in coin per month. The "O" mintmark of these coins is familiar to the coin collectors of the world. The huge structure has recently become the property of the Louisiana State Museum and now houses the museum's collection of historical documents. Open 9 a.m.-5 p.m. Tue-Sun. Admission to exhibits. (504) 568-6968.

27. Original Spanish Theater, 718 St. Peter. Built in 1791, this was the first Spanish theater in the U.S. Later a private home of the DeFlechie family, it has housed famous Pat O'Brien's (home of the "hurricane") since 1942.

28. Pete Fountain's, third floor of New Orleans Hilton Hotel, Poydras St. at Mississippi River. New Orleans Jazz played by New Orleans' own Pete Fountain and his Jazz Band. A French Quarter atmosphere with seating up to 500. One-hour shows. Call for rates. (504) 523-4374.

29. Pontalba Historical Puppetorium, 514 St. Peter St. Animated puppet show and exhibit is made up of 50 giant marionettes, depicting life and history in New Orleans. Admission. (504) 522-0344.

30. The Presbytere, on Chartres St. facing Jackson Square. Construction of the Presbytere was begun circa 1791. Now a property of the Louisiana State Museum, the old building (almost a twin of the Cabildo) contains exhibits of Newcomb pottery, historic costumes, furniture and many other items of interest. Changing exhibition gallery. Open 10 a.m.-6 p.m. Tue-Sun. Admission. (504) 568-6968.

31. Sky Line, adjacent to the New Orleans Convention Center on the East Bank of the Mississippi River and at 1229 Teche St. on the West Bank. Six-passenger gondolas suspended from cables 350 feet above the Mississippi River offer a bird's-eye view of New Orleans and the surrounding area, including Lake Pontchartrain.

Open daily, year round. Admission.
(504) 367-0300.

32. Steamboat Cruises, Toulouse St.
Wharf, Canal St. Wharf and Poydras St. Wharf.
Cruises include trips to the Audubon Zoo,
2-hour port tours, 5-hour explorations of nearby
bayous and swamplands, and various trips up the
Mississippi River into America's Heartland. Let
the steamboat Natchez, the paddlewheeler Cotton
Blossom, the paddlewheeler Creole Queen, the
Bayou Jean Lafitte, the riverboat President and
the paddlewheelers Mississippi Queen and Delta
Queen transport you back to antebellum
Louisiana. Check with nearest Tourist
Information Center for schedules.

33. Voodoo Museum, 724 Dumaine St.
This unique museum brings together the
old and the present day voodoo in New Orleans.
Featuring Marie Laveau, the Voodoo Queen,
and exciting occult displays. Open 10 a.m.-

10 p.m. or later daily. Voodoo tour 1 p.m. Tue-Sat,
includes the museum, Witchcraft Shop,
Mortuary Church, other attractions. Admission.
(504) 523-7685.

**34. Your Sound Promenade of the Vieux
Carré,** available at 626 Chartres St. Stroll to
an unforgettable rendezvous with New Orleans
of yesteryear. Listen to seldom-told personal
stories, intimate secrets and incomparable
sounds of the old city's proud, passionate,
fun-loving people. "Talking book tour"
recorded on two 90-minute cassettes.
Also available by writing P.O. Box 8876, New
Orleans, LA 70182, or by calling (504) 282-1932.

Tourist Information Center

New Orleans State and City Tourist Center,
529 St. Ann St. Open 10 a.m.-6 p.m. daily.
(504) 568-5661

 **Plantation Country**
Nestled along the majestic
Mississippi River lie stately antebellum
homes . . . plantations resplendently
restored to their original beauty and
elegance. Step in and explore our
history in these remembrances of a
bygone era.
Or discover the Art Deco architecture
of our Louisiana State Capitol building
as it towers above Baton Rouge,
reminding us that it is the tallest state
capitol in the nation.

Attractions

Cars of Yesteryear, 12137 Airline Hwy, Baton
Rouge. (U.S. 61), 3.5 miles south of I-12. These
35 vintage autos, all operational and in mint
condition, range in dates from 1915-1950. Group
tours only, 15 or more. Twenty-four hours notice
required. Admission. (504) 293-8070 or (504)
293-0581.

Catfish Town, at the foot of Government St.
along the Mississippi River levee, Baton Rouge.
Historic riverfront development features a

festival-like atmosphere with frequent special
entertainment. Within walking distance of major
points of interest in downtown Baton Rouge.
Filled with places to eat, drink, shop, browse and
have fun. Across from Riverside Centroplex
convention center.

Clinton, established 1824 to be the parish seat
of East Feliciana Parish, was a legal and
educational center in the 19th century. Fine
examples of antebellum and Victorian
architecture abound, and the courthouse and
Lawyers' Row are especially outstanding. Few
other early commercial buildings remain.
(504) 683-8577.

> **Audubon Regional Library,** c. 1860 Late
> Greek Revival, (504) 683-8753
>
> **Boatner-Record House,** c. 1830 Raised
> Cottage
>
> **Bonnie Burn,** c. 1858 Greek Revival,
> (504) 683-5207
>
> **Brame-Bennett House,** c. 1840 Greek
> Revival
>
> **Brickyard Store,** 1903
>
> **Cochran-DeLee Building,** c. 1836,
> (504) 683-9806
>
> **East Feliciana Courthouse,** 1840 Greek
> Revival, (504) 683-5145
>
> **First Baptist Church,** 1872
>
> **Hope Terrace,** c. 1840 Greek Revival

The Irwin House, c. 1906 Victorian, (504) 683-9481

Isidore Mayer-Hobgood House, c. 1910 Victorian

Lawyers' Row, c. 1840-1860 Greek Revival

Marston House, c. 1837 Greek Revival, (504) 683-3371

St. Andrew's Church, (Episcopal) 1871 Victorian Gothic

Silliman, 1850, 1860, c. 1894 Greek Revival

Stonehenge, c. 1837 Greek Revival

Wall House, c. 1839, c. 1895 Victorian, (504) 683-8402

Woodside, c. 1847 Gothic Cottage, (504) 683-5943

Cohn Memorial Arboretum, 12056 Foster Rd., Baton Rouge. Arboretum is located on 16 landscaped acres housing several major plant collections. More than 200 varieties of trees and shrubs native or adaptable to Louisiana are featured. Greenhouse has common and rare plants used in interior landscaping. Open 8 a.m.-5 p.m. weekdays, 9 a.m.-5 p.m. Sat-Sun. Free. (504) 775-1006.

Fun Fair Park, enter from the service road that intersects U.S. 61 at the first traffic light north of Florida Blvd. in Baton Rouge. Train rides, carnival rides and games. Hours are seasonal. Free. (504) 924-6266.

Godfrey's, 602 Main St., Plaquemine. Restaurant in a Victorian townhouse. Large two-story home was built in late 19th century. Has old teller's cage display from Bank of Melville, works of local artists. Open for lunch Sun-Fri. (504) 687-7578.

Governor's Mansion, 1001 Baton Rouge Expwy., Baton Rouge. Tours include the State Dining Room, State Meeting Room and State Reception Area. Tours 9-11 a.m. and 2-4 p.m., depending on daily mansion schedule. Tours by appointment only. Free. (504) 342-0926.

Greater Baton Rouge Zoo, Exit 8 off I-110, turn right to second light, turn right on Thomas Rd. More than 750 mammals and birds, many rare and endangered species. Set within 100 acres of wooded and landscaped grounds. Zoo-Choo rides, elephant shows, children's zoo. Open 10

a.m.-5 p.m. daily (CST), 10 a.m.-5 p.m. weekdays and 10 a.m.-6 p.m. weekends (DST). Admission. (504) 775-3877.

Jackson, established 1813 as the original seat of the parish of "Feliciana" (1815-1824). The greater part of the town is included as an Historic District on the National Register of Historic Places. (504) 683-8577.

Centenaria, 1840 Greek Revival

Centenary College State Commemorative Area, (504) 634-7925

East Louisiana State Hospital Center Building and Wings, 1848-1853 Greek Revival, (504) 634-2651

Feliciana Parish Courthouse, 1815-1817

Jackson First Baptist Church, c. 1860

Jackson Methodist Church, c. 1852

Milbank, c. 1835, (504) 634-4901

Millwood, c. 1840 Carolina I

Old Bank of Jackson (Jackson Town Hall), 1906, (504) 634-2637

Presbyterian Church, 1852

Roseneath, c. 1832 Greek Revival

St. Alban's Lodge, c. 1826

Lafitte's Landing Restaurant, on the Sunshine Bridge service road on the west bank of the Mississippi River, near Donaldsonville. Lafitte's Landing, originally Viala Plantation, was built circa 1800 and is said to have been frequented by the pirate Jean Lafitte. Restaurant has outstanding art collection and specializes in Cajun and Creole cuisine. Open 11 a.m.-3 p.m. and 6-10 p.m. Tue-Sat, 11 a.m.-8 p.m. Sun and 11 a.m.-3 p.m. Mon. (504) 473-1232.

Lagniappe Tours, 900 North Blvd., Baton Rouge. Professional tour guides offer van tours of the city and Plantation Country. (504) 387-2464.

Lake des Allemands Swamp Tours, about 3 miles south of Vacherie on La. 643. See alligators, ducks, egrets, squirrels, owls, nutria and other wildlife in their natural habitat. Call for time schedules. Morning and evening tours. (504) 265-3160.

Gillis W. Long Hansen's Disease Center, on River Road, Carville. This U.S. Public Health

Service Hospital is the only facility in the United States devoted to research, training and patient care in Hansen's disease. Located on the site of a 400-acre rice and sugar plantation, the hospital comprises over 100 buildings, including a 65-bed infirmary. Facility recognized internationally as one of the world's leading Hansen's disease research facilities. Open 8 a.m.-4:30 p.m. daily. Tours at 10 a.m. and 1 p.m. (504) 642-7771.

Milbank, 102 Bank St., Jackson. The oldest commercial building in Jackson, Milbank is a massive romantic antebellum mansion, a landmark in East Feliciana Parish for many years. Bed and breakfast, private dinner parties, weddings, receptions. Admission. (504) 634-5901.

Old South Jamboree, 1 mile west of Walker on U.S. 190. This old music hall comes to life the first Saturday of each month (8-10 p.m., occasional second show 10 p.m.-midnight). Country music at its best. Concessions. Admission. (504) 665-8874.

Pointe Coupee Bed & Breakfast, owned and operated by Mrs. Miller Armstrong, principally using the Bondy House at 304 Court St., the Hebert House at 401 Richey St. and the Claiborne House at 405 Richey St., all in New Roads. Transportation and tours of the False River and Pointe Coupee area provided, as well as overnight accommodations and tours for travelers and other visitors. Reservations. 605 E. Main St., New Roads, LA 70760. (504) 638-6254.

River Bend Energy Center, U.S. 61 south of St. Francisville. Located next to the River Bend nuclear generating station, the center offers demonstrations, audio-visual presentations and displays of the many forms and facets of energy. Open 8 a.m.-4 p.m. Mon-Fri. Free. (504) 635-3998.

St. Francisville Inn, 118 North Commerce, St. Francisville. Outstanding feature of the house, besides its Victorian Gothic architecture, is the original ceiling medallion in the parlor — the theme is Mardi Gras masks. Building circa 1880. Bed and breakfast. Open 11 a.m.-2 p.m. Tue-Sat for lunch, 11 a.m.-2 p.m. Sunday brunch. Also open 5-9 p.m. Tue-Sat for dinner. (504) 635-6502.

St. Jude Shrine and Rest Area, 1 mile south of Donaldsonville on La. 1. This delightful chapel and shrine honor the "patron saint of hopeless cases," and the grounds serve as a pleasant spot for picnicking and relaxation. Chapel available for special occasions by reservation. Open dawn to dusk daily. Free. (504) 473-6337 or (504) 473-7237.

Samuel Clemens Riverboat, Florida St. at the Mississippi River, Baton Rouge. The boat offers narrated sightseeing harbor cruises, luncheon cruises and private charters. While retaining the charm of the steamboat days, it offers all of today's modern conveniences. Also seasonal specials, souvenirs. Daily cruises at 10 a.m., noon and 2 p.m. Apr-Aug. Wed-Sun cruises Sep-Mar. Admission. (504) 381-9606.

State Capitol Building, State Capitol Dr., Baton Rouge. Building is 34 stories tall, the tallest state capitol building in the United States. Location of site of assassination of Huey Long. Observatory tower offers magnificent view of river and landscaped grounds. Open 8 a.m.-4:30 p.m. daily. Closed New Year's, Easter, Thanksgiving, Christmas. Free. (504) 342-7317.

U.S.S. Kidd, at foot of Government St. at Mississippi River, Baton Rouge. WWII Fletcher Class Destroyer, restored to its 1945 configuration. Its docking facility is the only one of its kind in the world and enables the ship to rise and fall with the river stage. Open 10 a.m.-6 p.m. Tue-Sun from Apr-Sep and 9 a.m.-4:30 Tue -Sun from Oct -Mar. Closed Christmas. Admission. (504) 383-9096.

IIIⓕIII Historic Places

Cabin Restaurant, La. 44 at La. 22, Burnside. Serves traditional River Road foods, especially seafood, in a unique setting of 150-year-old slave cabins that were gathered as a memorial to the rural farming community that surrounded the area. Many farm implements on display. Open 11 a.m.-3 p.m. Mon-Wed, 11 a.m.-9 p.m. Thu, 11 a.m.-10 p.m. Fri-Sat, 11 a.m.-6 p.m. Sun. (504) 473-3007.

Episcopal Church of the Nativity, off La. 77 in Rosedale (drive 2 blocks east on La. 76, then 1 block north on Laurel). Three gigantic live oaks stand vigil over this old frame church, built of cypress in 1859. (504) 638-8433.

The Lafayette Buildings, 342 and 348 Lafayette St., Baton Rouge. These fine old brick buildings with their iron columns and grillwork were constructed in the early 1800s, and the Marquis de Lafayette was entertained here during his tour of America on the 50th anniversary of

American independence. 348 Lafayette St. is private, but 342 contains the Lafayette Gallery, where paintings, prints and antiques may be purchased. By appointment only. (504) 383-7763.

Manresa Retreat House, on La. 44 in Convent. Built in 1831 to house Jefferson College, this memorable building now serves as a Jesuit retreat house. The retreat house is never open for tours.

Old State Capitol, on River Road at North Blvd., Baton Rouge. This impressive Gothic castle was built in 1847 and served as the capitol until 1932. Of particular interest is a massive spiral stairway which winds its way upward toward an impressive stained-glass dome. Closed indefinitely for renovation. (504) 342-6483.

Pentagon Barracks, Riverside Mall at State Capitol Dr., Baton Rouge. Built in 1823-24 to quarter U.S. Army personnel serving the post of Baton Rouge. Early drawings indicate the existence of a fifth building, although only four remain today. Many famous military men and public figures served the post or visited it before the outbreak of the Civil War in 1861. They included Lafayette, Zachary Taylor, Lee, Sheridan, Custer, Jefferson Davis and Lincoln. Buildings now house state offices.

Saint Francis of Pointe Coupee, La. 420 (Pointe Coupee Road), New Roads. This Catholic Church was built in 1760. When the shifting river threatened the building in 1895, the church was dismantled and reassembled at its present location. Open daily. Mass at 8 a.m. Sun or by appointment. (504) 638-9665.

St. Gabriel Catholic Church, on La. 75 in St. Gabriel. This delightful old weatherboarded church with its imposing steeple was built in 1769. Old St. Gabriel is no longer in use (the new church stands behind it).

St. Joseph's Cathedral, 412 North St., Baton Rouge. Built in 1853, the cathedral's interior has been renovated in a style which, while modern, is inspirational and magnificent. Its exterior remains unchanged. (504) 387-5928.

St. Stephen's Episcopal Church, 2 miles north of Innis on La. 418. Construction of this impressive Gothic Revival brick church for an Anglican congregation founded in 1848 was begun in 1850. (504) 492-2234.

Southern University, Baton Rouge. Oldest Negro college in the United States, features the sculpture of the "Red Stick" for which Baton Rouge is named (the spot on the bluff of the Mississippi River is the alleged landing spot of the first Europeans) and the Academic Building, which is on the National Register of Historic Places.

Stowell House, 511 W. Main St. in New Roads. Built in 1856 and open by appointment only. Free. (504) 638-8358.

Tourist Information Centers

State Tourist Center, north of St. Francisville on U.S. 61. Open 8:30 a.m.-5 p.m. daily. (504) 635-6962.

Louisiana Office of Tourism, 666 N. Foster Dr., Baton Rouge. Open 8 a.m.-4:30 p.m. Mon-Fri. (504) 925-3860.

State Capitol Tourist Information Center, State Capitol Building, State Capitol Dr., Baton Rouge. Open 8 a.m.-4:30 p.m. daily. Closed New Year's, Easter, Thanksgiving, Christmas. (504) 342-7317.

Baton Rouge Tourist Center, 100 St. James St. Open 9:30 a.m.-5 p.m. Mon-Fri, and 10 a.m.-5 p.m. Sat-Sun. (504) 383-1825.

Baton Rouge Tourist Center, 275 S. River Rd. (Catfish Town). Administrative offices located in Centroplex. Open 9:30 a.m.-5 p.m. daily. (504) 383-1825.

Gonzales Tourist Center, 728 E. Ascension Ave., located in the old railroad depot. Open 1-5 p.m. Wed-Fri. (504) 644-6000.

Pointe Coupee Tourist Center, 6 miles south of New Roads on La. 1. Open 10 a.m.-4 p.m. Tue-Sat, and 1-4 p.m. Sun. (504) 638-7171.

West Baton Rouge Tourist Information Centre, I-10 at La. 415, 2855 Frontage Rd., Port Allen. Open 9 a.m.-5 p.m. daily. Closed Thanksgiving, Christmas. (504) 344-2920.

Cajun Country

South Louisiana was settled by a people whose "joie de vivre" has flavored the swamps and bayous with lively music and spicy foods! These Cajuns, as the French-Acadian immigrants are known, have preserved their culture and heritage in a unique lifestyle which is celebrated daily.

Attractions

Academy of the Sacred Heart, Grand Coteau. Built in 1821, the academy is the second-oldest school in Louisiana. Building still serves as a boarding and day school for 300 girls from Louisiana and several other states. Centuries-old gardens, shrine of St. John Berchmans (only shrine in U.S. on the exact site of a miracle). Open 8 a.m.-4 p.m. daily. Free. (318) 662-5275.

Acadian Village, on Mouton Rd. just south of La. 342, Lafayette. A number of Acadian dwellings, a church and other antebellum buildings have been brought together here to represent an early "Cajun" bayou village. A sleepy bayou meanders past the historic structures. A gift shop offers Cajun crafts as well as books on the Acadians. Open 10 a.m.-5 p.m. daily. Admission. Group tours may be arranged by calling (318) 981-2364.

A la Bonne Veillée Guest House, Vermilion Parish La. 339 near Erath. This Louisiana French-style cottage, circa 1845-1860, has been home to families of prominent French Creole and Acadian merchants and civic leaders, even a steamboat captain. Now restored and furnished in period antiques, it is used as a guest house. Listed on the National Register of Historic Places. Admission. (318) 937-5495.

Bayou and Swamp Tours are located throughout the region. The tours vary greatly in length and content, so you are advised to inquire fully.

Annie Miller's Terrebonne Swamp & Marsh Tours, at Miller's Landing on Big Bayou Black, U.S. 90 west of Houma. The original swamp tour. From a comfortably cushioned boat you will cruise through bayous and wild marshlands filled with the wonders of nature. During early spring and summer you will see enormous flocks of egrets and herons, alligators and other wildlife species. Open daily from Feb 1-Nov 15. Tours last 2½ to 3 hours. Admission. (504) 879-3934.

Basin Boat Tours, Whiskey River Landing near Henderson. (318) 228-8567 or (318) 667-6135.

Atchafalaya Basin Backwater Adventure, La. 20 near U.S. 90, Gibson. Guided tours of the great Chacahoula Swamp, Pirogue rentals, camping. Tours at 11 a.m. and 4 p.m. daily. Tours last 2 or 4 hours. Admission. (504) 575-2371.

Atchafalaya Basin Boat Tour, leaving from McGee's Landing near Henderson. Take Exit 115 off I-10 to Henderson, go through town to the levee and turn right at the top of the levee. McGee's 2.25 miles farther. Tours at 10 a.m., 1 and 3 p.m. daily. Tours last about 1½ hours. Admission. (318) 228-8519 or (318) 228-2384.

Cypress Bayou Swamp Tours, 4340 Grand Caillou Rd., Houma. An exciting swampboat adventure deep into the wilderness of Terrebonne Parish. A tour guided and narrated by a bilingual native Houmas Indian. See exotic birds, flowers, wildlife and reptiles. Watch your guide hand-feed alligators. Accommodations for groups and handicapped. Reservations recommended. (504) 851-3569 or (504) 876-9435.

Swamp World, Houma. (504) 868-3361.

Broken Arrow Stables, La. 3013 at Segura Rd., New Iberia. Trail rides, hayrides, parties. Open 9 a.m.-dark daily. Admission. (318) 369-7669.

Brownell Memorial Park and Carillon Tower, located on La. 70 north of Morgan City. Features a carillon rising to 106 feet above its base, and 61 bronze bells cast in Holland. These musical bells and carillon are the second largest in the U.S., and are surrounded by the serenity and beauty of natural swamp situated on Lake Palourde. Open 9 a.m.-5 p.m. daily. Closed Christmas. Free. (504) 384-5118.

Cafe Vermilionville, 1304 W. Pinhook, Lafayette. This restaurant and lounge is housed in a fine old Acadian-style inn that was built circa 1800. Open 11 a.m.-10 p.m. Mon-Fri, 5:30-10 p.m. Sat, and 10:30 a.m.-2 p.m. Sun. (318) 237-0100.

Creole Antiques, Rt. 3, Sulphur. La. 27, south 4.5 miles to Cotton Vincent Road. American country antiques, primitives, linens, collectibles, handmade items. Open 9 a.m.-5 p.m. Mon-Sat and Sun by chance. Free. (318) 583-7529.

Creole Nature Trail, This spectacular driving tour begins in Sulphur and follows La. 27 and 82 through marshlands and swamplands and along the Gulf Coast. Some highlights of the tour aside from the flora and fauna are the Intracoastal Canal, Sabine Wildlife Reserve, Holly Beach, Rutherford Beach and the Rockefeller Wildlife Refuge. Pick up a tour map at the State Tourist Center on I-10 (near Texas border), or at the Lake Charles Tourist Center on I-10 in Lake Charles.

Delcambre Shrimp Boat Landing, La. 14 in Delcambre. Covered picnic area, fisherman's wharf, net repair shops, shrimp boats, seafood shops. Open daily, busiest during shrimping season.

Delta Downs, on La. 3063, Vinton. This fine racing facility offers thoroughbred and quarter horse racing with parimutuel wagering. Seasons ordinarily are Sep-Mar for thoroughbreds, Apr-Labor Day for quarter horses. Post time 7:05 p.m. Thu-Sat and 1:05 p.m. Sun. Admission. No minors. (318) 589-7441 or 1-800-551-7142 (Texas, Okla., Ark., Miss., Ala.) or 1-800-542-7112 (La.).

Evangeline Downs, I-49 (U.S. 167 North), Lafayette. Expansive 140-acre complex attracts leading thoroughbreds mid-Apr to mid-Sep, quarter horses Sep- Mar. Call for post times. Admission. (318) 896-3300 .

Grand Isle Resort, in the Gulf of Mexico at the terminus of La. 1. This island resort offers large beaches, pleasant lodges and fine seafood restaurants, camping with hookups, bird-watching, surfing and fishing. Crabbing and surf fishing are great, launches are available for your own boat, and charterboats are available. Grand Isle State Park (140 acres on the east end of Grand Isle) features a 400-foot fishing pier built out over the water affording day/night fishing. Picnicking and camping are also available.

Heritage Farm Village, on La. 35 at La. 365 in Branch. This expansive farm complex includes a Cajun house built in 1852 and the complex houses a fine museum of pioneer farm life in the Bayou Country. Restaurant. Open 9 a.m.-5 p.m. Mon-Sat. Admission. (318) 334-2949.

Jungle Gardens, La. 329 south of New Iberia at Avery Island. Developed by Edward Avery McIlhenny, the gardens feature camellias, azaleas and tropical plants in season. Enormous flocks of egrets and herons and other species protected here. Chinese Garden contains a fine Buddha dating from 1000 A.D. Open 9 a.m.-5 p.m. daily. Admission. (318) 365-8173.

Konriko Co. Store and Rice Mill, 309 Ann St., New Iberia. America's oldest rice mill presents a 22-minute slide presentation on the Cajun culture plus a tour of the rice mill and a large selection of local food and craft items. Allow 1 to 1½ hours. Open 9 a.m.-5 p.m. Mon-Sat. Admission. (318) 364-7242.

Lafayette Nature Station and Trails, Acadiana Park on E. Alexander St., Lafayette.

Facilities include three-story Nature Station and 40-acre nature trail system. Two naturalists are on hand to give information about the trails and to present slide talks, lectures and demonstrations. Open 9 a.m.-5 p.m. Mon-Fri and 11 a.m.-3 p.m. Sat-Sun. Free. (318) 261-8348.

Lafayette Planetarium, 637 Girard Park Dr., Lafayette. Complex optical instrument projects images of stars, planets and other celestial bodies onto a domed ceiling. On clear evenings, the Tuesday show is followed by a telescope session outdoors. Special shows scheduled from time to time. Shows at 4 p.m. Mon, 2 and 3:30 p.m. Sun and 8 p.m. (DST) or 7:30 p.m. (CST) Tue. Free. (318) 261-8350.

Lake Charles Beach, along Lakeshore Dr. and I-10 on the north shore of Lake Charles is a large and delightful white-sand beach. Bathhouses, easy parking. Free.

Laurel Valley Village, 6 miles below Thibodaux on Laurel Valley Rd. just off La. 308. Site of the largest, most intact remaining turn-of-the-century sugar plantation complex in the southern U.S. Efforts under way to restore the area and create a rural life museum depicting the lifestyle of the sugar-producing region. A National Historic Landmark. Tours by appointment. Admission. (504) 447-5216.

Live Oak Gardens, on La. 675 at Jefferson Island near New Iberia. Has 20 acres of beauti- fully landscaped gardens surrounding the completely restored Joseph Jefferson home, constructed in 1870. Audio-visual presentation, cafe overlooking Lake Peigneur, gift shop features gifts from exotic places. Open 9 a.m.-5 p.m. daily. Admission. (318) 367-3485.

Louisiana Oil and Gas Park, on La. 26 at I-10 near Jennings. Featured are a replica of Louisiana's first oil derrick (drilled here in 1901), an Acadian house and recreation island. Open 9 a.m.-8:30 p.m. daily. Free.

Louisiana State Arboretum, La. 3042, 8 miles north of Ville Platte. Established in 1961, it is one of the first state-supported arboretums in the Deep South. Excellent example of a Beech-Magnolia climax forest, plus other trees, shrubs and flowers. Has 600 acres plus nature trails. Open 9 a.m.-5 p.m. Mon-Sat, 1-5 p.m. Sun. Free. (318) 363-6287.

Maison Marseline, 442 E. Main St., New Iberia. An Eastlake Victorian Cottage open for tours 9 a.m.-4 p.m. Mon-Sat, and 10 a.m.-4 p.m. Sun. Admission. (318) 364-5922.

Mulate's Cajun Restaurant, La. 94, Breaux Bridge. Lively, down-home Cajun restaurant serving up good food, good Cajun music and good times. Authentic Cajun cuisine and live Cajun music. Open 11 a.m.-2 p.m. and 5-10 p.m. Tue-Fri, 5-10 p.m. Sat and 4-10 p.m. Sun. Music 8-10 p.m. Tue-Sat and 6-10 p.m. Sun. (318) 332-4648.

Original Swamp Gardens, on Myrtle St. 1 block north of U.S. 90 in Morgan City. A heritage park offers guided walking tours along raised pathways of this five-acre natural swamp depicting the history and settling of the Great Atchafalaya Basin and includes a wildlife zoo to complete the tour. Open daily except Mondays and legal holidays. Time schedule available. Admission. (504) 384-3343.

Prejean's Restaurant, 3480 U.S. 167 North, Lafayette, next to Evangeline Downs. Specialty is Cajun seafood, including boiled crawfish, crabs and shrimp, plus alligator. Cajun music and dancing, oyster bar. Decorated with original Cajun furnishings typical of the area. Open for lunch Mon-Fri, and dinner served daily. (318) 896-3247.

Steamboat Warehouse Restaurant, on Main St. at Bayou Courtableau in Washington. This fine old brick cotton warehouse was built in 1830, when Washington was a booming steamboat town. The warehouse now contains a great seafood restaurant (specializing in fresh river catfish) and a pleasant lounge. Open 5:30-11p.m. Tue-Sat. (318) 826-7227

Tabasco® Pepper Sauce Factory, La. 329 south of New Iberia at Avery Island. This is where the formula by which Tabasco sauce is made was perfected. Original frame building known as the "laboratory" was located on the home grounds of the Edmund McIlhenny family. Open 9-11:45 a.m. and 1-3:45 p.m. Mon-Fri, and 9-11:45 a.m. Sat. Bottling stops at 3:30 p.m. Mon-Fri. Free. (318) 365-8173.

Teche Queen, La. 182 in downtown New Iberia, docks on Bayou Teche in Bouligny Plaza. Paddlewheeler cruises at 10 a.m. and 2 p.m. daily, dinner cruises at 7 p.m. Wed and Sat. Admission. (318) 365-0581.

Trappey's Factory and Cajun Store, 900 E. Main St., New Iberia. See canning of pickled peppers and hot sauces. Free tours 9, 9:45 and 10:30 a.m. and 1, 1:45 and 2:30 p.m. Mon-Fri. Cajun Store open 9 a.m.-4:30 p.m. Mon-Sat. Closed major holidays. (318) 365-8281.

West Calcasieu Old Spanish Trail, Vinton. Self-guided tour of west Calcasieu Parish contains many points of interest, including Old Lyons House, Brimstone Museum, crawfish farm, rice farm and many others. (318) 589-2903.

 Historic Places

Carré Desautels, Washington, was built in 1903 for James J. Carriere, owner of three warehouses on Bayou Courtableau (River Opelousas), a son of steamboat captain and early mayor of Washington, Gerand Carriere. Last of the fine homes of the steamboat era in Washington, an excellent example of a Cape Cod / Queen Anne style. Later was home of inventor of the parking meter. Now used as a guest home. On the National Register of Historic Places. Open by appointment only. Admission. (318) 826-7330.

Christ Episcopal Church, on Main St. (La. 1) in Napoleonville. This small, brick Gothic building was consecrated in 1853 by the "fighting bishop of the Confederacy," Bishop-General Leonidas K. Polk. The church is ordinarily closed during the week. To inquire about services, call (504) 447-2910.

Episcopal Church of the Epiphany, 303 W. Main St., New Iberia. This handsome brick Gothic church was consecrated in 1858 by Bishop (and Confederate General) Leonidas K. Polk. Sunday services 7:30 a.m. and 10:30 a.m. (318) 369-9966.

Estorge House, 427 N. Market St., Opelousas. Restored and furnished with Louisiana antiques, the house dates to circa 1827. Bed and breakfast overnight accommodations. Tours 10 a.m.-5 p.m. daily. Closed major holidays. Admission. (318) 948-4592.

Evangeline Oak, on Port St. at Bayou Teche, St. Martinville, marks the landing place of the early settlers who traveled the slow, meandering waters of the Bayou Teche — Acadians from Nova Scotia, Canary Islanders from Spain, refugees from France during the French Revolution and the Creole families from New Orleans. This stately oak is the most famous tree in America.

Statue of Evangeline, beside St. Martin de Tours Catholic Church on Main St. (La. 31) in St. Martinville, was made famous by Longfellow's epic poem, "Evangeline." "The

Romance of Evangeline" was filmed here in 1929, and this statue was presented by the cast and crew.

Franklin Historic District, Exit 3211 off U.S. 90 and on La. 182, Franklin. Historic district composed of 420 properties that range from large plantation homes along Main Street to charming Victorian and turn-of-the-century cottages and bungalows. Driving tour ½ hour, to 1 hour, walking tour 1 to 3 hours. (318) 828-3631.

Statue of Hadrian, corner of Weeks and St. Peter streets in New Iberia, at Iberia Savings & Loan building. This seven-foot marble statue of the Emperor Hadrian, who ruled the Roman Empire from 117 to 138 A.D., was created in his lifetime, and it is assumed that he stood for the sculptor. Can be viewed by public at all times.

Hinckley House, 405 E. Dejean St., Washington. A Washington landmark and one of the older and more historically significant places in the area. House is surrounded by ancient live oak trees. Part of the Washington Historic District, which is in the National Register of Historic Places. Open 10 a.m.-5 p.m. daily by appointment or chance. Admission. (318) 826-3906.

House of History, on Main St. in Washington. Built in 1835 by the first mayor of Washington. Open 10 a.m.-5 p.m. daily. Admission. (318) 826-3670.

Jeanerette Driving Tour, scenic drive on La. 182 east from New Iberia to Jeanerette and Main St. of Jeanerette. Includes historic homes along Bayou Teche and LeJeune Bakery. Map available at New Iberia Tourist Information Center and Bicentennial Museum in Jeanerette. (318) 365-1540 or (318) 276-4293.

Lafourche Parish Courthouse, at Third and Green streets in Thibodaux. Completed in 1856, this is one of the best-preserved old public buildings in Louisiana.

New Iberia Driving and Walking Tour, Historic District of New Iberia. Includes Gebert Oak, Episcopal Church, Grotto, Mt. Carmel, Statue of Hadrian and Steamboat House. Map available at Tourist Information Center. (318) 365-1540 or (318) 365-6931.

Old Lyons House, 1335 Horridge St., Vinton. Elaborate Eastlake ornamentation of this delightful Queen Anne home makes it one of the most unique and beautiful homes in Southwest Louisiana. House was built in 1900 by the

prominent family of Samuel and Luvicy Lyons. Listed on National Register of Historic Places. Overnight accommodations. Tours by appointment only. (318) 589-2903.

Petite Caporal, on La. 1 in Golden Meadow. A 31-foot shrimp boat, named for Napoleon, is about 130 years old and is now on permanent display. Accessible at any hour. Free.

St. John's Episcopal Church, 718 Jackson St., Thibodaux. One of the oldest Episcopal churches west of the Mississippi River and the oldest Episcopal church building in Louisiana, consecrated in 1845. Adjoining graveyard includes tomb of Francis Tillou Nicholls, noted statesman and twice governor of Louisiana. Open by appointment only. (504) 447-2910.

St. Martin Parish Courthouse, Main St., St. Martinville, was built by slave labor about 1859. With its four Ionic columns, the building houses early records, written in Spanish and French, dating back to the 1730s.

St. Martin de Tours Catholic Church, on Main St. (La. 31) in St. Martinville. This church parish was established in 1765, and the present church, built in 1832, incorporates some sections of the original building. Inside are the original box-pews, an ornate baptismal font thought to have been a gift of Louis XVI, a replica of the grotto of Lourdes (built by a parishioner in the 1800s), and the elaborate old altar. (318) 394-6021.

Steamboat House, Washington, is of Dutch Colonial style. The three-story home has a full cellar, and the original red Belgian slate roof, copper gutter, batten shutters and French doors are in good condition. It was operated many years until the late 1930s as the Schmit Hotel. Acquired by Kenneth Deshotel in 1957, it was restored beautifully, furnished with antiques and converted into a home for his family. Open by appointment only. Admission. (318) 826-7330.

Turn-Of-The-Century House, 715 Second St., Morgan City. Beautifully restored turn-of-the-century home, which also houses artifacts, fabulous Mardi Gras exhibits and memorabilia. Original 1917 locally-filmed "Tarzan of the Apes" movie, 60 minutes. Open 9 a.m.-5 p.m. Mon-Fri, and 1-5 p.m. Sat-Sun. Admission. (504) 385-6159.

Wright-Andrus House, on Lake Dr. in Crowley, just west of La. 13. This fine old raised cottage was built in 1839 and contains an excellent collection of 18th and 19th century antiques. Open Mon-Fri by appointment. Admission. (318) 788-1879.

Tourist Information Centers

State Tourist Center, I-10 Eastbound, west of Vinton near Texas border. Open 8:30 a.m.-5 p.m. daily. (318) 589-7774.

Acadiana Tourist Information Center, 220 Academy St., Opelousas, east end of U.S. 190. Open 8 a.m.-4 p.m. weekdays, also 10 a.m.-4 p.m. weekends May-Aug. (318) 948-6263.

Atchafalaya Delta Tourist Commission Tourist Information Center, on Victor II Blvd. 2 blocks north of U.S. 90, Morgan City. Open 9 a.m.-5 p.m. Mon-Fri. (504) 385-5785.

Houma Tourist Center, South St. Charles St. at U.S. 90, Houma. Open 9 a.m.-5 p.m. Mon-Fri. (504) 868-2732.

Iberia Parish Tourist Information Center, La. 14 at U.S. 90 in New Iberia. Open 8 a.m.-noon and 1-5 p.m. daily. (318) 365-1540 or (318) 365-6931.

Lafayette Convention and Visitors Commission, 310 Sixteenth St. at U.S. 90, Lafayette. Open 8:30 a.m.-5 p.m. Mon-Fri, and 9 a.m.-5 p.m. Sat-Sun. (318) 232-3808.

Lake Charles Tourist Center, on Lake Shore Dr. at I-10 and the lake. Open 8 a.m.-5 p.m. Mon-Fri. (318) 436-9588.

Marksville Tourist Center, La. 1, Marksville. Open 11 a.m.-3 p.m. Tue-Sat, or by appointment. (318) 253-9550.

Morgan City Tourist Information Center, 725 Myrtle St., Morgan City. Open 8-11:30 a.m. and 1-4 p.m. Mon-Fri, and 9 a.m.-4 p.m. Sat-Sun. (504) 384-3343.

Washington Museum and Tourist Center, corner Main and DeJean streets, Washington. Open 10 a.m.-noon and 1-3 p.m. Mon-Fri. Also 10 a.m.-3 p.m. Sat-Sun in Jun-Aug. (318) 826-3626.

The Crossroads

A blending of north and south Louisiana, of historic remembrances and progressive outlooks, of rural countryside and city lights, a pleasant mix greets you in north central Louisiana.

Catch a prize-winning bass from Catahoula Lake, or explore historic Natchitoches and treat yourself to their famous meat pies.

Attractions

Alexandria Zoological Park, City Park Blvd. in Alexandria. Park, zoological garden, 9-hole golf course. Zoo open 9 a.m.-6 p.m. daily, summer months and 9 a.m.-5 p.m. daily, winter months. Free. Zoo (318) 473-1386.

Briarwood—Caroline Dormon Nature Preserve, 2 miles south of Saline on La. 9. Spectacular array of giant trees and native Louisiana flora, blooming flowers. Caroline Dormon was the first woman employed in forestry in the United States. Open 9 a.m.-5 p.m. Sat, noon-5 p.m. Sun in Apr, May, Aug and Nov. Admission. (318) 576-3379.

City Park Funland, City Park Blvd. in Alexandria. Adjacent to Alexandria Zoological Park. Amusements, rides. Funland opened seasonally. Fee for rides. (318) 445-2218.

Fort Claiborne Guest House, 801 Second St., Natchitoches. The structure which is now the guest house was built directly in front of the Fort Claiborne stockade, although perhaps not part of the fort. It has been dated to as early as 1810, possibly earlier. (318) 357-0064 or (318) 352-8957.

Kees Park, on La. 28 in Pineville. Swimming pool, picnic area, playgrounds and civic center. A picturesque old log cabin, barn and sweet potato house have been moved to the park and are open to the public as the Catahoula Homestead Museum during the annual Catahoula Lake Festival, held the last weekend in October.

Louisiana Outdoor Drama Association, at Red River (west bank) on La. 6, Natchitoches.

A different play is presented each year. Arrive before dark to enjoy the beautiful bluffs of Red River and to explore the earthen Confederate breastworks which still criss-cross the property. Concessions. For information concerning the play for a given season and for times, call the Natchitoches Tourist Center. Admission. (318) 352-8072.

Natchitoches National Fish Hatchery, 615 La. 1 South, Natchitoches. Operated by the U.S. Fish and Wildlife Service, it has 97 acres and rears striped bass, largemouth bass, channel catfish and redear sunfish for stocking waters in Louisiana and Arkansas. About 6 million fish are distributed annually. Aquarium has 20 tanks featuring many species of fish. Open 8 a.m.-4 p.m. daily. Closed New Year's, Christmas. Free. (318) 352-5324.

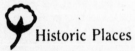 Historic Places

Alexandria National Cemetery, 209 Shamrock Ave. in Pineville. Established in 1867, this cemetery contains graves from the Indian, Mexican, Civil, Spanish-American and World Wars.

Burr Ferry Breastworks, just west of Burr Ferry on La. 8, east bank of Sabine River. These earthen breastworks were thrown up by Confederate troops late in the war, in anticipation of a Union advance up the Sabine. One section is contained in a small fenced park beside the river.

Christ Episcopal Church, on Courthouse Square in St. Joseph. Built in 1872 in late Gothic architectural style. The nearby Bondurant Home (private) now serves as the Christ Church Rectory. It was originally the second story of Pleasant View Plantation home, built in 1852. (318) 766-3518.

Fleur-de-Lis Bed and Breakfast Inn, 336 Second St., Natchitoches. Home was built around 1900 and is located in the National Historic Landmark District of the city. (318) 352-6621.

Front Street Buildings, 700 block of Front St., Natchitoches. Many of the businesses along Front Street are antebellum, but of particular interest are the Hughes Store (corner of Front and Horn) built in 1843 and featuring a rare wrought-iron spiral stairway in its courtyard,

and the Ducournau and La Coste Buildings, which have been restored to their original elegance, complete with carriageways and courtyards. 33 blocks in Natchitoches have been declared a National Historic Landmark District. Natchitoches is the oldest settlement in the Louisiana Purchase, founded in 1714.

Immaculate Conception Catholic Church, Second Street at Church St., Natchitoches. This handsome Catholic church was built in 1856. (318) 352-8072.

Lemee House, 310 Jefferson St., Natchitoches. This fine old home was built in 1830 and is furnished with fine antiques. By appointment. Admission. (318) 352-8072.

Mount Olivet Chapel, on Main St. (U.S. 165) in Pineville. This frame church, with a portico and two wooden columns, was built in 1857 and served as barracks for Union troops during the War Between the States.

Roque House, on River Bank Dr. beneath Front St. on Cane River Lake in Natchitoches. This rustic building, constructed circa 1803, is an excellent example of "bousillage" (a mud-and-moss mixture packed between cypress beams) construction. (318) 352-8072.

Rosalie Sugar Mill, south of Alexandria off U.S. 71 on La. 1208-A. Rosalie Plantation House, spared during the war because of owner's friendship with Gen. Sherman, is private. Behind the home and accessible to the public is the picturesque old sugar mill, built in 1852, which is listed on the National Register of Historic Places. Free.

Tensas Parish Library, on Plank Road, St. Joseph, is a magnificent town house built by a St. Joseph merchant about 1858, partially restored in 1964. Ground floor houses modern Tensas Parish Library, main floor contains the Plantation Museum, a collection of historical items depicting the 19th-century plantation system. Museum closed to public. Library open 8 a.m.-noon and 1-5 p.m. Mon, Wed and Fri, and 8 a.m.-noon Thu. (318) 766-3781.

Trinity Episcopal Church, Second St. at Trudeau, Natchitoches. Trinity was built in 1857 and consecrated by the "fighting bishop of the Confederacy," Bishop-General Leonidas K. Polk. By appointment. (318) 352-8072.

Tourist Information Centers

State Tourist Center, U.S. 84 in Vidalia. Open 8:30 a.m.-5 p.m. daily. (318) 336-7008.

Beauregard Tourist Center, 120 S. Washington St., DeRidder. Open 9 a.m.-5 p.m. Mon-Fri. (318) 463-5534.

Los Adaes Tourist Center, La. 6 West in Robeline. Open 8 a.m.-4 p.m. Tue -Sat. (318) 472-6582.

Natchitoches Parish Tourist Commission, 781 Front St., Natchitoches. Open 9 a.m.-5 p.m. Mon-Fri, 10 a.m.-2 p.m. Sat. (318) 352-8072.

Rapides Parish Convention and Visitors Bureau, 2020 W. MacArthur Dr., Alexandria. Open 8 a.m.-5 p.m. daily, winter, 8 a.m.-6 p.m. daily, summer. (318) 443-7049.

Vernon Parish Tourist and Recreation Commission, U.S. 171 North, Leesville. Open 8 a.m.-noon and 1-4:30 p.m. Mon-Fri, and 1-5 p.m. Sat-Sun. (318) 238-0783.

Sportsman's Paradise

Forests are fragrant with the scent of pines, and country streams flow through fertile river valleys. The plush heartland of North Louisiana is a scenic setting for fishermen, hunters, water sports enthusiasts and nature lovers.

Explore the ancient mounds of Poverty Point State Commemorative Area; visit the splendid American Rose Society's gardens; enjoy boating and skiing on Toledo Bend, the South's largest man-made lake; or thrill to the heat of the race at Louisiana Downs.

Attractions

Ambrose Mountain, a granite column on La. 154 near Sailes, marks the site where notorious Bonnie and Clyde were ambushed and killed in 1934 by Texas Rangers and a posse.

American Rose Society Gardens, Exit 5 off I-20 (west of Shreveport and east of Greenwood), follow signs to Jefferson-Paige Rd. This is America's largest garden devoted primarily to roses and is headquarters of America's largest plant society. In the midst of a 118-acre garden, the roses bloom from Apr through Nov, while other flowers and plants provide color all year. Gift shop. Open 8:30 a.m.-4:30 p.m. Mon-Fri (mid-Apr to Oct only) and from 8:30 a.m.-6 p.m. daily. Admission. (318) 938-5402.

Apocalypse Passion Play, just off I-20 (Exit 101) about 10 miles west of Monroe on La. 151 South, near entrance to Roselawn Memorial Gardens near Calhoun. Outdoor drama giving dramatic interpretation to major events in the life of Christ — His birth, teachings, death and resurrection. Performed 8:30 p.m. Thu-Sat, Jun-Aug and 8 p.m. Sat in Sep. Admission. (318) 644-2247.

Barnwell Cultural Center, featuring the R.S. Barnwell Memorial Garden & Art Center, located at 501 Clyde Fant Pkwy., Shreveport, on banks of Red River. Flower and art displays are exhibited by local clubs. Center houses garden activities and includes meeting rooms and a 7,850-square-foot domed botanical conservatory. Open 9 a.m.-4:30 p.m. Mon-Fri and 1-5 p.m. Sat-Sun. Free. (318) 226-6495.

Coushatta Depot, on U.S. 71 in Coushatta. Handmade quilts in traditional or customized designs are created in this old train station. Open 8 a.m.-4:30 p.m. Mon-Fri. Free. (318) 932-5721.

Critter's Creek, in Chennault Park, Monroe. Water slide, water coaster, go-carts, game room and more. Open 10 a.m.-3 p.m. Mon-Tue and Thu-Fri, 10 a.m.-7 p.m. Sat and noon-7 p.m. Sun from first Sat in May through May 31, then 10 a.m.-7 p.m. Mon-Tue and Thu-Sat and noon-7 p.m. Sun from Jun 1 through Labor Day. Closed Wed. Admission. (318) 343-4195.

Driskill Mountain, off La. 147 south of Arcadia, then north on La. 507. This is the highest point in the state, with an elevation of 535 feet above sea level.

Edgewood, on La. 33 near Farmerville. A steamboat-Gothic style mansion built by Jefferson Davis Baughman in 1902.

Emy-Lou Biedenharn Foundation, 2006 Riverside Dr., Monroe, provides a rare and varied experience for visitors. Its three parts are the Bible Research Center (museum-library), ELsong (home of Joe Biedenharn, first bottler of Coca-Cola) and ELsong Gardens (formal English gardens of year-round beauty). Guided tours. Open 10 a.m.-4 p.m. Tue-Fri and 2-5 p.m. Sat-Sun. Free. (318) 387-5281.

Town of Fisher, south of Many on U.S. 171. The homes, picket fences, commissary, opera house and depot of this turn-of-the-century sawmill town, founded in 1897, have been preserved, postcard perfect.

Ford Park, on South Cross Lake Dr. at Yarbrough Road, Shreveport. Newly renovated wooded park on the shore of Cross Lake offers picnic facilities, swimming on the beach area, fishing and a steam locomotive for kids to explore. Open 8 a.m.-sunset daily. Free. (318) 226-6446.

Fort Humbug, Shreveport. Enter from Fant Pkwy. or Youree Drive. Charred logs were placed to appear as cannon, thus "humbugging" Union scouts. Children's recreation area, complete with wooden cannon. Free. (318) 938-5613.

Garden of Prayer, off La. 33 via Parish Roads 822 and 505 near Ruston. This delightful little garden is maintained by the Rock Corner Baptist Church. Free.

Hamel's Park, at 3232 E. 70th St., Shreveport, at the foot of the 70th Street Bridge. Amusement park with rides and games, such as ferris wheel, bumper cars, Tilt-A-Whirl, Kiddie Barn, etc. Open 1-10 p.m. Sat and 1-6 p.m. Sun, spring and fall; 6-10 p.m. Wed-Fri, 1-10 p.m. Sat and 1-8 p.m. Sun, summer. Free. Admission for rides. (318) 869-3566.

Hodges Gardens, located 15 miles south of Many on U.S. 171, has 4,700 acres of gardens, greenhouses, plus 225-acre lake. Wild and cultivated flowers and plants all year. Giant terrazzo map commemorating the Louisiana Purchase. Excursion boat, wildlife, fishing boat rentals, picnic facilities. Open 8 a.m.-sunset daily. Closed New Year's, Christmas Eve, Christmas. Admission. (318) 586-3523.

Jacobs Nature Park, 2.8 miles west of Blanchard via Blanchard-Furrh Rd. A spacious, interpretive building is set in this 160-acre preserve, and through the park run miles of well-marked nature trails. Open 9 a.m.-5 p.m. Wed-Sat and 1-5 p.m. Sun. Free. (318) 929-2806.

Kepler Creek Lake, off La. 507, The "blue hole" behind the dam on the lake is a scenic spot that receives its color from the depth of the water. Fishing, boating, outdoor recreation.

Louisiana Downs Race Track, at 8000 U.S. 80 East in Bossier City. Thoroughbred racing and parimutuel wagering. Season is ordinarily Apr-Oct. Admission. No minors. For exact post times and seasons, call (318) 747-RACE. Outside Louisiana, call toll-free 1-800-551-RACE.

Louisiana Hayride, on La. 3 in Bossier City, 7 miles north of I-20. This is the famous country music show that launched the careers of Hank Williams, Elvis Presley, Johnny Horton, Jim Reeves and Johnny Cash. Restaurant open 5-10 p.m. Mon-Sat. Saturday night's 7:45 p.m. live show is followed by a dance at 10 p.m. Admission. (318) 742-7803.

Louisiana Legend, in Kiroli Park and the Twin City Queen at Forsythe Park in West Monroe. Exciting outdoor drama during Jun, Jul, Aug. Louisiana Legend at 8:30 p.m., Showboat boards at 7:30 p.m., sails at 8 p.m. Admission. (318) 387-5691.

Louisiana Purchase Gardens and Zoo, on Bernstein Drive, Monroe. Beautiful, modern zoo designed around points of historic interest and events involved in the shaping of the Louisiana Territory; features train and boat rides through the gardens and zoo. Open 10 a.m.-5:30 p.m. daily Apr-Oct and 10 a.m.-4:30 p.m. daily Nov - Mar. Admission. (318) 329-2400.

Louisiana Tech Arboretum, on La. Tech University south campus, east of Tech Farm Rd. in Ruston. 50-acre arboretum features a recreation area and the unique avenue of State Trees. Open 8 a.m.-5 p.m. Mon-Fri. Free. (318) 257-2879.

Northeast La. University, Visit Hanna Hall (geological and anthropological exhibits). Monroe. Open 8 a.m.-4:30 p.m. Mon-Fri. During summer months 8 a.m.-4 p.m. Mon-Fri. Free. (318) 342-4100.

Old Chautauqua Grounds, on U.S. 167 North, Ruston. The Chautauquas are no more, and the old resort hotel which once stood here is gone now, but the beautiful rose gardens and mineral springs of the Old Chautauqua Grounds still exist. Free.

Old Shreve Square, 100 block of Texas St. (beneath the Texas Street Bridge at the riverfront), Shreveport. These fabulous old Victorian buildings date to the Gay '90s and now contain restaurants, cafes and nightclubs.

Old Susannah's Country Square, I-20 Exit 108, West Monroe. Over 20 old-fashioned specialty shops featuring unique gifts and crafts — quaint and friendly, nestled in a country village setting. Open 10 a.m.-6 p.m. Mon-Sat, and 1-6 p.m. Sun. Free. (318) 396-2968.

Pioneer Heritage Center, on campus of LSU in Shreveport. A history laboratory museum comprising six authentic plantation structures of pioneer Northwest Louisiana. Trained volunteers interpret everyday life in the 1830s, the period of settlement and early development of the Red River region around Shreveport. Tourist groups by appointment. Open to general public on Sun, tours at 2, 3 and 4 p.m. Admission. (318) 797-5332.

Red Rock General Store, From I-20 (west of Monroe) take Exit 103 to U.S. 80 at Calhoun. Drive 500 yards east on U.S. 80, turn left on Brownlee Road and drive 5 miles. Browse and snack on old-fashioned goodies in this large country store, built in 1893. Antiques, miniatures, crafts and gee-gaws. Open 1-5 p.m. Sat-Sun (closed in Aug). Free. (318) 396-4319.

River Rose Paddlewheeler, 405 Clyde Fant Pkwy., across from Expo Hall, Shreveport. Authentic 150-passenger paddlewheeler that offers a variety of cruises on the historic Red River. Cruises Tue-Sun. Admission. (318) 424-7673.

Shreveport Symphony, performing in the exquisitely renovated Strand Theatre at Crockett and Louisiana Streets. Performances during the year feature a sensitive balance of the innovative and traditional designed for all musical tastes. Admission. (318) 869-2559.

The Symphony House, 2803 Woodlawn Ave., Shreveport. Built in 1872 by Col. Robert H. Lindsey, the home now serves as headquarters for the Shreveport Symphony Society. Open 9 a.m.-5 p.m. Mon-Fri. Free. (318) 869-2559.

Toledo Bend Reservoir, Stretched along the Louisiana-Texas border from Logansport to Toro. Perhaps the state's favorite "honey hole," 60 miles long and 15 miles wide, this 185,000-acre lake is renowned for excellent bass fishing. Marina, public parks, restaurants, boating, camping guides all available. (318) 256-5880.

Toro Hills Golf and Tennis Resort, between Many and Leesville on U.S. 171, facing entrance to Hodges Gardens. The 18-hole championship golf course is just one of the many leisure activities for tourists and conventioneers. Resort also features tennis courts, two adult pools, kids' pool, restaurants, lounges, hotel and golf shop. Hotel open 24 hours. Restaurant open 6 a.m.- 9 p.m. Admission. Toll-free in Louisiana 1-800-282-8560, elsewhere 1-800-551-8536.

Twin Gables Bed & Breakfast, 3 blocks from I-20 in downtown Ruston. Built in rural Lincoln Parish by the Knowles family in 1882, it was moved piece-by-piece to Ruston in 1890 after the arrival of the railroad. Individually furnished rooms with private baths. Manager in from 8 a.m.-noon daily. (318) 255-4452 or (318) 255-8677.

Water Town, 7670 W. 70th St., Shreveport, near I-20. 12-acre, water-related activities park for the entire family. Two speed slides, four body slides, two enclosed slide tubes, activity pool, kiddie pool, hot tubs, concessions, gift shop, video gallery, bath houses, lifeguards at all times, picnic area. Open mid-morning to late evening daily Jun-Aug, weekends Apr-May. Closed Labor Day weekend. Admission. (318) 938-5475.

Historic Places

All Saints Episcopal Church, on the Stonewall-Frierson Rd., 0.7 miles west of

Linwood Rd., just south of Shreveport in Stonewall. One of the few remaining antebellum chapels in Louisiana. Open by appointment only. Free. (318) 925-9885.

Claiborne Parish Courthouse, Homer. The present brick courthouse was accepted July 20, 1861, at an original cost of $12,304. It is a classic example of Greek Revival architecture, and is one of only four pre-Civil War courthouses in the state. Listed on the National Register of Historic Places.

Coates Bluff Postique, a re-creation of a 19th century post office. Located in the east end of Shreveport's main post office building at 2400 Texas Ave. Postique is constructed of lumber salvaged from one of the old millworks near Shreveport, using square nails, antique windows and light fixtures, plank floors and hitching rail and watering trough. Open 9 a.m.-1 p.m. and 1:30-4:15 p.m. Mon-Thu, and 9 a.m.-12:30 p.m. Fri. Free. (318) 226-5154.

Excelsior, on La. 133 in Oak Ridge. This fine old home, built in 1869 on Spanish Land Grant territory for a merchant, is of early Southern architecture with wood-on-wood gallery columns, a wide closed hallway and large rooms with paneled ceilings. The end rooms and kitchen originally were separate structures. Home houses Mib's Museum of antiques and memorabilia and is surrounded by pleasant gardens. Open by appointment or by chance. Admission. (318) 244-6490.

Keatchie Presbyterian Church, on La. 5 in Keatchie. Confederate soldiers wounded at the Battle of Mansfield were treated in this church, which was built in 1856.

Mount Lebanon Baptist Church, on La. 154 in Mount Lebanon. Built in 1837, this church contains slave-made pews with dividers which separated men and women. A chandelier from the home of William C.C. Claiborne (first American governor of Louisiana) hangs inside.

Planters Emporium, 107 Carroll St., Coushatta. Top quality antiques in this historic building, circa 1882. Upstairs houses "almost antiques." Building is on National Register of Historic Places. Tea room nearby, reservations. Foot of Red River Bridge, 2 miles off La. 1. Open 10 a.m.-4 p.m. Fri-Sat, or by appointment. (318) 932-5092 or (504) 344-8284.

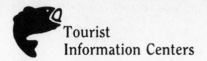

Tourist Information Centers

State Tourist Center, I-20 Westbound, near Mississippi border. Open 8:30 a.m.-5 p.m. daily. (318) 574-5674.

State Tourist Center, I-20 Eastbound, near Texas border, west of Greenwood. Open 8:30 a.m.-5 p.m. daily. Closed Easter, Thanksgiving, Christmas. (318) 938-5613.

State Tourist Center, 15 miles west of Many on La. 6 at Pendleton Bridge. Open 8 a.m.-4:30 p.m. daily. Closed Easter, Thanksgiving, Christmas. (318) 256-5185.

Many Tourist Center, south of La. 6 on U.S. 171. Open 8 a.m.-4 p.m. Mon-Fri. (318) 256-5880.

Monroe-West Monroe Convention and Visitors Bureau of Ouachita Parish, 1333 State Farm Dr., Monroe. Open 8 a.m.-5 p.m. Mon-Sat. Closed Sun. (318) 387-5691.

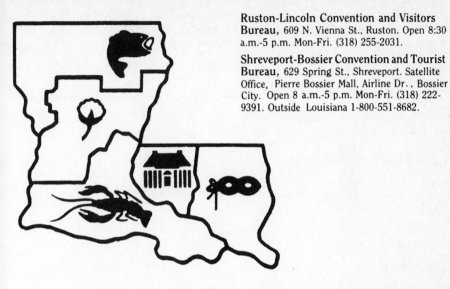

Ruston-Lincoln Convention and Visitors Bureau, 609 N. Vienna St., Ruston. Open 8:30 a.m.-5 p.m. Mon-Fri. (318) 255-2031.

Shreveport-Bossier Convention and Tourist Bureau, 629 Spring St., Shreveport. Satellite Office, Pierre Bossier Mall, Airline Dr., Bossier City. Open 8 a.m.-5 p.m. Mon-Fri. (318) 222-9391. Outside Louisiana 1-800-551-8682.

HIKING AND BACKPACKING

Hiking and Bicycling Trails

Red River Trail (Shreveport) — 4.5 miles
Jefferson Linear Park (Kenner) — 10 miles
Audubon Park (New Orleans) — 1.8 miles
Harahan Trail (New Orleans) — 12 miles

Hiking Trails

Port Hudson Commemorative Area (Baton Rouge) — 7 miles
Cypress-Black Bayou Recreation Area (Bossier City) — 3.5 miles
Sugar Cane Trail (Kisatchie National Forest) — 7.6 miles
Westwego Levee Hike (Westwego-New Orleans) — 10 miles

Algiers Levee Hike (Algiers) — 10 miles
Chalmette Trail (Scarsdale) — 16 miles

Nature Trails

Honey Island Nature Trail (Pearl River Wildlife Management Area)
Louisiana Nature Center (New Orleans) — 2.3 miles
Louisiana State Arboretum (Ville Platte) — 4 miles
Fontainebleau State Park (Mandeville) — 1 mile
Acadiana Park (Lafayette) — 3 miles

Backpacking Trails

Wild Azalea Trail (Kisatchie National Forest) — 31 miles
Chicot State Park (Ville Platte) — 7.5 miles

Definitions

Hiking and Bicycling Trails — *Hardsurfaced trails designed for bicycling, jogging and day hiking.*
Hiking Trails — *Trails designed for walking only and can generally provide an outdoors experience in a morning, afternoon or one full day. Overnight camping is usually found nearby.*

Nature Trails — *Trails designed for walking and interpretation of nature through the use of a printed guidebook or signs.*
Backpacking Trails — *Trails designed for an overnight experience where camping along the trail is allowed.*

For more information, write the New Orleans Group of the Sierra Club, 111 S. Hennessey St., New Orleans, LA 70119.

Canoeing

Southwestern Louisiana
Whiskey Chitto Creek — Calcasieu River
Six Mile Creek and Upper Whiskey Chitto Creek
Calcasieu River
Spring Creek
Anacoco Creek
Bayou Teche
Vermilion River
Bayou Tortue
Atchafalaya Basin
Atchafalaya Basin, Lake Grevenberg and Buffalo Cove

Southeastern Louisiana
Bogue Chitto River — Mississippi and Louisiana
Amite River
Tangipahoa River
Bogue Falaya River
Tchefuncte River
Tickfaw River

Central Louisiana
Kisatchie Bayou

Northern Louisiana
Bayou Dorcheat and Lake Bistineau
Bayou de L'outre
Chemin-A-Haut Bayou
Castor Creek in Caldwell Parish
Saline Bayou
Bayou D'Arbonne
Carney Creek
Bayou Bartholomew

For more information on canoeing in Louisiana, contact the Lafayette Natural History Museum and Planetarium, 637 Girard Park Dr., Lafayette, LA 70503, (318) 261-8350; or the New Orleans Group of the Sierra Club, 111 S. Hennessey St., New Orleans, LA 70119.

Tubing

Tubing the Tangipahoa
Independence, La Puma Beach (504) 878-6067
North Tangi Beach (504) 748-7239
Tickfaw, Cherokee Beach (504) 345-8485
Ponchatoula, Ponchatoula Beach (504) 386-6844

PRINCIPAL LOUISIANA ARTS ORGANIZATIONS

DANCE PRODUCTION GROUPS

Ballet Lyrique
P.O. Box 4209
Shreveport, LA 71104
Mr. Mills
Phone: 865-2947

Ballet South of New Orleans
6111 Elysian Fields Ave.
New Orleans, LA 70122
Ellen Hardeman
Phone: 283-6159

Baton Rouge Ballet Theatre
P. O. Box 64937
Baton Rouge, LA 70897
Margaret Stagg, Pres.
Phone: 927-7587

Crescent Ballet Company
3211 Taft Park Dr.
Metairie, LA 70002
Pat LeClero, Dir.
Phone: 885-2352

Delta Festival Ballet
4410 Clearview Dr.
Metairie, LA 70002
Kendal D. McDaniel, Pres.
Phone: 887-3446

Gonzales American Dance Theater
P. O. Box 417
Gonzales, LA 70737
Jackie Delong
Phone: 675-8185

Lafayette Festival Ballet
216 Devalcourt
Lafayette, LA 70506
Jeffrie Perkins Wall
Phone: 233-9972

Lake Charles Ballet Society
P.O. Box 5515
Lake Charles, LA 70601
Ida Winter Clark
Phone: 439-4018

Lake Charles Civic Ballet
904 Kirby St.
Lake Charles, LA 70601
Lady Leah Lafargue Hathaway
Phone: 433-1125

Louisiana Ballet Company
1765 Dallas Drive
Baton Rouge, LA 70806
Melanie Safer
Phone: 927-1730

Moving South Dance Company
100 Sycamore St.
Lafayette, LA 70506
Becky Valls
Phone: 988-5177

New Iberia Civic Ballet Co.
160 Duperier St.
New Iberia, LA 70560
Ms. Gail Freese
Phone: 365-1647

New Orleans Ballet Company
3110 St. Charles Ave.
New Orleans, LA 70115
Joan Friend
Phone: 895-2439

Southwest Dance Theatre
301 Shell Beach Dr.
Lake Charles, LA 70601
Sarah Quinn Jones
Phone: 433-3969

Shreveport Ballet Theatre
3811 Youree Dr.
Shreveport, LA 71105
Mrs. Walter Hawkins
Phone: 868-1087

Twin City Ballet Company
214 Haynes St.
West Monroe, LA 71201
Linda Lavender
Phone: 325-7179

MUSIC PRODUCTION GROUPS

Acadiana Symphony Orchestra
704 Lee Dr.
Lafayette, LA 70501
Mr. John Shennault
Phone: 233-7060

Baton Rouge Opera Guild
4484 W. Lakeshore Dr.
Baton Rouge, LA 70803
Mrs. Allison Kolb
Phone: 928-1639

The Baton Rouge Symphony
P.O. Box 103
Baton Rouge, LA 70821
Mr. Richard Mackie
Phone: 387-6166

Civic Symphony Orchestra
10041 Joel Ave.
River Ridge, LA 70123
Mr. Gordón O. Brown
Phone: 737-3827

Concert Choir of New Orleans
1020 St. Julien St., Apt. 118
Kenner, LA 70062
Mr. Mark Whitney
Phone: 467-5824

Jubilation
P.O. Box 4066
New Orleans, LA 70178
Mr. Leland P. Bennette
Phone: 831-9832

Lake Charles Civic Symphony
P.O. Box 3102
Lake Charles, LA 70601
Karl E. Boellert, Pres.
Phone: 478-6443 or 433-5237

Monroe Symphony Orchestra
P.O. Box 4353
Monroe, LA 71201
Jack May
Phone: 325-9462

Musica Da Camera
1035 Eleonora St.
New Orleans, LA 70115
Mr. Milton G. Scheuermann
Phone: 944-8758

New Leviathan Oriental Fox Trot
Orchestra
6 Jeri Ct.
New Orleans, LA 70121
Mr. Bruce Pollock
Phone: 835-6025

New Orleans Opera Association, Inc.
333 St. Charles Ave.
New Orleans, LA 70130
H. Lloyd Hawkins, Pres.
Phone: 529-2278

New Orleans Philharmonic Symphony
Orchestra
Suite 903, 203 Carondelet St.
New Orleans, LA 70130
Jim Hicks, Gen. Mgr.
Phone: 524-0404

Rapides Symphony Orchestra
4503 Willowwick Blvd.
Alexandria, LA 71301
LeDoux Provosty, Jr.
Phone: 445-3631

Shreveport Civic Opera
Civic Theater Box 4009
Shreveport, LA 71104
R. J. Murray
Phone: 868-0906

Shreveport Symphony
P.O. Box 4057
Shreveport, LA 71104
Russell Allen
Phone: 869-2559

Shreveport Symphony Opera
2803 Woodlawn
Shreveport, LA 71104
Phone: 869-2559

THEATRE GROUPS

Abbey Players Theatre
200 S. Main St.
Abbeville, LA 70510
Becky Stokes
Phone: 893-2442

Acadia Repertory Theater
P.O. Box 52248
Lafayette, LA 70505
Ms. Rose Anderson

Central Louisiana Community Theatre, Inc.
2019 Horseshoe Dr.
Alexandria, LA 71301
Mrs. Carolyn Pitts
Phone: 442-1376

Dashiki Project Theatre
P.O. Box 8323
New Orleans, LA 70182
Ted Gilliam
Phone: 283-4464

Diversity Players
912 Toulouse St.
New Orleans, LA 70112
Ms. Rose Summers
Phone: 581-5846

Experimental Theatre Company
4920 S. Bienville Ave.
New Orleans, La 70119
Charles Kerbs, Pres.
Phone: 482-0681

Free Southern Theatre
601 S. Scott St.
New Orleans, LA 70119
John O'Neal
Phone: 488-8521

Lafayette Community Theatre
529 Jefferson St.
Lafayette, LA 70501
Jack Reedy
Phone: 235-1532

Le Petit Theater De Terrebonne
P.O. Box 805
Houma, LA 70361
Gerald Daigle
Phone: 872-6842

Le Petit Theatre Du Vieux Carre
616 St. Peter St.
New Orleans, LA 70116
Mrs. George A. Broes, Pres.
Phone: 522-9958

Louisiana Outdoor Drama Association
P.O. Box 1714
Natchitoches, LA 71457
Phone: 357-1714

Off-Off-Off Broadway Players
620 Washington Ave.
New Orleans, LA 70130
Robert N. and Emily Cronin
Phone: 586-4521

Playwrights Theater of Louisiana
4855 W. Congress St.
Lafayette, LA 70506
Helen Jones

Thibodaux Playhouse, Inc.
P.O. Box 43
Thibodaux, LA 70301
Earline LeBlanc
Phone: 446-1896

Calendar of Louisiana Fairs, Festivals, and Celebrations

Louisiana's most famous party is of course the often wild Mardi Gras, a holiday that originally marked the solemn onset of Lent, but that is now better known for parades, beautifully decorated floats, masked balls, strange costumes, and huge crowds of shouting people. Mardi Gras, however, is only the beginning of fun in Louisiana. The calendar is packed with twelve months of events of all types--parades, music, food, exhibits--so many you can't possibly see them all!

Celebrations are arranged alphabetically under the months in which they occur, except for those related to the "floating" dates of Easter and Mardi Gras, and are followed by locations (the nearest town is given for events outside city limits), and the approximate dates. For exact information concerning dates and attractions, and especially before making a long trip to visit one of the listed events, write or call the appropriate contact in the event information list:

Louisiana Office of Tourism
P.O. Box 1111
Baton Rouge, LA 70821
(504) 925-3860

Mardi Gras
In addition to the mammoth celebration of Mardi Gras in New Orleans, other Louisiana cities, including Eunice, Houma, Lafayette, Mamou, New Roads, and Slidell, feature Fat Tuesday parades. Other Carnival-related events occur during this season.

Courrir de Mardi Gras la Pointe de l'Eglise--Church Point (Sunday prior to Mardi Gras)
La Grand Boucherie des Cajuns--St. Martinville (Sunday prior to Mardi Gras)
Lafayette Mardi Gras Festival--Lafayette Tchefuncte Mardi Gras Boat Parade--Madisonville (Sunday prior to Mardi Gras)

Easter
French Acadian Music Festival--Abbeville (second Saturday after Easter)
Hodges Gardens Predawn Easter Sunrise Services--Many (Easter morning)
New Orleans Spring Fiesta--New Orleans (first Friday after Easter through fourth Wednesday after Easter)

FRENCH MARKET

January
Battle of New Orleans Commemoration--
    Chalmette (early)
Louisiana Wildlife and Fur Festival--
    Cameron (second and third
    weekends)
Sugar Bowl Football Classic--New Orleans
    (January 1 or 2)

February
Bayou Ramble Antique Show and Sale--
    Opelousas (last full week)
Louisiana Boudin Festival--Broussard
    (second week)
Louisiana State University Livestock
    Shows--Baton Rouge
Mid-Winter Livestock Expo and Farm
    Machinery Show--Shreveport
    (second week)

March
Amite Oyster Day--Amite (third week)
Audubon Pilgrimage--St. Francisville
    (third week)
Bogalusa Dogwood Festival and Tour of
    Homes--Bogalusa (late)
Boggy Bayou Festival--Pine Prairie (mid-
    month)
East Feliciana Arts and Crafts Festival--
    Clinton (late)
Feliciana Festival--Clinton (last week)
LAA Annual Spring Arts and Crafts Show--
    Lafayette (first weekend)
Lafayette Azalea Trail--Lafayette (second
    week, seasonal)
Louisiana Nursery Festival--Forest Hill
    (third week)
New Growth Festival--A Celebration of
    Spring--Houma (late)
Rabbit Festival--Iowa (third week)
St. Joseph Day Celebration--Houma (mid-
    month)

St. Mary Parish Showcase--Franklin (last
    Sunday)
St. Patrick's Day Parade--Slidell (mid-
    month)
Spring Catahoula Dog Show--Denham Spring
    (late)
Tezcuco Plantation Civil War Reenactment
    -Burnside (early)
Trade Days on Cotile--Boyce (late)
USF & G Golf Tournament--New Orleans
    (mid-month)
Wcosta Spring Festival--Vinton (late)

April
Academy Conge--Grand Coteau (early)
American Legion Strawberry and Food
    Festival--Gonzales (late)
Artbreak Festival--Shreveport (late)
Battle of Mansfield--Mansfield (every
    five years; next in 1990)
Battle of Pleasant Hill Reenactment--
    Pleasant Hill (last weekend)
Blessing of the Shrimp Fleet--Chauvin
    (late)
Cajun Food and Fun Festival--Welsh (lat
Catfish Festival--Winnsboro (mid-month)
Cenlabration--Alexandria (late)
Claiborne Parish Jubilee--Homer (late
    April-early May)
Cochon de Lait Festival--Mansura (fourt
    weekend)
Coushatta Olde Time Country Festival--
    · Coushatta (late)
Crawfish Festival of St. Bernard--
    Chalmette (late)
Creole Festival--Jeanerette (late)
East Feliciana Spring Pilgrimage--Clint
    (late)
Farmerville Tour of Homes--Farmerville
    (last Sunday)
Firemen's Parade and Festival--Thibodau
    (last week)

ench Acadian Music Festival--Abbeville
(late)

ench Quarter Festival--New Orleans
(second weekend)

ant Parish Dogwood Festival--Pollock
(first Saturday)

liday in Dixie--Shreveport (mid-month)

ly Rosary Creole Festival--Houma (late)

dependence Italian Festival--
Independence (late)

uisiana Air Tour--statewide (late)

uisiana Forest Festival--Winnfield
(late)

uisiana Pine Tree Festival--Walker
(early)

uisiana Railroad Days Festival--
DeQuincy (second week)

adewood Arts Festival--Napoleonville
(mid-month)

ew Orleans Jazz and Heritage Festival--
New Orleans (end of April through
beginning of May)

le Country Bazaar--New Iberia (mid-
month)

ke Salad Festival--Oak Grove (early)

ntchatoula Strawberry Festival--
Pontchatoula (mid-month)

ver City Blues Festival--Baton Rouge
(late)

t. James River Road Food Festival--St.
James (early)

outhdown Spring Marketplace--Houma
(late)

Spring Fiesta--New Orleans (late)

Strawberry Festival--Gonzales (last full
weekend)

Washington Pilgrimage--Washington (last
weekend)

May

Allons Manger Food Festival--Hammond
(first Sunday)

Bossier City Arts and Crafts Festival--
Bossier City (mid-month)

Breaux Bridge Crawfish Festival--Breaux
Bridge (first weekend)

Cajun Country Outdoor Opry and Fais Do-
do--Houma (early)

Cajun Day--Mamou (last weekend)

Cheneyville Arts and Crafts Show and Tour
of Homes--Cheneyville (third
Saturday)

Contraband Days--Lake Charles (late April
through early May)

Fest-For-All--Baton Rouge (last weekend)

Festa Italiano--Shreveport (mid-month)

Festival of Festivals--Monroe (late)

Five Lakes Bluegrass Festival--Bush
(late)

Gator Festival--Baton Rouge (first
weekend)

Germanfest--Minden (second weekend)

The Great Amite River Catfish Festival--
    Denham Springs (mid-month)
Hammond Heritage Day--Hammond (first
    Sunday)
Hungarian Festival--Albany (early)
Italian Festival--Luling (second weekend)
Lasallette Rainbow of Fun Festival--
    Sulphur (late)
Louisiana Balloon Festival and Air Show--
    Hammond (mid-month)
Louisiana Passion Play--Calhoun (begins
    in May, running through
    September)
Louisiana Praline Festival--Houma (first
    weekend)
Lutcher-Grammercy Free Fair--Lutcher
    (early)
Madisonville Boat Races--Madisonville
    (late)
Mayhaw Festival--Marion (first weekend)
Mt. Lebanon Stagecoach Trail and Tour of
    Homes--Gibsland (first Sunday)
Nitram Park's Bluegrass Festival--Pitkin
    (late)
Pearl River Catfish Festival--Pearl River
    (mid-month)
River City Fest--Logansport (first
    weekend)
Rose Festival and Show--Shreveport (first
    week)
Sacred Heart Spring Festival--Oakdale
    (first weekend)
Sawmill Days--Fisher (fourth weekend)
Southeast Louisiana Dairy Festival and
    Livestock Show--Hammond (first
    Saturday)
Timberfest--Bastrop (first weekend)
Toledo Bend Trash Festival--Many
    (Memorial Day weekend)
Tomato Festival--Chalmette (first
    weekend)
West Louisiana Folk Arts & Crafts
    Festival--Leesville (early)

June
Acadian 500 Tricycle Race--New Iberia
    (second Sunday)
Angola Arts and Crafts Festival--Angola
    (late)
Antique Festival--Pontchatoula (mid-
    month)
Bayou Lacombe Crab Festival--Lacombe
Cajun Crab Festival--Henderson (first
    weekend)
Cajun Music Festival--Mamou (first
    weekend)
Cenlabration--Alexandria (end of May-
    beginning of June)
Corney Creek Festival and Governor's C
    Canoe Races--Bernice (first
    weekend)
Feliciana Peach Festival--Clinton (mid
    month)
Jambalaya Festival--Gonzales (second
    weekend)
Kentwood Dairy Festival--Kentwood (fir
    Saturday)
Lafete Louisiana--Baton Rouge (first
    weekend)
Le Bayou Teche Festival de Barbue--
    Franklin
Louisiana Blueberry Festival--Mansfiel
    (first weekend)
Louisiana Corn Festival--Bunkie (late)
Louisiana Peach Festival--Ruston (last
    two weeks)
Melrose Arts and Crafts Festival--
    Natchitoches (third weekend)
Okra Festival--Kenner (first weekend)
Spring Folk Festival--Gilbert (first
    Sunday)
Taste of Louisiana--Sulphur (mid-month
World's Champion Pirogue Races--Jean
    Lafitte (last Sunday)

July

Annual Beef Cook-Off--Opelousas (late)

Bastille Day--Kaplan (July 14)

Bastille Day--New Orleans (July 14)

Cajun Bastille Day--Baton Rouge (weekend
before July 14)

Cameron Parish Deep Sea Fishing Rodeo--
Grand Chenier Park (July 4
weekend)

Chitimacha Tribal Fair--Charenton (early)

Church Point Buggy Festival--Church Point
(July 4 weekend)

Creole Summer Festival--French Settlement
(third Sunday)

Depot Day in Pontchatoula--Pontchatoula
(second Saturday)

Erath 4th of July Fair and Festival--
Erath (July 4)

Family Festival--Eunice (July 4)

Festival International de Louisiane--
Lafayette (end of June-
beginning of July)

Golden Meadow International Tarpon Rodeo-
-Grand Isle (July 4 weekend)

Grand Isle International Tarpon Rodeo--
Grand Isle (last Thursday through
Saturday)

La Fete de la Nouvelle Orleans--New
Orleans (first two weeks)

Louisiana Catfish Festival--Des Allemands
(weekend after July 4)

Louisiana Freedom Festival--Elton (early)

Louisiana Heritage Festival--Monroe

Louisiana Oil Festival--Jennings

Louisiana Oyster Festival--Galliano
(third weekend)

Louisiana Paper Festival--Bogalusa
(early)

Louisiana Sauce Piquante Festival--French
Settlement (mid-month)

Louisiana Shakespeare Festival--Lake
Charles (late July-early August)

Louisiana Watermelon Festival--
Farmerville (last weekend)

Morgan City Fourth of July Fair and
Celebration--Morgan City (July 4
weekend)

New Orleans Food Festival--New Orleans
(July 4 weekend)

Northwestern Festival--Natchitoches
(third weekend)

Old-Fashioned Folk Festival--West Monroe
(third weekend)

St. Charles Parish Festival--
Norco/Destrehan (late)

Slidell Freedom Fair--Slidell (July 4
weekend)

Watermelon Festival--Franklinton (mid-
month)

August

Cajun Hunters Festival--Cut Off (late)

Calcasieu Cajun Festival--Sulphur (late)

Delcambre Shrimp Festival--Delcambre
(third weekend)

Empire South Pass Tarpon Rodeo--Empire
(third weekend)

Festival in the Forest--Many (early)

Fete des Acadiens--Lafayette (mid-month)

Lafitte Seafood Festival--Lafitte (early)

Le Bal de Maison--Lafayette (early)

South Lafourche Seafood Festival--
Galliano (second weekend)

September

Abbeville Kiwanis Tarpon Rodeo--Abbeville
(Labor Day weekend)

Abita Springs Water Festival--Abita
Springs (early)

Acadiana Fair and Trade Show--Lafayette

American Indian Pow Wow--Baton Rouge (early)

Ark-La-Miss Agri-Industrial Fair--West Monroe (early September through late October)

Backwood Village Folk Festival--Goldonna (mid-month)

Bayou Blue Food and Fun Festival--Houma (second weekend)

Bayou Lafourche Antique Show and Sale--Thibodaux

Beauregard Parish Pioneer Festival--DeRidder

Cajun Day Festival--Church Point

Cajun Festival--Vinton (third weekend)

Christian Family Festival--Pontchatoula (third weekend)

Festivals Acadiens--Lafayette (third weekend)

Greenwood Pioneer Days--Greenwood (Thursday through Saturday prior to Labor Day)

Gueydan Duck Festival--Gueydan (second weekend)

Harahan Railroad Fair--Harahan (mid-month)

Jackson Parish Junior Livestock Show--Jonesboro (last Saturday)

Kinder Sauce Piquante and Music Festival--Kinder (Labor Day weekend)

La Musique de la Prairie Mamou--Grand Mamou (weekend prior to Labor Day)

Lafourche Parish Agricultural Fair and Livestock Show--Raceland (last full weekend)

LaSalle Parish Fair--Jena (week after Labor Day)

Louisiana Downs Super Derby Festival--Bossier City/Shreveport (mid-month)

Louisiana Gumbo Festival of Chackbay--Chackbay (early)

Louisiana Shrimp and Petroleum Festival Morgan City (Labor Day weekend)

Louisiana Soybean Festival--Jonesville (second week)

Louisiana Sugar Cane Festival--New Iber (late)

Louisiana Wildfowl Carvers and Collecto Festival--New Orleans (last wee

North Louisiana Cotton Festival and Fai -Bastrop (third Tuesday through Saturday)

Oil Patch Festival--Haynesville (mid-month)

Original Red Beans and Rice Festival--Metairie (mid-month)

Pirogue Race--Houma (Labor Day)

Rayne Frog Festival--Rayne (third weekend)

Red River Parish Fair--Coushatta (late)

River City End of Summer Musical Extravaganza--Baton Rouge (ear

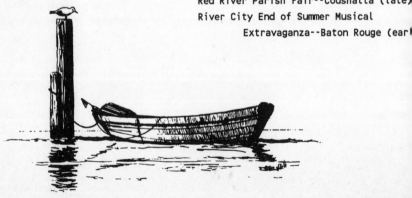

bine Parish Fair--Many (last full week)
. Andrews Parish Festival--Amelia
    (late)
. Helena Forest Festival--Greensburg
    (late)
idell Trade Fair--Slidell (late)
uthwest Louisiana State Fair and Trade
    Exposition--Lake Charles (late)
ink Creek Horseshoe Tournament--Swartz
    (second weekend)
ngipahoa Parish Fair--Amite (late
    September through early October)
ndebilt Autumn Festival--Houma (late)
nn Parish Fair--Winnfield (late
    September through early October)
lf Creek Arts and Crafts Festival--
    Sikes (third weekend)
deco Festival--Plaisance (early)

tober
len Parish Fair--Oberlin
lons aux Avoyelles Tour of Homes--
    Mansura (fourth Saturday)
douille Festival--LaPlace (last full
    weekend)
gola Prison Rodeo--Angola (every Sunday
    in October)
tique Show and Sale--Baton Rouge (first
    weekend)
cension Parish Fair--Prairieville
    (first weekend)
ton Rouge Antique Dealers Show and
    Sale--Baton Rouge
ton Rouge Fall Crafts Festival--Baton
    Rouge
auregard Parish Fair--DeRidder (fifth
    week after Labor Day)
ddo Parish Fair--Shreveport (early)
lcasieu-Cameron Bi-Parish Fair--Sulphur
    (first week)
tahoula Lake Festival--Pineville
    (fourth weekend)

Celebration Uptown--New Orleans (mid-
    month)
Children's Hospital Celebration--New
    Orleans (early)
Claiborne Parish Fair and Northwest
    Louisiana Dairy Festival--
    Haynesville (first week)
Cochon de Lait Festival--Luling (mid-
    month)
Cut Off Youth Center Fair--Cut Off (first
    weekend)
Delhi Fall Festival--Delhi (mid-month)
Donaldsonville Sunshine Festival--
    Donaldsonville (early)
Festa d'Italia--New Orleans (early)
Festival of Beauties--Youngsville (first
    full week)
Franklin Arts Festival--Franklin (first
    weekend)
French Food Festival--Larose (last full
    weekend)
French Louisiana Festival--Kenner (mid-
    month)
Greater Baton Rouge State Fair--Baton
    Rouge (late October through early
    November)
The Gumbo Festival--Bridge City (second
    full weekend)
International Acadian Festival--
    Plaquemine (third weekend)
International Alligator Festival--
    Franklin (third weekend)
International Rice Festival--Crowley
    (third weekend)
Jaycee Fair and Forestry Festival--Minden
    (early)
Jefferson Davis Parish Fair--Jennings
    (last weekend)
Keatchie Heritage Day--Keatchie (last
    weekend)
La Vie la Fourchaise Festival--Mathews
    (third weekend)

Lagniappe on the Bayou--Chauvin (second
full weekend)
Livingston Parish Fair--Livingston
(second full week)
Los Islenos Spanish Festival--St. Bernard
(mid-month)
Louisiana Art and Folk Festival--Columbia
(early)
Louisiana Cattle Festival and Fair--
Abbeville (first full weekend)
Louisiana Cotton Festival and Tournoi--
Ville Platte (second weekend)
Louisiana Dixie Darling Festival--Baton
Rouge (first weekend)
Louisiana Gulf Coast Oil Exposition--
Lafayette (third week,   Wednes-
day through Saturday; biennial,
odd years only)
Louisiana State Fair--Shreveport (seventh
Friday after Labor Day)
Louisiana Swine Festival--Basile (late
October through early November)
Louisiana Yambilee Festival--Opelousas
(last full weekend)
Marthaville Bluegrass Festival--
Marthaville (mid-month)
Natchitoches Historic Tour of Homes--
Natchitoches (second weekend)
Natchitoches Parish Fair--Natchitoches
(first week, beginning last
Wednesday of September)
North Louisiana Central District Fair--
Olla (mid-month)
North Louisiana State Fair--Ruston (first
or second week)
October Fete--Kaplan (mid-month)
Octoberfest--Jackson (mid-month)
Old Farmer's Day--Loranger (mid-month)
Ole Fashion Folk Festival--Monroe (first
ten days)
Pilot Club Flea Market, Arts and Crafts
Sale--Winnfield (early)
Plantation Day at Magnolia Mound--Baton
Rouge (late)

Pointe Coupee Fair and Festival--New
Roads
Potpourri Festival and Rodeo--Port Allen
(mid-month)
Poverty Point Festival--Delhi (mid-month)
Raceland Sauce Piquante Festival--
Raceland (first weekend)
Rapides Parish Fair--Alexandria (second
Tuesday)
Red River Revel--Shreveport (first
weekend)
St. Philomena, Cajun Country Festival--
Labadieville (early)
Six Flags Over Broadmoor--Houma (mid-
month)
Sorrento Boucherie--sorrento (second
weekend)
Tamale Fiesta--Zwolle (second weekend)
Tensas River Road Tour--St. Joseph
Terrebonne Parish Fair and Rodeo--Houma
(early)
Vermilion Fair and Fest--Kaplan (mid-
month)
Vidalia Chambre Festival--Vidalia (early)
Violet Oyster Festival--Violet (late)
Washington Parish Free Fair--Franklinton
(mid-month)
West Carroll Jaycee Fair--Oak Grove (mid
month)
West Louisiana Forestry Festival--
Leesville (first week)

November
Broussard Community Fair--Broussard
(weekend before Thanksgiving)
Cajun Sailing Regatta--Houma (early)
Catahoula Heritage Festival--Alexandria
(late October-early November)
Catahoula Lake Festival--Pineville (late
October-early November)
Christmas on the Bayou--Lafayette (late
Christmas Parade--Kenner (late)
DeRidder Arts and Crafts Festival--
DeRidder (late)

estrehan Plantation Fall Festival--
    Destrehan (second weekend)
estival de Grand Coteau--Arnaudville
    (first Sunday)
ambalaya Tours--Clinton (late)
afayette Arts and Crafts Festival--
    Lafayette (second weekend)
oreauville Harvest Fest--Loreauville
    (late)
ouisiana Cycling--Clinton (late)
ouisiana Folklife Festival--Baton Rouge
    (late October-early November)
ouisiana Pecan Festival--Colfax (first
    weekend)
amou Armistice Day Celebration--Mamou
    (November 11)
ississippi River Fair and Trade
    Exposition--New Orleans
ortheast Camelia Show--Monroe (seasonal)
abine Free-State Festival--Florien
    (second weekend)
t. Tammany Parish Fair--Covington
    (early)
outhdown Fall Festival--Houma (first
    weekend)
panish Heritage and Cultural Festival--
    Derico Island (early)
weet Adeline Craft Fair--Slidell (late)
heelbarrow Parade--Garyville (late)

ecember
onfires on the Levee--Lutcher-Grammercy
    area (Christmas Eve)
hristmas Comes Alive--Acadian Village,
    Lafayette (second week)
hristmas in the Country--Elizabeth
    (first Sunday)
hristmas in the Country--Lacombe
hristmas in Roseland--Shreveport (late
    November through December 31)
hristmas Lights and Set-Pieces--
    Natchitoches (all month)
hristmas Parade--Bossier City (first
    Friday night)

Christmas Parade--Eunice (first Saturday)
Christmas Parade--Many (second Saturday)
Christmas Parade--Sulphur (second week)
Christmas Parade--Vidalia (early)
A Creole Christmas in the French Quarter-
    New Orleans (entire month)
Destrehan Plantation Christmas Open
    House--Destrehan (first Sunday)
Hodges Gardens Christmas Festival of
    Lights--Many (early)
Houma Tour of Homes--Houma (early)
Independence Bowl--Shreveport (second
    Saturday)
Madewood Christmas Heritage Banquet--
    Napoleonville (mid-month)
Madisonville Santa Parade--Madisonville
    (second Sunday)
Merry Cajun Christmas--Lafayette (entire
    month)
Natchitoches Christmas Festival--
    Natchitoches (first Sunday)
Nineteenth Century Christmas at Mount
    Hope--Baton Rouge (early)
Oak Alley Plantation Christmas Bonfire
    Party--Vacherie (mid-month)
Plaquemine Parish Fair and Orange
    Festival--Fort Jackson (first
    weekend)
Santa on the Bayou--Lacombe (early)
Teche Queen "Christmas on the Bayou"--New
    Iberia (three weekends)
Winterfest--Monroe (December 1 through
    Christmas Day)

Louisiana Fairs, Festivals, and Celebrations
Event Information Contacts

January

Sugar Bowl Classic
New Orleans, La.
Mickey Holmes (504) 525-8573

Louisiana Fur and Wildlife Festival
Cameron, La.
Bonnie Conner (318) 775-5718

Battle of New Orleans (Reenactment)
Chalmette, La.
Ray Brende (504) 589-4429

Louisiana Boudin Festival
Broussard, La.
Martin Richard (318) 837-4505

February

Mid-Winter Livestock Expo and
Farm Machinery Show
Shreveport, La.
C. Ed Nelson (318) 635-1361

Frontier Days Celebration
Logansport, La.
Milton Smith (318) 697-5902

LSU Open Livestock Show
Baton Rouge, La.
Dr. W. H. Waters (504) 383-1404

International Crawfish Tasting/
Trade Show
Lafayette, La.
Lawrence Adams (318) 235-7072

Bayou Ramble Antique Show and Sale
Opelousas, La.
Bill Bourdier (318) 942-6963

March

Tezcuco Plantation Civil War
Reenactment
Burnside, La.
Debris Purifoy (504) 562-7042

LAA Annual Spring Arts and Crafts
Show
Lafayette, La.
C. Wooley (318) 269-0363

Boggy Bayou Festival
Pine Prairie, La.
Debbie Oge (318) 599-2690

St. Joseph Day Celebration
Houma, La.
Ray Marcello (504) 879-3535

USF & G Golf Classic
New Orleans, La.
Shirley Daniels (504) 529-3343

Amite Oyster Day
Amite, La.
George Dees (504) 748-7626

Rabbit Festival
Iowa, La.
Maxine Guthrey (318) 582-6120

Audubon Pilgrimage
St. Francisville, La.
Elizabeth K. Dart (504) 635-6330

Louisiana Redbud Festival
Vivian, La.
Chris Daniel (318) 375-3279

Louisiana Nursery Festival
Forest Hill, La.
Elizabeth Chamberlain (318) 659-4951

Antique Show and Sale
Jackson, La.
Olivia Acosta (504) 634-7155

Wcosta Spring Festival
Vinton, La.
Danny Cooper (318) 589-2903

New Growth Festival--A Celebration
Houma, La.
David Ellender (504) 876-4239

Trade Days on Cotile
Boyce, La.
Ralph C. Nielsen (318) 793-8995

Feliciana Arts and Crafts Festival
Clinton, La.
Cindy Mead (504) 683-3721

Spring Louisiana Catahoula Dog Show
Denham Springs, La.
(504) 665-6082

April

Poke Salad Festival
Oak Grove, La.
James H. Dumas (318) 428-3275

Crawfish Festival of St. Bernard
Chalmette, La.
Ruben Saavedra (504) 277-1026

Holiday in Dixie
Shreveport, La.
Judy O. Williams (318) 227-1515

Grant Parish Dogwood Festival
Pollock, La.
Elaine Beck (318) 765-3304

River City Blues Festival
Baton Rouge, La.
Rick Sabino (504) 344-3328

St. James River Road Food Festival
St. James, La.
Grace Graugnard (504) 265-4210

Academy Conge
Grand Coteau, La.
Ann Dreyfus (318) 662-5275

Louisiana Railroad Days Festival
DeQuincy, La.
Ranita Peterson (318) 786-8241

French Quarter Festival
New Orleans, La.
Sandra S. Dartus (504) 522-5730

Southdown Spring Marketplace
Houma, La.
Jody Waggenspack (504) 851-0154

Catfish Festival
Winnsboro, La.
E. Rudolph McIntyre (318) 435-4205

Ponchatoula Strawberry Festival
Ponchatoula, La.
Bobby Cortez (504) 386-6601

Firemen's Fair and Parade
Thibodaux, La.
Huey Guillot (504) 447-5308

Holy Rosary Creole Festival
Houma, La.
Dale Boudwin (504) 876-7652

Spring Fiesta
New Orleans, La.
(504) 581-1367

American Legion Strawberry and
Food Festival
Gonzales, La.
Ernest J. Cubbage (504) 644-4191

Louisiana Forest Festival
Winnfield, La.
Carolyn R. Phillips (318) 628-4528

Cajun Food and Fun Festival
Welsh, La.
Emerson Walker (318) 734-2769

Creole Festival
Jeanerette, La.
Iberia Tourist Commission
(318) 276-4850

Artbreak Festival
Shreveport, La.
Pam Atchison (318) 226-6446

Greater New Orleans
Jazz and Heritage Festival
New Orleans, La.
Anna Zimmerman (504) 522-4786

French Acadian Music Festival
Abbeville, La.
Robert P. Prejean (318) 893-1257

East Feliciana Spring Pilgrimage
Clinton, La.
Mildred P. Worrell (504) 683-5594

Battle of Pleasant Hill Reenactment
Pleasant Hill, La.
Dr. C. E. Poimboeuf (318) 796-3311

Independence Italian Festival
Independence, La.
Joseph A. Costa (504) 878-6371

Historic Washington Pilgrimage
Festival
Washington, La.
Mildred Nicholson (318) 826-3626

Blessing of the Shrimp Fleet
Chauvin, La.
Msgr. Frederic J. Brunet
(504) 594-5859

Claiborne Parish Jubilee
Homer, La.
Betty Fratus (318) 927-6651

Contraband Days
Lake Charles, La.
Lana Kate Brunet (318) 436-5508

Coushatta Olde Time Country Festival
Coushatta, La.
Rose Cox (318) 932-6904

May

Louisiana Praline Festival
Houma, La.
Winston English (504) 876-2047

River City Fest
Logansport, La.
Margaret McBride (318) 697-2593

Louisiana Passion Play
Calhoun, La.
James Burns (318) 644-2247

Sacred Heart Spring Festival
Oakdale, La.
Rev. John Poerio (318) 335-3780

Gator Festival
Baton Rouge, La.
(504) 293-7950

Hungarian Festival
Albany, La.
John Huszar (504) 345-8849

Stage Coach Trail Historical Day/
Homecoming Day
Mt. Lebanon, La.
Ms. P. F. Eaton (318) 834-6455

Southeast Louisiana Dairy Festival
Hammond, La.
E. E. Puls (504) 345-1524

West Louisiana Folk Arts and
Crafts Festival
Leesville, La.
Elize Howerton (318) 238-3244

Breaux Bridge Crawfish Festival
Breaux Bridge, La.
Allen Thibodaux (318) 332-5406

Rose Festival
Shreveport, La.
Harold S. Goldstein (318) 938-5402

Timberfest
Bastrop, La.
Kay Naff (318) 281-3794

Tomato Festival
Chalmette, La.
Rev. Warren Cooper (504) 271-3441

Mayhaw Festival
Marion, La.
Gail Durbin (318) 292-4319

Allons Manger Food Festival
Belle Rose, La.
Donald Savoie (504) 473-8437

Hammond Heritage Day
Hammond, La.
C. Phil Wagner III (504) 345-9344

Germanfest
Minden, La.
(318) 377-6366

Italian Festival
Luling, La.
Robert Monti (504) 785-9305

Festa Italiano
Shreveport, La.
Pat Coroaro (318) 221-1958

The Great Amite River
Catfish Festival
Denham Springs, La.
Randy Tullier (504) 644-4687

Pearl River Catfish Festival
Pearl River, La.
Ramon Monroe (504) 863-2501

Cajun Country Outdoor Opry
Houma, La.
Laverna B. Babin (504) 851-6596

Historic Cheneyville Tour of
Homes and Arts and Crafts Show
Cheneyville, La.
Betty P. Pearce (318) 279-2470

Nitram Park's Bluegrass Festival
Pitkin, La.
Johnnie Martin (318) 358-5183

Fest-For-All
Baton Rouge, La.
Richard A. Sabino (504) 344-3328

Sawmill Days
Fisher, La.
Viola Curruth (318) 256-2913

Five Lakes Bluegrass Festival
Bush, La.
Red Crawford (504) 886-3675

Festival of Festivals
Monroe, La.
Anita Akin (318) 387-5691

Le Bon Vivant
Marrero, La.
Harold Hebert (504) 341-9516

Toledo Bend Trash Festival
Anacoco, La.
Emmett or Coerry Smallwood
(318) 286-5565

Louisiana Balloon Festival and
Airshow
Hammond, La.
Kathy Pittman (504) 345-4457

Lasallette Rainbow of Fun Festival
Sulphur, La.
(318) 527-6722

June

Cenlabration
Alexandria, La.
Marsha Goff Cripps (318) 442-6671

Lafete Louisiana
Baton Rouge, La.
Amy Roll (504) 926-4546

Cajun Music Festival
Mamou, La.
Paul Tata (318) 468-5555

Corney Creek Festival
Bernice, La.
Linda Davis (318) 285-7546

Cajun Crab Festival
Henderson, La.
Shirley Haynes (318) 228-2006

Louisiana Blueberry Festival
Mansfield, La.
Monica Bell (318) 872-2746

Kentwood Dairy Festival
Kentwood, La.
Dianne Gill (504) 229-8607

Spring Folk Festival
Gilbert, La.
Mrs. Fay Montgomery (318) 435-5402

Okra Festival
Kenner, La.
Donna Edwards (504) 468-7221

Sportsmen's League Fishing Rodeo
Slidell, La.
Charles Chatnaignier
(504) 643-5273

Bayou Liberty Civic Club
Pirogue Races
Slidell, La.
A. L. Pichon, Jr. (504) 643-2581

Taste of Louisiana
Sulphur, La.
Algie Johnson (318) 527-9371

Louisiana Peach Festival
Ruston, La.
Regina Atkins (318) 527-9371

Antique Festival
Ponchatoula, La.
Stanley Cowen (504) 386-4970

Melrose Plantation Arts and
Crafts Festival
Melrose, La.
Dr. Ora V. Watson (318) 352-6472

Melrose Arts and Crafts Festival
Natchitoches, La.
Maxine Southerland (318) 352-4411

Jambalaya Festival
Gonzales, La.
Paul Leblanc (504) 647-3601

South Lafourche Cajun Festival
Galliano, La.
Huey L. Cheramie (504) 475-5108

Louisiana Corn Festival
Bunkie, La.
Jacquie Nibert (318) 346-2575

Feliciana Peach Festival
Clinton, La.
Ellen H. Fudge (504) 634-7793

Bayou Lacombe Crab Festival
Lacombe, La.
Marge Madere (504) 882-5792

Kay Cee Fishing Rodeo
Houma, La.
Donald J. Melancon (504) 879-1032

Possum's Unlimited Festival
Arcadia, La.
Rodney Cook (318) 263-2092

Angola Arts and Crafts Festival
Angola, La.
Ebba D. Wilson (504) 655-4411

July

Festival International de Louisiane
Lafayette, La.
Philippe Gustin (318) 233-1020

Erath 4th of July Fair and Festival
Erath, La.
Claudette Lacour (318) 937-5625

Louisiana Freedom Festival
Elton, La.
Avella Ackless (318) 584-2992

Louisiana Paper Festival
Bogalusa, La.
Peggy Triana (504) 735-1656

Chitimacha Tribal Fair
Charenton, La.
Patty Leblanc (318) 923-4973

Southwest Louisiana
Deep Sea Fishing Rodeo
Lake Charles, La.
Louis Vallee (318) 786-4004

Slidell Freedom Fest
Slidell, La.
Brad Champagne (504) 643-0496

Chruch Point Buggy Festival
Church Point, La.
Alcus Trahan (318) 684-5435

Food Festival
New Orleans, La.
John Putnam (504) 455-8247

La Fete de la Nouvelle Orleans
New Orleans, La.
Anne Bayard (504) 525-4143

Cajun Bastille Day
Baton Rouge, La.
Sherry Cole (504) 346-8888

Bastille Day
Kaplan, La.
Russell Campbell (318) 643-6448

Watermelon Festival
Franklinton, La.
Mary Hazen (504) 839-4695

Louisiana Catfish Festival
Des Allemands, La.
Rev. Paul Lamberty (504) 758-7542

Northwestern Folk Festival
Natchitoches, La.
Dr. Donald Hatley (318) 352-4332

Louisiana Oyster Festival
Galliano, La.
Beverly B. Eymard (504) 632-2224

Old-Fashioned Folk Festival
West Monroe, La.
Dianne Clower (318) 396-5000

International Grand Isle Tarpon Rodeo
Grand Isle, La.
Dr. Don Peterson (504) 288-3827

Louisiana Shakespeare Festival
Lake Charles, La.
Tom Munger (318) 439-8988

St. Charles Parish Festival
Norco/Destrehan, La.
Ralph D. St. Amant (504) 764-7166

Annual Beef Cook-Off
Opelousas, La.
Barbara Perrault (318) 942-2683

August

Tangipahoa Black Festival
Hammond, La.
George Perkins (504) 345-9134

South Lafourche Seafood Festival
Galliano, La.
Irvin Bouffanie (504) 632-4633

Delcambre Shrimp Festival
Delcambre, La.
Jacqueline Toups (318) 685-2653

Fete des Acadiens
Lafayette, La.
A. J. LeBlanc (318) 232-3797

Calcasieu Cajun Festival
Sulphur, La.
Jan McFarlain (318) 232-3797

Le Bal de Maison
Lafayette, La.
A. J. LeBlanc (318) 232-3797

Cajun Hunters Festival
Cut Off, La.
Rudy Guidry (504) 632-3043

September

Louisiana Shrimp and
Petroleum Festival and Fair
Morgan City, La.
Benny Villa (504) 385-0703

Duck Festival
Gueydan, La.
Nona Theriot (318) 536-6780

Kinder Sauce Piquante and
Music Festival
Kinder, La.
(318) 738-5578

Zydeco Festival
Plaisance, La.
Wilbert Guillory (318) 826-3431

Abita Springs Water Festival
Abita Springs, La.
Dick Granier (504) 892-1735

Labor Day Pirogue Race Festival
Houma, La.
Betty Reed (504) 868-2732

Lasalle Parish Fair
Jena, La.
Charles Williams (318) 992-5481

North Louisiana Cotton Festival and Fair
Bastrop, La.
Barbara VanCoevering (318) 281-9491

Backwood Village Folk Festival
Goldonna, La.
Sybil Womack (318) 727-9227

Bayou Lafourche Antique Show and Sale
Thibodaux, La.
Mrs. R. F. Grahm (504) 446-2450

Old Country Bazaar
Jeanerette, La.
Kate Fortier (318) 276-4293

Bayou Blue Food and Fun Festival
Houma, La.
Ronald Savoie (504) 873-7407

Cajun Day Festival
Church Point, La.
Theresa Cary (318) 684-2739

Harahan Railroad Fair
Harahan, La.
Carol Ferraro (504) 737-6383

Louisiana Downs Super Derby Festival
Bossier City/Shreveport, La.
Suzy Ryan (318) 868-8474

Cajun Festival
Vinton, La.
Clarence LeBlanc (318) 589-7358

Rayne Frog Festival
Rayne, La.
Hilda Hauie (318) 334-2332

Christian Family Festival
Ponchatoula, La.
Sonny Harmon (504) 386-4979

Louisiana Soybean Festival
Jonesville, La.
Sherry Floyd (318) 339-8536

Oil Patch Festival
Haynesville, La.
Emmett Wraten (318) 624-1733

Festivals Acadiens
Lafayette, La.
Beverly Corbell (318) 232-3737

Sikes Wolf Creek Handicraft
Arts Festival
Sikes, La.
Keith D. Bingham (318) 628-2266

Sabine Parish Fair
Many, La.
Betty Carrline (318) 256-6055

Red River Parish Fair
Coushatta, La.
Lem Jones (318) 932-4984

Pioneer Day Festival
Greenwood, La.
Tom Bryson (318) 938-1306

Southwest Louisiana State Fair and
Exposition
Lake Charles, La.
Jimmy Chance (318) 436-7575

Wildfowl Carvers Festival
New Orleans, La.
Edward M. Alba (318) 588-9143

St. Andrews Cajun Festival
Amelia, La.
Mr. and Mrs. Gerald Clements
(504) 631-2623

Jackson Parish Junior Livestock Show
Jonesboro, La.
Eddie D. White (318) 259-2452

St. Helena Forest Festival
Greensburg, La.
Tim Kirby (504) 222-6327

Slidell Trade Fair
Slidell, La.
Irma Cry (504) 643-5678

Claiborne Parish Fair/
Northwest Louisiana Dairy Festival
Haynesville, La.
Anita Bower (318) 624-1204

West Louisiana Forestry Festival
Leesville, La.
Thor Anderson (318) 239-0021

Tangipahoa Parish Fair
Amite, La.
Joyce Russell (504) 748-6268

Winn Parish Fair
Winnfield, La.
Carolyn R. Phillips (318) 628-4528

Ark-La-Miss Agri-Industrial Fair
West Monroe, La.
Curley Ketchell (318) 323-6621

October

Louisiana Cattle Festival and Fair
Abbeville, La.
Barbara T. DeBlanc (318) 893-6328

Raceland Sauce Piquante Festival
Raceland, La.
Kerry Babin (504) 537-3683

St. Philomena Cajun Country Festival
Labadieville, La.
Bonnie Nolan (504) 526-8322

Terrebonne Parish Fair and Rodeo
Houma, La.
LeeRoy J. Lirette (504) 876-1642

Annual Antique Show and Sale
Baton Rouge, La.
Carolyn Bennet (504) 387-2464

Calca ''Chew'' Food Festival/
Gumbeaux Gator Trail
Lake Charles, La.
R. Patrick Diamond (318) 478-2668

Festival of Beauties
Youngsville, La.
Dot Denais (318) 264-6029

St. Lukes Arts and Crafts Festival
Baton Rouge, La.
(504) 357-7835

Vidalia Chamber Festival
Vidalia, La.
Jean Walsworth (318) 336-7310

Donaldsonville Sunshine Festival
Donaldsonville, La.
Raymond Aucoin (504) 473-4814

Calcasieu Cameron Fair
Sulphur, La.
Algia Johnston (318) 527-9371

Allen Parish Fair
Oberlin, La.
Mitchel Brothers Amusements
(318) 639-4376

Jefferson Davis Parish Fair
Jennings, La.
T. L. Morgan (318) 824-1773

The Gumbo Festival
Bridge City, La.
Rev. Anthony J. Luminais
(504) 436-4712

Lafourche Parish Agricultural Fair
Thibodaux, La.
Dalton Landry (504) 446-1316

Lagnaippe on the Bayou
Chauvin, La.
Houston ''Sou'' Lirette (504) 594-5878

Sorrento Boucherie Festival
Sorrento, La.
J. M. ''Mac'' Phillipe (504) 675-5337

Tamale Fiesta
Zwolle, La.
Chris Loupe (318) 645-6988

Vermilion Fair and Fest
Kaplan, La.
Liz Stelly (318) 643-8075

Louisiana Cotton Festival
Ville Platte, La.
Mary Bergeron (318) 363-4521

Potpourri Festival and Rodeo
Port Allen, La.
Seamy Citadel (504) 344-2920

Festa d'Italia
New Orleans, La.
Frank Meselli (504) 891-1904

Louisiana Art and Folk Festival
Columbia, La.
Kem Gay (318) 649-2184

Slidell Food and Fun Fest
Slidell, La.
Joleen Megilligan (504) 643-6124

Annual Historic Tour of Natchitoches
Natchitoches, La.
Maxine Southerland (318) 352-8604

Natchitoches Pilgrimage
Natchitoches, La.
Betty Jones 9318) 352-4411

Kiawania Arts and Handicraft Show
Natchitoches, La.
Betty Jones (318) 352-4411

Octoberfest
Jackson, La.
Ms. Owen Kemp (504) 654-6868

Livingston Parish Fair
Livingston, La.
Clyde Palmer (504) 665-5575

Rapides Parish Fair
Alexandria, La.
Lou Altazan (318) 473-6605

Caddo Parish Fair and Livestock Show
Shreveport, La.
Winzer R. Andrews (318) 226-6805

International Rice Festival
Crowley, La.
Bill Williams (318) 783-3067

International Alligator Festival
Franklin, La.
Margie L. Luke (318) 828-3487

Six Flags Over Broadmoor
Houma, La.
Frank and Connie Benoit (504) 879-1071

International Acadian Festival
Plaquemine, La.
Joe Bryant (504) 687-7319

Louisiana Gumbo Festival of Chackbay
Chackbay, La.
Eddie Luquette (504) 633-7302

Cochon de Lait Festival
Luling, La.
(504) 785-8585

French Louisiana Festival
Kenner, La.
Dr. Don Landry (504) 469-2555

October Fete
Kaplan, La.
Bobby Breaux (318) 643-2588

La Vie Lafourchaise
Raceland, La.
Diane Baudoin (504) 537-7647

Celebration Uptown
New Orleans, La.
Nancy Frankel (504) 899-9511

Old Farmer's Day
Loranger, La.
Gerald Brunett (504) 878-9343

Cajun Country Outdoor Opry
Houma, La.
Laverna B. Babin (504) 851-6596

Louisiana Yambilee Festival
Opelousas, La.
Janel Duplechin (318) 948-8848

Washington Parish Free Fair
Franklinton, La.
(504) 732-4660

Louisiana Gulf Coast Oil Exposition
Lafayette, La.
Sally Ware (318) 235-4055

French Food Festival
Larose, La.
Ronald Pere (504) 693-7355

Andouille Festival
LaPlace, La.
John Peppo (504) 652-8034

Violet Oyster Festival
Violet, La.
Rev. Frank Lipps (504) 682-3046

Louisiana State Fair
Shreveport, La.
C. Ed Nelson (318) 635-1361

Louisiana Swine Festival
Basile, La.
Mary Jane LeJeune (318) 432-5437

Greater Baton Rouge State Fair
Baton Rouge, La.
J. H. Martin (504) 293-9901

Fall Folk Life Festival
Baton Rouge, La.
Rick Sabino (504) 344-8558

Plantation Day at Magnolia Mound
Baton Rouge, La.
Gwen Edwards (504) 343-4955

November

Catahoula Heritage Festival
Alexandria, La.
Bryan Saybe (318) 640-9009

Catahoula Lake Festival
Pineville, La.
Bryan Saybe (318) 640-9009

Louisiana Folklife Festival
Baton Rouge, La.
Bob Gates (504) 925-3930

St. Tammany Parish Fair
Covington, La.
Sandra McManus (504) 893-1719

Louisiana Pecan Festival
Colfax, La.
June M. Ingles (318) 627-5196

Southdown Fall Marketplace
Houma, La.
Jody Waggenspack (504) 851-0154

Morehouse Arts and Crafts Show
Bastrop, La.
Kay Naff (318) 281-3794

Festival de Grand Coteau
Grand Coteau, La.
John Slaughter (318) 622-3500

Destrehan Plantation Fall Festival
Destrehan, La.
Judy Keys (504) 764-9315

LAA Fall Arts and Crafts Fiesta
Lafayette, La.
C. Wooley (318) 269-0363

Broussard Community Fair
Broussard, La.
Lloyd Girouard (318) 837-6815

Arts and Crafts Show
DeRidder, La.
Mary Curran (318) 463-7297

Sweet Adeline Craft Fair
Slidell, La.
Maxine Gault (504) 468-1929

Loreauville Harvest Fest
Loreauville, La.
Marily Girouard (318) 365-2867

Jambalaya Tours
Clinton, La.
Dan Bieber (504) 292-1447

Annual Christmas Parade
Kenner, La.
Candy Nuccio (504) 468-7293

Christmas on the Bayou
Lafayette, La.
Marisol Ochoa (318) 232-3737

December

Christmas in Roseland
Shreveport, La.
Harold Goldstein (318) 938-5402

Winterfest
Morgan City, La.
Chris Garrette (318) 323-3461

Merry Cajun Christmas
Lafayette, La.
Nancy Broussard (318) 232-3808

A Creole Christmas in the
French Quarter
New Orleans, La.
Sandra S. Dartus (504) 522-5730

Victorian Christmas
Lafayette, La.
E. Straub (318) 234-2208

Christmas Festival of Lights
Natchitoches, La
Betty Jones (318) 352-4411

Christmas Festival
Houma, La.
Betty Reed (504) 868-2732

Ozone Camellia Club
Slidell, La.
Nicholas Kooney (504) 641-1129

Plaquemine Parish Fair and
Orange Festival
Pointe a la Hache, La.
Paula Cappiello (504) 564-2951

Nineteenth Century Christmas at
Mount Hope
Baton Rouge, La.
Mr. and Mrs. Jack Dease (504) 766-8600

Santa on the Bayou
Lacombe, La.
Sherry E. Wood (504) 764-9315

Christmas Lights and Set-Pieces
Natchitoches, La.
Betty Jones (318) 352-4411

Destrehan Christmas Open House
Destrehan, La.
(504) 764-9315

Teche Queen ''Christmas on the Bayou''
New Iberia, La.
Iberia Parish Tourist Commission
(318) 365-0581

Madewood Christmas Heritage Banquet
Napoleonville, La.
Joan Adams (504) 524-1988

Oak Alley Plantation Christmas
Bonfire Party
Vacherie, La.
Joanne Amort (504) 265-2151

HISTORY OF LOUISIANA

THE FIRST INHABITANTS

The Indians—so termed by Columbus who thought that he had discovered the East Indies—were originally of the Mongolian race. They had black, straight hair, dark skins and high cheek bones. They probably came over to the Continent of America by way of Bering Strait, although some might have been wafted across the Pacific upon rafts or boats. These early migrants and their descendants spread all over North and South America and developed different cultures and languages. In fact the hundreds of Indian languages, some seemingly unrelated, were almost as numerous as the tribes that settled in different parts of the two continents.

It was probably a long time after the Indians came to the Americas that any of them reached the Gulf Coast. Nobody knows exactly when, but the first Indians came to Louisiana about 3,000 years ago. The first arrivals were primitive. They used spears, harpoons, had no bows and arrows, and cooked by "stone boiling." They had no pottery, but would stretch a skin between four sticks and drop into the water or liquid held in its hollow, a hot stone which would set the liquid or food to boiling.

THE INDIAN VILLAGE AT POVERTY POINT*

* At the Louisiana State Exhibit Museum at Shreveport there is a diorama of the Poverty Point village, constructed by H. B. Wright with a technical assistance of Dr. C. H. Webb. The reconstruction is based on the report, "Poverty Point, A Late Archaic Site in West Carroll Parish, La.," published in 1956 by the Am. Museum of Natural History and written by J. A. Ford and Dr. Charles H. Webb, with collaboration of Dr. Junius B. Bird and Michael Beckman.

In July 1955 Dr. James A. Ford of the American Museum of Natural History announced the unearthing of a village in Northeast Louisiana that existed 2700 years ago. The ruins of the village site cover an area nearly a mile square on the Poverty Point Plantation, five miles northeast of the town of Epps in West Carroll Parish, and 45 miles west of Vicksburg, Miss.

By using the carbon-14 test and a study of river channels by geologists, it was estimated that the village was built and lived in between 800 and 600 B.C. This was when the culture of Greece was developing, before the beginning of the Roman Empire, and 200 years after Solomon built the temple at Jerusalem.

At this time too, most of the Indians in the United States consisted of small groups of from 25 to 30 people with few instances of the groups numbering as many as 100 or 200. Yet the Poverty Point settlement contained five or six thousand people, judging from the size of the village and the amount of construction. The Poverty Point village was erected long before any other communal dwellings appeared in North America, and long before the flourishing cities of the Aztecs, Toltecs, and Mayas had evolved.

Focal point of the ancient community was a great mound of earth 600 feet long and 70 feet high, the second highest Indian mound in North America. A mile north of the village is another large mound, 600 ft. long and 55 ft. high. Nearer the village is another mound 20 ft. high. These mounds were in the shape of a flying bird. The amount of earth used in building these three mounds comes to a half-million tons. Since all his dirt had to be dug with sticks and carried in baskets these Indians almost equalled the construction record of Cheops when he built the Great Pyramid.

The village itself was laid out in the shape of an octagon. Raised terraces 100 ft. wide were constructed of earth and a series of six terraces built. The people lived on these terraces. It required another half million tons of earth to form the terraces.

The inhabitants of Poverty Point were a people of an advanced stone age, and were the beginning of the American Neolithic period. Dr. Ford said that the Poverty Point culture represents the earliest southward movement of people with the Hopewell culture. As to the origin of this culture Dr. Ford believes it comes from Asia by way of the Bering Straits rather than from the high culture centers of Central and South America. Evidence supporting this theory is a fragment of a tubular pipe found at Poverty Point similar to pipes connected with magic cures in Northeast Asia for several milleniums.

Broken pottery was found at Poverty Point, which seems to contradict the theory that these early Indians did not or could not make pottery. But the pottery bits found evidently came from Florida and Georgia. These people travelled or traded for tremendous distances as they got iron ore from Arkansas and Missouri, flint from Illinois and Ohio, slate from Michigan, and stone from Kentucky and Tennessee. They had no bows and arrows and used spears and darts, also bolas—strings with weights at ends—for hunting.

These early Indians were followed by people 1200 or 1000 years ago with bows and arrows and pottery. Later, Indians arrived from Mexico, bringing agriculture, pipe smoking and erecting mounds for their dead. DuPratz who lived at Natchez around 1725 talked to an old Indian chief, and from his conversation we get the idea that their ancestors came originally from Mexico.

The Marksville Indians arrived about 800 years ago. They had metal—copper instruments made from copper from Lake Superior which they probably acquired by trading with Indians from up the valley. The Marksville Indians buried their dead in mounds and did some farming. They flattened the foreheads of their infants.

The year 1700, the time of the arrival of the white men, was the end of the prehistoric period. At that time many of the Indians of Louisiana lived in stockaded villages, showed an interest in religion, built temples, cultivated the land, made pottery and weaved baskets. The early pioneers were evidently peaceful as there is little evidence of war-like activities.

THE ABORIGINES

Other evidences of the early presence of human beings in what is now Louisiana were unearthed in 1933 by archaeologists of the U. S. National Museum working near Marksville. Indications are that the "Marksville" people engaged in agriculture, lived in permanent villages on or near river banks, and sometimes fortified such villages. They are believed to have been superior culturally to later Indian tribes encountered by the white explorers. After the "Marksville Period" came the period of the "Deasonville" and "Coles Creek" people whose cultural remains have been unearthed in eastern Louisiana. These people are believed to have been the ancestors of the Indians living in Louisiana at the time of the first European explorations.

INDIANS OF LOUISIANA

Students have divided the Indians of Louisiana into three linguistic groups—Tunican, Caddoan and Muskhogean. Each group may be subdivided into the lesser units or tribes enumerated below.

TUNICAN FAMILY

This group was comprised of the Tunican family proper (the Washa, Koroa and Chawasha tribes), the Opelousas, the Chitimacha, and the Atakapa tribes. Members of these tribes lived in the northeast corner of present-day Louisiana (the Koroa) and in the coastal region (Atakapa and Chitimacha). The Chitimacha culture was a notably advanced one, the members of this tribe being proficient in craftsmanship, both of basket-

ry and metal work. Their descendants still live on the Chitimacha reservation in St. Mary's Parish—the only Indian reservation in Louisiana at the present time.

A settlement since 1764, the Federal Government established the reservation in 1935. Located at Charenton near Baldwin, it comprises 265 acres and about 60 Chitimacha live there. For reservation privileges each person must have at least one-quarter Indian blood. The Indians receive regular government payments, have small farms and simply furnished homes. Most speak English, but the older ones prefer French. Some know a few words of their original Indian tongue.

The Chitimacha were a proud and noble tribe and their descendants constitute the Indian aristocracy of Louisiana.

The Atakapa and the related Opelousas were less advanced culturally. They even had the reputation (probably undeserved) of being cannibals.

The Washa, Chawasha and Koroa tribes were all small and either died out or became indistinct through intermarriage with larger tribes.

CADDOAN FAMILY

This group included the Yatasi, Doustioni, Kadohacho, Adai, Washita, and Natchitoche tribes. These tribes were located generally in the northwest corner of the state area on or near the banks of the Red River north of modern Alexandria. The group had a particularly difficult time after the coming of the whites since their location placed them in a no man's land between the rival French and Spanish empires. Eventually, after repeated difficulties with French, Spanish, and finally the neighboring Texans, the Caddoans fled by forced march in 1859 to Oklahoma, where their descendants still live.

MUSKHOGEAN FAMILY

This group was made up of the Muskhogean family proper (the Taensa, Okelousa, Payougoula, Quinipissa, Avoyel, Tangipahoa, Acolapissa, Houma and Choctaw tribes) and the related Natcheans, the former inhabiting the southeastern port of Louisiana, and the latter the east central area of the state. In 1700 the Muskhogeans lived in over 60 villages and numbered about 3,500. The Muskhogean tribe best remembered in American history is the Choctaw who lived north of Lake Pontchartrain. They were the first major tribe to form an alliance with the French in Louisiana. They aided the French on several occas-

MAJOR CONCENTRATIONS OF INDIAN TRIBES

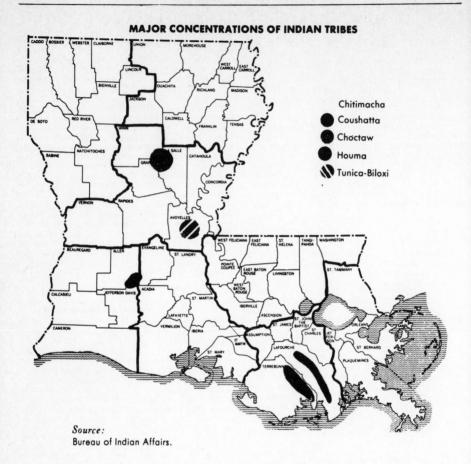

Source:
Bureau of Indian Affairs.

sions in fighting against their linguistic relatives, the Natchez. About 100 Choctaws are still living in Louisiana in La-Salle and St. Tammany Parishes. The other Muskhogean tribes either died out or lost their identity through intermarriage.

LOUISIANA INDIANS—GENERAL

With the possible exception of the Cad-

doans, whose northern location gave them access to buffalo hunting on the plains, all the Indians who lived in what is now Louisiana were of a semi-sedentary type, relying on agriculture and fishing for their main subsistence. Indian corn (maize) was the most important diet crop, though it was supplemented by beans, pumpkins and melons, which were also grown domestically, and by fish and game.

Indian settlements were always located on the banks of rivers or streams. There were several types of dwellings, depending on the resources available for construction in any given area. In the northern part of the state, houses usually had a frame of wooden poles and mud-plastered roofs covered with grass. Houses in the southern part were of palmetto leaves over a framework of poles. In each village one or more granaries were built above the ground on high posts where corn could be stored and protected from mice.

As of 1700, the Indians in what is now the State of Louisiana numbered about 13,000, or one to every four square miles. After decreasing almost to extinction, they reversed the trend after 1850. The 1940 census gives a total Indian population of 1,801 for the state, very few pureblooded. The 1950 census counted only 409, but the 1960 census showed 3,587 Indians in Louisiana, an increase of 777 per cent in ten years.

EUROPEAN EXPLORATION

Though details are obscure, the first explorer who might have seen what is now Louisiana was a Spaniard, Alvarez de Pineda, who reported a large river flowing into the Gulf of Mexico where he had sailed in 1519. Historians now believe that the river of his report was probably the Mobile, but it is possible that he passed and saw the mouth of the Mississippi. It is also possible that a party of Spanish sailors under Panfila de Narvaez came upon the mouth of the Mississippi in 1528.

In any event, Louisiana's white discoverers were Spanish. Hernando de Soto's party of exploration (1541-43) were the first white men to set foot on Louisiana soil and record their act. DeSoto's party was composed largely of noblemen who came in search of the fabled wealth of Florida. Landing in Florida, they fought their way through Georgia, Alabama and Mississippi, and crossed northern Louisiana into Arkansas. They discovered the Mississippi River in April 1541. After deSoto's death, May 21, 1542* his party under the command of Luis de Moscoso, wandered around what is now western Louisiana and eastern Texas for nearly a year. Finally they came back to the Mississippi and constructed boats, and sailed them down to the Gulf. Reaching

---

* One chronicler of the expedition wrote that deSoto died on the banks of the Mississippi River and that he was buried secretly at night in the trunk of a tree so that the Indians, who believed him to be immortal, would not know that he was dead. Fearing that the body might be found Moscoso removed and sank it to the bottom of the great river where the Red River joins the Mississippi. (Some modern historians believe that deSoto died near Deshay, Ark.)

---

there on July 19, 1543 they got to Tampico the next month.

Spanish exploration was largely a search by noble adventurers for quick riches. When it failed to yield these, the explorers lost enthusiasm. The history of the 17th century exploration in America concerns the French.

FRENCH EXPLORATION

France had been laying the foundations of a New World Empire in Canada since Cartier's expedition to the Gulf of St. Lawrence in 1534. The French approach to Louisiana exploration—after they ignored it for a century—was therefore from the north, and the first French names in the Louisiana story are really French Canadian.

In 1673, Louis Joliet, a French Canadian trader, and the missionary, Pére Marquette, arrived at the Wisconsin River from Quebec and descended by it to the Mississippi, on which they floated as far south as the mouth of the Arkansas River. Their expedition was undertaken under the auspices of the French Government in Quebec, in hopes of finding that the Mississippi flowed into the Pacific. When the explorers learned from Indians that it emptied instead into the Gulf of Mexico and that the Spanish were to the South, they returned to Canada with their disappointing news.

But this news was not so disappointing to Robert Cavelier de La Salle, a young Frenchman living in Canada, a protege of the French governor, Frontenac. La Salle went to France with his patron's encouragement, and enlisted the support of the French court for a project of exploration of the western portion of "New France." The idea of this far-seeing young man was to secure the Mississippi River for France and thus split the Spanish holdings in Texas and Florida. La Salle returned to Canada with royal backing, and organized an expedition which sailed down the Mississippi, reaching the territory of modern Louisiana in April 1682. On April 9th he took possession of the entire tributary system of the Mississippi for France, calling it Louisiana in honor of his king, Louis XIV. How much territory was included in this claim no one knew, but as further explorations were made, it came to include virtually all the territory of the present United States from the Appalachians to the Rockies and from Canada to Texas, the Gulf of Mexico with Florida on the east and Texas on the west belonging to Spain.

When La Salle returned to Canada, a new governor had succeeded his friend Frontenac. The new official did not see the value of La Salle's discoveries and had convinced the king that they were futile. La Salle was therefore forced to go to Paris once again to plead his case.

He succeeded in gaining the king's favor once more, and in 1684 he was sent out with a large party to explore and colonize the territory. His ships missed the mouth of the Mississippi and landed at what is now Matagorda Bay in Texas. A colony was set up here which was beset from the beginning by hardships. Worse there was dissension and mutiny. La Salle himself was murdered by one of his own men in 1687. Without his leadership the colony failed to withstand the combined attacks of smallpox, neighboring Indians, and the Spanish from Mexico.

But French imperial expansion, once under way, was not to be stopped. From 1689 to 1697, France was busy fighting England (William and Mary's War), but directly peace was made, French pressure from the North was again felt on the lower Mississippi.

This time the leader was Pierre le Moyne d'Iberville, third son of a powerful French Canadian family, who had distinguished himself as an officer in the French navy during the war just completed. Iberville was chosen by Louis XIV to establish the colony which La Salle had failed to do. He set sail from Brest on October 14, 1698, accompanied by his brother, Jean Baptiste le Moyne de Bienville and two hundred colonists, their wives and soldiers. The serious business of attaching Louisiana to France by actual colonization had begun.

IBERVILLE'S EXPEDITION

The ships reached Pensacola in January 1699. The Spanish had partially completed a fort there and had garrisoned it with soldiers to forestall French occupation. Having been refused permission to enter the harbor, Iberville sailed westward and established a temporary camp on Ship Island, south of modern Biloxi. He immediately began exploring for the Mississippi and on March 3, 1699, in the company of his brother and a small party, he began the ascent of the river.

On Friday, March 5th, they arrived at the site of modern New Orleans where they erected a cross and marked some trees. The party then continued upstream beyond Baton Rouge—so named for a red pole which they found set in the ground there by the Houma and Bayogoula tribes to mark the boundary of their respective hunting grounds. Reaching the mouth of the Red River, Iberville turned back and descended to his ships via Lakes Maurepas and Pontchartrain which he tactfully named in honor of the French Minister of Marine and Colonies, Count Pontchartrain, and the Count's son and successor, Jerome Maurepas, also called Pontchartrain. Bienville separated from his brother for the return trip, and went down the Mississippi to procure a letter addressed to LaSalle which had been left with the Indians 14 years before by Henry Tonti when he had come down the river to meet La Salle and failed because of the latter's death. This letter confirmed the conviction that the river they had just explored was indeed the Mississippi.

Iberville thought the lower banks of the Mississippi too marshy for settlement. He therefore selected the present sight of Biloxi for his headquarters, erecting Fort Maurepas there. Having made friends with the neighboring Indian tribes, Iberville sailed back to France to get further supplies and more colonists on the basis of his success so far.

In the meantime, Bienville, who remained in Biloxi, was instructed to explore the Mississippi River and surrounding territory. On one of these exploratory trips, in September 1699, Bienville encountered one of two English ships which had also been sent to explore the Mississippi. He informed the English Captain, Barr, that the river was not the Mississippi but another stream already possessed by the French in considerable strength—an assertion that does credit to his diplomatic adroitness if not to his honesty. The result was that Captain Barr turned back at a point on the river still known as English Turn and sailed away.

Iberville's mission to France was successful. He convinced the French Government that Spanish claims to Louisiana were not valid, and, more important, that strong efforts must be made to secure the territory against eventual English encroachments from the Atlantic Coast. Returning to Louisiana, he moved colonial headquarters from Biloxi to a point a few miles up the Mobile River from the present site of Mobile, where he built Fort Louis. In this location he could continue to control the mouth of the Mississippi and also keep watch on the Spanish at Pensacola. Thus strategically situated, he laid plans for a great French empire in the New World to be strengthened by commercial and military alliances with important Indian tribes as far up the Mississippi as the site of modern St. Louis. He planned and began a series of fortified trading posts along the river to facilitate the program. With such a system, making good use of Indian allies, he felt that New France could successfully resist and even eventually drive out the rival English from their colonies on the Atlantic. He thought they could prosper on Indian trade, and, he imagined, from mining.

Unfortunately for Iberville's grand plan, the French Government's attention was soon diverted from colonization by the War of the Spanish Succession (1701-1714). Iberville himself took part in this war against the English, and died of yellow fever at Havana on July 5, 1706.

Iberville's death left Bienville in charge. Because of the war and the lack of support from France, he could not carry out the ambitious project of his older brother with regard to colonization. A modest trade was built up with the Indians, and some colonists did arrive from time to time, but the colony's development was altogether too slow and unprofitable to satisfy the French Government.

In 1712, with the idea of decreasing expenses, the Government granted all trading rights in Louisiana to a French merchant, Antoine Crozat, for a period of 15 years. By the terms of the charter, the Government was to maintain forts and soldiers in the colony for a part of this period. Despite the return of peace in 1714 and a reshuffling of the officials in the colony's administration—Crozat replaced Bienville with Lamothe Cadillac in 1713—Louisiana failed to yield the entrepreneur a profit. On August 23, 1717, Crozat formally surrendered his rights in Louisiana back to the French government.

THE MISSISSIPPI BUBBLE

The same month in which Crozat withdrew, a charter for the control of Louisiana was granted by the government to a corporation called the Compagnie de la Louisiane ou d'Occident (later known as the Compagnie des Indes Occidentales), controlled by a remarkable Scotsman named John Law. Under Law's vigorous direction, the colony expanded. Bienville was reappointed governor and colonists were enticed in large numbers by glowing reports which Law circulated in France and Germany. Law's scheme of a French paper currency to be based on the colony's resources, which was to redeem French domestic finances seemed, for a short period, to be successful. A flurry of speculation unprecedented in the history of European finance shot the Compagnie's stock up to dazzling heights.

The hopes of the Company of the West centered on the profitable control of the Mississippi River. It was in this period (1718) that Bienville selected the site on the Mississippi River for a central commercial and military headquarters. He named it New Orleans in honor of the regent of France.

Concessions of land were made by Law's Compagnie to individuals who would undertake to colonize and develop them. In this way, for example, settlements were made at Natchitoches and Baton Rouge.

Under the Compagnie's administration, agriculture took on importance as the colonists came to realize that Law's boasted gold mines were imaginary and that they must gain a living in humbler fashion.

Yet despite these solid signs of progress, Law had over-reached himself. Beginning in February 1720, the frenzied speculation moved rapidly towards a financial panic which rocked all France and forced Law to flee in December 1720. The Mississippi Bubble had burst. The Compagnie, however, managed to weather the storm, and held the charter until 1731 with modest financial success. It established New Orleans as the seat of government in 1722, Bienville's choice of a capital site prevailing over that desired by the officers of the Compagnie at home who believed the central city should be located at Bayou Manchac.

THE BLACK CODE

Coincident with the beginnings of agriculture in the colony, the first Negro slaves had been introduced about 1719. From a total of 250 imported in that year, their number increased to near that of the whites by 1724, and they showed promise of overtaking the white population.

To meet the uneasiness which resulted from this condition, Governor Bienville in 1724 promulgated the Black Code—so-called because its provisions related mainly to Negroes. (It also excluded Jews from the colony and prohibited religious ceremonies not Roman Catholic). It was largely derived from the Spanish code then in force in Santo Domingo. Under the Code, which provided protection as well as discipline for the Negroes, mixed marriage and concubinage were prohibited under pain of severe penalties; Catholic religious instruction for Negro slaves was made mandatory; slave work was forbidden on Sundays and religious holidays; slave families were not to be broken up by sale; manumission was provided for; and food, clothing and protection were assured the slave under penalty to the negligent master. The masters were made responsible for what their slaves did under orders, corporal punishments were specified for various slave crimes, and Negroes were forbidden to carry weapons or gather in unauthorized assemblies.

BIENVILLE RECALLED

French colonial government, even under the Compagnie, featured a double administrative authority. The governor had military jurisdiction while another official—often, but not always, called the intendant—had charge of civil affairs. the result was that each man acted as a jealous spy upon the other. There was moreover, constant ill-feeling between native French officials in the colony and the French Canadians of whom Bienville, as governor, was the leader.

In 1726, as a result of charges of misappropriation made against him by French civil officials, Bienville was recalled to France where, despite a good defense of himself, he was dismissed from the Compagnie's service and replaced by the Sieur de Périer. The jealous tension between officials of which this incident is an example prevailed almost constantly throughout the period of French government in Louisiana.

Périer's administration, which lasted until 1733, was marked by increasing signs of permanency and stability of civilization in Louisiana. The Ursuline nuns arrived in 1727 to teach and to care for the sick. In December of 1728, the twenty-three fillies á la casette ("casket girls"—so-called because each was provided with a small, casket-like box containing a trousseau, furnished by the French government) arrived to marry colonists who wanted wives. They were sent over by the French authorities who wisely observed that the women already in the colony—mostly prostitutes and Indian concubines—must be replaced by respectable wives and mothers if the colony was to grow and become an asset to France.

END OF THE RULE OF THE COMPAGNIE

In spite of these definite signs of progress, the Compagnie's income from the colony was not sufficient to meet its expenses. A massacre of 250 Frenchmen at Fort Rosalie (modern Natchez) by the Natchez Indians on 28 November 1729, led to two expensive French-Natchez wars. Though the French were ultimately successful when Louis St. Denis annihilated the Natchez warriors near Natchitoches in 1731, the wars proved the last straw to the Compagnie which, as already mentioned, surrendered its charter in 1731. Louis XV's government took over the Compagnie's property and its responsibility in the colony. The Company of the West had failed financially but the colony had developed under its aegis from a scattering of 500 whites and 20 Negroes to a total of 5000 whites and 2500 Negroes in its various settlements.

LOUISIANA AS A CROWN COLONY 1731-1769

Compared to the progress made under the Compagnie, this period is not an eventful one. Bienville returned as governor in 1733, but was forced to devote most of this time to two large-scale, expensive, and generally unsuccessful expeditions against the Chickasaw Indians who had been threatening the colony. Moreover, a hurricane in 1740 ruined vital crops which had to be replaced by expensive importation, causing Louisiana to be an even greater drain on the French government's purse and further discouraging efforts for progress. Perhaps the most lastingly significant event of Bienville's third and last administration was the introduction of cotton as a crop in 1740. (Cotton had been planted as early as 1718 at Natchitoches.)

Bienville was succeeded by the Marquis de Vaudreuil who governed from 1743 to 1753. In retrospect, the most important event of his administration was the introduction of sugar cane by the Jesuits who imported it from Santo Domingo in 1751. (Sugar cane was grown in Louisiana before this time. Iberville brought a few stalks with him and planted a patch at the mouth of the Mississippi River. Bienville mentions sugar cane in his report in 1733.) Although it was to become Louisiana's chief crop, at that time sugar cane only served the unimportant purpose of making a poor alcoholic drink called tafia until 1795, when Etienne Bore first succeeded in clarifying and crystallizing sugar. In other respects, Vaudreuil's administration, and that of his successor de Kerlerec (1753-1763) were not notable for progress in Louisiana. The French and Indian War (called the Seven Years War in Europe which locked the British and French empires in struggle from 1755 to 1763, put a stop to the colony's peaceful development.

SPANISH DOMINATION 1762-1801

British victory in the French and Indian War resulted in the Treaty of Paris in 1763 which gave Canada, the part of the original Louisiana colony lying east of the Mississippi, and the Spanish colony of Florida to Britain. To Spain, in compensation for her aid in the war against England and her loss of Florida, France ceded the "Island of New Orleans" and all of the territory of Louisiana west of the Mississippi by the Treaty of Fontainbleu in 1762. (This treaty was signed a year before the Treaty of Paris, and it originally had ceded all Louisiana to Spain. It had to be modified when victorious Britain enforced her terms.)

The transfer to Spain was kept secret from the officials and people of Louisiana until the middle of 1764. When announced, it proved highly unpopular with them. Through Bienville—now an old man living in France—they petitioned Louis XV to undo the cession, but Louis, impressed by the constant expense and financial failures which studded the colony's history, refused. On March 5, 1766, Antonio de Ulloa arrived to govern in the name of the Spanish King.

10 MONTHS OF "INDEPENDENCE"

Ulloa was coldly received and almost ignored. He was not a forceful man and matters were hardly improved by his timid method of governing indirectly through the last of the French governors, Charles Phillipe Aubrey who remained in the colony after the cession to Spain. This unsatisfactory system, in addition to the much resented Spanish mercantilist commercial restriction of the colony's trade, led to an ultimatum from certain Creole leaders to Ulloa to either exhibit his credentials and rule, or get out. They hoped he would choose the latter course. The date was October 27, 1768. Ulloa sailed away to Cuba immediately. As the first New World colony to revolt against European rule, Louisiana became in effect an independent state for a period of ten months.

The leaders of the revolt had hopes that the French King might welcome them back, but these hopes were soon extinguished, for both the French and Spanish governments made it clear that Spain's claim to Louisiana would be enforced.

RESTORATION OF SPANISH RULE

Count Alexander O'Reilly arrived in Louisiana on August 18, 1769, ten months after the ousting of Ulloa, with 2000 soldiers. His mission was to re-establish Spanish control and prestige. O'Reilly, a young, exiled Irishman high in the favor of Charles III of Spain, was a man of action. His first official act as governor was to execute five—one was killed resisting arrest—of the leaders of the October Rebellion which had driven out Ulloa. He abolished the Superior Council, an inefficient feature of the old French government, and substituted the Cabildo, which exercised both judicial and administrative duties under the governor. He substituted Spanish law for French, the Spanish language for French as the official tongue, and enforced Spanish commercial regulations which, based on the prevailing mercantile theories of the day, limited Louisiana's trade to Spain and Cuba. Aside from these measures, O'Reilly's administration was not so despotic as historians used to believe. The Creoles were admitted to high office and allowed to lead their own lives in their own way even to speaking French. On the firm foundation of the government which he established, the colony continued to make progress throughout the period of Spanish control, which ended in 1801 when Napoleon regained Louisiana for France by the secret treaty of San Ildefonso.

During the Spanish rule, an important addition to Louisiana's population had been made—the Acadian migration. The Acadians, driven from Nova Scotia by the British, began arriving in Louisiana after 1760. It was a suitable refuge for them, because they shared a common French descent and the Catholic religion with the natives of the colony. By 1790 over 4,000 Acadians had come to Louisiana, settling in the southern part of the state, where some 300,000 of their descendants still live. Still another migration to Louisiana occurred in 1791 when a slave revolution in Santo Domingo drove out the whites, many of whom took refuge in Louisiana.

During the American Revolution the Spanish officials in Louisiana lent valuable aid to the American colonies, even though· such aid was of necessity unofficial until Spain declared war on England on June 16, 1779. The purpose, as in the case of France's aid to the colonies,

was not so much to help the Americans as it was to humble England. Munitions and supplies were shipped through New Orleans to the American forces fighting the British in the Ohio Valley. Governor Galvez allowed Americans to use New Orleans as a base for operations against the loyalists and British in West Florida.

As soon as Galvez, a young man in his twenties, learned that war had been declared on England, he planned to occupy East and West Florida for Spain. His first move must be against the British forces on the Mississippi River where they had forts at Manchac, Baton Rouge and Natchez. Galvez secured all the boats that he could and taking his soldiers of the regular army, the local militia and volunteers from up and down the river known as "the coast",* he managed to assemble 1400 men, among whom were Indians and Negroes.

On the day that the expedition was to start a storm sank some of the boats. Undaunted Galvez moved his small force up the river anyway. He surprised the first British outpost at Manchac and then approached Baton Rouge. Constructing emplacements he opened a bombardment. Captain Dixon, commandant of the British force, surrendered with 500 officers and men on Sept. 21, 1779.

Galvez then marched to Natchez and captured Fort Panmure. He later captured Pensacola and Mobile.

Although Baton Rouge was a small outpost of the British Empire, its capture by Galvez was an important event. It was a severe blow to the British interests in America. Galvez' accomplishments were perhaps the only useful contribution Spain made in the war against Britain.

AMERICAN PRESSURE BEGINS

Trade between American settlers in the Ohio Valley and Louisiana, though illegal under Spanish law, had become important just before the American Revolution. After the war, increased American migration to the Ohio country made it more so. Automatically, a control of or free access to the Mississippi and its mouth became highly important to western citizens of the United States. Tension became great, as Spain was forbidding American commerce at New Orleans, and occasionally seizing the boats and cargoes sent there by Tennessee and Kentucky traders. The conflict was temporarily resolved by the Treaty of 1795 between Spain and the U. S., by which Spain recognized the Mississippi as the western boundary of the U.S. For a

* A list of some of those serving under Galvez has been found in Seville, Spain, and a copy is at Howard Tilton Library in New Orleans. Those descendants who can prove their lineage are eligible to belong to the Sons of the American Revolution and other patriotic societies.

period of three years American commerce was allowed free use of the Mississippi and the important right to deposit and export goods at New Orleans was granted. These rights were extended at the end of that period, but the right of deposit was refused in 1802—a fact which nearly precipitated an unofficial American invasion of Louisiana; such was the recognized importance of the Mississippi River to the Americans.

THE TREATY OF SAN ILDEFONSO

In the meantime, though the Spanish governors continued to hold office, Louisiana had reverted to France by the secret Treaty of San Ildefonso between Napoleon's government and Spain, signed on October 1, 1800 and confirmed by a second treaty on March 21, 1801. Napoleon, envisioning a re-establishment of a French New World Empire, gained Louisiana by promising the Spanish King a large section of Italy, where the latter's son-in-law, the Duke of Parma, might rule as king. Napoleon also engaged never to dispose of any part of Louisiana unless it was to return it to Spain. Neither of his promises was kept, though he held the Spanish to theirs.

Unfortunately, the army which Napoleon planned to use in garrisoning Louisiana was wiped out before it ever arrived. It suffered the combined disasters of a native uprising and yellow fever in the French colony of Santo Domingo, which was to have been used as a relay station for the expedition to Louisiana. In addition to this setback, Napoleon became engaged in war with England in 1803. Because of his need for money, his fear of England's wresting Louisiana from him, and the impossibility of sending another expedition to occupy and defend it, Napoleon became willing to sell all of Louisiana to the United States. At this propitious moment, Jefferson, through his agents at Paris, Livingston and Monroe, offered to purchase the "island of New Orleans" in order to secure American interests there. Talleyrand acting for Napoleon, told the commissioner they could have all of Louisiana. On April 30, 1803, the Americans, amazed at the French offer, consummated the bargain by which, for approximately 15,000,-000 dollars, the United States more than doubled its size and gained over 80,000 inhabitants. On December 20, 1803, Pierre de Laussat, who had represented the French Republic for the twenty days it had ruled Louisiana after the departure of the Spanish handed the territory over to the United States represented by W. C. C. Claiborne, the new territorial governor, and General James Wilkinson.

LOUISIANA AS A TERRITORY
1803-1812

Despite a good deal of Creole resent-ment of the new American officials and their government, no time was lost in setting up the territorial government. By Act of Congress on March 25, 1804, the territory south of 33° (the northern border of modern Louisiana) was organized as the Territory of Orleans with Claiborne as Governor. The ill-defined expanse north of that line became the Territory of Louisiana. It was renamed the Territory of Missouri in 1812.

There was immediate disagreement with Spain over the western boundary, the United States claiming it had purchased all of the territory once included in French Louisiana, while Spain claimed West Florida and the Sabine region as belonging to her. For a time after 1800, both countries had agreed to regard the disputed area as neutral. The Florida Parishes of Louisiana (those lying East of the Mississippi and North of Lake Pontchartrain) threw off the Spanish yoke and set up the "Free and Independent State of West Florida" as a result of a successful revolution in 1810. They immediately applied for admission into the United States, and became part of the Louisiana Territory in October, 1810; President Madison taking the position that they were already under American rule as a result of the Louisiana Purchase. In 1819, the conflict with Spain was settled when President Monroe concluded the Treaty of Washington by which Spain sold both East and West Florida to the United States and granted the American claim to the Sabine boundary. By this act Louisiana received her present boundaries.

LOUISIANA IN THE UNION
1812-1861

The Census of 1810 reported a population of more than 75,000 in the Territory of Orleans. This was sufficient for statehood and a proposal to that effect was made in 1811 by Julien Poydras, the Territory's delegate to Congress. The Enabling Act of February 20, 1811, passed over violent opposition by the New England states whose representatives feared the power of their section would be diminished should too many Southern and Western states be admitted, authorized a territorial convention to meet at New Orleans in November 1811 and draw up a constitution. Forty-five delegates, headed by Poydras, drafted Louisiana's first constitution, patterning it after Kentucky's constitution, which provided for a Governor, a bicameral legislature, and a supreme court. It differed notably from other state constitutions in retaining the Napoleonic code rather than adopting the Common Law. Louisiana formally became a state on April 30, 1812.

Though Louisiana now ceased to play a colorful part in the intriguing story of European diplomacy, her history continued to be eventful.

The first steamboat to descend the Mississippi to New Orleans—the boat was called the **New Orleans**—arrived on January 12, 1812, and thus inaugurated that colorful era of the Mississippi steamboat, which brought so much prosperity to New Orleans. Three years later, on January 8, 1815, General Andrew Jackson defeated the British at Chalmette, near New Orleans, in a notable battle made even more so by the fact that it was fought fifteen days after peace had been signed at Ghent between Britain and America. (See **New Orleans** for a description of the Battle of New Orleans.)

More important than battles, if less spectacular, was the rapid growth of population, trade and agriculture in the state. From a population of around 75,000 in 1810, the state's inhabitants increased to over 150,000 in 1820, 350,000 in 1849, and more than 700,000 in 1860. People began to distribute themselves more evenly over the state as agriculture increased and provided the state with other income than commerce at New Orleans. A glance at the figures for sugar cane production will illustrate the growth of both cotton and sugar growing; In 1820, around 25,000 hogsheads of sugar were produced. In 1835, over 100,000; in 1845 more than 200,000, and in 1865, the peak year, more than 450,000 hogsheads were produced. This high rate of increase reflects improved agricultural methods and the use of steam equipment after 1830 as well as the growth of population. Commerce, particularly at New Orleans, kept pace with the state's rapid development in other fields, as evidenced by the figures for freight tonnage brought down the river to New Orleans—less than 70,000 in 1815 and almost 550,000 in 1840. About 250 steamboats plied the Mississippi in 1840, a tremendous increase since Nicholas Roosevelt's **New Orleans** made the first descent in 1811. Where the barges of the pre-steam period had required three to four months to carry their limited loads from Louisville to New Orleans, the steamboats of 1840 could make the trip in five or six days. Small wonder that population, agriculture and commerce flourished in the state which commanded the mouth of America's greatest river system. This was the period when Shreveport, Alexandria and Natchitoches arose as trading centers along the Red River after it was cleared for transportation by the valuable work of Captain Henry Shreve.

In 1845, a new constitution was adopted to meet the changing needs of the growing state. It provided for direct, popular election of the governor (he had been chosen by the House of Representatives under the 1812 Constitution), it eliminated property qualifications for voters and established a free public school system under a state superintendent of Public Education. Such democratic provisions reflect an Americanization of the state automatically resulting from her position as a focus of frontier migration.

THE MEXICAN WAR AND EXPANSION

Louisiana's location gave her an important part in the "Manifest Destiny" chapter of American history which includes the war with Mexico, the Annexation of Texas, and the curious "filibustering" expeditions aimed at fostering revolutions in the Spanish colonies in South America. Many Louisianians migrated to Texas and helped fight the Lone Star Republic's battles against Mexico. Many more served under General Zachary Taylor who, when the United States went to war in 1846, led his armies into Texas from Louisiana territory. In the '50's New Orleans was the center of such filibustering activity as Naraso Lopez' two futile expeditions against Cuba in 1850 and 1851 and William Walker's temporarily successful rebellion in Nicaragua in 1856.

SLAVERY, SECESSION AND CIVIL WAR

Since the days of Governor Bienville's "Black Code", Negro slavery had been a central factor in Louisiana history. Deplored by many Southerners in the 19th Century for both economic and ethical reasons (it became increasingly unprofitable as the 19th Century wore on because of the prohibitive capital investment in the labor supply), it nonetheless served as one means of racial adjustment generally suited to the production of Louisiana's staple crops.

The result of the abolitionist agitation which arose in the North in the 'thirties was that Southerners came to think less about the evils of slavery and more about the reasons for maintaining it. But so long as the abolitionists remained a minority, loyalty to the Union was as characteristic of Louisiana citizens as their conviction that immediate emancipation was dangerous. The State Legislature for example, passed a resolution in 1830 (during the South Carolina nullification crisis) condemning "nullification and secession as essentially revolutionary measures." Down to the very eve of the Civil War, the great majority of Louisiana citizens hoped that the Union might somehow be held together. The statue of Henry Clay which still stands in New Orleans was erected in 1856 out of gratitude for the great statesman's efforts to hold the Union together in the crisis of 1850. It is significant that the statue is erected to Clay rather than to Calhoun.

In the fateful four-cornered presidential election of 1860, Louisiana gave 22,681 votes to Breckinridge of the Southern Democrats, 20,204 to Bell of the more moderate Constitutional Union Party, and 7,625 to Douglas of the Northern Democrats. The vote indicates a comfortable majority of moderate opinion interested in compromise for the sake of the Union.

After the election of Lincoln and the secession of South Carolina, a state election was held to select a convention to determine Louisiana's action. When the convention met at Baton Rouge in January 1861, five states had already seceded, and there was nothing to do but follow. On January 27, the convention passed the Ordinance of Secession by a vote of 112 to 17. From that day until March 21, the state was called the "Independent Commonwealth of Louisiana." On March 21, the secession convention ratified the Provisional Constitution of the Confederate States and formally espoused its cause.

1861-1865

Directly the state seceded, the militia was called to service, Federal military installations and buildings such as the Mint and the Customhouse were seized, and the enlisting of troops begun. By November of 1861, more than 25,000 Louisiana citizens had gone North to serve in the Confederate armies on the Virginia battlefields under such distinguished Louisiana military leaders as Beauregard, Taylor and Bragg.

Louisiana's command of the Mississippi, which had made her an important factor in European and American diplomacy, caused her to play a vital part in Civil War strategy. With the double object of cutting the Confederacy off from her river supply line and of strengthening the blockade of the South, a Federal fleet of 43 vessels under the command of Admiral David Farragut, a former Louisianian, came up the Mississippi in April 1862. The fleet bombed Forts St. Philip and Jackson near the river's mouth and after passing through a formidable bombardment, 17 of the ships appeared before New Orleans on April 26.

On May 1, 15,000 Federal troops under General Benjamin F. Butler landed and occupied the city which had been inadequately garrisoned by 3000 militia under General Lovell. This was the first major blow to the Confederacy.

While Farragut continued up the river and seized Baton Rouge (driving Governor Moore and the other state officials to Opelousas), Butler began his unfortunate military administration of New Orleans where he achieved great heights of unpopularity by his arbitrary acts, alleged profiteering and his notorious "Woman Order." He was replaced by General Nathaniel Banks in December 1862.

Confederate forces in the state under General Dick Taylor (son of President Zachary Taylor), had been able to contain the inept General Butler in New Orleans, but failed to prevent General Banks from occupying most of Southern Louisiana and taking the temporary capital at Opelousas. When that city fell in March 1863, the state government was moved once more to Shreveport where it remained until the end of the war.

Alexandria fell to the Federals on May 1, 1863, and Port Hudson surrendered on July 9, 1863, after a long siege. While the Federal forces were engaged in these expeditions, General Dick Taylor recaptured much of Southern Louisiana. After the fall of Vicksburg on July 4, 1863, the strategic value of New Orleans to the Confederacy was much lessened.

However, General Taylor still kept up the fighting. As a matter of fact, when the war ended he was getting ready to take the offensive against the Federal troops in Louisiana. In 1864 his small army was successful in preventing the Federals from capturing Shreveport and the Red River Territory. Two Union armies, one going up the Red River and another Bayou Teche, got as far as Mansfield. There on April 8, 1864 they were defeated in a bloody engagement and driven back to Alexandria in disorderly retreat. After that there was little further fighting in the state.

During the Federal occupation of parts of Louisiana, the state government was headed in turn by Governors Thomas Moore and Henry W. Allen. Its jurisdiction was necessarily limited to the western part of the state for the most part. The rest of the state was ruled from New Orleans by Military Governors George Shepley from 1862 to 1864 and Michael Hahn from 1864 to 1865.

RECONSTRUCTION DURING AND AFTER THE WAR

Federal-held Louisiana was the first Confederate territory to be subject to Reconstruction. It began in New Orleans in 1862 when General Butler effected a partial emancipation of slaves by enlisting them in Federal regiments and encouraging them to leave their masters. This policy was modified by Banks who put the Negroes under discipline and made them work.

After George F. Shepley became military governor in August 1862, he staged an election for Congress in which the vote was limited to citizens who had taken the oath of allegiance. Michael Hahn and Benjamin F. Flanders were elected and occupied seats in the House of Representatives until their terms expired in 1863.

Slavery in Confederate-held territory was theoretically abolished by Lincoln's Emancipation Proclamation of January 1, 1863, but it continued in Federal-held territory until the first Reconstruction constitution for the state was put into effect in 1864.

Within the new Republican party which sprang up to control state politics in this chaotic period, there were two factions. The point at issue between radical and moderate Republicans was Negro suffrage. An election in January 1864 for "Free State" governor, resulted in the victory of the moderate Republican, Michael Hahn over his radical opponent, Benjamin Flanders. Lincoln, who favored the moderates all along, conferred the powers of military governor on Hahn under whose leadership a "Reconstruction Constitution" was drawn up in 1864. This document (which displeased the radicals both in Washington and Louisiana by failing to allow Negro suffrage), was rejected by Congress but served the state nevertheless until a second, more radical one was formed in 1868.

The last hope of Louisiana's Confederates vanished on May 26, 1865, when General Kirby Smith surrendered the Department of the Trans-Mississippi to Federal armies. Confederate Governor Allen issued a proclamation to the people of the state on June 2, 1865 advising them to cease all resistance, take the oath of allegiance, and endeavor to rebuild the prosperity of the state within the Union.

For a time there was hope of stable progress. President Johnson proclaimed amnesty in May 1865 for those former Confederates who had not been leaders in secession and the war. But by 1867, the radicals in Congress had overwhelmed Johnson's efforts for moderate reconstruction, and the Louisiana radicals, aided by Federal troops under General Sheridan, climbed into the saddle.

Under radical rule, both conservative and moderate officials were removed from office with little or no regard to law. The radical Benjamin Flanders was placed in the governor's chair by the Commander of the Federal army forces. Negroes were enrolled as voters under the terms of the Congressional Reconstruction Acts of 1867—acts designed to exclude ex-Confederates from political activity which consequently gave the suffrage to more colored than white voters.

This state of affairs was mirrored in the new constitutional convention of 1867. There were two Negro members for every one white. The constitution it wrote disfranchised almost all former Confederates, provided for interracial schools, abolished segregation of all types, and scheduled an election on the basis of the revised suffrage. With the adoption of this constitution by a popular vote of 51,737 to 39,076, Louisiana was re-admitted to the Union on June 25, 1868.

GOVERNOR WARMOTH AND AFTER

The election of 1868 inaugurated the sorriest decade in Louisiana's political history. Under Governor Henry Warmoth, his acting successor P. B. S. Pinchback, and finally William Pitt Kellogg, state politics were controlled by a combination of Federal force, and an ignorant electorate unscrupulously used by northern carpet-baggers and local turncoats. Corruption, tyranny and racial strife prevailed. Taxes rose 450% between 1868 and 1876 yet the bonded debt of the state went from $10,000,000 to $50,000,000 in the same period.

In the election of 1872, Governor Warmoth, who had become more conservative in his last year of office, supported the moderate John McEnery for governor. McEnery ran with the united backing of the Democrats and the Liberal Republicans against the radical, William Pitt Kellogg. Though McEnery received a majority of the votes he was deviously kept from taking office by the Radicals who had the backing of Congress, President Grant, and the Federal troops. In spite of this, the McEnery faction set up a rump in New Orleans, recognized as the true government in several parishes.

Opposition to carpetbag tyranny now began to be expressed in violence. At Colfax, Grant Parish, a bloody riot occurred in April 1873, when a band of white men from Grant and neighboring parishes sought to recapture the courthouse, from which white officials had been ousted during a Negro uprising. Three whites and 120 Negroes were killed but the Negroes were finally ejected.

Inevitably, the chaotic condition of the times gave rise to resistance groups and vigilantes. For several years secret organizations such as the nights of the White Camelia and the Ku Klux Klan had been opposing carpetbag rule with occasional resorts to violence and intimidation. By 1874, a more powerful organization, the White League, composed of some of the most conservative and respected men of the state, had been organized to fight for home rule and white control of politics. The most notable of several violent clashes between native whites and the alien faction was that which occurred on September 14, 1874 between Governor Kellog's Metropolitan Police—a virtual private army commanded by former Confederate General Longstreet—and the White League forces in New Orleans.

The White Leaguers, comprised of ex-Confederate soldiers and prominent citizens, numbered fifteen hundred under the command of General Fred Ogden. Having secured arms and two cannons they disposed themselves in military fashion, and advanced against General Longstreet's trained troops. Most of the action took place at the foot of Canal Street by the customhouse. On hearing the Confederate yell and after a few volleys the Metropolitans ran. 21 of the White Leaguers lost their lives and many more were wounded. Although this "battle of Canal Street" did not end carpetbag rule, it illustrates the desperate measures which otherwise peaceful men *were forced to adopt in those troubled times. It did not close the Reconstruction era, but it pointed to the end. A monument was erected to the memory of those who lost their lives in this fight against tyranny and oppression, and every year exercises are held to honor the martyrs who died there. The 14th of September is still regarded as a sort of state independence day by the people of Louisiana.

THE RETURN OF HOME RULE

In the campaign of 1876, the conservative forces had more hope of success than they had enjoyed for a decade. In the most orderly election since 1866, Democrat Francis Tillou Nicholls, a former Confederate general, was elected by a large majority over his Radical Republican opponent Stephen B. Packard. But because the state Returning Board was dominated by men of Radical sentiments, that body declared Packard the victor. The result was that both Packard and Nicholls were inaugurated as governor in January of 1877.

Fortunately for the whites and home rule, the Federal troops did not come to the aid of the Radicals as they had before. A sort of bargain between the forces of presidential candidate Hayes (who needed the Louisiana electoral vote to defeat his opponent Tilden) and the state's conservatives, resulted in the election of Hayes, who, in turn, recognized Nicholl's government as the legitimate one in Louisiana. (Similar arrangements were made in South Carolina and Florida.)

Without Federal backing, Packard's claim soon collapsed. Governor Nicholls became the unquestioned executive of the state, and, on April 20, 1877, President Hayes ordered the last of the Federal troops in Louisiana to withdraw. Reconstruction was over.

MODERN LOUISIANA—POLITICAL

One of the first political acts of the redeemed state was to adopt a new constitution—that of 1879—which increased the appointive powers of the governor and decreased the power of the legislature. This was done to lessen the danger of demagogy in politics. A strong court system was also provided to prevent a repetition of the disregard for law which characterized the previous decade.

This constitution served the state until 1898 when a new document was framed which stipulated property and educational qualifications for voters, restored powers to the legislature and decreased the power of the governor. In effect, this constitution established the one party system which has since prevailed in the state's politics.

The Constitution of 1898 remained in effect until 1913. In that year a new, provisional constitution was drawn up which was modified and made permanent by a convention in 1921. The new organic law, under which the state still operates, strengthened the judiciary (providing for a seven man Supreme Court with both original and appelate jurisdiction plus Courts of Appeal, District Courts and lesser courts), provided for improved education, a more efficient highway system and liberalized the suffrage.

In 1940, the Reorganization Act streamlined state administration by consolidating over eighty state boards and commissions into twenty departments.

The most memorable figure in state political history since the beginning of the century was the controversial Huey P. Long who served as governor from 1928 to 1931 and as U. S. Senator from 1931 until his assassination. Idolized by his supporters, Long could be ignored by no one during his undisputed rule of the state. His "Share the Wealth" program, a plan which was to assure every family a minimum income of $5,000 per year while prohibiting incomes of more than one million dollars annually—was important not merely to Louisiana politics. It became a movement of national significance when Long brought it before the nation while he was in the U. S. Senate. It must always be a question as to how far he would have gone with this plan in the field of national politics had he not been assassinated on September 8th, 1935 by Dr. Carl A. Weiss, the son-in-law of one of Long's political enemies.*

Long's conduct in state politics was often high-handed, but he had voters behind him. Long brought many needed improvements to the state. A new state capitol building, free schoolbooks for children, improvements in Louisiana State University, and the development of the state's highway and bridge system was made during Long's regime.

In 1940 a re-action set in against his followers who had governed the state for nine years, and a "reform" candidate Sam H. Jones won the governorship. He was succeeded in time by James H. Davis.

Earl K. Long became the dominant figure in state politics again with his election in 1948 as governor. In August of the same year his nephew, Russell B. Long—Huey P. Long's son—was nominated to the U. S. Senate.

Judge Robert Kennon was elected Governor 1952. Earl Long ran again in 1956 and was elected. James H. Davis was elected a second time in 1960.

A lawyer from Columbia and former floor leader in the House of Representatives under

Gov. Earl Long, John J. McKeithen gained the governorship in 1964 by defeating de Lesseps Morrison in a spirited runoff and then turning back a strong challenge by Republican Charlton Lyons of Shreveport.

Four years later, after pushing a Constitutional amendment through the Legislature to qualify, McKeithen was re-elected to a precedent-setting second term in office.

Cong. Edwin Edwards of Crowley was elected Governor in 1972, succeeding John J. McKeithen.

MODERN LOUISIANA—ECONOMIC AND SOCIAL

Economic and social recovery from the ravages of the Civil War was affected more slowly than political recovery.

One interesting phenomenon of this period was the famous Louisiana Lottery, established in 1868 by a group of citizens anxious to recoup fortunes lost in the war. In consideration of an annual payment of $40,000 to the state educational fund, the Lottery Company was granted a charter by the state for a period of twenty-five years. During most of this time it was the biggest business in Louisiana, and millions of dollars poured into the state from all over the country and from foreign countries. The lottery was conducted honestly, and to give its drawings standing, the concern employed Generals Beauregard and Ewell, two ex-Confederates, to superintend them. In 1892, despite the company's offer to pay the state $1,250,000 annually for a twenty-five-year extension of its charter, a vigorous reform group fought the granting of the charter. It was passed by the legislature but vetoed by Gov. Nicholls. Lotteries were then forbidden the use of the U. S. mails and later prohibited by the constitution of the State of Louisiana.

Improvement in the important field of transportation was begun only after 1870. In that year a program of levee construction on the Mississippi was inaugurated which has been continued ever since in spite of losses sustained by occasional floods.

The Port of New Orleans was immensely benefited in 1879 when Captain James B. Eads succeeded in constructing the first effective jetty system at the mouth of the Mississippi, thus controlling the shifting sandbars which by obstructing the entrance to the river had always impeded the city's full development as a port. In addition to port improvement, by 1883 New Orleans was connected with the rest of the country by five trunk railroad lines and a line extending to the Pacific Coast. The population of the state shows a steady increase in this period, going from 726,916 in 1879 to 1,118,588 in 1890, to 2,683,516 in 1950, and to 3,257,022 in 1960.

Since 1900, Louisiana has made enormous strides in industry and agriculture. The oil industry with all its ramifications has invigorated the state's economy, at no time more than in the fifteen years since the end of the second world war, years which have witnessed the important development of tideland oil exploitation on the Gulf Coast. Louisiana continues to be a large producer of sugar, cotton and rice—producing 75 per cent of all sugar cane grown in the country and 60 per cent of rice.

THE LOUISIANA PURCHASE

165 years ago (1803) the United States acquired Louisiana from France. This was the greatest real estate deal in all history for this vast empire of over 900,000 square miles—nearly 600 million acres—was bought for 15 million dollars (less the claims of some of our citizens against France for shipping losses in an undeclared naval war). This magnificent domain was acquired by peaceful means and without the shedding of a drop of blood—in striking contrast to the methods of the large empires of the past, which conquered their territory by force of arms.

Strange to say, although we paid only four cents an acre for this immense territory, including some of the finest agrarian land in the world, it seemed like a lot of money to many people at that time, particularly the thrifty New Englanders who opposed this expenditure.

France actually got $11,250,000, after deducting about three and three quarter million dollars for the American claimants. Including the interest of about $8,225,000, Louisiana cost the United States $23,225,000. It is interesting to note that the final accounting was not made until 1925 because the Government settled most of the claims which it had assumed in the purchase for 20¢ on a dollar and there was continuous bickering and litigation.

According to Bernard Devoto, American historian, in "The Course of An Empire," the United States earned a seven per cent return on the whole capital investment the first year after it had taken over the Port of New Orleans from the receipts of the customhouse there.

The Louisiana Purchase was due to the vision of one of the greatest Americans, Thomas Jefferson. Its consummation is one of the most significant events in history. Many famous battles and the rise and fall of empires have had less effect on the affairs of men than this great contract. It doubled the size of the country and put the United States in the position to become a world power.

The sale of Louisiana by Napoleon to the United States was the result of a complicated chain of events involving the rivalries of France and Spain as well as Great Britain, and latterly the interest of the United States. France ceded the territory known as Louisiana to Spain on

November 3, 1762, and the delivery of the province to Spain took place on April 21, 1764. It was under Spanish rule for nearly forty years.

In the meantime Spain began to decline as a world-power and the end of the century saw the rise of Napoleon. Napoleon with his ambition to rule the World forced Spain to recede Louisiana to France, which recession was made effective by the Treaty of San Ildefonso signed on October 1, 1800. It was a secret treaty and Napoleon gave in exchange Tuscany in Italy which was to be governed by the Spanish Duke of Parma. Napoleon also agreed not to sell or alienate any part of the Louisiana Territory. Napoleon swapped Tuscany, 9,000 square miles, with 1,000,000 inhabitants for Louisiana, 900,000 square miles and 80,000 inhabitants, but he knew the potential value of the land across the sea.

The Treaty was ratified in Madrid on March 21, 1801. The Treaty and confirmation were supposed to be secret, but Robert Livingston, our Minister to France, obtained a copy. Whether President Jefferson had a copy is not known, but he knew the contents of the treaty and became genuinely alarmed. He instructed Livingston to negotiate for the purchase of New Orleans—known then as the "Island of New Orleans"—and the portion of the territory east of the "island" of the western part of Florida. The whole land area which Jefferson deemed desirable did not exceed 2800 square miles.

In 1796 the United States signed a treaty with Spain in which that country agreed to allow to American citizens free navigation of the Mississippi River and the right to ship goods to the "Island of New Orleans," and to store them there or warehouse them for shipment abroad, without payment of export duty. But in October of 1802 Morales, the Spanish Intendant at New Orleans, suddenly forbade the Americans to land in any part of the Spanish province. This was not as arbitrary as it might seem now because in the treaty it was agreed that the citizens of the United States could use the Port for a period of three years; that if at the end of that time the Spanish Government wanted to revoke this permit, it could do so. Although it had been agreed that if the Spanish Governor denied the use of the Port to American shippers, that he would assign them another place for warehousing their goods on the West Bank of the Mississippi.

When Morales' withdrawal of the right to deposit became known indignation meetings were held in many cities up the Valley and business leaders and even Congressmen orated against Spain.

It was not generally known even at that time that the Louisiana Territory had been turned back to France in October 1800. The Spanish Intendant, Morales, still seemed to be in charge, and it was he who closed the Port to American shippers although it really belonged to France. At the time, Governor W. C. C. Claiborne of the Mississippi Territory endeavored to find out the cause of this order. Morales claimed that he was acting under orders of the Government of Spain, but the Governor General of the whole province, Salcedo, stated that the Intendant had acted on his own authority. Morales asserted that frauds were being committed by the Americans.

Historians have never been able to locate any of the alleged frauds. In any event members of the House and Senate of the Congress of the United States were much upset over these actions, and they demanded that our government seize New Orleans and teach his Catholic Majesty, the King of Spain, a lesson in warfare.

In the meantime, Thomas Jefferson was trying to arrange things diplomatically, and there was much discussion in the Congress, both in executive sessions of the Senate and House, whether Spain had the right to cede the Territory of Louisiana to France without the consent of America. Cooler heads prevailed and arguments in favor of a diplomatic procedure looking to a settlement were proposed by President Jefferson. Jefferson in his message to the Senate on January 11, 1803, said, "The cession of the Spanish province of Louisiana to France and perhaps of the Floridas and the late suspension of our right of deposit at New Orleans are of primary interest to the United States."

The so-called Mississippi question was debated hotly and continuously, and finally on February 14, 1803, Senator James Ross of Pennsylvania introduced a resolution that "the late infraction of their (U.S.) unquestionable rights is an aggression hostile to their honor and interest." And his resolution authorized the President to take immediate possession of the Island of New Orleans and to call into service any number of the militia of Georgia, South Carolina, Ohio, Kentucky, Tennessee or any other part of the Mississippi Territory, not exceeding 50,000 and to use them together with the military and naval forces of the Union for taking over the Port of New Orleans. The resolution further called for five million dollars for carrying it into effect. This resolution passed but it was never put into effect because the Louisiana Purchase was arranged for on April 30, 1803.

In January 1803, Jefferson nominated Robert R. Livingston, Minister Plenipotentiary, (Livingston was already in France as Minister) and James Monroe to be Minister Extraordinary and Plenipotentiary "to enter into a treaty with the First Consul of France for the purpose of enlarging and more exactly securing our right in the Mississippi River and in the territory east thereof." The resolution was passed by the House and the Senate on February 22, 1803 authorizing the acquisition of the Island on which New Orleans stands and part of Florida, an area of approximately 2800 square miles, and for this sum of two million dollars was appropriated which was to be used by the President within his discretion.

Livingston had been negotiating for the accession of Louisiana for many months with Talleyrand, who disclaimed France's possession of Louisiana, but nevertheless discussed the possibilities. In March 1803, he wrote Jefferson "with respect to negotiations for Louisiana, I think nothing will be effected here." But by this time conditions had changed.

Napoleon was not ignorant of the potential value of the Louisiana to the United States or any world power, but there were several reasons why he now thought it advisable to unload what was then a white elephant. The English Navy had some twenty warships in the Gulf and would no doubt soon attempt to seize Louisiana. He had just suffered a severe military loss in San Domingo where his large army succumbed to the yellow fever and the brilliant military genius of Tousaint l'Ouverteur. To colonize and defend Louisiana was not feasible at that time. He wanted to create a rival to Great Britain. And he could use ready cash. So on April 10 he sent for two of his ministers and asked their opinion of selling Louisiana to the United States. Information of this proposal filtered through court channels to Napoleon's brothers, Joseph and Lucien. They opposed the sale. They went immediately to see the Consul who invited them to come into the bathroom while he was taking his bath. Napoleon splashed them with water and laughed, stating that he knew what he was doing—literally throwing cold water on their proposal to retain Louisiana.

On April 11 Livingston was talking with Talleyrand who had always denied that France owned Louisiana. Talleyrand suddenly inquired whether the United States would purchase the whole of the Louisiana Territory Livingston assured Talleyrand that he did not want all of Louisiana but only the Island of New Orleans and the Floridas.

James Monroe arrived in Paris on the 12th of April. The next day Livingston gave a dinner party for him. Barbé-Marbois, the Minister of the Treasury, came late to the party and whispered to Livingston he would like to have him visit the ministry that same evening secretly. They conversed for an hour or so. Barbé-Marbois told Livingston that Napoleon had authorized him to sell not only New Orleans but the whole province of Louisiana. He asked for 100 million francs, or some 20 million dollars. Livingston wrote to Jefferson about the deal.

Realizing that it would take a month and a half to receive an answer, he and Monroe met with Barbé-Marbois almost daily. Finally he got the minister down to the rock bottom price of 15 million dollars. They closed the deal without waiting to hear from Washington and without authority to do so. The treaty was signed by Talleyrand, Monroe and Livingston on April 30, 1803. Actually it was signed on May 2, but it seems to have been antedated for no reason that we know now.

On hearing that a compact had been signed, Napoleon exclaimed: "I have just given England a maritime rival that will sooner or later lower her pride." When Spain learned of the agreement to sell she protested against the sale to Secretary Madison, stating that France had violated her terms not to alienate Louisiana.

Livingston said upon the signing of the treaty: "We have lived long, but this is the noblest day of our lives. The treaty which we have just signed has not been obtained by art or dictated by force.... From this date the United States will take their place among the powers of the first rank; the English lose all exclusive influence in the affairs of America."

Judge William C. Holmes of the New Orleans bar writes this description of the meeting in Paris of the actors in the sale of Louisiana.

"What was the scene of the climatic act of the exalted enterprise? It was the French court, displaying a magnificence of setting which surpassed in splendor, even in that early period of the consulate, that of any kingdom in Europe. Striding nervously back and forth, a short stocky man in his early middle years, speaking his lines crisply but in modulated tones, dressed in a blue broadcloth coat, with cream silk waistcoat, unbuttoned, his white covert breeches thrust tightly into tall sealskin boots—the first consul of France; and Prince Charles Maurice de Pericord Talleyrand, the crippled Minister of Foreign Affairs, leaning easily upon a goldheaded staff much like the crozier that supported him when he was a prince of the church—suave, sentient, scintillating —glittering in rose taffeta coat, pink silk waistcoat, and white silk breeches, with enormous silver buckles on his low-heeled slippers; Barbe-Marbois, in mauve velvet coat with cloth of gold waistcoat and cream-colored d o e s k i n breeches, white silk stockings, and varnished bootees—calm, confident—speaking slowly and deliberately; Joseph and Lucien Bonaparte standing anxiously to one side, suspended upon the words of their brother; Lord Whitworth, tall, erect, stiff in offended dignity, resplendent in red coat emblazoned with the orders of His Britannic Majesty wearing buff breeches and cream-colored silk stockings, with a jeweled sword hung from a gold sash; courtiers in flashing regalia in the background; and two quiet-voiced sombrely dressed citizens of another youthful republic across the Atlantic, their Excellencies, James Monroe, of Virginia, and Robert Livingston, of New York, lately aappointed Ambassadors Extraordinary and Ministers Plenipotentiary of the United States of America!"

The news of the purchase of the Louisiana Territory reached the United States on June 19, 1803. The mass of people were spontaneous in their approval.

In the Treaty of Purchase it was agreed that both parties had to ratify the treaty within six months, or not later than Nov. 10, 1803. President Jefferson called the Congress to meet on October 17th.

Not everyone thought that Louisiana was a great bargain. Hugh Murray, a geographer, in 1803, did not think so. He told in detail of a 500-mile wide belt of "desert" spreading east of the Rockies. He called it the American or Arkansas Desert, and declared it "entirely unsusceptible of cultivation." He did not like the drinking water in New Orleans and said eastern Arkansas was filled with "noisome swamps." He wrote off 300,000 square miles of the upper Missouri River basin as the home of "the ferocious and formidable grisly bear."

But the mid-westerners and Mississippi Valley people wanted Louisiana and cheered on the president. He came in for heavy criticism from eastern members of Congress and newspaper editors. The objectors said the new territory was too far away from established centers, that it cost too much, that Napoleon did not have a right to sell it and that the whole deal was unconstitutional. Senators Tracy of Connecticut and Pickering of Massachusetts charged that the purchase would admit new citizens into the United States without consent of the states already belonging to the Union (in 1803 in the whole Louisiana Territory there were less than 50,000 white persons). Representative Thomas Griffin of Virginia said that he feared "this Eden of the new world would prove a cemetery for the bodies of our citizens." He stated that the effect of the purchase would be to increase the wages of labor (sic) and decrease land values.

After much debate, some of it tinged with bitterness, the Senate ratified the Treaty on October 20, 1803. On the 25th the Senate authorized the President to take possession of the Louisiana Territory by a vote of 26 to 6. The bill authorizing the purchase of Louisiana passed the House on October 27th by a vote of 90 to 25. And on the 28th by a vote

of 89 to 23 it authorized the President to take possession of the Louisiana Territory. President Jefferson signed the Purchase Bill on October 31, 1803.

On November 4th the Senate authorized the "creation of stock to the amount of $11,250,000 and to make provision for the payment of same." It passed by a vote of 26 to 5. After the enabling act was passed the problem was to find a buyer for the bonds to be issued. Before the end of the year the great banking house of Baring Brothers of London agreed to underwrite 20-year bonds at a 6 per cent rate of interest for the total amount. Thus indirectly Napoleon got his money to fight the British from the British—one of the ironies of History.

On November 30, 1803, the Spanish officials and the French Prefect, Pierre Clement de Laussat, together with a few civil authorities and Army and Navy officials appeared at the Cabildo in New Orleans, and the Province of Louisiana was turned over to the French Republic.

On December 20, 1803, the United States of America in the same front room of the Cabildo took over formal possession of the Province of Louisiana. The American officials were Governor W. C. C. Claiborne and General James Wilkinson. The treaty was read aloud and the Prefect of the Republic of France, de Laussat, personally delivered to Governor Claiborne the keys to the City of New Orleans, tied with tri-color ribbons. Judge William C. Holmes describes the scene:

"Claiborne then made an address to the populace which had assembled in the Place d'/arms, now known as Jackson Square. The flag of the Republic of France was lowered in silence to a halfway point of the halyard, where it was met by the emblem of the United States, and as the flags of the two greatest republics on earth waved side by side, the crowd shouted huzzas and there was a military salute!"

That night de Laussat gave a great banquet and soiree where the citizens —French, Spanish and American—took part without distinction. Solemn toasts were drunk to the three nations. After coffee and liquers there was dancing— and as was the custom of those days— numerous card games of several kinds. At 1:00 A.M. supper was served. The ball lasted all night.

From the Louisiana Purchase Territory have been carved thirteen states or parts of states of the Union, as follows: .

Louisiana, Arkansas, Missouri, Iowa, Minnesota, North Dakota, South Dakota, Nebraska, Kansas, Oklahoma, Colorado, Wyoming and Montana.

The value of all this territory today is almost incalculable.

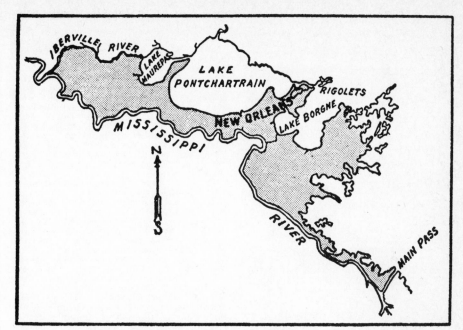

Map showing the "Island of New Orleans"—the part of Louisiana that Jefferson originally wanted to purchase.

OLD WORLD CULTURE STILL REMAINS ALIVE IN MANY SECTIONS OF STATE

Old World culture is not lost in Louisiana.

The ways and customs of early settlers have been preserved, not only in legend and architecture, but in entire isolated communities throughout the state.

Dr. Alvin Bertrand, professor of sociology at Louisiana State University, in 1955 defined, described and mapped tiny cultural islands where the ways and customs and, often, the language of the Old World are kept alive.

One third of Louisiana's population is of French descent, and one becomes accustomed to hearing the French accent through much of Louisiana.

But Dr. Bertrand has mapped areas of German, Irish, Spanish, Italian, Anglo-Saxon and Indian settlement.

Only an hour's ride from New Orleans is a small part of Spain.

Delacroix Island, as all cultural islands are, is isolated from the main thoroughfares. The original Spanish settlement there was accessible only to ox carts, and the community remained cut off from modifying influences.

In many of the homes, Spanish is still spoken by the older residents.

But the island, as are all cultural islands, is becoming engulfed in the tide of civilization.

In Plaquemines parish Slavonian citrus growers still preserve the language of the mother country. Many of the young settlers used to go to Yugoslavia for brides. Today they are becoming increasingly Americanized.

The remnants of once-proud Indian nations live on in LaSalle, St. Mary and St. Tammany parishes. There, too, the younger people are seeking jobs and wives in the outside world.

Dr. Bertrand says few pure-blood settlers remain.

His findings are published in the LSU bulletin "Many Louisianas."

He believes the findings will be useful in preparing many programs for the agriculture extension service at the university.

Although the small communities are destined to become Americanized, Dr. Bertrand says, the charm and culture of early America and old Europe will live on in Louisiana.

WHAT IS A CREOLE?

The word **Creole** means a pure white descendant of French or Spanish ancestry or of both. As an adjective it applies to their manners, usages, inventions, etc., as creole customs, creole lettuce, creole cooking and so forth.

Alexander Dimitry, New Orleans scholar, wrote: As early as 1520, Criollo (Creole) was invented by the Conquistadors to distinguish their pure-blooded off-springs, born in the colonies of South America or the Indies, from children of mixed blood born in the mother country."

The French adopted the Spanish word and changed it to "creole." Jean Bossu in his "Travels in North America" wrote in 1751: "The Creoles are those that are born here of a French man and French woman or of European parents."

THE ACADIANS IN LOUISIANA

During 1955 a year-round celebration was held in Louisiana commemorating the deportation of the Acadians from Nova Scotia 200 years ago. The Acadian Bicentennial Commission was organized and the State of Louisiana appropriated $100,000 to aid the celebration. Visitors from Canada were entertained in Louisiana and a delegation of Acadian descendants in Louisiana went to Canada. There were exhibits at various fairs held throughout the State during the year and several pageants brought to a climax the bicentennial celebration.

However, this celebration was something of an anomaly as far as Louisiana is concerned. While the Acadians were deported in 1755, beginning in September and ending in December, as far is known no Acadians reached Louisiana until 1764, nine years later.

Who are the Acadians?

No one knows exactly where the name of Acadia or Acadie comes from. It was applied to the peninsula on the eastern coast of Canada now known as Nova Scotia. Whether it was an Indian word or evolved from Arcadia because it was such a pleasant land we do not know. In any event the Acadians are those French people who settled in Nova Scotia in 1605 —the first white people to settle on the American Continent north of Mexico (which included Florida).

The earliest settlement in what is now the United States was St. Augustine in 1565. The oldest settlement in all the ter-

ritory north of the 30th parallel of latitude was that of Port Royal, now called Annapolis which was settled in 1605 by Poutrincourt. Poutrincourt brought with him as his apothecary Louis Hebert whose father was the apothecary of Catherine de Medici. This Louis Hebert was the progenitor of the thousands of Heberts living in Canada and the United States today. Soon other colonists were brought over from France. They were mostly peasants from Normandy and from Touraine. In the next thirty years several hundred additional families came to Acadie. The descendants of these few families in little over a hundred years numbered 10,000. The land was rich and fertile and they became prosperous and well to do.

England had obtained possession of Nova Scotia by the treaty of Utrecht in 1713. At various times her governors had attempted to force the French Acadians to take the oath of loyalty to England. The Acadians not only spoke a different language but they were Catholic in religion. They would not take the oath, claiming that they were "neutrals"—prisoners of war, so to speak. In fact, they were termed "French Neutrals" later by the English in their correspondence.

Finally, the English governor, Lawrence, decided that if these people would not swear to the oath of allegiance to the English King, that they had best be deported. Accordingly, in September 1755, the men were herded in their village churches, arrested and loaded on board ships waiting in the offing. In this process some of the families were separated. The soldiers burned the houses, took away their livestock, destroyed the orchards and laid waste the crops.

Recently, when millions of people were forced to leave their homes and millions more have been murdered by cruel dictators, the trials of the Acadians seem trivial and almost negligible when compared to the forced migration of millions in Russia, Germany, China, India and other countries.

Yet the deportation of the Acadians and their exile by force has been the subject of song and story. The tale of Evangeline by Longfellow moves us still.

Emile Louvriere has written a famous book in French termed "The Tragedy of A People," which won him the DeGoncourt prize for French composition and for excellence in literary expression, in which he tells the story of the expulsion of the Acadians. There are other books on the subject.

About 7,000 Acadians were deported in the Fall of 1755. These Acadian families were placed on ships and sent to various English colonies up and down the Atlantic Coast—Boston, New York, Philadelphia, Baltimore and Charleston. Some were landed at various ports in the Caribbean. Most of these deportees found their way back to Canada in a few years, while some were lost at sea, and some died from malnutrition and sickness.

However, no Acadians arrived in Louisiana until April 4, 1764. On this date D'Abbadie, the acting governor of the colony, noted in his diary that 20 Acadians had arrived from New York City. There were four families but they had no money as they had paid all of it for their passage down to New Orleans. (On April 6 D'Abbadie wrote his superior officers in France about the Acadians—for this reason the difference of two days in the date of the arrival of the Acadians has not been understood by some historians.)

After this there continued to arrive in Louisiana from various parts of the country and the Caribbean Islands small groups of Acadians. One of the largest contingents came from Baltimore in 1769.

In 1785 about 2,000 Acadians came from France where they had lived for a generation. This is known as the "grand migration." This group had gone to England from New England and then removed to St. Malo, France, where they were supported by the French Government. Finally in 1784 arrangements were made with the Spanish government to have them transported to Louisiana. Most of these settled along Bayou Teche or in the Attakapas country. The names of these immigrants and information about them is contained in a book recently published by the Louisiana State University Press.

From records available, it is probable that not more than 1,000 Acadians had arrived in Louisiana previous to 1784. The total number of Acadians who came here then could not have been more than 3,500. Today their descendants number from 200,000 to 300,000.

Some writers claim that a few Acadians settled in St. James and other parishes in 1756, reaching here overland from Georgia. This is improbable and would have been almost impossible. In the first place, it was the time of the French and Indian War. This lasted for seven years. Beginning in 1756 it did not end until 1763. During this time the English at war with France would not have permitted ships to sail down the coast bringing these French Acadian exiles to Louisiana. The migrants could not have come overland because not only was the war on and Indians on the warpath, but travel overland was practically impossible in those days. The exiles and their families would have had to traverse dense forests through which at that time there were no routes or trails from the Eastern seaboard to the Ohio or Mississippi rivers.

Besides such improbabilities there are no records to prove that any of these people arrived in Louisiana before 1764. There are two sources of records—first, the Catholic Church, and second, the Spanish Government which governed the province of Louisiana at that time. The Acadians were a very religious people and they were careful to record their marriages, baptisms and deaths. For instance, in St. James Parish, the first settlers would wait until a priest visited the area when several couples would get married at the same time and children of earlier marriages would be baptized. The Church has no records in any of its churches of sacraments administered to any Acadians before 1764.

The Acadians were industrious and a kindly and thrifty people. After arriving in Louisiana they worked hard and it wasn't long before they had gotten back the wealth they had lost by their forced migration. They did so well along the Mississippi River in St. James and Ascension Parishes that that section of the country was known as the Gold Coast in the early part of the Nineteenth Century.

FLAGS OVER LOUISIANA

It is probable that the banners of more sovereign nations have flown over what is now the State of Louisiana than any other state in the Union. Seven different flags have been hoisted over the land that now comprises the State or parts of it. One of these, it is true, was possibly not "sovereign" at all, and the other only to a limited degree; and both existed for a very short time. Strictly speaking, the flags of only five great nations have flown over Louisiana—France, Spain, Great Britain, the United States and the Confederate States of America. The other two "nations" were the Republic of West Florida and the State of Louisiana in 1861 before it joined the Confederate States.

If we consider the different periods of its history and the changes in the flags themselves, then the welkin of Louisiana has been pierced by many more flags. Spain in the course of her history has changed her standard several times. The flag of Spain in DeSoto's day with the arms of Castile was different from the Spanish flag at the end of the eighteenth century. The flag of France at the time of LaSalle was different from that of the Tri-Color of the Republic after the French Revolution.

When the Louisiana Territory was purchased from France the flag raised at the old Cabildo on December 20, 1803 consisted of fifteen stars and fifteen stripes. When Louisiana became a state in 1812, there were eighteen stars and eighteen stripes in the flag of the United States.

If we count then all the changes in flags we find that there were many different flags flown over this state. But the same might apply to other states.

Although Hernando DeSoto carried the banner of Spain to the Mississippi River

Spanish Flag of Leon and
Castile (DeSoto)–1541

French Fleur-de-Lis
(LaSalle)–1682

Bourbon Spain–1769

French Tri-Color–1803

West Florida Lone Star
–1810

Independent Louisiana
–1861

British Union Jack–1763

U.S. Flag of 15 Stars
–1803

Confederate Flag–1861

of Louisiana came under the Spanish flag.

In 1802 Spain ceded Louisiana back to France and the flag of France again flew over Louisiana. In 1803 the United States purchased Louisiana from France and on December 20, 1803, the French Tri-Color was lowered and the United States flag of fifteen stars and fifteen stripes was raised.

In 1810, the residents of West Florida, which included the present Florida Parishes with Baton Rouge as the capital, believing that the Louisiana Purchase treaty did not include them, declared themselves free and independent of Spain and formed the Republic of West Florida. On Sept. 26, 1810 they unfolded the Lone Star Flag. This consisted of a blue field with a single white star in the center. Governor Claiborne under instructions from President Madison sent soldiers into the Feliciana Parishes claiming them as part of the Territory of Orleans. The Republic of West Florida was peacefully dissolved in December, 1810, and the inhabitants acknowledged the sovereignty of the United States and saluted from then on the Stars and Stripes.

After Louisiana had seceded from the Union and before it joined the Confederacy, the legislature on Feb. 12, 1861, during the administration of Governor Thomas Overton Moore proclaimed Louisiana a sovereign power and adopted the national flag of Louisiana. This flag contained the colors of all previous Louisiana flags. It consisted of thirteen stripes—four blue, six white and three red—with a field of red in the upper left corner containing a single yellow star. Louisiana joined the Confederacy on March 21, 1861, and for four years the Stars and Bars flew over the State except as parts of it were occupied by Federal troops.

THE STATE FLAG OF LOUISIANA

The Louisiana Legislature adopted on July 1, 1912, a state flag for Louisiana. This is a blue field with a pelican, in white trimmed with gold, feeding its young. The words "union, justice and confidence" are beneath.

(and he may have been buried in it) and what was then part of the Louisiana Territory, he did not claim any of this for Spain. The first flag to be officially flown over Louisiana was the flag of France. It was raised by LaSalle at the mouth of the Mississippi River in 1682 when he took possession of Louisiana and named it for the king of France. The French flag flew over all the vast Louisiana Territory until it was ceded to Spain by secret treaty in 1762.

A year later, 1763, France ceded to England all of her territory east of the Mississippi River except the "Isle of New Orleans." The flag of England waved for sixteen yers over Fort Richmond at Baton Rouge, the capital of that time of the Florida Parishes and East Baton Rouge. In 1779 Galvez captured Baton Rouge for the Spaniards, and thus all

THE STATE SEAL

The Great Seal of the State of Louisiana was adopted in 1902. Governor W. W. Heard, complying with Section 3471 of the Revised Statutes, "in order to establish uniformity in the State seal and its use amongst the various departments of government", directed the Secretary of State to adopt an official seal for the state.

The report of the Secretary of State to Governor Heard on May 12, 1902, describes the seal as follows:

"A pelican with its head turned to the left, in a nest with three young; the pelican, following the tradition, in act of tearing its breast to feed its young; around the edge of the Seal to be inscribed 'Union Justice, &,, under the nest of the pelican to be inscribed 'Confidence'."

THE STATE BIRD

The Pelican adopted as the Louisiana State bird is known as the Eastern Brown Pelican (Pelecanus occidentalis), and nests from South Carolina to Brazil.

Pelicans are all famous for their large bills, the lower portion of which has a pouch which may be greatly extended. The birds depend almost entirely on fish for food, and scoop up quantities of water into the pouch as they seize their prey. The bill is then elevated, the water dribbles from the mandibles and the pouch contracts as the fish is swallowed. Five pounds of fish a day is the average consumption of a pelican at the age of one month, but this food is largely of no commercial value in fish markets.

THE STATE FLOWER

The large, creamy white bloom of the magnolia was officially designed the state flower of Louisiana by the Legislature on July 12, 1900, and was selected because there is such an abundant growth of magnolia trees throughout the state. The trees have evergreen foliage and the flower is unusually fragrant. The sepals of the flower are commonly three in number, the petals six to twelve. The cone-like fruit which remains after the petals have dropped from the flower consists of a number of carpels which are borne on a more or less conical receptacle and dehisce along the outer edge to allow the scarlet or brown seeds to escape.

PELICAN

THE STATE TREE

Despite the abundance, variety and beauty of the trees grown throughout Louisiana, no action was taken to designate a state tree until 1963 when the legislature made the baldcypress (Taxodium distichum) the official tree of the state. The tree, commonly called the "cypress," is grown in many areas of the state, particularly on poorly drained flood-plain sites and constitutes one of the most important timber trees. Its shape depends greatly upon the amount and duration of flooding in the area in which it is found, varying from columnar to conical, or bottle-shaped.

It has reddish-brown bark which is fibrous, thin and divided into small, flat ridges and shallow furrows, and its leaves generally are found to spread in flat planes in a feathery pattern on its branchlets. The Louisiana Forestry Commission declares that the "leaves fall attached to the branchlets. Apical branchlets usually have appressed, scale-like leaves. The globose cones are about one inch in diameter and may occur singly or in clusters."

OFFICIAL STATE SONG

The official state song of Louisiana is **Give Me Louisiana**, written by Doralice Fontane and adopted by the State Legislature in 1970.

Prior to this action, the official state song was **Song of Louisiana**, by Vashti Stopher. Legislative approval was granted in 1932.

The state's official march song, the result of legislative action in 1952, is **Louisiana, My Home Sweet Home**, by Castro Carazo.

WHAT IS A CAJUN?

According to the history books, a Cajun is a descendant of a hardy group of Nova Scotian exiles who settled along the bayous and marshes of South Louisiana. The name Cajun (they tell us) is a contraction of "Acadienne—Acadian." So much for the textbook!

In other parts of the world little girls are made of sugar and spice and everything nice, while little boys are made of snips and snails and puppy dog tails.

Little Cajun children are made of gumbo, boudin, and sauce piquante — crawfish stew and oreilles de cochon. A Cajun child is given bayous to fish in, marshes to trap in, room to grow in and churches to worship in.

A Cajun likes fiddles and accordions in his music, plenty of pepper in his courtbouillon, shrimp in his nets, speed in his horses, neighborliness in his neighbors, and love in his home.

A Cajun dislikes: People who don't laugh enough, fish enough, or enjoy enough of all the good things God has given to the Cajun Country.

He doesn't like to be hurried when he's resting or distracted when he's working. He doesn't like seeing people unhappy, and he'll do all he can, or give all he has to bring a smile to a face stricken with sadness.

A Cajun likes to dance and laugh and sing when his week of hard work has ended.

And just as Saturday night at the fais-do-do replenishes his store of energy and personal balance so that he can meet the next week's chores with vigor — Sunday at church refreshes his spiritual and moral values and keeps strong his always sustaining faith.

A Cajun can be stubborn as a mule and ornery as an alligator. If he sets his head on something, he'll fight a circle saw before he'll yield to your opinions.

You'd as well argue with a fence post as try to convince a Cajun.

And, as fun-loving as he is, a Cajun can work as hard and as long as any living man. He carved out Acadiana by hand from the swamp and marshes and uncultivated prairies.

But when the work is done and the argument is ended, a Cajun can sweep you right into a wonderful world of joie de vivre with an accordion chorus of "Joli Blanc" and a handful of happy little words five little words to be exact: "Laissez les bon temps roulle!" (Translated: Let the good times roll!)

Author Unknown

IMPORTANT DATES IN LOUISIANA HISTORY

1541 April. Hernando de Soto discovered the Mississippi River.

1542 May 21. De Soto died and was buried in the Mississippi River, below the mouth of Red River.

1543 July 19. De Soto's expedition, under the command of Luis de Moscoso reached the Gulf of Mexico, the first group of white men to descend the Mississippi to its mouth.

1673 Marquette and Joliet reached the Mississippi via the Wisconsin River on May 17, 1673, descended to the mouth of the Arkansas and after ascertaining that the Mississippi flows into the Gulf rather than the Pacific, returned to Canada by the end of September.

1682 La Salle's expedition from Quebec arrived at the mouth of the Mississippi and there, on April 9, La Salle erected a cross and took possession of the country, naming it Louisiana in honor of Louis XIV.

1687 La Salle was murdered on March 18 at what is now Matagorda Bay, Texas, where his second expedition had landed after failing to find the Mississippi on their voyage from France.

1699 Pierre Le Moyne, Sieur d'Iberville rediscovered the mouth of the Mississippi on March 2 and explored that river as far north as the mouth of the Red River, discovering and naming Baton Rouge from a red pole erected there to mark the boundaries of the hunting grounds of the Houma and Bayogoula tribes.

On May 4 Iberville sailed back to France to recruit more colonists and raise money, leaving Sauvole in command assisted by Bienville.

1700 Fort Iberville was established near Pointe à la Hache.

First Catholic church in the territory was established by the Jesuit Father du Ru at the settlement of the Houma Indians in West Feliciana Parish.

1701 Bienville succeeded Sauvole as governor on the latter's death on August 22.

1702 Bienville established Fort Louis de la Mobile on the Mobile River in January. This was to be the headquarters of the government of the territory.

1704 The **Pélican** arrived on July 24 from France with soldiers, workers and twenty-three girls sent out to marry colonists.

In September an epidemic of yellow

HISTORICAL MAP OF LOUISIANA

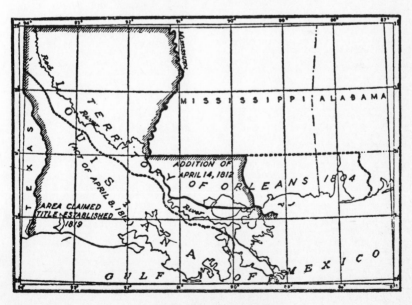

fever caused the deaths of more than thirty-five people, a serious blow to the struggling colony.

1706 Iberville died of yellow fever on July 9 at Havana where his duties in the war against England had taken him.

1712 Antoine Crozat was granted exclusive trading rights in Louisiana by the French government on September 14.

1715 Louis St. Denis founded Fort St. Jean Baptiste on the Red River at the site of modern Natchitoches. This was the first permanent settlement in the area of modern Louisiana.

1716 First Natchez war resulted from the murder of five Frenchmen by the Natchez. Bienville won by trickery.

1717 John Law's Company of the West received the charter for control of Louisiana from the French government in September after it had been relinquished by Crozat in August.

1718 In February, Bienville selected the site of a central headquarters on the Mississippi and named it New Orleans in honor of Phillipe d'Orléans, the Regent of France. By June the town had a total population of sixty-eight.

1719 In May, the name of Law's Company was changed by royal edict from the Company of the West to the Company of the Indies. Despite Law's energetic efforts however, the Company still failed to yield a profit and the stock in France began to fall in this year. This year also witnessed the first large importation of slaves as well as the arrival of about two hundred and fifty Germans sent by Law to work on his own estates.

1720 The population of the entire Louisiana colony was estimated at around six thousand persons. This included more than six hundred Negro slaves.

1722 Bienville's choice of a capital prevailed over that of the officials at home who wanted to continue at Biloxi, and Bienville established his official residence at New Orleans in August.

1723 In September a disastrous hurricane destroyed most of the buildings at New Orleans and ruined much of the crops. Bienville fought and subdued the Natchez for the second time in October.

1724 In March, the "Black Code" was promulgated in Louisiana. Bienville was recalled to France by officials of the Company who, discontented with the lack of profit shown by the colony, were influenced by his enemies.

1727 The Ursuline nuns arrived in New Orleans on August 6 and took up residence in Bienville's former house. They immediately opened a convent school where they gave instruction to Indians, Negresses and white girls.

1728 The first of the filles à la cassette (casket girls—called such because they were provided with a small casket by the government containing a trousseau) arrived in December. These were the first women of good character to be sent as wives to the colonists. They were taken in charge by the Ursuline nuns until their marriages.

1729 The massacre of 250 Frenchmen and the capture of many women, children and slaves at Fort Rosalie (Natchez) by the Natchez Indians on November 28, caused the fortification of New Orleans in December.

1730 A French expedition under Governor Périer, assisted by 350 Choctaw Indians, setting out on November 15 to fight the Natchez, eventually defeated them near Sicily Island, bringing back more than 400 prisoners to New Orleans in February 1731.

1731 The Natchez War was the final blow to the failing fortunes of the Company of the Indies, and they relinquished their charter to the King in November. Louisiana became a crown colony. Louis St. Denis routed the last of the Natchez who had been besieging Natchitoches, and killed almost all of them at a battle on Sang Pour Sang Hill near Cloutierville.
The colony's population was estimated at about 5000 whites and 2000 Negroes.

1732 A Royal Decree removed duties on all goods sent from Louisiana to France and from France to Louisiana, thus stimulating commerce.

1736 Jean Louis, a sailor, died on January 21st and left 10,000 livres to found a Charity Hospital in New Orleans. The contract for the hospital was let on June 10, 1736.
Bienville made an unsuccessful expedition against the hostile Chickasaw and the remnants of the Natchez in May. He was forced to retire to New Orleans because of the superior strength of the Chickasaw.

1739 In August, Bienville with 1200 white troops and twice that number of Choctaw allies made another attack on the Chickasaw. Though he failed to conquer them in battle, a permanent peace was ratified with them in April of the following year.

1740 Two hurricanes, on September 11 and 18, almost wiped out the French establishments at Biloxi and Mobile and caused near famine conditions in the entire colony because of the damage to crops.

1743 Bienville returned to France in May and never again came to Louisiana. He was succeeded by the Marquis de Vaudreuil. The first serious work on levee building was begun under Vaudreuil by virtue of an ordinance which he issued on October 18 forcing planters to build their levees before the following January on pain of confiscation of their lands.

1751 First sugar cane was introduced into Louisiana by the Jesuits of Santo Domingo.

1753 LeBlanc Villeneuve's play **Le Pére Indian** was presented at the governor's residence in New Orleans. It was the first theatrical production in the colony, and was performed by amateurs.

1762 On November 3, Louis XV gave Louisiana and New Orleans to Spain by the secret Treaty of Fontainbleau. Louis continued to possess Louisiana as far as its citizens and those of the outside world knew until 1764.

1763 The Treaty of Paris on February 10 confirmed the cession of Louisiana to Spain but modified the territory involved, since England, who had just defeated France in the Seven Years War, demanded and received the Florida Parishes. Baton Rouge became the capital of English Louisiana and was called New Richmond. On July 9, the Jesuits were expelled from Louisiana and their property, amounting to some nine hundred thousand livres, was confiscated and sold.

1764 On April 6, the first Acadian immigrants to Louisiana, four families, arrived from New York.
The Sieur Braud was granted the right to set up the first printing press in Louisiana at New Orleans.
In October the people of Louisiana were informed of the colony's transfer to Spain. Disliking this highhanded action, they petitioned Louis XV, through Bienville who was residing in France, to cancel the transfer. The King refused.

1766 Don Antonio de Ulloa arrived on March 5 to rule Louisiana in the name of the Spanish king.

1768 On October 28, a petition from Creole leaders of the province was presented to the Superior Council at New Orleans, enumerating grievances against Ulloa and demanding his departure. Ulloa sailed immediately for Cuba. Louisiana, governed by the Superior Council was in effect, an independent state.

1769 Count Alexander O'Reilly arrived in New Orleans on August 17 with 2000 troops and the mission of reestablishing Spanish rule.
On August 26, the leading inhabitants of the province took the oath of allegiance to the Spanish King.
On October 25, the five leading spirits of the 1768 Revolution against Ulloa were executed in New Orleans in a highhanded manner that has ever since blackened O'Reilly's name in Louisiana history.
A census made of New Orleans by O'Reilly's order in 1769 placed the population at 3,190.

1776 The Spanish governor Bernardo de Galvez permitted Oliver Pollock, an agent of the Continental Congress in New Orleans, and other American merchants there to send supplies to Americans fighting the British in western Pennsylvania and the Ohio Valley.

1777 On April 26, Galvez further demonstrated his partisanship for the American Revolution by seizing 11 richly laden English ships on the Mississippi.

1778 In January, Captain Willing of the American Army, using New Orleans as a base, conducted pillaging expeditions against Baton Rouge and Natchez, burning the plantations of English sympathizers along the way.

1779 The Spanish king entered the war against England and on July 8, authorized his subjects in Louisiana to begin operations against the English.
On September 21, Galvez attacked and captured Baton Rouge from the British.

1780 On March 14, Fort Charlotte (Mobile) surrendered to Galvez and with the taking of Pensacola the following year, the Spanish were in complete control of all the original Louisiana province.

1785 A census by Spanish officials placed the population of New Orleans at 4980 persons and of the entire province of Louisiana and West Florida at more than 32,000.

1788 New Orleans was ravaged by a fire on March 21 which destroyed nearly all the buildings except a few on the riverfront.
The fire had started from an altar taper in the private home of Don Vincente Nunez on Chartres Street.

1790 The Capuchin Father Antonio de Sedella attempted to establish the Inquisition of which he had been appointed Commissioner, but was arrested and deported by Governor Miro on April 29.

1791 A slave insurrection in Santo Domingo in August resulted in the deaths of many of the white and drove many of the survivors to refuge in Louisiana. Among them was a group of professional players headed by Louis Tabary who gave the first professional theatrical productions in New Orleans.

1793 A grand alliance was concluded on October 28 between the Spanish in Louisiana and the Cherokees, Chickasaws, Creeks and Alibamons aimed at defense of Spanish territory from American pressure.
April 25 Pope Pius VI established the Diocese of Louisiana, the second Catholic diocese in the United States.
The indigo crop was wiped out by caterpillars and never regained its importance.

1794 Over two hundred buildings in New Orleans were burned on December 8 in the city's second great fire.
On December 23, the New Orleans Church of St. Louis, which had been rebuilt after being destroyed in the fire of 1788, was dedicated as a cathedral.
In this year the first Louisiana news-

paper, **Le Moniteur de la Louisiane** was published at the press of Louis Duclot in New Orleans.

1795 In April an attempted slave insurrection in Pointe Coupée Parish misfired and twenty-three of the leaders were hanged. This "Black Rebellion" stemmed from slave unrest after the Santo Domingo uprising in 1791.

On July 17 Don Luis de Peñalver y Cardenas, the first bishop of Louisiana arrived in New Orleans. The St. Louis Cathedral was his seat.

On October 20, a treaty between Spain and the United States granted Americans free navigation of the Mississippi, the right of deposit at New Orleans, and established the 31st degree of latitude as the boundary between the Floridas and the United States.

The Cabildo was built in this year as the seat of Spanish colonial administration.

Etienne Boré performed the first successful granulation of sugar on his plantation in what is now Audubon Park in New Orleans.

1796 The Spanish Governor Carondelet established the first police force and system of street lighting in New Orleans.

1799 Tension between the western American settlers and the Spanish became high when the Intendant of Louisiana, Morales, discontinued the right of deposit at New Orleans and failed to designate an alternative place. The king reversed this ruling in 1800.

1800 The Treaty of San Ildefonso, signed on October 1, between Napoleon and Charles IV of Spain provided for the recession of Louisiana to France in exchange for Napoleon's promise to secure a kingdom in Italy for Charles' son-in-law, the Duke of Parma.

1801 On March 21, a second treaty between Napoleon and Charles was signed at Madrid confirming the Treaty of San Ildefonso. The cession was still kept secret however.

1802 Intendant Morales on October 16 again closed New Orleans to American commerce, an act which strengthened the American Government's resolve to acquire New Orleans. Once again the Spanish king restored the right but it was too late to stem the rising American demand for control of the Mississippi's mouth.

1803 Colonial Prefect Pierre Laussat arrived in New Orleans and announced for the first time on March 26 the transfer of Louisiana to France.

On April 30, James Monroe and Robert Livingston concluded the purchase of Louisiana from France for about $15,-000,000.

On November 30, Laussat received possession of Louisiana in the name of France and established a provisional government which was to last only

twenty days. Etienne Boré was appointed mayor of New Orleans.

On December 20, United States Commissioners W. C. C. Claiborne and General James Wilkinson accepted Louisiana from France in the name of the United States.

1804 The population of New Orleans was estimated at 8,056 and of the entire territory as 49,473.

On March 26, Louisiana was divided by act of Congress into the Territory of Orleans (the portion lying south of 33° latitude) and the District of Louisiana (the portion lying north of 33°). W. C. C. Claiborne was made governor of the Territory of Orleans by the same act.

1805 On February 17, New Orleans was incorporated as a city, and the first election was held for a Board of Aldermen.

On April 19, acts were approved by the Legislative Council to establish a University of Orleans and to incorporate a New Orleans Library Society. The university project was not realized until 1811.

In June, an Episcopal clergyman was chosen by fifty-three New Orleans Protestants and the first Protestant Church in New Orleans was incorporated by the Legislative Council.

Aaron Burr arrived on July 25 on his trip to organize his ill-defined "Western Conspiracy" against Mexico.

In December, Burr had organized his expedition, and General Wilkinson fortified New Orleans against Burr's coming down the Mississippi. The expedition was broken up near Natchez by Mississippi authorities.

1806 On November 6, American forces under General Wilkinson and Spanish forces under General Herrere, contending over disputed territory along the Sabine River agreed to regard the area as neutral ground until the dispute should be settled by their respective governments.

The town of Donaldsonville was founded in this year by William Donaldson.

1808 First public schools in Louisiana established in Pointe Coupée Parish.

1809 Nearly 6000 refugees who had fled from the Negro insurrection in Santo Domingo to Cuba, arrived in New Orleans after being virtually driven out of Cuba by the Spanish who resented them on account of Napoleon's invasion of Spain in this year

1810 The population of the Territory of Orleans was placed at 76,556.

On September 24, the residents of West Florida declared their independence from Spain, seized Baton Rouge from the Spanish officials, and set themselves up as the West Florida Republic. The territory was almost immediately taken over by the United States on the

grounds that it had been a part of the original Louisiana Purchase.

1811 On January 2, Julien Poydras, the territory's representative in Congress declared to the House of Representatives that the territory had the right to become a state.

In January, a slave revolt in the parishes of St. Charles and St. John the Baptist was suppressed by the militia with much bloodshed.

On February 20, President Madison signed the bill providing for Louisiana's statehood.

The College of Orleans was opened in this year and continued until 1826.

1812 The first steamboat to navigate the Mississippi, Nicholas Roosevelt's **New Orleans,** arrived at New Orleans from Pittsburg on January 10.

On January 22 the first state constitution was adopted.

On April 30, Louisiana was formally admitted to the Union as the 18th state in the Union.

1813 On March 15, Governor Claiborne issued a proclamation commanding the smugglers or "banditti" at Barataria to disperse. The pirates and smugglers commanded by the Lafitte brothers ignored the governor.

In April, legal prosecution of the Lafittes was begun in the United States District Court in New Orleans, for violation of the United States revenue laws but no convictions were obtained.

1815 General Andrew Jackson defeated the British regulars under General Pakenham at the Battle of New Orleans on January 8. This battle was fought 15 days after the conclusion of peace between Britain and the United States at Ghent.

1816 On March 23, General Jackson returned to New Orleans and was enthusiastically feted in the city.

1817 The New Orleans branch of the Bank of the United States was opened on January 1, and the following year the Bank of Louisiana was established with a capital of 2 million dollars.

1819 The United States and Spain signed the Treaty of Washington on February 22 by which Spain conceded the Sabine River as the western boundary of Louisiana.

1820 The United States census put the population of Louisiana at 153,407. New Orleans inhabitants numbered more than 41,000.

1821 On July 17, the United States received along the Sabine which had been the subject of the treaty with Spain in 1819.

The Sisters of the Sacred Heart established the Sacred Heart Academy for girls at Grand Coteau in St. Landry Parish. Jean Jacques Audubon established a studio in New Orleans.

1823 The first gas well in Louisiana was brought in near Natchitoches but was not thought to be of any value.
On May 8, illuminating gas was first used in New Orleans at the opening of James H. Caldwell's American Theater. In this year, the State Legislature granted licenses to six gambling establishments in New Orleans provided each should pay $5,000 towards the upkeep of the College of Orleans and Charity Hospital.

1824 Julien Poydras bequeathed a dowry fund of $30,000 each to West Baton Rouge and Pointe Coupée Parishes.

1825 On April 10, the Marquis de Lafayette arrived in New Orleans and was appropriately honored by the city.
The College of Louisiana was founded at Jackson. It later became the Centenary College when its property was purchased in 1845 by a group of private citizens and given by them to the Methodist Centenary College. It is now at Shreveport.

1827 The State Legislature voted a gift from the state of $10,000 for the relief of the family of Thomas Jefferson who had died in debt the previous year. The action reflects the gratitude of Louisiana to the man who, more than any other one person, was responsible for her entering the United States.

1829 The New Orleans Gas Light Company was incorporated by an act of the State Legislature.
Another act provided for a levee system along the entire river course within the state.
Louis Moreau Gottschalk, famous composer and pianist, was born in New Orleans on May 8.
On October 7, Governor Derbigny suffered a fatal accident when his horses ran away and he was thrown from his carriage.

1830 On January 4, the State Government was moved to Donaldsonville from New Orleans. However, the legislators missed the gaiety of the larger town, and the following year returned to the Crescent City. An unusually severe winter killed off the orange trees in the state.

1831 The House of Representatives of the state sent a memorial to the French people on March 24, congratulating them on the liberal revolution of July 1830.
On April 23, the first railroad west of the Alleghenies, the Pontchartrain Railroad, opened passenger and freight service between New Orleans and Milneburg. This company continued in operation until absorbed by the Louisville line in 1880.
On August 16 and 17, New Orleans suffered great damage from floods as a result of a Gulf storm.

1832 The old Charity Hospital building on Canal Street was bought by the state as a capitol building.

An unprecedented epidemic of cholera and yellow fever resulted in more than 5,000 deaths in New Orleans and even more throughout the state in this and the following year.

1833 Governor Roman's message to the Legislature on January 7 and the Legislature's Resolution of February 4 agreed in condemning the nullification stand of South Carolina and expressing loyalty to the firm stand of President Jackson.
On April 11, Captain Henry Miller Shreve began clearing the Great Raft from the Red River, thus preparing the way for navigation and for the growth of Shreveport which was to be named in his honor. A heavy shower of meteorites was recorded—"the year the stars fell."

1834 A riot in New Orleans resulted from the discovery of Madame Lalaurie's alleged cruelty to her slaves. She barely escaped the fury of the mob and succeeded in fleeing to France.

1835 The New Orleans and Carrollton Railroad, one of the earliest trolley lines in the country, was put into operation between Canal Street and the village of Carrollton.
The Medical College of Louisiana was founded in New Orleans by a group of prominent physicians. Tulane University grew out of this institution.

1836 As a result of ill-feeling between creoles and Americans, New Orleans was divided on March 8 into three independent municipalities, one comprising the Vieux Carré and the other two being above Canal Street.
Louisiana Historical Society was founded.

1837 Shreveport was founded.
As a result of the financial panic of 1837, fourteen New Orleans banks suspended payment and each of the three municipalities in the city issued its own emergency money.
Ralph Smith-Smith, a planter, began what is probably the first railroad west of the Mississippi, the Red River line which ran from Alexandria to Bayou Hauffpauer near Cheneyville for the purpose of transporting cotton and sugar to the Red River steamboats. America's most famous chess player, Paul Charles Morphy, was born in New Orleans on June 22.
New Orleans Picayune established.

1838 The first Mardi Gras parade took place in New Orleans on Shrove Tuesday. Henry Hobson Richardson, the first noted American architect, was born in St. James Parish on September 29. He built the famous Trinity Church in Boston and the Howard Library in New Orleans.

1839 The banks resumed specie payments and the financial crisis of 1837 was over.

1840 New Orleans with a population of

102,193 was rated as the fourth largest city in the Union.

Imprisonment for debt was abolished in this year by act of the Legislature.

1841 Another financial panic resulted in suspension of specie payments by the New Orleans banks.

1844 The National Art Gallery of Paintings was established in New Orleans where it flourished until the Civil War.

In July, an election was held for members of a Constitutional Convention to meet and revise the original document of 1812.

1845 On May 14, the new constitution was approved. It broadened the franchise, provided for popular election of the governor (he had previously been selected by the Legislature), and provided for free public schools.

General Zachary Taylor of Baton Rouge left New Orleans with a force of 1500 men in July as war with Mexico threatened.

John Slidell of New Orleans was appointed minister plenipotentiary to Mexico by President Polk on November 10. His mission to adjust the difficulties with Mexico so that war might be avoided was unsuccessful as the Mexican Government refused to receive him officially.

1846 The invention of the "multiple effect" process by Norbert Rillieux revolutionized the sugar refining industry.

The **New Orleans Picayune,** using the Pony Express, was the first newspaper to announce the Mexican War.

1847 The East Louisiana State Hospital for Mental Diseases was established at Jackson.

The Medical College of New Orleans added academic and scientific courses and was taken over by the state as the University of Louisiana.

1848 On November 7, General Zachary Taylor, hero of the Mexican War and planter from near Baton Rouge was elected President of the United States,

1849 Baton Rouge was made the capital of Louisiana, replacing New Orleans.

The Southern Yacht Club, the second in the country, was organized at New Orleans.

The famous Pontalba buildings were erected in New Orleans by the Baroness Pontalba who desired to beautify the Place d' Armes. James Gallier is reputed to have been the architect.

1850 A wealthy landowner, John McDonogh left a fortune of more than $750,-000 to establish public schools in New Orleans and Jefferson Parish. 35 public school buildings were later erected from this fund.

1851 Under the auspices of P. T. Barnum, Jenny Lind sang to enthusiastic New Orleans crowds.

1852 On July 31, a Constitutional Convention approved changes in the state organic law which reduced the residence requirements for office-holders, made all the judicial offices elective, and provided for annual meetings of the State Legislature. The Louisiana Institute for the Education of the Deaf and Dumb and Blind was founded at Baton Rouge. The three municipalities of New Orleans were again consolidated into one city which included the heretofore independent town of Lafayette.

1853 On April 7, Pierre Soulé, New Orleans attorney, was appointed by President Pierce as minister to Spain.

The New Orleans Academy of Sciences was founded.

The worst yellow fever epidemic in the history of the state killed more than 11,000 people in New Orleans, and devastated many rural districts.

1854 Lexington, the most famous thoroughbred racehorse in America, defeated New Orleans' Lecompte in the Great Post Stake on April 1 at the Metairie Course in New Orleans. In this period, New Orleans was the focal point of American horseracing.

1855 The Know-Nothing Party in Louisiana severed its connection with the national organization because of the latter's anti-Catholic bias.

1856 A disastrous hurricane and tidal wave killed more than 200 vacationists at Last Island on August 10. The tragedy is described in Lafcadio Hearn's novel, **Chita.**

1858 At the municipal election in June, there was grave danger of serious violence between a vigilance committee and the Native American Party. Between June 3 and 7, the opposing groups occupied and armed Jackson and Lafayette Squares respectively. There was no important violence and on June 7, the Native American Candidate, Gerard Stith, defeated Col. P. G. T. Beauregard.

1859 A strong gang of cattle rustlers was broken up by a group of 4,000 vigilantes in a fight near Lafayette in September. The famous French Opera House of New Orleans opened with **Guillaume Tell** on December 1st.

1860 On January 2, the Louisiana State Seminary of Learning was established at Alexandria. William Tecumseh Sherman, the future Federal general, was president. The institution remained at Alexandria until 1869 when it was transferred to Baton Rouge and renamed the Louisiana State University. In the election of 1860, Louisiana gave Breckinridge 22,681; Bell, 20,204, and Douglas, 7,675 votes.

On November 19, an audience at the French Opera House in New Orleans heard Adelina Patti, most famous opera star of the late 19th century, make her operatic debut.

In December, Governor Thomas Moore called a special session of the State

Legislature and, advising them that it was impossible for Louisiana to remain in the Union under a Republican president, called for a state convention to determine the state's action.

1861 On January 26, on the motion of John Perkins, Jr., of Madison, the Session Convention voted 112 to 17 to adopt the Ordinance of Secession. For nearly two months Louisiana was an independent state.

On January 30, the Convention elected six delegates to represent the state at the Confederate convention in Montgomery.

On March 21, the Secession Convention ratified the Confederate Constitution and formally joined the Confederacy.

On April 12, the first gun of the Civil War was fired at Fort Sumter by order of Major General P. G. T. Beauregard of St. Bernard Parish.

On November 8, Confederate Commissioners Slidell of New Orleans, and Mason of Virginia were removed illegally from a British ship, the Trent. The incident brought the United States and Britain to the verge of war.

1862 On March 17, Judah P. Benjamin of New Orleans, former U. S. Senator from Louisiana and recently Secretary of War in the Confederate Cabinet, was appointed Confederate Secretary of State by President Davis.

On April 16, a Federal fleet under Captain David Farragut appeared before the Confederate Forts Jackson and St. Philip at the mouth of the Mississippi and began a five-day bombardment. On April 25, New Orleans, insufficiently defended by less than 3000 militia, was captured by the Federal fleet and accompanying soldiers.

On May 1, General Bejamin F. Butler of the Federal Army began his arbitrary and unpopular military rule of New Orleans which was made the capital of Federal-held Louisiana.

In May, the Confederate capital was moved from Baton Rouge because of the approach of Farragut's fleet up the river, and transferred to Opelousas. Shortly thereafter it was moved once more to Shreveport where it was at the end of the war.

On June 7, William B. Mumford was executed by order of General Butler for tearing down a United States flag from the Mint in New Orleans on April 26.

On August 5, Confederate forces under General Breckinridge fought the indecisive Battle of Baton Rouge against Federal troops under General Williams.

1863 Confederate forces under General Dick Taylor were driven out of the Teche country by Federals under General Nathaniel Banks.

From May to July, Port Hudson endured a Federal siege which was aimed at gaining the center of control of the Mississippi. Port Hudson surrendered on July 9.

1864 On 25 January, General Henry W. Allen was installed as governor of Confederate Louisiana at Shreveport.

On March 4, the moderate Republican Michael Hahn, who was opposed to Negro suffrage, was inaugurated governor of Federal-held Louisiana at New Orleans.

On April 8, Confederate forces under General Taylor defeated General Banks at Sabine Hill near Mansfield.

Alexandria was fired by Federal troops on May 13 and largely destroyed.

On July 23, a new constitution was adopted by vote of those who had taken the Federal oath of allegiance. Although it abolished slavery in the state, it limited the suffrage to white males over twenty-one with a proviso that it could be extended, presumably to the Negroes, at the discretion of the Legislature.

1865 In January, President Jefferson Davis appointed Duncan F. Kenner of Ascension Parish as Confederate Minister to European powers to obtain recognition of the Confederacy, agreeing to the emancipation of the slaves as a last resort.

On May 8, General Dick Taylor surrendered the Confederate forces under his command in Louisiana to General Canby. On May 26, General Kirby-Smith surrendered the last Confederate forces in the field, the Department of the Trans-Mississippi.

On June 2, Confederate Governor Allen addressed a message to the people of Louisiana admonishing them to cease resistance and cooperate in rebuilding their land. He then fled to México to escape prosecution as one of the leaders of the Confederacy.

1866 On July 30, a serious race riot took place in New Orleans as the result of a meeting by radicals in the Mechanics Institute for the purpose of revising the constitution to insure Negro suffrage.

1867 On March 6, General Philip Sheridan assumed command of the Fifth Military District (Louisiana and Texas) with headquarters at New Orleans.

On June 3, General Sheridan removed the moderate Republican Governor J. Madison Wells from office and appointed the more radical Benjamin F. Flanders. He also removed other state officials and municipal officials in New Orleans.

The Knights of the White Camelia were organized at Franklin to oppose carpetbag rule.

1868 A new constitution was adopted on March 11. Framed by a convention in which Negroes outnumbered whites and ex-Confederates were excluded, this document embodied the principles of the Thirteenth and Fourteenth Amendments, and prohibited segregation in public places, including schools.

On June 25, on the basis of the new radical constitution, Louisiana was re-admitted to the Union.

On July 9, the Legislature ratified the Fourteenth amendment.

On August 11, the Louisiana Lottery was established to become a major industry in the state.

1869 The Fifteenth Amendment was ratified by the Legislature in February.

1870 On June 30, the **Robert E. Lee** and the **Natchez** left New Orleans on the most famous steamboat race in history. The **Robert E. Lee** arrived in St. Louis in 3 days, 18 hours and 14 minutes, beating the **Natchez** by 3 hours and 44 minutes.

1871 In August, two separate Republican conventions were held in the State, the more moderate group under Governor Warmoth and the radical, so-called "Custom House" faction under U.S. Marshal Stephen B. Packard. Both sides sent appeals on their behalf to President Grant.

1872 On Mardi Gras Day, Rex, King of Carnival, paraded for the first time. The Russian Grand Duke Alexis was present at the festivities.

In August, the Liberal Republicans under Warmoth, the new Reform Party, and the revived Democratic Party consolidated their forces behind John Mc-Enery to run for Governor against William Pitt Kellogg of the Radicals. On November 4, the McEnery faction received a majority of the votes, but was prevented from taking office however, by the Radical-dominated Returning Board who decided in favor of Kellogg. The radicals were backed by the Federal Government under President Grant.

On December 11, the McEnery ticket was declared the legal government by Governor Warmoth, but was forced to disband because Grant effectively supported the Kellogg faction despite a Congressional Committee's report that the McEnery Government was the de jure government of Louisiana.

1873 A race riot at Colfax on Easter Sunday resulted in the deaths of three white men and about 120 Negroes.

The first throughtrain service from Chicago to New Orleans was offered by the Mississippi Central. (The line was re-organized in 1875 as the Chicago, St. Louis and New Orleans and this in turn became part of the Illinois Central System in 1877.)

1874 Thirty-one parishes suffered terrible damage from a flood.

Carrolliton was incorporated into New Orleans as the Seventh District.

On April 27, The White League was first organized at Opelousas in a desperate attempt to correct abuses prevailing under the administration of Governor Kellogg. August 29-30, a Negro uprising at Coushatta was put down

by the White League. September 14, the "Battle of Canal Street," when the White League defeated the Metropolitan Police.

1875 On January 4, Governor Kellogg resorted to intimidation of the Legislature by Federal troops in order to maintain a Republican majority in the body. On March 24, a Congressional Committee, sent to investigate the recent state election which had resulted in Kellogg's using force to control the Legislature, effected the so-called Wheeler Compromise which seated Kellogg's opponents and in effect justified the Democratic stand concerning the election.

1876 The New Orleans Lawn Tennis Club, one of the first tennis clubs in the United States, was founded.

1877 On January 8, Francis T. Nicholls, Democratic candidate for governor and former Confederate general, was inaugurated Governor in New Orleans. Though he received a majority of the votes, his opponent, Stephen B. Packard was also declared elected by the Republicans and was also inaugurated in New Orleans. General Grant's refusal to back Packard's claims with Federal force, and President-elect Hayes' tacit agreement to withdraw Federal troops in exchange for Louisiana's electoral votes led to the complete collapse of Packard's claims.

On April 20, President Hayes ordered the withdrawal of the Federal troops. Reconstruction was over.

The **New Orleans Item** was founded.

1878 A disastrous yellow fever epidemic killed more than 3,800 in New Orleans and additional thousands throughout the state.

1879 On July 23, a new constitution was adopted which neutralized the Negro vote, corrected the deficiencies of the Constitution of 1868, and moved the capital to Baton Rouge.

Captain James B. Eads completed the first successful jetty system at the mouth of the Mississippi, thus controlling shifting sandbars and channels and enhancing New Orleans' prospects as a seaport.

1880 The Legislature enacted the first state poor law.

The **New Orleans States** was founded.

1882 Under the provisions of the 1879 Constitution, Baton Rouge became the new capital.

The Mississippi overflowed its banks and caused more than $12,000,000 in property damage in 16 Parishes.

1883 The first through train service from New Orleans to California began on February 5 over the lines of a series of companies which became part of the Southern Pacific System in 1885.

1884 The Louisiana State Normal College was established at Natchitoches.

The University of Louisiana became the Tulane University of Louisiana as the result of expansion made possible by a gift from Paul Tulane which aggregated more than a million dollars.

From December, 1884 until May, 1885 the World's Industrial and Cotton Centennial Exposition was held in New Orleans to celebrate a century of progress in cotton production.

1886 H. Sophie Newcomb College for girls was founded in New Orleans.

1887 The Howard Memorial Library was established in New Orleans.

1889 Jefferson Davis died on December 6 at Judge Charles Fenner's residence in New Orleans.

1890 The Louisiana State Penitentiary was established at Angola.

Louisiana legalized prize fighting, one of the first states to do so, and soon New Orleans became a center of the sport in this country.

1891 On March 14, a mob lynched 11 men who allegedly had murdered New Orleans Chief of Police David C. Hennessy on October 15 the previous year. The men were suspected of being members of the Italian Mafia.

1892 James J. Corbett knocked out John L. Sullivan in 21 rounds in New Orleans for the world championship.

1893 On February 20, General P. G. T. Beauregard died in New Orleans.

On March 20, President Cleveland appointed James B. Eustis of New Orleans as minister to France.

On April 6, Andy Bowen and Jack Burke fought 110 rounds to a draw in New Orleans in the longest prizefight in history. The fight lasted 7 hours and 19 minutes. On October 1, a hurricane devastated the area along the coast from the Mississippi Sound to Last Island. 2500 people were believed killed.

1894 The Leprosarium was established at Carville. Originally placed in charge of the Sisters of Charity, this institution was taken over by the Federal Government in 1921.

The Louisiana Industrial Institute and College was founded at Ruston. It became the Louisiana Polytechnic Institute in 1921.

1895 The Louisiana Lottery, prohibited by both state and Federal laws, removed from the country to Honduras. It finally expired in 1909.

1896 Several members of the City Council of New Orleans were convicted of bribery and sent to prison. The Citizens Reform League, organized to combat this corruption, was victorious at the city election on April 21.

The first rural free delivery in Louisiana, the second in the United States, was inaugurated on November 1 at Thibodaux.

1897 The Fisk Free Library was combined with the Lyceum Library and opened on January 18 in New Orleans as the Fisk Free and Public Library. It later became the New Orleans Public Library.

1898 On May 12, revisions to the State Constitutions were adopted which incorporated the "Grandfather clause" principle and certain educational and property qualifications for voting.

On December 29, a monument to the public school benefactor, John McDonogh was dedicated in New Orleans. Funds for this monument came exclusively from New Orleans school children.

1901 Oil was discovered near Jennings in August.

The Southwestern Louisiana Institute was established at Lafayette.

1902 The Central Louisiana State Hospital for Mental Diseases was founded near Pineville.

From September 27 to October 10, the New Orleans street-car employees struck for an 8-hour day and a 25¢ per hour minimum wage. Although public sympathy was largely with the strikers, they were unsuccessful.

1903 The Isidore Newman Manual Training School was established in New Orleans.

1904 The Jesuit Fathers founded Loyola Academy in New Orleans. It became Loyola University in 1912.

On December 20, Centennial Celebration of Louisiana's becoming a part of the U.S. was held.

1906 Louisiana College was founded at Pineville. Oil discoveries at Caddo Lake brought prosperity to Shreveport.

1909 The commercial mining of sulphur was begun at Sulphur in Calcasieu Parish using the new Frasch system for the first time. Until 1914, this field supplied 75 percent of the nation's sulphur. It was exhausted in 1924.

The last yellow fever epidemic in New Orleans occurred in this year. It was brought under control by the efforts of Dr. Quitman Kohnke who applied Dr. Carlos Finlay's new discovery that the mosquito carried the germ, and succeded in having mosquito-breeding cisterns in New Orleans screened.

1906 The United States Government completed the building of a 10-foot channel from Plaquemine to Morgan City and the Plaquemine Locks were thus opened, enabling through navigation from the Mississippi through Grand River to Atchafalaya River.

Ralph DePalma set a world automobile speed record by averaging 60 miles per hour for a distance of 50 miles at New Orleans.

1910 On December 12, President Taft appointed Edward Douglas White of Lafourche Parish Chief Justice of the United States Supreme Court. He held the position until his death on May 19, 1921.

On December 24, at an international aviation tournament held in New Orleans, a record for the mile was made at 57 seconds and at a record height of 7,125 feet. In a series of automobile-airplane races, a Packard car consistently defeated the airplane piloted by John Moisant.

Isaac Delgado bequeathed property to the city to maintain the Delgado Trades School.

1911 Loyola Academy was consolidated with the College of the Immaculate Conception and became Loyola University the following year.

1912 George Mestach made the second successful official air mail trip in the United States flying from New Orleans to Baton Rouge in one hour and 32 seconds on April 10.

1913 A tentative revision of the Constitution (confirmed by a convention in 1921 was decided upon by a convention which reported on November 22. The revised document made better provisions for public education, liberalized the suffrage, provided for a more efficient highway system, and reorganized the judiciary. The Legislature was given greater powers at the expense of the executive.

1914 Southern University, founded for Negroes in New Orleans in 1880, was moved to Scotlandville and became Southern University and Agricultural and Mechanical College.

The **Times Democrat** merged with the **Picayune** to become the **Times-Picayune.**

1915 The name "jazz" was given to that famous music of New Orleans orgin when it was introduced to Chicago in this year. On September 29, one of the worst hurricanes and floods in the state's history caused several deaths, many injuries and millions of dollars of property damage in New Orleans. Xavier College was founded at a preparatory school for Negroes by the Sisters of the Blessed Sacrament. It became, in 1925, Xavier University, the only Catholic institution of higher learning for Negroes in the United States.

1916 The discovery of the Monroe gas field caused Monroe to flourish.

Mosaic disease and root rot began to effect the sugar cane crop.

The State Federation of Labor was organized.

1918 Louisiana ratified the 18th (Prohibition) Amendment on August 3.

1919 The Homer oil field was brought in. The famous French Opera House, and scene of the Mardi Gras Balls, burned down on December 4.

1920 D. W. Pipes, Jr. and Elliott Jones of Houma brought in a few stalks of POJ cane that later saved the sugar industry of the state.

1921 A constitutional convention slightly modified and then confirmed the tentative document drawn up in 1913. Their work was adopted on June 18.

The Haynesville oil field was discovered.

1923 The Inner Harbor Navigational Canal was opened to traffic.

1925 Louisiana State University moved to its new buildings and campus at Baton Rouge.

Southeastern Louisiana College was founded at Hammond.

1926 The completion of a series of waterways from the Gulf made Lake Charles one of the state's three deep water ports.

1927 In April and May, the state suffered the greatest flood in its history. A record rainfall in the winter and spring caused the Mississippi to overflow its banks, break through the levees and flood a large part of the state. More than 1,300,000 acres of agricultural land was flooded and 300,000 people made homeless. New Orleans was saved from disaster by the blasting out of the levee at Poydras on April 29.

1928 Governor Huey P. Long was inaugurated.

On May 9, as a result of the recent flood, Congress passed the important Mississippi Valley Flood Control Act, appropriating $325,000,000 for flood control.

The State Legislature passed an act providing for free public school textbooks.

1929 On May 16, 15 state senators signed a round robin which blocked an attempt to impeach Governor Long.

1930 The extensive U. S. Veterans Administration Facilities were opened near Pineville.

Huey Long became U. S. Senator.

1932 The new Capitol building at Baton Rouge was dedicated on May 16.

1933 The $2,000,000 Harvey Locks, linking the Mississippi and the Intracoastal Waterway, were completed after four years of construction.

1934 In August, a barge tow carrying 1,400 tons of steel, made the first trip on that portion of the Intracoastal Waterway from New Orleans to Houston.

1935 In the first Sugar Bowl game, Tulane defeated Temple by 20 to 14 on January 1. The Rodessa oil field was brought in, in the summer.

Huey Long was assassinated in the State Capitol at Baton Rouge by Dr. Carl Weiss on September 8.

Dillard University was opened in New Orleans.

On December 13, the Bonnet Carré Spillway was dedicated. Part of the Mississippi Flood Control Project, it cost more than $13,000,000.

The Huey P. Long Bridge at New Orleans, costing more than $13,000,000, was dedicated on December 16.

1936 The State Department of Public Welfare was established on June 26.

1937 In January, the Bonnet Carré Spillway was used for the first time to hold the water level at New Orleans. President Roosevelt appointed Jefferson Caffery of Lafayette, Ambassador to Brazil on July 1.

1939 The New Charity Hospital in New Orleans opened in New Orleans.

1940 The bridge across the Mississippi at Baton Rouge was completed in August.

1948 July 1st International Trade Mart opened at New Orleans.

1951 August 22, discovery announced of a large sulphur deposit near the mouth of the Mississippi River.

1952 July 2 construction began of Alton Ochsner Medical Foundation Hospital on Jefferson Highway adjacent to New Orleans. Oct. 16 Samuel H. Kress Foundation donated a valuable Rennaisance art collection to the Delgado Museum at New Orleans.

1953 April 30 re-enactment at the Cabildo in New Orleans of the purchase of the Louisiana Territory on the 150th anniversary of the event. Oct. 15-17. The celebration at New Orleans of the sesqui-centennial of the purchase of Louisiana from France by the United States. Attended by Henri Bonnet, French ambassador, and ambassadors from other countries. On the 17th President Eisenhower visited the city and took part in the activities. Cecil de Mille was the narrator. Dec. 20. The transfer of Louisiana 150 years before was re-enacted at the Cabildo in New Orleans.

1954 Jan. 7th. Gen. Robert E. Lee's statue was restored to the top of the monument at Lee Circle after the shaft and base had been rebuilt. March 17. Contract was let for the borings at the site of the greater Mississippi River Bridge between New Orleans at Thalia Street and Algiers at Brignac street. April 16. The new Union Railroad Station was opened in New Orleans. May 1. The new charter of the city of New Orleans went into effect. June 11. The 50-million-dollar plant of the American Cyanimid Co. at the old Fortier Plantation in Jefferson Parish was dedicated.

1957 May 5 the new City Hall of New Orleans was dedicated. August 24 the Lake Pontchartrain Causeway was formally opened—the longest bridge in the world. Sept. 5 the Harvey Canal tunnel opened for traffic. June 27 "Audrey," one of the most destructive storms that ever raged over Louisiana, came in from the Gulf to kill 371 and injure 3880 persons in Cameron and Vermilion parishes, totally destroy 1300 homes, and causing damage to exceed $45,000,000.

1958 April 15 the Greater New Orleans Bridge opened for traffic May 21 segregation in streetcars and buses of New Orleans ended in compliance with the order of the Federal Court. Sept. 5 Louisiana State University in New Orleans opened its doors for the first time with an enrollment of 1500 freshmen students.

1960 April 19 Jimmie Davis elected Governor.
April 28 De Gaulle and his party were given a floodlit welcoming parade and military review, attended by 100,000 persons, as they arrived in New Orleans for a two-day visit.
Sept. 5 Earl Kemp Long died.
November 8 Representatives Hebert, Boggs, Willis, Brooks, Passman, Morrison, Thompson, McSween, were elected to Congress.

1961 Joe Waggoner won a special election in the 4th Cong. district for the U.S. House Seat left vacant by the death of Overton Brooks.

1962 March 29 New Orleans Parochial Schools ordered to desegregate by Archbishop.
April 3 Schiro elected Mayor.

1963 Jan. 1 Tulane accepted five Negroes, the first in its history.
Feb. 1 New Orleans D.A. Jim Garrison was convicted by a specially appointed court of defaming 8 New Orleans Criminal District Court Judges.
Sept. 3 Baton Rouge High Schools desegregated.
Oct. 4-10 Anti-bias demonstrations by Negro high school students in Plaquemines Parish, were broken up by police using tear gas and electric cattle prodders.
Dec. 30 The Justice Department ruled that states were to have possession of Tidelands formed after they had been admitted to the Union. In Louisiana some of the affected land had producing oil and gas wells.

1964 March 3 John McKeithen elected Governor.
Two Republicans won election to the State house and became the first Louisiana GOP legislators in the century.
June 8 The first Negro undergraduate enrolled at L.S.U.
June 16 Two barges rammed the Pontchartrain Causeway, causing a gap, and six persons were killed when their bus fell into the water.
October 3 Eighteen persons were killed and 115 injured in Larose by a tornado spun from Hurricane Hilda. Twelve persons were killed elsewhere in the State and the sugar crop was seriously damaged.
Nov. 3 Goldwater carried Louisiana in the Presidential election.
Representatives Hebert, Boggs, Willis, Waggoner, Passman, Morrison, Thompson, Long, were elected to the House. Code of ethics for State officials adopted in a referendum.
Nov. 8 Archbishop Joseph Francis Rummel of New Orleans died.
Nov. 23 The Supreme Court reversed the conviction of Orleans Parish D.A. Jim Garrison for criticizing 8 Criminal District Court Judges of Orleans Parish.

1965 Jan. 11 Negro football players boycotted the AFL ALL STAR Game to have been held in New Orleans, due to that city's racial bias.

March 4 Seventeen killed in gas pipeline explosion and fire north of Natchitoches.

April 1 Intensive Civil Rights campaign begins in Bogalusa.

July 1 Representative Theodore Ashton Thompson, 49, was killed in a car accident.

July 22 After months of violence in Bogalusa, Gov. McKeithen announced that he would appoint a 40 member biracial commission.

Sept. 9 Hurricane Betsy caused 61 deaths in Louisiana.

Sept. 29 Most Reverend Phillip M. Hannan named Archbishop of New Orleans.

Oct. 2 State Senator Edwin W. Edwards won the Democratic runoff primary to fill the 7th District Congressional Seat made vacant by Representative Thompson's death.

Nov. 6 Victor Schiro re-elected Mayor of New Orleans.

1966 Jan. 6 Harold Robert Perry, 49, a Negro, became Auxiliary Bishop of the Roman Catholic Archdiocese of New Orleans January 6th. The ceremony marked the first time since 1875 that a Negro had been elevated to the Bishropic in the United States.

Jan. 6 Ford Foundation Grant: 2,719,500.00 dollars was given to the New Orleans Public Schools for a five-year demonstration program in cooperation with Tulane and Dillard Universities.

Jan. 31 Centenary College in Shreveport, Louisiana, admitted four Negro students January 31st. They were the first Negroes to attend the College in its 140 years of operation.

March 11 Teachers Strike: A.F.T. Unions AFT Local 527 in New Orleans went on strike against the New Orleans Public School System March 11 to back up demands for bargaining election against National Education Association.

Nov. 1 New Orleans Gets N.F.L. Franchise: On November 1st, New Orleans was offered the 16th N.F.L. Franchise which was bought by a Syndicate whose principal owner (51%) was John W. Mecom, Jr., for 8,500,000.00 dollars.

1967 Mar. 22 Clay Shaw, retired New Orleans businessman was indicted on a charge of murder conspiracy in connection with the assassination of President John F. Kennedy.

May 1 Jack R. Thornton, a New Orleans photographer, was named winner of the Pulitzer Prize for news photography.

May 4 Edgar Labat, who with a fellow prisoner has served more time on death row than anyone else in history, was ordered released from Angola State Prison by the U.S. Supreme Court.

May 8 A state budget totalling $1.276 million for fiscal 1967-68 was introduced in the State Legislature.

June 23 The U.S. Attorney General was asked to probe labor-management problems in the Baton Rouge area as $250 million worth of construction came to a halt.

Nov. 4 Gov. John J. McKeithen was reelected to an unprecedented second four-year term by an overwhelming margin. McKeithen gained 81 percent of the vote over his opponent Congressman John R. Rarick.

1968 June 20 Presidential candidate George Wallace of Alabama brought his campaign to Louisiana, speaking in Baton Rouge where he raised some $60,000.

June 22 A poll revealed that an overwhelming majority of the candidates for posts as delegates from Louisiana to the Republican National Convention favored a ticket composed of Richard Nixon and Ronald Reagan.

June 24 Governor McKeithen and other state officials revealed four threats had been made on the governor's life in recent weeks. The threats were alleged to stem from the state's labor-management racketeering probe.

Dec. 6 Three men were sentenced to prison terms for trying to bribe LSU football players.

Dec. 9 Vice President Spiro Agnew visited New Orleans to deliver an address to Poverty Program officials.

Dec. 17 A thirty-day special session of the state legislature was adjourned following passage of a one-cent tax increase on a gallon of gasoline.

1969 Jan. 21 New Orleans businessman Clay Shaw went on trial on charges he was a conspirator in the assassination of President John F. Kennedy.

June 10 The Louisiana Legislature adjourned its regular thirty-day fiscal session. Legislative action included bills to raise the salaries of all state officials some 40 percent.

June 12 The Southern Baptist Convention, holding its annual meeting in New Orleans, called for bills by the U.S. Congress to allow prayers in public schools.

June 17 New Orleans District Attorney Jim Garrison's top aide resigned his post and announced he would oppose the controversial Garrison for reelection.

1970 Jan. 7 The U.S. Fifth Circuit Court of Appeals added three more Louisiana parishes -- Ascension, Iberville and Rapides -- to the list of school systems that must fully integrate by February 1.

Jan. 8 A team of surgeons performed Louisiana's first heart transplant on a 52-year-old man in Oschner Foundation Hospital.

Jan. 8 The Army charged a second Louisiana soldier, Sgt. Charles E. Hutto of Tallulah with murder in the alleged My Lai massacre in 1968. Similar charges were filed against Sgt. David Mitchell of St. Francisville in December.

Jan. 19 Governor McKeithen urged Louisianians to defy court orders which require bussing of their children to achieve racial integration in schools.

May 4 Dr. T. Harry Williams, Boyd Professor of history at Louisiana State University received the Pulitzer Prize for his highly acclaimed book, **Huey Long.**

Dec. 1 A multi-well oil platform in the Gulf of Mexico exploded, hurling some 55 workers into the sea and threatening to pollute much of Coastal Louisiana.

1971 The trials and conviction of State Attorney General Jack P. F. Gremillion.

A fire in the New Orleans Howard Johnson Motor Hotel killed six people.

Sept. 16 Hurricane Edith caused widespread devastation.

1972 Senator Allen J. Ellender died; J. Bennett Johnston elected to succeed Ellender.

Congressman Hale Boggs of New Orleans presumed dead after his plane crashed in the Alaskan wilderness.

Louisiana State Constitutional Convention called.

1973 Jan. 8 Sniper atop Howard Johnson Motor Hotel in downtown New Orleans terrorized city; one police official and seven bystanders were slain.

Sept. 28 Orleans Parish District Attorney Jim Garrison was acquitted in the New Orleans Pinball Bribery Case.

June 25 Thirty-two people died in a fire at the Upstairs Lounge in the New Orleans French Quarter.

Louisiana State Constitution Convention forged a new document after much debate.

Extensive flooding along the Mississippi River and Louisiana tributaries resulted in millions of dollars in damages.

1974 A shortage of foreign and domestic oil spurred a national energy crisis.

Former governor's aide Clyde Vidrine accused Gov. Edwin Edwards of selling high-level government positions for campaign contributions.

Sept. 8 Hurricane Carmen devastated the sugar cane crop.

Sixth Congressional District race resulted in a run-off between Republican Henson Moore and Democrat Jeff LaCaze.

1975 Louisiana Superdome in New Orleans opened.

Eastern Airlines flight 66 from New Orleans to New York crashed, killing 114 people, many from Louisiana.

The State of Louisiana won a 17-year battle over ownership of 15,000 acres of rich, undeveloped mineral lands in Vermilion Parish.

1976 Oct. 20 The Luling-Destrehan ferry, the *Prince George*, collided with the Norwegian tanker, *Frosta*, killing 78 people.

Citizens of New Orleans voted for a new City Council for the first time since 1969—

after a scheduled 1973 election was delayed over redistricting disputes.

Jimmy Carter was elected President of the United States and was the first Democratic party candidate to carry Louisiana since 1960.

Gov. Edwin Edwards admitted that his wife accepted a $10,000 gift from South Korean businessman Tongsun Park.

The Louisiana Legislature passed a right-to-work bill.

1977 Ernest N. ("Dutch") Morial was elected the first black mayor of New Orleans.

May 4 Rep. Richard A. Tonry resigned when fraudulent voting was uncovered in several precincts of Louisiana's First Congressional District.

The "Treasures of Tutankhamen" exhibit at the New Orleans Museum of Art drew thousands of visitors from the entire South.

The Port of New Orleans suffered from a 63-day strike by longshoremen, resulting in the loss of millions of dollars to the state economy.

May 24 Compulsory liability insurance bill passed by the State Legislature.

1978 New Orleans teachers strike for a 7 percent pay-raise.

Congress created six new federal judgeships for Louisiana.

Louisiana passed a "first-use" tax on natural gas.

Muhammed Ali regained the heavyweight boxing title in a match fought in the Superdome.

1979 David C. Treen was elected as the first Republican governor since Reconstruction.

A police strike caused the cancellation of Mardi Gras in New Orleans.

A gas shortage created long lines at gas stations across the state.

1980 April 13 Severe flooding isolated metropolitan New Orleans and parts of south Louisiana.

The federal "Brilab" investigation exposed Louisiana officials who accepted bribes in return for state contracts.

The Jefferson Island Salt Dome collapsed after it was punctured by oil drilling equipment.

Newly appointed L.S.U. football coach Robert "Bo" Rein died in an airplane crash.

The Louisiana seafood industry was threatened by a pentachlorophenol spill in the Mississippi River in St. Bernard Parish.

1981 Construction began at the New Orleans site of the 1984 Louisiana World Exposition.

Initial construction began for a new Mississippi River bridge at New Orleans.

Massive layoffs from the Kaiser Aluminum plant in St. Bernard Parish hurt the state economy.

1982 Pan Am flight 759 crashed at New

Orleans International Airport, killing 154 people. It was the second worst commercial air disaster in U.S. history.

Dutch Morial was reelected as mayor of New Orleans.

The derailment of 43 tank cars carrying toxic chemicals set off explosions and forced the evacuation of 2,700 people near Livingston, La.

Louisiana State Senate President Michael O'Keefe was tried and convicted on charges of malfeasance.

1983 Edwin W. Edwards was elected by a landslide to a third term as governor.

Louisiana football hero Billy Cannon was convicted on counterfeiting charges.

California feminist Ginny Foat was acquitted on murder charges in Jefferson Parish. The case received national media attention.

1984 The Louisiana World Exposition, a world's fair held along the New Orleans riverfront, attracted 7.3 million visitors to Louisiana.

Gov. Edwin Edwards began a third term in office.

St. John the Baptist parish public school employees went on strike for eight weeks. It was the longest school strike in Louisiana history.

1985 Gov. Edwin Edwards was tried on charges of racketeering and fraud in connection with the sale of hospital construction certificates. The trial ended with a hung jury.

Three hurricanes, Danny, Elena, and Juan, hit Louisiana.

The New Orleans Saints were sold for about $71 million to a consortium led by New Orleans automobile dealer Tom Benson.

The Tulane University basketball program was shut down after allegations of point shaving and illegal payments were exposed.

1986 The price of oil plunged to less than $10 a barrel.

In a second trial, Gov. Edwin Edwards and four co-defendants were acquitted of mailfraud and racketeering charges.

Democratic Rep. John Breaux was elected to the U.S. Senate, succeeding Russell B. Long.

The L. S. U. football team was Southeastern football champion and the basketball team went to the NCAA Final Four tournament.

1987 Pope John Paul II visited New Orleans on his tour of the United States.

A scandal involving the selling of pardons by the State Pardon Board resulted in the indictments of the State Pardon Board Chairman and a state legislator.

The office of State Superintendent of Education became an appointed rather than an elected position.

TOP NEWS STORIES
(Selected by the New Orleans *Times-Picayune*)

1982

1. The crash of Pan Am Flight 759, which killed 154 people and became the second worst commercial aviation disaster in U. S. history.

2. The recession's impact on the economy.

3. New Orleans Mayor Dutch Morial's re-election and subsequent political battles.

4. The widespread federal investigation into the alleged use of cocaine by professional athletes, including some members of the New Orleans Saints football team.

5. The derailment of 43 tank cars carrying toxic chemicals near Livingston, La., which set off explosions and forced about 2,700 people to evacuate.

6. The trade of Saints quarterback Archie Manning to the Houston Oilers.

7. The bitter weather of January 1982, which burst pipes and forced businesses and schools to close.

8. Accidents in plants and refineries upriver from New Orleans, which released chemicals into the air and the Mississippi River.

9. The land swap involving a tract of land next to the Louisiana Superdome for an Ohio developer's $300 million project. One of Morial's closest friends was revealed to be a partner.

10. Senate President Michael H. O'Keefe's conviction, which has been overturned pending a new trial, and his perjury indictment.

1983

1. Edwin W. Edwards's gubernatorial election landslide.
2. Economic suffering as the national recession bottomed out.
3. The home stretch to the opening of the 1984 world's fair in New Orleans.
4. The record freezes on Christmas weekend and near the end of the year.
5. The April 7 flood in New Orleans.
6. The execution of murderer Robert Wayne Williams in Louisiana's electric chair.
7. The conviction of Louisiana football hero Billy Cannon on counterfeiting charges.
8. Mayor Dutch Morial's successful backing of New Orleans candidates for state legislative seats, and the voters' rejection of a proposal to let him seek a third term.
9. The acquittal of California feminist Ginny Foat on murder charges in Jefferson Parish.
10. The New Orleans Saints' unsuccessful drive toward the National Football League playoffs.

1984

1. The Louisiana World Exposition, a world's fair held along the New Orleans riverfront, attracted 7.3 million visitors to Louisiana.
2. Gov. Edwin Edwards began a third term in office, accompanied by political controversy and investigation by a federal grand jury.
3. New Orleans voters rejected a 1 percent earnings tax designed to offset the city's estimated $60 million budget shortfall.
4. The New Orleans Saints pro football team finished a losing season, and owner John Mecom, Jr., announced that the team was for sale.
5. Two nuclear power plants, Waterford 3 and Grand Gulf, neared completion amid controversy about cost overruns and construction delays.
6. Longest school strike in Louisiana history, when 550 public-school employees in St. John the Baptist parish went on strike for eight weeks.
7. The shooting deaths of Mark Posey and Ray T. Liuzza in Uptown New Orleans.
8. The trial and aquittal of businessman Aaron Mintz, accused of murdering his wife, Pamela Mintz.
9. Riverfront development and a downtown building boom in New Orleans, with the anticipated construction of the Rouse Co. Riverwalk, additions to the Jackson Brewery site, and construction of six luxury hotels.
10. The Metairie Galleria, a $500 million hotel-office-apartment-shopping complex, won initial approval from the Jefferson Parish Council.

1985

1. The indictment and trial of Gov. Edwin Edwards on charges of racketeering and fraud in connection with the sale of hospital construction certificates. The trial ended with a hung jury.
2. The bleak outlook for the Louisiana economy because of a continued down-turn in the oil and gas industry.
3. Three hurricanes, Danny, Elena, and Juan, hit Louisiana.
4. State and local governments faced declining revenues as a result of statewide economic distress.

5. Education experts agree that Louisiana's schools are among the nation's poorest and that the state's economic problems are linked to educational shortcomings.
6. During a January freeze, 70,000 people in New Orleans were without power, and rotating blackouts were instituted throughout southeast Louisiana.
7. The New Orleans Saints were sold for about $71 million to a consortium led by New Orleans automobile dealer Tom Benson.
8. The Tulane basketball program was shut down after allegations of point shaving and illegal payments were exposed.
9. New Orleans Mayor Dutch Morial lost his bid to amend the City Charter so that he could seek a third consecutive term.
10. Two stories tied for the number 10 spot. Soviet sailor Miroslav Medvid tried unsuccessfully to escape from the grain ship Marshal Konev by leaping twice into the Mississippi River. Brian Busby, a convicted rapist, touched off a furor in Jefferson Parish when it was revealed that he was allowed to come and go at will, unguarded, from his cell in the parish prison.

1986

1. The Louisiana economy worsened, triggered by the collapse of oil prices, which plunged to less than $10 a barrel.
2. In a second trial, Gov. Edwin Edwards and four co-defendants were acquitted of mail-fraud and racketeering charges.
3. Councilman Sidney Barthelemy was elected mayor of New Orleans.
4. The commercial revival of the New Orleans riverfront, heralded by the opening of the Riverwalk and the second Jackson Brewery building.
5. The Port of New Orleans chose a new director, J. Ron Brinson, and weathered a week-long longshoremen's strike.
6. The Vatican confirmed the Pope John Paul II will visit New Orleans in September 1987.
7. Democratic Rep. John Breaux was elected to the U. S. Senate, succeeding Russell B. Long.
8. Optimism about the New Orleans Saints, inspired by a new coach, Jim Mora, and by new owner, Tom Benson.
9. Controversy about the implementation of tolls on the Greater New Orleans Bridge.
10. The L.S.U. football team was Southeastern Conference football champion and the basketball team went to the NCAA Final Four tournament. Athletic Director Bob Brodhead and football coach Bill Arnsparger resigned.

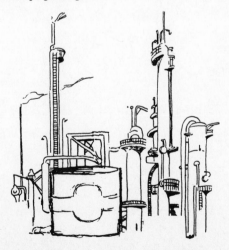

LOUISIANA WEATHER AND CLIMATE

In broader aspects, the climate of Louisiana is determined by the huge land mass to the north, its subtropical latitude, and the Gulf of Mexico to the south. The prevalent winds are from the south or southeast and consequently the influence of the warm moist air from the Gulf is quite great.

Summer weather is rather consistent. Physical conditions are favorable for the sporadic development of thundershowers which recur in spells with considerable regularity. Temperatures range from 85 degrees F. to 95 degrees F. during afternoons and 65 degrees F. to 75 degrees F. during early mornings. Temperature conditions in northern sections of the State are more of the continental type (greater diurnal range and both higher and lower extremes). Along the immediate Gulf Coast temperatures rarely exceed 100 degrees F., and such temperatures are infrequent for an extensive coastal area. In the northern parishes 100 degrees F. or higher has been reported in almost all years.

Occasional periods of hot and dry weather, characteristic of the continental climate of the Plains States, interrupt prevailing summer moist conditions. The State is also subject during summer and fall to tropical cyclones (tropical storms and hurricanes). These vicious visitors from the tropics bring high winds, heavy rainfall, and high tides to the coastal region. They usually lose much of their wind force shortly after moving inland, but heavy rains may continue far inland.

During the cooler seasons weather conditions are more variable as the State is covered alternately by warm tropical maritime air and cold polar continental air. The cold air, although modified by its southward movement through the Plains States, frequently causes large and rather sudden drops in temperature.

Average winter temperatures range from 55 degrees F. to 65 degrees F. in the afternoons to 40 degrees F. to 50 degrees F. during early morning hours; although both higher and lower readings are often observed. Freezing temperatures (32 degrees F. or lower) are recorded on 30 to 40 days in North and Central Louisiana during an average year and on 10 to 35 days in the Southern Parishes. Along the immediate coast and especially along the Mississippi River south of New Orleans, freezing temperatures are not recorded in every year.

EXTREME TEMPERATURE DATA FOR LOUISIANA

The highest temperature ever recorded at any Louisiana weather station was 114°F., at Plain Dealing, Bossier Parish, August 10, 1936. The lowest temperature ever recorded was -16°F., at Minden, Webster Parish, February 13, 1899. The greatest rainfall ever recorded at any Louisiana weather station during twenty-four hours was at the Sabine National Wildlife Refuge, 8 miles south-southwest of Hackberry, where 22.00 inches fell during parts of August 28 and 29, 1962.

Monthly extreme rainfalls are listed in the table below. The highest wind speed (fastest mile) ever recorded in Louisiana was 140 miles per hour at Burrwood, September 29, 1915. This extreme wind occurred in connection with an intense hurricane. Other speeds almost as high have been estimated in a few other hurricanes at points along the coast, but, in these cases, wind-measuring equipment was destroyed or damaged before the highest speed occurred.

Month		Deg. F	Day	Year	Location
January	Maximum	92	27	1914*	Donaldsonville
	Minimum	-8	27	1940	St. Joseph
February	Maximum	92	25	1918	Minden
	Minimum	-16	13	1899	Minden
March	Maximum	95	24	1929*	Ruston
	Minimum	10	3	1943	Arcadia
April	Maximum	98	4	1918*	Reserve
	Minimum	24	7	1971	Ashland
May	Maximum	105	30	1911	Abbeville
	Minimum	30	2	1925	Delhi
June	Maximum	110	20	1936	Dodson
	Minimum	41	5	1946	Pollock,
July	Maximum	111	29	1930*	Plain Dealing
	Minimum	50	15	1967*	Converse

August	Maximum	114	10	1936	Plain Dealing
	Minimum	45	24	1891*	Davis
September	Maximum	110	1	1951*	Lake Providence
	Minimum	30	30	1967*	Converse
October	Maximum	103	1	1938*	Plain Dealing
	Minimum	21	29	1952*	Chatham
November	Maximum	95	10	1915*	Robeline
	Minimum	10	19	1903	Collinston
December	Maximum	90	1	1913*	Donaldsonville
	Minimum	-1	23	1929	Plain Dealing

* Indicates also earlier dates of years

LOUISIANA WINTER RECORDS

Louisiana's winters of 1895, 1899 and 1983 were among the most severe ever experienced by the state, according to records of the state climatologist.

The lowest temperature recorded in Louisiana was -16 degrees F., in 1899. The longest freeze in the state's history came in 1983, when temperatures in Shreveport were below 33 degrees for 138 hours (December 22-26). December 1983 was also the coldest December on record. Furthermore, the National Weather Service office in Shreveport reported that the last fifteen days of the month, with an average temperature of twenty-five degrees, was the coldest fifteen-day period for the entire climatic record dating back to 1871.

Record snowfall in Louisiana was noted in 1895 when every parish received snow. Rayne holds the state record for snowfall, with 24 inches received in 1895. The same year, Baton Rouge received 12½ inches and Lake Charles, 22 inches.

AVERAGE SEASONAL PRECIPITATION—SEASONAL LOUISIANA STATIONS

	Dec-Feb	Mar-May	Jun-Aug	Sep-Nov	Annual
Alexandria	16.04	15.42	12.41	12.03	55.90
Amite	17.16	17.60	16.70	12.44	63.90
Bastrop	14.63	16.00	10.90	10.48	52.01
Baton Rouge	14.54	15.00	15.23	11.00	55.77
Bogalusa	16.21	16.59	15.68	11.63	60.11
Bunkie	16.79	17.37	14.08	12.64	60.88
Cotton Valley	13.08	14.67	11.37	10.68	49.80
Covington	16.08	16.28	16.45	12.47	61.28
Donaldsonville	15.56	15.13	17.37	12.30	60.36
Franklin	13.80	13.57	21.80	12.70	61.87
Grand Coteau	15.40	15.88	14.89	12.51	58.68
Hammond	16.45	17.50	16.17	13.12	63.24
Homer	13.43	15.24	11.53	10.89	51.09
Houma	14.29	14.23	20.71	14.66	63.89
Jennings	15.30	15.12	15.91	12.77	59.10
Lafayette	14.29	14.50	16.75	12.15	57.69
Lake Arthur	14.55	13.36	16.08	12.30	56.29
Lake Charles	13.21	12.25	15.13	12.44	53.03
Lake Providence	16.06	16.66	11.24	10.10	54.06
Leesville	14.85	14.87	13.25	11.10	54.07
Logansport	12.69	15.17	10.33	10.79	48.98
Melville	16.04	15.43	13.12	11.22	55.81
Minden	12.83	14.43	11.00	10.00	48.26
Monroe	14.09	15.20	10.39	9.88	49.56
Morgan City	14.15	13.83	20.36	14.19	62.53
Natchitoches	14.28	15.26	10.21	10.57	50.32
New Iberia	13.39	13.81	18.09	11.96	57.25

New Orleans (Moisant)	15.47	14.30	17.38	12.59	59.74
Plain Dealing	12.51	14.34	11.13	10.70	48.68
Ruston	14.34	15.90	10.98	10.93	52.15
Saint Joseph	15.75	16.44	10.13	9.93	52.25
Shreveport	11.35	13.18	9.62	9.69	43.84
Tallulah	15.78	17.00	11.38	9.27	53.43
Winnfield	14.95	16.59	12.47	11.32	55.33
Winnsboro	15.54	16.12	10.52	9.95	52.13

MONTHLY EXTREME RAINFALL TOTALS

Month	Year	Division	Location	Amount
January	1937	Central	Melville	18.87
February	1961	East-Central	Amite	20.99
March	1903	East-Central	Clinton	21.47
April	1980	Southeast	St. Bernard	24.06
May	1953	Central	Cheneyville	30.52
June	1886	Central	Alexandria	36.91
July	1908	South-Central	Franklin	29.28
August	1940	South-Central	Lafayette	37.99
September	1958	Southwest	Vinton	26.22
October	1937	Southeast	Belle Chasse	29.04
November	1948	Northeast	Winnsboro	23.37
December	1931	North-Central	Calhoun	26.34

ANNUAL AVERAGE PRECIPITATION

The table below shows annual average precipitation for Louisiana for each year since 1931, as measured at the NOAA National Weather Service Stations. At this time, precipitation measurements are made at more than 140 locations throughout the state. Figures given are sums of averages of precipitation in the nine climatic divisions of the state, weighted by the area of each division. In using these figures, one should always remember that the variations of precipitation between the different sections of Louisiana make a state average of little significance. The range of variation is illustrated in the first table showing the greatest and least annual total precipitation in each division since 1931.

The years of heaviest precipitation over the state were 1905, with 75.57 inches, according to old records on the basis of flat averages, and 1940, with 75.10 inches, on a weighted-average basis. The year of lightest precipitation was 1889 with a flat average of 35.83 inches.

The greatest rainfall recorded during one month was 37.99 inches at Lafayette, Lafayette Parish in August 1940.

The greatest rainfall recorded during one year was 111.28 inches at Morgan City, St. Mary Parish in 1946.

Source: Louisiana State Office of Climatology

Division	Greatest Annual Average Precipitation	Least Annual Average Precipitation
Northwest	72.78 (1946)	28.89 (1936)
North Central	73.57 (1968)	34.27 (1954)
Northeast	72.69 (1982)	34.47 (1952)
West Central	79.09 (1953)	32.90 (1954)
Central	80.26 (1940)	40.01 (1963)
East Central	85.40 (1961)	44.36 (1963)
Southwest	92.18 (1940)	36.95 (1954)
South Central	90.80 (1946)	42.72 (1962)
Southeast	77.28 (1961)	39.62 (1962)

ANNUAL AVERAGE PRECIPITATION

Year	Inches	Year	Inches
1931	51.79	1959	58.58
1932	61.85	1960	49.86
1933	56.26	1961	73.10
1934	59.06	1962	44.70
1935	57.21	1963	42.25
1936	45.40	1964	57.02
1937	58.00	1965	46.97
1938	51.71	1966	60.67
1939	51.13	1967	52.02
1940	76.02	1968	58.49
1941	61.15	1969	49.99
1942	57.58	1970	51.25
1943	51.92	1971	52.37
1944	62.28	1972	58.93
1945	62.43	1973	53.45
1946	73.97	1974	63.27
1947	61.12	1975	68.58
1948	54.95	1976	51.28
1949	61.76	1977	59.20
1950	60.76	1978	53.77
1951	48.76	1979	78.54
1952	49.35	1980	57.56
1953	66.21	1981	44.63
1954	43.76	1982	65.35
1955	57.80	1983	67.91
1956	50.64	1984	59.15
1957	67.07	1985	60.45
1958	58.13	1986	53.29

HURRICANES

The storm that American Indians referred to as "huracan" is a constant threat to the entire Gulf Coast area, including Louisiana. Caused when winds develop around a low-pressure center over the ocean to form a tropical storm (a system of winds rotating counterclockwise in the northern hemisphere, clockwise in the southern, around a calm center or eye), the tempest earns the name "hurricane" only when the winds reach a speed of 73 miles per hour.

Hurricanes and tropical storms follow erratic courses, often wandering around the ocean far from land for several days before disintegrating, and sometimes cutting a wide swath of flooding and destruction across land. The forward speed of the storms varies widely, as does the size; some hurricanes are spread over large areas, while some concentrate fierce winds and rain over a small path.

In Louisiana, the southern coastal area near the Mississippi River delta has historically been the most frequent victim of hurricanes. Since 1886, 23 hurricanes have struck the coastal region directly south of New Orleans; in the same time period, only 14 hit the southwestern coast near the Texas border. The lowest hurricane incidence has been recorded for the northwestern corner of the state, with only 3 of the oceanspawned storms reaching that distance since 1886.

The early Caribbean practice of naming a hurricane for the saint on whose feast day it occurred was never used in this country. Originally our method consisted of cumbersome latitude-longitude identifications. The advent of high-speed communications, together with the confusion that arose when more than one tropical storm was in progress in the same area,

1985— Ana, Bob, Claudette, David, Elena, Fabian, Gloria*, Henri, Isabel, Juan, Kate, Larry, Mindy, Nicholas, Odette, Peter, Rose, Sam, Theresa, Victor, Wanda.

1986— Andrew, Bonnie, Charley, Danielle, Earl, Frances, Georges, Hermine, Ivan, Jeanne, Karl, Lisa, Mitch, Nicole, Otto, Paula, Richard, Shary, Tomas, Virginie, Walter.

1987— Arlene, Bret, Cindy, Dennis, Emily, Floyd, Gert, Harvey, Irene, Jose, Katrina, Lenny, Maria, Nate, Ophellia, Phillippe, Rita, Stan, Tammy, Vince, Wilma.

1988— Alberto, Beryl, Chris, Debby, Ernesto, Florence, Gilbert, Helene, Issac, Joan, Keith, Leslie, Michael, Nadine, Oscar, Patty, Raphael, Sandy, Tony, Valerie, William.

1989— Allison, Barry, Chantal, Dean, Erin, Felix, Gabrielle, Hugo, Iris, Jerry, Karen, Luis, Marilyn, Noel, Opal, Pablo, Roxanne, Sebastien, Tanya, Van, Wendy.

1990— Arthur, Bertha, Cesar, Diana, Edouard, Fran, Gustav, Hortense, Isidore, Josephine, Klaus, Lili, Marco, Nana, Omar, Paloma, Rene, Sally, Teddy, Vicky, Wilfred.

1991— Ana, Bob, Claudette, David, Elena, Fabian, Gloria*, Henri, Isabel, Juan, Kate, Larry, Mindy, Nicholas, Odette, Peter, Rose, Sam, Theresa, Victor, Wanda.

1992— Andrew, Bonnie, Charley, Danielle, Earl, Frances, Georges, Hermine, Ivan, Jeanne, Karl, Lisa, Mitch, Nicole. Otto, Paula, Richard, Shary, Tomas, Virginie, Walter.

1993— Arlene, Bret, Cindy, Dennis, Emily, Floyd, Gert, Harvey, Irene, Jose, Katrina, Lenny, Maria, Nate, Ophellia, Phillippe, Rita, Stan, Tammy, Vince, Wilma.

1994— Alberto, Beryl, Chris, Debby, Ernesto, Florence, Gilbert, Helene, Issac, Joan, Keith, Leslie, Michael, Nadine, Oscar, Patty, Raphael, Sandy, Tony, Valerie, William.

(List is recycled every six years.)

* If a storm is large enough to have great historical significance its name may be retired from the list and another name of the same alphabetical rank substituted for it. At press time "Gloria", the name for a major 1985 storm, was being considered for retirement.

forced a change. For a time, tropical storms were designated by letters of the alphabet (A—1943) or the World War II phonetic alphabet (Able, Baker, Charlie); and it has been suggested that the storms be named from the International Civil Aviation Organization's phonetic system (Apha, Bravo, Cocoa), the letters of the Greek alphabet (Alpha, Beta, Gamma), the names of animals (Antelope, Bear, Coyote), and descriptive adjectives (Annoying, Blustery, Churning). It has also been suggested that the storms carry the names of well-known personalities, places, and things, and the names of mythological figures.

It appears that the feminization of tropical cyclones began during World War II, when weathermen plotting the movement of storms across vast theaters of operations identified them alphabetically, using the names of girls. George R. Stewart's novel *Storm* (Random House, 1941) may have been the first published account of this practice. Whatever the origin, the use of ladies' names for tropical storms and hurricanes was persistent until 1979, when complaints from women pushed a change of the nearly thirty-year-old Weather Service policy. In that year, a new listing of names, alternately male and female, was drawn up to refer to hurricanes.

Summary of the 1985 hurricane impact in coastal Louisiana as a result of Hurricanes Danny, Elena, and Juan.

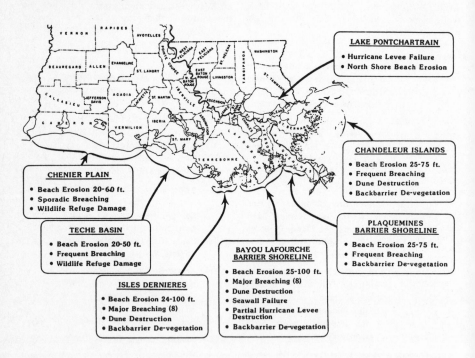

Hurricanes Danny, Elena, and Juan caused the most severe barrier island erosion problem in the state since the landfalls of Hurricanes Camille (1969) and Betsy (1965). With land loss rates in coastal Louisiana exceeding 50 square miles per year, preservation of the state's barrier shorelines has become critical.

Source: Louisiana Geological Survey and *Louisiana Conservationist*, January/February 1986

NOTABLE HURRICANES

September 19, 1947: Entered state through Lake Borgne, center passed directly over New Orleans and Baton Rouge. Damages $24 million, 12 fatalities.

June 28, 1957: "Audrey" entered coast in Cameron Parish. Massive storm surge over 10 ft. in depth penetrated 20 miles or more inland. Damages $150 million, 400 to 500 fatalities.

October 3, 1964: "Hilda" entered coast in St. Mary Parish, moved through Florida Parishes. Damages near $100 million, 37 fatalities, including 22 in tornado at Larose, Lafourche Parish.

September 9, 1965: "Betsy" entered coast near Grand Isle, moved generally parallel with Mississippi River. Damages $1.2 billion, 58 fatalities.

August 17, 1969: "Camille" entered coast in southern Mississippi. Large section of lower Plaquemines Parish inundated by storm surge. Louisiana damages $322 million, 9 fatalities.

September 16, 1971: "Edith" entered coast 30 miles east of Cameron. Damages $15 million, 1 fatality.

September 8, 1974: "Carmen" entered the state through Atchafalaya Bay; traveled in a northwesterly direction, and caused extensive damage to the sugar cane crop. 1 fatality.

September 5, 1977: "Babe" crossed the coast near Point au Fer. Caused wind and water damage to St. Mary, Iberia and St. Martin parishes. Estimated property damages were over $5 million.

July 10-11, 1979: "Bob" crossed coast east of Cocodrie. Bob was a minimal hurricane which caused one fatality and some minor wind damage.

August 15, 1985: "Danny" made landfall near Pecan Island in Vermilion Parish in southwest Louisiana. Top winds were about 90 mph and caused $20 million in damages. The storm surge eroded between 10 and 15 percent of Louisiana's barrier islands.

September 2, 1985: "Elena" entered the coast at Gulfport, Mississippi with highest winds at 125 mph. By the time she reached Washington Parish, Louisiana, top winds diminished to 90 mph. Four hundred thousand people in southeast Louisiana evacuated their homes early in the morning before landfall. Losses were estimated at $17 million.

October 27-31, 1985: "Juan" lingered over the Louisiana coast and coastal plain for five days, causing a 5-8 foot storm surge in southeast coastal parishes. Maximum winds reached 85 mph, with 8-13 inches of rain dumped over the southeastern part of the state. Twelve fatalities were associated with the storm which caused an estimated $304 million in damages to property and $250 million to crops.

TORNADOES

Year	Number of Tornadoes	Number of Tornado Days	Number of Deaths
1934	6	3	2
1935	7	5	9
1936	2	1	2
1937	2	2	1
1938	7	6	26
1939	7	4	10
1940	16	8	14
1941	7	7	4
1942	2	2	2
1943	5	3	5
1944	2	2	3
1945	6	3	4
1946	8	6	2
1947	9	7	24
1948	3	3	1
1949	8	7	3
1950	20	8	29
1951	10	8	0
1952	9	7	4
1953	20	12	13
1954	13	10	2
1955	3	3	0
1956	10	9	0
1957	30	16	14
1958	9	5	0
1959	11	11	0
1960	9	7	1
1961	25	15	6
1962	21	13	2
1963	9	7	0
1964	14	7	22
1965	26	10	0
1966	12	11	0
1967	19	9	0
1968	17	12	0
1969	18	12	1
1970	15	13	1
1971	20	10	12
1972	17	12	0
1973	30	20	1
1974	55	29	4
1975	54	21	3
1976	14	9	1
1977	42	24	1
1978	22	14	4
1979	9	8	0
1980	16	12	2
1981	21	13	0
1982	39	22	0
1983	64	28	5
1984	29	19	0
1985	20	11	0
1986	16	11	0

Total . . .885 . . . . . . .537 240
Averages 16.70 . . . . . .10.13 . . . . .4.53
per year

Source: Louisiana State Office of Climatology

PRECIPITATION NORMALS (INCHES)

STATION	JAN	FEB	MAR	APR	MAY	JUN	JUL	AUG	SEP	OCT	NOV	DEC	ANN
ALEXANDRIA	5.08	4.66	5.26	4.85	5.31	3.89	4.84	3.68	3.92	3.75	4.36	6.30	55.90
AMITE	5.44	5.90	5.66	6.46	5.48	4.51	7.33	4.86	5.18	2.68	4.58	5.82	63.90
ASHLAND 2 S	4.55	4.29	4.46	4.78	5.22	3.57	4.64	2.95	3.90	2.52	3.74	4.62	49.24
BASTROP	4.95	4.66	5.46	5.27	5.27	3.74	4.16	3.00	3.39	2.58	4.51	5.02	52.01
BATON ROUGE WSO R	4.58	4.97	4.59	5.59	4.82	3.11	7.07	5.05	4.42	2.63	3.95	4.99	55.77
BELAH FIRE TOWER	5.05	4.93	5.94	5.47	5.88	3.61	5.15	3.96	4.26	3.43	4.43	6.04	58.15
BOGALUSA	4.89	5.33	5.57	5.56	5.46	4.66	6.21	4.81	4.70	2.88	4.05	5.99	60.11
BUNKIE	5.36	4.80	5.44	5.63	6.30	4.49	5.22	4.42	4.17	3.58	4.89	6.63	60.88
CALHOUN EXP STATION	4.91	4.27	5.18	4.76	5.53	3.37	4.18	2.85	3.70	2.90	4.05	4.65	50.35
CARVILLE 2 SW	4.81	4.87	4.45	5.00	5.11	4.15	6.95	5.82	5.10	2.65	4.12	5.60	58.63
COTTON VALLEY	4.55	4.17	4.69	4.92	5.06	3.92	4.60	2.85	3.58	2.94	4.16	4.36	49.80
COVINGTON 4 NNW	4.87	5.32	5.71	5.33	5.24	4.64	6.65	5.16	5.39	2.96	4.12	5.89	61.28
CROWLEY EXP STATION	4.93	4.58	3.84	5.28	5.03	4.65	6.09	5.37	4.94	3.12	3.75	5.33	56.91
DE QUINCY 4 N	5.06	4.44	4.33	4.61	5.06	4.15	5.94	4.57	5.45	3.72	4.41	5.62	57.36
DE RIDDER	4.92	4.32	4.34	4.77	5.28	3.93	5.14	3.72	4.33	3.18	5.13	6.33	55.39
DONALDSONVILLE 3 E	4.78	4.93	4.83	5.01	5.29	3.65	7.54	6.18	5.42	2.69	4.19	5.85	60.36
ELIZABETH	5.31	4.73	5.20	5.24	5.98	4.54	5.07	4.29	4.68	3.81	4.64	6.89	60.38
FRANKLIN 3 NW	4.34	4.65	3.84	4.54	5.19	5.27	8.48	8.05	5.56	3.10	4.04	4.81	61.87
GLOSTER 1 W	4.38	3.57	4.06	4.61	5.24	3.38	4.02	2.74	3.86	2.85	3.64	4.34	46.69
GRAND COTEAU	5.00	4.96	4.78	5.35	5.75	4.42	6.13	4.34	4.89	3.59	4.03	5.44	58.68
GRAND ECORE	4.83	4.26	4.57	4.84	5.71	3.92	3.66	3.12	3.86	2.76	3.84	4.98	50.35
HACKBERRY 8 SSW	4.51	3.59	3.32	4.07	4.35	4.39	7.00	7.06	5.42	3.52	4.30	4.79	56.32
HAMMOND 3 NW	4.81	5.65	5.67	6.15	5.68	3.82	7.53	4.82	5.74	2.94	4.44	5.99	63.24
HOMER EXP STATION	4.62	4.25	4.50	5.26	5.48	3.78	4.70	3.05	4.12	2.57	4.20	4.56	51.09
HOSSTON	3.99	3.51	4.11	4.89	4.47	3.53	3.33	3.10	3.13	2.86	4.06	4.18	45.16
HOUMA	4.80	4.46	4.20	4.60	5.43	6.09	7.94	6.68	7.52	3.18	3.96	5.03	63.89
JEANERETTE EXP STA	4.42	4.35	3.88	4.42	4.98	5.10	7.82	6.47	5.12	3.53	3.64	5.24	58.97
JENNINGS	5.00	4.70	4.16	5.44	5.52	4.16	6.26	5.49	5.24	3.38	4.15	5.60	59.10
KEITHVILLE	4.54	3.92	4.23	4.52	5.20	3.68	3.72	2.42	3.78	2.59	3.96	4.20	46.76
KENTWOOD	5.39	5.18	5.78	6.17	6.14	4.49	7.15	5.03	4.74	2.79	4.78	5.91	63.55
KINDER 3 W	5.22	4.81	4.50	4.81	5.66	4.25	5.43	4.81	4.86	3.48	4.21	6.21	58.25
KORAN	4.40	4.01	4.13	4.44	5.50	3.55	3.60	2.68	3.21	2.67	3.99	4.42	46.60
LAFAYETTE FAA AIRPORT	4.72	4.55	4.16	5.10	5.24	4.18	7.19	5.38	5.35	3.20	3.60	5.02	57.69
LAKE ARTHUR 10 SW	4.57	4.53	3.36	4.60	5.40	3.85	6.27	5.96	4.73	3.35	4.22	5.45	56.29
LAKE CHARLES WSO	4.25	3.88	3.05	4.06	5.14	4.19	5.55	5.39	5.21	3.47	3.76	5.08	53.03
LAKE PROVIDENCE	5.42	5.07	6.17	5.27	5.22	3.59	4.57	3.08	3.13	2.64	4.33	5.57	54.06
LEESVILLE	4.66	4.51	4.54	5.02	5.31	4.16	5.47	3.62	3.70	3.05	4.35	5.68	54.07
LOGANSPORT 4 ENE	4.27	3.93	4.27	4.87	6.03	3.56	3.65	3.12	4.12	2.87	3.80	4.49	48.98
LONGVILLE	5.35	4.39	4.44	4.61	5.26	3.86	5.38	4.17	4.83	3.90	4.17	5.74	56.10
MELVILLE	5.14	5.13	4.65	5.25	5.53	3.93	5.18	4.01	4.26	2.89	4.07	5.77	55.81
MERMENTAU	4.99	5.10	3.91	5.63	5.49	4.02	6.64	5.59	5.23	3.68	3.86	5.66	59.80
MINDEN	4.36	4.03	4.38	4.61	5.44	3.76	4.25	2.99	3.28	2.52	4.20	4.44	48.26
MONROE FAA AIRPORT	4.84	4.41	5.21	4.95	5.04	3.30	4.53	2.56	3.49	2.42	3.97	4.84	49.56
MORGAN CITY	4.48	4.60	3.90	4.65	5.28	5.10	8.09	7.17	6.24	3.65	4.30	5.07	62.53
NATCHITOCHES	4.85	4.36	4.53	5.08	5.65	3.69	3.53	2.99	3.83	2.96	3.78	5.07	50.32
NEW IBERIA 5 NW	4.41	4.22	4.06	4.87	4.88	4.98	7.19	5.92	5.16	3.17	3.63	4.76	57.25
NEW ORLEANS MOISANT WSO	4.97	5.23	4.73	4.50	5.07	4.63	6.73	6.02	5.87	2.66	4.06	5.27	59.74
N O AUDUBON WSO R	4.90	5.19	4.68	4.68	5.06	5.39	7.17	6.67	5.98	2.52	4.01	5.30	61.55
NEW ORLEANS ALGIERS R	4.76	4.98	5.08	4.76	5.46	5.36	7.81	6.08	5.57	2.88	3.86	5.07	61.67
NEW ORLEANS CITRUS R	4.89	5.25	4.74	4.68	5.03	4.19	6.54	5.46	5.89	2.50	3.58	4.92	57.67
NEW ORLEANS DUBLIN R	4.67	4.76	4.31	4.26	4.80	4.92	6.76	6.24	5.65	2.33	3.54	4.55	56.79
NEW ORLEANS JOURDAN R	4.72	5.37	5.20	4.68	5.47	4.72	7.38	6.13	5.85	2.99	3.79	5.27	61.57
NEW ORLEANS LONDON R	4.72	5.14	4.88	4.61	4.90	4.73	6.69	5.89	5.76	2.59	3.86	5.03	58.80
OAKNOLIA	5.33	5.39	5.33	5.95	5.64	3.80	6.20	4.77	4.24	3.02	4.27	5.44	59.38
OBERLIN FIRE TOWER	5.49	5.00	4.90	4.98	6.33	4.11	5.74	4.31	5.42	3.85	4.51	6.08	60.72
OLLA 3 SSW	5.37	5.02	5.93	5.30	6.23	3.68	4.70	3.32	3.88	2.89	4.32	5.74	56.38
PARADIS 7 S	5.01	5.27	5.05	4.69	5.63	4.74	7.63	6.12	6.59	2.97	4.19	5.17	63.06
PEARL RIVER LOCK NO 1	4.92	5.07	5.85	5.46	5.20	4.16	6.64	5.20	5.53	2.72	4.41	5.78	60.94
PINE GROVE FIRE TOWER	5.88	5.86	6.08	6.52	6.11	4.26	7.78	5.57	4.94	3.20	4.83	6.46	67.49
PLAIN DEALING	4.28	3.86	4.26	5.34	4.74	3.72	4.08	3.33	3.47	2.99	4.24	4.37	48.68
RESERVE	5.13	5.58	5.15	4.51	5.29	4.31	6.50	5.70	5.95	3.01	4.07	5.62	60.82
RODESSA	3.96	3.74	4.45	5.22	4.57	3.69	3.15	2.67	3.32	3.03	4.23	4.20	46.23
RUSTON LA POLYTECH INS	5.07	4.37	4.93	5.03	5.94	3.55	4.59	2.84	4.10	2.72	4.11	4.90	52.15
SAINT JOSEPH EXP STA	5.41	4.69	6.09	5.17	5.18	3.06	3.91	3.16	2.98	2.88	4.07	5.65	52.25
SHERIDAN FIRE TOWER	5.61	5.93	6.21	6.27	6.24	4.86	7.31	6.02	4.98	3.18	4.53	6.59	67.73
SHREVEPORT WSO R	4.02	3.46	3.77	4.71	4.70	3.54	3.56	2.52	3.29	2.63	3.77	3.87	43.84
SIMMESPORT 1 SE	5.33	4.97	5.27	5.70	5.51	3.99	5.30	4.42	4.25	2.99	4.54	6.42	58.69
SPEARSVILLE FIRE TOWER	4.78	4.26	5.12	5.31	5.68	3.61	4.24	3.16	4.20	2.75	4.17	4.70	51.98
STERLINGTON LOCK	4.79	4.34	5.12	4.95	5.30	3.20	4.19	2.40	3.07	2.74	4.16	4.66	48.92
TALLULAH 2 SW	5.16	4.73	6.15	5.61	5.24	3.76	4.29	3.33	2.70	2.59	3.98	5.89	53.43
VERMILION LOCK	4.39	4.23	3.72	4.48	4.11	4.88	8.58	6.93	5.83	3.26	3.83	4.89	59.13
WINNFIELD 2 W	5.16	4.48	4.23	5.47	5.89	3.85	5.26	3.36	4.48	2.76	4.08	5.31	55.33
WINNSBORO	5.25	4.52	5.97	4.91	5.24	3.28	3.86	3.38	3.17	2.60	4.18	5.77	52.13
WINONA FIRE TOWER	5.39	4.79	5.36	5.67	5.91	3.79	5.45	3.94	4.33	3.08	4.43	5.65	57.79
WOODWORTH ST FOREST	5.20	4.92	5.34	5.33	5.74	3.69	5.50	4.11	4.18	3.50	5.11	6.94	59.56

Source: Louisiana State Office of Climatology

LOUISIANA WEATHER STATIONS

STATE-STATION NUMBER	STN TYP	NAME		LATITUDE DEG-MIN	LONGITUDE DEG-MIN	ELEVATION (FT)
16-0098	13	ALEXANDRIA		N 3119	W 09228	87
16-0205	13	AMITE		N 3043	W 09030	180
16-0349	12	ASHLAND 2 S		N 3207	W 09306	225
16-0537	13	BASTROP		N 3247	W 09154	140
16-0549	13	BATON ROUGE WSO	R	N 3032	W 09108	64
16-0639	13	BELAH FIRE TOWER		N 3138	W 09211	200
16-0945	13	BOGALUSA		N 3047	W 08952	103
16-1287	13	BUNKIE		N 3057	W 09210	80
16-1411	13	CALHOUN EXP STATION		N 3231	W 09220	180
16-1565	13	CARVILLE 2 SW		N 3012	W 09107	26
16-2121	13	COTTON VALLEY		N 3249	W 09325	230
16-2151	13	COVINGTON 4 NNW		N 3032	W 09007	40
16-2212	12	CROWLEY EXP STATION		N 3015	W 09222	25
16-2361	12	DE QUINCY 4 N		N 3031	W 09326	95
16-2367	12	DE RIDDER		N 3050	W 09318	180
16-2534	13	DONALDSONVILLE 3 E		N 3006	W 09056	20
16-2800	13	ELIZABETH		N 3052	W 09248	150
16-3313	13	FRANKLIN 3 NW		N 2949	W 09133	12
16-3657	12	GLOSTER 1 W		N 3212	W 09350	255
16-3800	13	GRAND COTEAU		N 3026	W 09202	55
16-3804	12	GRAND ECORE		N 3148	W 09306	150
16-3979	13	HACKBERRY 8 SSW		N 2953	W 09325	6
16-4034	13	HAMMOND 3 NW		N 3032	W 09029	45
16-4355	13	HOMER EXP STATION		N 3245	W 09304	380
16-4398	12	HOSSTON		N 3253	W 09353	200
16-4407	13	HOUMA		N 2935	W 09044	15
16-4674	12	JEANERETTE EXP STA		N 2957	W 09143	20
16-4700	13	JENNINGS		N 3015	W 09240	30

STATE-STATION NUMBER	STN TYP	NAME	LATITUDE DEG-MIN	LONGITUDE DEG-MIN	ELEVATION (FT)
16-4816	12	KEITHVILLE	N 3221	W 09350	200
16-4859	12	KENTWOOD	N 3056	W 09031	218
16-4884	12	KINDER 3 W	N 3030	W 09254	53
16-4931	12	KORAN	N 3225	W 09328	175
16-5026	13	LAFAYETTE FAA AIRPORT	N 3012	W 09159	38
16-5065	13	LAKE ARTHUR 10 SW	N 3000	W 09248	10
16-5078	13	LAKE CHARLES WSO	N 3007	W 09313	9
16-5090	13	LAKE PROVIDENCE	N 3249	W 09112	105
16-5266	13	LEESVILLE	N 3109	W 09316	240
16-5527	13	LOGANSPORT 4 ENE	N 3159	W 09357	210
16-5584	12	LONGVILLE	N 3036	W 09314	114
16-6117	13	MELVILLE	N 3041	W 09145	30
16-6142	12	MERMENTAU	N 3011	W 09235	16
16-6244	13	MINDEN	N 3236	W 09318	250
16-6303	13	MONROE FAA AIRPORT	N 3231	W 09203	78
16-6394	13	MORGAN CITY	N 2941	W 09111	5
16-6582	13	NATCHITOCHES	N 3146	W 09305	130
16-6657	13	NEW IBERIA 5 NW	N 3003	W 09153	25
16-6660	13	NEW ORLEANS MOISANT WSO	N 2959	W 09015	4
16-6664	13	N O AUDUBON WSO R	N 2955	W 09008	6
16-6666	12	NEW ORLEANS ALGIERS R	N 2956	W 09002	2
16-6668	12	NEW ORLEANS CITRUS R	N 3003	W 08959	0
16-6669	12	NEW ORLEANS DUBLIN R	N 2957	W 09008	22
16-6672	12	NEW ORLEANS JOURDAN R	N 2959	W 09001	10
16-6675	12	NEW ORLEANS LONDON R	N 2959	W 09004	12
16-6911	12	OAKNOLIA	N 3044	W 09059	130
16-6938	12	OBERLIN FIRE TOWER	N 3036	W 09247	67
16-6978	13	OLLA 3 SSW	N 3152	W 09216	100
16-7096	12	PARADIS 7 S	N 2947	W 09026	6
16-7161	12	PEARL RIVER LOCK NO 1	N 3027	W 08947	30
16-7304	12	PINE GROVE FIRE TOWER	N 3042	W 09045	190
16-7344	13	PLAIN DEALING	N 3254	W 09341	291
16-7767	13	RESERVE	N 3004	W 09034	13
16-7950	12	RODESSA	N 3258	W 09400	200
16-8067	13	RUSTON LA POLYTECH INS	N 3231	W 09239	275
16-8163	13	SAINT JOSEPH EXP STA	N 3157	W 09114	78
16-8405	12	SHERIDAN FIRE TOWER	N 3051	W 08959	330
16-8440	13	SHREVEPORT WSO R	N 3228	W 09349	254
16-8507	12	SIMMESPORT 1 SE	N 3059	W 09148	40
16-8669	12	SPEARSVILLE FIRE TOWER	N 3254	W 09234	200
16-8785	12	STERLINGTON LOCK	N 3242	W 09205	55
16-8923	13	TALLULAH 2 SW	N 3224	W 09113	85
16-9319	13	VERMILION LOCK	N 2947	W 09212	14
16-9803	13	WINNFIELD 2 W	N 3156	W 09241	160
16-9806	13	WINNSBORO	N 3209	W 09142	80
16-9809	12	WINONA FIRE TOWER	N 3202	W 09239	220
16-9865	12	WOODWORTH ST FOREST	N 3108	W 09228	90

11 = TEMPERATURE ONLY
12 = PRECIPITATION ONLY
13 = TEMP. & PRECIP.

AVERAGE ANNUAL PRECIPITATION
(1951-80 average)

Source: Louisiana State Office of Climatology

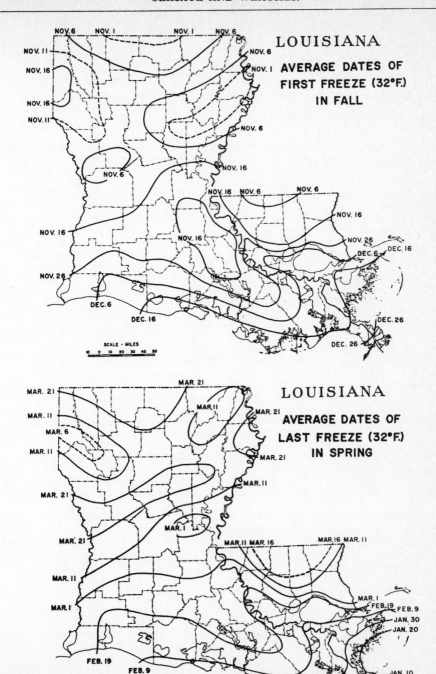

Population in Louisiana—1980

The 1980 federal census results for Louisiana confirm a pattern of growth that has been going on since the first recorded U. S. count in 1810. The final corrected and revised population figure is 4,206,312. This number is a healthy 15.5 percent above the 1970 count of 3,644,637, a growth rate which surpasses by good measure the U. S. national rate of increase of 11.4 percent. This steady and gradual growth places Louisiana as the nineteenth most populous state in the country, a move of two places since 1940, and ranks it eighth in the South (rate of increase is also eighth in the South). The Pelican State accounts for 1.86 percent of the total 1980 U.S. population of 226,546,000. With a total land area of 44,521 square miles (115,310 square kilometers), the state is relatively densely populated, at an average of 94.5 persons per square mile (36.5 per square kilometer) to the national 63.9 per square mile. Louisiana is a comparatively "young" state; the median age of 27.3 is over 2.5 years less than the national median age.

Louisiana's largest city, New Orleans, twenty-first in size in the U.S. and sixth in the South, has a 1980 population count of, 557,927, a 6.1 percent decrease since 1970. Two other Pelican State cities included in the top 100 are Baton Rouge at sixty-second with 219,419 (up 32.2 percent since 1970), and Shreveport at sixty-seventh with a population of 205,820 (a ten-year growth of 13.0 percent). The town with the greatest percentage increase in population since 1970 was not precisely a town at all, but what census officials refer to as a census designated place of CDP (a densely populated area that is not incorporated or given the powers and duties of municipalities); the area was Harvey, part of the New Orleans metropolitan area, with a growth rate of 257.8 percent. The incorporated area having the highest rate of increase was the town of Mandeville, part of booming St. Tammany Parish, with 166.3 percent. The area losing the most people over the 1970 to 1980 period was the census designated place North Fort Polk, with a drop of 79.3 percent, owing largely to the reduction of the military installation there; the town of Plain Dealing had the highest loss for incorporated areas with a drop of 42.7.

The three most heavily populated parishes in order were Orleans, 557,927; Jefferson, 454,592; and East Baton Rouge, 366,191. Besides being the most populous, Orleans is also the most urbanized (99.9 percent) and most densely populated (2801.6 persons per square mile or 1080.5 per square kilometer), an understandable figure owing to the fact that it is also the second smallest in land area in the state (the smallest is West Baton Rouge, with an area of 194 square miles or 502 square kilometers). The largest parish, Cameron (1,417 square miles or 3,670 square kilometers), is also the least dense (6.6 persons per square mile of 2.5 per square kilometer). The most ruralized parish is Assumption, with 85.7 percent of the population living outside of urban centers. St. Tammany Parish continued to have the highest rate of increase in the state, with a ten-year growth of 74.4 percent (the rate from 1960 to 1970 was 64.5 percent). Tensas Parish suffered a population decrease of 12.4 percent, the highest in the state; the same area lost 17.5 percent from 1960 to 1970.

In summation, the 1980 census appears to confirm trends that have been taking place throughout the twentieth century. Overall, the state of Louisiana is experiencing healthy growth, although some of this increase is to suburban centers at the expense of rural areas and older downtown urban areas (New Orleans proper is the best example of this).

Sources: Research Division, Louisiana Tech; 1980 U.S. Census

Mortality rates for lung cancer in Louisiana and New Orleans are among the highest in the nation, particularly among males. During the period from 1950 to 1969, Louisiana had the highest rate in the country for white males. Ten Louisiana parishes rank in the top 18 counties nationally. Six of these parishes border on the Mississippi River.

Source: *Louisiana Monthly Morbidity Report,* April/May, 1980.

POPULATION GROWTH
LOUISIANA AND THE UNITED STATES, 1810-1986

Year	Louisiana	United States	Louisiana as a Percent of United States	Decade Rates of Growth	
				Louisiana	United States
1810	76,556	7,239,881	1.06	--	36.4
1820	153,407	9,638,453	1.59	100.5	33.1
1830	215,739	12,866,020	1.68	40.6	33.5
1840	352,411	17,069,453	2.06	63.9	32.7
1850	517,762	23,191,876	2.23	46.9	35.9
1860	708,002	31,443,321	2.25	36.6	35.5
1870	726,915	39,818,449	1.82	2.7	22.7
1880	939,946	50,155,783	1.87	29.3	26.0
1890	1,118,588	62,947,714	1.78	19.0	25.5
1900	1,381,625	75,994,575	1.82	23.5	20.7
1910	1,656,388	91,972,266	1.80	19.9	20.0
1920	1,798,509	105,710,620	1.70	8.6	14.9
1930	2,101,593	122,775,046	1.71	16.8	16.1
1940	2,363,880	131,669,275	1.79	12.5	7.2
1950	2,683,516	150,697,361	1.78	13.5	14.4
1960	3,257,022	179,323,175	1.81	21.3	19.0
1970	3,644,637	203,304,000	1.79	11.9	13.3
1980	4,206,312	226,546,000	1.86	15.5	11.4
1986	5,633,588*	241,489,000*	2.30	33.9*	6.6*

*estimated

Sources: College of Administration and Business, Louisiana Tech
        U.S. Bureau of the Census
        Louisiana Department of Labor

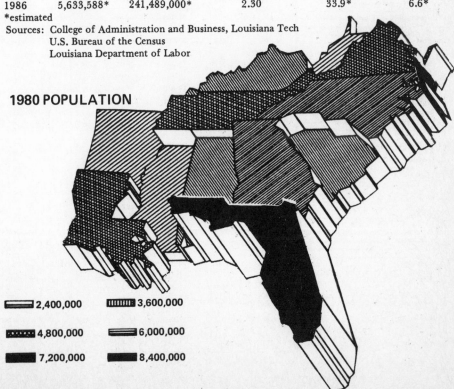

1980 POPULATION

2,400,000   3,600,000

4,800,000   6,000,000

7,200,000   8,400,000

Land Area and Population: 1980

Parishes	1980 land area		Population				
			1980			Percent change	
	Square miles	Square kilometers	Number	Per square mile	Per square kilometer	1970 to 1980	1960 to 1970
The State	44 521	115 310	4 205 900	94.5	36.5	15.4	11.9
Acadia	657	1 701	56 427	85.9	33.2	8.3	4.4
Allen	766	1 983	21 390	27.9	10.8	2.9	4.7
Ascension	296	767	50 068	169.1	65.3	35.0	32.8
Assumption	342	886	22 084	64.6	24.9	12.4	9.2
Avoyelles	846	2 192	41 393	48.9	18.9	9.6	0.4
Beauregard	1 163	3 012	29 692	25.5	9.9	29.7	19.3
Bienville	815	2 112	16 387	20.1	7.8	2.3	-4.2
Bossier	845	2 188	80 721	95.5	36.9	22.5	14.3
Caddo	894	2 316	252 358	282.3	109.0	9.6	2.8
Calcasieu	1 081	2 801	167 223	154.7	59.7	15.0	–
Caldwell	541	1 400	10 761	19.9	7.7	15.0	3.9
Cameron	1 417	3 670	9 336	6.6	2.5	13.9	18.6
Catahoula	732	1 896	12 287	16.8	6.5	4.4	3.0
Claiborne	765	1 981	17 095	22.3	8.6	0.4	-12.3
Concordia	717	1 857	22 981	32.1	12.4	1.8	10.3
De Soto	880	2 280	25 727	29.2	11.3	13.0	-6.1
East Baton Rouge	458	1 187	366 191	799.5	308.5	28.4	24.0
East Carroll	426	1 103	11 772	27.6	10.7	-8.6	-10.7
East Feliciana	455	1 179	19 015	41.8	16.1	7.7	-12.6
Evangeline	667	1 728	33 343	50.0	19.3	4.4	0.9
Franklin	636	1 646	24 141	38.0	14.7	0.8	-8.2
Grant	653	1 690	16 703	25.6	9.9	22.2	2.6
Iberia	589	1 526	63 752	108.2	41.8	11.1	11.1
Iberville	637	1 651	32 159	50.5	19.5	4.6	2.7
Jackson	578	1 498	17 321	30.0	11.6	8.5	0.9
Jefferson	347	900	454 592	1310.1	505.1	34.4	62.0
Jefferson Davis	655	1 697	32 168	49.1	19.0	8.8	-0.9
Lafayette	270	699	150 017	555.6	214.6	34.4	31.9
Lafourche	1 141	2 954	82 483	72.3	27.9	19.6	24.5
La Salle	638	1 652	17 004	26.7	10.3	27.9	2.2
Lincoln	472	1 223	39 763	84.2	32.5	17.6	18.5
Livingston	661	1 711	58 806	89.0	34.4	61.1	35.4
Madison	631	1 634	15 975	25.3	9.8	6.0	-8.4
Morehouse	807	2 089	34 803	43.1	16.7	7.2	-3.7
Natchitoches	1 264	3 273	39 863	31.5	12.2	13.2	-1.2
Orleans	199	516	557 515	2801.6	1080.5	-6.1	-5.4
Ouachita	627	1 623	139 241	222.1	85.8	20.7	13.5
Plaquemines	1 035	2 680	26 049	25.2	9.7	3.3	11.9
Pointe Coupee	566	1 466	24 045	42.5	16.4	9.3	-2.2
Rapides	1 341	3 474	135 282	100.9	38.9	14.6	6.0
Red River	394	1 020	10 433	26.5	10.2	13.1	-7.5
Richland	563	1 458	22 187	39.4	15.2	1.9	-8.6
Sabine	855	2 215	25 280	29.6	11.4	35.6	0.4
St. Bernard	486	1 260	64 097	131.9	50.9	25.2	59.0
St. Charles	286	742	37 259	130.3	50.2	26.1	39.3
St. Helena	409	1 060	9 827	24.0	9.3	-1.1	8.5
St. James	248	643	21 495	86.7	33.4	8.9	7.4
St. John the Baptist	213	551	31 924	149.9	57.9	34.1	29.1
St. Landry	936	2 424	84 128	89.9	34.7	4.7	-1.4
St. Martin	749	1 940	40 214	53.7	20.7	23.9	11.7
St. Mary	613	1 587	64 253	104.8	40.5	5.8	24.4
St. Tammany	873	2 262	110 869	127.0	49.0	74.4	64.5
Tangipahoa	783	2 029	80 698	103.1	39.8	22.5	10.8
Tensas	623	1 613	8 525	13.7	5.3	-12.4	-17.5
Terrebonne	1 367	3 541	94 393	69.1	26.7	24.1	25.1
Union	884	2 289	21 167	23.9	9.2	14.7	4.7
Vermilion	1 205	3 122	48 458	40.2	15.5	12.5	10.9
Vernon	1 332	3 449	53 475	40.1	15.5	-0.6	193.9
Washington	676	1 750	44 207	65.4	25.3	5.3	-4.6
Webster	602	1 560	43 631	72.5	28.0	9.2	0.6
West Baton Rouge	194	502	19 086	98.4	38.0	13.2	14.0
West Carroll	360	932	12 922	35.9	13.9	-0.8	-8.1
West Feliciana	406	1 051	12 186	30.0	11.6	13.2	-13.2
Winn	953	2 468	17 253	18.1	7.0	5.4	2.1

1986 LOUISIANA POPULATION ESTIMATES

PARISH	1986 TOTAL POP.	MALE POP.	FEMALE POP.	PARISH	1986 TOTAL POP.	MALE POP.	FEMALE POP.
ACADIA	60,595	29,237	31,358	MOREHOUSE	35,686	16,780	18,906
ALLEN	21,863	10,660	11,203	NATCHITOCHES	40,180	18,973	21,207
ASCENSION	60,082	29,584	30,498				
ASSUMPTION	24,009	11,892	12,117	ORLEANS	564,183	264,320	299,863
AVOYELLES	43,621	20,886	22,735	OUACHITA	144,883	68,921	75,962
				PLAQUEMINES	26,913	13,755	13,158
BEAUREGARD	33,153	16,782	16,371	POINTE COUPEE	25,351	12,171	13,180
BIENVILLE	16,743	8,062	8,681	RAPIDES	140,683	67,556	73,127
BOSSIER	92,994	46,079	46,915				
CADDO	276,009	129,365	146,644	RED RIVER	11,132	5,327	5,805
CALCASIEU	179,641	87,755	91,886	RICHLAND	23,249	11,078	12,171
				SABINE	28,168	13,712	14,456
CALDWELL	11,289	5,536	5,753	ST. BERNARD	69,387	33,778	35,609
CAMERON	10,306	5,198	5,108	ST. CHARLES	43,855	21,963	21,892
CATAHOULA	12,699	6,098	6,601				
CLAIBORNE	18,750	8,940	9,810	ST. HELENA	10,646	5,128	5,518
CONCORDIA	23,952	11,360	12,592	ST. JAMES	22,317	10,784	11,533
				ST. JOHN	43,321	21,466	21,855
DESOTO	28,133	13,476	14,657	ST. LANDRY	90,007	43,194	46,813
EAST BATON ROUGE	401,004	194,246	206,758	ST. MARTIN	47,524	23,206	24,318
EAST CARROLL	11,366	5,402	5,964				
EAST FELICIANA	20,625	10,585	10,040	ST. MARY	65,977	32,837	33,140
EVANGELINE	35,447	17,195	18,252	ST. TAMMANY	147,623	73,295	74,328
FRANKLIN	24,372	11,560	12,812	TANGIPAHOA	93,772	45,067	48,705
GRANT	18,387	8,920	9,467	TENSAS	8,294	3,897	4,397
IBERIA	70,725	34,570	36,155	TERREBONNE	104,184	52,061	52,123
IBERVILLE	33,522	16,352	17,170				
JACKSON	17,524	8,312	9,212	UNION	22,677	10,901	11,776
				VERMILION	54,558	26,493	28,065
JEFFERSON	486,060	237,975	248,085	VERNON	63,533	35,102	28,431
JEFFERSON DAVIS	33,620	16,259	17,361	WASHINGTON	47,706	22,761	24,945
LAFAYETTE	178,388	87,820	90,568	WEBSTER	46,272	22,178	24,094
LAFOURCHE	89,520	44,321	45,199				
LASALLE	17,782	8,578	9,204	WEST BATON ROUGE	21,059	10,340	10,719
				WEST CARROLL	13,106	6,324	6,782
LINCOLN	43,999	21,929	22,070	WEST FELICIANA	14,125	9,673	4,452
LIVINGSTON	75,066	37,293	37,773	WINN	17,342	8,338	9,004
MADISON	15,510	7,200	8,310				

STATE TOTAL: 4,574,469

Source: Louisiana Department of Labor, Office of Employment Security

Louisiana Population and Land Area

	1980	1970	1960	1950
Total population	4,206,312	3,644,637	3,257,022	2,683,516
Rank among states	19	20	20	21
Total land area (square miles)	44,521	44,930	45,106	45,162
Population per square mile	94.5	81.8	72.2	59.4

POPULATION

Name of Parish	1980	1970	1960	1950	1940	1930	1920	1910
Acadia	56,427	52,109	49,931	47,050	46,260	39,326	34,820	31,847
Allen	21,390	20,794	19,867	18,835	17,540	15,261	18,332	-------
Ascension	50,068	37,086	27,927	22,387	21,215	18,438	22,155	23,837
Assumption	22,084	19,654	17,991	17,278	18,541	15,996	17,912	24,128
Attakapas	- - - - - -	-------	-------	-------	-------	-------	-------	-------
Avoyelles	41,393	37,851	37,606	38,031	39,256	34,926	35,300	34,102
Beauregard	29,692	22,888	19,191	17,766	14,847	14,569	20,767	-------
Bienville	16,387	16,024	16,726	19,105	23,933	23,789	20,977	21,776
Bossier	80,721	64,703	57,622	40,139	33,162	28,388	22,266	21,788
Caddo	252,358	230,184	223,859	176,547	150,203	124,670	83,265	58,200
Calcasieu	167,223	145,415	145,475	89,635	56,506	41,963	32,870	62,767
Caldwell	10,761	9,354	9,004	10,293	12,040	10,430	9,514	8,593
Cameron	9,336	8,194	6,909	6,244	7,203	6,054	3,952	4,288
Carroll	- - - - - -	-------	-------	-------	-------	-------	-------	-------
Catahoula	12,287	11,769	11,421	11,834	14,618	12,451	11,074	10,415
Claiborne	17,095	17,024	19,407	25,063	29,855	32,285	27,885	25,050
Concordia	22,981	22,578	20,467	14,398	14,562	12,778	12,466	14,278
DeSoto	25,727	22,764	24,248	24,398	31,803	31,016	29,376	27,689
East Baton Rouge	366,191	285,167	230,058	158,236	88,415	68,208	44,513	34,580
East Carroll	11,722	12,884	14,433	16,302	19,023	15,815	11,231	11,637
East Feliciana	19,015	17,657	20,198	19,133	18,039	17,449	17,487	20,055
Evangeline	33,343	31,932	31,639	31,629	30,497	25,483	23,485	-------
Feliciana	- - - - - -	-------	-------	-------	-------	-------	-------	-------
Franklin	24,141	23,946	26,088	29,376	32,382	30,530	24,100	11,989
Grant	16,703	13,671	13,330	14,263	15,933	15,709	14,408	15,958
Iberia	63,752	57,397	51,657	40,059	37,183	28,192	26,855	31,262
Iberville	32,159	30,946	29,939	26,750	27,721	24,638	26,806	30,954
Jackson	17,321	15,963	15,828	15,434	17,807	13,808	14,486	13,818
Jefferson	454,592	338,229	208,769	103,873	50,427	40,032	21,563	18,247
Jefferson Davis	32,168	29,554	29,825	26,298	24,191	19,765	18,999	-------
Lafayette	150,017	111,745	84,656	57,743	43,941	38,827	9,858	28,733
Lafourche	82,483	68,941	55,381	42,209	38,615	32,419	30,841	33,111
LaSalle	17,004	13,295	13,011	12,717	10,959	11,668	30,344	9,402
Lincoln	39,763	33,800	28,535	25,782	24,790	22,822	16,962	18,485
Livingston	58,806	36,511	26,974	20,054	17,790	18,206	11,643	10,627
Madison	15,975	15,065	16,444	17,451	18,443	14,829	10,829	10,676
Morehouse	34,803	32,463	33,709	32,038	27,571	23,689	19,311	18,786
Natchitoches	39,863	35,219	35,653	38,144	40,997	38,477	38,602	36,455
Opelousas	- - - - - -	-------	-------	-------	-------	-------	-------	-------
Orleans	557,927	593,471	627,525	570,445	494,537	458,762	387,219	339,075
Ouachita	139,241	115,387	101,663	74,713	59,168	54,337	30,319	25,830
Plaquemines	26,049	25,225	22,545	14,239	12,318	9,607	10,194	12,524
Pointe Coupee	24,045	22,002	22,488	21,841	24,004	21,007	24,697	25,289
Rapides	135,282	118,078	111,351	90,648	73,370	65,455	59,444	44,545
Red River	10,433	9,226	9,978	12,113	15,881	16,078	15,301	11,402
Richland	22,187	21,774	23,824	26,672	28,829	26,374	20,860	15,769
Sabine	25,280	18,638	18,564	20,880	23,586	24,110	20,713	19,874
St. Bernard	64,097	51,185	32,186	11,087	7,280	6,512	4,968	5,277
St. Charles	37,259	29,550	21,219	13,363	12,321	12,111	8,586	11,207
St. Helena	9,827	9,937	9,162	9,013	9,542	8,492	8,427	9,172
St. James	21,495	19,733	18,369	15,334	16,596	15,338	21,228	23,009
St. John the Baptist	31,924	23,813	18,439	14,861	14,766	14,078	11,896	14,338
St. Landry	84,128	80,364	81,493	78,476	71,481	60,074	51,697	66,661
St. Martin	40,214	32,453	29,063	26,353	26,394	21,767	21,990	23,070
St. Mary	64,253	60,752	48,833	35,848	31,458	29,397	30,754	39,368
St. Tammany	110,869	63,585	38,643	26,988	23,624	20,929	20,645	18,917
Tangipahoa	80,698	65,875	59,434	53,218	45,519	46,227	31,440	29,160
Tensas	8,525	9,732	11,796	13,209	15,940	15,096	12,085	17,060
Terrebonne	94,393	76,049	60,771	43,328	35,880	29,816	26,974	28,320
Union	21,167	18,447	17,624	19,141	20,943	20,731	19,621	20,451
Vermilion	48,458	43,071	38,855	36,929	37,750	33,684	26,482	26,390
Vernon	53,475	53,794	18,301	18,974	19,142	20,047	20,493	17,384
Washington	44,207	41,987	44,015	38,371	34,443	29,904	24,164	18,886
Webster	43,631	39,939	39,701	35,704	33,676	29,458	24,707	19,186
West Baton Rouge	19,086	16,864	14,796	11,738	11,263	9,716	11,092	12,636
West Carroll	12,922	13,028	14,177	17,248	19,252	13,895	8,857	6,249
West Feliciana	12,186	11,376	12,395	10,169	11,720	10,924	12,303	13,449
Winn	17,253	16,369	16,034	16,119	16,923	14,766	16,119	18,357

OF PARISHES

1900	1890	1880	1870	1860	1850	1840	1830	1820	1810
23,483	13,231	-------	-------	-------	-------	-------	-------	-------	-------
-------	-------	-------	-------	-------	-------	-------	-------	-------	-------
24,142	19,546	16,895	11,677	11,484	10,752	6,951	5,426	3,728	2,219
21,620	19,629	17,010	13,234	15,879	10,638	7,141	5,669	3,576	2,472
-------	-------	-------	-------	-------	-------	-------	-------	12,063	-------
29,701	25,112	16,747	12,926	13,167	9,326	6,616	3,484	2,246	1,200
-------	-------	-------	-------	-------	-------	-------	-------	-------	-------
17,588	14,108	10,442	10,636	11,000	5,539	-------	-------	-------	-------
24,152	20,330	16,042	12,675	11,348	6,962	-------	-------	-------	-------
44,499	31,555	26,296	21,716	12,140	8,884	5,282	-------	-------	-------
30,482	20,176	12,484	6,733	5,928	3,914	2,067	-------	-------	-------
6,917	5,814	5,767	4,820	4,833	2,815	2,017	-------	-------	-------
3,952	2,828	2,416	1,591	-------	-------	-------	-------	-------	-------
-------	-------	-------	10,110	18,052	8,789	4,237	-------	-------	-------
16,351	12,902	10,277	8,475	11,651	7,132	4,955	2,581	2,287	1,164
23,029	20,312	18,837	20,240	16,848	7,471	6,185	1,764	-------	-------
13,559	14,871	14,914	9,977	13,850	7,768	9,414	4,642	2,624	2,896
25,063	19,860	15,603	14,962	13,298	8,023	-------	-------	-------	-------
31,153	25,922	19,966	17,816	16,046	11,977	8,138	6,698	4,808	1,463
11,373	12,362	12,134	-------	-------	-------	-------	-------	-------	-------
20,443	17,908	15,132	13,499	14,697	13,598	11,893	8,247	12,677	-------
-------	-------	-------	-------	-------	-------	-------	-------	-------	-------
-------	-------	-------	-------	-------	-------	-------	-------	12,732	-------
8,890	6,900	6,495	5,078	6,162	3,251	-------	-------	-------	-------
12,902	8,270	6,188	4,517	-------	-------	-------	-------	-------	-------
29,015	20,997	16,676	9,042	-------	-------	-------	-------	-------	-------
27,006	21,848	17,544	12,347	14,661	12,278	8,495	7,049	4,414	2,679
9,119	7,453	5,328	7,646	9,465	5,566	-------	-------	-------	-------
15,321	13,221	12,166	17,767	15,372	25,098	10,470	6,846	-------	-------
-------	-------	-------	-------	-------	-------	-------	-------	-------	-------
22,825	15,966	13,285	10,888	9,003	6,720	7,841	5,653	-------	-------
28,882	22,095	19,113	14,719	14,044	9,532	7,303	5,503	3,748	1,995
-------	-------	-------	-------	-------	-------	-------	-------	-------	-------
15,898	14,753	11,075	-------	-------	-------	-------	-------	-------	-------
8,100	5,769	5,258	4,026	4,431	3,385	-------	-------	-------	-------
12,322	14,135	18,906	8,600	14,133	8,773	-------	-------	-------	-------
16,634	16,786	14,206	9,387	10,357	3,913	-------	-------	-------	-------
33,216	25,836	19,707	18,265	16,699	14,228	14,350	7,905	7,486	2,870
-------	-------	-------	-------	-------	-------	-------	-------	10,085	-------
287,104	242,039	216,090	191,418	174,491	119,460	102,193	49,826	41,351	24,552
20,947	17,985	14,685	11,582	4,727	5,008	4,640	5,140	2,896	1,007
13,039	12,541	11,575	10,552	8,494	7,390	5,060	4,489	2,354	1,549
25,777	19,613	17,785	12,981	17,718	11,339	7,898	5,936	4,912	4,539
39,578	27,642	28,562	18,015	25,360	16,561	14,132	7,575	6,065	2,200
11,548	11,318	8,578	-------	-------	-------	-------	-------	-------	-------
11,116	10,230	8,440	5,110	-------	-------	-------	-------	-------	-------
15,421	9,390	7,344	6,456	5,828	4,515	-------	-------	-------	-------
5,031	4,326	4,405	3,553	4,076	3,802	3,237	3,356	2,635	1,020
9,072	7,373	7,161	4,867	5,297	5,120	4,700	5,147	3,862	3,291
8,479	8,062	7,504	5,423	7,180	4,561	3,525	4,028	3,026	-------
20,197	15,715	14,714	10,152	11,499	11,098	8,548	7,646	5,660	3,955
12,330	11,359	9,686	6,762	7,930	7,317	5,776	5,677	3,854	2,990
52,906	40,250	40,004	25,553	23,104	22,253	15,238	12,591	10,085	5,048
18,940	14,884	12,663	9,730	12,674	11,761	8,674	7,205	12,063	7,369
34,145	22,416	19,891	13,860	16,816	13,697	8,950	6,442	-------	-------
13,335	10,160	6,887	5,586	5,406	6,364	4,598	2,864	1,723	-------
17,625	12,655	9,638	7,928	-------	-------	-------	-------	-------	-------
19,070	16,647	17,815	12,419	16,078	9,040	-------	-------	-------	-------
24,464	20,167	17,957	12,451	12,091	7,724	4,410	2,121	-------	-------
18,520	17,304	13,526	11,685	10,389	8,203	1,838	-------	-------	-------
20,705	14,234	8,728	4,528	4,324	3,400	-------	-------	-------	-------
10,327	5,903	5,160	-------	-------	-------	-------	-------	-------	-------
9,628	6,700	5,190	3,330	4,708	3,408	2,649	2,286	2,517	-------
15,125	12,466	10,005	-------	-------	-------	-------	-------	-------	-------
10,285	8,863	7,667	5,114	7,312	6,720	4,638	3,084	2,338	-------
3,685	3,748	2,776	-------	-------	-------	-------	-------	-------	-------
15,994	15,062	12,809	10,499	11,671	13,245	10,910	8,629	-------	-------
9,648	7,082	5,846	4,954	6,876	-------	-------	-------	-------	-------

POPULATION OF ALL INCORPORATE

	1980	1970	1960	1950	1940	1930	1920	1910
Abbeville	12,391	10,996	10,414	9,338	6,672	4,356	3,461	2,907
Abita Springs	1,072	839	655	559	528	471	388	365
Addis	1,320	724	590	505	492	425	473	-------
Albany	857	700	557	-------	300	-------	-------	-------
Alexandria	51,565	41,557	40,279	34,913	27,066	23,025	17,510	11,213
Alexandria (SW)	- - - - -	3,151	2,782	-------	-------	-------	-------	-------
Allemands	2,920	2,318	1,167	-------	650	-------	-------	-------
Amelia	3,617	2,292	-------	-------	410	-------	-------	-------
Amite City	4,301	3,593	3,316	2,804	2,499	2,536	1,854	1,677
Anacoco	90	-------	-------	-------	-------	-------	-------	-------
Anandale	- - - - -	1,779	2,827	-------	-------	-------	-------	-------
Angie	311	317	254	230	187	207	230	346
Arabi	10,248	-------	-------	-------	-------	-------	-------	-------
Arcadia	3,403	2,970	2,547	2,241	1,601	1,809	1,280	1,079
Arnaudville	1,679	1,673	1,184	872	640	483	408	279
Ashland	307	211	-------	-------	210	-------	-------	-------
Athens	419	387	406	487	491	461	493	514
Atlanta	127	-------	-------	-------	-------	-------	-------	-------
Avondale	6,699	-------	-------	-------	-------	-------	-------	-------
Baker	12,865	8,281	4,823	762	150	-------	-------	-------
Baldwin	2,644	2,117	1,548	1,138	984	822	964	-------
Ball	3,405	-------	-------	-------	-------	-------	-------	-------
Barataria	1,123	-------	-------	-------	-------	-------	-------	-------
Basile	2,635	1,779	1,932	1,572	1,132	403	552	-------
Baskin	286	177	238	117	330	416	654	-------
Bastrop	15,527	14,713	15,193	12,769	6,626	5,121	1,216	854
Baton Rouge	219,419	165,963	152,419	125,629	34,719	30,729	21,782	14,897
Bayou Blue	2,729	-------	-------	-------	-------	-------	-------	-------
Bayou Cane	15,723	9,077	3,173	2,212	-------	-------	-------	-------
Bayou Vista	5,805	5,121	-------	-------	-------	-------	-------	-------
Belcher	436	-------	-------	-------	-------	-------	-------	-------
Belle Chasse	5,412	-------	-------	-------	-------	-------	-------	-------
Benton	1,864	1,493	1,336	741	519	402	-------	318
Bernice	1,956	1,794	1,641	1,524	1,071	965	662	781
Berwick	4,466	4,168	3,880	2,619	1,906	1,679	1,691	2,183
Bienville	249	287	305	445	357	381	478	606
Blanchard	1,128	806	-------	-------	200	-------	-------	-------
Bogalusa	16,976	18,412	21,423	17,798	14,604	14,029	8,245	-------
Bonita	503	533	574	504	422	507	310	273
Bossier City	50,817	41,595	32,776	15,470	5,786	4,003	1,094	775
Bourg	2,073	-------	-------	-------	-------	-------	-------	-------
Boyce	1,198	1,240	1,094	981	732	820	1,060	865
Breaux Bridge	5,922	4,942	3,303	2,492	1,668	1,399	1,171	1,339
Broadmoor	7,051	-------	-------	-------	-------	-------	-------	-------
Broussard	2,923	1,707	1,600	1,237	791	806	602	499
Brownsville -Bawcomville	7,252	-------	-------	-------	-------	-------	-------	-------
Brusly	1,762	1,282	544	493	433	345	400	390
Bryceland	94	65	89	123	139	176	243	-------
Bunkie	5,364	5,395	5,188	4,666	3,575	2,464	1,743	1,765
Buras-Triumph	4,137	4,113	4,908	1,799	750	-------	-------	-------
Calvin	263	286	232	-------	250	-------	-------	-------
Cameron	1,736	-------	-------	-------	-------	----- --	-------	-------
Campti	1,069	1,078	1,045	1,014	1,004	999	670	664
Cankton	303	-------	-------	-------	-------	-------	-------	-------
Carencro	3,712	2,302	1,519	1,587	914	684	630	609
Carlyss	1,806	-------	-------	-------	-------	-------	-------	-------
Carville	1,037	-------	-------	-------	-------	-------	-------	-------
Castor	195	178	142	171	244	256	-------	-------
Chalmette	33,847	-------	-------	-------	-------	-------	-------	-------
Chataignier	431	-------	-------	-------	-------	-------	-------	-------
Chatham	714	827	758	833	605	391	186	181
Chauvin	3,338	-------	-------	-------	-------	-------	-------	-------
Cheneyville	865	1,082	1,037	918	913	835	678	498
Choudrant	809	555	465	395	438	394	393	-------
Church Point	4,599	3,865	3,606	2,897	1,892	1,037	557	481
Claiborne	6,278	-------	-------	-------	-------	-------	-------	-------
Clarence	612	448	286	-------	94	-------	-------	-------
Clarks	931	889	940	-------	-------	-------	-------	-------
Clayton	1,204	1,103	882	657	(500)	-------	--------	-------
Clinton	1,919	1,884	1,568	1,383	998	702	701	918
Colfax	1,680	1,892	1,934	1,651	1,354	1,141	1,449	1,049
Collinston	439	397	497	546	482	473	354	333

AND UNINCORPORATED PLACES

1900	1890	1880	1870	1860	1850	1840	1830	1820	1810
1,536	637	255	545	----	----	----	----	----	----
----	----	----	----	----	----	----	----	----	----
----	----	----	----	----	----	----	----	----	----
5,648	2,861	1,800	1,218	1,461	672	----	----	----	----
----	----	----	----	----	----	----	----	----	----
----	----	----	----	----	----	----	----	----	----
1,547	1,510	1,120	910	----	----	----	----	----	----
----	----	----	----	----	----	----	----	----	----
----	----	----	----	----	----	----	----	----	----
----	----	----	----	----	----	----	----	----	----
954	862	----	----	----	----	----	----	----	----
327	----	149	----	----	----	----	----	----	----
----	----	----	----	----	----	----	----	----	----
----	----	----	----	----	----	----	----	----	----
----	----	----	----	----	----	----	----	----	----
----	----	----	----	----	----	----	----	----	----
----	----	----	----	----	----	----	----	----	----
----	----	----	----	----	----	----	----	----	----
----	----	----	----	----	----	----	----	----	----
787	----	822	521	----	----	----	----	----	----
11,269	10,478	7,197	6,498	5,428	3,905	2,269	----	----	----
----	----	----	----	----	----	----	----	----	----
----	----	----	----	----	----	----	----	----	----
----	----	----	----	----	----	----	----	----	----
----	----	----	----	----	----	----	----	----	----
----	----	----	----	----	----	----	----	----	----
713	769	796	----	----	----	----	----	----	----
263	----	----	----	----	----	----	----	----	----
----	----	----	----	----	----	----	----	----	----
----	----	----	----	----	----	----	----	----	----
----	----	----	----	----	----	----	----	----	----
----	----	----	----	----	----	----	----	----	----
832	301	----	----	----	----	----	----	----	----
654	654	443	----	----	----	----	----	----	----
----	----	----	----	----	----	----	----	----	----
290	----	----	----	----	----	----	----	----	----
----	----	----	----	----	----	----	----	----	----
----	315	216	----	----	----	----	----	----	----
----	----	----	----	----	----	----	----	----	----
873	299	----	----	----	----	----	----	----	----
----	----	----	----	----	----	----	----	----	----
----	----	----	----	----	----	----	----	----	----
----	310	101	----	----	----	----	----	----	----
----	----	----	----	----	----	----	----	----	----
445	289	----	----	----	----	----	----	----	----
----	----	----	----	----	----	----	----	----	----
----	----	----	----	----	----	----	----	----	----
----	----	----	----	----	----	----	----	----	----
----	----	----	----	----	----	----	----	----	----
----	----	----	----	----	----	----	----	----	----
278	----	----	----	----	----	----	----	----	----
----	----	----	----	----	----	----	----	----	----
----	----	----	----	----	----	----	----	----	----
----	----	----	----	----	----	----	----	----	----
----	----	----	----	----	----	----	----	----	----
960	974	1,129	----	----	----	----	----	----	----
190	161	----	----	----	----	----	----	----	----
----	----	----	----	----	----	----	----	----	----

	1980	1970	1960	1950	1940	1930	1920	1910
Columbia	687	1,000	1,021	920	947	760	434	500
Converse	449	375	291	311	314	291	-------	-------
Cooper Road	- - - - -	9,034	-------	-------	-------	-------	-------	-------
Cottonport	1,911	1,924	1,581	1,534	1,196	1,015	720	866
Cotton Valley	1,445	1,261	1,145	1,188	1,133	-------	-------	-------
Coushatta	2,084	1,492	1,663	1,788	1,289	959	962	564
Covington	7,892	7,170	6,754	5,113	4,123	3,208	2,942	2,601
Crowley	16,036	16,104	15,617	12,784	9,523	7,656	6,108	5,099
Crozier	1,150	-------	-------	-------	-------	-------	-------	-------
Cullen	1,869	1,956	2,194	-------	(1,400)	-------	-------	-------
Cut Off	5,049	-------	-------	-------	-------	-------	-------	-------
Delcambre	2,216	1,975	1,857	1,463	1,255	640	443	308
Delhi	3,290	2,887	2,514	1,861	1,192	1,043	980	685
Delta	295	153	111	150	183	-------	-------	-------
Denham Springs	8,563	6,752	5,991	2,053	1,233	1,002	500	574
De Quincy	3,966	3,448	3,928	3,837	3,252	3,589	1,873	715
De Ridder	11,057	8,030	7,188	5,799	3,750	3,747	3,535	2,100
Destrehan	2,382	-------	-------	-------	-------	-------	-------	-------
Dixie Inn	453	456	399	-------	(350)	-------	-------	-------
Dodson	469	457	512	375	442	436	410	845
Donaldsonville	7,901	7,367	6,082	4,150	3,889	3,788	3,745	4,090
Downsville	213	-------	-------	-------	-------	-------	-------	-------
Doyline	801	716	1,061	1,170	(600)	-------	-------	-------
Dry Prong	526	352	360	377	528	-------	-------	-------
Dubach	1,161	1,096	1,013	703	749	608	726	714
Dubberly	421	212	249	-------	(250)	-------	-------	-------
Duson	1,253	1,199	1,033	707	463	396	192	120
East Hodge	439	-------	-------	-------	-------	-------	-------	-------
Edgefield	312	201	-------	-------	-------	-------	-------	-------
Elizabeth	454	504	1,030	1,113	-------	-------	-------	-------
Elton	1,450	1,598	1,595	1.434	901	742	995	-------
Epps	672	448	411	308	391	-------	-------	-------
Erath	2,133	2,024	2,019	1,514	1,408	895	713	575
Eros	158	164	176	195	289	293	1,184	898
Estelle	12,724	-------	-------	-------	-------	-------	-------	-------
Estherwood	691	661	639	547	539	572	571	544
Eunice	12,479	11,390	11,326	8,184	5,242	3,597	3,272	1,684
Evergreen	272	307	325	382	384	298	262	299
Farmerville	3,768	3,416	2,727	2,173	1,428	1,137	632	598
Fenton	491	404	429	-------	(350)	-------	-------	-------
Ferriday	4,472	5,239	4,563	3,847	2,857	2,502	1,044	577
Fisher	325	-------	-------	-------	-------	-------	-------	-------
Florien	964	639	496	-------	266	-------	-------	-------
Folsom	319	249	225	166	(450)	-------	-------	-------
Fordoche	676	488	-------	-------	226	-------	-------	-------
Forest	299	221	-------	-------	(100)	-------	-------	-------
Forest Hill	494	370	302	365	302	304	-------	-------
Fort Polk North	1,644	-------	-------	-------	-------	-------	-------	-------
Franklin	9,584	9,325	8,673	6,144	4,274	3,271	3,504	3,857
Franklinton	4,119	3,562	3,141	2,342	1,579	963	964	814
French Settlement	761	-------	-------	-------	-------	-------	-------	-------
Galliano	5,159	-------	-------	-------	-------	-------	-------	-------
Garyville	2,856	2,474	2,389	1,850	(1,800)	-------	-------	-------
Georgetown	381	306	321	355	(150)	-------	-------	-------
Gibsland	1,354	1,380	1,150	1,085	1,023	1,090	798	1,065
Gilbert	800	746	472	452	428	496	442	-------
Gilliam	244	211	-------	-------	(750)	-------	-------	-------
Glenmora	1,479	1,651	1,477	1,566	1,452	1,875	2,298	-------
Golden Meadow	2,282	2,681	3,097	2,820	(300)	-------	-------	-------
Goldonna	526	337	292	364	256	250	-------	-------
Gonzales	7,287	4,512	3,252	1,642	857	462	-------	-------
Grambling	4,226	4,407	3,144	-------	(250)	-------	-------	-------
Gramercy	3,211	2,567	2,094	1,184	-------	-------	-------	-------
Grand Cane	252	284	322	286	377	393	378	485
Grand Coteau	1,165	1,301	1,165	1,103	662	580	470	392
Grand Isle	1,982	2,236	2,074	1,190	575	-------	-------	-------
Grayson	564	516	428	455	407	435	337	-------
Greensburg	662	652	512	423	389	262	286	268
Greenwood	1,043	212	-------	-------	(350)	-------	-------	-------
Gretna	20,615	24,875	21,967	13,813	10,879	9,584	7,197	-------
Grosse Tete	749	710	768	548	382	303	-------	-------
Gueydan	1,695	1,984	2,156	2,041	1,506	1,313	1,233	1,081
Hahnville	2,947	2,362	1,297	-------	(300)	-------	-------	-------
Hall Summit	276	190	-------	-------	-------	-------	-------	-------

1900	1890	1880	1870	1860	1850	1840	1830	1820	1810
382	352	219	......	......	......	......	......	......	......
......	......	......	......	......	......	......	......	......	......
......	......	......	......	......	......	......	......	......	......
505	......	......	......	......	......	......	......	......	......
......	......	......	......	......	......	......	......	......	......
600	619	488	......	......	......	......	......	......	......
1,205	976	567	585	......	......	......	......	......	......
4,214	240	......	......	......	......	......	......	......	......
......	......	......	......	......	......	......	......	......	......
......	......	......	......	......	......	......	......	......	......
......	......	......	......	......	......	......	......	......	......
507	620	315	......	......	......	......	......	......	......
......	320	399	......	......	......	......	......	......	......
......	......	......	......	......	......	......	......	......	......
......	......	......	......	......	......	......	......	......	......
......	......	......	......	......	......	......	......	......	......
......	......	......	......	......	......	......	......	......	......
......	......	......	......	......	......	......	......	......	......
4,105	3,121	2,600	1,573	......	......	......	......	......	......
......	......	......	......	......	......	......	......	......	......
......	......	......	......	......	......	......	......	......	......
......	......	......	......	......	......	......	......	......	......
......	......	......	......	......	......	......	......	......	......
......	......	......	......	......	......	......	......	......	......
......	......	......	......	......	......	......	......	......	......
......	......	......	......	......	......	......	......	......	......
......	......	......	......	......	......	......	......	......	......
......	......	......	......	......	......	......	......	......	......
215	......	......	......	......	......	......	......	......	......
......	......	......	......	......	......	......	......	......	......
......	......	......	......	......	......	......	......	......	......
......	......	......	......	......	......	......	......	......	......
316	......	......	......	......	......	......	......	......	......
322	......	......	......	......	......	......	......	......	......
458	472	712	272	......	......	......	......	......	......
......	......	......	......	......	......	......	......	......	......
......	......	......	......	......	......	......	......	......	......
......	......	......	......	......	......	......	......	......	......
......	......	......	......	......	......	......	......	......	......
......	......	......	......	......	......	......	......	......	......
......	......	......	......	......	......	......	......	......	......
......	......	......	......	......	......	......	......	......	......
2,692	2,127	1,702	......	......	......	......	......	......	......
236	97	......	......	......	......	......	......	......	......
......	......	......	......	......	......	......	......	......	......
......	......	......	......	......	......	......	......	......	......
......	......	......	......	......	......	......	......	......	......
558	......	......	......	......	......	......	......	......	......
......	......	......	......	......	......	......	......	......	......
......	......	......	......	......	......	......	......	......	......
......	......	......	......	......	......	......	......	......	......
......	......	......	......	......	......	......	......	......	......
......	......	......	......	......	......	......	......	......	......
......	......	......	......	......	......	......	......	......	......
385	351	......	......	......	......	......	......	......	......
521	333	302	470	......	......	......	......	......	......
......	......	......	......	......	......	......	......	......	......
......	......	......	......	......	......	......	......	......	......
315	280	297	160	......	......	......	......	......	......
......	......	......	......	......	......	......	......	......	......
......	......	......	......	......	......	......	......	......	......
......	......	......	......	......	......	......	......	......	......
376	......	......	......	......	......	......	......	......	......
......	......	......	......	......	......	......	......	......	......
......	......	......	......	......	......	......	......	......	......

	1980	1970	1960	1950	1940	1930	1920	1910
Hammond	15,043	12,487	10,563	8,010	6,033	6,072	3,855	2,942
Hammond East	1,937	1,342	-------	-------	-------	-------	-------	-------
Harahan	11,384	13,037	9.275	3,394	1,082	892	-------	-------
Harrisonburg	610	626	594	544	422	437	399	361
Harvey	22,709	6,347	-------	-------	-------	-------	-------	-------
Haughton	1,510	885	611	501	409	-------	-------	249
Haynesville	3,454	3,055	3,031	3,040	2,418	2,541	903	663
Heflin	279	-------	-------	-------	-------	-------	-------	-------
Henderson	1,560	-------	-------	-------	-------	-------	-------	-------
Hessmer	743	-------	-------	-------	-------	-------	-------	-------
Hodge	708	818	878	1,386	1,445	1,367	-------	-------
Hollywood	- - - - -	2,328	1,750	-------	-------	-------	-------	-------
Homer	4,307	4,483	4,665	4,749	3,497	2,909	3,305	1,855
Hornbeck	470	525	374	524	481	491	350	459
Hosston	480	428	-------	-------	-------	-------	-------	-------
Houma	32,602	30,922	22,561	11,506	9,052	6,531	5,160	5,024
Ida	306	370	-------	-------	-------	-------	-------	-------
Independence	1,684	1,770	1,941	1,606	1,498	1,700	1,032	1,004
Iota	1,326	1,271	1,245	1,162	1,000	827	802	769
Iowa	2,437	1,944	1,857	1,125	-------	-------	-------	-------
Jackson	3,133	4,697	1,824	6,772	5,384	3,966	2,320	2,146
Jamestown	131	153	-------	-------	-------	-------	-------	-------
Jeanerette	6,511	6,322	5,568	4,692	3,362	2,228	2,512	2,206
Jean Lafitte	936	-------	-------	-------	-------	-------	-------	-------
Jefferson	15,550	16,489	19,353	-------	-------	-------	-------	-------
Jena	4,332	2,431	2,098	1,438	946	1,007	520	680
Jennings	12,401	11,783	11,887	9,663	7,343	4,036	3,824	3,925
Jonesboro	5,061	5,072	3,848	3,097	2,639	1.949	837	1,134
Jonesville	2,828	2,761	2,347	1.954	2,080	1,123	1,029	287
Junction City	727	733	639	514	355	388	322	396
Kaplan	5,016	5,540	5,267	4,562	2,383	1,653	876	315
Keatchie	342	328	345	-------	-------	-------	-------	-------
Kenner	66,382	29,858	17,037	5,535	2,375	2,440	1,882	-------
Kentwood	2,667	2,736	2,607	2,417	1,854	1,726	3,059	3,609
Kilbourne	286	370	227	-------	-------	-------	-------	-------
Killian	611	-------	-------	-------	-------	-------	-------	-------
Kinder	2,603	2,307	2,299	2,003	1,415	962	1,148	635
Krotz Springs	1,374	1.435	1,057	866	630	449	247	-------
Labadieville	2,138	-------	-------	-------	-------	-------	-------	-------
Lacombe	5,146	-------	-------	-------	-------	-------	-------	-------
Lafayette	81,961	68,908	40,400	33,541	19,210	14,635	7,855	6,392
Lafayette (SW)	- - - - -	5,498	-------	-------	-------	-------	-------	-------
Lafitte	1,312	-------	-------	-------	-------	-------	-------	-------
Lake Arthur	3,615	3,551	3,541	2,849	2,131	1,602	1,882	1,093
Lake Charles	75,226	77,998	63,392	41,272	21,207	15,791	13,088	11,449
Lake Providence	6,361	6,183	5,781	4,123	3,711	2,867	1,917	1,568
Laplace	16,112	5,953	3,541	2,352	-------	-------	-------	-------
Larose	5,234	4,267	2,796	1,286	-------	-------	-------	-------
Lawtell	1,014	-------	-------	-------	-------	-------	-------	-------
Lecompte	1,661	1,518	1,485	1,433	1,311	1,247	1,034	1,058
Leesville	9,054	8,928	4,689	4,670	2,829	3,291	2,518	2,043
Leonville	1,143	512	526	514	451	408	325	-------
Lillie	172	160	-------	-------	-------	-------	-------	-------
Lisbon	138	151	229	-------	-------	-------	-------	-------
Little Farms	- - - - -	15,713	-------	-------	-------	-------	-------	-------
Livingston	1,260	1,398	1,183	-------	-------	-------	-------	-------
Livonia	980	611	430	-------	-------	-------	-------	-------
Lockport	2,424	2,398	2,221	1,388	877	866	803	669
Logansport	1,565	1,330	1,371	1,270	1,222	1,040	632	420
Lone Star	1,593	-------	-------	-------	-------	-------	-------	-------
Longstreet	281	182	283	224	263	308	146	-------
Loreauville	860	728	655	478	490	441	439	291
Lower Vacherie	3,189	-------	-------	-------	-------	-------	-------	-------
Lucky	370							
Luling	4,006	3,255	2,122	-------	-------	-------	-------	-------
Lutcher	4,730	3,911	3,274	2,198	2,167	1,481	1,700	-------
Madisonville	799	801	860	861	915	837	1,103	1,028
Mamou	3,194	3,275	2,938	2,254	1,379	800	649	-------
Mandeville	6,076	2,571	1,740	1,368	1,326	1,069	1,130	1,166
Mangham	867	544	521	554	572	714	462	470
Mansfield	6,485	6,432	5,839	4,440	4,065	3,837	2,564	1,799
Mansura	2,074	1,699	1,579	1,439	1,138	1,067	829	695
Many	3,988	3,112	3,164	1,681	1,474	1,239	663	683
Maringouin	1,291	1,365	1,168	898	708	518	399	447

1900	1890	1880	1870	1860	1850	1840	1830	1820	1810
1,511	692	277							
303	359	243							
1,157	1,132	718	80						
3,212	1,280	1,084	593						
2,012	1,276	880	934						
1,905	1,309	698							
1,539	412								
	172	90							
389									
		970							
1,313									
3,314	2,106								
6,680	3,442	838							
1,256	642		320	430					
1,148									
401									
688	281								
779	469	441							
1,029	1,012	753	541						
847	908	770	813						
408									
354	133	143							

	1980	1970	1960	1950	1940	1930	1920	1910
Marion	989	796	685	685	481	444	371	226
Marksville	5,113	4,519	4,257	3,635	1,811	1,527	1,185	1,076
Marrero	36,548	29,015	-------	-------	-------	-------	-------	-------
Martin	584	-------	-------	-------	-------	-------	-------	-------
Maurice	478	476	411	335	420	330	-------	-------
McNary	240	220	-------	267	151	211	1,318	-------
Melville	1,764	2,076	1,939	1,901	1,828	1,541	958	1,093
Mermentau	771	756	716	636	571	394	364	323
Mer Rouge	802	819	853	784	713	669	656	536
Merryville	1,286	1,286	1,232	1,383	1,216	2,626	2,963	-------
Metairie	164.160	136,477	-------	-------	-------	-------	-------	-------
Mimosa Park	3,737	1,624	-------	-------	-------	-------	-------	-------
Minden	15,084	13,996	12,785	9,787	6,677	5,623	6,105	3,092
Monroe	57,597	56,374	52,219	41,272	28,309	26,028	12,675	10,209
Montgomery	843	923	866	695	495	383	222	174
Montpelier	219	211	197	-------	-------	-------	-------	-------
Mooringsport	911	830	864	709	748	802	992	-------
Moreauville	853	807	815	835	815	600	867	728
Morgan City	16,114	16,586	13,540	9,759	6,969	5,985	5,429	5,477
Morganza	846	836	937	817	744	608	332	296
Morse	835	759	682	679	742	549	482	237
Moss Bluff	7,004	-------	-------	-------	-------	-------	-------	-------
Mound	40	78	107	105	145	-------	-------	-------
Mount Lebanon	105	102	-------	-------	-------	-------	-------	-------
Napeleonville	829	1,008	1,148	1,260	1,301	1,180	1,171	1,201
Natchez	527	-------	-------	-------	-------	-------	-------	-------
Natchitoches	16,664	15,974	13,924	9.914	6,812	4,547	3,388	2,532
Newellton	1,726	1,403	1,453	1,280	789	627	541	424
New Iberia	32,766	30,147	29,062	16,467	13,747	8,003	6,278	7,499
Newllano	2,213	1,800	264	277	-------	-------	-------	-------
New Orleans	557,927	593,471	627,525	570,445	494,537	458,762	387,219	339,075
New Roads	3,924	3,945	3,965	2,818	2,255	1,473	1,294	1,352
New Sarpy	2,249	1,643	1,259	-------	-------	-------	-------	-------
Noble	194	209	206	238	238	268	316	453
Norco	4,416	4,773	4,682	-------	-------	-------	-------	-------
North Hodge	573	640	680	-------	-------	-------	-------	-------
Norwood	421	348	427	414	-------	-------	-------	-------
Oakdale	7 155	7,301	6,618	5,598	3,933	3,188	4,016	-------
Oak Grove	2,214	1,980	1,797	1,796	1,654	1,241	700	398
Oak Ridge	257	276	287	287	373	260	318	332
Oberlin	1,764	1,857	1,794	1,544	962	790	623	232
Oil City	1,323	907	1,430	422	-------	-------	-------	-------
Olla	1,603	1,387	1,246	1,115	691	740	266	260
Opelousas	18,903	20,387	17,417	11,659	9,980	6,299	4,437	4,623
Paincourtville	2,004	-------	-------	-------	-------	-------	-------	-------
Palmetto	327	312	430	457	444	408	168	-------
Parks	545	491	413	460	460	409	766	466
Patterson	4,693	4,409	2,923	1,938	1,800	2,206	2,538	2,998
Pearl River	1,693	1,361	964	637	612	264	364	277
Pierre Part	3,153	-------	-------	-------	-------	-------	-------	-------
Pine Prairie	734	515	387	-------	-------	-------	-------	-------
Pineville	12,034	8,951	8,636	6,423	4,297	3,612	2,188	1,212
Pioneer	221	188	154	-------	-------	-------	-------	-------
Plain Dealing	1,213	1,300	1,357	1,321	1,085	1,142	655	474
Plaquemine	7,521	7,739	7,689	5,747	5,049	5,124	4,632	4.955
Plaquemine SW	1,467	1,224	1,272	-------	-------	-------	-------	-------
Plaucheville	196	224	228	227	367	366	335	380
Pleasant Hill	776	826	907	856	737	807	554	442
Pollock	399	341	366	421	317	376	353	675
Pontchatoula	5,469	4,545	4,727	4,090	4,001	2,898	955	1,055
Port Allen	6,114	5,728	5,026	3,097	1,898	1,524	920	-------
Port Barre	2,625	2,133	1,876	1,066	850	674	588	-------
Port Sulphur	3,318	3,022	2,868	-------	-------	-------	-------	-------
Port Vincent	450	387	340	-------	-------	-------	-------	-------
Powhatan	279	277	-------	-------	-------	-------	-------	-------
Poydras	5,722	-------	-------	-------	-------	-------	-------	-------
Prien	6,224	-------	-------	-------	-------	-------	-------	-------
Provencal	695	530	570	-------	-------	-------	-------	262
Quitman	231	169	185	204	212	207	177	215
Raceland	6,302	4,880	3,666	2,025	-------	-------	-------	-------
Rayne	9,066	9,510	8,634	6,485	4,974	3,710	2,720	2,247
Rayville	4,610	3,962	4,052	3,138	2,412	2,076	1,499	1,079
Reeves	199	214	151	106	120	139	243	-------

1900	1890	1880	1870	1860	1850	1840	1830	1820	1810
-------	-------	-------	-------	-------	-------	-------	-------	-------	-------
837	-------	-------	-------	-------	-------	-------	-------	-------	-------
-------	-------	-------	-------	-------	-------	-------	-------	-------	-------
-------	-------	-------	-------	-------	-------	-------	-------	-------	-------
-------	-------	-------	-------	-------	-------	-------	-------	-------	-------
-------	-------	-------	-------	-------	-------	-------	-------	-------	-------
517	361	-------	-------	-------	-------	-------	-------	-------	-------
465	-------	-------	-------	-------	-------	-------	-------	-------	-------
-------	-------	-------	-------	-------	-------	-------	-------	-------	-------
-------	-------	-------	-------	-------	-------	-------	-------	-------	-------
-------	-------	-------	-------	-------	-------	-------	-------	-------	-------
-------	-------	-------	-------	-------	-------	-------	-------	-------	-------
1,561	1,298	1,113	-------	-------	-------	-------	-------	-------	-------
5,428	3,256	2,070	1,949	-------	435	-------	-------	-------	-------
158	144	-------	-------	-------	-------	-------	-------	-------	-------
-------	-------	-------	-------	-------	-------	-------	-------	-------	-------
-------	-------	-------	-------	-------	-------	-------	-------	-------	-------
-------	-------	-------	-------	-------	-------	-------	-------	-------	-------
2,332	2,291	2,015	-------	-------	-------	-------	-------	-------	-------
-------	-------	-------	-------	-------	-------	-------	-------	-------	-------
-------	-------	-------	-------	-------	-------	-------	-------	-------	-------
-------	-------	-------	-------	-------	-------	-------	-------	-------	-------
-------	-------	-------	-------	-------	-------	-------	-------	-------	-------
-------	-------	-------	-------	-------	-------	-------	-------	-------	-------
945	723	497	-------	-------	-------	-------	-------	-------	-------
-------	-------	-------	-------	-------	-------	-------	-------	-------	-------
2,388	1,820	2,785	1,401	-------	-------	-------	-------	-------	-------
-------	-------	-------	-------	-------	-------	-------	-------	-------	-------
6,815	3,447	2,709	1,472	-------	-------	-------	-------	-------	-------
-------	-------	-------	-------	-------	-------	-------	-------	-------	-------
287,104	242,039	216,090	191,418	168,675	116,375	102,193	46,082	27,176	17,242
770	-------	-------	-------	-------	-------	-------	-------	-------	-------
-------	-------	-------	-------	-------	-------	-------	-------	-------	-------
-------	-------	-------	-------	-------	-------	-------	-------	-------	-------
-------	-------	-------	-------	-------	-------	-------	-------	-------	-------
-------	-------	-------	-------	-------	-------	-------	-------	-------	-------
-------	-------	-------	-------	-------	-------	-------	-------	-------	-------
-------	-------	-------	-------	-------	-------	-------	-------	-------	-------
348	296	-------	-------	-------	-------	-------	-------	-------	-------
213	-------	-------	-------	-------	-------	-------	-------	-------	-------
-------	-------	-------	-------	-------	-------	-------	-------	-------	-------
2,951	1,572	1,676	1,546	623	-------	-------	-------	-------	-------
-------	-------	-------	-------	-------	-------	-------	-------	-------	-------
-------	-------	-------	-------	-------	-------	-------	-------	-------	-------
-------	1,414	500	-------	-------	-------	-------	-------	-------	-------
-------	-------	-------	-------	-------	-------	-------	-------	-------	-------
-------	-------	-------	-------	-------	-------	-------	-------	-------	-------
617	540	763	414	-------	-------	-------	-------	-------	-------
-------	-------	-------	-------	-------	-------	-------	-------	-------	-------
258	-------	-------	-------	-------	-------	-------	-------	-------	-------
3,590	3,222	2,061	1,460	1,025	-------	-------	-------	-------	-------
-------	-- ----	-------	-------	-------	-------	-------	-------	-------	-------
300	-------	-------	-------	-------	-------	-------	-------	-------	-------
637	-------	-------	-------	-------	-------	-------	-------	-------	-------
711	459	293	-------	-------	-------	-------	-------	-------	-------
-------	-------	-------	-------	-------	-------	-------	-------	-------	-------
-------	-------	-------	-------	-------	-------	-------	-------	-------	-------
-------	-------	-------	-------	-------	-------	-------	-------	-------	-------
-------	-------	-------	-------	-------	-------	-------	-------	-------	-------
-------	-------	-------	-------	-------	-------	-------	-------	-------	-------
-------	-------	-------	-------	-------	-------	-------	-------	-------	-------
-------	-------	-------	-------	-------	-------	-------	-------	-------	-------
-------	-------	-------	-------	-------	-------	-------	-------	-------	-------
1,007	560	-------	-------	-------	-------	-------	-------	-------	-------
-------	366	216	-------	-------	-------	-------	-------	-------	-------
-------	-------	-------	-------	-------	-------	-------	-------	-------	-------

	1980	1970	1960	1950	1940	1930	1920	1910
Reserve	7,288	6,381	5,297	4,465	-------	-------	-------	-------
Richmond	505	-------	--------	-------	-------	-------	-------	-------
Richwood	1,223	-------	-------	-------	-------	-------	-------	-------
Ridgecrest	895	-------	-------	-------	-------	-------	-------	-------
Ringgold	1,655	1,731	953	1,007	1,006	618	335	-------
River Ridge	17,146	-------	-------	-------	-------	-------	-------	-------
Robeline	238	274	308	350	355	328	495	438
Rodessa	337	273	-------	-------	-------	-------	-------	-------
Rosedale	658	621	674	-------	-------	-------	-------	-------
Roseland	1,346	1,273	1,254	1,038	873	1,139	603	586
Rosepine	953	587	414	334	407	214	-------	325
Ruston	20,585	17,365	13,991	10,372	7,107	4,400	3,389	3,377
St. Francisville	1,471	1,603	1,661	936	821	830	673	966
St. Joseph	1,687	1,864	1,653	1,218	1,096	864	734	740
St. Martinville	7,695	7,153	6,468	4,614	3,501	2,455	2,465	2,318
Saint Rose	- - - - -	2,106	1,099	-------	-------	-------	-------	-------
Saline	293	307	329	357	381	346	390	346
Samtown	- - - - -	4,210	4,008	-------	-------	-------	-------	-------
Sarepta	831	882	737	-------	-------	-------	-------	-------
Scotlandville	15,113	22,557	-------	-------	-------	-------	-------	-------
Scott	2,239	1,334	902	688	407	344	324	239
Seymourville	2,891	2,506	1,788	-------	-------	-------	-------	-------
Shongaloo	163	173	-------	-------	-------	-------	-------	-------
Shreveport	205,820	182,064	164,372	127,206	98,167	76,655	43,874	28,015
Sibley	1,211	869	595	623	405	422	900	-------
Sicily Island	691	630	761	-------	-------	-------	-------	-------
Sikes	226	237	233	342	-------	-------	-------	-------
Simmesport	2,293	2,027	2,125	1,510	1,215	638	-------	-------
Simpson	534	491	-------	-------	-------	-------	-------	-------
Simsboro	553	412	363	-------	-------	-------	-------	282
Slaughter	729	580	403	290	306	327	215	287
Slidell	26,719	16,101	6,356	3,464	2,864	2,807	2,958	2,188
Sorrento	1,197	1,182	1,151	-------	-------	-------	-------	-------
South Fort Polk	12,498	15,600	-------	-------	-------	-------	-------	-------
South Mansfield	1,463	439	616	276	433	462	441	-------
Spearsville	181	197	-------	-------	-------	-------	-------	-------
Springfield	424	423	268	-------	-------	-------	-------	-------
Springhill	6,516	6,496	6,437	3,383	2,822	1,546	748	-------
Stanley	151	145	234	-------	-------	-------	-------	-------
Sterlington	1,400	1,118	-------	-------	-------	-------	-------	-------
Stonewall	1,175	-------	-------	-------	-------	-------	-------	-------
Sulphur	19,709	15,247	11,429	5,996	3,504	1,888	1,714	-------
Sulphur South	- - - - -	1,108	1,351	-------	-------	-------	-------	-------
Sun	404	-------	-------	-------	-------	-------	-------	-------
Sunset	2,300	1,675	1,307	1,080	630	520	433	377
Tallulah	11,634	9.643	9,413	7,758	5,712	3,332	1,316	847
Tangipahoa	493	469	465	353	319	304	252	394
Terrytown	23,548	13,832	-------	-------	-------	-------	-------	-------
Thibodaux	15,810	15,028	13,403	7,730	5,851	4.442	3,526	3,824
Tickfaw	571	370	317	-------	-------	-------	-------	-------
Timberlane	11,579	-------	-------	-------	-------	-------	-------	-------
Trout-Good Pine	1,033	-------	-------	-------	-------	-------	-------	-------
Tullos	776	600	594	732	589	707	-------	-------
Turkey Creek	366	280	279	-------	-------	-------	-------	-------
Urania	849	-------	-------	-------	-------	-------	-------	-------
Vacherie	2,169	2,145	-------	-------	-------	-------	-------	-------
Varnado	249	320	331	306	315	204	275	-------
Vidalia	5,936	5,538	4,313	1,614	1,318	1,141	1,246	1,345
Vienna	519	-------	-------	-------	-------	----- --	-------	-------
Ville Platte	9,201	9,692	7,512	6,633	3,721	1,722	1,364	603
Vinton	3,631	3,454	2,987	2,597	1,787	1,989	1,441	-------
Violet	11,678	-------	-------	-------	-------	-------	-------	-------
Vivian	4,146	4,046	2,624	2,426	2,460	1,646	1,864	826
Waggaman	9,004	-------	-------	-------	-------	-------	-------	-------
Walker	2,957	1,363	912	500	424	524	371	592
Wardville	- - - - -	1,087	1,086	-------	-------	-------	-------	-------
Washington	1,266	1,473	1,291	1,291	1,264	1,004	1,041	1,528
Waterproof	1,339	1,438	1,412	1,180	592	420	340	445
Welsh	3,515	3,203	3,332	2,416	1,822	1,514	1,456	1,250
West Ferriday	1,399	-------	-------	-------	-------	-------	-------	-------
Westlake	5,246	4,082	3,311	1,871	----	----	----	----
West Monroe	14,993	14,868	15,215	10,302	8,560	6,566	2,240	1,127
Westwego	12,663	11,402	9,815	8,328	4,992	3,987	----	----
White Castle	2,160	2,206	2,253	1,839	1,692	1,499	1,566	2,289

1900	1890	1880	1870	1860	1850	1840	1830	1820	1810
464	676								
	233	94							
1,324	767								
1,059	950	721							
717	473	486							
1,926	1,814	1,606	1,190						
16,013	11,979	8,009	4,607	2,190	1,728				
259									
1,129	364								
		1,340	519						
297		259	236						
3,253	2,078	1,515	1,922	1,039					
1,022	821	449							
163			135						
1,197	1,064	1,194	907						
298									
320	200								
775	447								
1,850	603								

	1980	1970	1960	1950	1940	1930	1920	1910
Wilson	656	606	----	----	----	----	----	762
Winnfield	7,311	7,142	7,022	5,629	4,512	3,721	2,975	2,925
Winnsboro	5,921	5,349	4,437	3,655	2,834	1,965	1,176	821
Wisner	1,424	1,339	1,254	738	617	692	----	----
Woodworth	412	409	320	392	----	----	----	----
Youngsville	1,053	1,002	946	769	647	536	361	328
Zachary	7,297	4,964	3,268	1,542	730	626	524	419
Zwolle	2,602	2,169	1,326	1,555	1,500	1,264	909	973

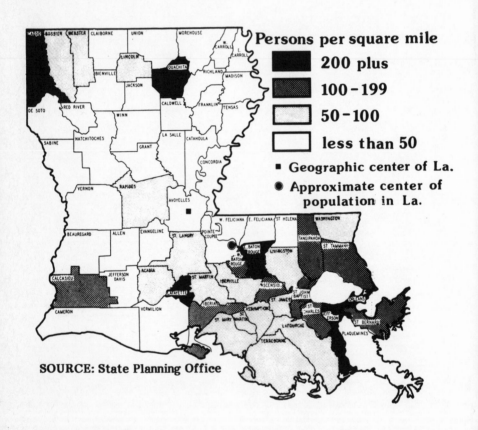

Persons per square mile

200 plus
100 - 199
50 - 100
less than 50

■ Geographic center of La.
● Approximate center of
population in La.

SOURCE: State Planning Office

1900	1890	1880	1870	1860	1850	1840	1830	1820	1810
----	----	----	-------	-------	-------	-------	-------	-------	-------
----	----	----	-------	-------	-------	-------	-------	-------	-------
----	----	----	-------	-------	-------	-------	-------	-------	-------
----	----	----	-------	-------	-------	-------	-------	-------	-------
200	----	----	-------	-------	-------	-------	-------	-------	-------
465	----	----	-------	-------	-------	-------	-------	-------	-------
276	----	----	-------	-------	-------	-------	-------	-------	-------

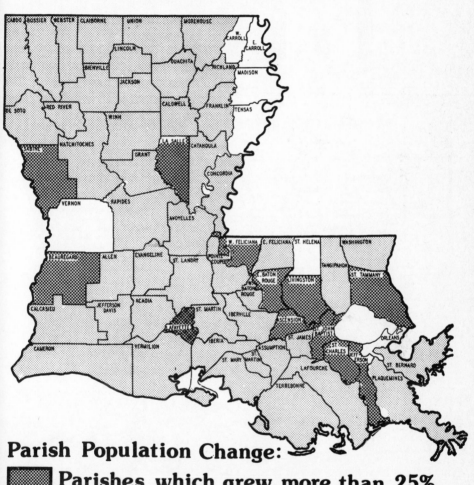

Parish Population Change:

Parishes which grew more than 25%.

Parishes which declined in population.

All Others (.6-24.6% growth).

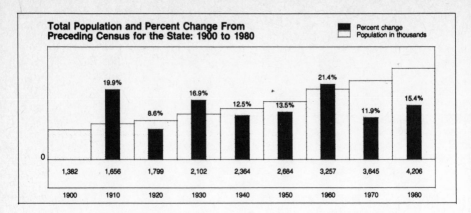

Total Population and Percent Change From Preceding Census for the State: 1900 to 1980

■ Percent change
□ Population in thousands

	19.9%	8.6%	16.9%	12.5%	13.5%	21.4%	11.9%	15.4%
1,382	1,656	1,799	2,102	2,364	2,684	3,257	3,645	4,206
1900	1910	1920	1930	1940	1950	1960	1970	1980

STATE METROPOLITAN STATISTICAL AREAS

BUREAU OF THE CENSUS

MSA boundaries are as defined on June 30, 1983   **U.S. Department of Commerce**

Population of Major Louisiana Cities—1940 to 1986

	1986 (est.)	1980	1970	1960	1950	1940
1. New Orleans	563,811	557,927	593,471	627,525	570,445	494,537
2. Baton Rouge	244,352	219,419	165,921	152,419	125,629	34,719
3. Shreveport	215,512	205,820	182,064	164,372	127,206	98,167
4. Metairie	164,160*	164,160	136,477	-------	-------	-------
5. Lafayette	92,113	81,961	69,908	40,400	33,541	19,210
6. Lake Charles	77,476	75,226	77,988	63,392	41,272	21,207
7. Kenner	75,577	66,382	29,858	17,037	5,535	2,375
8. Monroe	58,963	57,597	56,378	52,219	41,272	28,309
9. Bossier City	56,815	50,817	43,769	32,776	15,470	5,786
10. Alexandria	52,446	51,565	41,811	40,279	34,913	27,066
11. Marrero	36,548*	36,548	29,015	-------	-------	-------
12. Houma	34,594	32,602	30,922	22,561	11,506	9,052
13. New Iberia	34,426	32,766	30,147	29,062	16,467	13,747
14. Chalmette	33,847*	33,847	-------	-------	-------	-------
15. Slidell	27,387	26,718	16,101	6,356	3,464	2,864
16. Terrytown	23,548*	23,548	13,832	-------	-------	-------
17. Harvey	22,709*	22,709	6,347	-------	-------	-------
18. Ruston	21,810	20,585	17,365	13,991	10,372	7,107
19. Sulphur	21,124	19,709	14,959	11,429	5,996	3,504
20. Gretna	20,095	20,615	24,875	21,967	13,813	10,879
21. Opelousas	19,317	18,903	20,387	17,417	11,659	8,980
22. Natchitoches	17,244	16,664	15,974	13,924	9,914	6,812
23. River Ridge	17,146	17,146	15,713	-------	-------	-------
24. Morgan City	17,058	16,114	16,586	13,540	9,759	6,969
25. Bogalusa	16,682	16,976	18,412	21,423	17,798	14,604
26. Laplace	16,112	16,112	5,953	3,541	2,352	-------
27. Crowley	16,095	16,036	16,104	15,617	12,784	9,523
28. Thibodaux	15,849	15,810	15,028	14,403	7,730	5,851
29. Bayou Cane	15,723*	15,723	9,077	3,173	2,212	-------
30. Jefferson	15,550*	15,550	16,489	19,353	-------	-------

*The 1980 census figure. No data available for 1986.

1986 estimates prepared by the Research Division, College of Administration and Business, Louisiana Tech University.

1986 LOUISIANA POPULATION ESTIMATES	MAJOR LABOR MARKET AREAS	1986 TOTAL POPULATION	WHITE MALE	WHITE FEMALE	MINORITY MALE	MINORITY FEMALE
	ALEXANDRIA LMA (RAPIDES PARISH)	140,683	49,269	52,081	18,287	21,046
	BATON ROUGE LMA (ASCENSION, EAST BATON ROUGE, LIVINGSTON, & WEST BATON ROUGE PARISHES)	557,211	196,900	201,412	74,563	84,336
	HOUMA-THIBODAUX LMA (LAFOURCHE & TERREBONNE PARISHES)	193,704	81,071	81,579	15,311	15,743
	LAFAYETTE LMA (LAFAYETTE & ST. MARTIN PARISHES)	225,912	84,763	87,080	26,263	27,806
	LAKE CHARLES LMA (CALCASIEU PARISH)	179,641	68,690	70,890	19,065	20,996
	MONROE LMA (OUACHITA PARISH)	144,883	48,286	53,523	20,635	22,439
	NEW ORLEANS LMA (JEFFERSON, ORLEANS, ST. BERNARD, ST. CHARLES, ST. JOHN, & ST. TAMMANY PARISHES)	1,354,429	439,826	459,485	212,971	242,147
	SHREVEPORT LMA (BOSSIER, CADDO, PARISHES)	369,003	117,622	126,091	57,822	67,468
	STATE OF LOUISIANA	4,574,469	1,565,945	1,623,147	654,861	730,516

Source: Louisiana Department of Labor, Office of Employment Security

POPULATION OF STANDARD METROPOLITAN STATISTICAL AREAS (SMSA's)

Rank and Population of Incorporated Places of 5,000 or More in 1980 and 1970

Incorporated Places	Parishes	1980 rank	Population 1980	1970
New Orleans city	Orleans	1	557 515	593 471
Baton Rouge city	East Baton Rouge	2	219 419	'165 921
Shreveport city	Total	3	205 820	182 064
	Bossier (pt. in)		872	250
	Caddo (pt. in)		204 948	181 814
Lafayette city	Lafayette	4	81 961	68 908
Lake Charles city	Calcasieu	5	75 226	77 998
Kenner city	Jefferson	6	66 382	29 858
Monroe city	Ouachita	7	57 597	56 374
Alexandria city	Rapides	8	51 565	'41 811
Bossier City city	Bossier	9	50 817	'43 769
New Iberia city	Iberia	10	32 766	30 147
Houma city	Terrebonne	11	32 602	30 922
Slidell city	St. Tammany	12	26 718	16 101
Gretna city	Jefferson	13	20 615	24 875
Ruston city	Lincoln	14	20 585	17 365
Sulphur city	Calcasieu	15	19 709	'14 959
Opelousas city	St. Landry	16	18 903	'20 387
Bogalusa city	Washington	17	16 976	18 412
Natchitoches city	Natchitoches	18	16 664	15 974
Morgan City city	St. Mary	19	16 114	16 586
Crowley city	Acadia	20	16 036	16 104
Thibodaux city	Lafourche	21	15 810	'15 028
Bastrop city	Morehouse	22	15 527	14 713
Minden city	Webster	23	15 084	13 996
Hammond city	Tangipahoa	24	15 043	12 487
West Monroe city	Ouachita	25	14 993	14 868
Baker city	East Baton Rouge	26	12 865	8 281
Westwego city	Jefferson	27	12 663	11 402
Eunice city	Total	28	12 479	11 390
	Acadia (pt. in)		221	112
	St. Landry (pt. in)		l2 258	11 278
Jennings city	Jefferson Davis	29	12 401	11 783
Abbeville city	Vermilion	30	12 391	10 996
Pineville city	Rapides	31	12 034	8 951
Tallulah city	Madison	32	11 634	9 643
Harahan city	Jefferson	33	11 384	13 037
De Ridder city	Total	34	11 057	8 030
	Beauregard (pt. in)		11 057	8 030
	Vernon (pt. in)		—	...
Franklin city	St. Mary	35	9 584	9 325
Ville Platte town	Evangeline	36	9 201	9 692
Rayne city	Acadia	37	9 066	9 510
Leesville city	Vernon	38	9 054	8 928
Denham Springs city	Livingston	39	8 563	6 752
St. Martinville city	St. Martin	40	7 965	7 153
Donaldsonville city	Ascension	41	7 901	7 367
Covington city	St. Tammany	42	7 892	7 170
Plaquemine city	Iberville	43	7 521	7 739
Winnfield city	Winn	44	7 311	7 142
Zachary city	East Baton Rouge	45	7 297	4 964
Gonzales city	Ascension	46	7 287	4 512
Oakdale city	Allen	47	7 155	7 301
Springhill city	Webster	48	6 516	6 496
Jeanerette city	Iberia	49	6 511	6 322
Mansfield city	De Soto	50	6 485	6 432
Lake Providence town	East Carroll	51	6 361	6 183
Port Allen city	West Baton Rouge	52	6 114	5 728
Mandeville town	St. Tammany	53	6 076	'2 571
Vidalia town	Concordia	54	5 936	5 538
Breaux Bridge city	St. Martin	55	5 922	4 942
Winnsboro town	Franklin	56	5 921	5 349
Ponchatoula city	Tangipahoa	57	5 469	4 545
Bunkie town	Avoyelles	58	5 364	5 395
Westlake town	Calcasieu	59	5 246	4 082
Marksville town	Avoyelles	60	5 113	4 519
Jonesboro town	Jackson	61	5 061	5 072
Kaplan city	Vermilion	62	5 016	5 540

Component Parts	1980	1970	1960
ALEXANDRIA, LA.			
The area	151 985	131 749	124 681
Alexandria city	51 565	'41 811	40 279
Outside central city	100 420	'89 938	84 402
Grant Parish	16 703	13 671	13 330
Rapides Parish	135 282	118 078	111 351
BATON ROUGE, LA.			
The area	494 151	375 628	299 755
Baton Rouge city	219 419	'165 921	152 419
Outside central city	274 732	'209 707	147 336
Ascension Parish	50 068	37 086	27 927
East Baton Rouge Parish	366 191	285 167	230 058
Livingston Parish	58 806	36 511	26 974
West Baton Rouge Parish	19 086	16 864	14 796
LAFAYETTE, LA.			
The area	150 017	'111 643	84 656
Lafayette city	81 961	68 908	40 400
Outside central city	68 056	'42 735	44 256
Lafayette Parish	150 017	'111 643	84 656
LAKE CHARLES, LA.			
The area	167 223	145 415	145 475
Lake Charles city	75 226	77 998	63 392
Outside central city	91 997	67 417	82 083
Calcasieu Parish	167 223	145 415	145 475
MONROE, LA.			
The area	139 241	115 387	101 663
Monroe city	57 597	56 374	52 219
Outside central city	81 644	59 013	49 444
Ouachita Parish	139 241	115 387	101 663
NEW ORLEANS, LA.			
The area	187 073	046 470	907 123
New Orleans city	557 515	593 471	627 525
Outside central city	629 558	'452 999	279 598
Jefferson Parish	454 592	'338 229	208 769
Orleans Parish	557 515	593 471	627 525
St. Bernard Parish	64 097	51 185	32 186
St. Tammany Parish	110 869	63 585	38 643
SHREVEPORT, LA.			
The area	376 710	'336 000	321 182
Shreveport city	205 820	182 064	164 372
Outside central city	170 890	'153 936	156 810
Bossier Parish	80 721	'65 877	57 622
Caddo Parish	252 358	230 184	223 859
Webster Parish	43 631	39 939	39 701

Population of Parish Subdivisions: 1960 to 1980

Parish Subdivisions	1980	1970	1960
The State	4 205 900	'3 644 637	3 257 022
Acadia Parish[1]	56 427	52 109	49 931
Ward 1	12 211	11 499	10 460
Rayne city[1]	9 066	9 510	8 634
Ward 2	3 440	2 763	2 841
Ward 3	8 170	7 332	7 667
Church Point town[1]	4 599	3 865	3 606
Ward 4	5 953	5 338	5 191
Iota town	1 326	1 271	1 245
Ward 5	3 828	3 559	3 350
Estherwood village	691	661	639
Mermentau village	771	756	716
Morse village	835	759	682
Ward 6	19 763	19 333	18 171
Crowley city[1]	16 036	16 104	15 617
Ward 7	3 062	2 285	2 251
Eunice city (pt.)	221	,112	...
Allen Parish[2]	21 390	20 794	19 867
Ward 1	2 914	3 267	3 255
Oberlin town	1 764	i 857	1 794
Ward 2	5 242	4 804	4 738
Kinder town[2]	2 603	2 307	2 299
Ward 3	1 292	939	771
Reeves village	199	214	151
Ward 4	'1 575	1 411	1 218
Ward 5	10 367	10 373	9 885
Elizabeth town	454	504	...
Oakdale city[2]	7 155	7 301	6 618
Ascension Parish[3]	50 068	37 086	27 927
Ward 1	3 382	3 384	3 050
Donaldsonville city (pt.)[3]	2 323	2 073	1 475
Ward 2	1 672	1 440	1 124
Donaldsonville city (pt.)[3]	559	491	...
Ward 3	3 568	3 932	4 071
Donaldsonville city (pt.)	3 568	3 932	4 071
Ward 4	2 820	2 070	1 686
Donaldsonville city (pt.)[3]	1 451	871	536
Ward 5	1 796	1 626	1 516
Gonzales city (pt.)[3]	–	...	...
Ward 6	293	356	379
Ward 7	13 602	10 349	6 852
Gonzales city (pt.)[3]	7 287	4 512	3 252
Ward 8	8 450	5 367	3 333
Ward 9	6 188	3 216	1 953
Ward 10	8 297	5 346	3 963
Sorrento town	1 197	1 182	1 151
Assumption Parish[4]	22 084	19 654	17 991
Ward 1	2 282	...	...
Paincourtville (CDP) (pt.)	758	...	...
Ward 2	2 064	...	...
Ward 3	4 321	...	...
Labadieville (CDP)	2 138	...	...
Ward 4	1 785	...	...
Ward 5	1 914	...	...
Napoleonville town	829	1 008	1 148
Ward 6	2 363	...	...
Paincourtville (CDP) (pt.)	1 055	...	...
Ward 7	1 943	...	...
Paincourtville (CDP) (pt.)	191	...	...
Ward 8	2 049	...	...
Pierre Part (CDP) (pt.)	669	...	...
Ward 9	3 363	...	...
Pierre Part (CDP) (pt.)	2 484	...	...
Avoyelles Parish[5]	41 393	37 751	37 606
Ward 1	2 495	1 940	1 720
Ward 2	9 707	8 645	8 017
Marksville town[5]	5 113	4 519	4 257
Ward 3	4 207	3 366	2 998
Mansura town[5]	2 074	1 699	1 579
Ward 4	3 997	2 556	2 265
Hessmer village	743	454	433
Ward 5	1 562	1 302	1 157
Ward 6	1 721	1 612	1 879
Ward 7	3 104	2 812	3 012
Simmesport town	2 293	2 027	2 125
Ward 8	2 597	'2 572	2 710
Cottonport town (pt.)	98	'75	...
Plaucheville village	196	224	228
Ward 9	4 066	'4 010	4 295
Cottonport town (pt.)	1 795	'1 769	1 581
Evergreen town	272	307	325
Ward 10	6 386	6 654	6 939
Bunkie town[5]	5 364	5 395	5 188
Ward 11	2 251	'2 282	2 614
Cottonport town (pt.)	18	'18	...
Moreauville village	853	807	815
Beauregard Parish[6]	29 692	22 888	19 191
Ward 1	651	447	492
Ward 2	3 228	2 579	2 385
Merryville town	1 286	1 286	1 232
Ward 3[6]	16 474	...	...
De Ridder city (pt.)[6]	11 057	8 030	7 188
Ward 4	1 192	708	625
Ward 5	2 240	1 586	1 389
Ward 6	2 927	1 502	1 162
Ward 7[6]	1 928	...	...

Parish Subdivisions	1980	1970	1960
Beauregard Parish—Con.			
Ward 8[6]	1 052	...	...
Bienville Parish[7]	16 387	16 024	16 726
Ward 1	2 261	...	...
Arcadia town (pt.)[7]	1 401	(NA)	(NA)
Ward 2	2 610	...	...
Arcadia town (pt.)[7]	2 002	(NA)	(NA)
Bryceland village[7]	94	65	89
Ward 3	2 232	...	...
Gibsland town	1 354	1 380	1 150
Mount Lebanon town	105	102	...
Ward 4	2 285	...	...
Jamestown village	131	153	...
Ringgold town (pt.)[7]	809	(NA)	(NA)
Ward 5	1 999	...	...
Ringgold town (pt.)[7]	846	(NA)	(NA)
Ward 6	2 474	...	...
Bienville village	249	287	305
Castor village	195	'183	142
Ward 7	2 526	...	...
Lucky village[7]	370	...	...
Saline village	293	307	329
Bossier Parish[8]	80 721	'65 877	57 622
Ward 1	11 884	...	...
Bossier City city (pt.)[8]	11 243	(NA)	(NA)
Shreveport city (pt.)[8]	635	250	103
Ward 2	43 120	...	...
Benton town[8]	1 864	1 493	1 336
Bossier City city (pt.)[8]	36 277	(NA)	(NA)
Shreveport city (pt.)[8]	237	–	–
Ward 3	5 602	...	...
Plain Dealing town	1 213	'1 300	1 357
Ward 4	20 115	...	...
Bossier City city (pt.)[8]	3 297	(NA)	(NA)
Haughton town[8]	1 510	885	611
Caddo Parish[9]	252 358	230 184	223 859
Ward 1[9]	1 924	2 642	3 817
Belcher village[9]	436	'482	...
Gilliam village	244	211	...
Ward 2	7 848	7 266	8 009
Oil City town[9]	1 323	907	1 430
Vivian town[9]	4 146	4 046	2 624
Ward 3[9]	15 412	...	...
Blanchard village[9]	1 128	806	...
Mooringsport town[9]	911	830	864
Shreveport city (pt.)[9]	2 662	(NA)	(NA)
Ward 4[9]	172 319	...	...
Shreveport city (pt.)[9]	169 888	(NA)	(NA)
Ward 5[9]	15 914	...	...
Greenwood village[9]	1 043	212	...
Shreveport city (pt.)[9]	10 156	(NA)	(NA)
Ward 6	4 597	2 755	2 385
Shreveport city (pt.)[9]	27 545	...	...
Ward 7[9]	21 407	(NA)	(NA)
Shreveport city (pt.)[9]	3 965	...	...
Ward 8[9]	835	(NA)	(NA)
Shreveport city (pt.)[9]			
Ward 9	2 834	2 882	3 653
Hosston village[9]	480	428	...
Ida village[9]	306	370	...
Rodessa village	337	273	...
Calcasieu Parish[10]	167 223	145 415	145 475
Ward 1	10 126	4 180	2 772
Moss Bluff (CDP)	7 004	...	...
Ward 2	1 769	1 745	1 756
Ward 3	92 307	88 929	93 970
Lake Charles city[10]	75 226	77 998	63 392
Prien (CDP)	6 224	...	...
Ward 4	40 344	32 632	30 419
Carlyss (CDP)	1 806	...	...
Sulphur city[10]	19 709	'14 959	11 429
Westlake town[10]	5 246	4 082	3 311
Ward 5	2 713	2 165	1 923
Ward 6	8 118	6 615	6 824
De Quincy town	3 966	3 448	3 928
Ward 7	6 129	5 471	4 581
Vinton town	3 631	3 454	2 987
Ward 8	5 717	3 678	3 230
Iowa town	2 437	1 944	1 857
Caldwell Parish[11]	10 761	9 354	9 004
Ward 1	985	...	...
Ward 2	965	...	...
Ward 3	1 589	...	...
Ward 4	687	...	...
Columbia town	687	1 000	1 021
Ward 5	977	...	...
Ward 6	1 192	...	...
Ward 7	1 125	...	...
Grayson village (pt.)	551	516	428
Ward 8	868	...	...
Ward 9	1 034	...	...
Clarks village	931	889	940
Ward 10	1 339	...	...
Grayson village (pt.)	13	...	...

Parish Subdivisions	1980	1970	1960
Cameron Parish	9 336	8 194	6 909
Ward 1, Cow Island	532	566	611
Ward 2, Grand Chenier	1 256	1 166	879
Ward 3, Cameron	3 609	3 205	2 721
Cameron (CDP)	1 736	...	...
Ward 4, Grand Lake	1 522	1 218	1 036
Ward 5, Johnsons Bayou	816	704	479
Ward 6, Hackberry	1 601	1 335	1 183
Catahoula Parish[12]	12 287	11 769	11 421
Ward 1	1 263	...	...
Sicily Island village (pt.)[12]	131	(NA)	(NA)
Ward 2	1 469	...	...
Sicily Island village (pt.)	560	(NA)	(NA)
Ward 3	1 363	...	...
Ward 4	1 337	...	...
Harrisonburg village	610	626	594
Ward 5	1 499	...	...
Ward 6	1 838	...	...
Jonesville town (pt.)[12]	656	(NA)	(NA)
Ward 7	965	...	...
Jonesville town (pt.)	965	(NA)	(NA)
Ward 8	1 207	...	...
Jonesville town (pt.)	1 207	(NA)	(NA)
Ward 9	1 346	...	...
Claiborne Parish[13]	17 095	17 024	19 407
Ward 1	1 075	1 059	1 143
Ward 2	1 009	877	1 081
Haynesville town (pt.)[13]	61	...	...
Ward 3	4 524	4 387	5 115
Haynesville town (pt.)[13]	3 393	3 055	3 031
Ward 4	615	594	997
Ward 5	1 264	1 255	1 419
Athens village	419	387	406
Ward 6	1 050	884	1 027
Ward 7	6 262	6 464	6 841
Homer town[13]	4 307	4 483	4 665
Ward 8	892	1 073	1 352
Lisbon village	138	151	229
Ward 9	404	431	432
Junction City village (pt.)	119	159	138
Concordia Parish[14]	22 981	22 578	20 467
Ward 1	3 642	...	...
Ferriday town (pt.)	2 679	(NA)	(NA)
Ward 2	2 808	...	...
Ferriday town (pt.)[14]	1 793	(NA)	(NA)
West Ferriday (CDP) (pt.)	975	...	...
Ward 3	4 721	...	...
Vidalia town (pt.)	4 721	(NA)	(NA)
Ward 4	6 312	...	...
Ridgecrest town	895	1 076	...
Vidalia town (pt.)[14]	1 215	(NA)	(NA)
West Ferriday (CDP) (pt.)	375	...	...
Ward 5	5 498	...	...
Clayton village	1 204	1 103	882
West Ferriday (CDP) (pt.)	49	...	...
De Soto Parish[15]	25 727	22 764	24 248
Ward 1	1 694	1 359	1 551
Keatchie town	342	328	345
Longstreet village	281	182	283
Ward 2	3 798	2 781	2 825
Stonewall town[15]	1 175	...	...
Ward 3	1 609	1 688	1 920
Stanley village	151	145	234
Ward 4	11 001	9 776	9 551
Mansfield city	6 485	6 432	5 839
South Mansfield village[15]	1 463	439	616
Ward 5	1 315	1 220	1 717
Ward 6	1 637	1 611	1 945
Grand Cane village	252	284	322
Ward 7	1 306	1 458	1 773
Ward 8	3 367	2 871	2 966
Logansport town	1 565	1 330	1 371
East Baton Rouge Parish[16]	366 191	285 167	230 058
Ward 1	219 419	...	...
Baton Rouge city[16]	219 419	'165 921	152 419
Ward 2	71 366	...	...
Baker city[16]	12 865	8 281	4 823
Scotlandville (CDP)	15 113	'22 599	...
Zachary city[16]	7 297	4 964	3 268
Ward 3	75 406	...	...
East Carroll Parish	11 772	12 884	14 433
Ward 1	775	875	1 399
Ward 2	1 314	1 656	2 050
Ward 3	8 278	8 228	7 851
Lake Providence town	6 361	6 183	5 781
Ward 4	91	197	395
Ward 5	422	642	983
Ward 6	305	514	720
Ward 7	587	772	1 035
East Feliciana Parish[17]	19 015	17 657	20 198
Ward 1	2 709	1 136	1 172
Slaughter town	729	580	403
Ward 2	2 194	1 704	1 618
Ward 3	6 215	7 364	9 671
Jackson town	3 133	4 697	1 824
East Feliciana Parish—Con.			
Ward 4	1 423	1 370	1 374
Norwood village[17]	421	348	427
Wilson village	656	606	...
Ward 5	3 544	3 316	3 169
Clinton town[17]	1 919	1 884	1 568
Ward 6	1 235	1 007	1 179
Ward 7	764	699	872
Ward 8	931	1 061	1 143
Evangeline Parish[18]	33 343	31 932	31 639
Ward 1	17 470	17 164	16 606
Chataigner village[18]	431	...	...
Ville Platte town[18]	9 201	9 692	7 512
Ward 2	3 705	3 359	3 918
Basile town	2 635	1 779	1 932
Ward 3	6 435	6 585	6 320
Mamou town[18]	3 194	3 275	2 928
Ward 4	2 573	2 217	2 064
Pine Prairie village	734	515	387
Ward 5	3 160	2 607	2 731
Turkey Creek village	366	280	279
Franklin Parish[19]	24 141	23 946	26 088
Ward 1	3 129	2 910	3 270
Wisner town	1 424	1 339	1 254
Ward 2	2 291	2 333	2 642
Gilbert village	800	746	472
Ward 3	1 811	1 906	2 548
Ward 4	1 634	1 764	2 154
Ward 5	915	1 182	1 572
Ward 6	1 782	1 682	1 974
Baskin village[19]	286	177	238
Ward 7	10 182	9 471	8 702
Winnsboro town[19]	5 921	5 349	4 437
Ward 8	1 212	1 124	1 190
Ward 9	1 185	1 574	2 036
Grant Parish[20]	16 703	13 671	13 330
Ward 1	2 999	2 976	3 129
Colfax town[20]	1 680	1 892	1 934
Ward 2	3 400	2 476	2 172
Ward 3	2 110	1 566	1 540
Dry Prong village	526	352	360
Pollock town (pt.)[20]	4	...	...
Ward 4	533	341	329
Ward 5	1 092	842	1 000
Georgetown village[20]	381	306	321
Ward 6	1 111	907	831
Ward 7	2 598	2 258	2 332
Montgomery town	843	923	866
Ward 8	2 860	2 305	1 997
Pollock town (pt.)[20]	395	341	366
Iberia Parish[21]	63 752	57 397	51 657
Ward 1	13 597	...	...
Delcambre town (pt.)	678	775	830
New Iberia city (pt.)[21]	4 971	(NA)	(NA)
Ward 2	12 552	...	...
New Iberia city (pt.)	6 369	(NA)	(NA)
Ward 3	7 677	...	...
Jeanerette city[21]	6 511	6 322	5 568
Ward 4	11 066	...	...
Loreauville village[21]	860	728	655
New Iberia city (pt.)[21]	2 566	(NA)	(NA)
Ward 5	18 860	...	...
New Iberia city (pt.)	18 860	(NA)	(NA)
Iberville Parish[22]	32 159	30 746	29 939
Ward 1	5 815	'5 447	5 705
White Castle town[22]	2 160	2 206	2 253
Ward 2	8 878	'8 287	7 339
Plaquemine city (pt.)[22]	3 612	3 175	2 823
Plaquemine Southwest (CDP) (pt.)	1 407	1 224	1 272
Seymourville (CDP)	2 891	2 506	1 788
Ward 3	2 261	2 775	3 142
Plaquemine city (pt.)	2 261	2 775	3 142
Ward 4	2 592	1 597	1 363
Ward 5	1 590	1 618	1 726
Carville (CDP)	1 037	...	...
Ward 6	2 676	2 809	2 620
Ward 7	1 106	1 258	1 158
Grosse Tete village	2 111	'2 077	2 276
Rosedale village[22]	749	710	768
Ward 8	658	621	674
Plaquemine city (pt.)	3 884	3 480	3 507
Plaquemine Southwest (CDP) (pt.)	542	563	566
Ward 9	60	...	...
Maringouin town	2 352	'2 656	2 261
	1 291	1 365	1 168
Jackson Parish[23]	17 321	15 963	15 828
Ward 1	2 138	...	...
Quitman village	231	169	185
Ward 2	1 707	...	...
Eros village	158	164	176
Ward 3	1 517	...	...
Chatham town	714	827	758
Ward 4	1 883	...	...
Ward 5	2 248	...	...
Jonesboro town (pt.)	1 914	(NA)	(NA)
Ward 6	1 520	...	...

Parish Subdivisions	1980	1970	1960
Jackson Parish—Con			
Ward 6—Con			
Jonesboro town (pt.)	1 102	(NA)	(NA)
Ward 7	1 595	...	...
Jonesboro town (pt.)	978	(NA)	(NA)
Ward 8	1 637	...	...
Hodge village	708	818	878
Jonesboro town (pt.)	201	(NA)	(NA)
North Hodge village[23]	573	640	680
Ward 9	1 617	...	...
East Hodge village[23]	439	363	...
Jonesboro town (pt.)	426	(NA)	(NA)
Ward 10	1 459	...	...
Jonesboro town (pt.)[23]	440	(NA)	(NA)
Jefferson Parish[24]	454 592	338 229	208 769
Ward 1	32 013	24 732	9 900
Gretna city (pt.)	8 465	(NA)	(NA)
Terrytown (CDP)	23 548	13 832	...
Ward 2[24]	16 675	...	...
Gretna city (pt.)	5 096	(NA)	(NA)
Timberlane (CDP)	11 579	...	...
Ward 3[24]	27 075	...	...
Gretna city (pt.)	7 054	(NA)	(NA)
Harvey (CDP) (pt.)	19 858	3 153	...
Ward 4	73 844	51 064	38 799
Estelle (CDP)	12 724	...	...
Harvey (CDP) (pt.)	2 851	3 194	...
Marrero (CDP)	36 548	29 015	...
Westwego city	12 663	11 402	9 815
Ward 5	23 890	14 297	1 700
Avondale (CDP)	6 699	...	...
Waggaman (CDP)	9 004	...	...
Ward 6	4 480	4 403	4 216
Barataria (CDP)	1 123	...	...
Jean Lafitte town[24]	936	...	...
Lafitte (CDP)	1 312	1 223	...
Ward 7	15 550	17 347	19 488
Jefferson (CDP)	15 550	16 489	19 353
Ward 8[24]	72 079	...	...
Metairie (CDP) (pt.)	72 079	(NA)	...
Ward 9	114 258	78 339	51 399
Harahan city	11 384	13 037	9 275
Kenner city[24]	66 382	29 858	17 037
Metairie (CDP) (pt.)	19 346	(NA)	...
River Ridge (CDP)	17 146	15 713	...
Ward 10[24]	72 735	...	...
Metairie (CDP) (pt.)	72 735	(NA)	...
Ward 11	1 993	2 244	2 082
Grand Isle town	1 982	2 236	2 074
Jefferson Davis Parish[25]	32 168	29 554	29 825
Ward 1	5 023	4 781	4 818
Lake Arthur town	3 615	3 551	3 541
Ward 2	13 788	12 826	12 807
Jennings city[25]	12 401	11 783	11 887
Ward 3	1 281	1 073	1 060
Ward 4	2 267	2 400	2 519
Elton town	1 450	1 598	1 595
Ward 5	1 222	1 167	1 255
Fenton village	491	404	429
Ward 6	4 956	4 477	4 595
Welsh town	3 515	3 203	3 332
Ward 7	881	723	862
Ward 8	1 925	1 642	1 449
Ward 9	825	465	460
Lafayette Parish[26]	150 017	111 643	84 656
Ward 1	29 473	...	...
Carencro town[26]	3 712	2 302	1 519
Duson town (pt.)	1 007	(NA)	(NA)
Lafayette city (pt.)[26]	11 633	(NA)	(NA)
Scott town (pt.)[26]	1 191	(NA)	(NA)
Ward 2	34 276	...	...
Lafayette city (pt.)[26]	26 221	(NA)	(NA)
Ward 3	18 058	...	...
Lafayette city (pt.)	18 058	(NA)	(NA)
Ward 4	29 856	...	...
Broussard town[26]	2 923	1 707	1 600
Lafayette city (pt.)[26]	9 174	(NA)	(NA)
Youngsville village	1 053	1 002	946
Ward 5	38 354	...	...
Broadmoor (CDP)	7 051	...	...
Duson town (pt.)	246	(NA)	(NA)
Lafayette city (pt.)[26]	16 875	(NA)	(NA)
Scott town (pt.)[26]	1 048	(NA)	(NA)
Lafourche Parish[27]	82 483	68 941	55 381
Ward 1	7 754	4 104	1 982
Thibodaux city (pt.)[27]	1 208	47	...
Ward 2	16 174	16 055	14 008
Thibodaux city (pt.)[27]	14 011	14 981	13 403
Ward 3	10 414	7 561	5 752
Raceland (CDP) (pt.)	5 537	4 227	3 027
Ward 4	8 238	7 112	5 530
Larose (CDP) (pt.)	1 281	1 155	754
Lockport town[27]	2 424	2 398	2 221
Ward 5	2 262	1 762	2 101
Thibodaux city (pt.)[27]	591	...	...
Ward 6	5 323	4 323	3 267

Parish Subdivisions	1980	1970	1960
Lafourche Parish—Con.			
Ward 7	3 576	3 603	3 327
Des Allemands (CDP) (pt.)	377	225	...
Raceland (CDP) (pt.)	765	653	639
Ward 8	795	849	534
Ward 9	2 175	1 708	1 596
Larose (CDP) (pt.)	663	244	146
Ward 10	21 328	18 831	15 596
Cut Off (CDP)	5 049	...	...
Galliano (CDP)	5 159	...	...
Golden Meadow town	2 282	2 681	3 097
Larose (CDP) (pt.)	3 290	2 868	1 896
Ward 11	4 444	3 033	1 688
Bayou Blue (CDP) (pt.)	2 333	...	...
La Salle Parish[28]	17 004	13 295	13 011
Ward 1	1 543	...	...
Ward 2	2 020	...	...
Olla town[28]	1 603	1 387	1 246
Ward 3	1 788	...	...
Tullos town (pt.)[28]	776	600	594
Urania town[28]	849	874	...
Ward 4	1 310	...	...
Jena town (pt.)	251	(NA)	(NA)
Ward 5	2 676	...	...
Jena town (pt.)[28]	2 676	(NA)	(NA)
Ward 6	2 283	...	...
Jena town (pt.)	1 405	(NA)	(NA)
Trout–Good Pine (CDP) (pt.)	302	...	...
Ward 7	1 598	...	...
Trout–Good Pine (CDP) (pt.)	731	...	...
Ward 8	1 777	...	...
Ward 9	2 009	...	...
Jena town (pt.)	...	(NA)	(NA)
Lincoln Parish[29]	39 763	33 800	28 535
Ward 1	23 065	...	...
Ruston city (pt.)[29]	20 562	(NA)	(NA)
Ward 2	5 713	...	...
Grambling town[29]	4 226	4 407	3 144
Ward 3	3 138	...	...
Simsboro village	553	412	363
Ward 4	3 578	...	...
Dubach town	1 161	1 096	1 013
Vienna town[29]	519	59	(NA)
Ward 5	4 269	...	...
Choudrant village	809	555	465
Downsville village (pt.)[29]	56	...	...
Ruston city (pt.)	23	(NA)	(NA)
Livingston Parish[30]	58 806	36 511	26 974
Ward 1[30]	15 751	...	...
Walker town[30]	2 957	1 363	912
Ward 2[30]	23 581	...	...
Denham Springs city[30]	8 563	6 752	5 991
Port Vincent village	450	387	340
Ward 3[30]	5 807	...	...
French Settlement village[30]	761	670	...
Livingston town[30]	1 260	1 398	1 183
Ward 4[30]	13 667	...	...
Albany village[30]	857	700	557
Killian village[30]	611	293	...
Springfield town	424	423	268
Madison Parish[31]	15 975	15 065	16 444
Ward 1	1 737	...	...
Delta village	295	153	111
Mound village	40	78	107
Richmond village (pt.)[31]	...	...	...
Ward 2	1 733	...	...
Richmond village (pt.)	505	...	...
Tallulah city (pt.)[31]	451	(NA)	(NA)
Ward 3	2 300	...	...
Tallulah city (pt.)[31]	978	(NA)	(NA)
Ward 4	1 984	...	...
Tallulah city (pt.)[31]	1 984	(NA)	(NA)
Ward 5	2 198	...	...
Tallulah city (pt.)	2 198	(NA)	(NA)
Ward 6	1 936	...	...
Tallulah city (pt.)	1 936	(NA)	(NA)
Ward 7	2 075	...	...
Tallulah city (pt.)	2 075	(NA)	(NA)
Ward 8	2 012	...	...
Tallulah city (pt.)	2 012	(NA)	(NA)
Morehouse Parish[32]	34 803	32 463	33 709
Ward 1	972	620	711
Ward 2	1 183	943	861
Ward 3	2 220	1 800	1 382
Bastrop city (pt.)[32]	–	...	...
Ward 4	21 434	18 774	17 940
Bastrop city (pt.)[32]	15 527	14 713	15 193
Ward 5	1 235	1 690	2 357
Oak Ridge village[32]	257	276	287
Ward 6	3 561	3 633	4 450
Mer Rouge village	802	819	853
Ward 7	893	796	788
Ward 8	1 275	1 519	1 999
Collinston village	439	397	497
Ward 9	182	154	224
Ward 10	1 848	2 534	2 997
Bonita village	503	533	574

LOUISIANA ALMANAC

Parish Subdivisions

Parish Subdivisions	1980	1970	1960
Natchitoches Parish[33]	39 863	35 219	35 653
Ward 1	22 057	19 611	...
Natchitoches city[33]	16 664	15 974	13 924
Ward 2	7 111	5 701	...
Ashland village[33]	307	211	(NA)
Campti town[33]	1 069	1 078	1 045
Clarence village	612	448	286
Goldonna village[33]	526	337	292
Ward 3	5 679	5 053	...
Powhatan village	279	277	...
Provencal village	695	530	570
Robeline village	238	274	308
Ward 4	5 016	4 854	...
Natchez village[33]	527	...	...
Orleans Parish	557 515	593 471	627 525
New Orleans city	557 515	593 471	627 525
Ouachita Parish[34]	139 241	115 387	101 663
Ward 1	7 214	4 691	3 337
Sterlington town	1 400	1 118	...
Ward 2	9 857	2 931	1 850
Monroe city (pt.)	–	–	–
Ward 3	33 554	28 034	27 551
Monroe city (pt.)[34]	22 823	21 277	22 697
Richwood town[34]	1 223	...	...
Ward 4	2 328	1 437	1 226
Ward 5	35 790	33 147	28 326
Brownsville–Bawcomville (CDP)	7 252	...	...
Claiborne (CDP)	6 278	...	...
West Monroe city[34]	14 993	14 868	15 215
Ward 6	3 611	2 364	1 921
Ward 7	2 088	1 206	1 211
Ward 8	3 517	1 867	1 442
Ward 9	1 057	615	595
Ward 10	40 225	39 095	34 204
Monroe city (pt.)[34]	34 774	35 097	29 522
Plaquemines Parish	26 049	25 225	22 545
Ward 1	1 561	1 839	...
Ward 2	1 281	1 276	...
Ward 3	7 220	6 414	...
Buras–Triumph (CDP)	4 137	4 113	4 908
Ward 4	5 656	7 084	...
Port Sulphur (CDP)	3 318	3 022	2 868
Ward 5	10 331	8 612	...
Belle Chasse (CDP)	5 412	...	...
Pointe Coupee Parish[35]	24 045	22 002	22 488
Ward 1	1 273	1 289	1 603
Ward 2	1 317	1 633	1 826
Ward 3	987	994	1 051
Ward 4	1 711	1 683	2 012
Morganza village[35]	846	836	937
Ward 5	1 957	1 508	1 858
Ward 6	1 106	926	798
Ward 7	2 127	1 856	1 530
Ward 8	2 389	1 980	2 376
Ward 9	6 748	6 603	6 390
New Roads town	3 924	3 945	3 965
Ward 10	4 430	3 530	3 044
Fordoche village	676	488	...
Livonia village[35]	980	611	430
Rapides Parish[36]	135 282	118 078	111 351
Ward 1, Alexandria	55 898	53 910	52 781
Alexandria city (pt.)[36]	50 795	'41 631	40 279
Ward 2, Lamourie	3 954	3 574	3 575
Lecompte town (pt.)[36]	1	...	...
Woodworth village	412	409	320
Ward 3, Cheneyville	4 046	4 004	4 642
Cheneyville town	865	1 082	1 037
Lecompte town (pt.)[36]	1 660	1 518	1 485
Ward 4, Spring Hill	5 303	4 671	4 512
Forest Hill village[36]	494	370	302
Glenmora town	1 479	1 651	1 447
McNary village[36]	240	220	(NA)
Ward 5, Hineston	2 954	2 115	1 878
Ward 6, Calcasieu	2 057	1 644	1 646
Ward 7, Cotile	4 886	4 121	4 412
Boyce town	1 198	1 240	1 094
Ward 8, Rapides	12 228	10 739	7 339
Alexandria city (pt.)[36]	770	180	...
Ward 9, Pineville	15 783	14 746	16 304
Pineville city (pt.)[36]	10 636	8 884	8 631
Ward 10, Rigolette	20 654	14 117	10 447
Ball town[36]	3 405	...	...
Pineville city (pt.)[36]	1 398	67	5
Ward 11, Buckeye	7 519	4 437	3 815
Red River Parish[37]	10 433	9 226	9 978
Ward 1	1 828	...	...
Ward 2	1 501	...	...
Martin village[37]	584	...	...
Ward 3	1 395	...	...
Hall Summit village[37]	276	190	...
Ward 4	1 426	...	...
Ward 5	517	...	...
Coushatta town (pt.)[37]	...	(NA)	(NA)
Ward 6	989	...	...
Ward 7	1 426	...	...

Parish Subdivisions	1980	1970	1960
Red River Parish—Con.			
Ward 7—Con.			
Coushatta town (pt.)[37]	733	(NA)	(NA)
Edgefield village	312	201	...
Ward 8	1 351	...	...
Coushatta town (pt.)	1 351	(NA)	(NA)
Richland Parish[38]	22 187	21 774	23 824
Ward 1	6 039	5 876	5 694
Delhi town[38]	3 290	2 887	2 514
Ward 2	9 219	9 238	9 923
Rayville town[38]	4 610	3 962	4 052
Ward 3	2 081	1 787	1 960
Ward 4	2 128	2 058	2 608
Ward 5	1 883	1 863	2 167
Mangham town	867	544	521
Ward 6	316	451	850
Ward 7	521	501	622
Sabine Parish[39]	25 280	18 638	18 564
Ward 1	3 003	2 158	1 959
Florien village (pt.)[39]	953	639	496
Ward 2	1 153	681	888
Ward 3	1 955	1 141	893
Ward 4	8 576	6 317	6 089
Fisher village[39]	325	...	...
Florien village (pt.)[39]	11	...	...
Many town[39]	3 988	3 112	3 164
Ward 5	3 317	2 385	2 703
Zwolle town (pt.)	475	432	557
Ward 6	1 710	1 187	1 317
Converse village (pt.)	404	341	261
Noble village	194	209	206
Ward 7	1 434	1 473	1 574
Pleasant Hill village	776	826	907
Ward 8	2 801	2 160	1 956
Zwolle town (pt.)	2 127	1 737	769
Ward 9	787	632	538
Ward 10	544	504	647
Converse village (pt.)	45	34	30
St. Bernard Parish[40]	64 097	51 185	32 186
Ward A	4 809	...	...
Arabi (CDP) (pt.)	4 809	...	...
Ward B	4 906	...	...
Arabi (CDP) (pt.)	4 392	...	...
Chalmette (CDP) (pt.)	514	...	...
Ward C	5 218	...	...
Arabi (CDP) (pt.)	1 047	...	...
Chalmette (CDP) (pt.)	4 171	...	...
Ward D	6 221	...	...
Chalmette (CDP) (pt.)	6 221	...	...
Ward E	6 368	...	...
Chalmette (CDP) (pt.)	6 349	...	...
Ward F	5 550	...	...
Chalmette (CDP) (pt.)	5 550	...	...
Ward G	6 563	...	...
Chalmette (CDP) (pt.)	6 563	...	...
Ward H	7 332	...	...
Chalmette (CDP) (pt.)	4 479	...	...
Violet (CDP) (pt.)	2 853	...	...
Ward I	6 886	...	...
Violet (CDP) (pt.)	6 886	...	...
Ward J	6 259	...	...
Poydras (CDP) (pt.)	4 320	...	...
Violet (CDP) (pt.)	1 939	...	...
Ward K	3 985	...	...
Poydras (CDP) (pt.)	1 402	...	...
St. Charles Parish[41]	37 259	29 550	21 219
Ward 1	5 629	...	...
Hahnville (CDP)	2 947	'2 522	1 297
Luling (CDP) (pt.)	1 672	(NA)	(NA)
Ward 2	6 919	...	...
Lone Star (CDP) (pt.)	1 593	...	...
Luling (CDP) (pt.)	2 334	(NA)	(NA)
Ward 3	5 561	...	...
Destrehan (CDP)	2 382	...	...
New Sarpy (CDP) (pt.)	2 249	1 643	1 259
Norco (CDP) (pt.)	361	(NA)	(NA)
Ward 4	4 966	...	...
Des Allemands (CDP) (pt.)	2 543	2 093	1 167
Ward 5	4 589	...	...
Ward 6	4 710	...	...
New Sarpy (CDP) (pt.)	...	...	...
Norco (CDP) (pt.)	4 055	(NA)	(NA)
Ward 7	4 885	...	...
Lone Star (CDP) (pt.)	–	(NA)	(NA)
Luling (CDP) (pt.)	–	(NA)	(NA)
Mimosa Park (CDP)	3 737	1 624	...
St. Helena Parish[42]	9 827	9 937	9 162
Ward 1	716	745	778
Ward 2	2 170	2 585	2 278
Greensburg town (pt.)[42]	348	562	481
Ward 3	1 730	1 649	1 447
Greensburg town (pt.)[42]	314	90	31
Ward 4	1 955	1 969	1 718
Montpelier village	219	211	197
Ward 5	2 232	2 068	2 021
Ward 6	1 024	921	920

Parish Subdivisions	1980	1970	1960
St. James Parish[3]	21 495	19 733	18 369
Ward 1	2 947	..	...
Gramercy town (pt.)[3]	2 947	(NA)	(NA)
Ward 2	4 994	...	...
Gramercy town (pt.)	264	(NA)	(NA)
Lutcher town (pt.)[3]	4 730	(NA)	(NA)
Ward 3	1 982	...	...
Lutcher town (pt.)[3]	–	(NA)	(NA)
Ward 4	2 676	...	...
Ward 5	2 651	...	...
Ward 6	2 971	...	...
Lower Vacherie (CDP) (pt.)	150	...	...
Vacherie (CDP)	2 169	2 145	...
Ward 7	3 274	...	...
Lower Vacherie (CDP) (pt.)	3 039	...	...
St. John the Baptist Parish	31 924	23 813	18 439
Ward 1	2 424	1 716	1 623
Ward 2	366	1 563	1 423
Ward 3	1 252	1 368	1 397
Ward 4	17 032	9 286	5 268
Laplace (CDP) (pt.)	16 112	5 953	3 541
Reserve (CDP) (pt.)	3	...	...
Ward 5	7 369	6 667	5 446
Laplace (CDP) (pt.)	–	...	...
Reserve (CDP) (pt.)	7 285	6 381	5 297
Ward 6	3 481	3 213	3 282
Garyville (CDP)	2 856	2 474	2 389
St. Landry Parish[4]	84 128	80 364	81 493
Ward 1	31 839	...	...
Opelousas city[4]	18 903	'20 387	17 417
Port Barre town (pt.)[4]	142	77	39
Ward 2	7 339	...	...
Cankton village	303	260	...
Grand Coteau town[4]	1 165	1 301	1 165
Sunset town[4]	2 300	1 675	1 307
Ward 3	6 879	...	...
Arnaudville town (pt.)[4]	1 530	1 550	1 082
Leonville village[4]	1,143	512	526
Ward 4	11 644	...	...
Krotz Springs town	1 374	1 435	1 057
Melville town	1 764	'1 987	1 939
Palmetto village	327	312	430
Port Barre town (pt.)[4]	2 483	2 056	1 837
Ward 5	5 403	...	...
Washington town	1 266	1 473	1 291
Ward 6[4]	21 024	18 719	19 613
Eunice city (pt.)[4]	12 258	11 278	11 326
Lawtell (CDP)	1 014	...	...
St. Martin Parish[5]	40 214	32 453	29 063
Ward 1	8 198	...	...
St. Martinville city (pt.)[5]	4 079	(NA)	(NA)
Ward 2	4 567	...	...
St. Martinville city (pt.)[5]	3 023	(NA)	(NA)
Ward 3	5 040	...	...
Parks village	545	491	413
St. Martinville city (pt.)[5]	863	(NA)	(NA)
Ward 4	13 414	...	...
Breaux Bridge city[5]	5 922	4 942	3 303
Ward 5	8 995	...	...
Arnaudville town (pt.)	149	123	102
Henderson town[5]	1 560	...	...
St. Mary Parish[6]	64 253	60 752	48 833
Ward 1	3 449	2 938	2 554
Ward 2	907	957	1 142
Ward 3	13 093	13 210	12 321
Franklin city[6]	9 584	9 325	8 673
Ward 4	2 558	2 711	2 325
Ward 5	7 997	7 213	4 518
Bayou Vista (CDP) (pt.)	1 900	1 816	...
Patterson town[6]	4 693	4 409	2 923
Ward 6	18 625	18 870	15 715
Morgan City city[6]	16 114	16 586	13 540
Ward 7	1 641	1 555	1 508
Ward 8	8 379	7 736	5 181
Bayou Vista (CDP) (pt.)	3 905	3 305	...
Berwick town[6]	4 466	4 168	3 880
Ward 9	3 728	2 408	1 087
Amelia (CDP)	3 617	2 292	...
Ward 10	3 876	3 154	2 482
Baldwin town	2 644	2 117	1 548
St. Tammany Parish[7]	110 869	63 585	38 643
Ward 1	4 419	2 929	1 847
Madisonville town	799	801	860
Ward 2	6 303	4 126	3 452
Folsom village[7]	319	249	225
Ward 3	14 447	11 313	9 469
Covington city[7]	7 892	7 170	6 754
Ward 4	13 852	6 126	3 341
Lacombe (CDP) (pt.)	78	...	...
Mandeville town[7]	6 076	'2 571	1 740
Ward 5	2 064	1 500	1 445
Sun village[7]	404	288	224
Ward 6[7]	4 225	2 345	1 640
Ward 7	5 012	3 031	2 019
Lacombe (CDP) (pt.)	4 763	...	...
Ward 8	31 018	11 730	3 975
Pearl River town	1 693	1 361	964

Parish Subdivisions	1980	1970	1960
St. Tammany Parish — Con			
Ward 8 — Con.			
Slidell city (pt.)[7]	12 122	4 351	...
Ward 9[7]	26 767	18 736	10 339
Lacombe (CDP) (pt.)	305	...	...
Slidell city (pt.)[7]	14 596	11 750	6 356
Ward 10	2 762	1 749	1 116
Abita Springs town[7]	1 072	839	655
Tangipahoa Parish[6]	80 698	65 875	59 434
Ward 1	4 857	4 652	4 581
Kentwood town	2 667	2 736	2 607
Tangipahoa village	493	469	465
Ward 2	2 023	1 624	1 567
Ward 3	10 634	9 330	9 382
Amite City town[6]	4 301	3 593	3 316
Roseland town	1 346	1 273	1 254
Ward 4[6]	4 329	...	...
Ward 5[6]	4 198	...	...
Ward 6	13 542	10 377	8 677
East Hammond (CDP) (pt.)	162	...	...
Hammond city (pt.)[6]	392	442	...
Independence town[6]	1 684	1 770	1 941
Tickfaw village[6]	571	370	317
Ward 7	38 498	31 575	27 823
East Hammond (CDP) (pt.)	1 775	1 342	1 462
Hammond city (pt.)[6]	14 651	12 045	10 563
Ponchatoula city[6]	5 469	4 545	4 727
Ward 8	2 617	1 717	1 415
Tensas Parish[6]	8 525	9 732	11 796
Ward 1	1 249	...	...
Ward 2	1 726	...	...
Newellton town[6]	1 726	1 403	1 453
Ward 3	681	...	...
Ward 4	655	...	...
Ward 5	1 687	...	...
St. Joseph town	1 687	1 864	1 653
Ward 6	1 188	...	...
Ward 7	1 339	...	...
Waterproof town[6]	1 339	1 438	1 412
Terrebonne Parish[50]	94 393	76 049	60 771
Ward 1	14 124	9 635	5 040
Bayou Cane (CDP) (pt.)	3 272	10	...
Ward 2	2 802	1 345	1 738
Bayou Cane (CDP) (pt.)	383	...	...
Houma city (pt.)[50]	1 311	160	189
Ward 3	48 033	41 243	34 586
Bayou Blue (CDP) (pt.)	396	...	...
Bayou Cane (CDP) (pt.)	12 068	9 067	3 173
Houma city (pt.)	30 169	30 576	22 372
Ward 4	3 851	4 739	3 976
Houma city (pt.)[50]	48	186	...
Ward 5	3 706	2 053	1 499
Bourg (CDP) (pt.)[50]	2 073	...	...
Houma city (pt.)[50]	–	...	...
Ward 6	4 116	3 139	2 938
Ward 7	7 134	6 573	5 368
Chauvin (CDP)	3 338	...	...
Houma city (pt.)[50]	–	...	...
Ward 8	3 512	2 390	2 183
Ward 9	3 168	1 934	1 590
Houma city (pt.)[50]	1 074	...	...
Ward 10	3 947	2 998	1 853
Crozier (CDP)	1 150	...	...
Union Parish[51]	21 167	18 447	17 624
Ward 1	2 628	...	...
Farmerville town (pt.)	2 628	(NA)	(NA)
Ward 2	2 207	...	...
Marion village (pt.)[51]	887	(NA)	(NA)
Ward 3	2 234	...	...
Spearsville village	181	197	...
Ward 4	2 239	...	...
Bernice town (pt.)[51]	944	(NA)	(NA)
Ward 5	2 700	...	...
Downsville village (pt.)[51]	157	...	...
Ward 6	1 899	...	...
Marion village (pt.)[51]	102	(NA)	(NA)
Ward 7	2 386	...	...
Farmerville town (pt.)	1 140	(NA)	(NA)
Ward 8	2 530	...	...
Ward 9	2 344	...	...
Bernice town (pt.)[51]	1 012	(NA)	(NA)
Junction City village (pt.)	608	574	501
Lillie village	172	160	...
Vermilion Parish[52]	48 458	43 071	38 855
Ward 1	7 504	5 124	4 211
Delcambre town (pt.)	1 538	1 200	1 027
Erath town[53]	2 133	2 024	2 019
Ward 2	1 453	1 226	1 306
Ward 3	18 041	16 595	14 810
Abbeville city[52]	12 391	10 996	10 414
Ward 4	2 676	2 175	1 869
Maurice village	478	476	411
Ward 5	1 686	1 587	1 504
Ward 6	2 518	2 149	1 821
Ward 7	2 334	1 985	1 696
Ward 8	3 689	3 950	4 042

Parish Subdivisions	1980	1970	1960
Vermilion Parish—Con.			
Ward 8—Con.			
Gueydan town[52]	1 695	1 984	2 156
Ward 9	8 557	8 280	7 596
Kaplan city[52]	5 016	5 540	5 267
Vernon Parish[53]	53 475	53 794	18 301
Ward 1	17 596	21 767	7 070
Fort Polk North (CDP)	1 644	7 955	...
Leesville city[53]	9 054	8 928	4 689
Newllano village[53]	2 213	1 800	...
Ward 2	5 728	3 929	2 789
Anacoco village[53]	90	...	...
Hornbeck town	470	525	374
Ward 3	2 144	1 796	1 291
Ward 4	18 098	18 751	1 024
Fort Polk South (CDP)	12 498	15 600	...
Ward 5	2 308	2 260	2 075
Ward 6	1 380	1 102	958
Simpson village[53]	534	491	...
Ward 7	4 520	2 897	2 150
De Ridder city (pt.)[53]	–	...	...
Rosepine village	953	587	414
Ward 8	1 701	1 292	944
Washington Parish[54]	44 207	41 987	44 015
Ward 1	1 489	1 207	1 308
Ward 2	1 698	1 554	1 632
Ward 3	5 941	5 287	5 172
Franklinton town[54]	4 119	3 562	3 141
Ward 4	21 772	22 371	24 697
Bogalusa city	16 976	18 412	21 423
Ward 5	2 733	2 289	2 251
Varnado village	249	320	331
Ward 6	2 228	1 834	1 759
Ward 7	3 734	3 510	3 253
Angie village	311	317	254
Ward 8	3 077	2 581	2 741
Ward 9	1 535	1 354	1 202
Webster Parish[55]	43 631	39 939	39 701
Ward 1[55]	27 834	...	...
Dixie Inn village[55]	453	456	399
Doyline village	801	716	1 061
Dubberly village	421	212	249
Heflin village	279	314	289
Minden city[55]	15 084	13 996	12 785
Sibley village[55]	1 211	869	595
Ward 2[55]	15 797	...	...
Cotton Valley town[55]	1 445	1 261	1 145
Cullen town	1 869	1 956	2 194
Sarepta village	831	882	737
Shongaloo village	163	173	...
Springhill city[55]	6 516	6 496	6 437

Parish Subdivisions	1980	1970	1960
West Baton Rouge Parish[56]	19 086	16 864	14 796
Ward 1	1 753	1 523	1 105
Addis town (pt.)[56]	1 307	696	580
Ward 2	3 563	2 955	2 298
Addis town (pt.)	13	28	10
Brusly town	1 762	1 282	544
Ward 3	7 877	6 983	6 187
Port Allen city[56]	6 114	5 728	5 026
Ward 4	1 964	1 889	1 906
Ward 5	1 096	1 301	1 530
Ward 6	427	614	741
Ward 7	2 406	1 599	1 029
West Carroll Parish[57]	12 922	13 028	14 177
Ward 1	1 849	1 872	2 000
Epps village[57]	672	448	411
Ward 2	1 807	1 965	2 377
Pioneer village	221	188	154
Ward 3	2 827	2 718	3 052
Forest village	299	221	...
Ward 4	4 511	4 441	4 606
Oak Grove town[57]	2 214	1 980	1 797
Ward 5	1 928	2 032	2 142
Kilbourne village	286	370	227
West Feliciana Parish	12 186	'10 761	12 395
Ward 1	1 289	1 505	1 921
St. Francisville town (pt.)	1 284	1 452	1 661
Ward 2	837	740	756
Ward 3	1 361	1 330	1 709
St. Francisville town (pt.)	187	151	...
Ward 4	540	408	710
Ward 5	385	373	524
Ward 7	5 746	'4 682	4 671
Ward 8	482	556	611
Ward 9	964	627	740
Ward 10	582	540	753
Winn Parish[58]	17 253	16 369	16 034
Ward 1	8 961	8 393	8 114
Winnfield city[58]	7 311	7 142	7 022
Ward 2	1 135	1 376	1 362
Tullos town (pt.)	–	...	...
Ward 3	800	701	874
Sikes village	226	237	233
Ward 4	741	630	557
Ward 5	1 213	1 235	1 171
Ward 6	708	696	652
Atlanta village[58]	127	'197	(NA)
Ward 7	1 458	1 297	1 360
Dodson village	469	457	512
Ward 8	1 268	1 145	1 083
Calvin village[58]	263	286	232
Ward 9	491	443	382
Ward 10	478	453	479

Parish Subdivision Map Legend

TYPE STYLES	GEOGRAPHIC AREAS
CANADA	Foreign country
FLORIDA	State
LEE	Parish
Brent	Parish subdivision
MIAMI	Incorporated place
STAPLETON	Census designated place
Lake Wingra	Major water feature

Asterisk following place name indicates place is coextensive with a parish subdivision. Parish subdivision name is shown only when it differs from place name.

Note: All political boundaries are as of January 1, 1980. Boundaries of small areas may not be depicted exactly due to scale of map. Where boundaries coincide, boundary symbol of higher level geographic area is shown. Those places shown with parish subdivision symbol, but identified with type styles for incorporated or census designated places, are treated as parish subdivisions for census purposes.

MAP SECTIONS

NOTE: Louisiana parishes are the equivalent of counties in other States. The parish subdivisions are minor civil divisions (MCD's) known as police jury wards.

[1]ACADIA PARISH. Annexations were made by Rayne and Crowley cities and Church Point town.

[2]ALLEN PARISH. Annexations were made by Oakdale city and Kinder town.

[3]ASCENSION PARISH. Annexations were made by Donaldsonville and Gonzales cities.

[4]ASSUMPTION PARISH. The parish was redistricted. 1980 ward boundaries are not comparable with 1970 wards.

[5]AVOYELLES PARISH. Annexations were made by Marksville, Mansura, and Bunkie towns.

[6]BEAUREGARD PARISH. Annexations were made by De Ridder city. The parish was partially redistricted; Wards 3, 7, and 8 are not comparable in area to 1970.

[7]BIENVILLE PARISH. Annexations were made by Arcadia and Ringgold towns and Bryceland village. Lucky village was incorporated (1970 population: 297). The parish was redistricted; 1980 ward boundaries are not comparable with 1970 wards.

[8]BOSSIER PARISH. Annexations were made by Bossier City and Shreveport cities and Benton and Haughton towns. The parish was redistricted; 1980 ward boundaries are not comparable in area with 1970 wards.

[9]CADDO PARISH. Annexations were made by Shreveport city, Oil City, Vivian, and Mooringsport towns, and Blanchard, Greenwood, and Ida villages. Belcher village was not returned separately in 1970. The parish was partially redistricted; wards 3, 4, 5, 7, and 8 are not comparable in area to 1970.

[10]CALCASIEU PARISH. Annexations were made by Lake Charles and Sulphur cities. Area was annexed and detached by Westlake town.

[11]CALDWELL PARISH. The parish was redistricted; 1980 ward boundaries are not comparable with 1970 wards.

[12]CATAHOULA PARISH. Annexations were made by Jonesville town and Sicily Island village. The parish was redistricted; 1980 ward boundaries are not comparable with 1970 wards.

[13]CLAIBORNE PARISH. Haynesville town annexed into ward 2. Additional annexations were made by Haynesville. Area was annexed and detached by Homer town.

[14]CONCORDIA PARISH. Annexations were made by Ferriday and Vidalia towns. The parish was redistricted; 1980 ward boundaries are not comparable with 1970 wards.

[15]DE SOTO PARISH. Annexations were made by South Mansfield village. Stonewall town was incorporated (1970 population: 551).

[16]EAST BATON ROUGE PARISH. Annexations were made by Baton Rouge city which is coextensive with Ward 1. Annexations were also made by Baker and Zachary cities.

[17]EAST FELICIANA PARISH. Annexations were made by Clinton town and Norwood village.

[18]EVANGELINE PARISH. Annexations were made by Ville Platte and Mamou towns. Chataignier village was incorporated (1970 population: 365).

[19]FRANKLIN PARISH. Annexations were made by Winnsboro town and Baskin village.

[20]GRANT PARISH. Pollock town annexed into Ward 3. Additional annexations were made by Pollock, and by Colfax town and Georgetown village.

[21]IBERIA PARISH. Annexations were made by New Iberia and Jeanerette cities and Loreauville village. The parish was redistricted; 1980 ward boundaries are not comparable with 1970 wards.

[22]IBERVILLE PARISH. Annexations were made by Plaquemine city, White Castle town, and Rosedale village.

[23]JACKSON PARISH. Annexations were made by Jonesboro town and North Hodge and East Hodge villages. East Hodge village was not returned separately in 1970. The parish was redistricted; 1980 ward boundaries are not comparable with 1970 wards.

[24]JEFFERSON PARISH. Jean Lafitte town was incorporated (1970 population: 539). Annexations were made by Kenner city and Jean Lafitte town. Part of Ward 2 was added to Ward 3. The boundary was changed between Ward 8 and Ward 10.

[25]JEFFERSON DAVIS PARISH. Annexations were made by Jennings city.

[26]LAFAYETTE PARISH. Annexations were made by Lafayette city and Carencro, Scott, and Broussard towns. Area was detached by Carencro town. The parish was redistricted; 1980 ward boundaries are not comparable with 1970 wards.

[27]LAFOURCHE PARISH. Thibodaux city annexed into Ward 5. Additional annexations and detachments were made by Thibodaux. Annexations were also made by Lockport town.

[28]LA SALLE PARISH. Annexations were made by Olla, Tullos, and Jena towns. Urania town was not returned separately in 1970. The parish was redistricted; 1980 ward boundaries are not comparable with 1970 wards.

[29]LINCOLN PARISH. Annexations were made by Ruston city and Grambling and Vienna towns. Vienna town was reactivated. Downsville village was incorporated in Lincoln and Union parishes (1970 population: 160, total; 38 in Lincoln Parish). The parish was redistricted; 1980 ward boundaries are not comparable with 1970 wards.

[30]LIVINGSTON PARISH. Annexations were made by Denham Springs city, Walker and Livingston towns, and Killian village.

Corbin village was consolidated with Walker town (combined 1970 population: 1,552). French Settlement and Killian villages were not returned separately in 1970. The parish was redistricted: Wards 1, 8, and 11 were consolidated into new Ward 1 (combined 1970 population: 8,815); Wards 2 and 7 were consolidated into new Ward 2 (combined 1970 population: 13,414); Wards 3 and 9 were consolidated into new Ward 3 (combined 1970 population: 4,512); and Wards 4, 5, 6, and 10 were consolidated into the new Ward 4 (combined 1970 population: 9,770).

[31]MADISON PARISH. Annexations were made by Tallulah city. Richmond village was incorporated (1970 population: 56). The parish was redistricted; 1980 ward boundaries are not comparable with 1970 wards.

[32]MOREHOUSE PARISH. Bastrop city annexed into Ward 3. Additional annexations were made by Bastrop and by Oak Ridge village.

[33]NATCHITOCHES PARISH. Annexations were made by Natchitoches city, Campti town, and Ashland and Goldonna villages. Natchez village was incorporated (1970 population: 354).

[34]OUACHITA PARISH. Annexations were made by Monroe and West Monroe cities. Richwood town was incorporated (1970 population: 1,466).

[35]POINTE COUPEE PARISH. Annexations were made by Morganza and Livonia villages.

[36]RAPIDES PARISH. Ball town was incorporated (1970 population: 1,642). Annexations were made by Alexandria and Pineville cities, Lecompte and Ball towns, and Forest Hill and McNary villages. Area was detached by Alexandria and Pineville cities.

[37]RED RIVER PARISH. Annexations were made by Coushatta town and Hall Summit village. Martin village was incorporated (1970 population: 416). The parish was redistricted; the 1980 ward boundaries are not comparable with 1970 wards.

[38]RICHLAND PARISH. Annexations were made by Delhi and Rayville towns.

[39]SABINE PARISH. Florien village annexed into Ward 4. Additional annexations were made by Florien and by Many town. Fisher village was incorporated (1970 population: 191).

[40]ST. BERNARD PARISH. The parish was redistricted; 1980 ward boundaries are not comparable with 1970 wards.

[41]ST. CHARLES PARISH. The parish was redistricted; 1980 ward boundaries are not comparable with 1970 wards.

[42]ST. HELENA PARISH. Annexations were made by Greensburg town.

[43]ST. JAMES PARISH. Annexations were made by Gramercy and Lutcher towns. The parish was redistricted; 1980 ward boundaries are not comparable with 1970 wards.

[44]ST. LANDRY PARISH. Annexations were made by Opelousas and Eunice cities, Port Barre, Grand Coteau, and Arnaudville towns, and Leonville village. The parish was partially redistricted; the boundaries were changed for all wards except Ward 6.

[45]ST. MARTIN PARISH. Henderson town was incorporated (1970 population: 1,107). Annexations were made by St. Martinville and Breaux Bridge cities and Henderson town. The parish was redistricted; 1980 ward boundaries are not comparable with 1970 wards.

[46]ST. MARY PARISH. Annexations were made by Franklin and Morgan City cities and Patterson and Berwick towns.

[47]ST. TAMMANY PARISH. Annexations were made by Covington and Slidell cities, Mandeville and Abita Springs towns, and Folsom and Sun villages.

[48]TANGIPAHOA PARISH. Annexations were made by Hammond and Ponchatoula cities, Amite City town, and Tickfaw village. The parish was partially redistricted; part of Ward 5 was transferred to Ward 4.

[49]TENSAS PARISH. Annexations were made by Newellton and Waterproof towns. The parish was redistricted; 1980 ward boundaries are not comparable with 1970 wards.

[50]TERREBONNE PARISH. Houma city annexed into Wards 7 and 9. Additional annexations were made by Houma.

[51]UNION PARISH. Annexations were made by Bernice town and Marion village. Downsville village was incorporated in Lincoln and Union parishes (1970 population: 160 total; 122 in Union Parish). The parish was redistricted; 1980 ward boundaries are not comparable with 1970 wards.

[52]VERMILION PARISH. Annexations were made by Abbeville and Kaplan cities and Erath and Gueydan towns.

[53]VERNON PARISH. De Ridder city annexed into Vernon Parish. Additional annexations were made by Leesville city and Newllano and Simpson villages. Anacoco village was incorporated (1970 population: 498).

[54]WASHINGTON PARISH. Annexations were made by Franklinton town.

[55]WEBSTER PARISH. Annexations were made by Minden and Springhill cities, Cotton Valley town, and Dixie Inn and Sibley villages. The parish was redistricted; Wards 3, 4, and 5 were consolidated into new Ward 1 (1970 combined population: 23,866). Wards 1 and 2 were consolidated into new Ward 2 (1970 combined population: 16,073).

[56]WEST BATON ROUGE PARISH. Annexations were made by Port Allen city and Addis town.

[57]WEST CARROLL PARISH. Annexations were made by Oak Grove town and Epps village.

[58]WINN PARISH. Annexations were made by Winnfield city and Calvin village. Atlanta village was not returned separately in 1970.

Parish Subdivisions, Section 1

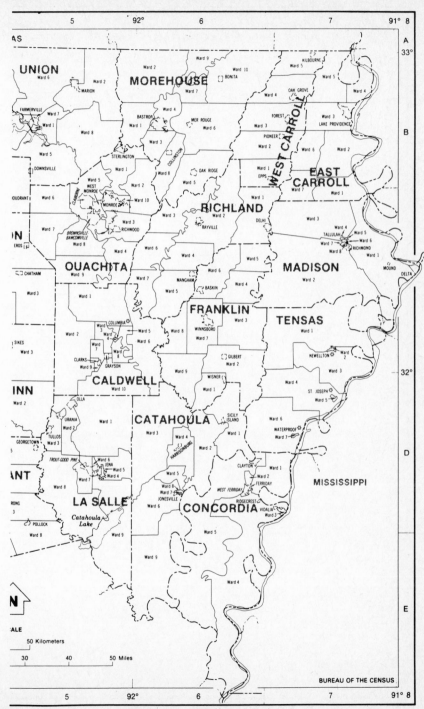

Parish Subdivisions, Section 1

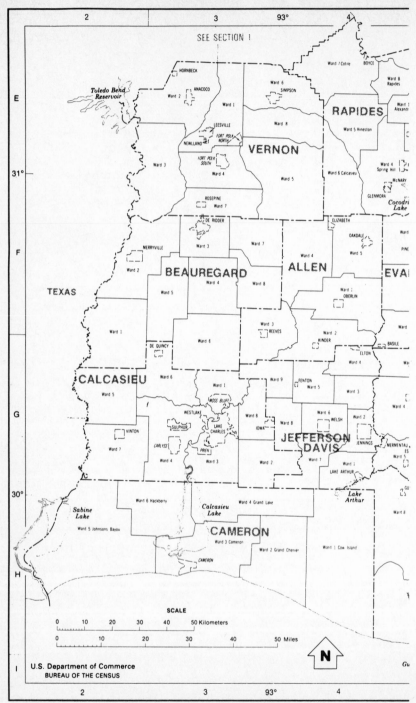

Parish Subdivisions, Section 2

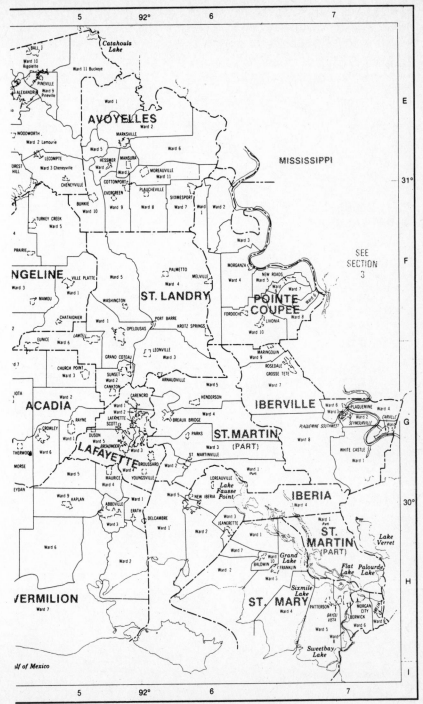

Parish Subdivisions, Section 2

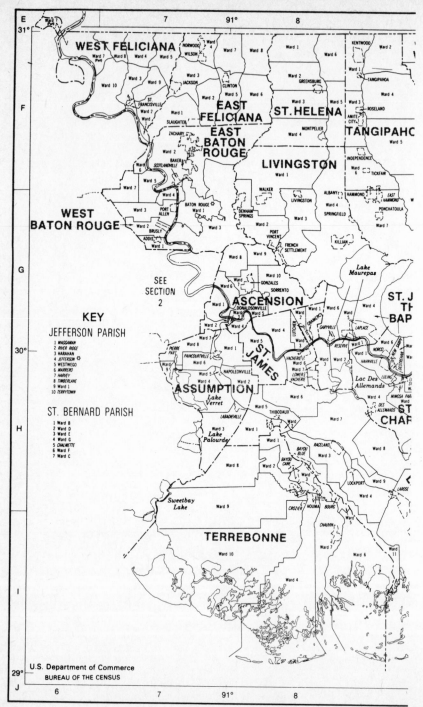

Parish Subdivisions, Section 3

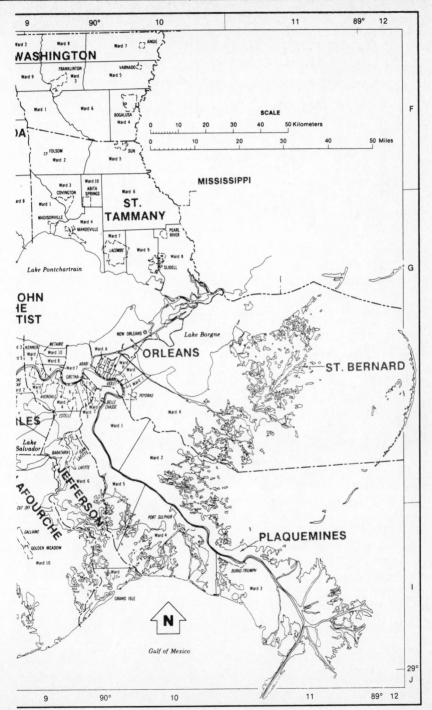

Parish Subdivisions, Section 3

Urbanized Areas

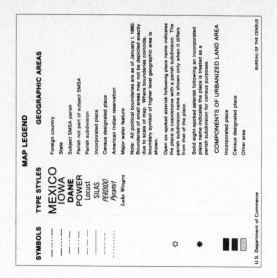

MAP LEGEND

SYMBOLS   **TYPE STYLES**   **GEOGRAPHIC AREAS**

	MEXICO	Foreign country
	IOWA	State
	DANE	Subject SMSA parish
	POWER	Parish not part of subject SMSA
	Locust	Parish subdivision
	SILAS	Incorporated place
	PERDIDO	Census designated place
	Pyramit	American Indian reservation
	Lake Wingra	Major water feature

Note: All political boundaries are as of January 1, 1980. Boundaries of small areas may not be depicted exactly due to scale of map. Where boundaries coincide, boundary symbol of higher level geographic area is shown.

Open six-spoked asterisk following place name indicates the place is coextensive with a parish subdivision. The parish subdivision name is shown only when it differs from that of the place.

Solid eight-spoked asterisk following an incorporated place name indicates the place is treated as a parish subdivision for census purposes.

COMPONENTS OF URBANIZED LAND AREA

Incorporated place
Census designated place
Other area

U.S. Department of Commerce   BUREAU OF THE CENSUS

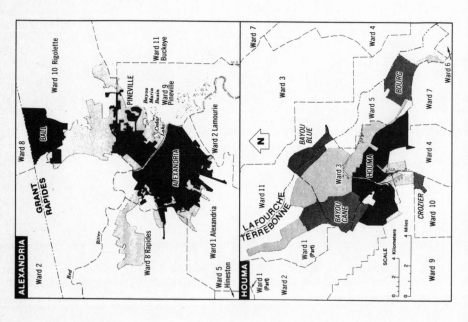

ALEXANDRIA

Ward 2 · GRANT RAPIDES · Ward 8 · Ward 10 Rigolette · PINEVILLE · Bayou Maria Basin · Cedar Lake · Ward 9 Pineville · Ward 11 Buckeye · BALL · ALEXANDRIA · Ward 2 Lamourie · Ward 8 Rapides · Red River · Ward 1 Alexandria · Ward 5 Hineston

HOUMA

Ward 7 · Ward 3 · Ward 4 · Ward 5 · BAYOU BLUE · BOURG · Ward 6 · Ward 7 · Ward 3 · HOUMA · LAFOURCHE · TERREBONNE · Ward 11 · BAYOU CANE · Ward 4 · CROZIER · Ward 10 · Ward 1 (Part) · Ward 2 · Ward 1 (Part) · Ward 9 · SCALE · 0 2 4 Kilometers · 0 2 4 Miles

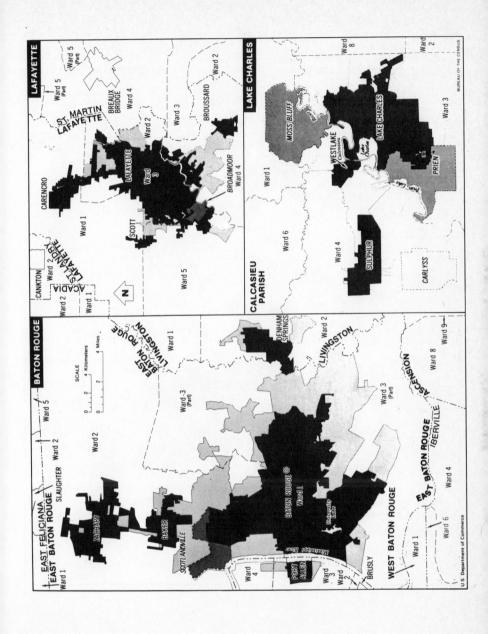

LAFAYETTE

BATON ROUGE

LAKE CHARLES

CALCASIEU PARISH

BUREAU OF THE CENSUS

U.S. Department of Commerce

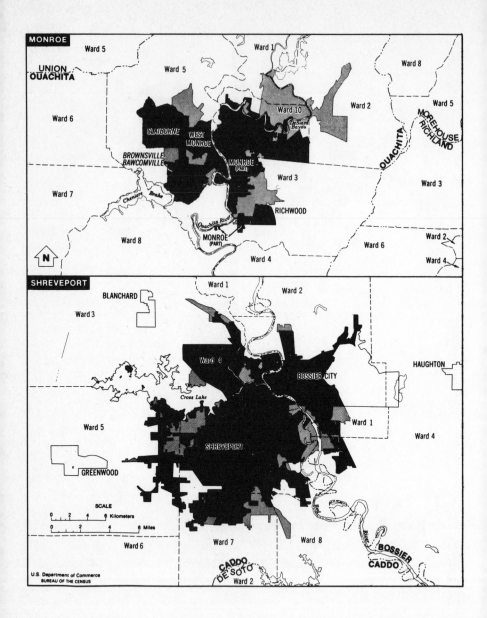

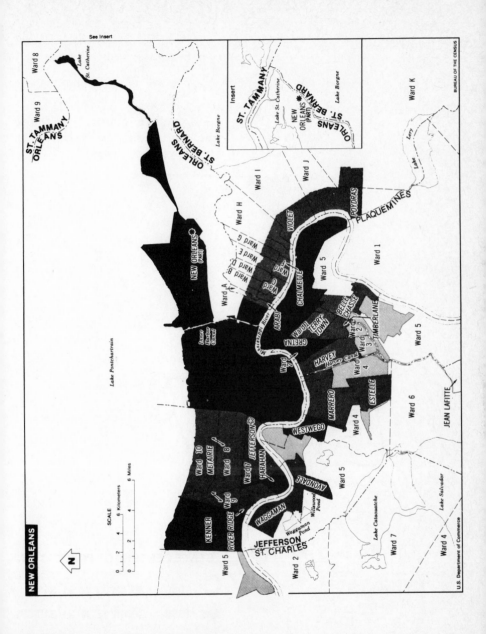

NEW ORLEANS

SCALE

0   2   4   6 Kilometers
0   2   4   6 Miles

BUREAU OF THE CENSUS

U.S. Department of Commerce

LOUISIANA POPULATION AND GEOGRAPHIC CENTERS

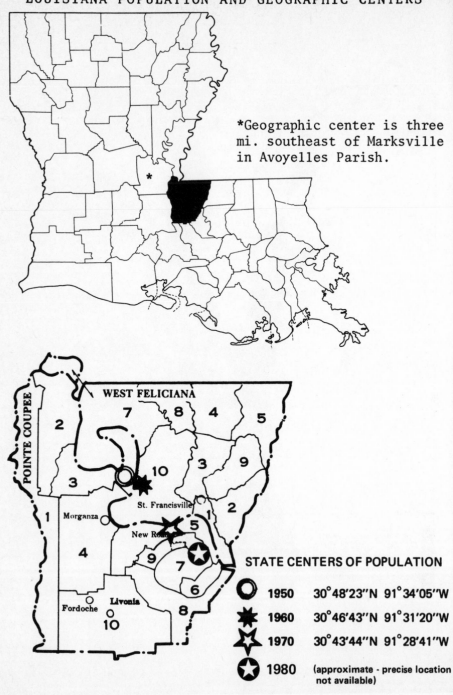

*Geographic center is three mi. southeast of Marksville in Avoyelles Parish.

STATE CENTERS OF POPULATION

⭕	1950	30°48'23"N	91°34'05"W
✴	1960	30°46'43"N	91°31'20"W
✰	1970	30°43'44"N	91°28'41"W
★	1980	(approximate - precise location not available)	

PARISHES HAVING A MINORITY POPULATION, OTHER THAN
BLACK, OF .5 PERCENT (.005) OR MORE.

PERCENT OF POPULATION

	TOTAL	1/AMERICAN INDIAN	2/ASIAN	3/OTHER	4/HISPANIC
Acadia	0	0	0	0	1.47
Allen	1.3	1.3	0	0	0
Ascension	0	0	0	0	2.11
Assumption	0	0	0	0	2.81
Avoyelles	0	0	0	0	1.27
Bossier	1.0	.2	.6	.2	1.91
Caddo	.6	.1	.4	.1	1.44
Calcasieu	.5	.2	.2	.1	1.61
Cameron	.6	.2	.3	.1	0
East Baton Rouge	1.2	.2	.8	.2	1.81
Evangeline	0	0	0	0	1.50
Iberia	0	0	0	0	3.52
Iberville	0	0	0	0	2.29
Jefferson	1.7	.3	1.3	.1	4.84
Jefferson Davis	0	0	0	0	1.93
Lafayette	.8	.1	.6	.1	2.57
Lafourche	1.5	1.2	.2	.1	2.34
LaSalle	1.2	.9	.3	0	0
Lincoln	1.0	.2	.4	.4	1.06
Livingston	0	0	0	0	1.29
Natchitoches	.6	.2	.2	.2	1.88
Orleans	1.5	.1	1.3	.1	3.44
Ouachita	.5	.1	.3	.1	.82
Plaquemines	2.0	1.2	.5	.3	2.20
Pointe Coupee	.5	.1	.3	.1	1.39
Rapides	.9	.3	.5	.1	1.16
Sabine	1.7	1.5	.1	.1	8.12
St. Bernard	.8	.4	.4	0	8.08
St. Charles	.5	.3	.2	0	2.51
St. John	0	0	0	0·	1.62
St. Landry	0	0	0	0	1.33
St. Martin	0	0	0	0	1.64
St. Mary	1.4	.5	.8	.1	2.25
St. Tammany	.7	.3	.3	.1	2.19
Tangipahoa	0	0	0	0	1.32
Terrebonne	3.6	3.3	.2	.1	1.53
Vermilion	0	0	0	0	1.55
Vernon	2.2	.5	1.6	.1	4.22
Webster	0	0	0	0	.75

1/ This category includes American Indians, Aleuts and Eskimos.

2/ This category includes Japanese, Chinese, Filipino, Korean, East or Asian Indian, Vietnamese, Hawaiian, Guamanian, and Samoan.

3/ This category includes all minority races other than Black and those listed.'

4/ Hispanics are included in all races. This Column not included in total.

Source: Louisiana Department of Labor, Office of Employment Security, 1987

White and Nonwhite Population in Louisiana

Year	Total Population	White	Nonwhite	Percent White	Percent Nonwhite
1840	352,411	158,457	193,954	45.0	55.0
1880	939,946	454,954	483,655	48.4	51.5
1890	1,118,588	558,395	559,193	49.9	50.1
1900	1,381,625	729,612	650,804	52.9	47.1
1910	1,656,388	941,086	713,874	56.8	43.1
1920	1,798,509	1,096,611	700,257	61.1	38.9
1930	2,101,593	1,322,712	776,326	62.9	36.9
1940	2,363,880	1,511,739	849,303	64.1	35.9
1950	2,683,516	1,796,683	882,428	66.95	32.9
1960	3,257,022	2,211,715	1,045,307	67.9	32.1
1970	3,644,637	2,552,572	1,088,734	70.1	29.9
1980	4,206,312	2,912,172	1,294,140	69.2	30.8

Places with No Black Residents: 1980
(*no blacks in 1970)

Dixie Inn--Webster
Dry Prong--Grant
Eros--Jackson
Forest--West Carroll*
Georgetown--Grant*
Golden Meadow--Lafourche*
Goldonna--Natchitoches*

Hornbeck--Vernon*
Jamestown--Bienville
Krotz Springs--St. Landry
Morse--Acadia
Noble--Sabine*
Pine Prairie--Evangeline*
Plaucheville--Avoyelles

Provencal--Natchitoches*
Reeves--Allen*
Ridgecrest--Concordia
Simpson--Vernon*
Spearsville--Union
Turkey Creek--Evangeline*

Source: College of Administration and Business, Louisiana Tech

Median Age
Louisiana and the United States

Year	Louisiana	United States
1900	19.4	22.9
1910	20.4	24.1
1920	21.7	25.3
1930	23.1	26.5
1940	25.5	29.0
1950	26.7	30.1
1960	25.3	29.5
1970	24.8	28.1
1980	27.3	30.0

Source: Statistical Abstract of the U.S.

PROJECTED POPULATION BY AGE FOR LOUISIANA TO 2000

	1985	1990	1995	2000
0-4	377,880	371,272	354,433	339,880
5-9	358,568	378,555	370,901	355,818
10-14	341,182	355,497	375,793	368,604
15-19	345,691	340,698	354,615	374,127
20-24	386,961	331,460	333,191	338,539
25-29	387,043	390,726	324,218	330,976
30-34	363,821	394,524	393,444	330,749
35-39	286,861	355,519	391,777	386,422
40-44	228,157	282,610	350,017	386,249
45-49	190,324	223,008	275,471	341,601
50-54	176,590	184,452	214,867	266,829
55-59	180,155	167,267	173,855	203,908
60-64	162,073	165,979	153,186	160,582
65-69	133,433	144,490	146,424	137,655
70-74	107,341	110,963	119,220	122,479
75+	157,032	164,406	182,157	184,802

Source: University of New Orleans,
Division of Business and Economic Research, January, 1976.

PARISHES OF LOUISIANA

In the State of Louisiana the subdivisions—in other states called "counties"—are known as **parishes.** This is because the original divisions fitted in with the ecclesiastical jurisdictions of the Roman Catholic Church whose districts, as we all know, are called parishes. When Louisiana was purchased from France in 1803, it was divided into two parts and what is now approximately the State of Louisiana was called the Orleans Territory. It was governed by a legislative council composed of the governor, W. C. C. Claiborne, and thirteen men of the Territory. On April 10, 1805, the Legislative Council divided the Orleans Territory into twelve **counties** Orleans, German Coast, Acadia [probably the Acadian Coast] Lafourche, Iberville, Pointe Coupee, Attakapas, Ope-

lousas, Natchitoches, Rapides, Ouachita, and Concordia. The boundaries of these were somewhat indefinite, but they coincided with the parishes established by the Church during the Spanish and French regimes. And so they were still called parishes by nearly every one.

On March 31, 1807, the territorial legislature passed an act which divided the Orleans Territory into nineteen **parishes,** but did not abolish the original twelve **counties.** These parishes were: City of New Orleans, St. Bernard, Plaquemines, St. Charles, St. John the Baptist, St. James, Ascension, The Parish of the Assumption, (Lafourche), Interior Lafourche, Iberville, Baton Rouge, Pointe Coupee, Concordia, Ouachita, Rapides, Avoyelles, Natchitoches, St. Landry, and

the Parish of the Attakapas, or St. Martin.
During this period both the term
county and parish were used. In 1811
Congress authorized the people of the
Orleans Territory to form a constitution
and a State's government for admission
into the Union. The Legislature of the
Orleans Territory provided that 45 representatives be apportioned from the original twelve counties. The Constitution was
adopted on January 22, 1812, and was
signed by these county representatives.
At the meeting of the first Legislature of
the State of Louisiana, after it was admitted to the Union, the State was divided by parishes into seven judicial districts,
and the word parish became to be generally accepted. In 1816 a map of Louisiana
published by William Darby showed 25
parishes. On several occasions up until
the adoption of another Constitution in
1845 the State Legislature used the word
county in several of its acts. Ever since
1845—over one hundred years ago—the
political subdivisions of Louisiana have
been known as parishes.

From the original nineteen parishes
there have been created 37 other parishes.
Eight parishes came from "West Florida"
which up until 1810 had been claimed by
Spain. These parishes have been ever
since called the "Florida Parishes." 48
parishes had been formed by 1857. Two
parishes were created in 1868 and nine
more created between that time and
1907. And by 1912 the last five parishes
of LaSalle, Beauregard, Evangeline, Allen and Jefferson Davis had been established.

It is interesting to note that two parishes, after an existence of several years,
were discontinued, so to speak. One was
Attakapas. This parish was created from
Attakapas County on March 31, 1807, but
on April 17, 1811, it was divided into St.
Martin and St. Mary Parishes. However,
even to this day people in southern Louisiana speak of the country along the
Teche as the Attakapas country. Attakapas is the name of an Indian tribe, said
to have been cannibals, who inhabited
this country before the coming of the
white man.

The other parish to lose its identity was
Warren, created from Concordia on March
20, 1811. It was dissolved and annexed to
the parishes of Ouachita and Concorida
in Feb. 14, 1814.

Carroll Parish was divided into East
and West Carroll in 1877. Feliciana
Parish was divided on Feb. 17, 1824 into
East and West Feliciana Parishes and
Lafourche Interior was changed on March
23, 1853 into Lafourche Parish.

Among the other proposed parishes for
which ordinances were drawn but which
parishes never came into existence were
Biloxi Parish to be formed from Feliciana
County on June 4, 1811.

An ordiance providing for the creation
of Pascagoula Parish from the County of

Feliciana, was introduced on January 4,
1811.

The creation of Dugdemonia Parish
(one wonders where the ugly name came
from), from the parishes of Catahoula,
Natchitoches and Rapides was proposed
on March 18, 1850.

Even as late as July 10, 1890, an act to
create the Parish of Troy from Catahoula
Parish was passed, but the parish was
never established.

The names of Louisiana parishes themselves tell much of the history of the
State. Many are of Indian origin, named
for the tribes which once lived in the
regions—Avoyelles, Caddo, Natchitoches,
Ouachita, Tensas. Or some have retained
the names which the Indian inhabitants
gave them—Calcasieu (crying eagle), Catahoula (beloved lake), Tangipahoa (ear
of corn).

Other names are reminiscent of French
occupation—Acadia, for the exiles who
settled in that parish, East and West
Baton Rouge (red stick), Plaquemines
(persimmons), and Terrebonne (good
earth). Some are named in honor of
French explorers—Iberville, Bienville, La-
Salle. From the Spanish occupation come
the names DeSoto, Iberia, Concordia and
Feliciana.

Other parishes are named for men who
have figured in American history or in
Louisiana history since it became a State
—Washington, Franklin, Claiborne, Jeffer-
son, Madison, Webster, Jefferson Davis,
Beauregard, Lincoln, Grant and Allen.

The designations of church parishes of the
French and Spanish eras in Louisiana are re-
tained by—St. James, St. John the Baptist, St.
Helena, St. Bernard, St. Charles, St. Martin,
St. Mary, St. Landry, Assumption and Ascen-
sion.

AREA AND POPULATION OF PARISHES
Largest Parishes
Total Area..Plaquemines......1986 sq.mi.
Land Area...Cameron..........1,417 sq. mi.
Water Area..St. Bernard......1408 sq.mi.
Population..Orleans..........　557,927
Smallest Parishes
Total Area..West Baton Rouge..209 sq.mi.
Land Area..West Baton Rouge ... 194 sq. mi.
Population..Tensas............　8,525

Note:　Several parishes have less than
　　　　five sq. mi. water areas.

FLORIDA PARISHES

The Florida Parishes are so-called because at one time they were part of
Florida territory claimed by Spain, which
extended from the Atlantic Ocean to the
Mississippi River below the 33rd Parallel
of Latitude, excluding the City of New
Orleans. In 1810 (Sept. 24th) the citizens
of West Florida rebelled and seized Baton
Rouge from the Spanish officials and set
themselves up as the West Florida Re-

public. A month later acting under orders of President Madison, Governor Claiborne took over the territory on the grounds that it had been part of the original Louisiana purchase. The following parishes were carved from the territory:

> East Baton Rouge
> East Feliciana
> Livingston
> St. Helena
> St. Tammany
> Tangipahoa
> Washington
> West Feliciana
> Eastern Part of Ascension

PARISH HISTORIES OF LOUISIANA

The broad canvas of the history of the country has been painted. The history of the United States—discoveries, conquests, colonies, states, Territories, wars, business cycles and social development—has been pretty well covered. There is not much new in the way of facts to be related—only generalizations and theorizings. But the history of minor divisions such as counties and cities, giving the details of names, dates and local events is a field that has scarcely been touched.

There are, of course, quite a number of local histories in the aggregate, but in the United States there are over 3,000 counties and over 4,000 towns and cities with populations over 2,500, and the total number of place histories is numbered in the hundreds.

In Louisiana, the state with a romantic and interesting history, the number of parish and city histories is remarkably few. There are only two or three histories of New Orleans—Kendall's and Rightor's, besides those treating of special subjects such as the Fire Department—and only nine or ten parishes have had histories written and printed about them.

Among the most complete is the History of Avoyelles Parish by Corinne Saucier—a 500-page book with maps and numerous illustrations. Sidney Marchand of Donaldsonville has written three books on Ascension Parish. There are small and incomplete histories of East Feliciana, Concordia, Caddo and one or two other towns and parishes.

Other parish histories are: "The Attakapas Country," a history of Lafayette Parish, by H. L. Griffin; "Cabanocey," a history of St. James Parish, by Lillian Bourgeois; "They Tasted Bayou Water," a history of Iberia Parish, by Maurine Bergerie; "No Man's Land," a history of the Natchitoches section, by Louis R. Nardini.

Several years ago St. Tammany Parish Fair Association at their Parish Fair had an interesting historical exhibit. The loan items were collected by Philip Burns, Jr. of Covington, and the display was quite a success.

A new history of St. Tammany Parish has been written by Judge Stephen Ellis, "St. Tammany Parish: L'Autre Cote du lac," and other parish groups are gathering historical material on their areas.

THE FREE STATE OF SABINE

The western boundary line of Louisiana for many years was indefinite. In fact, even before the United States bought Louisiana there was a continual conflict between the French and Spanish about the ownership of the land west of Natchitoches. Disputes about Louisiana's western boundary raged for a hundred years.

When the United States purchased Louisiana the Spanish claimed what is now Sabine Parish. In 1806 to substantiate their claim a Spanish army advanced as far as the Sabine River. American troops were on the east bank. The commanders of the armies compromised by agreeing that a certain strip of land about fifty miles wide along the Sabine River would be "neutral" ground and both armies withdrew.

Since by agreement no police power or armed force could enter this area, this neutral zone became the refuge for outcasts, thieves and murderers. Outlaws and criminals came from everywhere to live here, free from arrest or molestation by governmental authorities. The caves and forest glens were excellent hiding places for those robbers and desperadoes.

The two lanes of traffic that connected the East with San Antonio and other parts of Texas crossed this neutral ground. One was known as the San Antonio Trace and the other as Nolan's Trace. Nearly all the immense traffic that went between Texas and Louisiana had to go through the Free State of Sabine over those "traces."

Robberies and murders were numerous, and, as in the deserts of Arabia, people traveled in "caravans" armed and ready to fight.

In 1822 General Zachary Taylor established Fort Jessup on the San Antonio Trace about 20 miles from the Sabine River. General Taylor violated the agreement with Spain, but that country was too weak or indifferent to protest. His soldiers began to bring order into this lawless region. It was not until 1826 that the Sabine River was recognized as the Western boundary of the State of Louisiana, and the "Free State of Sabine" became part of the State of Louisiana and of the United States.

New Orleans, a city of charm and uniqueness, has at one time or another been the home of many famous people. Among the notables that were drawn to the Crescent City are Frances Xavier Cabrini, first American saint, Jean Lafitte, pirate and privateer, John James Audubon, naturalist, P.G.T. Beauregard, Confederate officer, Francis Parkinson Keyes, author, Lafcadio Hearn, author, and Tennessee Williams, playwright.

THE FOUNDING OF NEW ORLEANS

The Romans used to date everything ab.urbe condita—from the founding of the city. Although New Orleans was founded in comparatively recent historical times and its beginning is not lost in the myth of antiquity, yet there is uncertainty in the minds of some about the actual date of its establishment.

When referring to the founding of New Orleans we think of its settlement by Europeans. For on the spot where New Orleans now stands at various times Indian tribes lived in villages for generations, perhaps, before the coming of the white man. La Salle with twenty men came down the Mississippi River in 1682. On April 3rd, quoting from Gabriel Hanotaux:

"After a not very serious skirmish with the **Quinnipissas**, the explorers came upon the village of **Tangipaho**, a place which had been inhabited by about a score of people but which had been destroyed by the Oumas, and subsequently encamped on the left bank of the river some two leagues further down. Thus was discovered the site of the future city of New Orleans."

The location of New Orleans had early attracted the eyes of some explorers. In 1702 M. de Remonville proposed that a portage be created on the present site of the city. Bienville in 1707 and in 1708 had noted the location, and wanted to move the post located further down the river on the other side to that site. Crozat, who had "leased" Louisiana, in the winter of 1715-16 objected to the erection of a post at this place.

As a matter of fact there were a few white people living in what is now Orleans Parish before 1717. D'Artaguette reported that there were five to seven inhabitants living between the Mississippi River and Lake Pontchartrain in 1715, and Gayarre states that these five or seven people planted an arpent of corn in Gentilly in that year—the first white farmers in all Louisiana. Thus, it may be in one sense, that New Orleans was founded as early as 1715 or earlier.

It was to John Law, however, that New Orleans owed its birth. He named the city after his protector and regent, the Duke of Orleans.

According to Pere Charlevoix the establishment of New Orleans was decided on in the spring of 1717. On October 1, 1717 the Counseil de la Marine named Bonnaud as warehouse keeper and pay master (caissier) at New Orleans. On the same day, the company ordered the **Neptune** to proceed to Louisiana and to go up the Mississippi River. Charlevoix further says that de L'Epinay, the Governor of Louisiana, ordered Bienville to found New Orleans.

On October 24, 1717 the directors of the West India Company (with a capital of 100 million francs) headed by John Law, who had already taken over Louisiana from Crozat, met in Paris to discuss the details of the colonization of Louisiana. At this meeting a letter was read by D'Artaguette from Bienville, who had lived seventeen years in Louisiana, which told of a crescent bend in the Mississippi where Lake Pontchartrain almost touched the river by Bayou St. John, and half way by water between Natchez and Mobile and safe from tidal waves and hurricanes.

On October 25, 1717 the Company formally authorized the founding of New Orleans. Two hundred years later on October 25, 1917, the bicentenary of the founding of the City of New Orleans was celebrated at Paris. Champagny—**Etat Present de la Louisiane**—says: "The choice of 1718 seems quite indicated, but 1717, the date of the official founding in Paris can equally well be adopted. For cities, like humans, is not their baptism a sort of consecration of their existence? And especially in French territory, **par excellence** the country of administrative form, a city which has a paymaster and an adjutant can it not exist?"

However, the actual establishment of New Orleans did not take place until months later. According to Baron Marc de Villiers, "the city was not really founded—in the characteristically French sense of the word—until the arrival of the first public official. The first inhabitant of the future city, in fact, was a tax collector, who came ashore among the reeds and the cypresses and the alligators, with his cash-box, his registers and his account books. Once the French Government was officially on the spot, the tax payers might take up their abode in the district."

Now just when did Bienville or his men arrive at the site of New Orleans to begin the foundation of the city? Martin, considered an authority on Louisiana history, says (Vol. I, Chap. 9):

"On the 9th of February three of the company's ships arrived with as many companies of infantry and 69 colonists; Boisbrillant, who came in this fleet, was the bearer of Bienville's commission as governor of the province. Bienville dispatched Chateaugay with 50 men to take possession, of the Bay of St. Joseph. In the meanwhile Bienville visited the banks of the Mississippi to seek a spot for the principal settlement of the Providence. He chose that upon which the city of New Orleans now stands and left there 50 men to clear the ground and erect barracks."

As will be seen, this is an indefinite statement. It does not say that the company's ships arrived at New Orleans. They must have arrived at Biloxi.

Penicaut says the **Neptune** arrived filled with munitions and merchandise at New Orleans on February 9th. [Editor's note. **Penicaut, a ship's carpenter, was a sailor** and shipped when eighteen years old with Iberville from La Rochelle. He was un-educated, and probably dictated his nar-rative. Copying much verbatim from Charlevoix, he is otherwise unreliable as an historian. He went blind in 1721.]

On this same day Bienville received his commission as governor-general of Louis-iana, succeeding his old enemy, L'Epinay. This ship also brought him from the King of France the Cross of St. Louis. It was probably from this statement of Penicaut that Martin and others got the idea that the **Neptune** landed at the site of New Orleans on February 9th.

The Louisiana Historical Society in March 1917 passed a formal resolution that "the date for the founding of the City of New Orleans could with all se-curity of historical conviction be decided upon as February 9th, 10th and 11th, 1718."

Penicaut was mixed in his chronology. He confused the date of the arrival of the **Neptune** at Biloxi with the date of founding, and he was confused about the date of the order for the founding of New Orleans.

Villiers states that the date of the founding of New Orleans is somewhere between March 15 and April 15, 1718, and that Bienville named or "christened" the city then.

Lemaire, the map maker of the colony, on May 13, 1718 refused to mark the spot on the map.

Bernard de la Harpe, who was not at New Orleans at the time of the founding and therefore was not an eye witness, states that it occurred in May, 1718. He says: "At this time (Feb. 1718) M. de Bienville sought a fitting spot on the banks of the Mississippi . . . He left there 50 persons, carpenters and convicts [**faux sauliniers**—literally illicit salt makers. A felony in those times] to clear the land and build a few shelters." De Pailloux was the Commander.

Chevalier de Beausain, geographer ordi-nary of the king, in his original notes wrote: "February 1718. At this time M. de Bienville was looking for a site on the Mississippi at which to establish the prin-ciple office of the company."

This fits in with what LaHarpe says above, and allowing for time for explora-tions and bad weather, it could very well have been between the 14th and 16th of April 1718 when according to Villiers the founders finally encamped at the site of New Orleans.

La Harpe's description of the founding of the city reads, "In the month of May 1718, the establishment of New Orleans was started. It is situated at Latitude 20° 50' on level swampy ground suit-able only for the cultivation of rice. The river water seeps through the ground and as the crawfish are also very abun-dant, tobacco and vegetables grow there only with difficulty. Fog is very common

there and, the ground being thickly cov-ered with woods and canebrakes, the air is feverous. Furthermore, during the Summer one suffers from an infinity of mosquitoes." In that year (1718) accord-ing to La Harpe, a handful of settlers shared between them several apple trees and three plum trees.

On June 10, 1718, Bienville wrote that he had gone over to New Orleans, and that he was doing his best to build the city with so few workers. He boasts of having moved to the spot to further the work. He was chagrined to find so few people there. He must have stayed there some time, because DuPratz, who arrived at Dauphine Island on August 25th of that year, mentioned that Bienville was away at New Orleans.

Penicaut relates that about that time M. Hubert built a house near New Or-leans, and he mentions several other fami-lies that moved there from Dauphin Is-land. Du Pratz also mentions Hubert who gave him some advice about Louisiana and who moved later on with Du Pratz to Natchez.

Le Page Du Pratz arrived in Louisiana August 25, 1718. He came over with 800 other colonists on three ships. Some settled at New Orleans and some at Natchez. Du Pratz in his History of Lou-isiana states that when he got to Dauphin Island, "At my first arrival in Louisiana it [New Orleans] existed only in name; for on my landing I understood M. De Bienville, commandant general, was only gone to mark out the spot, whence he returned three days after our arrival at Isle Dauphine."

Four months later—about Jan. 1, 1719—Du Pratz, carrying a letter to M. Pail-loux, major-general who commanded at New Orleans, set out with his hired ser-vants and his effects for that post.

When he got to New Orleans he says, "I went to view a spot on St. John's Creek, about half a league distant from the place where the capital was to be founded, which was only marked out by a hut, covered with palmetto leaves, and which the commandant had caused to be built for his own lodging; and after him for M. Pailloux, whom he left comman-dant of that post."

It thus appears that while New Orleans was founded in 1718, there was very little there in that year. For in 1719, according to La Harpe, there were only four houses in New Orleans besides the Company's sheds which were covered with palmetto leaves. In 1719 a terrible hurricane and inundation occurred which stopped the work of construction.

On November 8, 1719, the Company or-dered Le Blond de la Tour, the chief engi-neer, to have one of his assistants look over the situation at New Orleans and to see whether the "city" should not be re-moved because of the terrible flood the previous spring.

Some time must have elapsed before the order of the Company was carried out, because de Pauger, an assistant engineer, says he arrived in New Orleans to lay it out on March 29, 1721. He found several huts among the bushes—quelques baraques parmy les broussailles.

De Pauger (Pauger Street is named after him) in a way was the real builder or founder of New Orleans. He first sounded the river at its mouth and found from 10 to 14 feet of water, making the channel deep enough for any ship of that day.

Bienville ordered de Pauger to draw plans for the city. When he arrived the "convicts," unwilling to work, fled to the woods and he appealed to de Pailloux for hands. The commandant put an officer and a few soldiers under de Pauger, and with these he finished clearing and laid out the plan of the city.

Then on April 14, 1721, he wrote to the Company of the Indies from New Orleans stating that he was sending the plan for the City of New Orleans which he had drawn up in conjunction with de Pailloux, on which he had marked the size of the sites intended for the persons on the list attached. (In some manner the plans were lost or held up for a while.)

Dumont says that the first circuit contained but four blocks surrounded by a parapet of ditches, the second eight blocks facing the river by five in depth.

De Pauger had to contend against the clerk of the Company, who hindered him in every way, insubordination and lazy workers. But he persevered and got his plan drawn up and the city started.

In 1721 a census of New Orleans, which included the surrounding lands up and down the river and across the river, showed that there were 293 men, 140 women, 96 children, 155 white servants, 514 Negro slaves and 51 Indian slaves. There were likewise 231 horned cattle and 28 horses.

D'Artaguette in a memorial to France says that New Orleans was really founded in 1722. For the men and "convicts" left under de Pailloux to clear the cane brake and begin building had done nothing.

It was not until 1722 that orders came from the Council in Paris to make New Orleans the official capital of the colony.

Charlevoix in Journal d'un Voyage fait par ordre du Roi on January 10, 1722, wrote:

"This City is the first to arise on the banks of one of the greatest rivers in the world. The eight hundred handsome dwellings and five churches credited [Sales talk to encourage emigrants, Ed.] to it by the Mercury two years ago are reduced today to about a hundred huts, arranged without a great deal of order, a large warehouse built of wood, two or three houses which would not adorn a town in France, and half of a wretched warehouse which had been assigned to

His Lordship and of which he had barely taken possession when they made him leave it, and lodged him in a tent; but what a pleasure, on the other hand, to see this future capital of a vast and beautiful country growing bit by bit, and to be able to say, not sighing like the hero of Virgil . . . but filled with the most well-founded hopes, " 'This savage and desolate place, which is still almost covered with trees and canebrakes, will one day be (and perhaps that day is not far off) an opulent city, and the Metropolis of a great and rich colony'." And on January 26, 1722, he wrote again:

"I have nothing to add to that which I said to you in my previous letter about the present situation of New Orleans. You can form the most accurate picture of it by imagining 200 people who were sent to found a city, and who made camp on the banks of a great river, where they thought only of getting shelter from the unhealthy open air until such time as a plan was drawn up, and who built houses. M. Pauger, whom I still have the honor to accompany, has just shown me a plan of his making: it is very handsome and very orderly; but it will not be as easy to carry it out as it was to put it on paper."

Father Matthius first held religious services in the Company's store under a tent, but soon a wooden church dedicated to St. Ignatius was erected. It is said that Bienville with his sword marked out the original site of the first wooden church in New Orleans, which is the same spot where the St. Louis Cathedral now stands. This church was blown down in 1723 and replaced a year later by a brick church.

In 1724 the streets of New Orleans were named. They extended from Esplanade to Bienville, from the river to Rampart. The first streets mentioned were the Rue de l'Arsenal, afterwards rue des Ursulines; St. Phillipe, du Maine, St. Anne; Orleans, St. Peter, Toulouse, St. Louis and Bienville.

The following description of New Orleans is taken from DuPratz' "History of Louisiana." Since he gave no date, it must have applied to a period several years after he had come to Louisiana.

"The place of arms is in the middle of that part of the town which faces the river; in the middle of the ground of the place of arms stands the parish church, called St. Louis, where the Capuchins officiate, whose house is to the left of the church. To the right stand the prison, or jail, and the guardhouse; both sides of the place of arms are taken up by two bodies or rows of barracks. This place stands all open to the river.

"All the streets are laid out both in length and breadth by the line, and intersect and cross each other at right angles. The streets divide the town into sixty-six isles; eleven along the river lengthwise, or in front, and six in depth; each of those isles is fifty square toises, and each again divided into twelve emplacements, or compartments for lodging as many families. The Intendant's house stands behind the barracks on the left; and the magazine or warehousegeneral behind the barracks on the right, on viewing the town from the river side. The Governor's house stands in the middle of that part of the town, from which we go from the place of arms to the habitation of the Jesuits, which is near the town. The house of the Ursuline Nuns is quite at the end of the town, to the right; as is also the hospital of the sick, of which the nuns have the inspection. What I have just described faces the river.

"On the banks of the river runs the causey, or mole, as well on the side of the town as on the opposite side, from the English Reach quite to the town, and about ten leagues beyond it; which makes about fifteen or sixteen leagues on each side the river; and which may be travelled in a coach or on horseback, on a bottom as smooth as a table.

"The greatest part of the houses is of brick; the rest are of timber and brick.

"The length of the causeys, I just mentioned, is sufficient to shew, that on these two sides of the Mississippi there are many habitations standing close together; each making a causey to secure his ground from inundations, which fail not to come every year with the spring; and at that time, if any ships happen to be in the harbour of New Orleans, they speedily set sail; because the prodigious quantity of dead wood, or trees torn up by the roots, which the river brings down, would lodge before the ship, and break the stoutest cables.

"At the end of St. John's Creek, on the banks of the Lake St. Louis, there is a redoubt, and a guard to defend it.

"From this creek to the town, a part of its banks is inhabited by planters; in like manner as are the long banks of another creek: the habitations of this last go under the name of Gentilly."

THE BATTLE OF NEW ORLEANS

The Battle of New Orleans was fought on the morning of January 8, 1815 at Chalmette.

It took place after the treaty of peace had been signed at Ghent by British and American commissioners on Dec. 24, 1814, but since methods of communication were slow in those days, the battle took place before it was learned that the hostilities were over. It was not until Feb. 17, 1815 that the War of 1812 were formally ended.

The Battle of New Orleans may be said to have been an unnecessary battle, but actually it had far-reaching consequences. Not only was it a brilliant victory for the Americans, but it stimulated nationalism, made a hero of Andrew Jackson and increased the influence of frontier democracy upon American social and political life.

The English realized that control of the Mississippi River was important, and in 1814 a British fleet sailed for the West Indies where it was joined by a large force of trained and experienced soldiers. The British forces numbered about 10,000 men, and the commander-in-chief of the expedition was Sir Edward Pakenham, brother-in-law of the Duke of Wellington. Under him war veterans of European campaigns against Napoleon, of proved ability, trained, disciplined and valorous.

Sailing from Jamaica, the British arrived in the Gulf of Mexico off the coast of Louisiana in the early part of December, and they approached the City of New Orleans through Lake Borgne.

On December 14th five small American gunboats protecting the water approaches to the city were captured, and 2,000 British troops landed at Fishermen's Village and came out to the Mississippi River to a point about seven miles below New Orleans. On December 23rd the British camped at the Villere, Lacoste and Delaronde Plantations for the night. If they had come right up to New Orleans, they might have been able to capture it as the defense had not been organized.

Andrew Jackson, Commander of the military district of the Gulf, was in New Orleans and had brought with him Kentucky and Tennessee militiamen. Working feverishly, he assembled a make-shift army consisting of Tennesseans, Kentuckians, people from the West Florida parishes, Acadians, Creoles, sailors, pirates, Indians and Negroes.

Jackson learned of the arrival of the British at the Villere Plantation from its owner, Major Villere, who, captured and then escaping, rode to New Orleans. The American general acted immediately. He struck at the British camp in a night attack, but because of the fog and darkness the attack was abandoned, and Jackson withdrew his forces to the Chalmette and McCarty Plantations, five miles below New Orleans. With the shallow 20-foot wide Rodrigues Canal in front of him, he built his defense line of earth and cotton bales. This line was approximately a mile long with the Mississippi River on the right hand side facing the enemy and an impassable swamp on the other. Jackson's men threw up a crude breastwork, and eight batteries were erected. The approach to the American line was across a flat open plain.

On December 28th Pakenham sent a strong force to attack the American line, but it withdrew until the artillery could be brought up.

On the morning of New Year's Day, 1815, the British batteries, numbering 24 guns, began a terrific bombardment accompanied by a shower of rockets. The

American batteries of 15 guns answered and fired with such accuracy that by noon the British guns were silenced. Two more attempts to break the line failed. Pakenham then decided to wait a week until his reserves arrived before attempting the final assault.

Early on the morning of January 8th, Pakenham launched a full frontal attack against the American position. Nearly 8,-000 British soldiers in their brilliant uniforms moved in serried array against the American position. Behind breastworks of cotton bales and earth, 5,000 Americans with their long rifles lived up to their reputation as marksmen. Twice the British lines advanced under murderous fire and twice they were thrown back. General Gibbs fell mortally wounded 20 yards from the American line. General Pakenham was likewise wounded in trying to rally his retreating men, and died a few hours later in the house now in ruins that faced the row of live oaks known today as the Pakenham Oaks.

The main action lasted only two and a half hours. The British lost 1900 men killed and wounded including many officers. The American loss was seven killed and six wounded. Thus ended one of the most remarkable battles in military annals.

Across the river a small force of British defeated the Americans, but as their main army had been defeated on the east side of the river, they had to retreat. The total British casualties were 2037, with 291 killed, and the total American losses on both sides of the river were 13 killed, 39 wounded and 19 missing. By the end of January the last of the British soldiers had gone aboard their ships and sailed away.

NEW ORLEANS—TODAY AND YESTERDAY

DRAINAGE

The average annual rainfall is 56.76 inches. The quantity of rain over 57 thousand acres amounts to more than 11 billion cubic feet of water weighing nearly 360 million tons. The Board maintains 9 recording rain gauges with a daily recording of rainfall.

Great canal systems convey the water and eleven great drainage pumping stations help to pump, some of it two or more times, before it is discharged into the tide level outfalls. Some of the canals are wood lined, some lined with masonry and covered. Some are of reinforced concrete and many are under the roadway streets. The largest open canals are more than 80 feet in width and when running full have more than nine feet of water.

New Orleans probably has the greatest aggregation of low lift pumps assembled anywhere in an equal area. The aggregate storm drainage pumping capacity of 17½ billion gallons per day is enough to empty a lake one mile wide, eight miles long and ten feet deep in 24 hours.

The drainage system of over 1400 miles of low-level canals and drains is constructed and operated so as to produce artificially the necessary slope. Sixteen major pumping stations drain 57,145 acres of land. All day weather and small storm flow goes into Lake Borgne, and the heavy flow of great storms into Lake Pontchartrain.

SEWERAGE SYSTEM

The construction of the sewer system was begun in June 1903, and it began operation in 1907. Before the installation of the sewerage system the city was filled with cess pools. In 1899 the cess pools numbered 67,000 (one for every house). At the end of 1925 the number had declined to 7,000 (one to every 15 houses) by 1939 there were still 13,000 cess pools or one to every 100 houses.

When the sewerage and drainage systems were planned they were separated because it was undesirable to discharge the sewage into tide or lake waters. Furthermore, a small flow of sewage in large water drains would not move rapidly enough, a condition which would cause objectionable conditions in the drains. Also, the uniting of the two systems would require a great amount of work, extra cost and many years of time.

A system of sewers was designed composed of main, submain and lateral sewers which lead to 22 pumping stations with a good "fall" from the high end of the sewers to the pumping stations. Most of the sewers drain by gravity to the pumping stations.

The sewage, consisting of polluted waste water from houses, factories, etc., is collected in a system entirely separated from the surface water or drainage system of pipes. There are 782 miles of sewers. Three discharge stations on this side of the river and one in Algiers pump the sewage through large cast iron discharge mains into the Mississippi River well downstream, where the continuous flow of the river brings it to the Gulf.

The largest pumping station by itself pumps 21 billion gallons a year—enough to make a lake of eight square miles and 12 feet deep. This vast quantity of water is lost in the immensity of the flow of the river. The sewage never reappears at the surface, and tests made further downstream have never indicated its presence in the river water.

MISSISSIPPI RIVER

Having a width of 2,200 feet at Canal Street, the river has a bankside depth of from 30 to 60 feet and a mid-stream depth of more than 100 to 180 feet. Levees at New Orleans are the finest in the world. The Bonnet Carre Spillway, 33 miles above the city, built by U. S. Army Engineers, gives New Orleans an even greater margin of safety. It extends 1½ miles along the Mississippi River and has a flowage capacity of 250,000 cubic feet per second, greater than that of Niagara Falls. If the water level in the river becomes dangerously high, this spillway may be opened to divert the floodwaters into Lake Pontchartrain and thence into the Gulf of Mexico.

INTRACOASTAL CANAL

This canal gives New Orleans direct water access westward to points in Louisiana and Texas as far as the Mexican border, and eastward through natural and artificial channels to Florida.

INDUSTRIAL CANAL

This 5½-mile canal connects the Mississippi River with Lake Pontchartrain, and provides access for deep-water shipping to the complex of industrial plants that line its banks. The canal is connected to the river by a lock permitting the passage of ocean-going vessels. It is also the connecting link between the Intracoastal Canal and the river, and serves the same purpose for the new Mississippi River-Gulf Outlet.

MISSISSIPPI RIVER-GULF OUTLET

Under Congressional authorization, the Corps of Engineers began dredging the Mississippi River-Gulf Outlet Channel in March, 1958. An interim channel 36 feet deep and 250 feet wide was completed in July, 1963, opening this new route for ocean-going ships. The full project depth of 36 feet and width of 500 feet have been achieved throughout the length of the project. The Port of New Orleans has built a bulk handling facility on the Mississippi River-Gulf Outlet and a new wallboard plant has been built nearby. The multi-million dollar bulk handling facility can speedily transfer bulk material between ships, barges, railroad cars or motor trucks—or move it to storage. The channel provides a 76-mile route to the Gulf, 40 miles shorter than by the river. It also provides thousands of acres of new industrial sites with deep-water access for ocean-going vessels.

LAKE PONTCHARTRAIN

Lake Pontchartrain, connecting with the Gulf of Mexico, offers boating, bathing and fishing. It covers an area of 610 square miles. A beautiful scenic driveway extends along its shores, where an outstanding resort and residential section is located. The Southern Yacht Club, second oldest in the U. S., is located on the lakefront in a modern clubhouse, adjacent to the New Orleans Yacht Club, yacht harbor, and the recently completed marina.

CAUSEWAY ACROSS LAKE PONTCHARTRAIN

Measuring a shore-to-shore distance of 23.83 miles, this bridge across Lake Pontchartrain, connecting Jefferson and St. Tammany Parishes, is the world's longest over-water highway bridge. Total expenditure for the causeway and its approaches was $51,000,000. It was opened in the fall of 1956. A second causeway parallels the first.

HUEY P. LONG BRIDGE

This railroad and vehicular toll-free bridge spans the Mississippi River. It is 4.4 miles long and its central pier from the bottom of its foundation 170 feet below mean Gulf level to the top of the superstructure is 409 feet high. Highway U. S. 90 (Old Spanish Trail) passes over this bridge to the west. The bridge was completed in 1935 at a cost of $13,000,000.

GREATER NEW ORLEANS BRIDGE

After years of conflict and controversy, a new bridge was constructed 400 feet north (that is, downstream) of the old one. Work was begun in 1981, and was completed in 1988.

INTERNATIONAL CENTER

The first two elements of the International Center—the INTERNATIONAL TRADE MART and THE RIVERGATE international exhibition facility—are at Eads Plaza where Canal Street meets the Mississippi River. The Trade Mart Tower is a 33-story building, financed through private capital. A 1,000-car parking garage is situated adjacent to the Tower Building. The total cost of the two structures was $16.5 million. The primary purpose of the Trade Mart Tower is to house firms and organizations which are directly connected or interested in foreign trade and the business of our great port. There is an observation tower on the 29th floor for which a small admission fee is charged. On the 33rd floor is a revolving lounge which offers a breath-taking view of the city.

THE RIVERGATE

The port's Rivergate convention - exhibition hall has blended port activity with the international exhibition business and has brought many thousands of visitors to the area.

Conventions and exhibitions attracting international traffic brought representation from many port users such as Japan, Argentina, Israel, Canada, Italy, and England.

The Rivergate is unique among exhibit halls in the country. It has 130,000 square feet of clear, unobstructed space. It can seat more than 17,500 persons for an assembly in the main hall, and the main hall can be used for 733 ten-by-ten-foot exhibit booths. The building has 15 meeting rooms with seating capacities from 115 to 1,400. Inside parking can accommodate 800 automobiles.

Adjacent to the International Trade Mart is the new River Center Complex, a cruise ship terminal whose facilities include the New Orleans Hilton, which is located next to the 1984 World's Fair site. (See Tourism section for more information on the World's Fair.)

EASTERN NEW ORLEANS

Fifty square miles, 32,000 acres, of land in this area adjacent to the NASA-Michoud plant is being developed as New Orleans East, and is considered the largest urban development in the United States under one ownership, representing one-fourth of the total area of the city. The area is served by three major U. S. highways, two railroads, the Intra-coastal Canal and the Mississippi River-Gulf Outlet. It is being developed for residential, commercial and heavy and light industrial areas with its own parks, schools and churches.

Lake Forest is another city within a city under development in the 5,000-acre area bisected by I-10 Highway between Paris Road and Downman Road which will offer 15,000 home sites in a community setting, landscaped with green areas, waterways, lagoons and an 18-hole golf course, complete with shopping centers, hospitals, s c h o o l s and churches, within minutes of the central business district.

AIRPORTS

Three airports serve New Orleans. New Orleans International Airport handles all scheduled airline passenger traffic, including jet service to virtually every major metropolitan area. A new $7.5 million terminal building was completed in 1959. The airport now boasts a 9,225-foot runway capable of handling the largest jet aircraft. New Orleans Airport, on Lake Pontchartrain, is devoted exclusively to private and corporate plane usage. A $50 million military installation, Alvin Callender Naval Air Station, is used by the air reserve units of the Navy, Air Force, Marines, Coast Guard and National Guard for training purposes.

UNION PASSENGER TERMINAL

Completed in 1954 at a cost of $16,000,-000, it combined six railroad stations located in various parts of the city. It is one of the first completely air-conditioned railroad terminals in the nation. Located in the central business district, it serves all passengers traveling by rail and has eliminated nearly 100 grade crossings in the city.

It is now the Amtrack Terminal for the New Orleans - New York, New Orleans - Chicago and the New Orleans - Los Angeles systems. In 1969, the Greyhound Corporation leased a portion of the terminal as a bus station.

POST OFFICE AND FEDERAL BUILDING

The U. S. Post Office, Post Office Garage, and Federal Office Building was completed on a site adjacent to the Union Passenger Terminal in 1961. This $15 million building consists of a two-story and basement Post Office, a one-story garage, and a 14-story office building, and is the largest government building of its kind in the South. It contains 552,000 square feet of usable area. The Passport Agency, U. S. Department of State, is located in Room 228, U. S. Custom House, 423 Canal Street.

CIVIC CENTER

This impressive Center includes an $8 million, 11-story City Hall with 431,278 square feet floor space; $4 million, 8-story State Office Building with 179,-000 square feet of floor space; $2 million State Supreme Court Building; $2.5 million Civil Courts Building; and a $2.5 million Main City Library, covering an area of 11 acres in the central business district. It is one of the most modern in the U. S. From City Hall one looks down Loyola Avenue to Basin Street to the Garden of the Americas where the Simon Bolivar monument, a gift from Venezuela, the Benito Juarez monument, a gift from Mexico, and the Francisco Morazan monument are located.

AUDITORIUM

Municipal Auditorium, within e a s y reach of all principal hotels, is the scene of many conventions, carnival balls and other events. Its arena seating capacity of 9,697 persons can be divided into two halls, one seating 2,959 persons and the other 4,944. There are 32,250 square feet of exhibit space on the main floor; other exhibit areas are the Annex Building with 26,408 square feet and the Scheuring Room with 10,000 square feet. The stage offers an area of 130 feet by 50 feet and has 37 lines. The orchestra pit measures 59 feet by 9 feet. There are also three separate meeting rooms. The air conditioned Auditorium is a memorial to veterans of World War I.

THEATRE

The New Orleans Theatre for the Performing Arts, built next to the older Municipal Auditorium, is the home of concerts, ballet, opera, recitals, and other performances. The Theatre fronts on Armstrong Park, a twelve-million-dollar, fourteen-acre complex of lagoons, bridges, promenades, and lights dedicated to the memory of "Satchmo."

Le Petit Theatre du Vieux Carre, located at the corner of St. Peter and Chartres Streets, is the oldest continually operating community theatre in the United States. Founded in 1916 as the New Orleans Chapter of the Drama League of America, the theatre moved to its present site in 1922.

CLIMATE AND HEALTH

New Orleans is both a summer and a winter resort. As extreme temperatures do not prevail, outdoor recreation is possible during any month. The normal daily average temperature for October through March is a comfortable 59.8 degrees. Cooled by the waters of Lake Pontchartrain on the north and the Gulf of Mexico on the south, the normal daily average temperature for April through September is 77.4 degrees. Seldom is freezing weather experienced. The temperature rises above 95 degrees on an average of only six days per year.

Annual average humidity at 1:00 p.m. is 63%; annual rainfall is 53.90 inches.

CITY PARK

Opportunities for recreation abound in the city's 150 recreational facilities. Audubon Park, once a famed plantation, contains 280 acres and the South's largest zoo.

City Park was once a plantation owned by the Allard family; later they sold the property to Mr. John McDonogh who in turn donated it to the City of New Orleans, and later it was developed into a beautiful park.

The Park has been under the jurisdiction of the Board of Commissioners of the New Orleans City Park since year 1891, at which time it was only 85 acres.

The present area of City Park is 1500 acres extending from City Park Avenue to Lake Pontchartrain.

Through the Monteleone Gate at Esplanade entrance of the Park is one of the largest and most attractive Floral Clocks in the United States; it has been stated by many Clock Watchers that this huge time piece is as accurate as the average wrist watch. Behind the Floral Clock is a boulevard banked with large magnolia and oak trees leading to Delgado Museum of Art.

To the left or south of the Delgado Museum is a dueling Oak where many a duel was fought in the early part of the Eighteenth Century.

At the attractive circular band stand of concrete construction during the summer months concerts are held and dancing schools give their reviews.

Across the street from Band Stand is a beautiful luminous fountain which was donated to City Park by the Jahncke Family.

West of the Band Stand on the shore of one of the lagoons, is the Peristyle, an attractive building of Greek architecture, which affords comfort to visitors who enjoy relaxation in City Park. Over 200 square dancing parties are held under the Peristyle annually.

A short distance from the Peristyle, on the opposite side of the street, is a swimming pool which was donated by Mr. William R. Irby.

Childrens' Storyland consists of numerous nursery rhyme characters expertly designed in a manner closely matching the actual story book characterization. The story of each Nursery Rhyme depicted in Storyland is told on tape recordings.

North of the swimming pool is the stadium which has a seating capacity of 27,000. Approximately fifty Prep H i g h School football games are played each season. The average attendance per game is 5,000. In the spring the stadium is used for track and field meets which averages about eighty meets per season; practically every school in the City of New Orleans participates.

A little further north is a landscaped garden of beauty. In the center of this garden is the Popp's Memorial Fountain, a large circular structure surrounded by 26 Greek columns. When this fountain is in operation the lighting effect in the pool creates a beautiful rainbow picture of spray. The fountain was donated by Mrs. John F. Popp and the balustrade by her sister Mrs. Isabel Grant.

Numerous lagoons interlacing with each other, the shores of which are lined with beautiful moss covered Oaks, afford a real southern picture. Boats and skiffs may be rented for a water trip through the lagoons. Fishing is also very popular in these lagoons and many times quantities of black bass, green trout and perch are caught.

In the front of City Park, among massive oaks, are the picnic grounds where thousands of family and school picnics are held. On these grounds are a number of rides such as merry-go-round, whip, caterpillar, miniature train, ponies, etc., for the children's entertainment, and four shelter houses with all convenient facilities. It was estimated that a crowd in excess of 80,000 people visited City Park on a 4th of July. This crowd represents about one-seventh of the total population of the City of New Orleans.

City Park has three eighteen-hole golf courses. About 125,000 rounds of golf are played on these courses annually.

Thirty-three tennis courts are open to the public for a small hourly fee. Night tennis may be played under arc lights that give a daytime appearance.

Twenty well kept baseball diamonds are enjoyed all year round. During the week there is no charge for the use of these diamonds. On Saturday and Sunday the diamonds may be reserved for which there is a charge of $2.00 for three hours of play.

It is estimated that there are approximately 22,000 trees in City Park, consisting of Oaks, Magnolias, Hackberries, Crepe Myrtles, Pines, Cedars and Golden Rains. The Golden Rain, common name for Koelreuteria Paniculata, blooms profusely during the autumn months.

In the front of the Park is the famous McDonogh Oak which has branches spreading one hundred and twenty-five feet.

BIRTHPLACE OF JAZZ

New Orleans is generally considered the birthplace of jazz. It is thought that jazz music first began to be recognized in New Orleans around the turn of the century. This traditional jazz is generally known as New Orleans or Dixieland jazz. Many of the great names of jazz started out in New Orleans, and New Orleans is an active center of jazz today.

Two unique establishments have recently come into being—Preservation Hall and Dixieland Hall—where jazz may be listened to without the usual embellishments of a club-type atmosphere or the serving of drinks or refreshments. These institutions normally have different bands each night and are supported by contributions rather than straight admission.

One of the forces that maintains jazz at a steady beat in the Crescent City is the New Orleans Jazz Club, which has been active for a number of years and gives special concerts and has jazz bands playing at its regular monthly meetings, to which visitors are welcome. The Jazz Club has also established the first Jazz Museum, which is located at 1017 Dumaine Street, where jazz lovers can see many instruments and other reminders of the early days of jazz and also have an opportunity to listen to recorded jazz music from a number of famous bands.

WORLD RENOWNED FESTIVITIES

Mardi Gras, the high point of the entertainment year, culminates weeks of lavish balls and pageantry with citywide masking and elaborate day and night parades. Thousands of visitors flock to New Orleans annually for this celebration. Other spectacular events of the year include a complete calendar of sports contests known as the Mid-Winter Sports Carnival, which is climaxed by the Sugar Bowl Football Classic on New Year's Day. The annual Spring Fiesta offers tours of homes, patios, and nearby plantations during the two weeks of the festival.

Musical activities held during the year include 15 symphony concerts by the New Orleans Philharmonic Symphony and 16 performances of eight operas by the New Orleans Opera House Association. Other musical events include: the Summer Pops Concert series; the New Orleans Jazz Club concerts; musicals, concerts and operas by the New Orleans Recreation Department.

MARDI GRAS

Mardi Gras is an ancient custom, dating from old Roman times and coming to Louisiana through her French Catholic ancestry. From the beginning of Louisiana colonization, the Latin custom of Mardi Gras has been marked with masquerade balls, and, most likely, spontaneous street dancing as well as purposeful feasting in preparation for the lean 40 days of Lent which, naturally, always follows.

Historically, the event has been one of revelry and abandonment. Somewhere along the line it became a bacchanalian fantasy with masqueraders becoming for this one day of the year exactly what they want to be. They ride on floats, they dance at fancy balls, they holler "Throw me something, Mister!" to passing float riders who toss trinkets to the crowds. They peek at each other through their fantastic finery—fantastic for its brilliance, grotesqueness, glitter, beauty, elegance, absurdity and whimsy. Yet, there are also those who neither dance, ride in parades nor dress in exotic apparel. They just come and look. And they all enjoy

Although Mardi Gras is actually only one day, Shrove Tuesday, in Louisiana it has come to mean the last two weeks or so of Carnival, immediately preceding Mardi Gras Day, during which the balls and parades staged by the private Mardi Gras "krewes" have built intensely to culminate in the monarchial meeting of Rex and Comus at the stroke of Mardi Gras midnight.

In cities outside Creole New Orleans, traditional "town-style" festivities may include only balls, parades, street masking, or any combination or all these activities. Crowds are large in every town ranging from more than a million in New Orleans and some 120,000 in Lafayette to the whole population—more or less—in smaller towns.

In these cities where the traditional, it unrestrained, style of Mardi Gras occurs, respective krewes—with names like Harlequins, High Priests of Mithras, Krewe of Thoth, Young Men

Illinois Club, Mystic Krewe of Comus, and, for ladies, Krewes like Pandora, Diana and Venus—wear eye-shattering costumes and stage extravagant ball, parade and tableau themes.

The flavor is different, though, in several outlying towns of that South Louisiana region known as Acadiana. In towns such as Church Point, Mamou, Ville Platte and Eunice here in Louisiana's bayou country, when masked riders dressed in rag-tag clothing mount snorting steeds and gallop madly off into the pre-dawn distance on this certain day of the year, they're not playing cowboys and they're not planning to rob the local homesteaders.

It's Mardi Gras Day, except in Church Point where it always occurs the Sunday before, and the name of the game is "Courrir du Mardi Gras," or "running of the Mardi Gras." The object of the wild ride through the countryside is to collect ingredients for a gigantic community gumbo. This is Mardi Gras "country-style."

RACING

The Fair Grounds race track opens its season each year on Thanksgiving Day. Racing is held at this famous track every day except Sunday for approximately 100 racing days each year. Many special races and handicaps are held during this season, which coincides with some of the greater attractions of the New Orleans calendar, including Mid-Winter Sports Carnival and the Mardi Gras season.

PRO FOOTBALL

On November 1, 1966, New Orleans was awarded a professional football franchise by the National Football League. The team, purchased for $8.5 million by Houston oilman John Mecom, was nicknamed the "Saints." The Saints play their home games in the Superdome. Former Houston Oilers coach Bum Phillips, who came on in 1981, shook up many long-time Saint aficionados by his startling trades and large-scale importation of former Oiler team members. New Orleans automobile dealer Tom Benson purchased the Saints in 1985. The present coach is Jim Mora. In 1987, with their first winning season ever, the Saints qualified for the National Football Conference playoffs.

SUPERDOME

Authorized by state constitutional amendment number ten on November 8, 1966, the Superdome immediately began to excite controversy throughout the state. After numer-ous attempts to halt the project and block construction, the state made a bond issue of $113,000,000, and actual construction began on August 11, 1971, on the edge of the Central Business District. After continuing disputes over finances and construction, the Superdome opened in August, 1975. The final budget for the building and grounds: $163,313,315.

Designed to be the premier sports center in the world, the Superdome can hold a vast number of spectators—from 20,000 for basketball to 80,000 for "expanded" football (movable stands quickly switch from one event to another). But the Superdome is by no means limited to sports. The largest unobstructed room in the world, the dome offers 470,000 square feet of open exhibition space. For entertainment events or concerts a "festival" arrangement allows seating for almost 100,000 people; the record attendance up to this time was set at the Rolling Stones concert in December, 1981, when 87,500 listeners packed the dome.

A special feature is the Superscreen TV System, six huge 26- by 22-foot color screens suspended from the ceiling to give fans close-up views of the action down on the field or stage. The Superdome is managed by Hyatt, which also runs a major hotel connected by a concourse right next door.

Superdome Facts

Total Land Area	52 Acres (building, garages & grounds)
Height	273 feet
Diameter of the Dome	680 feet clear span
Concrete	169,000 cubic yards
Structural Steel	20,000 tons
Air Conditioning	9,600 tons
Convention Rooms	40
Restrooms	88
Private Box Suites	64
Parking Garages	5,000 cars + 250 buses
Superscreen TV	6 sides, each 26' x 22'
Lighting	15,200 lighting fixtures
Scoreboards	4, each 8' x 88'
Electrical Wiring	400 miles
Anodized Aluminum Siding	of interior wiring More than 500,000 sq. ft.
Area of Roof	9.7 acres
Escalators	32
Elevators	9 plus 1 freight

ACADIA

HISTORY: Acadia Parish was originally part of St. Landry Parish. It was established as a separate parish on June 30, 1888. It was largely settled by the descendants of the Acadians, who were exiled from Nova Scotia and immigrated to Louisiana in the mid 18th century.

PARISH SEAT: Crowley
SQUARE MILE AREA............. 657
SCHOOLS .... Public 25
Private 9

RAIL LINES 2
CONGRESSIONAL DISTRICT 7
AIRPORTS 1

AGRICULTURE: Rice

INDUSTRY: Rice milling, garment manufacturing, commercial bags, and metal works.

TOURIST ATTRACTIONS: Blue Rose Museum and Heritage Farm Village.

PARKS and RECREATIONAL FACILITIES: Eight parks with various forms of recreation and picnic areas.

PARISH BUSINESS PATTERNS: Number of employees, 1983:

Agricultural services,............. 102
forestry, fisheries
Mining 555
Contract construction 892
Manufacturing................. 1,666
Transportation and other........ 984
public utilities

Wholesale trade.................. 1,079
Retail trade 2,239
Finance, insurance and............. 503
real estate
Services....................... 3,888
Public administration 566

PARISH PROFILES:
Median age, 1980 .... 27.0
Median family income, 1980 .... $15,792
Percent of families with income below poverty level, 1980 .... 18.5

General Hospitals, 1981 3
Patient Care Physicians, 1981 32

General Hospital Beds, 1981......... 176
Dentists, 1981...................... 13

Infant birth rate (per 1000 population), 1982................................ 20.3
Infant mortality rate (per 1000 live births), 1981.............................. 13
Death rate (per 1000 population), 1982..................................... 8.2
MAJOR CITIES (over 5,000 population): Crowley and Rayne

PARISH SEAT: Oberlin
SQUARE MILE AREA............. 766
SCHOOLS .... Public 10
Private 10

RAIL LINES 3
CONGRESSIONAL DISTRICT ... 7 and 8
CHURCHES...................... 50
AIRPORTS 1

ALLEN

HISTORY: On June 12,1912, Allen Parish was formed from the parish of Calcasieu. Named after Henry Watkins Allen, famous Confederate governor of Louisiana during the Civil War, it and Jefferson Davis Parish are the newest parishes in the state. At one time it was important as a great lumber producing region. Timber is still the major resource.

PARISH SEAT: Oberlin
SQUARE MILE AREA. 766
SCHOOLS .... Public 10
Private 10

RAIL LINES 3
CONGRESSIONAL DISTRICT 7 and 8
CHURCHES.................. 50
AIRPORTS 1

AGRICULTURE: Timber, rice, and soybeans.

INDUSTRY: Plywood plant, sawmills, and sulphate paper company.

PARKS and RECREATIONAL FACILITIES: Picnic and park areas; fishing in the Calcasieu River, bayous, creeks, and ponds, and in the Bear Creek Watershed Project.

PARISH BUSINESS PATTERNS: Number of employees, 1983:

Agricultural services,	41	Wholesale trade	61
forestry, fisheries		Retail trade	771
Mining	27	Finance, insurance and	170
Contract construction	198	real estate	
Manufacturing	451	Services	1,302
Transportation and other	270	Public administration	292
public utilities			

PARISH PROFILES:

Median age, 1980 .... 29.3
Median family income, 1980 .... $15,685
Percent of families with income below poverty level, 1980 .... 19.0

General Hospitals, 1981	2	General Hospital Beds, 1981	116
Patient Care Physicians, 1981	12	Dentists, 1981	7

Infant birth rate (per 1000 population), 1982 .... 16.2
Infant mortality rate (per 1000 live births), 1981 .... 8.0
Death rate (per 1000 population), 1982 .... 10.7

MAJOR CITIES (over 5,000 population): Oakdale

ASCENSION

HISTORY: Ascension is one of the original twelve "counties" of Louisiana and one of the original nineteen parishes. Although listed in 1805 as "Acadia," the real meaning was "Acadia Coast." On March 31, 1807, it was given its present name. The parish was settled first by the Acadians who came to Louisiana between 1764 and 1772. The historic Catholic church in Donaldsonville contains the oldest church records in the state, dating from 1772.

PARISH SEAT: Donaldsonville		RAIL LINES	3
SQUARE MILE AREA	296	CONGRESSIONAL DISTRICT	8
SCHOOLS	Public 15	CHURCHES	49
	Private 3		

AGRICULTURE: Sugarcane, soybeans, corn, strawberries, and livestock.

INDUSTRY: Petrochemical, lumber, and related wood products.

TOURIST ATTRACTIONS: Many antebellum homes, including Houmas House, Ashland-Belle Helene, and Hermitage, all beautiful old homes which give the visitor a glimpse into bygone days.

PARKS and RECREATIONAL FACILITIES: 7,120 acres of water and 103,700 acres in forests for ample boating, fishing, hunting, and other outdoor sports.

PARISH BUSINESS PATTERNS: Number of employees, 1983:

Agricultural services,	213	Wholesale trade	550
forestry, fisheries		Retail trade	2,396
Mining	148	Finance, insurance and	553
Contract construction	2,995	real estate	
Manufacturing	4,946	Services	3,768
Transportation and other	893	Public administration	357
public utilities			

PARISH PROFILES:

Median age, 1980 .... 25.5
Median family income, 1980 .... $21,572
Percent of families with income below poverty level, 1980 .... 12.3

General Hospitals, 1981 2   General Hospital Beds, 1981 85
Patient Care Physicians, 1981 15   Dentists, 1981 17

Infant birth rate (per 1000 population), 1982 .... 19.8
Infant mortality rate (per 1000 live births), 1981 .... 10.5
Death rate (per 1000 population), 1982 .... 6.4
MAJOR CITIES (over 5,000 population): Donaldsonville and Gonzales

Donaldsonville

Donaldsonville, the parish seat, serves the area as a business and commercial center. Many petro-chemical plants dot the riverfront, enhancing the economy. In its early history, large plantations arose on both sides of the river. Agriculture still plays a major role, although in recent years the trend has been toward industry and trade. At one time Donaldsonville was located at the confluence of the Mississippi River and Bayou Lafourche. Since then the levee has cut off the flow. The Sunshine Bridge links the east and west banks of the parish.

The history of Donaldsonville began in 1806, when William Donaldson established La Ville de Donaldson. Later called Lafourche and then Donaldsonville, it was incorporated in 1822 and served as the capital of the state from 1830-1831.

Gonzales

Gonzales, originally settled by the Acadians, is today a fast growing industrial center. The citizens are justly proud of the rapid growth and expansion. They call their city the "Jambalaya Capital of the World." Jambalaya is derived from the Spanish, "jamon," meaning ham. Today the recipe has been transformed to include succulent shrimp, crab, and chicken, and all of the spicy seasonings, and is served at the annual Jambalaya Festival and World Championship Jambalaya Cooking Contest, events which attract widespread attention.

ASSUMPTION

HISTORY: Created from one of the original twelve counties, Assumption Parish was named for the Assumption Catholic church at Plattenville, the oldest Catholic church in the state. The original church was erected in 1793, during the Spanish regime. The present building dates from 1856. The present boundaries were created in 1807 from a portion of Lafourche Parish. As is the case in most South Louisiana parishes, the early settlers were French. The earliest permanent settlements were made by Spanish and exiled Acadians along the historic Bayou Lafourche. Napoleonville is and has always been the parish seat. The present courthouse, in continuous use, was built in 1895. The town was officially incorporated on March 11, 1878, and named by a soldier who served under Napoleon Bonaparte.

PARISH SEAT: Napoleonville   RAIL LINES 2
SQUARE MILE AREA 342   CONGRESSIONAL DISTRICT 3
SCHOOLS .... Public 10   CHURCHES 16
                          Private 3

AGRICULTURE: Sugarcane, corn, vegetable farming, and beef cattle.

INDUSTRY: Sugarcane refining

TOURIST ATTRACTIONS: Annual spring Louisiana Heritage Tour, sponsored by the Foundation for Historical Louisiana; Madewood, a twenty room antebellum mansion built by Thomas Pugh in 1848, which sponsors the Madewood Arts Festival in the spring; Christ church (1853), of beautiful Gothic architectural construction with handmade brick and native cypress.

PARKS and RECREATIONAL FACILITIES: Fishing in Lake Verret and Bayou Corne

PARISH BUSINESS PATTERNS: Number of employees, 1983:
    Agricultural services, ... 206   Wholesale trade 117
      forestry, fisheries   Retail trade 567

Mining	170	Finance, insurance and	150
Contract construction	186	real estate	
Manufacturing	2,072	Services	1,052
Transportation and other public utilities	151	Public Administration	102

PARISH PROFILES:

Median age, 1980 . . . . 24.8

Median family income, 1980 . . . . $17,334

Percent of families with income below poverty level, 1980 . . . . 17.7

General Hospitals, 1981	1	General Hospital Beds, 1981	34
Patient Care Physicians, 1981	5	Dentists, 1981	3

Infant birth rate (per 1000 population), 1982 . . . . 22.2

Infant mortality rate (per 1000 live births), 1981 . . . . 15.2

Death rate (per 1000 population), 1982 . . . . 8.2

AVOYELLES

HISTORY: Established as a parish on March 31, 1807, this parish takes its name from the Avoyelles Indians, the original inhabitants of the area. Many Indian relics from prehistoric times may be found. The French and Spanish settlers came up the Red River in the mid 18th century. During the Civil War, fighting took place at Fort De Russy, a Confederate fortification three miles northeast of Marksville. Other skirmishes took place at Mansura.

PARISH SEAT: Marksville		RAIL LINES	2
SQUARE MILE AREA	846	CONGRESSIONAL DISTRICT	8
SCHOOLS	Public 21	CHURCHES	30
	Private 6	AIRPORTS	2

AGRICULTURE: Cotton, corn, soybeans, and wheat

INDUSTRY: Garon Manufacturing, Albertson Manufacturing, and Avoyelles Valve

TOURIST ATTRACTIONS: Marksville Prehistoric Indian Park, forty acres, is on a bluff overlooking Old River, a mile east of Marksville. The park is surrounded by an earthen embankment built as a fort by the Indians. Within the park are burial mounds and a natural history museum containing archaeological, cultural, and geological exhibits. Spring Bayou Reservation and Recreation Center.

PARISH BUSINESS PATTERNS: Number of employees, 1983:

Agricultural services, forestry, fisheries	86	Wholesale trade	353
		Retail trade	1,294
Mining	65	Finance, insurance and	378
Contract construction	802	real estate	
Manufacturing	735	Services	2,657
Transportation and other public utilities	353	Public Administration	327

PARISH PROFILES:

Median age, 1980 . . . . 29.3

Median family income, 1980 . . . . $11,987

Percent of families with income below poverty level, 1980 . . . . 25.5

General Hospitals, 1981 2   General Hospital Beds, 1981 106
Patient Care Physicians, 1981. 18   Dentists, 1981. 12

Infant birth rate (per 1000 population), 1982 . . . . 15.7
Infant mortality rate (per 1000 live births), 1981. . . . . 20.5
Death rate (per 1000 population), 1982 . . . . 10.1

MAJOR CITIES (over 5,000 population): Bunkie and Marksville

BEAUREGARD

HISTORY: Beauregard Parish, named after Louisiana's famous Confederate general, was created out of Calcasieu Parish on January 12, 1912. It is located on the Texas border. In early years, the region was largely uninhabited. Just before the Civil War, it was settled by Scotch-Irish descendants from the Carolinas. DeRidder was incorporated in 1903 and became the government seat in 1912.

PARISH SEAT: DeRidder   RAIL LINES 2
SQUARE MILE AREA. . . . . 1,163 CONGRESSIONAL DISTRICT. . . . . 4 and 7
SCHOOLS . . . . Public 11 CHURCHES. 90
                          Private 1   AIRPORTS 1

AGRICULTURE: Soybeans, forestry, livestock, dairy farming, and rice.

INDUSTRY: International Paper, Thermo-Con, DeRidder Dress Manufacturing and Ampecet Corp.

PARKS and RECREATIONAL FACILITIES: Four parks, six tennis courts, and other various recreational facilities.

PARISH BUSINESS PATTERNS: Number of employees, 1983:

Agricultural services, ... 31   Wholesale trade 146
  forestry, fisheries   Retail trade 1,225
Mining 111   Finance, insurance and 228
Contract construction 263   real estate
Manufacturing. 1,207   Services. 1,934
Transportation and other 438   Public Administration 485
  public utilities

PARISH PROFILES:
Median age, 1980. . . . . 27.7
Median family income, 1980 . . . . $17,417
Percent of families with income below poverty level, 1980 . . . . 14.0
Percent of families with income of $15,000 plus, 1970· 10.8
Percent of Civilian Labor Force unemployed, July, 1975 . . . . 5.l

General Hospitals, 1981 2   General Hospital Beds, 1981 146
Patient Care Physicians, 1981. 19   Dentists, 1981. 10

Infant birth rate (per 1000 population), 1982 . . . . 14.9
Infant mortality rate (per 1000 live births), 1981. . . . . 19.8
Death rate (per 1000 population), 1982. . . . . 6.7

MAJOR CITIES (over 5,000 population): DeRidder

BIENVILLE

HISTORY: Originally part of Natchitoches Parish, Bienville was established on March 14, 1848. It was named in honor of Jean Baptiste Sieur de Bienville, colonizer of Louisiana and founder of the city of New Orleans. The village of Mount Lebanon was settled in 1847 by immigrants from South Carolina. It was the site of the first Baptist Church in North Louisiana. The Baptist Convention organized and founded Mount Lebanon University in 1855. During the Civil War, the school was closed and the building used as a hospital. In later years, the college was moved to Pineville and reopened as Louisiana College.

PARISH SEAT: Arcadia
SQUARE MILE AREA. 815
SCHOOLS . . . . Public 10
                                    Private 1

CONGRESSIONAL DISTRICT. 5
CHURCHES. 60

PARISH BUSINESS PATTERNS: Number of employees, 1983:

Agricultural services, ... 8	Wholesale trade	53
forestry, fisheries	Retail trade	330
Mining 105	Finance, insurance and.	121
Contract construction 209	real estate	
Manufacturing. 1,202	Services.	845
Transportation and other 224	Public Administration	158
public utilities		

PARISH PROFILES:
Median age, 1980 . . . . 32.3
Median family income, 1980 . . . . $13,850
Percent of families with income below poverty level, 1980 . . . . 20.9

General Hospitals, 1981 1
Patient Care Physicians, 1981 6

General Hospital Beds, 1981 30
Dentists, 1981. 2

Infant birth rate (per 1000 population), 1982 . . . . 15.5
Infant mortality rate (per 1000 live births), 1981. . . . . 3.5
Death rate (per 1000 population), 1982 . . . . 9.5

BOSSIER

HISTORY: Bossier Parish was carved out of the great Natchitoches District on February 24, 1843. It was named after Pierre Evariste Bossier, a descendant of an early settler and a member of Congress when the parish was formed. Located in the rich valley of the Red River, the parish has long been known for its agriculture production. Barksdale Air Force Base, located in part within the city limits of Bossier City, has been a major factor in the growth of the parish.

PARISH SEAT: Benton
SQUARE MILE AREA. 845
SCHOOLS . . . . Public 30
                                    Private 3

RAIL LINES 1
CONGRESSIONAL DISTRICT. 4
CHURCHES. 77

AGRICULTURE: Cotton, soybeans, corn, hay, forestry, and beef cattle.

INDUSTRY: Playground equipment, mobile homes, oil field equipment and service, concrete and other diversified manufacturing.

TOURIST ATTRACTIONS: Louisiana Downs thoroughbred racing

PARKS and RECREATIONAL FACILITIES: Programs include swimming pools, recreational buildings, tennis courts, gymnasiums, fishing and boating in Lake Bistineau, Bodcau Reservoir, and numerous bayous.

PARISH BUSINESS PATTERNS: Number of employees, 1983:

Agricultural services, ... 219	Wholesale trade	1,103
forestry, fisheries	Retail trade	4,351
Mining 644	Finance, insurance and.	1,007
Contract construction 1,658	real estate	
Manufacturing. 1,829	Services.	6,736
Transportation and other 1,187	Public Administration	1,803
public utilities		

PARISH PROFILES:

Median age, 1980. . . . . 26.6
Median family income, 1980 . . . . $18,639
Percent of families with income below poverty level, 1980 . . . . 10.1

General Hospitals, 1981 1   General Hospital Beds, 1981 175
Patient Care Physicians, 1981 39   Dentists, 1981. 10

Infant birth rate (per 1000 population), 1982 . . . . 19.0
Infant mortality rate (per 1000 live births), 1981 . . . . 8.8
Death rate (per 1000 population), 1982 . . . . 5.6

MAJOR CITIES (over 5,000 population): Bossier City

Bossier City

Bossier City, with the motto "small enough to care—large enough to serve," is the major city of this northwest Louisiana parish. It was first called Bennett's Bluff (mid 19th century), with two stores located along the Red River—Bennett's Store and Cane's Store. Mrs. Bennett later married Mr. Cane, and the settlement, Cane's Landing, was chartered as a village in 1905. In 1907 it was incorporated as the town of Bossier City, today one of the fastest growing cities in North Louisiana.

CADDO

HISTORY: Caddo Parish, originally part of the Natchitoches District, came into existence on January 18, 1838. The parish takes its name from the Caddo Indians, who, in 1835, sold their territory (comprising all of Caddo Parish, parts of Arkansas and East Texas) to the United States for $80,000. Long before the early European explorers made their way into the territory, the tribes of the Caddo Nation were well established in the Red River valley. Along the western border of the parish, the mounds which marked the international boundary between the U. S. and the Republic of Texas still exist. These markers are five feet high and fifteen feet in diameter and were erected a mile apart. Caddo Parish was one of the few areas that remained in the hands of the Confederacy during the Civil War. From 1863-65 the new parish courthouse served as the wartime capitol. The last surrender of arms in the state occurred on the courthouse square in Shreveport.

PARISH SEAT: Shreveport   RAIL LINES 6
SQUARE MILE AREA. 894   CONGRESSIONAL DISTRICT. 4
SCHOOLS . . . . Public 73   CHURCHES. 379
                Private 27   AIRPORTS 3

AGRICULTURE: Cotton, soybeans, hay, timber, grain sorghums, corn, pecans, rice, and sweet potatoes.

INDUSTRY: Universal Oil Products; Beaird-Pouland; Western Electric; Riley Beaird, Inc.; Kast Metal Corp.; General Electric; Gould Battery; Bingham Willamette Co.; Brewster Co.; General Motors; Vivian Industrial Plastics; Roker Industries; Vivian Manufacturing.

TOURIST ATTRACTIONS: Louisiana State Fair; American Rose Society; Louisiana State Exhibit Museum; R. W. Norton Art Gallery; R. S. Barnwell Memorial Gardens and Art Center; Pioneer Museum; Oil and Indian Museum; SPAR Planetarium; Land's End, antebellum home, built in 1857 by Col. Henry Marshall on his plantation purchased in 1835.

PARKS and RECREATIONAL FACILITIES: Boating and fishing in Caddo and Cross lakes and numerous bayous; sixty parks with various recreational activities.

PARISH BUSINESS PATTERNS: Number of employees, 1983:

Agricultural services, ... 435   Wholesale trade 7,431
    forestry, fisheries   Retail trade 18,864

Mining 5,191	Finance, insurance and 6,346
Contract construction 6,558	real estate
Manufacturing. 17,356	Services. 34,033
Transportation and other 8,598	Public Administration 2,761
public utilities	

PARISH PROFILES:

Median age, 1980 . . . . 27.5
Median family income, 1980 . . . . $18,513
Percent of families with income below poverty level, 1980 . . . . 13.1

General Hospitals, 1981 7	General Hospital Beds, 1981. 350
Patient Care Physicians, 1981 685	Dentists, 1981. 145

Infant birth rate (per 1000 population), 1982. . . . . 18.4
Infant mortality rate (per 1000 live births), 1981 . . . . 13.7
Death rate (per 1000 population), 1982 . . . . 8.8

MAJOR CITIES (over 5,000 population): Shreveport

Shreveport

Shreveport, located in the northeast reaches of Louisiana, was incorporated in 1839. Once a small thriving river port, today the city is a large metropolitan area serving the Ark-La-Tex area of northeast Texas and southwest Arkansas, and has a combined estimated population of 1,800,000 people. Business booms in this oil, cotton, manufacturing, and commercial center. The city also is a major educational, medical, cultural and recreational center. Centenary College, Louisiana State University-Shreveport, Southern University and Baptist Christian College are among the institutions of higher learning.

The first inhabitants to arrive in the Caddo region were fur traders. In 1803, Larkin Edwards from Tennessee settled near an Indian village on Coates Bluff, at the eastern end of what is now Olive Street. He acted as interpreter for the Indians in their dealings with the traders. In 1835, as a reward for his services, the Caddo Indians gave him a block of land which now forms the heart of Shreveport.

In 1832, the U. S. government engaged Henry Miller Shreve to open the Red River for navigation. Shreve was a steamboat builder and inventor, and was familiar with what was then known as the Western rivers. In the spring of 1833, he began the task of opening the Red River of a massive jam of logs called "the great raft." Snags, tree trunks, and driftwood jammed the Red River from bank to bank for a distance of nearly 200 miles.

Most engineers said that clearing of this jam was impossible, but Captain Shreve undertook the impossible. With four steamboats, two of which were of the battering-ram type vessels of his own invention, and 159 men under his command, he attacked the "giant raft" on the morning of April 11, 1833. The job was finally finished in 1836. In his final report to Washington, Captain Shreve said, "There has also a town sprung up equal in population and surpassing any on the Red River in amount of business transactions." Thus, the way was open for the eventual growth of this large metropolitan center.

CALCASIEU

HISTORY: Organized as a parish on March 24, 1840, "Calcasieu," which means "crying eagle," is said to have been the name of an Attakapas Indian chief. As he went into battle, he gave a peculiar cry like an eagle. One of the first pioneers to arrive in the area was Charles Sallier, originally from the province of Savois, France. He married the daughter of Barthelemy LeBleu, who had arrived in 1771 from Bordeaux, France. The community became known as Charley's Lake. Those who settled between 1780 and 1819 acquired their property from the Indians or homesteaded what was then known as the Rio Hondo lands. During the Civil War, the Sabine River became an important hideout for blockade runners. Strong Confederate earthworks were built along the Sabine. A large sulphur deposit was discovered in the late 1860s near the present city of Sulphur. One of the world's largest sulphur industries was established at the site and flourished until the late 1920s. Soon after this, the development of the oil industry became significant when techniques for deep well drilling became known. With the advent of the deep water port, Calcasieu Parish has been destined for growth and development.

PARISH SEAT: Lake Charles
SQUARE MILE AREA. 1,081
SCHOOLS . . . . Public 66
Private 22

RAIL LINES 2
CONGRESSIONAL DISTRICT. 7
AIRPORTS 1

AGRICULTURE: Rice and beef cattle

INDUSTRY: Oil and related industries, chemical and petrochemical plants, the Port of Lake Charles.

TOURIST ATTRACTIONS: Delta Downs thoroughbred racing; Imperial Calcasieu Museum; Calcasieu Historical Museum; Peace Memorial Tower; Contraband Days, a festival commemorating the swashbuckling era of the buccaneer Jean Lafitte.

PARKS and RECREATIONAL FACILITIES: Niblett's Bluff State Park; Sam Houston State Park; one-and-one-fourth mile bathing beach bordering on Interstate 10; charter boats for deep sea fishing; fishing and boating in Lake Charles, Prien Lake, and numerous bayous.

PARISH BUSINESS PATTERNS: Number of employees, 1983:

Agricultural services, ... 429		Wholesale trade 3,032	
forestry, fisheries		Retail trade 10,954	
Mining 2,388		Finance, insurance and 2,631	
Contract construction 6,826		real estate	
Manufacturing. 10,158		Services. 16,197	
Transportation and other 4,621		Public Administration 2,432	
public utilities			

PARISH PROFILES:

Median age, 1980 · .31.4
Median family income, 1980 . . . .$21,316
Percent of families with income below poverty level, 1980 . . . . 9.9

General Hospitals, 1981 5
Patient Care Physicians, 1981 214

General Hospital Beds, 1981. 899
Dentists, 1981. 93

Infant birth rate (per 1000 population), 1982 . . . . .20.1
Infant mortality rate (per 1000 live births), 1981. . . . . 7.5
Death rate (per 1000 population), 1982. . . . . 6.4

MAJOR CITIES (over 5,000 population): Lake Charles, Sulphur, and Westlake

Lake Charles

Lake Charles began as a stopover on the Old Spanish Trail and as a "schooner port," which was tied in with the mythical stories of the famed buccaneer, Jean Lafitte. The present Port of Lake Charles is accessible to oceangoing vessels and is only thirty-four miles from the Gulf of Mexico—the shortest distance of the three deep water ports in Louisiana.

One of the first settlers to arrive was Charles Sallier. (See history.) The Salliers are credited with building the first home within the present city limits.

Lake Charles gained its first fame as a lumber producing area. The creation of the port provided the incentives for industrialization and has given the city a broad and stable basis for future growth and development.

Jacob Ryan, often called the "father of Lake Charles," was the town's first real estate man. It is said that he sold property by the rope length along the street which now bears his name (the main street of this modern city). Lake Charles, the cultural and education center of the area, is the home of McNeese State University.

CALDWELL

HISTORY: Caldwell Parish was established on March 6, 1838. It was formerly a part of Catahoula Parish. Settlements had been made in the district early in the 19th century, soon after the Louisiana Purchase.

PARISH SEAT: Columbia	RAIL LINES 1
SQUARE MILE AREA. 541	CONGRESSIONAL DISTRICT. 5
SCHOOLS 6	AIRPORTS 1

AGRICULTURE: Cotton, soybeans, timber, and beef cattle.

INDUSTRY: Forestry

PARKS and RECREATIONAL FACILITIES: Recreation center; fishing and boating in the surrounding lakes and Ouachita River.

PARISH BUSINESS PATTERNS: Number of employees, 1983:

Agricultural services, ... 11		Wholesale trade	34
forestry, fisheries		Retail trade	241
Mining 51		Finance, insurance and.	64
Contract construction 102		real estate	
Manufacturing. 130		Services.	939
Transportation and other 133		Public Administration	168
public utilities			

PARISH PROFILES:

Median age, 1980. . . . . .31.4
Median family income, 1980 . . . .$12,624
Percent of families with income below poverty level, 1980 . . . . 9.9

General Hospitals, 1981 2	General Hospital Beds, 1981. 90
Patient Care Physicians, 1981 4	Dentists, 1981. 4

Infant birth rate (per 1000 population), 1982 . . . . .11.5
Infant mortality (per 1000 live births), 1981 . . . . .18.2
Death rate (per 1000 population), 1982 . . . . 9.2

CAMERON

HISTORY: Cameron Parish, the largest in land area in the state, was organized on March 15, 1870. The parish reportedly took its name from Simon Cameron, Lincoln's secretary of war. Early records are sketchy, and comprise the history of several large southwest Louisiana parishes, including Vermilion and Calcasieu. Many of the early wooden courthouses have burned, thus destroying records. Early settlers' names include the Elenders, Deuhons, Faulks, Heberts, Smiths and Domingos. Early records of Grand Chenier include the names of Placide Labove, who settled in 1836, and John Smith, John Armstrong, John Sweeney, and James Welse, all settlers who came before 1850. The earliest inhabitants were the Attakapas Indians in the southwesternmost region of the area. Recollections of the early days tell of the enormous orange crops, with some trees producing 5,000 oranges. During the growing season, schooners came from Galveston, Texas to buy the crops. Despite the devastation caused by Hurricane "Audrey" and others, the parish has always been rebuilt and continues to grow and prosper.

PARISH SEAT: Cameron
SQUARE MILE AREA. . . . . . . Total, 1,417
    land, 1,457; water, 221
SCHOOLS 7

CONGRESSIONAL DISTRICT. 7
CHURCHES. 23

AGRICULTURE: Rice and corn

INDUSTRY: Menhaden companies, oil and related industries, fur and wildlife, fishing, shrimping, and vegetable farming.

TOURIST ATTRACTIONS: Seventy miles of sandy beaches on the Gulf of Mexico; hunting festival and fishing rodeo; Creole Nature Trail; Rockefeller Wildlife Refuge.

PARKS and RECREATIONAL FACILITIES: Boating and fishing in the bayous, Lacassine Reserve, and the Gulf of Mexico.

PARISH BUSINESS PATTERNS: Number of employees, 1983:

Agricultural services, ... 10		Wholesale trade 96	
forestry, fisheries		Retail trade 221	
Mining 1,048		Finance, insurance and 64	
Contract construction 337		real estate	
Manufacturing. 165		Services. 822	
Transportation and other 990		Public Administration 164	
public utilities			

PARISH PROFILES:
    Median age, 1980 . . . . 26.9
    Median family income, 1980 . . . . $20,562
    Percent of families with income below poverty level, 1980 . . . . 21.3

General Hospitals, 1981 1   General Hospital Beds, 1981. 27
Patient Care Physicians, 1981 3   Dentists, 1981 1

Infant birth rate, (per 1000 population), 1982 . . . . 17.8
Infant mortality (per 1000 live births), 1981 . . . . 16.0
Death rate (per 1000 population),1982 . . . . 6.3

CATAHOULA

HISTORY: Catahoula Parish, formed on March 23, 1808, derived its name from the Tensas Indian name, "cataoola," meaning big, clear lake. However, Catahoula Lake is now in LaSalle Parish, originally the western half of Catahoula Parish.

PARISH SEAT: Harrisonburg
SQUARE MILE AREA. 732
SCHOOLS 11

RAIL LINES 1
CONGRESSIONAL DISTRICT. 5
CHURCHES. 49

AGRICULTURE: Cotton, livestock, timber, and soybeans.

INDUSTRY: Timber and logging

TOURIST ATTRACTIONS: Catahoula Parish Museum houses prehistoric Indian artifacts and exhibits. Dogwood Trail in the spring; Soybean Festival.

PARKS and RECREATIONAL FACILITIES: One park with various recreational facilities; twenty freshwater lakes, excellent for fishing, skiing, and boating.

PARISH BUSINESS PATTERNS: Number of employees, 1983:

Agricultural services, ... 67	Wholesale trade 126	
forestry, fisheries	Retail trade 426	

Mining	63	Finance, insurance and	95
Contract construction	790	real estate	
Manufacturing	307	Services	794
Transportation and other public utilities	175	Public Administration	115

PARISH PROFILES:
Median age, 1980 . . . . 28.4
Median family income, 1980 . . . . $12,770
Percent of families with income below poverty level, 1980 . . . . 11.0

General Hospitals, 1981	1	General Hospital Beds, 1981	53
Patient Care Physicians, 1981	2	Dentists, 1981	1

Infant birth rate, (per 1000 population), 1982 . . . . 15.9
Infant mortality rate (per 1000 live births), 1981 . . . . 8.7
Death rate (per 1000 population), 1982. . . . . 7.1

CLAIBORNE

HISTORY: Named after the first governor of Louisiana, Claiborne joined the list of Louisiana parishes on March 11, 1828. Only a few years before, the first settlers arrived in this region, a wilderness of virgin forests at that time. The parish courthouse (in Homer) is a classic example of Greek Revival architecture (dating from 1861) and is one of the oldest public buildings in continuous use in the state. Claiborne Parish is the birthplace of T. H. Harris, superintendent of public education for several decades. Several Indian temple mounds are in the area. The first airmail in the South was delivered from Shreveport to Homer on July 21, 1920.

PARISH SEAT: Homer		RAIL LINES	1
SQUARE MILE AREA	765	CONGRESSIONAL DISTRICT	4
SCHOOLS	Public 10	CHURCHES	42
	Private 1	AIRPORTS	2

AGRICULTURE: Beef and dairy cattle, timber, and vegetable farming.

INDUSTRY: Oil and gas production; Butane-Propane Plant; plastics; glove manufacturing; draperies; furniture.

TOURIST ATTRACTIONS: Germantown Settlement and Ford Memorial Museum

PARKS and RECREATIONAL FACILITIES: Lake Claiborne State Park; boating and fishing in Corney Lake and various other sports facilities; scenic drives through the hilly country during the fall.

PARISH BUSINESS PATTERNS: Number of employees, 1983:

Agricultural services, forestry, fisheries	6	Wholesale trade	130
		Retail trade	623
Mining	595	Finance, insurance and real estate	162
Contract construction	202		
Manufacturing	731	Services	984
Transportation and other public utilities	313	Public Administration	384

PARISH PROFILES:
Median age, 1980 . . . . 33.2
Median family income, 1970 . . . . $14,538
Percent of families with income below poverty level, 1980 . . . . 25.8

General Hospitals, 1981 2   General Hospital Beds, 1981 89

Patient Care Physicians, 1981 9   Dentists, 1981 3

Infant birth rate (per 1000 population), 1982 . . . . 15.2

Infant mortality rate (per 1000 live births), 1981 . . . . 21.2

Death rate (per 1000 population), 1982 . . . . 12.4

CONCORDIA

HISTORY: Concordia was founded January 6, 1810. Some claim that the first white man to visit Concordia was Hernando de Soto in 1542. More than a hundred years later, LaSalle conferred with the Tensas and Natchez Indians here. He called it "new paradise." The actual settlement of the parish did not come until much later. The first land grant was made to Jose Vidal by Governor-General de Lemos, who called it "New Concordia." Gayarre, a noted historian, claims the name was inspired by the amicable agreement or "concord" arrived at by the Spaniard, Vidal, and American authorities in Natchez for the mutual surrender of fugitive slaves. Others say it was named for Concord, the magnificent residence built in Natchez by Governor Gayoso de Lemos. The mansion has since burned, but the stories of the lavish entertainment of the era continue to live.

PARISH SEAT: Vidalia   RAIL LINES 3

SQUARE MILE AREA. 717   CONGRESSIONAL DISTRICT. 5

SCHOOLS . . . . Public 11   CHURCHES. 20

                     Private 1   AIRPORTS 1

AGRICULTURE: Cotton and soybeans

INDUSTRY: Railroads

PARISH BUSINESS PATTERNS: Number of employees, 1983:

Agricultural services, ... 130   Wholesale trade 185

   forestry, fisheries   Retail trade 897

Mining 322   Finance, insurance and 156

Contract construction 428   real estate

Manufacturing. 176   Services. 1,365

Transportation and other 405   Public Administration 230

   public utilities

PARISH PROFILES:

Median age, 1980 . . . . 27.7

Median family income, 1980 . . . . $15,208

Percent of families with income below poverty level, 1980 . . . . 20.8

General Hospitals, 1981 1   General Hospital Beds, 1981 50

Patient Care Physicians, 1981 10   Dentists, 1981. 5

Infant birth rate (per 1000 population), 1982 . . . . 13.9

Infant mortality rate (per 1000 live births), 1981 . . . . 32.8

Death rate (per 1000 population), 1982 . . . . 7.6

MAJOR CITIES (over 5,000 population): Vidalia and Ferriday

DESOTO

HISTORY: DeSoto, which includes land from both Caddo and Natchitoches parishes, became a parish on April 1, 1843. The name honors Hernando de Soto, the Spanish explorer who discovered the Mississippi River in 1541. The first colonists were subjects of France and Spain, who later became citizens of the Republic of Texas. On the Sabine River, the Waterloo community seems to have existed since Louisiana became a state in 1812. The site probably shifted somewhat when Dr. Logan established the ferry crossing called Logan Port, which changed to Logansport in 1848. The progressive city of Mansfield serves as the seat of government, and the industrial, business, and medical center for the area.

PARISH SEAT: Mansfield

RAIL LINES 2

SQUARE MILE AREA. 880

CONGRESSIONAL DISTRICT. 4

SCHOOLS . . . . Public 11

CHURCHES. 69

Private 1

AIRPORTS 1

AGRICULTURE: Forestry

INDUSTRY: Nabors Trailers, Inc.; Hendrix Manufacturing; Anthony Forest Products; McNeil Garment Corp.; Rite Care Poultry.

TOURIST ATTRACTIONS: Mansfield State Commemorative Area, battle site and museum of the last major Confederate victory in the Civil War.

PARKS and RECREATIONAL FACILITIES: Various types of recreation, including swimming, golf, tennis, and ball fields.

PARISH BUSINESS PATTERNS: Number of employees, 1983:

Agricultural services, forestry, fisheries	47	Wholesale trade	168
Mining	218	Retail trade	888
Contract construction	704	Finance, insurance and real estate	255
Manufacturing.	1,098	Services.	1,533
Transportation and other public utilities	228	Public Administration	159

PARISH PROFILES:

Median age, 1980 . . . . 30.5

Median family income, 1980 . . . . $14,887

Percent of families with income below poverty level, 1980 . . . . 20.3

General Hospitals, 1981	1	General Hospital Beds, 1981	72
Patient Care Physicians, 1981	6	Dentists, 1981.	5

Infant birth rate (per 1000 population), 1982 . . . . 17.3

Infant mortality (per 1000 live births), 1981 . . . . 12.9

Death rate (per 1000 population), 1982 . . . . 7.7

MAJOR CITIES (over 5,000 population): Mansfield

EAST BATON ROUGE

HISTORY: Created on December 22, 1810, this area was settled by the French and ceded to Great Britain under the Treaty of Paris in 1763. It was captured by Galvez in 1779. In 1807, under the rule of Spain, it was claimed that this parish, together with the others in what is now referred to as the Florida Parishes, was still under the rule of Spain and not included in the boundaries of the Louisiana Purchase of 1803. The parishes in question rebelled against Spain and formed the West Florida Republic. This was immediately taken over by Governor Claiborne for the United States. During this early history, eight flags flew over the area.

In 1772, Penicaut, in his book on Louisiana, *Relation*, wrote "Five leagues above le Manchac we found very high banks, which are called bluffs in that country, and the savage tongue Istrouma which signifies Baton Rouge, (Red Stick) because there is in this place a reddened post, which the savages have placed to mark the division of the lands of two Indian nations, namely, that of the

Bayougoulas from which we came and the other about 30 leagues higher than Baton Rouge, called the Oumas." Some historians believe the red stick was a tall red cypress tree stripped of its bark.

Today, with the city of Baton Rouge the dominant center of business, culture, education and finance, the parish looks forward to more and more prosperity.

PARISH SEAT: Baton Rouge

SQUARE MILE AREA. 458

SCHOOLS . . . . Public 103
Private 31

RAIL LINES 3

CONGRESSIONAL DISTRICT. . . . . 6 and 8

AIRPORTS 1

AGRICULTURE: Soybeans, sugarcane, vegetable farming, beef cattle, and dairy farming.

INDUSTRY: Port of Baton Rouge, with diversified industrial plants; over 150 industries, including petrochemicals, machine shops, foundries, steel fabrication, brick, concrete, cabinet works, iron works, food and kindred products, lumber and kindred products.

TOURIST ATTRACTIONS: state Capitol; old state Capitol; public zoo and arboretum; Louisiana State University Rural Life Museum; several antebellum homes and buildings, including Magnolia Mound (late 1700s), Potts House (1850), the Pentagon (on the Capitol grounds), and U. S. National Cemetery at Port Hudson.

PARKS and RECREATIONAL FACILITIES: Seventy-eight parks, covering thousands of acres, with numerous facilities.

PARISH BUSINESS PATTERNS: Number of employees, 1983:

Agricultural services, forestry, fisheries	591	Wholesale trade	9,385
		Retail trade	31,562
Mining	495	Finance, insurance and real estate	10,449
Contract construction	17,622		
Manufacturing	16,180	Services	53,483
Transportation and other public utilities	9,056	Public Administration	16,786

PARISH PROFILES:

Median age, 1980. . . . . 26.1

Percent of families with income of $15,000 plus, 1970 . . . . 20.9

Percent of Civilian Labor Force unemployed, July, 1975 . . . . 7.9

General Hospitals, 1981 6

Patient Care Physicians, 1981 636

General Hospital Beds, 1981 775

Dentists, 1981. 221

Infant birth rate (per 1000 population), 1982 . . . . 17.5

Infant mortality rate (per 1000 live births), 1981 . . . . 15.4

Death rate (per 1000 population), 1982 . . . . 6.1

MAJOR CITIES (over 5,000 population): Baton Rouge, Baker, and Zachary

Baton Rouge

Baton Rouge is the site of the state Capitol, the parish seat of government and the key industrial city in the area, and the center of an immense chemical and petroleum complex on the Mississippi River. The metropolitan area is the second largest in the state. It was incorporated in 1817, and became the capital of the state in 1849. The expanding port ranks seventh among the major ports of the country and second in Louisiana. Both oceangoing vessels and barges are provided with modern facilities. Two large universities, Louisiana State University and Southern University, are located in Baton Rouge.

LSU began as the Louisiana Seminary of Learning and Military Academy in 1860 at Pineville. Fire destroyed the building in 1869 and it was moved to Baton Rouge. In 1870 the name was changed to Louisiana State University, and seven years later the Agricultural and Mechanical College, which had been established in New Orleans, became a part of the university. The old campus was located where the state Capitol grounds are today. In 1932 the transition to the present campus was completed. LSU is an old institution, rich in history and traditions, and looks forward to even greater expansion to meet the needs and challenges of the most remarkable era of progress in its history.

Southern University is located five miles north of Baton Rouge on a bluff overlooking the mighty Mississippi. It was opened in 1881 with twelve students and located in New Orleans. In 1892 it became a land grant college, and in 1914 moved to Baton Rouge. Southern is expanding its curriculum in several areas, particularly those of social impact and the sciences.

The capitol building, one of America's most beautiful, is thirty-four stories, 450 feet in height, erected on the site of the old campus of LSU. It was constructed in fourteen months, from January, 1931 to March, 1932, at a cost of $5,000,000. This magnificent building is visited by thousands each month. Its elaborateness lies in the intricate and costly artistic interpretations of the state itself, for the story of Louisiana is the decorative theme of every detail in the construction. Broad steps of Minnesota granite mark the entrance to the building. Many famous artists and sculptors decorated this building for which Louisiana is so proud. Former Governor Huey P. Long, under whose aegis it was built, is buried in front of the building. A twelve-foot bronze statue of him stands in the front.

Projected population figures show that this progressive city will have a phenomenal growth in future decades.

EAST CARROLL

HISTORY: The northeasternmost parish, bordering the Mississippi River, is East Carroll. The Carroll parishes, East and West, were formed in 1877 by division of the original Carroll (named after Charles Carroll of Carrollton, famous signer of the Declaration of Independence) established in 1832. East Carroll was officially organized on May 11, 1877. The area was thickly settled by English, Scotch, and Irish pioneers from the Carolinas, Georgia and Tennessee.

PARISH SEAT: Lake Providence   CONGRESSIONAL DISTRICT. 5
SQUARE MILE AREA. 426
SCHOOLS . . . . Public 6
                                       Private 2

AGRICULTURE: Forestry

PARISH BUSINESS PATTERNS: Number of employees, 1983:

Agricultural services, ... 280		Wholesale trade 146	
forestry, fisheries		Retail trade 321	
Mining . . . : 0		Finance, insurance and. 157	
Contract construction 124		real estate	
Manufacturing. 200		Services. 740	
Transportation and other 225		Public Administration 104	
public utilities			

PARISH PROFILES:
Median age, 1980 . . . . .24.5
Median family income, 1980 . . . .$10,388
Percent of families with income below poverty level, 1980 . . . . 34.5

General Hospitals, 1981 1   General Hospital Beds, 1981. 29
Patient Care Physicians, 1981 5   Dentists, 1981. 3

Infant birth rate (per 1000 population), 1982 . . . . .18.8
Infant mortality rate (per 1000 live births), 1981 . . . . 23.6
Death rate (per 1000 population), 1982 . . . . 9.3

MAJOR CITIES (over 5,000 population): Lake Providence

EAST FELICIANA

HISTORY: East Feliciana became a parish on February 27, 1824. It was formerly a part of the western district of Feliciana (meaning "happy land" in Spanish). The Felicianas, East and West, were part of the West Florida Revolution of 1810 and the territory of the Republic of West Florida. In the same year, it was taken over by the United States. The area is one of the oldest cotton sections of the state and was settled by homesteaders from most of the southern states.

PARISH SEAT: Clinton
SQUARE MILE AREA. 455
SCHOOLS . . . . Public 10
                                    Private 1

RAIL LINES 1
CONGRESSIONAL DISTRICT. 8
CHURCHES. 80

TOURIST ATTRACTIONS: Many antebellum homes, including Asphodel, Milbank, Marston House, and the historic parish courthouse.

PARKS and RECREATIONAL FACILITIES: Ten public parks, featuring recreational activities.

PARISH BUSINESS PATTERNS: Number of employees, 1983:

Agricultural services,	29	Wholesale trade	59
forestry, fisheries		Retail trade	303
Mining	56	Finance, insurance and	121
Contract construction	303	real estate	
Manufacturing.	355	Services.	2,944
Transportation and other	112	Public Administration	564
public utilities		establishments	

PARISH PROFILES:
Median age, 1980. . . . . 27.8
Median family income, 1980 . . . . $16,184
Percent of families with income below poverty level, 1980 . . . . 17.7

General Hospitals, 1981 1
Patient Care Physicians, 1981 24

General Hospital Beds, 1981 36
Dentists, 1981. 3

Infant birth rate (per 1000 population), 1982 . . . . 17.3
Infant mortality (per 1000 live births), 1981 . . . . 7.5
Death rate (per 1000 population), 1982 . . . . 7.5

EVANGELINE

HISTORY: Evangeline was created on June 15, 1910. It was appropriately named after the ill-fated heroine of Longfellow's poem. While the parish itself is new, the history of its people extends over a long period of time. Evangeline, a part of the celebrated Attakapas prairie region, was settled by exiled Acadians.

PARISH SEAT: Ville Platte
SQUARE MILE AREA. 667
SCHOOLS . . . . Public 14
                                    Private 2

RAIL LINES 3
CONGRESSIONAL DISTRICT. 8
CHURCHES. 26
AIRPORTS 1

AGRICULTURE: Rice, soybeans, beef cattle, sweet potatoes, cotton, dairy farming, forestry, corn, grain, vegetable farming, swine, hay, and catfish and crawfish farming.

INDUSTRY: Cabot Corp. (carbon black); Lithcote Corp. (railroad tank car processors); Valley Canning Co.; Mocon Industries, Inc.

TOURIST ATTRACTIONS: Louisiana Cotton Festival, featuring "tournoi" medieval jousting tournaments.

PARKS and RECREATIONAL FACILITIES: Chicot State Park; Crooked Creek Recreation Area; Mamou Youth Center.

PARISH BUSINESS PATTERNS: Number of employees, 1983:

Agricultural services, forestry, fisheries	176	Wholesale trade	156
Mining	152	Retail trade	1,256
Contract construction	383	Finance, insurance and real estate	291
Manufacturing	400	Services	2,581
Transportation and other public utilities	515	Public Administration	385

PARISH PROFILES:

Median age, 1980. . . . . 27.9
Median family income, 1980 . . . .$12,540
Percent of families with income below poverty level, 1980 . . . . 25.8

General Hospitals, 1981 2   General Hospital Beds, 1981 223
Patient Care Physicians, 1981 25   Dentists, 1981 6

Infant birth rate (per 1000 population), 1982. . . . . 15.7
Infant mortality rate (per 1000 live births), 1981. . . . . 8.7
Death rate (per 1000 population), 1982 . . . . 9.7

MAJOR CITIES (over 5,000 population): Ville Platte

Ville Platte

The center of business activity in the parish, Ville Platte, was first settled in the mid 19th century and presumably named because it was situated on the flatlands just south of the rolling hills north of Alexandria. The city was incorporated in March, 1858.

FRANKLIN

HISTORY: Established on March 1, 1843 and named after the great American, Benjamin Franklin, Franklin Parish was created from parts of three neighboring parishes, Catahoula, Ouachita and Madison. Franklin Parish owes its origin to an accident. Two keelboats on Little Boeuf River, laden with machinery, ran aground here. The machinery in one was said to be able to gin cotton at the breathtaking rate of four bales a day. The other boat held a massive iron contrivance that could "cut more cypress boards in a day than fifty men." After unsuccessful efforts to free the boats from the sandbar, the boatmen decided to pitch camp here, and a settlement was born.

PARISH SEAT: Winnsboro   CONGRESSIONAL DISTRICT. 5
SQUARE MILE AREA. 636   CHURCHES. 44
SCHOOLS . . . . Public 13
                                  Private 1

AGRICULTURE: Cotton, soybeans, and livestock.

INDUSTRY: Sustan garment factory, Mastercrafters (boat building), and Franklin Mobile Homes.

PARKS and RECREATIONAL FACILITIES: Landis and West Winnsboro parks.

PARISH BUSINESS PATTERNS: Number of employees, 1983:

Agricultural services, forestry, fisheries	109	Wholesale trade	251
Mining	14	Retail trade	901
Contract construction	271	Finance, insurance and real estate	192
Manufacturing	181	Services	1,517

Transportation and other 368	Public Administration 171
public utilities	

PARISH PROFILES:
Median age, 1980 .... 29.5
Median family income, 1980 .... $11,937
Percent of families with income below poverty level, 1980 .... 25.3

General Hospitals, 1981 1	General Hospital Beds, 1981 55
Patient Care Physicians, 1981. 8	Dentists, 1981. 4

Infant birth rate (per 1000 population), 1982 .... 15.1
Infant mortality rate (per 1000 live births), 1981. .... 20.4
Death rate (per 1000 population), 1982 .... 9.0

MAJOR CITIES (over 5,000 population): Winnsboro

GRANT

HISTORY: The postwar legislature created Grant Parish on March 1, 1869 from the southern part of Winn Parish and the northern part of Rapides. It was named after President Ulysses S. Grant. Colfax, the parish seat, was named after the vice-president. Much of the parish encompasses one of the large divisions of the Kisatchie National Forest, a vast reforestation project.

PARISH SEAT: Colfax	CONGRESSIONAL DISTRICT........ 5
SQUARE MILE AREA............ 653	CHURCHES.................. 54
SCHOOLS .... Public 8	

AGRICULTURE: Forestry, soybeans, beef cattle, pasture grass, corn, and vegetable farming.

INDUSTRY: Forest products, Ditto of California plant, and fertilizer plant.

TOURIST ATTRACTIONS: Dogwood Trail; Louisiana Pecan Festival; historical landmarks, including the Old Jail and McNeely Home.

PARKS and RECREATIONAL FACILITIES: Boating and fishing in Iatt, Nantachie and Stuart lakes.

PARISH BUSINESS PATTERNS: Number of employees, 1983:

Agricultural services, ... 12	Wholesale trade 24
forestry, fisheries	Retail trade 180
Mining 42	Finance, insurance and............. 43
Contract construction 207	real estate
Manufacturing. 756	Services. 824
Transportation and other 138	Public Administration 183
public utilities	

PARISH PROFILES:
Median age, 1980 .... 31.3
Median family income, 1980 .... $13,759
Percent of families with income below poverty level, 1980 .... 18.3

General Hospitals, 1981 0	General Hospital Beds, 1981 0
Patient Care Physicians, 1981 6	Dentists, 1981 1

Infant birth rate (per 1000 population), 1982 .... 13.0
Infant mortality rate (per 1000 live births), 1981. .... 3.7
Death rate (per 1000 population), 1982 .... 9.0

IBERIA

HISTORY: The parish of Iberia possesses a special charm, with its many points of interest attracting widespread attention. Organized as a parish on October 3, 1868, it is in the heart of the Evangeline country, rich in romantic history. Iberia Parish was first settled by Spanish colonists from Florida, who laid out the Old Spanish Trail to make a connecting route to their post at San Antonio, Texas. They named the area Iberia after the Iberian Peninsula (Spain). Later the French settled in the area, then the Acadians, and finally the Americans. Three of the largest salt mines in the world are located in the parish.

PARISH SEAT: New Iberia   RAIL LINES   2
SQUARE MILE AREA. 589   CONGRESSIONAL DISTRICT.   3
SCHOOLS . . . . Public 29
                         Private 4

AGRICULTURE: Sugarcane, timber, corn, rice, cotton, peppers, vegetable farming, and dairying.

INDUSTRY: Oil, gas, and related industries; salt and other natural resources; commercial fishing and trapping; hot sauce and pepper products.

TOURIST ATTRACTIONS: Sugarcane Festival; Avery Island Gardens and Bird Sanctuary; Rip Van Winkle's Live Oak Gardens; lovely old homes, including The Shadows (circa 1831-1834), Justine (1822) and Justine Bottle Museum, Dulcito, which dates from 1788, and many others; Loreauville Heritage Museum and village.

PARISH BUSINESS PATTERNS: Number of employees, 1983:

Agricultural services, ... 320	Wholesale trade 1,566
forestry, fisheries	Retail trade 3,963
Mining 3,234	Finance, insurance and 1,003
Contract construction 1,274	real estate
Manufacturing. 5,581	Services. 5,797
Transportation and other 2,676	Public Administration 539
public utilities	

PARISH PROFILES:
Median age, 1980 . . . . 25.9
Median family income, 1980 . . . . $19,268
Percent of families with income below poverty level, 1980 . . . . 11.8

General Hospitals, 1981 2   General Hospital Beds, 1981 215
Patient Care Physicians, 1981 62   Dentists, 1981. 32

Infant birth rate, (per 1000 population), 1982 . . . . 21.5
Infant mortality rate (per 1000 live births), 1981 . . . . 17.4
Death rate (per 1000 population), 1982 . . . . 7.3

MAJOR CITIES (over 5,000 population): New Iberia and Jeanerette

New Iberia

New Iberia, on the banks of the famous Bayou Teche, was first settled in the mid 18th century by a few French families, who were given permission by the Spanish government. It bears the ancient name of Spain—Iberia. Later the Canary Islanders were brought over during Galvez' administration. In 1788 the Spanish Government census report showed that New Iberia had a population of 190. The present city was not incorporated until 1836; the townsite laid out by Frederick H. Duperier, a sugar planter. New Iberia fell into the hands of Federal forces in 1863, during General Banks' Red River campaign. In 1868 New Iberia became the parish seat of government.

IBERVILLE

HISTORY: One of the original nineteen parishes, Iberville was created on March 31, 1807. It was named after Iberville, the great French explorer and brother of Bienville. Iberville made his first trip up the Mississippi River in 1699. A few miles south of Plaquemine, he found a large group of Bayougoulas Indians waiting to extend a welcome. The same year, Father Du Ru, a Jesuit missionary, established the first church and tried to convert the Indians. By 1769 there were only 376 residents, mostly at St. Gabriel. During the Civil War the parish was occupied by Union forces.

PARISH SEAT: Plaquemine   RAIL LINES 1
SQUARE MILE AREA. 637   CONGRESSIONAL DISTRICT. 8
SCHOOLS . . . . Public 17   CHURCHES. 40
                    Private 3

AGRICULTURE: Sugarcane, soybeans, corn, grain sorghum, pecans, beef cattle, and horse breeding.

INDUSTRY: Chemicals; Goodyear Tire & Rubber Co.; Georgia-Pacific; industrial fill materials; plastics.

PARISH BUSINESS PATTERNS: Number of employees, 1983:

Agricultural services, ... 54	Wholesale trade	256
forestry, fisheries	Retail trade	1,101
Mining 255	Finance, insurance and	290
Contract construction 1,622	real estate	
Manufacturing. 5,139	Services.	2,653
Transportation and other 764	Public Administration	1,029
public utilities		

PARISH PROFILES:
Median age, 1980 . . . . 26.3
Median family income, 1980 . . . . $17,340
Percent of families with income below poverty level, 1980 . . . . 18.7

General Hospitals, 1981 1   General Hospital Beds, 1981. 70
Patient Care Physicians, 1981 24   Dentists, 1981. 8

Infant birth rate, (per 1000 population), 1982 . . . . 19.7
Infant mortality rate (per 1000 live births), 1981 . . . . 10.2
Death rate (per 1000 population), 1982. . . . . 9.5

MAJOR CITIES (over 5,000 population): Plaquemine

JACKSON

HISTORY: Jackson Parish, named after the great president, Andrew Jackson, was created on February 27, 1845. It was formerly part of Claiborne Parish, which had in turn been part of the large Natchitoches Territory. The section was first settled by Spanish traders in 1776.

PARISH SEAT: Jonesboro   RAIL LINES 2
SQUARE MILE AREA. 578   CONGRESSIONAL DISTRICT. 5
SCHOOLS . . . . Public 10   AIRPORTS 1

AGRICULTURE: Forestry, beef cattle, poultry and egg farming, and vegetable farming.

INDUSTRY: Timber and related industries; Continental Forest Industries; Continental Can Company; printing ink company.

PARISH BUSINESS PATTERNS: Number of employees, 1983:

Agricultural services, ... 18	Wholesale trade	23
forestry, fisheries	Retail trade	695

Mining 12	Finance, insurance and 187
Contract construction 109	real estate
Manufacturing. 1,346	Services. 1,166
Transportation and other 165	Public Administration 167
public utilities	

PARISH PROFILES:

Median age, 1980. . . . . 32.0
Median family income, 1980 . . . . $13,919
Percent of families with income below poverty level, 1980 . . . . 18.9

General Hospitals, 1981 1	General Hospital Beds, 1981 67
Patient Care Physicians, 1981 7	Dentists, 1981. 3

Infant birth rate (per 1000 population), 1982 . . . . 13.3
Infant mortality rate (per 1000 live births), 1981. . . . . 18.1
Death rate (per 1000 population), 1982 . . . . 9.5

MAJOR CITIES (over 5,000 population): Jonesboro

JEFFERSON

HISTORY: Jefferson Parish, named after Thomas Jefferson, was created on February 11, 1825. The northern part of the parish adjoins New Orleans, and is a suburban residential section as well as a trade and industrial center. The parish stretches sixty miles to the south to the shores of the Gulf of Mexico at Grand Isle, a longtime seaside resort community and more recently, the base for oil and related industries. In between these two extremes are the quiet bayous, cypress swamps and wetlands, called the Barataria section, where the famed pirate, Jean Lafitte, once headquartered.

In 1803, when Louisiana became part of the U. S., this area was a wilderness paradise, roamed by Choctaw Indians. Several communities within the early boundaries were Lafayette (now the Garden District) and Carrollton, both of which are now within the limits of Orleans Parish. Jefferson Parish was under military occupation during the Civil War. It was not until 1877 that the parish once again governed itself.

PARISH SEAT: Gretna	RAIL LINES 2
SQUARE MILE AREA. . . . . . . Total, 347	CONGRESSIONAL DISTRICT. . . . . 1 and 3
SCHOOLS . . . . Public 83	CHURCHES. 162
Private 74	AIRPORTS 1

INDUSTRY: Numerous manufacturing and industrial plants, including shipyards, port facilities, oil and related firms, many trade centers; fishing, hunting and trapping.

TOURIST ATTRACTIONS: Jefferson Downs, thoroughbred racing; "haute cuisine" dining in the many famous restaurants.

PARKS and RECREATIONAL FACILITIES: Grand Isle State Park; fourteen community centers; numerous parks, picnic shelters, tennis courts and golf courses; fishing and boating on Lake Pontchartrain, many lakes, bayous, and the Gulf of Mexico.

PARISH BUSINESS PATTERNS: Number of employees, 1983:

Agricultural services, ... 361	Wholesale trade 14,906
forestry, fisheries	Retail trade 38,281
Mining 4,326	Finance, insurance and. 8,846
Contract construction 15,390	real estate
Manufacturing. 15,397	Services. 43,460
Transportation and other 14,925	Public Administration 4,402
public utilities	

PARISH PROFILES:
Median age, 1980 . . . . 27.9
Median family income, 1980 . . . . $21,920
Percent of families with income below poverty level, 1980 . . . . 7.8

General Hospitals, 1981 6   General Hospital Beds, 1981 830
Patient Care Physicians, 1981 983   Dentists, 1981 272

Infant birth rate (per 1000 population), 1982 . . . . 16.1
Infant mortality rate (per 1000 live births), 1981 . . . . 13.1
Death rate (per 1000 population), 1982 . . . . 6.2

MAJOR CITIES (over 5,000 population): Metairie, Gretna, Kenner, Harvey, Westwego, Marrero, Harahan, River Ridge, and Terrytown.

Metairie

This growing metropolis is the largest unincorporated city in the state and the second largest in the nation. It is situated on the south shore of Lake Pontchartrain, adjacent to New Orleans, and the progressive citizens are justly proud of the consistent growth and development. "Fat City" is a name given to the concentrated trade, restaurant and night club center near the intersection of Veterans Memorial Highway and Causeway Boulevard.

Hundreds of years ago, the spring floods sent water cascading through the bayous of the area, spilling into the lake. One of these was Bayou Choupique, which, after many years, built up a natural levee now called "the Metairie ridge." Today Metairie Road follows this course. There were plantations as early as 1723, but the settlers soon found that there was not enough dry land. Therefore, they broke it up into "metairies" or "little farms." Today many of the tree-shaded streets are lined with beautiful suburban homes and gardens.

Gretna

Gretna is located on the west bank of the river. It sprawls along and back from the river, its numerous industrial plants and dockside shipping terminals dominating the area. The town was founded in the early nineteenth century by Nicholas Noel Destrehan (1793-1848). The village was settled by German immigrants and called Mechanicsham. A few years later another wealthy landowner, John McDonogh (1779-1850), established a village a few miles east and called it McDonoghville. The two were incorporated as a town in 1913. At his death, McDonogh left his entire fortune to the schools of Baltimore, Maryland, New Orleans, and Jefferson Parish. The town finally gave way to the name Gretna, since it was a haven for quick marriages, day or night, as was the case in Gretna Green, Scotland, near the English border. Since 1884 Gretna has served as the parish seat.

Another population center in the parish is Kenner, with a remarkable growth rate. The city encompasses the New Orleans International Airport, Jefferson Downs thoroughbred racing and the Kenner Museum, which displays early memorabilia and history of the city. Harvey, Marrero and Westwego, with their tremendous commercial activity, are contributing factors in the growth of the entire parish. One of the key factors is the Harvey Canal, an outlet to the Gulf of Mexico and the site of major manufacturing and shipping centers. Other cities over 5,000 population include Harahan, River Ridge, and Terrytown, all with public-minded citizens who are contributing to the ongoing progress and prosperity of the parish.

JEFFERSON DAVIS

HISTORY: Named after the president of the Confederacy, Jefferson Davis Parish was formed on June 12, 1912. Prior to this date it comprised "Imperial Calcasieu" with Allen and Beauregard parishes. This division was a result of sixteen years of deliberation, and passed without a dissenting vote. The early population of the area was a mixture of Creoles, Acadians, and Americans, from many of the other southern states. The discovery of oil (the first in Louisiana on September 21, 1901) started the oil history of Louisiana. From that time the development of the area has been constant. Speaking for all of the citizens, a resident says, "It's a good place to live and work."

PARISH SEAT: Jennings
SQUARE MILE AREA.............. 655
SCHOOLS .... Public 15
                          Private 2

RAIL LINES 1
CONGRESSIONAL DISTRICT 7
CHURCHES....................... 41
AIRPORTS 2

AGRICULTURE: Rice, soybeans, oats, sweet potatoes, cotton, poultry & dairying, and catfish farming.

INDUSTRY: S.B.A. Shipyards; Zigler Shipyards; Jennings Manufacturing; Hunt Tool Co.; oil and related industries.

TOURIST ATTRACTIONS: Zigler Museum; replica of first productive oil well in the state; Acadian Handicraft Museum.

PARKS and RECREATIONAL FACILITIES: Lake Arthur beach; fishing and boating in the lakes and bayous.

PARISH BUSINESS PATTERNS: Number of employees, 1983:

Agricultural services,.............. 141
   forestry, fisheries
Mining 598
Contract construction 395
Manufacturing................... 738
Transportation and other......... 542
   public utilities

Wholesale trade 569
Retail trade 1,591
Finance, insurance and............. 340
   real estate
Services......................... 2,120
Public administration 321

PARISH PROFILES:
Median age, 1980 .... 27.3
Median family income, 1980 .... $17,657
Percent of families with income below poverty level, 1980 .... 15.3

General Hospitals, 1981 2
Patient Care Physicians, 1981 22

General Hospital Beds, 1981........ 120
Dentists, 1981....................... 12

Infant birth rate (per 1000 population), 1982.............................. 18.0
Infant mortality rate (per 1000 live births), 1981 .... 8.0
Death rate (per 1000 population), 1982 .... 6.7
MAJOR CITIES (over 5,000 population): Jennings

Jennings

The parish seat, Jennings, is the business, financial, medical, and cultural center of the parish. It is known today as the "Cradle of Louisiana Oil."

LAFAYETTE

HISTORY: Lafayette Parish, one of the smallest in square mile area in the state, was created on January 17, 1823. The earliest settlers to come into this rich agricultural region were Andrew Martin and the Mouton family. Salvator and Anne Mouton were exiled from Nova Scotia. The story is told that Anne and her children, fearing English persecution, fled into the forest and subsisted for ten days on roots and berries before escaping to a better life which ended in south central Louisiana. This is one of the many accounts which gives understanding to the rich heritage of the Acadians.

PARISH SEAT: Lafayette
SQUARE MILE AREA............. 270
SCHOOLS .... Public 38
                          Private 20

RAIL LINES 2
CONGRESSIONAL DISTRICT 7
CHURCHES....................... 71
AIRPORTS 1

AGRICULTURE: Rice, soybeans, sugarcane, beef cattle, vegetable and dairy farming.

INDUSTRY: Oil and related industries, wholesale and retail trade.

TOURIST ATTRACTIONS: Lafayette Museum; Acadian Village; Evangeline Downs (thoroughbred horse racing); the spring Azalea Trail, when the parish is ablaze with colors of the southern plantings.

PARKS and RECREATIONAL FACILITIES: Twenty-six public parks with various recreational facilities, including swimming pools, tennis courts, and golf courses.

PARISH BUSINESS PATTERNS: Number of employees, 1983:

Agricultural services, forestry, fisheries	407	Wholesale trade.	6,657
Mining.	17,253	Retail trade	15,642
Contract construction.	5,772	Finance, insurance and real estate	3,637
Manufacturing	3,999	Services.	23,839
Transportation and other public utilities	7,739	Public administration.	2,039

PARISH PROFILES:

Median age, 1980 .... 25.8
Median family income, 1980 .... $21,472
Percent of families with income below poverty level, 1980 .... 9.9

General Hospitals, 1981	3	General Hospital Beds, 1981	772
Patient Care Physicians, 1981	269	Dentists, 1981	86

Infant birth rate (per 1000 population), 1982................................ 20.6
Infant mortality rate (per 1000 live births), 1981........................... 12.8
Death rate (per 1000 population), 1982...................................... 5.6
MAJOR CITIES (over 5,000 population): Lafayette

Lafayette

Lafayette is the parish seat and the commercial trade center for a large area. It is referred to as the "Hub City of Southwest Louisiana." This region originated as a plantation settlement about the time of the American Revolution. Before that time it was inhabited by the feared Attakapas Indians. Vermilionville, as the settlement was first called, was laid out as the seat of the parish in 1824 by Jean Mouton, who donated land for the courthouse and the Catholic church. The city was incorporated in 1836. Today both the downtown area and the oil center are beehives of activity serving a large area of Louisiana. University of Southwestern Louisiana is located in Lafayette.

LAFOURCHE

HISTORY: Each parish in Louisiana has its own charm and uniqueness. Lafourche is no exception. It is considered to have the longest line village in the world—sixty-five miles of farms and homes fronting Bayou Lafourche, from Thibodaux to Leeville. One of the largest parishes in square mile area, Lafourche was among the original twelve counties, organized on April 10, 1805. From the French word meaning fork, it is named for Bayou Lafourche, a fork of the Mississippi River. The Washa, Chawasha and the Chitimacha Indian tribes were the first inhabitants. When the Acadians saw this fertile land, they immediately settled and began farming, fishing, trapping, and cooking, all in which they still excel.

PARISH SEAT: Thibodaux   CONGRESSIONAL DISTRICT 3
SQUARE MILE AREA 1,141
SCHOOLS .... Public 33
                          Private 12

AGRICULTURE: Sugarcane, corn, potatoes, rice, cotton, and fruit crops.

INDUSTRY: Oil and related industries; sugar refining and related industries; timber; seafood canning; boat building.

TOURIST ATTRACTIONS: Edward Douglass White State Commemorative Area; other antebellum homes.

PARKS and RECREATIONAL FACILITIES: Excellent boating and fishing on the many bayous and canals.

PARISH BUSINESS PATTERNS: Number of employees, 1983:

Agricultural services, forestry, fisheries	412	Wholesale trade	661
		Retail trade	3,359
Mining	1,500	Finance, insurance and real estate	931
Contract construction	1,146		
Manufacturing	2,448	Services	6,516
Transportation and other public utilities	4,381	Public administration	733

PARISH PROFILES:

Median age, 1980 . . . . 25.2
Median family income, 1980 . . . . $19,947
Percent of families with income below poverty level, 1980 . . . . 10.9

General Hospitals, 1981	3	General Hospital Beds, 1981	344
Patient Care Physicians, 1981	76	Dentists, 1981	41

Infant birth rate (per 1000 population), 1982. . . . . 18.2
Infant mortality rate (per 1000 live births), 1981 . . . . 10.6
Death rate (per 1000 population), 1982 . . . . 7.0
MAJOR CITIES (over 5,000 population): Thibodaux

Thibodaux

Thibodaux is the parish seat of Lafourche. It is said that the citizens have retained the best of the old while adopting the best of the new. With all of the industry, further development is assured. Thibodaux is the home of Nicholls State University. Edward Douglass White, father of the U. S. Supreme Court chief justice, was an early settler and served Louisiana as governor and as a U. S. congressman. The first courthouse, a one-story frame building, was built in 1808 where the municipal tower is now located.

LASALLE

HISTORY: LaSalle Parish was created out of Catahoula Parish on January 1, 1910. The new parish was named in honor of the great French explorer who took formal possession of "all the lands drained by the Mississippi and the tributaries thereof in the name of King Louis XIV in the year 1682." Of special interest is Henry E. Hardtner, of Urania Lumber Company in Urania, considered the father of reforestation in the South. LaSalle Parish is growing and the economy is good.

PARISH SEAT: Jena		CONGRESSIONAL DISTRICT	5
SQUARE MILE AREA	638	CHURCHES	69
SCHOOLS	11	AIRPORTS	2
RAIL LINES	3		

AGRICULTURE: Soybeans, cotton, corn, peas, sugarcane, potatoes, and hay.

INDUSTRY: Reforestation; oil production; copper wire and cable plant; particle board plant; plywood; garment factory.

TOURIST ATTRACTIONS: Indian Bluff, overlooking Catahoula Lake

PARKS and RECREATIONAL FACILITIES: Boating, fishing in Catahoula Lake and hunting (in season).

PARISH BUSINESS PATTERNS: Number of employees, 1983:

Agricultural services, ... 13	Wholesale trade 188
forestry, fisheries	Retail trade 482
Mining 722	Finance, insurance and............. 154
Contract construction 191	real estate
Manufacturing............,.......... 963	Services......................... 1,207
Transportation and other 198	Public administration 153
public utilities	

PARISH PROFILES:

Median age, 1980 .... 30.7
Median family income, 1980 .... $15,250
Percent of families with income below poverty level, 1980 .... 17.2

General Hospitals, 1981 2	General Hospital Beds, 1981......... 116
Patient Care Physicians, 1981 11	Dentists, 1981 5

Infant birth rate (per 1000 population), 1982............................... 14.2
Infant mortality rate (per 1000 live births), 1981 .... 8.0
Death rate (per 1000 population), 1982 .... 8.7

LINCOLN

HISTORY: Lincoln Parish was organized in 1872 and named after Abraham Lincoln, one of the nation's greatest presidents. Parts of Jackson, Claiborne, Bienville and Union parishes were combined to make the new parish. The area is rich in agricultural and forest lands. It is privileged to have one of the two state-operated schools for exceptional children.

PARISH SEAT: Ruston	RAIL LINES 2
SQUARE MILE AREA.............. 472	CONGRESSIONAL DISTRICT 5
SCHOOLS .... Public 14	CHURCHES........................ 87
Private 2	AIRPORTS 1

AGRICULTURE: Forestry, peaches, broilers, and beef cattle.

INDUSTRY: Forest, wood, and glass products.

PARKS and RECREATIONAL FACILITIES: Three public parks; year-round programs sponsored by the Ruston Parks and Recreation Board; several lakes, rivers, and bayous which offer excellent skiing, boating, and fishing.

PARISH BUSINESS PATTERNS: Number of employees, 1983:

Agricultural services, ... 255	Wholesale trade................... 1,077
forestry, fisheries	Retail trade 2,198
Mining 100	Finance, insurance and............. 770
Contract construction.......... 1,482	real estate
Manufacturing................. 1,618	Services......................... 5,202
Transportation and other 584	Public administration 340
public utilities	

PARISH PROFILES:

Median age, 1980 .... 23.5
Median family income, 1980 .... $16,660
Percent of families with income below poverty level, 1980 .... 14.7

General Hospitals, 1981 1	General Hospital Beds, 1981......... 148
Patient Care Physicians, 1981 32	Dentists, 1981 12

Infant birth rate (per 1000 population), 1982.............................. 12.6
Infant mortality rate (per 1000 live births), 1981.......................... 11.2
Death rate (per 1000 population), 1982..................................... 6.1
MAJOR CITIES (over 5,000 population): Ruston

Ruston

The geographic location of Ruston makes it an ideal trade center for north central Louisiana. The terrain consists of rolling hills, lush pastures and woodlands. Ruston was founded in 1883 by R. E. Russ, who ceded land to the Vicksburg, Shreveport and Pacific Railroad with the provision that a townsite be established. The city was incorporated in 1884.

Ruston serves the medical and educational needs of the area. Louisiana Tech University, in Ruston, has an enrollment of over 9,000 students. Grambling State University, five miles west, is nationally recognized for its academic, athletic, and band achievements.

The city is located on Interstate 20, which has resulted in accelerated growth in every area of community life.

LIVINGSTON

HISTORY: Livingston, one of the Florida Parishes, named after Edward Livingston, who formulated Louisiana's code of law, was created in 1832 from a part of St. Helena Parish. It is one of the earliest settled parishes of the state, as both French and Spanish colonists settled there in the early 1700s. In 1778 families from the Canary Islands settled on the Amite River. Interstate 12, which crosses the parish east and west, has contributed to the development of the parish in recent years.

PARISH SEAT: Livingston
SQUARE MILE AREA.............. 661
SCHOOLS .... Public 27
Private 1
RAIL LINES 1
CONGRESSIONAL DISTRICT 6
CHURCHES...................... 112

AGRICULTURE: Poultry, beef cattle, vegetable farming, dairying, and forestry.

INDUSTRY: Plywood; door works; pulpwood; iron works; Cellu-fibe manufacturing; aluminum.

PARKS and RECREATIONAL FACILITIES: Eight parks, with various activities; fishing and boating in the bayous and Lake Maurepas.

PARISH BUSINESS PATTERNS: Number of employees, 1983:

Agricultural services,.............. 24
forestry, fisheries
Mining 171
Contract construction 893
Manufacturing.................. 584
Transportation and other......... 300
public utilities
Wholesale trade 169
Retail trade 1,505
Finance, insurance and............. 313
real estate
Services......................... 2,670
Public administration 416

PARISH PROFILES:
Median age, 1980 .... 26.4
Median family income, 1980 .... $19,541
Percent of families with income below poverty level, 1980 .... 11.3

General Hospitals, 1981 1
Patient Care Physicians, 1981........ 9
General Hospital Beds, 1981.......... 52
Dentists, 1981...................... 13

Infant birth rate (per 1000 population), 1982............................... 18.1
Infant mortality rate (per 1000 live births), 1981.......................... 15.2
Death rate (per 1000 population), 1982..................................... 5.3
MAJOR CITIES (over 5,000 population): Denham Springs

MADISON

HISTORY: Madison Parish, named after the fourth president of the United States, was established on January 19, 1838. It was part of the Ouachita County, one of the original twelve counties. This section was home of the Tensas and Ouachita tribes. Many Indian mounds can be seen in the parish today.

The parish offers several medical and educational advantages, including a mental health clinic, Delta Recovery Center, vocational school, day care centers, and aircraft school.

PARISH SEAT: Tallulah
SQUARE MILE AREA.............. 631
SCHOOLS .... Public 7
                            Private 1

RAIL LINES........................ 2
CONGRESSIONAL DISTRICT 5
CHURCHES....................... 26
AIRPORTS 2

AGRICULTURE: Cotton and soybeans

INDUSTRY: Grain elevators; cotton gins; Valley Steel Mill; Chicago Mill and Lumber Company.

TOURIST ATTRACTIONS: Amusement park, and other playgrounds and swimming pools.

PARISH BUSINESS PATTERNS: Number of employees, 1983:

Agricultural services,............. 115
    forestry, fisheries
Mining 4
Contract construction 111
Manufacturing................... 264
Transportation and other......... 127
    public utilities

Wholesale trade 106
Retail trade 531
Finance, insurance and............. 151
    real estate
Services.......................... 1,085
Public administration 170

PARISH PROFILES:

Median age, 1980 .... 26.1
Median family income, 1980 .... $10,679
Percent of families with income below poverty level, 1980 .... 32.9

General Hospitals, 1981 1
Patient Care Physicians, 1981........ 5

General Hospital Beds, 1981.......... 25
Dentists, 1981 1

Infant birth rate (per 1000 population), 1982................................ 14.2
Infant mortality rate (per 1000 live births), 1981............................ 11.9
Death rate (per 1000 population), 1982...................................... 9.8

MAJOR CITIES (over 5,000 population): Tallulah

PARISH SEAT: Bastrop
SQUARE MILE AREA.............. 807
SCHOOLS .... Public 18
                            Private 5

RAIL LINES........................ 2
CONGRESSIONAL DISTRICT 5
AIRPORTS 1

MOREHOUSE

HISTORY: Morehouse lies mostly in the Mississippi River delta land, amply irrigated by numerous streams and bayous. It was originally a part of the Ouachita Territory, which extended from the Mississippi River to the Red River, encompassing a large part of northeast Louisiana. The first settlers arrived in 1796 under the colonization program of the Spanish governor, Baron De Carondelet. Baron De Carondelet granted twelve leagues square to the Dutch nobleman, Baron De Bastrop, with the provision that he bring 500 settlers to the area. Abraham Morehouse was one of these early settlers. The parish was formerly organized on March 25, 1844, and the parish and principal city named after the two founding fathers. In the 1890s the railroad arrived, bringing many more settlers and causing a more rapid movement of the economy.

PARISH SEAT: Bastrop
SQUARE MILE AREA. 807
SCHOOLS .... Public 18
                        Private 5

RAIL LINES 2
CONGRESSIONAL DISTRICT........ 5
AIRPORTS 1

AGRICULTURE: Cotton, rice, wheat, soybeans, corn, livestock, and timber.

INDUSTRY: International Paper Co.; Morehouse Garment Corp.; Baltz Manufacturing; Tidewater Manufacturing; Stauffer Chemical; Pellets, Inc.; grain elevators; cotton gins.

PARKS and RECREATIONAL FACILITIES: Chemin-A-Haut State Park; three recreation centers open year-round; several other neighborhood parks; excellent fishing in Bussey Brake Reservoir.

PARISH BUSINESS PATTERNS: Number of employees, 1983:

Agricultural services, ... 349 forestry, fisheries	Wholesale trade 169
Mining 27	Retail trade 1,040
Contract construction........'...... 1,077	Finance, insurance and............. 232 real estate
Manufacturing................. 1,747	Services......................... 2,010
Transportation and other......... 437 public utilities	Public administration 289

PARISH PROFILES:

Median age, 1980 .... 28.7
Median family income, 1980 .... $12,949
Percent of families with income below poverty level, 1980 .... 25.8

General Hospitals, 1981 1	General Hospital Beds, 1981........ 142
Patient Care Physicians, 1981 21	Dentists, 1981....................... 8

Infant birth rate (per 1000 population), 1982................................ 17.0
Infant mortality rate (per 1000 live births), 1981 .... 7.5
Death rate (per 1000 population), 1982....................................... 8.6

MAJOR CITIES (over 5,000 population): Bastrop

Bastrop

Bastrop, the parish seat, is the industrial center for the area. The first outpost was set up at Point Pleasant on Bayou Bartholomew. Soon a crossroads store was established. With the advent of the modern highways, the community moved a few miles east to present day Bastrop.

NATCHITOCHES

HISTORY: Natchitoches, established on March 31, 1807, was one of the original twelve counties in the state. It comprised, at that time, an enormous geographical area comprising nine parishes and parts of three others. The parish was settled by the French, and parts of it by the Spanish as early as 1717. Natchitoches, the principal city, is the oldest settlement in the Louisiana Purchase. It was originally laid out on the Red River Channel, which brought trade to the tiny city for 100 years. About 1825, the river changed its course and retreated about five miles east of town. The picturesque Cane River now divides the historical part of the parish. Interesting homes and landmarks are open during an annual historical pilgrimage. The restoration of the parish courthouse has been a recent addition to the rich heritage of the area.

PARISH SEAT: Natchitoches	RAIL LINES 1
SQUARE MILE AREA 1,264	CONGRESSIONAL DISTRICT 5
SCHOOLS .... Public 21	CHURCHES....................... 41
Private 9	AIRPORTS 1

AGRICULTURE: Cotton, soybeans, beef cattle, and pecans.

INDUSTRY: Paper, plywood, trailer manufacturing, cotton seed oil, bricks, and cement.

TOURIST ATTRACTIONS: "Louisiana Cavalier" drama; Christmas Lighting Festival; historical townhomes built along Front Street in Natchitoches (one dating from 1776); Annual Fall Tour of Historic Homes, held the second weekend in October, featuring many antebellum homes; Melrose Plantation; Bayou Folk Museum; Los Adaes Historical Park; Roque House Museum; the Creole Craft House and the grave of the Unknown Confederate Soldier at Rebel Park.

PARISH BUSINESS PATTERNS: Number of employees, 1983:

Agricultural services,	445	Wholesale trade	336
forestry, fisheries		Retail trade	1,842
Mining	104	Finance, insurance and	356
Contract construction	573	real estate	
Manufacturing	1,448	Services	3,713
Transportation and other	662	Public administration	468
public utilities			

PARISH PROFILES:

Median age, 1980 .... 27.0
Median family income, 1980 .... $13,393
Percent of families with income below poverty level, 1980 .... 21.8

General Hospitals, 1981 1   General Hospital Beds, 1981 84
Patient Care Physicians, 1981 24   Dentists, 1981 9

Infant birth rate (per 1000 population), 1982 .... 16.6
Infant mortality rate (per 1000 live births), 1981 .... 7.4
Death rate (per 1000 population), 1982 .... 7.3
MAJOR CITIES (over 5,000 population): Natchitoches

Natchitoches

When Manhattan Island was a small village and Bienville was yet to discover and name the present metropolis of New Orleans, Natchitoches was a busy outpost, having been established by St. Denis in 1714. This is the center of El Camino Real country, with many homes and landmarks preserved. The proud citizens claim, "We've got more history than anyone else in the state." Also included in the present busy trade center are Northwestern State University, founded in 1884, and the beautiful Grand Ecore Amphitheater, which features the outdoor musical drama, "Louisiana Cavalier," staged each summer and attracting widespread attention. Natchitoches is a quaint city where the old and the new stand side by side. Of special interest to thousands of visitors is the Annual Christmas Lighting Festival.

ORLEANS

For historical summary and current data, see Orleans Parish covered in another section.

OUACHITA

HISTORY: One of the original nineteen parishes, Ouachita was created on March 31, 1807. Meaning silver water, it was named for the Ouachita Indians. Many mounds are found in the Ouachita Valley. Hernando de Soto explored this rich territory in 1541. French settlers were here as early as 1720. Among the large grants made by the Spanish were those of the Baron De Bastrop and the Marquis de Maison Rouge. The original parish was later divided into eight other Louisiana parishes. Among the early planters were Samuel McEnery, who became governor of Louisiana, Josiah Franklin, James H. Stephens, George W. Copley, John Hamblen, E. K. Ross, Ferdinand Morgan, John T. Cabeen, Robert Layton, Hypolite Pargoud, John Pargoud, and Nepetagna Richardson.

PARISH SEAT: Monroe	RAIL LINES	3
SQUARE MILE AREA	627 CONGRESSIONAL DISTRICT	5
SCHOOLS	Public 38 CHURCHES	176
	Private 7 AIRPORTS	1

AGRICULTURE: Cotton, soybeans, livestock, forestry, horticultural crops, rice, corn, and grain.

INDUSTRY: More than one hundred diversified manufacturing plants, wholesale and retail trade.

TOURIST ATTRACTIONS: Louisiana Purchase Garden and Zoo; Masur Museum of Art; Strauss

Playhouse; Opera Club; Bible Research Center, including a rare collection of Bibles and religious manuscripts; other organizations of music, the arts, and ballet.

PARKS and RECREATIONAL FACILITIES: Several parks provide swimming, tennis, golf, and picnicking; the Ouachita River, area bayous, and lakes provide skiing, boating, and excellent fishing.

PARISH BUSINESS PATTERNS: Number of employees, 1983:

Agricultural services, forestry, fisheries	350	Wholesale trade	3,945
Mining	568	Retail trade	9,485
Contract construction	3,095	Finance, insurance and real estate	3,604
Manufacturing	7,025	Services	15,579
Transportation and other public utilities	3,130	Public administration	1,822

PARISH PROFILES:
Median age, 1980 .... 26.9
Median family income, 1980 .... $17,140
Percent of families with income below poverty level, 1980 .... 16.2

General Hospitals, 1981 4   General Hospital Beds, 1981 781
Patient Care Physicians, 1981 188   Dentists, 1981 60

Infant birth rate (per 1000 population), 1982 .... 16.3
Infant mortality rate (per 1000 live births), 1981 .... 14.4
Death rate (per 1000 population), 1982 .... 6.4
MAJOR CITIES (over 5,000 population): Monroe and West Monroe

Monroe

The twin cities of Monroe, the parish seat and West Monroe, situated on opposite banks of the Ouachita River, are today the hub of commerce in northeastern Louisiana, centrally located at the crossroads of railroad and highway systems. The earliest white inhabitants of the area were settlers who probably came up from French missions along the Mississippi in the Catahoula and Concordia country. They took up lands on the river and called the place "Prairie des Canots," the prairie of the canoes, probably because it was the landing place for the Indians of the region who came to trade with the hunters and trappers.

Juan Filhiol, who afterwards changed his name to John Filhiol, was the real founder of the city of Monroe. He gave the parish site for the present courthouse, stipulating that it was to be used "forever as a seat of justice." He also gave the present site of one parish school to be used as "a seat of learning."

On May 1, 1819, all of the citizens rushed to the riverfront to see the steamer, *James Monroe*, make a landing. That night the town held a big celebration and it was suggested that the name be changed from Fort Miro to Monroe after the steamer which had been christened for the then president of the U. S., James Monroe. John Filhiol remained commandant until 1800 when he resigned his office. He died at his plantation home (located in present West Monroe).

Monroe was incorporated in 1820. Today, with the cooperative effort of the community-spirited citizens, Monroe has become "The Pacemaker City." With its efficient local government, trading, and industrial opportunities, the growth and development will steadily expand in this cultural, recreational, and educational center. It is the home of Northeast Louisiana University, a fast growing center of education. The Civic Center Complex comprises three buildings, which include an exhibit hall, an arena, and a conference hall.

PLAQUEMINES

HISTORY: One of the original nineteen parishes, Plaquemines was organized March 31, 1807.

Plaquemines is a French and Mobile Indian dialect word meaning persimmons. Historically, the parish is important because all of the early commerce of the Mississippi Valley sailed through its confines. The earliest inhabitants were the cultures of the Tchefuncte and other tribes which Columbus later called Indians.

LaSalle is considered by historians to be the first white man to travel in the present day Plaquemines Parish. Approximately where Venice is today, he proclaimed the entire Mississippi Valley the property of King Louis XIV of France (1682). Several early forts bear witness to the danger of the early settlers. Fort De La Boulaye, founded in 1700, was the first settlement in the territory. It was located north of present day Phoenix. Other forts were Jackson, St. Philip, and Bourbon (now submerged under the river).

During the Civil War, after a bitter battle at Fort Jackson in April, 1862, when Farragut's fleet passed the fortifications, the subsequent capture of New Orleans was inevitable.

Today historical markers lead the visitor to many sites for a glimpse into much of the history of the Mississippi Valley. The river, railroad, and modern highways link the commerce of the parish (the largest in square mile area in the state) to all areas of the world.

PARISH SEAT: Point a la Hache
SQUARE MILE AREA 1,035
SCHOOLS .... Public 6
　　　　　　　　　　　　　　Private 7
RAIL LINES 2
CONGRESSIONAL DISTRICT 1
CHURCHES....................... 39
AIRPORTS 3
(Includes Callender Airbase)

AGRICULTURE: Citrus industry, dating from 1700, and creole tomatoes.

INDUSTRY: Oil and related industries, sulphur, manufacturing, and retail trade.

TOURIST ATTRACTIONS: Plaquemines Parish Fair and Orange Festival; Fort Jackson; Judge Perez Museum; several beautifully preserved antebellum homes.

PARKS and RECREATIONAL FACILITIES: Eleven parks with many facilities; fishing and boating in the area bayous and lakes.

PARISH BUSINESS PATTERNS: Number of employees, 1983:

Agricultural services, ... 67
　　forestry, fisheries
Mining........................ 4,435
Contract construction........... 2,548
Manufacturing................. 2,525
Transportation and other 2,104
　　public utilities
Wholesale trade.................. 1,295
Retail trade 932
Finance, insurance and............. 191
　　real estate
Services......................... 3,686
Public administration............. 2,249

PARISH PROFILES:
Median age, 1980 .... 25.4
Median family income, 1980 .... $19,884
Percent of families with income below poverty level, 1980 .... 12.5

General Hospitals, 1981 1
Patient Care Physicians, 1981........ 7
General Hospital Beds, 1981.......... 34
Dentists, 1981 6

Infant birth rate (per 1000 population), 1982.............................. 19.2
Infant mortality rate (per 1000 live births), 1981........................... 17.8
Death rate (per 1000 population), 1982.................................... 6.8

POINTE COUPEE

HISTORY: Established on March 13, 1807, this region was early explored by Iberville (1699). He cut a shallow waterway through a neck of high land circled by the Mississippi River and gave it the name Pointe Coupee, or "cut point." Canadian trappers came as early as 1708, and were joined by deserters of the French colony at Biloxi. In 1718 Bienville established a post here and gave large land grants to settlers. Later in the century Acadian refugees settled in the parish. Many fine plantation homes are still here. Julian Poydras, a representative in the U. S. Congress and a very wealthy citizen of the parish, entertained Louis Philippe when he was visiting Louisiana.

PARISH SEAT: New Roads
SQUARE MILE AREA.............. 566
SCHOOLS .... Public 10
Private 10
RAIL LINES 2
CONGRESSIONAL DISTRICT 8
CHURCHES........................ 38
AIRPORTS 1

AGRICULTURE: Soybeans, beef cattle, corn, grain, sugarcane, cotton, forestry, and horticulture crops.

INDUSTRY: Sugar mill, pecan shelling plant, Big Rivers Industry, chipping mill, cotton gin, garment factory, packing company, and grain elevator.

TOURIST ATTRACTIONS: Parlange (1750) and other lovely antebellum homes.

PARKS and RECREATIONAL FACILITIES: Boating, skiing, and fishing in False River, an oxbow lake formed from an earlier channel of the Mississippi River; fishing and hunting in the woodlands and bayous.

PARISH BUSINESS PATTERNS: Number of employees, 1983:
Agricultural services, ... 139
forestry, fisheries
Mining 468
Contract construction 522
Manufacturing.................. 145
Transportation and other......... 756
public utilities
Wholesale trade 160
Retail trade 806
Finance, insurance and............. 223
real estate
Services.......................... 1,573
Public administration 196

PARISH PROFILES:
Median age, 1980.. 27.7
Median family income, 1980 .... $15,958
Percent of families with income below poverty level, 1980 .... 23.1

General Hospitals, 1981 1
Patient Care Physicians, 1981........ 7
General Hospital Beds, 1981.......... 60
Dentists, 1981 3

Infant birth rate (per 1000 population), 1982.............................. 18.9
Infant mortality rate (per 1000 live births), 1981........................... 16.1
Death rate (per 1000 population), 1982..................................... 7.7

RAPIDES

HISTORY: Created on March 31, 1807, Rapides gets its name from a ledge of limestone which formerly crossed the Red River just above Alexandria, forming a rapids. In the center of Louisiana, and one of the largest parishes, St. Denis established in 1700 one of the earliest trading posts in the Louisiana Territory on the present site of Pineville. Later it became a French outpost, because the river was claimed by the Spanish as the boundary between Mexico and French Louisiana.

Today the parish is one of the seven metropolitan statistical areas in the state. The Louisiana Seminary of Learning, established in 1860, later became Louisiana State University in Baton Rouge. The parish claims the first railroad west of the Mississippi River, built from Alexandria to Lecompte in 1837.

The Rapides Parish Coliseum is a modern 65,000 square foot circular dome with an adjacent exhibit building equipped for all types of sports, games, and convention and trade shows.

PARISH SEAT: Alexandria
SQUARE MILE AREA 1,341
CONGRESSIONAL DISTRICT .... 5 & 8
CHURCHES...................... 190

SCHOOLS .... Public 51   AIRPORTS 3
                         Private 5

AGRICULTURE: Cotton, corn, sugarcane, soybeans, timber, and vegetable farming.

INDUSTRY: Dresser Industries (valves & gauges); Pineville Krafts (liner board); Proctor and Gamble (soap products); diversified manufacturing; wholesale and retail trade.

TOURIST ATTRACTIONS: Kent House (circa 1796-1800) in Alexandria and Loyd's Hall, near Meeker.

PARKS and RECREATIONAL FACILITIES: Hot wells, famous health resort; Buelow Lake (sponsoring the annual speed boat races); fishing locations, including Indian Creek Reservoir, and Cotile and Kinkaid lakes.

PARISH BUSINESS PATTERNS: Number of employees, 1983:

Agricultural services, forestry, fisheries	318	Wholesale trade	2,169
		Retail trade	7,538
Mining	236	Finance, insurance and real estate	2,256
Contract construction	2,678		
Manufacturing	3,176	Services	16,189
Transportation and other public utilities	2,584	Public administration	2,999

PARISH PROFILES:
Median age, 1980 .... 28.3
Median family income, 1980 .... $15,958
Percent of families with income below poverty level, 1980 .... 15.4

General Hospitals, 1981 4   General Hospital Beds, 1981 849
Patient Care Physicians, 1981 202   Dentists, 1981 56

Infant birth rate (per 1000 population), 1982 .... 16.6
Infant mortality rate (per 1000 live births), 1981 .... 15.1
Death rate (per 1000 population), 1982 .... 7.9
MAJOR CITIES (over 5,000 population): Alexandria and Pineville

Alexandria and Pineville

These twin cities, on opposite banks of the Red River, are the hub of business and commerce in the large Rapides Parish area. Heavy concentrations of federal and state institutions are located here. England Air Force Base is a landmark, along with institutions of higher learning, Louisiana State University Alexandria and Louisiana College.

The town of Alexandria was formally laid out about 1810 by Alexander Fulton, a wealthy landowner and merchant. The new town was named in honor of his infant daughter. During the following decade, with increasing steamboat traffic, the town developed into a busy shipping and trading center. Adjacent forests were cut down to provide lumber for fast growing New Orleans, and vast acreage was planted in cotton, sugarcane and other crops. Pineville, though it was the site of the original settlement, was not incorporated until 1878.

At the outbreak of the Civil War, Alexandria and Pineville were at the height of their antebellum prosperity. During General Banks' first invasion of the Red River Valley, in the spring and summer of 1864, both cities were occupied by Federal forces. In the absence of a strong military force, both submitted quietly.

At the crossroads of Louisiana, situated near the center of the state, the cities of Alexandria and Pineville are thriving business communities which serve the financial, medical, cultural, and commercial needs of all of the surrounding area.

RED RIVER

HISTORY: This parish was created on March 2, 1871 and was named for the Red River which flows through the entire length of the parish. The history is closely linked with the development and settlement of northwestern Louisiana.

PARISH SEAT: Coushatta
SQUARE MILE AREA.............. 394
SCHOOLS .... Public 5
                           Private 1

RAIL LINES 1
CONGRESSIONAL DISTRICT 4
AIRPORTS 1

AGRICULTURE: Cotton and soybeans

INDUSTRY: Dadco Fashions, Inc.; Sunbeam Corp.; Pineville Kraft Corp.

PARISH BUSINESS PATTERNS: Number of employees, 1983:

Agricultural services, ... 13
  forestry, fisheries
Mining 13
Contract construction 173
Manufacturing.................. 743
Transportation and other 89
  public utilities

Wholesale trade 69
Retail trade 274
Finance, insurance and.............. 80
  real estate
Services 714
Public administration 71

PARISH PROFILES:
Median age, 1980 .... 29.6
Median family income, 1980 .... $12,982
Percent of families with income below poverty level, 1980 .... 22.8

General Hospitals, 1981 1
Patient Care Physicians, 1981........ 6

General Hospital Beds, 1981......... 102
Dentists, 1981 1

Infant birth rate (per 1000 population), 1982............................... 17.4
Infant mortality rate (per 1000 live births), 1981........................... 29.9
Death rate (per 1000 population), 1982................................... 10.1

RICHLAND

HISTORY: Established on September 29, 1868, Richland Parish takes its name from the extreme fertility of the soil.

PARISH SEAT: Rayville
SQUARE MILE AREA.............. 563
SCHOOLS .... Public 12
                           Private 1

CONGRESSIONAL DISTRICT 5

AGRICULTURE: Cotton and timber

PARISH BUSINESS PATTERNS: Number of employees, 1983:

Agricultural services, ... 152
  forestry, fisheries
Mining 109
Contract construction 255
Manufacturing.................. 486
Transportation and other 261
  public utilities

Wholesale trade 335
Retail trade 809
Finance, insurance and.............. 264
  real estate
Services........................ 1,725
Public administration 174

PARISH PROFILES:
Median age, 1980 .... 29.5
Median family income, 1980 .... $12,112
Percent of families with income below poverty level, 1980 .... 28.6

General Hospitals, 1981 2   General Hospital Beds, 1981......... 118
Patient Care Physicians, 1981 17   Dentists, 1981 6

Infant birth rate (per 1000 population), 1982 .... 17.2
Infant mortality rate (per 1000 live births), 1981 .... 6.5
Death rate (per 1000 population), 1982 .... 9.9

SABINE

HISTORY: Established on March 7, 1843, Sabine Parish is rich in lore and history. Fort Jesup is a colorful reminder of Louisiana's history—when the land was the vast Louisiana Territory and eventually produced thirteen of the United States. During this transition period, the treaty of 1803 failed to define clearly the western boundary of Louisiana, with the result that America claimed eastern Texas and the Spanish claimed western Louisiana. From this confused state, there developed a no-man's-land east of the Sabine River. The section became known as "The Sabine Strip." Murders, robberies, and other crimes were commonplace until the boundary was fixed at the Sabine River by the Florida Purchase Treaty of 1819. Fort Jesup was built in 1822 by Lieutenant Colonel Zachary Taylor to keep order in this territory. A visit to Fort Jesup (one small kitchen remains out of the original eighty-two buildings) will give the visitor much history of the area.

Today the parish combines the old and the new. The growing resort area around Toledo Bend Reservoir, the largest manmade body of water in the South and the fifth largest in surface acres in the nation, covering 185,000 acres, is in the parish. El Camino Real, the early road to Mexico (circa 1720), crosses the parish. The annual Tamale Fiesta at Zwolle attracts many visitors, while the "Sawmill Days at Fisher" take visitors back in history.

PARISH SEAT: Many   CONGRESSIONAL DISTRICT 4
SQUARE MILE AREA.............. 855   CHURCHES....................... 12
SCHOOLS .... Public 14   AIRPORTS 1

AGRICULTURE: Poultry and beef cattle

INDUSTRY: Wood products (plywood, lumber, particle board and pulpwood); clothing manufacturing; Zwolle Tank Car Company.

TOURIST ATTRACTIONS: Fort Jesup State Monument; Hodges Gardens, open year-round, featuring a beautiful Christmas lighting celebration; Toledo Bend Reservoir, (year-round fishing, boating, and resort area, a sportsman's paradise); Toro Hills Resort; Village of Fisher; Old Sawmill Town; Block House Church Marker, site of the treaty setting up the boundary for the neutral strip.

PARKS and RECREATIONAL FACILITIES: Toledo Bend Reservoir and three public parks.

PARISH BUSINESS PATTERNS: Number of employees, 1983:
Agricultural services, ... 10   Wholesale trade 121
   forestry, fisheries   Retail trade 737
Mining 232   Finance, insurance and.............. 135
Contract construction 138   real estate
Manufacturing................. 1,255   Services........................... 1,425
Transportation and other......... 306   Public administration 157
   public utilities

PARISH PROFILES:
Median age, 1980 .... 32.1
Median family income, 1980 .... $13,519
Percent of families with income below poverty level, 1980 .... 18.9

General Hospitals, 1981 2   General Hospital Beds, 1981......... 105
Patient Care Physicians, 1981 11   Dentists, 1981 4

Infant birth rate (per 1000 population), 1982.............................. 15.1
Infant mortality rate (per 1000 live births), 1981.......................... 10.0
Death rate (per 1000 population), 1982.................................... 7.4

ST. BERNARD

HISTORY: Created on March 31, 1807, St. Bernard was once called "Terre aux Boeufs" because it was the last refuge of the country's wild oxen. The first settlers established plantations in St. Bernard in 1720. Under the Spanish rule, Canary Islanders, called "Islenos," were among the first to arrive. It was the first parish to grow indigo and sugarcane. For 150 years before the Civil War, palatial plantation homes were built by wealthy citizens of New Orleans, among them Galvez, the conquerer of the British at Baton Rouge and Pensacola. General Andrew Jackson defeated the British under General Pakenham at the Battle of New Orleans on January 8, 1815, fifteen days after the conclusion of the peace treaty between Britain and the United States. This battle was fought on the "plains of Chalmette," now a historic shrine. Today the parish offers many attractions to industries that prefer the convenience of nearby New Orleans, while availing the employees with advantages of living in an uncongested suburb.

PARISH SEAT: Chalmette
SQUARE MILE AREA.............. 486
SCHOOLS .... Public 17
                          Private 6
RAIL LINES 2
CONGRESSIONAL DISTRICT 1

AGRICULTURE: Farming, commercial fishing, and trapping.

INDUSTRY: Kaiser Aluminum and Chemical Corporation, oil refineries, frozen foods, other diversified businesses and dock facilities.

TOURIST ATTRACTIONS: Chalmette National Historical Park, Beauregard House Museum, and Chalmette National Military Cemetery.

PARKS and RECREATIONAL FACILITIES: Seven public parks with various activities; a fisherman's paradise in the many bayous and Lake Bourgne.

PARISH BUSINESS PATTERNS: Number of employees, 1983:
Agricultural services,.............. 49
  forestry, fisheries
Mining 212
Contract construction.......... 1,052
Manufacturing................. 3,265
Transportation and other........ 963
  public utilities
Wholesale trade 280
Retail trade 2,670
Finance, insurance and.............. 374
  real estate
Services......................... 3,518
Public administration 564

PARISH PROFILES:
Median age, 1980 .... 28.4
Median family income, 1980 .... $20,592
Percent of families with income below poverty level, 1980 .... 7.4

General Hospitals, 1981 2
Patient Care Physicians, 1981 23
General Hospital Beds, 1981......... 227
Dentists, 1981...................... 16

Infant birth rate (per 1000 population), 1982................................ 16.5
Infant mortality rate (per 1000 live births), 1981........................... 9.9
Death rate (per 1000 population), 1982.................................... 8.1
MAJOR CITIES (over 5,000 population): Chalmette

Chalmette

Chalmette, the seat of government, is the industrial, cultural, financial, and business center of the parish. Merchants are progressive, and civic-minded citizens have provided economic stability in the excellent opportunities to industry along the Mississippi River.

ST. CHARLES

HISTORY: Created on March 31, 1807, St. Charles is one of the oldest settlements in the state. When John Law's colonists, Germans from the Alsace-Lorraine region, failed in Arkansas, some were persuaded to settle on granted lands in what is now St. Charles Parish, later referred to as the "German Coast." Bayou des allemands is a reminder today of John Law's great colonization scheme. The German population soon mixed with French settlers from New Orleans. Hahnville was named for Governor Michael Hahn, who lived in the parish after the Civil War. Confederate General Richard Taylor was also a resident.

PARISH SEAT: Hahnville

SQUARE MILE AREA.............. 286

SCHOOLS .... Public 19
                          Private 2

RAIL LINES.......................... 4

CONGRESSIONAL DISTRICT 3

CHURCHES...................... 25

AGRICULTURE: Sugarcane

INDUSTRY: Petrochemical

TOURIST ATTRACTIONS: Destrehan Manor

PARKS and RECREATIONAL FACILITIES: Boating, tennis, and swimming facilities; planetarium associated with the St. Charles Parish Library.

PARISH BUSINESS PATTERNS: Number of employees, 1983:

Agricultural services, ... 5
    forestry, fisheries

Mining 196

Contract construction........... 6,051

Manufacturing................. 5,698

Transportation and other 2,228
    public utilities

Wholesale trade 830

Retail trade 1,463

Finance, insurance and............. 302
    real estate

Services......................... 3,642

Public administration 292

PARISH PROFILES:

Median age, 1980 .... 25.8

Median family income, 1980 .... $23,223

Percent of families with income below poverty level, 1980 .... 11.9

General Hospitals, 1981 1

Patient Care Physicians, 1981 15

General Hospital Beds, 1981.......... 50

Dentists, 1981 6

Infant birth rate (per 1000 population), 1982................................. 19.9

Infant mortality rate (per 1000 live births), 1981............................. 19.3

Death rate (per 1000 population), 1982....................................... 4.9

ST. HELENA

HISTORY: St. Helena, one of the Florida Parishes, was established on December 22, 1810. The early settlers were French and Spanish, but later English traders and Revolutionary War settlers from Georgia, the Carolinas, and Virginia came to this lush territory.

PARISH SEAT: Greensburg

SQUARE MILE AREA.............. 409

SCHOOLS......................... 7

CONGRESSIONAL DISTRICT 8

INDUSTRY: Forestry

PARISH BUSINESS PATTERNS: Number of employees, 1983:

Agricultural services,	2	Wholesale trade	34
forestry, fisheries		Retail trade	312
Mining	69	Finance, insurance and	44
Contract construction	73	real estate	
Manufacturing	153	Services	514
Transportation and other	107	Public administration	114
public utilities			

PARISH PROFILES:

Median age, 1980 .... 26.2
Median family income, 1980 .... $11,370
Percent of families with income below poverty level, 1980 .... 18.2

General Hospitals, 1981	1	General Hospital Beds, 1981	35
Patient Care Physicians, 1981	2	Dentists, 1981	1

Infant birth rate (per 1000 population), 1982 .... 14.4
Infant mortality rate (per 1000 live births), 1981 .... —
Death rate (per 1000 population), 1982 .... 7.6

ST. JAMES

HISTORY: St. James was one of the original nineteen parishes, and was created on March 31, 1807 by an act of the Orleans Territorial Legislature. The original seat of government was the community of St. James, on the west bank of the Mississippi River. In 1869 it was moved up to the east bank, near the Convent of the Sacred Heart. The site, now called Convent, is the present parish seat.

The only place in the world perique tobacco is grown is in this parish, on a three-hundred acre tract. It is in great demand by large tobacco interests. An Acadian exile, Pierre Chenet, nicknamed "Perique," was the first to successfully produce and market this aromatic type of tobacco still bearing his name. Its production has been in the same family for nearly two centuries.

Today St. James Parish, whose lands consist of rich soil, wooded lowlands, and marshes, can point with pride to continued development of its variety of natural resources and farm acreage. The mighty river that divides it is instrumental in the rapid growth of industry.

PARISH SEAT: Convent
SQUARE MILE AREA 248
SCHOOLS .... Public 12
                            Private 1
CONGRESSIONAL DISTRICT 8
CHURCHES 48

AGRICULTURE: Sugarcane, perique tobacco, soybeans, corn, hay, oats, and vegetable farming; fruit orchards; beef cattle; crawfish farming.

INDUSTRY: Oil and natural gas; oil refining; sugar refining; chemicals; fertilizer; Kaiser Aluminum

TOURIST ATTRACTIONS: Oak Alley, a magnificent Greek Revival plantation home built in 1836; Jefferson College, established in 1831, now Manresa Retreat Home; Our Lady of Lourdes Grotto at St. Michael's Catholic Church; Colomb House, a plantation home in miniature, built in 1835 by Christophe Colomb, Jr.; several other antebellum homes, including lovely Tezcuco, a raised cottage completed in 1855 (open to the public).

PARKS and RECREATIONAL FACILITIES: Hunting and fishing on scenic Blind River and in the abundant ponds and swamplands.

PARISH BUSINESS PATTERNS: Number of employees, 1983:

Agricultural services,	121	Wholesale trade	210
forestry, fisheries		Retail trade	705

Mining 64
Contract construction 254
Manufacturing 2,675
Transportation and other 699
 public utilities

Finance, insurance and 152
 real estate
Services 1,206
Public administration 236

PARISH PROFILES:
Median age, 1980 . . . . 24.8
Median family income, 1980 . . . . $21,044
Percent of families with income below poverty level, 1980 . . . . 14.5

General Hospitals, 1981 2
Patient Care Physicians, 1981 10

General Hospital Beds, 1981 9
Dentists, 1981 4

Infant birth rate (per 1000 population), 1982 . . . . 19.7
Infant mortality rate (per 1000 live births), 1981 . . . . 23.7
Death rate (per 1000 population), 1982 . . . . 8.5

ST. JOHN THE BAPTIST

HISTORY: St. John the Baptist was one of the original parishes, created on March 31, 1807. It was first settled by John Law's German colonists who came down from Arkansas, and many from the war-torn peasantry of Germany, who formed Louisiana's German Coast.

PARISH SEAT: Edgard
SQUARE MILE AREA 213
SCHOOLS . . . . Public 15
 Private 6

RAIL LINES 3
CONGRESSIONAL DISTRICT 8
CHURCHES 36

AGRICULTURE: Sugarcane

INDUSTRY: Dupont; Cargill; Bayside; Godchaux-Henderson Sugar Company; Marathon Oil Refinery.

TOURIST ATTRACTIONS: "San Francisco," built in 1849, was the setting for Frances Parkinson Keyes' book, *Steamboat Gothic*. Evergreen Plantation, on the west bank of the river, was built in the 1820s and has been the setting for several movies. Thousands attend the annual Andouille Festival to taste the spicy sausage which the first settlers brought to the area.

PARKS and RECREATIONAL FACILITIES: Three public parks; fishing and boating on Lake Maurepas, Les des allemands, Lake Pontchartrain, the river, and numerous bayous; 5,261 acres of wetlands, designated Manchac Wildlife Management Area.

PARISH BUSINESS PATTERNS: Number of employees, 1983:
Agricultural services, ... 40
 forestry, fisheries
Mining 95
Contract construction 489
Manufacturing 2,927
Transportation and other 501
 public utilities

Wholesale trade 665
Retail trade 1,052
Finance, insurance and 287
 real estate
Services 2,084
Public administration 209

PARISH PROFILES:
Median age, 1980 . . . . 25.0
Median family income, 1980 . . . . $21,818
Percent of families with income below poverty level, 1980 . . . . 12.1

General Hospitals, 1981 0	General Hospital Beds, 1981 0
Patient Care Physicians, 1981 7	Dentists, 1981 5

Infant birth rate (per 1000 population), 1982 .... 23.7
Infant mortality rate (per 1000 live births), 1981 .... 16.3
Death rate (per 1000 population), 1982 .... 6.5

MAJOR CITIES (over 5,000 population): LaPlace

LaPlace

LaPlace has experienced change and growth in the last decade. Its residential and business communities continue to expand at an unprecedented rate, reflecting the unusual industrial growth. LaPlace was named after Bazile LaPlace, a wealthy Frenchman who bought land in 1879 and formed LaPlace Plantation. It is the site of the famous Bonnet Carre' crevasse which began in 1872, lasted eleven years, and cut a wide channel from the river to Lake Pontchartrain.

ST. LANDRY

HISTORY: St. Landry Parish was established on April 10, 1805. It was named after St. Landry, the saint who founded the Hotel Dieu in Paris in the sixth century. Most of the inhabitants are descendants of the Acadians, but many French (some who came late in the 1600s), English, Scotch-Irish, and Germans later settled in the area, forming a potpourri of Americana. The citizens of the parish have preserved many of the early customs, such as the fais-do-do (lively dancing in the streets) and the early winter boucheries (hog killings) with much festivity involved. The Louisiana Yambilee Festival is an annual fall event.

PARISH SEAT: Opelousas	RAIL LINES 3
SQUARE MILE AREA 936	CONGRESSIONAL DISTRICT 8
SCHOOLS .... Public 44	
Private 13	

AGRICULTURE: Soybeans, beef cattle, rice, yams, cotton, dairy farming, and corn.

INDUSTRY: Diversified manufacturing, wholesale and retail trade.

TOURIST ATTRACTIONS: Historical marker at the site of Jim Bowie's home; antebellum homes in the Opelousas and Washington area, Washington once a thriving shipping port navigable through Bayou Courtbleau and the Atchafalaya River.

PARKS and RECREATIONAL FACILITIES: Fishing and boating in area bayous and lakes.

PARISH BUSINESS PATTERNS: Number of employees, 1983:

Agricultural services, ... 152	Wholesale trade 1,026
forestry, fisheries	Retail trade 3,718
Mining 1,383	Finance, insurance and 988
Contract construction 1,278	real estate
Manufacturing 2,183	Services 6,104
Transportation and other 1,128	Public administration 937
public utilities	

PARISH PROFILES:
Median age, 1980 .... 26.9
Median family income, 1980 .... $13,893
Percent of families with income below poverty level, 1980 .... 23.1

General Hospitals, 1981 3	General Hospital Beds, 1981 330
Patient Care Physicians, 1981 73	Dentists, 1981 16

Infant birth rate (per 1000 population), 1982 .... 18.5

Infant mortality rate (per 1000 live births), 1981 . . . . ,. 13.6
Death rate (per 1000 population), 1982 . . . . 8.4
MAJOR CITIES (over 5,000 population): Opelousas and Eunice

Opelousas

Named after the Indian tribe of the same name, Opelousas is one of the oldest settlements in Louisiana. In 1769 the Spaniards stationed a company of soldiers here. At that time there were few settlers besides the Indians. In 1803, when the United States took possession of Louisiana, Opelousas became the seat of the "county" or parish.

Opelousas was incorporated in 1821. During the Civil War it became the capital of the state for a short time. This was much conflict, rioting, and unrest during reconstruction.

From Opelousas, Jim Bowie, whose descendants still live in the parish, went forth to seek his fame and fortune. He died at the Alamo in San Antonio, while fighting for freedom in the Texas Revolution. The long dueling knife and the shorter hunting knife with the curved blade made him famous.

Eunice

Eunice is a growing city in the parish, named after the wife of C. C. Duson, the founder. The name means "happy victory." Founded in 1895, it is located in the heart of Acadiana, with hard working and fun loving citizens who say "venez-nous voir," meaning "Come see us!"

ST. MARTIN

HISTORY: St. Martin Parish was established as Attakapas Parish on March 31, 1807. It received its present name on April 17, 1811. It is in the center of the historic Teche country, the land of the Acadians and Evangeline. Even before the Acadians settled in this section, a "post" existed at St. Martinville. A number of officers of noble French and Spanish families remained after their appointments expired. Thus, for many years St. Martinville was the center of considerable culture. At one time, it was a summer resort for New Orleans society, and became known as "Le Petit Paris de la Louisiane." The same "joie de vivre" exists today.

PARISH SEAT: St. Martinville
SQUARE MILE AREA 749
SCHOOLS . . . . Public 17
Private 5

RAIL LINES 2
CONGRESSIONAL DISTRICT 7
CHURCHES 20

AGRICULTURE: Sugarcane, rice, and soybeans.

INDUSTRY: Martin Mills factory and St. Martin Parish Industrial Park, with diversified industry.

TOURIST ATTRACTIONS: Evangeline Oak; St. Martin de Tours Catholic Church and Evangeline statue; Duchamp Home; parish courthouse, whose earliest records date back to 1760 (cattle brands date in the 1730s); Oak and Pine Alley, a lovely drive; the biennial Crawfish Festival in Breaux Bridge.

PARK and RECREATIONAL FACILITIES: Three community parks and the Longfellow-Evangeline State Park, with Acadian House Museum.

PARISH BUSINESS PATTERNS: Number of employees, 1983:

Agricultural services, ... 10	Wholesale trade 384	
forestry, fisheries	Retail trade 1,670	
Mining 326	Finance, insurance and 244	
Contract construction 703	real estate	
Manufacturing 642	Services 1,949	
Transportation and other 291	Public administration 299	
public utilities		

PARISH PROFILES:
Median age, 1980 . . . . 25.3
Median family income, 1980 . . . . $16,612
Percent of families with income below poverty level, 1980 . . . . 16.9

General Hospitals, 1981 2   General Hospital Beds, 1981 55
Patient Care Physicians, 1981 12   Dentists, 1981 6

Infant birth rate (per 1000 population), 1982 .... 20.2
Infant mortality rate (per 1000 live births), 1981 .... 18.9
Death rate (per 1000 population), 1982 .... 7.4
MAJOR CITIES (over 5,000 population): St. Martinville and Breaux Bridge

St. Martinville

St. Martinville, along Bayou Teche, is a quiet, beautiful historic town in Acadian country. The Poste des Attakapas was established in 1756. In 1765 a colony of Acadians arrived. The same year the first Catholic church was established. The story of Evangeline, immortalized in Longfellow's poem, is centered around this immediate section. Some of the settlers around the post were supporters of the new French Republic, causing considerable friction between neighbors in 1803. The town was incorporated in 1817, and named for the fourth-century Bishop Martin.

ST. MARY

HISTORY: St. Mary Parish encompasses part of what was originally Attakapas County. The first settlers arrived at the turn of the nineteenth century, to find wilderness inhabited by the dreaded Attakapas Indians. The alluvial soil and numerous natural resources overshadowed the hardships, however, and the settlers remained.

The parish was officially organized in 1811. Berwick, on the west bank of the Atchafalaya River, was laid out as a townsite in 1797 by Thomas Berwick. The present boundaries of the parish date from 1868. In 1865 the French Acadians had come into the area to farm. Most settled along Bayous Teche and Boeuf. Soon afterward pioneers came from France and Spain, as well as Revolutionary War families from the eastern seaboard of the United States.

This beautiful section of the state has had a phenomenal population and industrial growth. It is known today as having the largest cypress mill in the world, the only known lighted seaplane landing strip in the nation, the largest commercial helicopter base in the world, being the biggest producer of carbon black, and its largest city, Morgan City, claims to be "the Shrimp Capital of the World."

PARISH SEAT: Franklin   RAIL LINES 1
SQUARE MILE AREA 613   CONGRESSIONAL DISTRICT 3
SCHOOLS .... Public 32   AIRPORTS 3
                         Private 8   (includes helicopter and seaplane bases)

AGRICULTURE: Sugarcane, rice, corn, and soybeans.

INDUSTRY: Oil and related industries, sugar refining, salt, carbon black, timber, shrimping, and fishing.

TOURIST ATTRACTIONS: Many antebellum homes, including Oaklawn Manor, built in the early 1800s, Albania (circa 1837-1842), Grevemberg House, which dates from 1851, and restored Frances, built in the early nineteenth century. All are open to the public.

PARKS and RECREATIONAL FACILITIES: Fishing and boating in the many fresh water bayous and lakes; deep sea fishing in the Gulf of Mexico. (all public waters.) Adjacent to Morgan City is Lake Palourde, with one of the finest power boat race courses in the U. S. Supervised youth recreational programs year-round.

PARISH BUSINESS PATTERNS: Number of employees, 1983:
Agricultural services, ... 323   Wholesale trade. 1,550
    forestry, fisheries   Retail trade 3,776
Mining. 5,366   Finance, insurance and 945

Contract construction.......... 2,384   real estate
Manufacturing................. 3,063   Services......................... 6,488
Transportation and other 5,964   Public administration 511
    public utilities

PARISH PROFILES:

Median age, 1980... 25.3
Median family income, 1980............................. $20,688
Percent of families with income below poverty level, 1980................... 12.6

General Hospitals, 1981 3   General Hospital Beds, 1981......... 300
Patient Care Physicians, 1981 43   Dentists, 1981...................... 20

Infant birth rate (per 1000 population), 1982............................... 20.4
Infant mortality rate (per 1000 live births), 1981............................ 11.0
Death rate (per 1000 population), 1982...................................... 6.5

MAJOR CITIES (over 5,000 population): Morgan City and Franklin

Morgan City

Morgan City is a thriving trade center because of its two major industries, oil and commercial shrimp-ing. It is at the confluence of the Atchafalaya River and the Intracoastal Canal, the gateway to the oil riches of the Gulf of Mexico. Each Labor Day weekend the city celebrates with a gigantic shrimp boil at the Louisiana Shrimp and Petroleum Festival. This is solemnized by the blessing of the fleet, a religious custom practiced in all South Louisiana fishing villages.

The city was incorporated in 1860, and named Brashear after its founder, Dr. Walter Brashear. In the 1850s the Brashear family divided their Tiger Island sugar plantation into lots to form the townsite. The name Morgan City was adopted in 1876 in tribute to Charles Morgan, a rail and steamboat magnate who first dredged the Atchafalaya Bay Ship Channel to accommodate ocean-going vessels. It is Louisiana's fourth official port of entry, and offers a short route to the Gulf for marine commerce.

Franklin

This small South Louisiana city possesses a special charm because much of its historic past is still evident in the oak-lined avenues and antebellum homes. The city was laid out in 1808 by Alexander Lewis of Pennsylvania, five years after the Louisiana Purchase and three years before the present parish was carved out of Attakapas County. It became the parish seat of government in 1811 and officially incorporated in 1830.

ST. TAMMANY

HISTORY: St. Tammany, one of the Florida Parishes, was established on December 22, 1810. It gets its name from a famous Delaware Indian Chief, renowned for his virtue and other saintly quali-ties. He lived during the American Revolution and had been chosen as the patron saint of the New Republic. St. Tammany Parish in the early days had a large Indian population, and when it was or-ganized, it honored the Indian chief. St. Tammany is in the "piney woods" section known as the Ozone Belt. The waters from the beautiful streams are spring fed and are said to have medicinal powers.

PARISH SEAT: Covington   RAIL LINES 1
SQUARE MILE AREA.............. 873   CONGRESSIONAL DISTRICT 1
SCHOOLS .... Public 38   AIRPORTS 1
             Private 12

INDUSTRY: Forestry

TOURIST ATTRACTIONS: Annual speed boat races on the Tchefuncte River; Abita Springs, famous for its ozone spring water.

PARKS and RECREATIONAL FACILITIES: Fishing and water skiing on Lake Pontchartrain and the Tchefuncte River; Bogue Falaya State Park; Fontainbleu State Park; Fairview Riverside State Park; Abita Springs Wayside Park. All state parks have many recreational facilities.

PARISH BUSINESS PATTERNS: Number of employees, 1983:

Agricultural services, ... 313	Wholesale trade 889
forestry, fisheries	Retail trade 6,675
Mining 147	Finance, insurance and 1,300
Contract construction. 1,921	real estate
Manufacturing 1,547	Services 8,778
Transportation and other 1,262	Public administration. 1,075
public utilities	

PARISH PROFILES:
Median age, 1980 .... 28.3
Median family income, 1980 .... $21,870
Percent of families with income below poverty level, 1980 .... 10.3

General Hospitals, 1981 3   General Hospital Beds, 1981......... 477
Patient Care Physicians, 1981 141   Dentists, 1981...................... 61

Infant birth rate (per 1000 population), 1982............................... 17.7
Infant mortality rate (per 1000 live births), 1981............................ 12.0
Death rate (per 1000 population), 1982...................................... 6.7

MAJOR CITIES (over 5,000 population): Slidell, Covington, and Mandeville

Slidell and Covington

Two cities in the parish, Covington, at the north end of Lake Pontchartrain Causeway, and Slidell, across Interstate 10 from New Orleans, are both growing trade centers as well as suburbs of the metropolitan New Orleans area. Both have ideal climates, being situated in the famous Ozone Belt, an area where nature has provided the purest air to be found anywhere in the world, created by the breezes through the tall pine forests. It is a mecca for nature lovers, with many facilities at nearby parks. The Slidell area is the fastest growing in the state and ranks among the top areas of extraordinary growth in the nation. It has over 50 civic, fraternal, and social organizations which offer countless opportunities to the civic-minded citizenry.

TANGIPAHOA

HISTORY: One of the Florida parishes, Tangipahoa Parish was established on March 6, 1869. Its name is derived from the Tangipahoa Indians, who lived in that section when the French first occupied Louisiana. The root of the word Tangipahoa is the Indian word for "ear of corn" or "cornstalk." Tangipahoa is the center of the strawberry industry in the South. Hundreds of carloads of the luscious fruit are shipped out annually. The topography of this parish, 51 miles long and 18 miles wide, is composed of flat lands to the south and rolling hills in the north.

PARISH SEAT: Amite	RAIL LINES 1
SQUARE MILE AREA.............. 783	CONGRESSIONAL DISTRICT 6
SCHOOLS .... Public 33	CHURCHES...................... 200
Private 10	AIRPORTS 1

AGRICULTURE: Strawberries, peppers, cucumbers, and tomatoes.

INDUSTRY: Iron mill, masonry, lumber, commercial catfish, crawfish and alligator farming, and candy.

TOURIST ATTRACTIONS: Country Market at Ponchatoula; Camp Moore Confederate Cemetery; Zemurray Gardens.

PARKS and RECREATIONAL FACILITIES: Boating and fishing in the rivers, bayous, creeks, swamps, and lakes.

PARISH BUSINESS PATTERNS: Number of employees, 1983:

Agricultural services, forestry, fisheries	166	Wholesale trade	924
Mining	74	Retail trade	4,984
Contract construction	1,103	Finance, insurance and real estate	879
Manufacturing	2,137	Services	7,107
Transportation and other public utilities	812	Public administration	883

PARISH PROFILES:

Median age, 1980 .... 26.0
Median family income, 1980 .... $14,315
Percent of families with income below poverty level, 1980 .... 21.4

General Hospitals, 1981	4	General Hospital Beds, 1981	76
Patient Care Physicians, 1981	52	Dentists, 1981	29

Infant birth rate (per 1000 population), 1982 .... 19.0
Infant mortality rate (per 1000 live births), 1981 .... 20.0
Death rate (per 1000 population), 1982 .... 8.6

MAJOR CITIES (over 5,000 population): Hammond and Pontchatoula

Hammond

Hammond is located at the crossroads of the South, at the intersection of Interstates 12 and 55. It is the home of Southeastern Louisiana University. With diversified wholesale and retail trade, it has much potential for future growth.

TENSAS

HISTORY: Established on March 17, 1843, Tensas Parish takes its name from the Tensas Indians who originally occupied that territory. LaSalle, the famous explorer who came down the river in 1682, mentions a large and powerful tribe of Indians called the "Taensas."

PARISH SEAT: St. Joseph   CONGRESSIONAL DISTRICT 5
SQUARE MILE AREA 623
SCHOOLS .... Public 6
                            Private 2

AGRICULTURE: Cotton and soybeans

INDUSTRY: Tensas Port Elevator, saw mill, and three cotton gins.

TOURIST ATTRACTIONS: Winter Quarters, the oldest house in the parish, dating from 1803, filled with antique furnishings and Civil War memorabilia; The Tensas Parish Library and Plantation Museum, situated in a townhouse dating from 1858, contains items related to early plantation life.

PARKS and RECREATIONAL FACILITIES: Lake Bruin State Park, with a scenic view of the Mississippi River and an oxbow lake (previously in the main channel of the everchanging course of the river).

PARISH BUSINESS PATTERNS: Number of employees, 1983:

Agricultural services, forestry, fisheries	244	Wholesale trade	134
		Retail trade	152

Mining 70
Contract construction 75
Manufacturing................... 51
Transportation and other 41
   public utilities

Finance, insurance and.............. 71
   real estate
Services 482
Public administration 96

PARISH PROFILES:
Median age, 1980 .... 28.8
Median family income, 1980 .... $10,447
Percent of families with income below poverty level, 1980.................... 34

General Hospitals, 1981 1
Patient Care Physicians, 1981........ 4

General Hospital Beds, 1981.......... 30
Dentists, 1981 1

Infant birth rate (per 1000 population), 1982.............................. 15.6
Infant mortality rate (per 1000 live births), 1981........................... 11.9
Death rate (per 1000 population), 1982.................................. 10.7

TERREBONNE

HISTORY: Terrebonne Parish, chronologically the twenty-sixth parish created, was established in April, 1822 from a portion of Lafourche Parish. The derivation of the name Terrebonne, "good land," seems fully justified because of the rich alluvial lands comprising the area. Of interesting note are the forerunners of the present highway system, which follow the paths of the numerous bayous. They were developed from the towpaths along each stream, used when there was not sufficient breeze to drive the sails upstream.

Prior to 1765 there were very few white settlers. Notable among them, however, was Captain Dautrine. In that year Acadians arrived in the area, coming via Santo Domingo. Early parish names include Royal, Belanger, Prevost, Marlbrough, Duplantis, and Grinage.

While the citizens enjoy a world of the slower lifestyle from the Spanish and French influence—savor each day and appreciate the simpler things of life—today Terrebonne Parish is recognized throughout the nation as one of the most important petroleum centers, and fishing, farming, and fur-trapping communities. This growth and development is sure to continue with forward looking usage of its wealth of natural resources.

PARISH SEAT: Houma
SQUARE MILE AREA 1,367
SCHOOLS .... Public 42
               Private 11

RAIL LINES 1
CONGRESSIONAL DISTRICT 3
CHURCHES........................ 31
AIRPORTS 1

AGRICULTURE: Sugarcane

INDUSTRY: Oil and gas production and related industries; sugar refining; commercial fishing and packing (shrimp, menhaden, oysters, crabs, finfish and industrial fish); shrimp drying; sulphur; diversified wholesale and retail trade.

TOURIST ATTRACTIONS: Antebellum homes, which include Ducros (1859), Magnolia (1850s), Southdown (1858), Crescent Farms (1834), and Ardoyne (open by appointment); Mardi Gras celebration; Louisiana Junior Miss Pageant (January).

PARKS and RECREATIONAL FACILITIES: Twelve city parks, ranging in size from one acre to thirty-five acres; a complete sports program under the direction of the Houma Recreational Depart-

PARISH BUSINESS PATTERNS: Number of employees, 1983:
Agricultural services,............. 333
   forestry, fisheries

Wholesale trade................... 3,108
Retail trade 7,250

Mining........................ 6,526	Finance, insurance and............ 1,471
Contract construction........... 2,213	real estate
Manufacturing................. 3,567	Services.................... 10,408
Transportation and other 4,059	Public administration 982
public utilities	

PARISH PROFILES:
Median age, 1980 .... 24.8
Median family income, 1980 .... $20,918
Percent of families with income below poverty level, 1980 .... 11.4

General Hospitals, 1981 2	General Hospital Beds, 1981......... 398
Patient Care Physicians, 1981 87	Dentists, 1981...................... 36

Infant birth rate (per 1000 population), 1982................................ 23.6
Infant mortality rate (per 1000 live births), 1981............................ 10.9
Death rate (per 1000 population), 1982...................................... 6.5
MAJOR CITIES (over 5,000 population): Houma

Houma

The parish seat of government, Houma, is located on the Intracoastal Canal and directly connected to the Gulf of Mexico by the Houma Navigation Channel. It is a good location for the visitor who wishes to view the sights and sounds of the bayou wonderland of South Louisiana. "Lagniappe on the Bayou" is celebrated each year at nearby Chauvin. Ask anyone to direct you to Cocodrie, Bourg, Montegut, or other choice places for hunting, fishing, delicious food, and to find "joie de vivre," which the progressive citizens still enjoy to the utmost.

UNION

HISTORY: Union Parish was established on March 13, 1839. Its name is derived from the sentiment of the time—"liberty and union, now and forever, one and inseparable." (From a speech by Daniel Webster.) Also, as Andrew Jackson said, "the Union must and shall be preserved."
Union is a center for watermelon farming. The annual Watermelon Festival is held each July.

PARISH SEAT: Farmerville	RAIL LINES 1
SQUARE MILE AREA.............. 884	CONGRESSIONAL DISTRICT 5
SCHOOLS .... Public 12	CHURCHES....................... 53
Private 1	AIRPORTS 1

AGRICULTURE: Dairy farming, beef cattle, watermelon, and vegetable farming.

INDUSTRY: Forestry, garment factory, and brush factory.

PARKS and RECREATIONAL FACILITIES: Lake D'Arbonne State Park, with many recreational facilities.

PARISH BUSINESS PATTERNS: Number of employees, 1983:

Agricultural services, ... 10	Wholesale trade 121
forestry, fisheries	Retail trade 448
Mining 32	Finance, insurance and.............. 133
Contract construction 255	real estate
Manufacturing.................. 591	Services.......................... 1,112
Transportation and other......... 440	Public administration 124
public utilities	

PARISH PROFILES:
Median age, 1980 .... 32.1

Median family income, 1980 . . . . $14,027
Percent of families with income below poverty level, 1980 . . . . , 17.5

General Hospitals, 1981 2   General Hospital Beds, 1981 60
Patient Care Physicians, 1981 8   Dentists, 1981 5

Infant birth rate (per 1000 population), 1982 . . . . 14.3
Infant mortality rate (per 1000 live births), 1981 . . . . 13.2
Death rate (per 1000 population), 1982 . . . . 10.4

VERMILION

HISTORY: Vermilion Parish was established on March 25, 1844, carved out of Lafayette Parish under the administration of Governor Mouton. Present day Perry (Perry's Bridge) was designated the parish seat at the same time, but has since been moved to Abbeville. The name is derived from the Vermilion River and Vermilion Bay, both named from the fact that the bluff along the lands of the course of the river is reddish, or vermilion in color. It offers summer and winter hunting and fishing in the many bayous and fifty miles fronting the Gulf of Mexico. An improved state highway leads to Pecan Island, where commercial and private hunting camps are located and hunters from all parts of the nation come to enjoy their favorite sport. The parish has an abundant supply of fresh water and fertile lands which offer an inviting and desirable spot for the location of new industries.

PARISH SEAT: Abbeville   RAIL LINES 1
SQUARE MILE AREA 1,205   CONGRESSIONAL DISTRICT 7
SCHOOLS . . . . Public 23   CHURCHES 25
                              Private 4   AIRPORTS 1

AGRICULTURE: Rice, sugarcane, beef cattle, soybeans, cotton, and sweet potatoes.

INDUSTRY: Oil, gas, and related industries, rice milling, cane syrup, fishing, and trapping.

TOURIST ATTRACTIONS: Madeleine Square, St. Marie Madeleine's Catholic Church.

PARKS and RECREATIONAL FACILITIES: Two parks with various facilities; fishing, boating and hunting on the thousands of acres of marshes, fields, and forests laced together by miles of bayous, lakes, and bays.

PARISH BUSINESS PATTERNS: Number of employees, 1983:

Agricultural services, ... 109   Wholesale trade 624
   forestry, fisheries   Retail trade 1,934
Mining 1,991   Finance, insurance and 445
Contract construction 891   real estate
Manufacturing 1,038   Services 3,448
Transportation and other 1,504   Public administration 477
   public utilities

PARISH PROFILES:
Median age, 1980 . . . . 28.0
Median family income, 1980 . . . . $16,951
Percent of families with income below poverty level, 1980 . . . . 14.1

General Hospitals, 1981 4   General Hospital Beds, 1981 250
Patient Care Physicians, 1981 29   Dentists, 1981 12

Infant birth rate (per 1000 population), 1982 . . . . 20.1

Infant mortality rate (per 1000 live births), 1981 . . . . 13.0
Death rate (per 1000 population), 1982 . . . . 8.6
MAJOR CITIES (over 5,000 population): Abbeville and Kaplan

Abbeville

Abbeville, with its tree-lined streets, centers today about St. Marie Madeleine's Catholic Church. The city was founded in 1843 by a French-born priest named Antoine Desire Megret. He purchased a tract of land for $900, and laid out the town of Abbeville. Some believe it was named for a city in France near his birthplace, others say it was named Abbe (for priest) and ville (for town). It was designated the parish seat in 1854. It is the home of the Louisiana Dairy Festival held annually, attracting thousands of visitors. The beautiful courthouse houses oil paintings of the surrounding countryside.

VERNON

HISTORY: Vernon Parish, named after George Washington's home, Mount Vernon, was created by an act of the Louisiana Legislature on March 30, 1871 from portions of the parishes of Natchitoches, Rapides, and Sabine.

PARISH SEAT: Leesville   RAIL LINES 1
SQUARE MILE AREA 1,332   CONGRESSIONAL DISTRICT 4
SCHOOLS . . . . Public 16

AGRICULTURE: Timber, vegetable farming, dairy farming, and beef cattle.

PARKS and RECREATIONAL FACILITIES: Excellent facilities for hunting, fishing, camping, and outdoor life at Toledo Bend Reservoir and Anacoco and Vernon lakes. Reforestation in the parish has resulted in more wildlife areas which provide good hunting.

PARISH BUSINESS PATTERNS: Number of employees, 1983:

Agricultural services, ... 28   Wholesale trade 180
  forestry, fisheries   Retail trade 1,958
Mining 6   Finance, insurance and 254
Contract construction 450   real estate
Manufacturing 251   Services 3,121
Transportation and other 437   Public administration 3,019
  public utilities

PARISH PROFILES:
Median age, 1980 . . . . 23.3
Median family income, 1980 . . . . $12,296
Percent of families with income below poverty level, 1980 . . . . 15.8

General Hospitals, 1981 2   General Hospital Beds, 1981 82
Patient Care Physicians, 1981 14   Dentists, 1981 4

Infant birth rate (per 1000 population), 1982 . . . . 24.1
Infant mortality rate (per 1000 live births), 1981 . . . . 11.5
Death rate (per 1000 population), 1982 . . . . 5.0
MAJOR CITIES (over 5,000 population): Leesville

Leesville

The parish seat, Leesville, was incorporated February 15, 1900. It is the business center of this western Louisiana parish. The civic-minded citizens have provided the city with several recreational areas, including Leesville Golf and Recreation Park. Near the city is Fort Polk, the fifth largest military installation in the nation, containing 311 square miles. The fort was built at a cost of $22 million in 1941 and named in honor of the Right Reverend Leonidas Polk, the first Episcopal Bishop of Louisiana, known as the "fighting Bishop of the Confederacy."

The area was designated as a permanent installation in 1968. Millions of dollars have been spent for the upkeep and expansion, which brings the present value to approximately $335 million. Northwestern State University in Natchitoches has recently completed a branch of the college on this military base.

WASHINGTON

HISTORY: Washington Parish, organized on March 6, 1819, was named after the country's first president. At one time, this Florida parish had one of the finest forests of long leaf yellow pine in the world. Much has been cut and has been reforested for a perpetual supply.

PARISH SEAT: Franklinton   CONGRESSIONAL DISTRICT 6
SQUARE MILE AREA.............. 676
SCHOOLS .... Public 12
                            Private 1

INDUSTRY: Forestry

PARISH BUSINESS PATTERNS: Number of employees, 1983:

Agricultural services,............. 142 forestry, fisheries	Wholesale trade 548
Mining 55	Retail trade 1,625
Contract construction 557	Finance, insurance and............. 460 real estate
Manufacturing................. 1,958	Services......................... 3,023
Transportation and other........ 624 public utilities	Public administration 534

PARISH PROFILES:
Median age, 1980... 29.7
Median family income, 1980... $13,641
Percent of families with income below poverty level, 1980 .... 20.4

General Hospitals, 1981 3   General Hospital Beds, 1981......... 258
Patient Care Physicians, 1981 42   Dentists, 1981...................... 14

Infant birth rate (per 1000 population), 1982............................... 17.0
Infant mortality rate (per 1000 live births), 1981........................... 11.3
Death rate (per 1000 population), 1982...................................... —
MAJOR CITIES (over 5,000 population): Bogalusa

WEBSTER

HISTORY: Webster Parish, established on February 27, 1871, was named after the great American orator, Daniel Webster. It is located in the beautiful rolling hill country of northwest Louisiana. Its population figures are included in the Standard Metropolitan Statistical Area of greater Shreveport.

PARISH SEAT: Minden   RAIL LINES 2
SQUARE MILE AREA.............. 602   CONGRESSIONAL DISTRICT 4
SCHOOLS .... Public 24   AIRPORTS 1
                            Private 1

AGRICULTURE: Forestry and cotton

INDUSTRY: Diversified manufacturing, including steel fabrication, wood and timber related industries, log hauling equipment, farm machinery, and plywood.

TOURIST ATTRACTIONS: Germantown Museum and Webster Parish Fair, held annually in October.

PARKS and RECREATIONAL FACILITIES: Lake Bistineau State Park; two recreational buildings for year-round events; Caney Lakes Recreational Area operated by the U. S. Forest Service.

PARISH BUSINESS PATTERNS: Number of employees, 1983:

Agricultural services, ... 92	Wholesale trade 342
forestry, fisheries	Retail trade 1,828
Mining 637	Finance, insurance and.............. 318
Contract construction 812	real estate
Manufacturing................. 3,169	Services.-,...................... 3,081
Transportation and other 560	Public administration 350
public utilities	

PARISH PROFILES:

Median age, 1980 .... 32.2
Median family income, 1980 .... $15,701
Percent of families with income below poverty level, 1980 .... 15.6

General Hospitals, 1981 2	General Hospital Beds, 1981......... 188
Patient Care Physicians, 1981 20	Dentists, 1981...................... 13

Infant birth rate (per 1000 population), 1982................................. 15.6
Infant mortality rate (per 1000 live births), 1981............................ 7.2
Death rate (per 1000 population), 1982...................................... 10.8

MAJOR CITIES (over 5,000 population): Minden and Springhill

Minden

Minden serves as the parish seat. It is a growing community, founded in 1836 by Charles H. Veeder. It is the business, finance, cultural, and recreational center for parish residents, situated at the hub of several major highways, including Interstate 20.

WEST BATON ROUGE

HISTORY: West Baton Rouge Parish was created on March 31, 1807. The earliest settlers arrived in the area before 1750. It is largely agricultural, but as East Baton Rouge Parish grows, so does this parish (the smallest in area in the state). It is situated on the west bank of the Mississippi River, across from metropolitan Baton Rouge. Indian mounds are evidence of early Indian culture.

PARISH SEAT: Port Allen	CONGRESSIONAL DISTRICT 8
SQUARE MILE AREA.............. 194	
SCHOOLS .... Public 10	
Private 2	

AGRICULTURE: Sugarcane

INDUSTRY: Port facilities with diversified industry

TOURIST ATTRACTIONS: West Baton Rouge Museum, located in the old courthouse; many picturesque, tree-lined avenues, plantation homes, churches, and cemeteries, which give the visitor a glimpse into bygone days.

PARISH BUSINESS PATTERNS: Number of employees, 1983:

Agricultural services, ... 52	Wholesale trade 713
forestry, fisheries	Retail trade 525
Mining 165	Finance, insurance and.............. 139
Contract construction 471	real estate
Manufacturing................. 1,008	Services........................ 1,295
Transportation and other 1,502	Public administration 338
public utilities	

PARISH PROFILES:
Median age, 1980 . . . . 25.4
Median family income, 1980 . . . . $19,093
Percent of families with income below poverty level, 1980 . . . . 15.6

General Hospitals, 1981 0   General Hospital Beds, 1981 0
Patient Care Physicians, 1981 2   Dentists, 1981 1

Infant birth rate (per 1000 population), 1982 . . . . 21.4
Infant mortality rate (per 1000 live births), 1981 . . . . 11.7
Death rate (per 1000 population), 1982 . . . . 6.9
MAJOR CITIES (over 5,000 population): Port Allen

WEST CARROLL

HISTORY: Organized on March 28, 1877, West Carroll was separated from East Carroll Parish when the original Carroll Parish was divided.

PARISH SEAT: Oak Grove   CONGRESSIONAL DISTRICT 5
SQUARE MILE AREA 360   AIRPORTS 1
SCHOOLS . . . . Public 7
                                      Private 1

AGRICULTURE: Cotton, soybeans, sweet potatoes, rice, tomatoes, and livestock.

TOURIST ATTRACTIONS: Poverty Point Commemorative State Park, located six miles northeast of Epps, the site of the earliest aboriginal culture group discovered in the lower Mississippi Valley, dating between 700 and 1700 B.C. The 400-acre site contains a complex of man-made earthen mounds.

PARKS and RECREATIONAL FACILITIES: Two public parks (Oak Grove and Epps).

PARISH BUSINESS PATTERNS: Number of employees, 1983:
Agricultural services, ... 49   Wholesale trade 71
    forestry, fisheries   Retail trade 352
Mining 40   Finance, insurance and 126
Contract construction 171   real estate
Manufacturing 225   Services 569
Transportation and other 127   Public administration 103
    public utilities

PARISH PROFILES:
Median age, 1980 . . . . 31.6
Median family income, 1980 . . . . $10,807
Percent of families with income below poverty level, 1980 . . . . 29.5

General Hospitals, 1981 1   General Hospital Beds, 1981 52
Patient Care Physicians, 1981 3   Dentists, 1981 2

Infant birth rate (per 1000 population), 1982 . . . . 17.3
Infant mortality rate (per 1000 live births), 1981 . . . . 11.7
Death rate (per 1000 population), 1982 . . . . 8.7

WEST FELICIANA

HISTORY: This beautiful, rural parish was created on February 17, 1824 by a division of the original Feliciana Parish. Time or progress has in no way diminished the quaint qualities of the parish. It is steeped in history, still in evidence in the many antebellum homes and buildings. Feliciana means "happyland."

John James Audubon, the famous naturalist, lived here for a short while and painted many of his Birds of America in the lovely woods near Oakley, while engaged there as a tutor in the 1820s.

Bayou Sara, below the bluffs of St. Francisville, was once a thriving river town. Called New Valencia by the Spaniards, it was one of the earliest towns in the Florida parishes, and established as a trading post in 1790. Before 1860 it was one of the largest points between Natchez, Mississippi and New Orleans when "cotton was king." The boll weevil, the demise of steamboat traffic, floods, and fire combined to bring about its decline. The town charter was revoked in 1926.

St. Francisville, the parish seat of government, is one of the most picturesque towns in the state and is the successor to Bayou Sara. The name is derived from a monastery built by Capuchin Friars in 1785 in honor of St. Francis of Assisi. Fort St. Reine, on the town's present site, existed as early as 1736.

Today the parish is building for the future while preserving its past, which makes it a special "happyland."

PARISH SEAT: St. Francisville   CONGRESSIONAL DISTRICT 8
SQUARE MILE AREA............. 406
SCHOOLS .... Public 3

AGRICULTURE: Forestry, vegetable farming, and beef cattle.

INDUSTRY: Paper mill and cannery

TOURIST ATTRACTIONS: Rosedown (circa 1835) and gardens, The Cottage (1795 and 1850), Catalpa and the Myrtles (1830), all open to the public year-round. Several other homes open during the Audubon Pilgrimage sponsored each March by the West Feliciana Historical Society; Locust Grove Cemetery, nearby. Oakley, a large house at Aubudon Memorial State Monument, built in 1799, predates the lovely architectural lines of Greek Revival structures built during the 1800s. It commands the center of a wooded area with picnic areas and nature trails.

PARKS and RECREATIONAL FACILITIES: Audubon Memorial State Monument

PARISH BUSINESS PATTERNS: Number of employees, 1983:

Agricultural services, ... 19	Wholesale trade 20
forestry, fisheries	Retail trade 188
Mining 19	Finance, insurance and............. 210
Contract construction........... 4,710	real estate
Manufacturing.................. 924	Services 814
Transportation and other........ 222	Public administration............. 1,816
public utilities	

PARISH PROFILES:
Median age, 1980 .... 28.7
Median family income, 1980 .... $14,289
Percent of families with income below poverty level, 1980 .... 27.7

General Hospitals, 1981 1   General Hospital Beds, 1981.......... 23
Patient Care Physicians, 1981........ 7   Dentists, 1981....................... 3

Infant birth rate (per 1000 population), 1982............................... 12.4
Infant mortality rate (per 1000 live births), 1981............................. —
Death rate (per 1000 population), 1982..................................... 4.6

WINN

HISTORY: Created on February 24, 1852, Winn Parish was named after Walter O. Winn, a prominent early Louisiana lawyer form Alexandria. The parish was originally a part of Natchitoches Parish. It is the birthplace of Huey P. Long and his brother, Earl K. Long, both longtime politicians and governors of Louisiana.

PARISH SEAT: Winnfield	CONGRESSIONAL DISTRICT 5
SQUARE MILE AREA.............. 953	AIRPORTS 1
SCHOOLS .... Public 9	

AGRICULTURE: Timber

INDUSTRY: Lumber (diversified into plywood, chips, timber treatment and veneer), creosote works, rock, charcoal, wearing apparel, and work gloves.

TOURIST ATTRACTIONS: Earl Kemp Long State Commemorative Area, located in the city of Winnfield, was established as a memorial to the one man ever to serve three terms as governor of the state. It is a one-acre park with an eight-foot bronze statue of Long.

PARKS and RECREATIONAL FACILITIES: Three public parks with various facilities.

PARISH BUSINESS PATTERNS: Number of employees, 1983:

Agricultural services, ... 13		Wholesale trade 114	
forestry, fisheries		Retail trade 514	
Mining 101		Finance, insurance and.............. 96	
Contract construction 182		real estate	
Manufacturing................ 1,579		Services......................... 1,131	
Transportation and other........ 175		Public administration 180	
public utilities			

PARISH PROFILES:

Median age, 1980 .... 31.2
Median family income, 1980 .... $12,445
Percent of families with income below poverty level, 1980 .... 21.6

General Hospitals, 1981 1	General Hospital Beds, 1981......... 103
Patient Care Physicians, 1981........ 8	Dentists, 1981....................... 4

Infant birth rate (per 1000 population), 1982............................... 15.5
Infant mortality rate (per 1000 live births), 1981............................ 18.4
Death rate (per 1000 population), 1982..................................... 10.1
MAJOR CITIES (over 5,000 population): Winnfield

Winnfield

Winnfield, the seat of government of the parish, also serves as the financial and business center of the area. A twenty-six acre new industrial park is located adjacent to the city.

GEOLOGY AND PHYSIOGRAPHY

Louisiana, shaped like a boot, with the toe pointing eastward, lies roughly between parallels 29° and 33° N. and meridians 89° and 94° W. and is bounded on the north by Arkansas, on the east by Mississippi, on the west by Texas, and on the south by the Gulf of Mexico. Somewhat larger than New York, the State has an area of 48,114 square miles, of which 3,593 are water.

Lying wholly within the Gulf Coastal Plain, Louisiana is the only State which extends in part over three major sections of that physiographic province: the East Gulf Coastal Plain, the Mississippi Alluvial Plain, and the West Gulf Coastal Plain. The more elevated areas east and west of the Alluvial Plain are known as the Upland Districts and consist of three main divisions: the Uplands of the Florida Parishes, north of Lake Pontchartrain and east of the Mississippi; the West Louisiana Uplands, west of the Red and Calcasieu Rivers; and the North Louisiana Uplands, a wedge-shaped area lying roughly between the Red and Ouachita Rivers. Near the coast, the delta formations of the Alluvial Plain lying east of Vermilion Bay and the low formations of the West Gulf Coastal Plain (Cameron-Vermilion Marshes or Wet Prairies) make up the Coastal-Delta Section. The higher arable portions of the Mississippi Alluvial Plain and the valleys of the Red and Ouachita Rivers are known as the Valley Lands.

The physiographic features of the State consist of pine hills, bluffs, prairies, coastal marshes, and alluvial plains. Rolling hill country, studded with long-leaf and shortleaf pine, is found in each of the upland regions. Ranging in elevation from 100 to 300 feet in the southernmost uplands, the hills rise to a maximum of a little more than 400 feet near the Arkansas boundary. Except for conspicuous differences of elevation at successive terraces, or where the hills border valleys, the uplands slope gently toward the coast, the average incline being about two feet to the mile. Two high points west of the Mississippi rise above 400 feet; the Kisatchie Hills on the Natchitoches-Vernon Parish line and an area in the southern part of Claiborne Parish. Picturesque hills, bluffs, and ravines occur along the streams and valleys, the most notable being Grand Ecore Bluff in Natchitoches Parish, the Tunica Hills in West Feliciana Parish, and the gorges known as Fluker's Cave and Fricke's Cave in St. Helena and Washington Parishes.

Bluffs border the Mississippi Alluvial Plain to the east and west of the river. On the east side the bluffs rise to an elevation of over 300 feet in the Tunica Hills east of Angola and end somewhat south of Baton Rouge at an elevation only slightly above the valley floor. West of the Alluvial Plain a lower chain of bluffs extends in a broken line from Oak Grove to Lafayette. The bluff lands slope away from the Mississippi Valley on each side, their drainage being away from the river.

The prairie lands in southwest Louisiana make up a flat sloping plain declining in elevation from 60 feet near Mamou to sea level at White Lake, the descent

ELEVATION EXTREMES

Highest Point: Driskill Mountain, Bienville Parish, 535 feet

Highest Town: Athens, Claiborne Parish, 469 feet

Lowest Point: New Orleans, Orleans Parish, 5 feet below mean sea level

Latitude, Longitude, and Elevation of
Major Louisiana Cities
(figures given at U.S. Geodetic Survey benchmarks)

	ELEVATION	LATITUDE	LONGITUDE
Alexandria	75′	31°18′30″.573	92°26′39″.044
Bogalusa	100′	30°46′20″	89°51′44″
Baton Rouge	50′	30°26′14″.325	91°10′25″.706
Clinton	180′	30°51′51″.48	91°01′01″.78
Gretna	5′	29°54′05″.192	90°03′59″.942
Opelousas	65′	30°31′59″.314	92°05′00″.928
St. Francisville	110′	30°46′30″.61	91°23′11″.16
Lafayette	40′	30°13′35″.38	92°00′50″.81
Lake Charles	15′	30°13′53″.270	93°12′51″.502
Monroe	80′	32°27′18″.75	92°06′55″.45
New Iberia	20′	29°50′44″.152	91°48′16″.118
New Orleans*	0′	29°56′57″.212	90°04′11″.587
Shreveport	200′	32°30′47″.320	93°44′59″.400

*Various portions of the city range from 14 ft. above to five feet below mean tide.

averaging a foot to the mile. There are no pronounced relief features.

THE MARSHES

A wide fringe of coastal marshes extends along the 1,700-mile coast line of Louisiana. Close growths of sedge, grass, and rushes make up a flat treeless plain dotted with thousands of shallow salt water lakes and lagoons. Except where the delta is encroaching on the seat, the marshes are bordered on the seaward side by barrier beaches, composed mainly of fine sand, which rise to a crest and support groves of live oak on their inner slopes. Sand and shell ridges, sometimes rising several feet above to general level, are to be found throughout the marshes. Called **Chénières** because of the oak groves usually found growing on them, they represent former barrier beaches. Good examples are Grand Chénière and Pecan Island in southwest Louisiana. Drainage of the marsh areas is effected by sloughs and drainage bayous. In the coastal region proper the marshes are generally salt or brackish, the transition from fresh water being very gradual.

In addition to the chênières, the "land islands" of Louisiana are positive topographic features of great importance both to topographers and geologists because they represent the surface expression of underlying salt masses. These "land islands" are usually a mile or more in diameter and rise to a maximum height of 196 feet (Avery Island) above the general level of the surrounding marshes.

In southwestern Louisiana, extending along a line bearing S. 49° E. from a place ten miles west of New Iberia to the mouth of Atchafalaya River, are five distinct surface mounds known as the "Five Islands" of Louisiana: Jefferson Island, Avery Island, Weeks Island, Côte Blanche, and Belle Isle.

The Mississippi Alluvial Plain extends southward along the river in a broad belt with an average width of about 50 miles. Narrow in the north, it widens considerably below Baton Rouge, where it swings southeastward to form the delta. From the Arkansas Line, where the elevation is 115 feet, the flood plain slopes gradually to sea level at the Gulf of Mexico, the drop in the river over its 569-mile course through the State being about 2½ inches to the mile. The variations in the topography of the Alluvial Plain consist mainly of a series of ridges and basins. Along the main river and its distributaries, or natural outlets the ridges are termed "natural levees." The arable lands of the high elevation sloping away from the river compose the "frontlands," the relief of which is altered in many places by meanders, cutoffs, and oxbow lakes. The intervening area between the frontlands and the bordering swamps is known as the "backlands," a region of fine silt and clay. When the level of the

backlands dips below the mean water table, swamps are found. They vary from shallow swamps, characterized by a variety of hardwoods, to deeper, more permanent, cypress-tupelo swamps. Since the drainage in the Alluvial Plain is away from the master streams, the swamps, as a rule, do not drain into the Mississippi River, but serve merely as catch-basins for overflow waters and rainfall. In the delta proper, there are, in addition to the swamps, wide expanses of treeless water areas—marshes, lagoons, and lakes. The low regions, including the alluvial lands and coast swamps, comprise about 20,000 square miles, or nearly half the area of the State.

RIVERS AND BAYOUS

The most important rivers in the State are the Mississippi, Red, Atchafalaya, Ouachita, Sabine, and Pearl. A peculiar feature of many streams is that they run upon a higher elevation than their flood plains. This is especially true of the Mississippi, which meanders through Louisiana between ridegs built up by successive depositions of silt. The river is of little value, therefore, as a drainage channel for the State, its only tributary on the west being Red River, and on the east, Bayou Sara and Thompson's Creek. Were it not for a continuous line of levees, one-third of the total area of the State would be flooded by the Mississippi whenever bankfull stage was exceeded.

Numerous bayous—flood distributaries and drainage streams for swamps—make up a drainage network for the State. Of these, Teche, Macon, Lafourche, and Boeuf are the largest. The bayous, in most instances, are distributaries rather than tributaries of streams, and as such act as auxiliary outlets. Those found in the catch-basin swamps along the Mississippi and in the Tensas River and Lake des Allemands areas serve as drainage outlets for overflow waters.

LAKES

Three classes of lakes occur. Coastal lagoons, existing as arms of the sea isolated behind barrier beaches or surrounded by deltaic ridges, are found in the delta. Lying at sea level, they have a slight tidal action, although storms and varying winds cause greater rises and falls than the regular tides. Barataria Bay and Lake Pontchartrain, Maurepas, and Salvador are typical of such lagoons. Oxbow lakes, resulting from cut-off meanders of the Mississippi River, are found throughout the Alluvial Plain. Their characteristic shape is that of a crescent, and their width that of the river from which they were cut off. The lakes found in the Red River Valley, of which Caddo, Bistineau, and Black are typical, were formed as a result of the damming of Red River by the Great Raft. Their level is dependent now upon that of Red River, high water resulting in a flooding of the lakes by backwater.

GEOLOGICAL FORMATIONS

Geologically considered, Louisiana is "new." Much of it consists of marine and alluvial sediments deposited after the principal structural features of surrounding regions had assumed their final form. Subsidence of the original structures was so great that few if any of the basic formations are visible. Most of such rocks as appear on the surface, as well as the cores brought up in the drilling of oil wells, show that the structures, even at great depths, are comparatively recent ones. Most observable evidence belongs to the Cenozoic era, the final and shortest major unit in geologic time.

Because the younger rocks conceal the older record, the history in the earlier eras of what is now Louisiana can be known only by inference from the evidence of adjacent States. It is certain, however, that this area had a long and varied history preceding the more recent era.

A long interval elapsed between the closing of the Mesozoic era and the accumulation of the earliest Tertiary deposits of Cenozoic age in Louisiana.

The dawn of Tertiary times in Louisiana showed this region occupying part of a large trough flooded by water and known as the Mississippi Embayment. Sedimentation and uplift contracted and ultimately obliterated the depressed area and resulted in continued and widespread advances and retreats of the invading Gulf waters.

The existing faults, folds, and salt domes were formed immediately following the completion of Miocene deposits of the Tertiary beds. The Gulf then receded far beyond the present shore line, erosion intensified, and the Quarternary period began with the entire region covered with a mantle of Pleistocene sands and gravel. The succeeding Recent period has been occupied largely with the removal of this debris.

The rocks exposed at the surface in Louisiana consist almost entirely of clay, sand, and marl beds. These materials, except for the flood-plain deposits along present-day streams, were laid down in the Gulf of Mexico or near gulf level, when that body of water was much larger than it is now and covered broad portions of the Gulf Coastal States. Some of the beds represent ancient deltas of the Mississippi River and of other large streams of the region; others represent deposits in marine water "offshore" from the ancient deltas.

The relationship and distribution of the beds indicate a progressive but gradual retreat of the Gulf and an accompanying rise of the northern part of the State. As the beds became dry land and rose higher and higher, stream erosion pro-

duced the hill lands. Due to these changes the oldest beds are found in the northern part of the State, with overlying and progressively younger beds southward. The youngest deposits are found along the coast and in the alluvial valleys of the present streams.

The chief structural features of the Louisiana geologic formations are the Sabine uplift, a prominent and broad uplift centering in northwestern Louisiana; the Monroe uplift, a similar structure in northeastern Louisiana; the Angelina-Caldwell flexure, a fold or line of weakness dating from Tertiary times, extending from Sabine Parish across north-central Louisiana to Caldwell Parish; the Mobile-Tunica flexure, a fold of rather recent formation, extending from near Mobile Bay, Alabama, westward to the Tunica Hills of the northern Feliciana Parishes of Louisiana; 11 interior salt domes in north Louisiana; and not less than 100 salt domes in the coastal area.

During the Cretaceous period near the close of the Mesozoic era, strata consisting of hard crystalline limestone, gypsum, salt, sulphur, and marls were deposited at the bottom of the inland sea in an area comprising a large part of Louisiana. These strata were nearly always accompanied by salt beds, which, when exposed by erosion, were bare of vegetation. The old salt works of Webster, Bienville, and Winn Parishes are proof of this; and enormous deposits of nearly pure salt were discovered in the 11 salt domes of that section.

The great pressure of the thick Tertiary and Quarternary deposits subsequently laid down along the coast is believed to have been a factor in driving upward the great columns of rock salt which form the numerous salt domes of the Louisiana coastal area.

The most widely accepted theory is that a prehistoric salt bed, similar to that of the Great Salt Lake in Utah, has been depressed and buried under the enormous accumulation, during millions of years, of the alluvial deposits of the Mississippi River. The great pressure of this deposit, which is estimated to be from 5 to 6 miles in depth, has caused the salt to become plastic and to seek relief by flowing upward through the surrounding rocks. In a few cases, the rising salt columns have perforated the entire 25,000 or more feet of superimposed strata; these outcrops, each usually with an overlying crust, are known as the "Five Islands," the salt mines of which produce most of Louisiana's rock salt.

Salt domes, or plugs, are an important element in the origin of the south Louisiana oil fields. The oil was formed in the bedded rocks as they were deposited, and finally accumulated in the porous and permeable sand layers. As a salt plug moved upward through the bedded rocks, it arched the beds above into dome-shaped structures, and where it cut through these beds they remained up-arched against the flank of the salt. If the domed beds or the beds abutting against the salt were oil-bearing sands, the oil would migrate up the slope of the beds and accumulate in the highest part of the dome above the salt, or in the upper end of the bed, against the side of the salt. In these places it would remain trapped until tapped by wells.

The salt core is sometimes topped with a cap, from a few feet to several hundred feet in thickness, consisting of various minerals, or combinations of minerals, such as limestone, gypsum, anhydrate, sulphur, galena, sphalerite, pyrite, and petroleum. Besides petroleum, the accompanying sandy strata contain vast quantities of natural gas.

The majority of the intruded salt masses have no surface expression, but a few have superficially manifested themselves by sunken areas. The absence of a surface expression has been the motivating reason for the rapid development and application of a new science, geophysical prospecting, which not only detects but measures and determines the shape, size, and location of these masses even when buried under thousands of feet of sediment and water.

On the flanks of the Sabine uplift, in northern Louisiana, are some oil pools localized chiefly by anticlinal structure, including high spots on the uplift and independent domes and anticlines grouped around it. Areal limitations of sand bodies and variation in permeability of reservoir rock, however, have been factors in determining the positions and extent of most of the pools of this district.

The powerful forces which produced the Sabine uplift caused many fractures and folds and gave north Louisiana the basis for its future drainage system. Similar forces produced the Monroe uplift in the northeastern part of the State, the two areas being separated by the immense Ouachita-Mississippi Basin. Extensive shallow swamps and coastal marshes in this basin furnished ideal conditions for preserving forest remains and other vegetable debris, which are represented today by the lignite deposits of North Louisiana.

Northwestern Louisiana slowly emerged, and rivers and creeks began sculpturing a topography similar to that of the present day. But again the scene changed, and another submergence took place. Muddy, shallow seas prevailed, and a heavy deposit of gray clays was placed over the former dry land. These clays rest upon the deeply eroded surfaces of the Wilcox, Claiborne, and Cockfield formations. They are of great economic importance, being the water-carrying beds for the springs and wells of North Louisiana. They enter into the composition of the soils of the creek bottoms, and the water coming from them is remarkably pure.

Deposits known as the Jackson formation rest upon the Cockfield formation.

Unlike the deposits mentioned above, which have a dip conforming to the Sabine uplift, the Jackson strata have a general southward dip conforming to the Angelina-Caldwell flexure. They run in a band about 30 miles wide across the southern portion of the hills of north Louisiana and outcrop in many places, frequently protruding like islands, especially along their northern boundary, through a thick cover of red, sandy clay formed later. The Jackson strata make up calcareous soils, which consist for the most part of tough, yellow, fossil-bearing marls grading into gray clays. Frequently, white and yellow limestone boulders are scattered over the outcrops; more rarely, limestone ledges a few feet in thickness cap the hills. Fossil bones of the Zeuglodon, a whalelike mammal, have b e e n found, and the formation is considered one of the best for the collection of upper Eocene fossils. Fossil Foraminifera are numerous both in kind and number.

The Vicksburg Oligocene deposits overlie the Jackson, but there is no difference in the topography of the territory they occupy, nor in their vegetation. They consist of fellow fossil-bearing marls and exhibit the same black prairies, but their fossils show them to belong to a later geological horizon.

South of the Vicksburg deposits are outcrops of the Catahoula formation, which form a prominent hilly belt across the State in the parishes of Vernon, Sabine. Natchitoches, Grant, La Salle, and Catahoula, terminating at Sicily Island. The belt is made up of sandstones, clay stones, and massive clays, which overtop the southern border of the Vicksburg marls. The area consists of steep hills and bluffs which frequently rise more than 150 feet above the surrounding country. The former plain structure has been preserved, however, as a plateau, in which the rivers have cut wide valleys with steep walls, and the tributaries, deep ravines.

Above the Catahoula formation, and completing the Miocene deposits, lie the Fleming clays and sands. The term "Fleming" at one time was used to refer to the 5,000 to 8,000 feet of sediments lying between the Citronelle gravels of the Pleistocene and the Discorbis zone of the Miocene. Lately "Fleming" is being used to name the clays and sands between the Discorbis zone and the Pliocene. As the study of microfauna and microfossils has progressed, tentative zones have been set up within the Fleming, such as the **Potamides matsoni** and **Rangia johnsoni** zones. The Fleming covers southern Calcasieu, southern Beauregard, central Allen and Evangeline, southern St. Landry, central Pointe Coupée, northern Livingston, and southern Tangipahoa and St. Tammany Parishes.

Little is known about the Pliocene, which lies between the Fleming and the Pleistocene. Interpretation is rendered difficult because the only described Pliocene microfauna available for correlation is a small one from the comparatively thin Caloosahatchee marl of southern Florida. Besides this, most of the knowledge of the Pliocene sediments of Louisiana comes from wells drilled on the piercement type domes, where the section is only partially represented. The horizon of the Pliocene covers southern Louisiana, and extends northward to end in a slanting line which cuts across southern Beauregard, Allen and Evangeline, central St. Landry and Pointe Coupée, southern West and East Feliciana, central St. Helena, northern Tangipahoa, and central Washington Parishes.

Pleistocene sands and gravels, known as the Drift, cover a vast surface area of the State. Strata are found at Avery Island, overlying the salt beds and underlying the Bluff strata. Excavations have revealed fossilized bones and some nearly complete skeletons of species of mastodon, elephant, horse, and species of mylodon, and megalonyx (giant sloths). Rising northward, the Drift becomes more or less abundant through the uplands of the State. It spreads a thin sheet over extreme north Louisiana, forms immense deposits centrally, and thins out again over the Catahoula deposits. Silicified corals, Favosites, and Cyathophyllum have been found among these gravels north of Alexandria.

Plant fossils are abundant in several of the Louisiana formations; the identifications include various extinct species of ferns, grasses, sedges, walnuts, oaks, elms, mulberries, figs, magnolias, laurels, hollies, heaths, dogwoods, and olives.

Blue clay, calcereous silts, and brown loams, deposited in or bordering the large bottoms during the Recent period by streams which immediately antedate those of the present time, may be classified together as the Port Hudson-Beaumont formations. Strictly speaking, they are not all alluvial. The clays were deposited as thick strata in sluggish, shallow estuaries running well up to Cairo, Illinois, along the Mississippi and up to Shreveport along the Red River Valley. The width of the ancient Mississippi flood plain extended almost to Monroe on the west and to Vicksburg on the east. At the present day, in spite of the fact that the rivers have been depositing their alluvium on top of the blue clay, large areas are still uncovered. When cultivated, these clays give rise to the famous "buckshot" soils.

The formation of Louisiana's bluffs accounts for the high uplands, 10 to 15 miles in width, which wall the Mississippi River. During the Pleistocene there were four epochs of alluviation, separated by distinct erosional intervals occurring in the Deltaic plain region of Louisiana. The deposits of this period have been correlated with interglacial stages, while the erosional intervals coincide with glacial advances. These four alluvial surfaces, called "Terrace," are named Praire, Montgomery, Bently, and Williana.

Each terrace starts as a thin layer of silt deposited along the banks in the back reaches of streams, but as the streams advance toward the coast the deposit becomes thicker and broader until it is a wide seaward-sloping surface, which forms a distinctive topographic belt more or less paralleling the alignment of the present coastal marshes. The older surfaces, such as the Bently and Williana, are more steeply inclined than the younger surfaces, which indicates continual regional tilting. This is partially due to the localized uplift along the Mobile-Tunica flexure.

A detailed study of the lower terraces has yet to be undertaken, and just how rich they may be in fossils is not known. The Prairie, or youngest terrace, however, is represented by buckshot clay, a dark colored, gummy soil containing calcareous and ferruginous concretions, fossil woods of oak, bamboo, hard pine, mulberry, hickory, cyprus, persimmon, tulip, poplar, elm and such northern species as white spruce, larch, and white cedar; fossil fruits and seeds of the buttercup, rose, grape, carrot, honeysuckle, and plaintain; and fossilized bones of the tapir, elephant, and peccary.

The limits of the Deltaic plain are very irregular, and it is practically impossible to give definite boundaries. This is partly due to the fact that bounding distributaries were inconsistent in position and subject to abandonment, bifurcation, and sudden relegation to an anterior position. Roughly, the delta spread between the Pearl and Sabine Rivers. Its northern boundary started in northern Calcasieu Parish; swept sharply north into southern Vernon and Rapides and Central Avoyelles Parishes; then dropped again to enter central Pointe Coupée, East and West Feliciana and St. Helena Parishes; and finally dropped still farther south to cross central Tangipahoa and St. Tammany Parishes.

In the marshes of the southern part of the State, the floods and tides of the Recent period have deposited mud, clay, and sand, with fossil shells similar to those of living species, on top of the blue clay of the Beaumont formation. These marshes are still in the process of formation and are overflowed daily by the tides. Near the rivers and along the banks of bayous that represent former river beds, the alluvium brought down by the floods has been piled upon this clay as deltaic fingers, elevating the adjacent surfaces above the level of the marshes and making arable land. In addition, wave-built barrier beaches are forming along the coast. Sand dunes rise along the crests of these beaches wherever they are exposed to the prevailing winds.

In Louisiana, except for the alluvial deposits at the mouth of the Mississippi, the shore line is receding at a rate of from 6 to 125 feet a year, irrespective of hurricanes, which can cause a retreat of several hundred feet in a few hours. Two factors cause this recession: (1) the regional tilting brought on by the weight of the growing Mississippi delta, which causes the lands about it to dip more sharply and become submerged; (2) the ease with which the low-lying shore is eroded, as is shown by the greater depth of the recession on those portions of the shore line which are more exposed to the prevailing winds and waves. Indeed, so noticeable and rapid has been the subsidence of the mainland, that many of the old plantations have become a region fit only for trapping, hunting and fishing.

Except in the delta, the shore line of southern Louisiana is generally sandy; there are numerous sand and shell ridges extending for miles parallel to the shore either in close proximity to the Gulf or some distance inland. Because of the recession of the coast line, similar ridges are now developing along the Gulf border, just above and below mean tide. Some distance out in the Gulf the same force is at work making the Sabine Shoals. Isle Derniére and Tambalier, Ship, Cat, and Chandeleur Islands will eventually become island ridges like Pecan Island and Grand Chêniére in southwest Louisiana or like the less elevated and less conspicuous sand and shell ridges that traverse Orleans Parish near the South shore of Lake Pontchartrain.

Equally interesting in this portion of the State are the numerous shallow lakes and bays. A complete series of beds showing a transition from purely salt to brackish, or even fresh-water, characterizes the submerged areas. The strictly marine Fulgur, Natica, and Arca shells give place successively to brackish water oysters and Mactra, Rangia, and fresh-water Unio, indicating that the land area of this part of Louisiana, during recent geological periods, has passed through a succession of stages similar to that in existence today. A number of extensive swamp areas have the appearance of being old lake beds from which the waters are nearly drained off. The water and oil wells of the region seldom fail to reveal masses of Rangia shells at some depth.

In some places there has been a continual loading and consequent depression of the Gulf's border, giving rise to uplifts in adjacent regions. The shifting of the mouth of the river and the resulting change of loading point has brought about a shifting of regions of depression and upheaval. If the region of uplift is some distance from the coast, the uplifting produces shallow sounds, bays, or lakes, according to its extent. These, when finally filled with clays derived from the sediments of inflowing rivers, pass from the sea-marsh stage into prairies.

Louisiana Gulf Coast

Louisiana has an interesting and complicated relationship with the Gulf of Mexico. The Mississippi River—which drains all or part of thirty one states of the U.S. (41 percent of the continental U.S.) and three Canadian provinces for a total area of 1.245 million square miles—discharges an average of about 640,000 cubic feet of water per second into the Gulf. Along with the water, the river carries approximately two million tons of silt into the Gulf every twenty-four hours. Several other major rivers and bayous—Pearl, Lafourche, Atchafalaya, and Sabine among others—empty along Louisiana's 7,721 miles of meandering shoreline (the coastline border is roughly four hundred miles long). The meeting of rivers, marsh wetlands, swamps, with Gulf water and jagged barrier islands is unique to Louisiana.

The Gulf of Mexico

The Gulf of Mexico, which forms the southern border of the entire state of Louisiana, is the fifth largest sea in the world. With a surface area of 582,100 square miles and an average depth of 5,297 feet, the Gulf is an important resource to Louisiana, supplying the state with seafood and recreational opportunities.

The Gulf collects about two-thirds of all waste material discharged into U.S. rivers and a substantial amount of river and coastal industrial wastes. Since the only outlet for the Gulf is the sixty-mile-wide Straits of Florida, pollution is a constant threat. However, the Marine Protection Research and Sanctuaries Act, passed in 1973, has led to over ninety-percent reduction in the amount of toxic waste dumped in the Gulf. Continuing improvements will ensure that the Gulf of Mexico is kept clean as possible, in order to preserve it as a resource for Louisiana and the coastal states.

Coastal Zone Land Loss

Louisiana's coastal zone, constructed by thousands of years of delta growth of the Mississippi River and accounting for 40 percent of the total coastal wetlands in the United States, is gradually diminishing. Extending across the southern portion of the state roughly below the east-west line formed by interstate highways 10 and 12, these wetlands are a valuable resource. The marsh and estuarine areas of South Louisiana provide the major nursery grounds for the fish and shellfish of the northern Gulf Coast; the fishing industry in this area lands one-quarter of the U.S. catch each year, and Louisiana alone is ranked number one in commercial catch poundage (1.4 billion pounds for a value of $178 million in 1980). Wetlands also support an enormous amount of wildlife for game fishing, waterfowl and small game hunting, and trapping for both pelts and meat (Louisiana leads the nation in fur and alligator harvest). Clearly, coastal zone wetlands are a key component of Louisiana industry and recreation.

However, this critically important area is in danger. In 1968, a study counted 2.5 million acres of marshland, 1.8 million acres of ponds and lakes, and 2.2 million acres of bays and estuaries; one-fifth of the marsh area has since then been lost to open salt water. Present estimates of annual wetland loss total 30,000 acres (46.9 square miles) per year, almost three times the rate figured ten years ago. The causes for this rapid loss of land area are a combination of factors both natural and man-made.

The primary natural problems are rising sea level, dropping land level, and erosion. The rise of sea level and subsidence of land are difficult to isolate from one another, but the combined effect is a drop in altitude of

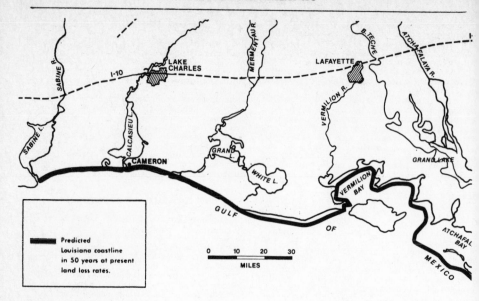

Predicted Louisiana coastline in 50 years at present land loss rates.

0 10 20 30
MILES

from two to five feet per century on the coast. While this subsidence seems insignificant, the low land surface elevations along the coastal zone mean that even a loss of a few hundredths of a foot can mean the flooding of thousands of acres of marsh. Erosion from both storms and common wave action is gradually wearing away the coast, because the rivers along the coastal area are no longer supplying the necessary sediment and sand to replace lost land. Barrier islands along the coast, remnants of old delta formations that form the "first line" of defense against coastal wave erosion, channel formation, and saltwater intrusion, are also gradually wearing away.

Mining of water, salt, petroleum, and gas may be contributing to settling of the land surface, but the greatest man-made effect on coastal areas is caused by the construction of levees and canals. Levees, which prevent coastal rivers (most importantly the Mississippi) from flooding during their spring high stages, also prevent them from regenerating nearby low-lying lands with distributions of sediment and silt. As the flood protection now stands, most of the silt carried by the Mississippi is dumped out of the mouth of the river, where it falls off the edge of the continental shelf into deep water. Canals are harmful to the wetlands because they destroy natural barriers between salt water and the marshland, thereby increasing erosion from the Gulf and inducing saltwater intrusion—the invading of fresh or brackish water areas by salt water—a process that is often fatal to freshwater plants and creatures. In addition, when canals are dredged to make them accessible to deep-draft vessels, the silt is usually piled up in what are called "spoil banks." These banks block the free flow of water through the marsh and interfere with the depositing of silt and nutrients, occasionally strangling the wetlands.

Some delta building is going on in Louisiana, most notably in Atchafalaya Bay, where about 4,500 acres of new delta marshes and wetlands are constructed each year by siltation. However, a careful conservation is necessary to preserve and protect Louisiana's remaining wetland resources.

Source: Center for Wetland Resources
Louisiana State University

FLOOD CONTROL

MISSISSIPPI RIVER

Without question America's greatest river, the Mississippi has made major contributions to the physical and economic growth of the nation. It is a navigation artery of great importance to the nation's transportation system, carrying an ever-growing commerce. Coursing through the heart of America, it supplies water for the cities and industries which have located along its banks. More and more the Mississippi's importance is emphasized as America continues to grow. This great river is truly one of the Nation's outstanding assets. Uncontrolled, it would be just as great a liability.

Discovered by DeSoto in 1541, the Mississippi River always has been a threat to the security of the valley through which it flows. Garciliaso de la Vega, in his history of the expedition begun by DeSoto, described the first recorded flood of the Mississippi as severe and of prolonged duration, beginning about the 10th of March, 1543, and cresting about 40 days later. By the end of May the river had returned to its banks, having been in flood for about 80 days. Since that time, explorers, traders, farmers, men of commerce, engineers have known—sometimes too well—the Mississippi in flood.

THE MISSISSIPPI DRAINAGE BASIN

The Mississippi River has the fourth largest drainage basin in the world, exceeded in size only by the watersheds of the Amazon, Congo and Nile Rivers. It drains 41% of 48 continental States of the United States. The basin covers more

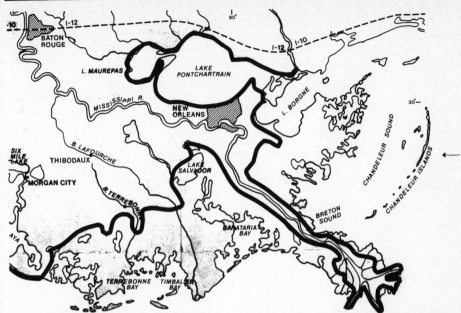

than 1,245,000 square miles, includes all or parts of 31 States and two Canadian Provinces, and roughly resembles a funnel which has its spout at the Gulf of Mexico. Waters from as far east as the State of New York and as far west as Montana contribute to flows in the lower river.

LOWER ALLUVIAL VALLEY

The lower alluvial valley of the Mississippi River is a relatively flat plain of about 35,000 square miles bordering on the river which would be overflowed during time of high water if it were not for the man-made protective works. This valley begins just below Cape Girardeau, Missouri, is roughly 600 miles in length, varies in width from 30 to 125 miles, and includes parts of seven states—Missouri, Illinois, Tennessee, Kentucky, Arkansas, Mississippi and Louisiana.

When the Mississippi River overflows, it deposits a part of the sediment it has been transporting. Most of the sediment is deposited adjacent to the river, forming low "natural levees," with decreasing amounts deposited away from the stream. For this reason, the banks of the river are generally 10 to 15 feet above the low-lands farther back from the river. This building of "natural levees" occurred, for the most part, before the present levee system was built. Because of the natural levees, drainage is generally away from the Mississippi River except where tributary streams join the river. This is an advantage in building flood control works, since it permits the construction of long, unbroken levee lines without interfering with drainage.

EARLY FLOOD CONTROL WORKS

Development of the First Levee System

The necessity of flood control was recognized immediately by the early settlers in the lower Mississippi River valley. When Bienville founded the city of New Orleans in 1717, his engineer, de la Tour, opposed the location of the city on the site selected because he knew that the settlement would be periodically overflowed by the river. Bienville overruled this objection, so de la Tour undertook the construction of the first levee system to be erected on the Mississippi. The work was not completed until 1727.

As settlements developed along the river, the levee system was extended. By 1735, the levee lines on both sides of the river extended from about 30 miles above New Orleans to about 12 miles below the city.

By 1812, when Louisiana was admitted to the Union, the levee system extended up the river to Baton Rouge on the east bank and to the vicinity of Morganza, 40 miles upriver from Baton Rouge, on the west bank. By 1844, in spite of several damaging floods, the levee system was continuous, except for a gap at Old River, from 20 miles below New Orleans to the mouth of the Arkansas River on the west bank and to Baton Rouge on the east bank.

Meanwhile, Federal efforts had been directed to improving the Mississippi for navigation. The first Federal operations occurred in 1820, when Congress appropriated funds for the preparation of a survey, maps and charts of the Ohio and Mississippi Rivers with a view to improving these rivers for navigation. River navigation was then well developed. The steamboat had made its appearance eight years before, and the need for navigation improvements on the Nation's major rivers was becoming increasingly apparent.

John C. Calhoun, presiding over a river improvement convention in Memphis in 1845, advanced the view that both flood protection and navigation improvements were national problems. The following year, he introduced a bill for the general improvement of the Mississippi. Although navigation was the primary objective, flood control was considered, and thus began to gain official recognition. In 1847, Thomas H. Benton, Abraham Lincoln, John C. Calhoun, and Horace Greeley attended conventions advocating flood control by the Federal Government.

A great flood occurred in 1849. The destruction from flood-waters below Red River was so great that this flood is recorded as one of the greatest ever experienced in this area. Several large crevasses occurred, with farm lands inundated for long periods and many sugar plantations ruined. The following year, another great flood occurred

These destructive floods created widespread distress in the lower Mississippi valley and focused national attention on the problem. The passage by Congress of the Swamp Acts of 1849 and 1850 was an expression of this interest.

These Acts granted to the States all unsold swamp and overflowed lands within the State borders and provided that funds derived from the sale of the lands should be applied to drainage, reclamation, and flood control projects. This attempt to secure flood protection failed because of the lack of coordination between the several States and the levee districts involved.

Financed solely by local interests, levee construction reached its highest point of development between 1851 and 1858. The levees constructed were not continuous, however, and they were inadequate in height and cross section. So, when the floods of 1858 and 1859 occurred, the levees were badly damaged.

During the War Between the States, flood control work came to a standstill and many levees were destroyed by floods or by the contending armies. By 1878, hundreds of miles of main line levee had disappeared entirely or had become valueless because of many crevasses.

Creation of Mississippi River Commission

The need for more substantial Federal participation in improvements of the river for navigation and flood control was generally recognized by 1879. The necessity for coordination of engineering operations through a centralized organization was also apparent. That year, on June 28th, Congress established the Mississippi River Commission, which had as its assigned duties ". . . to take into consideration and mature such plan or plans and estimates as will correct, permanently locate, and deepen the channel and protect the banks of the Mississippi River; improve and give safety and ease to the navigation thereof; prevent destructive floods; promote and facilitate commerce, trade, and the postal service . . ."

The Commission submitted its first report in 1880, recommending certain improvements for navigation and flood control. The following year, Congress appropriated one million dollars for the actual construction of improvement works under the jurisdiction of the Commission.

Levee work was begun by the Commission in 1882, marking the beginning of actual construction of a coordinated levee system for the lower Mississippi River. By 1906 the operations of the Commission were well advanced. Navigation improvement of the lower reaches of the river had been effected by dredging; bank protection by means of heavy willow mattresses had been successfully developed. Flood control benefits were only incidental, however. Although the law creating the Commission required it to prepare plans to prevent destructive floods, until 1917 the appropriation acts restricted levee construction and repair to such work as was considered a part of the navigation improvement plan.

The floods of 1912 and 1913 caused great damage. As a result the President directed the Mississippi River Commission to submit a special report on means for flood prevention. But no action was taken by Congress toward authorizing a comprehensive flood control plan for the entire alluvial valley, and operations under the Commission continued to be limited primarily to repairing levees and keeping the navigation channel open.

Development of Federal Flood Control Efforts

The flood of 1916 resulted in passage of the first Flood Control Act, approved March 1, 1917. This Act authorized the construction of levees for the control of floods and affirmed the policy of local cooperation. It provided that local interests should furnish rights-of-way and contribute a substantial percentage of the construction cost, and it charged local interests with the maintenance of completed works. It also authorized the Commission to spend Federal funds for work on tributaries as necessary to protect the upper limits of any alluvial basin from flooding. The second Flood Control Act, passed in 1923, further clarified the jurisdiction of the Mississippi River Commission.

The flood of 1927 was the most disastrous in the history of the lower Mississippi River Valley. An area of about

6,000 square miles was inundated. The total length of levee breached in main river lines exceeded five miles. Cities, towns, and farms were flooded. Crops were destroyed and industry paralyzed. Property damage amounted to about $236 million, which is equivalent to $930 million today; 214 lives were lost and 637,000 persons were displaced.

This disaster awakened the national conscience to the dire need for flood control in the lower valley. Out of it grew the Flood Control Act of 1928, which committed the Federal Government to a definite program of flood control. The present project dates from that Act.

The Act of 1928 authorized the expenditure of $325 million for construction of a Federal project to provide flood control in the alluvial valley of the lower Mississippi River and navigation from Cairo to New Orleans. Local interests were charged with furnishing rights-of-way for levees and maintaining them after construction.

PRESENT FLOOD CONTROL PLAN

The Project Flood

The flood control plan is designed to control the "project flood." It is a flood larger than the record flood of 1927.

At the outset it was obvious that the existing outlet capacity fell far short of what was required. Extensive meteorological and hydrological studies demonstrated that a maximum outflow rate of 3,000,000 cubic feet per second must be anticipated while the existing capacity was little more than half of this quantity. The solution evolved by the Corps of Engineers was to develop the flow capacity of the Atchafalaya Basin to the point where the combined capacity of the Basin and the Lower Mississippi would equal 3,000,000 cubic feet per second. This water flow is an enormous volume that would fill the Superdome in less than half a minute; it would flood the entire city of New Orleans to a depth of one foot in less than a half hour, and to eight feet in six hours.

Since the leveed channel at New Orleans is capable of handling only 1,250,000 cubic feet of water per second, about half of this floodflow would have to be diverted from the Mississippi into the Basin through two control structures. About one-fourth of the Mississippi's flow would be injected into the Atchafalaya Basin Floodway via the Old River Control Structure, located some 80 miles above Baton Rouge.

Another fourth of the River's flow would be removed from the River through the Morganza Control Structure and Floodway, some 30 miles south of Old River.

The majority of Red River's contribution to the flood would be routed down the West Atchafalaya Basin Floodway and the Atchafalaya River.

About half the flood would then be confined to the Atchafalaya Basin.

A great deal of the work needed to pass the "flood" has been completed. The mainline Mississippi River levees are in excellent condition. The Old River Control, Morganza, and Bonnet Carre Structures and Floodways have been completed.

The upper section of the Atchafalaya Floodway is made up of two separate sections. The West Atchafalaya Floodway, lying on a path parallel to the Atchafalaya River, is barricaded at the northern end by a "fuse plug" levee that is designed to fail when water in the Atchafalaya-Red River backwater area reaches flood stage. At this time (which should only occur under extreme conditions), the path would be open to the lower floodway. The second part is the Morganza Floodway, which is connected to the Mississippi 25 miles north of Baton Rouge by a massive control structure with 125 bays. During high stages on the Mississippi, these gates can be opened by a gantry crane, which will then allow the water to pass through the Morganza Floodway to just below Krotz Springs, where it joins the Atchafalaya Floodway.

The major work remaining is in the Atchafalaya Basin Floodway. In developing this Floodway, it was, of course, necessary to construct guide levees to confine floodflows. Unfortunately, in the southern portion of the Basin these levees had to be located in areas where foundation conditions are extremely poor and settlement and stability of the levee embankment are severe problems. As a result, after more than 40 years of construction, the levees are still deficient in grade through some of the lower part of Floodway, although it is now usable.

The Corps' answer was to construct wide stability berms where required so that the levees could be raised in one massive lift to a height above the flowline. Then subsequent lifts would be applied to keep the embankment above

LEGEND
I. Atchafalaya Basin Floodway
II. Red River Backwater Area
III. Drainage East of Atchafalaya Basin Floodway

Levees
Control Structures
West Atchafalaya Floodway
Morganza Floodway
Lower Floodway

the flowline and ultimately get it up to gross grade. Gross grade is an elevation equal to what the Corps calculates would provide the net grade after consolidation, shrinkage, and settlement. The net grade is two feet above the flowline.

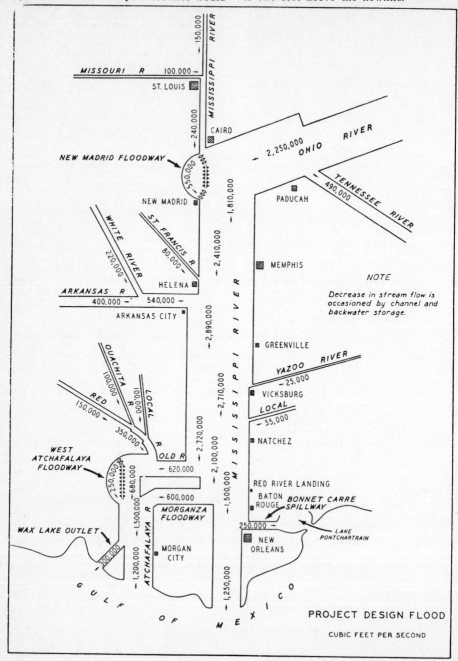

PROJECT DESIGN FLOOD

CUBIC FEET PER SECOND

NOTE

Decrease in stream flow is occasioned by channel and backwater storage.

Old River Control

One of the most important modifications to the project was made in 1954 when Congress authorized the feature for the control of flow at Old River to prevent the capture of the Mississippi by the Atchafalaya River. This work is unique in the history of river engineering in the United States.

Old River was a seven-mile stream that connected the Mississippi with the Red and Atchafalaya Rivers 80 miles above Baton Rouge. It was formed in 1831 when Captain Henry Shreve, a pioneer in the development of waterborne commerce in Louisiana, cut off one of the many loops of the Mississippi to shorten navigation. The upper portion eventually silted up, with the lower limb remaining as the link connecting the three rivers. The direction of flow in Old River varied, depending upon whether the Mississippi was high and the Red River low, in which case flow was to the west; or conversely, when the Red was high and the Mississippi low, flow was eastward. However, reversals in the direction of flow became less frequent as the Atchafalaya River began enlarging itself through the capture of increasingly greater amounts of the Mississippi's flow. In fact, no easterly flow occurred in Old River after 1945.

Changing conditions of the river were under observation by the Army Engineers for the better part of a century. In 1950 a major definitive study was begun, under the direction of the Mississippi River Commission, to determine the imminence of the threat of the Mississippi River to change its course to flow through the Atchafalaya River. The study included a complete review of all of the hydrologic, hydraulic, and geologic data that had been collected.

The findings left no doubt that the Atchafalaya River, if left alone, would become the main channel of the Mississippi below Old River.

That this could not be allowed to occur was obvious. Millions of dollars had been spent to protect the lower Mississippi Valley from floods through a network of levees and by the construction of massive floodways. Such a diversion would render many of these works useless and necessitate the construction of new flood control works costing many additional millions. The Mississippi River below Old River would become a salt-water estuary. This would have been a disaster of catastrophic proportions. Massive disruption adjacent to the Atchafalaya Basin would have resulted, and some towns would have ceased to exist. The vast industrial complex on the Mississippi below Baton Rouge, dependent as it is upon a bountiful supply of fresh water, would have been virtually destroyed.

After carefully studying all possible solutions, the Mississippi River Commission recommended that the uncontrolled link—Old River—be dammed and replaced with a controlled connection that would make it possible to divert the optimum amounts of water into the Atchafalaya Basin under normal and flood conditions.

After congressional authorization in 1954, construction began on the Old River control system. The first structures were the low-sill, to pass low and medium flows from the Mississippi to the Atchafalaya in a controlled manner, and the overbank, to pass flood flows to the Atchafalaya Floodway. Inflow and outflow channels were built to connect the structures with the Mississippi and Red-Atchafalaya systems. To force water through the controls, Old River had to be dammed. A huge closure standing 60 feet high and 1,500 feet wide was made of 2,160,000 cubic yards of sand from the bottom. In order to clear the way for river traffic, a lock was constructed just south of the junction of the Old and Mississippi rivers and connected with those arteries.

For ten years after the implementation of the Old River control plan, the Mississippi experienced no extremely high stages. However, heavy rainfall in late 1972 and early 1973 pushed the water level well above flood crest several times. The Old River controls held the river flow as they had been designed to do, but the low-sill structure suffered substantial damage. The turbulence of the water speeding by the low-sill washed away protective stone at the river bed and severely eroded the foundation.

Rehabilitation work began on the low-sill structure immediately. Repairs were made and studies instituted to determine the extent of the damage and the effect on future flood control. It was concluded that the low-sill was still operable, but at decidedly lower levels of stress, so in 1980 a new auxiliary structure was begun. The new control was completed in December 1987, and will be operated together with the existing controls to handle a total flow of about 700,000 cubic feet per second (more than 450 billion gallons per day).

BENEFITS FROM THE PROJECT

Because of the complicated nature of this comprehensive project and the large and diverse area affected, it is difficult to enumerate all the benefits resulting from its construction. When it is completed, it will give full flood protection to about 15,117,000 acres of land, partial protection to an additional 1,923,000 acres, and material benefit through major drainage improvement to about 2,700,000 acres. Also, it provides indirect flood control and navigation benefits to the entire central portion of the United States.

Since 1928 when the present project was authorized, there has been, with one exception, no failure of flood control works and no general overflow of the Valley, despite high waters that have reached record stages at some points within the Valley, notably during the years 1937, 1945, 1950, 1973, 1974, 1975, 1979, and 1983. Gradually more successful flood controls and techniques enacted by the U.S. Army Corps of Engineers have built confirmed public trust in the system of flood control works.

In addition to flood control, 9-foot minimum depths are being maintained in the river for navigation, providing a vital link in the Nation's transportation system. The river is the main stem of a vast network of inland waterways important to domestic and international trade, and over which such important commodities as petroleum, grain, chemicals, iron and steel products are transported. Each year the commerce increases. In fact, tonnages have doubled at about 10-year intervals since 1930.

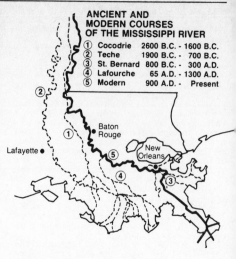

ANCIENT AND MODERN COURSES OF THE MISSISSIPPI RIVER

1. Cocodrie   2600 B.C. - 1600 B.C.
2. Teche   1900 B.C. - 700 B.C.
3. St. Bernard   800 B.C. - 300 A.D.
4. Lafourche   65 A.D. - 1300 A.D.
5. Modern   900 A.D. - Present

WIDTHS AND DEPTHS OF LOWER MISSISSIPPI RIVER
(depth is below water reference plane)

Station	Width Ft.	Depths, Ft.
Pilottown	3,500	25 ft. - 50 ft.
Ft. Jackson	2,300	5 ft. - 170 ft.
Pointe a la Hache	2,300	5 ft. - 70 ft.
Chalmette	2,400	5 ft. - 60 ft.
New Orleans Ferry	2,200	5 ft. - 150 ft.
Nine Mile Point	2,400	5 ft. - 160 ft.
Donaldsonville	2,800	5 ft. - 60 ft.
Baton Rouge	2,300	5 ft. - 50 ft.
Bayou Sara	3,200	5 ft. - 20 ft.
Vidalia	2,000	37 ft. - 78 ft.
St. Joseph	3,300	9 ft. - 54 ft.
Vicksburg	2,050	47 ft. - 105 ft.
Lake Providence	2,500	
Stack Island	2,500	3 ft. - 36 ft.

Widest: 7,600 ft. East Carroll Parish, Lat. 32° 40'
Narrowest: 1700 ft. Irvine Light, near Bayou Sara.
Deepest: 191 ft. opposite Gov. Nicholls St., New Orleans.
Shallowest: Dredged depth 9 feet in channels at many points.

LENGTHS OF PRINCIPAL RIVERS IN LOUISIANA

(Length represents distance to designated outflow from (a) original headwater of named river where name applies to entire length of channel, or (b) upper limit of channel so named, usually the junction of 2 tributaries or headwater streams)

River	Outflow	Length (miles)
Atchafalaya	Atchafalaya Bay	135
Calcasieu	Gulf of Mexico	102
Mississippi	Mouth of SW Pass	2,348
Pearl	Gulf of Mexico	490
Red	Mississippi River	1,222

Source: U.S. Army Engineer District, New Orleans

NAVIGABLE LOUISIANA RIVERS
(with minimum 5-foot draft)

River	Outflow	Navigable Length
Amite	Lake Maurepas	55
Atchafalaya*	Gulf of Mexico	63
Aux Chenes	Black Bay	20
Belle	Bayou Long	9
Black	Red River	237
(combined with Ouachita)		
Blind	Lake Maurepas	18
Blood	Tickfaw River	4
Bogue Falaya	Tchefuncte	4
Boeuf	Ouachita River	166
Calcasieu	Calcasieu Lake	71
Houston	Calcasieu River	20
Little	Red River	54.5
Little Atchafalaya	Upper Grand Lake	3
Lower Atchafalaya	Atchafalaya Bay	31
Lower Grand	Intracoastal Waterway	12
Mermentau	Gulf of Mexico	71.5
Mississippi	Head of Passes	305
Natalbany	Tickfaw River	10
Old	Lake Verret	5
Ouachita	Black River	237
(combined with Black)		
Pearl	Gulf of Mexico	104.8
Red	Atchafalaya River	369
Sabine	Sabine Lake	44
Tangipahoa	Lake Pontchartrain	14
Tchefuncte	Lake Pontchartrain	11
Tensas	Black River	137.8
Tickfaw	Lake Maurepas	26
Upper Grand	Atchafalaya Basin	20
Vermilion	Vermilion Bay	51

* Does not include Atchafalaya Basin, Main Channel

UNNAVIGABLE LOUISIANA RIVERS

Bogue Chitto	Pearl River
Cane	Red River
Comite	Amite River
Dugdemona	Little River
Lower Old	Mississippi River
Old	Mississippi River

Source: **U. S. Corps of Engineers** - New Orleans, La.; Vicksburg, Miss., Galveston, Tex.; Mobile, Ala.

BAYOUS OF LOUISIANA

Bayou	Location	Navigable Length	Bayou	Location	Navigable Length
Barataria	Barataria Bay	21	Grand Coteau	Field Lake	10
Bartholomew	Morehouse Parish	85.6	Green Island	Vermilion Bay	21
Bienvenue	Lake Borgne	14	Grosse Tete	Livonia	29
Big Carrion Crow	Four League Bay	23	Hog	Lower Mud Lake	14
Big Pigeon	Grand Lake	18	Lacassine	Lacassine Lake	26
Big Wax	Wax Lake Pass	24	Lacombe	St. Tammany Parish	12
Black	Houma	28	Lafourche	Napoleonville	79
Blue	Wax Lake	10	La Loutre	Yscloskey	29
Blue Hammock	Lake Mechant	10	La Rose	Atchafalaya Basin	10
Boeuf	Lake Palourde	13	Leopard	Wax Lake	12
Cheniere	Lake Washington	16	Little D'Arbonne	Unionville	20
Chevreuil	Lake des Allemands	10	Little Caillou	Bayou Terrebonne	33
Choupique	Lake Charles	14	Little Sorrel	Six Mile Lake	11
Cocodrie	Bayou Chene	10	Little Wax	Wax Lake	17
Colyell	Terrebonne Parish	11	Long	Black Bay	14
Courtablue	Atchafalaya River	26	Macon	Floyd	111.6
Cypremort	W. Cote Blanche Bay	15	Maringouin	Grand River	10
D'Arbonne	Corney Bayou	57	Natchitoches	Red River	12
de Cade	Lake de Cade	10	Nezpique	Mermentau River	25
des Allemands	Lake des Allemands	18	Oyster	Marsh Island	10
des Cannes	Mermentau River	15	Penchant	Bayou Shaffer	15
des Glaises	Alabama Bayou	14	Perot	Bayou Rigolettes	12
des Glaises	Atchafalaya River	28	Petit Amite	Blind River	12
du Large	Theriot	28	Plaquemine	Plaquemine	10
Dupont	Bayou Barataria	27	Plaquemine Brule	Bayou des Cannes	19
False	Field Lake	10	Queue de Tortue	Mermentau River	14
Ferblanc	Caminada Bay	13	Rigolettes	Little Lake	10
Freshwater	Intracoastal City	20	St. Denis	Little Lake	10
Grand	Bayou Chevreuil	15	Sorrel	Atchafalaya Basin	10
(Chegby, Cohabanosse)			Teche	Port Barre	125
Grand	Barataria Bay	10	Terrebonne	Houma	36
Grand	Bastion Bay	19	Terre aux Boeufs	Black Bay	18
Grand	Lake Verret	12	Twelve Mile	Big Willow Pass	23.8
Grand Caillou	Houma	36	Wilkinson	Lake Laurier	10

BAYOUS OF LOUISIANA WITH LESS THAN TEN MILES OF NAVIGABLE WATERS

Andre	Blanc	Cher Ami	Cypress	Dulac
Ash	Bloody	Cheri	Deadman's	Dulac
Auguste	Blue	Chevreau	Deep	du Nord
Austrian	Boeuf	Chicken	Deep Water	Dum Barr
Banan	Bois Connie	China	Deer	Dupont
Baptiste	Bonfouca	Chinaman	Deer Island	Dupre
Barre	Boston	Chitique	Defond	Dutch
Bartholomew	Bordeaux	Choctaw	De la Fleur	Dorcheat
Beauregard	Borre	Choctaw	De l'Ouest	Fast
Bedico	Boutte	Cholas	De l'Ouest	East Constance
Bee	Brant	Coffee Point	de Mar	East Little Constance
Belle Isle	Buckskin	Collicon	des Amoureaux	Echo
Berard	Burrwood	Constance	Des Ilettes	Eloi
Big Castaing	Butte La Rose	Contraband	Desir	Emile
Big Bull	Cane	Cook	des Oies	English
Big Charles	Cannon	Cooper	des Platins	English
Big Constance	Cantrell	Coposaw	de Suite	Eugene
Big Doctor's	Carlin	Coquette	de West	Felix
Big Goddel	Carlin	Couba	d'Inde	Ferrand
Big Hog	Carlin	Courant	Dosgris	Fifi
Big Lacassine	Castete	Crapaud	Dollar	Fish
Big Misale	Catahoula	Creole	Door Point	Fisher
Big Parasol	Cedar	Crocodile	Drum	Flat
Big Tensas	Chaland	Crocodile	Dry Cypress	Fontanelle
Biloxi	Charles Theriot	Crook Chene	Du Courant	Fordoche
Bird Island	Chauvin	Crooked	Dufrene	Foret
Black	Chene	Crooked	Dufrene	Fort
Black Jack	Chene	Cross	Duhuy	Fortier
Black Prince	Chene	Customhouse	Duhuy	Four Hundred Dollar
Blanc	Chene Blanc	Cutler	Duhuy	Four Island

Four Mile	Johnson's	L'Ourse	Palo	Sevin
Francais	John the Fool	L'Ourse	Pearl	Shaffer
Frenepiquant	Jones	Lucien	Pelton	Shark
Fucich	Joseph	Magazille	Petit Anse	Shrimp
Garci	Kelso	Mallett	Petit Liard	Shortway
Gaspar	la Chute	Manchac	Picnic	Snail
Gauche	La Fee	Mandeville	Pigeon	Snake
Gaullume	La Lagune	Maringouin	Plat	South
Gentilly	la Mer	Martinbox	Plumb	Stinking
Goreau	Lamoque	Mascot	Point au Chien	Stumpy
Gorofier	La Poule	Maxent	Pointe-en-pointe	Sword
Grand	Larompe	McCutcheon	Portage	Tambour
Grand	Lassene	Mercier	Portage	Tartellon
Grand	Laurier	Mersier	Portage	Taylor's
Grand Bank	le Boon	Middle	Possum	Tete de Ourse
Grand Bourbeaux	Le Carpe	Middle Fork Long	Postillion	Three Mile
Grand du Portage	L'Embarras	Milhomme	Pouailler	Thunder von Tranc
Grand Carrion Crow	Lem Hawkins	Mink	Quatre	Tigre
Grand Felicity	Lery	Misere	Quitman	Tortillion
Grand Liard	Liberty	Mississippi	Raccourci	Towhead
Gravenburg	Little	Moreau	Raquette	Treasure
Greque	Little Alabama	Mosquito	Rattlesnake	Trouble
Hackberry	Little Black	Myers	Redfish	Trove
Hasouse	Little Long	Myrtle	Rice	Tucker
Hermitage	Little Pigeon	Ne Touche Pas	Rigaud	Turkey
Heybours	Little Chenier	Nicholli	Robinson	Turtle
Hog	Little Chevreau	Nine Mile	Rochelle	Two Sisters
Hog	Little Coteau	Nobody's	Rollover	Upper Grand
Honey	Little Doctor's	North	Rosa	Vacherie
Huertes	Little Goddel	Oak	Round	Vacherie
Jack	Little Gonsoulin	Oaks	Rouville	Verret
Jack	Little Misale	Old Oyster	St. Honore	Villars
Jack Stout	Little Pecan	Onion	St. Jean Charles	Vincent
Jacques	Little Tensas	Orange	St. Malo	Washington
Jake	Live Oak	Oyster	Sale	Wax
Jake	Long	Oyster	Salt	Weeks
Jean La Crois	Long	Oyster	Sara	White
Jean Louis Robin	Long	Palaude	Sauveur	Wildcat
Jessie	Long	Palmetto	Schooner	Yellow
John Bop	Lorier	Palmetto	Segnette	Yscloskey

UNNAVIGABLE BAYOUS OF LOUISIANA

Alabama	Castor	Funny Louis	Little Corney	Serpent
Big Choctaw	Chemin-a-haut	Fusilier	Loggy	Sterling
Big Colewa	Cocodrie	Grappe	Luce	Tensas
Big Jessie	Corney	Jean de Jean	Paw Paw	Toro
Big Joe	Cross	Kelly	Posten	Vincent
Bodcau	De Loutre	Kisatchie	Provencal	Wauksha
Boggy	Dixie	Lafourche	Red Chute	Wilson
Brush	Flat Lick	Latenache	Saline	

Source: U. S. Corps of Engineers - New Orleans, La.; Vicksburg, Miss.

LOUISIANA RESERVOIR DATA

Name and Location	Drainage Area (Sq. Mi.)	Lake Data Elev. M.S.L.	Area Acres	Volume (Ac.-ft.)	Dependable Supply (Million G.P.D.)	Elev. Conservation Pool M.S.L.
Barnes Cr., Allen Parish	133	52.0	4,400	33,500	37.2	None
Bayou Bartholomew, Ouachita	1,737	75.0	6,300	35,500	89.3	61.0
Bayou Castor, DeSoto	96	220.0	4,800	75,000	28.5	201.9
Bayou D'Arbonne, Union*	1,585	80.0	15,250	130,000	80.0	None
Bayou D'Arbonne, Union	1,585	93.0	30,750	426,000	370.0	70.0
Bayou De L'Outre, Union*	390	81.5	4,970	70,000	103.9	56.0
Bayou Dorcheat, Webster	1,022	194.5	42,600	620,000	343.0	185.5
Bayou La Nana, Sabine	93	211.3	5,150	70,000	31.0	187.0
Bayou Na Bon Chasse, DeSoto	20	200.0	704	8,200	5.0	193.2
Bayou San Miguel, Sabine	200	180.0	8,650	130,000	49.0	None
Bayou San Patricio, Sabine	135	228.0	5,950	75,000	34.0	202.5
Bayou Sara, West Feliciana	97	163.3	5,350	118,300	90.0	128.0
Bayou Toro, Sabine	91	216.0	3,650	41,600	32.0	200.0
Bearhead, Calcasieu	103	80.0	7,170	74,000	79.9	60.0
Beckwith, Calcasieu	147	70.0	5,950	58,500	54.0	None
Beckwith, Beauregard	84	106.0	3,880	45,000	35.8	90.7
Big Creek, Grant	51	128.0	2,700	47,500	28.0	100.0
Big Creek, Tangipahoa	38	176.0	1,200	16,000	26.6	151.0
Black, Bossier	22	187.0	680	5,400	3.5	178.5
Black Bayou, Caddo*	231	183.0	3,960	17,750	23.0	None
Black Bayou, Caddo	231	190.5	7,100	57,500	68.0	None
Black Bayou, Ouachita	12	75.0	3,920	5,500	2.7	72.9
Black Lake, Red River, Natchitoches	630	137.5	21,200	277,500	239.0	110.0
Black Lake, No. 3, Red River, Natchitoches	535	140.0	8,250	84,900	89.3	131.1
Bogue Luna, Washington	49	183.0	2,620	49,000	22.8	160.0
Brown Creek, Rapides	13	111.0	775	10,700	10.8	97.5
Bundicks, Beauregard*	208	95.0	1,750	9,200	56.0	None
Bundicks, Beauregard	208	110.0	5,400	65,400	118.0	95.0
Caney, Jackson	42	200.0	4,970	79,600	27.0	172.0
Castor Creek, Rapides	25	96.0	2,550	26,000	29.0	None
Catahoula, Grant, LaSalle	2,672	34.0	27,000	133,000	752.0	None
Cedar Lake, Rapides	22	75.0	1,000	4,850	8.9	70.5
Cheniere Brake, Ouachita	140	81.0	6,050	94,000	61.6	60.5
Choudrant, Ouachita	142	102.0	3,430	39,500	43.5	80.0
Claiborne, Claiborne	133	185.0	6,400	100,000	62.0	165.0
Clement Creek, DeSoto	44	216.0	1,750	35,000	13.4	194.6
Cocodrie, Evangeline	240	75.0	19,500	285,000	210.0	55.0
Comite River, East Feliciana	88	219.2	5,700	106,500	82.5	168.0
Cotile, Rapides	41	105.6	1,775	25,000	20.9	88.5
Coulee Creek, Bienville, Jackson	12	180.0	1,330	20,600	6.0	169.0
Cypress Bayou, Bossier	149	177.0	2,690	17,000	8.5	169.5
Cypress, Bossier	149	197.0	7,330	118,500	51.0	174.0
Cypress, Caddo	65	201.1	4,300	61,000	34.0	188.0
Darling Creek, St. Helena	65	205.0	3,190	47,000	51.0	180.8
Dugdemona, Jackson	132	194.5	7,550	102,500	66.0	169.0
Dukedahl, Bienville, Jackson	18	192.5	1,340	17,600	8.8	178.5
Dukedahl-Coulee, Bienville, Jackson	30	183.0	2,250	32,800	15.8	170.0
Georgetown, Grant*	0.53	75.0	41	160	0.1	None
Goldonna, Natchitoches	280	140.5	12,500	160,000	115.0	111.0
Grand Bayou, Red River	334	146.0	5,100	66,000	40.0	122.0
Grand Cane, DeSoto	74	215.0	2,700	53,500	21.9	197.7
Halls & Berry Brake, Natchitoches	49*	135.0	6,075	49,500	30.0	121.0
Hays Creek, Washington	41	226.0	1,650	25,000	32.5	190.0
Hickory, Beauregard	111	48.2	2,250	20,000	30.7	24.0
Iatt Lake, Grant	243	93.0	12,500	126,500	70.0	80.0
Indian Creek, Rapides	23	90.0	3,150	30,000	18.0	79.0
Kepler Creek, Bienville*	46.5	176.5	1,925	16,800	20.0	None
Kiesche, Winn	57	125.0	1,870	20,600	20.0	110.0
Kisatchie, Natchitoches	278.0	130.0	5,800	65,000	60.0	110.0
Lake Bistineau, Bossier, Bienville	1,450	154.5	46,100	870,000	421.6	141.0
Lake Vernon, Vernon	112	243.0	4,250	27,000	88.0	None
Lawrence, Washington	44	207.9	2,030	28,000	34.8	181.9
Longleaf, Rapides	499	156.5	12,300	199,000	215.0	127.5
Longleaf, Rapides	499	164.5	16,100	300,000	270.0	127.5
Mansfield Cow Bayou, DeSoto	8	273.0	930	15,700	4.0	267.1
Mid Fk B. D'Arbonne, Claiborne	80	199.0	4,100	65,500	32.2	180.0
Nantachie, Grant	77	100.0	1,950	17,200	9.5	None
Nantachie, Grant	77	114.0	4,750	59,500	34.5	89.5
Natalbany, St. Helena	29	158.0	2,440	31,000	20.6	135.5
Rambin, DeSoto	31	172.0	2,650	50,000	13.0	140.0
Saline, Red River-Winn	232	140.0	1,730	12,000	22.0	None
Saline, Red River-Winn	232	150.0	3,950	40,000	62.0	130.0
Saline, Bienville	205	160.0	2,800	22,000	35.9	None
Saline, Bienville	164	190.0	7,450	96,400	52.0	170.0
Sandy Creek, East Feliciana	29	186.4	2,225	33,000	21.3	166.2
Sibley, Natchitoches*	40	115.0	2,175	19,500	8.3	None
Sibley, Natchitoches*	40	120.0	2,775	29,200	13.0	None
Silver Creek, Washington	93	226.0	3,500	68,000	77.0	199.2
Sizzile Creek, Allen	164	129.0	7,300	90,000	130.0	107.5
Smithport, DeSoto*	205	131.6	2,950	11,500	13.0	None
Smithport, DeSoto	205	147.0	7,900	92,000	48.2	131.0
Spring Creek, Rapides	67	116.7	2,240	40,000	56.8	91.5
Tchefuncte, Washington and Tangipahoa	25	189.8	1,220	18,000	19.6	172.0
Tenmile Creek, Allen	101	126.0	5,500	72,000	68.4	106.1
Thompson Creek, E. & W. Feliciana	77	186.0	3,900	92,900	72.5	144.0
Tickfaw, St. Helena	114	197.5	1,300	12,500	55.0	None
Turkey Creek, Catahoula	163	50.0	4,600	50,500	34.0	None
Twelvemile Creek, St. Helena	29	167.2	1,960	24,000	23.3	150.9
Upper Cypress No. 1, Bossier*	2.23	306.8	101	850	0.8	None
Upper Cypress No. 2, Bossier*	1.54	304.8	95	720	0.55	None
Valentine, Rapides	36	92.0	2,100	26,000	29.5	79.0
Winnfield, Winn	654	120.0	22,400	255,000	162.0	100.8
Winnfield, Winn	654	110.0	11,100	89,600	75.0	None

*Existing (Others are potential)

LOUISIANA ISLANDS

Total Islands	Acreage by Size				
	10-99 acres	100-499 acres	500-999 acres	1000 or more acres	Total Acreage
2,482	1,401	751	166	164	1,279,282

Acreage by Percent Developed			Acreage by Ownership and State				
Total Acreage	None-25	26-100	Total Acreage	Federal	State	Public	Private
141,255	141,255		1,213,186	4,965	107,260	1,800	1,099,161

LOUISIANA LAKES

Name	Map No.	Surface area (sq mi)	Name	Map No.	Surface area (sq mi)
Pontchartrain, Lake	210	621	Opelousas Bay	164	6.8
Toledo Bend Reservoir	49	284	Boudreaux, Lake	234	6.7
Maurepas, Lake	209	91	Eagle Lake	33	6.68
Sabine Lake	112	87	Vernon Lake	51	6.6
White Lake	153	81	Decade, Lake	222	6.5
Salvador, Lake	290	70	Raccourci Old River	203	6.5
Calcasieu Lake	119	67	Adams Bay	326	6.4
Grand Lake	189	64	Black Bayou Reservoir	18	6.2
Caddo Lake	19	51	Name unknown	292	6.2
Grand Lake	133	50	Arthur, Lake	152	6.0
Catahoula Lake	66	42	Lac aux Siene	88	5.23
Sabine Reservoir	114	41	Flat Lake	192	5.2
Six Mile Lake	191	30	Turkey Creek Lake	43	4.84
Rockefeller Refuge	145	28	Millers Lake	101	4.69
Bistineau, Lake	24	26.9	Name unknown	206	4.63
Lacassine Refuge	125	25	Smithport Lake	48	4.6
Fausse Point, Lake	175	24	False River	204	4.55
Bayou D'Arbonne, Lake	7	23.83	Honey Brake Lake	73	4.44
Lac Des Allemands	213	23	Sweetbay Lake	197	4.2
Verret, Lake	214	22	Anacoco Lake	52	4.06
Black Lake	47	20.17	Cheniere Brake	28	4.06
Little Lake	268	20.1	Wax Lake	199	3.9
Palourde, Lake	194	18	Mud Lake	118	3.85
Cataouatche, Lake	287	14.5	Collicon Lake	140	3.8
Wallace Lake	23	14.45	Misere, Lake	127	3.8
Saline Lake	46	14.0	Bruin Lake	40	3.66
Cross Lake	21	13.81	Petit Lac Des Allemands	263	3.6
Mechant, Lake	228	13.4	Name unknown	154	3.5
Iatt Lake	57	11.1	Black Lake	116	3.4
Claiborne, Lake	9	10	Larto Lake	75	3.4
Cocodrie Lake	95	9.53	Sibley Lake	53	3.40
St. Catherine, Lake	212	9.2	Bayou de la Bay	87	3.36
De Cade, Lake	233	7.6	St. John, Lake	76	3.31
Name unknown	195	7.4	Fields, Lake	264	3.3
Lery, Lake	345	6.85	Big Mar	297	3.18

LOUISIANA LAKES

Name	Map No.	Surface area (sq mi)	Name	Map No.	Surface area (sq mi)
Yucatan Lake	38	3.12	Black River Lake	82	1.78
Saline Lake	67	3.08	Charles, Lake	109	1.74
Kepler Lake	25	3.01	Bayou de Siard	29	1.72
Corney Lake	8	3.00	Shad Lake	74	1.67
Cotile Reservoir	58	2.8	Concordia, Lake	78	1.64
Sweet Lake	122	2.8	Big Constance Lake	148	1.6
Name unknown	83	2.77	Fearman Lake	161	1.6
Bundick Lake	93	2.73	Grassy Lake	193	1.6
Lower Mud Lake	124	2.7	Cocodrie Lake	81	1.54
Black Bayou Lake	30	2.57	Prien Lake	110	1.53
Chicot, Lake	98	2.54	Name unknown	286	1.5
Boeuf, Lake	262	2.5	Name unknown	312	1.5
Little Lake	211	2.5	Peigneur, Lake	174	1.5
Bob Taylors Pond	339	2.47	Name unknown	165	1.43
Nantachie Lake	56	2.47	Catfish Lake	130	1.36
Catfish Lake	272	2.4	Bay Charlie	246	1.3
Grand Lake	303	2.4	Bay Pomme d'Or	329	1.3
Bayou du Lac	89	2.30	Carrion Crow Lake	221	1.3
Dauterive Lake	172	2.3	Cuatro Caballo, Lake	307	1.3
Name unknown	123	2.3	Deep Lake	146	1.3
Bay Sansbois	319	2.2	Dog Lake	245	1.3
Mud Lake	230	2.2	Hermitage, Lake	315	1.3
Name unknown	150	2.2	Hospital Bay	333	1.3
Theriot, Lake	232	2.2	Long Lake	266	1.3
Washington, Lake	323	2.2	Name unknown	277	1.3
Cane River Lake	54	2.11	Penchant, Lake	226	1.3
Providence, Lake	3	1.92	Petit, Lake	304	1.3
Bay Jacques	336	1.9	Name unknown	105	1.26
Boeuf River Reservoir	32	1.9	Gassoway Lake	1	1.25
Hackberry Lake	244	1.9	Chicot, Lake	170	1.2
Spanish Lake	173	1.89	Laurier, Lake	316	1.2
St. Joseph, Lake	39	1.87	Name unknown	265	1.2
Round Lake	294	1.85	Name unknown	293	1.2
Marengo Bend	79	1.81	Yellow Cotton Bay	334	1.2
Laurier, Lake	281	1.8	Albemarle Crevasse	4	1.17

LOUISIANA LAKES

Name	Map No.	Surface area (sq mi)	Name	Map No.	Surface area (sq mi)
Bateman Lake	196	1.1	Amedee, Lake	348	1.0
Bay Denesse	331	1.1	Duck Lake	190	1.0
Bay Lanaux	321	1.1	Five, Lake	317	1.0
Scofield Bay	328	1.1	Hamilton Lake	198	1.0
Upper Mud Lake	131	1.1	Moss Lake	107	1.0
Willow Lake	120	1.1	Name unknown	158	1.0
Rodney Lake	41	1.04	Name unknown	343	1.0

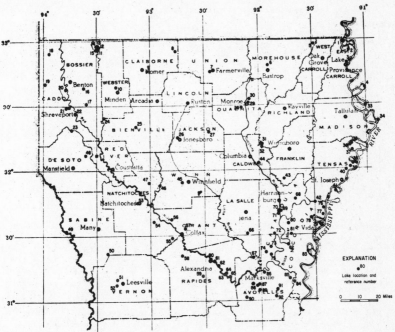

Location of lakes in northern Louisiana.

ARTIFICIAL RESERVOIRS

There are important distinctions between artificial reservoirs and natural lakes, although many reservoirs have the outward appearances of natural lakes. For one thing, reservoirs are so constructed that they contain very little dead storage; most of the water is above the level of the lowest outlet and can be released, if need be. On the other hand, almost all the water in natural lakes is dead storage, or below the level of the natural outlet. Bayou Bodcau with a surface area of 33 square miles is the largest artificial reservoir in Louisiana.

TOLEDO BEND LAKE

Toledo Bend Lake, sprawling 70 miles along the Louisiana-Texas border 17 miles northwest of Leesville and covering 186,000 acres, is the nation's fourth largest man-made lake. There are 1200 miles of shoreline.

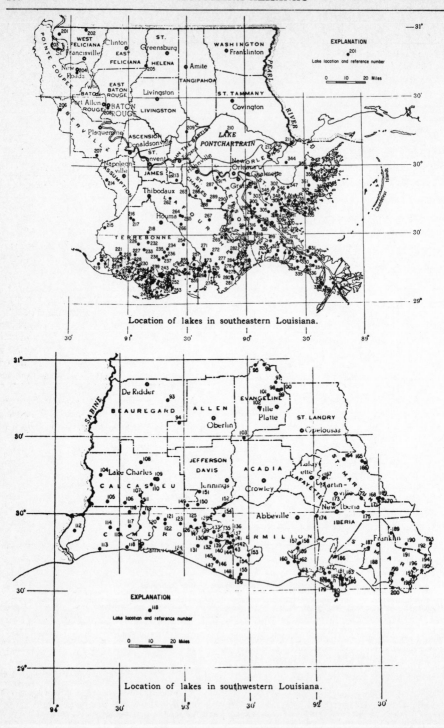

Location of lakes in southeastern Louisiana.

Location of lakes in southwestern Louisiana.

Water Area

Lakes, Bays & Ponds	3,173,366 Acres
Bayous & Passes	163,454 Acres
Canals & Channels	42,104 Acres
Total Water Areas	3,378,924 Acres

Water Volume

Lakes, Bays & Ponds	20,452,231 Acre-ft.
Bayous & Passes	2,338,521 Acre-ft.
Canals & Channels	349,744 Acre-ft.
Total Water Volume	23,140,496 Acre-ft.

Length of Bayous & Passes	7,227.4 Miles
Length of Canals & Channels	4,572.6 Miles
Length of Shoreline	30,511 Miles
Length of Coastline	390 Miles

Marsh Type	Acres
Fresh	1.0 million
Intermediate	.7 million
Brackish	1.3 million
Saline	1.0 million
Total acres of coastal marsh	4.0 million

Major vegetative species found in each marsh type are: fresh - *Panicum hemitomon, Sagittaria falcata, Eleocharis sp.*, and *Alternanthera philoxeroides*; intermediate - *Spartina patens, Phragmites communis* and *Sagittaria falcata*; brackish - *Spartina patens* and *Distichlis spicata*; saline - *Spartina alterniflora, Distichlis spicata* and *Juncus roemerianus*.

Offshore

Major problems in Louisiana's offshore area include weather chemical dumping and obstructions to navigation and shrimp trawling.

Another problem, primarily legal, related to the offshore areas is the location of the boundary between offshore and inshore waters. This boundary is not well defined along the central and eastern parts of the coast.

There are approximately 1,170 square miles of offshore waters (from the coastline to 3 miles offshore) under the jurisdiction of the State of Louisiana. Except for the area in the vicinity of the Mississippi River mouth, these offshore waters are shallow—less than 30 feet in depth.

The high productivity of these offshore waters in principally due to the nutrient rich waters of the fresh water rivers which empty into the Gulf.

FLOODED BOTTOMLAND HARDWOODS

While seasonally flooded bottomland hardwoods may not be considered by some as true wetlands, they are none-the-less extremely important to wintering waterfowl, fur animals, and also play a vital role in freshwater fish production. Flooding brings about additional benefits by stimulating growth and seed production of desirable mast producting hardwoods.

MARSH

There are approximately 4 million acres of coastal marshlands in Louisiana and approximately 1 million acres of swamps in south Louisiana. Most of this is fair to excellent furbearer and alligator habitat except saline marsh. The only species that tolerate very saline conditions are marsh raccoons and isolated populations of muskrat. One of the most productive segments of the coastal marsh is the brackish type which is subjected to the freshwater input and a mixing of brackish water from the Gulf. Historically high populations of muskrats have occurred throughout the marsh where these conditions are most prevalent, such as the fringe of Vermilion Bay, the marshes of Terrebonne, as well as the upper segments of marshes adjacent to Barataria Bay and interior marshes of St. Bernard Parish. In addition to these excellent producing marshes, the prairie marshes of southwest Louisiana and the Atchafalaya Basin produce high numbers of furbearers on an annual basis.

Saltwater

The saline marshes of Louisiana are relatively poor producers of furbearers and alligators with only limited occurrences of species mentioned earlier. Many acres of fresh and intermediate marshes have been changed along the Louisiana coast as a result of saltwater intrusion caused by manmade and natural change. As a result some excellent fur producing marshes have been eliminated.

Brackish and Intermediate

Considering all fish and wildlife resources combined, the brackish marshes are the most productive. The intermediate marsh is also very productive and usually is located on the upper fringe of the brackish marsh and varies in acreage depending upon the amount of fresh water input. The intermediate and brackish marshes support plant communities which are heavily utilized by furbearers and waterfowl. Outstanding among the most desired plants produced in this zone is three-cornered grass, millet, spike rush and a wide variety of other aquatic plants important to the furbearers as well as the waterfowl. With these marshes, a fair population of white-tailed deer also occur.

Fresh

The fresh marshes carry the highest population of the American alligator and also produce large quantities of nutria, raccoon, and mink. These marshes are being reduced in size in Louisiana due to the saltwater intrusion and interruption of fresh water flow into the marshes. This change has been occurring for the past 200 years as the highlands along the Mississippi River and all of the other bayous that flow into the marshes have been settled. Agricultural invasion in the form of sugar cane and rice fields, and cow pastures, and in recent years industrial development of and adjacent to the coastal marshes brought about by the petro-chemical industries have converted many marshlands and changed the edaphic conditions. The fresh marshes are very important for waterfowl, furbearers and white-tailed deer; and many of the natural ridges and levees which penetrate into the marsh interior provide good habitat for squirrels and rabbits.

Wildlife Resources

The diverse habitat types found in Louisiana produce an abundance of wildlife. These species are utilized in many ways, some by the trappers for the fur industry, some by sport hunters and still others by non-consumptive users, such as naturalists, students and thousands of people that simply enjoy watching wildlife, whatever kind. The latest available survey revealed that big game hunters spent an average of approximately 10 days hunting deer, while squirrel and rabbit hunters spent approximately 8 days hunting. Duck hunters each spent an average of 12.5 days in the field. Thus, the importance of these resources is apparent.

Game Species

MAMMALS

Deer

The deer population of the State is estimated to be 475,000 animals. The Department currently estimates the deer kill to be approximately 130,000 animals, taken by 190,000 licensed hunters. This figure does not include hunters under 16 or over 60 years of age.

Squirrel

The Louisiana squirrel population fluctuates from year to year depending on hardwood mast abundance for the previous year. Squirrels occur statewide wherever the timber is of the size and maturity to provide adequate food. However, the largest populations are expected to be found in any of the Delta type of hardwood areas. We estimate that about 30 percent of the population is harvested annually. The Department estimates that, approximately 3½ million squirrels are harvested annually by over 200,000 hunters.

Rabbits

Approximately 25 percent of our state rabbit population is harvested annually by the hunter. The latest kill survey, conducted for the 1985-86 season, indicated 1,500,000 were harvested by 150,000 hunters.

Black Bear

Louisiana's black bear population consists of remnant groups derived from native stock or re-introduced from outside the state during the 1960's. Bears are found in the Atchafalaya Basin, the Tensas River bottom in Madison and Tensas Parish, the Tunica Hills in West Feliciana Parish and in the coastal parishes of Iberia and St. Mary.

Other Mammals

Opossums and raccoons are hunted throughout the state in the wide variety of habitats in which these animals occur. Bobcat, gray fox, and red fox are listed as protected quadrupeds and cannot be taken by gun. However, they are prized species among fur trappers, and are also very popular with our state's houndsmen for "chase only" activities.

Furbearers and the Alligator

The Fur and Refuge Division of the Department is responsible for the management of furbearer species of wildlife in Louisiana. This includes all of the recognized furbearers indigenous to our state as well as the American alligator. Louisiana has for many years led the nation in the production of wild fur and averaged harvesting $11 million overall in fur annually during the 10 year period (1976-77 through 1985-86). The 1972 alligator season, conducted in Cameron Parish, was the first season following 10 years of closure. The open area was gradually expanded to a statewide harvest in 1981 and since then the average annual alligator harvest has been approximately 17,000 skins worth over $2 million (1981-1986). Approximately 90% of the total pelts harvested in Louisiana were taken from the coastal marshes; however, many species such as raccoon, opossum, fox and bobcat are important in upland habitat. In the coastal marshes, muskrat, nutria, raccoon, mink and otter comprise the bulk of the fur harvest. A breakdown by species and monetary value is presented in Table II on page 25.

Furbearers like game species of wildlife can be harvested annually on a sustained yield basis. This sustained yield concept also applies to the alligator with a much more closely regulated harvest. Muskrat and nutria numbers can be controlled with trapping and, thus, overpopulation and habitat damage avoided. With many furbearing species, the potential for outbreaks of density dependent diseases, such as distemper and rabies, can be reduced by maintaining optimum numbers of animals and thus, reducing contact and spread of contagious diseases.

While controlling population density, trapping also produces income to landowners and thus provides an incentive to maintain fur animal habitat. The Department annually establishes an open trapping season during the months of December, January and February. The alligator season is usually conducted during the month of September. Severance taxes, paid to the Department on fur and alligator skins shipped out of the state, help maintain accurate records on production. Furbearer and alligator population densities vary widely in the coastal marshes depending on marsh type and habitat quality. Upland furbearer population densities also vary with the quality of habitat.

In addition to having the responsibility of managing the statewide fur resources, the division also manages 500,000 acres of coastal marshes that are owned or managed by the Department and conducts vigorous trapping programs on these areas. These areas were originally obtained through donations and purchases for waterfowl refuges or wildlife management areas. Many of the management programs for waterfowl are also beneficial for furbearers. Adequate trapping of muskrat and nutria is essential because of their ability to destroy marsh by overutilization of vegetation. This happens when too many animals occupy a given area of land. If such damage goes unchecked it can add to the loss of coastal marsh from other causes. Some people oppose trapping and usually do not understand the need to manage wildlife.

Shellfish

Oysters: The Louisiana oyster industry, as is true of its counterpart along the Atlantic and Gulf coasts of the United States, relies almost totally on one species, *Crassostrea virginica* Gmelin. The American oyster has long been an important fishery resource in the state of Louisiana. Since 1880, attempts to record commercial oyster landings have been made by various state and federal agencies. The lowest catch was recorded in 1880 with a total of 1,189,000 pounds of meat. The 1984 oyster landings were a record catch amounting to 13,700,000 pounds. The oyster landings for 1986 amounted to 12,700,000 pounds of meat.

In Louisiana, the fisheries have developed to a large extent into a culture type industry. Cultivation in this instance means utilization of the environment to best produce a quality product. During the 1840's and 50's became apparent to Louisiana fishermen that oysters obtained from certain waters had a nicer configuration, were better tasting, larger, and consequently were in greater demand than oysters apparently of the same age but in other locations. These oysters became a delicacy and the demand soon out stripped the supply. To compensate for this, fishermen began moving small oysters into these choicer growing areas. At this point in time, the early fishermen had enough foresight to recommend legislation which would incorporate certain ground into private ownership (leased from the state), and the remaining natural reefs at the time were placed under state control. It is difficult to conceive of an oyster fisheries based solely on public grounds. Louisiana's oyster grounds have, from that period to the present, been divided into two regions; state controlled and those set aside to be leased to private individuals. Approximately 264,000 acres were under lease in July 1979 (Survey Section, Division of Oysters, Water Bottoms and Seafoods) which are dispersed throughout the estuarine system from the Mississippi/Louisiana line on the east to offshore Vermilion Bay on the western extremity. The state has under its jurisdiction approximately 690,000 acres within "redline" areas. Of this 690,000 acres, 16,453 are maintained within managerial sections referred to as "Seed Ground Reservations," and 6,737 acres are incorporated into a "Public Reef" located in Calcasieu Lake on the extreme western boundary of the state. "Seed Ground Reservations", generally entire bays, are spread out along the coast and are harvested on alternate years unless biological evidence indicates otherwise. Of the remaining 600,000 plus acres under state managerial supervision, only about 200,000 acres are fished annually for oysters.

The Department has a legislative responsibility to manage those areas under their control to provide a ready source of seed oysters (RS 56, Part VII, Subpart D, Section 456.) Commercial fishermen generally enter the "Oyster Seed Grounds" when they are open in September (by law the first Wednesday after Labor Day). Those commercial fishermen that are bedding (relocating oysters) are primarily interested in the small (1 to 3 inch) seed oysters which are approximately a year old. Depending on market conditions, oysters 3 inches and larger may be bedded, although in the majority of cases, commercial size oysters are culled for direct sale. The seed oysters will be moved onto private bedding grounds (leases), generally in more saline waters resulting in better growth, but at the same time increasing the incidence of mortality. These oysters generally remain on the bedding grounds 3 to 5 months or longer, depending on the commercial market. However, those oysters that remain in high salinity areas throughout the summer generally encounter high mortalities from oyster drill predation and fungus infection.

During the early days of the Louisiana oyster industry, around the time of the Civil War, seed oysters were gathered, transplanted and harvested by the bare hands of fishermen wading in waist-deep water. During the late 1880's tongs appeared as the tools used in oyster culture. Oyster tongs were constructed by hinging two rakelike tools with curved teeth that formed a basket. In 1905, the first pair of oyster dredges were installed and this is the predominant method used today. During the 1977-1978 harvesting season, the Department licensed 395 vessels for dredging. An average number of employees on a vessel consists of 3 people. In addition to those larger boats dredging, the Department manages Calcasieu Lake as public tonging reef, and during the same period licensed 1,152 to tong oysters in Calcasieu Lake.

Clams: The fact that Louisiana has large localized populations of the hard clam (*Mercenaria compochiensis*) has been known and documented for some years now. The hard clam industry is the largest commercial clam industry in the United States. Approximately 17,000 fishermen and 13,300 vessels are engaged in the industry and are producing clams in 16 states. Due to lack of a local market and the fact that few Louisianians eat clams, a commercial clam fisheries was never established. However, the clam industry on the Atlantic coast ran into supply problems in 1976 and thus it became economically feasible to harvest and ship Louisiana clams to the east coast market.

In 1977, a prominent Louisiana oyster corporation, the Pausina Oyster Corporation, obtained a permit to experimentally harvest clams in Louisiana. They explored the coastal waters for a fishable population, and, in addition, designed and developed gear to feasibly fish the clams present in Louisiana. As of the end of calendar year 1977, they had harvested approximately 10,000 bushels of clams. Since that period there has been no harvesting of *mercenaria* in Louisiana's waters. There has been some recent interest in developing a fisheries for the Marsh Clam *(Rangia Cuneata)* for consumption. However, there has been a problem with off taste to contend with.

Crustaceans

Shrimp: The important saltwater commercial species of Louisiana shrimp are: brown shrimp *(Penaeus aztecus),* white shrimp *(Penaeus setiferus),* and seabobs *(Xiphopenaeus kroyeri).* The white and brown shrimp are found in Louisiana's coastal marshes and estuaries the seabob is found primarily in the near offshore waters. Over the past 20 years annual harvest of the brown shrimp has been approximately 48 million pounds (heads on); annual harvest of white shrimp has been approximately 44 million pounds. Seabob catches are much smaller, averaging about 1.4 million pounds per year; however, seabobs do provide an important source of income at certain times of the year when catches of the other species decline. White and brown shrimp are found along the entire coast of Louisiana.

Crabs: The only crab currently of commercial importance in Louisiana is the blue crab, *Callinectes sapidus* Rathbun.

Approximately 7.3 million acres of coastal Louisiana marsh produce blue crabs. These may be divided into three types: 1) Salt marsh, 2) brackish marsh and 3) fresh marsh. Brackish marshes are probably the most abundant, followed by fresh.

These areas are productive because of high nutrient levels, slow tidal fluctuations, and large expanses of grasslands.

Serious problems presently existing are due primarily to manmade causes. The most serious is the cessation of fresh water intrusion, caused by leveeing of the major rivers in the guise of flood control. Compounding this factor is the dredging of the marsh for petroleum exploitation, navigation purposes or "flood control". This causes rapid deterioration of marshes because of salt water intrusion, erosion, and loss of productive grasslands.

Annual commercial harvest-varied from 288,000 pounds in 1880 to over 33 million pounds in 1986. Annual average landings during the last 40 years of approximately 16 million pounds.

This crustacean is found from fresh waters of the Atchafalaya Basin to offshore waters of Gulf of Mexico.

Most numerous in shallow, brackish estuarine areas.

LOUISIANA NATURAL HERITAGE PROGRAM

The Louisiana Natural Heritage Program (LNHP) was established in 1986 as a cooperative venture of the Louisiana Department of Natural Resources and the Nature Conservancy, a national nonprofit conservation organization dedicated to the identification and protection of ecologically significant natural lands. The goal of LNHP is the identification of Louisiana's significant natural areas through a statewide inventory of natural features, and to design a system to conserve the resources that represent the natural diversity of the state. The LNHP is the only comprehensive computerized ecological inventory of the state's outstanding natural communities and of rare, threatened, and endangered species' habitats.

Federally endangered or threatened species of vertebrates from Louisiana and adjacent waters.

Common	Scientific Name
Mammals	
Cougar	*Felis concolor corvi*
Manatee	*Trichechus manatus*
Seal, Caribbean monk	*Monachus tropicalis*
Whale, finback	*Balaenoptera physalus*
Whale, sei	*Balaenoptera boralis*
Whale, sperm	*Physeter macrocephalus*
Wolf, red	*Canis rufus*
Herps	
Alligator, American[1]	*Alligator mississippiensis*
Turtle, green sea	*Chelonia mydas*
Turtle, hawksbill sea	*Eretmochelys imbricata*
Turtle, Atlantic Ridley	*Lepidochelys kempi*
Turtle, leatherback sea	*Dermochelys coriacea*
Turtle, loggerhead	*Caretta caretta*
Birds	
Crane, Whooping	*Grus americana*
Curlew, Eskimo[2]	*Numenius borealis*
Eagle, Bald	*Haliaeetus leucocephalus*
Falcon, Peregrine	*Falco peregrinus*
Pelican, Brown	*Pelecanus occidentalis*
Plover, Piping	*Charadrius melodus*
Prairie-chicken, Greater[3]	*Tympanuchus cupido*
Stork, Wood	*Mycteria americana*
Tern, Least	*Sterna antillarium*
Warbler, Bachman's	*Vermivora bachmanii*
Woodpecker, Ivory-billed[2]	*Campephilus principalis*
Woodpecker, Red-cockaded	*Picoides borealis*

[1]threatened due to similarity of appearance
[2]possibly extinct
[3]extirpated from Louisiana

FISH

The waterways of the state, including the rivers, bayous, and the Gulf of Mexico, abound in fish of all sorts and are a great source of pleasure as well as income for professionals in any season.

With the exception of oil and gas, Louisiana's fisheries are its largest industry. The state's three principal species of shrimp produce 60 to 80 million pounds annually, oysters 10 to 15 million pounds annually and total production of all species is 700 million to 1 billion, 100 million pounds.

Fish Habitat

Disregarding cold water fisheries, Louisiana has the most diversified fisheries habitat in the nation. The varied type habitats include salty gulf waters, coastal estuarine areas that contain salt, brackish and fresh waters; and, the various freshwater lakes, farm ponds rivers and streams widely scattered throughout the state.

Each of these habitat types has characteristics and components that are peculiar to that particular ecosystem. These habitats are characterized by varying productivity and production potentials. Fisheries habitat must be viewed as being the primary consideration in the management and perpetuation of our rich fisheries resources.

Lakes

IMPOUNDMENTS

The total fish habitats in Louisiana comprises 2,907,364 acres of water areas. In addition there are 3,676,320 acres of marshlands which have excellent fish populations but these areas will be discussed under marsh habitat. Of this area, 245,000 acres are comprised of man-made impoundments, 46,756 acres are oxbow lakes, and 448,621 acres are backwater and/or natural lakes. Also of these water areas there are +40,300 miles of rivers, bayous, and creeks. The most prominent rivers in the state are the Mississippi, Atchafalaya, Red, Sabine, and Ouachita. Fish populations of the man-made impoundments consist primarily of largemouth bass, crappie, bream, catfishes, and usually low numbers of gar and buffalo fishes, carp, and freshwater drum with the primary forage fish being small bream, various minnows, gizzard, and threadfin shad. In the oxbow and backwater lakes, the fish population make-up is primarily the same as the man-made impoundments but support a greater population of all fishes, particularly buffalo fishes, catfishes, freshwater drum, carp and gar.

OXBOWS AND BACKWATER AREAS

As previously stated, the backwater and oxbow lakes support the highest poundage of fishes. This is due primarily to the basic fertility of the soil types in which these water bottoms are located. Most of the impoundments in the state are located in relatively infertile soil areas and therefore support lesser pounds per acre in fish. The major rivers or more sluggish bayous support higher populations of fish than the more upland streams due to the fertility of the flood plains in which they lie.

Extensive land clearings and increases in agricultural lands in the portion of the state where most of the oxbow and backwater lakes occur have caused great increases in turbidity in these lakes due to runoff from these denuded areas. This factor along with associated pesticides used on agricultural crops that find their way into these water bodies have caused substantial decreases in the fish populations in recent years. The losses brought about from these occurrences in many systems are irreversible. Another factor that has caused reduction in fish populations most in the state streams and bayous has been the channelization of these streams for improved drainage either for flood control or agriculture land drainage. This practice caused a reduction in fish populations by destroying the fishes cover. A major problem that exists with man-made impoundments is poor lake basin design and shallow infertile waters that have over the years produced excessive growths of aquatic vegetation. This vegetation not only causes fishermen access problems but also plays a major role in fish populations becoming out of balance.

Salt Water Fish

		Fresh Water Fish	
Speckled trout	Sail fish	Perch	Gars
Red fish	Bonita	Sunfish	Trout
Red snappers	Porpoise	Buffalo	Catfish
Sheepshead	Rays	Bass	Choupique
Flounder	Devilfish	Pike	Crayfish
Spanish mackerel	Alligator gar		
Bluefish	Bony gar		
Mullet	Portuguese		
Croakers	Man-of-War		
Drum	Sea horse		
Ling	Sea cat or Hardhead		
Blockfish	Dog fish		
White trout	Spade fish		
King mackerel	Shrimp		
Tarpon	Crabs—Oysters		
Yellow jack			

Fish Resources

Louisiana has an abundance of both fresh and saltwater resources and offers some of the finest year-round sports fishing and probably the most productive commercial fisheries in the United States. There are 3.2 million people and more than a third of these people fish. A Gallup poll recently indicated the fishing was the number three form of recreation in the nation.

Freshwater

SPORT FISHING

Finfish

The principal freshwater sport fishes include largemouth bass, spotted bass, crappie, bream (bluegill, redear, warmouth, etc.), white bass, catfishes, and the recently introduced striped bass. All of these fishes occur statewide. Most people prefer to catch largemouth bass but the greatest fishing pressure on freshwater species is exerted on crappie with bream second. Harvest rates of these fish are highly variable. Catch rates from man-made impoundments (i.e., Toledo Bend, D'Arbonne, Bistineau) vary from 0.4 pounds per hour to 1.2 pounds per hour, while the catch rate in backwater lakes (Spring Bayou, Sunk Lake, Grassy Lake) and oxbow lakes (Old River, False River, Lake Bruin) are somewhat higher due to increased fertility of these areas. The total pounds produced per acre depend upon the region of the state where the water body is located and the fertility of the surrounding lands. The most productive areas of the state are the backwater lakes. A study of seven such lakes by Lambou (1959) showed an average of 397 pounds of all species of fish per acre with sport fish comprising 103 pounds. The population of seven (7) Mississippi River oxbow lakes sampled by Lambou (1954 and 1955) averaged 202 pounds of fish per acre with game fish comprising 73 pounds per acre. Lambou (1959) in the study fish populations of Louisiana impoundments found an average of 73 total pounds of fish per acre.

Sport Crustaceans

Some sport fishing for crawfish is done in flooded fields managed for crawfish production. Crawfishing is an outdoor sport unique to Louisiana. Crawfish are found in swamps and marshes throughout the state with the best wild populations occurring in the overflow basins of the Atchafalaya, Red and Pearl Rivers. Crawfish are usually caught with baited traps or nets and provide recreation for thousands of Louisiana citizens. The average person in Louisiana participates in crawfishing 0.49 times during the summer months.

Sport Amphibians

Frogging is another sport enjoyed by many people in Louisiana. Bullfrogs are found near water throughout the state. By law these amphibians must be caught with "frog grabs" or by hand and a headlight is usually used. There is no estimate available as to numbers harvested or the pounds per acre averaged.

Saltwater

SPORT FISH

Louisiana historically has been a major saltwater sportfishing state because of its proximity to the Gulf of Mexico. However, interest in saltwater sportfishing increased tremendously with the advent of offshore oil production and improved boats and motors. This was brought about because many saltwater sport fish concentrated in these "so-called" artificial reefs. The principal offshore saltwater species include bonita, cobia, bluefish, dolphin, jackfish, pompano, marlin, sailfish, tuna, wahoo, barracuda, snapper, mackerel, grouper, and even sharks. Speckled trout, redfish, and flounder are caught primarily in the more brackish coastal lakes bays and near offshore waters. Billfish fishing off the Louisiana coast occurs near the continental shelf and beyond in the deeper Gulf. In recent years this type activity has increased with the discovery of the Destin Rip beginning near the mouth of the Mississippi River. There are no estimates available on harvest rates in pounds per acre of these fish because of the difficulty in sampling and obtaining these data.

Approximately 25,000 saltwater sportfishermen participate in sport shrimping. The actual number in pounds harvested are not available since these people take shrimp for home consumption. Practically all of this sport shrimp occurs during the inside (waters) shrimping season. These people are allowed to catch 100 pounds of shrimp per day. Also, several saltwater sportfishermen participate in sport oystering. Two sacks of oysters can be taken per boat per day during open season from the public grounds by tonging.

BIRDS

Louisiana has an unusually wide variety of birds at almost any season of the year, due in part to the semi-tropical temperature climate, and also to its geographical position. Most of the transitory birds of the Mississippi Valley that migrate to the tropics are to be seen in the state at certain times of the year. Other birds, such as the ducks and geese, spend the entire year, others stay throughout the summer. Thus, the birds found in Louisiana may be grouped under four general headings:

Transistory—Those birds passing through the state at various seasons of the year:

American redstart
Blackburnian warbler
Bobolink
Pectoral sandpiper
Rose-breasted grosbeck
Scarlet tanager

Migratory—Summer—Those birds found in Louisiana during the summer, migrating usually from Central and South America:

Avocet
Black-necked stilt
Catbird
Chimney swift
Crested flycatcher
Green heron
Kingbird
Man-O'-War bird
Nighthawk
Orchard Oriole
Prothonotary Warbler
Purple martin
Roseate Spoonbill
Ruby-throated hummingbird
Snowy egret
Warbling vireo
White ibis
Wood stork
Yellow-billed tropic bird

Migratory—Winter—Those birds found in Louisiana during the winter, migrating from the north:

American bittern	Hermit thrush
American pipit	Horned grebe
Blue heron	Hudsonian
Brown creeper	curlew
Cedar waxwing	Jacksnipe
Coot	King rail
Crane	Woodcock
Double-crested	Merganser
cormorant	Marsh wren
Dewitcher	Osprey
Duck hawk	Palm warbler
Duck—baldpate	Robin
canvasback	Sandpiper
mallard	Short-billed
pintail	wren
ring-necked	Song sparrow
ruddy duck	Sopsucker
scaup	Swan
shoveller	Whooping crane
teal	Willit
Geese—blue goose	Winter wren
snow goose	

Permanent Residents—Those that live in the state and nest here:

Bald eagle	La. prairie
Black skimmer	chicken
Bluebird	La. water thrush
Bob white	Mockingbird
Boat-tailed	Oyster catchers
Grackle	Red-winged
Brown Pelican	blackbird
Brown thrasher	Owl
Carolina wren	Screech owl
Caspian tern	Southern blue
Chickadee	jay
Clapper rail	Southern red-
Crow	shouldered
Cooper hawk	hawk
Cowbird	Swallow-tailed
Killdeer	kite
Kingfisher	Turkey vultures
Laughing gull	Wild turkey
La. cardinal	Woodpecker
Purple gallinule	Yellow throat
La. heron	

BIRDS

Quail

The statewide bobwhite quail population may fluctuate annually due primarily to climatic conditions, which in turn affect quail reproduction and food production. The 1985-1986 harvest survey revealed that 400,000 quail were harvested by 29,000 hunters. Quail are found throughout the State with the exception of the marsh. The highest population, as far as accessibility to the hunter is concerned, is found in the longleaf pine region of Central and West Louisiana. Populations in other parts of the state may be as high as those in the longleaf pine region but accessibility to the hunter is poor.

Turkey

The Department is continuing its program to stock all suitable turkey habitat with turkey. This has been a very successful endeavor. It was estimated that approximately 6,500 birds were harvested in 1986. The highest populations are found in those areas where an open hunting season is allowed for the 1986 spring gobbler season. Those areas are all of Madison and Tensas Parishes, and part of Franklin Parish. Part or all of the Parishes of Vernon, Natchitoches, Grant, Winn, Bienville, Jackson, Union, Lincoln, Red River and Rapides; part or all of the Parishes of St. Helena, Washington, Livingston, East Baton Rouge, St. Tammany and Tangipahoa; part of Pointe Coupee; eastern part of East Carroll Parish; and parts of Assumption, Iberia and Iberville Parishes.

Doves

Doves occur statewide as resident nesters and as winter migrants. During the 1985-86 dove season, according to the Department survey, there were 2,000,000 birds harvested by 100,000 hunters.

Waterfowl

Louisiana is an important wintering area for North America's ducks and geese. Every fall, waterfowl migrate from the Canadian nesting grounds down the Mississippi Flyway to Louisiana. Many migrants continue their journey to South America, while millions of birds spend the winter in our agricultural areas, swamps, and coastal marshes. An aerial waterfowl survey conducted in January 1987 indicated 2,548,000 ducks and 283,000 coots utilizing the Coastal Zone and Catahoula Lake.

Waterfowl are an economically important natural resource to the people of Louisiana. Millions of dollars are generated into the economy through waterfowl related activities. Duck hunting is one of the most significant sporting activities in the state. In 1985-1986, 96,109 adult hunters harvested 1,215,392 ducks, and each adult hunter bagged an average of 12.02 ducks during the season.

Goose hunting is another popular sporting activity in Louisiana. The majority of hunting occurs in agricultural areas of northeast and southwest Louisiana. In 1985-1986, goose hunters harvested 92,207 birds. Each adult hunter spent an average of 7.95 days afield, with an average seasonal harvest of 1.03 birds.

Waterfowl bird watching is another economically important activity persued in coastal Louisiana. State refuge lands provide excellent opportunities for the viewing of waterfowl and other wetland species.

Most waterfowl species migrate to Louisiana during the fall and winter months. Two resident species found in the state year round are the mottled duck and woodduck. The mottled duck utilizes southern agricultural areas and coastal marshes, while the woodduck is found predominantly in wooded lakes, bayous, and sloughs.

The fulvous tree duck (Mexican squeeler) is another migrant found in Louisiana. This species nests in the rice fields of southwest Louisiana beginning in mid-July then leaves and winters in south Texas and Mexico.

The Louisiana Department of Wildlife and Fisheries is charged with the responsibility of managing, regulating, and perpetuating waterfowl resources in Louisiana, and state operated refuges provide 500,000 acres of waterfowl habitat. These areas will become increasingly important to waterfowl in the future, since many coastal marshes are deteriorating at a rapid rate due to both man-made and natural causes. Wise use and management of our remaining wetlands will ensure the well-being of our waterfowl resources.

Woodcock

The 1985-86 woodcock harvest was estimated by the Department at 263,000 birds taken by 34,000 hunters. Woodcock reach their peak numbers during the months of December, January and February. The total number of birds that visit the state are not known but research conducted on the bird shows that approximately 80 percent of the continental woodcock population migrates into Louisiana. Birds are prevalent in the bottomland forest and along streams and creek bottoms in the uplands. Other game birds occurring in the State and sought by some hunters are rail, snipe and gallinules.

ROCKEFELLER WILDLIFE REFUGE

Rockefeller Wildlife is located in the coastal marshes of southwestern Louisiana in Cameron and Vermilion parishes. It encompasses 84,000 acres and is owned and operated by the Louisiana Department of Wildlife and Fisheries. The refuge plays host to hundreds of thousands of ducks, geese, coots, and numerous wading birds each year. It also serves as a resting area for many of the transient birds that winter in Central and South America. The refuge is also a very important fisheries nursery area.

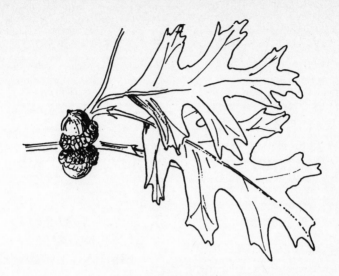

1987-88
WILDLIFE MANAGEMENT
AREA REGULATIONS

GENERAL

The following rules and regulations concerning the management, protection and harvest of wildlife have been officially approved and adopted by the Louisiana Wildlife and Fisheries Commission in accordance with the authority provided in Louisiana Revised Statutes of 1950, Section 109 of Title 56. Failure to comply with these regulations will subject individual to citation and/or expulsion from the management area.

Wildlife management area seasons can be altered or closed anytime by the Department in emergency situations (floods, fire or other critical circumstances).

Lands within WMA boundaries will have same seasons and regulations as the management area with which they are associated.

Dumping garbage or trash on WMAs except in designated locations is prohibited.

Disorderly conduct or hunting under influence of alcoholic beverages, chemicals and other similar substances is prohibited.

Deer seasons are for legal buck deer unless otherwise specified.

Requests for WMA maps may be directed to any district office: P.O. Box 915, Minden, 71055, Phone (318) 377-3575; P.O. Box 4004, Monroe, 71211, Phone (318) 343-4044; P.O. Box 278, Tioga, 71477, Phone (318) 487-5885; P.O. Box 426, Ferriday, 71334, Phone (318) 757-4571; 1213 North Lakeshore Drive, Lake Charles, 70601, Phone (318) 491-2575; P.O. Box 585, Opelousas, 70571-0585, Phone (318) 942-7553; P.O. Box 15570, Baton Rouge, 70895, Phone (504) 342-5875; or 400 Royal Street, New Orleans, 70130, Phone (504) 568-5615.

PERMITS

DAILY: When required, may be obtained at the permit stations on or near each WMA. Hunters must check out daily one-half hour after the end of legal shooting time.

SEASON: Basic resident and non-resident hunting licenses serve as season permits on WMAs when required, EXCEPT additional permits required on Fort Polk and Peason Ridge WMAs. Persons under 16 and those 60 or over need no season permits EXCEPT on Peason Ridge WMA and Fort Polk WMA. When permits are required, hunters may enter an area one (1) hour before legal shooting time and must be off the area one-half (½) hour after legal shooting time EXCEPT when daily permits are required and otherwise specified. Archery license required for all bow hunters over 16 and under 60 years of age.

SPECIAL SEASON: For handicapped hunters only, Dec. 5-6. Sherburne WMA shall be open exclusively to handicapped persons who have applied for and received in advance the necessary permits from any District office.

TRAPPING: Permits to take furbearers from WMAs may be obtained at district offices. Other special trapping exceptions are listed under respective WMA season schedules. Unless otherwise noted, WMA trapping seasons are the same as outside seasons. All traps must be run daily. Traps with teeth are illegal. Each trapper must submit an annual trapping report to the district office where his permit was obtained. Non-compliance will result in forfeiture of trapping privileges on the WMAs. Permits may be obtained only between hours of 8:00 am-4:30 pm on normal working days at district offices.

RACCOON HUNTING: NIGHTTIME EXPERIMENTAL-Raccoon hunters with dogs must submit an annual report of their kill to the district office where their permit was obtained. Non-compliance will result in forfeiture of hunting privileges on WMAs. A licensed hunter may take raccoon or opossum, one per person, during daylight hours only, during the open squirrel season on WMAs. Raccoon bag limit one per person per night for raccoon hunters during "take season" with dogs on WMAs EXCEPT no limit on Ouachita and Russell Sage (EXPERIMENTAL). Permits are required and may be obtained at district offices only between hours of 8:00 am-4:30 pm on normal working days.

COMMERCIAL FISHING: Permits are required of all commercial fishermen using Grassy Lake, Pearl River, Pomme de Terre and Spring Bayou WMAs. Drag seines (except minnow and bait seines) are prohibited EXCEPT experimental bait seines permitted on Saline WMA north of La. 28 in diversion canal. Commercial fishing is prohibited during regular waterfowl season on Grand Bay, Silver Lake and Lower Sunk Lake on Three Rivers WMA. Commercial fishing is prohibited on Salvador and Pointe-Au-Chien Wildlife Management Areas. EXCEPT shrimping allowed on Pointe-Au-Chien only in Cut Off Canal during daytime and nighttime. Trawling allowed in Wonder Lake during daytime only. Non-compliance with permit regulations will result in revocation of commercial fishing privileges.

SPORT-FISHING: Sport fishing, crawfishing and frogging are permitted on WMAs when in compliance with current laws and regulations EXCEPT nighttime frogging prohibited on Salvador and Pointe-Au-Chien.

FIREARMS

Firearms having live ammunition in the chamber, magazine, cylinder or clip when attached to firearms, are not allowed in or on vehicles including boats, motorcycles, ATVs and ATCs on WMAs. Firearms may not be carried on any area before or after permitted hours except in authorized camping areas.

Firearms, bows and arrows are not permitted on WMAs during closed seasons EXCEPT on designated shooting ranges. Bows and broadhead arrows are not permitted on WMAs EXCEPT during regular archery season or EXCEPT as permitted for bowfishing.

Encased or broken down firearms and any game harvested may be transported through the areas by the most direct route provided that no other route exists (see respective WMA season schedule for specific regulations).

Loaded firearms are not permitted near WMA check stations.

Rifles and handguns larger than .22 caliber rimfire, shotgun slugs or shot larger than BB cannot be carried onto any WMA EXCEPT during deer season.

Target shooting and other forms of practice shooting are prohibited on WMAs EXCEPT as otherwise specified.

Discharging of firearms on or hunting from improved roads or their rights-of-way is prohibited.

METHODS OF TAKING GAME

Organized drivers and standers making use of noises or noisemaking devices are not permitted on WMAs.

Baiting is prohibited on all WMAs (hogs included). Unmarked hogs may be taken on certain WMAs only during prescribed seasons and only with guns or bow and arrow legal for specified seasons in progress. Proper licenses and permits are required for hunting the game species for which the area is open at the time.

Hunters who kill deer on WMAs where daily permits are required must have deer checked at the check station on same day of kill.

Deer hunting on WMAs is restricted to still hunting only. No WMA will be open for deer during early still hunt season unless specified in the regulation pamphlet.

Construction of and hunting from permanent tree stands or permanent blinds on WMAs is prohibited.

Tree climbing spurs are also prohibited. Any permanent stand or permanent blind will be destroyed.

A permanent blind or stand is defined as any structure and/or material, including vegetation, used for concealment while hunting, that is not completely dismantled or removed from the wildlife management area daily.

All waterfowl hunters must dismantle blind and remove decoys within 30 minutes after close of shooting hours on each respective area. Unattended decoys will be confiscated and forfeited to the Department of Wildlife and Fisheries and disposed of by the Department. This action is necessary to prevent preemption of hunting space.

Hunters shall not hunt, take or pursue game birds or animals from moving vehicles on any WMA.

Spotlighting (shining) from vehicles, is prohibited on all WMA's. (NEW)

The use of horses and mules is prohibited for hunting or trapping on WMAs, EXCEPT for quail hunting or EXCEPT as otherwise specified.

All hunters EXCEPT waterfowl hunters (including archers and small game hunters) on WMAs must display 400 square inches of "Hunter Orange" during open gun season for deer. ALSO all non-hunters afield during hunting seasons are encouraged to display "Hunter Orange".

ARCHERY SEASON FOR DEER: Still hunting only. The entire archery season is open to either-sex deer EXCEPT as otherwise specified on individual WMAs. Archery seasons, restricted on Pointe-Au-Chien and Salvador WMAs, and closed on WMAs when special seasons for handicapped hunters are in progress.

Either-sex deer may be taken on WMAs at any time during archery season EXCEPT when bucks only seasons are in progress on the respective WMAs. Archers must abide by bucks only regulations and other restrictions when such seasons are in progress.

MUZZLELOADER SEASON FOR DEER: December 5-6 on Alexander Forest, Fort Polk, Georgia Pacific, Grassy Lake, Pearl River and Spring Bayou. December 12-13 on Alexander Forest, Attakapas, Fort Polk, Loggy Bayou, Pearl River, Russell Sage and West Bay. All muzzleloader seasons on WMAs are either sex, season permit. Legal muzzleloader firearms are single barrel rifles; .44 caliber minimum, or shotguns 10 gauge or smaller, either of which must load exclusively from the muzzle, use black powder or approved substitute only, take single ball or slug only, have exposed percussion caps or flintlock, and be fitted only with iron sights.

CAMPING

Camping on WMAs, including trailers, houseboats, recreation vehicles and tents is permitted only in designated areas and for a period not to exceed sixteen (16) consecutive days. Camping area use limited exclusively to outdoor recreational activities.

Houseboats are prohibited from overnight mooring within WMAs EXCEPT on streambanks adjacent to Department-owned boat launching ramps and/or designated camping areas.

On Atchafalaya Delta WMA and Pass-a-Loutre WMA, camp boats may be moored in specially designated areas throughout the waterfowl season. At all other times of the year mooring period limited to a period not to exceed sixteen (16) consecutive days. Permits are required for overnight mooring of houseboats on Pass-a-Loutre and Atchafalaya Delta Wildlife Management Areas. Permits may be obtained from headquarters on respective WMAs.

No refuse or garbage may be dumped from these boats while vessel is within the WMA boundary.

Firearms may not be kept loaded or discharged in a camping area.

Campsites must be cleaned by occupants prior to leaving and all refuse placed in designated locations.

Non-compliance with camping regulations will subject occupant to immediate expulsion and/or citation.

Damage to or removal of trees, shrubs and wild plants on WMAs without prior approval is prohibited.

Swimming prohibited within 100 yards of boat launching ramps.

DOGS

EXCEPT for bird hunting, duck hunting, nighttime experimental raccoon hunting, squirrel and rabbit hunting, when allowed, having or using dogs on any WMA is prohibited. Only recognizable breeds of bird dogs and retrievers are permitted for quail and migratory bird hunting. Only beagle hounds which do not exceed 15 inches at the front shoulders and which have recognizable characteristics of the breed may be used on WMAs having experimental rabbit seasons.

VEHICLES

Vehicles with a wheel-tire combination having a radius of 17 inches or more from the center of the hub (measured horizontal to the ground), are prohibited on specified WMAs.

Tractor or implement tires with farm tread designs R1, R2, and R4 known commonly as spade or lug grip types are prohibited on all vehicles. (NEW).

Airboats, aircraft and hover craft are prohibited on all WMAs.

Driving or parking vehicles on food or cover plots and strips is prohibited.

Motorized vehicles including ATVs, ATCs and motorcycles are restricted entirely to designated roads and trails as shown on WMA maps which are available at all District Offices. (See page 15 for addresses).

ATVs, ATCs and motorcycles cannot be left overnight on WMAs EXCEPT on designated camping areas.

1987-88
HUNTING AND SPORT FISHING LICENSES

MANDATORY HUNTER SAFETY TRAINING

All persons born on or after September 1, 1969 must show proof of satisfactorily completing a Hunter Safety course approved by the Department of Wildlife and Fisheries in order to purchase a Basic Hunting License.

GENERAL

HUNTING: 1987-88 SEASON

1. Basic Resident Fishing and Hunting License Expires June 30, 1988 .... $16.00
2. Resident (All person ages 16-59 inclusive).
   a. Basic Season (Excluding Big Game) 10.50
   b. Big Game (Required of all Bear, Deer and Turkey Hunters in addition to basic license)................................ 10.50
   c. Archery License....................................... 10.50
   d. Combination: Hunting and Big Game 21.00
   e. Combination: Basic Hunting, Big Game, Basic Fishing and Saltwater Fishing 32.00
3. Non-Resident
   a. Basic Season (Excluding Big Game) 75.50
   b. (3-day) 40.50
   c. Big Game (Required of all Bear, Deer and Turkey Hunters in addition to basic license)................................ 40.50
   d. Archery License....................................... 10.50
   e. Non-Resident Migratory Game Bird - 3 day trip 25.00

Commercial Hunting Preserve (Pen raised birds only) (Expires June 30) 200.00

Game Breeder (Expires December 31)
Raising and selling wild game birds and/or wild game quadrupeds... 25.00

FISHING

1. Universal Fishing License (Cane pole/hook and line license)..... 2.50 Expires June 30, 1988
2. Resident Basic Fishing License Expires June 30, 1988 .... 5.50
3. Non-Resident Basic Fishing License Expires June 30, 1988 ...... 15.50
4. Non-Resident, seven consecutive days..................... 10.50
5. Resident Saltwater Angler's License (Required in addition to basic license) Expires June 30, 1988............................ 5.50
6. Non-Resident Season Saltwater Angler's License (Required in addition to basic license) Expires June 30, 1988.................. 25.50
7. Non-Resident 7-Day Trip Saltwater Angler's License (Required in addition to basic seven day trip license) Expires June 30, 1988 .... 15.50

Additionally sport fishermen using the gear listed below must in addition to their basic fishing license purchase the applicable gear fee.

1. Crab Traps - Limited to 10 traps
   Resident - $1.00 per trap up to $10.00 .... 10.00
   Non-Resident 20.00
2. Gill Nets - Limited to 150 feet maximum
   Resident... 25.00
   Non-Resident 50.00
3. Hoop Nets - Limited to Five nets maximum
   Resident... 20.00
   Non-Resident 40.00
4. Slat Traps - Limited to Five traps maximum
   Resident... 20.00
   Non-Resident 40.00
5. Trammel Nets - Limited to 150 Feet maximum
   Resident... 25.00
   Non-Resident 50.00

6. Seines - Limited to 150 Feet maximum
   Resident... 25.00
   Non-Resident 50.00
7. Trawls - Up to 16 Feet
   Resident... 25.00
   Non-Resident 50.00
   Above 16 feet to 25 feet (Valid until 5-01-88)
   Resident... 40.00
   Non-Resident.. 80.00

8. Oyster Tong - Per Tong
   Resident... 5.00
   Non-Resident 10.00

Exception and Exemption—Hunting and Fishing License fees:
1. Texas, Arkansas, Mississippi, Alabama and Florida reciprocal agreement. Residents of these five states pay the same fee to hunt and fish in Louisiana that Louisiana residents pay to hunt and fish in Texas, Arkansas, Mississippi, Alabama and Florida.
2. Residents and non-residents under sixteen years of age and residents sixty years of age and older who have resided within the state for two years prior to application, shall not be required to obtain licenses, permits or pay fees to fish and hunt. PROOF OF AGE MUST BE CARRIED ON PERSON.
3. All hunters born on or after September 1, 1969 are required to complete a firearm and hunter education course prior to receiving a hunting license.
4. Person in the Armed forces of the United States, on active military duty, shall for license purposes be allowed to purchase and use resident licenses.

5. Veterans having a permanent service connected disability classification of fifty percent or more and who are Louisiana residents or resident persons who are blind, paraplegic, or multiple amputees shall upon identification, and proof of disability satisfactorily to the department, be issued licenses without the payment of any fees thereof.

Hunting Permits—Jean Lafitte National Historical Park

Beginning on October 9, 1987, the Barataria Unit of Jean Lafitte National Historical Park instituted a hunting permit system. The permits are free and are issued on a daily basis at the Barataria Unit Maintenance Area on LA 45 from 1:30 p.m. until 10:00 p.m., and at the Bayou Segnette State Park boat launch from 2:30 p.m. until 11:00 p.m. Hunters can obtain permits either for a same-day hunt or for the next day only. Hunters will be required to present proof of identity upon application, and to surrender their valid state license which will be returned at the end of the hunt. Hunting in the Barataria Unit will be conducted in accordance with applicable state and federal regulations, including the steel shot regulations in force across Louisiana.

ACT 295 of the 1984 Louisiana Legislature requires that all recreational anglers fishing south of the officially established "Saltwater Line" for saltwater species (see maps below) have in their possession a Louisiana Saltwater Fishing License IN ADDITION TO a regular Louisiana Fishing License EXCEPT that those persons exempted from purchasing a regular Louisiana Fishing License are also exempted from purchasing a Louisiana Saltwater Fishing License.

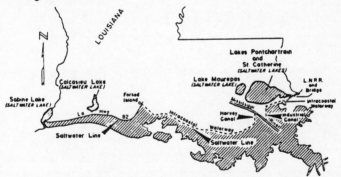

LOUISIANA SALTWATER LINE DEFINITION:

Title 56, Section 322-Louisiana Highway 82 from the Texas-Louisiana boundary to its junction with the Intracoastal Waterway at Forked Island, the Intracoastal Waterway from Forked Island to Bayou Barataria to the Harvey Canal, the Harvey Canal to the Mississippi River, the Mississippi River to the Industrial Canal, the Industrial Canal to the Intracoastal Waterway, the Intracoastal Waterway to the Rigolets to the Louisville & Nashville Railroad bridge, the Louisville & Nashville railroad right of way to the Mississippi state line.

The areas south of the above described line, plus saltwater lakes known as Sabine Lake, Calcasieu Lake, including Calcasieu Ship Channel, Lake Maurepas, Lake Pontchartrain, Lake St. Catherine, shall be designated as saltwater areas.

SALTWATER FISHING LICENSES EFFECTIVE JULY 1, 1984

Alligator Harvest in Louisiana, 1972-1986

Year	Hunters	Tags Issued	No. Taken	Success (%)	Avg. t.l. (ft)	Value of skins	Avg./foot	Acres Hunted	Approx. Amount Meat Sold (lbs)	Approx. Value of Meat
1972	59	1,961	1,350	68.8	6'11'	$ 75,505	$ 8.10	274,700		
1973	107	3,243	2,921	90.1	7'0'	$ 268,994	$13.13	534,600		
1975	191	4,645	4,420	95.2	7'5'	$ 258,791	$ 7.88	812,700		
1976	198	4,767	4,389	92.1	7'1'	$ 512,240	$16.55	807,500		
1977	236	5,760	5,474	95.0	7'4'	$ 488,499	$12.23	976,900		
1979	708	17,516	16,300	93.0	7'0'	$1,711,500	$15.00	2,585,600	100,000 (bone-in)	$ 125,000
1980	796	19,134	17,692	92.5	6'8'	$1,609,972	$13.00	3,243,100	100,000 (bone-in)	$ 125,000
1981	913	15,534	14,870	95.7	6'11'	$1,821,575	$17.50	3,494,800	100,000 (bone-in)	$ 125,000
1982	1,184	18,188	17,142	94.2	6'10'	$1,621,633	$13.50	3,993,600	100,000 (bone-in)	$ 125,000
1983	945	17,130	16,154	94.3	6'11'	$1,452,568	$13.00	3,498,700	100,000 (bone-in)	$ 125,000
1984	1,104	18,386	17,389	94.6	7'0'	$2,556,183	$21.00	3,526,400	100,000 (bone-in)	$ 125,000
1985	1,076	17,466	16,691	95.6	7'1'	$2,482,619	$21.00	3,494,600	150,000 (deboned)	$ 675,000
1986*	1,207	20,267	19,500	96.0	7'0'	$3,139,500	$23.00	3,500,000	250,000 (deboned)	$1,125,000

*Approximate as of 29 January 1987

ENVIRONMENTAL MANAGEMENT

The management and control of aquatic vegetation is an extremely important part
of the manipulation of Louisiana's aquatic ecosystem. Control of acquatic vegetation
is essential to the maintenance and enhancement of fish management and to the
utilization of the state's fish and wildlife resources. Benefits of the control program
include improved navigation of waterways, agricultural and flood control drainage, and
assured public access to waterways used for recreational purposes.

The water hyacinth is the most serious aquatic pest plant in Louisiana. It is estimated that the water hyacinth control program maintains 3,059,366 acres of wetlands
and open water areas, free of hyacinth infestation. The Louisiana Department of Wildlife and Fisheries controls this problem plant with the application of approved herbi-
cides and with biological agents, such as hyacinth weevils and plant pathogens. These
agents have been extensively tested prior to release and will not harm any desirable
plants in Louisiana.

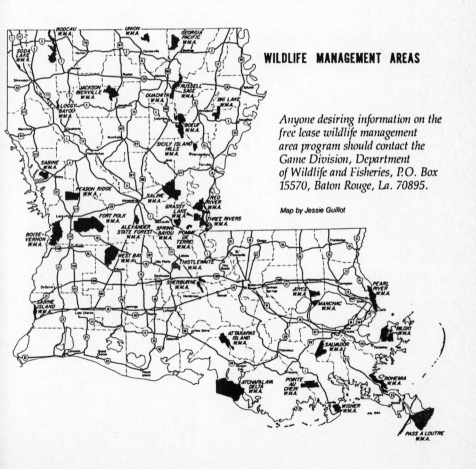

WILDLIFE MANAGEMENT AREAS

*Anyone desiring information on the
free lease wildlife management
area program should contact the
Game Division, Department
of Wildlife and Fisheries, P.O. Box
15570, Baton Rouge, La. 70895.*

Map by Jessie Guillot

LAND OWNED OR LEASED BY LOUISIANA DEPARTMENT OF WILDLIFE & FISHERIES FOR PUBLIC USE — WILDLIFE MANAGEMENT AREAS

Name of Area	Acreage	Location	Deer	Squirrel	Rabbit	Turkey	Waterfowl	Quail	Doves	Woodcock	Snipe	Bass	Bream	Crappie	Catfish	Buffalo	Gaspergou	Salt Water Species	Camping Area	Boat Ramps
			Hunting									Fishing — Sport			Fishing — Commercial					
Alexander Forest	7,875	Rapides Parish, 10 miles south of Alexandria, off U.S. Highway 167, and one mile east of Woodworth	X	X	X		X	X	X	X		X	X	X	X				X	X
Atchafalaya Delta	126,375	St. Mary Parish - Atchafalaya Bay — 18 miles S.W. of Morgan City		X	X		X			X	X	X	X	X	X	X		X	X	
Attakapas	25,500	St. Mary, St. Martin, and Iberia Parishes, 20 miles N.W. of Morgan City	X	X	X		X					X	X	X	X	X	X		X	
Big Lake	14,711	Franklin, Madison, and Tensas Parishes, 12 miles east of Gilbert, Highways 4 and 710.	X	X	X	X	X		X			X	X	X	X	X				
Biloxi	39,583	St. Bernard Parish, Hopedale. 9 miles south; Shell Beach 6 miles southwest Hwy. 46	X	X	X	X	X	X	X	X		X	X	X	X			X		
Bodcau	32,471	Bossier-Webster Parishes, from Bellevue north to La-Ark line Hwy. 157	X	X	X	X	X	X	X	X	X		X						X	
Boeuf	38,444	Caldwell Parish, 10 miles southeast of Columbia, Highway 559	X	X	X	X	X	X		X		X	X	X	X	X	X		X	
Bohemia	33,000	Plaquemines Parish, 4 miles south of East Point-a-la-Hache	X	X	X		X	X	X	X	X	X	X	X	X	X	X		X	X

Area	Acres	Location	1	2	3	4	5	6	7	8	9	10	11	12	13	14	15	16	17
Boise-Vernon	54,269	Vernon Parish, 20 miles west of Leesville, south of La. Hwy. 8	X	X	X	X	X	X											X
Cities Service	13,374	Ouachita Parish—6 miles northeast of Monroe, Hwy. 34	X	X	X	X	X	X											
Fort Polk	109,855	Vernon Parish, 10 miles east of Leesville, off Highway 28 (north) and U.S. Highway 71 (west) Highway 10 (south)	X	X					X	X									
Georgia Pacific	27,361	Morehouse Parish, 5 miles northwest of Bastrop, west Hwy. 139	X	X	X	X	X	X											
Grassy Lake	13,608	Avoyelles Parish, 2 miles north of Bordelonville, Highway 29	X	X			X		X	X	X	X					X	X	X
Jackson-Bienville	31,000	Jackson-Bienville Parishes, 12 miles southwest of Ruston, Hwy. 167	X	X	X	X	X	X										X	
Joyce	13,659	Tangipahoa Parish, 5 miles south of Hammond, 1 mile south of Pontchatoula Highways I-55, U.S. 51	X	X	X		X												
Loggy Bayou	3,689	Bossier Parish—20 miles southeast of Bossier City off U.S. Hwy. 71	X	X	X	X	X	X										X	X
Manchac	8,325	St. John the Baptist Parish, 17 miles northeast of LaPlace, and east of U.S. Hwy. 51	X	X			X	X	X								X		X
Ouachita	8,745	Ouachita Parish, 12 miles south of Monroe, on La. Hwy. 841	X	X	X	X	X												
Pass-A-Loutre	66,000	Plaquemines Parish, 10 miles south of Venice, access by boat on Mississippi River	X		X		X	X	X	X								X	
Pearl River	32,813	St. Tammany Parish, 6 miles east of Slidell	X	X	X	X	X	X	X	X	X						X	X	X

LAND OWNED OR LEASED BY LOUISIANA DEPARTMENT OF WILDLIFE & FISHERIES FOR PUBLIC USE— WILDLIFE MANAGEMENT AREAS—Continued

Name of Area	Acreage	Location	Deer	Squirrel	Rabbit	Turkey	Waterfowl	Quail	Doves	Woodcock	Snipe	Bass	Bream	Crappie	Catfish	Buffalo	Gaspergou	Salt Water Species	Camping Area	Boat Ramps
			\<Hunting\>									\<Sport Fishing\>						\<Commercial\>	\<Facilities\>	
Peason Ridge	33,488	Vernon, Natchitoches, Sabine Parishes, 15 miles north of Leesville, Hwy. 117	X	X	X	X		X	X	X										
Pointe-au-Chien	29,000	Terrebonne and Lafourche Parishes		X	X	X	X	X	X	X	X	X	X	X						
Pomme-de-Terre	6,004	Avoyelles Parish, 6 miles east of Moreauville on La. Hwy. 451	X	X	X		X			X	X	X	X	X	X	X	X		X	X
Red River	28,325	Concordia Parish, 3 miles west of Shaw off Hwy. 15	X	X	X		X			X	X	X	X	X	X	X	X		X	
Russell Sage	17,280	10 miles east of Monroe, U.S. Hwy. 80	X	X	X		X	X	X			X	X	X	X				X	
Sabine	14,780	5 miles west of Many, La. 5 miles off Highway 171	X	X	X	X		X	X	X									X	
Sabine Island	8,100	Calcasieu Parish, 5 miles west of Vinton. Take La. Hwy. 109 to Nibblets Bluff	X	X	X							X	X		X	X	X			
Saline	60,276	Catahoula-LaSalle Parishes, 20 miles northeast of Alexandria, Hwy. 28	X	X	X	X	X			X		X	X	X	X	X	X		X	X

Area	Acreage	Location													
Salvador	31,000	St. Charles Parish, 10 miles southwest of New Orleans	X	X	X				X	X				
Sherburne	10,230	Pointe Coupee and St. Martin Parishes, 5 miles southeast of Krotz Springs, Highway 975 off both I-10 and U.S. 190.	X	X	X	X	X	X	X	X	X	X	X	X	X X
Sicily Island Hills	6,369	Catahoula Parish, 6 miles west of Sicily Island, La. Hwys. 8, 913 and 915	X	X	X	X	X	X	X	X	X	X	X	X	X
Soda Lake	1,200	Caddo Parish, 15 miles north of Shreveport, La. Highway 1			X						X				
Spring Bayou	12,158	Avoyelles Parish, 3 miles southeast of Marksville, La. Hwy. 452	X	X	X	X	X	X	X	X	X	X	X	X	X X
Thistlethwaite	11,100	St. Landry Parish, 2 miles north of Washington, off Highway 10	X	X	X	X	X								
Three Rivers	24,982	Concordia Parish, 50 miles south of Vidalia on La. Hwy. 15	X	X	X	X	X	X	X	X	X	X	X	X	X X
Union	12,196	Union Parish, 4 miles northwest of Marion, Hwy. 551	X	X	X	X			X					
West Bay	55,185	Allen Parish, 3 miles west of Oakdale Hwy. 10, 7 miles west of Oberlin, Hwy. 26	X	X	X	X	X	X						X	
Wisner	21,621	Lafourche Parish, 8 miles south of Leesville and 5 miles west of Grand Isle, Highway 1			X		X			X			X		X

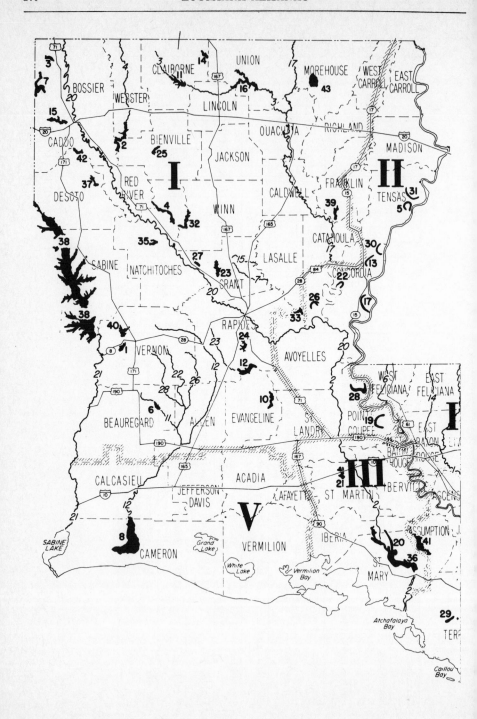

LAKES

1. ANACOCO	22. HORSESHOE
2. BISTINEAU	23. IATT
3. BLACK BAYOU	24. INDIAN CREEK
4. BLACK-CLEAR	25. KEPLER
5. BRUIN	26. LARTO
6. BUNDICK	27. NANTACHIE
7. CADDO	28. OLD RIVER
8. CALCASIEU	29. PENCHANT
9. CATAOUATCHE	30. ST. JOHN
10. CHICOT	31. ST. JOSEPH
11. CLAIBORNE	32. SALINE
12. COCODRIE	33. SALINE
13. CONCORDIA	34. SALVADOR
14. CORNEY	35. SIBLEY
15. CROSS	36. SIX MILE
16. D'ARBONNE	37. SMITHPORT
17. DEER PARK	38. TOLEDO BEND
18. DES ALLEMANDS	39. TURKEY CREEK
19. FALSE RIVER	40. VERNON
20. GRAND	41. VERRET
21. HENDERSON	42. WALLACE
	43. BUSSEY

STREAMS

1. AMITE RIVER
2. ATCHAFALAYA RIVER
3. BAYOU D'ARBONNE
4. BAYOU DORCHEAT
5. BAYOU LACOMBE
6. BAYOU SARA
7. BIG CREEK
8. BLIND RIVER
9. BLOOD RIVER
10. BOGUE CHITTO RIVER
11. BUNDICK CREEK
12. CALCASIEU RIVER
13. CHAPPEPEELA CREEK
14. COMITE RIVER
15. FISH CREEK
16. NATALBANY RIVER
17. OUACHITA RIVER
18. PEARL RIVER
19. PUSHEPATAPA CREEK
20. RED RIVER
21. SABINE RIVER
22. SIX MILE CREEK
23. SPRING CREEK
24. TANGIPAHOA RIVER
25. TCHEFUNCTE RIVER
26. TEN MILE CREEK
27. TICKFAW RIVER
28. WHISKEY CHITTO CREEK

DIRECTORY OF PUBLIC LAUNCH RAMPS AND LOCATIONS

IN ALLEN PARISH:
Calcasieu River — 1½ miles NW of Oakdale on State Road 10.
Whiskey Chitto River — 9.8 miles NW of Oberlin on SR 26.
Calcasieu River — 3.4 miles NW of Oberlin on SR 26.

IN ASCENSION PARISH:
Bayou Francois — in Gonzales on U.S. Hwy 61.
Mississippi River — in Donaldsonville on La. Hwy 1.

IN ASSUMPTION PARISH:
Lake Verret — 5 miles S of Pierre Pass on La. Hwy 70.
Lake Verret — on La. Hwy 401 at Lake Verret.

IN AVOYELLES PARISH:
Spring Bayou — about 3 miles E of Marksville.
Big Creek — 15 miles N of Marksville on La. Hwy 115.
Old River — 2 miles N of Mansura on La. Hwy 1.

IN BIENVILLE PARISH:
Lake Bistineau — 4 miles NW of Ringgold on the east side of the lake.
Lake Kepler — just off La. Hwy 507 at the spillway.

IN BOSSIER PARISH:
Bayou Bodcau — at Wenks Landing just off La. Hwy 7 near Sarepta.
Bayou Bodcau — at the damsite just off La. Hwy 157 near Bellevue.
Ivan Lake — just off La. Hwy 160 near Ivan.

IN BEAUREGARD PARISH:
Bundicks Lake — just off La. Hwy 394 near Dry Creek.

IN CADDO PARISH:
Caddo Lake — 3 miles S of Oil City and ½ mile W of La. Hwy 1.
Cross Lake — 2½ miles W of Shreveport on South Lakeshore Drive.

IN CALCASIEU PARISH:
Calcasieu River — at the foot of I-10 bridge in Lake Charles.
Prien Lake — in the City of Lake Charles on Lock Lane.

IN CALDWELL PARISH:
Long Lake — about 30 miles S of Monroe and 5 miles E of Columbia.

IN CAMERON PARISH:
Mermentau River — 30 miles E of Cameron-Grand Chenier Park.
Sabine Pass — immediately N of La. Hwy 82 on the east side of Sabine Lake.
Calcasieu Ship Channel — adjacent to the Cameron Ferry.

IN CATAHOULA PARISH:
Youngblood Landing — in Saline Bayou on Larto Lake on the Saline Wildlife Management Area.
Ouachita River — in Harrisonburg in the E bank of the Ouachita.
Saline Bayou — 14 miles S of La. Hwy 28 on the Saline WMA.
Black River — right in Jonesville.
Bayou Louis — right in Sicily Island.

IN CLAIBORNE PARISH:
Lake Claiborne — 10 miles SE of Homer and 1 mile N of La. Hwy. 146.

IN CONCORDIA PARISH:
Cocodrie Lake — 3 miles E of Lismore on La. Hwy 565.
Deer Park Lake — 15 miles S of Vidalia just off La. Hwy 15.
Lake Concordia — on La. Hwy 568 about 5 miles NE of Ferriday.

IN EAST CARROLL PARISH:
Lake Providence — just N of Lake Providence city limits on La. Hwy 45.

IN EVANGELINE PARISH:
Lake Chicot — just off La. Hwy 106 S of Cheneyville.
Lake Chicot — on La. Hwy 375 S of Cheneyville.
Lake Chicot — 2½ miles S of La. Hwy 106 below the spillway.

IN FRANKLIN PARISH:
Bayou Macon — ½ mile W of La. Hwy 572 in Lorelein.
Tensas River — 10 miles SE of Wisner off La. Hwy 562.

IN GRANT PARISH:
Nantachie Lake — 4 miles S of Montgomery and 1 mile N of La. Hwy 71 on La. Hwy 1240.
Little River — 10 miles SE of La. Hwy 8 from Fishville.
Iatt Lake — just off La. Hwy 122 S of Montgomery.
Iatt Lake — just off La. Hwy 71 at the spillway.

IN IBERIA PARISH:
Delcambre Canal — launch adjacent to Delcambre.
Commercial Canal — E bank of Commercial Canal about 5 miles S of New Iberia.
Lake Dauterive — on La. Hwy 345 at Lake Dauterive.

IN JEFFERSON PARISH:
Intracoastal Canal — 3 miles S of Crown Point on La. Hwy 45.

IN JEFFERSON DAVIS PARISH:
Dredge Canal — 2 blocks W of Main Street in Lake Arthur.

IN LAFAYETTE PARISH:
Vermilion River — at the intersection of Surrey Street and Vermilion Road in Lafayette.
Vermilion River — on West Bayou Parkway at Coulee Mine.

IN LASALLE PARISH:
Muddy Bayou — launch on Muddy Bayou on the Saline WMA.

IN LINCOLN PARISH:
Lake D'Arbonne — just N of La. Hwy 151 at Lincoln Landing.

IN LIVINGSTON PARISH:
Amite River — just off La. Hwy 42 in Port Vincent.

IN NATCHITOCHES PARISH:
Cane River Lake — 3.2 miles S of SR 1 in Natchez on SR 110 in Bermuda.
Sibley Lake — right on SR 1 in the City of Natchitoches.
Clear Lake — 4 miles NE and 1 mile S of La. Hwy 9 from Campti.
Clear Lake — 6 miles E and 1 mile N of La. Hwy 480 from Campti.
Black Lake — just off La. Hwy 480 E of Campti.

IN ORLEANS PARISH:
West End — multi-complex on Lake Pontchartrain at West End.
Industrial Canal — multi-complex on Lake Pontchartrain at Seabrook Bridge and Industrial Canal.
Rigolets — on Rigolets Pass at Fort Pike just off US Hwy 90.

IN OUACHITA PARISH:
Cheniere Lake — S side of lake at Park Area I just off La. Hwy 34.
Cheniere Lake — N side of lake at Park Area IV just off I-20.

IN POINTE COUPEE PARISH:
False River — in New Roads city limits just off La. Hwy 980.

IN ST. LANDRY PARISH:
Half-Moon Bayou — 3 miles W of Melville on La. Hwy 10.

IN ST. MARTIN PARISH:
Bayou Benoit — 20 miles S of Henderson on West Atchafalaya Guide Levee.
Lake Martin — 4 miles N of Parks city limits on La. Hwy 31.
Butte-LaRose River — 5 miles S of Henderson E of West Atchafalaya Guide Levee.
Lake Dauterive — 25 miles S of Henderson on West Atchafalaya Guide Levee.

IN ST. MARY PARISH:
Intracoastal Canal — West side of the lower Atchafalaya River about 3.5 miles S of Berwick.

IN ST. TAMMANY PARISH:
Davis Landing — on the Pearl River via access road off La. Hwy 1033, near Slidell.
Crawford's Landing — on Pearl River via access road off La. Hwy 1033, near Slidell.
Indian Village Landing — 5 miles west of US Hwy 90 just off US Hwy 190 East, near Slidell.
Bayou Castine — in Mandeville on Jackson Avenue at Lakeshore Drive.

IN UNION PARISH:
Ouachita River — in Ouachita City, just off La. Hwy 143.
Lake D'Arbonne — north side of the lake at the spillway just off La. Hwy 2.
Lake D'Arbonne — south side of lake at spillway, just off La. Hwy 15.
Lake D'Arbonne — at Hog Pen Landing on Corney Arm just off La. Hwy 2.

IN VERNON PARISH:
Anacoco Lake — 8.7 miles W of US Hwy 171 in Leesville.
Anacoco Lake — 8 miles W of Leesville on La. Hwy 8 and 2 miles S on La. Hwy 464 from La. Hwy 8 and 464 intersection.
Lake Vernon — 4 miles W and 3 miles N of Leesville off La. Hwy 8.

IN WASHINGTON PARISH:
Pearl River (Angie) — approximately 6 miles E of Angie city limits.
Pearl River — in Bogalusa just off La. Hwy 26.
Bogue Chitto — in Franklinton just off La. Hwy 16.
Bayou Chene Blanc — in Franklinton just off La. Hwy 16.

IN WEBSTER PARISH:
Bayou Dorcheat — 5 miles W of Minden just off La. Hwy 80.

Source: Department of Wildlife and Fisheries

Louisiana Attractions

(GMA)*GAME MANAGEMENT AREA
(KNF)†KISATCHIE NATIONAL FOREST

🐾 NORTHEAST

Site	Camping	Freshwater Fishing	Saltwater Fishing	Deer Hunting	Waterfowl Hunting	Small Game Hunting	Launch Ramp	Bait & Tackle	Boat Rental	Charter Boat	Guide Service	Motel	Restaurant	Water Skiing	Swimming	Hiking	Canoeing	Bicycling	Sail Boating	Site Location
Bayou Desiard	●	●					●				●	●	●	●		●				Monroe
Bussey Lake	●	●		●	●	●	●									●				Approx 15 mi N Bastrop
Caldwell Wildlife Area	●	●		●																Fort Necessity
Chemin-A-Haut	●	●												●	●		●			12 mi N of Bastrop
Cheniere Brake	●	●		●	●	●	●					●	●	●		●	●	●		4 mi W of Monroe
D'Arbonne Lake	●	●		●	●	●	●				●	●	●	●		●	●	●		Farmerville
Lake Brun	●	●		●		●	●					●					●			5 mi N of St. Joseph
Lake Means	●	●		●		●	●													Sicily Island
Lake Providence	●	●		●	●	●	●				●	●	●	●		●	●	●		Lake Providence
Lake St. Joseph	●	●		●		●	●											●		St. Joseph
Ouachita River	●	●		●		●	●					●	●	●						Monroe
Russell Sage (GMA)*	●	●		●	●	●	●									●	●			5 mi E of Monroe
Tensas River	●	●		●								●				●				Madison Parish
Turkey Creek Lake	●	●		●		●	●						●			●	●			La. 875, W of Wisner

🐾 NORTHWEST

Site	Camping	Freshwater Fishing	Saltwater Fishing	Deer Hunting	Waterfowl Hunting	Small Game Hunting	Launch Ramp	Bait & Tackle	Boat Rental	Charter Boat	Guide Service	Motel	Restaurant	Water Skiing	Swimming	Hiking	Canoeing	Bicycling	Sail Boating	Site Location
Black Bayou Lake	●	●		●	●	●	●									●				5 mi E of Vivian
Black Lake	●	●		●	●	●	●			●	●						●			La. 480, 6 mi E of Campti
Caddo Lake	●	●		●	●	●	●			●	●	●	●	●	●		●			Mooringsport
Clear Lake	●	●		●	●	●	●			●										La. 480, 6 mi E of Campti
Corney Lake	●	●		●		●	●													La. 9, N of Summerfield
Cross Lake	●	●		●		●	●				●	●	●	●	●		●	●		Shreveport
Jackson-Bienville (GMA)*	●	●		●													●			Hodge
Kepler Creek Lake	●	●		●		●	●						●	●		●	●			5 mi N of Castor

Caney (GMA)*—(KNF)† — 5 mi N of Homer

Name	Location
Lake Bistineau	12 mi W of Minden
Lake Claiborne	Homer
Lakes Edwards & Smithport	La. 509 W of Abington
Saline Lake	6 mi W of Clarence
Toledo Bend Reservoir	U.S. 171 S Logansport
Wallace Lake	7 mi S of Shreveport
CENTRAL	
Anacoco Lake	5 mi W of Leesville
Big Creek	Fishville
Black River	Jonesville
Catahoula — (KNF)†	Winnfield
Catahoula Lake	30 mi NE of Alexandria
Chicot Lake	8 mi N of Ville Platte
Cocodrie Lake	25 mi SE of Alexandria
Concordia (GMA)*	Ferriday
Cotile Recreation Area	Approx 15 mi NW of Alexandria
Fish Creek	10 mi W of Pollock
Ft. Polk (GMA)* — (KNF)†	Leesville
Horseshoe Lake	Avoyelles Parish, Big Bend area
Iatt Lake	5 mi NE of Colfax
Kitterling Bay-Leyman's Lake-Walker Lake Complex	(Complex) 12 mi E of Pollock
Lake Concordia	Ferriday
Lake Louis	Harrisonburg
Lake St. John	Spokane
Larto Lake	26 mi S of Jonesville
Little River	Jonesville
Lutcher Moore (GMA)*	Burr Ferry
Miller's Lake	Ville Platte
Nantachie Lake	U.S. 71
Old River	Mansura
Red Dirt — (KNF)†	Kisatchie

Water	Location
Red River (GMA)*	Shaw
Sabine (GMA)*	5 mi N of Many
Saline (GMA)*	La. 28, 25 mi E of Alexandria
Saline Bayou	La. 28, E of Alexandria
Saline Lake	20 mi SW of Winnfield
Sibley Lake	Natchitoches
Spring Bayou	Marksville
Spring Bayou (GMA)*	Marksville
Toledo Bend Reservoir	Many
Valentine Lake	5 mi S of Gardner
Vernon Lake	U.S. 171, 15 mi N of Leesville
Whiskey Chitto Creek	La. 26, La. 113, Vernon Beauregard & Allen Parishes
Yucatan Lake	7 mi E of Newellton

SOUTHEAST

Water	Location
Amite River	East Baton Rouge Parish
Bogue Chitto River	Washington—St. Tammany
Bonnet Carre Spillway	39 mi. W of New Orleans
Cocodrie	Cocodrie
Empire	Empire
False River	New Roads
Grand Isle	Grand Isle
Lac Des Allemands	Kraemer
Lake Borgne	New Orleans
Lake Maurepas	Maurepas
Lake Pontchartrain	New Orleans
Lake Salvador	5 mi W of Barataria
Old River	14 mi N of New Roads
Pass Manchac	30 mi NW of New Orleans
Tangipahoa River	Tangipahoa Parish
Tcheluncte River	Tangipahoa—St. Tammany
Tickfaw River	Livingston Parish—St. Helena

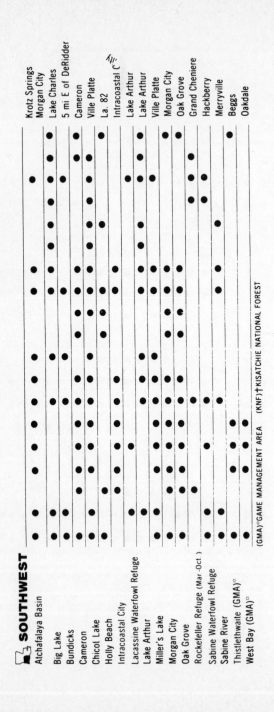

SOUTHWEST

Atchafalaya Basin
Big Lake
Bundicks
Cameron
Chicot Lake
Holly Beach
Intracoastal City
Lacassine Waterfowl Refuge
Lake Arthur
Miller's Lake
Morgan City
Oak Grove
Rockefeller Refuge (Mar.-Oct.)
Sabine Waterfowl Refuge
Sabine River
Thistlethwaite (GMA)°
West Bay (GMA)°

Krotz Springs
Morgan City
Lake Charles
5 mi E of DeRidder
Cameron
Ville Platte
La. 82
Intracoastal C...
Lake Arthur
Lake Arthur
Ville Platte
Morgan City
Oak Grove
Grand Cheniere
Hackberry
Merryville
Beggs
Oakdale

(GMA)°°GAME MANAGEMENT AREA   (KNF)†KISATCHIE NATIONAL FOREST

SHRIMP DRYING

Although the first dried shrimp were shipped to Oriental communities on the Pacific coast, abundant harvest soon enabled distribution to such far-flung markets as the Far East, Philippines, Hawaii, and, to a lesser extent, the West Indies and South America.

At the industry's zenith, an estimated 75 platforms existed in Louisiana. As late as 1962, 23 such camps remained. Today only seven are known by the authors, and the art of shrimp-drying is a dying one.

Early records indicate the first crude drying platform was built in Barataria Bay at a site later called Cabinash. Initial efforts were to sun-dry oysters. When this proved impractical, the men began to dry shrimp.

Gerald Atkins, writing in the *Louisiana Conservationist*, reports that in the early 1800s, Oriental immigrants purchased several small islands in Barataria Bay to be used as sites for shrimp platforms.

The industry was well established in 1885, when Yee Foo was issued Patent Number 310-811 for a process to sun-dry shrimp. Actually his preservative technique was not new; it had been practiced in China for centuries. The patent simply documented this method of food preservation.

Early platforms were dominated by Orientals, who made their home on the site. They often did so to avoid trouble with immigration authorities, since many entered this country illegally. In fact, according to legend, large numbers were smuggled into Louisiana by commercial fishermen, who placed the aliens in barrels and brought them into the coastal waters unnoticed. Along with the Chinese, a melange of other ethnic groups made up platform crews.

The platforms were supplied, of course, by shrimp fishermen. Initially the shrimp were caught by haul seines, but in 1917, the otter trawl revolutionized shrimping. The haul seine required shallow water, a large crew, and was limited to the summer and fall months. Otter trawls, on the other hand, could be used over a much larger area and required fewer men. Their widespread adoption opened new fishing grounds and expanded the shrimping industry. By 1920, Louisiana's shrimp catch totaled 32 million pounds.

The sun-dried shrimp industry's demand for small, cheap shrimp was also responsible for another net, today's highly controversial *poupier*, or butterfly, net. Mounted on boats and wharves, the 15-foot-long mesh bags are rigged on seven- to twelve-foot square, iron-pipe frames.

With more sophisticated equipment, numerous platforms began operating in Atchafalaya, Barataria, Caillou, Terrebonne, and Timbalier Bays. In the industry's heyday, an estimated 75 platforms were operating. (Because of their isolation, an accurate count was never made.) Many were destroyed in the hurricane of 1915 and never rebuilt. Of those that survived, one of the largest and oldest is Manila Village. Mr. Chin Bow Wing, current owner, recounts much of the change that first expanded Manila Village into a thriving community, then reduced it to what it is today: a small shack surrounded by assorted pilings.

Located in the upper reaches of Barataria Bay, Manila Village served the seine crews and Lafitte skiff fishermen quite well. A newspaper account states that the village was a Spanish attempt to establish a Fillipino colony and was first used for sun-drying shrimp about 1873. The platform became an important hamlet, at one time large enough to have its own post office.

Such settlements generally consisted of small, rude shacks of rough, unpainted cypress boards, which served as warehouse, storehouse, and living quarters. These buildings were rectangular and varied from typical shotgun houses to large general stores. Some structures and the wharf—used as an unloading site for unprocessed shrimp—were built over water on hand-driven pilings. Pilings also supported the large wooden platforms utilized in the cooking, drying, and thrashing procedure.

A cypress platform was built eight to ten feet high, so that air could circulate freely around the structure. The floor undulated, with ridges three to four feet high and six feet wide, with some 30 feet from crest to crest. The crests allowed quicker drying and rapid runoff during rainy periods. At the top of each crest was a chain of interconnected A-shaped frames, which supported tarpaulins. When rain threatened, the drying shrimp were raked under the stands, and the tarps were lowered to keep the shrimp from spoiling.

Seine crews brought their catch to the platforms and transferred shrimp directly from boat into wash tubs for weighing. After weighing, the "green" shrimp were moved to large metal baskets mounted on copper and cypress boiling kettles called "brine tanks." These baskets were hinged so that they could be raised and lowered into the boiling brine.

In preparing sun-dried shrimp, the raw crustaceans were boiled about 15 minutes. Manila Village used the little sea bob (*Xiphopanaeus kroyer*), for which there was less commercial demand. They were cooked just long enough to insure easy removal of shell after drying. Then the shrimp were spread onto the platform, where they were exposed to sun for a period of one day, if the day were clear and hot, and for several days under cloudy, wet weather.

After drying, heads and shells were removed. Laborers wrapped their brogan shoes with cloths or sacks and tramped or "danced the shrimp." Small amounts could be flailed with a bundle of branches or a large homemade "flyswatter," then sifted or winnowed to remove the loose hulls. The shrimp were next shaken on hardware cloth or poured from a height during a brisk wind.

A later development was the rotating-drum shell-huller, patented in 1922 by Fred Chauvin and Shelly Bergeron.

For shipment, dried shrimp were packed in 125- to 230-pound lots in barrels or coffee sacks, each representing 800 to 1,400 pounds of raw shrimp. The product was either exported to Latin or Asiatic markets or sold in the United States as a snack item or gumbo ingredient.

Although limited to a small region, and never utilizing more than 30 percent of the catch, sun-dried shrimp provided a unique economic activity. Such competition as freezing and canning has today rendered the centuries-old method of preservation passe.

Basa Basa, Bayou Brouilleau, Cabinash, Camp Dewey, Chenier Dufon, Manila Village... all that is left of many of these colorful villages are a few relict landscape features.

SOURCE: Donald W. Davis and Randall A. Detro, *Aquanotes*, Vol. 5, Issue 3, June 1976.

Estimated Monetary Value of Hunting in Louisiana

SPECIES	ESTIMATED NO. HUNTERS	TOTAL HUNTING TRIPS MADE	VALUE OF TRIP	TOTAL VALUE
Deer	198,000	2,655,000	$25.00	$ 66,375,000
Squirrel	237,000	2,220,000	11.00	24,420,000
Rabbit	157,000	800,000	11.00	8,800,000
Quail	32,000	220,000	11.00	2,420,000
Dove	114,000	800,000	11.00	8,800,000
Waterfowl, (Ducks, Geese, Coots) ...	131,000	1,400,000	15.00	21,000,000
Turkey	15,600	118,000	25.00	2,950,000
Gallinule	4,300	20,000	11.00	220,000
Rail	7,400	35,000	11.00	385,000
Snipe	21,800	200,000	11.00	2,200,000
Woodcock	50,000	250,000	11.00	2,750,000
Raccoon	41,000	800,000	7.00	5,600,000
Fox	10,000	100,000	7.00	700,000
Bobcat	5,200	50,000	7.00	350,000
			TOTAL VALUE	$146,277,000

Estimates computed from 1984-85 mail survey by Louisiana Department of Wildlife and Fisheries and National Hunting and Fishing Survey 1980.

Fur

The production of wild fur in Louisiana has long been of substantial economic importance to Louisiana citizens. An average of 10,709 trappers produced an annual harvest worth approximately $11,192,457 during the past 10 years (1976-77 through 1985-86). The average number of alligator hunters licensed each year since the harvest has been opened statewide has been 1,072 (1981-1986).

NUMBER AND DOLLAR VALUE OF PELTS TAKEN IN LOUISIANA: 1947-48 SEASON TO 1986-87 SEASON

Season	Number	Value	Season	Number	Value
1947-48	6,144,060	11,315,990.	1967-68	2,130,473	2,858,324.
1948-49	3,200,387	4,182,293.	1968-69	3,469,040	6,063,514.
1949-50	2,451,283	2,956,478.	1969-70	3,002,043	5,965,700.
1950-51	2,879,322	5,957,247.	1970-71	2,090,761	4,512,968.
1951-52	1,299,482	2,265,514.	1971-72	1,732,682	5,691,398.
1952-53	1,531,427	2,825,554.	1972-73	2,180,332	9,628,831.
1953-54	1,453,056	1,835,983.	1973-74	2,304,916	11,932,453.
1954-55	1,920,303	3,418,679.	1974-75	2,038,379	9,655,195.
1955-56	2,370,698	2,644,986.	1975-76	2,533,500	12,456,562.
1956-57	2,278,939	2,683,979.	1976-77	3,246,988	24,122,144.
1957-58	2,829,108	2,742,242.	1977-78	2,635,001	12,804,437.
1958-59	1,930,029	$ 2,351,278.	1978-79	1,964,937	11,527,684.
1959-60	2,381,506	3,296,347.	1979-80	2,256,671	16,467,773.
1960-61	1,791,226	2,164,208.	1980-81	2,245,679	17,929,823.
1961-62	1,717,871	2,428,267.	1981-82	1,616,131	8,148,407.
1962-63	1,945,756	3,216,248.	1982-83	1,343,553	5,037,592.
1963-64	1,633,933	2,641,594.	1983-84	1,371,660	4,334,267.
1964-65	1,872,545	3,172,037.	1984-85	1,656,157	7,487,283.
1965-66	1,699,330	4,614,371.	1985-86	1,051,428	4,230,500.
1966-67	1,993,873	3,648,012.	1986-87	1,438,394	6,676,488.

LICENSES SOLD

Year	La. Totals	National Totals	Year	La. Totals	National Totals
1937-1971	$6,974,540.14	$417,611,125.45	1980	1,688,270.49	89,000,000.00
1972	648,366.94	34,455,000.00	1981	1,615,753.00	83,394,000.00
1973	765,592.62	41,045,000.00	1982	2,316,438.00	116,960,000.00
1974	887,714.94	47,385,000.00	1983	2,155,101.00	107,060,000.00
1975	990,227.92	53,470,000.00	1984	1,786,844.00	88,450,000.00
1976	1,084,564.17	58,600,000.00	1985	1,637,712.00	79,099,600.00
1977	1,536,407.00	84,400,000.00	1986	2,153,264.00	107,471,100.00
1978	1,164,273.00	62,900,000.00			
1979	1,570,589.00	82,200,000.00	Totals	$28,975,658.22	$1,553,500,825.45

Comparative Takes of Fur Animals in Louisiana
10 Year Average (1976-77 through 1985-86 seasons)

	No. of Pelts	Approx. Price to Trapper	Value
Nutria (Eastern)	810,010	$ 4.79	$ 3,879,947.90
Nutria (Western)	370,809	6.34	2,350,929.06
	1,180,819		$ 6,230,876.96
Muskrat (Eastern)	341,313	3.74	$ 1,276,510.62
Muskrat (Western)	118,350	4.72	558,612.00
	459,663		$ 1,835,122.62
Raccoon (Upland)	134,345	12.35	$ 1,683,342.85
Raccoon (Coastal)	68,936	6.32	435,675.52
	203,281		$ 2,119,018.37
Mink	38,760	10.54	$ 408,530.40
Opossum	36,606	1.92	70,283.52
Otter	7,039	28.57	201,104.23
Skunk	286	1.90	543.40
Red Fox	1,279	33.56	42,923.24
Gray Fox	3,165	31.02	98,178.30
Bobcat	2,963	51.39	152,268.57
Beaver	1,089	5.22	5,684.58
Coyote	1,812	15.41	27,922.92
Total Pelts	1,936,762		$11,192,457.11
Nutria Meat	920,700 lbs.	.05	$ 46,035.00
Raccoon Meat	777,005 lbs.	.44	341,882.20
Opossum Meat	58,123 lbs.	.25	14,530.75
	1,755,828 lbs.		$ 402,447.95

TOTAL PELTS AND MEAT..................................... $11,594,905.06

AGRICULTURE

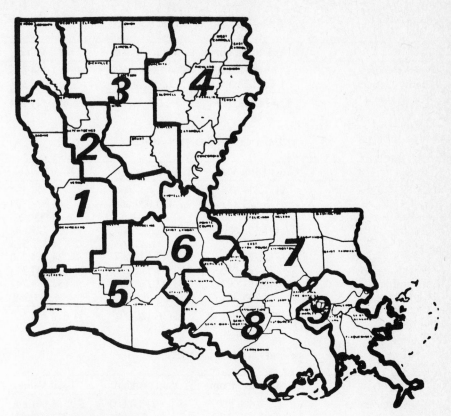

Type of Farming Areas

1. Western Dairy, Poultry, Livestock, and Pine Area
2. Red River Cotton, Cattle, and Soybean Area
3. North Central Dairy, Poultry, and Pine Area
4. Mississippi Delta Cotton, Soybeans, and Beef Area
5. Southwest Rice, Soybean, Beef, and Dairy Area
6. Central Mixed Farming Area
7. Southeast Dairy, Poultry, Truck, and Pine Area
8. Sugar Cane Area
9. Truck and Fruit Area

FARM INCOME

1986 PROGRESS REPORT

Area	Gross Farm Income	Value Added	Total Value
Animal Science	$ 891,117,961	$ 736,126,692	$1,627,244,653
Plant Science	1,532,074,178	3,537,005,413	5,069,079,591
TOTAL	$2,423,192,139	$4,273,132,105	$6,696,324,244

ANIMAL COMMODITIES—1986

Animal	Gross Farm Value	Value Added	Total Value
Cattle & Calves	$155,317,152	$ 15,000,000	$ 170,317,152
Milk	115,823,133	170,000,000	285,823,133
Horses	39,904,350	—0—	39,904,350
Poultry	191,553,682	132,172,000	323,725,682
Sheep	1,073,910	53,663	1,127,573
Swine	12,223,243	22,491,097	34,714,340
Freshwater Fish	55,289,040	59,152,272	114,441,312
Marine Fish	315,194,082	337,257,660	652,451,742
Fur	4,739,369	—0—	4,739,369
TOTAL	$891,117,961	$736,126,692	$1,627,244,653

PLANT COMMODITIES

Commodity	Gross Farm Income	Value Added	Total Value
Christmas Trees	$ 2,400,800	$ 2,400,800	$ 4,801,600
Cotton	201,339,840	20,133,984	221,473,824
Forestry, FOB Mill	441,390,830	3,294,834,779	3,736,225,609
Fruit Crops	4,320,938	509,281	4,830,219
Feed Grain Crops	126,329,946	13,950,699	140,280,645
Hay, Sold	17,098,625	————	17,098,625
Home Gardens	141,149,250	————	141,149,250
Nursery Stocks & Ornamentals	27,861,408	————	27,861,408
Peanuts	104,500	10,450	114,950
Pecans	9,589,445	958,945	10,548,390
Rice	151,520,714	51,409,989	202,930,703
Sod Production	8,660,734	6,282,845	14,943,579
Soybeans	168,391,605	16,839,161	185,230,766
Sugarcane	171,260,243	109,494,254	280,754,497
Sweet Potatoes	19,712,650	6,564,310	26,276,960
Tobacco	54,000	————	54,000
Vegetables, Commercial	40,888,650	13,615,916	54,504,566
TOTAL	$1,532,074,178	$3,537,005,413	$5,069,079,591

ANIMAL COMMODITIES 1982-1986

Year	Gross Farm Value	Value Added	Total Value
1982	$884,876,616	$580,097,270	$1,424,973,886
1983	832,715,157	546,492,186	1,370,207,343
1984	811,835,654	536,216,541	1,348,052,196
1985	841,800,014	576,224,082	1,418,024,096
1986	891,117,961	736,126,692	1,627,244,653

PLANT COMMODITIES—1982-1986

Year	Gross Farm Income	Value Added	Total Value
1982	$1,670,476,606	$2,505,892,903	$4,176,369,509
1983	1,853,885,169	4,332,971,989	6,186,857,158
1984	1,921,335,418	3,706,530,846	5,627,866,264
1985	1,556,097,287	3,325,675,389	4,881,772,676
1986	1,532,074,178	3,537,005,413	5,069,079,591

PROGRESS MEASURED IN DOLLARS FOR 5 YEARS
PLANT AND ANIMAL COMMODITIES

Year	Gross Farm Income	Value Added	Total Values
1982	$2,515,353,222	$3,085,990,173	$5,601,343,395
1983	2,677,600,326	4,879,464,175	7,557,064,501
1984	2,733,171,072	4,242,747,387	6,975,918,459
1985	2,397,897,301	3,901,899,471	6,299,796,772
1986	2,423,192,139	4,273,132,105	6,696,324,244

PRICES OF COMMODITY PRODUCTS
ANIMAL COMMODITIES

Commodity	Unit	Price
Steers		
300-400 lbs.	cwt.	$ 64.00
400-500 lbs.	cwt.	61.00
500-600 lbs.	cwt.	60.00
Average All Steers	cwt.	62.00
Heifers		
300-400 lbs.	cwt.	58.00
400-500 lbs.	cwt.	56.00
500-600 lbs.	cwt.	54.00
Average All Heifers	cwt.	56.00
Cows		
Slaughter, Commercial	cwt.	36.00
Stocker, Good	cwt.	42.00
Cow and calf (Good)	pair	475.00
Bulls		
Commercial	cwt.	45.00
Dairy Cows		
Milk Cows	head	475.00
Milk	cwt.	11.75
Horses (2 yr. Quarter and Other stock horse breeds)	head	1,000.00
Horses (Thoroughbreds—2 yr.)	head	2,500.00
Brood Mares (Quarter-Paints, etc.)	head	1,000.00
Thoroughbreds (Mares)	head	3,000.00
Stallions (Quarters, etc.)	head	15,000.00
Thoroughbreds (Stallions)	head	50,000.00
Chickens, All	lb.	.40
Eggs	doz.	.60
Sheep		
Stocker	head	47.50
Slaughter	head	25.00
Lambs	cwt.	61.00
Wool	cwt.	56.00
Hogs, Finished Slaughter	cwt.	52.22
Brood Sows (culls)	cwt.	45.15
Feeder Pigs	cwt.	81.25
Boars	cwt.	36.25
Freshwater Fisheries		
Crawfish	lb.	.50
Catfish	lb.	.62
Fishbait		
Marine Fisheries		
Shrimp	lb.	2.00
Menhaden	lb.	.035
Oysters	sack	13.00
Crabs	lb.	.40
Commercial finfish	lb.	.75

PLANT COMMODITIES

Commodity	Unit	Price
Beans		
Lima	bu. (32 lbs.)	$ 16.00
Snap	bu. (30 lbs.)	9.50
Beets	cwt.	18.00
Blueberries	lb.	.75
Broccoli	carton (20 lbs.)	7.00
Cabbage	sack (50 lbs.)	5.00
Cantaloupe	cwt.	26.00
Cauliflower	carton (20 lbs.)	8.00
Carrots	cwt.	22.00
Christmas Trees	ea. (6-8 ft.)	
	Wholesale	10.00
	Retail	20.00
Collards	doz. bunches	4.00
Corn		
Field	bu.	1.45
Sweet	doz. ears	1.00
Cotton		
Lint	lb.	.55
Seed	lb.	.035
Cucumber	bu. (50 lbs.)	7.00
Eggplant	bu. (33 lbs.)	6.00
Figs	lb.	.50
Garlic	lb.	1.00
Grain Sorghum	cwt.	2.92
Hay		
Alfalfa	ton	100.00
Grass	ton	50.00
Home Garden	each	450.00
Mirliton	lb.	.35
Mustard	doz. bunches	4.00
Nursery & Ornamentals	acre	3,500.00
Onions	bag (50 lbs.)	7.00
Oats	bu.	1.40
Okra		
Fresh	bu.	10.00
Processing	cwt.	11.00
Oranges		
Louisiana Sweet	bu.	No Production
Navel	bu.	No Production
Satsuma	bu.	No Production
Parsley	doz. bunches	1.20
Peaches	bu.	No Production
Pears	bu.	6.00

Peas, Southern	bu. (24 lbs.)	8.00
Peanuts	lb.	.20
Pecan		
Improved	lb.	.85
Native	lb.	.45
Peppers		
Bell	bu.	7.00
Cayenne	cwt.	20.00
Italian	cwt.	27.00
Tabasco, green	cwt.	55.00
Tabasco, red	cwt.	60.00
Potatoes		
Irish	cwt.	9.00
Sweet (canning)	bu. (50 lbs.)	2.00
Sweet (fresh)	bu. (50 lbs.)	4.00
Pumpkin	cwt.	5.00
Rice	cwt.	7.20
Shallots	doz. bunches	1.75
Sod Production	acre	2,900.00
Soybeans	bu.	4.77
Squash	bu. (45 lbs.)	8.00
Strawberries	flats	8.00
Sugar (raw)	cwt.	21.78
Tobacco	lb.	1.80
Tomatoes		
Field	lugs (20 lbs.)	6.00
Turnip	doz. bunches	4.00
Watermelon	cwt.	7.00
Wheat	bu.	2.40

ANIMAL ENTERPRISES
1986

BEEF CATTLE

Cattle and calves, not including dairy cattle, numbered about 1.12 million on July 1 in Louisiana. Beef cows numbered about 550,000 head. Declines from the previous year paralleled the national decline. Cattle over-wintered in 1986-87 will be off by about 50 percent due to cost of calves in the fall of 1986 and winter grass production costs.

Gross farm value was $150 million with an added value of about $11 million. Total value of all cattle and calves was about $164 million when revenue of slaughtered dairy cows and calves is added.

DAIRYING

In 1986 the number of dairy farms in Louisiana declined by 12.5 percent to 791. Total mature dairy cows were estimated at 77,518, making the average herd size 98 adult cows. Total milk production was approximately 833 million pounds with an on-farm value of $113 million. The average price received by dairymen was $13.60 per hundredweight (cwt).

Processing and retail sales within the state added $170 million to the value of the milk produced, yielding a total income of $283 million. The value of cull dairy cows and dairy calves was an estimated $16 million.

Statistical Data

	1985	1986	Change
1. No. of farms	904	791	−113
Estimated no. of cows	88,910	77,518	−11,392
Total prod. for year (million pounds)	912	833	−79
Avg. prod./comm. cow	10,257	10,746	+489
Avg. prod. cows on DHI	12,500	12,861	+361
2. No. of people working on farms	2,755	2,531	−244
3. No. people emp. between farm and consumer	3,590	3,770	+180
4. Price to farmers (per cwt.)	13.50	13.60	+10
Consumer price in store (per gallon)	2.35	2.35	0
(per pound)	$.275	$.275	0

5. Cost of production

1976	$ 9.50/cwt.	1982	$12.70/cwt.
1977	$ 9.40/cwt.	1983	$13.20/cwt.
1978	$10.00/cwt.	1984	$13.40/cwt.
1979	$10.75/cwt.	1985	$13.20/cwt.
1980	$12.05/cwt.	1986	$12.90/cwt.
1981	$12.90/cwt.		

HORSES

The horse industry has increased in importance as an economic stimulus for Louisiana. Although 80 percent of the horse owners list recreation and pleasure as their primary reason for horse ownership, the expenditures associated with the horse industry have been a major contributor to the economy and a significant source of government revenue.

The population of horses in Louisiana is more than 250,000, owned by an estimated 80,000 people. Although only 15 to 20 percent of the horse owners derive an income from horses, the average horse owner spends about $2,000 per year on such things as feed, equipment, tack, veterinary supplies and services. This results in an estimated $500 million that the horse industry contributes to the economy.

Approximately 7,958 horse producers derive an income from the horse business. These producers own 36,328 mares, which produced 18,901 colts that were sold in 1986 for $31.7 million. These producers own 1,329 stallions, which were bred to 18,913 outside mares, generating income from stud fees of $7.9 million for their owners. The total income generated from horse production by breeders in 1986 was $39.9 million. This is a small portion of the overall effect of the horse industry on the economy of Louisiana.

The racing industry in Louisiana generates a tremendous cash flow, especially among service-related organizations such as restaurants, motels, service stations and other related businesses. These activities have increased the number of jobs in Louisiana and the land values in areas where horses are concentrated. As a result, approximately 57,000 people are employed directly or indirectly with the horse industry and receive all or part of their income from horses. The money generated directly at the race tracks as a result of pari-mutuel handle and concessions resulted in pari-mutuel taxes and fees in excess of $23 million.

Horse shows, rodeos and youth programs have also had a substantial influence on the Louisiana horse industry. All major breed associations have an active youth program and actively conduct and promote horse shows. An estimated 500 horse shows, rodeos and youth horse activities are conducted each year, generating about $4,000 in expenditures per activity. With the increasing development of racing, showing and youth programs, Louisiana horses have become a major contributor to the state's economy. They also provide satisfaction and enjoyment.

POULTRY

The commercial poultry industry in Louisiana is composed of hens for production of table eggs, broiler breeders for production of hatching eggs, pullet growout and broiler growout. Broiler growout is estimated at 2.2 million birds per week. This includes some broilers grown in Louisiana and processed in a neighboring state. There are three broiler processing plants in Louisiana and all production is near one of these plants. Plants are located in Hammond, Natchitoches and Arcadia. All broiler growout is under a contract arrangement between farmers and the processing plant. Increased demand for poultry products and increased consumption by consumers indicate a real potential for growth of the Louisiana broiler industry.

Approximately 2.5 million hens produce 50 million dozen table eggs annually in Louisiana. Although some production is by contractual arrangements with a processor, most production is by relatively large independently owned operations.

In addition to commercial production, many families own a small poultry flock (including game birds) for home consumption. In most cases these flocks are considered a hobby, and little income is derived.

SHEEP

Breeding sheep numbers in Louisiana for 1986 were estimated at 22,523, slightly below 1985.

Beauregard, Vermilion, Acadia, Evangeline, St. Landry, Calcasieu, Jefferson Davis, Allen and St. Martin were the top producing parishes. Thirty-three parishes reported sheep being produced by 1,287 purebred and commercial producers.

About 17,900 lambs and 3,971 cull sheep were marketed by producers in 1986.

Approximately 146,149 pounds of wool were produced in Louisiana (an average of 5.69 pounds of wool per sheep). A total of 101,389 pounds of wool were marketed in the 1986 Louisiana Wool Growers Association wool pool for a value of $57,568.00 ($.5678/lb of wool).

Gross farm increase from sheep for 1986 was $1,073,260. Value added (processing, shipping, etc.) amounted to $53,663. Total estimated value of 1986 sheep production in Louisiana was $1,126,923. This increase over the 1985 income was caused by stronger lamb and wool prices and higher production.

Youth programs play a major role in the Louisiana sheep industry. In 1986, there were 1,900 boys and girls enrolled in the 4-H market lamb and breeding sheep projects. The Louisiana Sheep Producers Association and four breed associations (Louisiana Suffolk Association, Louisiana Hampshire Association, Louisiana Southdown Association and the Louisiana Dorset Club) work jointly to promote sheep production and develop educational programs to motivate and involve producers and youths.

SWINE

The number of pork producers in Louisiana remained fairly stable, with only a slight decrese in 1986 as compared to 1985. The number of hog producers in 1986 was 1,450. This included 640 feeder pig producers and 810 slaughter hog producers. The number of feeder pig producers increased about 12 percent; number of slaughter hog producers decreased by about 12 percent. Even though the number of slaughter hog producers decreased slightly in 1986, several new hog operations were built and existing producers increased the breeding herd production in litter size sold to 6.3.

The total breeding herd decreased slightly over 1985 and was reported at 10,789 sows. This included 3,734 sows producing feeder pigs and 7,055 sows producing market hogs and seedstock. The total Louisiana pig crop sold increased from 133,349 in 1985 to 136,323 in 1986. This figure indicates an average litter size sold at market of about 6.3 pigs per sow per farrowing. However, the better and larger commercial producers averaged about 7.5 pigs marketed per sow per farrowing. The number of feeder pigs sold in 1986 was 48,962 head. The number of slaughter hogs sold was 87,361 head. There were 3,116 cull sows sold.

Feeder pig sales produced $1,962,272 in 1986, with slaughter hog sales bringing $9,791,248. The value of cull sows sold was $401,873. The gross farm value of live hogs sold was $12,155,393, an increase of about 13 percent. The increase resulted from selling hogs at a higher price. The average price for live market hogs in 1986 was $52.22 per hundredweight as compared to $44.66 in 1985.

The added value for pork processed and sold was $22,491,097, a substantial increase from 1985. About 88 percent of the market hogs were sold to and processed by out-of-state packers.

PLANT ENTERPRISES
1986

VEGETABLES—COMMERCIAL

The commercial vegetable acreage increased by about 5 percent, from 19,574 to 20,541 acres. The estimated farm value increased from $33,426,001 to $40,888,650 in 1986, an increase of about 23 percent.

There was considerable interest in commercial vegetable production in 1986, partly because of the depressed conditions in agronomic crops. The increase in vegetables reported came primarily from Morehouse Parish where cucumbers and squash were grown and marketed through a packing facility established last year. There is still a lot of interest in vegetables as an alternative crop, but greater understanding of the marketing structure and the ability to access these markets are needed before the vegetable acreage can increase significantly.

COTTON

Approximately 7,619 producers harvested 570,000 acres of cotton in 1986. Yield was estimated at 573 pounds of lint per acre. This provided a statewide production of 680,000 bales. Estimated value of the crop including seed was $201,339,840.

Satisfactory stands were obtained by most producers, and the crop appeared to be developing rapidly and on its way to producing a good crop. A drought in mid-season reduced plant size on about all non-irrigated cotton and became a concern for many. As a result, much of the crop matured several weeks early and yields were reduced. Harvest weather was, for the most part, satisfactory and the harvest season progressed normally.

FEED GRAIN CROPS

Corn

Corn acreage increased to 427,072 acres in 1986, an increase of 84 percent. Good corn yields in 1984 and 1985 and optimism over higher profits from grain crops than from soybeans contributed to this increase. Corn was produced by 2,742 growers who averaged 109 bushels per acre. Total production of 46.7 million bushels was valued at $67.4 million.

Adoption of new hybrids and better cultural practices, along with good weather and ample rainfall, contributed to the high yields. Problems associated with elevators receiving high moisture corn occurred. Facilities at present cannot dry corn as fast as growers can harvest the crop. This has resulted in some large moisture discounts and has made the price received by growers much lower than previously experienced.

Grain Sorghum

Grain sorghum acreage decreased from 417,760 acres harvested in 1985 to 361,129 acres harvested in 1986. Yields declined somewhat from 3,944 pounds per acre in 1985 to 3,752 pounds per acre in 1986. Total production of 13.55 million hundredweight compared to 16.47 million hundredweight in 1985. The crop was valued at $40.17 million and was produced by 2,732 growers.

The decreased yields were caused by several factors including drought conditions during grain filling in some parts of the state as well as stand reductions caused by green stink bug infestations, especially in southern Louisiana. Ratoon crop production was also down somewhat in 1985.

The acreage planted to grain sorghum should decrease again in 1987. Much of this decrease will be caused by limited cross compliance in effect for program crops this year. This will prevent producers with other program crops from planting grain sorghum outside of the program or risk losing benefits.

Oats

Oats were harvested from 10,361 acres by 363 producers in 1986. The total production of 659,119 bushels resulted from an average yield of 64 bushels/acre and was an increase of 193,815 bushels above the 1985 production. An acreage increase of 3,203 acres provided the extra production since yield declined from the 65 bushels/acre of 1985. Poor stands and poor weather at planting, as well as in the spring, contributed to the yield decline. The total production for 1986 had a gross farm value of $922,765.

Wheat

Wheat production increased slightly in 1986 because of a yield increase from 34 bushels/acre in 1985 to 35 bushels/acre in 1986 and a harvested acreage increased from 210,000 acres in 1985 to 214,003 acres in 1986. The total production of 7.4 million bushels was an increase over the 7.1 million bushels of 1985. The 1986 crop was valued at $17,834,433 and was produced by 2,203 growers. The decline in crop value from the $23.4 million 1985 crop reflects a substantial decline in prices.

FORESTRY

The projected sawlog harvest increased by 18 percent in 1986 compared with 1985 for a total cut of 1,418,197,735 board feet.

The Louisiana pulpwood harvest for 1986 was projected to increase 20 percent from 1985, resulting in a cut of 4,771,186 cords.

Prices paid for pine sawlog stumpage averaged $127 per thousand board feet, a 10 percent decrease from the previous year. Prices decreased during the year. The January 1986 average was $153/M Bd. Ft. compared with December 1986 state average of $91/M Bd. Ft.

Average prices for oak sawlogs and other hardwoods did not change significantly, but some good quality oak sold for better prices in 1986.

Pulpwood stumpage prices for 1986 averaged $12.04 per cord for pine, $3.76 for soft hardwood and $3.25 for hard hardwoods. Wood chips averaged $27.27 per ton for pine.

With wood-using industries in 47 of Louisiana's 64 parishes and with 61 parishes commercially producing wood, the economic impact of forestry radiated throughout both urban and rural areas. In 1986 the 113,000 Louisiana private forest landowners were projected to receive $220 million from the sale of pulpwood and sawtimber. Timber harvesting contractors and their employees earned $221 million for harvesting the trees and moving the wood to the mills. In addition the 169 Christmas tree growers received $2.56 million from their 1986 crop of 151,850 trees.

An additional 24,900 individuals received income directly from manufacturing of Louisiana forest products. This payroll and income derived from money generated by the wood products industry amounted to an estimated $3.7 billion in 1986.

This makes the Louisiana forest products industry the second largest employer in Louisiana, ahead of oil and slightly behind chemicals. Forestry is still Louisiana's number one crop.

FRUIT CROPS

Strawberries

Louisiana produced about 600 acres of strawberries in 1986, up slightly from the 1985 acreage. The number of strawberry producers remained at about 300. Gross income was $3,856,864. Acreage is expected to remain steady or perhaps decline slightly because of increased production costs and competition from other markets from other states.

Citrus

Citrus acreage is beginning to increase in Louisiana following the drastic declines caused by the killing freezes of the 1980s. The current citrus acreage in Louisiana is approximately 500 acres, down 75 percent from the previous years. Of this acreage, none is presently old enough to be in production. Acreage is expected to increase, however, as producers anticipate mild winter patterns. No gross farm value is given for citrus in 1986.

Peaches

Peach acreage in Louisiana continues an upward trend despite a 95 percent loss in the 1986 crop because of a late spring freeze. Per acre profits of peaches make it one of the most attractive crops for Louisiana producers, particularly for small acreages. About 160 producers traditionally produce an average yield of 286 bushels per acre with a gross farm income totaling more than $5 million. This year's gross farm income was $343,695.

Blueberries

Rabbiteye blueberry production in Louisiana continues to show a strong upward trend. There are currently about 400 acres of commercial blueberries in Louisiana with an expected 10 to 20 percent increase in acreage in 1987.

Blueberry marketing consists primarily of pick-your-own operations, but there is an effort to establish other markets through a cooperative effort with Mississippi in establishing a Mississippi/Louisiana marketing cooperative. The gross farm income from blueberries this year was $581,560.

Miscellaneous

The planting of miscellaneous fruits in small home orchards and small commercial plantings to supply local markets continues to gain popularity. More and more homeowners are planting high maintenance fruits such as peaches and plums as a supplement to income and their dietary needs. Newer and more widely adapted varieties are now available and make it easier and more enjoyable for homeowners to grow and produce their own fruit. Their gross income from miscellaneous fruit is estimated at $48,100.

HAY SOLD

Hay is produced both for sale and for feeding on the farm where it is produced. In 1986, hay for sale was produced on 570 acres of alfalfa and 105,501 acres of grass with average yields of 4.00 tons/acre for alfalfa and 3.20 tons/acre for grasses. The total production for sale of 2,280 tons of alfalfa and 337,412 tons of grass hay generated a gross farm income of $228,000 for 11 alfalfa producers and $16,870,625 for 2,691 grass hay producers. Total hay production for sale and on-farm use was 781,000 tons from 300,000 acres. It had a gross farm value of $39,050,000.

HOME VEGETABLE GARDENS

The gross value of home vegetable gardens in Louisiana was estimated at $141,149,250 in 1986. There were 313,665 gardens statewide, a 2.2 percent decrease. Families find that they can trim their food budgets and improve nutrition, as well as gain other benefits, by gardening and then add the savings to the home budget. Thirty-eight percent of Louisiana home gardens are in the urban areas around New Orleans, Baton Rouge and Shreveport. Freshness, quality, exercise and aesthetic values are still very important factors to gardeners. Because of the economic situation, interest in home gardens should increase in 1987.

NURSERY STOCK AND ORNAMENTALS

Total value of nursery stock and ornamentals during 1986 was $27.8 million. This represents a reduced farm value reflecting the depressed economy of the area in which the state's nursery markets are located.

PEANUTS

Peanuts are supported by a government program which includes in its provisions a marketing quota. In Louisiana there is no interest in growing peanuts outside the program. Since only a few growers have an allotment (Morehouse Parish), it is from these producers that the state's production is derived. In 1986 27 growers planted 262 acres. Average yields were 1994 pounds per acre, for a total production of 261 tons—a sharp drop from the 1,110 tons for 1985. Severe drought in August hurt yields on this crop. The total crop value was $104,000.

PECANS

The 1986 pecan crop was about 18 million pounds, up slightly from 1985. Because of excellent harvesting conditions and excellent prices, the Louisiana pecan grower received excellent returns for the 1986 pecan crop. Quality was excellent as a result of the harvesting conditions. The gross farm income for pecans in Louisiana was $9,589,445.

RICE

Louisiana had 425,321 acres of rice produced by 3,272 growers in 1986, a decrease from 455,847 acres produced in 1985. The acreage decrease occurred because the rice marketing loan program in effect in 1986 made it financially difficult to grow rice outside of the U.S.D.A. program which dictated planting only 65 percent of base acreage. A per acre average yield of 4,871 pounds was produced in 1986, a record high yield for Louisiana. This was up from the previous record high of 4,618 pounds per acre produced in 1985. The yield increase was caused by improved management and favorable growing conditions. The stubble crop acreage was at an all-time high in southwest Louisiana, which also contributed to the record yield level.

The estimated gross value of the 1986 crop was $149.2 million. Processing will add roughly $50.6 million to the value, so the total value of the crop will be about $199.8 million.

Rice acreage in 1987 should be similar to that planted in 1986. The rice program for the 1987 crop is basically unchanged. The 35 percent acreage reduction program will encourage production within the permitted acreage; virtually no rice will be produced outside of the program.

Both domestic use and exports should grow in 1987 but not as dramatically as in 1986. The marketing loan program has served to increase exports as well as domestic consumption and should continue to do so as long as it is in force.

SOD PRODUCTION

This is the third year to report sod production of fine turfgrass. There are 21 sod farms with 2,986 acres in production. This estimate indicates an 18.6 percent increase in sod acreage over last year. Most turfgrass produced is centipede grass. A distant second is St. Augustine grass, followed by hybrid bermuda. Other grasses of minor consequence include zoysia, carpetgrass and common bermuda.

The 1986 gross farm value for harvestable sod is estimated at $8,660,734. Several hundred more acres are presently growing and will be sold in 1987.

Interest in production of fine turf sod is growing. Sod demand fluctuates, primarily with construction. This industry is suitable for large scale production and mechanization and thus interests agronomic producers not satisfied with their present commodity situation. Traditional crop farmers are considering sod production to enhance their cash flow situations. Marketing is a significant limiting factor. Some specialized equipment and irrigation are needed.

SOYBEANS

Harvested acreage in 1986 was 1.95 million acres, down from the 2.43 million of 1985 and the 2.75 million acres of 1984. Reasons for this decline are poor net income caused by low prices and adverse weather conditions. The need to rotate to grain crops to combat diseases, insects, nematodes and weeds has also been a factor.

Approximately 9,500 soybean growers averaged 18 bushels per acre for a total production of 35 million bushels, down from the 45 million of 1985 and the 72 million bushels in 1984. The total value of the crop is estimated at $185,000,000.

Part of the 1986 crop was planted earlier than normal. This caused some problems with dwarfing out. Most of the remainder was planted by June 15. Continuous rains in June and early July followed by drought and heat stress in late July and August caused stunting of plants, pod abortion and delays in maturity. There were also high infestations of the southern green stink bug and many fields which were diagnosed as having viral infections. These may also have contributed to maturity problems. As a result, yields were 4-5 bushels under the normal state average and growers again sustained huge financial losses from soybeans. Acreage is expected to drop further in 1987.

SUGARCANE

Sugarcane was grown commercially in 15 parishes by about 715 producers in 1986. Some 246,000 acres were produced for sugar, and another 21,000 acres were harvested for seed cane. The average yield of cane was about 30.4 gross tons per acre. This represents about a 14 percent increase in gross tonnage over 1985.

Sugar prices were somewhat higher than in 1985 because of reduced sugar imports. No sugar was sold above the market stabilization price of 21.78 cents per pound. Per capita consumption was 60.9 pounds, down 1.1 pounds from 1985.

Sugar production per acre increased in 1986 to about 5,447 pounds, up 16.4 percent from 1985 production figures of 4,680 pounds per acre. The world price of sugar, as in 1985, ranged from about 5 to 7 cents per pound, well below production costs in every sugar-producing country.

The stable prices in 1986 and the reduced import quotas for 1987 should encourage growth of the Louisiana acreage by about 6 to 7 percent for 1987. World surpluses are expected to continue for the next crop year.

SWEET POTATOES

The 17,332 acres of sweet potatoes planted in 1986 represent an approximate 10 percent reduction from 1985. This reduction was caused primarily by the low price received for the 1985 crop and the loss experienced by sweet potato producers in 1985 because of the excessively wet harvest season. The average price received for processing potatoes was $2/bushel. This accounts for approximately 70 percent of the crop.

Most of the sweet potatoes for fresh market (approximately 30 percent of the crop) are sold to shippers who then wash, grade, pack and sell on the national market. The average price growers received for fresh market potatoes was $4/bushel when sold to packers and shippers. The average price the shipper received was estimated at $8/bushel even though the price increased to $12/bushel f.o.b. for Thanksgiving and Christmas. The value of the crop to the growers and grower-shippers is estimated at $19,712,650, up significantly from 1985. Generally the acreage increases following a year when price is favorable. Therefore, if farmers can get financing, there could be a slight increase in acreage this year. There is a small carryover of stored sweet potatoes which usually encourages a strong early "green" market in July. However, the price received for the Louisiana crop is determined to a large extent by the size of the crop North Carolina has each year.

TOBACCO

Tobacco production in Louisiana decreased from 35,000 pounds in 1985 to 30,000 pounds in 1986. The decline resulted from a drop from 35 acres in 1985 to 30 acres in 1986 while yields remained at 1,000 pounds per acre. The crop had a gross farm value of $54,000 and was grown by 12 producers.

Source: Louisiana Cooperative Extension Service

FRENCH MARKET

EDUCATION

HISTORY OF EDUCATION IN LOUISIANA

The first school in Louisiana was the Ursuline Convent for girls which was established 1727. The curriculum, limited to reading, writing, needlework and catechism was later expanded to include such subjects as history, geography, English, and mathematics. From 1734 until 1824 the Ursuline Convent was located on Chartres Street. In 1824 the convent was moved to more spacious quarters between Dauphine Street and the levee where it remained until 1912. In 1912 the school was moved to State Street; its present location. To the Ursulines is attributed the distinction of establishing the first convent in the Mississippi valley and the first, and for many years the only girls' school in Louisiana.

There is a record of a request made by Bienville to the crown in 1742 for the establishment of a college in Louisiana, but such a venture was probably considered too impractical at such a time and the request was refused. The territory of Louisiana was large while the French colonists were widely scattered and relatively few in number.

During this period a great many small private schools sprang up both in the city and throughout the territory. In 1772 the Spanish crown established a public school which offered Latin, grammar, reading, and writing. However free education was unpopular; pride forbade many from accepting charity even in the form of education, and public school attendance was a virtual announcement of poverty.

A year after Louisiana was purchased by the United States a public school established in New Orleans but it also suffered from the stigma of poverty. In 1805 plans were made for the establishment of the College of Orleans—to be supported by lotteries, later by appropriations. Although the College of Orleans enjoyed a rather short life, it indicated the need for higher education in the state.

In 1819 the College of Rapides and the Academy of Natchitoches were founded and the following year the College of Baton Rouge. In 1821 the Academy of the Sacred Heart was established at Grand Coteau.

The establishment in 1824 of the College of Ouachita instituted a new departure in the field of education in Louisiana for it was the first nonsectarian college. In the same year the College of Louisiana was established at Jackson with state appropriations. The Jackson College was somewhat more English in character than any of its predecessors. Also, in 1824 the Convent of St. Michael's at Convent was founded under the auspices of the Order of the Sacred Heart.

The Academy of Covington was founded in 1828, the Clinton Female Academy in 1830. In 1831, Jefferson College was founded, also non-sectarian. Jefferson College enjoyed a brief period of success, although it incurred the animosity of those who believed a religious education as important as a purely academic one. Around 1844 a fire destroyed many of the school buildings and thereafter Jefferson College suffered gradual decline. In the same year (1831) Franklin College in Opelousas was established by an act of the legislature.

During this period an effort was made to provide education for the indigent in an acceptable form. There grew up a great many rather small schools and academies which were subsidized by the state in return for admitting a certain percentage of indigent children. Among them were Montpelier (1883); Academy of Claiborne (1836); Ouachita Female Academy (1837); Academy of West Baton Rouge (1837); Avoyelles Academy (1837); Catahoula Academy (1840); Covington Female Academy (1837); Spring Creek Academy (1838); Caddo Academy (1838); Franklinton Academy (1838); Pine Grove Academy (1838); Plaquemines Academy (1839); Minden Female Seminary (1839); Vermillionville Academy (1840); and the Union Male and Female Academy (1840).

In 1845 funds were provided for free public schools in New Orleans, and in 1847 the first bill was passed providing for free education throughout the state. The system was supported by a state tax on property, as well as poll tax receipts.

In 1845 a merger of Mississippi College with Louisiana College formed Centenary College then at Jackson, now in Shreveport. In 1949 the Jesuits founded the College of Immaculate Conception in New Orleans. The Holy Cross nuns established St. Basil's Academy at Plaquemine (1856) and the Academy of the Immaculate Conception (1858) at Opelousas.

In 1850 New Orleans received 750,000 dollars for public education from the estate of John McDonogh from which 35 public schools were built. St. Mary's College in New Orleans opened in 1855. In 1853 the legislature passed a bill providing for a State Seminary of Learning which opened its doors in 1860. Colonel William T. Sherman, later a general in the Union army, served as its first president. In 1869, the University was moved to Baton Rouge, renamed La. State University, and in 1877 the Agricultural and Mechanical College merged with it.

During Reconstruction education for white children probably suffered but Negro education advanced tremendously. These Negro institutions for higher learning were established: Flint Medical College was established in the 1870's, Leland University (Baptist) in 1870; Southern University in 1879; Straight University (Congregationalist) in 1870; Union Normal School in 1879, later became New Orleans University (Methodist).

In 1884 Tulane University was founded with the money donated by Paul Tulane, and in 1886 H. Sophie Newcomb College was established as a part of Tulane. The Louisiana State Normal School at Nat-

chitoches (now The Northwestern State College of La.) was established in 1884.

Around the turn of the century and in more recent times several schools and universities have been established. Louisiana Polytechnic Institute at Ruston in 1894; Southwestern Louisiana Institute at Lafayette (now the University of Southwestern Louisiana) in 1901; Louisiana College at Pineville in 1906; Loyola in New Orleans in 1904; Xavier University (Negro) in New Orleans in 1915; the Baptist Bible Institute in New Orleans in 1917; Southeastern Louisiana College at Hammond in 1925; and New Orleans University and Straight merged in 1935 to form Dillard University for Negroes.

LOUISIANA COLLEGES AND UNIVERSITIES

LOUISIANA STATE UNIVERSITY AND AGRICULTURAL AND MECHANICAL COLLEGE

Louisiana State University has evolved into a state-wide system of higher education, with seven campuses throughout the state and various adult education and extension programs in every parish.

LSU began as the Louisiana State Seminary of Learning and Military Academy, which opened for its first session on January 2, 1860, at Pineville, La. William Tecumseh Sherman, later famed for his Civil War exploits, was the first president. The Seminary was moved to Baton Rouge in 1869 and fire destroyed the original building. In 1870 the name was changed to Louisiana State University and seven years later the University was merged with the Agricultural and Mechanical College, which previously had been located in New Orleans.

This merger and subsequent increased legislative support led to the building of a "greater university," planning for which was begun in 1914. Construction of the present campus was begun in 1923 and put into use in 1925. Not until 1932 did the University completely abandon the old campus, which was located where the State Capitol gorunds are today.

The major academic divisions were founded as follows: Agricultural and Mechanical College, 1874; Law School, 1906; College of Arts and Sciences, College of Agriculture, College of Engineering, and College of Education, 1908; General Extension Division, 1924; College of Commerce 1928; School of Medicine, Library School, College of Chem-

istry and Physics, School of Music, School of Geology, and School of Journalism, and Graduate School, all 1931; Junior Division, 1933; School of Social Welfare, 1937; University College, 1951; LSU in New Orleans, 1958; LSU in Alexandria, 1959.

The campus is located on a 1,944-acre tract on the southern edge of Baton Rouge, with the principal buildings being grouped on a 300-acre plateau one half mile east of the Mississippi River. The architectural treatment is based on the domestic style of northern Italy (tan stucco, red tiled roofs), with buildings housing most of the classrooms and administrative offices being grouped around a double quadrangle and connected by collonaded passageways.

In New Orleans, the LSU System operates the LSU Medical Center and the University of New Orleans, a four-year institution with both undergraduate and graduate programs. Another school of medicine and LSU at Shreveport (a four-year branch) are located in Shreveport.

LSU at Alexandria, a two-year division, offers freshman and sophomore courses in liberal arts and business administration and conducts terminal programs leading to associates in nursing and in arts.

LSU at Eunice is a two-year division of the System established in 1967 and offers lower division curricula.

The LSU Law Center, originally established in 1906, became a separate school from Louisiana State University in 1977. The facility's new name is the Paul M. Hebert Law Center.

UNIVERSITY OF NEW ORLEANS

Louisiana State University in New Orleans was established by the Legislature in 1956, as a means of extending undergraduate facilities of Louisiana State University to the Greater New Orleans Metropolitan Area. A 99-year lease on its 178-acre site on Lake Pontchartrain, the site of a former Naval Air Station was obtained in late 1957 from the Board of Levee Commissioners of the New Orleans Levee District. The first freshman class, numbering approximately 1500 students, began attending classes on September 5, 1958, in the renovated buildings of the old air station.

A sophomore curriculum was added in September 1958, and a junior curriculum the following year. In the autumn of 1961, LSUNO offered a full four-year college curriculum, and it graduated its first senior class in June of 1962.

LSU MEDICAL CENTER

Established in New Orleans in 1931, the Louisiana State University Medical Center is now one of the nation's outstanding health-science training and research facilities. Now housed in every section of the state, the Medical Center, through its six professional schools and the hospitals with which they are affiliated, offers educational and training opportunities in the complete range of study encompassing the total spectrum of the health sciences, including the undergraduate, graduate, post-graduate and residency levels. Enrollment totals some 1600.

UNIVERSITY OF SOUTHWESTERN LOUISIANA

Established as Southwestern Louisiana Industrial Institute in 1898, the institution first offered instruction at the college level in 1916. It underwent a change of name in 1921, adopting the somewhat ostentatious title of Southwestern Louisiana Institute of Liberal and Technical Learning, and in 1960 was rechristened the University of Southwestern Louisiana.

The university now offers undergraduate instruction in liberal arts, agriculture, commerce, education, engineering and nursing, along with a graduate program. Recent additions to the curricula include degree programs in computer science and statistics, medical record science and vocational rehabilitation.

USL covers 735 acres, including three farms, and has a physical plant valued in excess of $20 million.

LOUISIANA TECH UNIVERSITY

Located at Ruston, the grounds of Louisiana Tech University comprise 50 acres within the city limits in addition to 29 acres for a demonstration farm, and 610 acres outside the city limits about a half mile away from the School of Agriculture and Forestry. The school opened on Sept. 23, 1895, in one two-story building.

The institution now has a physical plant valued at $25 million spread over 892 acres.

Long known as Louisiana Polytechnic Institute, the institution was granted university status by the legislature in 1970.

McNEESE STATE UNIVERSITY

The McNeese State University at Lake Charles was organized in 1938 as the Lake Charles Junior College. In 1940 its name was changed by the Board of Supervisors to John McNeese Jr. College. It operated for a time as a branch of L.S.U. In 1950 by an act of the Legislature it became a State College with a four-year course and placed under the supervision of the Board of Education.

McNeese, formally recognized as a university in 1970 by legislative action, is divided into five academic divisions and one department.

NICHOLLS STATE UNIVERSITY

Francis T. Nicholls Junior College of Louisiana State University was established in 1948 and eight years later became an independent, four-year state college. Legislative action in 1970 elevated the institution to university status.

Nicholls, a coeducational institution, offers undergraduate programs in liberal arts and teacher education. A Graduate Division, established in 1965, coordinates programs at the master's level in elementary and secondary education. school administration and supervision and guidance leading to the M.A. and M. Ed. A master's degree program in business administration was begun in 1968.

Located at Thibodaux, the campus encompasses 170 acres and has a physical plant valued at some $8 million.

NORTHEAST LOUISIANA UNIVERSITY

Located at Monroe, Northeast evolved from a junior college and experienced several name changes before becoming a full-fledged university in 1970.

Originally established as Ouachita Parish Junior College in 1928, the institution first opened its doors to students in 1931. It was renamed Northeast Center of Louisiana State University in 1934 and later became Northeast Junior College of LSU. It was made a separate four-year college in 1950 and experienced unusual growth before achieving university status.

Northeast offers undergraduate programs in liberal arts, business administration, education, pharmacy and pure and applied sciences. Graduate training is available in most departments.

Situated on a 160-acre site, the university's physical plant is valued at more than $20 million.

SOUTHEASTERN LOUISIANA UNIVERSITY

Southeastern Louisiana University, a four-year state institution, is located on a 375 acre campus in Hammond's northern outskirts. The university grants nationally-recognized Bachelor of Arts, Bachelor of Science, and Bachelor of Music degrees for academic work completed in Arts and Sciences. Teacher Training, Music, Business Administration, Social Sciences, Health and Physical Education, Home Economics, Agriculture, and Industrial Arts. Pre-professional courses preparing students for professional schools are also offered. Students may work in one of three divisions —Applied Sciences, Education, Liberal Arts.

Enrollment at Southeastern is more than 5,400. To provide for this student registration the college has 22 permanent buildings and some 20 odd temporary structures and Veteran's apartments. The buildings have a replacement value of $20,000,000.

Southeastern's dairy, chicken farm and beef cattle pastures are located on 752 acres, formerly U.S. Airport property.

An act of the legislature in 1970 bestowed upon Southeastern university status.

NORTHWESTERN STATE UNIVERSITY

Northwestern State University at Natchitoches, founded July 1884, is the oldest of Louisiana's state colleges. From 1885 to 1918, NSC operated as a Norman School and offered two years of work for the training of teachers; in 1918 the school became Louisiana State Normal College, offering four years of academic work.

The functions and curricula of the College having been greatly widened by 1944, the State Normal College took a new name—Northwestern State College of Louisiana—which was more indicative of its new and broader role. The College now consists of four undergraduate schools—Applied Arts and Sciences, Education, and Nursing—the Graduate School which was established in 1954.

Legislative action in 1970 elevated Northwestern to university status.

GRAMBLING UNIVERSITY

Established in 1901 as a Negro institution, Grambling has received widespread attention as a producer of outstanding athletes for the professional ranks.

Located just West of Ruston at the town of Grambling, the institution presently enrolls almost 4,000 men and women students in a variety of disciplines.

Baccalaureate degrees are available in industrial arts, institutional management, agriculture, agribusiness, liberal arts, business administration, elementary education, secondary education and health and physical education. Grambling also offers a curriculum in pre-nursing and a two-year secretarial training course.

SOUTHERN UNIVERSITY

Southern University consists of three campuses, the main campus at Baton Rouge, established in 1881, a branch institution in New Orleans, which opened in 1959, and a two-year branch in Shreveport, begun in 1967. The student bodies are predominantly Negro.

The Baton Rouge campus, long recognized as the largest predominantly Negro institution in the nation, enrolls almost 8,000 students and offers a wide range of programs at the bachelor's and master's levels. Master's degree programs are offered in social studies, industrial arts, home economics education, English, music, guidance counseling, education, business education, chemistry and biology. The Baton Rouge campus also offers a program in law.

Southern-New Orleans enrolls more than 1,500 students and its curricula include degree programs in business and the sciences.

TULANE UNIVERSITY OF LOUISIANA

Tulane University of Louisiana, which had its beginning in 1834 as the Medical College of Louisiana, comprises the College of Arts and Sciences, the H. Sophie Newcomb College for Women, the School of Architecture, the College of Commerce and Business Administration, the College of Law, the School of Medicine, the school of Social Work, the College of Engineering, the Graduate School. the Division of Graduate Medicine, the Summer Session, the Middle American Research Institute, and University College, which is the evening division of the university.

The College of Engineering includes the Department of Chemical, Civil, Electrical and Mechanical Engineering, and Newcomb College, which is the oldest coordinate college in the United States, includes the School of Art and School of Music.

Other units of Tulane include the Institute of Comparative Law, the Law-Science Institute, both within the College of Law; the Urban Life Research Institute, and the Division of Economic and Business Research, within the College of Commerce and Business Administration.

Organized in 1834, the Medical College of Louisiana was chartered in 1835 and a year later issued the first degrees in medicine and science ever conferred in Louisiana or the Southwest.

The greatest epoch in the educational history of the State of Louisiana be-

gan with a donation by Paul Tulane in 1882 of his New Orleans property for higher education. In 1884 the administrators of the Tulane Educational Fund received from the Legislature of Louisiana complete and perpetual control of the University of Louisiana. By this same act the name of the institution was changed to the Tulane University of Louisiana.

In 1886, Mrs. Josephine Louise Newcomb donated to the Tulane Educational Fund the sum of $100,000 to be used in establishing the H. Sophie Newcomb Memorial College for Women as a coordinate college of the university, named in honor of her only child who died in 1870. By her will in 1901 the university became the residuary legatee, and received an additional bequest for Newcomb College of about $2,700,000. At that time the college had the largest endowment among all women's colleges in the United States. These gifts enabled the administrators to round out the ideal of a university by advantages which had before been offered only to men.

LOUISIANA COLLEGE

Louisiana College is a private, coeducational, liberal arts college, owned by the Louisiana Baptist Convention and controlled by a Board of Trustees chosen by the Convention.

The college is fully accredited by the Southern Association of Colleges and Secondary Schools, and holds membership in the Association of American Colleges and the American Council of Education.

Louisiana College, founded at Pineville, Rapides Parish, Louisiana, October 3, 1906, was the successor of two earlier Louisiana Baptist Schools—Mt. Lebanon University and Keatchie Female College. Mt. Lebanon, located at Mt. Lebanon, Bienville Parish, was founded in 1852 by the North Louisiana Baptist Convention as a college for men. Keatchie College, located at Keatchie, DeSota Parish, in 1857, was founded by the Grand Cane Association of Baptist churches. After a varied history beset by financial difficulties, both schools came under control of the State Baptist Convention in 1899. An Education Commission was selected by the State Convention to administer the schools with the understanding that both would be succeeded by a more centrally located college as soon as a suitable campus could be selected. When Louisiana College was opened in 1906, Mt. Lebanon College was closed, followed by Keatchie a few years later.

Louisiana College was administered by the Education Commission until 1921, when the Commission was replaced by a Board of Trustees, as called for in a new charter.

Louisiana College is located in Pineville on the north side of the Red River, about one and one-half miles from the business district of Alexandria. The Pineville-Alexandria community is located in the center of the state and is easily accessible by highway, railroad, or air service.

The campus comprises an 81-acre tract, covered by native pines, oaks, and other trees.

CENTENARY COLLEGE

Centenary College, located at Shreveport is one of the oldest colleges in the Southwest. In fact, it is the oldest college west of the Mississippi River. Centenary College was originally located at Jackson, Louisiana, and was chartered in 1825, under the auspices of the Methodists. Among its students were Jefferson Davis and Judah P. Benjamin.

OUR LADY OF HOLY CROSS COLLEGE

Our Lady of Holy Cross College is a private, coeducational, four-year liberal arts college, owned by the Marianite Sisters of Holy Cross and controlled by a Board of Trustees chosen by the Sisters.

The Marianites have been involved actively in education for over one hundred years. These Sisters first arrived in New Orleans in 1848 and within a few years established many secondary and elementary schools. To prepare the women who came to the Congregation of Marianites for the teaching profession a Normal school was established in 1916 at the Academy of Holy Angels and was authorized by the General Assembly of Louisiana to confer degrees and to grant diplomas. From 1922 to 1938 the college functioned as a two-year Normal school approved by the Louisiana Department of Education. In July, 1938 the State Department approved the four-year teacher education program. The college conferred its first baccalaureate degree in July, 1942.

Within a few years the necessity of meeting the needs arising from the rapidly increasing enrollment gave rise to the separation of college and high school which were on the same grounds. Consequently, in April, 1960, the Holy Angels College Department moved to its present location in Aurora Gardens on the West Bank of the Mississippi River. Here the beautiful Southern mansion building of white pillars and red brick was dedicated on April 4, 1960 by Joseph Francis Rummel, Archbishop of New Orleans.

Our Lady of Holy Cross College opened its doors to the public in 1962. Today the scope of the college has expanded to meet the ever growing demands of the Civic community. Today the College continues to function in air-conditioned buildings on the forty acres of land donated by Mr. and Mrs. Ernest B. Norman, Sr.

LOYOLA UNIVERSITY OF THE SOUTH

Loyola University in New Orleans is a co-educational Catholic university founded and administered by the Jesuit Fathers and open to students of all faiths.

The Jesuit Fathers were among the earliest settlers of New Orleans and Louisiana. They have been credited with the introduction of sugar cane to the area, paving the way for one of the state's most important industries.

On February 1, 1840, the Jesuits established a college preparatory academy and the College of the Immaculate Conception in New Orleans at the corner of Baronne and Common streets. In 1904 they opened an academy and college on St. Charles Avenue opposite Audubon Park and the associated institutions were known as Loyola College. In 1911 the College of the Immaculate Conception was united with Loyola College on the present Loyola campus. At the same time, the Loyola Academy and the Academy of the Immaculate Conception were united to become Jesuit High School.

Loyola College was expanded to become Loyola University in the fall of 1911 and on June 10, 1912, was duly incorporated by the General Assembly of Louisiana and empowered to grant all university degrees.

Today the university stands as the largest Catholic university in the South with six fully accredited colleges offering more than 500 courses of study in approximately 45 degree programs.

The university's 18-acre campus is located in uptown New Orleans in an area of fine homes and quiet oak-lined streets. Buildings are mainly of Tudor-Gothic architecture and the entrance of the university, consisting of Marquette Hall, flanked across an emerald lawn by Holy Name of Jesus Church and Thomas Hall, is a familiar and impressive New Orleans view.

In recent years there have been a number of new buildings added to the campus, including the main library, costing approximately $900,000 and completed in 1950 and the Loyola Field House, costing $600,000, which seats 6500 persons and is the scene of the Sugar Bowl basketball tournament. It was completed in 1954.

of more than 12 blocks and contains besides the Administration Building which is constructed of Indiana limestone, a 100,000 volume library, gymnasium, sciences building, lounge, fine arts building, music building, dormitories, and a convent for the 35 sisters who conduct the university's affairs. The entire plant is valued at approximately $5 million. The faculty, including both religious and lay professors, number 105. There were 1,422 students at the university during the 1970-71 scholastic year.

Xavier's College of Pharmacy, founded in 1937, until two years ago was the only such college for Negroes in the south. The Fine Arts department is noted around the world for the excellence of its graduates and for the encouragement of arts among Negroes. The Music Department, which produces the yearly Xavier Grand Opera, kept grand opera alive in New Orleans during the decade or more between the last visit of the Metropolitan Opera and the founding of the New Orleans Opera. In 1954 Xavier amended its charter to admit white students as well as colored and thus, at this time, has no restrictions as to race, creed or sex. Xavier's students are drawn from more than 30 states and from at least four foreign countries. Among its 3500 graduates are men and women who have distinguished themselves by outstanding achievements in the sciences and arts as well as in the field of education.

XAVIER UNIVERSITY

Founded in 1915 by the Sisters of the Blessed Sacrament, an order of Roman Catholic women dedicated to missionary work among the Colored People and Indians of the United States, Xavier University of Louisiana is the only predominantly-Negro Catholic university in the United States. Located at Palmetto and Pine Streets, New Orleans, the campus covers an area

NEW ORLEANS BAPTIST THEOLOGICAL SEMINARY

Organized in 1917 under the name of Baptist Bible Institute, the New Orleans Baptist Theological Seminary became the official title in 1946 at the mandate of the Southern Baptist Convention which owns and controls the institution. From its beginning in Oct. 1918 until Sept. 1953 the Seminary was located at 1220 Washington Ave., which was purchased from the Sophie Newcomb College. In 1947 a 75-acre tract was purchased on Gentilly Boulevard for $250,000 on which buildings costing some $8,000,000 have been erected. Besides the administration building and other main buildings, the campus structures include 300 apartments, 5 residence halls, 30 faculty residences, a gymnasium and a children's building.

NOTRE DAME SEMINARY

Notre Dame Seminary at New Orleans opened its doors to students for the priesthood in 1923, after a million dollars had been subscribed and the building completed. On its beautiful grounds at 2901 So. Carollton Ave., embracing ten squares a large addition to the Seminary, Philosophy Hall was completed in 1955. A million-dollar gift was made by the Archdiocesan parishes for this purpose. The addition comprises a large library section for 35,000 volumes, a spacious auditorium, two lecture halls and rooms for 175 persons.

Notre Dame Seminary offers undergraduates work in the specialized fields of philosophy, history and religion. Students are prepared not only for the specific duties of priesthood but for education, secular as well as religious.

DILLARD UNIVERSITY

Dillard University is the successor to New Orleans University, founded in 1869 for Negro higher education by the Freedmen's Bureau, and Straight University founded and maintained at a later date by the American Missionary Society of New York. These universities were merged in 1935 to form Dillard University, named after Dr. James H. Dillard, a former professor at Tulane University, and later administrator of the John F. Slater Fund, established to aid in the advancement and promote the welfare of the Negro race.

Dillard University is located on Gentilly Road, New Orleans. Its campus is 63 acres in extent and its buildings and landscaping together make it one of the most beautiful in the South. The Stern Science Hall cost over $600,000. The Lawless Memorial Chapel cost $525,000. Value of property, buildings and equipment over $6 million. The total endowment is $6.5 mllion.

DELGADO MUSEUM OF ART

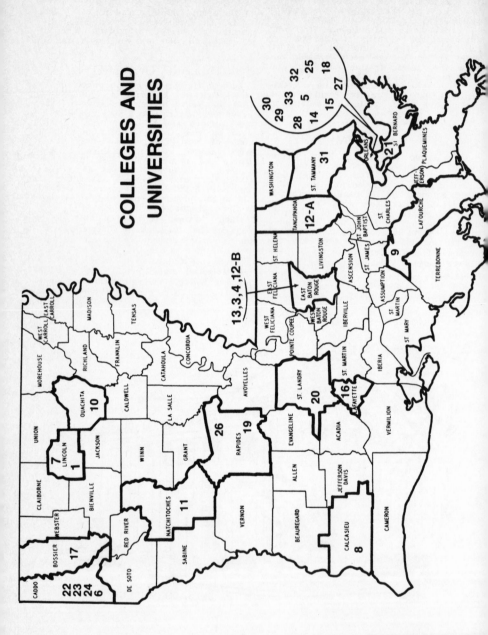

COLLEGES AND UNIVERSITIES

COLLEGES AND UNIVERSITIES

College or University	President	Registrar	Head of School of Education	Mailing Address	Telephone	Fall 1987 Enrollment
FOUR-YEAR PUBLIC						
1. Grambling State University, 1901 (1-A-S-D)	Dr. Joseph B. Johnson	Irene Thomas	Dr. Burnett Joiner	P.O. Drawer 607 Grambling 71245	(318) 247-3811	5,000
2. Louisiana State University System, 1860	Dr. Allen A. Copping			99 University Lakeshore Drive Baton Rouge 70803	(504) 388-2111	
3. LSU and A & M College, 1860 (2-A-S-D-R)	Dr. James H. Wharton Chancellor	Dr. O. Carruth McGehee	Dr. Charles W. Smith	Baton Rouge 70803	(504) 388-3202	27,707
4. Paul M. Hebert Law Center, 1977 (2-B-S-D-R)	William D. Hawkland Chancellor	Beth W. Loup		LSU, Baton Rouge 70803-1002	(504) 388-8491	700
5. LSU Medical Center, 1932 (2-S-M-D)*	Dr. Perry G. Rigby Chancellor	Susan A. Doucet Mr. Edmund A. Vidacovich		1440 Canal Street, Suite #1510 New Orleans 70112-2784	(504) 568-4800	2,500
6. LSU—Shreveport, 1967 (2-A-S-R)	Dr. E. Grady Bogue Chancellor	Kathleen G. Plante	Dr. B. E. Tabarlet	8515 Youree Drive Shreveport 71115	(318) 797-5000	4,300
7. Louisiana Tech University, 1895 (1-A-S-D-Q)	Dr. Daniel D. Reneau	Dr. Harold Pace	Dr. Jerry W. Andrews	P.O. Box 3168 Tech Station Ruston 71272	(318) 257-0211	10,200
8. McNeese State University, 1939 (1-A-S-D-R)	Dr. Robert D. Hebert	Linda Y. Finley	Dr. James M. Brown, Jr.	Lake Charles 70609	(318) 437-5000	8,000
9. Nicholls State University, 1948 (1-A-S-D-R)	Dr. Donald J. Ayo	S. Dan Montz, Jr.	Dr. Philip C. Bergeron, Jr.	University Station Thibodaux 70310	(504) 446-8111	6,950
10. Northeast Louisiana University, 1931 (1-A-S-D-R)	Dr. Dwight D. Vines	Barry M. Delcambre	Dr. Bob N. Cage	700 University Avenue Monroe 71209	(318) 342-2011	10,500
11. Northwestern State University of Louisiana, 1885 (1-A-S-D-R)	Dr. Robert A. Alost	Lynda Tabor	Dr. Edward Graham	College Avenue Natchitoches 71457	(318) 357-6441	6,000
12-A. Southeastern Louisiana University, 1925 (1-A-S-D-R)	Dr. G. Warren Smith	Dr. Randall Webb	Dr. Ronald Zaccari	P.O. Box 784 University Station Hammond 70402	(504) 549-2000	8,000
12-B. Southern University System, 1959	Dr. Joffre T. Whisenton			Southern Branch Post Office Baton Rouge 70813	(504) 771-4680	

COLLEGES AND UNIVERSITIES—Continued

College or University	President	Registrar	Head of School of Education	Mailing Address	Telephone	Fall 1987 Enrollment
13. Southern University and Agricultural and Mechanical System, 1881 (3-A-S-D-R)	Dr. Joffre T. Whisenton Dr. Wesley C. McClure Chancellor	Cleo Carroll, Jr.	Dr. Elaine Lewnau	Southern Branch Post Office Baton Rouge 70813	(504) 771-2011	9,500
14. Southern University at New Orleans, 1959 (3-A-S-R)	Dr. Dolores R. Spikes Chancellor	Dr. Melvin L. Hodges	Dr. Marilyn Ray	6400 Press Drive New Orleans 70126	(504) 282-4401	3,200
15. University of New Orleans, 1958 (2-A-D-R)	Dr. Gregory M. St. L. O'Brien Chancellor	S. Mark Strickland	Dr. David E. Kapel	Lakefront New Orleans 70148	(504) 286-6000	15,950
16. University of Southwestern Louisiana, 1901 (1-A-S-D-R)	Dr. Ray P. Authement	Wiltz P. Champagne	Dr. Robert Alciatore	USL Drawer 41008 Lafayette 70504	(318) 231-6000	15,500
TWO-YEAR PUBLIC						
17. Bossier Parish Community College, 1967 (4-A-R-S)	Dr. Douglas Peterson	Patty Hensley	Kathy McCallister	2719 Airline Drive N. Bossier City 71111	(318) 746-9851	2,250
18. Delgado Community College, 1970 (1-S-R)	Dr. Harry Boyer	Dr. K. Sippola City Park Campus Dr. Robert Evans West Bank Campus		501 City Park Avenue New Orleans 70119	(504) 483-4114	8,500
19. LSU—Alexandria, 1960 (2-S-R)	Dr. James W. Firnberg Chancellor	Richard Averitt		LSUA Campus Alexandria 71302-9633	(318) 445-3672	2,005
20. LSU—Eunice, 1967 (2-A-S-R)	Dr. Anthony Mumphrey Chancellor	Edith A. Cones		P.O. Box 1129 Eunice 70535	(318) 457-7311	1,750
21. St. Bernard Parish Community College, 1968 (4-A-R-S)	Dr. Daniel D. Daste Chancellor	Dr. Hugh Craft		1100 East Judge Perez Drive Chalmette 70043	(504) 277-1142	1,525
22. Southern University, Shreveport-Bossier City, 1967 (3-S-R)	Dr. Robert H. Smith Chancellor	Clifton Jones	Dr. Mary L. Wilson	3050 Martin L. King Jr. Drive Shreveport 71107	(318) 674-3300	800
FOUR-YEAR NONPUBLIC						
23. Baptist Christian College, 1961 (A-D-R)	Dr. Phillip Martin Dr. J. G. Tharpe Chancellor	Wanda C. Chappell	Dr. Edith Tharpe	3031 Hollywood Shreveport 71108	(318) 631-8875	275

	President			Address	Phone	Enrollment
24. Centenary College of Louisiana, 1825, Methodist (A-S-D-R)	Dr. Donald A. Webb	Johnson R. Watts	Dr. Robert N. Hallquist	P.O. Box 41188 Shreveport 71134-1188	(318) 869-5011	900
25. Dillard University, 1869 (A-S-D-R)	Dr. Samuel D. Cook	Dr. C. L. Reynolds	Dr. Jude T. Sorapuru	2601 Gentilly Boulevard New Orleans 70122	(504) 283-8822	1,280
26. Louisiana College, 1906, Baptist (A-S-D-R)	Dr. Robert L. Lynn	Ronald L. Ellis	Dr. Thomas W. Kelly	1140 College Drive Pineville 71359	(318) 487-7011	1,250
27. Loyola University of New Orleans, 1912, Catholic (A-S-D-R)	Rev. James C. Carter, S.J.	Dr. Bobs M. Tusa	Dr. Justin E. Levitov	6363 St. Charles Avenue New Orleans 70118	(504) 865-2011	5,210
28. New Orleans Baptist Theological Seminary, 1917 (S-D-R)	Dr. Landrum P. Leavell II	Dr. Bart C. Neal	Dr. Joe H. Cothen	3939 Gentilly Boulevard New Orleans 70126-4858	(504) 282-4455	2,000
29. Notre Dame Seminary School of Theology, 1923, Catholic— Men (S-D-R)	Rev. Monsignor Gregory M. Aymond	Margaret Ann Breaux	Rev. William S. Swann	2901 South Carrollton Avenue New Orleans 70118-4391	(504) 866-7426	100
30. Our Lady of Holy Cross College, 1938, Catholic (A-S-R)	Sr. Mary Charles Clement, M.S.C	Sr. Ann Louise Arno, M.S.C.	Dr. Judith Miranti	4123 Woodland Drive New Orleans 70114	(504) 394-7744	700
31. St. Joseph Seminary College, 1891, Catholic— Men (S-D-R)	Very Rev. Pius C. Lartigue, O.S.B.	Thomas Siegrist, Sp.E.		St. Benedict 70457	(504) 892-1800	85
32. Tulane University, 1834 (A-B-S-M-D-R)	Dr. Eamon M. Kelly	Earl D. Retif	Dr. Jean A. King	6823 St. Charles Avenue New Orleans 70118	(504) 865-5201	10,302
33. Xavier University of Louisiana, 1917, Catholic (A-S-D-R)	Dr. Norman C. Francis	Marlene Robinson	Dr. Antoine Garibaldi	7325 Palmetto Street New Orleans 70125	(504) 486-7411	2,000

Year designates the founding date of the institution based on first student enrollment and first classes held.

(1) Under the control and supervision of Board of Trustees for State Colleges and Universities.
(2) Under the control and supervision of Louisiana State University Board of Supervisors.
(3) Under the control and supervision of Southern University Board of Supervisors.
(4) Under the control and supervision of State Board of Elementary and Secondary Education.
(A) Accredited for teacher training by the Louisiana Department of Education.
(B) Accredited by American Bar Association and Association of American Law Schools.
(S) Accredited by the Southern Association of Colleges and Schools.
(M) Accredited by the Association of American Medical Colleges.
(D) Dormitory Facilities.
(R) Operating on regular semester system.
(Q) Operating on quarter system.

* Schools included in the Louisiana State University Medical Center are School of Allied Health, School of Dentistry, School of Nursing, School of Medicine—New Orleans, School of Medicine—Shreveport, and Graduate School.

Louisiana Elementary and Secondary Education

STATE DEPARTMENT OF EDUCATION

State Department of Education
P.O. Box 44064
Baton Rouge, LA 70804

Education Building Location:
626 North Fourth Street
Information: (504) 342-4411
LA Public Assistance Line: 1-800-272-9872

State Superintendent of Public Education
(504) 342-3602

TOTAL PUBLIC REGISTRATION, 1985-86

PARISH	WHITE	NONWHITE	K-8	9-12	SPEC. ED.	TOTAL	DESCENDING RANK
ACADIA	7,870	2,743	7,855	2,514	244	10,613	21
ALLEN	3,665	1,266	3,513	1,350	68	4,931	42
ASCENSION	8,524	3,773	8,202	3,517	578	12,297	19
ASSUMPTION	2,928	2,192	3,676	1,237	207	5,120	41
AVOYELLES	5,627	2,939	5,864	2,468	234	8,566	26
BEAUREGARD	5,968	1,215	5,151	1,996	36	7,183	31
BIENVILLE	1,609	1,906	2,239	941	335	3,515	54
BOSSIER	15,534	5,634	14,047	5,505	1,616	21,168	10
CADDO	23,450	28,251	35,332	14,096	2,273	51,701	4
CALCASIEU	24,130	9,877	23,150	9,642	1,215	34,007	5
CALDWELL	1,724	548	1,738	525	9	2,272	62
CAMERON	1,966	129	1,534	561	0	2,095	63
CATAHOULA	1,817	980	2,076	717	4	2,797	59
CLAIBORNE	1,319	2,057	2,387	988	1	3,376	56
CONCORDIA	2,608	2,595	3,703	1,263	237	5,203	40
DESOTO	3,174	3,167	4,454	1,689	198	6,341	35
EAST BATON ROUGE	28,417	31,928	40,219	17,851	2,275	60,345	2
EAST CARROLL	270	2,212	1,810	616	56	2,482	60
EAST FELICIANA	1,347	2,334	2,688	925	68	3,681	52
EVANGELINE	4,740	2,549	5,354	1,586	349	7,289	30
FRANKLIN	3,168	2,418	4,128	1,359	99	5,586	37
GRANT	3,220	740	2,712	1,152	96	3,960	48
IBERIA	10,179	5,911	11,467	3,918	705	16,090	16
IBERVILLE	2,088	3,916	4,341	1,515	148	6,004	36
JACKSON	2,061	1,276	2,424	881	32	3,337	57
JEFFERSON	33,615	24,206	39,075	13,971	4,775	57,821	3
JEFFERSON DAVIS	5,458	2,012	5,352	2,066	52	7,470	29
LAFAYETTE	19,185	8,829	19,728	7,350	936	28,014	6
LAFOURCHE	13,586	3,898	12,070	5,063	351	17,484	14
LASALLE	2,983	458	2,516	902	23	3,441	55
LINCOLN	3,960	3,161	5,115	1,798	208	7,121	32
LIVINGSTON	15,339	1,238	11,853	4,531	193	16,577	15
MADISON	714	2,880	2,597	940	57	3,594	53
MOREHOUSE	2,738	4,157	5,006	1,758	131	6,895	33
NATCHITOCHES	4,168	4,017	5,908	1,978	299	8,185	28
ORLEANS	7,730	77,648	59,148	20,777	5,453	85,378	1
OUACHITA	14,049	4,092	11,986	4,541	1,614	18,141	12
PLAQUEMINES	3,093	1,697	3,393	1,294	103	4,790	44
POINTE COUPEE	1,211	2,498	2,721	912	76	3,709	51
RAPIDES	14,599	9,637	16,213	6,330	1,693	24,236	8
RED RIVER	931	1,007	1,443	467	28	1,938	64
RICHLAND	2,499	2,389	3,613	1,226	49	4,888	43
SABINE	3,038	2,181	3,728	1,475	16	5,219	39
ST. BERNARD	8,743	972	6,629	2,985	101	9,715	23
ST. CHARLES	5,335	3,007	6,053	2,209	80	8,342	27
ST. HELENA	641	1,641	1,486	672	124	2,282	61
ST. JAMES	1,523	2,975	3,021	1,407	70	4,498	46
ST. JOHN THE BAPTIST	2,625	3,822	4,441	1,778	228	6,447	34
ST. LANDRY	8,538	9,760	13,074	4,508	716	18,298	11
ST. MARTIN	5,379	3,831	6,608	2,332	270	9,210	24
ST. MARY	7,142	5,924	9,423	3,281	362	13,066	18
ST. TAMMANY	21,843	4,449	18,662	7,243	387	26,292	7
TANGIPAHOA	9,588	7,967	12,426	4,680	449	17,555	13
TENSAS	359	1,223	1,099	436	47	1,582	66
TERREBONNE	14,971	6,531	15,328	5,020	1,154	21,502	9
UNION	2,885	1,672	3,268	1,195	94	4,557	45
VERMILION	7,947	1,993	7,231	2,511	198	9,940	22
VERNON	9,502	3,711	10,029	2,927	257	13,213	17
WASHINGTON	3,195	2,324	3,875	1,486	158	5,519	38
WEBSTER	5,521	3,512	6,451	2,468	114	9,033	25

PARISH	WHITE	NONWHITE	K-8	9-12	SPEC. ED.	TOTAL	DESCENDING RANK
WEST BATON ROUGE	1,958	1,874	2,547	1,071	214	3,832	50
WEST CARROLL	2,247	692	2,178	714	47	2,939	58
WEST FELICIANA	959	977	1,336	490	110	1,936	65
WINN	2,554	1,400	2,834	1,046	74	3,954	49
CITY OF MONROE	2,077	8,977	8,576	2,337	141	11,054	20
CITY OF BOGALUSA	2,633	1,586	2,979	1,094	146	4,219	47
LOUISIANA	444,464	359,381	561,083	210,081	32,681	803,845	

TOTAL NONPUBLIC REGISTRATION, 1985-86

PARISH	WHITE	NONWHITE	K-8	9-12	SPEC. ED.	TOTAL
ACADIA	1,854	91	1,613	332	0	1,945
ALLEN	0	0	0	0	0	0
ASCENSION	1,387	111	1,191	307	0	1,498
ASSUMPTION	0	0	0	0	0	0
AVOYELLES	868	123	881	110	0	991
BEAUREGARD	0	0	0	0	0	0
BIENVILLE	0	0	0	0	0	0
BOSSIER	195	21	216	0	0	216
CADDO	3,242	784	2,989	1,004	33	4,026
CALCASIEU	2,304	748	2,469	547	36	3,052
CALDWELL	0	0	0	0	0	0
CAMERON	0	0	0	0	0	0
CATAHOULA	0	0	0	0	0	0
CLAIBORNE	324	0	222	102	0	324
CONCORDIA	371	0	251	120	0	371
DESOTO	154	0	113	41	0	154
EAST BATON ROUGE	14,856	1,864	12,344	4,270	106	16,720
EAST CARROLL	373	23	285	111	0	396
EAST FELICIANA	536	0	367	169	0	536
EVANGELINE	856	0	590	266	0	856
FRANKLIN	0	0	0	0	0	0
GRANT	0	0	0	0	0	0
IBERIA	1,275	284	1,190	369	0	1,559
IBERVILLE	828	12	670	170	0	840
JACKSON	0	0	0	0	0	0
JEFFERSON	25,778	2,079	21,354	6,109	394	27,857
JEFFERSON DAVIS	435	31	405	61	0	466
LAFAYETTE	4,991	917	4,462	1,446	0	5,908
LAFOURCHE	2,550	94	2,048	596	0	2,644
LASALLE	0	0	0	0	0	0
LINCOLN	795	0	527	268	0	795
LIVINGSTON	279	6	225	60	0	285
MADISON	380	2	258	124	0	382
MOREHOUSE	853	117	735	182	53	970
NATCHITOCHES	420	14	262	172	0	434
ORLEANS	19,954	14,364	21,832	12,094	392	34,318
OUACHITA	1,285	32	829	488	0	1,317
PLAQUEMINES	1,441	227	1,249	402	17	1,668
POINTE COUPEE	1,497	155	1,149	503	0	1,652
RAPIDES	2,840	312	2,619	446	87	3,152
RED RIVER	283	2	174	111	0	285
RICHLAND	331	4	208	127	0	335
SABINE	0	0	0	0	0	0
ST. BERNARD	2,851	70	2,827	94	0	2,921
ST. CHARLES	651	72	723	0	0	723
ST. HELENA	0	0	0	0	0	0
ST. JAMES	352	19	371	0	0	371
ST. JOHN THE BAPTIST	1,928	87	1,544	471	0	2,015
ST. LANDRY	2,112	274	1,678	708	0	2,386
ST. MARTIN	798	225	836	187	0	1,023
ST. MARY	1,436	133	1,163	406	0	1,569
ST. TAMMANY	4,254	178	3,071	1,312	49	4,432
TANGIPAHOA	2,425	80	2,095	410	0	2,505
TENSAS	0	0	0	0	0	0
TERREBONNE	2,570	140	2,110	600	0	2,710
UNION	72	0	48	24	0	72
VERMILION	1,112	60	932	240	0	1,172
VERNON	0	0	0	0	0	0
WASHINGTON	0	0	0	0	0	0
WEBSTER	269	0	180	89	0	269
WEST BATON ROUGE	447	35	482	0	0	482
WEST CARROLL	0	0	0	0	0	0
WEST FELICIANA	0	0	0	0	0	0
WINN	0	0	0	0	0	0
CITY OF MONROE	1,085	212	826	471	0	1,297
CITY OF BOGALUSA	260	6	266	0	0	266
LOUISIANA	116,157	24,008	102,879	36,119	1,167	140,165

NONPUBLIC SCHOOLS

Nonpublic schools in Louisiana are made up in large part by Catholic parochial schools, which are grouped into six superintended dioceses. Other private schools are independent commercial academies or are affiliated with religious groups other than Roman Catholics. Religious groups with affiliated Louisiana private schools include Assemblies of God, Baptists, Bible Churches, Churches of Christ, Churches of God, Episcopals, Lutherans, Methodists, Presbyterians, and Seventh Day Adventists.

SUPERINTENDENTS OF CATHOLIC DIOCESAN SCHOOL BOARDS

Alexandria Diocese
Sr. Marjorie Hebert, MSC
Superintendent
P.O. Box 7417
Alexandria 71306
(318)445-2401

Baton Rouge Diocese
Sr. Mary Michaeline Green, O.P.
Superintendent
P.O. Box 2028
Baton Rouge 70821
(504)387-0561

Houma-Thibodaux Diocese
Sister Immaculata Paisant, M.S.C.
Superintendent
P.O. Box 9077
Houma 70361
(504)868-7720

Lafayette Diocese
Sr. Myra Banquer, MSC
Superintendent
P.O. Drawer E
Lafayette 70502-8005
(318)261-5529

Lake Charles Diocese
Sister Gloria Cain, SSND
Superintendent
4029 Avenue G
Lake Charles 70601
(318)439-7418

New Orleans Archdiocese
Howard J. Jenkins
Archdiocesan Superintendent
7887 Walmsley Avenue
New Orleans 70125
(504)861-9521

Shreveport Diocese
Miss Noel Byrd
Superintendent
2500 Line Avenue
Shreveport 71104
(318)222-2006

PARISHES IN EACH CATHOLIC DIOCESE

Alexandria Diocese	Shreveport Diocese	Baton Rouge Diocese	Houma-Thibodaux Diocese	Lake Charles Diocese
Avoyelles	Bienville	Ascension	Jefferson*	Allen
Caldwell	Bossier	Assumption	Lafourche**	Beauregard
Catahoula	Caddo	East Baton Rouge	St. Mary**	Calcasieu
Concordia	Claiborne	East Feliciana	Terrebonne	Cameron
Franklin	DeSoto	Iberville		Jefferson Davis
Grant	East Carroll	Livingston	**Lafayette Diocese**	
LaSalle	Jackson	Pointe Coupee	Acadia	**New Orleans Archdiocese**
Madison	Lincoln	St. Helena	Evangeline	
Natchitoches	Morehouse	St. James	Iberia	Jefferson*
Rapides	Ouachita	Tangipahoa	Lafayette	Orleans
Tensas	Red River	West Baton Rouge	St. Landry	Plaquemines
Vernon	Richland	West Feliciana	St. Martin**	St. Bernard
Winn	Sabine		St. Mary	St. Charles
	Union		Vermilion	St. John
	Webster		Washington	St. Tammany
	West Carroll		City of Bogalusa	
	City of Monroe			

* The city of Grand Isle is in the Houma-Thibodaux Diocese and the rest of Jefferson is in the New Orleans Archdiocese. **The portion of St. Mary Parish east of the Atchafalaya River is in the Houma-Thibodaux Diocese and the portion west of the Atchafalaya River is in the Lafayette Diocese.

Comparison of Louisiana and the U.S.: Enrollment and Attendance[a]

	Louisiana	U.S.	Louisiana's Rank
Public school enrollment, Estimates, Fall 1985	792,700.00	39,534,826.00	17
Fall 1984 enrollment in public schools as percent of school-age population, 1984	83.84	87.85	44
Nonpublic school enrollment as percent of total school enrollment, Fall 1980	16.97	10.80	5
Average daily attendance as percent of fall enrollment, 1985-86	90.05	92.53	42
Average daily attendance as percent of average daily membership, 1985-86	94.35	NA	25

[a] Source: Rates and ranks were taken from the National Education Association's Rankings of the States, 1985 and 1986. Rankings include the 50 states and the District of Columbia.

LOUISIANA STUDENT REGISTRATION, 1985-86

PUBLIC STUDENT REGISTRATION, ACTUAL 1985-86, PROJECTED 1986-90

	K	1	2	3	4	5	6	7	8	SPECIAL ED. ELEMENTARY	K-8 TOTAL
1985-86	69907.0	74703.0	64478.0	63052.0	59336.0	57496.0	55029.0	61132.0	55950.0	21966.0	583049.0
1986-87	NA	83053.8	70353.3	62549.7	62317.4	58119.4	56976.2	57082.3	55699.5	NA	506151.6
1987-88	NA	83173.0	73070.7	68087.9	61905.4	60697.1	57875.2	59995.9	52510.0	NA	517315.2
1988-89	NA	85770.3	73175.6	70717.8	67386.5	60295.8	60442.1	60942.5	55190.2	NA	533920.8
1989-90	NA	83951.5	75460.7	70819.3	69989.4	65634.4	60042.5	63645.5	56061.0	NA	517315.2

(CONTINUED)

	9	10	11	12	SPECIAL ED. SECONDARY	9-12 TOTAL	K-12 GRAND TOTAL	GRADUATES
1985-86	64888.0	55665.0	48039.0	41489.0	10715.0	220796.0	803845.0	38428.0
1986-87	60378.4	56933.7	47750.2	40949.8	NA	206012.1	712163.7 *	38251.2
1987-88	59180.7	54014.5	47385.9	41284.8	NA	201865.9	719181.1 *	38564.1
1988-89	55791.8	52943.0	44956.2	40969.8	NA	194660.8	728581.6 *	38269.8
1989-90	58639.5	49911.3	44064.4	38869.1	NA	191484.3	737088.6 *	36307.6

* THE TOTALS FOR THE PROJECTIONS DO NOT INCLUDE KINDERGARTEN OR SPECIAL EDUCATION STUDENTS.

NONPUBLIC STUDENT REGISTRATION, ACTUAL 1985-86, PROJECTED 1986-90

	K	1	2	3	4	5	6	7	8	SPECIAL ED. ELEMENTARY	K-8 TOTAL
1985-86	13086.0	12844.0	12023.0	11698.0	10704.0	10846.0	10598.0	10500.0	10580.0	926.0	103805.0
1986-87	NA	15110.4	13434.4	11338.1	11149.5	10413.3	10578.4	10248.2	9783.2	NA	92055.5
1987-88	NA	15285.5	13983.1	12636.3	10726.9	10740.3	10036.3	10098.1	9500.5	NA	93107.0
1988-89	NA	15723.0	14145.2	13152.5	11955.2	10333.2	10351.5	9580.6	9459.9	NA	94701.1
1989-90	NA	15179.6	14550.0	13304.9	12443.5	11516.4	9959.1	9881.5	8975.1	NA	95810.1

(CONTINUED)

	9	10	11	12	SPECIAL ED. SECONDARY	9-12 TOTAL	K-12 GRAND TOTAL	GRADUATES
1984-85	9718.0	9417.0	8713.0	8271.0	241.0	36360.0	140165.0	8405.0
1986-87	8679.0	8789.8	8551.3	8044.0	NA	34064.1	126119.6 *	7698.1
1987-88	8103.4	7983.8	8063.7	7982.6	NA	32133.5	125240.5 *	7639.3
1988-89	7952.0	7454.3	7324.3	7527.4	NA	30258.0	124959.1 *	7203.7
1989-90	7835.6	7315.0	6838.5	6837.2	NA	28826.3	124636.4 *	6543.2

*THE TOTALS FOR THE PROJECTIONS DO NOT INCLUDE KINDERGARTEN OR SPECIAL EDUCATION STUDENTS.

STUDENT REGISTRATION, ETHNICITY AND SEX

	PUBLIC			NONPUBLIC		
	MALE	FEMALE	TOTAL	MALE	FEMALE	TOTAL
AM. INDIAN	1,626	1,461	3,087	79	79	158
ASIAN	4,986	4,376	9,362	469	468	937
BLACK	173,557	165,783	339,340	9,840	11,353	21,193
HISPANIC	4,078	3,514	7,592	844	876	1,720
WHITE	230,615	213,849	444,464	57,894	58,263	116,157
TOTAL	414,862	388,983	803,845	69,126	71,039	140,165

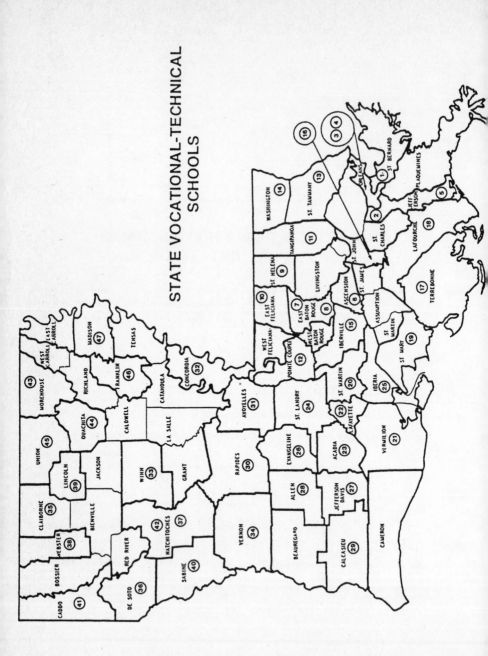

STATE VOCATIONAL-TECHNICAL SCHOOLS

STATE VOCATIONAL-TECHNICAL SCHOOLS

School	Director	Mailing Address	Telephone
Region 1			
1. Elaine P. Nunez Vocational-Technical School	John J. Kane	3700 LaFontaine Street, Chalmette 70043	(504)277-8111
Branch: Port Sulphur Vo-Tech School	John J. Kane	P.O. Drawer 944, Port Sulphur 70083	(504)277-8111
2. Jefferson Parish Vocational-Technical School	John L. D'Aubin	5200 Blair Drive, Metairie 70001	(504)733-5250
3. New Orleans Regional Vocational-Technical Institute	Justin M. Lemaitre	980 Navarre Avenue, New Orleans 70124	(504)483-4666
4. Sidney N. Collier Vocational-Technical School	Levi Lewis Sr.	3727 Louisa Street, New Orleans 70126	(504)945-8080
5. Jefferson Parish West Bank Vocational-Technical School	Estella F. Lain (Acting)	475 Manhattan Boulevard, Harvey 70058	(504)361-6464
Region 2			
6. Ascension Parish Vocational-Technical School	Charles A. Tassin Sr.	P.O. Box 38, Sorrento 70778	(504)342-4261
7. Baton Rouge Vocational-Technical Institute	Robert R. Buck	3250 North Acadian Thruway, Baton Rouge 70805	(504)355-5621
8. J.M. Frazier Sr. Vocational-Technical School	Burton J. Brumfield	555 Julia Street, Baton Rouge 70802	(504)342-6828
Branch: Port Side Vo-Tech School	Burton J. Brumfield	3233 Rosedale Road, Port Allen 70767	(504)342-6828
9. Florida Parishes Vocational School	James Meadows	P.O. Box 130, Greensburg 70441	(504)222-4251
10. Folkes Vocational-Technical School	James V. Soileau	P.O. Box 808, Jackson 70748	(504)634-2636
11. Hammond Area Vocational School	Vacancy	P.O. Box 489, Hammond 70404	(504)345-0731
12. Memorial Area Vocational School	Cosby D. Joiner	P.O. Box 725, New Roads 70760	(504)342-7471
13. Slidell Vocational-Technical School	George W. Foster	P.O. Box 827, Slidell 70459-0827	(504)643-9610
14. Sullivan Vocational-Technical Institute	Michael J. Murphy	1710 Sullivan Drive, Bogalusa 70427	(504)735-8291
15. Westside Vocational-Technical School	Alfred S. Bell	P.O. Box 733, Plaquemine 70764-0733	(504)344-2895
Region 3			
16. River Parishes Vocational-Technical School	Paul Fair Jr.	P.O. Drawer AQ, Reserve 70084	(504)536-4418
17. South Louisiana Vocational-Technical Institute	F. Travis Lavigne Jr.	P.O. Box 5033, Houma 70361	(504)873-7773
Branch: Golden Meadow Branch Vo-Tech School	F. Travis Lavigne Jr.	P.O. Drawer J, Galliano 70354	(504)873-7773
Branch: LA Marine and Petroleum Institute	F. Travis Lavigne Jr.	P.O. Box 10251, Station I, Houma 70363	(504)873-7773

STATE VOCATIONAL-TECHNICAL SCHOOLS - Continued

School	Director	Mailing Address	Telephone
Region 3			
18. Thibodaux Area Vocational-Technical School	Kenneth A. Callahan	P.O. Box 1831, Thibodaux 70302-1831	(504)446-8243
19. Young Memorial Vocational-Technical School	Lyman J. Wilson	P.O. Box 2148, Morgan City 70381	(504)384-6526
Region 4			
20. Evangeline Vocational-Technical School	Prosper Chretien	P.O. Box 68, St. Martinville 70582	(318)394-6466
21. Gulf Area Vocational-Technical School	Ray Lavergne	P.O. Box 878, Abbeville 70510	(318)893-4984
22. Lafayette Regional Vocational-Technical Institute	Shelton J. Cobb	P.O. Box 4909, Lafayette 70502-4909	(318)235-5541
23. Southwest Louisiana Vocational-Technical Institute	Richard A. Arnaud	P.O. Box 820, Crowley 70527-0820	(318)783-3723
24. T.H. Harris Vocational-Technical School	Ceasar Veazie Jr.	P.O. Box 713, Opelousas 70570	(318)942-4902
25. Teche Area Vocational-Technical School	Henry G. Segura	P.O. Box 1057, New Iberia 70561-1057	(318)365-6672
26. Ville Platte Vocational-Technical School	Charles B. Coreil	P.O. Box 296, Ville Platte 70586	(318)363-2197
Region 5			
27. Jefferson Davis Vocational-Technical School	Nolan H. Ackoury	P.O. Box 1327, Jennings 70546-1327	(318)824-4811
28. Oakdale Vocational-Technical School	Charles R. Baggett	P.O. Box EM, Oakdale 71463	(318)335-3944
29. Sowela Technical Institute	Earl Lee Hammett	P.O. Box 16950, Lake Charles 70616	(318)491-2698
Region 6			
30. Alexandria Vocational-Technical Institute	Ms. Patricia Juneau	4311 S. MacArthur Drive, Alexandria 71302	(318)487-5443
31. Avoyelles Vocational-Technical Institute	Ward Nash	P.O. Box 307, Cottonport 71327	(318)876-2401
32. Concordia Vocational-Technical School	Arthur Ray King	P.O. Box 152, Ferriday 71334	(318)757-6501
33. Huey P. Long Memorial Vocational School	Donald R. Purser	303 South Jones Street, Winnfield 71483	(318)628-4342
34. Lamar Salter Vocational-Technical School	Alferd Davis	Route 2, Box 25, Leesville 71446	(318)537-3135

STATE VOCATIONAL-TECHNICAL SCHOOLS - Continued

School	Director	Mailing Address	Telephone
Region 7			
35. Claiborne Vocational-Technical School	James H. Horton	3001 Minden Road, Homer 71040	(318)927-2034
36. Mansfield Branch Vocational-Technical School	Donnie Robison	P.O. Box 1236, Mansfield 71052	(318)872-2243
Branch: Coushatta Branch Campus	Donnie Robison	P.O. Box 755, Coushatta 71019	(318)932-3417
37. Natchitoches-Central Area Vocational-Technical School	Ms. Dolores Tucker	P.O. Box 657, Natchitoches 71457	(318)357-0822
38. Northwest Louisiana Vocational-Technical School	James E. McMichael	P.O. Box 835, Minden 71055-0835	(318)377-6832
39. Ruston Vocational-Technical School	Floyd L. Ellerman	P.O. Box 1070, Ruston 71273-1070	(318)255-6152
40. Sabine Valley Vocational-Technical School	David Crittenden	P.O. Box 790, Many 71449	(318)256-5663
41. Shreveport-Bossier Vocational-Technical Institute	Sam Merritt	P.O. Box 78527, Shreveport 71137-8527	(318)226-7811
42. Vocational Curriculum Development and Research Center*	David Poston	P.O. Box 1159, Natchitoches 71457	(318)352-5348
Region 8			
43. Bastrop Vocational-Technical School	Don R. Wood	P.O. Box 1120, Bastrop 71221-1120	(318)281-8954
44. Delta-Ouachita Vocational-Technical Institute	Dean Adkins	609 Vocational Parkway, West Monroe 71291	(318)396-7431
45. North Central Area Vocational-Technical School	Ms. Noreen Smith	P.O. Box 548, Farmerville 71241	(318)368-3179
46. Northeast Louisiana Vocational School	Kenneth Bridges	P.O. Box 672, Winnsboro 71295	(318)435-5096
47. Tallulah Vocational-Technical School	Patrick T. Murphy	P.O. Drawer 1740, Tallulah 71284-1740	(318)574-4820
Branch: Lake Providence Vo-Tech School	Patrick Murphy	P.O. Box 368, Lake Providence 71254	(318)574-4820

* Instructional programs not offered

LOUISIANA HIGH SCHOOL GRADUATES, 1986

Comparisons of Louisiana and National SAT
Scores for College-Bound Seniors, 1975-1986[a]

Year	SAT Math Score		SAT Verbal Score	
	Louisiana	National	Louisiana	National
1975-76	501	472	464	431
1976-77	505	470	466	429
1977-78	501	468	464	429
1978-79	495	467	460	427
1979-80	499	466	462	424
1980-81	494	466	461	424
1981-82	505	467	470	426
1982-83	502	468	469	425
1983-84	508	471	472	426
1984-85	503	475	473	431
1985-86	507	475	474	431

[a]Source: Data taken from College Entrance Examination Board of Princeton, New Jersey, *State SAT Scores 1976 through 1984 and College Board ATP Summary Report, Louisiana, 1985-86.*

NUMBER OF HIGH SCHOOL GRADUATES—1985-86

GROUP	SUMMER SESSION LAST SUMMER			MIDTERM THIS SCHOOL YEAR			END OF SESSION THIS SCHOOL YEAR			GRAND TOTAL		
	MALE	FEMALE	TOTAL	MALE	FEMALE	TOTAL	MALE	FEMALE	TOTAL	MALE	FEMALE	TOTAL
PUBLIC												
AM. INDIAN	3	0	3	1	2	3	93	77	170	97	79	176
ASIAN	5	2	7	7	6	13	178	124	302	190	132	322
BLACK	203	160	363	198	182	380	6,283	7,634	13,917	6,684	7,976	14,660
HISPANIC	2	2	4	12	9	21	126	141	267	140	152	292
WHITE	219	115	334	208	208	416	10,738	11,490	22,228	11,165	11,813	22,978
TOTAL	432	279	711	426	407	833	17,418	19,466	36,884	18,276	20,152	38,428
NONPUBLIC												
AM. INDIAN	0	0	0	0	0	0	5	3	8	5	3	8
ASIAN	0	0	0	0	0	0	15	15	30	15	15	30
BLACK	7	1	8	9	0	9	402	511	913	418	512	930
HISPANIC	1	0	1	0	0	0	41	68	109	42	68	110
WHITE	45	28	73	16	23	39	3,382	3,833	7,215	3,443	3,884	7,327
TOTAL	53	29	82	25	23	48	3,845	4,430	8,275	3,923	4,482	8,405
TOTAL PUBLIC AND NONPUBLIC												
AM. INDIAN	3	0	3	1	2	3	98	80	178	102	82	184
ASIAN	5	2	7	7	6	13	193	139	332	205	147	352
BLACK	210	161	371	207	182	389	6,685	8,145	14,830	7,102	8,488	15,590
HISPANIC	3	2	5	12	9	21	167	209	376	182	220	402
WHITE	264	143	407	224	231	455	14,120	15,323	29,443	14,608	15,697	30,305
TOTAL	485	308	793	451	430	881	21,263	23,896	45,159	22,199	24,634	46,833

APPROVED SPECIAL STATE SCHOOLS

Parish	School	Pupil Registration	Contact Person	Address	Telephone
East Baton Rouge	Louisiana School for the Deaf* +	455	Dr. Harvey J. Corson, Superintendent	2888 Brightside Lane P.O. Box 3074 Baton Rouge 70821	(504)769-8160
	Louisiana School for the Visually Impaired* +	95	Dr. Richard Day, Superintendent	1120 Government Street P.O. Box 4328 Baton Rouge 70821	(504)342-4756
	Down Syndrome Project**	30	Susan Batson	3365 Dalrymple Drive Baton Rouge 70802	(504)342-1257
Natchitoches	Louisiana School for Math, Science, and the Arts++	403	Dr. Richard Brown, Director	715 College Avenue Natchitoches 71457	(318)357-0606
Orleans	Human Development Center (LSUMC)	32	Dr. Bob Crow	1100 Florida Avenue New Orleans 70119	(504)942-8200
Ouachita	Northeast Louisiana Special Education Center*	40	Dr. Aline Cicardo, Superintendent	800 Claiborne Monroe 71201	(318)362-5152
Rapides	Louisiana Special Education Center* +	70	Dr. Aline Cicardo, Superintendent	P.O. Drawer 7797 Alexandria 71306	(318)487-5484

* Operated by Board of Elementary and Secondary Education
** Operated by State
+ Residential
++ Independent Residential State School operated by a Board of Directors

State and Federal Expenditures for Special Education, 1975–86[a]

Fiscal Year	State Expenditures	Federal Expenditures	Total Expenditures
1975–76	45,240,398	2,090,877	47,331,275
1976–77	50,726,050	4,070,828	54,796,878
1977–78	65,161,131	6,552,921	71,714,052
1978–79	75,929,655	15,944,240	91,873,895
1979–80	92,586,079	21,244,965	113,831,044
1980–81	97,204,327	22,382,895	119,587,222
1981–82	130,467,163	23,456,764	153,923,927
1982–83	148,872,431	19,086,871	167,959,302
1983–84	153,091,839	22,564,590	175,656,429
1984–85	165,423,833	24,255,120	189,678,953
1985–86	168,858,739	26,881,888	195,740,627

[a] Source: These figures were supplied by the Division of Special Education in the Louisiana State Department of Education.

APPROVED PROPRIETARY SCHOOLS IN LOUISIANA

Legislative Act 311 of 1972 provided for the establishment of the Advisory Commission on Proprietary Schools, its membership, powers and duties; the licensing and regulating of schools selling courses of instruction in the state, including all persons selling such courses; the procedures therefore, and the penalties for all violations. Proprietary Schools are referred to as those classified nonpublic, which sell or offer for sale mostly post-secondary instruction which leads to an occupation. All approved schools are bonded and have complied with the provisions of the law. Application must be submitted annually with final approving authority vested with the Louisiana State Board of Elementary and Secondary Education.

City	Name of School	Administrator	Mailing Address	Telephone
Alexandria	Commercial College of Alexandria	Ralph White	3349 Masonic Drive, 71301	(318)442-1864
	Delta Career College - Electronics Div.	John F. McCray	5905 Highway 28 West, 71303	(318)442-4818
	Delta Career College - Medical Div.	John F. McCray	110 Bolton Avenue, 71301	(318)442-9337
	Delta School of Commerce	John F. McCray	1239 Jackson Street, 71301	(318)442-9586
	H & R Block Income Tax School	Robert Fowler	3312-B Jackson Street, 71301	(318)455-5671
	Louisiana Business College	Daniel Ritz	5003 Masonic Drive, Suite A,	(318)445-0475
Baton Rouge	AEW College of Photography		921 N. Lobdell Blvd., Suite D, 70806	(504)924-4421
	American College	Monty Miller	2840 Florida Boulevard, 70802	(504)346-8545
	Bartender's Academy	Janice Thigpen	4864 Constitution Avenue #1B, 70808	(504)924-1901
	Baton Rouge School of Computers, Inc.	Betty Truxillo	9255 Interline Avenue, 70809	(504)923-2525
	Camelot Career College	Ronnie L. Williams	2618 Wooddale Blvd., Suite A, 70806	(504)828-3005
	Carroll Institute of Polygraphy	William Carroll III	4560 North Boulevard, Suite 115, 70806	(504)927-6907
	Commercial College	Ken Osborne	5677 Florida Boulevard, 70806	(504)927-3470
	Corporate Institute of Travel	Jesse E. LeBlanc III	3111 S. Sherwood Forest, 70816	(504)292-5446
	Delta College, Inc.	Bill Clark	7290 Exchange Place, 70806	(504)927-7780
	Diesel Driving Academy, Inc., (SACS)	Philip O. Johnson	8136 Airline Highway, 70815	(504)929-9990
	HART Institute	Dale Christensen	2300 Government Street, 70806	(504)387-4536
	H & R Block Income Tax School	Larry Carver	1825 South Sherwood Forest Boulevard, 70816	(504)273-2835
			4669 Plank Road, 70805	(504)357-9770
			6250 Florida Boulevard, 70806	(504)273-3399
	Ibelco Personal Development School	Ida Hall	1723 Dallas Drive, Suite C, 70806	(504)924-4852
	International Bartending Institute	Warren J. LaCoste	4864 Constitution Avenue, Suite 1B, 70808	(504)923-1190
	International Technical Institute, Inc.	Joey Martin	13944 Airline Highway, 70817	(504)292-4230
	John Casablancas Modeling & Career Center	Dolly-Dean Martinez	3535 S.Sherwood Forest Blvd.,Suite 201, 70816	(504)292-2424
	Louisiana Accounting Education Foundation	Vincent Brenner	LNB Building, Suite 726, 70801	(504)388-6202
	Louisiana Art Institute	Norma Routt	7707 Waco Drive, 70806	(504)924-5329
	Louisiana Bartending Institute	Anthony Palermo	4626 Jamestown Avenue, Suite 2, 70808	(504)925-9288
	Louisiana Court Reporting College	Lori Cobb		
		Martha Montelongo	8146 One Calais, Suite 103-104, 70809	(504)767-3162
	National Truck Driver Education Institute	Carlos Gonzales	P.O. Box 66334, 70896	(504)261-1694

APPROVED PROPRIETARY SCHOOLS IN LOUISIANA-(Continued)

City	Name of School	Administrator	Mailing Address	Telephone
Baton Rouge (cont.)	North American Education Center	Andrew James	7600 Airline, 70814	(504)924-7118
	Radio Shack Computer Center #7586	Wayne Wilcox	7007 Florida Blvd., 70806	(504)928-5260
	Southland School of Taxidermy	Huey Tortorice	2603 Osceola Street, 70805	(504)356-2903
	Spencer College	Sharon Burke	2902 Florida Boulevard, 70806	(504)383-7701
	Technical Learning Center	Uhland Carter	5966 Heidel Avenue, 70805	(504)357-9921
	Virginia Schools	Karen Everhart	4173 Government Street, 70806	(504)344-3838
	WKG-TV Video Electronics College	Lionel Thibodeaux	141 Ocean Drive, 70806	(504)928-0632
Bossier City	Bossier Occupational Training Center	David Broussard	2026 Texas Street, 71111	(318)742-4011
	Career Institute of Bossier	David Broussard	2026 Texas Street, 71111	(318)742-1771
	H & R Block Income Tax School	Glen Taylor	183 Bossier Center, 71111	(318)746-3211
Chalmette	H & R Block Income Tax School	Nancy Arnold	8400 West Judge Perez, 70043	(504)244-4431
	Sea School	Duane Herbert	210 West Urguhart, 70043	(504)277-6319
Denham Springs	Legal Training Center	Kathy Underwood	P.O. Box 1175, 70727-1175	(504)665-0005
Gretna	Belinda Constant School of Reporting	Belinda Constant	1700 Stumpf Blvd., Suite 74, 70053	(504)361-7755
	Creative Floral Design School of N.O.	Jeanne Safley	714 Lafayette Street, 70053	(504)366-7676
	Delta College, Inc.	Bill Clark	511 Westbank Expressway, 70058	(504)362-5445
Jefferson	AACEP, Inc.	Jessie Barfield	P.O. Box 10523, 70181	(504)737-0128
Kenner	Institute of Electronic Technology	Julian Thompson	3921 Florida Street, 70065	(504)469-8601
	International Bartending Institute	Daphne Roundtree	2327 Veterans Boulevard, Suite E, 70062	(504)468-8068
	Louisiana Bartending Institute	Tony Palermo	2327 Veterans Boulevard, Suite B, 70002	(504)467-1344
	New Orleans Exam Prep Center	Betty K. Wallace	1600 20th Street, 70062	(504)469-9013
Lafayette	Acadiana Technical College	Lester Mitchell	102 Savonne Drive, Scott, 70583	(318)235-7327
	Delta School of Nursing Assistant Division	Larry Gremillion	815 Congress Street, 70501	(318)235-1147
	Delta Schools, Inc.	Peggy Fassio	4549 Johnston St., 70503	(318)988-2211
	H & R Block Income Tax School	Harold Pritchard	317 Frontage Road, 70501	(318)235-8507
	Images, Inc.	Gwendolyn Fontenot	104 Merchants Boulevard, Suite 4, 70508	(318)232-6945
	International Bartending Institute	Shawn Butz	P.O. Box 30970, 502 Belle Downs St., 70503	(318)232-8535
	Louisiana Bartending Institute	Monique Abed-Champagen	850 Kaliste Saloom, 70508	(318)232-8535
	Southern Technical College of Lafayette, Inc.	C.W. Stewart	105 Patriot Street, 70508	(318)981-4010
	Travel Affair Inc. School of Travel Instruction	Gwendolyn Bourgeois	623 W. Pinhook Road, 70503	(318)235-7572
Lake Charles	Delta School of Business	Gary Holt	517 Broad Street, 70601	(318)439-5765
	Acadiana Technical College	Lester Mitchell	1015 6th Avenue, 70601	(318)433-4488
	H & R Block Income Tax School	Shelia Bellais	3309 Ryan Street, 70601	(318)478-6500
	Institute of Electronic Technology	Mark Montgomery	3505 5th Avenue, 70605	(318)478-8095
	Outrigger Marine Driving Academy	Olen Clark	P.O. Box 6709, 70601	(318)439-5940

City	Name of School	Administrator	Mailing Address	Telephone
LaPlace	Martin International, Inc. of Delaware	Walter Martin	408 Belmont Drive, 70068	(504)652-3087
LaRose	LaRose Exam Prep Center	T.B. Houston Jr.	Highway 1 & Oak D Street, 70373	(504)693-7553
Mandeville	Fashion Steps Modeling Company	Chanelle Chatelain	4480 Highway 22, 70448	(504)626-5210
	Owner Builder Systems, Inc.	David McDonald	P.O. Box 1149, 70448	(504)626-7695
Marrero	H & R Block Income Tax School	Nancy Arnold	1701 Barataria Boulevard, 70072	(504)340-0048
	Phillips Junior College	Linda Meredith	5201 Westbank Expressway, 70072	(504)348-1182
	Westbank Business College	Brent Henley	4633 Westbank Expressway, 70072	(504)347-8411
Meraux	Glamour Modeling School	Karen Berthalot	4801 E. Judge Perez, 70075	(504)279-3764
Metairie	Biggers College	Virgene Biggers	601 Papworth Avenue, Suite 200, 70005	(504)831-3333
	Cameron College (SACS)	Eleanor Cameron	2629 North Causeway, 70002	(504)
	Darcor	Dennis Richards	4405 North I-10 Service Road, 70002	(504)888-6297
	Dealer's Choice School of Dealing	Nicholas Crefasi	4209 Lime Street, 70006	(504)887-5527
	Delta College, Inc.	Randall Wagley	734 Martin Behrman Avenue, 70005	(504)838-8823
	Eastern College of Health Vocations	Susan Dalto	2748 Metairie Lawn Drive, 70002	(504)834-8644
	Franklin College of Court Reporting	Mary Franklin	4441 Utica Street, Suite 200, 70002	(504)454-0102
	H & R Block Income Tax School	Carol Brister	3314 Transcontinental Drive, 70002	(504)887-0727
	International Bartending Institute	Kenneth A. Wallace	1900 Veterans Boulevard, 70005	(504)887-0800
	John Casablancas Modeling and Career Center	Connie Plaisance	3619 18th Street, Suite C, 70002	(504)885-1500
	John Robert Powers School of New Orleans	Nanette Planas	4241 Veterans Boulevard, 70002	(504)445-7575
	Joker's Wild School of Dealing	Yvonne P. Todd	3780 Veterans Boulevard, 70002	(504)887-9272
	New Orleans School of Dog Grooming	Loretta Voiron	4201 Lime Street, 70006	(504)887-6967
	Professional Bartenders School, Inc.	Marti Boyer	2400 David Drive, 70003	(504)455-1123
	Professional Reporters College of Court Reporting	Mildred J. Griffin	5041 Wade Drive, 70003	(504)455-0923
	R.E.I.S. Training Center	Harold Zlatnicky	3605 Division Street, 70002	(504)888-6848
	Radio Shack Computer Center #7686	Barbara Cordon	3750 Veterans Boulevard, 70002	(504)454-3681
	Russell Papania School of Floral Art	Russell Papania	4409 Chastant Street, 70006	(504)888-1212
Monroe	Delta School of Nursing Assistant Division	Clint Moran	102 South Grand, 71201	(318)322-8870
	H & R Block Income Tax School	James Wilde	1202 North 18th Street, 71201	(318)387-5601
	Louisiana Business College	Joyce Beaty	4500 Millhaven Road, 71203	(318)325-8261
	Quality Employment Health Care Service	Bessie Hoard	3631 Curry Street, 71203	(318)388-2208
	Robinson Business College	Emily Robinson	604 Jack McEnery Street, 71201	(318)323-7515
	Southern Technical College of Monroe(SACS)	Jerry Krise	1811 Auburn Avenue, 71202	(318)323-1500

APPROVED PROPRIETARY SCHOOLS IN LOUISIANA-(Continued)

City	Name of School	Administrator	Mailing Address	Telephone
Morgan City	Morgan City Exam Prep Center	Rudy Sistrunk	1112 7th Street, 70380	(504)385-3228
New Iberia	Delta Schools Inc.	Patsy Clemens	412 West Admiral Doyle, 70560	(318)365-7348
New Orleans	American College	Ronald Witt	2025 Canal Street, Suite 210, 70112	(504)522-8824
	American International Travel School	Norman L. Augusta	921 Canal Street, Suite 720, 70112	(504)525-0101
	Americo Technical Institute	Danny Bedford	264 Harbor Circle, 70126	(504)246-4105
	Andy Garza Floral School	Andy Garza	1301 Dealers Avenue, 70123	(504)275-3892
	Audubon College	Marvin Weindorff	3901 Tulane Avenue, 70119	(504)486-6141
	Barbizon School of Modeling	Linda Bennett	921 Canal Street, Suite 1117, 70112	(504)581-3737
	Bayou Technical Institute	Albert Murphy Jr.	7818 Earhart Blvd., 70125	(504)486-6628
	Cameron College	Eleanor Cameron	P.O. Box 19288, 70179	(504)821-5881
	CareerCom College of Business	Richard Swanson	7166 Crowder Blvd., 70127	(504)242-2109
	Coastal Training Institute	Voc White	2001 Canal Street, Suite 101, 70112	(504)522-2400
	Crescent City Tech	Edward Venanzi	6600 Plaza Drive, Suite 105, 70127	(504)245-1604
	Crescent City Bartending School	Ronald Richard	209 North Broad Avenue, 70119	(504)822-3362
	Delta International	Bonnie Broel	1508 St. Charles Avenue, 70130	(504)525-1000
	Dryades Street YMCA School of Commerce	Stanley Robinson	2220 Dryades Street, 70113	(504)522-8811
	Food Service Institute	David Schaffer	1115 St. Mary Street, 70130	(504)524-8636
	Future Reporters	Louise Partee	1414 Jefferson Avenue, 70115	(504)891-3077
	Gartrell School of Travel	Robert Gartrell	431 Gravier Street, 70130	(504)525-3649
	H & R Block Income Tax School	Nancy Arnold	9954 Lake Forest Blvd., 70127	(504)244-4400
		Carol Brister	3502 Magazine Street, 70115	(504)887-0800
		Nancy Arnold	7190 Downman Road, 70125	(504)244-4431
	Jackie M., The School for Professional Modeling	Jackie Maysonave	4139 Toulouse Street, 70119	(504)282-0476
	Laboratory Assistance Program	Wanda Serino	3301 Tulane Avenue, 70119	(504)822-6412
	Louisiana School of Floral Design	Mary Holleman	5921 Alost Street, 70126	(504)242-8807
	Lucas Travel School	Patricia Korchek	921 Canal Street, Suite 720, 70112	(504)525-0101
	Meadows Draughon College	Sharon Burke	8700 Lake Forest Blvd., Suite 112, 70127	(504)244-0212
	New Orleans Art Institute	Mike Willmon	6055 Magazine Street, 70118	(504)899-2081
	O'Henry's Bartending Institute	Henry Rosenblat	623 South Carrollton Avenue, 70118	(504)866-0002
	Orleans Regional Security Institute	Wade Schindler	1500 Sugar Bowl Drive, 70112	(504)587-3170
	Page Navigation School	Robert Page	205 South Galvez Street, 70119	(504)822-2391
	Phillips Junior College	Georjean Crosley	1333 South Clearview Parkway, 70121	(504)734-0123
	Refrigeration School of New Orleans	Godfrey Adams	1201 Mazant Street, 70117	(504)949-2712
	Rutledge College of Charlotte	Larry Pate	2609 Canal Street, 70119	(504)822-6111

City	Name of School	Administrator	Mailing Address	Telephone
New Orleans (cont.)	Stanley Kaplan Education Center	Christopher Wells	3839 Ulloa Street, Suite 2C, 70119	(504)486-7273
	Vocational Training Center (NAITS)	William Fisher	3900 General Taylor Street, 70125	(504)
	Walker, M.F., and Associates	M.F. Walker	616 Baronne Street, Suite 102, 70113	(504)595-8954
New Sarpy	South East Training Center, Inc.	Eugene Oncale	3348 Rivers Road, 70078	(504)764-6409
Shreveport	American College	Arthur Lovett	820 Cotton Street, 71101	(318)424-1000
	American School of Business	Jerry Wood	701 Professional Drive, 71105	(318)798-3333
	Ayers Institute	Raymond Vay Jr.	1431 Wilkinson Street, 71103	(318)221-1853
	Barbizon School of Modeling	Edward Beakey	3010 Knight Street, Suite 150, 71105	(318)865-6593
	Commercial College	Brent Henley	2640 Youree Drive, 71104	(318)865-6571
	Computerland of Shreveport Training Center	Wilson D. Grant	1314 Shreveport Barksdale Highway, 71105	(318)869-1256
	Diesel Driving Academy, Inc.	Phillip Johnson	P.O. Box 36949, 71133-6949	(318)636-6300
	Draughon Business College	Terry F. Shultz	2924 Knight Street, Suite 318, 71105	(318)868-6060
	H & R Block Income Tax School	Glen Taylor	4424 Youree Drive, 71105	(318)869-3448
	K-9 Specialists	Paul Nelson	175 Overton Brooks Road, 71106	(318)686-7017
	LA School of Professions	Ernest Lampkins	4140 Hollywood Drive, 71109	(318)631-9818
	Mister Lynn's Inc.	Glenda Martin	3007 Knight Street, Suite 126, 71105	(318)868-2728
	National College of Technology	W.C. Taylor	P.O. Box 36768, 71133	(318)227-9108
	Southern Technical College of Shreveport	Thomas DuPriest	3004 Knight Street, 71105	(318)869-3800
	United Engines, Inc.	Glen Smith	7255 Greenwood Road, 71119	(318)635-8022
Slidell	The Travel School	Edwin Polk	1680 Old Spanish Trail, 70458	(504)641-4422
St. Gabriel	Hunt Correction Institute	Herb Carter	P.O. Box 174, Highway 74, 70776	(504)642-3306
	Louisiana Correctional Institute for Women (NCACS, AICS)	Herb Carter	P.O. Box 26, Highway 74, 70776	(504)642-5529
Vidalia	Louisiana Business College (AICS)	Carlton Coon	901 Carter Street, 71373	(318)336-9636

APPROVED NURSING SCHOOLS

School	Mailing Address	Telephone
BACCALAUREATE DEGREE		
Dillard University	2601 Gentilly Boulevard, New Orleans 70122	(504) 283-8822
Louisiana State University	420 South Prieur Street, New Orleans 70112	(504) 568-6570
	420 South Prieur Street, New Orleans 70112	(504) 568-6271
McNeese State University	Lake Charles 70609	(318) 477-2520
Northeast Louisiana University	700 University Avenue, Monroe 71209	(318) 342-3063
Northwestern State University of Louisiana	1800 Warrington Place, Shreveport 71101	(318) 424-5133
	1427 Kings Highway, Shreveport 71103	(318) 674-6252
Southeastern Louisiana University	Box 781, Hammond 70402	(504) 549-2156
University of Southwestern Louisiana	Box 490, Lafayette 70504	(318) 231-6808
Nicholls State University*	Box 2143, Thibodaux 70310	(504) 446-8111
ASSOCIATE DEGREE		
Louisiana State University at Alexandria	Alexandria 71303	(318) 445-3672
Louisiana State University at Eunice	P. O. Box 1129, Eunice 70535	(318) 457-7311
Louisiana State University Medical Center	420 South Prieur Street, New Orleans 70112	(504) 568-6689
	420 South Prieur Street, New Orleans 70112	(504) 568-6271
Louisiana Tech University	P. O. Box 6458, Ruston 71272	(318) 257-2572
Nicholls State University	Box 2143, Thibodaux 70310	(504) 446-8111
Northwestern State University of Louisiana	1427 Kings Highway, Shreveport 71101	(318) 226-3543
	1427 Kings Highway, Shreveport 71101	(318) 674-6252
DIPLOMA		
Charity Hospital School of Nursing	450 South Claiborne Avenue, New Orleans 70112	(504) 568-6461
Our Lady of the Lake Medical Center	5000 Hennesy Boulevard, Baton Rouge 70809	(504) 769-3100
Touro Infirmary School of Nursing	3450 Chestnut Street, New Orleans 70115	(504) 897-8610

*Granted initial approval in May.

APPROVED FLIGHT TRAINING SCHOOLS

	Name of School	Mailing Address	Telephone
Baton Rouge	Metro Aviation, Inc.*	9181A Plank Road, 70811	(504) 357-2348
Lafayette	Cypress Aviation, Inc.	P. O. Box 53323, 70505	(318) 261-0530
Lake Charles	Transit Aviation, Inc.*	P. O. Box 5933, 70606	(318) 478-7722
Natchitoches	Northwestern State University of Louisiana*	Natchitoches 71457	(318) 357-5102
New Iberia	Pelican Aviation Corporation*	P. O. Box 2008, 70560	(318) 365-5451
New Orleans	Airtaix Aviation, Inc.*	Room 120, Lakefront Airport, 70126	(504) 242-3214
	New Orleans Aviation, Inc.*	Walter Wedell Hanger, Lakefront Airport, 70126	(504) 246-7070
	R. W. Aviation	P. O. Box 7117, Aero Hanger, Lakefront Airport, 70126	(504) 246-6543
Ruston	Louisiana Tech University*	6445 Tech Station, 71272	(318) 257-2691
Shreveport	Air American, Inc.*	1408 Airport Drive, 71107	(318) 221-2208
	Greater Shreveport Air Service, Inc.*	1504 Airport Drive, 71107	(318) 424-5269
	Louisiana Tech University—Barksdale*	P. O. Box 128, 71110	(318) 746-8472
	Southern Aviation Corporation*	1450 Airport Drive, 71107	(318) 221-4391
Thibodaux	Nicholls Aviation, Inc.*	P. O. Box 1222, 70301	(504) 447-3386

*Approved for Veterans Education

James I. Riddle, Chief
General Aviation District Office
FAA Bldg., Lakefront Airport
New Orleans, LA 70126, (504) 241-2506

Ansel M. Winham, Chief
General Aviation District Office
Terminal Bldg., Downtown Airport
Shreveport, LA 71107, (318) 226-5379

PUBLIC LIBRARIES

Name	Location and/or Mailing Address	Telephone
Louisiana State Library	760 Riverside Mall, P. O. Box 131, Baton Rouge 70821	(504) 342-4923
Acadia Parish	1125 North Parkerson Avenue, P. O. Drawer 1509, Crowley 70526	(318) 788-1880
Allen Parish	Sixth Avenue, P. O. Box 400, Oberlin 70655	(318) 639-4338
Ascension Parish	218 Railroad Avenue, P. O. Box 588, Donaldsonville 70346	(504) 473-8052
Assumption Parish	108 Jefferson Street, P. O. Drawer A, Napoleonville 70390	(504) 369-7070
Audubon Regional	Woodville Street, P. O. Box 565A, Clinton 70722	(504) 683-8753
Avoyelles Parish	101 North Washington Street, Marksville 71351	(318) 253-7559
Beauregard Parish	205 South Washington Avenue, P. O. Box 647, DeRidder 70634	(318) 463-6217
Bienville Parish	604 South Maple Street, Arcadia 71001	(318) 263-2930
Bossier Parish	Sixth and Sibley Streets, P. O. Box 399, Benton 71006	(318) 965-2751
Caddo Parish		
Calcasieu Parish	411 Pujo Street, Lake Charles 70601	(318) 433-1045
Caldwell Parish	Corner East Pearl and Jackson Streets, P. O. Box 828, Columbia 71418	(318) 649-2259
Cameron Parish	Marshall Street, P. O. Box P, Cameron 70631	(318) 775-5421
Catahoula Parish	Bushley Street, P. O. Box 218, Harrisonburg 71340	(318) 744-5271
Claiborne Parish	512 North Main Street, Homer 71040	(318) 927-3845
Concordia Parish	709 North Third Street, Ferriday 71334	(318) 757-3550
DeSoto Parish	P. O. Box 513, Mansfield 71052	(318) 872-6100
East Baton Rouge Parish	7711 Goodwood Boulevard, Baton Rouge 70806	(504) 389-3360
East Carroll Parish	P. O. Box 349, Lake Providence 71254	(318) 559-2615
Evangeline Parish	242 West Main Street, P. O. Box 40, Ville Platte 70586	(318) 363-1369
Franklin Parish	209 Main Street, Winnsboro 71295	(318) 435-4336
Grant Parish	300 Main Street, Colfax 71417	(318) 627-9920
Iberia Parish	445 East Main Street, P. O. Box 1089, New Iberia 70560	(318) 367-2584
Iberville Parish	1501 J. Gerald Berret Boulevard, P. O. Box 736, Plaquemine 70764	(504) 344-6948
Jackson Parish	614 South Polk, Jonesboro 71251	(318) 259-2069
Jefferson Parish	3420 North Causeway Boulevard, P. O. Box 7490, Metairie 70010	(504) 834-5850
Jefferson Davis Parish	526 North Main Street, P. O. Box 356, Jennings 70546	(318) 824-1210
Jennings	303 Cary Avenue, Jennings 70546	(318) 824-4367
Lafayette	301 West Congress Street, P. O. Box 3427, Lafayette 70502	(318) 233-0587
Lafourche Parish	303 West 5th Street, P. O. Box 998, Thibodaux 70301	(504) 446-1163
LaSalle Parish	221 North First Street, P. O. Drawer P, Jena 71342	(318) 992-5675
Lincoln Parish	509 West Alabama Street, P. O. Box 637, Ruston 71270	(318) 255-1920
Livingston Parish	Courthouse Building, Livingston 70754	(504) 686-2436

Madison Parish	403 North Mulberry Street, P. O. Box 312, Tallulah 71282	(318) 574-4308
Morehouse Parish	108 East Jefferson Avenue, P. O. Box 232, Bastrop 71220	(318) 281-3683
Morgan City	220 Everett Street, P. O. Box 988, Morgan City 70380	(504) 385-1666
Natchitoches Parish	431 Jefferson Street, Natchitoches 71457	(318) 352-2415
Opelousas-Eunice	249 East Grolee Street, P. O. Box 249, Opelousas 70570	(318) 948-3693
Orleans Parish	219 Loyola Avenue, New Orleans 70140	(504) 524-7382
Ouachita Parish	1800 Stubbs Avenue, Monroe 71201	(318) 387-1950
Plaquemines Parish	203 Louisiana Highway 23, South, Buras 70041	(504) 657-7121
Pointe Coupee Parish	201 Claiborne Street, New Roads 70760	(504) 638-7593
Rapides Parish	411 Washington Street, Alexandria 71301	(318) 445-2411
Red River Parish	Carroll Street, P. O. Drawer H, Coushatta 71019	(318) 932-5614
Richland Parish	910 Louisa Street, Rayville 71269	(318) 728-4806
Sabine Parish	750 East Main Street, Many 71449	(318) 256-2212
St. Bernard Parish	1125 East St. Bernard Highway, Chalmette 70043	(504) 279-0448
St. Charles Parish	298 Lakewood Drive, P. O. Box 975, Luling 70070	(504) 785-8464
St. James Parish	1542 Front Street, Route 1, Box 32-C, Lutcher 70071	(504) 869-3618
St. John Parish	1334 West Airline Highway, LaPlace 70068	(504) 652-6857
St. Landry Parish	(See Opelousas-Eunice)	
St. Martin Parish	105 South New Market Street, P. O. Box 79, St. Martinville 70582	(318) 394-4086
St. Mary Parish	206 Iberia Street, Franklin 70538	(318) 828-5364
St. Tammany Parish	402 North Jefferson Avenue, P. O. Box 1000, Covington 70433	(504) 892-0812
Shreve Memorial	424 Texas Street, P. O. Box 21523, Shreveport 71120	(318) 226-5897
Tangipahoa Parish	200 East Mulberry Street, P. O. Box 578, Amite 70422	(504) 748-7151
Tensas Parish	Plank Road, P. O. Box 228, St. Joseph 71366	(318) 766-3781
Terrebonne Parish	424 Roussell Street, P. O. Box 510, Houma 70361	(504) 876-5861
Union Parish	202 West Jackson Street, Farmerville 71241	(318) 368-9226
Vermilion Parish	200 North Street, P. O. Drawer 640, Abbeville 70510	(318) 893-2655
Vernon Parish	301 Courthouse Street, P. O. Box 310, Leesville 71446	(318) 239-2027
Washington Parish	825 Free Street, Franklinton 70438	(504) 839-5336
Webster Parish	521 East and West Streets, Minden 71055	(318) 377-1411
West Baton Rouge Parish	830 North Alexander, Port Allen 70767	(504) 343-3484
West Carroll Parish	Highway 17 and Marietta, P. O. Box 703, Oak Grove 71263	(318) 428-2697
Winn Parish	204 West Main Street, Winnfield 71483	(318) 628-4478

Public School Libraries, 1975-86

Session	Number of Libraries	Librarians	
		Full-Time	Part-Time
1975-76	1,316.0	1,040.0	153.0
1976-77	1,332.0	1,081.0	140.0
1977-78	1,354.0	1,110.0	117.0
1978-79	1,370.0	1,150.0	126.0
1979-80	1,383.0	1,153.0	146.0
1980-81	1,378.0	1,160.0	117.0
1981-82	1,332.0	1,134.0	121.0
1982-83	1,332.0	1,171.0	95.0
1983-84	1,359.0	1,117.0	123.0
1984-85	1,374.0	1,162.0	121.0
1985-86	1,286.0	1,192.0	104.0

1986-87 MINIMUM SALARY SCHEDULE FOR TEACHERS

Yrs. of Exp.	2 Years' Coll.	3 Years' Coll.	Bach. Degree	Master's Degree	Master's Plus 30*	Specialist Ed.	Ph.D. Ed.D. Degree
0	$ 9,229	$ 9,817	$12,171	$12,464	$12,464	$12,907	$13,495
1	9,375	9,965	12,464	12,758	12,758	13,200	13,787
2	9,523	10,110	12,758	13,053	13,053	13,495	14,083
3	9,817	10,405	13,053	13,346	13,346	13,787	14,525
4	10,110	10,700	13,346	13,641	13,641	14,083	14,990
5	10,405	10,994	13,641	14,083	14,155	14,603	15,451
6	10,700	11,287	13,936	14,525	14,679	15,142	15,915
7	10,994	11,729	14,230	14,990	15,221	15,684	16,378
8	11,436	12,171	14,525	15,452	15,761	16,223	16,841
9	11,876	12,612	14,990	15,915	16,300	16,765	17,304
10	12,318	13,053	15,452	16,378	16,841	17,304	17,769
11				16,841	17,382	17,844	18,232
12					17,924	18,383	18,671

*Master's Degree Plus 30 Graduate Hours

"Talking Book" Service

The Louisiana State Library has a "talking book" service to enable blind, near blind, or physically disabled people to enjoy books. Recorded material is available for those who cannot read standard printed material, including people who have muscle paralysis, muscle or nerve deterioration, palsy, or multiple sclerosis. Information can be obtained from the New Orleans Public Library or the Louisiana State Library Department for the Blind and Physically Handicapped (Box 131, Baton Rouge, LA 70821).

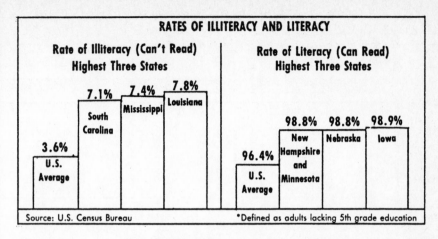

RATES OF ILLITERACY AND LITERACY

Rate of Illiteracy (Can't Read) Highest Three States

- 3.6% U.S. Average
- 7.1% South Carolina
- 7.4% Mississippi
- 7.8% Louisiana

Rate of Literacy (Can Read) Highest Three States

- 96.4% U.S. Average
- 98.8% New Hampshire and Minnesota
- 98.8% Nebraska
- 98.9% Iowa

Source: U.S. Census Bureau   *Defined as adults lacking 5th grade education

EDUCATION'S INFLUENCE ON INCOME

Adult Heads of Family (Age 25+)	Median Family Income
College: 5 Years of More	$46,656
College: 4 Years Completed	40,724
College: 1 to 3 Years	30,665
High School: 4 Years Completed	26,528
High School: 1 to 3 Years	19,162
Elementary School: Completed	17,169
Elementary School: Not Completed	13,319

Source: U.S. Department of Commerce, 1985

Expenditure of All State Revenues
(State Resources and Federal Grants) by Education Functions[a]

Session	Department of Education	Other Education	Vo-Tech Schools and Centers	Institutions of Higher Education	Total
1984-85	$1,570,842,874	$38,931,701	$66,297,176	$786,632,792	$2,462,704,543
Percent of All State Revenues (Including Federal Grants)	22.31%	0.55%	0.94%	11.17%	34.97%
1985-86	1,573,636,747	59,358,421	64,989,438	840,738,939	2,538,723,545
Percent of All State Revenues (Including Federal Grants)	21.54%	0.81%	0.89%	11.51%	34.75%

[a] Source: <u>Executive Budget of the State of Louisiana</u>, <u>1985-86</u> and <u>1986-87</u>. These are budgeted figures and not actual expenditures.

MUSEUMS, EXHIBITION SPACES AND HISTORICAL SITES

Persons who desire to take large groups on a field trip should write or call beforehand.

Location (City)	Name of Facility	Mailing Address	Telephone	Days and Hours Open	Charges	Nature of Facility
Alexandria	Alexandria Museum and Visual Arts Center	P.O. Box 1028 71309-1028	(318) 443-3458	Tue.-Fri. 9:00-5:00 Sat. 10:00-2:00	Free	Art Museum
	Alexandria Zoological Park	P.O. Box 31 71301-0031	(318) 473-1387	Sept.-May Mon.-Sun. 9:00-5:00 June-Aug. Mon.-Sun. 9:00-6:00	Free	Zoology Museum, Zoological Gardens, Children's Zoo
	James C. Bolton Library	LSU—Alexandria 71302-9633	(318) 473-6438	Mon.-Fri. 8:00-4:30 Sat. 8:30-12:30	Free	Library
	Kent House	3601 Bayou Rapides 71303	(318) 487-5998	Mon.-Sat. 9:00-5:00 Sun. 1:00-5:00	Adults $2.50 Children $1.00 Members free Group discounts	Museum, Historic House/Building(s)
Alto	Altus Museum	P.O. Box 104 71216-0104	(318) 248-2367	Mon.-Tue. 10:00-4:00 Thu.-Fri. 10:00-4:00	Donations accepted	Art Museum
Baker	Baker Heritage Center	P.O. Box 707 70714-0707	(504) 774-1776	Tue.-Fri. 10:00-4:00 Sat. 1:00-4:00		History Museum
Bastrop	Snyder Museum and Creative Arts Center	1620 East Madison Avenue 71220	(318) 281-8760	Mon.-Fri. 9:00-4:30	Free	History Museum
Baton Rouge	Anglo-American Art Museum—LSU	Memorial Tower Louisiana State University 70803	(504) 388-4003	Mon.-Fri. 8:00-4:30 Sat. 10:00-4:00 Sun. 1:00-4:00	Free	Art Museum
	Arts and Humanities Council of Greater Baton Rouge	427 Laurel Street 70801	(504) 344-8558	Mon.-Fri. 9:00-5:00	Free	Fire-fighting Museum
	House Arts Advisory Commission	P.O. Box 94062 70804	(504) 342-7393	Mon.-Fri. 8:00-5:00	Free	Art Agency
	L. H. Cohn Sr. Memorial Plant Arboretum	12056 Foster Road 70811	(504) 775-1006	Mon.-Fri. 8:00-5:00 Sat.-Sun. 9:00-5:00	Free Donations accepted	Museum, Arboretums, Botanical and Aquatic Gardens

Location (City)	Name of Facility	Mailing Address	Telephone	Days and Hours Open	Charges	Nature of Facility
	Louisiana Arts and Science Center	P.O. Box 3373 70821	(504) 344-9463	Mon.-Fri. 10:00-3:00 Sat. 10:00-4:00 Sun. 1:00-4:00	Adults $1.50 Sr. Citizen/Students $.75 Children $.75 Members free School groups free	Art Museum, Planetarium
	Louisiana Division of Archives, Records Management and History	P.O. Box 94125 70804	(504) 342-5440	Mon.-Fri. 8:00-4:30	Free	Library, Archives
	Magnolia Mound	2161 Nicholson Drive 70802	(504) 343-4955	Tue.-Sat. 10:00-4:00 Sun. 1:00-4:00	Adults $3.50 Sr. Citizen $2.50 Students $1.50 Children $.75 Group discounts Members free	Museum, Historic Site
	Museum of Geoscience — LSU	Geology Building, Room 313 70803	(504) 388-2931	By appointment Mon.-Fri. 8:30-4:30	Free	Geology, Mineralogy and Paleontology Museum
	Museum of Natural Science — LSU	Louisiana State University 70803-3216	(504) 388-2855	Mon.-Fri. 8:00-4:00 Sat. 9:30-1:00	Free	Natural History and Natural Science Museum
	Old Arsenal State Commemorative Area	P.O. Box 44121 70804-4121	(504) 342-5097	Wed.-Mon. 10:00-4:30	Adults $2.00 Children $1.00 School groups free	History Museum
	Rural Life Museum — LSU	6200 Burden Lane 70808	(504) 766-8241	By appointment Mon.-Fri. 8:30-4:00	Donations accepted	History Museum
	U.S.S. Kidd DD661	P.O. Box 44242 70804	(504) 383-9096	Oct.-May Mon.-Sun. 9:00-4:30 June-Sept. Mon.-Sun. 10:00-5:30	Adults $3.00 Children $2.00 Group discounts Members free	Maritime, Naval and Whaling Museum, Historic Ships
	Union Art Gallery — LSU	Box B.U., LSU 70803	(504) 388-5117	Mon.-Fri. 9:00-9:00 Sat.-Sun. 11:00-9:00	Free	Art and Cultural Center

MUSEUMS, EXHIBITION SPACES AND HISTORICAL SITES—Continued

City	Name	Address	Phone	Hours	Admission	Type
Benton	Bossier Parish Nature Study Center	Linton Road 71006	(318) 965-0679	Mon.-Fri. 8:30-4:00	Free	Museum, Arboretums, Botanical and Aquatic Gardens
Bogalusa	Bogalusa Indian and Pioneer Museums	1637 Avenue F 70427-1179	(504) 732-4008	By appointment Sat.-Sun. 1:00-4:00	Free	History Museum
Chalmette	Jean Lafitte National Historic Park—Chalmette Unit	St. Bernard Highway 70043	(504) 589-4428	Mon.-Sun. 8:00-5:00	Free Donations accepted	Military Museum
Cloutierville	Bayou Folk Museum	Route 1, Box 60 71416	(318) 379-2546	March-Nov. Tue.-Fri. 10:00-5:00 Sat.-Sun. 1:00-5:00	Adults $2.00 Children $1.00	Museum, Historic House/Building(s)
Columbia	Louisiana Art and Folk Center and Museum	P.O. Box 196 71418	(318) 649-6722	Tue.-Sat. 9:00-5:00	Donations accepted School groups free	Museum, Crafts
Covington	St. Tammany Art Association	P.O. Box 704 70434	(504) 892-8650	Mon.-Sat. 10:00-4:00 Sun. 1:00-4:00	Free	Agency, Art Association
Crowley	Crowley Art Association	P.O. Box 2003 70527-2003	(318) 783-3747	Tue.-Fri. 10:00-4:00 Sat. 10:00-1:00	Free Donations accepted	Art and Cultural Center
Epps	Poverty Point State Commemorative Area	HC 60, Box 208-A 71237	(318) 926-5492	Mon.-Sun. 8:00-5:00	Adults $2.00 Children $1.00 School groups free	Archaeology Museum, Archaeological Sites
Fort Polk	Fort Polk Military Museum	P.O. Drawer R 71459	(318) 535-7905	Mon.-Fri. 8:00-4.30 Sat.-Sun. 8:00-5:00	Free	Military Museum
Gonzales	Tee Joe Gonzales Museum	728 East Ascension Street 70737	(504) 644-6000	Wed.-Fri. 1:00-5:00	Free Donations accepted	Museum, Historic House/Building(s)
Hammond	Hammond Cultural Foundation	P.O. Box 2974 70401	(504) 542-9546	Tue.-Fri. 12:00-4:00	Free	Art and Cultural Center
Homer	Herbert S. Ford Memorial Museum	519 South Main Street 71040	(318) 927-3271	Mon.-Fri. 8:30-4:00 Sun. 2:00-5:00	Adults $1.00 Children $.50 Donations accepted Members free	History Museum
Jackson	Centenary State Commemorative Area	P.O. Box 574 70748	(504) 635-3739	Closed; under development		Commemorative Areas/ Cemeteries
Jena	LaSalle Museum Association	P.O. Box 1019 71342	(318) 992-4475	By appointment	Free	Museum, Historic House/Building(s)
Jennings	Zigler Museum	411 Clara Street 70546	(318) 824-0114	Tue.-Sat. 9:00-5:00 Sun. 1:00-5:00	Free Donations accepted	Art Museum

Location (City)	Name of Facility	Mailing Address	Telephone	Days and Hours Open	Charges	Nature of Facility
Lafayette	Lafayette Art Association Gallery	700 Lee Avenue 70501	(318) 269-0363	By appointment Mon.-Fri. 10:00-5:00	Free	Arts Center
	Lafayette Museum Association	1122 Lafayette Street 70501	(318) 234-2208	Tue.-Sat. 9:00-5:00 Sun. 3:00-5:00	Adults $2.00 Children $1.00 Group discounts School groups free	Museum, Historic House/Building(s)
	Lafayette Natural History Museum	637 Girard Park Drive 70503	(318) 261-8350	Mon., Wed., Fri. 9:00-5:00 Tue., Thu. 9:00-9:00 Sat.-Sun. 1:00-5:00	Free Donations accepted School groups free	Natural History and Natural Science Museum
	University Art Museum—USL	USL Drawer 42571 70504	(318) 231-5326	Mon.-Fri. 9:00-4:00 Sun. 2:00-5:00	Free	Art Museum
Lake Charles	Frazar Memorial Library— McNeese St. Univ.	Frazar Memorial Library 70609	(318) 437-5716	Mon.-Thu. 7:45-11:00 Fri. 7:45-5:00 Sat. 11:00-5:00 Sun. 2:00-10:00	Free	Library
	Imperial Calcasieu Museum	204 West Sallier Street 70601	(318) 439-3797	Mon.-Fri. 10:00-5:00 Sat. 10:00-12:00 Sun. 2:00-5:00	Free Donations accepted	Museum, Historic House/Building(s)
Mansfield	Mansfield State Commemorative Area	Route 2, Box 459 71052	(318) 872-1474	Winter Thu.-Mon. 9:00-5:00 Summer Thu.-Mon. 9:00-7:00	Adults $2.00 Students $1.00 School groups free	Military Museum
Many	Fort Jesup State Commemorative Area	Route 2 71449	(318) 256-5480	Mon.-Sun. 9:00-5:00	Adults $2.00 Children $1.00 School groups free	Museum, Historic House/Building(s)
Marksville	Hypolite Bordelon Home	P.O. Box 585 71351	(318) 253-9550	By appointment Tue.-Sat. 11:00-3:00	Donations accepted	Museum, Historic House/Building(s)
	Marksville State Commemorative Area	700 Allen Street 71351	(318) 253-9546	Mon.-Sun. 9:00-5:00	Adults $2.00 Children $1.00 School groups free	History Museum
Marrero	Jean Lafitte National Historic Park—Barataria Unit	7400 Highway 45 70072	(504) 348-2923	Mon.-Sun. 8:00-5:00	Free	Site, Nature Center

MUSEUMS, EXHIBITION SPACES AND HISTORICAL SITES—Continued

Location	Name	Address	Phone	Hours	Fees	Type
Marthaville	Rebel State Commemorative Area	P.O. Box 127 71450	(318) 472-6255	Thu.-Mon. 9:00-5:00	Free	Museum, Folk Arts
Monroe	Masur Museum of Art	1400 South Grand Street 71202	(318) 329-2237	Tue.-Thu. 10:00-6:00 Fri.-Sun. 2:00-5:00	Free	Art Museum
Morgan City	Morgan City Museum	P.O. Box 1218 70381	(504) 385-6159	Mon.-Fri. 9:00-5:00 Sat.-Sun. 1:00-5:00	Adults $2.00 Sr. Citizen/Children $1.00 Group discounts Members free	Museum, Historic House/Building(s)
Natchitoches	Fort St. Jean Baptiste State Commemorative Area	P.O. Box 1127 71458-1127	(318) 357-0001	Thu.-Sun. 8:00-5:00	Free	Museum, Historic Site
	Williamson Museum — NW St. Univ.	Dept. of History, Social Sciences and Social Work 71497	(318) 357-4364	By appointment Mon.-Fri. 8:00-4:00	Free	Anthropology and Ethnology Museum
New Iberia	Shadows-on-the-Teche	P.O. Box 254 70561-0254	(318) 369-6446	Mon.-Sun. 9:00-4:30	Adults $4.00 Students $2.00 Group discounts Members free	Museum, Historic House/Building(s)
New Orleans	Audubon Park and Zoological Gardens	P.O. Box 4327 70178	(504) 861-2537	Daily 9:30-5:00	Adults $5.00 Children $2.50 Sr. Citizens $2.00 Group discounts Members free	Zoology Museum, Zoological Gardens, Children's Zoo
	Beauregard-Keyes House	1113 Chartres Street 70116	(504) 523-7257	Mon.-Sat. 10:00-3:00	Adults $3.00 Sr. Citizen/Students $2.00 Children $1.00 Group discounts	Museum, Historic House/Building(s)
	Contemporary Arts Center	P.O. Box 30498 70190	(504) 523-1216	Tue.-Sun. 12:00-5:00	Non-members $2.00 Donations accepted Group discounts Members free	Art and Cultural Center
	Fort Pike State Commemorative Area	Route 6, Box 194 70129	(504) 662-5703	Mon.-Sun. 9:00-5:00	Adults $2.00 Children $1.00 School groups free	Museum, Historic House/Building(s)

Location (City)	Name of Facility	Mailing Address	Telephone	Days and Hours Open	Charges	Nature of Facility
	Gallier House Museum	1118-1132 Royal Street 70116	(504) 523-6722	Mon.-Sat. 10:00-4:30	Adults $3.00 Sr. Citizen/Students $2.50 Children $1.00 Group discounts Members free	Decorative Arts Museum
	Hermann-Grima Historic House	820 St. Louis Street 70112	(504) 525-5661	Mon.-Sat. 10:00-4:00	Adults $3.00 Students/Children $2.00 Group discounts	Museum, Historic Site
	Historic New Orleans Collection	533 Royal Street 70130	(504) 523-4662	Tue.-Sat. 10:00-4:45	Free Donations accepted Group discounts	History Museum
	Jean Lafitte National Historic Park — French Quarter Unit	c/o Municipal Auditorium 70116	(504) 589-2636	Sept.-May Mon.-Sun. 9:00-5:00 June-Aug. Mon.-Sun. 9:00-6:00	Free	Site, Interpretive Center
	Longue Vue House and Gardens	7 Bamboo Road 70124	(504) 488-5488	Tue.-Fri. 10:00-4:30 Sat.-Sun. 1:00-5:00	Adults $5.00 Students/Children $3.00 Garden only: Adults $2.00 Students/Children $1.00 Group discounts Members free	Decorative Arts Museum
	Louisiana Nature and Science Center, Inc.	11000 Lake Forest Boulevard 70127	(504) 246-5672	Tue.-Fri. 9:00-5:00 Sat.-Sun. 12:00-5:00	Adults $2.00 Sr. Citizen/Children $1.00 Families $5.00 Members free	Museum, Nature Center
	Louisiana State Museum	P.O. Box 2458 70176-2458	(504) 568-6968	Tue.-Sun. 10:00-6:00	$2.00 per building School groups free Members free	History Museum
	Middle American Research Institute and Museum	Tulane University 70118	(504) 865-5110	Mon.-Fri. 9:00-4:30	Free	Art Museum

MUSEUMS, EXHIBITION SPACES AND HISTORICAL SITES—Continued

Location	Name	Address	Phone	Hours	Admission	Type
	New Orleans Museum of Art	P.O. Box 19123 70179-0123	(504) 488-2631	Tue.-Sun. 10:00-5:00	Adults $3.00 Sr. Citizen/Children $1.50 Members free	Art Museum
New Roads	Pointe Coupee Museum and Tourism Center	Route 1, Box 70 M 70760	(504) 638-7171	Tue.-Sun. 1:00-4:00	Free	Museum, Historic House/Building(s)
Newellton	Winter Quarter State Commemorative Area	Route 1, Box 91 71357	(318) 467-5439	Thu.-Mon. 9:00-5:00	Adults $2.00 Children $1.00 School groups free	Museum, Historic Site
Oil City	Caddo-Pine Island Oil and Historical Society	P.O. Box 897 71061	(318) 995-6845	Mon.-Fri. 9:00-5:00 Sat. 1:00-5:00	Adults $1.00 Children $.50 School groups free Members free	History Museum
Plaquemines	Plaquemines Lock State Commemorative Area	P.O. Box 107 70764	(504) 687-8159	Closed; under development		Maritime, Naval and Whaling Museum, Historic Ships
Port Allen	West Baton Rouge Museum	845 North Jefferson 70767	(504) 383-2392	By appointment Tue.-Sat. 10:00-4:30 Sun. 2:00-5:00	Free	History Museum
Ruston	Lincoln Parish Museum and Historical Society	609 North Vienna 71270	(318) 251-0018	Tue.-Fri. 9:00-4:30 Sat.-Sun. 2:00-5:00	Donations accepted	History Museum
	Louisiana Tech. (Univ.) Museum	Box 3089, Tech Station 71272	(318) 257-2130	By appointment Mon.-Fri. 9:00-12:00	Free	Natural History and Natural Science Museum
	Louisiana Tech. University Art Gallery	School of Art and Architecture 71272	(318) 257-3077	Mon.-Fri. 9:00-4:00 Sun. 2:00-5:00	Free	Museum, Art Gallery
	Museum of Fashion and Textiles— LA Tech.	P.O. Box 3167, Tech Station 71272	(318) 257-3676		Free Donations accepted	Textile Museum
Shreveport	Grindstone Bluff Museum	P.O. Box 7965 71107	(318) 425-5646	By appointment	Free	Archaeology Museum, Archaeological Sites
	Louisiana State Exhibit Museum	P.O. Box 9067 71109	(318) 227-5196	Mon.-Sun. 9:00-5:00	Free	History Museum
	Meadows Museum of Art— Centenary Col.	2911 Centenary Boulevard 71104-3335	(318) 869-5169	Tue.-Fri. 1:00-5:00 Sat.-Sun. 2:00-5:00	Free	Art Museum

Location (City)	Name of Facility	Mailing Address	Telephone	Days and Hours Open	Charges	Nature of Facility
	Museum of Life Sciences— LSU-S	8515 Youree Drive 71115	(318) 226-7174	Mon.-Fri. 8:00-5:00	Free	Natural History and Natural Science Museum
	Pioneer Heritage Center— LSU-S	8515 Youree Drive 71115	(318) 797-5332	By appointment Sun. 1:30-4:30	Adults $1.00 School groups free	Folkways Museum
	Spring Street Museum	P.O. Box 6134 71106	(318) 424-0964	By appointment Oct.-June Sat.-Sun. 1:30-4:30	Adults $1.00	History Museum
	Stoner Art Center	516 Stoner Avenue 71101	(318) 222-1780	Tue.-Sat. 12:00-5:00 Sun. 1:00-4:00	Free	Art and Cultural Center
	W. B. Jacobs Memorial Nature Park	Route 9, Box 168 71107	(318) 929-2806	Wed.-Sat. 8:00-5:00 Sun. 1:00-5:00	Free	Site, Nature Center
Slidell	Slidell Museum	P.O. Box 1564 70459	(504) 646-4380	Mon.-Fri. 12:00-4:00	Free Donations accepted	Museum, Children's Museum
St. Francisville	Audubon State Commemorative Area	P.O. Box 546 70775-0546	(504) 635-3739	Mon.-Sun. 9:00-5:00	Adults $2.00 Children $1.00 Sr. Citizens free $40.00 per bus	Museum, Historic House/Building(s)
	Locust Grove State Commemorative Area	P.O. Box 546 70775	(504) 635-3739	Mon.-Sun. 9:00-5:00	Free	Commemorative Areas/ Cemeteries
St. Martinville	Longfellow Evangeline State Commemorative Area	P.O. Box 497 70582	(318) 394-3754	Mon.-Sun. 9:00-5:00	$2.00 per car $40.00 per bus School groups free	Museum, Historic House/Building(s)
Sulphur	Brimstone Historical Society and Museum	P.O. Box 242 70664	(318) 527-7142	Mon.-Fri. 9:30-5:00	Free	Museum, Historic House/Building(s)
Tangipahoa	Camp Moore State Commemorative Area	P.O. Box 15 70465	(504) 229-8200	Mon.-Sun. 9:00-5:00	Adults $2.00 Children $1.00	History Museum
Thibodaux	E. D. White State Commemorative Area	Box 234, Route 2 70301	(504) 447-3473	Wed.-Sun. 9:00-5:00	Adults $1.00 Students $.50	History Museum
Ville Platte	Louisiana State Arboretum	Route 3, Box 489 70586	(318) 363-6287	Mon.-Sun. dawn to dusk	Free	Museum, Arboretums, Botanical and Aquatic Gardens

MUSEUMS, EXHIBITION SPACES AND HISTORICAL SITES—Continued

Zachary	McHugh House Museum	4524 Virginia Street 70791	(504) 654-3042	Mon.-Sun. 1:00-5:00	Adults $1.00 Donations accepted Group discounts School groups free	Museum, Historic House/Building(s)
	Pt. Hudson State Commemorative Area	Route 1, Box 196 70791	(504) 654-3775	Thu.-Sun. 8:00-5:00	Free	Commemorative Areas/Cemeteries

Source: Louisiana Association of Museums

FINANCIAL SUPPORT

Based on responses from 43 institutions.

Financial Support represents unearned income including grants and appropriations. More than one-third ($3,328,667) of the respondents' total unearned income came from the state in 1986. Other sources include Corporate Support ($949,715), Foundation Support ($837,950), Other Private Support ($1,147,439), Federal Government Support ($437,194), Local Government Support ($1,708264) and Other Support ($441,810).

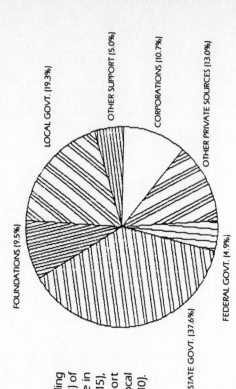

FOUNDATIONS (9.5%)

LOCAL GOVT. (19.3%)

OTHER SUPPORT (5.0%)

CORPORATIONS (10.7%)

OTHER PRIVATE SOURCES (13.0%)

FEDERAL GOVT. (4.9%)

STATE GOVT. (37.6%)

Source: Louisiana Association of Museums

Other Louisiana Museums and Educational Sites

Kenner	Kenner City Museum	1922 Third Street (La. 48)	Historical Museum
Lafayette	Acadiana Park	East Alexander Street	Nature Museum Prehistoric Site
	Acadian Village	H. Mouton Road (off La. 342)	Historical Museum
Lake Providence	Louisiana Cotton Museum	U.S. 65	Historical Museum
Monroe	Masur Museum of Art	1400 South Grand	Art Gallery
New Orleans	Pharmaceutical Museum	514 Chartres	Historical Museum
	Ursuline Convent	2635 State Street	Historical Museum Research Library
Patterson	Louisiana Aviation Museum	La. 182	Historical Museum
Pontchatoula	Tally Ho Railroad Museum	Old Highway 51	Historical Museum Nature Park
Scott	Beau Cajun Art Gallery	1012 St. Mary Street	Art and Antique Museum

LOUISIANA SUPERLATIVES

(NOTE: Readers are asked to submit information for possible use
in the section, LOUISIANA SUPERLATIVES. Any submissions used will be credited to the respondent.)

ACADIAN MUSICAL RECORDING
The first record of Acadian music was made by Joseph F. Falcon in 1928. "Allons a Lafayette" was released by the Columbia Recording Company. (Submitted by Ovey Broussard)

ACADIANS, FIRST
On April 6, 1764, the first four Acadian families arrived in Louisiana from New York.

ACUPUNCTURE
The first use of acupuncture as anesthesia in the South occurred at Touro Infirmary in New Orleans, December 27, 1972.

AIRPLANE
In 1910 Louis Taulhan made the first airplane flight in Louisiana at a spring exhibition at New Orleans' City Park race track.

AIRPORT
The only state-supported airport in Louisiana is the Harry P. Williams Memorial Airport in St. Mary Parish near Patterson.

AIRPORT
Louisiana's first public airport was built in Mansfield, 1926.

ALAMO SURVIVOR
The only man to escape from the Alamo, Moses Rose, died in Logansport in 1850.

WHERE JAZZ WAS BORN

SECOND LARGEST SEAPORT IN THE UNITED STATES

ALKYLAMINES PLANT

Air Products & Chemicals, Inc., in St. Gabriel, is the world's largest alkylamines plant.

AMENDMENT, FOURTEENTH

The first Supreme Court test of the 14th amendment was the Slaughterhouse Case in New Orleans, 1873.

APARTMENT BUILDINGS

The Pontalba Buildings, facing Jackson Square in New Orleans, are believed to be the first apartment buildings in the nation.

ARBORETUM

Chicot State Park, near Ville Platte, encompasses about 300 acres and includes the nation's first state-operated arboretum.

ARCHITECTURE, AFRICAN

Melrose Plantation, located on the Cane River near Natchitoches, is the site of the African House, the only authentic example of early African architecture in North America. (Submitted by Claude Kenneson)

BANKS, NATIONAL

On December 31, 1986, the Hibernia National Bank in New Orleans was the largest national bank in the state.

BANKS AND SAVINGS & LOANS

On December 31, 1986, the Dixie Savings & Loan in New Orleans was the largest savings and loan association in the state.

BANKS, STATE

On December 31, 1986, Guaranty Bank and Trust Company in Lafayette was the largest state bank.

BASKETBALL

The New Orleans Jazz drew a crowd of 26,500, the largest number to ever see an NBA game.

BLACK UNIVERSITY

The largest predominantly black university in the United States is Southern University in Baton Rouge.

BOTTLE MUSEUM

The Justine Bottle Museum, near New Iberia, is believed to be the only bottle museum in the South.

BOXING MATCH

The longest boxing match in history (7 hours and 19 minutes) was held at New Orleans, April 6, 1893, between Andy Bowen and Jack Burke. The fight went 100 rounds to a draw.

CAMELLIAS

The world's most complete collection of camellias, nearly 1000 varieties, may be found in the gardens on Avery Island in Iberia Parish. (Submitted by Claude Kenneson)

CATHEDRAL, OLDEST

Originally built in 1718, the St. Louis Cathedral in New Orleans is the oldest cathedral in the U. S. The present structure, the third one on the site, dates from 1789.

CATHOLIC DIOCESE

On April 25, 1793, Pope Pius VI established the Diocese of Louisiana, the second oldest in the U. S.

CHAMBER DIVE, DEEPEST

The deepest chamber dive (1600 feet) successfully completed in the U. S. was made by six Navy divers at Belle Chasse, completed May 21, 1973.

CHAPEL, SMALLEST

The smallest chapel in the world is the Chapel of the Madonna, located on State Highway 168 between Point Pleasant and Bayou Goula. It measures six feet wide and eight feet long. (Submitted by Claude Kenneson)

CHECKERS

Alfred Barrow of New Orleans is the National Checkers champion.

CITY, HIGHEST

Athens, in Claiborne Parish, 469 feet above sea level.

CITY, OLDEST

In 1714-15 Louis St. Denis founded Fort St. Jean Baptiste at the present site of Natchitoches, the first permanent settlement in Louisiana.

CIVIL WAR

By order of Major-General P.G.T. Beauregard of St. Bernard Parish, the first shot of the Civil War was fired in defense of the city of Charleston at Fort Sumter, on April 12, 1861.

CIVIL WAR BATTLE

Mansfield Battle Park, in De Soto Parish, was the site of the last major Confederate victory in the Civil War. On April 8, 1864, Confederate General Richard "Dick" Taylor routed the forces of Union General Nathaniel Banks to end the northern Red River campaign. (Submitted by Claude Kenneson)

COLLEGE, FIRST

The University of Orleans, chartered in 1803, was the first school of higher learning in Louisiana.

COLLEGE, FIRST MEDICAL

The Medical College of Louisiana (1834) was the first Medical School in the South.

COLLEGE, OLDEST

Centenary College in Shreveport (originally located at Jackson) is the oldest college still in existence west of the Mississippi River (chartered in

1825).

CONGRESSIONAL ELECTION

The Henson Moore-Jeff LaCaze 6th District congressional election was the closest in the nation's history. Moore led by 44 votes, and because of a voting machine malfunction a new election was held.

CONGRESSWOMAN, FIRST

U. S. Representative Lindy Boggs took her seat March 28, 1973, to become the first woman ever elected to Congress from Louisiana.

COTTON, PERMANENT PRESS

Dr. J. David Reid, formerly with the U. S. Department of Agriculture in New Orleans, is considered the "father of wash-and-wear," the pioneer in the field of durable-press fabrics.

COURT TRIALS

The longest court trial in the history of the nation was the Myra Clark Gaines case, 1836-1891.

CRAWFISH

Ninety-nine percent of all crawfish produced in the U. S. come from Louisiana.

CYPRESS

The largest cypress mill in the world is located in St. Mary Parish.

DREDGING, SOUTHWEST PASS

In 1974, at Southwest Pass of the Mississippi River, the U. S. Corps of Engineers performed the largest concentrated dredging effort in history. In a normal year approximately 13,400,000 cubic yards are dredged; the fiscal year ending June, 1974, showed 63,600,000 cubic yards dredged. Nationwide, all maintenance dredging by the Corps of Engineers is approximately 290,000,000 cubic yards. (Submitted by H. R. Vick)

DRUNKEN DRIVING ARRESTS

The national record for most arrests in eight hours is 43 by the New Orleans Alcohol Safety Enforcement Section, September 22-23, 1972.

DRAMA, FIRST WRITTEN

Fete du Petit-Ble, by Paul LeBlanc de Villeneuve, 1814, was the first drama published in Louisiana.

ECOLOGICAL PATTERN

Louisiana lies entirely within the gulf coastal plain, extending in part over three major physiographic provinces and two major ecotones, an ecological pattern unique in the world. It has the largest variety of plant and animal species of any of the gulf states.

EDUCATION, MENTALLY RETARDED

Delta Kappa Gamma gave Mrs. Louise Simon Davis the first award as a "woman pioneer" in the field of education for the mentally retarded.

ELECTIONS

In 1975, Louisiana pioneered the first statewide nonpartisan elections in the nation.

FACTORY, OLDEST

Gullett Gin Company in Amite, manufacturer of gin material and equipment, is the oldest factory in the state.

FIRE, WORST

The state's most destructive fire occurred in New Orleans in 1788. More than 800 houses (including nearly every building of importance) were destroyed after a taper, lighted in observance of Good Friday, ignited a curtain and started the conflagration.

FISHING BOATS

Delhi Manufacturing Corporation is the world's largest builder of fishing boats. (Submitted by Claude Kenneson)

FISHING RODEO

Grand Isle Tarpon Rodeo, established in 1928, is the oldest fishing tournament in the U. S.

FORESTRY

Louisiana was the first state in the nation to plant trees under the Forest Incentives Program (1974).

FORT, OLDEST

Fort De La Boulaye, founded in 1700, was the first settlement on the lower Mississippi River. It was located just north of the present town of Phoenix in St. Bernard Parish.

GAS FIELD

The first natural gas field in Louisiana was discovered in 1823, at a depth of 400 feet.

GAS LIGHT

On May 8, 1823, the American Theatre (on Camp Street between Gravier and Poydras in New Orleans) displayed the first gas light in Louisiana.

GAS WELL

Working with hand forged tools designed by a visiting French engineer during a search for water in 1823, drillers accidentally discovered Louisiana's first gas well at Natchez Plantation.

GEOGRAPHIC CENTER

The geographic center of Louisiana is located three miles southeast of Marksville in Avoyelles Parish.

GEOGRAPHICAL NOTES

Louisiana, named by the explorer in honor of King Louis XIV of France, was admitted to the Union as a state in 1812. The state is 280 miles long, 275 miles wide and contains a land area of 44,930 sq. mi. Inland water bodies totaling 3,593 sq. mi. give the state a total area of 48,523 sq. mi., 31st in size nationally.

GEOGRAPHY, HIGHEST POINT

The highest point in Louisiana is Driskill Mountain (535 feet) in Bienville Parish.

GEOGRAPHY, LOWEST POINT

The lowest point in Louisiana (five feet below sea level) is in Orleans Parish.

GOLF, BLIND CHAMPION

Pat Browne, a New Orleans lawyer, is the champion of the National Blind Golfers Association.

GOVERNOR, SMALLEST WINNING PERCENTAGE

The smallest winning percentage ever to elect a governor in Louisiana was 32.7% by Charles E. ("Buddy") Roemer III on September 24, 1987. Roemer forced a runoff with incumbent governor Edwin Edwards which was scheduled for November 20, but Edwards withdrew from the race the following day, thus automatically electing Roemer.

GRAIN ELEVATOR
The Port of New Orleans built the first export grain elevator in 1917.

GRAIN EXPORT AREA
Multiple grain elevators near New Orleans have made it the world's largest grain export area.

GRAIN SHIPMENT
At the Port of New Orleans, in 1974, the M/V Furness Bridge, a 965-foot OBO carrier, loaded 65,000 long tons of grain bound for Rotterdam. This is believed to be the largest single load of grain, or of any other commodity, ever handled at the port.

HANGING, FIRST WOMAN
Ada Bonner LeBoeuf was the first woman ever hanged for murder in Louisiana (the 25th in the U. S.). She, with Dr. Thomas Dreher, was accused and convicted of murdering her husband, James LeBoeuf, on July 1, 1927. They were hanged February 1, 1929, in the St. Mary Parish Jail, Franklin.

HEALTH
The oldest Health Maintenance Organization in the nation was started in Baton Rouge in 1924 by Standard Oil (now Exxon).

HELIPORT, LARGEST
The world's largest commercial heliport is based in Morgan City. Owned by Petroleum Helicopters, Inc., it has landing pads for 46 helicopters, complete fuel, maintenance facilities and passenger waiting room accommodations.

HISTORY, FIRST PRINTED
The first printed history in Louisiana was *History of Louisiana* by Francois-Xavier Martin, in two volumes, at New Orleans in 1827.

HUNGARIAN SETTLEMENT
The oldest Hungarian settlement in the nation is located in Albany. (Submitted by Claude Kenneson)

INDIANS
The Chitimacha Indian Reservation in St. Mary Parish was the first Indian reservation in the nation to be designated a Bicentennial Community.

INDUSTRY
The Port of Orleans is the state's largest single industry with an estimated impact of $9.3 billion.

ISLANDS
Louisiana's 2,482 islands cover almost 1.3 million acres, the third in total islands in the nation and the second in total acreage.

JAZZ, ORIGIN
The name "jazz" was first given to music of New Orleans origin in 1915.

JETTY, FIRST
Captain James B. Eads completed the first successful jetty system at the mouth of the Mississippi River in 1879.

LAKES
The largest lake in the state is Lake Pontchartrain, with a 621 sq. mi. area. Of natural origin, it has a maximum depth of 15 feet and a shoreline of 117 miles.

LAW
Louisiana is the only state in the Union whose jurisdiction is based on civil law. All other states in the nation are under the common law code.

LAW SERVICES
Louisiana began the first prepaid law services program in the United States.

LEGISLATIVE SESSION, SHORTEST
Louisiana's shortest legislative session (one hour) occurred August 10, 1959.

LEPROSARIUM
Carville, the only leprosarium on the U. S. mainland, was founded in 1894.

LEPROSY
The world's first successful transmission of leprosy to a laboratory animal (armadillo) was performed by Dr. Eleanor E. Storrs at New Iberia in 1971.

LEVEES
The first levees constructed along the Mississippi River were reputed to have been at Bayou Goula in Iberville Parish.

LIBRARIES
The first free public library in Louisiana was founded by Judah Touro at New Orleans in 1824. (Submitted by Colin Hamer)

LIBRARY SCHOOLS
The Graduate School of Library Science at LSU in Baton Rouge is the first library school in North America to be accredited under the new standards of the American Library Association.

MAIN STREET
Bayou Lafourche is called "the longest main street in the world" stretching sixty-five miles from Thibodaux to Leeville in Lafourche Parish. (Submitted by Claude Kenneson)

MANUFACTURERS, LARGEST
Manufacturers in the state employing more than 5,000 workers are AT & T Consumer Products, Shreveport; Avondale Shipyards, Inc., Avondale; and Avondale Shipyards, Modular Construction Division, Avondale.

MARDI GRAS, FIRST PARADE
The first Mardi Gras parade took place on Shrove Tuesday in 1838, New Orleans.

MARDI GRAS FLOATS, LARGEST
Two "super" floats, both 3 stories high, were built by Blaine Kern for the Bacchus parade, 1975.

MARDI GRAS, OLDEST BLACK ORGANIZATION
The oldest black carnival organization in New Orleans, and reputedly in the world, is the Original Illinois Club, founded in 1894.

MARDI GRAS, REX
Rex, King of Carnival, paraded for the first time on Mardi Gras, 1872.

MARSH BUGGY
The marsh buggy was perfected by Andrew Cheramie and used for the first time in Louisiana.

MASONS
The first lodge in Louisiana was "Loge Parfaite," Union No. 29, organized on March 30, 1794, by the Grand Lodge of South Carolina.

MASONS
First English speaking, Louisiana Lodge No. 1, 1807.

MATCHES
A Kenner match company, Trans-Match, Inc., produces 60 million woodstick matches daily, one-half of the wooden matches sold in the U. S.

MEDICAL JOURNAL
New Orleans Medical & Surgical Journal (now the *Journal of Louisiana Medical Society*) is considered the oldest medical publication in the South.

MISSISSIPPI RIVER
The Mississippi River is the widest (7600 feet) at East Carroll Parish; the narrowest (1250 feet) at the Irvine Light, near Bayou Sara; the deepest (214 feet) opposite Gov. Nicholls St. in New Orleans; and the shallowest (9 feet) dredged depth in channels at many points.

MUSEUMS
Ranking first in the South and fifth in the nation are the holdings of the Museum of Natural Science and affiliated research collections of the Museum of Zoology, housed in Foster Hall at LSU, Baton Rouge.

NEWSPAPER, FIRST
The first newspaper in Louisiana was *Le Moniteur de la Louisiane*, established in 1794.

NUTTALL OAK, LARGEST
Located in Morehouse Parish, this Nuttall oak is 21 feet 6 inches in circumference, 115 feet in height, and has an 84 foot crown.

OAK
The national champion Overcup Oak is located on the Calcasieu River bottom in Vernon Parish near Simpson.

OAK, LARGEST
The largest Live Oak in Louisiana, the Seven Sisters (girth: 36 feet, 10 inches) is located on the estate of Mr. and Mrs. Tom L. Doby, Jr., at Lewisburg, near Mandeville.

OIL, DEEPEST DRILLING RIG
When completed in 1978, Shell Oil Company's 1,270 foot tall drilling platform will be the world's deepest offshore facility. It is located 15 miles southeast of the mouth of the Mississippi River.

OIL, DEEPEST DRY HOLE
The state's deepest dry hole is in St. Bernard Parish, in Lake Borgne, drilled by Placid Oil Company to a depth of 25,600 feet.

OIL, DEEPEST PRODUCER
The world's deepest producing offshore well is Hunt Oil No. 1, State Lease 3523, Grand Isle, 22,115 feet deep, producing from 20,500 feet.

OIL REFINERY
Marathon Oil Company's facility at Garyville is the largest refinery ever built in a single construction phase in the nation.

OIL REFINERY, LARGEST
The EXXON Refinery at Baton Rouge is the largest oil refinery (in capacity) on the North American continent.

OIL WELL, DEEPEST
The state's deepest well, at 25,600 feet, was drilled in 1970 in Lake Borgne, St. Bernard Parish.

OIL WELL, FIRST
Louisiana's first oil well was drilled near Jennings in August, 1901.

OIL WELL, OFFSHORE
In 1947, Kerr-McGee Corporation, with offshore operations based in Morgan City, drilled the first commercial producing oil well out of sight of land.

OIL WELL FIRE, WORST
The most destructive and most expensive oil well fire in history was at the Shell Oil Company, Platform B, Bay Marchand, at 9:45 a.m. from December 1, 1970 to April 16, 1971, (137 days, 11 wells, $36 million dollar cost).

OLDEST RESIDENT
Mrs. Lou Saulsberry of Epps is believed to have been the oldest Louisianian. Born a slave in Richland Parish on March 15, 1847, she died at the age of 125.

OPERA
Opera was first performed in the United States at New Orleans in 1796.

ORANGE GROVE
First on record planted in Buras in 1860 by Florentine Buras.

OVERWATER SPAN
The Lake Pontchartrain Causeway is the longest overwater span in the world. The southbound lane is 23.86 miles (125,980.8 feet); the northbound lane is 23.87 miles (126,033.6 feet).

OYSTER EATING RECORD
Mickey Rigdon of Metairie holds the Louisiana record for oyster eating, 236 in 30 minutes.

PARISHES
Louisiana is the only state in the nation which is divided into parishes, not counties—dating from the earliest boundaries set using existing Catholic Diocese boundaries. (Submitted by Claude Kenneson)

PARISH, CONSTRUCTION
The largest single construction permit recorded in Louisiana totaled $93,090,000 for the building of the Superdome in New Orleans.

PARISH, LARGEST IN AREA
Total area—Plaquemines, 1986 sq. mi.; land area—Cameron, 1441 sq. mi.; water area—St. Bernard, 1408 sq. mi.

PARISH, SMALLEST IN AREA
Total area—West Baton Rouge, 209 sq. mi.; land area—Orleans, 197 sq. mi.

PARISH, LARGEST IN POPULATION
Orleans, 561,200 residents
PARISH, SMALLEST IN POPULATION
Tensas, 8,400 residents
PARISH FAIRS
Washington Parish Fair is the largest in Louisiana, and the 3rd largest "county" fair in the nation.
PEACE MEMORIAL
The Louisiana Memorial to Peace in Lake Charles serves as home for more than 5,000 purple martins, and is the world's largest birdhouse.
PEPPERS, HOTTEST
The world's hottest variety of pepper is the Capsicum, of which the tabasco pepper is a member. It is grown on Avery Island by the McIlhenny Company.
PETROLEUM TECHNOLOGY
Lafourche Parish began the first high school petroleum technology course in the nation during the 1973-1974 school year.
PHARMACIST, FIRST
The first registered pharmacist in the United States was Louis Dufilhol. His drugstore is now a museum in New Orleans.
PIROGUE RACING
Merlin Frickey of Westwego won the 1978 World Champion Pirogue Racing Title.
PLYWOOD
Louisiana is the leading U. S. producer of southern pine plywood.
POEM, FIRST PUBLISHED
The first poem published by a Louisianian in Louisiana was *La Prise du Morne du Baton Rouge*, by Julien Poydras, in New Orleans in 1799. Only one known copy still exists.
POPULATION, UNINCORPORATED CITIES
Metairie, population 136,477, is the largest unincorporated city in the state and the second largest in the nation.
PORT OF NEW ORLEANS
New Orleans is the largest port on the Gulf of Mexico, the second largest in the United States and the third largest in the world in volume of cargo handled.
PORT OF NEW ORLEANS
New Orleans is the No. 1 U. S. port in trade with Latin America.
PORTS, DEEP WATER
Baton Rouge's port facility is the nation's farthest inland deep water port, the fourth largest port in the nation, ranking behind New York, New Orleans and Houston.
POSTAL SERVICE
The first airmail in the South was delivered from Shreveport to Homer on July 21, 1920.
POST OFFICE
The only building adapted for use by the U. S. Government in the interest of preservation is the post office in St. Martinville, built in 1876 as the Durande residence.
POST OFFICE

The first Rural Free Delivery route in Louisiana, the second in the United States, was established at Thibodaux on November 1, 1896. (Submitted by P. J. Oneil, Jr.)
POVERTY POINT
Poverty Point, a 2,600-year-old Indian city situated near Epps in West Carroll Parish, is the oldest known habitat of man in the lower Mississippi Valley. Its central mound, containing 35 times the cubic volume of the Great Pyramid of Egypt, measures 640 feet by 710 feet at its base and is nearly 70 feet high.
PRINTING
The first newspaper printed on offset press in the U. S. was the Opelousas *Daily World*.
PRINTING PRESS
Monsieur Braud of New Orleans was granted the right to set up the first printing press in Louisiana in 1764.
PROTESTANT SERMON
In 1803, at a point near the present city of Vidalia, Reverend Lorenzo Dow, a circuit riding Methodist preacher, delivered the first Protestant sermon on Louisiana Territory soil.
PUBLISHING COMPANIES
The oldest book publishing company in Louisiana is Pelican Publishing Company, established in 1926.
RACING
The Fair Grounds in New Orleans was the first track to introduce a mechanical starting gate and the first to glass-enclose and steam heat the grandstand, 1924.
RAILROAD, TO CALIFORNIA
The first through train service to California from New Orleans began in 1883. The line eventually became the Southern Pacific.
RAILROAD, TO CHICAGO
The first through train service to Chicago from New Orleans began in 1873. The line eventually became the Illinois Central.
RAILROAD, LONGEST
Missouri Pacific, 760.2 miles.
RAILROAD, SHORTEST
Feliciana Eastern, 0.5 miles.
RAILROAD BRIDGE
The world's longest railroad bridge crosses the Mississippi River by way of the Huey P. Long bridge in Jefferson Parish near New Orleans.
RAILROADS
The largest single piece of equipment ever hauled by American railroads was a fractionating column used in petrochemical operations. The 235-foot long piece of equipment was manufactured in Shreveport and delivered to Houston, Texas.
RAILROADS
The first railroad west of the Allegheny Mountains was the Pontchartrain Railroad between New Orleans and Milneburg, opened April 23, 1831.
RAIN
The heaviest rainfall ever recorded at a Louisiana weather station during a 24-hour period was at the

Sabine National Wildlife Refuge where 22 inches fell August 28 and 29, 1962.

RAIN

The heaviest precipitation for one year in Louisiana was 75.57 inches, reported in 1905.

RAIN

The lightest precipitation for one year in Louisiana was 38.34 inches, reported in 1924.

RAINIEST MAJOR CITY IN U. S.

The rainiest major city in the U. S. is New Orleans, with an annual rate of 54 inches.

REFINERY, LUBRICANTS & WAX

The CIT-CON refinery at Lake Charles is the largest refiner of lubricants and wax in the nation. (Submitted by Claude Kenneson)

RESTAURANT, OLDEST

Antoine's in New Orleans, established in 1840, is the state's oldest continuously operating restaurant.

REVOLT AGAINST A FOREIGN POWER

In 1768 Louisiana was the first colony in North America to revolt against a foreign power, Spain. On October 29, the speech of Nicolas LaFreniere in the Superior Council gave a rationale for the revolt and expulsion of Ulloa, the Spanish Governor.

RICE

The largest rice milling company in the world is located in Vermilion Parish.

RIVER PILOT, OLDEST

Captain George J. Spence holds the record as the oldest river pilot on the Mississippi River. He manned 10,000 ships in his 53 years of service.

RIVER TRAVEL

Captain Henry Shreve, for whom Shreveport is named, was the first man to pilot a steamboat, the "Enterprise," up the Red River to Natchitoches.

SALT

Louisiana is the nation's number 1 salt-producing state, with 24 percent of domestic production.

SALT MINE

Discovered in 1862, the salt mine at Avery Island is the oldest in the Western Hemisphere.

SALT MINE

Second largest in North America at Belle Isle.

SCHOOL, FIRST

The first school in Louisiana was the Ursuline Convent for girls, established in 1727 at New Orleans.

SCHOOLS, FIRST FREE PUBLIC

The May 14, 1845 state constitution provided for the first free public schools in Louisiana.

SCHOOLS, FIRST PUBLIC

The first public schools in Louisiana were established in Pointe Coupee Parish in 1808.

SEPARATE BUT EQUAL DOCTRINE

First decision on "separate but equal doctrine" was decided in Louisiana case, "Plessy *vs.* Ferguson," on May 18,1896. What is generally not known is that the Louisiana Supreme Court held for Plessy, but the U. S. Supreme Court reversed this decision and thus established the separate but equal doctrine.

SHALLOTS

Louisiana produces about 90 percent of the nation's true shallots, sometimes called "multiplying onions."

SHIPBUILDING

Avondale Shipyards is the only U. S. builder of the LASH design vessel.

SHIPS

The "Delta Queen" is the last inland overnight passenger paddlewheeler in the nation.

SHIPS, FASTEST SURFACE-EFFECT SHIP

Textron's Bell Aerospace Division in New Orleans developed the U. S. Navy SES-100B, a 100-ton surface-effect ship which established a world record of more than 80 knots (92 miles per hour) in 1974.

SHRIMP

First canned commercially at Grand Terre Island in 1867 by the Dunbar family.

SHRIMP DRYING PRODUCTION

The only area in the U. S. to produce dried shrimp is the coastal area of Louisiana.

SNOWFALL, HEAVIEST

The heaviest snowfall ever recorded in Louisiana was 24 inches, at Rayne, in 1895.

SPANISH MISSION

The only Spanish mission in Louisiana, San Miguel de Los Adais, was established in 1717 in Sabine Parish.

STAMPS

The highest price ever paid for a philatelic item was $380,000 for two one-penny Mauritius stamps of 1847, purchased by the Raymond H. Weill Company of New Orleans.

STATE CAPITOL, TALLEST

Louisiana state capitol in Baton Rouge, 34 floors, 450 feet high.

STATE, CLEANEST

In 1976, in the "Keep America Beautiful" drive, Louisiana was named the "cleanest state in the nation."

STATUES

America's first statue honoring a woman, Margaret Haughery, was erected at New Orleans in 1884.

STEAMBOAT, FIRST

The first steamboat to navigate the Mississippi, Nicholas Roosevelt's "New Orleans," arrived at New Orleans from Pittsburgh on January 10, 1812.

STRAWBERRIES

The first strawberries sold in the South were raised at Magnolia Lane Plantation near New Orleans.

STREET RAILWAY

The last mulecar in Louisiana in Burnside, 1922.

STREET RAILWAY

First mulecar in Louisiana in New Orleans, January, 1835.

STREET RAILWAY

First electric car in New Orleans, February 1, 1893; in Baton Rouge, April 5, 1893.

STREET RAILWAY

The Street Railway in Monroe was the first municipally-owned line in the U. S., 1906.

STYRENE MONOMER PLANT

The COS-MAR plant near Baton Rouge is the world's largest producer of styrene monomer at a single location.

SUBMARINES

The world's first iron submarine, "The Pioneer," was built in a machine shop in New Orleans in 1861.

SUGAR

First granulated by Etienne de Bore in 1795 on the site of Audubon Park, New Orleans.

SUGAR BOWL GAME, FIRST

In 1935, Tulane 20, Temple 14.

SUGAR CANE

Sugar cane was first introduced into Louisiana in 1751.

SULPHUR

The first sulphur deposit in the U. S. was discovered in Louisiana in 1869 in Calcasieu Parish.

SULPHUR

The world's largest sulphur warehouse is located at Port Sulphur. (*Louisiana: The Land and Its People*)

SUPERDOME

The Superdome in New Orleans is the largest enclosed stadium-arena in the world.

SURGERY

Sarah Jackson, age 103, is believed to be the oldest patient ever to survive major surgery, performed at Sara Mayo Hospital in New Orleans, June, 1973.

SWEET POTATOES, LARGEST PRODUCER

St. Landry Parish is the largest producer of sweet potatoes of any governmental unit in the world.

SWIMMER

Ernest C. Hunt swam 22 miles across Lake Pontchartrain (from Mandeville to Spanish Fort) in 15 hours, 5 minutes on Labor Day, 1923.

SYRUP PLANT

The world's largest syrup plant is Steen's Syrup Mill in Abbeville.

TALLEST STRUCTURE

The tallest structure in the state is the KNOE-TV tower at Monroe (1,986 feet).

TELEPHONE COMPANY, LARGEST

South Central Bell Telephone Company with 356,536 miles of cable.

TELEPHONE COMPANY, SMALLEST

The Chatham Telephone Company and the Union Telephone Company are the smallest telephone companies in the state with 3 miles of cable each.

TELEVISION

On December 18, 1948, WDSU in New Orleans signed on the air as the first television station in Louisiana.

TEMPERATURE, HIGHEST

The highest temperature ever recorded in Louisiana was 114°F. at Plain Dealing on August 10, 1936.

TEMPERATURE, LOWEST

The lowest temperature ever recorded in Louisiana was minus 16°F. at Minden on February 13, 1899.

TENNIS CLUB, OLDEST

The New Orleans Lawn Tennis Club, one of the first in the nation, is the oldest tennis club in Louisiana, established in 1876.

THEATER

The first theater established in the U. S. was in New Orleans.

THEATRE, COMMUNITY

New Orleans' LePetit Theatre, whose history dates from 1919, is recognized as the oldest community theatre in America.

THEATRE, FIRST PERFORMANCE

LeBlanc Villeneuve's play, *Le Pere Indian*, was the first theatrical production in Louisiana, performed by amateurs in 1753.

TOBACCO, PERIQUE

St. James Parish is the only area in the world where perique tobacco is grown.

TRADEMARK

The second oldest food trademark in the U. S. Patent Office is "Tabasco," the pepper sauce bottled on Avery Island by the McIlhenny Company.

TRAFFIC CITATIONS

The national record for traffic citations is 117, by New Orleans Alcohol Safety Enforcement Section, September 22-23, 1972.

TREES

A chinquapin tree (Castanea pumila) measuring 11 feet, 10 inches, located in Red River Parish, holds the state and national championship in the LFA champion tree listing.

TV TOWER, TALLEST

The tallest TV tower in the state is used by KNOE-TV in Monroe (1,986 feet).

TWINE MILL

Largest in the world is the International Harvester Factory in New Orleans. It produces enough twine yearly to circle the globe 65 times.

U. S. AMBASSADOR

Mrs. Anne L. Armstrong, a native of New Orleans, became the second American woman ambassador to a major embassy, Great Britain, in January, 1976.

U. S. REPRESENTATIVE, LONGEST TERM

F. Edward Hebert, New Orleans, congressman from Louisiana District One; January 3, 1941-July 31, 1976 (35 years, 6 months and 28 days).

U. S. REPRESENTATIVE, SHORTEST TERM

George Sheridan, Lake Providence, March 3, 1875; served one day.

U. S. SENATE, LONGEST TERM

Allen Ellender, Houma; January 3, 1937-July 27, 1972, 35 years, 6 months.

U. S. SENATE, SHORTEST TERM

Pierre Soule, New Orleans; served one month, February 3, 1847-March 3, 1847.

WATERBORNE COMMERCE

Waterborne trade at the Port of Orleans in 1976 amounted to an estimated 155 million tons valued at $9,294,000,000.

WETLANDS

Louisiana has over seven million acres in wetlands and estuarine water, more than any other state in the nation.

WHEAT-RYE HYBRID

In April, 1975, the world's first export of a wheat-rye hybrid grain called triticale was loaded at the St. Charles grain elevator at Destrehan.

WIND SPEED

The highest wind speed ever recorded in Louisiana was 140 miles per hour at Burrwood, September 29, 1915.

WOMAN FOUNDER

Tangipahoa is the only town known to have been founded by a woman, Mrs. Rhoda Holly Singleton Mixon, in 1806.

WOMAN MAYOR

Mrs. Lula Venable Coleman of Jena was the first woman mayor in Louisiana.

WOMAN POLITICIAN

Lucille May Grace was Louisiana's first woman ever elected to a state office, Register of the State Land Office, in 1932.

WOMAN STATE TROOPER, FIRST

Cindy Kay Bell became Louisiana's first woman state trooper on October 10, 1974.

YACHT CLUB

The Southern Yacht Club, in New Orleans, is the oldest yacht club in the state and second oldest in the nation. Its charter dates from 1849.

YELLOW FEVER

Last epidemic in the state occurred in 1909.

YELLOW FEVER, WORST EPIDEMIC

The worst yellow fever epidemic in the state killed 11,000 people in New Orleans and devastated many rural districts in 1853.

TALLEST BUILDINGS IN LOUISIANA

	Hgt.	Flrs.		Hgt.	Flrs.
One Shell Square, New Orleans	697'	51	Superdome, New Orleans	273'	
Place St. Charles, New Orleans	645'	53	Beck Building, Shreveport	266'	20
1001 Building, New Orleans	531'	45	1555 Poydras Bldg., New Orleans	262'	22
Energy Center, New Orleans	506'	39	Two Lakeway Center, Metairie	259'	19
Sheraton Hotel, New Orleans	488'	49	Heritage Plaza, Metairie	245'	18
Texaco Center, New Orleans	460'	33	Chevron Place, New Orleans	238'	21
State Capitol, Baton Rouge	450'	34	Hilton Hotel, Baton Rouge	230'	21
Marriott Hotel, New Orleans	450'	42	Masonic Temple, New Orleans	228'	18
Bank of New Orleans, New Orleans	438'	31	First National Bank Bldg., Shreveport	227'	16
Canal Place One, New Orleans	433'	32	American Bank Bldg., Shreveport	222'	16
International Trade Mart, New Orleans	407'	33	National Bank of Commerce, New Orleans	220'	18
One Poydras Plaza, New Orleans	367'	28	Per Marquette Building, New Orleans		18
Hilton Hotel, New Orleans	365'	29	Commerce Building, New Orleans		18
Louisiana & Southern Life Insurance Bldg., New Orleans	362'	28	Mid-South Towers, Shreveport	213'	15
Hyatt-Regency Hotel, New Orleans	360'	27	Commercial National Bank, Shreveport	210'	15
Hibernia Bank, New Orleans	355'	23	Texaco Building, New Orleans	207'	17
Pan American Life Center, New Orleans	342'	28	Imperial Executive Twin Towers, Metairie	204'	14
American Bank Bldg., Baton Rouge	330'	24	Hale Boggs Federal Complex, New Orleans	204'	14
National American Bank, New Orleans	330'	23	First National Bank, Lafayette	197'	15
1515 Poydras Bldg., New Orleans	327'	27	One Lakeway Center, Metairie	193'	14
Louisiana Towers, Shreveport	302'	22	Petroleum Tower, Shreveport	187'	14
Poydras Center, New Orleans	300'	28	International Hotel, New Orleans	184'	17
Canal-LaSalle Bldg., New Orleans	288'	24	Lake Marina Towers, New Orleans	180'	19
225 Baronne Bldg., New Orleans	280'	28	Veterans Administration Hospital, Shreveport	176'	14
Amoco Bldg., New Orleans	280'	20	Campanile, LSU Campus, Baton Rouge	175'	
Charity Hospital, New Orleans	279'	19			
Louisiana Bank, Baton Rouge	277'	21			
1615 Poydras Bldg., New Orleans	276'	23			
Lykes Center, New Orleans	276'	22			

LONGEST BRIDGES IN LOUISIANA

Bridge	Location (parish)	Length in Miles	Length in Feet
Lake Pontchartrain Causeway	Orleans and St. Tammany	23.87 (N) 23.86 (S)	126,033.6 125,980.8
LaPlace-Frenier, I-10 and I-55	St. John and Tangipahoa	23.08	121,891.0
Atchafalaya Floodway Crossing, I-10	Iberville, St. Martin, and West Baton Rouge	17.90	94,512.0
Bonnet Carre Spillway, I-10	St. Charles	12.16	64,204.8
Bonnet Carre Spillway, I-10	St. Charles	9.67	51,057.0
Lake Pontchartrain Bridge, I-10	Orleans and St. Tammany	5.41	28,564.8
Lake Pontchartrain Bridge, LA - US 11	Orleans and St. Tammany	4.73	24,974.4
Broad Street, I-10	Orleans	4.12	21,753.6
Morganza Floodway Bridge, LA - US 190	Pointe Coupee	3.56	18,796.0
Reserve Relief Canal Bridge, I-10	St. John the Baptist	3.49	18,427.2
Mississippi River Bridge, I-10	East and West Baton Rouge	2.68	14,150.4
Pendelton Bridge at Toledo Bend, LA 6	Sabine (and state of Texas)	2.50	13,200.0
Chippewa Street—Monte Sano. Bayou, I-110	East Baton Rouge	2.18	11,510.4
Mississippi River Bridge, Greater New Orleans	Orleans	2.10	11,088.0
Luling-Destrehan Bridge, I-310	St. Charles	2.03	10,700.0
Ouachita River Bridge, I-20	Ouachita	1.83	9,662.4
Mississippi River Bridge, Huey P. Long, LA - US 90	Jefferson	1.74	9,187.2
Calcasieu River Bridge, I-210	Calcasieu	1.70	8,976.0
Prien Lake, I-20	Calcasieu	1.61	8,501.0
Mississippi River Bridge, Vicksburg, Mississippi	Madison (and state of Mississippi)	1.60	8,448.0
Mississippi River Bridge, Sunshine Bridge	Ascension and St. James	1.56	8,236.8
Calcasieu River Bridge, I-10	Calcasieu	1.44	7,603.2
Atchafalaya River Bridge, US 90	St. Mary	1.31	6,902.0
Inner Harbor Navigation Canal, I-10	Orleans	1.27	6,715.0
Calcasieu River, I-10	Calcasieu	1.25	6,607.0
Intracoastal Waterway Bridge, LA 47	Orleans	1.24	6,622.0
Inner Harbor Canal Bridge, I-10	Orleans	1.20	6,336.0
Mississippi River Bridge, I-20	Madison (and State of Mississippi)	1.20	6,317.0
Bonnet Carre Spillway Bridge, LA - US 61	St. Charles	1.14	6,019.2
East Pearl River Bridge, I-10	St. Tammany	.96	4,987.0
Bayou Barataria, LA 314	Jefferson	.88	4,624.0
Mississippi River Bridge, US 65, Natchez	Concordia (and state of Mississippi)	.80	4,224.0
Morganza Spillway Bridge, LA 1	Pointe Coupee	.78	4,118.4

LOUISIANA LIVE OAKS

The Live Oak Society, under the direction of Dr. Edwin L. Stephens of Lafayette, was organized in 1934. The membership is composed of the trees themselves, each being represented by an owner or sponsor. There are presently over 400 registered members. The purpose of the organization is to promote the culture, distribution and appreciation of the Live Oak. To qualify for membership, the tree must be more than 100 years old, determined by a girth of at least 17½ feet, measured four feet from the ground, or documentation of age.

The largest oak has the honor of being the President of the Society, and on May 11, 1968, the Seven Sisters Oak was installed as President. It is located in Lewisburg and sponsored by its owners, Mr. and Mrs. Thomas L. Doby, Jr.

The Evangeline Oak, in St. Martinville, is probably the most famous Live Oak in Louisiana. The Gebert Oak, in New Iberia, is a truly magnificent specimen of the Society and has been used as a gauge in judging the ages of other trees.

Another magnificent tree, the Schaefer Oak, whose girth grew 17 inches from 1935 to 1945, is located on Frenchman Street in New Orleans. Many large oaks in Audubon Park and City Park in New Orleans provide beauty and pleasure to tourist and native alike. Another stately oak is on the grounds of St. John's Cathedral in Lafayette. Six huge oaks in Covington were recently presented as members. Several lovely trees in St. Martinville are sponsored by Mr. Tony Barras.

The following is a selected list of some of the largest members of the Society.

Name of Oak	Location	Girth	
Seven Sisters	Lewisburg	36'	10"
Arnaud Robert	Cecelia, St. Martin Parish	33'	10"
Frederick Point	Bayou du Large, Terrebonne Parish	32'	
Reformation	Metairie	30'	
Lorenzo Dow	East Feliciana Parish	30'	
Grandpere	Jefferson Parish	29'	4"
Bowie	Little Bayou, Vermilion Parish	28'	8"
LaBauve	Troul	28'	
Faucheaux	Thibodaux	28'	
Martha Washington	Audubon Park, New Orleans	27'	6"
Felix and Frankie's	St. Martin Parish	27'	5"
Patterson	Patterson	27'	
Holly Garden	Baton Rouge	27'	
Tony Barras	St. Martinville	25'	10"
Granberry	Lewisburg	25'	6"
Langlois	New Roads	25'	
Deda	St. Tammany Parish	24'	3"
Back Brusly	Brusly	24'	
Etienne de Bore	Audubon Park, New Orleans	23'	10"

Source: Live Oak Society; Louisiana Garden Club Federation

BROWN PELICAN

THE STATE GOVERNMENT

The Government of the state of Louisiana, is divided into three departments—legislative, executive and judicial.

The legislative power of the state is vested in a general assembly. The executive department, of which the governor is the chief magistrate. The judicial power is vested in a supreme court, courts of appeal and district courts. These departments all function under the authority and in accordance with the provisions of the state constitution and the bill of rights, which follow, in general, the lines of the constitution of the United States.

THE LOUISIANA LEGISLATURE

The legislature-or the general assembly-is composed of two houses: the Senate, which limits number of members to 39, and the House of Representatives, with a member limit of 105.

From 1812 until 1879 the legislature met in annual session except the years between 1845 and 1852 when its sessions were biennial. During the 75-year period from 1879 through 1954 the legislature met in biennial 60-day calendar sessions. In 1954 it returned to the annual session with those in odd-numbered years being restricted to budgetary matters.

General Assembly meets in Baton Rouge, at the State Capitol, the sessions beginning on the second Monday in May of the even-numbered years. The regular sessions of the Legislature are limited to 60 days unless emergency matters require their extension, in which case extensions can be made in the same manner as special sessions can be called, i.e., by proclamation of the Governor or by two-thirds vote of both the Senate and the House.

The members of the general assembly are elected by the qualified electors of the districts which they represent. For the election of senators to the state legislature, the state is divided into thirty-nine senatorial districts. The districts are made up of complete parishes, or a group of parishes, or, as in the case of Orleans, by parts of a parish.

There are one hundred and five districts in the House of Representatives. The most populous parishes elect several representatives and the least populous parishes comprise a portion of a district.

According to the constitution, each representative and senator must be at least 18 years of age and a registered voter. He or she must be a citizen of Louisiana for at least 2 years, and a resident of the district from which elected at least 1 year immediately preceding the election. All legislators are elected for concurrent terms of four years.

A bill introduced in the general assembly does not become a law until after it has received a majority vote in both houses and is signed by the governor or allowed to become a law by the governor without his signature or is passed by a two-thirds vote of both houses over the governor's veto. No bill can become a law which conflicts with the state or national constitutions. Should it appear that an amendment to the state constitution is desirable, the amendment must be submitted to the vote of the qualified electors of the state, whose vote decides whether or not the amendment shall be made. To submit an amendment to the people a two-thirds vote in both houses is required. All appropriation bills must originate in the house, although the senate may amend such bills.

THE COMMITTEES OF THE LEGISLATURE

Each house has fifteen standing committees, as follows:

House of Representatives
Administration of Criminal Justice
Agriculture
Appropriations
Civil Law and Procedure
Commerce
Education
Health and Welfare
House and Governmental Affairs
Judiciary
Labor and Industrial Relations
Municipal and Parochial Affairs
Natural Resources
Retirement
Transportation, Highways and Public Works
Ways and Means

Senate
Agriculture
Commerce
Education
Finance
Health and Welfare
Judiciary A
Judiciary B
Judiciary C
Labor and Industrial Relations
Local and Municipal Affairs
Natural Resources
Retirement
Revenue and Fiscal Affairs
Senate and Governmental Affairs
Transportation, Highways and Public Works

THE JUDICIARY
The Supreme Court

The highest court in the state is the supreme court which is composed of the chief justice and six associate justices who are elected for terms of 14 years from six supreme court districts in which the state is divided. The first supreme court district which includes Orleans and three other parishes elects two justices. The justice oldest in point of service becomes the chief justice. When the supreme court is sitting enbanc, four justices must control or render a decision. If for any reason four cannot control, or if a vacancy exists which the court is not authorized to fill, the court can call in a judge from the court of appeals. Supreme court justices must be citizens of the state who are qualified electors and not less than 35 years of age. They must be learned in the law and must have practiced law in Louisiana for at least ten years and must be a resident of the district from which elected for at least two years immediately prior to the election.

Courts of Appeal

There are four courts of appeal in Louisiana which exercise only civil and probate jurisdiction. A judge of the court of appeal must be a citizen of the state and a qualified elector, learned in the law, and have practiced law in Louisiana for at least six years, and been a resident in the district from which elected at least two years immediately prior to election. The judges of the court of appeal serve terms of 12 years.

District Courts

The court of general jurisdiction of both civil and criminal cases is the district court. There are 39 judicial districts in Louisiana. In addition to the civil district courts and criminal district courts in New Orleans there are juvenile and family courts, minor courts of various sorts, city courts, mayor's courts and justice of the peace courts.

The court officials are the district attorneys, clerks of court, sheriffs, municipal police and constables, coroners.

THE SECRETARY OF STATE

The office of secretary of state was established by the constitution of 1812 under which the secretary of state was appointed by the Governor for a term of four years. The constitution of 1852 made the office elective.

THE QUALIFICATIONS FOR GOVERNOR

The qualifications for Governor are threefold. He must be at least 25 years of age, a citizen of the United States and a resident of the state for at least 5 years preceding the election and hold no federal office.

THE OFFICE OF LIEUTENANT-GOVERNOR

The office of lieutenant-governor was established by the constitution of 1845, and since that time the lieutenant-governor has been elected for a term of four years. The same qualifications apply as for the governor. Although he is part of the executive branch his principal function is to preside over the senate in which capacity he appoints committees and has the deciding vote in the event of a tie.

THE ATTORNEY GENERAL

The attorney general has been a constitutional officer since 1812 and until the adoption of the constitution of 1852 he was appointed by the governor to serve a two-year term. Since 1852 the attorney general has been elected for a four-year term.

QUALIFICATIONS OF VOTERS

In order to vote in Louisiana a person must be 18 years of age, a citizen of the U. S. and be registered 30 days prior to an election. The Registrar of Voters is selected by the police jury except in Orleans, Jefferson and Plaquemines Parish where they are appointed by the Commission Council.

POLICE JURY

With the exception of Orleans, Plaquemines, St. Bernard, East Baton Rouge and Jefferson Parishes, each parish is governed by a police jury. However, other officials such as the sheriff, clerk of court, the assessor, the school board and the coroner are not controlled by the police jury. Police jurors are elected from wards for terms of four years.

PARISH ELECTIVE OFFICERS

The elective officers are the sheriff, the coroner, the clerk of court, the assessor. Members of the board of education are elected for six years and all the other officers for four.

STATE GOVERNMENT

ELECTED

Governor   *Charles E. ("Buddy") Roemer III*
State Capitol
P. O. Box 44004
Baton Rouge 70804
(504) 342-7015

Lieutenant Governor   *Paul Hardy*
P. O. Box 44243
Baton Rouge 70804
(504) 342-7009

Secretary of State   *W. Fox McKeithen*
P. O. Box 44125
Baton Rouge 70804
(504) 342-5710

Attorney General   *William J. Guste, Jr.*
P. O. Box 44005
Baton Rouge 70804
(504) 342-7013

Treasurer   *Mary Landrieu*
P. O. Box 44154
Baton Rouge 70804
(504) 342-7227

Commissioner of
  Agriculture   *Bob Odom*
P. O. Box 44302
Baton Rouge 70804
(504) 342-7011

Commissioner of
  Insurance   *Doug Green*
P. O. Box 44214
Baton Rouge 70804
(504) 342-5322

Commissioner of
  Elections   *Jerry M. Fowler*
P. O. Box 44095
Baton Rouge 70804
(504) 342-5885

APPOINTED

Commissioner of
  Administration   *Brian E. Kendrick*
P. O. Box 44095
Baton Rouge 70804
(504) 342-7000

Secretary of Commerce
P. O. Box 44185
Baton Rouge 70804
(504) 342-5359

Secretary of Corrections
P. O. Box 44304
Baton Rouge 70804
(504) 342-6740

Secretary of Culture,
  Recreation and Tourism
P. O. Box 44361
Baton Rouge 70804
(504) 925-3800

Secretary of Health and
  Human Resources
P. O. Box 3776
Baton Rouge 70821
(504) 342-6711

Secretary of Labor
P. O. Box 44094
Baton Rouge 70804
(504) 342-3111

Secretary of Natural
  Resources
P. O. Box 44396
Baton Rouge 70804
(504) 342-4500

Secretary of Revenue
  and Taxation
P. O. Box 201
Baton Rouge 70821
(504) 925-7537

Secretary of Transportation
  and Development
P. O. Box 44245
Baton Rouge 70804
(504) 342-6732

Secretary of Urban and
  Community Affairs
P. O. Box 44455
Baton Rouge 70804
(504) 925-3703

Superintendent of
  Education
P. O. Box 44064
Baton Rouge 70804
(504) 342-3602

Louisiana Senatorial Districts

District Number	District Description*	Senator
1	Jefferson—Wards 1 (pcts. 5A thru 6) & 6; Plaquemines; St. Bernard	Samuel B. Nunez, Jr.
2	Orleans—Ward 9 (pcts. 1 thru 10, 17, 22, & 32 thru 45A)	Jon Johnson
3	Orleans—Wards 6 (pcts. 8 & 9), 7 (pcts. 1 thru 18, 20 & 37), 8 & 9 (pcts. 11 thru 16, 18 thru 21 & 23 thru 31E)	Dennis Bagneris
4	Orleans—Wards 1 (pcts. 1 & 2), 2 (pcts. 1 thru 5), 3, 4, 5, 6 (pcts. 1 thru 7) & 7 (pcts. 19, 20A thru 36A & 38 thru 42)	Bernard J. Bagert, Jr.
5	Orleans—Wards 1 (pcts. 5, 6, & 7), 2 (pcts. 6, 6A & 7), 10 thru 13, 14 (pcts. 23, 24, 24A, 26 & 26A), 16 (pct. 9) & 17 (pcts. 10 & 12 thru 14)	William J. Jefferson
6	Jefferson—Wards 7 (pcts. 1 thru 16 & 19), 8 (pcts. 1 thru 11, 13 thru 16, 18 & 22) & 10 (pcts. 1 thru 16 & 40)	John Joseph Hainkel, Jr.
	Orleans—Wards 14 (pcts. 1 thru 22 & 25), 16 (pcts. 1 thru 8) & 17 (pcts. 1 thru 9, 11, 15 thru 21)	
7	Jefferson—Wards 1 (pcts. 1 thru 5), 2, & 3 (pcts. 2 3, 6, & 8); Orleans—Ward 15	Fritz H. Windhorst
8	Jefferson—Wards 3 (pcts. 1, 4, 5, 7 & 9), 4 & 5	Chris Ullo
9	Jefferson—Wards 7 (pcts. 17 & 18), 8 (pcts. 12, 17, 19, 20, 21 & 23 thru 50), 9 (pcts. 10A & 10G) & 10 (pcts. 17 thru 39, 41, 42 & 43)	J. Ken Hollis
10	Jefferson—Ward 9 (pcts. 1 thru 9K, 10B thru 10F & 10H thru 31K)	Francis E. "Hank" Lauricella
11	St. Tammany—Wards 1, 3, 4, 7, 8 (pcts. 2 thru 9) & 9	Gerry E. Hinton
	Tangipahoa—Wards 6 (pcts. 2 & 2A), 7 (pcts. 2, 10, 15, 16, 18, 18A & 19) & 8	
12	St. Helena; St. Tammany—Wards 2, 5, 6, 8 (pct. 1) & 10; Tangipahoa—Wards 1 thru 5 & 6 (pcts. 1 & 3 thru 8); Washington	Benjamin B. "Sixty" Rayburn
13	East Baton Rouge—Wards 2 (pcts. 4A thru 9B, 13A thru 15, 17A, 17B, 21 & 22) & 3 (pcts. 1A thru 1D, 14A, 14B & 14C); Livingston—Wards 1, 2 (pcts. 1, 1A, 2, 3, 3A & 5), 4, 8 & 11 (pcts. 3 & parts of pcts. 1 & 1A); Tangipahoa—Ward 7 (pct. 1, 1A, 3 thru 9A, 11 thru 14 & 17)	Mike Cross
14	East Baton Rouge—Wards 1 (pcts. 1A thru 5, 10, 11, 15A thru 29, 31A, 31B, 45, 50A thru 51B, 58A, 58B, 61, 62, 67, 84A thru 86B, 91, 92A, 92B, 94A thru 95B) & 2 (pcts. 1A, 1B, 11A thru 12B, 16A, 16B, 20, 23A & 23B)	Cleo Fields
15	East Baton Rouge—Wards 1 (pcts. 6, 7, 8, 13A thru 14B, 30, 32, 33, 35 thru 44, 46A thru 48B, 54A, 54B, 56A, 56B, 57, 59, 63 thru 66, 68 thru 70, 75A thru 78B, 82A thru 83B & 93) & 3 (pct. 5)	Larry Bankston
16	East Baton Rouge—Wards 1 (pcts. 34A, 34B, 49A, 49B, 52A thru 53D, 55A, 55B, 60A, 60B, 71A thru 74C, 79, 80, 81 & 87 thru 90) & 3 (pcts. 2 thru 4D, 8A thru 13B & 17A thru 22D)	Kenneth E. Osterberger
17	East Feliciana; Iberville; Pointe Coupee; West Baton Rouge; West Feliciana	John Enoul Jumonville, Jr.

18	Ascension; Assumption—Wards 1 (pct. 1 & part of pct. 2) & 7 (parts of pcts. 1 & 1A); Livingston—Wards 2 (pcts. 4, 4A, 6 & 6A), 3, 5, 6, 7, 9, 10 & 11 (pct. 2 & parts of pcts. 1 & 1A); St. James; St. John the Baptist—Dist. 1	Joseph A. Sevario III
19	Lafourche—Wards 1, 2, 3, & 5 thru 8; St. Charles; St. John the Baptist—Dists. 2 thru 7	Ron J. Landry
20	Jefferson—Ward 11; Lafourche—Wards 4, 9, 10, & 11; Terrebonne—Wards 2 thru 7 & 10	Leonard J. Chabert
21	Assumption—Wards 1 (part of pct. 2), 2 thru 6, 7 (pct. 2 & parts of pcts. 1 & 1A), 8 & 9; St. Martin—Dist. 1 (pcts. 2 & 5); St. Mary; Terrebonne—Wards 1, 8, & 9	M. J. "Mike" Foster
22	Iberia; St. Martin—Dists. 1 (pcts. 1, 3, & 4) & 2 thru 9	Oswald A. Decuir
23	Lafayette—Dists. A (pcts. 7-A & 7-B), B (pcts. 16, 17-18 & 19-20), C (pcts. 27 thru 31-32 & 34A thru 36) & D thru G	Allen Bares
24	Lafayette—Dists. A (pcts. 1-A thru 6), B (pcts. 8-9 thru 15 & 21-22 thru 24), & C (pcts. 25-26, 33-A & 33-B); St. Landry—Wards 1 thru 5 & 6 (pcts. 1, 3, 4, 11 & 17)	Armand J. Brinkhaus
25	Acadia; Vermilion	Cecil J. Picard
26	Calcasieu—Wards 3 (pcts. 22 thru 25, 31, 32 & 35 thru 38B) & 4 thru 7; Cameron	Jack Dowland
27	Calcasieu; Wards 1, 2, 3 (pcts. 1 thru 21, 26 thru 30, 33, 34, 39, 41 & 42) & 8; Jefferson Davis	William L. McLeod, Jr.
28	Allen; Avoyelles, Evangeline; St. Landry—Ward 6 (pcts. 2, 5 thru 10 & 12 thru 16)	John Saunders
29	Rapides—Wards 1 thru 9	"Joe" McPherson
30	Beauregard; Sabine; Vernon	Bryan A. Poston
31	Grant; Natchitoches; Rapides—Ward 10; Red River; Winn	Donald G. Kelly
32	Caldwell; Catahoula; Concordia; Franklin; LaSalle; Rapides—Ward 11; Tensas	Steve Thompson
33	East Carroll; Madison; Morehouse; Ouachita—Wards 1 (pcts. 1 & 2), 2 (pct. 1) & 4; Richland; West Carroll	Willie Crain
34	Ouachita—Wards 1 (pcts. 3, 4 & 5), 2 (pcts. 2A & 2L), 3, 5 (pcts. 1 thru 4, 6, 8 thru 12, 15 & parts of pcts. 16A & 16L) & 10	Lawson L. Swearingen, Jr.
35	Claiborne—Wards 1, 2, 7, 8 & 9; Jackson; Lincoln; Ouachita—Wards 5 (pcts. 5, 7, 13, 14 & parts of pcts. 16A & 16L) & 6 thru 9; Union	Randy Ewing
36	Bienville; Bossier—Wards 1, 3, & 4; Claiborne—Wards 3 thru 6; Webster	Foster L. Campbell, Jr.
37	Bossier—Ward 2; Caddo—Wards 4 (pcts. 6 thru 24, 26 thru 29, 47, 48, 49, 56A, 56B, 62, 63, 64, 66 & 72) & 8 (pcts. 1 & 2)	Sydney Nelson
38	Caddo—Wards 4 (pcts. 4, 35, 36, 38, 50 thru 53, 59, 68A, 68B, 69 & 70), 5, 6, 7, & 8 (pct. 3); DeSoto	Richard G. Neeson
39	Caddo—Wards 1, 2, 3, 4, (pcts. 1, 2, 3A, 3B, 5, 25, 30 thru 34, 37, 39 thru 46, 54, 55, 57 & 58, 60, 61, 65, 67, 71 & 73) & 9	Gregory Tarver

Louisiana Representative Districts

District Number	District Description*	Representative
1	Caddo—Wards 1, 2, 3 (pcts. 1 thru 3B & 5), 4 (pct. 5), 5 (pcts. 2, 4, 5A & 5B) & 9	Roy Hopkins
2	Caddo—Wards 3 (pct. 4), 4 (pcts. 1, 31, 39, 40, 41, 44, 45, 54, 57, 65, 67, 71, & 73)	Alphonse Jackson, Jr.
3	Caddo—Ward 4 (pcts. 3A, 3B, 23, 25, 34, 38, 42, 43, 46, 50, 51, 58, 60, & 61)	Willie Singleton
4	Caddo—Wards 4 (pcts. 2, 30, 35, 36, 52, 53, 55, 59, 69, & 70), 5 (pcts. 1A & 1B) & 7 (pcts. 1A, 1B & 2)	Robert P. Waddell
5	Caddo—Wards 4 (pcts. 4, 11, 12, 16, 22, 24, 26, 49, 56A, 56B, 62, 63, 68A, 68B & 72), 7 (pcts. 3A, 3B, 4 & 6) & 8 (pcts. 1 & 2)	Roy Brun
6	Caddo—Ward 4 (pcts. 6 thru 10, 13, 14, 15, 17, thru 21, 27, 28, 29, 32, 33, 37, 47, 48, 64 & 66)	Arthur W. "Art" Sour, Jr.
7	Caddo—Wards 5 (pct. 3), 6, 7 (pcts. 5A, 5B, 7A & 7B) & 8 (pct. 3)	John McFerren
	DeSoto—Wards 1 thru 4, 6, & 8	
8	Bossier—Wards 1 (part of pct. 1) & 2 (pcts. 2 thru 17 & 19)	Robert R. Adley
9	Bossier—Wards 1 (pcts. 2A, 2B, 3 & part of pct. 1), 2 (pcts. 1 & 18), 3 & 4	Billy Montgomery
	Webster—Ward 1 (pct. 24)	
10	Webster—Wards 1 (pcts. 1 thru 23 & 25 thru 28) & 2	Bruce Bolin
11	Bienville—Ward 2; Claiborne; Union	Kenneth Volentine
12	Lincoln	William R. Sumlin, Jr.
13	Bienville—Wards 1 & 3 thru 7	Rodney Alexander
	Jackson—Wards 1, 2, (parts of pcts. 1 & 2) & 4 thru 10; Winn—Wards 1 thru 9, 10 (pct. 3) & 12 (pct. 1)	
14	Morehouse—Wards 1, 3, & 4 (pcts. 1A thru 11, 14 & 15); Ouachita—Wards 1 & 2	John C. Ensminger
15	Ouachita—Wards 4, 5 (pcts. 1 thru 9, 11 thru 15 & parts of pcts. 16A & 16L) & 6 thru 9	Charles Anding
16	Ouachita—Wards 5 (pcts. 10A, 10M & parts of pcts. 16A & 16L) & 10 (pcts. 1 thru 12 & 14A thru 16)	Jimmy N. Dimos
17	Ouachita—Wards 3 & 10 (pcts. 13A & 13M)	Charles D. Jones
18	East Carroll; Morehouse—Wards 2, 4 (pcts. 12A, 12B & 13) & 5 thru 10; West Carroll	Jess Smith
19	Madison; Richland; Tensas—Wards 1 & 2	Francis Coleman Thompson
20	Caldwell; Franklin; Jackson—Wards 2 (pcts. 3, 4, & parts of pcts. 1 & 2) & 3; Winn—Wards 10 (pcts. 1 & 2), 11 & 12 (pcts. 2 & 3)	Noble Ellington
21	Catahoula; Concordia; Tensas—Wards 3 thru 7	Al Ater
22	Grant; LaSalle; Rapides—Wards 7 & 10 (pcts. 3 & 11)	Dale Smith
23	Natchitoches	Jimmy D. Long
24	DeSoto—Wards 5 & 7; Red River; Sabine	Joe R. Salter
25	Rapides—Wards 1 (pcts. 6, 7, 8, 16 thru 19, 22, 27, 31, 35, & part of pct. 36), 2, 3, 4, & 8 (pcts. 1, 2 & 3)	Charles DeWitt
26	Rapides—Wards 1 (pcts. 1 thru 5, 9 thru 15, 20, 21, 23 thru 26, 28, 29, 30, 32, 33, 34 & part of pct. 36) & 8 (pct. 4)	Charles Herring

27	Rapides—Wards 9, 10 (pcts. 1, 2, & 4 thru 10, 12, & 13) & 11	Carl N. Gunter, Jr.
28	Avoyelles	Raymond J. Laborde
29	Pointe Coupee; West Baton Rouge—Wards 2 (pct. 2) & 3 thru 7	Clyde W. Kimball
30	Beauregard—Ward 2 Rapides—Wards 5 & 6 Vernon—Wards 1, 2, 3, 5, 6, & 8	Claude Leach, Jr.
31	Beauregard—Ward 3 Vernon—Wards 4 & 7	C. Allen Bradley, Jr.
32	Allen; Beauregard—Wards 1 & 4 thru 8; Calcasieu—Wards 5 & 6 (pcts. 1 thru 4, 7 & 8)	James David Cain
33	Calcasieu—Wards 4 (pcts. 1 thru 8, 11 thru 16, 18 & 19), 6 (pcts. 5 & 6) & 7	Dennis Stine
34	Calcasieu—Ward 3 (pcts. 1 thru 6, 11, 16, 17, 25 thru 29, 33, 35, 39, 41 & 42)	Wilford Carter
35	Calcasieu—Wards 1, 3, (pcts. 7 thru 10, 12, 14, 15, 18 thru 23 & 34) & 4 (pcts. 9, 10 & 17)	Vic Stelly
36	Calcasieu—Ward 3 (pcts. 24, 30, 31, 32 & 36 thru 38B); Cameron	Randy Roach
37	Calcasieu—Wards 2 & 8; Jefferson Davis	James P. Martin
38	Evangeline; St. Landry—Wards 1 (pcts. 2 & 19), 4 (pcts. 8, 9 & 10) & 5 (pcts. 2 thru 5)	Danny Lemoine
39	Lafayette—Dists. A (pcts. 1-A thru 2-B), B (pcts. 8-9 thru 16, 21-22 & part of pct. 17-18), C (pct. 25-26) & E (part of pct. 55) St. Landry—Wards 2, 3, & 4 (pcts. 5, 12, & 13)	Raymond "Lala" LaLonde
40	St. Landry—Wards 1 (pcts. 1, 3 thru 18 & 20 thru 29), 4 (pcts. 1 thru 4, 6, 7, 11, & 14), 5 (pcts. 1, 6, & 7) & 6 (pct. 4)	Armand Castille
41	Acadia—Wards 2, 3, 4 & 7 St. Landry—Ward 6 (pcts. 1, 2, 3 & 5 thru 17)	Darrett Sittig
42	Acadia—Wards 1, 5 & 6 Lafayette—Dist. B (pcts. 23A, 23B & 24)	Chris John
43	Lafayette—Dists. B (pct. 19-20), D (pcts. 48A & 48B), E (pcts. 56A, 56B, 58A thru 61 & part of pct. 55), F (pcts. 62A, 62B, 62C, 65E, 67A-68 thru 72C) & G (pcts. 76, 77 & parts of pcts. 73A & 73B)	Odon Bacque, Jr.
44	Lafayette—Dists. C (pcts. 30, 31-32, 34A, 34B, 36 & part of pct. 29), D (pcts. 37A, 37B, 38, 43 thru 47, 49+ & 50), F (pcts. 63A, 63B & 64++) & G (pcts. 74-75C, 75A, 75B, 78A-79 thru 83 & parts of pcts. 73A & 73B)	Ron Gomez
45	Lafayette—Dists. A (pcts. 3 thru 7B), B (part of pct. 17-18), C (pcts. 27, 28, 33A, 33B, 35 & part of pct. 29), D (pcts. 39 thru 42), E (pcts. 51A-52 thru 54 & 57) & F (pct. 66)	Kathleen Babineaux Blanco
46	St. Martin—Dists. 1 (pcts. 1, 3, & 4) & 2 thru 9	Harry L. Benoit
47	Vermilion—Dists. 1, 2, 3 (part of pct. 14), 4, 5, 6 (pcts. 12, 32 & part of pct. 39), 7, 9 (pcts. 34, 39, 71 & 72) & 10 thru 14	Sam Theriot
48	Iberia—Dists. 1 thru 7, 8 (pcts. 1A & 1B), 9 (pcts. 1, 2A & 2B), 10 (pct. 4) & 13 (pct. 4)	Elias Ackel, Jr.

49	Iberia—Dists. 8 (pcts. 2 & 3), 9 (pct. 3), 10 (pcts. 1, 2, & 3), 11, 12, 13 (pcts. 1, 2 & 3) & 14; St. Mary—Wards 1, 2, 3 (pct. 6) & 7; Vermilion—Dists. 3 (pcts. 13, 15, 18 & part of pct. 14), 6 (pct. 21 & part of pct. 39), 8 & 9 (pct. 21)	Ted M. Haik, Jr.
50	St. Martin—Dist. 1 (pcts. 2 & 5); St. Mary—Wards 3 (pcts. 1 thru 5 & 7), 4, 5, 6 (pcts. 5 & 6), 8 & 10.	Vincent Joseph "V.J." Bella
51	Assumption—Wards 1 (part of pct. 2), 2, 3, 4 (pcts. 1 & part of pct. 3) & 5 (part of pct. 2); St. Mary—Wards 6 (pcts. 1 thru 4 & 7 thru 10) & 9; Terrebonne—Wards 3 (pct. 12), 4, 8, 9 & 10	John Joseph Siracusa
52	Lafourche—Ward 11 (pct. 3); Terrebonne—Wards 1, 2, & 3 (pcts. 4, 13A-I thru 14J-Z & 16 thru 24)	Huntington Blair Downer, Jr.
53	Lafourche—Ward 11 (pcts. 1); Terrebonne—Wards 3 (pcts. 1A-J thru 3, 5 thru 11M-Z & 15), 5, 6, & 7	Johnny Glover
54	Jefferson—Ward 11; Lafourche—Wards 4, 7 thru 10 & 11 (pct. 2)	Jesse P. Guidry
55	Lafourche—Wards 1, 2, 3, 5 & 6	Warren Triche, Jr.
56	St. Charles; St. John the Baptist—Dist. 1	Ralph R. Miller
57	St. James—Dists. 1, 2, 3 & 4 (pcts. 1 & 2); St. John the Baptist—Dists. 2 thru 7	Joseph Accardo, Jr.
58	Ascension—Dists. 1, 2, 3, & 4 (pcts. 2A & 2B); Assumption—Wards 1 (pct. 1 & part of pct. 2), 6 (pcts. 1 & 1A) & 7 (parts of pcts. 1 & 1A); Iberville—Wards 4 & 5; St. James—Dists. 4 (pct. 3), 5, 6 & 7	Melvin Irvin, Jr.
59	Ascension—Dists. 4 (pcts. 1A, 1B, 3 & 4), 5, 6 & 7; Livingston—Wards 3 (parts of pcts. 1 & 2), 4 (parts of pcts. 2, 2A & 3), 5, 6 & 10	John "Juba" Diez
60	Assumption—Wards 4 (pct. 2 & part of pct. 3), 5 (pcts. 1, 3 & part of pct. 2), 6 (pct. 2), 7 (pct. 2 & parts of pcts. 1 & 1A), 8 & 9; Iberville—Wards 1, 2, 3 & 6 thru 9; West Baton Rouge—Wards 1 & 2 (pct. 1)	Charles Melancon
61	East Baton Rouge—Ward 1 (pcts. 10, 14A, 14B, 18 thru 23, 27 thru 30, 32, 37, 38A, 38B, 62, 63, 70, 85A & 85B)	Raymond Jetson
62	East Baton Rouge—Ward 2 (pcts. 5A thru 6B & 21); East Feliciana; West Feliciana	John D. Travis
63	East Baton Rouge—Wards 1 (pcts. 84A, 84B, 86A, 86B, 91, 92A, 92B, & 94A thru 95B) & 2 (pcts. 13A, 13B, 16A, 16B, 20, 22, 23A & 23B)	Melvin "Kip" Holden
64	East Baton Rouge—Wards 2 (pcts. 4A thru 4D, 7A thru 12B, 14A thru 15, 17A & 17B) & 3 (pcts. 1A thru 1D)	Mike McCleary
65	East Baton Rouge—Wards 1 (pcts. 55A, 55B, 71A thru 71D, 77, 83A, 83B, 87 & 88) & 3 (pcts. 8A thru 9D, 12A, 12B, 14A, 14B & 14C)	Donald Ray Kennard
66	East Baton Rouge—Wards 1 (pcts. 24, 25, 26, 31A, 31B, 36A thru 36D, 50A, 50B, 54A, 54B, 58A, 58B, 61, 78A, 78B, 82A thru 82D & 93) & 2 (pcts. 1A & 1B)	Louis "Woody" Jenkins
67	East Baton Rouge—Ward 1 (pcts. 1A thru 6, 11, 13A, 13B, 15A thru 17, 45 thru 46D, 51A, 51B, 67 & 68)	Joseph A. Delpit
68	East Baton Rouge—Wards 1 (pcts. 7, 8, 34A, 34B, 35, 39 thru 42, 44, 47A thru 48B, 56A, 56B, 57, 59, 64, 65, 66, 73A, 73B & 76A thru 76D) & 3 (pcts. 13A, 13B & 17A thru 17D)	Sean Reilly

69	East Baton Rouge—Wards 1 (pcts. 33, 49A, 49B, 52A thru 53D, 60A, 60B, 72A, 72B, 72C, 74A, 74B, 74C, 79, 80, 81 & 90) & 3 (pcts. 2 thru 3D, 11A thru 11D & 22A thru 22D)	E. Clark Gaudin
70	East Baton Rouge—Wards 1 (pcts. 43, 69A, 69B, 75A thru 75D & 89) & 3 (pcts. 4A thru 5, 21A thru 22D); Livingston—Ward 3 (parts of pcts. 1 & 2) & 7	Carl Crane
71	Livingston—Wards 1, 2, 4 (pct. 1 & parts of pcts. 2, 2A & 3), 8, 9, & 11	Bernard Carrier
72	St. Helena; Tangipahoa—Wards 1, 2, 3 & 6	Buster Guzzardo
73	Tangipahoa—Wards 7 & 8	Dennis Paul Hebert
74	St. Tammany—Wards 2, 3 (pcts. 1B, 3, 3A, 4B & 5B), 5, 6, 8 (pct. 1), 9 (pct. 1B) & 10; Tangipahoa—Wards 4 & 5; Washington—Wards 1, 2, & 9	R. H. "Bill" Strain
75	Washington—Wards 3 thru 8	Jerry Thomas
76	St. Tammany—Wards 8 (pcts. 2 thru 9) & 9 (pcts. 1, 1A, 2, 3, 5, 7, 8 & 9)	Edward Cecil Scogin
77	St. Tammany—Wards 1, 3 (pcts. 1, 2, 4, 4A, 5 & 5A), 4, 7 & 9 (pcts. 4, 6 & 10)	Edward Deano
78	Jefferson—Ward 9 (pcts. 1, 2, 2A, 3 thru 3I, 10C, 10D, 10E, 11, 11A, 12, 12A, 13 & 13A)	Robert T. Garrity, Jr.
79	Jefferson—Wards 9 (pcts. 19K thru 23K, 25K thru 28K & 31K) & 10 (pcts. 25, 32 thru 36, 39 & 42)	Kernan A. "Skip" Hand
80	Jefferson—Wards 8 (pcts. 21, 25, 28, 29, 32, 48, 49 & 50) & 10 (pcts. 13, 15 thru 20, 22 & 41)	Charles Lancaster
81	Jefferson—Wards 8 (pcts. 1 thru 19 & 47) & 10 (pcts. 1 thru 12, 14 & 40)	Charles V. Cusimano
82	Jefferson—Wards 7 & 8 (pcts. 20, 22, 23, 24, 26, 27, 30, 31, 33, 34, 35, 37 thru 40, 43, 44 & 45)	Quentin Dastugue
83	Jefferson—Wards 4 (pcts. 11 thru 18) & 5	John A. Alario, Jr.
84	Jefferson—Wards 4 (pcts. 5, 7 thru 7D, 10 & 10A) & 6 (pcts. 1, 3 & 4)	Steve J. Theriot
85	Jefferson—Wards 1 (pcts. 1 thru 5), 2 (pcts. 1 thru 5) & 3 (pcts. 1 thru 4, 6 & 9)	Joseph Toomy
86	Jefferson—Ward 1 (pcts. 5A thru 6) Orleans—Ward 15 (pcts. 14D, 14G, 17 & 18 thru 19C)	Terry Gee
87	Jefferson—Wards 3 (pcts. 5, 7 & 8) & 4 (pcts. 1 thru 4, 5A, 5B, 6, 8, 9 & 9A)	Nuncio J. Damico
88	Jefferson—Wards 8 (pcts. 36, 41, 42 & 46), 9 (pcts. 10A, 10B, 10F, 10G & 10H) & 10 (pcts. 21, 23, 24, 26 thru 31, 37, 38 & 43)	James J. Donelon
89	Orleans—Wards 14 & 16 (pcts. 1 thru 8)	James St. Raymond
90	Orleans—Wards 10 (pcts. 3 thru 8), 11 (pcts. 1 thru 9), 12 (pcts. 1 thru 6) & 13 (pcts. 1 thru 14A)	Mitch Landrieu
91	Orleans—Wards 10 (pcts. 9 thru 12), 11 (pcts. 10 thru 19), 12 (pcts. 7 thru 20) & 13 (pcts. 15 & 16)	Diana Elizabeth Bajoie
92	Jefferson—Ward 9 (pcts. 1K, 2K, 3K thru 9K, 10K, 11K, 12K, 13K thru 18K, 24K, 29K & 30K)	Glenn Ansardi
93	Orleans—Wards 1, 2, 3 (pcts. 1 thru 6), 4 (pcts. 2, 3 & 4), 5 (pcts. 1, 2 & 3), 6 (pcts. 1 & 2) & 10 (pcts. 13 & 14)	Rev. Avery C. Alexander
94	Orleans—Wards 4 (pcts. 5 thru 23), 5 (pcts. 8 thru 19), 6 (pcts. 8 & 9) & 17 (pcts. 17 thru 21)	Charles Emile Bruneau, Jr.

95	Orleans—Wards 3 (pcts. 7 thru 20), 16 (pct. 9) & 17 (pcts. 1 thru 16)	**Irma Muse Dixon**
96	Orleans—Wards 5 (pcts. 4 thru 7), 6 (pcts. 4 thru 7) & 7 (pcts. 1 thru 7, 10 thru 20, 27A, 28, 28A & 30)	**Charles R. Jones**
97	Orleans—Wards 7 (pcts. 8, 9, 9A, 20A thru 24, 26, 26A, 27, 27B & 29), 8 (pcts. 1 thru 14) & 9 (pcts. 12 thru 15, 20 & 24)	**Arthur A. Morrell**
98	Orleans—Wards 7 (pcts. 25 & 31 thru 42), 8 (pcts. 15 thru 30) & 9 (pcts. 31B thru 31E, 42, 42A & 42B)	**Garey Forster**
99	Orleans—Ward 9 (pcts. 1 thru 11, 16, 17, 18, 22, 26 & 26A)	**Sherman Copeland**
100	Orleans—Ward 9 (pcts. 32, 37 thru 40A, 42C thru 44B & 44J thru 44M)	**Louis Ivon**
101	Orleans—Ward 9 (pcts. 19, 21, 23, 25, 25A, 27 thru 31A & 33 thru 36C)	**Naomi White Warren**
102	Orleans—Ward 15 (pcts. 1 thru 14C, 14E, 14F, 15 thru 16, 17A & 17B)	**Francis C. Heitmeier**
103	Orleans—Ward 9 (pcts. 40B thru 41D, 44C thru 44I, 45 & 45A); St. Bernard—Wards A, B (pcts. 2 & 3), C (pct. 3), D (pct. 3) & E (pcts. 1 & 2)	**Kenneth Odinet**
104	St. Bernard—Wards B (pct. 1), C (pcts. 1 & 2), D (pcts. 1, 2, 4 & 5), E (pct. 3), F thru I & J (pcts. 1, 2 & 3)	**Tommy Warner**
105	Jefferson—Wards 2 (pct. 6) & 6 (pcts. 2 & 5); Plaquemines; St. Bernard—Wards J (pct. 4) & K	**Frank J. Patti**

High Pay for Louisiana State Officials

Louisiana's elected and appointed officials and administrators have for several years been among the highest paid in the United States, according to figures compiled by the Council of State Governments. Of the nine major statewide elective positions in Louisiana, all have salaries in the top ten among similar positions of other states (all but two are in the top five). This is surprising in view of the fact that Louisiana is in the lower third of states with regard to per capita income.

Salaries of Major Elective Positions

Position	Salary	Rank in U.S.
Governor	$73,440	6
Lieutenant Governor	63,367	1
Secretary of State	60,169	3
Attorney General	60,169	2
Treasurer	60,169	1
Superintendent of Education	60,169	6
Commissioner of Agriculture	60,169	3
Commissioner of Insurance	60,169	3
Commissioner of Elections	60,169	2

Sources: Book of States, *1982–83*
Louisiana Department of State

PASSAGE OF A BILL.

Introduction in the House

First reading

Second reading and reference to committee

Committee hearing

Second reading and reference to committee

Report of committee

Referred to Legislative Bureau

Report of Legislative Bureau

Conference committee attempts to iron out differences between the two houses and may submit a compromise report

Bill sent to a conference committee composed of members of both houses

If House rejects changes

If conference committee reaches an agreement

Report of conference committee sent to both houses

If no agreement reached bill dies in conference committee

If one or both houses reject compromise bill fails

This chart traces a bill introduced in the House. A bill introduced in the Senate would follow this same procedure shown in the chart with Senate and House action reversed. The submission of the bill to the Legislative Bureau would come before final passage in the House.

a complicated procedure

mittee aring

Report of committee

Third reading

Debate and amendment by entire House

Vote on final passage

TO SENATE

Sent to Senate

If bill passes

If bill fails to pass

May be reconsidered

ng

Third reading

Debate and amendment by entire Senate

Vote on final passage

May receive no further consideration

If bill passed in different form

TO HOUSE

If bill passed both houses in identical form

If bill passes, it is returned to House

If bill fails to pass

And House ccepts changes

May be reconsidered

Enrolled and sent to Governor

Enrolled and sent to Governor

houses accept , bill is enrolled o the Governor

May receive no further consideration

LAW BOOK

BILL BECOMES LAW
- If Governor signs
- If Governor does not sign
- If vetoed bill is repassed in each house by a two-thirds vote of the elected membership

If Governor vetoes the bill, it is returned to the house in which it originated. Veto session can be convened by mail ballot of legislators if Legislature has adjourned.

HOW TO CONTACT YOUR LEGISLATORS

To have messages delivered to legislators or contact them at their desks, phone:

House: (504) 342-6945
Senate: (504) 343-2020

To write to legislators at the state capitol:

Senators:　P.O. Box 94183
Baton Rouge, LA 70804

Representatives: P.O. Box 94281 or 94062
Baton Rouge, LA 70804

INFORMATION

The House of Representatives provides a Public Update Legislative System (PULS) to answer questions during the session, such as description and status of proposed legislation, when committees meet and their agenda.

Phone:　In-state (toll free): 1-800-272-8186
Baton Rouge only:　　342-2456

The Governor's Office provides a Governor's Tie Line year-round. During legislative sessions, you may express your opinions on legislative proposals to the governor or your legislators, or find out if the governor has signed or vetoed particular bills.

Phone:　In-state (toll free): 1-800-272-9868
Baton Rouge only:　　342-3000

Citizens may obtain copies of House and Senate bills (original or as amended), daily House and Senate journals, status of bills, and the order of the day from the Senate Bill Room outside the Senate committee hall in the basement of the capitol.

Copies of legislative bills and other documents may be ordered by phone through the PULS line or the Governor's Tie Line. (See above.)

Beginning this session, the House and Senate are charging for legislative documents at 10 cents a page, or a fixed price for sets of documents for the entire regular session.

Public Service Commission

Suite 1630 One American Place, Baton Rouge, LA 70825
(504) 342-4404

Chairman . . . . . . John F. Schwegmann

MEMBERS

Public Service Commission District

1st	John F. Schwegmann	.Term expires 12/31/90
2nd	George Ackel	.Term expires 12/31/88
3rd	Louis Lambert	.Term expires 12/31/92
4th	Thomas E. "Tommy" Powell	.Term expires 12/31/92
5th	Don Owen	.Term expires 12/31/90

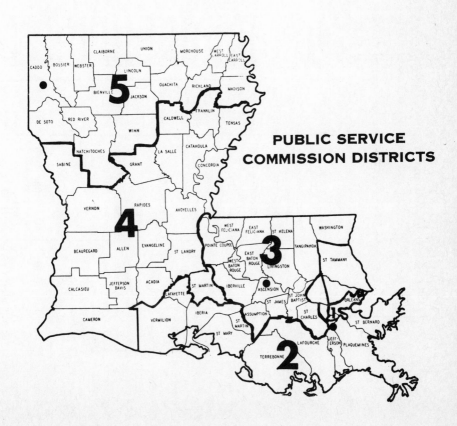

PUBLIC SERVICE
COMMISSION DISTRICTS

State of Louisiana—Parish Officials Elected November 21, 1987
Sheriffs and Ex-Officio Tax Collectors—1988-1991*

(Article VII, Section 89 of 1921 Constitution; Article V, Sections 27 and 32 of 1974 Constitution)

PARISH	NAME	ADDRESS	PHONE
Acadia	Kenneth Goss	Crowley 70526	783-5616
Allen	John Claiborne Durio	Oberlin 70655	639-4353
Ascension	Harold L. Tridico	Donaldsonville 70346	†473-8671
Assumption	Anthony G. Falterman	Napoleonville 70390	†369-7281
Avoyelles	Bill Belt	Marksville 71351	253-7515
Beauregard	Bolivar Bishop	DeRidder 70634	463-3281
Bienville	"Joe" Story	Arcadia 71001	263-2215
Bossier	Larry Deen	Benton 71006	965-2203
Caddo	Don Hathaway	Shreveport 71101	226-6555
Calcasieu	Wayne McElveen	Lake Charles 70601	491-3700
Caldwell	Floyd "Slim" Hodges	Columbia 71418	649-2345
Cameron	James R. "Sono" Savoie	Cameron 70631	775-5111
Catahoula	Thomas L. "Sonny" Jackson	Harrisonburg 71340	744-5411
Claiborne	J. R. "Snapp" Oakes	Homer 71040	927-2011
Concordia	Hubert Lee McGlothin	Vidalia 71373	336-5231
DeSoto	Floyd "Frenchie" Lambert	Mansfield 71052	872-3956
E. Baton Rouge	Elmer Litchfield	Baton Rouge 70801	†389-5000
E. Carroll	Dale Rinicker	Lake Providence 71254	559-2800
E. Feliciana	Joe A. Fudge	Clinton 70722	†683-5309

PARISH	NAME	ADDRESS	PHONE
Evangeline	Floyd Soileau	Ville Platte 70586	363-2161
Franklin	Eugene Parker	Winnsboro 71295	435-4505
Grant	L. R. "Pop" Hataway	Colfax 71417	627-3261
Iberia	Errol "RoMo" Romero	New Iberia 70560	369-3711
Iberville	Freddie Pitre, Sr.	Plaquemine 70764	†687-3555
Jackson	Van Beasley	Jonesboro 71251	259-9021
Jefferson	Harry Lee	Gretna 70053	†367-6611
Jefferson Davis	Dallas Cormier	Jennings 70546	824-3850
Lafayette	"Don" Breaux	Lafayette 70501	232-9211
Lafourche	Duffy J. Breaux	Thibodaux 70301	†447-7282
LaSalle	Wayne McGuffee	Jena 71342	992-2151
Lincoln	Wayne Houck	Ruston 71270	255-3030
Livingston	Odom Graves	Livingston 70754	†686-2241
Madison	B. B. Harmon	Tallulah 71282	574-1831
Morehouse	Frank E. Carroll	Bastrop 71220	281-4141
Natchitoches	Norm Fletcher	Natchitoches 71457	352-6432
Orleans— Civil Sheriff	Paul R. Valteau	New Orleans 70112	†523-6143
Criminal Sheriff	Charles C. Foti, Jr.	New Orleans 70112	†822-8000
Ouachita	Laymon Godwin	Monroe 71201	388-2222
Plaquemines	Ernest D. Wooten Schoenberger	Pointe-a-la-Hache 70082	†564-2525
Pointe Coupee	Preston Chustz	New Roads 70760	†638-8737
Rapides	Grady L. Kelley, Jr.	Alexandria 71301	445-6201

Parish	Official	City & Zip	Phone
Red River	"Buddy" Huckabay	Coushatta 71019	932-5753
Richland	Lorell Graham	Rayville 71269	728-2071
Sabine	James Alfice Brumley, Jr.	Many 71449	256-9241
St. Bernard	Jack A. Stephens	Chalmette 70043	†271-2501
St. Charles	"Johnny" Marino	Hahnville 70057	†783-6807
St. Helena	Eugene Holland	Greensburg 70441	†222-4413
St. James	Joesph S. Nassar	Convent 70723	†562-3562
St. John the Baptist	Lloyd B. Johnson	Edgard 70049	†497-3321
St. Landry	Howard Zerangue	Opelousas 70570	948-6516
St. Martin	Charles A. Fuselier	St. Martinville 70582	394-3071
St. Mary	Huey Bourgeois	Franklin 70538	828-1960
St. Tammany	P. J. "Pat" Camulette	Covington 70433	†892-4141
Tangipahoa	Ed Layrisson	Amite 70422	†748-8147
Tensas	Fred E. Scott	St. Joseph 71366	766-3961
Terrebonne	Jerry J. Larpenter	Houma 70360	†876-2500
Union	Larry Averitt	Farmerville 71241	368-3124
Vermilion	Raywood LeMaire	Abbeville 70510	893-0871
Vernon	Frank A. Howard	Leesville 71446	238-1311
Washington	B. B. "Benny" Rayburn, Jr.	Franklinton 70438	†839-3434
Webster	Royce "Doc" McMahen	Minden 71055	377-1515
W. Baton Rouge	Belvin F. Bergeron	Port Allen 70767	†343-9234
W. Carroll	Gary Keith Bennett	Oak Grove 71263	428-2331
W. Feliciana	W. M. "Bill" Daniel	St. Francisville 70775	†635-3241
Winn	Wiley Warren	Winnfield 71483	628-4611

*Terms expire June 30, 1991
**Terms expire May 5, 1990
†Area code 504-all others 318

Clerks of Court—1988-1991*

(Article VII, Sections 66 and 89 of 1921 Constitution; Article V, Sections 28 and 32 of 1974 Constitution)

PARISH	NAME	ADDRESS	PHONE	PARISH	NAME	ADDRESS	PHONE
Acadia	J. Andrus "Andy" Barousse	Crowley 70526	783-0953	Jefferson	Raoul "Skip" Galan	Gretna 70053	†367-6611
Allen	Robert L. Thomas	Oberlin 70655	639-4351	Jefferson Davis	Gay B. Huff	Jennings 70546	824-1160
Ascension	Kermit A. "Hart" Bourque	Donaldsonville 70346	†473-9866	Lafayette	Dan Guilliot	Lafayette 70501	233-0150
Assumption	Lawrence "Bud" Bergeron	Napoleonville 70390	†369-6653	Lafourche	Bobby A. Theriot	Thibodaux 70301	†447-4841
Avoyelles	Sammy Couvillon	Marksville 71351	253-9203	LaSalle	Joseph D. "Joe" Nugent	Jena 71342	992-2158
Beauregard	Robert B. Nichols	DeRidder 70634	463-8595	Lincoln	Sue Sanderson	Ruston 71270	255-3535
Bienville	Frances N. Joyner	Arcadia 71001	263-2123	Livingston	Lucius W. Patterson	Livingston 70754	†686-2216
Bossier	Wilna Mabry	Benton 71006	965-2336	Madison	J. K. "Billy" Post, Jr.	Tallulah 71282	574-0655
Caddo	W. Orie Hunter, Jr.	Shreveport 71101	226-6795	Morehouse	A. T. "Speedy" Goodnight	Bastrop 71220	281-3343
Calcasieu	Kathy Johnson	Lake Charles 70601	433-5221	Natchitoches	Irby L. Knotts, Jr.	Natchitoches 71457	352-8152
Caldwell	Eugene Dunn	Columbia 71418	649-2272	**Orleans—Civil Dist. Ct.	Dan Foley	New Orleans 70112	†827-9260
Cameron	A. R. Hodgkins, Jr.	Cameron 70631	775-5316	**Orleans—Criminal Dist Court	Edwin A. Lombard	New Orleans 70112	†586-3061
Catahoula	Debbie B. Theriot	Harrisonburg 71340	744-5497	Ouachita	"Bill" Hodge	Monroe 71201	323-8441
Claiborne	Betty Ann Gladney	Homer 71040	927-9601	Plaquemines	Allen L. Lobrano	Pointe-a-la-Hache 70082	†333-4377
Concordia	Clyde R. Webber, Jr.	Vidalia 71373	336-4204	Pointe Coupee	I. G. Olinde	New Roads 70760	†638-9596
DeSoto	W. Alvin Porter, Jr.	Mansfield 71052	872-3110	Rapides	Robert L. "Bob" Stewart	Alexandria 71301	445-2781
E. Baton Rouge	Mike Cannon	Baton Rouge 70801	†389-3960	Red River	Emmett V. Womack	Coushatta 71019	932-4961
E. Carroll	Edna Bishop Brock	Lake Providence 71254	559-2399	Richland	Ramona N. Haire	Rayville 71269	728-4142
E. Feliciana	Debbie D. Hudnall	Clinton 70722	†683-5145	Sabine	Dollie Moore Knippers	Many 71449	256-2091
Evangeline	Walter Lee	Ville Platte 70586	363-5671	St. Bernard	Sidney D. Torres	Chalmette 70043	†271-3434
Franklin	Faye T. Elkin	Winnsboro 71295	435-5133				
Grant	J. ElRay Lemoine	Colfax 71417	627-3246				
Iberia	Patrick Saunier	New Iberia 70560	365-7282				
Iberville	J. Gerald Dupont	Plaquemine 70764	†687-6373				
Jackson	Ann B. Walsworth	Jonesboro 71251	259-2424				

Parish	Official	City/Zip	Phone
St. Charles ..	Charles J. Oubre, Jr.	Hahnville 70057	†783-6632
St. Helena ...	Carl Lathan Johnson........	Greensburg 70441 ..	†222-4514
St. James ...	Edmond E. Kinler, Jr.	Convent 70723	†562-7431
St. John the Baptist ...	Harold L. Montegut..	Edgard 70049	†497-3331
St. Landry ...	Patti Hebert Kempf ...	Opelousas 70570	942-5606
St. Martin...	James A. Theriot	St. Martinville 70582	394-3792
St. Mary	Cliff Dressel	Franklin 70538	828-4100
St. Tammany	Lucy Reid Rausch ...	Covington 70433.....	†892-5214
Tangipahoa..	Carmon Moore.......	Amite 70422	†748-4146
Tensas....	James A. Kitchen	St. Joseph 71366 ...	766-3921
Terrebonne..	I. Robert "Bobby" Boudreaux	Houma 70360	†868-5660
Union........	Joe A. Brantley.......	Farmerville 71241 ..	368-3055
Vermilion	Russell R. Gaspard ..	Abbeville 70510	893-3641
Vernon	Donald M. "Donnie" Perkins	Leesville 71446	238-1884
Washington ...	Dewaine Seal	Franklinton 70438 ..	†839-4582
Webster	Henry S. Matthews ..	Minden 71055	377-6453
W. Baton Rouge	Thomas J. "Tom" LeBlanc	Port Allen 70767 ...	†383-0378
W. Carroll ...	Marvin N. Oldham ...	Oak Grove 71263 ..	428-3281
W. Feliciana...	Mary Nell Marchive..	St. Francisville 70775	†635-3794
Winn	Donald E. "Don" Kelley	Winnfield 71483 ...	628-3515

*Terms expire June 30, 1991
**Terms expire May 5, 1990
†Area Code 504—all others 818

Assessors—January 1, 1988-December 31, 1988*

(Article XIV, Sections 9 and 20 of 1921 Constitution; Article VII, Section 24 of 1974 Constitution)

PARISH	NAME	ADDRESS	PHONE
Acadia	Russel L. Benoit	Crowley 70526	783-2177
Allen	Richard Karam	Oberlin 70655	639-4391
Ascension	Gerald M. McCrory, Jr.	Donaldsonville 70346	†473-9239
Assumption	Joe S. Daigle	Napoleonville 70390	†369-6385
Avoyelles	Lee Thevenot	Marksville 71351	253-7677
Beauregard	Roy D. Miller	DeRidder 70634	463-8945
Bienville	J. M. Lamkin, Jr.	Arcadia 71001	263-2214
Bossier	James W. "Bill" Little	Benton 71006	965-2213
Caddo	Charles R. Henington	Shreveport 71101	226-6704
Calcasieu	Kenneth Wayne Darnsteadt	Lake Charles 70601	436-7282
Caldwell	Sue H. Hopper	Columbia 71418	649-2636
Cameron	Robert E. Conner	Cameron 70631	775-5416
Catahoula	Carmon F. Walker	Harrisonburg 71340	744-5291
Claiborne	J. Weldon Kilpatrick	Homer 71040	927-3022
Concordia	Monelle M. Moseley	Vidalia 71373	336-5122
DeSoto	Hugh B. Bennett, Jr.	Mansfield 71052	872-3610
East Baton Rouge	Frank Granger III	Baton Rouge 70801	†389-3920
East Carroll	Leonard R. Kennedy	Lake Providence 71254	559-2850
East Felician	Carl E. Bunch	Clinton 70722	†683-8945

PARISH	NAME	ADDRESS	PHONE
Evangeline	Weber Lee "Bee" Deshotels	Ville Platte 70586	363-4310
Franklin	J. W. Dean	Winnsboro 71295	435-5390
Grant	Randell A. Fletcher	Colfax 71417	627-5471
Iberia	Elton J. Barras	New Iberia 70560	364-1823
Iberville	James H. "Jimmy" DuPont	Plaquemine 70764	†687-3568
Jackson	Eddie G. Gatlin	Jonesboro 71251	259-2151
Jefferson	Lawrence E. Chehardy	Gretna 70053	†362-4100
Jefferson Davis	Curtis J. Hanks	Jennings 70546	824-3451
Lafayette	L. Ellis Dupleix, Jr.	Lafayette 70501	232-9832
Lafourche	Leroy Martin	Thibodaux 70301	†447-7242
LaSalle	Jimmy Dean	Jena 71342	992-8256
Lincoln	Jewette Farley	Ruston 71270	255-0404
Livingston	Charles A. "Bubbie" Abels	Livingston 70754	†686-7278
Madison	James D. "Jim" Sevier	Tallulah 71282	574-0117
Morehouse	Michael Wooden	Bastrop 71220	281-1802
Natchitoches	Don E. Hargis	Natchitoches 71457	352-2377
*Orleans Board of Assessors			
District 1	Kenneth Carter	New Orleans 70112	†586-4305
District 2	Claude Mauberret, Jr.	New Orleans 70112	†586-4310
District 3	Erroll Williams	New Orleans 70112	†586-4312
District 4	Ronald G. Burke	New Orleans 70112	†586-4317

District 5	Thomas Arnold	New Orleans 70112	†586-4318
District 6	Janice Degan	New Orleans 70112	†586-4320
District 7	Edward H. Heaton		
Ouachita	Rich Bailey	Monroe 71201	388-1341
Plaquemines	Robert R. Gravolet	Pointe-a-la-Hache 70082	†333-4331
Pointe Coupe	Joseph P. Jewell, Jr.	New Roads 70760	†638-7077
Rapides	Charles Slay	Alexandria 71301	445-7301
Red River	Ivy True Price	Coushatta 71019	932-4922
Richland	W. H. "Dub" Hallack	Rayville 71269	728-4491
Sabine	Conrad L. Cathey	Many 71449	256-3482
St. Bernard	Maurice L. Vinsanau	Chalmette 70043	†279-6379
St. Charles	Clyde "Rock" Gisclair	Hahnville 70057	†783-6281
St. Helena	Chaney Phillips	Greensburg 70441	†222-4540
St. James	Ellis J. Bourgeois	Convent 70723	†562-7431
St. John the Baptist	Henry Hotard, Jr.	Edgard 70049	†652-5311
St. Landry	Al Savoy	Opelousas 70570	942-3166
St. Martin	Mitchel B. "Mike" LeBlanc	St. Martinville 70582	394-3351
St. Mary	Sherel A. Martin, Jr.	Franklin 70538	828-4100
St. Tammany	Kirk R. Wascom	Covington 70433	†892-6150
Tangipahoa	J. D. Addison	Amite 70422	†748-7181
Tensas	Irby S. Gamble	St. Joseph 71366	766-3501
Terrebonne	George L. Hebert, Jr.	Houma 70360	†876-6620
Union	M. L. Graham, Jr.	Farmerville 71241	368-3232
Vermilion	Daniel J. Broussard, Sr.	Abbeville 70510	893-2837
Vernon	Eugene W. Cavanaugh	Leesville 71446	239-2167
Washington	Curtis M. Thomas	Franklinton 70438	†839-2280
Webster	Kerry Burns	Minden 71055	377-9311
West Baton Rouge	N. F. "Nim" Pecquet, Jr.	Port Allen 70767	†344-6777
West Carroll	Don Harris	Oak Grove 71263	428-2371
West Feliciana	W. D. Spillman	St. Francisville 70775	†635-3350
Winn	"Jimmy" Howard	Winnfield 71483	628-3267

*Terms expire December 31, 1988
†Area Code 504—all others 318

Coroners—1988-1991*

(Article VII, Sections 70 and 89 of 1921 Constitution; Article V, Section 29 of 1974 Constitution)

PARISH	NAME	ADDRESS	PHONE	PARISH	NAME	ADDRESS	PHONE
Acadia	Mark H. Dawson	Iota 70543	783-8532	Iberville	C. E. Blunck, Jr.	Plaquemine 70764	†687-3524
Allen	James L. Lowry	Kinder 70648	738-5654	Jackson	Richard Johnson	Quitman 71268	259-2628
Ascension	John F. Fraiche		†644-2119	Jefferson	Charles Brown Odom	Metairie 70005	891-3778
Assumption	Nelson A. Cox	Gonzales 70737 Napoleonville 70390	†369-6485	Jefferson Davis	George W. "Smokey" Speight, Jr.	Jennings 70546	824-2230
Avoyelles	F. P. Bordelon, Jr.	Marksville 71351	253-7800	Lafayette	Robert B. Thompson	Lafayette 70501	233-1115
Beauregard	Etienne R. Brown	DeRidder 70634	463-6068	Lafourche	John A. Heidingsfelder	Raceland 70394	†537-5241
Bienville	Maida F. Wimberly	Ringgold 71068	894-5264	LaSalle	I. C. Turnley, Jr.	Jena 71342	992-2166
Bossier	Michael Ellis	Bossier City 71111	742-0579	Lincoln	Rel Gray	Ruston 71270	255-3690
Caddo	George N. McCormick II	Shreveport 71101	226-6881	Livingston	Edwin Walker	Denham Springs 70726	†665-5149
Calcasieu	Charles M. Smith	Sulphur 70663	527-6385	Madison	Thomas A. Neumann	Tallulah 71282	574-3575
Caldwell	Harry Winters	Columbia 71418	649-6157	Morehouse	Francis D. Elias	Bastrop 71220	281-2431
Cameron	Cecil W. Clark	Cameron 70631	775-5102	Natchitoches	Charles E. Cook	Natchitoches 71457	352-2024
Catahoula	William C. Coney	Jonesville 71343	339-8387	Orleans	Dr. Frank Minyard**	New Orleans 70116	†586-4061
Claiborne	Donald K. Haynes	Homer 71040	927-3571	Ouachita	Claude K. Smith	Monroe 71201	325-4874
Concordia	William T. Polk	Vidalia 71373	336-4215	Plaquemines	William B. Barrett	Buras 70041	†657-7171
DeSoto	Jack L. Grindle	Mansfield 71052	872-0516	Pointe Coupee	Robert N. Helm	New Roads 70760	†638-8774
E. Baton Rouge	Hypolite T. Landry, Jr., M.D.	Baton Rouge 70801	†389-3047	Rapides	Wesley R. Dyer	Pineville 71360	640-2553
E. Carroll	F. M. Terral	Lake Providence 71254	559-2814	Red River	Richard L. Hanna	Coushatta 71019	932-5734
E. Feliciana	John F. Piker	Clinton 70722	†683-5109	Richland	W. David Thompson	Rayville 71269	728-2046
Evangeline	Charles Edward Fontenot	Ville Platte 70586	363-5521	Sabine	Clarence E. Poimboeuf	Pleasant Hill 71065	796-3311
Franklin	Hollis T. Rogers Jr.	Winnsboro 71295	435-4571	St. Bernard	William Wolfe	Chalmette 70043	†277-5515
Grant	Bruce L. Craig	Pollock 71467	765-3750				
Iberia	Joseph C. Musso	New Iberia 70560	364-4506				

Parish	Official	City	Phone
St. Charles ..	David J. Vial	Luling 70070.......	†785-6204
St. Helena ..	L. E. Stringer	Greensburg 70441 ...	†222-6376
St. James ...	Carl J. Poche	Lutcher 70071.......	†869-3493
St. John The Baptist	Christy Montegut	LaPlace 70068	†652-9504
St. Landry ..	Sylvan J. Manuel	Opelousas 70570	948-8206
St. Martin...	Kenneth L. Fournet..	St. Martinville 70582	394-3066
St. Mary	Evariste J. Trahan...	Morgan City 70380	†384-7210
St. Tammany	Ludwig C. Heintz	Covington 70433....	†892-2339
Tangipahoa..	Russel T. Ribando	Hammond 70404	†386-6161
Tensas	Joseph R. Whitaker ..	Newellton 71357.....	467-5131
Terrebonne..	Victor E. Tedesco III	Houma 70361	†868-0268
Union........	J. E. Booth	Farmerville 71241 ..	368-3053
Vermilion ...	Ardly Hebert........	Abbeville 70510 ...	893-2163
Vernon	Shellie J. Jones	Leesville 71446....	239-0220
Washington..	Roger Casama	Bogalusa 70427	†732-5447
Webster	Charles D. Hancock, Jr.	Minden 71055 ...	377-4143
W. Baton Rouge	Guy Otwell	Port Allen 70767 ...	†387-2802
W. Carroll ...	James R. Riley	Oak Grove 71263 ...	428-2341
W. Feliciana ..	Alfred R. Gould	St. Francisville 70775	†635-3256
Winn	Randolph Layne Williams	Winnfield 71483	628-2734

*Terms expire March, 1991
**Terms expire May 5, 1990
†Temporary Appointment
† Area Code 504—all others 318

Registrars of Voters (Appointed)

(Article VIII, Section 18 of 1921 Constitution: Article XI, Section 5 of 1974 Constitution)

PARISH	NAME	ADDRESS	PHONE
Acadia	Martin W. Venable	Crowley 70526	783-4862
Allen	Raynella R. Ortego	Oberlin 70655	639-4966
Ascension	Robert Poche	Donaldsonville 70346	†644-3885
Assumption	Sherry Delcambre	Napoleonville 70390	†369-7347
Avoyelles	Huron J. Roy	Marksville 71351	253-7129
Beauregard	Evelina H. Smith	DeRidder 70634	463-7955
Bienville	Paula K. Stewart	Arcadia 71001	263-2778
Bossier	William Thomas Johnston	Benton 71006	965-2301
Caddo	A. W. Fulco	Shreveport 71101	226-6891
Calcasieu	Margaret Hulin	Lake Charles 70601	437-3572
Caldwell	Mrs. Viola G. Roberts	Columbia 71418	649-7364
Cameron	Ruby Kelley	Cameron 70631	775-5493
Catahoula	Sue D. Manning	Harrisonburg 71340	744-5745
Claiborne	Patricia Brunson Sanders	Homer 71040	927-3332
Concordia	J. P. House	Vidalia 71373	336-7770
DeSoto	Linda S. Lilley	Mansfield 71052	872-1149
E. Baton Rouge	Nathaniel D. Bankston	Baton Rouge 70801	†389-3940
E. Carroll	Jimmie C. Hattaway	Lake Providence 71254	559-2015

PARISH	NAME	ADDRESS	PHONE
E. Feliciana	Edwin Lea McGehee	Clinton 70722	†683-5171
Evangeline	Herbert Fontenot, Jr.	Ville Platte 70586	363-5538
Franklin	Mrs. W. A. Hatton	Winnsboro 71295	435-4489
Grant	Lorraine Sellers	Colfax 71417	627-9938
Iberia	Mrs. Mildred L. Adams	New Iberia 70561-0341	369-4407
Iberville	Eunice Albert	Plaquemine 70764	†687-5201
Jackson	Mrs. Vicki J. Stewart	Jonesboro 71251	259-2486
Jefferson	Sam Altobello	Jefferson 70181	†736-6191
Jefferson Davis	Lee James Clement	Jennings 70546	824-0834
Lafayette	Steven Bernard	Lafayette 70501	232-9193
Lafourche	Sterling C. Diaz	Thibodaux 70301	†447-3256
LaSalle	John S. Allen	Jena 71342	992-2254
Lincoln	Lillian H. Fallin	Ruston 71270	255-3557
Livingston	Mrs. Wynona L. Graves	Livingston 70754	†686-7236
Madison	Mrs. Myrtis Bishop	Tallulah 71282	574-2193
Morehouse	Sandra R. Thomas	Bastrop 71220	281-1434
Natchitoches	James McKnight	Natchitoches 71457	352-2464
Orleans	Antonio E. Papale	New Orleans 70112	†525-6321
Ouachita	Everett Zeagler	Monroe 71201	322-5651
Plaquemines	Betty C. Ballay	Port Sulphur 70083	†682-0081
Pointe Coupee	Quintin Gustin	New Roads 70760	†638-9708
Rapides	B. G. Dyess	Alexandria 71301	473-6770

Parish	Official	City & ZIP	Phone
Red River	Mrs. Mary R. Crawford	Coushatta 71019	932-5027
Richland	(Mrs.) Audrey S. McGlothin	Rayville 71269	728-3582
Sabine	Elmo N. Langton	Many 71449	256-3697
St. Bernard	Louis C. Riess	Chalmette 70043	†277-6371
St. Charles	J. Leonard Zeringue	Hahnville 70057	†783-2731
St. Helena	Mrs. Barbara F. Bates	Greensburg 70441	†222-4440
St. James	Mrs. Annie Evelyn Gravois	Convent 70723	†562-7431
St. John the Baptist	Betty T. Madere	Edgard 70049	†497-3425
St. Landry	John Alcee Moreau	Opelousas 70570	948-4472
St. Martin	Patrick Olivier	St. Martinville 70582	394-4496
St. Mary	Mrs. Arlene R. Norris	Franklin 70538	828-4100
St. Tammany	Yvonne Allison	Covington 70433	†898-2572
Tangipahoa	Cade Williams	Amite 70422	†748-3215
Tensas	Earl Morris	St. Joseph 71366	766-3931
Terrebonne	Mrs. Peggy D. Henry	Houma 70360	†868-3000
Union	John R. Hicks	Farmerville 71241	368-8660
Vermilion	Corbet J. Domingue	Abbeville 70510	893-3783
Vernon	Sandra T. Perkins	Leesville 71446	239-3690
Washington	Mrs. Gladys Johnson	Franklinton 70438	†839-3593
Webster	Virginia M. Franklin	Minden 71055	377-9272
W. Baton Rouge	Mrs. Sybil Newsham	Port Allen 70767	†383-6130
W. Carroll	Peggy Henderson	Oak Grove 71263	428-2381
W. Feliciana	Anne H. Bennett	St. Francisville 70775	†635-6161
Winn	Mrs. Barbara Martin Clark	Winnfield 71483	628-6133

†Area code 504—all others 318

1986 ELECTION FOR
U. S. SENATOR FROM LOUISIANA

Source: *Louisiana Business Journal*

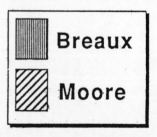

Louisiana's Choice In Presidential Elections, 1948-1984

Year	Candidate	Party	Percent of Vote
1948	Thurmond	State's Rights	49.1%
1952	Stevenson	Democratic	52.9
1956	Eisenhower*	Republican	53.3
1960	Kennedy*	Democratic	50.4
1964	Goldwater	Republican	56.8
1968	Wallace	American	48.3
1972	Nixon*	Republican	65.2
1976	Carter*	Democratic	51.5
1980	Reagan*	Republican	51.2
1984	Reagan*	Republican	60.8

* Elected.

Louisiana Voter Participation In Presidential Elections, 1948-1984

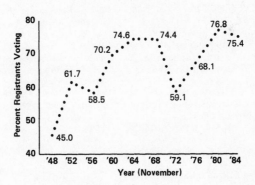

Source: Public Affairs Research Council

CONGRESSIONAL DISTRICTS,

1st Congressional District

Jefferson—Wards 1, 2 (pct. 1), 3 (pcts. 1, 2, 4, & 5), 4 (pcts. 1, 2, 3, 7A, 7B, 7C, 7D, 10A, and 11 thru 18), 5, 7, 8, 9, & 10; Orleans—Wards 4 (pcts. 7 thru 23), 5 (pcts. 13 thru 19), 7 (pcts. 39 thru 42), & 17 (pcts. 17 thru 21); St. Tammany

2nd Congressional District

Orleans—Wards 1, 2, 3, 4, (pcts. 2 thru 6), 5 (pcts. 1 thru 12), 6, 7 (pcts. 1, 2, 4 thru 38A), 8, 9, 10, 11, 12, 13, 14, 15, 16, & 17 (pcts. 1 thru 16)

3rd Congressional District

Assumption; Iberia; Jefferson—Wards 2 (pcts. 2 thru 6), 3 (pcts. 3 & 6 thru 9), 4 (pcts. 4 thru 10), 6, & 11; Lafourche, Plaquemines; St. Bernard; St. Charles, St. Martin (pcts. 5 & 6); St. Mary; Terrebonne

4th Congressional District

Beauregard—Ward 3; Bossier; Caddo; Claiborne; DeSoto; Red River; Sabine; Vernon; Webster

5th Congressional District

Bienville; Caldwell; Catahoula; Concordia; East Carroll; Franklin; Grant; Jackson; LaSalle; Lincoln; Madison; Morehouse; Natchitoches; Ouachita; Rapides—Wards 10 (pcts. 1, 2, 3, 5 thru 8 & 10) & 11; Richland; Tensas; Union; West Carroll; Winn

6th Congressional District

East Baton Rouge—Wards 1 (pcts. 1, 3 thru 8, 10, 11, 13 thru 84, 87 thru 90, & 93), 2 (pcts. 1, 4 thru 7, 9, 11 thru 17, 20, 21, and 23), & 3; Livingston; Tangipahoa; Washington

7th Congressional District

Acadia; Allen—Wards 1, 2 & 3; Beauregard—Wards 1, 2 & 4 thru 8; Calcasieu; Cameron; Jefferson Davis; Lafayette; St. Martin—Wards 1 (pcts. 1 thru 4 & 7) & 2 thru 5; Vermilion

8th Congressional District

Allen—Wards 4 & 5; Ascension; Avoyelles; East Baton Rouge—Wards 1 (pcts. 85, 86, 91, & 92) & 2 (pcts. 3, 18 & 22); East Feliciana; Evangeline; Iberville; Pointe Coupee; Rapides—Wards 1, 2, 3, 4, 5, 6, 7, 8, 9, & 10 (pcts. 4 & 9); St. Helena; St. James; St. John the Baptist; St. Landry; West Baton Rouge; West Feliciana

LOUISIANA PRESIDENTIAL VOTE

1908 - - Bryan (Dem.), 63,568; Taft (Rep.), 8,958; Debs (Socialist), 2,538

1912 - - Wilson (Dem.), 60,971; Roosevelt (Prog.), 9,323; Taft (Rep.), 3,834; Debs (Socialist), 5,249

1916 - - Wilson (Dem.), 79,875; Hughes (Rep.), 6,466; Roosevelt (Prog.), 6,349; Benson (Socialist), 292

1920 - - Cox (Dem.), 87,519; Harding (Rep.), 38,538

1924 - - Davis (Dem.), 93,218; Coolidge (Rep.), 24,670; LaFollette (Prog.), 4,063

1928 - - Smith (Dem.), 164,655; Hoover (Rep.), 51,160

1932 - - Roosevelt (Dem.), 249,418; Hoover (Rep.), 18,863

1936 - - Roosevelt (Dem.), 292,894; Landon (Rep.), 36,791

1940 - - Roosevelt (Dem.), 319,751; Willkie (Rep.), 52,446

1944 - - Roosevelt (Dem.), 281,564; Dewey (Rep.), 67,750

1948 - - Thurmond (States Rights), 204,290; Truman (Dem.), 136,344; Dewey (Rep.), 72,657; Wallace (Prog.), 3,035

1952 - - Stevenson (Dem.), 345,027; Eisenhower (Rep.), 306,925

1956 - - Eisenhower (Rep.), 329,047; Stevenson (Dem.), 243,977; Andrews (States Rights), 44,520

1960 - - Kennedy (Dem.), 407,339; Nixon (Rep.), 230,980; unpledged (States Rights), 169,572

1964 - - Goldwater (Rep.), 509,225; Johnson (Dem.), 367,068

1968 - - Wallace (Am. Ind.), 530,300; Humphrey (Dem.), 309,615; Nixon (Rep.), 248,478

1972—Nixon (Rep.), 687,752; McGovern (Dem.), 299,424; Schmitz (Amer.), 52,873; Jenness (Soc. Work.), 14,873

1976—Carter (Dem.), 660,338; Ford (Rep.), 591,057; Maddox (Amer.), 10,058; Hall (Comm.), 7,417; McCarthy (Ind.), 6,588; McBride (Lib.), 3,325; Camejo (Soc. Work.), 2,240

1980—Reagan (Rep.), 792,853; Carter (Dem.), 708,453; Anderson (Ind.), 26,345; Rarick (Amer. Ind.), 10,333; Clark (Lib.), 8,240; Commoner (Cit.) 1,584; DeBerry (Soc. Work.), 783

1984—Reagan (Rep.), 1,037,299; Mondale (Dem.), 651,586; Johnson (Cit.), 9,502; LaRouche (Ind.), 3,552; Bergland (Lib.), Serrette (New All.), Mason (Soc.), 4,883

LOUISIANA ELECTIONS OF UNITED STATES SENATORS AND REPRESENTATIVES

DEMOCRATIC PRIMARIES, 1968
First Primary
U. S. Senate

Russell B. Long	494,467
Maurice P. Blache	73,791
Total Vote	568,258

U. S. House of Representatives

District 1
F. Edward Hebert	45,749
Carlton H. Pecot	7,628
Total Vote	53,377

District 2
Hale Boggs	49,336
Cy D. F. Courtney	15,900
Total Vote	65,236

District 3
Edwin E. Willis	33,007
Patrick T. Caffery	27,505
Warren J. Moity	5,374
Caesar LaBauve, Jr.	4,670
Total Vote	70,556

District 4
J. D. Waggonner, Jr.	71,029
Leon Tarver, Jr.	20,167
Andrew C. Pappas	1,152
Total Vote	92,348

District 5
Otto E. Passman	45,652
Anthony Brocato	18,848
Total Vote	64,500

District 6
John R. Rarick	52,686
Ossie B. Brown	22,617
Joseph F. Keogh	21,009
J. D. DeBlieux	11,688
Total Vote	108,000

District 8
Speedy O. Long	50,878
James N. Lee	22,305
Gilbert Harrison, Sr.	10,663
Total Vote	83,846

Second Primary

District 3
Patrick T. Caffery	48,864
Edwin E. Willis	36,005
Total Vote	84,869

District 6
John R. Rarick	67,119
Ossie B. Brown	41,456
Total Vote	108,575

GENERAL ELECTION, 1968

U. S. Senate
Russell B. Long (Dem)	518,586

U. S. House of Representatives

District 1
F. Edward Hebert (Dem)	70,658

District 2
Hale Boggs (Dem)	81,537
David C. Treen (Rep)	77,633
Total Vote	159,170

District 3
Patrick T. Caffery (Dem)	39,215

District 4
J. D. Waggonner, Jr. (Dem)	63,788

District 5
Otto E. Passman (Dem)	34,901

District 6
John R. Rarick (Dem)	100,461
Loyd Rockhold (Rep)	26,267
Total Vote	126,728

District 7
Edwin W. Edwards (Dem)	79,709
Vance Plauche (Rep)	14,126
Total Vote	93,835

District 8
Speedy O. Long (Dem)	41,086

DEMOCRATIC PRIMARY, 1970
U. S. House of Representatives

District 1
F. Edward Hebert	59,512
Florence Jennison	6,382
Total Vote	65,894

District 3
Patrick T. Caffery	75,394
Jules Mollere	18,607
Warren J. Moity	3,831
Total Vote	97,832

District 5
Otto E. Passman	47,172
Paul H. Kidd	15,391
David I. Patten	13,855
Total Vote	76,418

District 6
John R. Rarick	57,835
Jesse Bankston	40,451
Total Vote	98,286

District 7
Edwin W. Edwards	57,277
Robert B. Thompson	13,943
Sidney Sylvester	6,221
Alexander Sas Jaworsky	5,471
Warren J. Moity	2,592
Charles Washington	429
Total Vote	85,933

District 8
Speedy O. Long	59,032
John K. Snyder	24,112
Total Vote	83,144

GENERAL ELECTION, 1970
U. S. House of Representatives

District 1
F. Edward Hebert (Dem)	66,284
Luke J. Fontana (Ind)	9,602
Total Vote	75,886

District 2
Hale Boggs (Dem)	51,812
Robert E. Lee (Rep)	19,703
Benjamin E. Smith (Ind)	3,279
Total Vote	74,794

District 3
Patrick T. Caffery (Dem)	48,677

District 4
J.D. Waggonner, Jr. (Dem)	44,848

District 5
Otto E. Passman (Dem)	31,087

District 6
John R. Rarick (Dem)	36,632

District 7
Edwin W. Edwards (Dem)	24,517

District 8
Speedy O. Long (Dem)	26,607

DEMOCRATIC PRIMARIES, 1972
First Primary

U. S. Senate
J. Bennett Johnston	623,076
Frank T. Allen	88,198
Allen J. Ellender	73,088
Total Vote	784,362

U. S. House of Representatives

District 2
Hale Boggs	68,749
Jules W. Hillery	8,210
Joseph B. Smith	5,252
Total Vote	82,211

District 3
Carl W. Bauer	26,965
J. Louis Watkins, Jr.	26,703
Goerge T. Oubre	16,239
L. C. Montgomery, Jr.	15,812
Newton D. Thompson	7,137
Laurence Autin	4,443
Henry R. Burke, Sr.	3,877
Anthony Catanese	876
J. Robert Hoepffner	707
Total Vote	102,759

District 5
Otto E. Passman	67,976
Charles M. Brown	34,314
David I. Patten	9,299
Total Vote	111,589

District 6
John R. Rarick	69,274
Lamar Gibson	25,267
James J. Berdou	13,783
James A. Edwards	5,306
Total Vote	113,630

District 7[1]
John B. Breaux	46,615
Gary Tyler	25,262
D. A. de la Houssaye	11,051
Basile Miller	6,870
Eddie Ackal	6,649
William S. Boyd	5,966
Total Vote	102,413

District 7
John B. Breaux	49,670
Gary Tyler	31,158
D. A. de la Houssaye	12,073
Eddie Ackal	11,737
Basile Miller	7,148
William S. Boyd	5,691
Total Vote	117,477

District 8
Gillis W. Long	61,452
Armand J. Brinkhaus	31,934
J. E. Jumonville	15,995
Huey P. Coleman	3,690
Philip N. Pecquet	2,287
Total Vote	115,358

Second Primary

District 7
John B. Breaux	52,359
Gary Tyler	42,729
Total Vote	95,088

GENERAL ELECTION, 1972

U. S. Senate
J. Bennett Johnston (Dem)	598,987

LOUISIANA ELECTIONS OF UNITED STATES SENATORS AND REPRESENTATIVES

John J. McKeithen (Ind) 250,161
Ben C. Toledano (Rep).. 206,846
Hall M. Lyons (Amer)... 28,910
Total Vote..... 1,084,904

U. S. House of Representatives

District 1
F. Edward Hebert (Dem). 78,156
District 2
Hale Boggs (Dem)....... 68,093
District 3
David C. Treen (Rep)... 71,090
J. Louis Watkins,Jr.(Dem)60,521
Total Vote........ 131,611
District 4
J. D. Waggonner,Jr.(Dem) 74,397
District 5
Otto E. Passman (Dem).. 64,027
District 6
John R. Rarick (Dem)... 84,275
District 7
John B. Breaux (Dem)... 71,901
District 8
Gillis W. Long (Dem)... 62,607
R. S. Abramson (Amer).. 17,844
Roy C. Strickland (Rep) 15,517
Total Vote........ 95,968

DEMOCRATIC PRIMARY, 1973[2]
U. S. House of Representatives
District 2
Lindy Boggs............ 41,520
Harwood Coppel.......... 12,208
Joseph B. Smith......... 1,343
Jules W. Hillery........ 999
Rodney Fertel........... 781
Total Vote....... 56,851

GENERAL ELECTION, 1973[2]
U. S. House of Representatives
District 2
Lindy Boggs (Dem)....... 43,255
Robert E. Lee (Rep)..... 10,315
Total Vote........ 53,570

DEMOCRATIC PRIMARIES, 1974
First Primary
U. S. Senate
Russell B. Long........ 520,606
Sherman A. Bernard..... 131,540
Annie Smart............ 44,341
Total Vote........ 696,487

U. S. House of Representatives

District 1
F. Edward Hebert....... 65,443
William A. Fontenot.... 13,626
Florence Jennison...... 2,156
Total Vote........ 81,225
District 2
Lindy Boggs............ 64,466
Charles E. Clark....... 6,840
Rodney Fertel.......... 2,428
Total Vote........ 73,734
District 5
Otto E. Passman....... 64,831
Frank T. Allen......... 21,566
Total Vote........ 86,397
District 6
John R. Rarick......... 48,672
Jeff LaCaze............ 38,293
Greg Eaton............. 18,781
Ramsey Gilchrist...... 1,959
Total Vote........ 107,705

District 7
John B. Breaux........ 71,848
J. Vernon Hebert....... 10,289
Total Vote........ 82,137

Second Primary
District 6
Jeff LaCaze............ 60,533
John R. Rarick........ 56,710
Total Vote........ 117,243

REPUBLICAN PRIMARY, 1974
U. S. House of Representatives
District 5
Ross P. Shirah......... 304
Robert M. Ross......... 193
Total Vote........ 497

GENERAL ELECTION, 1974
U. S. Senate
Russell B. Long (Dem).. 434,643
U. S. House of Representatives
District 1
F. Edward Hebert (Dem). 48,452
District 2
Lindy Boggs (Dem)...... 53,802
Diane Morphos (Rep).... 9,632
Jules W. Hillery (Ind). 2,322
Total Vote 65,756
District 3
David C. Treen (Rep)... 55,574
Charles Grisbaum,Jr.(Dem)39,412
Total Vote 94,986
District 4
J. D. Waggonner,Jr.(Dem) 47,371
District 5
Otto E. Passman (Dem).. 43.068
District 6[3]
Henson Moore (Rep)..... 60,969
Jeff LaCaze (Dem)...... 60,925
Total Vote....... 121,894
District 6[4]
Henson Moore (Rep)..... 74,804
Jeff LaCaze (Dem)...... 63,360
Total Vote........ 138,164
District 7
John B. Breaux (Dem)... 59,406
Jeremy Millett (Ind)... 7,131
Total Vote 66,537
District 8
Gillis W. Long (Dem)... 41,704

DEMOCRATIC PRIMARIES, 1976

First Primary

U. S. House of Representatives

District 1

James A. Moreau......... 38,429
Richard A. Tonry....... 18,837
David F. Dixon......... 12,659
Salvadore Gutierrez,Jr... 10,343
William Bergeron....... 6,335
Albert Laplace Dart..... 682
Sanford Krasnoff........ 475
Total Vote........ 87,760

District 2

Lindy Boggs............ 48,312

Matt Miller............. 6,896
Travis J. Chiasson....... 2,874
Total Vote......... 58,082

District 3

David Scheuermann,Sr..... 35,869
Warren J. Moity, Sr...... 18,044
Total Vote......... 53,913

District 5

Jerry Huckaby............ 45,700
Otto E. Passman......... 40,697
Total Vote......... 86,397

District 6

J. D. DeBlieux.......... 59,253
Bobby Pailette, Sr....... 23,087
Total Vote......... 82,340

Second Primary

District 1[5]

Richard A. Tonry........ 48,798
James A. Moreau......... 48,446
Total Vote......... 97,244

GENERAL ELECTION, 1976

U. S. House of Representatives

District 1

Richard A. Tonry (Dem)... 61,652
Bob Livingston (Rep)..... 56,679
John R. Rarick (Ind)..... 12,227
Total Vote..........130,558

District 2

Lindy Boggs (Dem)....... 85,923
Jules W. Hillery........ 6,904
Total Vote......... 92,827

District 3

David C. Treen (Rep).... 109,135
David Scheuermann,Sr.(Dem)39,728
Total Vote......... 148,863

District 4
J. D. Waggonner (Dem)... 76,406

District 5

Jerry Huckaby (Dem)...... 83,696
Frank Spooner (Rep)...... 75,574
Total Vote..........159,270

District 6

Henson Moore (Rep)...... 99,780
J. D. DeBlieux (Dem).... 53,212
Total Vote......... 152,992

District 7

John B. Breaux (Dem).... 117,196
Charles F. Huff (Rep)... 23,414
Total Vote......... 140,610

[1]For unexpired term of Edwin W. Edwards ending January 3, 1973
[2]For unexpired term of Hale Boggs ending January 3, 1975
[3]Election nullified due to voting machine malfunction
[4]Repeat election for nullified election
[5]Vote fraud charges led to resignation of Tonry; vote returns certified November 20, 1976

District 8

Gillis W. Long (Dem)....	106,285
Kent Courtney (Ind).....	6,526
Total Vote........	112,811

SPECIAL ELECTION, 1977

District 1

Robt. L. Livingston(Rep)..	56,121
Ron Faucheux (Dem)........	40,802
Sanford Krasnoff(Nom.Pap.)	12,665
Total Vote........	109,588

OPEN PRIMARY, 1978

U. S. Senate

J. Bennett Johnston....	498,773
Woody Jenkins..........	340,896
Total Vote........	839,669

U.S. House of Representatives

District 1

Bob Livingston........	89,469
Sanford Krasnoff......	14,373
Total Vote........	103,842

District 2

Lindy Boggs...........	57,056
Christine Gauvreau....	4,348
William King..........	4,063
Total Vote........	65,467

District 3

David Treen..........	Unopposed

District 4

Buddy Leach...........	35,010
Jimmy Wilson..........	34,841
Buddy Roemer..........	33,302
Loy Weaver...........	17,396
Mickey Prestridge....	3,363
John O. Robinson.....	2,766
J. Charles Crowder....	1,708
Robert H. Briggs......	938
Sophie Thompson......	748
Total Vote........	130,072

District 5

Jerry Huckaby........	66,276
Jim Brown............	38,969
Bill Johnson.........	16,194
Martha Madden........	3,698
L.D. Knox............	2,157
Total Vote........	127,294

District 6

W. Henson Moore......	102,430
Bobby G. Pailette, Sr..	10,256
Total Vote........	112,686

District 7

John B. Breaux.......	78,297
Mike Thompson........	42,247
Johnny Myers.........	9,126
Total Vote........	129,670

District 8

Gillis W.Long.........	80,666
Robert Mitchell.......	20,547
Total Vote........	101,213

GENERAL ELECTION, 1978

U.S. House of Representatives

District 4

Claude "Buddy" Leach...	65,583
Jimmy Wilson...........	65,317
Total Vote........	130,900

SPECIAL ELECTION, 1980

U.S. House of Representatives

District 3

W.J. "Billy" Tauzin (Dem).............	62,108
James J. Donelon (Rep)	54,815
Total vote.......................	116,923

OPEN PRIMARY, 1980

U.S. Senate

Russell B. Long (Dem)	484,770
Louis "Woody" Jenkins (Dem)	325,922
Jerry C. Bardwell (Rep).............	13,739
Robert Max Ross (Rep)...............	10,208
Naomi Bracey (Ind).................	6,374
Total vote.......................	841,013

U.S. House of Representatives

District 1

Robert L. "Bob" Livingston (Rep)	81,777
Michael J. Musmeci, Sr. (Dem).........	8,277
Tristan P. Junius (Ind)................	2,501
Total vote.......................	92,555

District 2

Lindy Boggs (Dem)	45,091
Bob Couhig (Rep)	25,521
Clyde F. Bel, Jr. (Dem)................	3,571
Total vote.......................	74,183

District 3

W.J. "Billy" Tauzin (Dem).............	80,455
Bob Namer (Dem)	14,074
Total vote.......................	94,529

District 4

Claude "Buddy" Leach (Dem).........	35,847
Buddy Roemer (Dem).................	33,049
Jimmy Wilson (Rep).................	29,992
Foster Campbell (Dem)...............	14,666
Forrest Dunn (Dem)	8,208
C. Kay Carter (Dem)	1,329
Total vote.......................	123,091

District 5

Jerry Huckaby (Dem)	93,519
L.D. "None of the Above" Knox (Dem)	11,748
Total vote.......................	105,267

District 6

W. Henson Moore (Rep).............	118,540
Alice Brooks (Dem).................	12,149
Total vote.......................	130,689

District 7

John B. Breaux (Dem)..............	unopposed

District 8

Gillis W. Long (Dem)...............	75,433
Clyde C. Holloway (Rep).............	27,816
Robert H. Mitchell (Rep).............	6,243
Total vote.......................	109,492

GENERAL ELECTION, 1980

U.S. House of Representatives

District 4

Buddy Roemer (Dem).................	103,625
Claude "Buddy" Leach (Dem).........	58,705
Total vote.......................	162,330

OPEN PRIMARY, 1982

U.S. House of Representatives

District 1

Robert L. "Bob" Livingston (Rep)	77,102
Murphy O. Green (Ind)	6,691
Suzanne Weiss (Ind).................	6,028
Total vote.......................	89,821

District 2

Lindy Boggs (Dem)	44,968
"Captain" Roger C. Johnson (Dem).....	13,404
Total vote.......................	58,372

District 3

W.J. "Billy" Tauzin(Dem)	unopposed

District 4

Buddy Roemer (Dem).............	unopposed

District 5

Jerry Huckaby (Dem)	71,571
Donald M. Greene (Dem)	6,081
L.D. Knox (Ind)	4,771
R.T. "Ronnie" King (Dem)...........	3,082
Total vote.......................	85,505

District 6

W. Henson Moore (Rep)..............	65,269
James D. Agnew (Ind)..............	19,354
Total vote.......................	84,623

District 7

John B. Breaux (Dem).............	62,722
"Johnny" Myers (Dem)	16,688
Total vote.......................	79,410

District 8

Gillis W. Long (Dem)..............	71,103
Edward G. "Ned" Randolph, Jr. (Dem)	46,656
Rosemary Rougon Rummler (Ind)......	1,467
Total vote.......................	119,226

OPEN PRIMARY, 1984

U.S. Senate

J. Bennett Johnston (Dem)	838,181
Robert Ross (Rep)..............	86,546
Larry Cooper (Rep).............	52,746
Total vote.......................	977,473

OPEN PRIMARY, 1986

U.S. House of Representatives

District 1

Robert L. "Bob" Livingston (Rep)..	unopposed

District 2

Lindy Boggs (Dem)	105,661
Roger Johnson (Rep).............	8,474
Other.......................	2,387
Total vote................	116,522

District 3

W. J. "Billy" Tauzin (Dem)	unopposed

District 4

Buddy Roemer (Dem)	unopposed

District 5

Jerry Huckaby (Dem)	96,200
Thomas Brady (Dem).............	32,284
Fred Huenafeld (Dem)	11,966
Total vote................	140,450

District 6

Richard Baker (Rep).............	76,833
Thomas Hudson (Dem)...........	67,774
Willis Blackwell (Dem)...........	6,120
Total vote................	150,727

GENERAL ELECTION, 1986

U.S. Senate

John B. Breaux (Dem)...........	723,586
W. Henson Moore (Rep)	646,311
Total vote................	1,369,897

U.S. House of Representatives

District 7

James A. Hayes (Dem)...........	109,205
Margaret Lowenthal (Dem)	82,293
Total vote................	191,498

District 8

Clyde Holloway (Rep)	102,276
Faye Williams (Dem)	96,864
Total vote................	199,140

1987 GUBERNATORIAL ELECTION

United States Congressman Charles E. ("Buddy") Roemer III defeated incumbent governor Edwin W. Edwards in the October 24, 1987 primary election. Edwards conceded the race in the early morning hours of October 25 when it became clear that he ran second to Roemer at the polls. Roemer received 33 percent of the statewide votes, while Edwards received 28 percent of the vote. Edwards' concession brought to a dramatic conclusion the bitterly fought eight-man race.

The proportion of voters registered as Democrats continues to decline. Since 1983, the proportion of registered Democrats has dropped from 83.5 percent to the present 77.4 percent, the proportion of Republicans increased from 9.1 percent to 14.0 percent, and the pro-

portion of other parties or independent rose from 7.4 percent to 8.6 percent. The increase in black voter registration continued slowly. Blacks now comprise 25.7 percent of the registered voters, a 6.36 percent increase over 1983.

Of the 2,191,428 voters registered in Louisiana, 1,588,730 voters, or 71.1 percent of those registered, participated in the election. St. James Parish had the highest voter participation rate at 85.4 percent and Orleans Parish the lowest, at 61.4 percent.

Roemer ran stronger than Edwards in all but one of the state's seven metropolitan areas. Edwards polled 27.1 percent of the metropolitan vote compared to 28 percent of the statewide vote, while Roemer received 32 percent compared to 33 percent statewide.

LOUISIANA GUBERNATORIAL ELECTIONS

POPULAR VOTE, 1812

William C. C. Claiborne..	2,757
Jacques Villere..........	945
Jean. Noel Destrehan......	168
Francois Livaudais.......	2
Evariste Lauve..........	1
Callaux LaFontaine.......	1
Total Vote......	3,874

LEGISLATURE VOTE, 1812

William C.C. Claiborne(Rep)	33
Jacques Villere (Rep)....	6
Total Vote..........	39

POPULAR VOTE, 1816

Jacques Villere..........	2,314
Joshua Lewis.............	2,145
Total Vote..........	4,459

LEGISLATURE VOTE, 1816

Jacques Villere (Rep)....	43
Joshua Lewis (Rep).......	3
Total Vote..........	46

POPULAR VOTE, 1820

Thomas B. Robertson......	1,903

POPULAR VOTE, 1820 (cont.)

Peter Derbigny...........	1,187
Abner L. Duncan..........	1,031
Jean Noel Destrehan......	627
Total Vote..........	4,748

LEGISLATURE VOTE, 1820

Thomas B. Robertson......	49
blank....................	2
Total Vote..........	51

POPULAR VOTE, 1824

Henry Johnson...........	2,847
Jacques Villere..........	1,841
Bernard Marigny..........	1,427
Philemon Thomas..........	236
Thomas Butler............	134
Total Vote..........	6,485

LEGISLATURE VOTE, 1824

Henry Johnson (Amer).....	41
Jacques Villere..........	16
Total Vote..........	57

POPULAR VOTE 1828

Pierre Derbigny..........	3,372
Thomas Butler............	1,562
Bernard Marigny..........	1,196

Philemon Thomas..........	1,151
Total Vote..........	7,281

LEGISLATURE VOTE, 1828

Pierre Derbigny..........	55
Thomas Butler............	1
blank....................	1
Total Vote..........	57

POPULAR VOTE, 1830

A. B. Roman.............	3,638
William S. Hamilton......	2,701
Armand Beauvais..........	1,478
David A. Randall........	463
Total Vote..........	8,280

LEGISLATURE VOTE, 1830

A. B. Roman.............	59
blank....................	2
Total Vote..........	61

POPULAR VOTE, 1834

Edvard D. White (Whig)..	6,973
John B. Dawson (Dem)....	4,149
Total Vote........	11,122

LOUISIANA GUBERNATORIAL ELECTIONS

LEGISLATURE VOTE, 1834

Edward D. White (Whig)..	58
scattering..............	3
Total Vote........	61

POPULAR VOTE, 1838

A. B. Roman(Whig).......	7,590
Dennis Prieur (Dem).....	6,782
Total Vote........	14,372

LEGISLATURE VOTE, 1838

A. B. Roman.............	49
Dennis Prieur..........	2
scattering.............	5
Total Vote........	56

POPULAR VOTE, 1842

Alexander Mouton (Dem)..	9,669
Henry Johnson (Whig)....	8,104
Total Vote........	17,773

LEGISLATURE VOTE, 1842

Alexander Mouton........	60
Henry Johnson..........	2
blank..................	9
Total Vote........	71

POPULAR VOTE, 1846

Isaac Johnson (Dem).....	12,629
William DeBuys (Whig)...	10,138
Charles Derbigny........	598
(Native Amer)	
Total Vote........	23,365

POPULAR VOTE, 1848

Joseph Walker (Dem).....	14,485
Alexander Declouet (Whig)	13,807
Total Vote........	28,292

POPULAR VOTE, 1852

Paul O. Hebert (Dem)...	17,813
Louis Bordelon (Whig)...	15,781
Total Vote........	33,594

POPULAR VOTE, 1855

Robert C. Wickliffe(Dem)	23,952
Charles Derbigny........	19,755
(Know-Nothing)	
Total Vote........	43,707

POPULAR VOTE, 1859

Thomas O. Moore (Dem)...	16,306
Thomas J. Wells.........	10,805
(Know-Nothing)	
Total Vote........	27,111

GENERAL ELECTION, 1863
UNION PORTION

Michael Hahn (Adm)······	6,158
J. Q. A. Fellows (Cons)··	2,720
Benjamin Flanders ······	1,847
(Free State)	
Total Vote········	10,725

CONFEDERATE PORTION

Henry Watkins Allen·····	
Unanimous Vote	

GENERAL ELECTION, 1865

James Madison Wells·····	22,312
Henry Watkins Allen·····	5,497
Total Vote········	27,809

GENERAL ELECTION, 1868

Henry Clay Warmoth......	64,941
James G. Taliaferro.....	38,046
Total Vote........	102,987

GENERAL ELECTION, 1872

William Pitt Kellog....	72,890
John McEnery...........	55,249
Total Vote........	128,139

GENERAL ELECTION, 1876

Francis T. Nicholls(Dem)	84,487
S. B. Packard (Rep)....	76,477
Total Vote........	160,964

GENERAL ELECTION, 1879

Louis A. Wiltz (Dem)...	74,769
Taylor Beattie (Rep)...	40,764
Total Vote........	115,533

GENERAL ELECTION, 1884

Samuel D. McEnery (Dem)	88,794
John A. Stevenson (Rep)	43,502
Total Vote........	132,296

GENERAL ELECTION, 1888

Francis T. Nicholls(Dem)	137,257
Henry Clay Warmoth (Rep)	51,471
Total Vote........	188,728

GENERAL ELECTION, 1892

Murphy J. Foster.......	79,388
Samuel D. McEnery......	47,037
A. H. Lecnard..........	29,459
John E. Breaux.........	12,359
R. H. Tannehill........	9,792
Total Vote........	178,035

GENERAL ELECTION, 1896

Murphy J. Foster.......	116,216
J. M. Pharr............	90,138
A. B. Booth............	176
Total Vote........	206,530

GENERAL ELECTION, 1900

Wm. Wright Heard (Dem).	60,206
Eugene S. Reems (Rep)..	2,449
Don Caffery, Jr. (Peo).	4,938
Don Caffery, Jr. (Ind).	9,277
Total Vote........	76,870

GENERAL ELECTION, 1904

Newton C. Blanchard.(Dem)	48,345
W. J. Behan (Rep)......	5,877
Total Vote........	54,222

DEMOCRATIC PRIMARY, 1908

Jared Y. Sanders.......	60,176
Theodore S. Wilkinson..	46,729
Total Vote........	106,905

GENERAL ELECTION, 1908

Jared Y. Sanders(Dem)...	60,066
Henry N. Pharr (Rep)....	7,617
J. W. Barnes (Soc)......	1,247
Total Vote........	68,930

DEMOCRATIC PRIMARY, 1912

Luther E. Hall..........	53,407
John T. Michel..........	46,201
J. B. Aswell............	23,800
Total Vote........	123,408

REPUBLICAN PRIMARY, 1912

Hugh S. Suthon.........	1,003
Charles J. Bell........	607
Total Vote........	1,610

GENERAL ELECTION, 1912

Luther E. Hall(Dem)....	50,581
H. S. Suthon (Rep).....	4,961
J. R. Jones (Ind)......	984
Total Vote........	56,526

DEMOCRATIC PRIMARY, 1916

Ruffin G. Pleasant.....	84,407
Thomas C. Barrett......	30,112
Total Vote........	114,519

GENERAL ELECTION, 1916

Ruffin G. Pleasant(Dem)	80,801
John M. Parker(Prog)...	48,068
Horace Noonan (Ind)....	351
John M. Parker (Ind)...	17
J. A. Barousse (Ind)...	5
Total Vote........	129,242

DEMOCRATIC PRIMARY, 1920

John M. Parker..........	77,868
Frank P. Stubbs........	65,585
Total Vote........	143,553

GENERAL ELECTION, 1920

John M. Parker (Dem)...	53,792
J. Stewart Thompson(Rep)	1,306
Total Vote........	55,098

FIRST DEMOCRATIC PRIMARY, 1924

Hewitt Bouanchaud......	84,162
Henry L. Fuqua.........	81,382
Huey P. Long...........	73,985
Total Vote........	239,529

SECOND DEMOCRATIC PRIMARY, 1924

Henry L. Fuqua.........	125,880
*Withdrew, no second primary	
Hewitt Bouanchaud......	92,006
Total Vote........	217,886

LOUISIANA GUBERNATORIAL ELECTIONS

GENERAL ELECTION, 1924

Henry L. Fuqua (Dem) ...	66,203
James S. Millikin(Rep).	1,420
Total Vote	67,623

DEMOCRATIC PRIMARY, 1928

Huey P. Long	126,842
Riley J. Wilson	81,747*
O. H. Simpson..........	80,326
Total Vote.......	288,915

GENERAL ELECTION, 1928

Huey P. Long (Dem).....	92,941
Etienne J. Caire(Rep)..	3,733
Total Vote.......	96,674

DEMOCRATIC PRIMARY, 1932

Oscar K. Allen.........	214,699
Dudley J. LeBlanc......	110,048
George S. Guion........	53,756
William C. Boone.......	
William L. Clark, Jr...	1,346
Total Vote.......	379,849

GENERAL ELECTION, 1932

Oscar K. Allen (Dem)...	110,193
scattering.............	59
Total Vote.......	110,252

DEMOCRATIC PRIMARY, 1936

R. W. Leche............	368,115
Frank J. Looney........	160,566
Irving Ward-Steinman....	7,026
Total Vote........	535,707

FIRST DEMOCRATIC PRIMARY, 1940

Earl K. Long...........	226,385
Sam H. Jones...........	154,936
James A. Noe...........	116,564
James H. Morrison......	48,243
Henry V. Moseley.......	7,595
Total Vote.......	553,723

SECOND DEMOCRATIC PRIMARY, 1940

Sam H. Jones...........	284,437
Earl K. Long...........	265,403
Total Vote.......	549,840

DEMOCRATIC PRIMARY, 1944

Jimmie H. Davis........	167,434
Lewis L. Morgan........	131,682*
James H. Morrison......	76,081
Dudley J. LeBlanc......	40,392
Sam S. Caldwell........	34,335
Ernest Clements........	20,404
Vincent Moseley........	7,385
Lee Lanier.............	1,641
Total Vote.......	479,354

FIRST DEMOCRATIC PRIMARY, 1948

Earl K. Long...........	267,253
Sam H. Jones...........	147,329
Robert F. Kennon.......	127,569
James H. Morrison......	101,754
Total Vote.......	643,905

SECOND DEMOCRATIC PRIMARY, 1948

Earl K. Long...........	432,528
Sam H. Jones...........	223,971
Total Vote.......	656,499

FIRST DEMOCRATIC PRIMARY, 1952

Carlos G. Spaht........	173,987
Robert F. Kennon.......	163,434
Hale Boggs.............	142,542
James M. McLemore.....	116,405
William J. Dodd........	90,925
Dudley J. LeBlanc......	62,906
Kermit A. Parker.......	5,470
Lucille May Grace......	4,832
Cliff Liles.............	1,233
Total Vote.......	761,734

SECOND DEMOCRATIC PRIMARY, 1952

Robert F. Kennon.......	482,302
Carlos G. Spaht........	302,743
Total Vote.......	785,045

DEMOCRATIC PRIMARY, 1956

Earl K. Long...........	421,681
deLesseps S. Morrison..	191,576
Frederick T. Preaus....	95,955
Francis C. Grevemberg..	62,309
James M. McLemore......	45,188
Total Vote.......	816,709

FIRST DEMOCRATIC PRIMARY, 1960

deLesseps S. Morrison..	278,956
Jimmie H. Davis........	213,551
William M. Rainach.....	143,095
James A. Noe...........	97,654
William J. Dodd........	85,436
Mack P. Stewart, Jr....	6,383
Allen G. LaCombe.......	4,917
A. Roswell Thompson....	4,200
Holt M. Allen.........	4,106
John B. Krey, Jr.......	2,587
Gale Berry.............	1,724
Total Vote.......	842,609

SECOND DEMOCRATIC PRIMARY, 1960

Jimmie H. Davis........	487,681
deLesseps S. Morrison..	414,110
Total Vote.......	901,791

FIRST DEMOCRATIC PRIMARY, 1964

deLesseps S. Morrison..	299,702
John J. McKeithen......	157,304
Gillis W. Long.........	137,778
Robert F. Kennon.......	127,870
Shelby M. Jackson......	103,949
Louis J. Michot, Jr....	37,463
Claude Kirkpatrick.....	28,578
Wilford L. Thompson,Sr.	6,454
Hugh P. Lasseigne......	4,034
A. Roswell Thompson....	3,343
Total Vote.......	906,475

SECOND DEMOCRATIC PRIMARY, 1964

John J. McKeithen......	492,905
deLesseps S. Morrison..	451,161
Total Vote.......	944,066

DEMOCRATIC PRIMARY, 1968

John J. McKeithen......	836,304
John R. Rarick.........	179,846
Cy D. F. Courtney......	8,698
Frank J. Ahern.........	7,152
A. Roswell Thompson....	5,102
Total Vote.....	1,037,102

FIRST DEMOCRATIC PRIMARY, 1971

Edwin W. Edwards.......	276,397
J. Bennett Johnston....	208,820
Gillis W. Long.........	164,276
Jimmie H. Davis........	138,656
John G. Schwegmann.....	92,072
C. C. Aycock..........	88,475
Samuel Bell, Sr........	72,486
Speedy O. Long........	61,359
Frank T. Salter, Jr...	32,203
James W. Moore........	9,408
Warren J. Moity........	8,965
David L. Chandler.....	7,244
Huey P. Coleman........	4,833
Harold Lee Bethune,II..	3,032
Wilford L. Thompson,Sr.	2,535
A. Roswell Thompson....	1,924
Jimmy Strain...........	1,258
Total Vote.....	1,173,943

SECOND DEMOCRATIC PRIMARY, 1971

Edwin W. Edwards.......	584,262
J. Bennett Johnston....	579,744
Total Vote.....	1,164,036

REPUBLICAN PRIMARY, 1971

David C. Treen........	9,732
Robert Ross............	839
Total Vote........	10,571

GENERAL ELECTION, 1972

Edwin W. Edwards (Dem).	641,146
David C. Treen (Rep)...	480,424
Total Vote.....	1,121,570

OPEN PRIMARY, 1975

Edwin W. Edwards (Dem)...	750,107
Robert Jones (Dem).......	292,220
Wade O. Martin (Dem).....	146,368
Ken Lewis (Dem).........	5,307
A. Roswell Thompson (Dem)	4,664
Cecilia Pizzo (Dem)......	4,338
Total Vote.....	1,203,004

Open Primary, 1979

Dave Treen (R)	297,469
Louis Lambert (D)........	282,708
James E. Fitzmorris(D).....	280,412
Paul Hardy (D)...........	227,026
E. L. "Bubba" Henry (D)..	135,769
Edgar G. Mouton (D)......	124,333
Luther Divine Knox (D)......	6,327
Ken Lewis (D).............	5,942
Greg Nelson..............	4,783
Total Vote..........	1,364,769

General Election, 1979

Dave Treen (R)	690,691
Louis Lambert (D)........	681,134
Total Vote..........	1,371,825

Open Primary, 1983
Edwin W. Edwards (D)
. 1,006,561
David C. Treen (R) . .588,508
Robert M. Ross (R). . . 7,625
Ken Lewis (D). 4,128
Charlie Moore 2,391
Floyd W. Smith, Jr. (D)
. . . . 2,314
Michele A. Smith 2,299
Joseph T. Robino 1,048
Michael J. Musmeci (D) .1,031

Total Vote 1,615,905

Source: Official Promulgation, Secretary of State.

OLD STATE CAPITOL

LOUISIANA'S NATIVE AMERICAN PLACE NAMES

Acadia (Parish)
Everyone knows that the term Cajun stems from the word *Acadian*. But few know that *Acadian* is an Indian word, from the Micmac (Maine) language of the northeast meaning "place of bounty," or "where something abounds."

Atchafalaya (Bay, River, Swamp)
From Choctaw, meaning "long river."

Avoyelles (Parish)
"Flint people" or "people of the rock." This is the French spelling for the name of an Indian tribe. The name is believed to refer to their role as middlemen in supplying flint to Gulf Coast tribes.

Bayou Funny Louis (River)
Choctaw. From *fani*, "squirrel," and *lusa*, "black." "Black squirrel creek."

Bogalusa (River, Town)
The Indian word is from *bok* and *lusa*, and means "black creek" or "black stream." The Bogalusa flows into the Pearl River at Louisiana's border with Mississippi.

Caddo (Lake, Parish)
In the language of the Caddo, *kadohadacho* means "real chiefs." The *Kadohadacho* Confederacy consisted of several tribes from Louisiana and Texas who shared a common language. The principal Caddo village on Caddo Lake was Shachidini, or "Timber Hill."

Calcasieu (Lake, River)
This name is apparently a French spelling from the Attakapan meaning "crying (screaming) eagle." *Katosh* means "eagle"; *yok* means "to cry." This name was given to an Attakapan war chief.

Chinchuba (Creek)
From the Choctaw *hachunchuba*, meaning "alligator."

Source: John B. Tenney, *Louisiana Conservationist*, July/August 1987

1987
Vote for Governor By Parish[a]

Parish	Total	Brown Number	Brown Percent	Edwards Number	Edwards Percent	Livingston Number	Livingston Percent	Roemer Number	Roemer Percent	Tauzin Number	Tauzin Percent	Others[b] Number	Others[b] Percent
Acadia	26,417	2,195	8.3%	8,650	32.7%	3,197	12.1%	7,607	28.8%	4,268	16.2%	500	1.9%
Allen	9,652	850	8.8	2,948	30.5	1,312	13.6	3,334	34.5	858	8.9	350	3.6
Ascension	23,567	2,342	9.9	6,648	28.2	3,025	12.8	8,180	34.7	3,172	13.5	200	0.8
Assumption	11,043	588	5.3	3,456	31.3	832	7.5	2,067	18.7	3,822	34.6	278	2.5
Avoyelles	17,509	1,615	9.2	5,336	30.5	1,994	11.4	5,900	33.7	1,609	9.2	1,055	6.0
Beauregard	11,517	840	7.3	1,810	15.7	2,091	18.2	5,471	47.5	806	7.0	499	4.3
Bienville	8,376	447	5.3	2,943	35.1	457	5.5	4,189	50.0	147	1.8	193	2.3
Bossier	28,144	430	1.5	3,999	14.2	1,499	5.3	21,551	76.6	387	1.4	278	1.0
Caddo	84,223	1,354	1.6	19,714	23.4	4,819	5.7	55,846	66.3	2,122	2.5	368	0.4
Calcasieu	59,997	4,826	8.0	13,728	22.9	9,691	16.2	23,901	39.8	7,276	12.1	575	1.0
Caldwell	5,347	1,118	20.9	976	18.3	1,038	19.4	1,932	36.1	158	3.0	125	2.3
Cameron	5,081	448	8.8	1,505	29.6	484	9.5	1,778	35.0	776	15.3	90	1.8
Catahoula	6,149	1,319	21.5	1,527	24.8	753	12.2	2,129	34.6	220	3.6	201	3.3
Claiborne	7,017	326	4.6	2,407	34.3	345	4.9	3,683	52.5	87	1.2	169	2.4
Concordia	9,082	2,077	22.9	2,731	30.1	1,263	13.9	2,468	27.2	313	3.4	230	2.5
DeSoto	10,968	411	3.7	3,812	34.8	355	3.2	6,036	55.0	161	1.5	193	1.8
East Baton Rouge	132,857	11,136	8.4	31,322	23.6	27,058	20.4	54,089	40.7	8,445	6.4	807	0.6
East Carroll	4,210	511	12.1	1,977	47.0	575	13.7	861	20.5	146	3.5	140	3.3
East Feliciana	8,064	613	7.6	3,587	44.5	1,271	15.8	2,012	25.0	456	5.7	125	1.6
Evangeline	16,121	1,542	9.6	4,696	29.1	1,656	10.3	5,270	32.7	2,409	14.9	548	3.4
Franklin	10,363	2,052	19.8	2,614	25.2	1,486	14.3	3,754	36.2	213	2.1	244	2.4
Grant	7,799	708	9.1	1,610	20.6	1,369	17.6	3,328	42.7	264	3.4	520	6.7
Iberia	27,351	2,021	7.4	5,891	21.5	4,586	16.8	7,676	28.1	6,675	24.4	502	1.8
Iberville	16,738	1,515	9.1	6,972	41.7	1,440	8.6	4,272	25.5	2,240	13.4	299	1.8
Jackson	7,869	745	9.5	2,189	27.8	1,180	15.0	3,395	43.1	178	2.3	182	2.3
Jefferson	141,326	16,662	11.8	33,642	23.8	49,351	34.9	30,066	21.3	10,886	7.7	719	0.5
Jefferson Davis	13,597	1,236	9.1	3,571	26.3	2,015	14.8	4,290	31.6	2,192	16.1	293	2.2
Lafayette	56,245	4,968	8.8	13,038	23.2	10,552	18.8	18,150	32.3	8,372	14.9	1,165	2.1
Lafourche	33,013	1,361	4.1	6,034	18.3	4,171	12.6	4,367	13.2	16,623	50.4	457	1.4
LaSalle	7,581	1,032	13.6	1,037	13.7	1,132	14.9	3,540	46.7	169	2.2	671	8.9
Lincoln	13,874	666	4.8	3,627	26.1	1,894	13.7	7,040	50.7	398	2.9	249	1.8
Livingston	29,520	2,946	10.0	7,802	26.4	5,107	17.3	11,418	38.7	1,926	6.5	321	1.1
Madison	5,386	568	10.5	2,173	40.3	719	13.3	1,282	23.8	420	7.8	224	4.2
Morehouse	11,819	1,823	15.4	2,841	24.0	2,561	21.7	3,813	32.3	514	4.3	267	2.3
Natchitoches	14,880	548	3.7	4,613	31.0	1,425	9.6	7,106	47.8	611	4.1	577	3.9
Orleans	151,062	16,525	10.9	68,155	45.1	34,483	22.8	22,389	14.8	8,134	5.4	1,376	0.9
Ouachita	46,681	4,923	10.5	10,144	21.7	11,753	25.2	17,383	37.2	1,771	3.8	707	1.5

Parish	Total		%		%		%		%		%		%
Plaquemines	10,017	1,347	13.4	3,538	35.3	2,303	23.0	1,752	17.5	1,019	10.2	58	0.6
Pointe Coupee	11,173	895	8.0	4,626	41.4	1,177	10.5	3,199	28.6	1,130	10.1	146	1.3
Rapides	45,215	3,966	8.8	10,592	23.4	9,745	21.6	16,958	37.5	1,859	4.1	2,095	4.6
Red River	5,362	134	2.5	1,641	30.6	200	3.7	3,106	57.9	157	2.9	124	2.3
Richland	8,682	1,303	15.0	2,379	27.4	1,664	19.2	2,888	33.3	210	2.4	238	2.7
Sabine	9,776	251	2.6	1,892	19.4	634	6.5	6,599	67.5	175	1.8	225	2.3
St. Bernard	31,829	3,240	10.2	9,731	30.6	10,538	33.1	5,262	16.5	2,826	8.9	232	0.7
St. Charles	17,164	1,691	9.9	4,828	28.1	3,331	19.4	3,439	20.0	3,759	21.9	116	0.7
St. Helena	6,141	581	9.5	2,839	46.2	636	10.4	1,645	26.8	330	5.4	110	1.8
St. James	11,477	1,145	10.0	4,676	40.7	873	7.6	2,031	17.7	2,676	23.3	76	0.7
St. John	16,030	2,101	13.1	6,011	37.5	2,518	15.7	3,397	21.2	1,860	11.6	143	0.9
St. Landry	35,439	2,436	6.9	13,307	37.5	4,176	11.8	10,507	29.6	4,630	13.1	383	1.1
St. Martin	19,769	1,602	8.1	7,031	35.6	2,517	12.7	3,916	19.8	3,746	18.9	957	4.8
St. Mary	23,276	1,841	7.9	5,456	23.4	2,967	12.7	6,195	26.6	6,202	26.6	615	2.6
St. Tammany	48,009	4,401	9.2	9,493	19.8	19,651	40.9	12,319	25.7	1,940	4.0	205	0.4
Tangipahoa	32,182	3,475	10.8	10,239	31.8	5,637	17.5	10,859	33.7	1,680	5.2	292	0.9
Tensas	3,558	441	12.4	1,506	42.3	607	17.1	762	21.4	83	2.3	159	4.5
Terrebonne	32,623	1,969	6.0	6,947	21.3	5,751	17.6	6,346	19.5	11,107	34.0	503	1.5
Union	10,096	1,288	12.8	2,429	24.1	1,698	16.8	4,202	41.6	248	2.5	231	2.3
Vermilion	24,851	2,142	8.6	7,516	30.2	2,986	12.0	5,963	24.0	5,741	23.1	503	2.0
Vernon	13,865	862	6.2	2,721	19.6	1,666	12.0	7,557	54.5	497	3.6	562	4.1
Washington	18,520	2,664	14.4	5,827	31.5	3,061	16.5	5,704	30.8	1,057	5.7	207	1.1
Webster	16,789	433	2.6	3,969	23.6	864	5.1	10,896	64.9	273	1.6	354	2.1
West Baton Rouge	8,533	709	8.3	3,269	38.3	949	11.1	2,630	30.8	877	10.3	99	1.2
West Carroll	5,396	961	17.8	1,408	26.1	1,014	18.8	1,751	32.4	144	2.7	118	2.2
West Feliciana	4,350	353	8.1	1,903	43.7	628	14.4	990	22.8	434	10.0	42	1.0
Winn	8,163	705	8.6	2,302	28.2	1,050	12.9	3,632	44.5	195	2.4	279	3.4
Total	1,558,730	138,223	8.9%	437,801	28.1%	287,780	18.5%	516,078	33.1%	154,079	9.9%	24,269	1.6%

a May not add to 100% due to rounding.
b Includes candidates Amedee, Lewis and Long.
SOURCE: Official Promulgation, Secretary of State.

Statewide Vote on 1987 Constitutional Amendments

Amendment	Total Votes	Votes For	Percent For
1. Appointment of temporary lower court judges	723,621	426,461	58.9%
2. Constitutional Wildlife and Fisheries Conservation Fund	703,431	473,618	67.3
3. Actuarial funding, retirement systems	732,985	498,757	68.0
4. Legislature or BESE authority over state school aid program	694,016	385,267	55.5
5. Nominees, New Orleans City Civil Service Commission*	683,920	353,518	51.7

* Voter approval was required and received both statewide and in New Orleans.
SOURCE: Official Promulgation, Secretary of State.

Table provided by Public Affairs Research Council of Louisiana, Inc.

Previous Voting on Proposed Amendments to 1974 Louisiana Constitution

Date	Number of Amendments		Average Percent of Registrants Voting
	Proposed	Approved	
November 7, 1978	1	1	29.9%
October 27, 1979	3	3	37.5
November 4, 1980	4	4	55.7
September 11, 1982	8	4	24.9
October 22, 1983	3	3	44.2
November 6, 1984	5	0	53.7
September 27, 1986	7	2	39.3

1987
Voter Participation, Gubernatorial Election

Parish	Number Registered	Number Voting	Percent Voting	Rank*
Acadia	35,365	26,417	74.7%	33
Allen	12,644	9,652	76.3	20
Ascension	30,459	23,567	77.4	14
Assumption	13,946	11,043	79.2	9
Avoyelles	23,568	17,509	74.3	35
Beauregard	16,195	11,517	71.1	46
Bienville	10,537	8,376	79.5	8
Bossier	37,536	28,144	75.0	29
Caddo	119,949	84,223	70.2	54
Calcasieu	88,894	59,997	67.5	60
Caldwell	6,944	5,347	77.0	17
Cameron	6,523	5,081	77.9	13
Catahoula	7,774	6,149	79.1	10
Claiborne	9,315	7,017	75.3	27
Concordia	12,811	9,082	70.9	48
DeSoto	14,640	10,968	74.9	31
East Baton Rouge	187,410	132,857	70.9	49
East Carroll	6,140	4,210	68.6	57
East Feliciana	10,600	8,064	76.1	22
Evangeline	22,240	16,121	72.5	42
Franklin	14,203	10,363	73.0	39
Grant	10,410	7,799	74.9	30
Iberia	36,264	27,351	75.4	25
Iberville	19,784	16,738	84.6	2
Jackson	9,586	7,869	82.1	3
Jefferson	202,800	141,326	69.7	55
Jefferson Davis	18,675	13,597	72.8	40
Lafayette	82,731	56,245	68.0	58
Lafourche	43,436	33,013	76.0	23
LaSalle	9,464	7,581	80.1	5
Lincoln	19,595	13,874	70.8	50
Livingston	37,849	29,520	78.0	12
Madison	8,212	5,386	65.6	63
Morehouse	16,832	11,819	70.2	53
Natchitoches	20,192	14,880	73.7	36
Orleans	246,157	151,062	61.4	64
Ouachita	66,191	46,681	70.5	51
Plaquemines	14,951	10,017	67.0	61
Pointe Coupee	14,821	11,173	75.4	26
Rapides	66,651	45,215	67.8	59
Red River	6,715	5,362	79.9	6
Richland	12,043	8,682	72.1	44
Sabine	13,518	9,776	72.3	43
St. Bernard	41,657	31,829	76.4	19
St. Charles	22,711	17,164	75.6	24
St. Helena	7,947	6,141	77.3	16
St. James	13,438	11,477	85.4	1
St. John the Baptist	22,072	16,030	72.6	41
St. Landry	48,096	35,439	73.7	37
St. Martin	25,687	19,769	77.0	18
St. Mary	33,572	23,276	69.3	56
St. Tammany	72,312	48,009	66.4	62
Tangipahoa	44,817	32,182	71.8	45
Tensas	4,847	3,558	73.4	38
Terrebonne	43,573	32,623	74.9	32
Union	12,839	10,096	78.6	11
Vermilion	30,621	24,851	81.2	4
Vernon	19,515	13,865	71.0	47
Washington	26,337	18,520	70.3	52
Webster	22,530	16,789	74.5	34
West Baton Rouge	11,331	8,533	75.3	28
West Carroll	7,086	5,396	76.2	21
West Feliciana	5,629	4,350	77.3	15
Winn	10,241	8,163	79.7	7
Total	2,191,428	1,558,730	71.1%	

* In the case of ties, calculations were extended to determine rank.
SOURCE: Louisiana Department of Elections and Registration, and Official Promulgation, Secretary of State.

Table provided by Public Affairs Research Council of Louisiana, Inc.

Characteristics of Voter Registration, October 1987

Parish	Total Registered	Democrat		Party Affiliation Republican		Other		Blacks Registered	
		Number	Percent	Number	Percent	Number	Percent	Number	Percent
Acadia	35,365	32,237	91.2%	1,998	5.6%	1,130	3.2%	6,041	17.1%
Allen	12,644	11,515	91.1	702	5.6	427	3.4	2,392	18.9
Ascension	30,459	25,808	84.7	2,356	7.7	2,295	7.5	6,575	21.6
Assumption	13,946	12,800	91.8	657	4.7	489	3.5	4,357	31.2
Avoyelles	23,568	21,127	89.6	1,196	5.1	1,245	5.3	5,364	22.8
Beauregard	16,195	13,008	80.3	1,604	9.9	1,583	9.8	1,967	12.1
Bienville	10,537	9,573	90.9	688	6.5	276	2.6	4,287	40.7
Bossier	37,536	24,291	64.7	8,289	22.1	4,956	13.2	5,130	13.7
Caddo	119,949	82,544	68.8	25,677	21.4	11,728	9.8	35,147	29.3
Calcasieu	88,894	72,134	81.1	9,464	10.6	7,296	8.2	18,075	20.3
Caldwell	6,944	5,921	85.3	705	10.2	318	4.6	1,075	15.5
Cameron	6,523	5,717	87.6	311	4.8	495	7.6	362	5.5
Catahoula	7,774	6,951	89.4	567	7.3	256	3.3	1,801	23.2
Claiborne	9,315	7,761	83.3	975	10.5	579	6.2	3,871	41.6
Concordia	12,811	10,981	85.7	1,061	8.3	769	6.0	4,118	32.1
DeSoto	14,640	12,267	83.8	1,088	7.4	1,285	8.8	5,016	34.3
East Baton Rouge	187,410	130,060	69.4	38,116	20.3	19,234	10.3	50,499	26.9
East Carroll	6,140	5,222	85.0	493	8.0	425	6.9	3,360	54.7
East Feliciana	10,600	9,059	85.5	859	8.1	682	6.4	3,307	31.2
Evangeline	22,240	21,061	94.7	838	3.8	341	1.5	5,357	24.1
Franklin	14,203	12,759	89.8	1,089	7.7	355	2.5	3,775	26.6
Grant	10,410	8,843	84.9	913	8.8	654	6.3	1,401	13.5
Iberia	36,264	29,590	81.6	4,086	11.3	2,588	7.1	9,366	25.8
Iberville	19,784	18,473	93.4	681	3.4	630	3.2	8,705	44.0
Jackson	9,586	8,318	86.8	845	8.8	423	4.4	2,597	27.1
Jefferson	202,800	134,560	66.4	45,287	22.3	22,953	11.3	24,062	11.9
Jefferson Davis	18,675	15,853	84.9	1,261	6.8	1,561	8.4	3,204	17.2
Lafayette	82,731	55,907	67.6	15,456	18.7	11,368	13.7	14,642	17.7
Lafourche	43,436	37,352	86.0	3,299	7.6	2,785	6.4	3,714	8.6
LaSalle	9,464	8,116	85.8	819	8.7	529	5.6	712	7.5
Lincoln	19,595	14,166	72.3	3,561	18.2	1,868	9.5	6,924	35.3
Livingston	37,849	30,711	81.1	3,494	9.2	3,644	9.6	2,225	5.9
Madison	8,212	6,445	78.5	1,144	13.9	623	7.6	4,202	51.2
Morehouse	16,832	13,257	78.8	2,123	12.6	1,452	8.6	5,841	34.7
Natchitoches	20,192	16,593	82.2	1,992	9.9	1,607	8.0	6,741	33.4
Orleans	246,157	191,198	77.7	34,222	13.9	20,737	8.4	130,187	52.9

Ouachita	66,191	45,754	69.1	12,681	19.2	7,756	11.7	17,026	25.7
Plaquemines	14,951	12,673	84.8	1,453	9.7	825	5.5	2,813	18.8
Pointe Coupee	14,821	13,572	91.6	696	4.7	553	3.7	5,786	39.0
Rapides	66,651	50,514	75.8	10,251	15.4	5,886	8.8	14,446	21.7
Red River	6,715	5,878	87.5	376	5.6	461	6.9	2,252	33.5
Richland	12,043	9,951	82.6	1,308	10.9	784	6.5	3,704	30.8
Sabine	13,518	11,729	86.8	1,115	8.2	674	5.0	1,925	14.2
St. Bernard	41,657	36,328	87.2	3,464	8.3	1,865	4.5	1,640	3.9
St. Charles	22,711	17,892	78.8	2,995	13.2	1,824	8.0	5,354	23.6
St. Helena	7,947	7,140	89.8	434	5.5	373	4.7	3,901	49.1
St. James	13,438	12,443	92.6	522	3.9	473	3.5	6,185	46.0
St. John	22,072	17,642	79.9	2,281	10.3	2,149	9.7	7,976	36.1
St. Landry	48,096	42,468	88.3	3,364	7.0	2,264	4.7	18,752	39.0
St. Martin	25,687	23,345	90.9	1,504	5.9	838	3.3	7,907	30.8
St. Mary	33,572	25,942	77.3	4,007	11.9	3,623	10.8	9,573	28.5
St. Tammany	72,312	42,881	59.3	19,196	26.5	10,235	14.2	6,515	9.0
Tangipahoa	44,817	36,126	80.6	4,624	10.3	4,067	9.1	10,938	24.4
Tensas	4,847	4,177	86.2	529	10.9	141	2.9	2,359	48.7
Terrebonne	43,573	33,424	76.7	5,778	13.3	4,371	10.0	6,752	15.5
Union	12,839	10,967	85.4	1,325	10.3	547	4.3	3,279	25.5
Vermilion	30,621	26,998	88.2	1,563	5.1	2,060	6.7	3,736	12.2
Vernon	19,515	15,591	79.9	1,819	9.3	2,105	10.8	1,644	8.4
Washington	26,337	23,277	88.4	1,836	7.0	1,224	4.6	6,881	26.1
Webster	22,530	18,826	83.6	2,122	9.4	1,582	7.0	6,117	27.2
West Baton Rouge	11,331	10,044	88.6	568	5.0	719	6.3	4,030	35.6
West Carroll	7,086	5,910	83.4	897	12.7	279	3.9	1,003	14.2
West Feliciana	5,629	4,742	84.2	439	7.8	448	8.0	2,471	43.9
Winn	10,241	8,715	85.1	700	6.8	826	8.1	2,512	24.5
Total	2,191,428	1,697,127	77.4%	305,763	14.0%	188,538	8.6%	563,876	25.7%

SOURCE: Louisiana Department of Elections and Registration.

Table provided by Public Affairs Research Council of Louisiana, Inc.

LOUISIANA'S NATIVE AMERICAN PLACE NAMES

Houma (Town)
Choctaw. "Red." This town was named for the Houma (or "Red") Indians wh
settled in the area during the early 1700s. The Houma used the red crayfish as the
war emblem.

Keatchie (Town)
This Indian word means "panther."

Mississippi (River)
Algonquian for "large river." From *misi*, "big," and *sipi*, "river." Because of th
prevalence of Indian trade from and to the north, the Algonquian name came int
widespread use throughout the south, and in time displaced the names for the riv
used by local tribes.

Natalbany (River)
"Lone bear." This river empties into Lake Maurepas.

Natchez (Town)
Louisiana's Natchez is south of Natchitoches. It means "timber land" or "timbe
forest." Some experts believe it stems from the Caddo *Na'htcha* for wood fore
and from *da'htcha'hi*, for timber.

Opelousas (Town)
Choctaw. For "black hair" or "black legs (leggings)." This was the name for
small tribe inhabiting the area around St. Landry Parish.

Ouachita (Parish, River)
The Indian name means "silver water."

Ponchatoula (Town)
From the Indian word for "falling hair," referring to Spanish moss which is pre
valent in the area.

Powhatan (Town)
Algonquian; for "falls in a current of water," or "at the falls."

Roanoke (Town)
This Indian name appears to have been brought in from the east, probably fro
Virginia. *Roanoke* or *roanoak* was the name given to a form of shell money mad
from beads of several types.

Tallulah (Town)
Tallula in Choctaw means "bell," from *tali*, "metal," and *ula*, "sounding."

Tammany (St. Tammany Parish)
Because of the many Indians inhabiting the area, present day St. Tammany Paris
was named in honor of the famous Delaware chief, *Tamanend* or *St. Tammany.*

Source: John B. Tenney, *Louisiana Conservationist*, July/August 1987

Trend In Party Affiliation Of Registered Voters

Year	Total Registered Voters	Democrats		Republicans		Others	
		Number Registered	Percent of Total	Number Registered	Percent of Total	Number Registered	Percent of Total
1984	2,244,469	1,807,622	80.5	255,709	11.4	181,138	8.1
1985	2,145,476	1,700,892	79.3	273,864	12.8	170,720	8.0
1986	2,179,317	1,704,570	78.2	293,990	13.5	180,757	8.3
1987	2,191,428	1,697,127	77.4	305,763	14.0	188,538	8.6

SOURCE: Louisiana Department of Elections and Registration; Public Affairs Research Council of Louisiana.

Trend In Black Registered Voters, 1963-1987

Year	Total Registered Voters	Number Blacks Registered	Percent Black Registrants of Total	Percent Increase of Black Registrants Over Prior Four Years
1963	1,182,676	160,533	13.6%	—
1967	1,381,354	269,437	19.5	67.8%
1971	1,633,181	347,098	21.3	28.8
1975	1,798,032	408,696	22.7	17.7
1979	1,936,804	453,016	23.4	10.8
1983	2,135,771	530,170	24.8	17.0
1987	2,191,428	563,876*	25.7	6.36

*It should be noted that under state law race cannot be required for registration, and some registrants did not indicate their race.
SOURCE: Louisiana Department of Elections and Registration; Public Affairs Research Council of Louisiana.

Gubernatorial Election
Qualifications, Terms & Salaries

Office*	Length of Term, Term Begins	Salary	Minimum Age	U.S. Citizenship	State Residence	Domiciled In District	Special Qualifications
Governor	4 years, begins noon, 2nd Monday, in March following election	$73,440	25	5 years	5 years		Be an elector
Lieutenant Governor	"	$63,367	"	"	"		"
Secretary of State	"	$60,169	"	"	"		"
Attorney General	"	"	"	"	"		Be an elector, admitted to practice of law in Louisiana 5 years
Treasurer	"	"	"	"	"		Be an elector
Commissioner of Insurance	"	"	"	"	"		"
Commissioner of Agriculture	"	"	"	"	"		"
Commissioner of Elections	"	"	"	"	"		"
State Board of Elementary and Secondary Education Members, Districts 1, 3, 4, 6, 7 & 8	"	$50/diem					
State Senators, Districts 1 - 39	4 years, begins 2nd Monday in March	$16,800 + $75/diem	18		2 years	1 year	"
State Representatives, Districts 1 - 105	"		"		"	"	"
Sheriffs**	4 years, begins July 1 after general election	Varies by parish	"				Be a qualified elector

Office	Term			Qualifications
Clerks of Court**	"			Be a qualified elector
Assessors**	4 years, begins January 1, 1985			Be a qualified elector
Coroners**	4 years, begins 4th Monday in March			Be a licensed physician unless no licensed physician will accept the position
Police Jurors***	4 years, begins 2nd Monday in January***	"	2 years	1 year	Be an elector
Justices of the Peace	4 years, begins 4th Monday in March	Varies by parish****		Be a qualified elector, a freeholder, of good moral character, able to read and write the English language correctly
Constables	"	Varies by parish*****		Be a qualified elector, of good moral character, able to read and write the English language correctly
Regular municipal elections where applicable	"			!
Special elections where applicable	"			
Democratic State Central Committee Members	4 years, begins noon 2nd Sat. in January	"		Be a registered Democrat
Democratic Parish Executive Committee Members**	4 years, begins within 30 days after general election	"		"
Republican State Central Committee Members	4 years, begins noon 2nd Sat. in January	"		Be a registered Republican
Republican Parish Executive Committee Members**	4 years, begins within 30 days after general election	"		"

SOURCE: Louisiana Department of Elections and Registration; Public Affairs Research Council of Louisiana.

LOUISIANA OFFICIALS OF THE PAST

GOVERNORS OF LOUISIANA UNDER FRENCH RULE

Marquise de Sauvolle 1699-1701
Bienville 1701-1712
Lamothe Cadillac 1713-1716
Bienville (acting) 1716-1717
De L'Epinay 1717-1718
Bienville 1718-1726
Boisbriant (ad interim) 1724-1726
Perier 1726-1733
Bienville 1733-1743
Marquise de Vaudreuil 1743-1753
Baron de Kerlerec 1753-1763
D'Abadie (acting) 1763-1765
Phillipe Aubry (acting) 1765-1769

UNDER SPANISH RULE

Antoine de Ulloa 1766-1768
Alexander O'Reilly 1769-1770
Luis de Unzaga 1770-1777
Bernardo de Galvez 1777-1785
Estevan Miro 1785-1791
Baron de Carondelet 1791-1797
Gayoso de Lemos 1797-1799
Francois Bouligny (acting) 1799
Sebastian y Caso Calvo 1799-1801
Juan Manuel y de Salcedo 1801-1803

SECOND FRENCH PERIOD
(20 days duration)

Pierre de Laussat 1803

TERRITORY OF LOUISIANA

W. C. C. Claiborne 1804-1812

STATE OF LOUISIANA

W. C. C. Claiborne 1812-1816
Jacques Villere 1816-1820

Thomas Bolling Robertson......1820-1824
Henry S. Thibodaux
  (acting governor)............ 1824
Henry Johnson 1824-1828
Pierre Derbigny (died in office) 1828-1829
A Beauvais (President of the
  Senate, acting governor) 1829-1830
Jacques Dupre 1830-1831
Andre Bienvenu Roman 1831-1835
Edward White 1835-1839
Andre Bienvenu Roman 1839-1843
Alexandre Mouton 1843-1846
Isaac Johnson 1846-1850
Joseph Walker 1850-1853
Paul O. Hebert 1853-1856
Robert Charles Wickliffe 1856-1860
Thomas Overton Moore 1860-1862
Gen. G. F. Shepley, Military
  Governor 1862-1864

GOVERNORS OF LOUISIANA

Henry Watkins Allen (under
  Confederate government) 1864-1865
Michael Hahn (under Federal
  government) 1864-1865
James Madison Wells 1865-1867
Benjamin Flanders, under
  military authority 1867-1868
Joshua Baker, under military
  authority 1868

Henry Clay Warmoth 1868-1873
John McEnery (counted out
  by the Returning Board) 1873
P. B. S. Pinchback (Lieutenant
  Governor, acting gov.) 1873
William Pitt Kellogg, Governor
  de jure 1873-1877
Stephen Packard (claims to
  office rejected) 1877
Francis T. Nicholls 1877-1880
Louis Alfred Wiltz (died in
  office) 1880-1881
Samuel Douglas McEnery,
  Lieut Governor suc-
  ceeded him as Governor 1881-1884
Samuel Douglas McEnery 1884-1888
Francis T. Nicholls 1888-1892
Murphy James Foster 1892-1900
William Wright Heard 1900-1904
N. C. Blanchard 1904-1908
J. Y. Sanders.................1908-1912
L. E. Hall....................1912-1916
R G. Pleasant.................1916-1920
John M. Parker 1920-1924
Henry L. Fuqua (died in
  office) 1924-1926
O. H. Simpson, Lieutenant
  Governor, succeeded as
  Governor 1926-1928
Huey P. Long (Resigned) 1928-1931
Alvin A. King (Acting) 1931-1932
O. K. Allen (Died) 1932-1936
James A. Noe (Acting) 1936
Richard W. Leche (Resigned) ..1936-1939
Earl K. Long (Acting) 1939-1940
Sam Houston Jones 1940-1944
James H. Davis 1944-1948
Earl K. Long 1948-1952
Robt. F. Kennon 1952-1956
Earl K. Long 1956-1960
James H. Davis 1960-1964
John J. McKeithen 1964-1972
Edwin Edwards...................1972-1980
Dave Treen 1980-1984
Edwin Edwards 1984-1988
Charles E. "Buddy" Roemer III. . . 1988-

LIEUTENANT GOVERNORS— EX OFFICIO PRESIDENTS OF THE SENATE

Trasimond Landry 1846-1849
Jean Baptiste Plauche 1850-1852
William Wood Farmer 1852-1853
  (died in office)
Robert Charles Wickliffe 1854-1855
Charles Homere Mouton 1856
  (resigned)
William F. Griffin 1857-1859
Henry M. Hyams 1860-1864
Benjamine W. Pearce 1864
J. Madison Wells (de facto;
  succeeded by Michael Hahn,
  governor de jure) 1864
Charles Smith 1864
Charles W. Boyce 1864
Louis Gastinel 1864
Victor Burthe 1865
Albert Voorhies 1866-1868

Oscar J. Dunn 1868-1871
(died in office)
P. B. S. Pinchback 1871
C. C. Antoine 1872-1876
Louis Alfred Wiltz 1877-1880
Samuel Dougles McEnery
(succeeded Gov. L. A. Wiltz
as governor) 1880-1881
Dr. W. A. Robertson 1881
George L. Walton 1881-1882
Robert C. Davey 1884-1888
Clay Knobloch 1884-1888
James Jeffries 1888-1892
Charles Parlange (appointed
Justice, Supreme Court) 1892
H. R. Lott 1894
R. H. Snyder 1896-1900
Albert Estopinal 1900-1904
Jared Y. Sanders 1904-1908
Paul M. Lambremont 1908-1912
Thomas C. Barrett 1912-1916
Fernand Mouton 1916-1920
Hewitt Bouanchaud (resigned
April 12, 1924—appointed
to La. Tax Commission) 1920-1924
Delos R. Johnson, (Succeeded
Hewitt Bouanchaud on
April 12, 1924) 1924
Oramel H. Simpson (Suc-
ceeded Gov. Fuqua Oct. 11,
1926 as Governor 1924-1926
Philip H. Gilbert (Succeeded
O. H. Simpson) 1926-1928
Paul M. Cyr 1928-1931
Alvin O. King (Sworn in Oct.
14, 1931; became governor
Jan. 26, 1932, succeeding
Huey P. Long) 1931-1932
John B. Fornet (Elected to
Supreme Court—sworn in
Jan. 2, 1935) 1932-1935
Thomas C. Wingate (Sworn in
Jan. 2, 1935; resigned Feb.
26, 1935) 1935
James A. Noe (Sworn in Feb.
26, 1935; became Gov. Jan.
28, 1936, succeeding O. K.
Allen) 1935-1936
Richard W. Leche 1936-1939
Earl K. Long (Became gov-
ernor June 26, 1939, suc-
ceeding Richard W. Leche............1939
Coleman Lindsey (Succeeded
Earl K. Long) 1939-1940
Marc M. Mouton 1940-1944
J. Emile Verret 1944-1948
William J. Dodd 1948-1952
C. E. Barham 1952-1956
Luther E Frazar 1956-1960
C. C. "Taddy" Aycock 1960-1972
James E. Fitzmorris, Jr.............1972-1980
Robert L. Freeman 1980-1988
Paul Hardy. 1988-

PRESIDENTS OF THE LEGISLATIVE
COUNCILS—TERRITORY OF
ORLEANS
Julien Poydras 1804-1805
Jean Noel Destrehan 1806
Pierre Sauve 1807
Julien Poydras 1808
J. D. Degouton Bellechasse ...1809-1810
Jean Noel Destrehan 1810-1812

PRESIDENTS OF THE SENATE
Julien Poydras 1812-1813
Fulmar Skipwith 1814-1815
Nathaniel Meriam 1816-1819
Julien Poydras 1820-1821
Bernard Marigny 1822
H. S. Thibodeaux 1823-1826
A. Beauvais 1827-1829
Isaac A. Smith 1830-1831
Charles Derbigny 1832-1837
Joseph E. Johnston 1838
Jacques Dupre 1838
Felix Garcia 1839-1845

TERRITORIAL ATTORNEYS-GENERAL
John Mahlon Dickens 1804-1806
James Brown 1807-1808
Francois Xavier Martin 1809
Louis Moreau Lislet................1810-1811

ATTORNEYS-GENERAL OF THE
STATE OF LOUISIANA
(Appointed by the Governor)
Francois X. Martin 1812-1816
Louis Moreau Lislet 1817-1818
Thos. Bolling Robertson 1819-1820
Etienne Mazureau 1820-1823
Isaac T. Preston 1923-1829
Alonzo Morphy 1829
George Eustis 1830-1832
Etienne Mazureau 1832-1840
Christian Roselius 1841-1842
Isaac T. Preston 1843-1845
William A. Elmore 1846-1850
Isaac Johnson 1850-1852
(Office made elective,
constitution of 1852)
Isaac E. Moise 1853-1855
E. Warren Moise 1855-1859
Thomas J. Semmes 1860-1862
F. C. Goode 1862-1864
Andrew S. Herron 1865
B. S. Lynch 1865-1867
Simon Belden 1868-1871
A. P. Field 1872-1876
William H. Hunt 1876
Hiram B. Steele 1876
Horatio N. Ogden 1877-1879
James C. Egan 1880-1884
Milton J. Cunningham 1884-1888
Walter H. Rogers 1888-1892
Milton J. Cunningham 1892-1900
Walter Guion 1901-1912
Ruffin G. Pleasant 1912-1916
Adolph V. Coco 1916-1924
Percy Saint 1924-1932
Gaston L. Porterie 1932-1938
Lessley P. Gardiner 1938-1940
Eugene Stanley 1940-1944
Fred S. LeBlanc 1944-1948
Boliver E. Kemp, Jr. 1948-1952
Fred S. LeBlanc 1952-1956
Jack P. F. Gremillion................1956-1972
William Guste 1972-

TERRITORIAL
SECRETARIES OF STATE
James Brown 1803-1804
John Graham 1805-1809
Thomas Bolling Robertson 1810-1811

SECRETARIES OF STATE
Louis B. Macarty...................1812-1816

Etienne Mazureau 1817-1820
Pierre Bourisgay Derbigny 1821-1828
George Waggaman 1829-1832
George Eustis 1833-1834

Martin Blache 1835-1836
Wm. Charles Cole Claiborne, Jr..........1837
Alfred E. Forstall 1838
Henry Adams Bullard 1839
Levi Pierce 1839-1844
Rober Carter Nicholas....................1845
Xenon Le Doux, Jr. 1845
Charles Gayarre 1846-1852
(Under the Constitution of 1852 this office was made elective)
Andrew S. Herron 1853-1859
Kling D. Hardy 1860-1864
S. Wrotnozki 1864
J. Hamilton Hardy 1867
George E. Bovee 1868-1871
Francis J. Herron 1871
Jack Wharton............................1871
P. J. Deslonde 1873-1876
Will A. Strong 1877-1884
Oscar Arroyo 1884-1888
Leonard F. Mason 1888-1892
Thomas S. Adams 1892-1896
John T. Michel 1896-1912
Alvin E. Hebert 1912-1914
W. F. Millsaps 1914-1916
James J. Bailey 1916-1930
Alice Lee Grosjean 1931-1932
E. A. Conway......................1932-1940
James A. Gremillion 1940-1944
Wade Omer Martin, Jr..........1944-1976
Paul J. Hardy **1976-1980**
James H. Brown. **1980-1988**
W. Fox McKeithen **1988-**

COMMISSIONERS OF AGRICULTURE

T. J. Bird 1884-1890
T. S. Adams 1890-1892
H. C. Newsom 1892-1894
A. V. Cartèr 1894-1896
J. G. Lee 1896-1899
Leon Jastremski 1899-1900
J. G. Lee 1900-1906
Charles Schuler 1906-1911
E. O. Bruner 1911-1916
Harry D. Wilson 1916-194F
Millard S. Perkins 1948-1948
W. E. Anderson 1948-1952
Dave L. Pearce 1952-1956
S. J. McCrory.....................1956-1960
Dave L. Pearce................1960-1976
Gilbert Dozier........................**1976-1980**
Bob Odom..........................**1980-**

STATE SUPERINTENDENTS OF PUBLIC EDUCATION
(1847-1982)

Alexander Dimitry 1847-1851
Robert Carter Nicholas 1851-1853
John N. Carrigan 1853-1855
Samuel Bard 1855-1857
W. T. Hamilton....................1857-1859
Henry Avery 1859-1861
W. H. N. McGruder................1862-1865

John MacNair* 1863-1865
Robert M. Lusher..................1865-1868
Thomas W. Conway...............1868-1872
W. G. Brown (Black)...............1872-1876
Robert M. Lusher..................1877-1879
Edwin H. Fay 1880-1884
Warren Easton 1884-1888
Joseph A. Breaux 1888-1890
W. H. Jack 1890-1892
A. D. Lafargue.....................1892-1896
Joseph V. Calhoun.................1896-1904
James B. Aswell....................1904-1908
Thomas H. Harris 1908-1940
John E. Coxe......................1940-1948
Shelby M. Jackson 1948-1964
William J. Dodd 1964-1972
Louis J. Michot....................1972-1976
J. Kelly Nix 1976-1984
Thomas G. Clausen **1984-1988**

*Appointed by the Federal Government.
**Last elected Superintendent of Education.

PUBLIC SERVICE COMMISSIONERS

	Term Ended
R. N. Sims	April, 1901
W. L. Foster	December, 1906
Overton Cade	December, 1908
C. L. DeFuentes	December, 1910
J. J. Meredith	December, 1912
Henry Schreiber	September, 1918
B. A. Briges	December, 1918
John T. Michel	November, 1921
Shelby Taylor	December, 1926
Huey P. Long ..(Became Governor May, 1928)
Dudley J. LeBlanc	November, 1932
Francis Williams	December, 1934
H. G. Fields	December, 1936
James P. O'Conner, Jr.	December, 1940
John S. Patton	December, 1942
James H. Davis (Became Governor May, 1944)
Lamar T. Loe	December, 1948
Harvey Broyles	December, 1954
Wade O. Martin	August, 1956
E. P. Roy	December, 1956
John McKeithen(Became Governor May, 1964)
Nat B. Knight	December, 1976
Ernest E. Clements	December, 1974
John S. Hunt	December, 1972
Ed Kennon.	**December, 1984**
George J. Ackel	**December, 1988**
John F. Schwegmann	**December, 1990**
Louis Lambert.	**December, 1992**
Thomas E. Powell.	**December, 1992**
Don Owen	**December, 1990**

TEZCUCO

SENATORS TO THE UNITED STATES CONGRESS FROM LOUISIANA

Name	Home.	Dates Served
Allen B. McGruder.............	Opelousas.............	Nov. 18, 1812-Mar. 3, 1813
John N. Destrehan*............	Destrehan............	
Thomas Posey..................	Attakapas............	Dec. 7, 1812-Feb. 4, 1813
James Brown...................	New Orleans..........	Feb. 5, 1813-Mar. 3, 1817
Elegius Fromentin.............	New Orleans..........	Mar. 4, 1813-Mar. 3, 1819
William C. C. Claiborne*......	New Orleans..........	
Henry Johnson.................	Donaldsonville........	Feb. 26, 1818-May 27, 1824
James Brown...................	New Orleans..........	Mar. 4, 1819-Dec. 10, 1823
Dominique Bouligny............	New Orleans..........	Dec. 21, 1824-Mar. 3, 1829
Josiah S. Johnston............	Alexandria...........	Mar. 12, 1824-May 19, 1833
Edward Livingston.............	New Orleans..........	Mar. 4, 1829-May 24, 1831
George A. Waggaman............	New Orleans..........	Nov. 15, 1831-Mar. 3, 1835
Alexander Porter.............	Attakapas............	Jan. 6, 1834-Jan. 5, 1837
Alexander Mouton..............	Vermilionville.......	Feb. 2, 1837-Mar. 1, 1842
Robert C. Nicholas...........	Donaldsonville.......	Mar. 4, 1836-Mar. 3, 1841
Charles E. A. Gayarre*........	New Orleans..........	
Charles M. Conrad.............	New Orleans..........	Apr. 14, 1842-Mar. 3, 1843
Alexander Barrow.............	Baton Rouge..........	Mar. 4, 1841-Dec. 29. 1846
Henry Johnson.................	New River............	Mar. 4, 1844-Mar. 3, 1849
Alexander Porter*............	Attakapas............	
Pierre Soule..................	New Orleans..........	Feb. 3, 1847-Mar. 3, 1847
Solomon W. Downs..............	Monroe...............	Mar. 4, 1847-Mar. 3, 1853
Pierre Soule..................	New Orleans..........	Mar. 4, 1849-Apr. 11, 1853
John Slidell..................	New Orleans..........	Dec. 5, 1853-Feb. 4, 1861
Judah P. Benjamin.............	New Orleans..........	Mar. 4, 1853-Feb. 4, 1861
John S. Harris...............	Vidalia..............	July 17, 1868-Mar. 3, 1871
William Pitt Kellogg..........	New Orleans..........	July 17, 1868-Nov. 1, 1872
J. Rodman West...............	New Orleans..........	Mar. 4, 1871-Mar. 3, 1877
James B. Eustis**.............	New Orleans..........	
William Pitt Kellogg..........	New Orleans..........	Nov. 30, 1877-Mar. 3, 1883
James B. Eustis..............	New Orleans..........	Jan. 12, 1876-Mar. .3, 1879
Benjamin F. Jonas.............	New Orleans..........	Mar. 4, 1879-Mar. 3, 1885
Randall L. Gibson.............	New Orleans..........	Mar. 4, 1883-Dec. 15, 1892
James B. Eustis..............	New Orleans..........	Mar. 4, 1885-Mar. 3, 1891
Donelson Caffery.............	Franklin.............	Jan. 14, 1893-Mar. 3, 1901
Edward Douglass White........	New Orleans..........	Mar. 4, 1891-Mar. 12, 1894
Newton C. Blanchard..........	Shreveport...........	Mar. 12, 1894-Mar. 3, 1897
Samuel D. McEnery............	New Orleans..........	Mar. 4, 1897-June 28, 1910
Murphy J. Foster.............	Franklin.............	Mar. 4, 1901-Mar. 3, 1913
John R. Thornton.............	Alexandria...........	Dec. 12, 1910-Mar. 3, 1915
Joseph E. Ransdell...........	Lake Providence.......	Mar. 4, 1913-Mar. 3, 1931
Robert F. Broussard..........	New Iberia...........	Mar. 4, 1915-Apr. 12, 1918
Walter Guion.................	Napoleonville........	Apr. 24, 1918-Nov. 5, 1918
Edward J. Gay.................	Plaquemine...........	Dec. 2, 1918-Mar. 3, 1921
Edwin S. Broussard...........	New Iberia...........	Mar. 4, 1921-Mar. 3, 1933
Huey P. Long.................	New Orleans..........	Jan. 25, 1932-Sept 10, 1935
John H. Overton..............	Alexandria...........	Mar. 4. 1933-May 14, 1948
Rose McConnell Long..........	New Orleans..........	Feb. 10, 1936-Jan. 3, 1937
Allen J. Ellender............	Houma................	Jan. 3, 1937-July 27, 1972
William C. Feazel............	West Monroe..........	May 24, 1948-Dec. 30, 1948
Russell B. Long.	Shreveport.	Dec. 31, 1948-Jan. 2, 1987
Elaine Edwards	Crowley	Aug. 7, 1972-Nov. 13, 1972
J. Bennett Johnston.	Shreveport.	Nov. 14, 1972-
John Breaux.	Crowley	Jan. 3, 1987-

*Never qualified for office
**Contested election, no action taken in 44th Congress

Source: Biographical Directory of the American Congress, 1774-1971

REPRESENTATIVES TO THE UNITED STATES CONGRESS FROM LOUISIANA

Name	Home	Dates Served
Daniel Clark*...................	New Orleans..........	Dec. 1, 1806-Mar. 3, 1809
Julien de L. Poydras*..........	New Orleans..........	Mar. 4, 1809-Mar. 3, 1811
Allen B. McGruder**............	Opelousas............	
Elegius Fromentin**............	New Orleans..........	

District 1

Thomas Robertson...............	New Orleans..........	Dec. 23, 1812-Apr. 20, 1818
Thomas Butler..................	St. Francisville......	Nov. 16, 1818-Mar. 3, 1821
Josiah S. Johnston.............	Alexandria...........	Mar. 4, 1821-Mar. 3, 1823
Edward Livingston..............	New Orleans..........	Mar. 4, 1823-Mar. 3, 1829
Edward D. White................	Donaldsonville.......	Mar. 4, 1829-Nov. 15, 1834
Henry Johnson..................	Donaldsonville.......	Dec. 1, 1834-Mar. 3, 1839
Edward D. White................	Thibodaux............	Mar. 4, 1839-Mar. 3, 1843
John Slidell...................	New Orleans..........	Mar. 4, 1843-Nov. 10, 1845
Emile LaSere...................	New Orleans..........	Jan. 29, 1846-Mar. 3, 1851
Louis St. Martin...............	New Orleans..........	Mar. 4, 1851-Mar. 3, 1853
William Dunbar.................	New Orleans..........	Mar. 4, 1853-Mar. 3, 1855
George Eustis, Jr..............	New Orleans..........	Mar. 4, 1855-Mar. 3, 1859
John E. Bouligny...............	New Orleans..........	Mar. 4, 1859-Mar. 3, 1861
Benjamin F. Flanders***........	New Orleans..........	Feb. 17, 1863-Mar. 3, 1863
J. Hale Sypher.................	New Orleans..........	July 18, 1868-Mar. 3, 1869
J. Hale Sypher****.............	New Orleans..........	Dec. 5, 1870-Mar. 3, 1875
Randall L. Gibson..............	New Orleans..........	Mar. 4, 1875-Mar. 3, 1883
Carleton Hunt..................	New Orleans..........	Mar. 4, 1883-Mar. 3, 1885
Louis St. Martin...............	New Orleans..........	Mar. 4, 1885-Mar. 3, 1887
Theodore S. Wilkinson..........	Plaquemines Parish....	Mar. 4, 1887-Mar. 3, 1891
Adolph Meyer...................	New Orleans..........	Mar. 4, 1891-Mar. 8, 1908
Albert Estopinal...............	Estopinal............	Dec. 7, 1908-Apr. 28, 1919
James O'Connor.................	New Orleans..........	June 10, 1919-Mar. 3, 1931
Joachim O. Fernandez...........	New Orleans..........	Mar. 4, 1931-Jan. 3, 1941
F. Edward Hebert...............	New Orleans..........	Jan. 3, 1941-Jan. 3, 1976
Richard A. Tonry*****..........	Chalmette............	Jan. 3, 1976-May 4, 1976
Robert L. Livingston...........	New Orleans..........	Sep. 7, 1977-

District 2

Henry Gurley...................	Baton Rouge..........	Mar. 4, 1823-Mar. 3, 1831
Philemon Thomas................	Baton Rouge..........	Mar. 4, 1831-Mar. 3, 1835
Eleazer W. Ripley..............	Jackson..............	Mar. 4, 1835-Mar. 3, 1839
Thomas W. Chinn................	Baton Rouge..........	Mar. 4, 1839-Mar. 3, 1841
John B. Dawson.................	St. Francisville.....	Mar. 4, 1841-Mar. 3, 1843
Alcee L. LaBranche.............	New Orleans..........	Mar. 4, 1843-Mar. 3, 1845
Bannon G. Thibodeaux...........	Thibodaux............	Mar. 4, 1845-Mar. 3, 1849
Charles M. Conrad..............	New Orleans..........	Mar. 4, 1849-Aug. 17, 1850
Henry A. Bullard...............	New Orleans..........	Dec. 5, 1850-Mar. 3, 1851
J. Aristide Landry.............	Donaldsonville.......	Mar. 4, 1851-Mar. 3, 1853
Theodore G. Hunt...............	New Orleans..........	Mar. 4, 1853-Mar. 3, 1855
Miles Taylor...................	Donaldsonville.......	Mar. 4, 1855-Feb. 5, 1861
Michael Hahn***................	New Orleans..........	Feb. 17, 1863-Mar. 3, 1863
James Mann.....................	New Orleans..........	July 18, 1868-Aug. 26, 1868
Lionel A. Sheldon..............	New Orleans..........	Apr. 8, 1869-Mar. 3, 1875
E. John Ellis..................	New Orleans..........	Mar. 4, 1875-Mar. 3, 1885
Michael Hahn...................	New Orleans..........	Mar. 4, 1885-Mar. 15, 1886
Nathaniel D. Wallace...........	New Orleans..........	Dec. 9, 1886-Mar. 3, 1887

* Delegate from Orleans Territory
** Agent only, not voting delegate, granted floor privileges Mar. 6, 1812
*** Took office by resolution of Congress upon presentation of credentials
**** Contested election
***** Resigned because of vote fraud

Matthew D. Lagan...............	New Orleans...........	Mar. 4, 1887-Mar. 3, 1889
Hamilton D. Coleman............	New Orleans...........	Mar. 4, 1889-Mar. 3, 1891
Matthew D. Lagan...............	New Orleans...........	Mar. 4, 1891-Mar. 3, 1893
Robert C. Davey................	New Orleans...........	Mar. 4, 1893-Mar. 3, 1895
Charles F. Buck................	New Orleans...........	Mar. 4, 1895-Mar. 3, 1897
Robert C. Davey................	New Orleans...........	Mar. 4, 1897-Dec. 26, 1908
Samuel L. Gilmore..............	New Orleans...........	Apr. 22, 1909-July 18, 1910
H. Garland Dupre...............	New Orleans...........	Dec. 12, 1910-Feb. 21, 1924
J. Zach Spearing...............	New Orleans...........	May 15, 1924-Mar. 3, 1931
Paul H. Maloney................	New Orleans...........	Mar. 4, 1931-Dec. 15, 1940
T. Hale Boggs..................	New Orleans...........	Jan. 3, 1941-Jan. 3, 1943
Paul H. Maloney................	New Orleans...........	Jan. 3, 1943-Jan. 3, 1947
T. Hale Boggs*.................	New Orleans...........	Jan. 3, 1947-Jan. 3, 1973
Lindy Boggs....................	New Orleans...........	Mar. 28, 1973-

District 3

William L. Brent...............	St. Martinville.......	Mar. 4, 1823-Mar. 3, 1829
Walter H. Overton..............	Alexandria............	Mar. 4, 1829-Mar. 3, 1831
Henry A. Bullard...............	Alexandria............	Mar. 4, 1831-Jan. 4, 1834
Rice Garland...................	Opelousas.............	Apr. 28, 1834-Aug. 31, 1840
John Moore.....................	Franklin..............	Dec. 17, 1840-Mar. 3, 1843
Pierre E. J. B. Bossier........	Natchitoches..........	Mar. 4, 1843-Apr. 21, 1844
Isaac E. Morse.................	St. Martinville.......	Dec. 2, 1844-Mar. 3, 1851
John Moore.....................	New Iberia............	Mar. 4, 1851-Mar. 3, 1853
Roland Jones...................	Shreveport............	Mar. 4, 1853-Mar. 3, 1855
John M. Sandidge...............	Pineville.............	Mar. 4, 1855-Mar. 3, 1859
John M. Landrum................	Shreveport............	Mar. 4, 1859-Mar. 3, 1861
Michel Vidal...................	Opelousas.............	July 18, 1868-Mar. 3, 1869
Chester B. Darrall.............	Brashear..............	July 6, 1870-Feb. 20, 1878
Joseph H. Acklen...............	Pattersonville........	Feb. 20, 1878-Mar. 3, 1881
Chester B. Darrall.............	Morgan City...........	Mar. 4, 1881-Mar. 3, 1883
William Pitt Kellogg...........	New Orleans...........	Mar. 4, 1883-Mar. 3, 1885
Edward J. Gay..................	Plaquemine............	Mar. 4, 1885-May 30, 1889
Andrew Price...................	Thibodaux.............	Dec. 2, 1889-Mar. 3, 1897
Robert F. Broussard............	New Iberia............	Mar. 4, 1897-Mar. 3, 1915
Whitmell P. Martin.............	Thibodaux.............	Mar. 4, 1915-Apr. 6, 1929
Numa F. Montet.................	Thibodaux.............	Oct. 14, 1929-Jan. 3, 1937
Robert L. Mouton...............	Lafayette.............	Jan. 3, 1937-Jan. 3, 1941
James Domengeaux**.............	Lafayette.............	Jan. 3, 1941-Apr. 15, 1944
James Domengeaux...............	Lafayette.............	Nov. 7, 1944-Jan. 3, 1949
Edwin E. Willis................	St. Martinville.......	Jan. 3, 1949-Jan. 3, 1969
Patrick T. Caffery.............	New Iberia............	Jan. 3, 1969-Jan. 3, 1973
David C. Treen ....Metairie.. Jan. 3, 1973-Mar. 10, 1980
W. J. "Billy" Tauzin ....Metairie........................... May 22, 1980-

District 4

John B. Dawson.................	St. Francisville......	Mar. 4, 1843-Mar. 3, 1845
John H. Harmanson..............	Simmesport............	Mar. 4, 1845-Oct. 24, 1850
Alexander G. Penn..............	Covington.............	Dec. 30, 1850-Mar. 3, 1853
John Perkins, Jr...............	Ashwood...............	Mar. 4, 1853-Mar. 3, 1855
Thomas G. Davidson.............	East Feliciana Parish.	Mar. 4, 1855-Feb. 5, 1861
Joseph P. Newsham..............	St. Francisville......	July 18, 1968-Mar. 3, 1869
Joseph P. Newsham***...........	St. Francisville......	May 23, 1870-Mar. 3, 1871
James McCleery****.............	Shreveport............	

```
    * Seat officially declared vacant
   ** Resigned to enter service
  *** Successfully contested election
 **** Never qualified for office
```

Aleck Boarman...................	Shreveport...........	Dec.	3, 1872-Mar. 3, 1873
Samuel Peters*.................			
George L. Smith................	Shreveport...........	Dec.	3, 1873-Mar. 3, 1875
William M. Levy...............	Natchitoches.........	Mar.	4, 1875-Mar. 3, 1877
Joseph B. Elam................	Mansfield............	Mar.	4, 1877-Mar. 3, 1881
Newton C. Blanchard...........	Shreveport...........	Mar.	4, 1881-Mar. 12, 1894
Henry W. Ogden................	Benton...............	May	12, 1894-Mar. 3, 1899
Phanor Breazeale..............	Natchitoches.........	Mar.	4, 1899-Mar. 3, 1905
John T. Watkins...............	Minden...............	Mar.	4, 1905-Mar. 3, 1921
John N. Sandlin...............	Minden...............	Mar.	4, 1921-Jan. 3, 1937
Overton Brooks................	Shreveport...........	Jan.	3, 1937-Sep. 16, 1961
Joe D. Waggonner	Plain Dealing	Sept.	16, 1961-Jan. 3, 197
Claude "Buddy" Leach	Leesville	Jan.	3, 1979-Jan. 3, 198
Charles E. "Buddy" Roemer III***	Bossier City.	Jan.	3, 1981-Mar. 14, 198

District 5

W. Jasper Blackburn...........	Homer................	July	18, 1868-Mar. 3, 1869
Frank Morey...................	Monroe...............	Dec.	6, 1870-June 8, 1876
William B. Spencer............	Vidalia..............	June	8, 1876-Mar. 3, 1877
John E. Leonard...............	Lake Providence......	Mar.	4, 1877-Mar. 15, 1878
John S. Young.................	Homer................	Dec.	2, 1878-Mar. 3, 1879
J. Floyd King.................	Vidalia..............	Mar.	4, 1879-Mar. 3, 1887
Cherubusco Newton.............	Bastrop..............	Mar.	3, 1887-Mar. 3, 1889
Charles J. Boatner............	Monroe...............	Mar.	4, 1889-Mar. 20, 1896
Charles J. Boatner**..........	Monroe...............	Dec.	10, 1896-Mar. 3, 1897
Samuel T. Baird...............	Bastrop..............	Mar.	4, 1897-Apr. 22, 1899
Joseph E. Ransdell............	Lake Providence......	Dec.	4, 1899-Mar. 3, 1913
J. Walter Elder...............	Monroe...............	Mar.	4, 1913-Mar. 3, 1915
Riley J. Wilson...............	Harrisonburg.........	Mar.	4, 1915-Jan. 3, 1937
Newt V. Mills.................	Mer Rouge............	Jan.	3, 1937-Jan. 3, 1943
Charles E. McKenzie...........	Monroe...............	Jan.	3, 1943-Jan. 3, 1947
Otto E. Passman...............	Monroe...............	Jan.	3, 1947-Jan. 3, 1976
Jerry Huckaby.	Ringgold.	Jan.	3, 1977-

District 6

Charles E. Nash...............	Washington...........	Mar.	4, 1875-Mar. 3, 1877
Edward W. Robertson...........	Baton Rouge..........	Mar.	4, 1877-Mar. 3, 1883
Andrew S. Herron*.............			
Edward T. Lewis...............	Opelousas............	Dec.	3, 1883-Mar. 3, 1885
Alfred B. Irion...............	Marksville...........	Mar.	4, 1885-Mar. 3, 1887
Edward W. Robertson...........	Baton Rouge..........	Mar.	4, 1887-Aug. 2, 1887
Samuel M. Robertson...........	Baton Rouge..........	Dec.	5, 1887-Mar. 3, 1907
George K. Favrot..............	Baton Rouge..........	Mar.	4, 1907-Mar. 3, 1909
Robert C. Wickliffe...........	St. Francisville.....	Mar.	4, 1909-June 11, 1912
Lewis L. Morgan...............	Covington............	Dec.	2, 1912-Mar. 3, 1917
Jared Y. Sanders..............	Bogalusa.............	Mar.	4, 1917-Mar. 3, 1921
George K. Favrot..............	Baton Rouge..........	Mar.	4, 1921-Mar. 3, 1925
Bolivar E. Kemp...............	Amite................	Mar.	4, 1925-June 19, 1933
Jared Y. Sanders, Jr..........	Baton Rouge..........	May	21, 1934-Jan. 3, 1937
John K. Griffith..............	Slidell..............	Jan.	3, 1937-Jan. 3, 1941
Jared Y. Sanders, Jr..........	Baton Rouge..........	Jan.	3, 1941-Jan. 3, 1943
James H. Morrison.............	Hammond..............	Jan.	3, 1943-Jan. 3, 1967
John R. Rarick................	St. Francisville.....	Jan.	3, 1967-Jan. 3, 1975
W. Henson Moore.	Baton Rouge	Jan.	3, 1975-Jan. 3, 198
Richard Baker.	Baton Rouge	Jan.	3, 1987-

   * Never qualified for office
  ** Successfully contested election
***Special election to be called to fill this seat until
   January 3, 1989:

District 7

Arsene P. Pujo.................	Lake Charles..........	Mar. 4, 1903-Mar.	3, 1913
Ladislas Lazaro................	Washington...........	Mar. 4, 1913-Mar.	30, 1927
Rene L. DeRouen................	Ville Platte..........	Dec. 5, 1927-Jan.	3, 1941
Vance Plauche..................	Lake Charles..........	Jan. 3, 1941-Jan.	3, 1943
Henry D. Larcade, Jr..........	Opelousas.............	Jan. 3, 1943-Jan.	3, 1953
T. Ashton Thompson............	Ville Platte..........	Jan. 3, 1953-July	1, 1965
Edwin W. Edwards..............	Crowley..............	Oct. 18, 1965-May	9, 1972
John B. Breaux	**Crowley**	**Oct. 12, 1972-Jan.**	**3, 1987**
James Hayes.	**Lafayette**	**Jan. 3, 1987-**	

District 8

James B. Aswell................	Natchitoches..........	Mar. 4, 1913-Mar.	16, 1931
John H. Overton................	Alexandria...........	Dec. 7, 1931-Mar.	3, 1933
Cleveland Dear.................	Alexandria...........	Mar. 4, 1933-Jan.	3, 1937
A. Leonard Allen..............	Winnfield............	Jan. 3, 1937-Jan.	3, 1953
George S. Long.................	Pineville............	Jan. 3, 1953-Mar.	22, 1958
Harold B. McSween.............	Alexandria...........	Jan. 3, 1959-Jan.	3, 1963
Gillis W. Long................	Winnfield............	Jan. 3, 1963-Jan.	3, 1965
Speedy O. Long................	Jena................	Jan. 3, 1965-Jan.	3, 1973
Gillis W. Long	**Winnfield**	**Jan. 3, 1973-Jan.**	**20, 1985**
Cathy Long	**Winnfield**	**Apr. 3, 1985-Jan.**	**3, 1987**
Clyde Holloway	**Forest Hill**	**Jan. 3, 1987-**	

At Large

George A. Sheridan*..........	Lake Providence.......	Mar. 3, 1875-Mar.	3, 1875

* Successfully contested election, took seat Mar. 3, 1875, served one day

Sources: *Biographical Directory of the American Congress, 1774-1971* and Louisiana Office of the Secretary of State

PENTAGON

THE SUPERIOR COURT OF THE TERRITORY OF ORLEANS

Name	Dates Served
Ephraim Kirby......... Mar	1804-Oct 2, 1804
John B. Prevost....... Mar	1804-Nov 14, 1808
William Sprigg........ Jan 17,	1806-Nov 10, 1806
George Matthews....... Jan 19,	1806-Mar 1, 1813
Joshua Lewis.......... Nov 10,	1806-Mar 1, 1813
John Thompson......... Nov 14,	1808-Mar 21, 1810
Francois-X. Martin.... Mar 21,	1810-Mar 1, 1813

THE SUPREME COURT OF THE STATE OF LOUISIANA

Name	Dates Served
Dominick A. Hall...... Mar	1, 1813-Jul 3, 1813
George Matthews....... Mar	1, 1813-Nov 14, 1836
Pierre Derbigny....... Mar	9, 1813-Dec 15, 1820
Francois-X. Martin.... Feb	1, 1815-Mar 19, 1846
Alexander Porter, Jr.. Jan	2, 1821-Dec 16, 1833
Henry Adams Bullard... Feb	4, 1834-Feb 1, 1839
Henry Carleton........ Apr	1, 1837-Feb 1, 1839
Pierre Adolphe Rose... Mar	4, 1839-Jun 30, 1839
George Eustis........ Mar	4, 1839-May 30, 1839
George Strawbridge.... Aug	3, 1839-Dec 1, 1839
Alonzo Morphy......... Aug 31,	1839-Mar 19, 1846
Edward Simon.......... Jan	1, 1840-Mar 19, 1846
Rice Garland.......... Jan	1, 1840-Mar 19, 1846
Henry A. Bullard...... Jan	1, 1840-Mar 19, 1846
*GEORGE EUSTIS......... Mar 19,	1846-May 4, 1853
Pierre Adolphe Rost... Mar 19,	1846-May 4, 1853
George Rogers King.... Mar 19,	1846-Mar 1, 1850
Thomas Slidell........ Mar 19,	1846-May 4, 1853
Isaac T. Preston...... Mar	1, 1850-Jul 5, 1852
William Dunbar....... Sep	1, 1852-May 4, 1853
*THOMAS SLIDELL........ May	4, 1853-Jun 18, 1855
Cornelius Voorhies.... May	4, 1853-Apr 27, 1859
Alexander M. Buchanan. May	4, 1853-May 6, 1862
Abner Nash Ogden...... May	4, 1853-Jun 30, 1855
James G. Campbell..... May	4, 1853-Oct 17, 1854
Henry M. Spofford..... Nov	6, 1854-Nov 1, 1858
James N. Lea......... Jul 23,	1855-Apr 6, 1857
*EDWIN T. MERRICK..... Aug	1, 1855-Apr 1, 1865
James L. Cole......... May	4, 1857-Mar 12, 1860
Thomas T. Land....... Nov	1, 1858-Apr 1, 1865
Albert Voorhies...... May	3, 1859-Apr 1, 1865
Albert Duffel......... Mar 12,	1860-Apr 1, 1865
Peter F. Bonford.....	1863- 1864
Thomas C. Manning....	1864- 1865
*WILLIAM B. HYMAN...... Apr	1, 1865-Nov 1, 1868
Zenon Labauve........ Apr	1, 1865-Nov 1, 1868
John H. Ilsley....... Apr	1, 1865-Nov 1, 1868
Rufus K. Howell...... Apr	1, 1865-Jan 9, 1877
Robert B. Jones...... Apr	1, 1865-Jul 1, 1866
James G. Taliaferro.. Jul	1, 1866-Nov 3, 1876
*JOHN T. LUDELING..... Nov	1, 1868-Jan 9, 1877
William G. Wyly...... Nov	1, 1868-Nov 3, 1876
William Wirt Howe.... Nov	1, 1868-Dec 3, 1872
John H. Kennard...... Dec	3, 1872-Feb 1, 1873
Philip H. Morgan..... Feb	1, 1873-Jan 9, 1877
John E. Leonard..... Nov	3, 1876-Jan 9, 1877
John Edward King..... Jan	9, 1877-Jan 9, 1877
*THOMAS C. MANNING..... Jan	9, 1877-Apr 5, 1880
Robert H. Marr....... Jan	9, 1877-Apr 5, 1880
Alcibiades DeBlanc.... Jan	9, 1877-Apr 5, 1880
William B. Egan...... Jan	9, 1877-Nov 30, 1878
William B. Spencer.... Jan	9, 1877-Apr 5, 1880
Edward D. White....... Jan 11,	1879-Apr 5, 1880
*EDWARD BERMUDEZ....... Apr	5, 1880-Apr 5, 1892
Felix P. Poche....... Apr	5, 1880-Apr 5, 1890
Robert B. Todd....... Apr	5, 1880-Jun 11, 1888
William B. Levy...... Apr	5, 1880-Nov 5, 1882
Charles E. Fenner..... Apr	5, 1880-Sep 1, 1893
Thomas C. Manning.... Dec	1, 1882-Apr 19, 1886
Lynn B. Watkins....... Apr 19,	1886-Mar 2, 1901

Name	Dates Served
Samuel D. McEnery..... Jun 11,	1888-Mar 4, 1897
Joseph A. Breaux...... Apr	5, 1890-Apr 4, 1904
*FRANCIS T. NICHOLLS... Apr	5, 1892-Apr 4, 1904
Charles Parlange...... Sep	1, 1893-Jan 1, 1894
Henry Carleton Miller. Feb	1, 1894-Mar 4, 1899
Newton C. Blanchard... Mar	4, 1897-Oct 17, 1903
Frank Adair Monroe.... Mar 22,	1899-Apr 4, 1914
Olivier O. Provosty... Mar 16,	1901-Jan 1, 1922
Alfred D. Land....... Oct 17,	1903-Jun 4, 1917
Francis T. Nicholls... Apr	4, 1904-Mar 18, 1911
*JOSEPH A. BREAUX..... Apr	5, 1904-Apr 5, 1914
Walter B. Sommerville. Mar 18,	1911-Oct 15, 1921
*FRANK ADAIR MONROE.... Apr	5, 1914-Jan 2, 1922
Charles A. O'Niell.... Apr	6, 1914-Dec 30, 1922
**Paul Leche......... Jun 12,	1917-Dec 7, 1918
Ben C. Dawkins........ Dec 10,	1918-May 17, 1924
Winston Overton...... Jul	5, 1921-Sep 9, 1934
John R. Land.......... Oct 13,	1921-Apr 18, 1941
Joshua G. Baker....... Oct 15,	1921-Nov 27, 1922
*OLIVIER O. PROVOSTY... Jan	2, 1922-Dec 30, 1922
John St. Paul........ Jan	2, 1922-Apr 30, 1934
Wynne G. Rogers....... Nov 27,	1922-Sep 15, 1946
David N. Thompson.... Dec	5, 1922-Dec 1, 1930
**Paul Leche.......... Dec	5, 1922-Jan 27, 1923
*CHARLES A. O'NIELL.... Dec 30,	1922-Sep 7, 1949
Robert R. Reid........ Jan	2, 1923-Jan 14, 1923
Harney F. Brunot...... Jun	4, 1923-Dec 31, 1936
**Paul Leche......... Oct	1, 1923-Oct 1, 1923
Frederick M. Odom..... Jan	1, 1931-Dec 20, 1944
Archibald T. Higgins.. Sep 19,	1934-Oct 3, 1945
John B. Fournet...... Jan	2, 1935-Sep 7, 1949
Amos L. Ponder, Jr.... Jan	4, 1937-Oct 19, 1959
**E. Howard McCaleb..... May 23,	1941-Jan 1, 1943
Joe B. Hamiter........ Jan	1, 1943-Aug 1, 1970
Frank W. Hawthorne.... Jan	1, 1945-Jan 2, 1968
**Robert F. Kennon..... Oct 15,	1945-Dec 31, 1946
E. Howard McCaleb..... Jan	1, 1947-Dec 31, 1970
Nat W. Bond.......... Jun	2, 1947-Feb 18, 1948
Harold A. Moise...... May 10,	1948-Sep 26, 1958
*JOHN B. FOURNET...... Sep	7, 1949-Jul 31, 1970
**J. Cleveland Fruge... Sep	8, 1949-Dec 12, 1949
Sam A. LeBlanc....... Dec 12,	1949-Dec 31, 1954
James D. Simon...... Jan	1, 1955-Aug 23, 1960
Walter B. Hamlin...... Dec 15,	1958-Dec 26, 1972
Rene A. Viosca........ Oct 19,	1959-Nov 7, 1960
Joe W. Sanders....... Nov	7, 1960-Mar 14, 1973
Frank Summers........ Dec 12,	1960--Jan 1,1979
*Louis H. Yarrut...... Jan	2, 1968-Feb 12, 1968
Mack E. Barham....... Feb 12,	1968--Sep15,1975
**Edward L. Gladney..... Apr	1, 1968
*JOE B. HAMITER........ Aug	1, 1970-Dec 31, 1970
Albert Tate, Jr.......	.Aug 1, 1970-Nov 3, 1979
** H. W. Ayres	.Oct 7, 1970-Apr 30, 1975
** Edward L. Gladney . . .	.Dec 1, 1970
* E. HOWARD McCALEB.	.Dec 31, 1970-Dec 22, 1972
John A. Dixon, Jr. . . .	.Jan 4, 1971-Feb 29, 1980
* WALTER B. HAMLIN.	.Dec 26, 1972-Mar 13, 1973
Pascal Calogero, Jr . . .	.Jan 15, 1973-
Walter F. Marcus, Jr. .	.Mar 13, 1973-
* JOE W. SANDERS . . .	.Mar 14, 1973-Dec 31, 1978
** James E. Bolin.	.Oct 8, 1975-Dec 7, 1975
James L. Dennis. . . .	.Dec 3, 1975-
* FRANK SUMMERS . . .	.Jan 1, 1979-Feb 29, 1980
Fred Blanche, Jr. . . .	.Jan 1, 1979-May 16, 1986
Jack C. Watson	.Nov 19, 1979-
* JOHN A. DIXON, JR. . .	.Mar 1, 1980-
Harry T. Lemmon. . . .	.May 1, 1980-
Luther F. Cole.	.May 19, 1986-

*Term served as chief justice
**Temporary assignment
Source: Judicial Administrator, State Supreme Court

WIVES OF LOUISIANA GOVERNORS

Governor	Term of Office	Maiden Name of Wives
William C. C. Claiborne........	1812-1816........	Eliza Lewis; Clarisse Duralde Suzette Bosque
Jacques Philippe Villere.......	1816-1820........	Jeanne Henriette Fazende
Thomas Bolling Robertson.......	1820-1824........	Lelia Skipwith
Henry Schuyler Thibodaux.......	1824-	Miss Lejeune; Brigitte Bellanger
Henry S. Johnson..............	1824-1828........	Elizabeth Key
Pierre Derbigny...............	1828-1829........	Felicite Odile de Hault de Lassus
Armand Beauvais...............	1829-1830........	
Jacques Dupre.................	1830-1831........	Theotiste Roy
Andre Bienvenu Roman..........	1831-1835........ 1839-1843	Aimee Francoise Parent
Edward Douglass White.........	1835-1839........	Catherine S. Ringgold
Alexandre Mouton..............	1843-1846........	Zelia Rousseau
Isaac Johnson.................	1846-1850........	Charlotte McDermott
Joseph Marshall Walker........	1850-1853........	Catherine Carter
Paul Octave Hebert............	1853-1856........	Cora Wills Vaughn; Penelope Lynch
Robert Charles Wickliffe......	1856-1860........	Anna Dawson; Anna Davis Anderson
Thomas Overton Moore..........	1860-1862........	Bertha Leonard
Gen. G. F. Shepley............	1862	
Henry Watkins Allen...........	1864-1865........	Salome Crane
Michael Hahn..................	1864-1865........	Not married
James Madison Wells...........	1865-1867........	Mary Ann Scott
Benjamin Flanders.............	1867-1868........	Susan H. Sawyer
Joshua Baker..................	1868	Fanny Assherton; Catherine Patton
Henry Clay Warmoth............	1868-1873........	Sally Durand
Pinckney B. S. Pinchback......	1873	Nina Emily Hawthorne
William Pitt Kellogg..........	1873-1877........	Mary Emily Wills
Francis T. Nicholls...........	1877-1880........ 1888-1892	Caroline Zilpha Guion
Louis Alfred Wiltz............	1880-1881........	Mildred Bienvenue
Samual Douglas McEnery........	1881-1888........	Elizabeth Phillips
Murphy James Foster..........	1892-1896........ 1896-1900	Rosa Rosetta Ker
William Wright Heard..........	1900-1904........	Isabelle Manning
Newton Crain Blanchard........	1904-1908........	Emily Barret; Charlotte Tracy
Jared Young Sanders...........	1908-1912........	Ada V. Shaw; Emma Dickinson
Luther Egbert Hall...........	1912-1916........	Clara Wendell
Ruffin G. Pleasant...........	1916-1920........	Ann Ector
John Milliken Parker..........	1920-1924........	Cecile Airey
Henry Luce Fuqua..............	1924-1926........	Laura Matta
Oramel H. Simpson.............	1926-1928........	Louise Pickett
Huey Pierce Long..............	1928-1931........	Rose McConnell
Alvin Olin King...............	1931-1932........	Willie Lee Voris
Oscar K. Allen................	1932-1936........	Florence Love
James Albert Noe..............	1936	Anna Gray
Richard Webster Leche.........	1936-1939........	Elton Reynolds
Earl Kemp Long................	1939-1940........ 1948-1952 1956-1960	Blanche B. Revere
Sam Houston Jones.............	1940-1944........	Louise Gambrell Boyer
James H. Davis................	1944-1948........ 1960-1964	Alverne Adams
Robert F. Kennon..............	1952-1956........	Eugenia Sentell
John J. McKeithen.............	1964-1972........	Marjorie Funderburk
Edwin W. Edwards	1972-1980.......	Elaine Schwartzenburg
David C. Treen	1980-1984.......	Dolores Brisbi
Edwin W. Edwards	1984-1988.......	Elaine Schwartzenburg
Charles E. "Buddy" Roemer III. . .	1988-	Patti Crocker

Source: Mrs. Elaine Edwards

THE CAPITOL

Louisiana's State Capitol, one of America's most beautiful, is the tallest building in the South. Thirty-four stories, 450 feet in height, it is erected on the site of the old campus of Louisiana State University, which now is converted into 27 acres of landscaped grounds. The Capitol was constructed in 14 months, from January 1, 1931 to March 1, 1932, at a cost of $5,000,000.

A magnificent building, visited by 30,000 persons each month, the Capitol's elaborateness lies in intricate and costly artistic interpretations of the state itself, for the story of Louisiana is the decorative theme of every detail and object that went into its construction. Yet the building is efficiently designed and provides 249,000 square feet—nearly six acres—of floor space for use of government agencies.

In the front of the building, broad steps of Minnesota granite are flanked by statuary of Lorado Taft, groups called "The Patriots" and "The Pioneers."

Famous artists and sculptors decorated the building—among them Lorado Taft, Jules Guerin, Angela Gregory, Adolph Weinman and Ulric Ellerheusen.

The Memorial Hall is the most sumptuous chamber of the building. Of huge proportions, 35 by 120 feet, the hall has a floor of polished lava from Mount Vesuvius. In the center of the floor is a huge bronze plaque on which is outlined in relief a map of Louisiana.

From the observation tower, almost 450 feet above the earth, it is possible to see the surrounding country for a distance of 30 miles.

Immediately in front of the Capitol is a perfectly patterned garden. Three giant century-old oaks worked into the landscape of the right break the symmetry of the garden, but on the left smaller trees overcome the unbalance. Flower beds make bright spots of color. Former Governor Huey P. Long, under whose aegis the Capitol was built, is buried in front of the Capitol, and a 12-ft. bronze statue by Charles Keck stands there.

*For further information consult *The Louisiana Capitol* by Vincent Kubly or *The Pelican Guide to the Louisiana Capitol*, by Ellen Roy Jolly and Jim Calhoun, both published by Pelican Publishing Company.

LOUISIANA LAW
LOUISIANA CIVIL LAW

Louisiana is the only state in the Union whose jurisdiction is based on the civil law. The other states are common law states. Briefly described, civil law is a code law or written law, common law is unwritten or case law; The Civil law is written law made up of systematic bodies of law composed of the broad general basic principles. While Civil law is drafted by authorities in the various fields of law and it must always be adopted by the legislative bodies.

Equally important is the fact that in the deciding issues presented to the court the judges interpret each of the separate facts presented to them in the light of the law itself, without the necessity of reference to or reliance upon prior interpretations of the same law in other cases regardless of any similarity of facts. One of the basic concepts of the civil law system is that the courts interpret the law applicable to each case. They rely almost totally on the written law as it may apply to each case.

Under the common law cases are decided on the basis of prior determination and earlier rulings of courts and judges. It should be pointed out that the real distinctions between civil law and common law as applied in the United States are becoming less rare in recent times than was true when Louisiana first became a state. In Louisiana today lawyers cite previous decided-cases in almost every case brought before the courts, and in almost every decision rendered the courts rely to some extent at least on the courts' interpretation of the law in prior cases. But the fact that the courts are not required to do so and are in no sense bound by such prior case law should not be lost sight of.

SUMMARY OF
LOUISIANA LAWS
OF GENERAL INTEREST

The following outline is designed to furnish general information only; when confronted with a specific problem, readers are advised to consult an attorney.

MARRIAGE:

Minimum age for marriage as to females is sixteen, and for males, eighteen. Minors must have the consent of their parents in order for the license to issue.

So-called common law marriages—i. e., those without the performance of a ceremony—are not recognized in Louisiana.

In all of the Parishes of Louisiana except the Parish of Orleans, licenses are issued by the clerks of court; in the Parish of Orleans licenses are obtained at the Board of Health, or they may be issued by the Judges of the City Court. The law authorizes the issuance of the license only at the domicile of one of the parties.

Parties applying for a license to marry must present a certificate by a licensed physician setting forth that they are free of venereal disease. The physical examination must have been made not more than ten days prior to the application for the license.

To obtain a marriage certificate both parties must present copies of their birth certificates and medical certificates at time of application.

The law requires a certified copy of the original birth certificate. Baptismal papers will not be accepted in lieu of birth records.

If no birth certificate is on file, Legislative Act 160 provides that "a letter signed by the proper registration authority with his seal or stamp affixed thereto must be surrendered to the officer issuing the marriage license in lieu of a birth certificate." The letter must state, in essence, that a thorough search was made and no birth record was found.

No license can be issued to authorize the following marriages, and even if it should the marriage would be void; between persons in the ascending or descending line, between brothers and sisters, aunts and nephews, uncles and nieces, or first cousins.

Those authorized to perform marriages are the following: minsters of the gospel, priests of any religious sect, parish judges, and justices of the peace. The license must be specifically directed to one of these persons.

Seventy-two hours must elapse between the issuance of the license and the performance of the ceremony. However, this delay may be shortened if in the opinion of the officer performing the marriage there is serious and grave reason to do so, and if he also first obtains the written consent of the Board of Health in the Parish of Orleans, or of the Clerk of Court in the other Parishes of Louisiana.

DIVORCE:

An immediate divorce can be had (1) by either spouse when the parties have been living separate and apart for six months, or (2) by one on the ground of adultery of the other, or (3) by one spouse when the other has been convicted of a felony and sentenced to death or hard labor. Separation from bed and board is granted on grounds of abandonment, habitual intemperance, cruel treatment, and other statutory causes. When a judgment of separation from bed and board is granted, final divorce can be obtained after the lapse of one year, provided there has been no intervening reconciliation of the parties.

In the event of divorce on the grounds of six months' separation, either spouse, if not at fault and if without sufficient means for support, may be granted alimony by the court out of the property and earnings of the other spouse (however, it shall not exceed one-third of the income of the paying spouse). In determining the entitlement and amount of alimony after divorce, the court shall consider the income, means, and assets of the spouses; the liquidity of such assets; the financial obligations of the spouses, including their earning capacity; the effect of caring for children of the marriage upon the custodial spouse's earning capacity; the time necessary for the recipient to acquire appropriate education, training, or employment; the health and age of the parties and their obligations to support or care for dependent children; and any other circumstances that the court deems relevant. During the pendency of the suit for divorce or separation, if the spouse has not a sufficient income for maintenance, the judge may allow the claimant spouse a sum for that spouse's support, proportioned to the needs of the claimant spouse and the means of the other spouse. The court may award alimony in lump sum rather than periodic payments, and this award may include property.

Custody of the child or children shall be granted to the husband or the wife, or to both jointly by agreement of both the husband and wife, in accordance with the best interest of the child or children; however, an award of joint custody may be granted only when the husband and wife are both domiciled in the State of Louisiana. No preference shall be given on the basis of the sex of the parent in cases where custody is awarded to only one parent. If one parent does not receive whole or partial custody, he or she is nevertheless entitled to visit them at reasonable times and places, which if necessary the court will fix.

Louisiana courts have jurisdiction in divorce or separation procedures if one or both spouses are Louisiana domiciliaries, and "except as otherwise provided by law," if the grounds were committed in Louisiana, or while the marriage was domiciled in Louisiana.

There is a presumption of domicile if a spouse has established and maintained residence in this state for a period of twelve months. On the other hand, a person who has moved to Louisiana need not wait for the passage of the twelve-month period if his intention and acts are such that he can thereby establish domicile without the benefit of the presumption.

COMMUNITY PROPERTY SYSTEM

Separate property is that which one spouse already has when the marital community arises; that which one spouse may receive during marriage by gift or inheritance; property acquired by a spouse with separate things or with separate and community things when the value of the community things is inconsequential in comparison with the value of the separate things used; damages awarded to a spouse in an action for breach of contract against the other spouse or for the loss sustained as a result of fraud or bad faith in the management of community property by the other spouse; damages or other indemnity awarded to a spouse in connection with the management of his separate property; and things acquired by a spouse as a result of a voluntary partition of the community during the existence of a community property regime.

Community property generally embraces all other property which the spouses, or either of them, acquire during marriage. The Code defines it as property acquired during the existence of the legal regime through the effort, skill, or industry of either spouse.

If community funds are used to improve the separate property of a spouse, or if separate funds are employed for the acquisition or betterment of community property, an adjustment is made in the settlement of the community on its termination.

A community property system can be ended by the death of either the husband or wife, by a legal separation, by a divorce, by a contract between the husband and the wife or by a court judgment setting up a separate property system instead of a community property system. Although the patrimony of each spouse includes only an undivided one-half of the mass of the community property, each spouse has by provision of law the right to manage and to dispose of the entire mass and the things that compose it, subject to certain exceptions as provided in the code. However, a spouse may not alienate, incumber, or lease to a third person his undivided interest in the community or in particular things of the community prior to the termination of the regime.

Even though the husband and wife both own community property, some of it can be sold by one of them alone and some of it cannot be sold, mortgaged or leased unless the husband and wife both agree. For example, both husband and wife are needed for the sale, mortgage or lease of real estate, of furniture located in their family home, of a community business or of things registered in both of their names. Both spouses must also be in agreement before expensive gifts can be given. In some instances, either the husband or wife alone can sell, mortgage, or lease community property even if the other disagrees. For example, things that do not have a registered title can be sold by either one of them. Also things that are registered in one name alone can be sold by just the one in whose name it is registered.

INHERITANCE:

A variety of forms for wills is provided, the simplest form being the holographic will, which must be wholly written, dated, and signed in the handwriting of the testator. Other forms for wills are available to suit particular needs and circumstances. Careful drafting by an experienced counsellor is always advisable in order to protect and fulfill the wishes of the maker of the will.

A unique feature of Louisiana law is its doctrine of forced heirship. This doctrine, of course, only comes into play when the decedent leaves a will; it requires that he leave at least a certain portion of his estate to his children. If decedent leaves one child, he is entitled to a minimum of one-third; if he leaves two or more children, they must receive one-half. Children cannot be deprived of this inheritance by a will, except upon certain statutory grounds provided in the code. (The legitimacy of the relationship between the decedent and children is irrelevant.)

If there is no will, the children of the decedent inherit his entire estate. If the deceased leaves no descendants but is survived by a father, mother, or both, and by a brother or sister, or both, or descendants from them, the brothers and sisters or their descendants succeed to the separate property of the deceased subject to a usufruct in favor of the surviving parent or parents. If both parents survive the deceased, the usufruct shall be joint and successive. And if there be no children and no brothers and sisters, but a surviving parent or parents, the latter will succeed to the separate property to the exclusion of other ascendants and other collaterals.

The rules just stated always apply to the disposition of the decedent's separate property in the absence of a will. With respect to the decedent's interest in the community p r o p e r t y, however, special rules exist favoring the surviving spouse of the marriage. If the decedent has not disposed of his share of the community property by testament, the surviving spouse has the usufruct over so much of that share as is inherited by descendants, whether or not those descendants are issue of the marriage with the surviving spouse. This usufruct ends if the surviving spouse remarries, unless the usufruct is confirmed by testament for life or a shorter period. If there are no children or descendants surviving, and no will, the surviving spouse inherits the decedent's share of the community property. A surviving spouse not judicially separated will also succeed to the decedent's separate property when he leaves no descendants, parents, or siblings or their descendants, inheriting ahead of other ascendants and collaterals.

Adopted persons have rights as forced heirs along with any natural forced heirs. The Civil Code has many particular provisions concerning inheritance, such as those regarding division between brothers and sisters of the whole and the half blood, representation by children and their parents in the successions of grandparents, and other rules too detailed to mention here.

LIMITATIONS AND PRESCRIPTIONS:

Actions for damages for personal injuries, death, or damage to property all must be brought within one year.

Likewise, actions by laborers or workmen for unpaid wages must be brought within one year.

A three-year limitation is applicable to suits for rent, demands by physicians or attorneys for their fees, and actions on open accounts for merchandise or goods purchased.

Promissory notes prescribe in five years.

Actions on contracts generally must be brought within ten years.

A partial payment upon an indebtedness or an oral acknowledgement and promise to pay will interrupt the limitations upon an indebtedness before prescription accrues. Once the limitation has run, only a written promise or acknowledgment will remove the bar.

Mineral servitudes are lost in ten years for non-user. They may be interrupted by appropriate written acknowledgement by the land owner, or by actual drilling even though such drilling results in a dry hole. This prescription does not run against minors.

Royalty rights prescribe in ten years unless there is actual production within this period. This limitation does run against minors.

Land may be acquired by ten years adverse possession where the possessor bought under an apparently valid title and was in good faith, having no knowledge of any defects. Once having commenced to run, the ten-year period will not be lengthened by the subsequent inheritance of ownership by a minor. Otherwise, the acquisitive period of adverse possession is suspended during minority. The age of majority is now eighteen.

Thirty years open and adverse possession is sufficient to establish title to land by prescription without regard to good faith or an apparently valid title.

In certain instances, successive purchases can add the adverse possession of former owners to their own in order to make out the full period required for prescription.

THE LOUISIANA ADOPTION LAW

The legal adoption of children placed by a licensed agency or by the Department of Public Welfare is quite a simple procedure. When the child has been in the home six months and the agency gives permission, your attorney should file a petition for adoption in the Juvenile or District Court for your parish or in the parish where the agency is located. Some agencies require that petitions be filed in New Orleans by their own attorneys, believing that attorneys who are specialists in this work can be more sure that the adoption is legally sound.

The Department of Public Welfare is required by law to report to the Court the facts about your adoption, but where the child has been placed by an agency, this information is u s u a l l y gathered without a worker from the Welfare Department having to visit your home. The parents of your child are not notified of the hearing and do not appear. Their rights to the child have been legally ended before the child comes to your home.

There will be a private hearing in the judge's office 30 to 60 days after your petition is filed. Except in very rare cas-

es, you will then receive your final adopt-
tion papers.

CIVIL SERVICE RULES
GOVERNING POLITICAL ACTIVITIES

The Civil Service Law by protecting classified
employees from discrimination or disciplinary
action because of their political opinions or
affiliations preserves the political freedom of
each employee, enabling him to vote for the candidate of his choice without fear of punishment
or reprisal. To achieve this, the law provides for
serious penalties for the coercion or intimidation
of, favoritism toward or discrimination against
a classified employee because of his political
views but not without placing certain restrictions on the political activity of employees in the
classified service. The evident purpose of these
restrictions is to promote efficiency and integ-
rity in the public service and to insure that the
funds and energy of the classified employee shall
not be used to the detriment of efficient government administration.

Specific prohibitions governing Civil Service
employees include the following:

Take no part in the management or affairs
of any political faction or party or in any political
campaign and more particularly —

Do not solicit votes or contributions

Do not make a political contribution

Do not make a public political statement or
address

Do not wear a campaign badge, ribbon or insig-
nia

Do not distribute political campaign cards,
buttons or posters

Do not influence or attempt to influence the
vote of another

Do not become a candidate for office, serve as
a member of any political committee or take part
in the management or affairs of a political party
or organization.

Do not publicly display political campaign lite-
rature or placards on personal property.

RECIPROCAL SUPPORT LAW

Louisiana was the 41st state to adopt a
reciprocal support law. It can be enforced against men and women who leave
the state, leaving their families without
means of support. Their salaries can be
garnished or they can be haled into court
in any one of forty states reciprocating
with each other and forced to pay alimony or to support their families. Illegit-
imate children are likewise entitled to
assistance.

WORKMEN'S COMPENSATION LAW

Employees working in factories, mills,
construction, building operation and haz-
ardous occupations in Louisiana are covered by the Workmen's Compensation
Law. If a person is injured in an accident
(including death) the disability benefits
shall be as follows:

For injury producing temporary total disability to engage in any gainful work, sixty-six
and two-thirds percent of wages during the period of such disability.

For injury producing permanent total disability to engage in any gainful work, sixty-six

and two-thirds percent of wages during the period of such disability.

For injury causing death within two years of
the accident, legal dependents of the deceased
shall be granted a weekly sum to be determined
in each case. For legal dependents only partially dependent on the deceased party, weekly
payments will be determined on the basis of
the deceased party's contribution to support at
the time of injury.

If the deceased employee leaves no legal
dependents, the lump sum of twenty thousand
dollars shall be paid to each surviving parent of
the employee.

Employers are also required to furnish to
the employee all necessary medical expenses,
prosthetic devices, or additional expenses incurred due to the injury. In the event of death,
the employer is required to pay, in addition to
all other expenses, the reasonable costs for burial, not to exceed three thousand dollars.

In the case of personal injury (including death) resulting therefrom, all claims
for payments will be barred forever unless made within one year after the accident. The attorney fees are filed by the
court and shall not in any case exceed
20%. Excessive fees or gratuities, or solic-
itation for accident compensation are subject to fine and imprisonment.

It is unlawful for any employer to collect from any of his employee directly or
indirectly any payment toward the pre-
mium for liability insurance.

Source: Office of the Attorney General,
         Kendall L. Vicks

LICENSE CODE

Ever wonder about those letters bisecting
your auto license? They represent the State
Highway Patrol Troop locations, each letter
being the designation of a troop. The letter "X"
represents licenses issued in Baton Rouge by
mail. The other 13 represent these troop head-
quarters: "A" Baton Rouge; "B" New Orleans;
"C" New Iberia and Franklin; "D" Lake Charles;
"E" Alexandria and Natchitoches; "F" Monroe;
"G" Shreveport; "H" Leesville; "I" Lafayette;
"K" Opelousas; "L" Covington, Bogalusa and
Hammond.

LOUISIANA CORRECTIONAL INSTITUTIONS

LOUISIANA TRAINING INSTITUTE - PINEVILLE

This institution was established in 1926 for juvenile girls adjudged to be delinquent or neglected in their community. The decision for sending these girls to this agency is made by either a juvenile court or district courts sitting as juvenile courts. The institution encompasses forty acres of beautifully landscaped grounds with pine and hardwood trees. The property is located ten miles north of Alexandria on Highway No. 175.

This institution operates programs that are conducive to instill in each student high moral principles, a faith and confidence in herself as well as her neignbor, and to return each girl to her community a better adjusted and useful citizen.

Courses taught in the school include:

1. Home Economics - Includes meal preparation, sewing, laundry care, interior decorating, and personal hygiene.

2. Nurses Aide Training - This course is given to girls who show interest in the social service field. A registered nurse is the instructor for this activity.

3. Special Tutorial Service - A special educational teacher is employed to provide this study on an hourly basis. Girls are selected to attend that have handicaps or exceptionalities that make it difficult for them to function in regular class rooms.

4. Business Education - Courses are taught in shorthand, typing, clerical practice, and use of business machines.

5. Guidance Counseling - A guidance counselor is employed to provide individual and group counseling to all the girls within the institution.

LOUISIANA TRAINING INSTITUTE - MONROE

Louisiana Training Institute, a boys correctional unit, in located in North Louisiana at Monroe. Students sent to this institute come

STATE OF LOUISIANA DEPARTMENT OF CORRECTIONS

1. Headquarters
2. Louisiana Correctional & Industrial School
3. Louisiana State Penitentiary
4. La. Training Institute
5. La. Training Institute
6. La. Training Institute
7. Louisiana Correctional Institute for Women
8. Hunt Correctional Institution
9. Dixon Correctional Institution
10. Wade Correctional Center
11. Washington Correctional Center

WORK RELEASE CENTERS
12. Jackson Barracks
13. Beauregard

from the northern and central portion of the state. The home for these neglected and delinquent boys was originally named, State Reform School, in 1904.

There are 683 acres, of which 50 acres are taken up by the campus and its buildings and streets. The remaining acreage is devoted to farm and pasture. There are fifty-four buildings, including dairy, farm and recreational units.

Southside High School is an academic facility of the institution. This school offers instructions in all twelve grade levels. Southside achieved distinction during the 1969-70 school year by receiving accreditation by the Southern Association of Colleges and Schools. In addition to the regular graded and non-graded sections, the school offers instruction in remdial work to students with profound learning problems relating to severe academic retardation or mental retardation.

LOUISIANA CORRECTIONAL AND INDUSTRIAL SCHOOL - DEQUINCY

This institution, located at DeQuincy in Beauregard Parish, was opened in September 1958. The unit was created to offer better rehabilitational opportunities for first offenders, selected from the inmate population of the Louisiana State Penitentiary. The facility has a maximum capacity of 928.

The philosophy of this unit is to educate and train all the inmates to become citizens who can make a contribution to society and to their own life. Periodic in-training programs are held for the employees with regard to methods and prodedures on maintaining discipline and order, and reminding the employees of their involvement in re-shaping human lives. This institution has fully implemented programs in education, recreation and a well-rounded work program.

LOUISIANA STATE PENITENTIARY - ANGOLA

Composed of 18,000 acres, the Penitentiary is situated in one of the most rugged areas of the state. The land, acquired in 1901 (8,000 acres) and in 1922 (10,000 acres), is located on the eastern bank of the Mississippi River. Three-fourths of the western boundary of the prison is located in a half moon of the river. The eastern boundary is composed of the rough terrain known as the Tunica Hills. This location is about 65 miles north of Baton Rouge. The facility has a maximum capacity of 4,637.

The philosophy and aims at the Penitentiary are based upon the belief in the individual worth of a man and his innate ability to change. A fundamental concern is why an individual committed a crime, rather than with the act itself.

LOUISIANA CORRECTIONAL INSTITUTE FOR WOMEN

This unit is located about 15 miles south of Baton Rouge at St. Gabriel. It has a maximum capacity of 414 inmates.

All the old buildings were condemned and a complete new unit was built in 1973-1974 by the State of Louisiana.

Inmate labor is utilized as clerical, food service, and maintenance. There is a garment factory that employs approximately sixty women inmates. This industry is included in the Agri-Business Program of Louisiana State Penitentiary.

LOUISIANA TRAINING INSTITUTE - BATON ROUGE

This institution, comprising 830 acres, is located fifteen miles north of Baton Rouge. This unit was formerly an institution for both male and female children of the colored race, confined by the courts because of negligence or delinquency. On September 3, 1969, all juvenile institutions in the state were ordered to desegregate. This order was immediately carried out with successful results.

HUNT CORRECTIONAL INSTITUTION

Located in St. Gabriel, this unit was opened in 1979. It is a medium security facility which includes a diagnostic center and an impact program for adults. Its maximum capacity is 1,843.

DIXON CORRECTIONAL INSTITUTION

This medium security facility, located in Jackson, was opened in 1976. It has a maximum inmate capacity of 924.

WADE CORRECTIONAL CENTER

Located in Homer, this medium security unit was opened in 1980. It houses a maximum of 1,181 inmates and includes a medical section and protection unit.

WASHINGTON CORRECTIONAL INSTITUTION

Located in Angie, this medium security facility was opened in 1983. It has a maximum capacity of 1,120 inmates and includes a medical section.

WORK TRAINING FACILITY—NORTH (CAMP BEAUREGARD)

This minimum security facility, located in Rapides Parish, is a work-release unit. It was opened in 1970 and has a maximum capacity of 450.

WORK TRAINING FACILITY—SOUTH (JACKSON BARRACKS)

Located in Orleans Parish, this minimum security facility is a work-release unit. It was opened in 1976 and has a maximum capacity of 300.

Crime in Louisiana

Area	Murder and non-negligent man-slaughter	Forci-ble rape	Robbery	Aggra-vated assault	Burglary	Larceny-theft	Motor vehicle theft
United States Total	17,521	80,710	461,725	663,891	2,879,250	6,482,621	1,014,056
Rate per 100,000 inhabitants	8.1	37.2	212.9	306.1	1,327.4	2,988.7	467.5
LOUISIANA Standard Metropolitan Statistical Area							
Area actually reporting	459	1,426	9,286	16,017	51,716	119,784	17,941
Estimated totals	477	1,510	9,597	17,194	55,218	129,826	18,726
Other cities							
Area actually reporting	22	57	195	1,183	3,400	9,002	353
Estimated totals	35	91	312	1,891	5,434	14,388	564
Rural							
Area actually reporting	43	139	110	1,760	3,463	6,523	397
Estimated totals	63	205	162	2,591	5,099	9,604	585
State total	575	1,806	10,071	21,676	65,751	153,818	19,875
Rate per 100,000 inhabitants	12.8	40.1	223.8	481.6	1,460.8	3,417.4	441.6

Crime Index for Major Louisiana Cities

	Murder and non-negligent man-slaughter	Forcible rape	Robbery	Aggra-vated assault	Burglary	Larceny-theft	Motor vehicle theft
Alexandria	20	28	86	335	1,312	3,222	200
Bastrop	1	16	7	33	139	592	21
Baton Rouge	51	181	1,224	3,635	9,610	18,775	2,166
Bogalusa	1	12	22	104	323	662	45
Bossier City	5	27	71	344	640	2,550	217
Crowley	2	2	12	48	243	246	25
Gretna	1	8	110	148	455	1,118	164
Harahan		1	3	16	93	305	24
Houma	3	11	36	172	532	1,403	66
Jennings.............		1	5	107	141	423	13
Lafayette............	12	75	232	839	2,067	6,523	323
Lake Charles	5	9	58	152	1,016	3,293	180
Leesville............	2	3	12	98	132	507	14
Minden	1	1	8	133	149	196	14
Monroe.............	3	32	69	761	1,093	2,367	151
Morgan City	1	2	15	22	373	489	42
Natchitoches......	1	3	13	126	217	440	16
New Iberia........		3	44	17	358	1,007	31
New Orleans	197	456	5,165	3,347	11,561	26,697	9,466
Pineville............	1	1	4	12	127	406	18
Ruston	1		2	63	118	697	20
Shreveport	45	109	651	1,202	5,170	13,019	820
Tallulah	1	6	7	109	153	211	5
West Monroe	1	8	6	52	157	807	18
Westwego	1	2	18	36	108	325	41

Supreme Court of Louisiana

Chief Justice: John A. Dixon, Jr.	Second District
Associate Justices:	
Pascal F. Calogero, Jr.	First District
James L. Dennis	Fourth District
Jack C. Watson	Third District
Walter F. Marcus, Jr.	First District
Luther F. Cole	Fifth District
Harry T. Lemmon	Sixth District
Clerk of Court: Frans J. Labranche	

SUPREME COURT OF LOUISIANA
THREE YEAR TREND IN ACTIVITY

	1984	1985	1986
APPEALS:			
Filed	47	40	34
Dismissed	0	0	0
Opionions Rendered			
with written opinions	80	24	19
per curiam affirmances	30	16	4
WRITS:			
Applications Filed	2,126	2,314	2,507
Granted	453	563	520
to be argued	106	130	113
with orders	347	433	407
Dismissed	10	8	16
Not Considered	28	1	29
Denied	1,774	1,637	1,764
Opinions Rendered	87	96	123
REHEARINGS:			
Applied for	90	73	90
Granted	6	4	10
Denied	103	67	83
Opions Rendered	8	1	7
ORIGINAL JURISDICTION:			
Petitions Filed	16	23	23
Opinions Rendered	15	9	13
OTHER MATTERS:			
Filed	25	39	17
Opinions Rendered	0	1	0
OTHER PER CURIAM OPINIONS RENDERED	6	2	6
TOTAL FILINGS:	2,304	2,489	2,671
Per Justice	329	356	382
TOTAL OPINIONS RENDERED	226	149	172

Source: *Annual Report 1986.* The Judicial Council of the Supreme Court of Louisiana

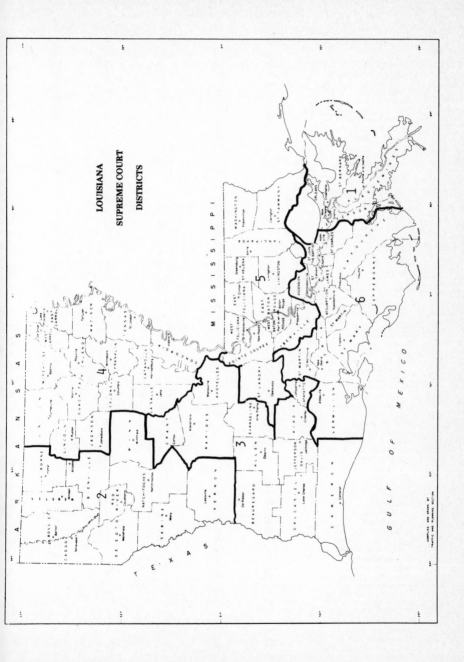

LOUISIANA
SUPREME COURT
DISTRICTS

LOUISIANA COURTS OF APPEAL
THREE YEAR TREND IN ACTIVITY

	TOTAL 1984	TOTAL 1985	TOTAL 1986	CIVIL 1986	CRIMINAL 1986
FIRST CIRCUIT					
Appeals Filed	1,115	974	1,024	815	209
Motions Filed	43	31	33	27	6
Writs Filed (except Pro Se)	320	403	371	214	157
Writs Refused	280	309	248	141	107
Writs Granted	61	85	123	84	39
Pro Se Writs Filed	99	174	276	55	221
Pro Se Writs Refused	59	120	225	47	178
Pro Se Writs Granted	35	45	42	3	39
Appeals Dismissed	155	158	195	172	23
Opinions Rendered	766	873	926	762	164
Rehearings Acted Upon	82	171	152	137	15
Appeals Pending					
Argued But Not Decided	11	14	7	7	0
To Be Argued	888	831	800	679	121
SECOND CIRCUIT:					
Appeals Filed	570	542	590	388	202
Motions Filed	47	8	7	4	3
Writs Filed (except Pro Se)	181	255	259	72	187
Writs Refused	114	204	185	48	137
Writs Granted	47	68	76	22	54
Pro Se Writs Filed	71	89	136	0	136
Pro Se Writs Refused	32	45	82	0	82
Pro Se Writs Granted	32	32	43	0	43
Appeals Dismissed	40	47	54	45	9
Opinions Rendered	515	510	490	286	204
Rehearings Acted Upon	133	116	90	52	38
Appeals Pending					
Argued But Not Decided	57	47	60	40	20
To Be Argued	234	233	302	200	102
THIRD CIRCUIT:					
Appeals Filed	865	831	823	659	164
Motions Filed	37	21	16	13	3
Writs Filed (except Pro Se)	268	293	306	138	168
Writs Refused	188	168	187	88	99
Writs Granted	99	87	112	60	52
Pro Se Writs Filed	38	118	160	4	156
Pro Se Writs Refused	34	83	96	4	92
Pro Se Writs Granted	0	21	32	0	32
Appeals Dismissed	104	108	124	114	10
Opinions Rendered[1]	623	651	886	740	146
Rehearings Acted Upon	131	127	133	119	14
Appeals Pending					
Argued But Not Decided	15	5	37	33	4
To Be Argued	749	849	656	551	105
FOURTH CIRCUIT					
Appeals Filed	858	726	761	465	296
Motions Filed	33	17	16	12	4
Writs Filed (except Pro Se)[2]	504	412	435	269	166
Writs Refused	299	284	302	191	111
Writs Granted	135	123	139	85	54
Pro Se Writs Filed	162	544	808	1	807
Pro Se Writs Refused	132	385	582	1	581
Pro Se Writs Granted	23	151	201	0	201
Appeals Dismissed	98	70	79	60	19
Opinions Rendered	730	640	893	528	365
Rehearings Acted Upon	166	166	177	156	21
Appeals Pending					
Argued But Not Decided	96	158	66	44	22
To Be Argued	583	513	453	275	178
FIFTH CIRCUIT:					
Appeals Filed	462	505	497	371	126
Motions Filed	20	12	19	17	2
Writs Filed (except Pro Se)	180	204	191	139	52
Writs Refused	141	143	135	102	33
Writs Granted	53	52	59	45	14
Pro Se Writs Filed	19	46	74	3	71
Pro Se Writs Refused	18	31	42	4	38
Pro Se Writs Granted	2	9	22	0	22

	TOTAL 1984	TOTAL 1985	TOTAL 1986	CIVIL 1986	CRIMINAL 1986
Appeals Dismissed	98	91	83	62	21
Opinions Rendered[3]	345	514	406	313	93
Rehearings Acted Upon	62	103	82	73	9
Appeals Pending					
Argued But Not Decided	43	60	63	49	14
To Be Argued	246	145	176	137	39
TOTAL FOR ALL CIRCUITS:					
Appeals Filed	3,870	3,578	3,695	2,698	997
Motions Filed	180	89	91	73	18
Writs Filed (except Pro Se)	1,453	1,567	1,562	832	730
Writs Refused	1,022	1,108	1,057	570	487
Writs Granted	395	415	509	296	213
Pro Se Writs Filed	389	971	1,454	63	1,391
Pro Se Writs Refused	275	664	1,027	56	971
Pro Se Writs Granted	92	258	340	3	337
Appeals Dismissed	495	474	535	453	82
Opinions Rendered	2,979	3,188	3,601	2,629	972
Rehearings Acted Upon	574	683	634	537	97
Appeals Pending					
Argued But Not Decided	222	284	233	173	60
To Be Argued	2,700	2,571	2,387	1,842	545

1. This total includes 51 Civil Opinions written by 5th Cir. Judges, and 112 Civil and 13 Criminal Opinions written by other Judges Pro Tempore.

2. Pro Se Writs not separated until July 1, 1984, for the Fourth Circuit.
3. This total does not include 51 Civil Opinions written on 3rd Cir. filings.

LOUISIANA COURTS OF APPEAL CIRCUITS & DISTRICTS

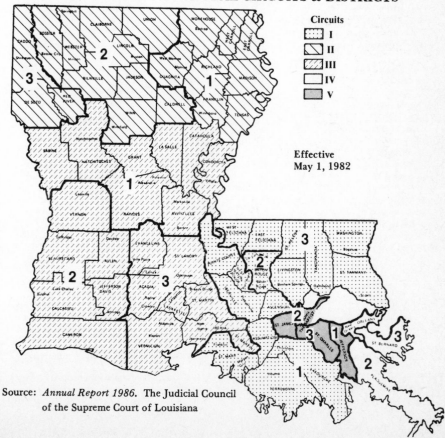

Circuits
- I
- II
- III
- IV
- V

Effective
May 1, 1982

Source: *Annual Report 1986.* The Judicial Council of the Supreme Court of Louisiana

LOUISIANA DISTRICT COURTS
THREE YEAR TREND IN ACTIVITY

District	Parishes within District	Total Cases Filed		
		1984	1985	1986
1	Caddo	18,177	18,666	21,785
2	Bienville, Claiborne, Jackson	9,423	10,499	9,989
3	Lincoln, Union	8,419	8,607	6,704
4	Morehouse, Ouachita	22,251	23,229	20,902
5	Franklin, Richland, W. Carroll	8,440	9,323	8,390
6	E. Carroll, Madison, Tensas	8,309	8,355	6,097
7	Catahoula, Concordia	8,655	9,117	8,007
8	Winn	2,504	3,653	1,884
9	Rapides	16,916	18,950	16,405
10	Natchitoches	8,625	9,166	7,495
11	De Soto, Sabine	8,231	9,007	7,201
12	Avoyelles	4,887	4,381	4,211
13	Evangeline	4,095	4,211	3,314
14	Calcasieu	23,957	22,096	17,464
15	Acadia, Lafayette, Vermilion	37,755	35,166	31,466
16	Iberia, St. Martin, St. Mary	26,788	29,657	26,729
17	Lafourche	16,413	16,240	13,623
18	Iberville, Point Couppe, W. Baton Rouge	16,992	15,440	14,313
19	E. Baton Rouge	25,216	30,354	33,164
20	E. Feliciana, W. Feliciana	5,222	5,864	4,420
21	Livingston, St. Helena, Tangipahoa	22,122	24,145	23,252
22	St. Tammany, Washington	22,444	28,037	26,153
23	Ascension*, Assumption, St. James	8,898	9,517	8,801
24	Jefferson*	18,114	19,546	21,322
25	Plaquemines	8,176	8,816	6,093
26	Bossier, Webster	16,095	16,504	14,098
27	St. Landry	11,276	11,542	8,702
28	LaSalle	3,218	3,624	3,078
29	St. Charles, St. John†	23,598	13,678	10,793
30	Vernon	11,387	10,659	8,494
31	Jefferson Davis	4,585	4,172	4,302
32	Terrebonne	14,105	12,735	11,504
33	Allen	4,746	4,304	2,826
34	St. Bernard	12,225	13,124	11,346
35	Grant	3,646	4,089	4,053
36	Beauregard	5,541	5,056	3,451
37	Caldwell	2,517	2,435	2,176
38	Cameron	4,966	4,777	3,366
39	Red River	3,027	4,101	2,889
40	St. John†		14,964	12,462
	Orleans**			
	Civil	21,582	22,289	23,536
	Criminal	5,843	7,309	5,916
	District Totals	27,425	29,598	29,452
	Statewide Total	509,386	537,404	482,176

*Violations of traffic laws and criminal misdemeanors are processed by First and Second Parish Courts.

**Violations of traffic laws are processed by New Orleans Traffic Court; minor misdemeanors are processed in New Orleans Municipal Court.

†Became 40th JDC on January 1, 1985.

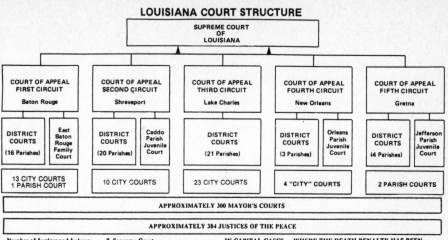

LOUISIANA COURT STRUCTURE

SUPREME COURT OF LOUISIANA

COURT OF APPEAL FIRST CIRCUIT	COURT OF APPEAL SECOND CIRCUIT	COURT OF APPEAL THIRD CIRCUIT	COURT OF APPEAL FOURTH CIRCUIT	COURT OF APPEAL FIFTH CIRCUIT
Baton Rouge	Shreveport	Lake Charles	New Orleans	Gretna

DISTRICT COURTS (16 Parishes)	East Baton Rouge Family Court	DISTRICT COURTS (20 Parishes)	Caddo Parish Juvenile Court	DISTRICT COURTS (21 Parishes)	DISTRICT COURTS (3 Parishes)	Orleans Parish Juvenile Court	DISTRICT COURTS (4 Parishes)	Jefferson Parish Juvenile Court
13 CITY COURTS 1 PARISH COURT		10 CITY COURTS		23 CITY COURTS	4 "CITY" COURTS		2 PARISH COURTS	

APPROXIMATELY 300 MAYOR'S COURTS

APPROXIMATELY 384 JUSTICES OF THE PEACE

Number of Justices and Judges:
  7 Supreme Court
  48 Courts of Appeal
  192 District, Family and Juvenile
  71 City and Parish Courts
  318 TOTAL

IN CAPITAL CASES — WHERE THE DEATH PENALTY HAS BEEN IMPOSED — APPEAL IS DIRECTLY TO THE SUPREME COURT FROM THE DISTRICT.

Source: *Annual Report 1986.* The Judicial Council of the Supreme Court of Louisiana

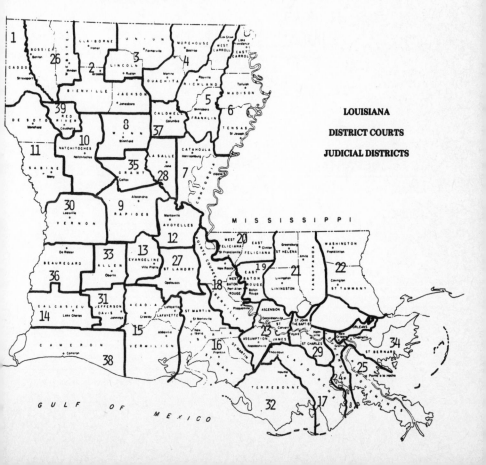

LOUISIANA

DISTRICT COURTS

JUDICIAL DISTRICTS

STATE FINANCE

TOTAL DEPARTMENT COLLECTIONS

TOTAL REVENUE COLLECTIONS
PERCENT OF CHANGE
FROM PRIOR FISCAL YEAR

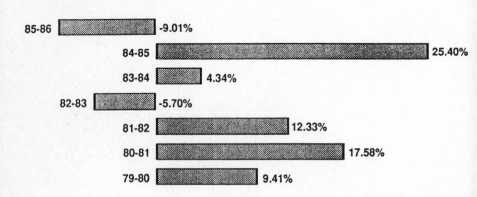

85-86		-9.01%
84-85		25.40%
83-84		4.34%
82-83		-5.70%
81-82		12.33%
80-81		17.58%
79-80		9.41%

TOTAL DEPARTMENT COLLECTIONS

Fiscal Year	Total Collections	% Change
1985-86	$3,169,228,485.40	−9.01
1984-85	3,482,893,487.27	25.40
1983-84	2,777,535,437.10	4.34
1982-83	2,662,087,740.84	−5.70
1981-82	2,822,877,909.32*	12.33
1980-81	2,512,990,869.77*	17.58
1979-80	2,137,176,437.74*	9.41

*Does not include accrued revenues.

Source: *Annual Report Fiscal Year 1985-86.* Louisiana Department of Revenue and Taxation

COLLECTION TRENDS

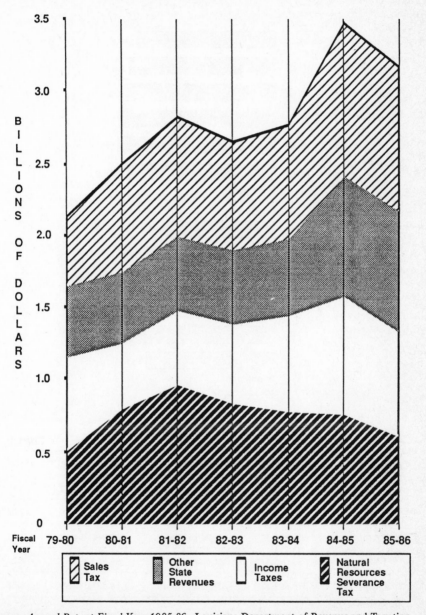

Source: *Annual Report Fiscal Year 1985-86.* Louisiana Department of Revenue and Taxation

LIQUORS–ALCOHOLIC BEVERAGE TAXES

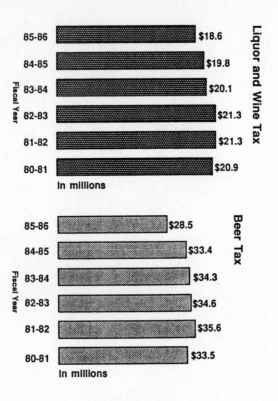

Fiscal Year	Beer Tax	Liquor and Wine Tax	Total	% Change
1985-86	$28,505,625.13	$18,594,772.13	$47,100,397.26	–11.44
1984-85	33,406,360.61	19,775,989.02	53,182,349.63	–2.17
1983-84	34,280,564.38	20,078,689.57	54,359,253.95	–2.84
1982-83	34,604,233.26	21,345,530.93	55,949,764.19	–1.75
1981-82	35,635,690.47*	21,309,302.06*	56,944,992.53*	4.64
1980-81	33,516,609.33*	20,905,140.63*	54,421,749.96*	6.82

*Does not include accrued revenues.

Source: *Annual Report Fiscal Year 1985-86.* Louisiana Department of Revenue and Taxation

CORPORATION FRANCHISE TAX

Corporation franchise tax collections rose from $200.1 million to $231.6 million, an increase of 15.74 percent, in fiscal year 1985-86, following a dramatic 69 percent increase the previous year as a result of a tax increase passed in the March 1984 Extraordinary Session of the Louisiana Legislature.

Effective July 1, 1984, the corporation franchise tax rate was increased from $1.50 per each $1,000 of capital stock, surplus, undivided profits, and borrowed capital (taxable base) to $1.50 for each $1,000 of taxable base up to $300,000 and $3 for each $1,000 of taxable base over $300,000. The minimum amount of tax paid by a corporation is $10 per year. Corporation franchise tax, administered by the Income and Corporation Franchise Taxes Section, is levied on any corporation doing business or qualified to do business in Louisiana, unless specifically exempted by statute.

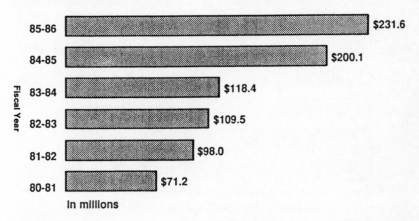

Fiscal Year

85-86	$231.6
84-85	$200.1
83-84	$118.4
82-83	$109.5
81-82	$98.0
80-81	$71.2

In millions

Fiscal Year	Amount Collected	% Change
1985-86	$231,618,168.85	15.74
1984-85	200,114,309.93	69.01
1983-84	118,402,976.32	8.11
1982-83	109,522,055.03	11.81
1981-82	97,954,666.76*	37.61
1980-81	71,183,427.78*	9.02

*Does not include accrued revenues.

Source: *Annual Report Fiscal Year 1985-86.* Louisiana Department of Revenue and Taxation

SALES TAX

In 1985-86, Louisiana sales tax provided the largest percentage of the Department's total collections, 31.47 percent, despite a decline of 5.75 percent. It earned this number one position last year as a result of the increase in the sales tax rate from three to four percent and a sharp decline in the natural resources tax collections. It easily retained the position as natural resources collections declined an additional 18.82 percent this fiscal year.

The four percent sales tax is imposed on: retail sales of tangible personal property; goods used or stored for use in Louisiana; leases and rentals of tangible personal property; and sales of certain services. Numerous exemptions are provided by statute.

Under House Current Resolution 55 of the 1986 Regular Session of the Louisiana Legislature, a one percent sales tax is levied on all items specifically exempted in the sales tax law for the period July 1, 1986—June 30, 1987. Also effective July 1, 1986, vendor's compensation to dealers remitting state sales tax is reduced from 1.5 percent to 1.1 percent.

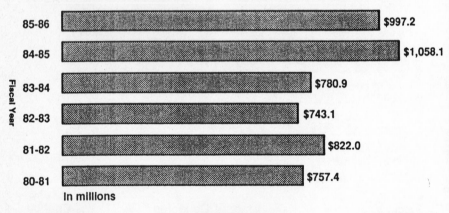

Fiscal Year

85-86	$997.2
84-85	$1,058.1
83-84	$780.9
82-83	$743.1
81-82	$822.0
80-81	$757.4

In millions

Fiscal Year	Amount Collected	% Change
1985-86	$997,200,787.58	–5.75
1984-85	1,058,062,691.82	35.49
1983-84	780,929,243.85	5.10
1982-83	743,068,525.34	–9.60
1981-82	821,981,861.34*	8.53
1980-81	757,385,725.07*	16.88

*Does not include accrued revenues.

Source: *Annual Report Fiscal Year 1985-86.* Louisiana Department of Revenue and Taxation

SALES TAX NET CASH COLLECTIONS
by Parish

Acadia	5,636,988.36		Morehouse	2,630,979.63
Allen	975,743.93		Natchitoches	3,409,397.82
Ascension	6,544,655.70		Orleans	134,089,786.13
Assumption	937,682.46		Ouachita	31,918,226.27
Avoyelles	1,889,389.21		Plaquemines	4,474,877.16
Beauregard	3,132,091.98		Pointe Coupee	962,423.82
Bienville	561,568.93		Rapides	19,612,878.99
Bossier	10,645,022.69		Red River	462,874.65
Caddo	58,216,380.43		Richland	1,308,776.58
Calcasieu	30,226,292.33		Sabine	1,617,411.57
Caldwell	530,487.38		St. Bernard	5,783,200.29
Cameron	1,202,561.65		St. Charles	4,166,518.56
Catahoula	608,652.10		St. Helena	188,778.66
Claiborne	1,081,258.34		St. James	1,737,331.54
Concordia	1,551,901.40		St. John the Baptist	3,229,516.07
DeSoto	1,830,655.50		St. Landry	6,338,607.29
East Baton Rouge	94,792,783.80		St. Martin	2,699,121.60
East Carroll	652,166.21		St. Mary	8,686,337.73
East Feliciana	718,275.50		St. Tammany	14,289,317.87
Evangeline	1,872,701.89		Tangipahoa	7,535,031.52
Franklin	1,220,891.65		Tensas	278,034.75
Grant	272,364.58		Terrebonne	14,840,197.20
Iberia	9,354,243.69		Union	904,239.55
Iberville	4,522,481.82		Vermilion	3,728,218.38
Jackson	976,922.89		Vernon	3,176,901.08
Jefferson	100,945,671.19		Washington	2,685,340.35
Jefferson Davis	2,618,064.73		Webster	3,859,508.23
Lafayette	48,141,902.72		West Baton Rouge	2,161,406.28
Lafourche	7,040,659.23		West Carroll	540,227.89
LaSalle	1,023,485.75		West Feliciana	1,966,720.31
Lincoln	5,223,424.89		Winn	1,258,775.63
Livingston	3,360,472.28		Out-of-State	309,388,766.32
Madison	714,581.79		**Total**	**$1,008,952,156.72**

Source: *Annual Report Fiscal Year 1985-86.* Louisiana Department of Revenue and Taxation

SALES TAX COLLECTIONS
of Motor Vehicles

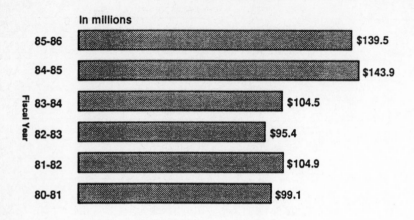

In millions

Fiscal Year	
85-86	$139.5
84-85	$143.9
83-84	$104.5
82-83	$95.4
81-82	$104.9
80-81	$99.1

INDIVIDUAL INCOME TAX

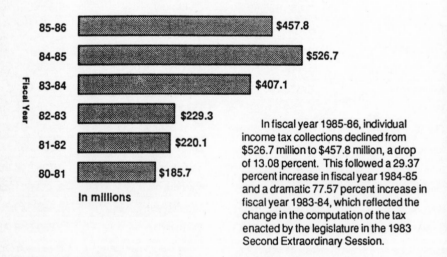

Fiscal Year	
85-86	$457.8
84-85	$526.7
83-84	$407.1
82-83	$229.3
81-82	$220.1
80-81	$185.7

In millions

In fiscal year 1985-86, individual income tax collections declined from $526.7 million to $457.8 million, a drop of 13.08 percent. This followed a 29.37 percent increase in fiscal year 1984-85 and a dramatic 77.57 percent increase in fiscal year 1983-84, which reflected the change in the computation of the tax enacted by the legislature in the 1983 Second Extraordinary Session.

Source: *Annual Report Fiscal Year 1985-86.* Louisiana Department of Revenue and Taxation

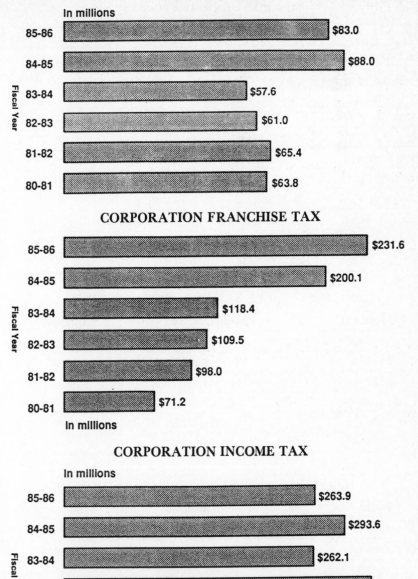

TOBACCO TAX

In millions

Fiscal Year	
85-86	$83.0
84-85	$88.0
83-84	$57.6
82-83	$61.0
81-82	$65.4
80-81	$63.8

CORPORATION FRANCHISE TAX

Fiscal Year	
85-86	$231.6
84-85	$200.1
83-84	$118.4
82-83	$109.5
81-82	$98.0
80-81	$71.2

In millions

CORPORATION INCOME TAX

In millions

Fiscal Year	
85-86	$263.9
84-85	$293.6
83-84	$262.1
82-83	$321.4
81-82	$292.0
80-81	$266.6

Source: *Annual Report Fiscal Year 1985-86.* Louisiana Department of Revenue and Taxation

PETROLEUM PRODUCTS
Motor Fuel Consumption

	1984-85		1985-86
Gross Gallons Taxed:		**Gross Gallons Taxed:**	
Gasoline	1,975,184,151	Gasoline	1,928,699,475
Highway Diesel	347,676,606	Highway Diesel	338,637,695
Highway LPG	7,585,674	Highway LPG	5,842,214
Total	2,330,446,431	Total	2,273,179,384
Gallons Refunded	52,379,695	**Gallons Refunded**	135,461,968
Net Gallons Taxed:		**Net Gallons Taxed:**	
Gasoline	1,922,804,456	Gasoline	1,793,237,507
Highway Diesel	347,676,606	Highway Diesel	338,637,695
Highway LPG	7,585,674	Highway LPG	5,842,214
Total	2,278,066,736	Total	2,137,717,416

MOTOR VEHICLE SALES TAX COLLECTION

Fiscal Year	Amount Collected	% Change
1985-86	$139,450,780.68	–3.08
1984-85	143,883,568.17	37.66
1983-84	104,517,666.10	9.51
1982-83	95,442,276.80	–9.04
1981-82	104,930,127.68	5.93
1980-81	99,051,814.69	8.41

TOBACCO PRODUCT TAXES COLLECTION

Fiscal Year	Amount Collected	% Change
1985-86	$82,992,177.13	-5.67
1984-85	87,985,121.01	52.64
1983-84	57,643,730.15	-5.48
1982-83	60,987,272.63	-6.68
1981-82	65,356,277.42*	2.43
1980-81	63,807,459.05*	4.63

*Does not include accrued revenues.

Source: *Annual Report Fiscal Year 1985-86.* Louisiana Department of Revenue and Taxation

SUMMARY OF REVENUE SOURCES ACCRUED

During June 1983, a policy change was implemented by the Division of Administration which converted the state's method of accounting to a modified accrual basis of accounting. Under this policy, "revenues associated with the economic activity of a particular fiscal year must be recognized (accrued) and reported in that year: (a) when the revenues are collected during the fiscal year to which they are associated, or (b) when the revenues are collected within forty-five days after the end of the fiscal year to which they are associated."

Accrual amounts are determined by using the actual collections for each tax for the period July 3, 1985, through August 14, 1985. The following table lists the taxes, their net cash collections, the amounts accrued to fiscal years 1985 and 1986, and the total net collections for fiscal year 1986, which appear in the Comparative Revenue Collections Statement of this report.

Revenue Source	Net Cash Collections	Less Adjustment for Accrued Taxes 7/3/85-8/14/85	Revenues Accrued to FY 1986	Total Net Collections FY 1986
Contractor Fee, Non-Resident	7,520.00	0.00	1,650.00	9,170.00
Corporation Franchise Tax	230,965,288.91	2,324,739.67	2,977,619.61	231,618,168.85
Electric Cooperative Fee	39,458.11	18,934.11	10,449.70	30,973.70
Gift Tax	2,567,531.12	209,083.33	62,598.72	2,421,046.51
Hazardous Waste Disposal Tax	3,092,902.00	987,191.83	714,752.15	2,820,462.32
Income Taxes				
Corporation	276,396,157.52	20,984,528.02	8,457,394.26	263,869,023.76
Individual	474,308,127.05	61,851,000.99	45,321,918.40	457,779,044.46
Inheritance and Estate Transfer Tax	36,886,787.32	3,713,120.48	5,277,951.79	38,451,618.63
Liquors - Alcoholic Beverage Taxes				
Alcoholic Beverage	18,549,536.46	1,380,496.94	1,425,732.61	18,594,772.13
Retail Alcoholic Beverage	13,201,944.05	2,289,638.71	119,809.02	11,032,114.36
State Beer	27,740,653.06	2,353,039.42	3,118,011.49	28,505,625.13
Minerals-Oil and Gas				
Pipeline Safety Inspection Fee	751,183.85	0.00	105,484.85	856,668.70
Natural Resources Taxes				
General Severance	665,153,307.92	112,200,559.70	64,505,077.00	617,457,825.22
Reforestation Severance	109,157.42	1,442.62	20,576.95	128,291.75
Occupational License Tax	123,466.62	15,417.61	1,149.87	109,198.88
Petroleum Products Taxes				
Gasoline Tax and Inspection Fee	283,091,010.73	22,229,077.76	20,636,676.28	281,498,609.25
Special Fuels	55,073,300.56	6,100,319.37	5,847,510.36	54,820,491.55
Public Utilities Taxes				
Inspection and Supervision Fee	2,766,140.42	10,443.51	12,385.55	2,768,082.46
Motor Carrier Fee	155.00	0.00	0.00	155.00
Natural Gas Franchise	11,022,856.43	2,482,098.41	2,738,967.36	11,279,725.38
Transportation and Communication	28,775,884.28	7,219,681.77	6,663,009.87	28,219,212.38
Sales Tax	1,008,952,156.72	92,440,252.95	80,688,883.81	997,200,787.58
Soft Drinks Tax	11,593,282.05	1,186,246.20	1,396,097.75	11,803,133.60
Soft Drink Permit Fee	-506.82	10.00	4,912.05	4,395.23
Tobacco Tax	83,743,146.96	4,315,734.40	3,557,289.57	82,984,702.13
Tobacco Permit Fee	7,440.00	25.00	60.00	7,475.00
Unclaimed Property	3,045,087.12	0.00	0.00	3,045,087.12
Total	$3,237,962,974.86	$344,313,082.80	$253,565,969.02	$3,147,315,861.08

Source: *Annual Report Fiscal Year 1985-86.* Louisiana Department of Revenue and Taxation

NATURAL RESOURCES
Collections by Resource

Resource	1985-86	1984-85	% Change
Oil/Condensate	486,223,883.09	623,226,158.75	−21.98
Gas	120,272,997.05	126,168,282.51	−4.67
Minerals	3,512,970.24	4,241,280.35	−17.17
Timber/Pulpwood	7,447,974.84	7,021,439.02	6.12
Reforestation	128,291.75	95,592.66	30.52
Total	$617,586,116.97	$760,752,753.29	−18.82

OIL/CONDENSATE AND NATURAL GAS PRODUCTION
AND NET CASH COLLECTIONS (Does not include accrued revenues.)

Year	Oil/Condensate Tax Collections (Dollars)	Oil/Condensate Production (Barrels)	Natural Gas Tax Collections (Dollars)	Natural Gas Production (MCFs)
1985-86	$533,761,390.59	186,743,286.43	$119,819,142.98	1,740,016,533.00
1984-85	606,909,815.97	181,208,017.89	124,847,347.91	1,840,044,177.39
1983-84	666,845,430.85	189,662,280.13	136,337,169.62	1,989,605,857.00
1982-83	719,725,489.89	186,883,693.33	138,363,571.89	1,975,467,139.00
1981-82	809,285,811.93	197,968,513.76	159,424,740.93	2,290,214,109.00
1980-81	639,024,418.95	209,963,775.50	160,872,591.05	2,363,366,389.00
1979-80	335,017,133.47	209,158,801.43	174,308,230.58	2,558,384,379.00
1978-79	261,942,795.10	242,412,166.36	191,764,975.60	2,798,454,541.00
1977-78	259,613,666.82	269,112,519.36	202,031,301.80	2,926,564,328.00
1976-77	269,874,158.46	295,457,801.18	210,372,381.15	3,066,449,864.00
1975-76	275,928,253.21	326,217,542.62	225,791,583.52	3,321,032,842.00
1974-75	282,483,486.72	364,522,502.89	250,940,363.57	3,730,912,260.00
1973-74	186,060,926.59	440,660,860.75	192,213,660.23	4,238,244,668.00

COMPARATIVE REVENUE COLLECTIONS

State Revenues	1985-86	1984-85	% Change
Contractor Fee, Non-Resident	9,170.00	0.00	0.00
Corporation Franchise Tax	231,618,168.85	200,114,309.93	15.74
Electric Cooperative Fee	30,973.70	31,511.91	−1.71
Gift Tax	2,421,046.51	2,344,458.85	3.27
Hazardous Waste Disposal Tax	2,820,462.32	4,942,912.86	−42.94
Income Taxes			
Corporation	263,869,023.76	293,597,811.45	−10.13
Individual	457,779,044.46	526,683,982.79	−13.08
Inheritance and Estate Transfer Tax	38,451,618.63	31,790,122.46	20.95
Liquors-Alcoholic Beverage Taxes			
Alcoholic Beverage	18,594,772.13	19,775,989.02	−5.97
Retail Alcoholic Beverage	11,032,114.36	20,322,464.69	−45.71
State Beer	28,505,625.13	33,406,360.61	−14.67
Minerals-Oil and Gas			
Pipeline Safety Inspection Fee	856,668.70	0.00	0.00
Natural Resources Taxes			
General Severance	617,457,825.22	760,657,160.63	−18.83
Reforestation Severance	128,291.75	95,592.66	34.21
Occupational License Tax	109,198.88	305,914.80	−64.30
Petroleum Products Taxes			
Gasoline	280,767,533.41	306,299,666.19	−8.34
Inspection Fee (Gasoline)	731,075.84	785,144.57	−6.89
Special Fuels	54,820,491.55	55,479,056.58	−1.19
Public Utilities Taxes			
Inspection and Supervision Fee	2,768,082.46	1,216,550.31	127.54
Motor Carrier Fee*	155.00	35.71	334.05
Natural Gas Franchise	11,279,725.38	11,858,553.14	−4.88
Transportation and Communication	28,219,212.38	30,226,377.86	−6.64
Sales Tax	997,200,787.58	1,058,062,691.82	−5.75
Soft Drinks Tax	11,803,133.60	11,045,119.18	6.86
Soft Drink Permit Fee	4,395.23	2,075.93	111.72
Tobacco Tax	82,984,702.13	87,984,191.01	−5.68
Tobacco Tax Permit Fee	7,475.00	930.00	703.76
Unclaimed Property	3,045,087.12	2,513,126.52	21.17
Total	3,147,315,861.08	3,459,542,111.48	−9.03
Other Taxes			
Beer Tax			
Parishes and Municipalities	5,110,877.39	5,354,879.19	−4.56
Hotel/Motel Room Occupancy Tax			
Louisiana Stadium and Exposition District	11,709,266.81	12,668,334.54	−7.57
New Orleans Exhibition Hall Authority	5,092,480.12	5,328,162.06	−4.42
Total Other Taxes	21,912,624.32	23,351,375.79	−6.16
Grand Total	$3,169,228,485.40	$3,482,893,487.27	−9.01

* Transferred to the Department of Public Safety

NATURAL RESOURCES
Net Cash Distribution by Parish

Parish	Total tax collected	Tax collected on all timber products	Tax collected on all other products	Oil tax	Gas tax	Gas or LPG tax	Sulphur tax	Timber tax	Shell tax	Gravel tax	Sand tax
Acadia	17,802,554.46	49,991.02	17,752,563.44	14,210,600.74	3,541,075.65	858.60	0.00	45,836.14	0.00	0.00	28.45
Allen	3,706,349.48	281,279.92	3,425,069.56	3,148,820.14	263,337.68	0.00	0.00	166,250.92	0.00	234.47	12,677.27
Ascension	1,368,505.81	17,060.25	1,371,445.56	1,238,121.33	131,740.72	0.00	0.00	5,269.66	0.00	0.00	0.00
Assumption	2,796,992.94	3,230.34	2,793,762.60	1,778,727.77	981,848.68	0.00	0.00	2,094.35	0.00	0.00	0.00
Avoyelles	1,449,826.58	20,702.52	1,429,124.06	1,427,366.28	1,757.78	0.00	0.00	12,194.30	0.00	0.00	0.00
Beauregard	6,006,395.11	357,572.18	5,648,822.93	5,357,598.75	268,673.95	0.00	0.00	99,173.47	0.00	19,633.69	2,716.54
Bienville	2,498,342.38	322,159.11	2,176,183.27	630,682.88	1,544,465.55	0.00	0.00	174,879.40	0.00	1,034.84	0.00
Bossier	6,014,742.50	217,994.05	5,796,748.45	4,939,918.66	855,467.82	0.00	0.00	152,180.19	0.00	1,361.97	0.00
Caddo	8,326,278.28	61,438.80	8,264,839.48	7,325,862.38	938,902.85	0.00	0.00	29,865.00	0.00	0.00	12.65
Calcasieu	14,769,424.05	94,268.61	14,675,155.44	13,044,239.19	1,622,448.36	0.00	0.00	20,272.88	0.00	0.00	995.74
Caldwell	1,150,574.98	138,327.28	1,012,247.70	195,447.89	815,745.09	0.00	0.00	83,820.52	0.00	54.72	0.00
Cameron	42,366,549.15	212.50	42,366,336.65	33,327,675.99	9,037,200.89	0.00	0.00	81.13	0.00	0.00	0.00
Catahoula	4,231,937.10	25,264.76	4,206,672.34	4,193,190.96	54.42	0.00	0.00	16,481.44	0.00	11,178.28	2,258.66
Claiborne	14,494,450.39	228,211.85	14,266,238.54	12,554,324.47	1,709,979.95	0.00	0.00	139,235.41	0.00	1,934.12	0.00
Concordia	8,185,027.72	13,951.81	8,171,075.91	8,080,345.48	90,730.43	0.00	0.00	9,670.16	0.00	0.00	0.00
DeSoto	2,818,931.42	257,460.93	2,561,470.49	1,171,379.77	1,387,574.10	0.00	0.00	140,589.94	0.00	2,516.62	0.00
East Baton Rouge	15,549,843.70	18,745.48	15,531,098.22	13,117,819.41	2,381,062.87	0.00	0.00	12,591.68	0.00	12,729.20	19,486.74
East Carroll	8,002.81	6,592.09	1,410.72	1,410.72	0.00	0.00	0.00	4,669.59	0.00	0.00	0.00
East Feliciana	263,435.75	121,744.24	141,691.51	86,113.84	5,889.87	0.00	0.00	86,902.52	0.00	32,430.44	17,257.36
Evangeline	5,193,461.08	56,400.32	5,137,060.76	4,638,556.23	498,504.53	0.00	0.00	37,016.01	0.00	0.00	0.00
Franklin	393,306.85	3,772.17	389,534.68	242,928.28	146,011.32	0.00	0.00	2,135.38	0.00	595.08	0.00
Grant	569,348.16	389,292.65	200,055.51	145,156.38	54,044.72	0.00	0.00	285,587.13	0.00	737.07	117.34
Iberia	25,394,093.95	17.08	25,394,076.87	14,345,766.72	10,803,005.66	0.00	0.00	0.00	0.00	0.00	0.00
Iberville	13,643,688.10	14,651.96	13,629,036.14	13,161,397.19	464,108.65	0.00	0.00	13,657.12	0.00	0.00	0.00
Jackson	1,674,283.75	289,121.16	1,385,162.59	562,055.40	818,975.40	0.00	0.00	130,935.66	0.00	874.11	671.93
Jefferson	19,235,826.56	0.00	19,235,826.56	16,018,667.57	2,236,090.72	0.00	889,005.36	0.00	25,309.04	0.00	427.45
Jefferson Davis	11,055,144.27	12,252.66	11,042,891.61	8,533,925.10	2,500,970.71	0.00	0.00	10,140.57	0.00	147.89	64,836.69
Lafayette	9,421,192.44	0.00	9,421,192.44	6,683,760.94	2,726,338.26	0.00	0.00	0.00	0.00	0.00	7,847.91
Latourche	40,537,509.24	6,583.09	40,530,926.15	34,255,076.06	6,275,850.09	0.00	0.00	5,918.04	0.00	0.00	11,093.24
LaSalle	11,708,687.91	279,020.09	11,429,667.82	11,323,858.98	89,533.11	0.00	0.00	174,737.95	0.00	13,648.81	2,626.92

Parish										
Lincoln	3,770,461.52	131,194.98	3,639,266.54	1,498,522.20	2,137,526.01	0.00	0.00	43,067.56	0.00	3,218.33	0.00
Livingston	10,925,027.99	166,977.23	10,758,050.76	10,109,510.01	614,917.62	0.00	0.00	91,119.38	0.00	17,726.50	15,896.63
Madison	38,021.27	19,243.37	18,777.90	16,585.34	2,192.56	0.00	0.00	13,716.82	0.00	0.00	0.00
Morehouse	223,819.71	141,400.44	82,419.27	12,784.71	69,634.56	0.00	0.00	121,207.29	0.00	0.00	0.00
Natchitoches	8,778,491.30	559,929.36	8,218,561.94	3,009,712.57	5,208,228.44	0.00	0.00	360,952.21	0.00	620.93	0.00
Orleans	173,954.02	14.31	173,939.71	6,913.09	167,026.62	0.00	0.00	14.31	0.00	0.00	0.00
Ouachita	1,996,968.26	119,373.50	1,877,594.76	866,489.93	973,001.48	0.00	0.00	66,045.68	0.00	13,597.75	24,505.60
Plaquemines	122,848,175.69	99.90	122,848,075.79	113,769,718.34	7,673,849.08	0.00	1,396,388.52	99.90	0.00	0.00	8,000.00
Point Coupee	11,235,007.38	10,260.24	11,224,727.14	6,729,804.44	4,494,922.70	0.00	0.00	6,735.83	0.00	0.00	0.00
Rapides	1,344,309.43	371,698.75	972,610.68	856,004.79	23,028.76	0.00	0.00	197,051.71	0.00	48,484.97	43,092.16
Red River	911,198.16	131,854.45	779,343.71	516,279.93	252,782.98	0.00	0.00	87,544.41	0.00	5,456.35	3,824.45
Richland	4,167,228.30	2,835.20	4,164,393.10	4,022,288.38	142,000.26	0.00	0.00	2,271.88	0.00	0.00	104.46
Sabine	2,023,420.03	532,836.43	1,490,583.60	868,728.30	621,102.52	0.00	0.00	364,236.67	0.00	42.34	94.49
St Bernard	18,851,955.79	0.00	18,851,955.79	17,535,995.90	1,295,915.53	0.00	0.00	0.00	0.00	0.00	20,044.36
St Charles	20,668,754.77	38.29	20,668,716.48	19,390,670.53	1,258,071.04	0.00	0.00	0.00	6,625.41	0.00	13,349.50
St Helena	2,492,977.22	117,760.37	2,375,216.85	2,205,464.63	5,299.90	0.00	0.00	54,237.22	0.00	110,265.43	54,196.89
St James	2,884,309.94	731.35	2,883,578.59	1,619,230.01	1,264,348.58	0.00	0.00	731.35	0.00	0.00	0.00
St John	1,520,273.33	2,149.11	1,518,124.22	1,401,069.76	103,970.54	0.00	0.00	2,142.81	10,032.49	0.00	2,251.43
St Landry	6,029,547.08	24,163.60	6,005,383.48	5,138,576.21	866,134.57	672.70	0.00	19,064.25	0.00	0.00	0.00
St Martin	20,484,161.21	1,542.03	20,482,619.18	19,063,055.74	1,401,574.99	0.00	0.00	954.62	0.00	166.22	8,451.06
St Mary	29,022,200.40	81.15	29,022,119.25	19,772,962.37	9,028,818.11	1,232.31	0.00	0.00	122,686.16	0.00	1,662.42
St Tammany	437,681.05	143,571.15	294,109.90	9,772.48	15,267.49	0.00	0.00	81,552.65	118,166.78	52,488.23	98,414.92
Tangipahoa	357,277.41	156,759.81	200,517.60	184,224.71	0.00	0.00	0.00	99,492.45	1,608.62	10,400.73	4,283.54
Tensas	1,734,620.59	29,353.45	1,705,267.14	1,573,141.21	132,114.05	0.00	0.00	19,886.28	0.00	11.88	0.00
Terrebonne	44,768,845.12	691.82	44,768,153.30	32,719,495.54	12,040,222.26	8,435.59	0.00	691.82	0.00	0.00	0.00
Union	1,904,413.03	350,941.99	1,553,471.04	998,731.61	552,070.45	0.00	0.00	211,369.13	0.00	2,313.24	355.74
Vermilion	40,126,110.52	1,782.43	40,124,328.09	26,070,108.23	14,052,246.12	1,971.74	0.00	1,754.66	0.00	0.00	0.00
Vernon	560,260.63	441,025.45	119,235.18	79,020.74	10,055.57	0.00	0.00	218,751.11	0.00	17,060.69	13,098.18
Washington	496,432.24	154,662.73	341,769.51	9,006.78	247,818.53	0.00	0.00	98,467.47	0.00	75,248.01	9,696.19
Webster	7,722,049.54	142,865.92	7,579,183.62	5,522,881.78	1,964,134.38	0.00	0.00	96,308.33	0.00	32,277.33	59,890.13
West Baton Rouge	2,432,638.92	2,081.06	2,430,557.86	1,595,660.67	832,046.03	0.00	0.00	2,039.34	0.00	0.00	2,851.16
West Carroll	19,403.23	1,215.48	18,187.75	0.00	18,187.75	0.00	0.00	953.80	0.00	0.00	0.00
West Feliciana	365,903.87	28,296.08	337,607.79	260,288.84	54,646.83	0.00	0.00	16,044.04	0.00	12,467.89	10,204.23
Winn	1,271,859.47	575,803.57	696,055.90	584,095.32	104,404.84	0.00	0.00	421,064.19	0.00	93.96	0.00
State Totals	665,262,465.34	7,650,573.92	657,611,891.42	533,761,380.59	118,818,142.98	13,170.85	2,285,393.86	4,563,767.93	204,428.50	502,052.09	537,322.43

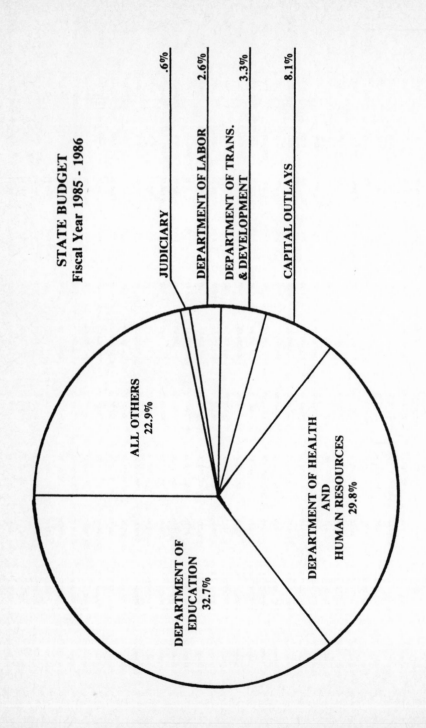

STATE BUDGET
Fiscal Year 1985 - 1986

JUDICIARY .6%

DEPARTMENT OF LABOR 2.6%

DEPARTMENT OF TRANS. & DEVELOPMENT 3.3%

CAPITAL OUTLAYS 8.1%

ALL OTHERS 22.9%

DEPARTMENT OF EDUCATION 32.7%

DEPARTMENT OF HEALTH AND HUMAN RESOURCES 29.8%

State General Fund Revenues, Fiscal 1985-86 and Fiscal 1986-87 (In Millions)[a]

	Fiscal 1985-86 (Actual)	Fiscal 1986-87 (Est. 11/7/86)	Annual Change Amount	Percent
Department of Revenue				
Alcoholic Beverage Tax	$ 19.2	$ 18.0	$ -1.2	-6.3%
Alcohol Retail Sales Tax[b]	13.6	0.0	-13.6	-100.0
Beer Tax	33.1	30.0	-3.1	-9.4
Corporation Franchise Tax	228.3	229.3	1.0	0.4
Gasoline Tax	285.2	321.6	36.4	12.8
Gift Tax	2.5	2.0	-0.5	-20.0
Hazardous Waste Tax	3.4	3.0	-0.4	-11.8
Corporate Income Tax	288.3	239.0	-49.3	-17.1
Individual Income Tax	510.8	486.8	-24.0	-4.7
Inheritance Tax	31.1	36.9	5.8	18.6
Inspection Fees (Gasoline)	0.8	0.8	0.0	0.0
Natural Gas Franchise Tax	11.5	10.4	-1.1	-9.6
Public Utilities Tax	29.8	31.1	1.3	4.4
Sales Tax	1,034.8	1,116.5	81.7	7.9
Severance Tax	657.7	425.0	-232.7	-35.4
Soft Drinks Tax	11.6	11.8	0.2	1.7
Special Fuels Tax	54.5	55.3	0.8	1.5
Supervision & Inspection Fees	2.6	2.0	-0.6	-23.1
Tobacco Tax	84.5	84.0	-0.5	-0.6
Unknown Owners	1.8	8.2	6.4	355.6
Amnesty Program[c]	1.5	0.0	-1.5	-100.0
Total	$3,306.7[d]	$3,111.7	$-195.0	-5.9%
Department of Natural Resources				
Royalties	$ 369.6	$ 256.4	$-113.2	-30.6%
Rentals	20.5	12.0	-8.5	-41.5
Bonuses	29.8	14.0	-15.8	-53.0
Conservation Fund	7.3	4.0	-3.3	-45.2
Rockefeller Fund	10.7	7.0	-3.7	-34.6
Marsh Island, Russell Sage Fund	0.7	0.1	-0.6	-85.7
State Land Office Fees	2.1	0.3	-1.8	-85.7
Total	$ 440.7	$ 293.8	$-146.9	-33.3%
Department of Treasury				
Excise License Insurance Tax	$ 140.0	$ 144.0	$ 4.0	2.9%
Insurance Rating Commission	3.1	3.1	0.0	0.0
Interest Earnings	74.0	57.2	-16.8	-22.7
Various Agency Receipts[d]	86.9	100.2	13.3	15.3
Wildlife & Fisheries Fees	13.0	12.0	-1.0	-7.7
Total	$ 317.0	$ 316.5	$ -0.5	-0.2%
Department of Public Safety				
Alcoholic Beverage Permits	$ 2.1	$ 2.1	$ 0.0	0.0%
Certificate of Title	17.3	17.6	0.3	1.7
Vehicle Sales Tax	136.4	140.3	3.9	2.9
Total	$ 198.9	$ 206.8	$ 7.9	4.0%
Total Taxes, Licenses & Fees	$4,263.3	$3,928.8	$-334.5	-7.8%

a Revenues affecting general fund directly or indirectly.
b Repealed.
c Program expired.
d Includes banking fees and recovered fund balances.
SOURCE: Revised estimates by Legislative Fiscal Office as of November 7, 1986.

Total State Expenditures, Fiscal 1985-86 and Fiscal 1986-87
(In Millions)*

General Appropriations Act (No. 16 of 1985 and No. 17 of 1986)	Budgeted 1985-86[a]	Appropriated 1986-87[b]	Annual Change Amount	Annual Change Percent	Executive Order Cut Amount	Executive Order Cut Revised Total	Revised Annual Change Amount	Revised Annual Change Percent
Judiciary	$ 44.5	$ 47.4	$ 2.9	6.6%	$ 0.0	$ 47.4	$ 2.9	6.6%
Executive	121.3	111.2[c]	-10.2	-8.4	-6.5	104.7	-16.7	-13.7
Agriculture	29.0	116.1[c]	87.1	300.3	-2.5	113.6	84.6	291.7
Justice	8.9	8.8	-0.1	-0.9	-0.6	8.2	-0.7	-7.9
Insurance	4.6	4.3	-0.3	-6.6	-0.5	3.8	-0.8	-16.6
Elections	14.4	16.5	2.1	15.0	-1.2	15.4	1.0	7.0
Lieutenant Governor	0.5	0.4	-0.1	-23.6	-0.1	0.3	-0.2	-31.0
State	4.7	5.2	0.6	11.8	-0.6	4.7	0.0	-0.2
Treasury[d]	15.3	15.4	0.1	0.9	-0.1	15.4	0.1	0.5
Public Service	4.3	3.9	-0.3	-7.6	-0.2	3.8	-0.5	-11.6
Commerce	17.2	55.8[e]	38.6	224.1	-4.4	51.5	34.2	198.6
Culture, Recreation & Tourism[f]	28.1	23.7	-4.4	-15.6	-1.4	22.3	-5.8	-20.7
Transportation & Development	258.9	249.5	-9.4	-3.6	-17.9	231.6	-27.3	-10.5
Public Safety	168.8	178.5	9.8	5.3	-11.6	166.9	-1.8	-1.1
Health & Human Resources	2,081.8	2,219.0	137.2	6.6	-82.0	2,136.9	55.2	2.7
Corrections	185.3	187.1	1.9	1.0	0.0	187.1	1.8	1.0
Natural Resources	89.2	35.7[c]	-53.4	-59.9	-1.0	34.8	-54.4	-61.0
Revenue & Taxation	32.4	42.3	9.9	30.6	-0.2	42.2	9.8	30.1
Environmental Quality	25.8	19.2	-6.6	-25.6	-0.1	19.1	-6.7	-26.1
Labor	187.1	190.4	3.3	1.8	-0.1	190.3	3.2	1.7
Urban & Community Affairs	35.7	39.0	3.3	9.2	-0.1	38.9	3.2	8.8
Wildlife & Fisheries	35.1	36.1	1.0	2.8	0.0	36.1	1.0	2.8
Civil Service	5.8	5.9	0.1	2.2	-0.6	5.3	-0.4	-7.7

	Budgeted 1985-86[a]	Appropriated 1986-87[b]	Annual Change Amount	Annual Change Percent	Executive Order Cut Amount	Executive Order Cut Revised Total	Revised Annual Change Amount	Revised Annual Change Percent
Retirement	43.3	48.1	4.9	11.3	0.0	48.1	4.9	11.3
Elementary & Secondary Education	1,623.0	1,504.6	-118.4	-7.3	-59.3	1,445.2	-177.8	-11.0
Other Education	79.4	76.0	-3.4	-4.2	-1.7	74.3	-5.1	-6.4
Vo-Tech Schools	68.1	49.9	-18.2	-26.7	-2.3	47.6	-20.5	-30.1
Higher Education	819.0	820.8	1.8	0.2	-26.0	794.9	-24.1	-2.9
Miscellaneous	54.5	43.5	-11.0	-20.3	-4.3	39.1	-15.4	-28.2
Other Requirements	15.4	16.0	0.5	3.4	-0.2	15.7	0.3	1.8
Total	$6,101.4	$6,170.7	$ 69.3	1.1%	$-225.3	$5,945.4	$-156.0	-2.6%
Other Appropriations or Dedications								
Capital Outlay (not bonds)	$ 630.0	$ 565.6	$ -64.4	-10.2%	0.0	$ 565.6	$ -64.4	-10.2%
Debt Service	363.4	387.5	24.0	6.6	0.0	387.5	24.0	6.6
Legislature	30.3	28.5	-1.7	-5.7	0.0	28.5	-1.7	-5.7
Revenue Sharing	86.5[g]	90.0	3.5	4.1	0.0	90.0	3.5	4.1
Ancillary (Group Insurance)	63.8[h]	63.8	0.0	0.1	0.0	63.8	0.0	0.1
Interim Emergency Board	6.5[h]	6.6	0.1	1.0	0.0	6.6	0.1	1.0
Judgments	25.0[i]	25.0	0.0	0.0	0.0	25.0	0.0	0.0
Total	$1,205.5	$1,167.0	$-38.5	-3.2%	$ 0.0	$1,167.0	$ -38.5	-3.2%
Grand Total	$7,307.0	$7,337.8	$ 30.8	0.4%	$-225.3	$7,112.5	$194.5	-2.7%

* Totals may not add due to rounding.

a Includes $79.8 million in executive order cuts.

b Includes cancellation of priority cuts A through E, gubernatorial vetoes of cuts, and appropriation of $100 million undedicated 8 (g) money and interest earnings appropriated from 8 (g) dedicated money.

c Forestry transferred from Department of Natural Resources to Department of Agriculture and Forestry. Agriculture also includes $3 million from 8 (g) money for Agricultural Products Development Fund and $80 million for gasohol subsidies.

d As shown in Executive Budget. Department of Treasury includes Patient Compensation Fund and funds to pay small judgments.

e Includes $37 million in 8 (g) money appropriated to four economic development funds.

f Transferred to Office of the Governor.

g $3.53 million withheld from New Orleans allocation in lieu of repayment of state loan for World's Fair expenses.

h Actual amount spent was $4.337 million.

i Estimated.

SOURCE: Legislative Fiscal Office and Division of Administration.

STATE OF LOUISIANA
GENERAL REVENUES BY SOURCE - ALL FUNDS
LAST TEN FISCAL YEARS (EXPRESSED IN THOUSANDS)

	1976-1977	1977-1978	1978-1979	1979-1980
TAXES AND PERMITS:				
AD VALOREM TAX	$ 147	$ 83	$ 8	$
ALCOHOLIC BEVERAGE AND BEER TAX	47,116	49,563	52,304	53,060
ANHYDROUS AMONIA PERMITS	35	32	26	24
CORPORATION FRANCHISE TAX	46,669	51,341	54,225	65,292
POWER GENERATION TAX	196	21	40	15
EXCISE LICENSE TAX	42,231	49,087	57,988	61,377
GASOLINE TAX	156,913	164,933	172,011	165,090
GIFT TAX	3,445	328	503	769
HOTEL - MOTEL OCCUPANCY TAX	114	140	182	217
INCOME TAX	228,862	379,232	454,798	496,776
INHERITANCE TAX	16,552	15,881	23,225	21,922
INSPECTION FEES - PETROLEUM PRODUCT	739	762	800	788
INSPECTION AND SUPERVISION FEES	473	528	582	685
LIQUEFIED PETROLEUM GAS PERMITS	166	173	170	172
LUBRICATING OIL TAX	4			
MOTOR CARRIER REGULATORY TAX	1,133	1,386	1,578	140
NATURAL GAS FRANCHISE TAX	4,629	4,935	4,759	6,300
OCCUPATIONAL LICENSE TAX	17,573	19,647	22,086	25,822
PUBLIC UTILITIES TAX	12,136	14,119	16,616	23,529
REFORESTATION			126	78
SALES TAX	481,676	565,411	676,630	739,347
SEVERANCE TAX	492,938	474,189	466,316	522,784
SOFT DRINK TAX	6,001	7,195	7,872	8,692
SPECIAL FUELS TAX	16,226	18,701	21,216	22,403
TOBACCO TAX	56,954	59,011	58,557	60,984
UNCLAIMED PROPERTY	840	746	732	627
VEHICLE LICENSE TAX	27,571	36,928	43,172	44,206
TOTAL TAX AND PERMITS	1,661,339	1,914,372	2,136,522	2,321,099
MINERAL RESOURCES:				
ROYALTIES	153,386	180,786	196,078	236,287
RENTALS, LEASES AND FEES	19,142	15,119	19,357	23,772
BONUSES	46,572	89,418	47,094	275,637
TOTAL MINERAL RESOURCES	219,100	285,323	262,529	535,696
OTHER RECEIPTS:				
INTEREST ON INVESTMENTS	41,829	54,041	87,409	139,753
WILDLIFE AND FISHERIES FEES	7,774	8,259	8,331	9,123
INSURANCE RATING COMMISSION FEES	3,301	3,975	4,548	3,204
OFFICE OF FINANCIAL INSTITUTIONS	1,453	1,648	1,843	1,998
OTHER FEES AND MISCELLANEOUS RECEIPTS	3,538	11,696	12,722	17,536
(INCOME NOT AVAILABLE)	8,575	17,442	15,645	31,326
(MEANS OF FINANCING)	146,091	161,040	194,691	192,343
PROCEEDS OF BOND SALES	214,245	257,640	297,075	271,095
INTERAGENCY RECEIPTS	141,408	162,129	183,994	194,918
TOTAL - OTHER RECEIPTS	568,214	677,870	806,258	861,296
FEDERAL REVENUE SHARING	46,918	45,940	45,609	42,696
FEDERAL GRANTS	800,153	1,008,425	1,056,489	1,232,741
TOTAL FEDERAL REVENUE	847,071	1,054,365	1,102,098	1,275,437
GRAND TOTAL	$ 3,295,724	$ 3,931,930	$ 4,307,407	$ 4,993,528

1980-1981	1981-1982	1982-1983	1983-1984	1984-1985	1985-1986
$ 1	$	$	$	$	$
56,669	59,899	58,321	56,818	75,983	60,360
27	30		22	36	35
71,184	97,955	109,522	118,403	200,114	231,618
31	23	31	32	32	31
68,623	76,118	95,748	82,357	123,153	143,692
163,921	164,581	159,985	165,961	150,134	137,564
1,185	843	1,468	1,847	2,345	2,352
255	264	247	262	367	343
452,274	512,090	550,633	669,201	820,282	721,451
23,332	26,314	34,042	38,173	31,790	38,375
757	731	704	832	785	731
824	864	990	1,140	1,217	2,444
322	-6			391	358
169	195	8			
7,759	9,199	11,416	11,924	11,259	11,280
29,021	3,097	555	682	306	109
23,513	27,273	28,432	25,650	30,226	28,213
73	56	141	105	96	128
858,605	928,767	847,188	895,534	1,202,669	1,135,007
813,000	955,021	849,596	789,426	760,657	617,458
6,816	9,718	9,999	10,654	11,045	11,791
23,871	25,508	26,120	29,869	27,688	27,410
63,808	65,536	60,987	57,644	87,984	82,985
1,688	923	961	2,201	2,513	3,045
61,905	52,660	54,300	75,258	70,166	68,547
2,729,633	3,017,659	2,901,394	3,033,995	3,611,238	3,325,327
348,013	545,262	481,724	498,020	429,403	356,285
40,119	61,600	40,520	23,833	23,461	28,346
128,983	122,828	41,879	52,786	59,712	25,950
517,115	729,690	564,123	574,639	512,576	410,581
181,660	230,243	195,305	101,049	79,678	72,929
9,525	10,789	11,326	11,424	14,589	12,776
3,417	3,169	3,280	3,028	2,912	3,160
2,468	2,665	2,842	2,981	3,342	3,444
26,256	54,669	1,678,509	1,706,748	2,108,303	2,187,580
31,153	36,284	38,310	42,201	45,973	46,268
213,341	596,258	913,349	840,888	878,617	954,809
310,610	323,175	365,675	239,030	453,780	324,705
220,542	246,127	253,762	281,570	291,599	284,100
998,972	1,503,379	3,462,358	3,228,919	3,878,793	3,889,771
20,790					
1,310,075	1,236,983	1,375,097	1,383,087	1,547,244	1,691,239
1,330,865	1,236,983	1,375,097	1,383,087	1,547,244	1,691,239
$ 5,576,585	$ 6,487,711	$ 8,302,972	$ 8,220,640	$ 9,549,851	9,316,918

Source: *State of Louisiana Comprehensive Annual Financial Report*

STATE OF LOUISIANA GENERAL GOVERNMENTAL EXPENDITURES BY FUNCTION
LAST TEN FISCAL YEARS
(EXPRESSED IN THOUSANDS)

	1976-77	1977-78	1978-79	1979-80	1980-81	1981-82	1982-83(2)	1983-84(2)	1984-85(2)	1985-86 (3)
GENERAL GOVERNMENT	$ 144,017	$ 256,904	$ 265,328	$ 343,752	$ 368,065	$ 385,016	$ 440,807	$ 525,571	$ 560,546	$ 537,340
CULTURE, RECREATION AND TOURISM	12,820	12,984	15,717	20,453	24,235	25,815	22,053	23,304	24,833	23,715
TRANSPORTATION AND DEVELOPMENT	511,370	188,000	236,975	260,381	303,473	416,171	317,794	242,412	235,194	222,532
PUBLIC SAFETY	59,314	67,203	64,994	67,920	81,140	95,752	86,926	89,110	85,686	103,832
HEALTH AND WELFARE	783,858	887,591	1,041,796	1,207,711	1,397,971	1,578,335	1,747,364	1,838,989	1,883,353	2,049,765
CORRECTIONS	48,125	55,387	65,176	80,628	103,248	121,650	138,015	154,746	169,184	189,028
CONSERVATION	33,250	35,535	41,093	58,476	78,475	83,560	80,552	90,718	84,538	83,706
EDUCATION	1,087,774	1,261,866	1,346,004	1,552,309	1,802,610	2,329,624	1,513,204	1,552,396	1,682,552	1,717,752
AID TO LOCAL GOVERNMENT	211,029	225,644	254,166	256,432	327,180	326,867	315,950	355,603	389,094	326,704
DEBT SERVICE	91,628	133,496	172,926	164,115	175,533	207,226	387,474	303,019	317,880	374,667
CAPITAL OUTLAY(1)	146,478	455,891	427,629	546,030	683,227	723,400	816,020	860,200	713,214	809,877
OTHER	44,614	53,565	29,432	28,808	31,162	25,984	50,606	29,148	25,186	17,039
AUXILIARY							10,536	11,693	14,468	
INTERNAL SERVICE FUNDS							234,543	227,718	221,674	270,819
OTHER NON-BUDGETED							809,842	674,088	522,701	534,162
PENSIONS TRUST							370,076	418,907	485,181	517,846
LEVEE DISTRICTS							32,196	39,541	45,384	52,143
HARBORS AND PORTS							44,477	50,511	62,420	67,260
SUB-TOTAL EXPENDITURES	3,174,277	3,634,066	3,961,236	4,587,015	5,376,319	6,319,400	7,418,435	7,487,674	7,523,088	7,898,187
COLLEGES AND UNIVERSITIES							986,303	1,038,553	1,091,964	1,139,638
TOTAL EXPENDITURES	$ 3,174,277	$ 3,634,066	$ 3,961,236	$ 4,587,015	$ 5,376,319	$ 6,319,400	$ 8,404,738	$ 8,526,227	$ 8,615,052	$ 9,037,825

(1) CONSTRUCTION PROGRAM INCLUDED IN CAPITAL OUTLAY.
(2) EXPENDITURES REFLECT ALL EXPENDITURES AND ENCUMBRANCES. Prior to 1982-83 ONLY THE EXPENDITURES AND ENCUMBRANCES FOR THE GOVERNMENTAL FUND TYPES AND COLLEGE AND UNIVERSITY FUND TYPES, THE AUXILIARY FUND AND NON-BUDGETED EXPENDITURES FOR SPECIAL PURPOSE, DEBT SERVICE AND CAPITAL OUTLAY FUNDS were reflected.
(3) 1985-1986 REFLECT ONLY EXPENDITURES. ENCUMBRANCES HAVE BEEN OMITTED FROM THE ANNUAL FINANCIAL REPORTS.

STATE OF LOUISIANA
DEBT SERVICE REQUIREMENTS TO MATURITY
GENERAL OBLIGATION BONDS WHICH ARE SELF SUPPORTING
OR PAID FROM SPECIAL TAXES
TOTAL PRINCIPAL AND INTEREST

FISCAL YEAR	SOUTH LOUISIANA PORT COMMISSION	LAKE PROVIDENCE PORT COMMISSION	GREATER BATON ROUGE PORT COMMISSION	PORT OF NEW ORLEANS BONDS	HIGHWAY BONDS	TOTAL REQUIREMENT
1986 - 1987	$ 958,930	$ 56,404	$ 948,257	$ 3,944,367	$ 3,374,651	$ 9,282,609
1987 - 1988	960,500	55,751	952,958	3,921,607	3,232,158	9,122,974
1988 - 1989	965,480	55,064	951,957	3,788,960	1,549,839	7,311,300
1989 - 1990	968,570	25,300	955,257	3,936,823	275,800	6,161,750
1990 - 1991	974,502	24,565	957,805	3,752,151	137,050	5,846,073
1991 - 1992	978,313	28,815	964,512	3,254,725	312,850	5,539,215
1992 - 1993		27,795	970,293	3,458,838	237,350	4,694,276
1993 - 1994		26,775	970,232	3,438,688		4,435,695
1994 - 1995		25,755	713,042	3,463,313		4,202,110
1995 - 1996		24,715	467,275	3,458,413		3,950,403
1996 - 1997		23,675	464,500	2,503,225		2,991,400
1997 - 1998		27,625	466,288	2,524,150		3,018,063
1998 - 1999		26,313	467,550	1,079,225		1,573,088
1999 - 2000			463,375	1,073,625		1,537,000
2000 - 2001			463,763			463,763
2001 - 2002			463,625			463,625
2002 - 2003			462,963			462,963
	$ 5,806,295	$ 428,552	$ 12,103,652	$ 43,598,110	$ 9,119,698	$ 71,056,307

Source: *State of Louisiana Comprehensive Annual Financial Report*

Per Capita State and Local Expenditures, 1985

| | Amount | | Louisiana Rank |
	Louisiana	U.S.	50 States
Total Direct			
General Expenditures	$1,691.77	$1,641.34	23
Total Education	526.97	540.09	29
Higher Education	198.00	200.73	30
Welfare	245.10	282.71	21
Hospitals	119.24	67.12	2
Highways	152.14	139.37	31

Source: U.S. Bureau of the Census, *State Government Finance in 1985*,
Series GF 85, No. 3.

Selected Per Capita State Government Revenues, 1985

| | Amount | | Louisiana Rank |
	Louisiana	U.S.	50 States
Total	$1,820.14	$1,843.45	26
Federal Taxes	350.99	354.74	28—combined federal and local taxes
Local Taxes	2.73	22.90	
Individual Income	177.54	267.28	37
General Sales	266.06	292.42	27
Motor Fuel Sales	80.75	56.07	N/A

Source: U.S. Bureau of the Census, *State Government Finance in 1985*,
Series GF 85, No. 3.

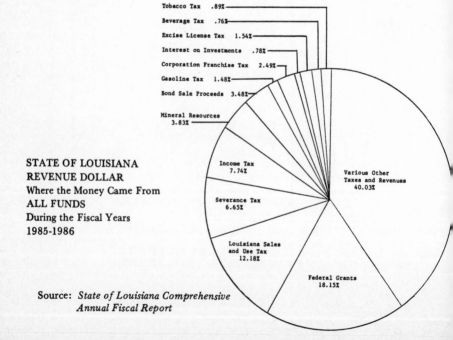

STATE OF LOUISIANA
REVENUE DOLLAR
Where the Money Came From
ALL FUNDS
During the Fiscal Years
1985-1986

Tobacco Tax .89%
Beverage Tax .76%
Excise License Tax 1.54%
Interest on Investments .78%
Corporation Franchise Tax 2.49%
Gasoline Tax 1.48%
Bond Sale Proceeds 3.48%
Mineral Resources 3.83%
Income Tax 7.74%
Severance Tax 6.65%
Louisiana Sales and Use Tax 12.18%
Federal Grants 18.15%
Various Other Taxes and Revenues 40.03%

Source: *State of Louisiana Comprehensive Annual Fiscal Report*

Louisiana's Annual Capital Budgeting Cycle

Deadline	Source	Action Required by State Law	Action Submitted To:
November 1	State departments, agencies, legislators, local governments	Submit annual requests, including proposed projects for the next five years, and the status of ongoing projects.	Division of Administration (Facility Planning and Control), Legislative Fiscal Office
November - February	Division of Administration—Facility Planning and Control, Budget Office, State Planning	Evaluate requests, analyze availability of funding, and prepare the five-year program.	Governor
March 1	Governor	Submit preliminary capital outlay recommendation to include a summary of maximum funding and an appendix showing rejected projects and the reasons for rejection.	Appropriate legislative committees
April (seventh day of session)	Governor	Submit capital outlay program, to include availability of funding and the status of ongoing, uncompleted projects, and the proposed capital outlay budget act for the first year of the five-year program.	Legislature
July (by end of session)	Legislature	Adopt a capital outlay bill for the next fiscal year and a concurrent resolution adopting the remaining four years of the five-year program.	Governor and Division of Administration
September (within 60 days after passage of the capital outlay bill)	Governor and Division of Administration	Prepare a revised five-year capital outlay program which reflects projects approved in the capital outlay bill.	Legislative Fiscal Office and the public

SOURCE: LSA-R.S. 39:61.

Louisiana Zip Code Directory

This list is a guide to zip codes in Louisiana. For codes of addresses located in large Louisiana cities or areas not included in the directory, call your local post office. (The indication (1st) after some post offices means that they are first class post offices.)

Post Office	Zip Code	Post Office	Zip Code	Post Office	Zip Code
Abbeville	70510	Belle Rose	70341	Clarence	71414
Main Office Boxes	70511	Belmont	71406	Clarks	71415
Forked Island	70510	Bentley	71407	Clayton	71326
Intracoastal City	70510	Benton	71006	Clinton	70722
Abita Springs	70420	Bernice	71222	Cloutierville	71416
Acme	71316	Berwick	70342	Colfax	71417
Addis	70710	Bethany	71007	Collinston	71229
Aimwell	71401	Bienville	71008	Columbia	71418
Akers	70421	Big Bend	71318	Convent	70723
Albany	70711	Blanchard	71009	Converse	71419
Alco	71446	Blanks	70717	Cottonport	71327
Alexandria	713	Bogalusa	70427	Cotton Valley	71018
A	71301	Bonita	71223	Coushatta	71019
Downtown	71301	Boothville	70038	Covington	70433
England AFB	71311	Bordelonville	71320	Main Office Boxes	70434
South Park	71307	Bossier City	711	Creole	70632
Alto	71216	Main Office Boxes	71171	Creston	71020
Ama	70031	Plantation Park		Crowley	70526
Amelia	70340	DLBU	71113	Main Office Boxes	70527
Amite	70422	Bourg	70343	Crowville	71230
Anacoco	71403	Boutte	70039	Cullen	71021
Angie	70426	Boyce	71409	Cut Off	70345
Varnado	70426	Braithwaite	70040	Cypress	71420
Angola	70712	Branch	70516	Darrow	70725
Arabi	70032	Breaux Bridge	70517	Davant	70046
Arcadia	71001	Bridge City	70094	Delcambre	70528
Archibald	71218	Brittany	70718	Delhi	71232
Arnaudville	70512	Broussard	70518	Delta	71233
Ashland	71002	Brusly	70719	Denham Springs	70726
Athens	71003	Bryceland	71014	Main Office Boxes	70727
Atlanta	71404	Buckeye	71321	De Quincy	70633
Avery Island	70513	Bueche	70720	De Ridder	70634
Bains	70713	Bunkie	71322	Derry	71421
Baker	70714	Buras	70041	Des Allemands	70030
Main Office Boxes	70704	Burnside	70738	Destrehan	70047
Baldwin	70514	Bush	70431	Deville	71328
Ball	71405	Cade	70519	Dixie	71107
Barataria	70036	Calcasieu	71433	Dodson	71422
Barksdale AFB	71110	Calhoun	71225	Donaldsonville	70346
Basile	70515	Calvin	71410	Donner	70352
Baskin	71219	Cameron	70631	Downsville	71234
Bastrop	71220	Campti	71411	Doyline	71023
Main Office Boxes	71221	Carencro	70520	Dry Creek	70637
Batchelor	70715	Carlisle	70042	Dry Prong	71423
Baton Rouge	708	Carville	70721	Dubach	71235
Audubon	70806	Caspiana	71015	Dubberly	71024
Broadview	70815	Castor	71016	Dulac	70353
Capitol	70804	Catahoula	70582	Dunn	71236
Central	70811	Cecilia	70521	Duplessis	70728
Highland Road	70808	Center Point	71323	Dupont	71329
Istrouma	70805	Centerville	70522	Duson	70529
Scotlandville	70807	Chalmette	70043	East Point	71025
Southeast	70808	Main Office Boxes	70044	Echo	71330
Southern	70813	Charenton	70523	Edgard	70049
South Sherwood	70826	Chase	71324	Effie	71331
University	70803	Chataignier	70524	Egan	70531
Zion City	70811	Chatham	71226	Elizabeth	70638
Bayou Chicot	70586	Chauvin	70344	Elmer	71424
Bayou Gauta	70716	Cheneyville	71325	Elm Grove	71051
Belcher	71004	Chestnut	71070	Elton	70532
Bell City	70630	Chopin	71412	Empire	70050
Belle Chasse	70037	Choudrant	71227	England AFB	71311
Money Order Unit	70037	Church Point	70525	Enterprise	71425

Post Office	Zip Code	Post Office	Zip Code	Post Office	Zip Code
Eola	71322	Oakwood	70053	Kurthwood	71443
Epps	71237	Grosse Tete	70740	Labadieville	70372
Erath	70533	Gueydan	70542	Labarre	70751
Eros	71238	Hackberry	70645	Lacamp	71444
Erwinville	70729	Hahnville	70057	Lacassine	70650
Estherwood	70534	Hall Summit	71034	Lacombe	70445
Ethel	70730	Hamburg	71339	Lafayette	705
Eunice	70535	Hammond	70401	Jefferson	70502
Evangeline	70537	Main Office Boxes	70404	Oil Center	70505
Evans	70639	Univ. of Soe La	70402	Southside	70503
Evergreen	71333	College	70401	Southwestern	
Extension	71239	Hanna	71035	University	70504
Fairbanks	71240	Harahan	70123	Lafitte	70067
Farmerville	71241	Hardwood	70742	Lake Arthur	70549
Felixville	70722	Harmon	71036	Lake Charles	706
Fenton	70640	Harrisonburg	71340	Drew	70605
Ferriday	71334	Harvey	70058	East Side	70601
Fields	70641	Main Office Boxes	70059	McNesse	
Fisher	71426	Haughton	71037	University	70609
Flatwoods	71427	Hayes	70646	Moss Bluff	70611
Flora	71428	Haynesville	71038	Lakeland	70752
Florien	71429	Hebert	71436	Lake Providence	71254
Fluker	70436	Heflin	71039	La Place	70068
Folsom	70437	Henderson	70517	Main Office Boxes	70069
Forbing	71106	Hessmer	71341	Larose	70373
Fordoche	70732	Hester	70743	Larto	71344
Forest	71242	Hicks	71437	Lawtell	70550
Forest Hill	71430	Hineston	71438	Leander	71445
Forked Island	70510	Hodge	71247	Lebeau	71345
Fort Necessity	71243	Holden	70744	Le Blanc	70651
Fort Polk	71459	Holly Ridge	71248	Lecompte	71346
Franklin	70538	Homer	71040	Leesville	71446
Franklinton	70438	Hornbeck	71439	Main Office Boxes	71496
French Settlement	70733	Hosston	71043	Alco	71446
Frierson	71027	Houma	703	Fort Polk	71459
Frogmore	71335	Main Office Boxes	70361	North Fort Polk	
Fullerton	70642	Husser	70442	Univ.	71459
Galliano	70354	Iberville	70746	Tower Park	71446
Garden City	70540	Ida	71044	Le Moyen	71347
Gardner	71431	Independence	70443	Lena	71447
Garyville	70051	Innis	70747	Leonville	70551
Geismar	70734	Intracoastal City	70510	Lettsworth	70753
Georgetown	71432	Iota	70543	Libuse	71348
Gheens	70355	Iowa	70647	Lillie	71256
Gibsland	71028	Jackson	70748	Linville	71257
Gibson	70356	Jamestown	71045	Lisbon	71048
Gilbert	71336	Jarreau	70749	Livingston	70754
Gilliam	71029	Jaenerette	70544	Livonia	70755
Girard	71244	Jefferson	70121	Lockport	70374
Glenmora	71433	Jena	71342	Logansport	71049
Gloster	71030	Jennings	70546	Longleaf	71448
Glynn	70736	Jigger	71249	Longstreet	71050
Golden Meadow	70357	Jones	71250	Longville	70652
Goldonna	71031	Jonesboro	71251	Loranger	70446
Gonzales	70737	Jonesville	71343	Loreauville	70552
Main Office Boxes	70707	Joyce	71440	Lottie	70756
Gorum	71434	Junction City	71749	Louisiana Tech	71272
Goudeau	71338	Kaplan	70548	Luling	70070
Grambling	71245	Keatchie	71046	Lutcher	70071
Gramercy	70052	Keithville	71047	Lydia	70569
Grand Cane	71032	Kelly	71441	Madisonville	70447
Grand Chenier	70643	Kenner	700	Mamou	70554
Grand Coteau	70541	Main Office Boxes	70063	Mandeville	70448
Grand Isle	70358	Chateau Estates		Mangham	71259
Grant	70644	DLBU	70064	Mansfield	71052
Gray	70359	Kentwood	70444	Mansura	71350
Grayson	71435	Kilbourne	71253	Many	71449
Greensburg	70441	Killona	70066	Maringouin	70757
Greenwell Springs	70739	Kinder	70648	Marion	71260
Greenwood	71033	Kolin	71360	Marksville	71351
Gretna	70053	Kramer	70371	Marrero	70072
Main Office Boxes	70054	Krotz Springs	70750	Main Office Boxes	70073

Post Office	Zip Code
Marthaville	71450
Mathews	70375
Maurepas	70449
Maur'ce	70555
McNeese University	70609
Melder	71451
Melrose	71452
Melville	71353
Meraux	70075
Mermentau	70556
Mer Rouge	71261
Merryville	70653
Metairie	700
Johnson St.	70001
Modu	70002
Modu	70005
Park Manor	70003
Midland	70557
Milton	70558
Minden	71055
Main Office Boxes	71058
Mira	71059
Mitchell	71453
Mittie	70654
Modeste	70376
Monroe	712
Downtown	71201
Louisville	71207
Northeast Louisiana Univ.	71209
Station 2	71201
Montegut	70377
Monterey	71354
Montgomery	71454
Mooringsport	71060
Mora	71455
Moreauville	71355
Morgan City	70380
Main Office Boxes	70381
Downtown	70381
Morganza	70759
Morrow	71356
Morse	70559
Mound	71262
Mount Airy	70076
Mount Hermon	70450
Napoleonville	70390
Natalbany	70451
Natchez	71456
Natchitoches	71457
Main Office Boxes	71458
Northwestern State Univ.	71497
Northwestern	71457
Negreet	71460
Newellton	71357
New Iberia	70560
Main Office Boxes	70561
Newllano	71461
New Orleans	701
A	70114
B	70115
Broadmoor	70125
Bywater	70117
Carrollton	70118
Chef Menteur	70126
Custom House	70116
Gentilly	70122
Harahan	70123
International Trade Mart	70130

Post Office	Zip Code
Jefferson	70121
Lafayette Square	70130
Lakeview	70124
Michoud	70129
Mid City	70119
MODU	70113
Moisant Airport	70141
Vieux Carre	70172
New Roads	70760
New Sarpy	70078
Nicholls University	70310
Noble	71462
Norco	70079
Northeast Louisiana Univ.	71209
North Fort Polk Univ.	71459
Northwestern State Univ.	71497
Norwood	70761
Oakdale	71463
Oak Grove	71263
Oak Ridge	71264
Oberlin	70655
Oil City	71061
Olinkraft	71291
Olla	71465
Opelousas	70570
Main Office Boxes	70571
Oscar	70762
Otis	71466
Paincourtville	70391
Palmetto	71358
Paradis	70080
Parks	70582
Patterson	70392
Paulina	70763
Pearl River	70452
Pelican	71063
Perry	70575
Pierre Part	70339
Pilottown	70081
Pine Grove	70453
Pine Prairie	70576
Pineville	71360
Main Office Boxes	71361
Pioneer	71266
Pitkin	70656
Plain Dealing	71064
Plaquemine	70764
Main Office Boxes	70765
Plattenville	70393
Plaucheville	71362
Pleasant Hill	71065
Point Clair	70721
Pointe A La Hache	70082
Pollock	71467
Ponchatoula	70454
Port Allen	70767
Port Barre	70577
Port Sulphur	70083
Powhatan	71066
Prairieville	70769
Pride	70770
Princeton	71067
Provencal	71468
Quitman	71268
Raceland	70394
Ragley	70657
Rayne	70578
Rayville	71269
Reddell	70580

Post Office	Zip Code
Reeves	70658
Reserve	70084
Mount Airy	70076
Rhinehart	71363
Ringgold	71068
Roanoke	70581
Robeline	71469
Robert	70455
Rodessa	71069
Rosa	71364
Rosedale	70772
Roseland	70456
Rosepine	70659
Rougon	70773
Ruby	71365
Ruston	71270
Main Office Boxes	71273
Louisiana Tech	71272
Saint Amant	70774
Saint Benedict	70457
Saint Bernard	70085
Saint Francisville	70775
Saint Gabriel	70776
Saint Gertrude	70433
Saint James	70086
Saint Joseph	71366
Saint Landry	71367
Saint Martinville	70582
Saint Maurice	71471
Saint Rose	70087
Saline	71070
Sarepta	71071
Schriever	70395
Scott	70583
Shongaloo	71072
Shreveport	711
Dixie	71107
Forbing	71106
Barksdale AFB	71110
Cedar Grove	71106
Centenary	71104
Cooper Road	71107
Downtown	71101
Industrial	71107
Jewella	71109
Morningside	71108
Southfield	71105
South Park	71118
Sibley	71073
Sicily Island	71368
Sieper	71472
Sikes	71473
Simmesport	71369
Simpson	71474
Simsboro	71275
Singer	70660
Slagle	71475
Slaughter	70777
Slidell	704
Main Office Boxes	70459
Sondheimer	71276
Sorrento	70778
Southern	70813
Spearsville	71277
Spencer	71278
Springfield	70462
Springhill	71075
Starks	70661
Start	71279
Sterlington	71280
Stonewall	71078
Sugartown	70662

Post Office	Zip Code	Post Office	Zip Code	Post Office	Zip Code
Sulphur	70663	Trout	71371	Waterproof	71375
Main Office Boxes	70664	Tullos	71479	Watson	70786
Summerfield	71079	Tunica	70782	Waverly	71232
Sun	70463	Turkey Creek	70585	Welsh	70591
Sunset	70584	Uncle Sam	70792	Westlake	70669
Sunshine	70780	Univ. of Soe La.	70402	West Monroe	71291
Swartz	71281	Urania	71480	Main Office Boxes	71294
Talisheek	70464	Vacherio	70090	Olinkraft	71291
Tallulah	71282	Varnado	70467	Westwego	70094
Main Office Boxes	71284	Venice	70091	Weyanoke	70787
Tangipahoa	70465	Ventress	70783	White Castle	70788
Taylor	71080	Verda	71481	Whiteville	71322
Temple	71476	Vick	71372	Wildsville	71377
Terry	71285	Vidalia	71373	Wilson	70789
Theriot	70397	Ville Platte	70586	Winnfield	71483
Thibodaux	70301	Bayou Chicot	70586	Winnsboro	71295
Main Office Boxes	70302	Vinton	70668	Wisner	71378
Nicholls University	70310	Violet	70092	Woodworth	71485
Tickfaw	70466	Vivian	71082	Youngsville	70592
Tioga	71477	Wakefield	70784	Zachary	70791
Torbert	70781	Walker	70785	Zion City	70811
Transylvania	71286	Warden	71289	Zwolle	71486
Trees	71081	Washington	70589		

STATE ABBREVIATIONS

Alabama	AL	Kentucky	KY	Ohio	OH
Alaska	AK	Louisiana	LA	Oklahoma	OK
Arizona	AZ	Maine	ME	Oregon	OR
Arkansas	AR	Maryland	MD	Pennsylvania	PA
California	CA	Massachusetts	MA	Puerto Rico	PR
Colorado	CO	Michigan	MI	Rhode Island	RI
Connecticut	CT	Minnesota	MN	South Carolina	SC
Delaware	DE	Mississippi	MS	South Dakota	SD
Dist. of Col	DC	Missouri	MO	Tennessee	TN
Florida	FL	Montana	MT	Texas	TX
Georgia	GA	Nebraska	NE	Utah	UT
Guam	GU	Nevada	NV	Vermont	VT
Hawaii	HI	New Hampshire	NH	Virginia	VA
Idaho	ID	New Jersey	NJ	Virgin Islands	VI
Illinois	IL	New Mexico	NM	Washington	WA
Indiana	IN	New York	NY	West Virginia	WV
Iowa	IA	North Carolina	NC	Wisconsin	WI
Kansas	KS	North Dakota	ND	Wyoming	WY

SPORTS
LSU FUTURE FOOTBALL SCHEDULES
1988   1989

1988	1989
9/ 3 TEXAS A&M (H)	9/ 2 Texas A&M (a)
9/17 Tennessee (a)*	9/16 FLORIDA STATE (H)
9/24 Ohio State (a)	9/30 OHIO STATE (H)
10/ 1 Florida (a)*	10/ 7 FLORIDA (H)*
10/ 8 AUBURN (H)*	10/14 Auburn (a)*
10/15 KENTUCKY (H)*	10/21 Kentucky (a)*
10/29 OLE MISS (H)*	10/28 TENNESSEE (H)*
11/ 5 Alabama (a)*	11/ 4 Ole Miss (a)*
11/12 Mississippi State (a)*	11/11 ALABAMA (H)*
11/19 MIAMI (FLA.) (H)	11/18 MISSISSIPPI STATE (H)*
11/26 TULANE (H)	11/25 Tulane (a)

*Southeastern Conference
game

LSU ATHLETIC HALL OF FAME

FOOTBALL: Ruffin G. Pleasant, Edward Robertson, G. E. (Doc) Fenton, J. J. Seip, R. B. Howell, Lawrence Dupont, Tom Dutton, Clarence (Fatty) Ives, Newton C. Helm, W. E. (Bill) Pitcher, Norman Stevens, Charley Mason, Guy Nesom, Abe Mickal, Jesse Fatherree, Marvin (Moose) Stewart, Gaynell Tinsley, Charles (Pinky) Rohm, Ken Kavanaugh, Steve Van Buren, Clyde Lindsey, Y. A. Tittle, Abner Wimberly, Kenny Konz, Jerry Marchand, Sid Fournet, Joe Tuminello, Jimmy Taylor, Fred Miller, Percy Brown, Billy Cannon, Butch Helveston, Doug Moreau, Roy Winston, Jerry Stovall, Charles "Bo" Strange, Tommy Casanova, Johnny Robinson, George Bevan, Tyler Lafauci

BASKETBALL: Malcolm (Sparky) Wade, Joe Dean, Bob Pettit

TRACK: Sidney Bowman, Nathan (Buddy) Blair, Glenn (Slats) Hardin, Jack Torrance, Al Moreau, Matt Gordy, Billy Brown, Oris (Arky) Erwin, Billy Hardin, Robert Lowther, R. Delmon McNabb, Joseph T. Butler, Sr., Harry Carpenter

BOXING: Henry Glaze, J. L. Golsan, Heston Daniel, Wilbert Moss, Edsel (Tad) Thrash, Calvin Clary, Robert L. (Bobby) Freeman, Al Michael

GOLF: Fred Haas, Jr., Henry Castillo, B. R. (Mac) McClendon, Gardner E. Dickinson, Jr., Al Michael

SWIMMING: Bob Percy, Rick Meador

TENNIS: Steve Faulk

ATHLETIC COUNCIL: James F. Broussard

BASEBALL: Joe Bill Adcock, Alvin Dark

SUGAR BOWL

1935 Tulane 20, Temple 14	1962 Alabama 10, Arkansas 3
1936 TCU 3, LSU 2	1963 Mississippi 17, Arkansas 13
1937 Santa Clara 21, LSU 14	1964 Alabama 12, Mississippi 7
1938 Santa Clara 6, LSU 0	1965 LSU 13, Syracuse 10
1939 TCU 15, Carnegie Tech 7	1966 Missouri 20, Florida 18
1940 Texas A&M 14, Tulane 13	1967 Alabama 34, Nebraska 7
1941 Boston College 19, Tennessee 13	1968 LSU 20, Wyoming 13
1942 Fordham 2, Missouri 0	1969 Texas 36, Tennessee 13
1943 Tennessee 14, Tulsa 7	1970 Mississippi 27, Arkansas 22
1944 Georgia Tech 20, Tulsa 18	1971 Tennessee 34, Air Force 13
1945 Duke 29, Alabama 26	1972 Oklahoma 40, Auburn 22
1946 Okla. A&M 33, St. Mary's 13	1972 Oklahoma 14, Penn State 0
1947 Georgia 20, North Carolina 10	1973 Notre Dame 24, Alabama 23
1948 Texas 27, Alabama 7	1974 Nebraska 13, Florida 10
1949 Oklahoma 14, N. Carolina 6	1975 Alabama 13, Penn State 6
1950 Oklahoma 35, LSU 0	1977 Pitt 27, Georgia 3
1951 Kentucky 13, Oklahoma 7	1978 Alabama 35, Ohio State 6
1952 Maryland 29, Tennessee 13	1979 Alabama 14, Penn State 7
1953 Ga. Tech 24, Mississippi 7	1980 Alabama 24, Arkansas 9
1954 Ga. Tech 42, W. Virginia 19	1981 Georgia 17, Notre Dama 10
1955 Navy 21, Mississippi 0	1982 Pitt 24, Georgia 20
1956 Ga. Tech 7, Pittsburgh 0	1983 Penn State 27, Georgia 23
1957 Baylor 13, Tennessee 7	1984 Auburn 9, Michigan 7
1958 Mississippi 39, Texas 7	1985 Nebraska 28, LSU 10
1959 LSU 7, Clemson 0	1986 Tennessee 35, Miami (FLA.)
1960 Mississippi 21, LSU 0	1987 Nebraska 30, LSU 15
1961 Mississippi 14, Rice 6	1988 Auburn 16, Syracuse 16

LSU's BOWL RECORD (14-12-1)

Date	Game	Opponent	Score
January 1, 1936	Sugar	TCU	2-3
January 1, 1937	Sugar	Santa Clara	14-21
January 1, 1938	Sugar	Santa Clara	0-6
January 1, 1944	Orange	Texas A&M	19-14
January 1, 1947	Cotton	Arkansas	0-0
January 1, 1950	Sugar	Oklahoma	0-35
January 1, 1959	Sugar	Clemson	7-0
January 1, 1960	Sugar	Mississippi	0-21
January 1, 1962	Orange	Colorado	25-7
January 1, 1963	Cotton	Texas	13-0
December 21, 1963	Bluebonnet	Baylor	7-14
January 1, 1965	Sugar	Syracuse	13-10
January 1, 1966	Cotton	Arkansas	14-7
January 1, 1968	Sugar	Wyoming	20-13
December 30, 1968	Peach	Florida State	31-27
January 1, 1971	Orange	Nebraska	12-17
December 18, 1971	Sun	Iowa State	33-15
December 30, 1972	Bluebonnet	Tennessee	17-24
January 1, 1974	Orange	Penn State	9-16
December 31, 1977	Sun	Stanford	14-24
December 23, 1978	Liberty	Missouri	15-20
December 22, 1979	Tangerine	Wake Forest	34-10
January 1, 1983	Orange	Nebraska	20-21
January 1, 1984	Sugar	Nebraska	28-10
December 29, 1985	Liberty	Baylor	21-7
January 1, 1987	Sugar	Nebraska	30-15
December 31, 1987	Gator	South Carolina	30-13

1987 LOUISIANA FOOTBALL SCORES

GRAMBLING (5-6)

24	Alcorn State	28
21	Central State	37
21	Bethune-Cookman	14
28	at Prairie View	7
51	at Tenn. State	9
45	Miss. Valley	14
17	at Jackson State	31
30	Texas Southern	9
7	at Alabama State	17
13	at S.C. State	15
21	Southern	27

LA. TECH (3-8)

3	at Baylor	13
7	Northeast	44
13	at Miss. State	14
16	at Kansas	11
18	at UT-Chattanooga	20
7	McNeese State	3
3	at Arkansas State	37
23	Northwestern	0
3	at Texas A&M	32
10	SW Missouri State	13
5	at N. Texas State	10

LSU (9-1-1)

17	at Texas A&M	3
56	Fullerton State	12
49	Rice	16
13	Ohio State	13
13	Florida	10
26	at Georgia	23
34	Kentucky	9
42	at Ole Miss	13
10	Alabama	22
34	Miss. State	14
41	at Tulane	36

McNEESE STATE (2-9)

31	Northern Iowa	34
3	at Northwestern	39
20	S. F. Austin	8
16	N. Texas State	38
0	Arkansas State	17
3	at Louisiana Tech	7
13	at New Mexico State	32
10	at Northeast	37
10	SW Texas State	24
7	Nicholls State	29
44	at Lamar	36

NICHOLLS STATE (5-5-1)

17	St. Cloud State	3
17	Troy State	17
21	at SW Missouri State	9
14	at Northeast	26
14	Alcorn State	3
27	at Southern	21
21	S. F. Austin	24
16	SW Texas State	31
17	at Akron	23
28	Northwestern	31
29	at McNeese State	7

NORTHEAST (9-2)

44	at Louisiana Tech	7
44	at SW Texas State	7
26	Nicholls State	14
33	Northwestern	31
28	Lamar	48
26	Ga. Southern	17
7	USL	17
37	McNeese State	10
34	at Southern Miss.	24
24	N. Texas State	23
31	Arkansas State	21

NORTHWESTERN (6-5)

23	at Arkansas State	20
39	McNeese State	3
13	North Texas State	15
31	at Northeast	33
3	at USL	13
24	at SW Texas State	21
0	Louisiana Tech	23
7	at Sam Houston	34
31	at Nicholls State	28
26	Jackson State	24
33	at S. F. Austin	21

SOUTHERN (7-4)

14	at Alabama State	10
33	Texas Southern	13
14	at Prairie View	0
17	at Miss. Valley	14
21	Nicholls State	27
0	at Jackson State	14
17	Alcorn State	19
14	Tenn. State	7
17	at Florida A&M	24
8	SW Missouri State	6
27	Grambling	21

TULANE (6-5)

40	at Louisville	42
25	Iowa State	12
24	at Southern Miss.	31
31	Ole Miss	24
27	Vanderbilt	17
36	at Memphis State	45
57	Virginia Tech	38
14	at Florida State	73
30	at Miss. State	19
38	USL	10
36	LSU	41

USL (6-5)

3	at Miss. State	31
21	Nevada-Las Vegas	10
0	at Oklahoma State	36
10	at Alabama	38
13	Northwestern	3
14	at Ole Miss	24
17	at Northeast	7
31	Memphis State	7
10	at Tulane	38
35	Colorado State	28
37	Southern Miss	30

Source: *The Morning Advocate*, Baton Rouge, La.

Note: The football program at Southeast Louisiana University has been discontinued.

PRO FOOTBALL HALL OF FAME
LOUISIANA HONOREES

Name	Team	Position	Final Season
Steve Van Buren	LSU	halfback	1943
Y. A. Tittle	LSU	quarterback	1947
Jim Taylor	LSU	fullback	1957

LSU FOOTBALL RECORDS

1893 (0-1-0)
Coach: C. E. Coates
Captain: R. G. Pleasant

0	Tulane	34
0		34

1894 (2-1-0)
Coach: A. P. Simmons
Captain: S. M. D. 'Clark

36	Natchez AC	0
6	Mississippi	26
30	Centenary	0
72		26

1895 (3-0-0)
Coach: A. P. Simmons
Captain: J. E. Snider

8	Tulane	4
16	Centenary	6
12	Alabama	6
36		16

1896 (6-0-0)
Coach: A. W. Jeardeau
Captain: E. A. Scott

46	Centenary	0
6	Tulane	0
12	Mississippi	4
14	Texas	0
52	Miss. State	0
6	Southern AC	0
136		4

1897 (1-1-0)
Coach: A. W. Jeardeau
Captain: E. A. Scott

28	Montgomery AC	6
0	Cincinnati	26
28		32

1898 (1-0-0)
Coach: E. A. Chavanne

37	Tulane	0
37		0

1899 (1-4-0)
Coach: J. P. Gregg
Captain: H. F. Aby

0	Mississippi	11
0	Sewanee	34
0	Texas	29
0	Texas A & M	52
38	Tulane	0
38		126

1900 (2-2-0)
Coach: E. A. Chavanne
Captain: I. H. Schwing

70	Millsaps	0
0	Tulane	29
5	Millsaps	6
10	LSU Alumni	0
85		35

1901 (5-1-0)
Coach: W. S. Borland
Captain: E. L. Gorham

57	La. Tech	0
46	Mississippi	0
11	Tulane	0
0	Auburn	28
38	YMCA (N.O.)	0
15	Arkansas	0
167		28

1902 (6-1-0)
Coach: W. S. Borland
Captain: H. E. Landry

42	S.W. (La.)	0
5	Texas	0
5	Auburn	0
6	Mississippi	0
5	Vanderbilt	27
6	Miss. State	0
11	Alabama	0
80		27

1903 (4-5-0)
Coach: W. S. Borland
Captain: J. J. Coleman

16	LSU Alumni	0
33	Eagles (N.O.)	0
16	La. Tech	0
5	Shreveport AC	0
0	Miss. State	11
0	Alabama	18
0	Auburn	12
0	Cumberland	41
0	Mississippi	11
70		93

1904 (3-4-0)
Coach: D. A. Killian
Captain: E. L. Klock

17	La. Tech	0
0	Shreveport AC	16
0	La. Tech	6
5	Mississippi	0
16	Nashville Med	0
0	Tulane	5
0	Alabama	11
38		38

1905 (3-0-0)
Coach: D. A. Killian
Captain: F. M. Edwards

16	La. Tech	0
5	Tulane	0
15	Miss. State	0
36		0

1906 (2-2-2)
Coach: D. A. Killian
Captain: E. E. Weil

5	Monroe AC	0
0	Mississippi	9
0	Miss. State	0
17	La. Tech	0
12	Texas A&M	21
6	Arkansas	6
40		36

1907 (7-3-0)
Coach: E. R. Wingard
Captain: S. W. Brannon

28	La. Tech	0
5	Texas	12
5	Texas A & M	11
57	Howard	0
17	Arkansas	12
23	Miss. State	11
23	Mississippi	0
4	Alabama	6
48	Baylor	0
56	Havana U.	0
266		52

1908 (10-0-0)
Coach: E. R. Wingard
Captain: M. H. Gandy

41	YMGC (N. O.)	0
81	Jackson Br. NO.	5
26	Texas A & M	0
55	S.W. (Tenn.)	0
10	Auburn	2
50	Miss. State	0
89	Baylor	0
32	Haskell	0
22	La. Tech	0
36	Arkansas	4
442		11

1909 (6-2-0)
Coaches: J. G. Pritchard
J. W. Mayhew
Captain: R. L. Stovall

70	Jackson Br. NO	0
10	Mississippi	0
15	Miss. State	0
6	Sewanee	15
23	La. Tech	0
0	Arkansas	16
52	Transylvania	0
12	Alabama	6
188		37

1910 (1-5-0)
Coach: J. W. Mayhew
Captain: J. J. Seip

40	Miss. College	0
0	Miss. State	3
5	Sewanee	31
0	Vanderbilt	22
0	Texas	12
0	Arkansas	51
45		119

1911 (6-3-0)
Coach: J. K. Dwyer
Captain: A. J. Thomas

42	S.W. (La.)	0
46	La. Normal	0
40	Miss. College	0
40	Meteor AC	0
6	Baylor	0
0	Miss. State	6
6	S.W. (Tenn.)	17
0	Arkansas	11
6	Tulane	0
186		34

1912 (4-3-0)
Coach: J. K. Dwyer
Captain: C. S. Reiley

85	S.W. (La.)	3
45	Miss. College	0
7	Mississippi	10
0	Miss. State	7
0	Auburn	7
7	Arkansas	6
21	Tulane	3
165		36

1913 (6-1-2)
Coach: J. K. Dwyer
Captain: T. W. Dutton

20	La. Tech	2
26	S.W. (La.)	0
45	Jefferson Col.	6
50	Baylor	0
0	Auburn	7
12	Arkansas	7
0	Miss. State	0
40	Tulane	0
7	Texas A&M	7
200		29

1914 (4-4-1)
Coach: E. T. McDonald
Captain: G. B. Spencer

54	S.W. (La.)	0
60	La. Tech	0
14	Miss. College	0

0	Mississippi	21
14	Jefferson Col.	13
9	Texas A & M	63
12	Arkansas	20
0	Haskell	31
0	Tulane	0
163		148

1915 (6-2-0)
Coach: E. T. McDonald
Captain: A. J. Reid

42	Jefferson Col.	0
14	Miss. Col.	0
28	Mississippi	0
7	Ga. Tech	36
10	Miss. State	0
13	Arkansas	7
0	Rice	6
12	Tulane	0
126		49

1916 (7-1-2)
Coach: E. T. McDonald
I. R. Pray, D. X. Bible
Captain: P. Cooper

24	S.W. (La.)	0
59	Jefferson Col.	0
13	Texas A & M	0
50	Miss. College	7
0	Sewanee	7
17	Arkansas	7
13	Miss. State	3
41	Mississippi	0
7	Rice	7
14	Tulane	14
238		45

1917 (3-5-0)
Coach: W. Sutton
Captain: A. O'Quinn

20	S.W. (La.)	6
52	Mississippi	7
0	Sewanee	3
0	Texas A & M	27
0	Arkansas	14
34	Miss. College	0
0	Miss. State	9
6	Tulane	28
112		94

1919 (6-2-0)
Coach: I. R. Pray
Captain: T. W. Dutton

39	S.W. (La.)	0
38	Jefferson Col.	0
13	Mississippi	0
20	Arkansas	0
0	Miss. State	6
24	Miss. College	0
0	Alabama	23
27	Tulane	6
161		35

1920 (5-3-1)
Coach: Branch Bocock
Captain: R. L. Benoit

81	Jefferson Col.	0
34	La. Normal	0
40	Spring Hill	0
0	Texas A & M	0
7	Miss. State	12
41	Miss. College	9
3	Arkansas	0
0	Alabama	21
0	Tulane	21
206		63

1921 (6-1-1)
Coach: Branch Bocock
Captain: F. L. Spencer

78	La. Normal	0
6	Texas A & M	0

41	Spring Hill	7
7	Alabama	7
10	Arkansas	7
21	Mississippi	0
0	Tulane	21
17	Miss. State	14
180		56

1922 (3-7-0)
Coach: I. R. Pray
Captain: E. L. Ewen

13	La. Normal	0
0	Loyola	7
0	S. M. U.	51
0	Texas A & M	47
6	Arkansas	40
25	Spring Hill	7
0	Rutgers	25
3	Alabama	47
0	Miss. State	7
25	Tulane	14
72		245

1923 (3-5-1)
Coach: Mike Donahue
Captain: E. L. Ewen

40	La. Normal	0
7	S.W. (La.)	3
33	Spring Hill	0
0	Texas A & M	28
13	Arkansas	26
0	Miss. College	0
3	Alabama	30
0	Tulane	20
7	Miss. State	14
103		121

1924 (5-4-0)
Coach: Mike Donahue
Captain: C. C. Campbell

7	Spring Hill	6
31	S.W. (La.)	7
20	Indiana	14
12	Rice	0
0	Auburn	3
7	Arkansas	10
7	Ga. Tech	28
40	La. Normal	0
0	Tulane	13
124		81

1925 (5-3-1)
Coach: Mike Donahue
Captain: J. E. Steele

27	La. Normal	0
38	S.W. (La.)	0
0	Alabama	42
6	LSU Freshmen	0
0	Tennessee	0
0	Arkansas	12
6	Rice	0
13	Loyola	0
0	Tulane	16
90		70

1926 (6-3-0)
Coach: Mike Donahue
Captain: L. T. Godfrey

47	La. Normal	0
34	S.W. (La.)	0
7	Tennessee	14
10	Auburn	0
6	Miss. State	7
0	Alabama	24
14	Arkansas	0
3	Mississippi	0
7	Tulane	0
128		45

1927 (4-4-1)
Coach: Mike Donahue
Captain: L. T. Godfrey

45	La. Tech	0
52	S.W. (La.)	0
0	Alabama	0
9	Auburn	0
9	Miss. State	7
0	Arkansas	28
7	Mississippi	12
0	Ga. Tech	23
6	Tulane	13
128		83

1928 (6-2-1)
Coach: Russ Cohen
Captain: Jess Tinsley

46	S.W. (La.)	0
41	La. College	0
31	Miss. State	0
30	Spring Hill	7
0	Arkansas	7
19	Mississippi	6
13	Georgia	12
0	Tulane	0
0	Alabama	13
180		45

1929 (6-3-0)
Coach: Russ Cohen
Captain: Frank Ellis

58	La. College	0
58	S.W. (La.)	0
27	Sewanee	14
31	Miss. State	6
53	La. Tech	7
0	Arkansas	32
6	Duke	32
13	Mississippi	6
0	Tulane	21
246		118

1930 (6-4-0)
Coach: Russ Cohen
Captain: W. Reeves

76	S. D. Wesleyan	0
71	La. Tech	0
85	S.W. (La.)	0
6	S. Carolina	7
6	Miss. State	8
12	Sewanee	0
27	Arkansas	12
6	Mississippi	0
0	Alabama	33
7	Tulane	12
296		72

1931 (5-4-0)
Coach: Russ Cohen
Captain: Ed Khoury

0	T. C. U.	3
35	Spring Hill	0
19	S. Carolina	12
31	Miss. State	0
13	Arkansas	6
6	Sewanee	12
0	Army	20
26	Mississippi	3
7	Tulane	34
137		90

1932 (6-3-1)
Coach: L. M. Jones
Captain: Walter Fleming

3	T. C. U.	3
8	Rice	10
80	Spring Hill	0
24	Miss. State	0
14	Arkansas	0
38	Sewanee	0
6	S. Carolina	0
0	Centenary	6
14	Tulane	0
0	Oregon	12
187		31

1933 (7-0-3)
Coach: Biff Jones
Captain: Jack Torrance

13	Rice	0
40	Millsaps	0
0	Centenary	0
20	Arkansas	0
7	Vanderbilt	7
30	So. Carolina	7
31	Mississippi	0
21	Miss. State	6
7	Tulane	7
7	Tennessee	0
176		27

1934 (7-2-2)
Coach: Biff Jones
Captain: Bertis Yates

9	Rice	9
14	SMU	14
20	Auburn	6
16	Arkansas	0
29	Vanderbilt	0
25	Miss. State	3
6	George Wash.	0
14	Mississippi	0
12	Tulane	13
13	Tennessee	19
14	Oregon	13
172		77

1935 (9-1-0)
Coach: B. H. Moore
Captain: Jeff Barrett

7	Rice	10
18	Texas	6
32	Manhattan	0
13	Arkansas	7
7	Vanderbilt	2
6	Auburn	0
28	Miss. State	13
13	Georgia	0
56	S.W. (La.)	0
41	Tulane	0
221		38

Sugar Bowl
2	TCU	3

1936 (9-0-1)
Coach: B. H. Moore
Captain: Bill May

20	Rice	7
6	Texas	6
47	Georgia	7
13	Mississippi	0
19	Arkansas	7
19	Vanderbilt	0
12	Miss. State	0
19	Auburn	6
93	S.W. (La.)	0
33	Tulane	0
281		33

Sugar Bowl
14	Santa Clara	21

1937 (9-1-0)
Coach: B. H. Moore
Captain: Arthur Morton

19	Florida	0
9	Texas	0
13	Rice	0
13	Mississippi	0
6	Vanderbilt	7
52	Loyola (N.O.)	6
41	Miss. State	0
9	Auburn	7
52	La. Normal	0
20	Tulane	7
234		27

Sugar Bowl
0	Santa Clara	6

1938 (6-4-0)
Coach: B. H. Moore
Captain: Ben Friend

7	Mississippi	20
20	Texas	0
3	Rice	0
47	Loyola (N.O.)	6
7	Vanderbilt	0
6	Tennessee	14
32	Miss. State	7
6	Auburn	28
32	S.W. (La.)	0
0	Tulane	14
160		89

1939 (4-5-0)
Coach: B. H. Moore
Captain: Young Bussey

7	Mississippi	14
26	Holy Cross	7
7	Rice	0
20	Loyola (N.O.)	0
12	Vanderbilt	6
0	Tennessee	20
12	Miss. State	15
7	Auburn	21
20	Tulane	33
111		116

1940 (6-4-0)
Coach: B. H. Moore
Captain: Charles Anastasio

39	La. Tech	7
6	Mississippi	19
25	Holy Cross	0
0	Rice	23
20	Mercer	0
7	Vanderbilt	0
0	Tennessee	28
7	Miss. State	22
21	Auburn	13
14	Tulane	0
139		112

1941 (4-4-2)
Coach: B. H. Moore
Captain: Leo Bird

25	La. Tech	0
13	Holy Cross	19
0	Texas	34
0	Miss. State	0
27	Rice	0
10	Florida	7
6	Tennessee	13
12	Mississippi	13
7	Auburn	7
19	Tulane	0
119		93

1942 (7-3-0)
Coach: B. H. Moore
Captain: Willie Miller

40	La. Normal	0
16	Texas A & M	7
14	Rice	27
16	Miss. State	6
21	Mississippi	7
34	Georgia Navy	0
0	Tennessee	26
26	Fordham	13
7	Auburn	25
18	Tulane	6
192		117

1943 (5-3-0)
Coach: B. H. Moore
Captain: Steve Van Buren

34	Georgia	27
20	Rice	7
13	Texas A & M	28
28	La. Army STU	7
27	Georgia	6
14	T. C. U.	0
7	Ga. Tech	42
0	Tulane	27
143		144

Orange Bowl
19	Texas A & M	14

1944 (2-5-1)
Coach: B. H. Moore
Captain: Al Cavigga

27	Alabama	27
13	Rice	14
0	Texas A & M	7
6	Miss. State	13
15	Georgia	7
0	Tennessee	13
6	Ga. Tech	14
25	Tulane	6
92		101

1945 (7-2-0)
Coach: B. H. Moore
Captain: Andy Kosmac

42	Rice	0
7	Alabama	26
31	Texas A & M	12
32	Georgia	0
39	Vanderbilt	7
32	Mississippi	13
20	Miss. State	27
9	Ga. Tech	7
33	Tulane	0
245		92

1946 (9-1-0)
Coach: B. H. Moore
Captain: Dilton Richmond

7	Rice	6
13	Miss. State	6
33	Texas A & M	9
7	Ga. Tech	26
14	Vanderbilt	0
34	Mississippi	21
31	Alabama	21
20	Miami (Fla.)	7
40	Fordham	0
41	Tulane	27
240		123

Cotton Bowl
0	Arkansas	0

1947 (5-3-1)
Coach: B. H. Moore
Captain: Jim Cason

21	Rice	14
19	Georgia	35
19	Texas A&M	13
14	Boston College	13
19	Vanderbilt	13
18	Mississippi	20
21	Miss. State	6
12	Alabama	41
6	Tulane	6
149		161

1948 (3-7-0)
Coach: Gus Tinsley
Captain: Ed Claunch

0	Texas	33
26	Rice	13
14	Texas A & M	13
0	Georgia	22
7	North Carolina	34
19	Mississippi	49
7	Vanderbilt	48
0	Miss. State	7
26	Alabama	6
0	Tulane	46
99		271

1949 (8-2-0)
Coach: Gus Tinsley
Captain: Melvin Lyle

0	Kentucky	19
14	Rice	7
34	Texas A & M	0
0	Georgia	7
13	N. Carolina	7
34	Mississippi	7
33	Vanderbilt	13
34	Miss. State	7
48	Southeastern	7
21	Tulane	0
231		74

Sugar Bowl

0	Oklahoma	35

1950 (4-5-2)

Coach: Gus Tinsley
Captain: Ebert Van Buren

0	Kentucky	14
19	Col. of Pacific	0
20	Rice	35
0	Ga. Tech	13
13	Georgia	13
40	Mississippi	14
33	Vanderbilt	7
7	Miss. State	13
13	Villanova	7
14	Tulane	14
6	Texas	21
165		151

1951 (7-3-1)

Coach: Gus Tinsley
Captains: Ray Potter,
Chester Freeman

13	Miss. Southern	0
13	Alabama	7
7	Rice	6
7	Ga. Tech	25
7	Georgia	0
0	Maryland	27
6	Mississippi	6
13	Vanderbilt	20
3	Miss. State	0
45	Villanova	7
14	Tulane	13
128		111

1952 (3-7-0)

Coach: Gus Tinsley
Captains: Norm Stevens,
Joe Modicut, Bill Lansing, Leroy Labat, Jim
Sanford, Ralph McLeod

14	Texas	35
20	Alabama	21
27	Rice	7
34	Kentucky	7
14	Georgia	27
6	Maryland	34
0	Mississippi	28
3	Tennessee	22
14	Miss. State	33
16	Tulane	0
148		214

1953 (5-3-3)

Coach: Gus Tinsley
Captains: Jerry Marchand,
Charley Oakley

20	Texas	7
7	Alabama	7
42	Boston College	6
6	Kentucky	6
14	Georgia	6
21	Florida	21
16	Mississippi	27
14	Tennessee	32
13	Miss. State	26
9	Arkansas	8
32	Tulane	13
194		159

1954 (5-6-0)

Coach: Gus Tinsley
Captain: Sid Fournet

6	Texas	20
0	Alabama	12
6	Kentucky	7
20	Ga. Tech	30
20	Texas Tech	13
20	Florida	7
6	Mississippi	21
26	Chattanooga	19
0	Miss. State	25
7	Arkansas	6
14	Tulane	13
125		173

1955 (3-5-2)

Coach: Paul Dietzel
Captains: Joe Tuminello,
O. K. Ferguson

19	Kentucky	7
0	Texas A & M	28
20	Rice	20
0	Ga. Tech	7
14	Florida	18
26	Mississippi	29
0	Maryland	13
34	Miss. State	7
13	Arkansas	7
13	Tulane	13
139		149

1956 (3-7-0)

Coach: Paul Dietzel
Captain: Don Scully

6	Texas A & M	9
14	Rice	23
7	Ga. Tech	39
0	Kentucky	14
6	Florida	21
17	Mississippi	46
13	Okla. A & M	0
13	Miss. State	32
21	Arkansas	7
7	Tulane	6
104		197

1957 (5-5-0)

Coach: Paul Dietzel
Captain: Alvin Aucoin

14	Rice	20
28	Alabama	0
19	Texas Tech	14
20	Georgia Tech	13
21	Kentucky	0
14	Florida	22
0	Vanderbilt	7
12	Mississippi	14
6	Miss. State	14
25	Tulane	6
159		110

1958 (10-0-0)

Coach: Paul Dietzel
Captain: Billy Hendrix

26	Rice	6
13	Alabama	3
20	Hardin-Simmons	6
41	Miami	0
32	Kentucky	7
10	Florida	7
14	Mississippi	0
50	Duke	18
7	Miss. State	6
62	Tulane	0
275		53

Sugar Bowl

7	Clemson	0

1959 (9-1-0)

Coach: Paul Dietzel
Captain: Lynn LeBlanc

26	Rice	3
10	TCU	0
22	Baylor	0
27	Miami	3
9	Kentucky	0
9	Florida	0
7	Mississippi	3
13	Tennessee	14
27	Miss. State	0
14	Tulane	6
164		29

Sugar Bowl

0	Mississippi	21

1960 (5-4-1)

Coach: Paul Dietzel
Captain: Charles Strange

9	Texas A & M	0
3	Baylor	7
2	Ga. Tech	0
0	Kentucky	3
10	Florida	13
6	Mississippi	6
35	So. Carolina	6
7	Miss. State	3
16	Wake Forest	0
17	Tulane	6
105		50

1961 (9-1-0)

Coach: Paul Dietzel
Captain: Roy Winston

3	Rice	16
16	Texas A & M	7
10	Ga. Tech	0
42	So. Carolina	0
24	Kentucky	14
23	Florida	0
10	Mississippi	7
30	No. Carolina	0
14	Miss. State	6
62	Tulane	0
234		50

Orange Bowl

25	Colorado	7

1962 (8-1-1)

Coach: Charles McClendon
Captain: Fred Miller

21	Texas A & M	0
6	Rice	6
10	Ga. Tech	7
17	Miami (Fla.)	3
7	Kentucky	0
23	Florida	0
7	Mississippi	15
5	TCU	0
28	Miss. State	0
38	Tulane	3
162		34

Cotton Bowl

13	Texas	0

1963 (7-3-0)

Coach: Charles McClendon
Captain: Bill Truax

14	Texas A & M	6
12	Rice	21
7	Ga. Tech	6
3	Miami	0
28	Kentucky	7
14	Florida	0
3	Mississippi	37
28	TCU	14
6	Miss. State	7
20	Tulane	0
135		98

Bluebonnet Bowl

7	Baylor	14

1964 (7-2-1)

Coach: Charles McClendon
Captain: Richard Granier

9	Texas A & M ..	6
3	Rice	0
20	No. Carolina	3
27	Kentucky	7
3	Tennessee	3
11	Mississippi	10
9	Alabama	17
14	Miss. State	10
13	Tulane	3
6	Florida	20
115		79

Sugar Bowl

13	Syracuse	10

1965 (7-3-0)

Coach: Charles McClendon
Captains: Billy Ezell and John Aaron

10	Texas A & M	0
42	Rice	14
7	Florida	14
34	Miami	27
31	Kentucky	21
21	So. Carolina	7
0	Mississippi	23
7	Alabama	31
37	Miss. State	20
62	Tulane	0
251		157

Cotton Bowl

14	Arkansas	7

1966 (5-4-1)

Coach: Charles McClendon
Captains: L'nard Neumann and Gawain DiBetta

28	South Carolina ..	12
15	Rice	17
10	Miami	8
7	Texas A & M ...	7
30	Kentucky	0
7	Florida	28
0	Mississippi	17
0	Alabama	21
17	Miss. State	7
21	Tulane	7
135		124

1967 (6-3-1)

Coach: Charles McClendon
Captains: Barry Wilson and Benny Griffin

20	Rice	14
17	Texas A & M ...	6
37	Florida	6
15	Miami	17
30	Kentucky	7
14	Tennessee	17
13	Mississippi	13
6	Alabama	7
55	Miss. State	0
41	Tulane	27
248		114

Sugar Bowl

20	Wyoming	13

1968 (7-3-0)

Coach: Charles McClendon
Captains: Barton Frye and Jerry Guillot

13	Texas A & M ...	12
21	Rice	7
48	Baylor	16
0	Miami	30
13	Kentucky	3
10	TCU	7
24	Mississippi	27
7	Alabama	16
20	Miss. State	16
34	Tulane	10
190		144

Peach Bowl

31	Florida State	27

1969 (9-1-0)

Coach: Charles McClendon
Captains: George Bevan and Robert Ryder

35	Texas A&M	6
42	Rice	0
63	Baylor	8
20	Miami	0
37	Kentucky	10
21	Auburn	20
23	Mississippi	26
20	Alabama	15
61	Miss. State	6
27	Tulane	0
349		91

1970 (9-2-0)

Coach: Charles McClendon
Captains: Buddy Lee and John Sage

18	Texas A & M	20
24	Rice	0
31	Baylor	10
34	Pacific	0
14	Kentucky	7
17	Auburn	9
14	Alabama	9
38	Miss. State	7
0	Notre Dame	3
26	Tulane	14
61	Ole Miss	17
277		96

Orange Bowl

12	Nebraska	17

1971 (9-3-0)

Coach: Charles McClendon
Captains: Louis Cascio and Mike Demarie

21	Colorado	31
37	Texas A&M	0
38	Wisconsin	28
38	Rice	3
48	Florida	7
17	Kentucky	13
22	Ole Miss	24
7	Alabama	14
28	Miss. State	3
28	Notre Dame	8
36	Tulane	7
320		138

Sun Bowl

33	Iowa State	15

1972 (9-2-1)

Coach: Charles McClendon
Captains: Paul Lyons & Pepper Rutland

31	Pacific (H)	13
42	Texas A&M (H)	17
27	Wisconsin (H)	7
12	Rice (A)	6
35	Auburn (H)	7
10	Kentucky (H)	0
17	Mississippi (H)	16
21	Alabama (Birmingham)	35
28	Miss. State (H)	14
3	Florida (A)	3
9	Tulane (A)	3
235		121

Astro-Bluebonnet Bowl

17	Tennessee	24

1973 (9-3-0)

Coach: Charles McClendon
Captains: Tyler Lafauci & Binks Miciotto

17	Colorado (H)	6
28	Texas A&M (H)	23
24	Rice (H)	9
24	Florida (H)	3
20	Auburn (A)	6
28	Kentucky (H)	21
33	South Carolina (A)	29
51	Mississippi (Jackson, Ms.)	14
26	Miss. State (H)	7
7	Alabama (H)	21
0	Tulane (A)	14
258		153

Orange Bowl

9	Penn State	16

1974 (5-5-1)

Coach: Charles McClendon
Captains: Brad Boyd & Steve Lelekacs

42	Colorado (H)	14
14	Texas A&M (H)	21
10	Rice (A)	10
14	Florida (A)	24
20	Tennessee (H)	10
13	Kentucky (A)	20
24	Mississippi (H)	0
0	Alabama (Birmingham)	30
6	Miss. State (Jackson)	7
24	Tulane (H)	22
35	Utah (H)	10
202		168

1975 (5-6-0)

Coach: Charles McClendon
Captains: Greg Bienvenu &
          Steve Cassidy

7	Nebraska (A)	10
8	Texas A & M (H)	39
16	Rice (Shreveport)	13
6	Florida (H)	34
10	Tennessee (A)	24
17	Kentucky (H)	14
24	South Carolina (H)	6
13	Mississippi (Jackson)	17
10	Alabama (H)	23
*6	Miss. State (H)	16
42	Tulane (A)	6
159		202

*Forfeited to LSU by NCAA

1976 (7-3-1)

Coach: Charles McClendon
Captains: Roy Stuart & Butch Knight

6	Nebraska (H)	6
28	Oregon State (H)	11
31	Rice (H)	0
23	Florida (A)	28
33	Vanderbilt (H)	20
7	Kentucky (A)	21
45	Mississippi (H)	0
17	Alabama (Birmingham)	28
*13	Miss. State (Jackson)	21
17	Tulane (H)	7
35	Utah (H)	7
255		149

1977 (8-4-0)

Coach: Charles McClendon
Captains: Kelly Simmons & Steve Ripple

21	Indiana (A)	24
77	Rice (H)	0
36	Florida (H)	14
28	Vanderbilt (A)	15
13	Kentucky (H)	33
56	Oregon (H)	17
28	Mississippi (A)	21
3	Alabama (H)	24
27	Mississippi State (H)	24
20	Tulane (A)	17
66	Wyoming (H)	7
375		196

SUN BOWL

14	Stanford	24

1978 (8-4-0)

Coach: Charles McClendon
Captains: Ch. Alexander & Thad Minaldi

24	Indiana (H)	17
13	Wake Forest (H)	11
37	Rice (A)	7
34	Florida (A)	21
17	Georgia (H)	24
21	Kentucky (A)	0
30	Ole Miss (H)	8
10	Alabama (A)	31
14	Mississippi State (A)	16
40	Tulane (H)	21
24	Wyoming (H)	17
264		173

Liberty Bowl

15	Missouri	20

1979 (7-5-0)

Coach: Charles McClendon
Captains: John Ed Bradley, Willie Teal,
          Rusty Brown

44	Colorado (A)	0
47	Rice (H)	3
12	USC (H)	17
20	Florida (H)	3
14	Georgia (A)	21
23	Kentucky (H)	19
19	Florida State (H)	24
28	Ole Miss (A)	24
0	Alabama (H)	3
21	Mississippi State (H)	3
13	Tulane (A)	24
241		141

Tangerine Bowl

34	Wake Forest	10

1980 (7-4-0)

Coach: Jerry Stovall
Captains: Hokie Gajan & Lyman White

0	Florida State (H)	16
21	Kansas State (H)	0
23	Colorado (H)	20
7	Rice (A)	17
24	Florida (A)	7
21	Auburn (H)	17
17	Kentucky (A)	10
38	Ole Miss (H)	16
7	Alabama (A)	28
31	Mississippi St. (A)	55
24	Tulane (H)	7
213		193

1981 (3-7-1)

Coach: Jerry Stovall
Captains: James Britt & Tom Tully

7	Alabama (H)	24
9	Notre Dame (A)	27
27	Oregon St. (H)	24
28	Rice (H)	14
10	Florida (H)	24
7	Auburn (A)	19
24	Kentucky (H)	10
14	Florida St. (H)	38
27	Mississippi (A)	27
9	Mississippi St. (H)	17
7	Tulane (A)	48
169		272

1982 (8-3-1)

Coach: Jerry Stovall
Captains: Alan Risher & James Britt

45	Oregon State (H)	7
52	Rice (H)	13
24	Florida (A)	13
24	Tennessee (H)	24
34	Kentucky (A)	10
14	South Carolina (H)	6
45	Mississippi (H)	8
20	Alabama (A)	10
24	Mississippi State (A)	27
55	Florida State (H)	21
28	Tulane (H)	31
365		170

Orange Bowl

20	Nebraska	21

1983 (4-7-0)

Coach: Jerry Stovall
Captains: John Fritchie & Mike
  Gambrell

35	Florida State (H)	40
24	Rice (A)	10
40	Washington (H)	14
17	Florida (H)	31
6	Tennessee (A)	20
13	Kentucky (H)	21
20	South Carolina (H)	6
24	Mississippi (A)	27
26	Alabama (H)	32
26	Miss. State (H)	45
20	Tulane (A)	7
251		253

1984 (8-3-1)

Coach: Bill Arnsparger
Captains: Gregg Dubroc, Liffort
  Hobley, Kevin Langford, Jeff
  Wickersham

21	Florida (A)	21
47	Wichita State (H)	7
27	Arizona (H)	26
23	USC (A)	3
34	Vanderbilt (H)	27
36	Kentucky (A)	10
22	Notre Dame (H)	30
32	Mississippi (H)	29
16	Alabama (A)	14
14	Miss. State (A)	16
33	Tulane (H)	15
305		198

Sugar Bowl

10	Nebraska	28

1985 (9-2-1)

Coach: Bill Arnsparger
Captains: Shawn Burks, Dalton Hilliard,
  Jeff Wickersham, Karl Wilson

23	North Carolina (A)	13
17	Colorado State (H)	3
0	Florida (H)	20
49	Vanderbilt (A)	7
10	Kentucky (H)	0
14	Mississippi (A)	0
14	Alabama (H)	14
17	Miss. State (H)	15
10	Notre Dame (A)	7
31	Tulane (A)	19
35	East Carolina (H)	15
220		113

Liberty Bowl

7	Baylor	21

1986 (9-3-0)
SEC CHAMPION

Coach: Bill Arnsparger
Captains: Eric Andolsek, Michael
  Brooks, John Hazard, Karl Wilson

35	Texas A&M (H)	17
12	Miami (Ohio) (H)	21
28	Florida (A)	17
23	Georgia (H)	14
25	Kentucky (A)	16
30	North Carolina (H)	3
19	Mississippi (H)	21
14	Alabama (A)	10
47	Miss. State (A)	0
21	Notre Dame (H)	19
37	Tulane (H)	17
291		155

U S F&G Sugar Bowl

15	Nebraska	30

1987 (10-1-1)

Coach: Mike Archer
Captains: Wendell Davis, Tommy
  Clapp, Eric Andolsek, Nicky
  Hazard

17	Texas A&M (A)	3
56	Fullerton State (H)	12
49	Rice (H)	16
13	Ohio State (H)	13
13	Florida (H)	10
26	Georgia (A)	23
34	Kentucky (H)	9
42	Ole Miss (A)	13
10	Alabama (H)	22
34	Miss. State (H)	14
41	Tulane (A)	36
322		158

Gator Bowl

30	South Carolina	13

Mississippi River Facts

☐ The Mississippi River is the longest river on the North American continent.

☐ Only the Amazon and Congo rivers carry more water and drain more land than the Mississippi.

☐ Mississippi River tributaries extend from New York to Wyoming and Montana.

☐ The average flow on the Mississippi downstream from the Old River Outflow Channel is approximately 460,000 cubic feet per second.

☐ In a record year, (1973) the Mississippi carried 729,000 cubic feet per second.

☐ The Mississippi River basin drains 41% of the continental United States and a small portion of Canada.

LOUISIANA'S GOAL—CLEAN WATER

Olen D. Curtis and Bradley E. Spicer[1]

Everyone is interested in having ample clean water to meet the present and future needs of all people. Louisiana people are blessed with streams, lakes and underground water supplies which are essential for health, recreation, agriculture and wildlife. Agriculturists have always had a keen interest in soil and water conservation, but this interest—along with measures to assure the means to maintain high water quality—must intensify.

In 1972 Congress added Section 208 to the Federal Water Pollution Control Act PL92-500.

The Clean Water Act, as the law is known, provides for a basic change in methods used to control the discharge of pollutants into surface water. The act requires each state to develop a control program that addresses point source pollutants such as industrial waste and sewage waste discharged into surface waters. It also requires states to identify nonpoint sources of pollution.

SITUATION

Principal nonpoint source pollutants are carried into lakes and streams in runoff water from urban areas, agricultural and forested areas, and mining and construction sites. Soil loss from disturbed soils on mining and construction sites usually means that sediments are carried by water into lakes or streams.

In Louisiana, the water quality planning program for agricultural nonpoint source pollutants emphasizes assessing pollution problems caused by runoff from farm lands. The primary pollutants are sediments, resulting from soil erosion. Other agricultural pollutants include pesticides and fertilizer nutrients. Fertilizer nutrients and pesticides ride piggyback on the soil particles carried by runoff water. Controlling soil erosion not only reduces soil loss but greatly reduces the loss of fertilizer nutrients from fields, and also reduces pesticide pollution in streams.

[1] Specialist, Louisiana Cooperative Extension Service; Soil Scientist, USDA Soil Conservation on IPA Assignment to Louisiana Department of Agriculture, respectively.

Tulane Football

1893 (1-2-0)

0 Southern AC....12
34 L. S. U. 0
4 Mississippi 12

1894 (0-4-0)

0 Texas...........12
6 Alabama....... 8
2 Mississippi...... 8
6 Sewanee........12

1895 (4-2-0)

4 L. S. U. 8
22 Alabama 0
0 Texas 16
28 Mississippi 4
16 Sou. AC Jrs. .. 0
12 Alumni 0

1896 (2-2-0)

48 Vicksburg AC... 0
4 Texas.......... 12
10 Mississippi..... 0
0 L. S. U........ 6

1897
(No Team)

1898 (1-1-0)

14 Mississippi...... 9
0 L. S. U.........37

1899 (0-6-1)

0 Southern AC ... 0
0 Sewanee 22
0 Texas 11
0 Texas 32
0 Mississippi 17
0 Texas A&M 22
0 L. S. U. 38

1900 (5-0-0)

23 Southern AC.... 0
0 Alabama....... 0
29 L. S. U. 0
35 Millsaps 0
12 Mississippi..... 0

1901 (5-1-0)

11 Meridian 0
0 Mobile 2
24 Miss. State 6
23 L. S. U. 0
35 Y. M. C. A. ... 0
25 Mississippi 11

1902 (1-4-2)

26 Alumni 0
0 Auburn 0
11 Miss. State 11
5 Texas A&M 17
5 Vanderbilt 23
0 Texas 6
0 Mississippi 10

1903 (2-2-1)

46 Meridian A. A.. 0
0 Shreveport A.A. 23
0 Cumberland U.. 28
18 Richmond 5
0 Miss. State 0

1904 (5-2-0)

11 La. Polytech 0
10 Miss. State 0
10 Marion 0
0 Sewanee 18
5 L. S. U. 0
22 Mississippi 0
0 Alabama 5

1905 (0-1-0)

0 L. S. U. 5

1906 (0-4-1)

0 Howard 0
0 Mississippi 17
0 Sewanee 35
0 Texas A&M 18
0 Arkansas 22

1907 (3-2-0)

13 Howard 0
12 Drury 0
12 Arkansas.......17
28 Centre......... 9
6 Texas A&M ... 18

1908 (7-1-0)

10 Centre 0
11 Y. M. C. A..... 0
10 Mississippi..... 0
33 Miss. State..... 0
10 Baylor......... 2
28 Texas..........16
0 Baylor......... 6
11 Washington.... 0

1909 (4-3-2)

11 Y. M. C. A..... 0
5 Mississippi...... 0
0 Centre......... 6
2 Miss. State..... 9
6 Cincinnati..... 0
10 Texas..........10
5 Alabama...... 5
0 Texas Souw.....18
0 Cuba (Jan. 1)...11

1910 (0-7-0)

0 Mississippi......16
0 Centre..........35
3 Ky. State......10
0 Miss. State.....10
3 Alabama...... 5
0 Texas A&M ...17
0 Auburn........33

1911 (5-3-1)

27 La. State Normal 0
45 La. Institute.... 0
10 Miss. College.... 0
10 Howard College. 0
3 Sewanee........ 9
5 Miss. State..... 4
5 Wash. & Lee.... 5
0 L. S. U........ 5
0 Alabama......22

1912 (5-3-0)

37 Jefferson....... 0
95 S'western (La.).. 0
10 Miss. College.... 6
47 Howard College. 0
0 Alabama...... 7
27 Miss. State.....24
0 Texas A&M.....41
3 L. S. U........21

1913 (3-5-0)

13 Jefferson...... 0
3 Miss. College...32
0 Alabama......26
12 St. Louis...... 6
0 Miss. State.....32
31 Southwestern... 9
0 L. S. U........40
0 Alabama......26

1914 (3-3-1)

33 Southwestern... 0
82 Centenary...... 0
24 Jefferson....... 7
0 Alabama......58
6 Mississippi....21
0 Miss. State....61
0 L. S. U........ 0

1915 (4-4-0)

24 St. Paul....... 0
13 S'western (La.).. 0
35 Spring Hill......18
0 Alabama......16
8 Mississippi....20
32 Howard College. 3
7 Florida.........14
0 L. S. U.........12

1916 (4-3-1)

14 Spring Hill...... 0
39 Jefferson....... 3
13 Mississippi..... 0
0 Ga. Tech......45
13 Rice...........23
33 Alabama....... 0
14 L. S. U........14
0 Georgetown....61

1917 (5-3-0)

32 Jefferson....... 0
28 Spring Hill..... 0
52 Florida......... 0
18 Wash. Artillery.. 0
0 Texas A&M.....35
0 Ga. Tech......48
0 Rice...........16
28 L. S. U......... 6

1918 (2-1-1)

13 Camp Shelby... 6
7 Camp
Beauregard... 0
7 Camp Pike.....10
0 Pensacola Av.... 0

1919 (6-2-1)

27 Jefferson....... 0
73 S'western (La.).. 0
21 Spring Hill..... 0
27 Mississippi.....12
49 Miss. College... 0
14 Florida......... 2
7 Georgia........ 7
6 L. S. U........27
0 Wash. & Lee.... 7

1920 (6-2-1)

79 Southwestern... 0
29 Miss. College... 0
0 Rice........... 0
32 Mississippi..... 0
0 Michigan.......21
14 Florida......... 0
6 Miss. State..... 0
21 L. S. U........ 0
0 Detroit......... 7

1921 (4-6-0)

0 Miss. College....14
28 Mississippi...... 0
7 Rice........... 6
7 Miss. State..... 0
10 Detroit........14
0 Auburn........14
6 Washington.....14
21 L. S. U........ 0
0 Centre.........21
7 Alabama.......14

1922 (4-4-0)

30 Miss. College... 0
30 Spring Hill......10
18 Camp Benning.. 0
26 Miss. State..... 0
12 North Carolina..19
0 Auburn........19
6 Florida........27
14 L. S. U.........25

1923 (6-3-1)

20 Southwestern... 2
18 Miss. College.... 3
0 Texas..........33
13 La. Polytech.... 7
0 Vanderbilt......17
2 Tennessee......13
6 Auburn........ 6
19 Mississippi..... 0
20 L. S. U........ 0
19 Washington U.. 8

1924 (8-1-0)

14 Southwestern ... 0
32 Miss. College....7
42 La. Polytech....14
21 Vanderbilt 13
33 Spring Hill 0
6 Miss. State 14
14 Auburn 6
26 Tennessee 7
18 L. S. U........ 0

1925 (9-0-1)

77 La. College..... 0
0 Missouri......... 6
26 Mississippi..... 7
25 Miss. State..... 3
18 Northwestern... 7
13 Auburn........ 0
37 La. Polytech.... 9
14 Sewanee....... 0
16 L. S. U........ 0
14 Centenary...... 0

1926 (3-5-1)

47 La. Polytech.... 0
0 Missouri........ 0
6 Ga. Tech....... 9
0 N. Y. U........21
0 Auburn......... 2
6 Mississippi..... 0
0 Miss. State....14
19 Sewanee....... 0
0 L. S. U........ 7

1927 (2-5-1)

19 Mississippi..... 7
6 Ga. Tech.......13
6 Miss. State.....13
0 Vanderbilt......32
0 Georgia........31
6 Auburn........ 0
6 Sewanee.......12
13 L. S. U........ 6

1928 (6-3-1)
```
65 La. Normal .... 0
51 Miss. State ..... 6
 0 Ga. Tech ...... 12
 6 Vanderbilt ..... 13
14 Georgia ....... 20
27 Millsaps ........ 0
13 Auburn ....... 12
41 Sewanee ........ 6
47 La. College ..... 7
 0 L S. U ......... 0
```

1929 (9-0-0)
```
40 La. Normal .... 6
13 Texas A&M .... 10
60 Southwestern ... 0
20 Ga. Tech ...... 14
34 Miss. State .... 0
21 Georgia ....... 15
52 Auburn ........ 0
18 Sewanee ...... 0
21 L. S. U ........ 0
```

1930 (8-1-0)
```
84 Southwestern ... 0
 0 Northwestern .. 14
19 Texas A&M ..... 9
21 B'ham Southern. 0
28 Ga. Tech ...... 0
53 Miss. State .... 0
21 Auburn ........ 0
25 Georgia ........ 0
12 L. S. U ........ 7
```

1931 (11-0-0)
```
31 Mississippi .... 0
 7 Texas A&M ..... 0
40 Spring Hill ..... 0
19 Vanderbilt ...... 0
33 Ga. Tech ...... 0
59 Miss. State .... 7
27 Auburn ........ 0
20 Georgia ........ 7
40 Sewanee ....... 0
34 L. S. U ........ 7
28 Wash. State ... 14
```

1932 (6-2-1)
```
26 Texas A&M .... 14
34 Georgia ....... 25
 6 Vanderbilt ..... 6
 7 Auburn ....... 19
 6 S. Carolina .... 0
20 Ga. Tech ...... 14
 6 Kentucky ...... 3
26 Sewanee ....... 0
 0 L. S. U ....... 14
```

1933 (6-3-1)
```
 6 Texas A&M .... 13
13 Georgia ....... 26
20 Maryland ...... 0
 7 Ga. Tech ...... 0
 7 Auburn ....... 13
 7 Colgate ........ 0
33 Miss. State .... 0
34 Kentucky ..... 0
26 Sewanee ....... 9
 7 La. State ...... 7
```

1934 (9-1-0)
```
41 Chattanooga .... 0
13 Auburn ........ 0
28 Florida ........ 12
 7 Georgia ........ 6
20 Ga. Tech ...... 12
 6 Mississippi ..... 0
 6 Colgate ....... 20
20 Kentucky ..... 7
32 Sewanee ....... 0
13 La. State ...... 12
```

1935 (6-4-0)
```
44 V. M. I ........ 0
 0 Auburn ....... 10
19 Florida ........ 7
 0 Minnesota ..... 20
33 Sewanee ........ 0
14 Colgate ........ 6
13 Georgia ....... 26
20 Kentucky ..... 13
13 La. Normal .... 0
 0 La. State ..... 41
```

1936 (6-3-1)
```
 7 Mississippi ..... 6
 0 Auburn ........ 0
19 Centenary ..... 0
28 Colgate ........ 6
21 N. Carolina .... 7
22 La. Tech ...... 13
 7 Alabama ...... 34
 6 Georgia ....... 12
53 Sewanee ........ 6
 0 La. State ..... 33
```

1937 (5-4-1)
```
 7 Clemson ......... 0
 0 Auburn .......... 0
84 Miss. College ... 0
 7 Colgate ......... 6
 0 N. Carolina .... 13
14 Mississippi ...... 7
 6 Alabama ........ 9
 6 Georgia ........ 7
33 Sewanee ........ 7
 7 La. State ...... 20
```

1938 (7-2-1)
```
10 Clemson ....... 13
 0 Auburn ......... 0
17 N. Carolina .... 14
26 Rice Institute .. 17
51 Mercer ......... 0
27 Miss. State ..... 0
 0 Alabama ........ 3
28 Georgia ........ 6
38 Sewanee ....... 0
14 La. State ....... 0
```

1939 (8-0-1)
```
 7 Clemson ........ 6
12 Auburn ........ 0
 7 Fordham ....... 0
14 N. Carolina ... 14
18 Mississippi .... 6
13 Alabama ....... 0
25 Columbia ...... 0
52 Sewanee ...... 0
33 La. State ...... 20
```

1940 (5-5-0)
```
 7 Boston College 27
14 Auburn ........ 20
 7 Fordham ...... 20
15 Rice Institute .. 6
14 N. Carolina ... 13
13 Clemson ....... 0
 6 Alabama ...... 13
21 Georgia ....... 13
47 La. Normal .... 0
 0 La. State ...... 14
```

1941 (5-4-0)
```
21 Boston College.. 7
32 Auburn ........ 0
 9 Rice Institute .. 10
52 N. Carolina .... 6
13 Mississippi .... 20
34 Vanderbilt ..... 14
14 Alabama ...... 19
45 New York U ... 0
 0 La. State ...... 19
```

1942 (4-5-0)
```
27 Sou. California .. 13
13 Auburn ........ 27
18 Rice Institute... 7
 0 Georgia ....... 40
29 N. Carolina ... 14
28 Vanderbilt ..... 21
 0 Miss. State .... 21
 0 Ga. Pre-Flight.. 7
 6 La. State ...... 18
```

1943 (3-3-0)
```
 7 Memphis
     NATTC ..... 41
33 Rice Institute .. 0
12 Sou. Meth. U ... 6
13 Ga. Pre-Flight .. 33
 0 Ga. Tech ...... 33
27 La. State ...... 0
```

1944 (4-3-0)
```
 0 Notre Dame ... 26
21 Rice Institute .. 0
16 Auburn ........ 13
27 Sou. Meth. U ... 7
 7 Ga. Tech ...... 34
36 Clemson ...... 20
 6 La. State ...... 25
```

1945 (2-6-1)
```
 6 Florida ......... 6
 7 Rice Institute .. 13
14 Auburn ........ 20
19 Sou. Meth ...... 7
14 Miss. State .... 13
 7 Ga. Tech ...... 41
20 Clemson ...... 47
 6 Notre Dame ... 32
 0 La. State ...... 33
```

1946 (3-7-0)
```
 6 Alabama ....... 7
27 Florida ........ 13
 6 Rice Institute .. 25
32 Auburn ........ 0
 7 Miss. State .... 14
54 Clemson ...... 13
 7 Ga. Tech ...... 35
 0 Notre Dame ... 41
27 La. State ...... 41
13 Sou. California .. 20
```

1947 (2-5-2)
```
21 Alabama ....... 20
 0 Ga. Tech ...... 20
 0 Rice Institute .. 33
14 Mississippi .... 27
40 Auburn ......... 0
 0 Miss. State .... 20
 7 Florida ......... 7
 6 Notre Dame ... 59
 6 L. S. U. ....... 6
```

1948 (9-1-0)
```
21 Alabama ....... 14
 7 Ga. Tech. ...... 13
14 S. Carolina ..... 7
20 Mississippi ..... 7
21 Auburn ......... 6
 9 Miss. State ..... 0
28 V. M. I. ....... 7
35 Baylor ........ 13
 6 Cincinnati ...... 0
46 L. S. U. ....... 0
```

1949 (7-2-1)
```
28 Alabama ....... 14
10 Ga. Tech. ...... 0
40 S. E. La. ....... 0
 7 Notre Dame ... 46
14 Auburn ....... 6
54 Miss. State ... 0
21 Navy ........ 21
41 Vanderbilt ..... 14
28 Virginia ...... 14
 0 L. S. U. ..... 21
```

1950 (6-2-1)
```
14 Alabama ..... 26
64 La. College ... 0
 9 Notre Dame .. 13
27 Mississippi ... 20
28 Auburn ....... 0
27 Navy ......... 0
42 Virginia ..... 18
35 Vanderbilt ... 0
14 L. S. U. ..... 14
```

1951 (4-6-0)
```
21 Miami (Fla.) .. 7
14 Baylor ....... 27
20 Holy Cross ... 14
 6 Mississippi ... 25
 0 Auburn ...... 21
 7 Miss. State ... 10
 0 Kentucky ..... 37
14 Vanderbilt ... 10
48 S. E. La. .... 14
13 L. S. U. ..... 14
```

1952 (5-5-0)
```
16 Georgia ...... 21
35 Santa Clara ... 0
 0 Ga Tech ..... 14
21 Mississippi ... 20
21 Auburn ...... 6
34 Miss. State ... 21
 6 Kentucky .... 27
16 Vanderbilt .... 7
46 La. College ... 14
 0 L. S. U. ..... 16
```

1953 (1-8-1)
```
54 The Citadel ... 6
14 Georgia ...... 16
 7 Michigan ..... 26
13 Ga. Tech .... 27
14 Mississippi ... 45
 7 Auburn ...... 34
 0 Army ......... 0
 0 Miss. State ... 21
 7 Vanderbilt .... 21
13 L. S. U. ..... 32
```

1954 (1-6-3)
```
 0 Ga. Tech .... 28
12 Memphis St. .. 13
 7 N. Carolina ... 7
 0 Miss. State ... 14
 7 Mississippi ... 34
 0 Georgia ...... 7
 0 Auburn ...... 27
 0 Alabama ...... 0
 6 Vanderbilt .... 0
13 L. S. U. ..... 14
```

1955 (5-4-1)
```
20 V. M. I. ...... 7
21 Texas ........ 35
21 Northwestern .. 0
 0 Miss. State ... 14
13 Mississippi ... 27
14 Georgia ...... 0
27 Auburn ...... 13
27 Alabama ...... 0
 7 Vanderbilt ... 20
13 L. S. U. ..... 13
```

1956 (6-4-0)

21	V. P. I.	14
6	Texas	7
20	Northwestern	13
21	Navy	6
10	Mississippi	3
0	Ga. Tech	40
20	Miss. State	14
7	Alabama	13
13	Vanderbilt	6
6	L. S. U.	7

1957 (2-8-0)

13	V. P. I.	14
6	Texas	20
20	Marquette	6
6	Georgia	13
0	Mississippi	50
13	Ga. Tech	20
6	Miss. State	27
7	Alabama	0
14	Army	20
6	L. S. U.	25

1958 (3-7-0)

14	Florida	34
20	Texas	21
0	Ga. Tech	14
8	Mississippi	19
14	Navy	6
9	Kansas	14
27	Texas Tech	0
13	Alabama	7
0	Vanderbilt	12
0	L. S. U.	62

1959 (3-6-1)

0	Florida	30
7	Miami	26
6	Wake Forest	0
25	Detroit	0
7	Mississippi	53
13	Ga. Tech	21
17	Texas Tech	7
7	Alabama	19
6	Vanderbilt	6
6	L. S. U.	14

1960 (3-6-1)

7	California	3
6	Alabama	6
7	Rice	10
13	Mississippi	26
6	Ga. Tech	14
40	Wm. & Mary	8
21	Texas Tech	35
6	Florida	21
20	Vanderbilt	0
6	L. S. U.	17

1961 (2-8-0)

7	Stanford	9
0	Alabama	9
3	Florida	14
28	Va. Tech	14
0	Ole Miss	41
0	Ga. Tech	35
6	Clemson	21
0	Miami	6
17	Vanderbilt	14
0	L. S. U.	62

1962 (0-10-0)

3	Stanford	6
6	Alabama	44
8	Texas	35
6	Miss. State	35
0	Mississippi	21
12	Ga. Tech	42
22	Va. Tech	24
16	Tennessee	28
0	Vanderbilt	20
3	L. S. U.	38

1963 (1-8-1)

0	Texas	21
0	Alabama	28
0	Miami (Fla)	10
10	Miss. State	31
0	Mississippi	21
3	Ga. Tech	17
20	So. Carolina	7
0	Tennessee	26
10	Vanderbilt	10
0	L. S. U.	20

1964 (3-7-0)

0	Texas	31
6	Alabama	36
6	Miss. State	17
9	Mississippi	14
6	Ga. Tech	7
25	V. M. I.	6
0	Miami (Fla.)	21
7	Vanderbilt	2
3	L. S. U.	13
17	Duke	0

1965 (2-8-0)

0	Texas	31
0	Alabama	27
24	Miami	16
10	Ga. Tech	13
7	Mississippi	24
17	Miss. State	15
0	Vanderbilt	13
0	Stanford	16
13	Florida	51
0	L. S. U.	62

1966 (5-4-1)

13	V. P. I.	0
21	Texas A&M	13
14	Stanford	33
20	Virginia	6
28	Cincinnati	21
17	Ga. Tech	35
13	Vanderbilt	12
10	Miami (Fla.)	10
10	Florida	31
7	L. S. U.	21

1967 (3-7-0)

3	Miami (O.)	14
36	N. Carolina	11
14	Miami (Fla.)	34
0	Florida	35
10	Air Force	13
23	Ga. Tech	12
27	Vanderbilt	14
14	Tennessee	35
10	Virginia	14
27	L. S. U.	41

1968 (2-8-0)

7	Houston	54
3	Texas A&M	35
14	Tampa	17
3	Florida	24
28	Boston College	14
19	Georgia Tech	23
7	Vanderbilt	21
25	Tulsa	15
47	Virginia	63
10	L. S. U.	34

1969 (3-7-0)

0	Georgia	35
17	West Virginia	35
24	Boston College	28
17	Florida	18
26	Pittsburgh	22
0	Notre Dame	37
23	Vanderbilt	26
14	Georgia Tech	7
31	Virginia	0
0	L. S. U.	27

1970 (8-4-0)

14	Texas Tech	21
17	Georgia	14
23	Illinois	9
6	Cincinnati	3
3	Air Force	24
24	N. Carolina	17
6	Georgia Tech	20
10	Vanderbilt	7
31	Miami, Fla.	16
31	N. C. State	0
14	L. S. U.	26
17	Colorado	3

1971 (3-8-0)

15	Texas Tech	9
7	Georgia	17
11	Rice	14
3	William & Mary	14
37	North Carolina	29
33	Pittsburgh	8
16	Georgia Tech	24
9	Vanderbilt	13
7	Ohio U.	30
7	Notre Dame	21
7	L. S. U.	36

1972 (6-5-0)

10	Boston College	0
24	Georgia	13
7	Michigan	41
38	Pittsburgh	6
21	Miami (Fla)	24
19	West Virginia	31
7	Georgia Tech	21
18	Kentucky	7
44	Ohio U.	6
21	Vanderbilt	7
3	L. S. U.	9

1973 (9-2-0)

21	Boston College	16
42	V. M. I.	0
24	Pittsburgh	6
24	Duke	17
16	North Carolina	0
23	Georgia Tech	14
7	Kentucky	34
17	Navy	15
24	Vanderbilt	3
9	Maryland	42
14	L. S. U.	0

Astro-Blubonnet Bowl
Tulane 7-University of
Houston 47

1974 (5-6-0)

17	S.W.Louisiana	16
31	Army	14
17	West Virginia	14
10	Air Force	3
30	Citadel	3
7	Georgia Tech	27
7	Kentucky	30
3	Boston Col	27
22	Vanderbilt	30
22	L.S.U.	24
10	Mississippi	26

1975 (4-7-0)

17	Clemson	13
14	Mississippi	3
13	Syracuse	31
3	Vanderbilt	6
17	Boston College	7
16	West Virginia	14
0	Goergia Tech	23
10	Kentucky	23
12	Air Force	13
15	North Carolina	17
6	L.S.U.	42

1976 (2-9-0)

14	Cincinnati	21
7	Ole Miss	34
3	Boston College	27
24	Vanderbilt	13
0	Syracuse	3
23	Army	10
16	Georgia Tech	28
7	Memphis State	14
28	West Virginia	32
20	Rutgers	29
7	L.S.U.	17

1977 (3-8-0)

9	Memphis State	27
17	Stanford	21
23	SMU	28
36	Vanderbilt	7
28	Boston College	30
16	Cincinnati	13
14	Georgia Tech	38
0	Pittsburgh	48
13	Miami	10
8	Rutgers	47
17	L.S.U	20

1978 (4-7-0)

7	Maryland	31
6	Pittsburgh	24
17	Georgia Tech	27
14	Stanford	17
38	Vanderbilt	3
9	Boston College	3
41	Memphis State	24
20	Miami (Fla.)	16
3	Ole Miss	13
21	L.S.U.	40

1979 (9-3-0)		
33	Stanford	10
17	Rice	21
33	TCU	19
24	SMU	17
42	Vanderbilt	14
20	USM	19
17	West Virginia	27
12	Georgia Tech	7
43	Boston College	8
49	Ole Miss	15
24	L.S.U.	13
6*	Penn. State	9

1980 (7-5-0)		
14	USM	17
14	Stanford	19
35	Rice	14
26	Ole Miss	24
21	SMU	31
43	Vanderbilt	21
28	Air Force	7
31	Georgia Tech	14
24	Kentucky	22
21	Memphis State	16
7	L.S.U.	24
15*	Arkansas	34

1981 (6-5-0)		
18	Ole Miss	19
5	Clemson	13
3	U.S.M.	21
16	Rice	20
14	Vanderbilt	10
31	Air Force	13
27	Ga. Tech	10
13	Cincinnati	17
14	Maryland	7
24	Memphis State	7
48	L.S.U.	7

1982 (4-7-0)		
21	Miss. State	30
7	SMU	51
30	Rice	6
21	Vanderbilt	24
13	Ga. Tech	19
10	USM	22
17	Memphis St	10
30	Baylor	15
14	Ole Miss	45
7	Florida	21
31	LSU	28

1983 (4-7-0)		
9	Miss. State	14
*27	Ole Miss	23
*34	Florida State	28
14	Kentucky	26
17	Vanderbilt	30
25	Memphis State	28
17	SW Louisiana	15
14	Southern Miss	7
18	Baylor	24
10	Virginia Tech	26
7	Louisiana State	20
*Forfeit		

1984 (3-8-0)		
3	Miss. State	30
21	Florida	63
26	Kentucky	30
14	Ole Miss	19
27	Vanderbilt	23
35	Southern Miss	7
6	Florida State	27
6	Virginia Tech	13
10	Pittsburgh	21
14	Memphis State	9
15	Louisiana State	33

1985 (1-10)		
12	Florida State	38
13	Texas Christian	30
11	Kentucky	16
10	Mississippi	27
17	Vanderbilt	24
21	Memphis State	38
27	Mississippi State	31
3	Georgia	58
27	Southwestern La.	17
6	Southern Miss	24
10	Louisiana State	31

1986 (4-7)		
31	Texas Christian	48
35	Vanderbilt	17
10	Ole Miss	35
20	Wichita State	21
21	Florida State	54
27	Mississippi State	34
35	Southern Miss	20
42	Southwestern La.	39
12	Louisville	23
15	Memphis State	6
17	LSU	37

1987 (6-6)		
40	Louisville	42
25	Iowa State	12
24	Southern Miss	31
31	Ole Miss	24
27	Vanderbilt	17
36	Memphis State	45
57	Virginia Tech	38
14	Florida State	73
30	Miss. State	19
38	USL	10
36	LSU	41
Independence Bowl		
12	Univ. of Washington	24

TULANE TEAM NICKNAME

Olive and Blue ... Greenbacks ... Green Wave

From 1893 to 1919, the athletic teams of Tulane were known as the Olive and Blue. In 1919 the college newspaper, the Hullabaloo, began calling the football team the Greenbacks.

On October 20, 1920, Earl Sparling, a Tulane student from Oklahoma City who was editor of the student newspaper, wrote a football song which appeared in the paper. The song was entitled "The Rolling Green Wave." Although the name was not immediately adopted, it began to receive acceptance, and on November 19, 1920, a report of the Tulane-Mississippi A&M game in the student newspaper referred to it as the "Green Wave." By the end of the season it seemed to have been accepted by the Hullabaloo and most of the daily newspapers, although as late as 1923 the name Greenbacks was still being alternately used with Green Wave.

At one time Tulane's mascot was a pelican depicted riding on a surf board. The "Greenie" was adopted in 1955, created by John Chase, a local cartoonist who drew the covers of the Tulane football programs and those of many teams throughout the South.

Dr. Rix Yard became Tulane's athletic director in 1963. He and others felt Tulane needed a more virile symbol for its teams. Working through Elton Endacott, the manager of the Tulane Bookstore, several sketches were submitted by Art Evans, art director for the Angelus-Pacific Company in Fullerton, Cal. Evans has created mascots for many of the nation's colleges, including the Purdue "Boilermaker" and the Southern California "Trojan." The angry-looking Green Wave finally came into being in 1964, and has been the symbol of Tulane's athletic teams ever since.

NATIONAL COLLEGE FOOTBALL HALL OF FAME
LOUISIANA HONOREES

Name	Team	Position	Final Season
Chris Cagle	USL, Army	Halfback	1929
G. Dalrymple	Tulane	End	1931
Monk Simons	Tulane	Halfback	1934
Abe Mickal	LSU	Halfback	1934
Gaynell Tinsley	LSU	End	1935
Ken Kavanaugh	LSU	End	1939

LSU PLAYERS IN PRO FOOTBALL

Alexander, Charles—Bengals 1979-85
Alexander, Dan—Jets, 1977-
Atiyeh, George—Gold, Invaders 1983; Bulls, 1984

Baggett, Billy—Texans 1952
Barnes, Walter—Eagles 1948-51
Barrett, Jeff—Dodgers 1936-38
Bordelon, Kenny—Saints 1976-83
Branch, Mel—Texans 1960-62; Chiefs 1963-65; Dolphins 1966-68
Britt, James—Falcons 1983-
Brodnax, J. W.—Broncos 1960
Burks, Shawn—Redskins 1986-
Burrell, Clinton—Browns, 1979-85
Bussey, Young—Bears 1940-41

Cannon, Billy—Oilers 1960-63; Raiders 1964-69; Chiefs 1970
Cantrelle, Art—49ers 1976
Capone, Warren—Cowboys 1975; Buccaneers 1976; Saints 1976
Cassanova, Tommy—Bengals 1972-1977
Carson, Carlos—Chiefs 1980-
Cason, Jimmy—49ers 1948-52, 54; Rams 1955-56
Champagne, Ed—Rams 1947-50
Coates, Ray—Giants 1948-49
Coffee, Pat—Cardinals 1937-38
Collins, Albin Harrel (Rip)—Cardinals 1949; Colts 1950; Packers 1951
Collins, Ray—49ers 1950-52; Giants 1954; Texans 1960-61
Crass, Bill—Cardinals 1937

Dale, Jeffery—Chargers 1985-
Daniel, Eugene—Colts 1984-
Dardar, Ramsey—Cardinals 1983-84
Davis, Brad—Falcons, 1975-76
Davis, Tommy—49ers 1959-70
Demarie, John—Browns 1967-76; Seahawks, 1976
Duhe, A. J.—Dolphins 1977-84

Elko, Bill—Chargers 1983-84
Estay, Ronnie—Eskimos 1972-1982; Federals 1983-84
Estes, Don—Chargers 1966

Fournet, Sid—Rams 1955-56; Steelers 1957; Texans 1960-61; Titans 1962; Jets 1963; Broncos 1964
Friend, Ben—Rams 1939
Fussell, Tom—Patriots 1967

Gajan, Hokie—Saints 1981-
Garlington, John—Browns 1968-1977
Gaubatz, Dennis—Lions 1963-64; Colts 1965-69
Glamp, Joe—Steelers 1947-49
Gorinski, Walt—Steelers 1946
Graves, White—Patriots 1965-67; Bengals 1968
Gros, Earl—Packers 1962-63; Eagles 1964-66; Steelers 1967-69; Saints 1970

Hamilton, Andy—Chiefs 1972-74; Saints 1975
Harris, Bo—Bengals, 1975-83
Harris, Wendell—Colts 1962-65; Giants 1966-67
Hilliard, Dalton—Saints 1986-
Hodgins, Norm—Bears 1974; Packers 1975

Jackson Rusty—Rams 1976; Bills 1978
Jackson, Steve—Raiders 1977-1978
James, Garry—Lions 1986-
Joiner, Tim—Oilers 1983-84
Jones, Bert—Colts 1973-1981; Rams, 1982
Jones, LeRoid—Edmonton, 1981
Jones, W. A. "Dub"—Seahawks 1946; Dodgers 1946-47; Rams 1948-49; Browns 1949-55

Kavanaugh, Ken, Sr.—Bears 1940-41, 1945-50
Konz, Kenny—Browns 1953-59

LaFleur, Greg—Cardinals 1981-86; Colts 1986-
Lang, Gene—Broncos 1984-
Land, Fred—49ers 1948

Lee, Buddy—Bears 1971
Leggett, Earl—Bears 1957-60; 1962-65; Rams 1966; Saints 1967-68
Leisk, Wardell—Dodgers 1937

Malancon, Rydell—Falcons 1984-85
Marshall, Leonard—Giants 1983-
Martin, Eric—Saints 1985-
Masters, Billy—Bills 1966-70; Broncos 1970-74; Chiefs 1975-77
May, Bill—Cardinals 1937-38
McCormick, Dave—49ers 1966, Saints 1967-68
McDaniel, Orlando—Broncos 1982
Miller, Fred—Colts 1963-72; Redskins 1973
Miller, Paul—Rams 1954-57; Texans 1960-61; Chargers 1962
Montgomery, Bill—Cardinals 1946
Moreau, Doug—Dolphins 1968-69
Morgan, Mike—Eagles 1964-67; Redskins 1968
Myles, Jesse—Broncos 1983-84

Neal, Ed—Packers 1945-51; Bears 1951
Neck, Tommy—Bears 1962-63
Nunnery, R. B.—Texans 1960

Porter, Tracy—Lions 1981-83; Colts 1984
Prudhomme, Remi—Bills 1966-67; Chiefs 1968-69; Saints 1971-72

Quinn, Marcus—Ottawa 1981; Saints 1982; Invaders 1983-84; Bandits 1985

Rabb, Warren—Lions 1960; Bills 1961-62
Ray, Eddie—Patriots 1970; Chargers 1971; Falcons 1972-76; Seahawks 1976
Reed, Joe (Rock)—Cardinals 1937-39
Reid, Joe—Rams 1951; Texans 1952
Reynolds, M. C.—Cardinals 1958-59; Redskins 1960; Bills 1961; Raiders 1961
Richards, Bobby—Eagles 1962-65; Falcons 1966-67
Rice, George—Oilers 1966-69
Risher, Alan—Wranglers 1983-85; Buccaneers 1985-86
Robinson, Johnny—Texans 1960-62; Chiefs 1963-71
Robiskie, Terry—Raiders 1977-79; Dolphins 1980-81
Rogers, Steve—Saints 1975
Rukas, Justin—Dodgers 1936

Sandifer, Dan—Redskins 1948-49; Lions 1950; 49ers 1950; Eagles 1950-51; Packers 1952-53; Cardinals 1953
Schroll, Bill—Bills 1949; Lions 1950; Packers 1951
Scott, Malcolm—Giants 1983; Saints 1986
Schurtz, Hubert—Steelers 1948
Stovall, Jerry—Cardinals 1963-71
Sykes, Gene—Bills 1963-65; Broncos 1967

Tarsovic, George—Steelers 1952-53, 1956-63; Eagles 1963-65; Broncos 1967
Taylor, Jimmy—Packers 1958-66; Saints 1967
Teal, Willie—Vikings 1980-
Tinsley, Gaynell—Cardinals 1937-40
Tinsley, Jess—Cardinals 1929-33
Tittle, Y. A.—Colts 1948-51; 49ers 1951-60; Giants 1961-64
Torrance, Jack—Bears 1939-40
Toth, Zollile—Yankees 1950-51; Texans 1952; Colts 1954-54
Truax, Billy—Rams 1964-70; Cowboys 1971-74
Turner, Mike—Stallions 1983-85
Turner, Willie—Montreal 1981

Van Buren, Ebert—Eagles 1951-53
Van Buren, Steve—Eagles 1944-51

White, Lyman—Falcons 1981-82
Williams, Chris—Bills 1981-83
Williams, Mike—Chargers 1975-83
Wimberly. Abner—Rams 1949; Packers 1950-52
Winston, Roy—Vikings 1962-77
Woodley, David—Dolphins 1980-83; Steelers 1984-85

Zaunbrecher, Godfrey—Vikings 1970-74; Packers 1975

Active players in boldface

NEW ORLEANS SAINTS HALL OF FAME

Members of the New Orleans Saints Hall of Fame are selected by a board of sportswriters and sportscasters. The Hall of Fame was established in 1988 by the city of Kenner.

Inductees

1988   Danny Abramowicz, all-time leading pass receiver

Archie Manning, all-time leading quarterback

BASKETBALL

PETE MARAVICH
All-Time College Scoring Champion
LSU, 1967-70
Career Statistics

G	FG	FGA	PCT.	FT	FTA	PCT.	RB	A	PF	TP	AVE.
83	1387	3166	.438	893	1152	.775	528	423	250	3667	44.2

NATIONAL CONSECUTIVE FREE THROW RECORD
DARYL MOREAU (6'2", 175 pounds)
De La Salle High School, New Orleans

January 17, 1978-January 9, 1979—126 consecutive free throws made

1977-78 Season

Opponent	Made	Miss
Jesuit	8	0
Chalmette	7	0
Bro. Martin	6	0
St. Augustine	6	0
Jesuit	5	0
Rummel	2	0
Total	34	0

1978-79 Season
Pre-District

Warren Easton	4	0
Terrebonne	5	0
Ehret	12	0
Bonnabel	8	0
East Jefferson	8	0
Kennedy	4	0
Country Day	10	0
Cohen	6	0

Holy Cross	6	0
Warren Easton	3	0
Fortier	6	0
Chalmette	2	0

District

Shaw	6	0
Bro. Martin	7	0
Jesuit	5	1
Total	92	1

L.O.W.A. OFFICIAL FISH RECORDS
1987

FRESH WATER

BASS, HYBRID

15-0	Richard Thompson	June 1983
11-12	J D Murphy	March 1979
10-8	Wilton J Pino Jr	Dec 1979
8-2	Scott Boyett	March 1985
6-10	Sadie Easom	April 1983
3-8	Harris Allemand Sr.	May 1982

BASS, LARGEMOUTH

12-0	Harold C. Dunaway	Feb 1975
11-13	Jack O'Connor	April 1972
11-11	Elwin Husser	Nov. 1958
11-9	Jake J Crater	May 1971
11-8	Richard R. Brasher Jr.	Feb 1976
11-6	Zeke Davis	March 1962
11-2	James Strickland	Jan 1974
11-1	John T Allen II	May 1973
11-1	Donald A. Daniel Jr	Masy 1983
11-0	Robert Berry	March 1969

BASS, LARGEMOUTH
(caught on fly rod)

8-12	Vernon H Sonnier	March 1979
8-8	Nesbitt W Hagood III	April 1971
7-6	Dr. James W. Lorio	Dec. 1975
7-3	Roland Thibodeaux	March 1976
7-0	Rene J. Russo	April 1976
6-11	Gordon L King Sr.	Oct. 1965
6-9	Shelby Bordelon	March 1975
6-8	J.S. Drew	June 1962
6-6	Leonard Kleinpeter	March 1982
6-4	William I. Lake Jr.	March 1981

BASS, SPOTTED
(Kentucky)

4-14	Vernon C. Johnson Jr	Aug. 1976
4-6	Jim Farr	Feb 1976
4-6	Dalton T. Fayard	April 1976
4-4	Ben M. Strange Jr.	July 1976
4-3	Carroll Perkins	Oct. 1939
4-0	Bill Varnado	March 1978
3-15	Charles J. Kennedy	May 1976
3-14	Jeff Hughes	Nov. 1975
3-13	Charles J. Kennedy	Feb. 1972
3-10	Charles J. Kennedy	May 1976

BASS, STRIPED

37-0	John E. Dowden	Sept 1983
33-8	Robert L. Frisby	April 1982
33-3	James Kent Jr.	Feb. 1980
32-12	Mrs. Gloria Andrus	April 1979
30-9	Charles E. Slaughter Sr.	April 1982
30-4	Paul Blanchet	Jan 1978
28-2	Patrick Stringer	April 1979
27-1	James Teasley	March 1977
25-4	Robert Andries	March 1976
25-2	Ellen Strickland	April 1979

BASS, WHITE

4-12	Randy L. Dubuc	Feb. 1986
3-14	Sam Parrish	Feb. 1969
3-8	Kenny DeJean	Feb. 1986
3-3	M.L. Rabb	Aug. 1985
3-1	Linus Beard	Feb. 1978
3-0	DeWitt Cooper Jr.	Aug. 1980
2-14	C.L. Teel	May 1978
2-13	Ervin Murphy	Feb. 1979
2-11	J.A. Oliver	Nov. 1982
2-9	Mrs. Ouida Glynn Geter	April 1976
2-9	Elton J. Landry	Nov. 1980

BOWFIN

20-8	Brian Fant	April 1976
18-15	Hollis E. Moore	April 1976
17-8	Julius E. Aaron	Feb. 1973
17-0	K. R. McCullough	May 1976
16-8	Ike Dunlap	May 1974
16-8	Mark King	Aug 1976
16-1	Francis J Gautreau	Nov 1975
14-12	Mary T Boose	April 1975
14-4	Perry A. Dixon	June 1980
14-0	Robert L. Thurmond	Jan. 1981

BREAM

2-8	Grant M Kelly	Sept 1959
2-8	J W. Parker Jr	June 1961
2-5	Lloyd G. Hoover	April 1970
2-4	J.W. Parker Jr	May 1960
2-4	Tommy Frazier	April 1974
2-3	Joe Hudson	June 1973
2-2	Otis Marshall	May 1966
2-2	Henry C. Shaw	June 1978
2-1	Dee Murphy	April 1957
2-1	Kent Hollenshead	June 1976

BUFFALO

70-5	Delbert Sisk	April 1980
55-0	Donnie L. Goleman	July 1981
52-0	Tommy Descant	July 1976
46-8	Victor Zagone Jr.	Feb. 1971
42-0	Merv LeBlanc	July 1982
40-0	Ray Rhymes Jr.	July 1975
30-0	Rick Meador	Feb. 1981
26-4	Arnold Watson	May 1974
26-0	V Bonny Collura	July 1976
24-0	Robert Prator	Aug 1973

CARP

35-0	James D Rogers Jr.	April 1981
33-0	James E Strange	May 1978
29-8	Glenn Bond Jr.	Feb. 1980
27-0	Edgar Coltharp Sr.	June 1975
16-0	Amy Ann Smith	July 1986
15-4	G. Morgan Ford	April 1976
15-0	Edgar Coltharp Sr	June 1975

CATFISH

84-0	Tommy P Soileau	Jan. 1981
78-0	Edd Deshotels	Aug. 1980
62-0	James W. Hibben	March 1970
60-0	Jimmy B. Duff	March 1982
52-3	Darrell J. Farris	Jan. 1970
52-0	James W. Hibben	Jan. 1970
46-0	E F Witteborg	June 1966
43-0	Milton Blackwell	Aug. 1975
40-8	Warren Babin	March 1978
40-0	Eugene J. Canal Jr.	Jan. 1980
40-0	Mrs. Iona Blount	Dec. 1984

CRAPPIE
(sacalait)

6-0	Lettie Robertson	Nov 1969
4-4	Welzie Garrett	April 1950
4-2	David Lowery	April 1985
4-0	Ronald P. Cobbs	June 1971
3-14	Pat Cullen	March 1960
3-13	Nellie Keller	Feb 1964
3-12	L.M. Owens	Feb. 1973
3-12	John Kelly	Feb. 1986
3-8	Robert L. Nelson	Feb. 1971
3-8	Mike C. Thompson	Feb. 1985

CHAIN PICKEREL

5-12	Chris H Marien	May 1977
5-11	Jerry Haynie	July 1985
5-9	Edward R Nelson	Nov 1976
5-9	George C. Wallace	March 1977
5-4	Ross F. Miller	Aug. 1976
5-4	Walter Nutter	Oct 1976
4-12	Jack Kurfiss	Feb. 1980
4-8	Anthony E. Hough	Feb 1976
4-7	Tommy Harris	May 1976
4-6	Kenneth Ray McCullough	May 1977

REDFIN PICKEREL

1-8	Keith W. Henderson Sr.	Nov. 1974
0-10	Harry H Anderson	June 1983
0-10	Sidney Gonsoulin	July 1983
0-6	Niles M. Robichaux	Jan. 1980
0-4	Gerald Foret	Dec 1979

WARMOUTH
(goggle-eye)

1-8	Allen Polk	Sept. 1973
1-8	Harry H. Anderson	July 1983
1-6	Glenn R. Battle	June 1971
1-6	Lloyd David Sexton	July 1975
1-6	Mickey Montalbano	April 1976
1-6	Harry H. Anderson	July 1983
1-5	Leonard Gremillion Jr.	April 1974
1-5	Dr James W. Lorio	Aug. 1973
1-5	John J. Guarisco	June 1976
1-3	Dr. James W Lorio	Aug. 1971
1-3	Dr James W Lorio	Sept 1973
1-3	Charles Lea	May 1974
1-3	Sonny Guice	May 1974
1-3	Norman Guidry	July 1984

SALT WATER

AMBERJACK

130-8	Mike Lane	April 1977
120-0	Steven Hebert	Sept. 1982
118-10	Aubry Dauterive	July 1982
114-4	Jay Davidson	July 1985
113-8	Larry Hitter	July 1984
106-12	Milton J. Mouton	Aug. 1975
105-0	Aubrey Dauterive	Sept. 1983
101-4	Michael James Hebert	Aug. 1981
100-0	Duane Thomas Corley	Aug. 1979
98-6	Chuck Duhon	Sept 1982

BARRACUDA

50-0	A.C. Mills	Aug. 1970
48-8	Rhonda Green	July 1981
48-0	Dr. Thomas F. Kramer	Oct. 1975
47-8	Lester L. Jay	Aug. 1972
44-8	Jep. E. Turner Jr.	Sept. 1968
43-12	C.W. Gladney Jr.	Aug. 1977
42-0	Bob Marino	July 1972
42-0	Ruse A. Smith	June 1980
41-8	Harry Barbay	July 1976
40-0	J.J. Jones	Sept. 1966

BLACK JACK

21-5	Wayne McElveen	July 1982
14-0	Dr. John Tassin	July 1977
12-6	Jim Davidson	July 1982
11-10	H.W. Busch	July 1982
11-5	Rhett Pitre	July 1983
11-2	Rhett Pitre	June 1979
10-6	Johnny Johnson	June 1983
10-4	Ruse Smith	July 1983
9-14	Ruse Smith	July 1983
7-14	Greg Savoy	June 1983

BLUEFISH

21-14	Steve Van Every	July 1982
18-0	Jerry Quick	June 1984
16-8	Leon Kolmaister	Sept 1971
16-4	Joseph Steverson	Mar 1971
15-4	Richard Soileau	Sept 1984
14-12	Mrs. Dorothy Lane	July 1972
13-8	Gary Oberg	Aug. 1974
13-1	Rodney A. Pierce	Mar. 1978
12-15	Tim Sebastian	Oct. 1976
12-15	Joseph C. Schouest, Sr.	Sept. 1975

BONITO

29-12	Sidney Gonsoulin	July 1974
26-8	Al "Teppy" Daboval Jr.	July 1973
24-12	Joseph W. Gex	June 1970
24-9	Stirling Couch	July 1949
24-8	Erin M. Burks	Aug. 1971
24-5	Jill Bertucci	Aug. 1976
23-0	Charles Andres III	July 1949
20-0	Mrs. Lester Plaisance	July 1959
19-8	John Duffy Jr.	Aug. 1977
18-0	Mark Landrieu	July 1974

BROADBILL SWORDFISH

310-0	Tom Dantin	July 1980
284-8	Dr. Richard M. Landry	June 1978
166-12	Dr. Thomas Ellender	June 1980
138-12	Gerald M. Kapp	Oct. 1979
112-8	Geo. M. Snellings, III	July 1969
96-8	Leroy J. Breaux Jr.	June 1980
89-0	H. Vernon Myers, Jr.	Oct. 1979
69-8	Gerald Guidry	June 1980
68-8	Gerald M. Kapp	June 1980
59-8	Lawrence A. Durant	July 1977

COBIA

105-5	Douglas Lachico	May 1980
96-0	Charlie Hardison	June 1973
95-0	Dr. Roger Peak	ept. 1983
86-0	Steve Cassidy	May 1981
85-0	Randolph Lawton Reid	May 1984
84-5	Ronnie Babin	July 1983
84-0	Jim Delatte	May 1978
83-0	Louis "Boo" LeBlanc	May 1978
82-12	Alphonse S. Hebert Sr.	Nov. 1967
82-8	Harry Morris	May 1966

CROAKER
(Atlantic)

8-0	Douglas J. Bernard	Aug. 1972
5-5	Eugene Lefort Jr.	Aug. 1970
5-4	Eugene Lefort Jr	Oct. 1970
5-3	Melvin Backes	Feb 1978
5-2	Lloyd J. Babin	Oct. 1969
5-0	William Sparacello	Aug. 1972
4-14	Joseph D. Toups Jr	June 1966
4-11	Judge Alvin Oser	Aug 1973
4-10	Eugene Lefort Jr.	Oct. 1970
4-9	Eugene Lefort Jr.	Oct. 1970
4-9	Eugene Lefort Jr.	Oct. 1970

DOLPHIN

71-4	Robert Prest IV	June 1976
66-5	Harris Callais	June 1979
62-8	Mike Pratt	June 1973
60-12	Henry F. Page	June 1973
60-12	James R. Eichorn Jr.	June 1985
59-12	Stuart W. Wilson	June 1969
56-12	Wayne Plaisance	June 1968
56-3	David Brenham	June 1973
55-8	Buck Gladden III	May 1985
55-6	Herbert Malone	June 1980

DRUM

77-0	Timmy Joseph Darcey	April 1975
68-0	Charles Bienvenu	June 1983
61-15	Walton J. Theriot	June 1974
61-0	Gabe Schexnider	June 1970
59-0	Thomas Hoover	March 1983
59-0	A.V. Dixon Jr.	April 1983
58-3	Laddie Portier	Aug. 1974
58-3	Greg Green	July 1986
56-9	Davis Doucet	July 1974
56-0	Ricky Lanza	July 1981

FLOUNDER

12-2	Clarence Craig	Feb 1969
11-8	Jeff Patout	Aug 1981
11-1	Clarence Craig	Nov. 1967
11-0	Lee W Coulon	Nov 1967
11-0	George E. Stevens	Nov. 1967
11-0	Henry Schomaker	Dec. 1968
10-12	Mrs. Joseph Fousse Jr.	Nov. 1970
10-12	Richard A. Weisen Jr.	Aug 1980
10-0	Richard J. Boll Jr.	July 1965
10-0	Mrs. Joseph Hebert	Nov 1974

HORSE EYE JACKFISH

22-5	Earl Gothreaux	July 1982
21-6	Dr. Eric L. Lensgraf	June 1986
20-13	Dr. Ken Ritter Jr.	Aug. 1983
20-3	Doug Gothreaux	June 1986
19-8	John Bell	July 1985
19-7	M.B. Slocum	June 1986
19-0	Tim Pitre	July 1977
18-11	Michael Savoy	July 1985
18-10	Patrick Savoy	June 1980
18-3	Al Daboval Jr.	June 1986

JACK CREVALLE

54-4	Bill Dahringer	Aug. 1982
52-11	Robert M. Schultz Sr	Dec. 1985
52-8	Robert C. Buuck Sr.	Oct. 1984
51-8	Glenn P. Templet	June 1982
51-4	Daniel C. Ross	Aug. 1984
50-2	Robert M. Schultz Sr.	July 1986
47-8	Thomas C. Rhodes	Jan. 1981
44-8	Jeffry Blaine Lea	Sept. 1977
44-4	Dr Eric Lensgraf	July 1984
44-0	Dean S. Beard	April 1977

MACKEREL, KING

82-0	W.D. Lamb	Dec. 1980
78-4	Debra R. Sabastian	Nov 1981
76-12	Robert T. Barnes	Dec. 1979
75-4	Terry Levy	Dec. 1979
75-0	Dwight G. Bardwell	Nov. 1981
74-6	Henry A. Bolen Jr.	Nov. 1981
74-4	James A. Crumly	Dec. 1980
74-0	David C. Bouza	Dec. 1979
74-0	John A. Robinson III	Oct. 1981
73-8	Donny Classert	Nov 1979
73-8	Philip J. David Sr.	Feb. 1980

MACKEREL, SPANISH

10-9	Mike LeBlanc	Aug 1972
9-8	Rodney C. Robert	June 1980
9-1	James P. Antill	Aug. 1971
9-0	W.J "Bill" Bowen	Oct 1978
8-9	Warren Fisher Jr.	Oct 1974
8-7	David J. Danos	Aug 1976
8-4	Anthony C. D'Antonio	Nov 1970
8-2	Mrs. Earlise Lefort	July 1975
8-1	Pat Matherne	Aug 1973
8-0	Earl E. Wall	Aug 1973

MAKO SHARK

412-0	Carroll Goulas	July 1980
400-0	Jules E. Guglielmo Sr	July 1972
365-8	Marvin G. Heebe	Mar. 1976
358-8	O.R. Payne	July 1973
315-8	Carl Sibley	May 1983
280-0	Leander H. Perez Jr.	Aug. 1967
268-0	Mrs. Alma L. Burks	July 1971
265-8	Richard Landry	May 1975
261-0	H.L. Herrin Jr.	June 1978
259-8	J W. Duffy	May 1970

MARLIN, BLUE

1018-8	Linda Koerner	July 1977
738-0	Archie Lowery	July 1980
699-0	Berry Grubbs	Sept. 1978
695-8	Robert T. Hatcher Jr.	July 1980
686-0	Alvin E. DuVernay Jr.	Aug. 1969
681-8	Clint Shackelford	June 1986
665-8	Karen Savage	July 1979
665-0	James P. Solari	July 1980
657-0	Dick Strohe	June 1980
654-4	Judy Prejeant	June 1985

MARLIN, WHITE

134-0	Dennis L. Good	July 1967
110-8	George M. Snelling III	May 1968
109-11	Carl E. Hursman	June 1984
103-4	Sidney Gonsoulin	Aug. 1973
103-0	Mrs. Al R. Childress Jr	May 1967
102-6	Chalin O. Perez Jr.	July 1977
102-0	Paul C. Boyer	June 1979
101-0	Alfred Hitter Jr.	June 1979
100-8	Paul Pumilia	June 1983
100-0	William L. Manning	July 1968

POMPANO

8-8	Buddy Pons	Dec 1969
7-11	Louis Thornton	Nov 1986
7-8	Buddy Pons	Dec 1979
6-14	Leon Kolmaister	Nov 1975
6-13	Hugh R. Babylon	Dec 1970
6-10	Clement Andollina	Dec 1970
6-8	U.S Allan	Jan 1971
6-6	Lynn Matthews	Dec 1975
6-4	Felix C. Byxbe	Dec 1970
6-4	Lamar J. Callaway	Nov 1971

POMPANO
(African)

36-4	Jack Lawton	July 1980
36-0	Sonny Hackett	Oct. 1983
31-2	Huey A. Lynch	Aug 1971
30-8	H.W. "Bill" Busch	Sept 1979
27-6	Dr Frank Savoy	May 1980
27-1	Harold Moreaux	Nov 1975
27-0	John Beyt III	Sept 1977
23-2	Clyde H. Martin	Sept 1975
22-11	Jeff Patout	Nov 1975
22-0	Dr. Darryl Elias	Oct. 1977

RAINBOW RUNNER

16-2	Marion Tucker	July 1983
15-15	Tom McAndrew	June 1979
15-8	Donita O'Neal	June 1984
14-8	Gayle Boudreaux	Aug. 1980
13-8	Harry Hawkins	July 1983
12-11	Charlie Grey	June 1978
12-2	Myron Fischer	May 1978
11-4	Frank Lynn Palmisano	June 1984
11-1	Melanie O'Brien	July 1985
10-15	Warren Bogan	Aug. 1986

REDFISH

56-8	O.L. Cornish	Sept. 1963
52-2	Ira J. Breaux	Aug 1977
51-8	Philip A. Robinson	June 1967
51-4	Robert E. Bailey	Feb. 1982
47-15	Eldon Hutchinson	July 1986
47-8	John E. Dakin Jr.	Dec. 1975
47-4	Richard J. Davis	July 1981
46-8	Joe W. Burns	Feb. 1981
46-0	James T. Brady	Sept. 1972
46-0	Mrs. Pauline G. Rohm	May 1974
46-0	Johnny Ledet Jr.	Aug. 1976

SAILFISH

96-0	John Lauricella	Oct. 1953
90-8	Richard A. Wikenhauser	June 1979
85-12	Cheyenne Williams	June 1981
85-0	Arnold O. Domin	July 1965
84-4	Grant A. Rodriguez Jr.	May 1975
83-4	W. McKerall O'Neil Jr.	June 1974
82-2	Frank Tutzauer	June 1971
80-0	Dennis L. Good	Oct. 1967
78-9	Dr. Jerry R. Smith	June 1984
78-0	Don Locasio	July 1971

SHEEPSHEAD

21-4	Wayne J. Desselle	April 1982
14-12	John N. Bourg	May 1970
14-4	Eugene Lefort Jr.	Mar. 1970
12-4	James Summersgill Jr.	July 1972
12-2	Dudley J. Bourg	Feb. 1974
11-14	Mrs. Bruce Matherne	Feb. 1974
11-13	George P. Bourg	Aug. 1972
11-8	Mrs. Aubrey Bares	1955
11-8	Steve Troesch	Dec. 1956
11-6	Eugene Lefort Jr.	May 1971

SNAPPER, CUBERA

121-8	Mike Hebert	July 1982
99-8	Joe Beatty	July 1986
97-8	Louis Mere Jr	July 1986
87-0	Louis Mere Jr	July 1986
79-0	Tommy N. Stoker	June 1979
74-0	Jim Meriwether	Oct. 1963
72-8	Patrick Savoy	July 1983

SNAPPER, RED

39-2	Mrs Jesse B. Lane	May 1975
38-3	Allen M. Kahoe	June 1977
37-10	C. Lee Mason	Aug. 1981
36-0	Charlie Joseph Begnaud	April 1982
35-7	John L. DiMiceli Jr.	July 1977
35-6	Bobby Green	July 1983
35-2	Paul C. Boyer	June 1977
35-0	Marvin E. Griffin	Aug. 1967
35-0	Bill Barnhill	Aug. 1971
35-0	Dr. Joseph A. Tusa	Aug. 1975

SPADEFISH

9-4	Benny Avera	Dec. 1969
8-8	Schuyler Thibodeaux	April 1972
8-6	Wilson Couch	June 1972
8-3	Charles Sebastian	Aug. 1963
8-0	Davey A. Landry	Sept. 1983
7-12	James M. Lee	Jan. 1981
7-11	Charles L. Crawford Jr.	Dec. 1979
7-8	Hilary Blanchard	June 1976
7-5	Charles G. Donewar III	May 1976
7-5	Stephen C. Randazzo	March 1981
7-5	James H. Dufrene Jr.	June 1984

SPEARFISH

78-0	Larry Bulot	July 1964
47-8	Jack Cooper	June 1984
27-15	Stephanie Slatten	July 1974
21-12	Pat Manuel	July 1981
20-4	Mrs. Guy C. Billups Jr.	1969
17-10	William A. Summers Jr.	July 1981
17-6	Barry Barger	Aug. 1977
12-4	W. H. Schnauder	July 1984
7-8	Kyle T. Marks	June 1977

TARPON

222-12	Pat Parra	June 1979
218-0	James R. Eichorn Jr	Oct 1984
211-8	George J. Huber	Sept. 1978
206-0	Johnny A. Guidry	July 1973
205-12	Ray Grezaffi	Sept. 1978
205-0	Wesley J. Thibodeaux	Aug. 1980
204-0	Michael Mathieu	Aug. 1982
200-12	Joseph C. Schouest Sr.	Oct. 1981
200-0	Joe Schouest Jr.	Sept. 1977
200-0	Barron M. Whipple	Aug. 1982
200-0	Eugene Schouest	Sept. 1982

TRIPLETAIL

39-8	Mrs. Jimmy Toups	July 1959
39-0	Jimmy Frickey	July 1977
33-12	Mrs. Mary G. Blackmon	Aug. 1970
33-12	Jeff Toups	July 1973
33-0	Bob Moran	June 1953
32-0	Jimmy Toups	July 1970
29-0	Mrs Jimmy Toups	July 1970
28-8	Lawrence Federico Jr.	Aug. 1971
26-8	Mrs. Jimmy Toups	July 1970
25-4	Mrs. Clavena Cognevich	Aug. 1970

TROUT, SPECKLED

12-6	Leon Mattes	May 1950
10-12	Randolph D. Green	Aug. 1970
10-10	John Kaparis	May 1979
10-0	David G. Buccola	May 1974
9-14	James L. LeMay	April 1970
9-14	Edward J. Goodwin Jr.	May 1977
9-12	John W. Burns	Mar. 1968
9-12	Anthony J. Bianca	Aug. 1970
9-11	Nicholas J. Dimaio Sr.	May 1975
9-8	Richard F. Muller Jr.	June 1970

TROUT, WHITE

11-0	Donald H. Marion	Sept. 1973
10-8	James Gomez	Jan. 1973
9-13	Ferdinand Von Behren III	Jan. 1976
9-2	Claude McCall	Feb. 1978
8-12	Richard Landry	Feb. 1975
8-8	Martin Vinet	May 1977
8-4	Dale Schlottman	Aug. 1975
8-0	Mickey Montalbano	Feb. 1981
7-10	Franklin V. Endom Jr.	Feb. 1975
7-4	Jimmy Hill	Mar. 1975

TUNA, BLACKFIN

31-0	James D. Busby	July 1977
30-8	Jeff Patout	Aug. 1984
30-8	Walter Puckett	April 1985
30-4	Domennic Corrent Jr.	June 1984
30-3	Johnny Johnson	May 1982
29-13	John Ryan	May 1986
29-12	Dorothy Perkins	July 1978
28-9	Prentiss Perkins	June 1986
28-9	Allen Stuart	June 1986
28-8	Chris Sadler	June 1984

TUNA, BLUEFIN

891-0	Darlene Fischer	May 1981
859-0	Jack A. Brown	June 1971
834-0	Arnold Boudreaux	May 1977
831-12	Roy V. Eskine	May 1972
826-0	Dr. John Melton	June 1978
803-0	Roy O'Neal	June 1984
780-8	Pierre Villere	May 1977
665-0	Steve Edgett	May 1975
580-0	Jack A. Brown	June 1971
526-4	Jack Kimmerly	May 1975

TUNA, YELLOWFIN
(Allison)

221-8	Dr. Charles Terrell	June 1982
211-10	Charles M. Drost	June 1980
203-4	Chris Barker	June 1986
201-8	Alvin E. DuVernay	June 1971
200-12	Arnold J. Boudreaux	May 1980
199-8	William A. Good	July 1969
198-9	Mrs. Judi Burrus	June 1977
196-8	Guy C. Billups Jr	May 1966
196-0	Clyde V. Hawk	June 1968
195-8	Wayne Cestia	June 1983

WAHOO

139-4	Myron J. Fischer	April 1976
124-8	Salvadore Perino Jr.	May 1974
110-4	Erin Burks	May 1976
110-0	Mrs. Homer J. Moore Jr.	1964
108-4	Edison Chouest	May 1977
103-0	William H. Barrett Jr.	July 1973
101-8	H.D. Bacon IV	Aug. 1977
99-11	Priscilla Claverie	June 1980
97-4	Dan Doerle	June 1986
97-0	Mrs. Merle Couch	April 1978
97-0	Jan Pitre Aymond	Aug. 1985

Louisiana's official fish records are maintained by the Louisiana Outdoor Writers Association in 15 freshwater and 35 saltwater categories. LOWA awards a certificate to fishermen who make a catch that places in the Top Ten in each category.

Record applications should be mailed to Joe Macaluso, The State-Times, P.O. Box 588, Baton Rouge 70821. Application forms also may be obtained upon request by sending a stamped, self-addressed envelope to the same address.

HORSE RACING HISTORY AT THE FAIR GROUNDS

The history of racing in New Orleans began in 1820 at Live Oak Plantation by Francois Livaudais. In 1825 Jackson Race Track opened near Chalmette, followed by the Eclipse Course near what is now Audubon Park (1837). Metairie Race Course opened in 1838 and was eventually bought (1872) and converted into the present Metairie cemetery. The Fair Grounds Course was inaugurated in 1872 by the Louisiana Jockey Club. Two famous horses, Pan Zareta and Black Gold are buried in the infield. A highlight occurred in 1939 when Eddie Arcaro won the Rex Handicap.

LOUISIANA DERBY WINNERS

1920	Damask	E. Ambrose
1923	Amole	J. D. Mooney
1924	Black Gold	J. D. Mooney
1925	Quatrain	H. Stutts
1926	Bagenbaggage	F. Blind
1927	Boo	G. Johnson
1928	Jack Higgins	C. F. Allen
1929	Calf Roper	F. Coltiletti
1930	Michigan Boy	J. Shelton
1931	Spanish Play	C. Landolt
1932	Lucky Tom	A. Pascuma
1933	Col. Hatfield	C. Meyer
1934	Hickory Lad	J. Westrope
1935	McCarthy	P. Keester
1936	Rushaway	J. Longden
1937	Grey Count	C. Corbett
1938	Wise Fox	J. Longden
1939	Day Off	E. Arcaro
1943	Amber Light	J. Longden
1944	Olympic Zenith	N. Jemas
1946	Pellicle	A. LoTurco
1947	Carolyn A	R. Nash
1948	Bovard	W. Saunders
1949	Rookwood	J. Delahoussaye
1950	Greek Ship	C. Errico
1951	Whirling Bat	P. Anderson
1952	Gushing Oil	A. Popara
1953	Matagorda	P. J. Bailey
1954	Gigantic	R. McLaughlin
1955	Roman Patrol	D. Dodson
1956	Reaping Right	R. L. Baird
1957	Federal Hill	W. Carstens
1958	Royal Union	J. Heckmann
1959	Master Palynch	R. Broussard
1960	Tony Graff	W. Chambers
1961	Bass Clef	R. Baldwin
1962	Admiral's Voyage	R. Broussard
1963	City Line	R. L. Baird
1964	Grecian Princess	K. Broussard
1965	Dapper Delegate	J. Heckman
1966	Blue Skyer	R. Broussard
1967	Ask the Fare	D. Holmes
1968	Kentucky Sherry	J. Combest
1969	King of the Castle	C. H. Marquez
1970	Jim's Alibhi	R. Baldwin
1971	Northfields	W. Blum
1972	No Le Hace	P. Rubbicco
1973	Leo's Pisces	B. Breen
1974	**Sellout**	**M. Castaneda**
1975	**Master Derby**	**D. McHargue**
1976	**Johnny Appleseed**	**M. Castaneda**
1977	**Clever-Tell**	**R. Broussard**
1978	**Esops Foibles**	**C. McCarron**
1979	**Golden Act**	**S. Hawley**
1980	**Prince Valliant**	**M. Gonzales**
1981	**Woodchopper**	**J. Velasquez**
1982	**El Baba**	**D. Brumfield**
1983	**Balboa Native**	**J. Velasquez**

1984	**Taylor's Special**	**S. Maple**
1985	**Violado**	**S. Vasquez**
1986	**Country Light**	**P. Day**
1987	**J. Y.'s Pet**	**P. Day**

NEW ORLEANS HANDICAP WINNERS

1925	Quatrain	F. Legere
1926	Nurmi	J. Thomas
1927	Cotlogomor	C. Allen
1928	Justice F	A. Pascuma
1929	Vermajo	A. Pascuma
1930	Donnay	E. Steffen
1931	Jimmy Moran	E. James
1932	Spanish Play	C. Landolt
1933	Rocky News	J. Kacala
1934	Slapped	B. Haas
1935	Jesting	S. Young
1936	Julia Grant	H. Spears
1937	Skeeter	F. Ritz
1938	Novelette	V. Nodarse
1939	Chance Sweet	J. F. Oros
1940	Rough Diamond	A. Sorsen
1943	Marriage	A. Craig
1944	Marriage	J. Higley
1946	Hillyer Court	W. L. Johnson
1947	Earshot	F. Moon
1948	Star Reward	S. Brooks
1949	My Request	C. Erickson
1950	Red Camelia	P. Milligan
1951	Mount Marcy	K. Church
1952	Oil Capitol	K. Church
1953	Smoke Screen	G. Porch
1954	Grover B	P. J. Bailey
1955	Sea O Erin	K. Church
1956	Find	E. Guerin
1957	Kingmaker	S. Boulmetis
1958	Tenacious	R. Broussard
1959	Tenacious	R. Broussard
1960	Tudor Era	R. L. Stevenson
1961	Greek Star	R. Broussard
1962	Yorktown	J. Nichols
1963	Endymion	J. Nichols
1964	Green Hornet	R. Broussard
1965	Valiant Man	R. Ussery
1966	Just About	L. Moyers
1967	Cabildo	J. Combest
1968	Diplomat Way	L. Moyers
1969	Miracle Hill	D. F. Whited
1970	Etony	P. Rubbicco
1971	Rio Bravo	F. Valdizan
1972	Urgent Message	G. St. Leon
1973	Combat Ready	L. Moyers
1974	**Smooth Dancer**	**Larry Adams**
1975	**Lord Rebeau**	**C. Martuez**
1976	**Master Derby**	**D. Margue**
1977	**Tudor Tambourine**	**A. Trosclair**
1978	**Life's Hope**	**C. McCarron**
1979	**A Letter to Harry**	**E. Delahoussaye**
1980	**Pool Court**	**R. Ardoin**
1981	**Sun Catcher**	**A. Guajardo**
1982	**It's the One**	**W. Guerra**
1983	**Listcapade**	**E. J. Perrodin**
1984	**Wild Again**	**P. Day**
1985	**Westheimer**	**L. Snyder**
1986	**Herat**	**R. Meza**
1987	**Honor Medal**	**R. Baze**

LOUISIANA FUTURITY WINNERS

Year	Horse	Owner/Trainer
1963	Mr. Burke	J. Heckmann
1964	Mush McGinnis	P. Bohenko
1965	Bogue Falaya	L. Moyers
	Near Music	J. Lopez
1966	Cazenove (f)*	R. Gallimore
	Backbiter (c&g)**	G. Overton
1967	Bush Gypsy (f)	H. Romero
	Torque Gauge (f)	W. Fleming
	Hart the Herald (c&g)	L. Moyers
1968	Heck's Pride (f)	R. L. Baird
	Dillie Juror (f)	J. A. Martinez
	Cosmic Corner (c&g)	N. Menard
	Ray's Law (c&g)	J. Manuel
1969	Tina Kate (f)	J. A. Martinez
	Jumpstep (c&g)	D. E. Whited
	Debbie Pal (c&g)	J. A. Martinez
1970	Eight Year (f)	N. Menard
	Jayme M. (f)	D. Copling
	Tall Tall (c&g)	D. Niblick
	Joey Bob (c&g)	J. Nichols
1971	Sister Moon (f)	E. Delahoussaye
	Hold Taga (c&g)	K. Bourque
	Marvin Vessier (c&g)	L. P. Suire
1972	Fly 'n Win (f)	E. Delahoussaye
	Young Tickey (f)	J. Alleman
	Speedy Pro (c&g)	R. Sibille
	David M. (c&g)	L. Munster
1973	Exact Fare (c&g)	S. Vail
	Creole Cross (c&g)	S. Adams
	Pet Tale (f)	T. Dupre
	Plus Pluit (f)	C. Perret
1974	Creole Cookin (f)	P. Rubbico
	Dr. Jerrell (c&g)	J. Anderson
1975	Kitassy (f)	A. Trosclair
	Olympian Minstrel (c&g)	J. Power
1976	Corn Soup (f)	A. Trosclair
	Scotty's Gin (c&g)	L. Melancon
1977	Miss Poodle Pup (f)	R. Ardoin
	Dr. Dean (c&g)	W. Soirez
1978	Porpourie (f)	R. Ardoin
	Smooth & Daring (c&g)	A. Trosclair
1979	Greenback Gert (f)	N. Menard
	Lumber Man (c&g)	K. Bourque
1980	D. J.'s Pet (f)	A. Guajardo
	Reason's Tattoo (f)	R. Romero
	Brazen Ruller (c&g)	B. Walker
	Smooth Wood (c&g)	M. Holland
1981	Daring Style (f)	E. J. Perrodin
	Fly Miss Fly (f)	W. Talley
	Tommy Bolo (c&g)	E. J. Perrodin
1982	Amoriah (f)	L. Munster
	Best You've Seen (f)	D. Copling
	Joe's Intent (c&g)	J. Faul
	Judge Lindsey (c&g)	D. Whited
1983	Everloving Mama (f)	R. Franklin
	Cruzin Smooth (f)	R. Romero
	K'N'T' Omara's Boy (c&g)	J. Court
	Piece of Pacific (c&g)	N. Menard
1984	Solo From Rio (f)	K. Boussard, Jr.
	Opal's Claim (f)	K. Boussard, Jr.
	Pacific Sun (c&g)	C. Simon
1985	Best In Class (f)	R. Ardoin
	Eustoo (c&g)	T. Hebert
	Beau Voyage (c&g)	J. Imparato
1986	Beth's Girl (f)	A. Dupuy
	Tricky N' Clever (f)	K. Bourque
	Courtin' Ann (c&g)	A. Dupuy

* filly   ** colt and gelding
Source: New Orleans Fair Grounds

Members of the Louisiana Sports Hall of Fame

Joe Adcock	Doc Fenton	Bill Lee	Harry Rabenhorst
Joe Aillet	Peggy Flournoy	Bob Love	Willis Reed
Bill Banker	Ralph Garr	Johnny Lynch	Dutch Reinhardt
Bernie Bierman	Paul Geisler	Ted Lyons	Ham Richardson
Buddy Blair	Larry Gilbert	Charles McClendon	Eddie Robinson
Tommy Bolt	Matt Gordy	Max McGee	Johnny Robinson
Sid Bowman	Tad Gormley	Jimmy McGonagill	Roland Romero
Frank Brian	Eric Guerin	Bo McMillin	Glynn Saulters
Lou Brock	Freddie Haas	Carl Maddox	Clark Shaughnessy
Billy Brown	Jake Hanna	Faize Mahfouz	Monk Simons
Joe Brown	Slats Hardin	Pete Maravich	Jackie Smith
Willie Brown	Jay Hebert	Tommy Mason	Bobby Spell
Buck Buchanan	Lionel Hebert	Abe Mickal	Jerry Stovall
Chris Cagle	Charley Hennigan	J. D. Mooney	Dave Styron
Billy Cannon	Ed Head	Bernie Moore	Don Styron
Tony Canzoneri	Pete Herman	Al Moreau	Jimmy Taylor
Tommy Casanova	Bob Hopkins	Jackie Moreland	Red Thomas
Jim Corbett	Cal Hubbard	A. W. Mumford	Gaynell Tinsley
Clifford Ann Creed	Dana Jenkins	Mel Ott	Y. A. Tittle
John David Crow	Bert Jones	Mel Parnell	Emmett Toppino
Jerry Dalrymple	Biff Jones	Willie Pastrano	Jack Torrance
Al Dark	Dub Jones	John Pennell	Harry Turpin
Willie Davis	Ken Kavanaugh	Jimmy Perrin	Steve Van Buren
Bill Dickey	Dwight Lamar	Bob Pettit	Sparky Wade
Atley Donald	Maxie Lambright	Howie Pollet	Tank Younger
Tom Dutton	Hank Lauricella	H. Lee Prather	Don Zimmerman
Eddie Dyer	Lester Lautenschlaeger	Eddie Price	

U S F&G GOLF CLASSIC

Year	Champion	Total No. Strokes	Amount of Winnings
1958	Billy Casper	278	$ 2,800
1959	Bill Collins	280	2,800
1960	Dow Finsterwald	270	3,500
1961	Doug Sanders	272	4,300
1962	Bo Wininger	281	4,300
1963	Bo Wininger	279	6,400
1964	Mason Rudolph	283	7,500
1965	Dick Mayer	273	20,000
1966	Frank Beard	276	20,000
1967	George Knudson	277	20,000
1968	George Archer	271	20,000
1969	Larry Hinson	275	20,000
1970	Miller Barber	278	25,000
1971	Frank Beard	276	25,000
1972	Gary Player	279	25,000
1973	Jack Nicklaus	280	25,000
1974	Lee Trevino	267	30,000
1975*	Billy Casper	271	30,000
1976	Larry Ziegler	274	35,000
1977	Jim Simons	273	35,000
1978	Lon Hinkle	271	40,000
1979	Hubert Green	273	45,000
1980	Tom Watson	273	45,000
1981	Tom Watson	270	63,000
1982	Scott Hoch	206*	54,000
1983	Bill Rogers	274	72,000
1984	Bob Eastwood	.272	72,000
1985	Steve Ballesteros	.205	72,000
1986	Calvin Peete	.269	90,000
1987	Ben Crenshaw	.268	90,000

*54 holes (shortened tournament)

Track and Field
Men's State Collegiate Track Records

EVENT	T/D	RECORD HOLDER
100-meter dash	10.08	Brian Cooper, (McNeese), 1987
200-meter dash	20.21	Brian Cooper, (McNeese), 1987
400-meter dash	5.15	Theron Lewis, (Southern), 1966
800-meter run	1:46.95	Michael Lolis, (Southern), 1987
1500-meter run	3:42.04	Bobby Beck, (LSU), 1984
5000-meter run	13:51.00	Roger Barker, (La. Tech), 1980
3000-meter steeplechase	8:39.72	Marv Dobbins, (LSU), 1979
110-meter high hurdles	13.12	Rod Milburn, (Southern), 1972
400-meter hurdles	49.61	Bernard Williams, (LSU), 1986
400-meter relay	39.03	Northwestern State (Mario Johnson, Ray Brown, Edgar Washington, Mark Duper), 1982
1600-meter relay	3:03.64	Southern (Anthony Gates, Robert Johnson, Everett Mason, Theron Lewis), 1965
Long jump	27-7¼ (WA)	Andre Ester, (Northeast), 1987
	26-11	Brian Cooper, (McNeese), 1987
Triple jump	53-8	Eric Barber, (Northwestern), 1985
High jump	7-6½	Neal Guidry, (Southwestern), 1987
Pole vault	18-5¼	Greg Duplantis, (LSU), 1986
Shot put	69-3¾	John Campbell, (La. Tech), 1985
Discus	199-3	Bruce Navarre, (Northeast), 1981
Javelin	271-0	Steve Stockton, (Northwestern), 1983

Source: Bob Anderson, Sports Information Director, Northeast Louisiana University.

COMMUNICATIONS
COMMERCIAL BROADCAST STATIONS ON THE AIR

Year	Total	AM	FM	TV	Year	Total	AM	FM	TV
1955	78	58	12	8	1964	107	85	10	12
1956	86	63	12	11	1965	108	86	10	12
1957	92	71	10	11	1970	121	90	14	17
1958	100	78	10	12	1972	131	89	23	19
1959	100	80	8	12	1974	133	88	27	18
1960	99	78	9	12	1976	165	90	56	19
1961	99	79	8	12	1981	192	94	76	22
1962	99	80	8	11	1985	206	102	81	23
1963	104	83	9	12	1986	208	97	88	23

*This column includes FM stations associated with AM stations.

Source: Federal Communications Commission, South Central Bell

TELEVISION STATIONS

Alexandria

KALB TV (5) NBC
605 Washington
71301
P. O. Box 951
71306

KLAX TV (31) ABC
1811 England Dr.
P. O. Box 8818
71306

KLPA TV (25) PBS
7860 Anselmo Ln.
Baton Rouge
70810

Baton Rouge

WAFB TV (9) CBS
844 Government St.
70802
P. O. Box 2671
70821

WBRZ TV (2) ABC
1650 Highland Road
70802
P. O. Box 2906
70821

WLPB TV (27) PBS
7860 Anselmo Ln.
70810

WRBT TV (33) NBC
5220 Essen Lane
70808
P. O. Box 14685
70898

Destrehan

Sunbelt Cablevision, LTD.
1900- A Ormond Blvd.
70047

Golden Meadow

Callais Cablevision
Callais Lane
P. O. Box 788
70357

Harahan

WCOX TV (2)
Cox Cable Jefferson Parish
338 Edwards
70123-4195

Houma

Vision Cable of Houma
104 Lois Rd.
70360

Lafayette

Acadiana Open
Channel Inc. (5)
124 E. Main St.
P. O. Box 5159
70502

KADN TV (15)
1500 Eraste Landry Road
70506

KATC TV (3) ABC
1103 Eraste Landry Road
P. O. Box 93133
70509

KLFY TV (10) CBS
2410 Eraste Landry Road
P. O. Box 90665
70509

KLPB TV (24) PBS
7860 Anselmo Ln.
Baton Rouge
70810

Lake Charles

KLTL TV (18) PBS
7860 Anselmo Ln.
Baton Rouge
70810

KPLC TV (7) NBC
320 Division St.
P. O. Box 1488
70602

KVHP TV (29)
129 W. Prien Lake Rd.
70601

Laplace

Riverland Cablevision
136 Farm Road
70068

Luling

St. Charles Cable TV
1500 Paul Mallard Rd.
70070

Monroe

KLTM TV (13) PBS
1860 Anselmo Ln.
Baton Rouge
70810

KNOE TV (8) CBS
1400 Oliver Road
71201
P. O. Box 4067
71211

KTVE TV (10) NBC
2909 Kilpatrick Blvd.
71201

New Orleans

Cox Cable
2120 Canal St.
70112

WDSU-TV (6) NBC
520 Royal St.
70130

WGNO-TV (26)
World Trade Center
Suite 2800
2 Canal St.
70130

WLAE TV (32) PBS
2929 S. Carrollton Ave.
70118

WNOL TV (38)
1661 Canal St.
70112

WVUE TV (8) ABC
1025 S. Jefferson Davis Pkwy
70125

WWL TV (4) CBS
1024 N. Rampart St.
70116

WYES TV (12) PBS
916 Navarre
70124

St. Bernard

Cablevision of St. Bernard
7509 E. St. Bernard Hwy.
70092
P. O. Box 1458
70044

Slidell

St. Tammany Cablevision (10)
Route 5, Ben Thomas Road
70460
P. O. Box 890
70459

Shreveport

Cablevision of
Shreveport, Inc.
6529 Quilen Rd.
71108

KLTS TV (24) PBS
7860 Anselmo Ln.
Baton Rouge
70810

KMSS TV (33)
3519 Jewella Ave.
P. O. Box 30033
71130

KSLA TV (12) CBS
1812 Fairfield Ave.
71104
P. O. Box 4812
71134

KTAL TV (6) NBC
3150 N. Market
P. O. Box 7428
71107

KTBS TV (3) ABC
312 E. Kings Hwy.
71104
P. O. Box 44227
71134

West Monroe

KARD TV (14) ABC
701 Parkwood Dr.
71291

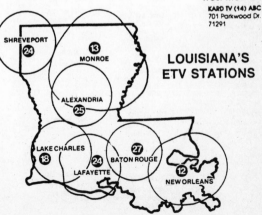

LOUISIANA'S
ETV STATIONS

RADIO STATIONS

Abbeville
KROF AM 960
FM 104.9
Highway 167
P. O. Box 610
70511-0610

Alexandria
KALB AM 580
KZMZ FM 96.9
601 Washington
P. O. Box 471
71301

KDBS AM 1410
KRRV FM 100.3
1515 Jackson St.
P. O. Box 591
71301

KQID FM 93
KSYL AM 970
1115 Texas Ave.
P. O. Box 7057
71303

Amite
WABL AM 1570
Bankston Road
P. O. Box 787
70422

Bastrop
KJBS FM 100
KVOB AM 1340
121 Haynie St.
71220

KTRY AM 730
FM 94.3
Shelton Road
P. O. Box 1075
71220

Baton Rouge
WFMF FM 102.5
WJBO AM 1150
444 Florida St.
70801
P. O. Box 496
70821

WGGZ FM 98.1
844 Government St.
70802
P. O. Box 2671
70821

WIBR AM 1300
1815 Lafiton Lane
Port Allen
70767
P. O. Box 1226
70821

WKJN FM 103
3029 S. Sherwood Forest
Suite 200
70816

WLUX AM 1550
8919 World Ministry Blvd.
70810
P. O. Box 2550
70821

Bayou Vista
KDLP AM 1170
KQKI FM 95.3
10 Pluto St.
70380
P. O. Box 847
70381

Belle Chasse
KAGY AM 1510
P. O. Box 220
1402 Belle Chasse
Hwy. S.
70037

Bogalusa
WBOX AM 920
FM 92.7
Old Varnado Highway
P. O. Box 280
70427

WIKC AM 1490
607 Rio Grande
P. O. Box 638
70427

Boyce
KBCE FM 102
Highway 1 South
P. O. Box 69
71409

Columbia
KCTO AM 1540
FM 103.1
Radio Road
P. O. Box 1319
71418

Coushatta
KRRP AM 950
Jordan Ferry Road
P. O. Box 910
71019

WQXY FM 100.7
WXAM AM 910
100 St. James St.
Suite K100
70802

WRKF FM 89.3
3050 Valley Creek Dr.
70808

WTKL AM 1260
4854 Constitution Ave.
70808
P. O. Box 14856
70898

WXOK AM 1460
6819 Cezanne Ave.
70806
P. O. Box 66475
70896

WYNK AM 1380
FM 101.5
854 Main St.
70802
P. O. Box 2541
70821

Covington
WARB AM 730
Hammond Highway
70433
P. O. Box 568
70434

Crowley
KPWS AM 1560
KAJN FM 102.9
110 W. 3rd St.
P. O. Box 1469
70527-1469

KSIG AM 1450
320 N. Parkerson Ave.
P. O. Box 228
70526

Denham Springs
WBIU AM 1210
601 Hatchell Ln.
70726
P. O. Box 68
70727-0068

DeRidder
KDLA AM 1010
KEAZ FM 101.7
Highway 171 North
P. O. Box 46
70634

KROK FM 92.1
P. O. Box 1180
70634

Donaldsonville
KKAY AM 1590
FM 104.9
Highway 1
P. O. Box 797
70346

Dubach/Ruston
KPCH FM 97.7
P. O. Box 977
Ruston
71270

Erwinville
KPAE FM 91.5
13028 U.S. Highway 190 West
Port Allen
70767

Eunice
KEUN AM 1490
211 South Second St.
P. O. Box 1049
70535

KJJB FM 105.5
105 South Second St.
70535

Farmerville
KTDL AM 1470
KWJM FM 92.7
113 North Main St.
71241

Ferriday
KFNV AM 1600
FM 107.1
917 South 4th St.
P. O. Box 592
71334

Franklin
KFRA AM 1390
KFMV FM 105.5
103 Wilson St.
P. O. Box 1111
70538

Franklinton
WFCG AM 1110
N. Fairground Road
P. O. Box 604
70438

Golden Meadow
KLEB AM 1600
KBAU FM 94.3
315 Callais Ln.
70357

Gonzales
WSLG AM 1090
Highway 74
P. O. Box 236
70737

Hammond
WFPR AM 1400
WHMD FM 107.1
200 E. Thomas
P. O. Box 1829
70404

WKJN FM 103.3
Highway 51 North
P. O. Box 3067
70404-3067

Harvey
KGLA AM 1540
P. O. Box 428
70073

Haynesville
KLVU AM 1580
FM 105.5
1803 N. 1st E. St.
71038

Houma
KJIN AM 1490
KCIL FM 107.5
906 Belanger St.
P. O. Box 2068
70360

KTIB AM 640
KHOM FM 104.1
2306 W. Main
Station 2 Box 728
70360

Jena
KCKW AM 1480
KJNA FM 99.3
Second and Elm Sts.
P. O. Box 1340
71342

Jennings
KJEF AM 1290
FM 92.7
122 N. Market St.
P. O. Box 1248
70546

Jonesboro
KTOC AM 920
FM 104.9
1300½ Gansville Rd.
P. O. Box 690
71251

Kaplan
KMDL FM 97.7
400 East 1st St.
70548

Lafayette
KFXZ FM 106.3
106 Vincent St.
P. O. Box 519
Maurice 70555

KJCB AM 770
413 Jefferson St.
70501

KPEL AM 1420
KTDY FM 99.9
1749 Bertrand Dr.
P. O. Box 52046
70505

KRKR AM 1330
123 E. Main St.
P. O. Box 3030
70502

KSMB FM 94.5
202 Galbert Road
70506
P. O. Box 3345
70502

KXKW AM 1520
202-A Galbert Road
70506
P. O. Box J
70502

Lake Charles
KAOK AM 1400
645 15th St.
P. O. Drawer S
70602

KLCL AM 1470
KHLA FM 99.5
P. O. Box 3067
70602

KXCZ AM 1580
KBIU FM 103.7
311 Alamo St.
P. O. Box 1725
70602

KYKZ FM 96.1
716 Hodges ST.
P. O. Box 999
70602

Lake Providence

KLPL AM 1050
FM 92.7
Hwy. 65 North
P. O. Box 469
71254

Laplace

WCKW AM 1010
FM 92.3
U. S. Highway 61
70068
P. O. Box 970
70069-0970

Leesville

KLLA AM 1570
KJAE FM 92.7
Texas Highway
P. O. Box 1323
71446

KVVP FM 105
Highway 8
P. O. Drawer K
71446

Mansfield

KDXI AM 1360
KJVC FM 92.7
Radio Station Road
P. O. Box 740
71052

Many

KWLA AM 1400
KWLV FM 107.1
595 San Antonio
71449

Marksville

KAPB AM 730
KWLB FM 97.7
100 Chester
P. O. Box 7
71351

Metairie

WSHO AM 800
4900 Veterans Highway
Suite 702
70006

Minden

KASO AM 1240
FM 95.3
410 Lakeshore Dr.
P. O. Box 1240
71055

Monroe

KNOE AM 540
FM 101.9
1400 Oliver Road
71201
P. O. Box 4067
71211

KWEZ AM 1440
KJLO FM 104.1
Hwy. 165 N.
P. O. Box 4808
71211

Moreauville

KLIL FM 92.1
Highway 1
P. O. Box 365
71355

Morgan City

KMRC AM 1430
KFXY FM 96.7
409 Duke St.
P. O. Box 1430
70381-1430

Natchitoches

KNOC AM 1450
KDBH FM 97.7
720 Front St.
P. O. Box 607
71457

KZBL FM 95.9
1115 Washington St.
P. O. Box 567
71457

New Iberia

KANE AM 1240
2316 E. Main St.
70560

KNIR AM 1360
KDEA FM 99.1
145 W. Main St.
P. O. Box 1360 (AM)
P. O. Box 2218 (FM)
70561

New Orleans

WBOK AM 1230
3301½ Tulane Ave.
70119

WBYU FM 96
1001 Howard Ave.
42nd Floor
70113

WEZB FM 97.1
601 Loyola
Poydras Plaza
70113
P. O. Box 53447
70153

WNOE AM 1060
FM 101.1
529 Bienville
70130

WMKJ AM 1280
WQUE FM 93.3
1440 Canal St.
70112

WRBH FM 88.3
5926 S. Front St.
70115

WRNO FM 99.5
4539 I-10 Service Rd.
Metairie
70006

WSMB AM 1350
921 Canal St.
70112

WTIX AM 690
332 Carondelet
70130

WVOG AM 600
125 N. Galvez
70119

WWIW AM 1450
1515 St. Charles
70130

WWL AM 870
WAJY FM 101.9
1024 N. Rampart St.
70116

WWOZ FM 90.7
Armstrong Park
Jazz Complex
70116
P.O. Box 51840
70151

WYAT AM 990
WLTS FM 105.3
1639 Gentilly Blvd.
70119

WYLD AM 940
FM 98.5
2906 Tulane Ave.
70119

New Roads

KCLF AM 1500
P. O. Drawer 350
70760

KQXL FM 106.3
7707 Waco Ave.
Baton Rouge
70806

Oakdale

KICR AM 900
231 E. Fifth St.
P. O. Box 571
71463

Oak Grove

KWCL AM 1280
FM 96.7
Hwy. 2 East
P. O. Drawer K
71263

Opelousas

KSLO AM 1230
KOGM FM 107.1
232 North Court
P. O. Box 1150
70571-1150

Pineville

KISY FM 98.3
92 West Shamrock
71360

Rayville

KIXLA AM 990
Hwy. 80 West
P. O. Box 990
71269

Ruston

KRUS AM 1490
KXKZ FM 107.5
500 North Monroe St.
P. O. Box 430
71273-0430

Shreveport

KBCL AM 1070
2375 Airline Dr.
Bossier City
71111

KCIJ AM 980
4102 Deramus St.
P. O. Box 197
71161

KCOZ FM 100.1
725 Austin Place
71101

KDAQ FM 90
8515 Youree Dr.
71115

KDKS FM 92.1
1000 Grimmett Dr.
71107

KEEL AM 710
KITT FM 93.7
710 Spring St.
P. O. Box 20007
71120

KFLO AM 1300
318 Lane Bldg.
71101

KLMB AM 1480
P. O. Box 21480
71120-1480

KOKA AM 1550
KVKI FM 96.5
1300 Grimmett Dr.
71107

KRMD AM 1340
FM 101.1
3109 Alexander St.
71104-4615
P. O. Box 41011
71134-1011

KTAL FM 98.1
3150 N. Market St.
P. O. Box 7428
71107

KTUX FM 99
4615 Monkhouse
71109

Pineville

KWKH AM 1130
FM 94.5
6341 Westport
P. O. Box 31130
71130

Slidell

WSDL AM 1560
Coastal Blvd.
70458
P. O. Box 1175
70459

Springhill

KBSF AM 1460
KTKC FM 92.7
226 N. Main St.
P. O. Box 127
71075

Sulphur

KEZM AM 1310
320 W. Parish Road
P. O. Box 324
70663

KTQQ FM 101
P. O. Box 2418
70663

Thibodaux

KTIB AM 640
108 Green St.
P. O. Box 682
70301

KXOR FM 106.3
106 Ridgefield Road
70301

Ville Platte

KVPI AM 1050
FM 93.5
P. O. Drawer J
70586

Vivian

KNCB AM 1320
Highway 1 North
P. O. Box 1072
71082

Washington

KNEK AM 1190
P. O. Box 598
70589

West Monroe

KNAN FM 106.1
2716 N. 7th St.
71291

KMBS AM 1310
613 N. 5th St.
71291

KYEA FM 98.3
516 Martin St.
71291

Wilson

WQCK FM 92.7
P. O. Box 7934
Clinton
70722

Winnfield

KVCL AM 1270
P. O. Box 548
71483

Winnsboro

KMAR AM 1570
FM 95.9
Lone Cedar Road
P. O. Box 312
71295

NEWSPAPERS

Daily (D)
Bi-Weekly (BW)
Weekly (W)

Semi-Weekly (SW)
Monthly (M)

Abbeville

The Meridional (D)
318 N. Main St.
P. O. Box 400
70510

Alexandria

Alexandria Daily Town Talk (D)
1201 Third St.
P. O. Box 7558
71306

Alexandria News Weekly (W)
706 Lee St.
P. O. Box 608
71301

Amite

Tangi Talk (W)
110 S. W. Central Ave.
70422

The News-Digest (W)
133 E. Oak St.
P. O. Box 698
70422

Arabi

St. Bernard Voice (W)
234 Mehle Ave.
P. O. Box 88
70032

Arcadia

Bienville Democrat-Ringgold Record (W)
723 N. Railroad Ave.
P. O. Box 29
71001

Baker

The Observer (W)
5240 Groom Rd.
P. O. Box 539
70704

Basile

Basile Weekly (W)
610 Stagg St.
P. O. Drawer 578
70515

Bastrop

The Bastrop Daily Enterprise (D)
119 East Hickory Ave.
71220
P. O. Box 311
71221

Baton Rouge

Morning Advocate (D)
525 Lafayette St.
70801
P. O. Box 588
70821

State-Times (D)
525 Lafayette St.
70801
P. O. Box 588
70821

Baton Rouge Community Leader (W)
1010 N. Boulevard
70802

Baton Rouge Post (W)
326 S. 11th St.
70802

Weekly Press (W)
8154 Scenic Highway
P. O. Box 73579
70807

Belle Chasse

Plaquemines Gazette (W)
Plaquemines Watchman (W)
801 Belle Chasse Hwy. N.
P. O. Box 700
70037

Benton

The Bossier Banner-Progress (W)
Highway 3
P. O. Box 248
71006

Bogalusa

Daily News (D)
525 Avenue V
P. O. Box 820
70427

Bossier City

Bossier Press-Tribune (W)
409 Barksdale Blvd.
P. O. Box 6267
71171

Boutte

Louisiana Sportsman (M)
U.S. Highway 90
P.O. Box 1199
70039

River Parishes Guide (SW)

U. S. Highway 90
P. O. Box 1199
70039

Breaux Bridge

Breaux Bridge Banner (W)
111 N. Main St.
70517

Bunkie

The Bunkie Record (W)
Evergreen Hwy.
P. O. Box 179
71322

Cameron

Cameron Parish Pilot (W)
P. O. Box J
70631

Chalmette

The St. Bernard News (W)
3010 Lausat St.
Metairie
70001

Church Point

The Church Point News (W)
118 E. Plaquemine St.
70525

Clinton

The Watchman (W)
109 W. St. Helena
P. O. Box 368
70722

Colfax

The Chronicle (W)
505 2nd
P. O. Box 248
71417

Columbia

Caldwell Watchman-Progress (W)
215 Kentucky St.
P. O. Box 1269
71418

Coushatta

The Coushatta Citizen (W)
1703 Ringgold Ave
P. O. Drawer F
71019

Covington

The St. Tammany Farmer (W)
321 N. New Hampshire St.
70433
P. O. Box 269
70434

St. Tammany News-Banner (SW)
Highway 190
70433
P. O. Drawer 90
70434

Crowley

Crowley Post-Signal (D)
602 N. Parkerson Ave.
P. O. Box 1589
70527

Delhi

Delhi Dispatch (W)
111 Broadway St.
P. O. Box 608
71232

Denham Springs

Denham Springs-Livingston Parish News (SW)
688 Hatchell Lane
P. O. Box 1529
70727

DeQuincy

DeQuincy News (W)
P. O. Box 995
70633

DeRidder

Beauregard Daily News (D)
903 W. First St.
P. O. Box 698
70634

Donaldsonville

The Chief (W)
118 Railroad Ave.
P. O. Box 309
70346

Eunice

The Eunice News (D)
251 N. Second St.
P. O. Box 989
70535

Farmerville

The Gazette (W)
102 Washington St.
P. O. Box 722
71241

Ferriday

Concordia Sentinel (SW)
421 N. First St.
P. O. Box 312
71334

Fort Polk

Guardian
Public Affairs Office
71459-500

Franklin

Banner Tribune (D)
111 Wilson St.
70538

Franklinton

The Era Leader (W)
1044 Main St.
P. O. Drawer A
70438

Gonzales

Community Mirror (W)
205 W. Worthey
P. O. Box 38
70737

Gonzales Weekly (W)
205 W. Worthy Road
P. O. Box 38
70737

Gretna

West Bank Guide (W)
Jefferson Parish Times &
Democrat (W)
401 Whitney Ave.
70053

Gueydan

Gueydan Journal (W)
P. O. Box 536
70542

Hammond

Daily Star (D)
725 S. Morrison Blvd.
70403
P. O. Box 1149
70404

Hammond Vindicator (W)
105 S. Cate
70401
P. O. Box 2848
70404

Homer

The Guardian-Journal (W)
620 N. Main St.
P. O. Box 119
71040

Haynesville

The Haynesville News (W)
113 S. 1st East St.
P. O. Box 269
71038

Houma

Houma Daily Courier (D)
3030 Barrow St.
70360

Jeanerette

Jeanerette Enterprise (W)
806 E. Main St.
P. O. Box 327
70544

Jena

The Jena Times
Olla-Tullos Signal(W)
108 E. Third
P. O. Drawer M
71342

Jennings

The Jennings Daily News (D)
238 Market St.
P. O. Box 910
70546

Jonesboro

Jackson Independent (W)
624 Hudson Ave.
P. O. Box 520
71251

Jonesville

Catahoula News-Booster (W)
103 Third St.
P. O. Box 188
71343

Kaplan

Kaplan Herald (W)
116 N. Cushing Ave.
P. O. Box 236
70548

Kentwood

Kentwood Ledger (W)
Highway 51 South
P. O. Box AD
70444

Kentwood News (W)
210 Avenue F
P. O. Box K
70444

Kinder

Kinder Courier-News (W)
100 Fourth St.
P. O. Drawer AK
70648

Lafayette

The Daily Advertiser (D)
221 Jefferson St.
P. O. Box 3268
70502

The Times of Acadiana (W)
201 Jefferson St.
70501
P. O. Drawer 3528
70502

Lake Arthur

Lake Arthur Sun-Times (W)
214 Arthur Ave.
P. O. Box 670
70549

Lake Charles

Lake Charles American
Press (D)
327 Broad St.
P. O. Box 2893
70602

Lake Providence

Banner Democrat (W)
313 Lake St.
71254

Laplace

L'Observateur (W)
121 W. Sixth St.
P. O. Drawer B
70069-1101

River Parishes Sun (SW)
1120A W. Airline Hwy.
70068

Larose

Lafourche Gazette (W)
502 E. Main St.
P. O. Drawer G
Larose
70373

Leesville

Leesville Daily Leader (D)
206 E. Texas St.
P. O. Box 619
71446

Senior Advocate (M)
P. O. Box 275
71496-0275

Livingston

Livingston Leader (W)
Hwy. 190
P. O. Box 146
Livingston
70754

Logansport

Interstate Progress (W)
Main St.
P. O. Box 158
71049

Lutcher

News-Examiner (W)
312 Texas St.
P. O. Drawer 460
70071

Mamou

Mamou Acadian Press (W)
620-A 6th St.
P. O. Box 360
70554

Mansfield

The Enterprise (W)
202 Adams St.
P. O. Box 840
71052

Many

The Sabine Index (W)
850 San Antonio Ave.
P. O. Box 850
71449-0850

Marksville

Weekly News (W)
215 N. Washington
71351

Metairie

CityBusiness (BW)
111 Veterans Blvd., Suite 750
70005

Minden

Minden Press-Herald (D)
203 Gleason
P. O. Drawer 1339
71058

Monroe

News-Star-World (D)
411 N. 4th St.
71201
P. O. Box 1502
71210

Free Press (W)
104 N. 10th St.
71201
P. O. Box 112
71210

Monroe Dispatch (W)
2301 DeSiard St.
71201
P. O. Box 4823
71211

Morgan City

The Daily Review (D)
1014 Front St.
P. O. Box 948
70381

St. Mary Journal (BW)
1014 Front St.
70380

Napoleonville

Assumption Pioneer (W)
501 Assumption St.
P. O. Drawer 428
70390

Natchitoches

The Louisiana Business
Journal (M)
455 Second Street
71457

Natchitoches Times (SW)
904 Highway 1 South
P. O. Box 448
71457

New Iberia

The Daily Iberian (D)
926 E. Main St.
P. O. Box 1270
70560

New Orleans

Daily Record (D)
Audubon Building
931 Canal St., Suite 518
70112
P. O. Drawer 53367
70153

Gambit (W)
Maison Blanche Building
921 Canal St., Suite 740
70112

Louisiana Weekly (W)
616 Baronne St.
70113
P. O. Box 53008
70153

New Orleans Tribune (M)
2335 Esplanade Ave.
70119

The Times-Picayune (D)
3800 Howard Ave.
70140

New Roads

Pointe Coupee Banner (W)
123 St. Mary St.
70760

Pointe Coupee Democrat (W)
208A W. Main St.
P. O. Box 37
70760

Norco

St. Charles Herald (W)
24 Barreca St.
P. O. Box 159
70079

Oakdale

Oakdale Journal (W)
122 E. Sixth Ave.
P. O. Box 668
71463

Oak Grove

West Carroll Gazette (W)
307 Marietta St.
P. O. Box 1007
71263

Opelousas

The Daily World (D)
Highway I-49 South
P. O. Box 1179
70570

**Opelousas &
St. Landry Today (SW)**
3151 I-49 South
P. O. Box 1526
70570

Plaquemine

**Plaquemine Post/
South (SW)**
1114 Belleview Road
P. O. Box 589
70764-0589

Bayou Country (W)
635 Fort St.
P. O. Box 693
70764-0693

Ponchatoula

The Enterprise (W)
240 East Pine
P. O. Box 218
70454

Ponchatoula Times (W)
167 East Pine St.
P. O. Box 743
70454

Port Allen

West Side Journal (W)
668 North Jefferson
P. O. Box 260
70767

Rayne

**Rayne Acadian
Tribune (SW)**
108 N. Adams St.
P. O. Box 260
70578

Rayne Independent (W)
201 E. S. First St.
P. O. Box 428
70578

Rayville

Richland Beacon News (W)
105 N. Louisa St.
P. O. Box 209
71269

Richland Journal (W)
311 S. Benedette St.
P. O. Box 873
71269

Ringgold

Ringgold Progress
Mill St.
P. O. Box 708
71068

Ruston

Daily Leader (D)
208 W. Park Ave.
P. O. Box 520
71270

Morning Paper (W)
306 South Monroe
71270

St. Francisville

The Democrat (W)
Johnson St.
P. O. Drawer 1876
70775

St. Joseph

Tensas Gazette (W)
209 Newton
P. O. Box 25
71366

St. Martinville

Teche News (W)
214 North Main St.
P. O. Box 69
70582

Shreveport

Shreveport Journal (D)
222 Lake St.
71101
P. O. Box 31110
71130

The Times (D)
222 Lake St.
71101
P. O. Box 30222
71130-0222

Shreveport Business (M)
4415 Thornhill
71106

Shreveport Sun (W)
2224 Jewella Road
P. O. Box 9328
71109

South Towne Courier (W)
409 Barksdale Blvd.
P. O. Box 6267
Bossier City
71111

UpState Newsweekly (W)
4415 Thornhill
71106

Slidell

St. Tammany Sun Times (SW)
1441 Shortcut Hwy.
70458
P. O. Box 490
70459

The Daily Sentry News (D)
3648 Pontchartrain Dr.
70458
P. O. Box 910
70459

Springhill

**Springhill Press & News
Journal (W)**
127 Main St.
P. O. Box 668
71075

Sulphur

Southwest Daily News (D)
716 E. Napoleon St.
P. O. Box 99
70663

Tallulah

Madison Journal (W)
300 S. Chestnut St.
71282

Thibodaux

The Daily Comet (D)
705 W. 5th St.
P. O. Box 5238
70301

Vacherie

The Enterprise (W)
Waguespack Mall
Hwy. 20 So.
P. O. Drawer 208
70090

Vidalia

Concordia Sentinel (SW)
1620 Carter
P. O. Box 430
Ferriday
71373

Ville Platte

The Gazette (SW)
145 Court Street
P. O. Box 220
70586

Vinton

Vinton News (W)
P. O. Box 946
70668

Vivian

The Caddo Citizen (W)
Hwy. 1N
P. O. Box 312
71082

Welsh

Welsh Citizen (W)
119 S. Elm St.
P. O. Box 796
70591

Westlake

**Westlake/Moss Bluff News
(W)**
905 McKinley St.
P. O. Box 127
70669

West Monroe

The Citizen (SW)
810 Natchitoches St.
P. O. Box 758
71291

White Castle

The White Castle Times (W)
1114 Belleview Road
P. O. Box 589
Plaquemine
70764-0589

Winnfield

Winn Parish Enterprise (W)
Lafayette St.
P. O. Box 750
71483

Winnsboro

Franklin Sun (W)
604 Prairie St.
P. O. Box 550
71295

Zachary

**The Plainsman
News (W)**
4833 Main St.
P. O. Box 279
70791

UNIVERSITY BROADCAST STATIONS

Alexandria

KLSA FM 90.7
Louisiana State University
Alexandria
Hwy 715
71302

Baton Rouge

KLSU FM 91.1
Louisiana State University
106 East Stadium Dr.
70803

Grambling

KGRM FM 91.3
Grambling State University
P. O. Drawer K
71245

TV (4)
Grambling State University
P. O. Drawer K
71245

Hammond

KSLU FM 90.9
Southeastern Louisiana Univ.
University Station
P. O. Box 783
70402

Lafayette

KRVS FM 88.7
University of Southwestern
Louisiana
P. O. Box 42171
70504

Monroe

KNLU FM 88.7
Northeast Louisiana Univ.
Stubbs Hall, Room 128
71209

Natchitoches

KNWD FM 91.7
Northwestern State Univ.
71497

New Orleans

WLDC AM 640
Loyola University
6363 St. Charles Ave.
70118

WLDC TV (2)
Loyola University
6363 St. Charles
70118

WBSN FM 89.1
Loyola University
3939 Gentilly Blvd.
70126

WTUL FM 91.5
Tulane University
6823 St. Charles
70118

WWNO FM 90
University of New Orleans
New Orleans Lakefront
70148

Ruston

KLPI FM 89.1
Louisiana Tech University
P. O. Box 8638
71272-0045

Shreveport

KSCL FM 91.3
Centenary College
2911 Centenary Blvd.
71104
P. O. Box 41188
71134-1188

UNIVERSITY NEWSPAPERS

Alexandria

Paper Tiger
LSU in Alexandria
71302

Baton Rouge

Daily Reveille
LSU
B-1 Coates Hall
70803

Southern Digest
Southern University
Branch Post Office
70803

Eunice

Bayou Bengal
LSU in Eunice
70535

Hammond

Lion's Roar
Southeastern Louisiana
University
University Station
P. O. Box 877
70402

Lafayette

Vermilion
University of Southwestern
Louisiana
P. O. Box 44813
70504

Lake Charles

Contraband
McNeese State University
P. O. Box 9A
70609

Monroe

Pow Wow
Northeast Louisiana
University
700 University Ave.
Sub. Room 249
71209

Natchitoches

Current Sauce
Northwestern State
University
71457

New Orleans

Courtboullion
Dillard University
2601 Gentilly Blvd.
70122

Maroon
Loyola University
6363 St. Charles Ave.
70118

SUNO Observer
Southern University of
New Orleans
6400 Press Dr.
70126

Hullabaloo
Tulane University
6823 St. Charles
University Center
70118

Driftwood
University of New Orleans
New Orleans Lakefront
70148

Xavier Herald
Xavier University of
Louisiana
7325 Palmetto St.
70125

Pineville

Wildcat
Louisiana College
1140 College Blvd.
P. O. Box 948
71359

Ruston

The Tech Talk
Louisiana Tech University
146 Keeny Hall
P. O. Box 10258
71272-0045

Shreveport

The Conglomerate
Centenary College
2911 Centenary Blvd.
71104
P. O. Box 41188
71134-1188

Almagest
LSU in Shreveport
8515 Youree Dr.
71115

Susbo Voice
Southern University
Shreveport-Bossier City
Campus
3050 Martin Luther King Dr.
71107

Thibodaux

The Nicholls Worth
Nicholls State University
Louisiana Hwy. 1
NSU. Box 2036
70310

Louisiana Labor Force Summary (Annual Averages)

Year	Total Civilian Labor Force	Employed	Unemployed	Unemployment Rate (percent)
1975	1,455,000	1,349,000	106,000	7.4
1976	1,498,000	1,396,000	102,000	6.8
1977	1,571,000	1,462,000	109,000	7.0
1978	1,623,000	1,510,000	113,000	7.0
1979	1,679,000	1,567,000	112,000	6.7
1980	1,788,000	1,667,000	121,000	6.7
1981	1,853,000	1,697,000	156,000	8.4
1982	1,856,000	1,664,000	192,000	10.3
1983	1,913,000	1,688,000	225,000	11.8
1984	1,943,000	1,748,000	195,000	10.0
1985	1,986,000	1,758,000	228,000	11.5
1986	1,988,000	1,727,000	261,000	13.1

Source: Department of Labor

Louisiana Non-agricultural Wage and Salary Employment by Industrial Sector
(in thousands)

Sector	Actual 1984[a]	Actual 1985[b]	Projected 1986	Projected 1987	Average Annual Growth Rates 1984	1985	1986	1987
Mining	81.1	78.5	75.2	75.3	0.5%	−3.2%	−4.2%	0.1%
Oil & Gas Extraction	78.0	75.3	72.0	72.0	0.6%	−3.5%	−4.4%	0.0%
Non-metallic Materials	3.1	3.2	3.2	3.3	−3.1%	3.2%	0.0%	3.1%
Construction	118.8	113.0	117.6	121.5	3.1%	−4.9%	4.1%	3.3%
Manufacturing	181.9	175.1	177.7	181.5	1.0%	−3.7%	1.5%	2.1%
Durable Goods	83.1	81.0	82.3	84.3	4.0%	−2.5%	1.6%	2.4%
Lumber & Wood	13.5	12.7	12.7	12.2	3.1%	−5.9%	0.0%	−3.9%
Furniture & Fixtures	0.8	1.0	1.0	1.0	0.0%	25.0%	0.0%	0.0%
Stone, Clay & Glass	8.1	7.8	8.1	8.3	5.2%	−3.7%	3.8%	2.5%
Primary Metals	3.6	4.0	3.7	3.9	−2.7%	11.1%	−7.5%	5.4%
Fabricated Metals	12.9	12.3	12.3	12.4	−3.7%	−4.7%	0.0%	0.8%
Machinery, ex. Electrical	9.9	9.8	10.0	10.4	1.0%	−1.0%	2.0%	4.0%
Electric & Electronic Machinery	10.3	9.0	9.6	10.3	24.1%	−12.6%	6.7%	7.3%
Transportation Equipment	21.4	21.9	22.4	23.3	1.4%	2.3%	2.3%	4.0%
Other Durable Goods	2.5	2.5	2.5	2.5	19.0%	0.0%	0.0%	0.0%
Nondurable Goods	98.8	94.1	95.4	97.2	−1.3%	−4.8%	1.4%	1.9%
Food & Kindred Products	21.8	21.6	20.7	20.6	−6.8%	−0.9%	−4.2%	−0.5%
Apparel & Textiles	9.4	8.7	9.0	9.2	11.9%	−7.4%	3.4%	2.2%
Paper & Allied Products	11.7	10.8	11.1	11.5	1.7%	−7.7%	2.8%	3.6%
Printing & Publishing	10.0	10.1	10.3	10.3	2.0%	1.0%	2.0%	0.0%
Chemical & Allied Products	29.1	27.6	28.6	29.6	−4.0%	−5.2%	3.6%	3.5%
Petroleum & Coal Products	13.0	11.9	12.0	12.2	−0.8%	−8.5%	0.8%	1.7%
Other Nondurables	3.7	3.4	3.7	3.8	0.0%	−8.1%	8.8%	2.7%
Transportation & Public Utilities	118.1	114.2	113.2	114.0	−0.1%	−3.3%	−0.9%	0.7%
Railroad Transportation	7.4	7.1	6.9	7.1	4.2%	−4.1%	−2.8%	2.9%
Transportation, ex. Railroads	68.3	65.9	64.5	64.3	−1.2%	−3.5%	−2.1%	−0.3%
Communications & Public Utilities	42.4	41.2	41.8	42.6	1.0%	−2.8%	1.5%	1.9%
Wholesale & Retail Trade	380.9	381.6	389.3	396.9	3.1%	0.2%	2.0%	2.0%
Wholesale Trade	94.5	94.5	94.9	95.4	0.2%	0.0%	0.4%	0.5%
Retail Trade	286.4	287.1	294.4	301.5	4.1%	0.2%	2.5%	2.4%
Gen. Merchandise, Apparel, Appliances	59.5	57.6	59.5	60.6	1.2%	−3.2%	3.3%	1.8%
Food Stores	52.7	55.6	56.3	58.0	4.2%	5.5%	1.3%	3.0%
Auto Dealers & Service Stations	32.2	32.9	33.6	35.0	4.2%	2.2%	2.1%	4.2%
Eating & Drinking Places	86.7	85.9	87.9	89.8	5.1%	−0.9%	2.3%	2.2%
Other Retail Trade	55.3	55.1	57.1	58.1	5.9%	−0.4%	3.6%	1.8%
Finance, Insurance, Real Estate	83.1	84.3	85.0	86.5	1.3%	1.4%	0.8%	1.8%
Banking	27.4	27.4	27.7	28.1	1.1%	0.0%	1.1%	1.4%
Services	312.1	320.0	321.3	327.3	2.5%	2.5%	0.4%	1.9%
Hotels & Other Lodging Places	22.5	21.3	22.3	22.8	5.6%	−5.3%	4.7%	2.2%
Other Services	289.6	298.7	299.0	304.5	2.2%	3.1%	0.1%	1.8%
Government	320.6	325.6	324.6	325.3	1.8%	1.6%	−0.3%	0.2%
Federal	34.4	35.7	35.4	35.8	1.2%	3.8%	−0.8%	1.1%
State & Local	286.2	289.9	289.2	289.5	1.9%	1.3%	−0.2%	0.1%
State	101.5	98.9	98.2	98.5	−0.4%	−2.6%	−0.7%	0.3%
Local	184.7	191.0	191.0	191.0	3.1%	3.4%	0.0%	0.0%
TOTAL	1596.7	1592.3	1603.9	1628.3	2.0%	−0.3%	0.7%	1.5%

[a] Louisiana Department of Employment Security. Data are annual averages as of March 1985.
Totals may not equal sum of parts because of rounding errors.
[b] Labor Market Information, Louisiana Department of Employment Security, September 1985 data.

Source: *Louisiana Economic Outlook.* Louisiana State University, College of Business Administration

Composition of Personal Income, Louisiana, 1966-1986

Sector	66	67	68	69	70	71	72	73	74	75
Farm	57	60	66	64	59	57	65	69	71	71
Ag. Services	17	18	19	22	24	28	31	35	38	39
Mining	376	405	433	470	482	510	549	585	690	826
Construction	556	612	671	622	621	649	713	771	943	1,063
Manufacturing	1,044	1,134	1,242	1,335	1,358	1,439	1,562	1,721	1,906	2,109
Transp. & Public Utilities	558	586	635	689	744	779	848	958	1,098	1,181
Wholesale Trade	366	397	447	484	517	562	614	681	780	880
Retail Trade	567	610	666	721	758	819	904	1,011	1,115	1,235
Fin.,Ins.,& Real Estate	226	245	271	298	323	346	386	431	481	546
Services	613	699	772	842	910	994	1,092	1,227	1,373	1,567
Government	1,065	1,176	1,300	1,485	1,631	1,760	1,932	2,060	2,235	2,508
Other Labor Income	292	334	390	413	484	545	632	716	846	1,021
Proprietor Income	852	910	972	911	938	1,041	1,123	1,330	1,526	1,400
Div.,Int.,Rent,& Royalties	1,140	1,230	1,277	1,287	1,370	1,445	1,555	1,747	2,185	2,378
Transfer Payments	704	814	904	1,017	1,240	1,420	1,568	1,807	2,108	2,573
Social Insurance	-227	-266	-296	-333	-357	-401	-446	-536	-636	-719
Residence Adjustments	-8	-5	-6	0	-2	-4	-5	-5	-3	2
Totals	8,198	8,957	9,764	10,328	11,099	11,988	13,124	14,607	16,755	18,680

Source: *Survey of Current Business,* U.S. Department of Commerce, Bureau of Economic Analysis

Growth in Louisiana State Employment

As of	Total Classified and Unclassified State Employees	Governor
June 30, 1977	69,999	Edwin W. Edwards
June 30, 1978	71,870	
June 30, 1979	76,016	
June 30, 1980	79,058	David C. Treen
June 30, 1981	83,703	
June 30, 1982	86,708	
June 30, 1983	88,027	
June 30, 1984	87,900	Edwin W. Edwards
June 30, 1985	89,989	
June 30, 1986	88,425	
June 30, 1987	84,733	
Percent Increase, 1977-1987	21.0%	

Source: Louisiana State Department of Civil Service.

(in Millions of Dollars)

76	77	78	79	80	81	82	83	84	85	86
72	75	82	89	100	353	378	462	428	314	350
44	43	55	70	73	109	113	114	163	183	184
947	1,117	1,339	1,542	2,002	2,919	3,136	2,663	2,792	2,917	2,322
1,394	1,484	1,798	2,087	2,455	3,185	2,980	2,925	3,375	3,082	2,704
2,428	2,749	3,108	3,480	3,915	5,421	5,306	4,990	5,184	5,238	5,056
1,314	1,476	1,761	2,050	2,328	3,139	3,271	3,245	3,355	3,375	3,229
991	1,123	1,331	1,550	1,760	2,201	2,218	2,130	2,233	2,248	2,108
1,428	1,624	1,856	2,060	2,266	2,921	3,062	3,279	3,739	3,775	3,729
599	672	782	894	1,016	1,356	1,448	1,653	1,799	1,905	2,024
1,755	2,023	2,366	2,727	3,217	5,074	5,652	6,139	7,536	7,936	8,127
2,698	2,923	3,209	3,524	4,076	4,781	5,355	5,613	5,958	6,242	6,308
1,254	1,461	1,731	2,023	2,406	2,649	2,913	3,081	3,093	3,106	3,007
1,691	1,766	1,755	2,206	2,112	1,932	1,786	2,217	3,755	3,882	4,093
2,537	3,014	3,600	4,155	4,852	6,271	7,265	7,736	7,204	7,756	7,927
2,861	3,130	3,365	3,771	4,409	5,153	5,778	6,499	7,429	8,057	8,722
-815	-889	-1,032	-1,210	-1,325	1,751	1,864	1,898	2,001	2,147	2,117
23	17	0	-8	-17	-3	13	25	-350	-339	-290
21,221	23,809	27,106	31,009	35,645	41,129	44,112	45,576	48,843	50,540	50,382

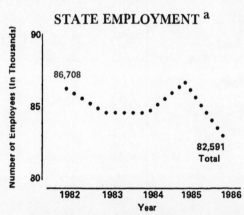

STATE EMPLOYMENT [a]

Number of Employees (In Thousands)

86,708

82,591
Total

1982 1983 1984 1985 1986
Year

[a] Does not include employees in the state civil
service system, judicial employees or about
3,000 grant-funded employees in the LSU
system.
*Total as of June 30 of each year except for
1986 which is as of March 31, the latest available date.

Total Personal and Per Capita Income in Louisiana Selected Years

Year	Total (millions)	Per Capita (dollars)	Year	Total (millions)	Per Capita (dollars)
1965	$ 7,361.9	$ 2,106	1975	$ 18,296.9	$ 4,808
1966	8,197.9	2,309	1976	21,160.6	5,355
1967	8,956.7	2,501	1977	23,737.9	5,911
1968	9,764.5	2,710	1978	27,126.5	6,660
1969	10,274.8	2,839	1979	130,791.2	7,439
1970	11,034.1	3,023	1980	35,764.9	8,472
1971	11,913.6	3,227	1981	40,994.9	9,517
1972	13,040.0	3,493	1982	44,112	8,755
1973	14,515.2	3,875	1983	45,576	9,064
1974	16,451.3	4,373	1984	48,233	10,808

Source: U.S. Bureau of the Census, State Government Finance in 1985, Series GF85, No. 3

Most Rapidly Growing Occupations in Louisiana: 1978-1990

Rank	Occupation	1978 (Number)	1990 (Number)	Change, 1978-1990 (Number)	Change, 1978-1990 (Percent)
1	Sales Clerks and Workers	86,748	115,620	28,839	33.3
2	Janitors	50,520	71,329	20,809	41.2
3	Food Preparers	19,404	38,818	19,414	100.1
4	Helpers—Trades	28,855	44,485	15,630	54.1
5	Waiters	15,463	30,111	14,648	94.7
6	Nurses Aid and Orderlies	23,331	37,676	14,345	61.5
7	General Clerks, Office	34,026	46,710	12,684	37.3
8	Cashiers	28,886	41,457	12,571	43.5
9	Cooks	17,869	29,267	11,398	63.8
10	Secretaries	31,579	42,512	10,933	34.6
11	Truck Drivers	30,634	40,649	10,015	32.7
12	Blue Collar Supervisors	25,985	34,973	8,988	34.6
13	Kitchen Helpers	11,720	20,032	8,312	70.9
14	Welders	16,204	24,131	7,927	48.9
15	Professional Nurses	12,765	19,686	6,891	54.3
16	Carpenters	13,712	20,450	6,738	49.1
17	Accountants	13,179	19,879	6,700	50.8
18	Licensed Practical Nurses	9,636	15,545	5,909	61.3
19	Guards	14,054	21,353	5,873	51.9
20	Assemblers	8,636	14,184	5,548	64.2
21	Plumbers and Pipefitters	10,920	16,435	5,515	50.5
22	Typists	14,289	19,551	5,262	36.8
23	Maintenance Repairs, General Utility	14,939	20,183	5,244	35.1
24	Heavy Equipment Operators	8,832	14,028	5,196	58.8
25	Receptionists	8,953	14,004	5,051	56.4
26	Waiter Assistants	5,262	14,242	4,980	94.6
27	Roustabouts	12,783	17,638	4,855	38.0
28	Electricians	11,420	16,235	4,815	42.2
29	Auto Mechanics	12,912	17,660	4,748	36.8
30	Restaurant and Cafe Managers	6,297	11,012	4,715	74.9
31	Store Managers	14,688	19,400	4,712	32.1

Source: *Louisiana Business Review,* Fall 1983

CONSUMER PRICE INDEX

The Consumer Price Index, sometimes called the "Cost of Living Index," is a statistical measure of *change*, over time, in the prices of goods and services in major expenditure groups—such as food, housing, apparel, transportation, medical care, and entertainment—typically purchased by urban consumers. The CPI for All Urban Consumers includes, in addition to wage earners and clerical workers, groups such as professional, managerial, and technical workers, the self-employed, short-term workers, the unemployed, and retirees and others not in the labor force.

Prices are gathered from 85 areas across the country. The year 1967 is used as the base period. While the CPI may provide a broad outline of price fluctuations, it cannot reflect individual buying trends or regional experiences.

Annual Averages

Year	All Urban Consumers		Urban Wage and Clerical Workers	
	Index	% Change from prior year	Index	% Change from prior year
1967	100.0	-	100.0	-
1968	104.2	+ 4.2	104.2	+ 4.2
1969	109.8	+ 5.4	109.8	+ 5.4
1970	116.3	+ 5.9	116.3	+ 5.9
1971	121.3	+ 4.3	121.3	+ 4.3
1972	125.3	+ 3.3	125.3	+ 3.3
1973	133.1	+ 6.2	133.1	+ 6.2
1974	147.7	+11.0	147.7	+11.0
1975	161.2	+ 9.1	161.2	+ 9.1
1976	170.5	+ 5.8	170.5	+ 5.8
1977	181.5	+ 6.5	181.5	+ 6.5
1978	195.4	+ 7.6	195.3	+ 7.6
1979	217.4	+11.3	217.7	+11.5
1980	246.8	+13.5	247.0	+13.5
1981	272.4	+10.4	272.3	+10.2
1982	289.1	+ 6.1	288.6	+ 6.0
1983	298.4	+ 3.8	297.4	+ 3.0
1984	311.1	+ 4.0	307.6	+ 3.4
1985	322.2	+ 3.8	318.5	+ 3.6
1986	328.4	+ 1.1	323.4	+ 1.5

Source: U.S. Department of Labor, Bureau of Labor Statistics

To compute percent change:

$$\frac{\text{current period} - \text{prior period}}{\text{prior period}} \times 100 = \text{\% Change}$$

STATE EMPLOYMENT TRENDS

The last year of employment growth in Louisiana was in 1984 when non-agricultural wage and salary employment reached 1,601,500. Nineteen eighty-seven marked the third straight year of employment declines in the state, with 105,000 jobs lost since the 1984 peak.

The unemployment rate peaked at 14.9 percent in January 1987, leading the nation in unemployment for the entire year. By July, the rate had dropped significantly to 10.7 percent. This was partly due to the beginning of an economic recovery in midsummer; but the rate reduction was also attributable to some 88,700 people leaving the Louisiana labor force since September 1984. These people either left the state to work in more prosperous areas or stayed in Louisiana but did not work or look for work because of discouragement over job prospects.

The decline in oil prices and the uncertainty over their future course is responsible for employment declines in Louisiana. But according to forecasts from the Louisiana Econometric Model (LEM), the Louisiana economy will experience modest growth through 1988-89.

Three factors contribute to this positive forecast. First and foremost, a recovery in oil prices, rising from $18.50 per barrel in 1987 to $21 in 1989, could lead to mining employment rising to a plateau of almost 64,000 workers by the end of 1989.

A second factor providing impetus to the economy will be the continued growth of the national economy, and a third positive element will be the continuing decline in the value of the dollar. Both factors will provide some positive support to the state's manufacturing sector—in particular to the chemical and petroleum refining industries, which together generate almost one-half of Louisiana's value-added manufacturing.

Source: *The Louisiana Economic Outlook for 1988 and 1989.* LSU College of Business Administration.

Louisiana Personal Income, Population, and Per Capita Income

Category	Actual[a]		Projected			Average Annual Growth Rates			
	1985	1986	1987	1988	1989	1986	1987	1988	1989
Personal Income (billions)	$50.54	$50.38	$51.23	$53.79	$56.91	-0.3%	1.7%	5.0%	5.8%
Real Personal Income (billions of 1982 dollars)	$45.44	$44.15	$43.37	$43.73	$44.08	-2.8%	-1.8%	0.8%	0.8%
Population (millions)	4.49	4.50	4.53	4.55	4.58	0.2%	0.7%	0.4%	0.7%
Per Capita Income	$11,267	$11,193	$11,309	$11,822	$12,425	-0.7%	1.0%	4.5%	4.5%
Real Per Capita Income (1982 dollars)	$10,132	$9,810	$9,574	$9,604	$9,624	-3.2%	-3.0%	0.3%	0.2%

a - Regional Economic Information Service, Bureau of Economic Analysis, U.S. Department of Commerce.

Total Non-agricultural Wage and Salary Employment
Louisiana Metropolitan Areas
(in thousands)

Sector	Actual			Projected		Average Annual Growth Rates			
	1985a	1986a	1987b	1988	1989	1986	1987	1988	1989
Alexandria	45.0	45.4	45.7	46.1	46.9	0.8%	0.7%	0.8%	1.7%
Baton Rouge	216.2	213.4	214.2	215.4	216.9	-1.2%	0.4%	0.6%	0.7%
Lafayette	98.8	88.5	84.0	85.9	88.1	-10.0%	-5.1%	2.3%	2.6%
Lake Charles	59.0	57.6	59.2	60.3	61.2	-2.3%	2.8%	1.9%	1.5%
Monroe	56.1	55.8	54.5	55.0	55.6	-0.5%	-2.3%	0.9%	1.1%
New Orleans	533.5	520.2	510.1	513.1	516.6	-7.5%	-1.9%	0.6%	0.7%
Shreveport	142.5	134.7	131.0	132.3	133.0	-5.5%	-2.7%	1.0%	0.5%

a - Louisiana Department of Employment Security.
b - Labor Market Information, Louisiana Department of Employment Security

Composition of Employment in Major Metropolitan Areas in Louisiana
Percent of Total Non-agricultural Employment   1987

Metropolitan Area	Contract Construction	Manufacturing	Mining	Transportation, Public Utilities, and Communications	Wholesale and Retail Trade	Finance, Insurance, and Real Estate	Services	Gov't.
Alexandria	5.7%	7.4%	—	5.2%	23.6%	5.7%	24.2%	28.0%
Baton Rouge	9.3%	8.8%	0.4%	5.0%	24.6%	6.3%	19.7%	25.7%
Lafayette	3.7%	6.8%	14.2%	7.7%	26.3%	4.6%	21.1%	15.5%
Lake Charles	8.9%	17.9%	2.5%	6.4%	23.6%	4.5%	17.9%	18.2%
Monroe	5.5%	13.0%	1.1%	4.8%	27.1%	8.3%	20.9%	19.3%
New Orleans	4.6%	8.6%	3.4%	8.3%	26.0%	6.5%	25.9%	16.6%
Shreveport	5.8%	14.1%	2.6%	6.1%	22.9%	5.8%	23.7%	19.0%

Source: LSU College of Business Administration, *The Louisiana Economic Outlook for 1988 and 1989.*

Louisiana Chambers of Commerce

LOCATION	NAME	ADDRESS	PHONE
Abbeville	Greater Abbeville C of C	P. O. Box 507, 70511-0507	(318) 893-2491
Alexandria	Greater Alexandria/Pineville C of C	P. O. Box 992, 71309	(318) 442-6671
Amite	Amite C of C	P. O. Box 383, 70422	(504) 748-5537
Bastrop	Bastrop-Morehouse C of C	P. O. Box 1175, 71220	(318) 281-3794
Baton Rouge	Greater Baton Rouge C of C	P. O. Box 3217, 70821	(504) 381-7125
Bogalusa	Bogalusa C of C	608 Willis Ave., 70427	(504) 735-5731
Bossier City	Bossier C of C	710 Benton Rd., 71111	(318) 746-0252
Breaux Bridge	Breaux Bridge Area C of C	Rt. 3, P. O. Box 88, 70517	(318) 332-6655
Bunkie	Bunkie C of C	P. O. Box 70, 71332	(318) 346-2575
Chalmette	St. Bernard Parish Police Jury C of C	8201 W. Judge Perez Dr., 70043	(504) 277-6371
Coushatta	Coushatta-Red River C of C	P. O. Box 333, 71019	(318) 932-3289
Covington	St. Tammy West C of C	P. O. Box 1179, 70434	(504) 892-3216
Crowley	Crowley C of C & Agriculture	P. O. Box 2127, 70527	(318) 788-0177
Cut Off	South Lafourche C of C	P. O. Box 116, 70345	(504) 632-5804
Denham Springs	Greater Denham Springs C of C	P. O. Box 591, 70726	(504) 665-8155
DeRidder	Greater DeRidder Area C of C	P. O. Box 309, 70634-0309	(318) 463-5533
Donaldsonville	Donaldsonville Area C of C	P. O. Box 646, 70346	(504) 473-4814
Eunice	Eunice C of C	P. O. Box 508, 70535	(318) 457-2565
Farmerville	Union Parish C of C	P. O. Drawer 67, 71241	(318) 368-3947
Franklin	West St. Mary Parish Area C of C	P. O. Box 38, 70538	(318) 828-5608
Gonzales	Greater Gonzales C of C	P. O. Box 1204, 70737	(504) 647-7487
Grand Isle	Grand Isle Tourist Commission, Inc.	La. Hwy. 1, 70358	(504) 787-3421
Hammond	Hammond C of C	P. O. Box 1458, 70404	(504) 345-4457
Houma	Houma-Terrebonne C of C	P. O. Box 328, 70361	(504) 876-5600
Jackson	Feliciana C of C	P. O. Box 667, 70748	(504) 634-7155
Jeanerette	Jeanerette C of C	P. O. Box 31, 70544	(318) 276-4293
Jena	LaSalle Parish Development Board	P. O. Box 122, 71342	(318) 992-4441
Jennings	Greater Jennings C of C	P. O. Box 1209, 70546	(318) 824-0933
Jonesboro	Jackson Parish C of C	520 S. Polk, 71251	(318) 259-4693
Kaplan	Kaplan Area C of C	P. O. Box 639, 70548	(318) 643-2400
Lafayette	Greater Lafayette C of C, Inc.	P. O. Drawer 51307, 70505	(318) 233-2705
Lake Charles	The Chamber/Southwest Louisiana	P. O. Box 3109, 70602-3109	(318) 433-3632

Lake Providence	Lake Providence C of C	P. O. Box 642, 71254	(318) 559-3995
Leesville	Leesville/Vernone C of C	P. O. Box 1228, 71446	(318) 238-0349
Logansport	Logansport C of C	P. O. Box 320, 71049	(318) 697-4472
Mandeville	Mandeville C of C	P. O. Box 22, 70448	(504) 626-8186
Mansfield	DeSoto Parish C of C	P. O. Box 591, 71052	(318) 872-1310
Many	Sabine Parish C of C	920 Fisher Road, 71449	(318) 256-3523
Mathews	Central Lafourche C of C	P. O. Box 94, 70375	(504) 537-6189
Minden	Minden C of C	P. O. Box 819, 71058-0819	(318) 377-4240
Monroe	Monroe C of C	300 Washington St., Ste. 104, Washington Plz., 71201	(318) 323-3461
Morgan City	E. St. Mary Area C of C	P. O. Box 2606, 70381	(504) 384-3830
Natchitoches	Natchitoches Area C of C	P. O. Box 3, 71458	(318) 352-4411
New Iberia	Greater Iberia C of C	P. O. Box 27, 70561-0027	(318) 364-1836
New Orleans	The Chamber/New Orleans and the River Region	P. O. Box 30240, 70190	(504) 527-6900
New Roads	Greater Pointe Coupee C of C	P. O. Box 555, 70760	(504) 638-3500
Oak Grove	Oak Grove C of C	P. O. Drawer 1336, 71263	(318) 428-3489
Olla	Olla C of C	P. O. Box 223, 71465	(318) 495-5151
Opelousas	Opelousas-St. Landry C of C	P. O. Box 109, 70570	(318) 942-2683
Plaquemine	Plaquemine-Sherville	P. O. Box 248, 70764	(504) 687-3560
Ponchatoula	Ponchatoula C of C	P. O. Box 306, 70454	(504) 386-2533
Rayne	Rayne C of C & Agriculture	P. O. Box 383, 70578	(318) 334-2332
Ruston	Ruston-Lincoln C of C	P. O. Box 150, 71273-0150	(318) 255-2031
Saint Martinville	Saint Martinville C of C	P. O. Box 436, 70582	(318) 394-7578
Shreveport	Shreveport C of C	P. O. Box 20074, 71120	(318) 226-8521
Slidell	Slidell C of C	118 W. Hall Ave., 70460	(504) 643-5678
Springhill	Springhill-Cullen C of C	400 N. Giles St., 71075	(318) 539-4717
Sulphur	West Calcasieu Association of Commerce	P. O. Box 2657, 70664	(318) 527-7142
Tallulah	Madison Parish C of C	P. O. Box 669, 71284-0669	(318) 574-5627
Thibodaux	Thibodaux C of C	P. O. Box 467, 70302	(504) 446-1187
Vidalia	Vidalia C of C	P. O. Box 267, 71373	(318) 336-7310
Ville Platte	Ville Platte C of C	P. O. Box 331, 70586	(318) 363-1878
Walker	Walker C of C	P. O. Box 217, 70785	(504) 664-3123
West Monroe	West Monroe C of C	P. O. Box 427, 71291	(318) 325-1961
Winnfield	Winn C of C	P. O. Box 565, 71483	(318) 628-4461
Winnsboro	Winnsboro Franklin Parish C of C	P. O. Box 876, 71295	(318) 435-4488
Zachary	Zachary C of C	P. O. Box 493, 70791	(504) 654-6777

Source: Johnson's 1986 Worldwide Chamber of Commerce Directory

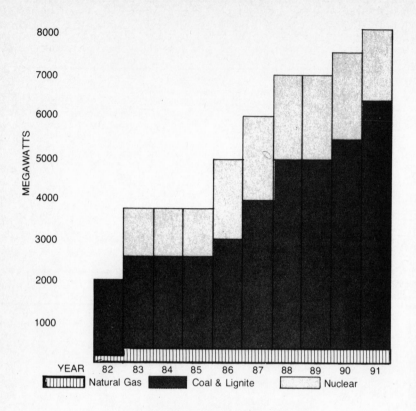

PROJECTED NEW ELECTRICAL GENERATING CAPACITY IN LOUISIANA BY FUEL TYPE, 1982-1991

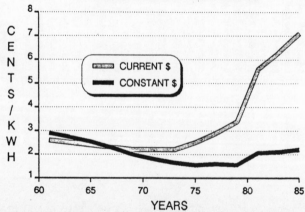

RESIDENTIAL ELECTRICITY PRICES
TOTAL ALL LA ELECTRIC UTILITIES

Source: Louisiana Dept. of Natural Resources,
Louisiana Energy Statistics 1960-1985

TRANSPORTATION

LOUISIANA HIGHWAYS

In the 1920's Louisiana roads were rural in character. Disjointed stretches of soil and gravel roads, interspersed with isolated patches of urban areas, sprinkled agricultural Louisiana. Then in the 1930's, the Department of Highways constructed a badly needed system of cross-state, hard-surfaced roadways. These 18-foot concrete roads were a tremendous boon to the economy. People could travel from farm to market with greater ease, safer, cheaper and at a swifter pace.

After World War II, Louisiana witnessed the greatest industrial boom in its history. Attracted by the state's rich natural resources, new industry flocked here to locate. Domestic business expanded. Suddenly, thousands of new jobs were created and new families around the nation poured into this new industrial frontier of America. Even within the state, people left the farms and rural areas for lucrative jobs around the urban areas. Cities spilled over into mushrooming suburbs, and these fringe areas became cities themselves. Quiet, tranquil pre-war towns surged with new activity. All over Louisiana, the story was the same—the economy was flourishing.

This great development brought on new highway problems. The number of trucks and automobiles spiraled upward. Existing bridges and roadways could not adequately handle the tremendous impact. Farm to market roads were pounded to fragments by the heavier, faster and increased traffic volumes. Thousands of gravel mileage needed hard surfacing. Most of the two-lane 18-foot state highways suddenly become obsolete. These had to be widened or made into four lanes. And in the expanding urban areas, even the four-lane thoroughfares could not cope with bumper-to-bumper traffic. Six and eight lanes were needed here.

Finally, it became apparent that more multiple lanes would not adequately serve modern needs. The answer was what highway engineers had long known and advocated—control of access. In 1956, Congress approved a new cross-country system of controlled Interstate and Defense Highways. Immediately Louisiana sprang into action on plans for this huge new system.

The State's share of the Interstate will be 718 miles.

Constructed to the highest engineering standards, Louisiana's Interstate will be completely free of traffic obstructions of any kind. There will be no stop signs, no traffic signals or cross movement of vehicles at grade level. Traffic flow will be completely free.

Entry and exit will be over elaborate interchanges and over-passes. When completed, a motorist theoretically can enter the Interstate in Louisiana and travel all the way to California without slackening speed.

Time consuming delays of bumper-to-bumper traffic on crowded conventional highways will be eliminated. Thousands of lives will be saved because of the emphasis on safety and the elaborate engineering design. Each motorist will realize big annual savings in operating costs.

LOUISIANA DEPT. OF HIGHWAYS DEDICATED REVENUES—
SOURCES AND DISTRIBUTION

GASOLINE

4 cents per gallon	To the general highway fund
2 cents per gallon	One cent to the general highway fund One cent to the Parish One Cent Gasoline Fund
1 cent per gallon	To the Louisiana Bond Security and Redemption Fund
1 cent per gallon	1/2 cent to the Long Range Highway Fund 1/20 to the Board of Commissioners Lake Charles Harbor and Terminal District 9/20 to the Board of Commissioners of the Port of New Orleans

The full amount of taxes collected on gasoline remaining after the above dedicated disbursements have been made shall go to the Bond Security and Redemption Fund. After all state obligations have been met, the remainder shall be paid into the Louisiana Highway, Flood Control, and Drainage Priority Fund.

SPECIAL FUELS

16 cents per gallon	To the Bond Security and Redemption Fund

After all state obligations have been met, one-half of the taxes collected shall go to the Louisiana Highway, Flood Control, and Drainage Priority Fund. The remainder of taxes collected shall go into the state general fund.

Sources: Louisiana Revised Statutes; 47:727, 47:801, 1987

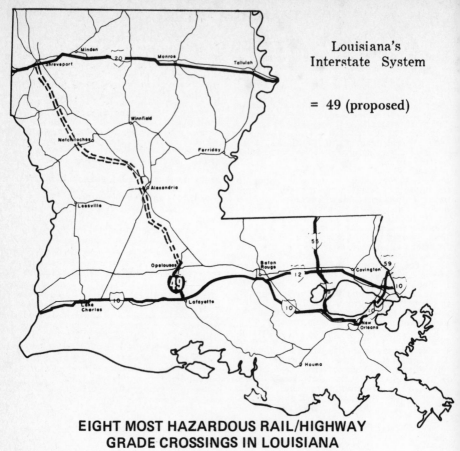

Louisiana's
Interstate System

= 49 (proposed)

EIGHT MOST HAZARDOUS RAIL/HIGHWAY
GRADE CROSSINGS IN LOUISIANA
(In Descending Order)

Location	*Railroad*	*Current Warning Devices*
LA. 46 (St. Claude Ave.) New Orleans	Southern R.R.	Flashing Lights & Bells
LA. 49 (Williams Blvd.) Kenner	Illinois Central Gulf	Flashing Lights & Bells
U.S. 165 (East Madison) Bastrop	AR & LA Missouri R.R.	Signs
LA. 72 Bossier City	St. Louis Southwestern R.R.	Signs
LA. 20 Vacherie	Missouri Pacific	Flashing Lights w/Gates & Bells (now under construction)
U.S. 61 (Airline Highway) Baton Rouge	Illinois Central Gulf	Flashing Lights & Bells
U.S. 79 (Texas Avenue) Shreveport	Kansas City Southern	No Warning Devices
LA. 18 (River Road) Avondale	Missouri Pacific	Signs

RECOMMENDED AIRPORT SYSTEM BY 1995

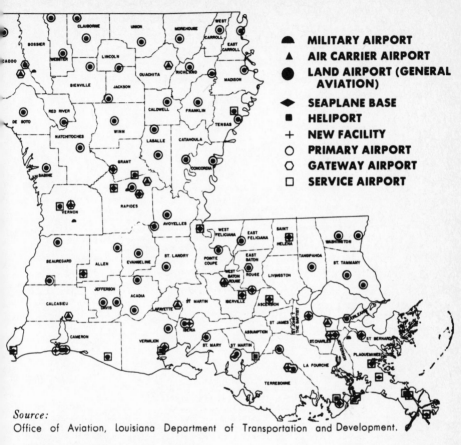

Source:
Office of Aviation, Louisiana Department of Transportation and Development.

Landing Facilities in Louisiana

Airports

Publically owned/public use	—	63
Privately owned/public use	—	27
Privately owned/private use	—	116
Total	—	206

Heliports

Publically owned/private use	—	1
Privately owned/private use	—	134
Restricted/Hospitals	—	52
Total	—	187

Seaplane Bases

Privately owned/public use	—	4
Privately owned/private use	—	13
Total	—	17

Total Facilities   — 410

Source: Louisiana Department of
         Transportation and Development

**State Police Emergency Toll-Free DWI
Emergency Hotline: 1-800-525-5555**

State Police Troop Headquarters

Troop A, Baton Rouge: (504) 292-8200
Troop B, New Orleans: (504) 438-4830
Troop C, Gray: (504) 568-5964
Troop D, Lake Charles: (318) 491-2511
Troop E, Alexandria: (318) 487-5911
Troop F, Monroe: (318) 345-0000
Troop G, Bossier City: (318) 226-7651
Troop H, Leesville: (318) 239-3414
Troop I, Lafayette: (318) 235-4522
Troop K, Opelousas: (318) 942-6515
Troop L, Covington: (504) 892-5151

FINANCIAL INSTITUTIONS

CONSOLIDATED STATEMENT

OF TWO HUNDRED THIRTY

STATE BANKS LOCATED IN THE SIXTH AND ELEVENTH

FEDERAL RESERVE DISTRICTS IN LOUISIANA

AS OF DECEMBER 31, 1986

ASSETS

Cash and balances due from depository institutions:	
Noninterest-bearing	$ 1,086,177
Interest-bearing	432,624
Securities	4,360,190
Federal Funds sold/securities purchased under agreements to resell	1,170,498
Net loans	9,058,720
Assets held in trading accounts	15,297
Premises and fixed assets	416,563
Other real estate owned	236,770
Investments in unconsolidated subsidiaries/associated companies	190
Customers' liability to this bank on acceptances outstanding	1,079
Intangible assets	13,359
Other assets	363,062
TOTAL ASSETS	$17,154,529

LIABILITIES

Deposits:	
Noninterest bearing	$ 2,819,777
Interest bearing	12,435,559
Federal funds purchased/securities sold under agreements to repurchase	355,674
Demand notes issued to the U.S. Treasury	20,197
Other borrowed money	27,141
Mortgage indebtedness and obligations under capitalized leases	16,209
Bank's liability on acceptances executed and outstanding	1,079
Notes and debentures subordinated to deposits	14,241
Other liabilities	168,331
TOTAL LIABILITIES	$15,858,208
Limited life preferred stock	-0-

EQUITY CAPITAL

Perpetual preferred stock	$ 1,360
Common stock	225,148
Surplus	593,848
Undivided profits and capital reserves	475,965
TOTAL EQUITY CAPITAL	$ 1,296,321
TOTAL LIABILITIES, LIMITED LIFE PREFERRED STOCK, AND EQUITY CAPITAL	$17,154,529

Source: Office of Financial Institutions

LOUISIANA STATE BANKS AND ASSETS, 1949 - 1986

Year	No. of Banks	Total Assets	% Annual Asset Growth	Average Assets Per Bank (In Millions)
1949	127	$ 577,653,415	——	$ 4.5
1950	129	610,525,358	10.6	4.7
1951	130	684,143,117	12.1	5.3
1952	130	742,013,788	8.5	5.7
1953	132	795,270,957	7.2	6.0
1954	132	822,057,267	3.4	6.2
1955	134	871,703,216	6.0	6.5
1956	139	1,012,163,488	16.1	7.3
1957	141	1,051,927,291	3.9	7.5
1958	145	1,075,492,253	2.2	7.4
1959	145	1,163,629,632	8.2	8.0
1960	148	1,167,694,436	0.3	7.9
1961	150	1,234,403,355	5.7	8.2
1962	153	1,318,020,811	6.8	8.6
1963	155	1,442,825,559	9.5	9.3
1964	162	1,633,093,084	13.2	10.1
1965	167	1,875,907,164	14.9	11.2
1966	173	2,188,194,403	16.6	12.6
1967	179	2,459,822,555	12.4	13.7
1968	181	2,754,769,390	12.0	15.2
1969	182	2,992,720,996	8.6	16.4
1970	182*	3,330,779,061	11.3	18.3
1971	186	3,983,359,937	19.6	21.4
1972	188	4,654,141,408	16.8	24.8
1973	194	5,317,791,007	14.3	27.4
1974	197	6,028,177,006	13.4	30.6
1975	201	6,649,516,769	10.3	33.1
1976	200	7,391,521,000	11.2	37.0
1977	201	8,307,546,000	12.4	41.3
1978	202	9,425,938,000	13.5	46.7
1979	207	11,052,537,000	17.3	53.4
1980	216	13,001,424,000	17.6	60.2
1981	221	15,376,144,000	18.3	69.6
1982	226	16,681,318,000	8.5	73.8
1983	226	17,187,106,000	3.0	N/A
1984	237	18,200,584,000	5.9	N/A
1985	233	18,180,986,000	- 0.1	N/A
1986	230	17,154,529,000	- 5.6	N/A

Source: State Office of Financial Institutions

Louisiana State-Chartered Credit Unions Annual Summaries

Year	Number	Total Resources	Total Outstanding Loans
1983	98	200,268,765	151,649,088
1984	94	228,081,518	189,481,966
1985	91	289,149,884	200,148,450
1986	91	370,440,706	227,630,606

Source: State Office of Financial Institutions

CONSOLIDATED STATEMENT

Of the Ninety of the Ninety-One State Chartered Credit Unions

Located in the State of Louisiana

As of December 31, 1986

ASSETS

Unsecured loans...$	78,681,915
New auto loans...	48,558,357
First mortgage real estate.....................................	26,496,575
Other real estate..	10,603,390
Agricultural loan..	18,058
Commercial loans...	336,782
All other loans to members....................................	57,616,077
Other loans...	5,319,452
TOTAL LOANS...$	227,630,606
Allowance for loan losses.....................................	-115,170
Cash..	7,682,766
U.S. Government obligations...................................	564,899
Federal agency securities.....................................	800,612
Mutual funds..	1,886,251
Corporate central credit unions...............................	50,855,957
Commercial banks..	19,792,514
S&L's and mutual savings banks................................	44,630,446
NCUA share insurance capitalization deposits..................	2,279,444
NON-NCUA insurance capitalization deposits....................	284,658
Credit unions...	928,847
Loans to credit unions..	20
Other investments...	2,435,598
Allowance for investment losses...............................	-3,008
Land & building...	4,981,334
Other fixed assets..	2,325,658
Other assets..	3,479,274
TOTAL ASSETS...$	370,440,706

LIABILITIES AND EQUITY

Promissory notes..	-0-
Reverse repurchase agreements.................................	-0-
Other notes payable and interest on notes payable.............	1,829,561
Accounts payable..	683,679
Accrued and/or undistributed interest payable on deposits.....	54,447
Accrued dividends payable on shares...........................	2,901,986
Other liabilities...	886,128
Share certificates..	36,982,426
Share drafts..	7,738,658
IRA/Keogh & retirement accounts...............................	19,087,627
All other shares..	268,025,480
Permanent capital shares......................................	2,373,147
TOTAL SHARES..$	340,563,139
Member deposits...	20,217
Non-member deposits...	-0-
TOTAL SHARES & DEPOSITS.................................$	340,583,356
Regular reserve...	15,786,848
Investment valuation reserve..................................	30,706
Other reserves..	2,947,997
Undivided earnings..	11,091,798
Net income..	
TOTAL LIABILITIES & EQUITY..............................$	370,440,706

The Twenty-Five Largest National Banks in Louisiana

Name and Location	Assets on December 31, 1986
Hibernia National Bank, New Orleans	$2,813,793
Whitney National Bank, New Orleans	2,565,603
First National Bank of Commerce, New Orleans	2,350,724
Louisiana National Bank, Baton Rouge	1,498,554
First National Bank of Shreveport	1,244,051
Commercial National Bank, Shreveport	1,119,418
Hibernia National Bank, Baton Rouge	837,349
Calcasieu Marine National Bank, Lake Charles	737,039
City National Bank of Baton Rouge	569,021
Ouachita National Bank, Monroe	529,793
First National Bank of Jefferson Parish, Gretna	440,949
First National Bank of Lafayette	363,475
Whitney National Bank in Jefferson Parish, Metairie	351,934
First National Bank, Covington	318,973
Hibernia National Bank of Jefferson Parish	256,464
First National Bank of Houma	252,235
First National Bank of Lake Charles	185,699
Security First National Bank, Alexandria	185,377
Lakeside National Bank, Lake Charles	166,102
Gulf National Bank of Lake Charles	158,662
Citizens National Bank, Hammond	149,985
First National Bank of St. Landry Parish, Opelousas	143,016
First National Bank of West Monroe	137,755
First National Bank of St. Mary Parish, Morgan City	132,127
Hibernia National Bank, Lafayette	121,888

Source: *Sheshunoff Banks of Louisiana 1987*

The Twenty-Five Largest State Banks, Savings Banks, and Bank and Trust Companies in Louisiana

Name and Location	Assets on December 31, 1986
Guaranty Bank and Trust Company, Lafayette	$713,556
American Bank and Trust Company, Baton Rouge	689,149
Capital Bank and Trust Company, Baton Rouge	499,301
Central Bank, Monroe	463,316
Louisiana Bank and Trust Company, Shreveport	437,443
Guaranty Bank and Trust Company, Alexandria	421,999
The Jefferson Guaranty Bank, Metairie	393,815
Rapides Bank and Trust Company, Alexandria	392,529
American Bank and Trust Company, New Orleans	389,583
Terrebonne Bank and Trust Company, Houma	300,474
Pioneer Bank and Trust Company, Shreveport	297,488
Citizens Bank and Trust Company, Thibodaux	267,121
Raceland Bank and Trust Company, Raceland	230,101
Bank of Gonzales, Gonzales	197,295
First Bank, Slidell	189,566
Concordia Bank and Trust Company, Vidalia	189,056
American Bank and Trust Company, Monroe	182,103
First Guaranty Bank, Hammond	176,378
St. Landry Bank and Trust Company, Opelousas	173,755
Ruston State Bank and Trust Company, Ruston	172,400
Baton Rouge Bank and Trust Company, Baton Rouge	160,614
Metairie Bank and Trust Company, Metairie	155,579
Bank of New Roads, New Roads	144,133
Bank of Commerce and Trust Company, Crowley	138,997
St. Bernard Bank and Trust Company, Arabi	129,005

Source: State Office of Financial Institutions

The Twenty-five Largest Savings and Loan and Homestead Associations in Louisiana

Name and Location	Assets on December 31, 1986
Dixie Savings and Loan Association, New Orleans	$1,578,125,000
Pelican Homestead and Savings Association, New Orleans	982,215,741
St. Bernard Savings and Loan, Chalmette	868,817,000
Louisiana Savings Association, Lake Charles	582,658,534
Security Homestead Association, New Orleans	571,788,440
Fidelity Homestead Association, New Orleans	413,266,923
French Market Homestead, Metairie	335,641,511
South Savings and Loan, Slidell	331,083,559
Iberia Savings and Loan Association, New Iberia	294,889,064
Southern Savings Association, New Orleans	276,330,224
Dryades Savings and Loan Association, New Orleans	209,229,307
Greater New Orleans Homestead Association, Metairie	263,953,977
Jefferson Savings and Loan Association, Metairie	239,573,071
Lafayette Building Association, Lafayette	236,204,137
Fifth District Savings and Loan, New Orleans	186,344,705
Acadia Savings and Loan Association, Crowley	186,214,661
First Financial of Louisiana Savings and Loan, Donaldsonville	183,026,634
Home Savings and Loan Association, Lafayette	177,275,129
Delta Savings and Loan Association, Kenner	171,050,136
Citizens Homestead Association, New Orleans	116,972,622
Columbia Homestead Association, Metairie	98,864,479
Eureka Homestead Society, New Orleans	90,862,125
Guaranty Savings and Homestead Association, New Orleans	87,087,383
St. Landry Homestead Association, Opelousas	83,346,824
American Savings and Loan Association, New Orleans	78,595,860

Louisiana Savings and Loan Institutions
Annual Summaries

Year	Number	Total Resources	Total Outstanding Mortgages
1979	74	$4,974,629,516	$4,589,322,980
1980	75	5,771,799,355	4,709,334,008
1981	71	5,727,410,345	4,972,009,744
1982	66	6,068,840,814	5,104,892,479
1983	58	7,614,712,926	5,446,085,434
1984	56	8,450,427,580	5,826,759,234
1985	54	8,783,282,280	5,870,353,650
1986	54	9,866,751,369	6,666,226,759

Source: State Office of Financial Institutions

Property Assessment by Parish

Parish	TABLE NO. 50 COMPARATIVE STATEMENT SHOWING TOTAL ASSESSMENTS BY PARISHES FOR THE YEARS 1982-1985 (1983-1986 in the Parish of Orleans)			
	1982	1983	1984	1985
Acadia	$ 111,783,010	$ 114,661,410	$ 114,403,140	$ 120,895,070
Allen	47,218,060	47,835,730	49,436,030	51,191,110
Ascension	190,439,860	195,202,070	199,123,020	204,331,670
Assumption	76,642,100	84,042,600	85,045,320	85,301,900
Avoyelles	73,237,150	75,177,930	76,123,570	78,153,670
Beauregard	85,984,101	89,295,557	91,888,111	95,451,668
Bienville	98,930,730	115,957,910	117,665,910	120,506,020
Bossier	195,739,650	213,173,240	220,346,180	233,272,540
Caddo	786,037,980	807,264,930	823,231,200	876,529,580
Calcasieu	598,756,460	653,448,470	612,922,920	629,203,320
Caldwell	21,904,950	22,275,020	22,931,490	24,122,720
Cameron	113,908,220	129,413,850	129,838,670	139,515,030
Catahoula	26,828,580	27,084,420	27,246,500	27,635,490
Claiborne	55,499,140	62,120,530	65,685,660	67,626,060
Concordia	50,339,530	53,927,900	56,387,750	59,187,210
DeSoto	55,062,575	60,469,502	62,811,576	69,150,126
East Baton Rouge	1,294,985,740	1,337,019,630	1,404,848,370	1,509,217,910
East Carroll	28,315,212	29,400,052	30,142,682	30,727,396
East Feliciana	39,722,640	41,269,270	44,293,660	45,164,600
Evangeline	46,229,720	46,986,470	47,174,990	48,182,640
Franklin	24,688,339	25,452,970	26,684,527	27,748,312
Grant	193,862,564	206,700,912	214,068,414	223,163,741
Iberia	206,082,041	207,030,660	213,818,526	217,316,720
Iberville	38,706,900	40,670,010	45,244,690	46,620,900
Jackson	1,400,729,221	1,494,413,723	1,560,135,494	1,615,775,541
Jefferson	104,297,110	109,639,170	109,927,760	110,374,090
Jefferson Davis	619,813,460	659,619,970	680,539,903	687,277,470
Lafayette	244,986,860	271,350,130	275,402,020	289,234,190
Lafourche	38,312,950	38,697,540	41,544,890	42,676,068
LaSalle	100,002,690	108,749,950	109,207,450	116,610,750
Lincoln	90,331,450	93,168,190	98,728,480	102,728,810
Livingston	35,813,710	35,400,045	35,133,577	35,874,570
Madison	97,182,020	96,656,520	99,410,100	101,984,330
Morehouse	80,786,730	82,968,030	85,071,300	90,580,730
Natchitoches	339,837,745	365,869,420	380,550,295	414,340,220
Orleans — 1st District	194,838,428	199,121,731	214,914,003	215,954,324
2nd District	480,923,583	494,471,612	510,450,500	543,376,362
3rd District	58,808,351	59,312,721	60,501,630	61,230,856
4th District	116,863,340	123,116,260	130,072,470	133,680,790
5th District	162,252,119	163,139,916	164,679,186	166,648,497
6th District	95,090,184	97,809,126	98,370,300	101,288,334
7th District	388,702,343	394,740,119	409,959,851	441,499,482
Ouachita	366,950,930	447,136,550	459,675,190	465,557,185
Plaquemines	95,537,071	100,591,758	96,742,776	106,756,305
Pointe Coupee	280,666,225	284,093,067	320,613,436	329,295,921
Rapides	22,802,550	23,956,510	25,121,970	27,030,580
Red River	51,433,470	52,077,060	53,610,080	55,200,710
Richland	51,419,765	54,789,636	56,540,006	59,407,980
Sabine	173,437,968	169,745,401	172,219,369	180,032,964
St. Bernard	252,692,670	261,378,961	268,489,784	278,072,179
St. Charles	25,470,550	26,533,110	28,652,200	30,252,890
St. Helena	123,097,500	130,630,890	125,509,325	120,275,675
St. James	98,263,741	103,383,627	112,845,862	117,030,159
St. John the Baptist	218,453,140	224,933,950	228,402,960	237,055,500
St. Landry	97,373,580	98,233,840	104,955,000	112,211,220
St. Martin	278,791,865	307,755,750	303,987,271	307,899,207
St. Mary	283,145,339	293,789,485	316,130,369	344,177,359
St. Tammany	160,306,189	162,810,557	170,381,795	181,635,679
Tangipahoa	23,616,630	24,253,420	25,052,410	25,436,170
Tensas	366,345,720	403,553,130	415,825,780	417,242,075
Terrebonne	59,234,470	60,975,250	62,700,230	64,904,650
Union	195,424,850	201,176,960	206,309,220	216,025,050
Vermilion	55,495,850	58,403,400	60,554,990	63,767,850
Vernon	75,332,810	78,582,580	80,219,840	81,711,420
Washington	83,512,601	89,334,812	93,660,582	99,828,320
Webster	91,152,000	94,350,950	98,615,930	101,891,360
West Baton Rouge	34,919,010	37,258,780	40,801,170	42,514,980
West Carroll	41,965,690	41,084,724	40,998,076	39,767,560
West Feliciana	40,906,250	42,431,980	42,375,790	43,454,230
Winn				
TOTALS	$ 12,833,355,600	$ 13,525,657,414	$ 13,939,218,686	$ 14,538,907,405

Source: The Louisiana Tax Commission

PLANT LIFE

WILDFLOWERS

The geographical position of the state is partly responsible for the abundance of native flowers, and flowers of both eastern and western America are to be found here.

A great many species of iris are found in southern Louisiana, having a wide range of color—blues, whites, yellows and reds. There is also disparity in the size of the various species, from the giant iris which often reaches a height of about four feet to the smaller iris fulva, usually about seven inches tall. Most iris seems to grow best in rich bottomlands and in mucky ditches and marshes.

A wild flower of special interest is the pitcher plant. Its hollow leaves are a trap for insects which are caught and partially digested by the plant.

Spanish dagger is a well-known native of the region and is probably most impressive in the summer when in bloom. Its blossoms are bell-shaped, straw-colored flowers and grow in a tall spike formation.

Many and varied are the species of the orchid family growing wild in Louisiana, such as the snake mouth, yellow fringed orchid, ladies' tresses and the crane fly orchid.

The passion flower, so called because early French Catholics saw in the design of the flower a symbol of the death of Christ, is a lovely vine which blooms during the fall and summer.

The wild violets of Louisiana are almost as numerous as the iris, and it is doubtful if anyone knows how many species actually do exist. For the most part, they bloom in the spring—some varieties in sandy soil while others require more fertile places.

A hardy wild flower often seen along the highways is the hibiscus, and in the same family, the poppy mallow, and the marsh mallow.

Along the water ways of Louisiana, are often seen the yellow lotus or "water chinquapin" known in parts of the state as a graine-a-volée. This plant is unusual in that the flowers do not rest on the water but extend several inches above it. The water hemlock grows around the water's edge and occasionally in shallow water. The most hardy and persistent of all water plants is the water hyacinth which grows in profusion in many southern bayous and slow moving streams.

The ubiquitous Spanish moss, interestingly enough, is not a parasite as is commonly supposed but an air feeding plant which uses trees as an anchor. It has small whitish flowers which bloom in the spring and reproduces by cell division.

Other wild flowers prevalent in the state are:

Lantana	Aster
Wild hyacinth	Goldenrod
Spider lily	Yellow aster
Buttercup	Gayfeather
Wild azalea	Blue sage
Red honeysuckle	Indian fire
Yellow jessamine	Wild verbena
Bull-thistle	Blue phlox
Bur-marigold	Morning glory
Coreopsis	Butterfly weed
Field daisy	Buckeye

PROJECT WILDFLOWER

Project Wildflower began in 1983 as a program to seed grassy and weed-filled areas along the Louisiana interstate system and along parish and state roads with native wildflowers. Sponsored by the Louisiana Department of Transportation and Development and operated by the Lafayette Natural History Museum, Project Wildflower's most visible payoff is beautification and litter abatement. As has been demonstrated in other states, the planting of wildflowers along rights-of-way cuts government spending on highway maintainence and enhances the state's tourist indusry.

There are three seed outlets around the state where interested citizens can obtain seeds for planting and learn more about native Louisiana plants. The Lafayette Natural History Museum and Planetarium, CENLA Pride in Alexandria (a chapter of Keep America Beautiful), and the Louisiana Nature and Science Center in New Orleans provide seed mixes. Any business, organization, or individual wishing to know more about Project Wildflower may contact the Lafayette Natural History Museum, 637 Girard Park Drive, Lafayette, LA 70503, (318) 261-8350.

GARDEN FLOWERS OF LOUISIANA
(Cultivated)

JANUARY

Camellias	Japanese Magnolia
Azaleas	Sweet alyssum
Pansies	Calendulas
Flowering quince	Brush honeysuckle
Sweet olive	Eranthemum
White hyacinths	Purple solanum
Narcissus	Nasturtiums
Sweet peas	Petunias
Violets	Baby's breath
(Cultivated)	Guava

Daffodils   Lobelia

FEBRUARY

Roman hyacinths	Yellow jasmine
Narcissus	Wood violets
Bridal wreath	Periwinkle
Camellias	White azaleas
Japanese magnolia	Roman hyacinths
Azaleas	Pear trees
Daffodils	White flag lilies
Snow drops	Calla lilies

Bignonia
Honeysuckle bush
Sweet olive
Quince
Eranthemum
Bridal wreath

Narcissus
Sweet alyssum
White flowering quince
Magnolia Conspicua

MARCH

Dogwood
Jack-in-the-pulpit
Pink honeysuckle
Crabapple
Perennial phlox
Geraniums
Roses
Sweet alyssum
Eranthemums
Verbena
Bridal wreath
Calla lilies
Iris
Sweet Peas
Azuratum
Red bud
Parsley haw

Wisteria
Pansies
Calendula
Nasturtiums
Flowering almond Stick
Flowering Quince
Daffodils
Azaleas
Camellias
Cherry laurel
Pear trees
Johnny Jump-ups
Bush honeysuckle
Peach
White verbena

APRIL

Crab apple
Dogwood
Violets
Yellow jasmine
Calendulas
Pansies
Johnny-Jump-Ups
Lantana
Azureatum
Lavendar perennial phlox
Azalea
Camellias
Periwinkle
Bridal wreath
Sweet olive
Japanese magnolia
Red bud
Sweet peas
Nicotiana

Amaryllis
Wisteria
Roses
Lupin
Cornflowers
Cerisa
Pomegranate
Mock orange
Bottle brush
Thistles
Pittosporum
Merica
Stock
Mountain laurel
Daisies
Amsonia
Anchusa
Plumbago
Queen's Anne's lace

MAY

Forget-me-not
Blue salvia
Phlox
Yellow day lilies
Oleanders
Roses
Purple clematis
Confederate jasmine
Daisies
Moss verbena
Hydrangeas
Lavendar
Parkinsonia
Gardenias
Sultana
Larkspur
Nasturtiums
Nicotiania

Queen Anne's lace
St. John's wart
Ginger lilies
Azureatum
Petunias
Hollyhocks
Cosmos
Coryopsis
Cashmere bouquet
Parrots feather
Feverfew
Asters
Buddleia
Snowdrop
Cannas
Arctotis
Peruvian lily

JUNE

Gardenias

Daisies

Crepe myrtle
Oleanders
Moss verbena
Phlox
Pinks
Altheas
Lily of the Nile
Hollyhocks
Gladioli
Hydrangeas
Azureatum
Nasturtiums

Mimosa
Radiance roses
Sultana
Parkinsonia
Buddleia
Zinnias
Balsam
Purple salvia
Rain lilies
Snake tongue
Montbretia

JULY

Montbretia
Oleanders
Buddleia
Althea
Crepe myrtle
Hidden lilies
Vinca
Torenia
Ophiopagon

Perennial phlox
Hydrangea
Justicia
Rosa Montana
Cleome
Rain lilies
Four o'clock
Colladiums

AUGUST

Altheas
Crepe myrtles
Zinnia
Torenia
Roses
Butterfly lilies
Butterfly lilac
Tithonia
Hidden lily

Lirope
Otheopagon
Cleomé
Dahlias
Hyacinth Bean vine
White clematis
Spider lilies

SEPTEMBER

Torenias
Roses
Buddleia
Plumbago
Purple salvia
Rosa Montana
Altheas
Hidden lily
Ophiopagan
Clerodendron
Dahlias

Celosia
Butterfly lily
Vinca
Guernsey lilies
Lycorus lilies
Hybiscus
Angels' trumpet
Crotelaria
Duranta
Night jasmine

OCTOBER

Guernsey lilies
Roses
Buddleia
Torenias
Blue salvia
Rosa Montana
Physostegia
Globe amaranth
Butterfly lily

Marigolds
Tithonia
Sassanqua
Crotelaria
Dahlias
Goldenrod
Azureatum
Lantana

NOVEMBER

Crysanthemums
"Michaelmas daisies" or Wild Asters
Japanese Tea

Crotons
Datura lily
Gordonia
Sassanqua

DECEMBER

Camellias
Roman hyacinths
Poinsettia
Roses

Yellow day lily
Azaleas
Sweet-olive
Sassanqua

LOUISIANA FOREST INDUSTRY

A forest is a community of plants and animals in which trees are the dominant plant members.

The historical development of the forest and the practice of forestry in Louisiana have paralleled that of the United States. From the arrival of the early settlers until the time of the Civil War the impact of man on the total forested area of the State was gradual. It has been estimated that at the close of the Civil War some seventy-five percent of the State was still forested.

By 1860 the State of Pennsylvania led the nation in lumber production, a position it held for a decade. Then came the rise of southern lumber production, and by 1890 lumbering was approaching its peak in the south and on the west coast.

During World War I and the early 1920s the migration away from the farm to the cities began. Demand for labor, high wages, depression, drought, exhausted soils, and vastly improved agricultural methods all contributed to this exodus—an exodus that appears to be slowing and perhaps ending today. Abandoned farmland has been gradually revegetated—either naturally or by man's plantings. Forest fires and burned areas have been curbed with reasonable success.

By the early 1960s, Louisiana was growing twice as much timber as was harvested—staying well ahead of demand. Between 1947 and 1969 production of pulpwood quadrupled, lumber increased twenty-five percent.

A southern pine plywood industry, born in 1963, produced sixteen percent of this nation's plywood in 1969. In 1981, Louisiana was the third largest producer of plywood in the nation.

Lumber, the chief structural material for home building, is in great demand today. The government's increasing housing goals of many millions of units, however, suggests that current lumber output should double or triple by the end of the century.

In 1981, Louisiana produced the third largest quantity of pulpwood in the country.

Increased incentives for Louisiana's small forest landowners must be a prime objective of the industry-sponsored "Third Forest" plan. This project seeks to double timber growth in the south by the year 2000 with a new forest of super trees to cope with the burgeoning demands for material, aesthetic, and recreational needs.

Of the total of 14.5 million acres of forest land in Louisiana, 67 percent is privately owned by more than 114 thousand people; 26 percent is owned by forest industry; and 7 percent is publicly owned. Louisiana's forest area has declined 4.5 percent since 1974; the present total is 13,872,600 acres. This figure is approximately 2,000,000 acres less than the 1964 total, or a 13 percent decline. The predominant reason for this decline is conversion to agriculture; however, urban expansion, mineral development, and rights-of-way for roads and utilities have also had a significant impact.

The estimated 1978 value of the timber resource (value received by the landowners) on this forest land is more than $205 million. This does not include the land, water, mineral, wildlife, recreational, or other values of these woodlands. The importance of forests cannot be measured entirely in monetary values. Their value must also be expressed in terms of the welfare, security and happiness of all people, because we depend upon them for more than 5 thousand necessities and luxuries of life.

In terms of total, value-added dollars, trees are Louisiana's number one crop. They generate more economic impact for the nation than all the state's other agricultural products combined. This impact amounted to $3.7 billion in 1985. The forest industry employs approximately 24,000 people and is the second leading manufacturing employer in the state.

The Louisiana Forestry Commission was established in 1944 by legislative act and the state forester is appointed by the seven-member Commission. During recent reorganization of state government, the name of the state forestry agency was changed to the Office of Forestry, one of the agencies in the Department of Natural Resources. However, the seven-member Louisiana Forestry Commission remains as policy-making board for the Office of Forestry. The Office of Forestry's fundamental purpose is to protect and develop the forest resources of Louisiana, public and private.

HISTORICAL HIGHLIGHTS

1869—Lumber production 76 million board feet
1898—Urania Lumber Co. organized by Henry Hardtner
1904—Reforestation begins at Urania
1904—Lumber production 2½ billion board feet
1904—First forestry act
1908—Great Southern Lumber Company began operations
1908—Conservation Commission Act 144
1910—First severance tax
1913—First forestry act
1913—Lumber production 4.2 billion board feet
1913—First Reforestation contract
1915—First fire protection funds
1917—Cut-over land conference, New Orleans
1918—R. D. Forbes, first State Forester
1921—R. D. Forbes, first Director, Southern Forest Experiment Station
1921—Caroline Dorman, appointed instructor of forestry
1922—First pine plantation, Great Southern Lumber Company, Washington Parish
1922—First fire tower constructed, Great Southern Lands, Washington Parish
1922—First fire tower constructed
1923—V. H. Sonderegger, Supt. of Forestry, takes pulpwood to eastern paper companies
1923—Louisiana divided into two districts
1923—Alexander State Forest established
1926—Severance tax established
1926—Fire protection pay by landowner inaugurated
1926—State divided into eight districts
1928—One million seedlings produced at Alexander State Forest
1933—Twenty forestry CCC camps established in Louisiana
1934—First forest survey
1940—Murray Brashears, State Forester, begins new forestry concept
1944—Louisiana Forestry Commission established
1946—Nurseries established at Oberlin and Sibley
1947—James E. Mixon, State Forester
1948—Big Forestry Plan—legislation doubled protection funding
1951—LFA Tree Farm Program begins
1951—Hardwood Management begins
1952—Statewide disastrous fire season
1954—New timber land and severance tax law
1954—Interstate fire protection compact established
1956—Soil Bank Program started
1956—Southern Forest Fire Prevention Conference in New Orleans
1956—New Baton Rouge Central Office building constructed
1957—Nursery established at Columbia
1959—Nursery established at Beauregard
1961—Beginning of tree seed orchard in Beauregard
1963—Cypress tree established as state tree
1964—Pine plywood industry established
1969—"Third Forest" report and concept begins
1970—Indian Creek Lake established
1971—Prison trainee center established at Alexander State Forest
1971—State divided into eleven districts
1972—Treetime USA—New Orleans National Tree planting Conference
1973—1½ million acres of woodland flooded
1973—State Forest, Indian Creek Recreation Area opened
1974—Louisiana first state to plant trees under Forest Incentives Program
1975—Tornadoes cause extensive damage to Alexander State Forest
1977—In a reorganization of the state government, the state's forestry agency becomes the
     Louisiana Office of Forestry in the Department of Natural Resources.

TIMBER SEVERED BY SPECIES AND PARISH - 1986
(SAWTIMBER - BOARD FEET, DOYLE SCALE; PULPWOOD - STANDARD CORDS)

PARISH	SAWTIMBER		PULPWOOD	
	PINE	HARDWOODS	PINE	HARDWOODS
ACADIA	7,399,146	977,574	6,893.64	2,871.57
ALLEN	49,782,858	3,877,899	109,806.82	54,983.55
ASCENSION	286,481	874,959	10,982.99	10,438.19
ASSUMPTION	0	1,300,867	0.00	8,282.06
AVOYELLES	414,278	4,915,665	1,808.76	26,492.06
BEAUREGARD	44,008,220	7,217,624	338,522.64	32,083.57
BIENVILLE	49,046,734	5,395,332	166,469.91	50,056.67
BOSSIER	43,635,630	1,219,785	62,001.04	44,149.32
CADDO	7,595,711	1,563,144	36,949.13	17,457.03
CALCASIEU	7,128,330	1,728,410	49,725.53	7,003.23
CALDWELL	23,608,173	3,559,229	54,886.28	34,239.52
CAMERON	0	0	0.00	449.03
CATAHOULA	4,491,093	3,126,681	10,716.12	22,149.52
CLAIBORNE	34,552,098	6,693,381	105,754.18	39,738.17
CONCORDIA	0	7,429,640	0.00	29,651.79
DESOTO	37,966,598	4,628,242	141,861.19	51,546.51
EAST BATON ROUGE	1,829,459	2,956,430	7,968.93	4,692.27
EAST CARROLL	0	1,787,945	0.00	14,187.12
EAST FELICIANA	17,463,619	6,107,107	39,107.14	18,999.07
EVANGELINE	10,375,869	670,513	37,556.92	17,967.18
FRANKLIN	797,243	2,774,168	562.32	6,496.88
GRANT	66,029,678	2,764,065	98,101.60	41,750.02
IBERIA	0	0	0.00	0.00
IBERVILLE	0	3,536,270	0.00	1,240.88
JACKSON	36,334,889	7,868,728	209,869.21	59,223.78
JEFFERSON	0	0	0.00	0.00
JEFF DAVIS	1,227,134	739,147	3,858.49	1,663.53
LAFAYETTE	0	0	0.00	0.00
LAFOURCHE	0	2,084,860	0.00	766.16
LASALLE	49,510,474	1,911,821	143,907.71	21,353.45
LINCOLN	13,025,613	707,447	96,865.21	33,315.85

LIVINGSTON	34,184,681	2,283,077	88,231.60	18,928.24
MADISON	3,648	8,905,581		13,597.93
MOREHOUSE	34,981,101	1,230,109	22,055.55	32,703.04
NATCHITOCHES	71,882,109	4,021,542	179,566.31	55,196.83
ORLEANS	0	0	0.00	0.00
OUACHITA	16,153,066	2,817,069	59,286.74	33,848.00
PLAQUEMINES	0	11,267	0.00	67.11
POINTE COUPEE	0	3,149,799	0.00	3,390.84
RAPIDES	75,733,164	4,503,187	232,936.22	26,640.17
RED RIVER	20,919,341	936,794	42,014.71	14,691.26
RICHLAND	407,720	1,595,395	82.51	1,892.77
SABINE	132,059,054	4,408,212	192,262.79	74,430.26
ST. BERNARD	0	0	0.00	0.00
ST. CHARLES	0	0	0.00	191.92
ST. HELENA	20,374,815	2,077,607	96,682.65	21,853.61
ST. JAMES	0	0	0.00	0.00
ST. JOHN	0	197,698	0.00	42.23
ST. LANDRY	74,725	12,112,692	195.07	23,434.93
ST. MARTIN	0	330,266	0.00	1,109.58
ST. MARY	0	0	0.00	0.00
ST. TAMMANY	29,964,611	431,339	96,364.78	2,214.39
TANGIPAHOA	38,940,270	2,248,179	84,279.64	12,071.57
TENSAS	0	8,468,222	14.77	48,200.26
TERREBONNE	0	364,864	0.00	0.00
UNION	58,084,474	5,724,973	147,469.64	81,770.78
VERMILION	0	0	0.00	0.00
VERNON	65,239,198	9,424,222	291,076.64	57,821.67
WASHINGTON	25,019,075	1,015,261	62,608.99	9,083.38
WEBSTER	29,315,703	2,977,575	50,518.56	29,059.03
WEST BATON ROUGE	0	1,494,829	0.00	152.12
WEST CARROLL	12,620	189,168	252.88	563.03
WEST FELICIANA	1,469,330	4,853,703	2,247.17	17,970.13
WINN	90,778,393	8,731,766	156,167.60	61,523.91
TOTAL VOLUME	1,251,930,210	182,921,333	3,538,478.08	1,295,696.97

Source: Louisiana Department of National Resources, Office of Forestry.

LOUISIANA STATE FIRE TOTALS
FIRES BY MAJOR PROPERTY USE
1986

RESIDENTIAL PROPERTY   6,663

   (Single family dwellings,
   apartments, mobile homes,
   hotels, motels, etc.)

PUBLIC AND MERCANTILE PROPERTY   929

   (Stores, restaurants, institutions, churches, public
   facilities and education.)

INDUSTRIAL AND OTHER BUILDINGS   835

   (Basic industry, manufacturing,
   residential garages, storage,
   vacant and under construction.)

MOBILE PROPERTY   4,965

   (Automobiles, trucks, trains,
   buses, airplanes and boats.)

OUTSIDE AND OTHER PROPERTY   8,289

   (Dumpsters, trash, grass,
   trees, etc.)
                                     ———————

TOTAL FIRES   21,681

These totals do not include fire incidents from the City of New Orleans
Fire Department, because these figures were generated from the Louisiana
Fire Incident Reporting System and the New Orleans Fire Department is not
yet on this system.

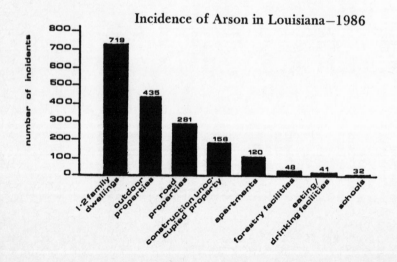

Incidence of Arson in Louisiana—1986

number of incidents

1-2 family dwellings: 719
outdoor properties: 435
road properties: 281
construction unoccupied property: 158
apartments: 120
forestry facilities: 48
eating/drinking facilities: 41
schools: 32

LOUISIANA FIRE LOSSES

YEAR	FIRES	SUSPICIOUS OR INCENDIARY LOSS IN DOLLARS	ESTIMATED LOSS IN DOLLARS	PERCENT LOSS SUSPICIOUS OR INCENDIARY
1941	2,866	20,016	2,320,206	.86
1942	3,128	46,519	2,430,591	1.91
1943	3,994	51,752	4,703,527	1.10
1944	2,752	14,436	4,445,834	.32
1945	3,145	12,128	4,981,989	.24
1946	4,122	6,167	7,102,800	.09
1947	4,951	21,380	7,461,137	.29
1948	5,180	21,143	6,479,849	.33
1949	5,164	88,810	7,391,118	1.20
1950	5,386	39,839	7,337,692	.54
1951	6,211	84,197	9,991,170	.84
1952	6,086	386,280	9,115,649	4.24
1953	5,829	96,738	9,135,309	1.06
1954	5,360	395,641	9,841,948	4.02
1955	5,350	146,374	9,947,774	1.47
1956	6,292	130,074	14,769,798	.88
1957	6,338	130,280	11,813,905	1.10
1958	7,140	282,165	16,743,229	1.69
1959	7,046	854,100	14,318,144	5.97
1960	8,041	1,501,342	18,058,574	8.31
1961	8,011	341,457	13,351,493	2.56
1962	9,630	895,623	19,587,469	4.57
1963	10,299	776,980	22,855,748	3.40
1964	10,307	713,638	19,030,269	3.75
1965	10,469	1,933,240	36,736,523	5.26
1966	9,092	1,181,913	24,438,839	4.84
1967	8,781	1,560,441	49,207,010	3.17
1968	8,749	1,832,307	31,291,789	5.86
1969	8,135	8,547,300	37,618,575	22.72
1970	8,367	4,105,989	48,021,954	8.55
1971	7,660	3,141,701	29,906,195	10.51
1972	8,558	7,571,835	35,689,861	21.22
1973	9,625	5,633,979	41,830,260	13.47
1974	9,616	5,758,410	58,375,469	9.86
1975	10,188	6,666,787	49,160,354	13.56
1976	10,877	8,810,801	63,985,681	13.77
1977	10,987	7,038,463	113,070,182	6.22
1978.	11,098	9,815,513	83,466,079	11.76
1979	11,079	10,484,201	94,559,368	11.09
1980˙	14,094	16,886,498	142,267,081	11.87
Fiscal Year 1981-82	23,439*	15,606,853	132,679,908	11.76
1983	23,268	19,159,864	134,409,279	14.25
1984	28,454	6,891,200	146,828,996	4.69
1985	27,210	32,211,498	185,202,956	17.39
1986	26,193	20,401,492	135,062,271	15.10

*It should be noted that in 1981 Louisiana joined the National Fire Incident Reporting System (NFIRS); thereby collecting uniform fire incident and fire casualty data. We feel that now we are obtaining a more complete and accurate statistical picture.

Source: 1987 Annual Report, Office of State Fire Marshal

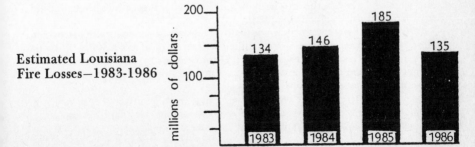

Estimated Louisiana Fire Losses—1983-1986

THE MINERAL INDUSTRY OF LOUISIANA

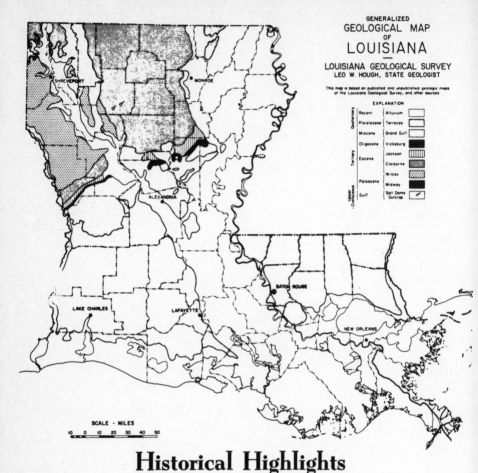

Historical Highlights
Of the Oil and Gas Industry in Louisiana

ABOUT 1868—The Louisiana Oil and Coal Company drilled a well about 15 miles west of Lake Charles in search of oil but was unsuccessful although it did reveal very extensive sulphur deposits.

1870—A night watchman at an ice plant in Shreveport accidentally discovered natural gas emanating from a well drilled in search of artesian water when he struck a match. Gas from the well was piped to the plant to provide illumination— the first use in the state of the fuel that today heats the vast majority of Louisiana homes and places of business.

Sept. 21, 1901—The Heywood well six miles from Jennings was brought in, producing the first oil discovered in the state in commercial quantities and marking what is recognized as the birth of the industry in the state.

1906—The Louisiana Legislature passed the first state oil and gas conservation law.

1908—The first natural gas pipeline was laid in Louisiana. It brought gas from the Caddo field to Shreveport.

1909—The new refinery in Baton Rouge (which is the Exxon refinery of today) went on stream. Today it is, in terms of capacity, the largest oil refinery on the North American continent. This is also the year in which construction began on Louisiana's first long distance oil pipeline which by 1910 was transporting crude oil from Caddo Parish to the Baton Rouge refinery.

ABOUT 1910—The first over-water drilling in America occurred on Caddo Lake near Shreveport.

1913—A major discovery occurred in Northwest Louisiana when the Bull Bayou Field was brought in.

1916—The discovery well in the Monroe Gas Field, one of the largest ever discovered, was brought in.

1921—The prolific Haynesville Gas Field was discovered.

1940—The oil and gas industry came to Central Louisiana in a big way with discovery of the Olla Field in LaSalle Parish.

1942—The Lake St. John Field on the eastern border of Louisiana was discovered.

Nov. 14, 1947—The first oil well out of sight of land was brought in in the Gulf of Mexico about 45 miles south of Morgan City in the Ship Shoal Block 32 field, marking the birth of the offshore oil and gas industry.

1948—The Main Pass Field came in near the mouth of the Mississippi River.

1949—Three major fields were discovered in the Gulf of Mexico off the Louisiana coast. They were the Eugene Island, Bay Marchand and Vermilion Fields.

1950—The South Pass Field in the Gulf of Mexico was discovered.

1954—The westernmost boundary of Louisiana's offshore oil and gas industry was established with discovery of the West Cameron Field.

1959—Severance taxes on oil and gas rose above the $100 million mark in Louisiana for the first time. Annual severance tax collections rose to a peak $539 million in 1975 before beginning a decline.

1970—Louisiana's natural gas reserves dropped for the first time since gas was discovered in significant quantities in the state.

1971—Louisiana oil production peaked at 799,731,000 barrels and reserves began to decline.

1973—The offshore industry unveiled Clean Gulf Associates, a cooperative stockpiling of the most sophisticated oil spill containment and cleanup equipment available. The equipment is on call today in several coastal cities of South Louisiana.

1974—Lease and royalty income paid by the oil and gas industry to the state of Louisiana soared to an all-time record $209,384,451.83.

1975—Gerald R. Ford became the first President of the United States to visit an offshore oil platform when he came to Louisiana on April 23. His comment: "We just have to get more and more of these."

1982-Lease and royalty income paid by the oil and gas industry to the state of Louisiana soared to an all-time record $624,529,812. Oil and gas severance taxes in Louisiana hit an all-time record $971,677,140. About 165,000 citizens of Louisiana earned their living in the oil and gas industry.

1986—The Bay Marchand Field produced its 500,000,000th barrel of oil, making it one of the greatest producers in the U.S.

Source: La. Division, Mid-Continent Oil & Gas Division

LOUISIANA OIL AND GAS PRODUCTION (1984)

Production Onshore and in State Waters in the Gulf of Mexico

TOTAL CRUDE	151,398,713	bbls.
North Louisiana	29,590,376	
South Louisiana onshore	96,690,421	
South Louisiana offshore	25,117,916	

TOTAL CONDENSATE	35,844,231	bbls.
North Louisiana	3,140,006	
South Louisiana onshore	30,785,661	
South Louisiana offshore	1,918,564	

TOTAL NATURAL AND CASINGHEAD GAS	2,095,597,000	MCF
North Louisiana	386,892,055	
South Louisiana onshore	1,390,697,247	
South Louisiana offshore	318,007,698	

Average Daily Production

Crude oil	414,790	bbls.
Condensate	98,203	bbls.
Natural and Casinghead Gas	5,741,361	MCF

Production in Federal Waters in the Gulf of Mexico

Crude	286,179,678	bbls.
Condensate	31,844,944	bbls.
Natural and Casinghead Gas	3,578,740,570	MCF

Average Daily Production

Crude oil	784,053	bbls.
Condensate	87,246	bbls.
Natural and Casinghead Gas	9,804,768	MCF

Total Louisiana Production (Onshore, Offshore and Federal Zone)

Crude oil	437,578,391	bbls.
Condensate	67,689,175	bbls.
Natural and Casinghead Gas	5,674,337,570	MCF

Proved Reserves of Louisiana Oil and Gas (Onshore, Offshore and Federal Zone, as of January 1, 1986)

Crude Oil	2,661,000,000	bbls.
Decrease from Previous Year	19,000,000	bbls.
Natural Gas	41,085,000,000	MCF
Decrease from Previous Year	1,263,000,000	MCF

TOTAL WELLS DRILLED

Year	Total Wells	North Louisiana	South Louisiana	Offshore
1956	3875	1702	1747	426
1957	3858	1446	1738	671
1958	3523	1384	1720	416
1959	3781	1517	1853	411
1960	3707	1452	1765	460
1961	4040	1826	1690	524
1962	4988	2411	1869	708
1963	5282	2861	1731	690
1964	5344	2923	1571	850
1965	5132	2631	1636	865
1966	3936	1383	1587	963
1967	3185	1114	1204	867
1968	3478	947	1463	1068
1969	3174	875	1464	835
1970	2948	763	1347	838
1971	2935	992	1142	801
1972	3065	1116	1144	805
1973	2705	835	1108	759
1974	2809	1200	1017	592
1975	2951	1146	1091	714
1976	3172	1285	1115	772
1977	3323	1603	942	778
1978	3876	1796	1280	800
1979	4124	2063	1236	825
1980	4970	2735	1285	950
1981	5379	3382	1302	695
1982	5005	3022	1331	652
1983	4742	2800	1200	742
1984	6480	4000	1470	1010

PRODUCING WELLS IN LOUISIANA AS OF JANUARY 1986

	OIL	GAS
Total Wells	26,872	14,759
North Louisiana	19,611	11,434
South Louisiana onshore	6,250	2,819
South Louisiana offshore	1,011	506

LOUISIANA LEASE AND ROYALTY INCOME

Year	Total
1946	$ 9,785,686.60
1947	18,598,106.99
1948	32,354,203.72
1949	19,372,458.31
1950	20,753,081.73
1951	21,853,545.45
1952	29,714,695.99
1953	30,373,805.99
1954	70,385,900.79
1955	116,262,194.79
1956	92,787,189.93
1957	78,381,232.38
1958	55,419,191.15
1959	126,191,819.04
1960	66,105,335.77
1961	76,173,780.48
1962	87,850,562.30
1963	109,375,050.19
1964	112,675,943.68
1965	118,036,442.16
1966	154,142,606.10
1967	$135,965,066.57
1968	150,108,735.78
1969	156,268,176.97
1970	147,323,684.41
1971	160,752,766.08
1972	146,269,110.42
1973	138,167,418.82
1974	209,384,451.83
1975	174,751,193.30
1976	189,212,955.21
1977	223,331,123.17
1978	283,326,000.00
1979	265,879,945.22
1980	545,914,446.27
1981	391,404,031.00
1982	624,529,812.54
1983	545,206,481.00
1984	497,959,159.00
1985	526,300,000.00
1986	405,300,000.00

(Department of Natural Resources)

Louisiana Energy Consumption and Production

Sector	Actual		Projected			Average Annual Growth Rates			
	1983	1984	1985	1986	1987	1984	1985	1986	1987
Energy Consumption									
Electricity[a]									
Residential	18,234	19,015	18,324	18,343	18,854	4.3%	-3.6%	0.1%	2.8%
Commercial & Industrial	35,288	37,943	36,294	36,553	37,902	7.5%	-4.3%	0.7%	3.7%
Natural Gas[b]									
Residential	68,304	70,392[c]	73,902	77,783	81,743	3.1%	5.0%	5.3%	5.1%
Commercial	34,906	35,273[c]	35,362	35,832	36,332	1.1%	0.3%	1.3%	1.4%
Industrial	986,899	1,055,982[c]	1,057,038	1,097,205	1,158,649	7.1%	0.1%	3.8%	5.6%
Energy Supply									
Natural Gas Production[d]	2,004	2,064	1,976	1,934	1,890	3.0%	-4.3%	-2.1%	-2.3%
Oil & Condensate Production[e]	181,351	188,044	186,000	178,000	175,000	3.7%	-1.1%	-4.3%	-1.7%
Active Rigs (monthly average)	223	258	249	238	235	15.7%	-3.5%	-4.4%	-1.3%

a - Millions of kilowatt hours   b - Millions of cubic feet   c - Estimated   d - Billions of cubic feet   e - Thousands of barrels

1985 Louisiana Economic Outlook

OIL AND GAS SEVERANCE TAXES *

Fiscal Year	Total	Fiscal Year	Total
1953-54	$ 76,094,730	1970-71	$ 249,079,291
1954-55	75,865,959	1971-72	236,484,125
1955-56	83,475,385	1972-73	259,454,515
1956-57	95,266,813	1973-74	380,767,316
1957-58	94,074,315	1974-75	539,571,517
1958-59	123,098,506	1975-76	507,139,740
1959-60	132,552,912	1976-77	485,339,599
1960-61	143,545,609	1977-78	466,346,422
1961-62	146,201,197	1978-79	458,009,265
1962-63	159,485,491	1979-80	513,150,906
1963-64	169,630,150	1980-81	803,146,949
1964-65	174,523,196	1981-82	971,677,140
1965-66	200,261,245	1982-83	859,930,363
1966-67	213,773,395	1983-84	803,182,600
1967-68	233,070,145	1984-85	731,759,504
1968-69	234,567,908	1985-86	653,580,534
1969-70	243,115,993		

* Oil, natural gas, natural gasoline and condensate taxes; Department of Revenue and Taxation

PETROLEUM PRODUCTS TAXES *

Fiscal Year	Total	Fiscal Year	Total
1953-54	$ 47,417,256	1970-71	$ 128,235,120
1954-55	50,094,293	1971-72	138,651,309
1955-56	55,660,780	1972-73	150,775,462
1956-57	59,412,423	1973-74	150,405,321
1957-58	61,694,338	1974-75	152,729,860
1958-59	61,127,603	1975-76	164,932,780
1959-60	66,686,416	1976-77	172,965,445
1960-61	66,123,770	1977-78	183,633,000
1961-62	68,873,716	1978-79	193,226,764
1962-63	71,873,978	1979-80	187,478,012
1963-64	75,632,744	1980-81	187,791,790
1964-65	80,135,285	1981-82	191,316,601
1965-66	88,067,843	1982-83	186,549,799
1966-67	92,911,362	1983-84	192,454,050
1967-68	92,457,134	1984-85	363,209,157
1968-69	107,705,882	1985-86	337,389,822
1969-70	123,482,076		

* Gasoline and Special Fuels; Department of Revenue and Taxation

TOTAL WORKERS IN THE OIL AND GAS INDUSTRY IN LOUISIANA

Year	Production	Refining	Chemicals	Oil, Product Pipelines	Gas Utilities	Marketing	Total
1956	40,200	15,500	16,600	1,400	5,600	12,450	87,200
1957	42,300	15,700	16,700	1,500	5,800	13,100	90,750
1958	41,350	15,450	17,100	1,400	6,000	13,200	90,450
1959	42,100	13,500	16,800	1,320	6,380	13,440	88,840
1960	40,300	13,400	16,400	1,250	6,400	13,150	90,900
1961	40,300	12,800	16,300	1,100	6,300	13,050	89,850
1962	40,400	12,000	16,100	950	6,250	13,600	89,300
1963	40,400	11,400	16,500	1,000	6,200	13,400	88,900
1964	43,100	10,400	17,100	950	6,150	14,100	91,800
1965	45,800	10,400	17,500	900	6,100	14,600	95,300
1966	47,200	9,200	20,200	900	6,050	14,550	98,650
1967	47,100	9,800	21,500	900	5,750	15,600	100,650
1968	47,200	10,500	22,300	900	5,800	15,800	102,500
1969	48,300	9,700	23,500	900	5,900	15,900	104,200
1970	47,300	9,600	23,700	900	5,950	15,750	102,700
1971	48,000	9,600	23,900	900	6,200	15,700	103,400
1972	49,200	9,500	24,300	900	6,100	15,900	105,900
1973	49,800	9,600	25,300	900	6,100	14,500	106,200
1974	49,900	9,900	26,800	900	6,800	13,600	107,900
1975	54,800	9,600	27,300	950	6,500	14,700	113,850
1976	58,200	9,700	29,300	900	6,000	14,400	118,500
1977	61,300	9,300	31,100	900	5,800	15,400	123,800
1978	70,100	10,800	31,800	1,000	5,600	15,600	134,900
1979	71,400	11,500	33,200	1,100	5,900	15,700	138,800
1980	83,300	12,100	33,500	1,200	5,900	14,744	150,944
1981	93,500	15,100	32,300	1,200	6,800	16,100	165,000
1982	95,300	12,600	33,800	1,000	7,000	15,600	165,300
1983	77,300	12,300	30,300	1,300	7,400	14,100	142,700
1984	78,000	12,000	29,100	1,300	7,100	14,100	141,600
1985	78,500	11,700	28,300	1,200	6,700	13,900	140,300

(Louisiana Department of Labor)

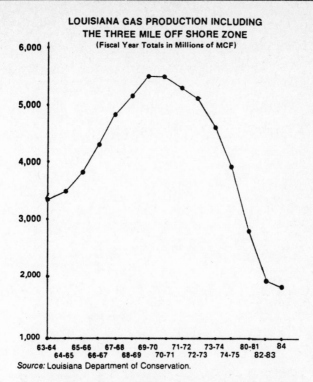

LOUISIANA GAS PRODUCTION INCLUDING
THE THREE MILE OFF SHORE ZONE
(Fiscal Year Totals in Millions of MCF)

Source: Louisiana Department of Conservation.

COMPARATIVE COST OF DRILLING AND EQUIPPING WELLS
(1984)

Oil Wells

	Cost per Foot	Average Depth	Cost per Well
LOUISIANA	$140.14	3,574 feet	$ 500,858
North Louisiana	39.78	1,875 feet	74,583
South Louisiana	116.70	8,004 feet	934,060
Offshore	297.69	9,894 feet	2,945,327
UNITED STATES	66.31	3,952 feet	262,065

Gas Wells

	Cost per Foot	Average Depth	Cost per Well
LOUISIANA	$186.23	7,171 feet	$1,335,437
North Louisiana	69.91	4,126 feet	288,433
South Louisiana	157.75	11,705 feet	1,846,490
Offshore	325.83	9,956 feet	3,243,969
UNITED STATES	88.80	5,516 feet	489,808

Dry Holes

	Cost per Foot	Average Depth	Cost per Well
LOUISIANA	$115.14	7,079 feet	$ 815,109
North Louisiana	24.40	3,725 feet	90,877
South Louisiana	93.08	10,929 feet	1,017,316
Offshore	284.43	10,587 feet	3,011,285
UNITED STATES	67.17	4,900 feet	329,155

(Joint Association Study of Industry Drilling Costs)

THE PETROLEUM PRICE PICTURE

Year	U. S. Average Crude Oil Price	U. S. Average Gasoline Price at Refinery	U. S. Average Four Principle Refinery Products*	U. S. Consumer Price Index (1967 = 100)
1963	$ 2.97 per bbl.	11.35¢ per gal.	$3.79 per bbl.	91.7
1964	2.97	11.27	3.71	92.9
1965	2.96	11.52	3.83	94.5
1966	2.882	11.59	3.84	97.2
1967	2.913	11.84	3.92	100.0
1968	2.94	11.55	3.84	104.2
1969	3.077	11.80	3.89	109.8
1970	3.18	12.33	4.28	116.3
1971	3.38	12.70	4.59	121.3
1972	3.39	12.70	4.57	125.3
1973	3.89	14.72	5.25	133.1
1974	6.73	25.53	9.36	147.7
1975	7.52	30.27	11.35	161.2
1976	8.13	33.82	12.41	170.5
1977	8.57	36.99	13.95	181.5
1978	8.96	39.22	14.16	195.4
1979	12.64	56.84	20.79	217.4
1980	21.59	87.40	30.57	246.8
1981	31.84	101.63	37.29	272.3
1982	28.50	92.90	34.62	288.6
1983	26.13	83.75	31.64	297.4
1984	25.88	77.87	30.60	311.1
1985	24.07	81.11	30.69	322.2
1986	12.65	47.74	18.47	328.4

(Source: National Petroleum News Factbook; Louisiana Department of Labor)   * Gasoline, kerosene, light fuel, heavy fuel.

RANK OF RELIGIOUS DENOMINATIONS IN LOUISIANA

Ranking, denomination	Churches	Adherents
1- Roman Catholic Church	633	1,330,713
2- Southern Baptist Convention	1,344	652,246
3- National Baptist Convention-USA Inc.	xxx	430,000
4- United Methodist Church	589	169,328
5- Episcopal Church	96	38,554
6- Presbyterian Church (USA)	133	32,234
7- United Pentecostal Church International	240	30,000
8- Assemblies of God	210	30,000
9- Christian Methodist Episcopal Church	123	27,056
10- Churches of Christ	226	22,931
11- Lutheran Church-Missouri Synod	58	20,429
12- American Baptist Association	85	15,140
13- Mormons (Church of Jesus Christ of Latter Day Saints)	45	11,581
14- Baptist Missionary Association	51	11,067
15- African Methodist Episcopal Zion Church	20	10,369
16- Church of God (Anderson, Ind.)	63	9,708
17- Reform Judaism	13	8,217
18- Seventh-Day Adventists	45	7,811
19- Evangelical Lutheran Church in America	18	5,761
20- Church of God (Cleveland, Tenn.)	68	5,750
21- Church of Nazarene	57	5,729
22- Christian Church/Disciples of Christ	25	5,667
23- United Church of Christ	18	3,545
24- Christian Churches/Churches of Christ	29	3,221
25- The Salvation Army	8	2,400
26- Free Methodist Church of North America	14	1,722
27- Presbyterian Church in America	13	1,594
28- Southern Methodist Church	20	1,239
29- American Baptist Churches in the USA	3	1,125
30- Reorganized Church/Latter Day Saints	9	892
31- Unitarian Universalist Association	7	885
32- Cumberland Presbyterian Church	7	779
33- Conservative Judaism	3	552
34- Christian Brethren	6	330
35- International Church of the Foursquare Gospel	2	277
36- Wisconsin Evangelical Lutheran Synod	4	277
37- Church of God in Christ/Mennonite	2	275
38- Church of God (Abrahamic Faith)	4	273
39- Evangelical Methodist Church	3	171
40- Pentecostal Holiness Church, USA	2	154
41- The Mennonite Church	1	120
42- Metropolitan Community Churches	1	120
43- Church of the Brethren (Dunkers)	1	119
44- North American Baptist Conference	1	85
45- Christian & Missionary Alliance	2	73
46- Society of Friends-USA/Quakers	2	47
47- Armenian Apostolic Church of America	1	40
48- Advent Christian Church	1	37
49- Fire Baptized Holiness Church (Wesleyan)	1	2
TOTALS	4,310	2,898,645

Source: Wesley Jackson, Religion Editor, New Orleans *Times-Picayune*

The following is a list of denominations, cults, sects, and religious societies currently active in Louisiana:

Advent Christian Church
  African Methodist Episcopal
African Methodist Episcopal Zion
American Baptist Association
American Baptist Churches-USA
  American Episcopal Church
  American Muslim Mission
  American Orthodox Church
  Anglican Orthodox Church
  Antiochian Orthodox Christian Archdiocese of North America

  "Apostolic" Churches
  Apostolic Overcoming Holy Church of God
  "Apostolic-Pentecostal" Churches
  Armenian Apostolic Church of America
Assemblies of God
  Baha'i World Faith
Baptist Missionary Association of America
  "Bible Churches"
  "Bible Missionary" Churches
  "Bible Way" Churches
  Buddhist Fellowship of America
  "Charismatic" Churches
Christian & Missionary Alliance
Christian Brethren
Christian Church/Disciples of Christ
Christian Church/Churches of Christ
  Christian Congregation (Monroe, N.C.)
  "Christian Fellowship" Churches
  "Christian Methodist" Churches

Christian Methodist Episcopal
  Christ's Sanctified Holy Church
  Church of Christ, Holiness-USA
  Church of Christ Holiness, Triumph Overcoming
  Church of Christ, Scientist (Christian Science)
Church of God (Anderson, Ind.)
Church of God (Cleveland, Tenn.)
  "Church of God and Christ"
  Church of God in Christ
Church of God in Christ/Mennonite
Church of God of Prophecy
Church of God/Abrahamic Faith
  "Church of Jesus Christ"
Church of Jesus Christ of Latter-Day Saints/Mormons
  Church of Our Lord Jesus Christ of the Apostolic Faith
Church of the Brethren (Dunkers)
  Church of the Living God
  Church of The Lord Jesus Christ of the Apostolic Faith
Church of the Nazarene
Churches of Christ
  "Colored Baptist" Churches
  "Congregational" Churches
  "Congregational Christian"
  Congregational Methodist Church
Conservative Judaism
  Coptic Orthodox Church
  "Covenant" Churches
Cumberland Presbyterian Church
  Divine Science
  Eastern Orthodox Church
  Eastern Rite Catholics
  Eckankar (ECK)
Episcopal Church
EST
  Evangelical Presbyterian Church
  Evangelical and Reformed Church
  "Evangelical" Churches
  Evangelical Lutheran Church in America
Evangelical Methodist Church
Fire Baptized Holiness Church
  First Congregational Methodist-USA
  Foundation Faith of God

Free Methodist Church of North America
  Full Gospel Fellowship
  German Seamen's Mission
  Greek Orthodox Church, Archdiocese of North and South America
  Hindus/India-based religions
  "Holiness" Churches
  Holy Orthodox Catholic Church
  "Independent" Baptist Churches
  Independent Fundamentalists
  "Independent Methodists"
  "Interdenominational" Churches
International Foursquare Gospel Church
  Jehovah's Witnesses
  Korean Christian Church
  Krishna Consciousness (Hare Krishna)
  Liberal Catholic Church
Lutheran Church-Missouri Synod
  Norwegian Seamen's Church
Mennonite Church
  Metaphysical Science
  Methodist Protestant Church
Metropolitan Community Churches
  "Missionary Baptist."
  Muslims (Sunni/Shiite)
  National Baptist Convention-America
  National Baptist Convention-USA, Inc.
  Nichiren Shoshu Buddhism (USA)
  "Non-denominational" Churches
North American Baptist Conference
  "New Covenant" Churches
  "New Testament" Churches
  Orthodox Church in America
  Orthodox Judaism
Pentecostal Holiness Church, International
  "Plant of Renown" Churches
Presbyterian Church in America
Presbyterian Church (USA)
  Primitive Baptists
  Progressive National Baptist Convention
  "Rastafarians"
  Reformed Baptists
Reform Judaism
  Reorganized Church of Jesus Christ of Latter Day Saints
  Roman Catholic Church
  Salvation Army
Seventh-Day Adventists
  Seventh-Day Baptists
  Sikhs (American) and Sikhs (East Indian)
Society of Friends-USA (Quakers)
Southern Baptist Convention
Southern Methodist Church
  Spiritualist Churches
  Syrian Orthodox Church of Antioch
"Traditional" Judaism
  Traditionalist Catholics (Lefebvrist)
  Transcendental Meditation (TM)
  Triumph Church and Kingdom of God in Christ International
  Unification Church ("Moonies")
Unitarian Universalist Association
United Church of Christ
  "United" Churches
  United Free Will Baptist Church
United Methodist Church
  United Pentecostal Church, Inc.
  Unity School of Christianity
Universal Bible Teaching Ministries
  Universal Church of Lord Jesus Christ
  Volunteers of America
  Wesleyan Church
Wisconsin Evangelical Lutheran Synod
  World Church of the Living God
  Worldwide Church of God
  Zoroastrians

Source: Wesley Jackson, Religion Editor, New Orleans *Times-Picayune*

HEALTH, VITAL STATISTICS AND HOSPITALS
LOUISIANA HOSPITALS

HEALTH CARE AND HUMAN SERVICES PROGRAM

The Department of Health and Human Resources, the largest state agency in Louisiana, is charged with maximizing Louisiana's human resources through services aimed at meeting the citizens' social, medical, economic and health needs.

The Department of Health and Human Resources includes the following offices: Office of Management and Finance, Office of Charity Hospital at New Orleans, Office of Family Security, Office of Health Services and Environmental Quality, Office of Human Development, Office of Mental Health and Substance Abuse, Office of Mental Retardation and Office of Hospitals.

The Office of Management and Finance (OMF) is a management support system of DHHR composed of five ancillary sections and four operational bureaus. OMF's function is to provide accounting, budgeting, property procurement, data support and processing, personnel management and development and grants management services to all Offices in the department.

The Office of Charity Hospital at New Orleans (CHNO) provides medical care to the state's indigent population. Through its affiliation with LSU and Tulane Medical Schools, CHNO is the major teaching hospital in Louisiana.

Charity Hospital has become a consultation and tertiary care center for today's statewide system of general acute care hospitals.

The Office of Family Security (OFS) is responsible for meeting the physical, emotional and social needs of the low income citizenry through the following programs: Assistance Payments, Medical Assistance, Food Stamps and Child Support Enforcement Services.

Services provided include Aid to Families with Dependent Children, Disability Determinations, General Assistance, Refugee Assistance, Disaster Assistance and Supplementary S.S.I.; Diagnostic and Treatment, Pharmaceutical, Medical, Hospital and Long Term Care; food; and parent location and enforcement of support obligations.

The Office of Health Services and Environmental Quality (OHSEQ) is responsible for protecting and preserving the citizens' health through the operation of public health units and the development of environmental quality programs.

The 62 health units throughout the state provide personal health services, medical social services, nutrition, child health, dental health and communicable disease control.

The Office of Human Development (OHD) has been recently reorganized to include Human Services, Youth Services, Rehabilitative Services and Client Service and Placement (Title XX Social Services).

Human Services provides services to designated groups including the Aging, Women, Handicapped and Children; Youth Services provides services to delinquent children and children in need of supervision; Rehabilitation Services administers the Vocational Rehabilitation, Blind Services, Exceptional Children's Act and the Commission on the Deaf. Title XX Social Services include day care, work training programs, homemaker services, child protection, adoption and foster care.

The Office of Mental Health and Substance Abuse (OMHSA) is responsible for the prevention, detection, treatment, rehabilitation and follow-up care of mental and emotional illness and for implementing drug abuse and alcoholism programs.

Mental Health services are provided at 37 clinics and outreach programs, four hospitals and a comprehensive mental health center. Substance Abuse treatment is provided primarily through 42 outpatient clinics and some of the state hospitals.

The Office of Mental Retardation (OMR) provides comprehensive care and training for the mentally retarded citizens of the state. The Office administers eight residential facilities, contracts with over 55 organizations for day and respite care and monitors and assists 14 group homes in the community.

Concentrated efforts have been made recently to develop more adequate facilities to treat the state's mentally retarded and reduce the enrollment in out-of-state facilities.

The Office of Hospitals (OH) is responsible for providing medical treatment and health care services for the indigent population. The Office consists of three bureaus: General Hospitals (eight in the state), Special Hospitals (two—a geriatric hospital and an inmate hospital) and Emergency Medical Services.

Through affiliation with medical schools and other training institutions, each of the state hospitals are able to provide programs for physician training.

PRINCIPAL CAUSES OF DEATH BY PARISH OF RESIDENCE
Louisiana, 1985

PARISH	TOTAL		Diseases of Heart (390-398, 402, 404-429)		Malignant Neoplasms (140-208)		Cerebrovascular Diseases (430-438)		Accidents and Adverse Effects (800-949)		Chronic Obstructive Pulmonary Diseases and Allied Conditions (490-496)	
	NUMB.	RATE*	NUMB.	RATE*	NUMB.	RATE*	NUMB.	RATE*	NUMB.	RATE*	NUMB.	RATE
TOTAL	37041	826.7	13184	294.2	8235	183.8	2653	59.2	2064	46.1	1047	23.4
ACADIA	574	960.9	211	353.2	115	192.5	55	92.1	25	41.9	25	41.9
ALLEN	237	1091.1	115	529.4	41	188.7	15	69.1	11	50.6	8	36.8
ASCENSION	384	664.2	121	209.3	98	169.5	33	57.1	24	41.5	9	15.6
ASSUMPTION	183	780.8	70	298.7	35	149.3	15	64.0	19	81.1	7	29.9
AVOYELLES	458	1065.4	181	421.1	80	186.1	24	55.8	27	62.8	14	32.6
BEAUREGARD	268	826.7	106	327.0	56	172.7	27	83.3	13	40.1	6	18.5
BIENVILLE	200	1199.3	58	347.8	56	335.8	18	107.9	8	48.0	4	24.0
BOSSIER	535	593.4	193	214.1	140	155.3	33	36.6	41	45.5	11	12.2
CADDO	2544	939.4	974	359.7	552	203.8	189	69.8	102	37.7	69	25.5
CALCASIEU	1434	811.1	551	311.7	336	190.1	91	51.5	79	44.7	47	26.6
CALDWELL	127	1137.9	70	627.2	19	170.2	10	89.6	6	53.8	4	35.8
CAMERON	73	726.2	20	199.0	19	189.0	8	79.6	6	59.7	-	-
CATAHOULA	120	951.2	50	396.4	26	206.1	11	87.2	10	79.3	1	7.9
CLAIBORNE	228	1237.8	97	526.4	48	260.6	18	97.7	9	48.9	4	21.7
CONCORDIA	217	916.7	71	299.9	51	215.4	24	101.4	12	50.7	4	16.9
DESOTO	307	1109.8	97	350.7	63	227.7	36	130.1	24	86.8	7	25.3
E BATON ROUGE	2562	655.4	833	213.1	613	156.8	143	36.6	136	34.8	57	14.6
EAST CARROLL	143	1250.4	37	323.5	26	227.4	18	157.4	10	87.4	2	17.5
E FELICIANA	171	846.3	67	331.6	42	207.9	14	69.3	12	59.4	2	9.9
EVANGELINE	360	1027.8	132	376.9	70	199.9	24	68.5	25	71.4	15	42.8
FRANKLIN	278	1145.8	110	453.4	48	197.8	31	127.8	15	61.8	7	28.9
GRANT	197	1099.0	81	451.9	40	223.1	15	83.7	8	44.6	5	27.9
IBERIA	507	735.8	160	232.2	122	177.0	33	47.9	33	47.9	12	17.4
IBERVILLE	296	889.6	92	276.5	58	174.3	27	81.1	24	72.1	9	27.0
JACKSON	193	1096.7	61	346.6	48	272.8	21	119.3	10	56.8	4	22.7
JEFFERSON	3246	681.9	1095	230.0	827	173.7	217	45.6	164	34.5	95	20.0
JEFF DAVIS	311	931.4	101	302.5	82	245.6	15	44.9	17	50.9	11	32.9
LAFAYETTE	1030	604.5	354	207.7	247	145.0	76	44.6	58	34.0	34	20.0
LAFOURCHE	561	644.3	211	242.3	121	139.0	47	54.0	41	47.1	9	10.3
LASALLE	169	966.7	62	354.4	34	194.5	20	114.4	7	40.0	4	22.9
LINCOLN	311	719.0	101	233.5	70	161.8	48	111.0	16	37.0	6	13.9
LIVINGSTON	397	557.2	132	185.3	87	122.1	26	36.5	36	50.5	16	22.5
MADISON	177	1138.6	89	572.5	36	231.6	14	90.1	8	51.5	2	12.9
MOREHOUSE	354	999.4	127	358.5	75	211.7	38	107.3	14	39.5	12	33.9
NATCHITOCHES	397	995.8	158	396.3	83	208.2	43	107.9	17	42.6	13	32.6
ORLEANS	6059	1073.6	2007	355.6	1370	242.7	411	72.8	227	40.2	142	25.2
OUACHITA	1223	852.8	469	327.0	255	177.8	63	43.9	54	37.7	32	22.3
PLAQUEMINES	179	670.9	50	187.4	40	149.9	14	52.5	20	75.0	4	15.0
POINTE COUPEE	228	908.3	88	350.6	46	183.3	17	67.7	15	59.8	7	27.9
RAPIDES	1205	864.9	501	359.6	240	172.3	78	56.0	54	38.8	47	33.7
RED RIVER	130	1188.5	57	521.1	26	237.7	10	91.4	12	109.7	3	27.4
RICHLAND	258	1114.7	103	445.0	50	216.0	20	86.4	13	56.2	15	64.8
SABINE	247	901.0	121	441.4	38	138.6	16	58.4	18	65.7	9	32.8
ST BERNARD	530	778.9	218	320.4	112	164.6	28	41.1	25	36.7	16	23.5
ST CHARLES	247	582.8	86	202.9	57	134.5	12	28.3	15	35.4	9	21.2
ST HELENA	77	736.4	26	248.7	11	105.2	5	47.8	7	66.9	3	28.7
ST JAMES	164	740.0	58	261.7	34	153.4	11	49.6	12	54.1	9	40.6
ST JOHN	214	527.7	62	152.9	50	123.3	14	34.5	21	51.8	7	17.3
ST LANDRY	909	1026.4	325	367.0	190	214.5	65	73.4	61	68.9	32	36.1
ST MARTIN	315	690.9	114	250.0	75	164.5	26	57.0	20	43.9	9	19.7
ST MARY	491	750.2	172	262.8	112	171.1	27	41.3	56	85.6	11	16.8
ST TAMMANY	907	659.0	320	232.5	207	150.4	58	42.1	64	46.5	26	18.9
TANGIPAHOA	734	812.6	254	281.2	159	176.0	60	66.4	38	42.1	25	27.7
TENSAS	102	1217.8	37	441.7	15	179.1	12	143.3	3	35.8	4	47.8
TERREBONNE	642	635.2	219	216.7	129	127.6	36	35.6	60	59.4	19	18.8
UNION	259	1157.9	98	438.1	54	241.4	14	62.6	21	93.9	11	49.
VERMILION	433	816.3	162	305.4	108	203.6	34	64.1	36	67.9	11	20.
VERNON	342	558.9	89	145.4	63	102.9	24	39.2	46	75.2	11	18.
WASHINGTON	510	1075.0	184	387.9	101	212.9	43	90.6	33	69.6	15	31.
WEBSTER	562	1098.1	178	389.4	123	269.1	31	67.8	24	52.5	11	24.
W BATON ROUGE	140	676.4	42	202.9	31	149.8	13	62.8	11	53.1	8	38.
WEST CARROLL	156	1201.3	53	408.1	28	215.6	16	123.2	7	53.9	5	38.
W FELICIANA	57	414.5	17	123.6	11	80.0	4	29.1	2	14.5	3	21.
WINN	209	1223.9	84	491.9	35	205.0	14	82.0	15	87.8	7	41.
UNKNOWN***	23		2		1		-		7		1	
OUT OF STATE**	1135		334		251		72		180		29	

* RATE PER 100,000 POPULATION
** NOT INCLUDED IN STATE TOTALS
*** PARISH OF RESIDENCE UNKNOWN, ASSUMED LOUISIANA RESIDENT

Source: *Vital Statistics of Louisiana: Public Health Statistics.* Louisiana Department of Health and Human Resources

BIRTH, DEATHS, INFANT DEATHS, AND STILLBIRTHS
LOUISIANA, 1950 - 1984

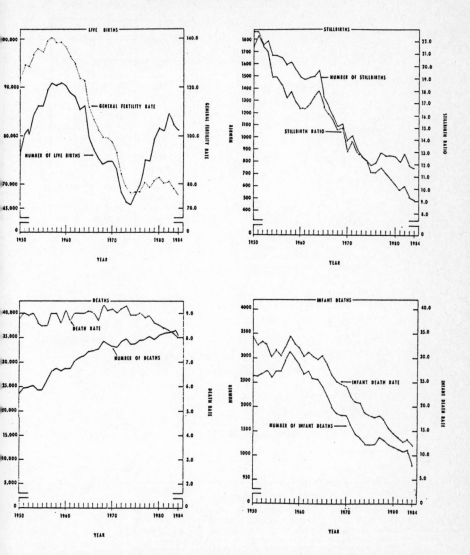

General Fertility Rate equals Live Births per 1,000 females 14-44. Stillbirth Ratio equals Spontaneous Fetal Deaths per 1,000 Live Births. Death Rate equals Deaths per 1,000 Population. Infant Death Rate equals Infant Deaths per 1,000 Live Births.

INFANT MORTALITY RATES, BY RACE
UNITED STATES AND LOUISIANA, 1950 - 1984

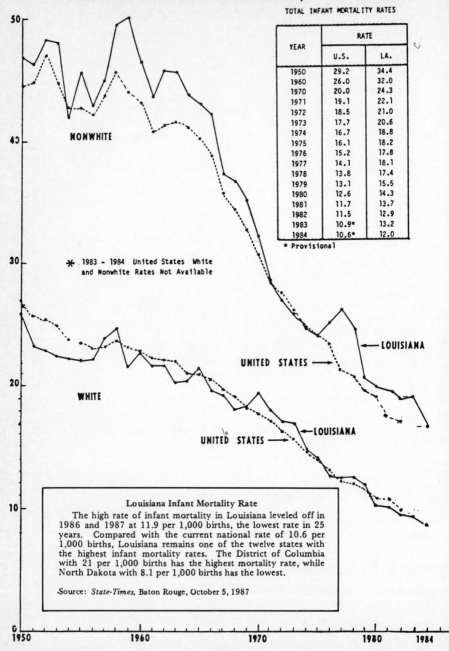

TOTAL INFANT MORTALITY RATES

YEAR	RATE	
	U.S.	LA.
1950	29.2	34.4
1960	26.0	32.0
1970	20.0	24.3
1971	19.1	22.1
1972	18.5	21.0
1973	17.7	20.6
1974	16.7	18.8
1975	16.1	18.2
1976	15.2	17.8
1977	14.1	18.1
1978	13.8	17.4
1979	13.1	15.5
1980	12.6	14.3
1981	11.7	13.7
1982	11.5	12.9
1983	10.9*	13.2
1984	10.6*	12.0

* Provisional

* 1983 - 1984 United States White and Nonwhite Rates Not Available

Louisiana Infant Mortality Rate
The high rate of infant mortality in Louisiana leveled off in 1986 and 1987 at 11.9 per 1,000 births, the lowest rate in 25 years. Compared with the current national rate of 10.6 per 1,000 births, Louisiana remains one of the twelve states with the highest infant mortality rates. The District of Columbia with 21 per 1,000 births has the highest mortality rate, while North Dakota with 8.1 per 1,000 births has the lowest.

Source: *State-Times*, Baton Rouge, October 5, 1987

BIRTHS, DEATHS, AND NATURAL INCREASE
LOUISIANA, 1950 - 1984

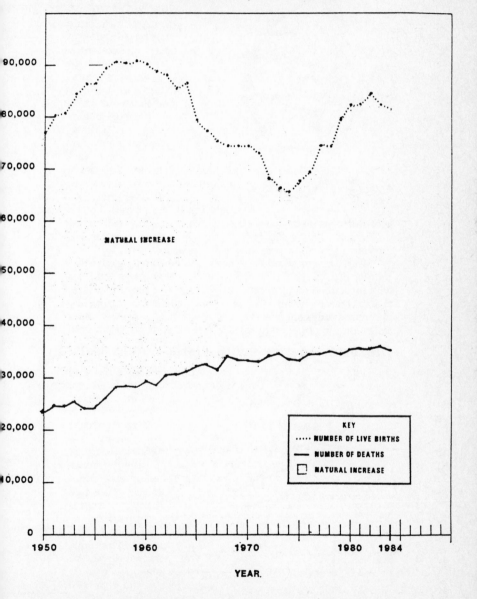

KEY
..... NUMBER OF LIVE BIRTHS
——— NUMBER OF DEATHS
☐ NATURAL INCREASE

YEAR.

Skipping medication can be dangerous

Persons who are on medication for elevated blood pressure and chest pain should never skip a dose of medication. Even if you are feeling "fine," you need to continue your medication in order to successfully manage high blood pressure. Otherwise, you may find that your blood pressure begins to fluctuate. If you experience any side effects (such as feeling depressed) which discourage you from taking your medication, consult your personal physician. Many times, your physician can substitute this medication with a similar one which will be less problematic. Never *stop* taking any medication, whether it is for your high blood pressure or for your heart.

Heart patients should also be careful when taking over-the-counter drugs, such as decongestants. These drugs can react with prescribed medications, causing elevated blood pressure, abnormal heart rhythms or anxiety and agitation. If you are taking cardiac drugs and feel the need to also take over-the-counter drugs for a minor ailment, please consult your physician first.

Most emergency room visits unnecessary

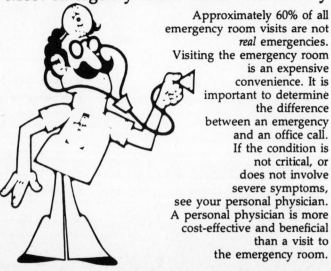

Approximately 60% of all emergency room visits are not *real* emergencies. Visiting the emergency room is an expensive convenience. It is important to determine the difference between an emergency and an office call. If the condition is not critical, or does not involve severe symptoms, see your personal physician. A personal physician is more cost-effective and beneficial than a visit to the emergency room.

NAMES APPEARING MOST FREQUENTLY ON BIRTH CERTIFICATES
LOUISIANA RESIDENTS, 1960, 1970, 1980, AND 1986

GIRLS

RANK	1960 NAME	1960 NUMBER	1970 NAME	1970 NUMBER	1980 NAME	1980 NUMBER	1986 NAME	1986 NUMBER
1	MARY	1207	ANGELA	608	JENNIFER	988	ASHLEY	1271
2	CYNTHIA	831	MICHELLE	554	AMANDA	747	JESSICA	919
3	DONNA	741	LISA	530	JESSICA	677	BRITTANY	709
4	LINDA	726	MELISSA	522	MELISSA	479	AMANDA	609
5	PATRICIA	706	KIMBERLY	520	TIFFANY	457	JENNIFER	529
6	LISA	671	JENNIFER	506	KIMBERLY	450	SARAH	471
7	KAREN	649	MARY	486	CRYSTAL	418	LAUREN	432
8	DEBRA	628	TAMMY	473	ASHLEY	396	HEATHER	386
9	SANDRA	620	SHANNON	420	APRIL	383	MEGAN	369
10	BRENDA	594	STEPHANIE	386	HEATHER	343	TIFFANY	360
11	PAMELA	544	NICOLE	343	AMY	329	KIMBERLY	330
12	DEBORAH	508	AMY	331	MICHELLE	324	AMBER	329
13	SUSAN	495	KAREN	329	SARAH	315	COURTNEY	296
14	SHARON	485	TRACY	313	NICOLE	314	STEPHANIE	283
15	BARBARA	428	PAMELA	280	ANGELA	303	DANIELLE	282

NAMES APPEARING MOST FREQUENTLY ON BIRTH CERTIFICATES
LOUISIANA RESIDENTS, 1960, 1970, 1980, AND 1986

BOYS

RANK	1960 NAME	NUMBER	1970 NAME	NUMBER	1980 NAME	NUMBER	1986 NAME	NUMBER
1	MICHAEL	1705	MICHAEL	1301	MICHAEL	1187	CHRISTOPHER	1230
2	JAMES	1415	JAMES	1101	CHRISTOPHER	1031	MICHAEL	873
3	DAVID	1333	JOHN	1073	JASON	963	JOSHUA	851
4	JOHN	1300	ROBERT	876	JOHN	838	BRANDON	813
5	ROBERT	1053	DAVID	816	JAMES	789	MATTHEW	696
6	CHARLES	829	CHRISTOPHER	731	JOSHUA	732	JOHN	650
7	JOSEPH	766	KEVIN	624	DAVID	691	JAMES	610
8	MARK	762	CHARLES	603	JOSEPH	620	DAVID	558
9	KENNETH	748	WILLIAM	594	BRANDON	610	JUSTIN	557
10	WILLIAM	718	JOSEPH	571	ROBERT	575	JOSEPH	540
11	DONALD	591	MARK	462	JEREMY	538	JEREMY	502
12	RICHARD	571	RICHARD	445	JUSTIN	496	ROBERT	476
13	RONALD	517	BRIAN	425	WILLIAM	491	RYAN	465
14	GREGORY	511	ANTHONY	408	NICHOLAS	448	DANIEL	455
15	KEVIN	478	KENNETH	401	JONATHAN	439	JONATHAN	447

How much do you smoke?

None?

The bronchi and blood vessels appear as small round holes in this normal lung.

½ pack?

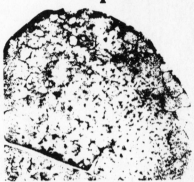

Small holes in upper lung typical of early emphysema.

1 pack?

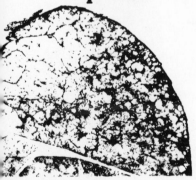

A later stage showing larger holes in the lung.

2 or more?

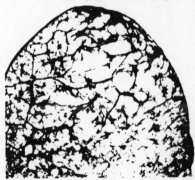

Many large holes representing far advanced emphysema.

Photos of whole lung sections show changes of pulmonary emphysema as related to smoking habits. Auerbach, O., et al. Relation of smoking and age to emphysema. New Eng J Med 286:853-7, 1972.

U.S. Department of Health, Education, and Welfare.
Public Health Service.

A person choking on food will die in 4 minutes – you can save a life using the HEIMLICH MANEUVER*

Food-choking is caused by a piece of food lodging in the throat creating a blockage of the airway, making it impossible for the victim to breathe or speak. The victim will die of strangulation in four minutes if you do not act to save him.

Using the Heimlich Maneuver* (described in the accompanying diagrams), you exert pressure that forces the diaphragm upward, compresses the air in the lungs, and expels the object blocking the breathing passage.

The victim should see a physician immediately after the rescue. Performing the Maneuver* could result in injury to the victim. However, he will survive only if his airway is quickly cleared.

If no help is at hand, victims should attempt to perform the Heimlich Maneuver* on themselves by pressing their own fist upward into the abdomen as described.

WHAT TO LOOK FOR

The victim of food-choking:

1. Can Not Speak or Breathe.

HEIMLICH MANEUVER*

RESCUER STANDING
Victim standing or sitting

☐ Stand behind the victim and wrap your arms around his waist.

☐ Place your fist thumb side against the victim's abdomen, slightly above the navel and below the rib cage.

☐ Grasp your fist with your other hand and press into the victim's abdomen with a **quick upward thrust**.

☐ Repeat several times if necessary.

When the victim is sitting, the rescuer stands behind the victim's chair and performs the maneuver in the same manner.

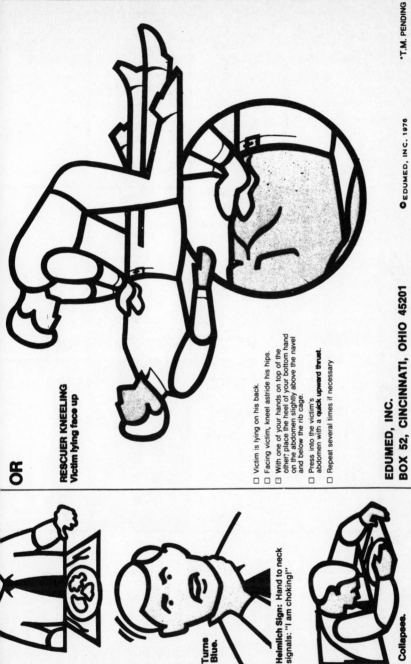

OR

RESCUER KNEELING
Victim lying face up

- ☐ Victim is lying on his back.
- ☐ Facing victim, kneel astride his hips.
- ☐ With one of your hands on top of the other, place the heel of your bottom hand on the abdomen slightly above the navel and below the rib cage.
- ☐ Press into the victim's abdomen with a **quick upward thrust.**
- ☐ Repeat several times if necessary

EDUMED, INC.
BOX 52, CINCINNATI, OHIO 45201

©EDUMED, INC. 1976

*T.M. PENDING

2. Turns Blue.

Heimlich Sign: Hand to neck signals: "I am choking!"

3. Collapses.

AMERICAN DRUGGIST
COUNTERDOSES FOR THE HOME

DO THIS FIRST

- **CALL A PHYSICIAN—IMMEDIATELY!**
- Keep the patient warm.
- Determine if the patient has taken

  (1) A POISON
  (2) AN OVERDOSE

- While waiting for physician, give appropriate counterdose below.
- But do not force any liquids on the patient—if he is unconscious.
- And do not induce vomiting if patient is having convulsions, or if patient is unconscious.

To Find The Correct Counterdose

- In one of the lists printed at left, find substance causing the trouble.
- Next to that substance is a number. This refers to counterdose bearing same number in the section below.

POISONS

Acids · 16
After-Shave Lotion · 8
Camphor · 1
Carbon Monoxide · 11
Chlorine Bleach · 15
Cologne, Perfume · 8
Detergents · 15
Disinfectant
  with chlorine · 15
  with carbolic acid · 3
Food Poisoning · 6
Furniture Polish · 14
Gasoline, Kerosene · 14
Household Ammonia · 13
Insect & Rat Poisons
  with arsenic · 2
  with sodium fluoride · 10
  with phosphorus · 12
  with strychnine · 5
Lighter Fluid · 14
Lye · 13

Keep All Poisons And Medicines Out Of Reach Of Children!

1
- Induce vomiting with
  - Finger in throat. OR
  - 1 tablespoon of syrup of ipecac, followed by a glass of water, OR
  - Teaspoonful of mustard in half glass of water.

2
- Give glass of milk. OR 1 tablespoonful of activated charcoal mixed with a little water.
- Induce vomiting (see #1) but not with syrup of ipecac if charcoal was given.

3
- Induce vomiting. (See #1)
- Then give 4 tablespoons of castor oil.
- Next give glass of milk OR the white of 2 raw eggs.

4
- Induce vomiting (see #1) if patient is conscious.
- Give glass of milk. OR activated charcoal in water.
- Give 2 tablespoons of epsom salt in 2 glasses of water.
- Keep patient awake

5
- Give glass of milk, or activated charcoal in water.
- Induce vomiting (#1) if not in convulsions. Do not use ipecac if charcoal was given.
- Keep patient quiet.

Oil of Wintergreen · 8
Pine Oil · 14
Rubbing Alcohol · 8
Turpentine · 14

OVERDOSES

Alcohol · 8
Aspirin · 8
Barbiturates · 9
Belladonna · 5
Bromides · 6
Codeine · 4
Headache & Cold Compounds · 8
Iron Compounds · 7
Morphine, Opium · 4
Paregoric · 4
'Pep' Medicines · 2
Sleeping Medicines · 9
Tranquilizers · 9

6
· Induce vomiting. (See #1)
· Next give 2 tablespoons of epsom salt in 2 glasses of water—except in cases where diarrhea is severe.

7
· Induce vomiting. (See #1)
· Give 2 teaspoons of bicarbonate of soda in a glass of warm water.
· Finally give glass of milk.

8
· Give a glass of milk.
· Next induce vomiting. (#1)
· Give 2 teaspoons of bicarbonate of soda in a glass of warm water.

9
· Give activated charcoal in water.
· Induce vomiting (see #1) but not with ipecac.
· Give 2 tablespoons of epsom salt in 2 glasses of water.

10
· Give glass of milk or lime water.
· Then induce vomiting. (See #1)

11
· Carry victim into fresh air.
· Make patient lie down.
· Give artificial respiration if necessary.

12
· Induce vomiting. (See #1):
· Don't let vomit touch victim's skin or yours.
· Then give 4 oz mineral oil. Positively do NOT give vegetable or animal oil.
· Also give 1 tablespoon of bicarbonate of soda in a quart of warm water.

13
· Give 2 tablespoons of vinegar in 2 glasses of water.
· Then give the white of 2 raw eggs....or 2 ounces of vegetable oil.
· Do NOT induce vomiting!

14
· Give water or milk.
· Then give 4 tablespoons of vegetable oil.
· Do NOT induce vomiting!

15
· Give patient one or two glasses of milk.

16
· Give large quantity of water.
· Give 2 tablespoons of milk of magnesia, or a similar antacid.
· Do NOT induce vomiting!

EMERGENCY PHONE NUMBERS

PHYSICIAN

POISON CONTROL CENTER

PHARMACIST

POLICE

HOSPITAL

AMBULANCE

FIRE

Post This Chart On The Back Of Your Medicine Cabinet Door —Or On The Back Of Your Bathroom Door.

Poison Control Centers

Toll-free: 800-535-0525

LSU Medical Center
Dept. of Pharmacology
P.O. Box 33932
Shreveport 71130

Monroe
(318) 325-6454
School of Pharmacy
Northeast Louisiana University
P.O. Box 1901
Monroe 71301

Lake Charles
(318) 478-6800
Lake Charles Memorial Hospital
170 Oak Park Boulevard
P.O. Drawer M
Lake Charles 70601

In any city, hospital emergency rooms are the best sources of information on how to deal with accidental poisonings.

INCUBATION PERIODS OF VARIOUS DISEASES

Disease	Incubation Period	Rash
Diphtheria	2-5 days	—
Scarlet fever	1-5 days	1st day
Measles	10-15 days	4th day
Rubella	14-21 days	1st day
Mumps	7-26 days	—
Whooping-cough	2-21 days	—
Chicken-pox	14-21 days	1st day
Smallpox	7-16 days	3rd day
Virus influenza	1-4 days	—
Gastroenteritis	6-24 hours	—
Infectious hepatitis	15-35 days	—
Serum hepatitis	2-4+ months	—
Poliomyelitis	7-21 days	—
Meningococcic meningitis	2-10 days	—
Brucellosis	7-14 days	—
Typhoid fever	3-38 days	—
Typhus	8-16 days	5th day
Bacillary dysentery	1-7 days	—
Gonorrhea	1-8 days	—
Malaria	variable	—
Yellow fever	3-6 days	—
Relapsing fever	3-12 days	—
Plague	2-10 days	—
Syphillis	1-6 weeks	—

BLOOD GROUPS

Recipient's Serum	Red Cells of Donor: Agglutinogens in Capitals				Per cent Population in Group
	1. AB	2. A	3. B	4. O	
Group Agglutinin					
1. AB O	—	—	—	—	7%
2. A β	+	—	+	—	40%
3. B α	+	+	—	—	10%
4. O αβ	+	+	+	—	43%
(After Moss)					

+ represents agglutination, therefore incompatibility.

— represents non-agglutination; not necessarily compatible until corpuscles and serum of donor are cross-tested with serum and corpuscles of recipient and agglutination absent.

ANTIDOTE AND FIRST AID FOR POISONING

An emergency always exists if someone swallows poison. **Do not delay contacting hospital or physician to obtain advice concerning first aid materials that are not readily available. If necessary, summon police or rescue squad for assistance.** Keep telephone numbers immediately available. Even after emergency measures have been taken, **always** consult physician. A delayed reaction could be fatal.

●It is important to dilute or remove poisons as soon as possible. Keep Syrup of Ipecac (available from most pharmacies or poison centers) in your home to induce vomiting if recommended by physician or indicated on product label. If Syrup of Ipecac is not available; try to make patient vomit by tickling back of throat with finger, spoon, or similar blunt object after giving water

HOWEVER....

● Vomiting is **not** recommended in all cases. Never induce vomiting in a patient who is unconscious or convulsing. Do not induce vomiting if swallowed substance is acidic or corrosive or petroleum distillate products.

● If poison is from a container; take container with intact label to medical facility treating patient. If poisonous substance is a plant or other unlabeled substance, be prepared to identify suspected substance. Save evidence such as portions of ingested materials from vomitus which may help identify plant or object involved.

CALORIES AND CHOLESTEROL

aver..average   sl......slice
C........cup   sm.....small
lg......large   sq.....square
med..medium   T..tablespoon
oz.....ounce   wh.....whole

H—high cholesterol
M—medium cholesterol
L—low cholesterol
O—no cholesterol

CANDIES AND NUTS

Caramels	1 med	75	M
Chocolate Bar	1 sm	300	H
Chocolate			
Creams	1 med	75	H
Fudge	1 sq	110	L
Hard Candy	1 oz	110	O
Marshmallows	1 lg	25	O
Almonds	12	100	O
Chestnuts	8	50	O
Filberts	12	100	O
Peanuts	10	100	O
Peanut Butter	1 T	100	O
Pecans	8	50	O
Popcorn, butter	1 C	150	M
Walnuts	4	100	O

DESSERTS

COOKIES

Brownies	1 sq	50	H
Butter	6 sm	100	H
Chocolate Chip	3 sm	65	M
Oatmeal	2 sm	50	M
Vanilla Wafers	3 sm	50	L
Angel Food	aver	100	O
Cheese Cake	1 sm	350	H
Chocolate Cake	aver	250	H
Coffee Cake	aver	150	M
Cup Cake	aver	100	M
Custard	½ C	125	H
Danish Pastry	aver	200	H
Doughnut	aver	150	H
Eclairs	aver	275	H
Fruitcake	1 sm	250	L
Gelatin, sweet	aver	100	O
Ice Cream,			
scoop	1	150	M
Lady Fingers	1	25	L
Pie, 1 crust	aver	250	M
Pie, 2 crusts	aver	350	M
Pound Cake	aver	200	H
Sherbet, scoop	1	100	O
Sponge Cake	aver	125	M
Sundae, fancy	aver	400	H
White Cake	aver	200	M

DAIRY PRODUCTS AND EGGS

American			
Cheese	1 oz	105	H
Bleu Cheese	1 oz	95	H
Butter	1 T	100	H
Buttermilk	1 C	85	M
Camembert	1½ oz	125	M
Cheddar			
Cheese	1 oz	105	H
Cottage Cheese	½ C	105	L
Cream Cheese	1 oz	105	H
Cream, light	1 T	30	H
Cream, heavy	1 T	50	H
Goat Milk	1 C	165	H
Milk, whole	1 C	165	H
Milk, skim	1 C	85	O
Milk, evap	1 C	200	H
Milk,			
dried skim	1 T	25	O
Parmesan,			
grated	1 T	25	M
Sour Cream	1 T	50	H
Swiss Cheese	1 oz	100	M
Whipped Cream	1 T	50	H
Yogurt, skim	1 C	115	L

EGGS

Boiled	1 med	70	H
Fried	1 med	100	H
Omelet, butter	2 eggs	185	H
Scrambled	aver	150	H
White	1 med	15	O
Yolk	1 med	55	H

BEVERAGES

Ale	8 oz	100	O
Beer, Bock	8 oz	175	O
Beer, Lager	8 oz	110	O
Bourbon	1½ oz	100	O
Brandy	1½ oz	75	O
Cider	1 C	100	O
Chocolate Milk	1 C	225	H
Cocoa, milk	1 C	235	H
Coffee, black	1 C	0	O
Fruit Punch	6 oz	150	O
Grapefruit			
Juice	6 oz	75	O
Ice Cream Soda	1	350	M
Liqueurs	1 oz	80	O
Malted Milk	1	400	H
Manhattan	3½ oz	175	O
Martini, dry	3½ oz	125	O
Orange Juice	6 oz	75	O
Pineapple Juice	1 C	125	O
Scotch	1½ oz	100	O
Soda drinks	6 oz	75	O
Tea, black	1 C	0	O
Tomato Juice	6 oz	50	O
Tom Collins	3½ oz	225	O
Vegetable Juice	6 oz	75	O
Whiskey Sour	3½ oz	225	O
Wine, dry	3½ oz	70	O
Wine, sweet	3½ oz	125	O

BREADS, CEREALS, FLOUR, PASTA

BISCUITS

Bkg. Powder	1 lg	55	O
Buttermilk	1 lg	110	M
Eng. Muffin	aver	150	L
Shortcake	aver	175	M
Yeast	1 lg	100	M

BREADS

Bran	1 sl	75	L
Cinnamon	1 sl	200	L
Cornbread	1 sm	200	M
Date, nut	1 sl	90	M
Egg	1 sl	75	H
French	1 sl	50	L
Gluten	1 sl	75	L
Graham	1 sl	75	O
Protein	1 sl	40	O
Raisin	1 sl	75	O
Rye	1 sl	75	O
White	1 sl	65	O
Wh. Wheat	1 sl	65	O

CRACKERS

Cheese	3 sm	50	H
Graham, lg	1 sq	25	L
Rye, sm.	5 sq	50	O
Soda, sm	4 sq	50	O

CEREALS

Bran Flakes	¾ C	100	O
Corn Flakes	1 C	100	O
Corn Grits	1 C	120	M
Cream of			
Wheat	¾ C	100	L
Oatmeal	1 C	150	O
Rice Flakes	1 C	120	O

FLOURS

All Purpose	1 C	400	O
Biscuit	½ C	265	L
Buckwheat	1 C	480	O
Corn Meal	1 C	480	O
Corn Starch	1 T	30	O
Soy, med fat	1 C	230	O
Wheat Germ	1 C	400	O
Wh. Wheat	1 C	400	O

PASTA

Egg Noodles	1 C	105	O
Macaroni	1 C	200	O
Noodles	1 C	150	O
Spaghetti	1 C	220	O

RICE

Brown	1 C	130	O
Converted	1 C	130	O
White	1 C	200	O
Wild	1 C	110	O

ROLLS

Bagel	1	110	L
Cinnamon	aver	100	M
Hard	1	100	L
Hot Dog	1	125	M
Plain	1	100	O
Parkerhouse	1	100	M
Popovers	1	75	H
Sweet	1	125	O

OTHERS

Blintzes	aver	175	H
Pancakes	1 sm	100	M
Muffin	1	125	M
Waffles	1	225	M

FRUITS

FRESH FRUITS

Apples	1 sm	75	O
Apricot	5 med	100	O
Avocado	1 sm	425	M
Banana	1 med	100	O
Blueberries	1 C	80	O
Cantaloupe	½ med	40	O
Cherries,			
unpitted	1 C	95	O
Dates, pitted	½ C	250	O
Figs	aver	30	O
Fruit Cocktail	½ C	65	O
Grapefruit	½ sm	50	O
Grapes,			
Concord	1 C	85	O
Grapes, gr.			
seedless	1 C	90	O
Lemon Juice	1 T	4	O
Oranges	1 med	75	O
Peaches	aver	45	O
Pears	aver	95	O
Persimmons	aver	95	O
Pineapples	1 C	75	O
Strawberries	1 C	55	O
Watermelon, sl.	1 med	100	O

DRIED FRUIT

Apricot, halves	3	50	O
Coconut,			
shredded	2 T	50	M
Figs	aver	50	O
Prunes	4	100	O

Raisins	1 C	430	O
FROZEN FRUITS			
One third of 9-10 oz package			
Apricots		100	O
Blueberries		105	O
Boysenberries		95	O
Cherries		110	O
Peaches, sliced		90	O
Raspberries		100	O
Strawberries		115	O

LAMB, BEEF, PORK

BEEF

Brains	6 oz	200	H
Corned	4 oz	250	H
Ground	3 oz	310	H
Heart	3 oz	100	L
Liver, beef	4 oz	150	H
Liver, calf	4 oz	160	H
Pot Roast	4 oz	250	H
Roast	4 oz	200	H
Steak	4 oz	200	H
Tongue, canned	1 C	250	H
Tongue, fresh	2 sl	100	H
Tripe	4 oz	175	M

VEAL

Chop	1 med	150	L
Cutlet	4 oz	125	L
Loaf	4 oz	250	M
Roast	4 oz	150	M
Steak	4 oz	250	L
Stew	4 oz	250	L
Sweetbread	4 oz	125	H

LAMB

Chop, broiled	aver	250	H
Chop, fried	aver	325	H
Kidney	4 oz	150	H
Liver	4 oz	155	H
Roast	4 oz	200	H
Stew	1 C	250	H
Tongue	3 sl	150	H

PORK

Bacon, strips	3	100	L
Bacon Fat	1 T	50	M
Chop, broiled	aver	225	H
Chop, fried	aver	250	H
Ham, boiled	4 oz	350	H
Ham	1 sl	100	H
Ham, smoked	4 oz	450	H
Kidney	4 oz	130	H
Liver	4 oz	150	H
Loin Roast	1 sl	100	H
Sausage, links	2	150	H
Spareribs	6	250	H

OTHER MEATS

Bologna	2 oz	125	H
Frankfurter	aver	125	H
Liverwurst	1 sl	75	H
Rabbit	4 oz	175	L
Salami	1 oz	125	H

SUGAR AND SPICE

Brown Sugar	1 T	15	O
Capers	1 T	3	O
Catsup	1 T	25	O
Cranberry Sauce	3 T	100	O
Dill Pickles	aver	15	O
French Dressing	1 T	100	L
Granulated Sugar	1 T	18	O
Honey	1 T	65	O
Jam, Jellies	1 T	50	O

Maple Sugar	1 T	18	O
Maple Syrup	1 T	60	O
Mayonnaise	1 T	100	M
Molasses	1 T	50	O
Mustard	1 T	10	O
Olives	6 sm	50	O
Olive Oil	1 T	125	O
Tomato Sauce	¼ C	50	O
White Sauce	1 T	25	H

SOUPS

Beef Bouillon	1 C	25	L
Beef Broth	1 C	35	L
Bean Soup	1 C	225	L
Celery, creamed	1 C	200	M
Chicken	1 C	100	L
Chicken Rice	1 C	125	L
Chili with Beans	½ C	175	M
Clam Chowder	1 C	100	O
Noodle	1 C	125	O
Onion	1 C	100	L
Pea	1 C	140	O
Tomato, plain	1 C	100	O
Vegetable	1 C	100	O

POULTRY

CHICKEN

A La King	½ C	375	H
Broiled	½ med	200	L
Canned	4 oz	200	L
Creamed	½ C	150	H
Fat	1 T	45	L
Fried	½ med	325	M
Fricassee	4 oz	225	L
Giblets	4 oz	150	H
Livers	4 oz	150	H
Pot Pie	4 oz	350	M
Roast	4 oz	200	L
Salad	4 oz	225	L
Stew	½ med	225	L
Capon, roast	4 oz	225	L
Duck, roast	4 oz	300	M
Guinea Hen	4 oz	175	L
Goose fat	1 T	145	L
Goose Liver	4 oz	150	H
Goose, roast	4 oz	325	L
Pheasant	4 oz	175	L
Quail, broiled	4 oz	175	M
Squab	1	150	L
Turkey, canned	4 oz	300	L
Turkey hash	4 oz	175	L
Turkey, roast	4 oz	250	L

SEAFOOD

FISH

Bass	4 oz	100	L
Cod	4 oz	100	L
Finnan Haddie	4 oz	125	L
Flounder	4 oz	150	L
Haddock	4 oz	180	L
Hake	4 oz	125	L
Halibut	4 oz	200	L
Herring	4 oz	225	L
Herring, pickled	4 oz	150	L
Mackerel	4 oz	150	L
Perch	4 oz	100	L
Salmon, broiled	4 oz	140	L
Salmon, canned	½ C	200	L
Sardines, canned	4	100	L

Sole	4 oz	125	L
Trout	8 oz	225	L
Tuna, canned	4 oz	125	L
OTHER SEAFOOD			
Abalone	aver	100	L
Caviar	1 T	50	H
Clams, steamed	12	100	L
Clams, fried	2	200	H
Crabs	½ C	65	M
Crab Cocktail	½ C	90	H
Lobster	½ C	65	H
Lobster Newburg	aver	350	H
Mussels	12	125	L
Oysters	6 med	50	H
Oysters, fried	6 med	250	H
Scallops	4 oz	90	L
Shrimps, average	10	100	H
Shrimp, canned	4 oz	145	H
Shrimp Creole	aver	175	H
Shrimp, fried	6 med	250	H

VEGETABLES

Artichokes	1 lg	95	O
Asparagus	12	25	O
Beans, Baked	1 C	200	O
Beans, Kidney	1 C	225	O
Beans, Lima	1 C	150	O
Beans, Green	1 C	25	O
Beets	1 C	70	O
Broccoli	1 C	45	O
Brussels Sprouts	1 C	60	O
Cabbage, raw	1 C	35	O
Cabbage, cooked	1 C	45	O
Carrots	1 med	25	O
Carrots, cooked	1 C	50	O
Cauliflower	1 C	30	O
Celery	1 stalk	15	O
Corn	1 ear	100	O
Cucumbers	1 aver	20	O
Eggplants	1 C	50	O
Leeks	1 C	40	O
Lentils	1 C	110	O
Lettuce	1 head	50	O
Mushrooms	1 C	30	O
Onions, cooked	1 lg	50	O
Peas, cooked	1 C	110	O
Peppers, green	1 lg	25	O
Potatoes, boiled	1 med	125	O
Potato Chips	10 med	100	O
Potato, Fr. fried	6	100	M
Sauerkraut	1 C	50	O
Soybeans	1 C	200	O
Spinach, boiled	1 C	100	O
Squash, Hubbard	1 C	100	O
Squash, Summer	1 C	35	O
Tomatoes	1 med	25	O
Turnips	1 C	45	O
Yams, baked	1 aver	200	O
Watercress	1 C	10	O
Zucchini	1 C	45	O

CALORIE REQUIREMENTS FOR VARIOUS ACTIVITIES

Type of activity: *Calories per hour*

Sedentary activities, such as: Reading; writing;   80 to 100.
eating; watching television or movies; listening
to the radio; sewing; playing cards; and typing,
officework, and other activities done while sitting
that require little or no arm movement.

Light activities, such as: Preparing and cooking   110 to 160.
food; doing dishes; dusting; handwashing small
articles of clothing; ironing; walking slowly;
personal care; officework and other activities
done while standing that require some arm
movement; and rapid typing and other activities
done while sitting that are more strenuous.

Moderate activities, such as: Making beds, mop-   170 to 240.
ping and scrubbing; sweeping; light polishing
and waxing; laundering by machine; light gardening and carpentry work; walking moderately
fast; other activities done while standing that
require moderate arm movement; and activities
done while sitting that require more vigorous
arm movement.

Vigorous activities, such as: Heavy scrubbing and   250 to 350.
waxing; handwashing large articles of clothing;
hanging out clothes; stripping beds; walking
fast; bowling; golfing; and gardening.

Strenuous activities, such as: Swimming; playing   350 or more.
tennis; running; bicycling; dancing; skiing; and
playing football.

Source: U. S. Department of Agriculture
        YOU AND YOUR WEIGHT

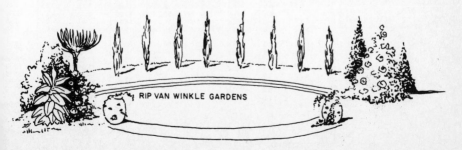

RIP VAN WINKLE GARDENS

Expectation of Life

EXPECTATION OF LIFE AND EXPECTED DEATHS, BY RACE, SEX, AND AGE: 1983

AGE IN 1983 (years)	EXPECTATION OF LIFE IN YEARS					EXPECTED DEATHS PER 1,000 ALIVE AT SPECIFIED AGE				
	Total	White		Black		Total	White		Black	
		Male	Female	Male	Female		Male	Female	Male	Female
At birth	74.6	71.7	78.7	65.4	73.6	11.15	10.79	8.60	21.05	17.23
1	74.5	71.5	78.4	65.9	73.9	.75	.80	.59	1.22	.92
2	73.5	70.5	77.4	64.9	72.9	.59	.60	.47	1.00	.76
3	72.6	69.6	76.4	64.0	72.0	.47	.47	.37	.81	.62
4	71.6	68.6	75.5	63.0	71.0	.39	.39	.31	.66	.51
5	70.6	67.6	74.5	62.1	70.1	.33	.35	.26	.54	.42
6	69.7	66.6	73.5	61.1	69.1	.30	.33	.23	.45	.34
7	68.7	65.7	72.5	60.1	68.1	.26	.30	.20	.38	.29
8	67.7	64.7	71.5	59.2	67.2	.23	.27	.18	.33	.25
9	66.7	63.7	70.6	58.2	66.2	.20	.22	.16	.30	.23
10	65.7	62.7	69.6	57.2	65.2	.18	.19	.14	.30	.22
11	64.7	61.7	68.6	56.2	64.2	.18	.18	.14	.32	.23
12	63.7	60.7	67.6	55.2	63.2	.22	.25	.17	.38	.25
13	62.8	59.8	66.6	54.3	62.2	.31	.39	.21	.48	.27
14	61.8	58.8	65.6	53.3	61.2	.44	.60	.28	.61	.31
15	60.8	57.8	64.6	52.3	60.3	.59	.83	.36	.75	.36
16	59.8	56.9	63.7	51.4	59.3	.73	1.04	.43	.91	.41
17	58.9	55.9	62.7	50.4	58.3	.84	1.22	.49	1.10	.47
18	57.9	55.0	61.7	49.5	57.3	.92	1.34	.51	1.32	.54
19	57.0	54.1	60.7	48.5	56.4	.97	1.41	.51	1.55	.61
20	56.0	53.1	59.8	47.6	55.4	1.02	1.47	.50	1.81	.69
21	55.1	52.2	58.8	46.7	54.4	1.07	1.53	.50	2.06	.77
22	54.2	51.3	57.8	45.8	53.5	1.10	1.57	.50	2.27	.84
23	53.2	50.4	56.9	44.9	52.5	1.12	1.58	.51	2.42	.90
24	52.3	49.4	55.9	44.0	51.6	1.13	1.57	.52	2.53	.94
25	51.3	48.5	54.9	43.1	50.6	1.13	1.55	.53	2.62	.98
26	50.4	47.6	54.0	42.2	49.7	1.14	1.52	.54	2.74	1.04
27	49.4	46.7	53.0	41.3	48.7	1.14	1.51	.55	2.88	1.09
28	48.5	45.7	52.0	40.4	47.8	1.16	1.50	.56	3.05	1.16
29	47.6	44.8	51.0	39.6	46.8	1.18	1.51	.57	3.26	1.24
30	46.6	43.9	50.1	38.7	45.9	1.21	1.52	.59	3.49	1.33
31	45.7	42.9	49.1	37.8	45.0	1.24	1.54	.61	3.72	1.43
32	44.7	42.0	48.1	37.0	44.0	1.28	1.57	.65	3.93	1.53
33	43.8	41.1	47.2	36.1	43.1	1.33	1.61	.69	4.12	1.65
34	42.8	40.1	46.2	35.3	42.2	1.38	1.66	.74	4.30	1.77
35	41.9	39.2	45.2	34.4	41.2	1.46	1.73	.81	4.50	1.91
36	41.0	38.3	44.3	33.6	40.3	1.54	1.82	.88	4.73	2.07
37	40.0	37.3	43.3	32.7	39.4	1.64	1.92	.96	4.99	2.24
38	39.1	36.4	42.3	31.9	38.5	1.76	2.04	1.05	5.26	2.42
39	38.2	35.5	41.4	31.0	37.6	1.89	2.18	1.15	5.57	2.61
40	37.2	34.6	40.4	30.2	36.7	2.05	2.35	1.27	5.89	2.81
41	36.3	33.6	39.5	29.4	35.8	2.23	2.55	1.40	6.26	3.05
42	35.4	32.7	38.5	28.6	34.9	2.44	2.78	1.55	6.75	3.33
43	34.5	31.8	37.6	27.8	34.0	2.69	3.06	1.71	7.40	3.67
44	33.6	30.9	36.7	27.0	33.1	2.97	3.39	1.90	8.16	4.05
45	32.7	30.0	35.7`	26.2	32.2	3.29	3.76	2.10	9.02	4.47
46	31.8	29.1	34.8	25.4	31.4	3.64	4.17	2.33	9.90	4.92
47	30.9	28.2	33.9	24.7	30.5	4.02	4.64	2.58	10.74	5.39
48	30.0	27.4	33.0	23.9	29.7	4.45	5.17	2.88	11.51	5.89
49	29.1	26.5	32.1	23.2	28.9	4.91	5.77	3.20	12.23	6.41
50	28.3	25.7	31.2	22.5	28.1	5.42	6.42	3.56	12.97	6.98
51	27.4	24.8	30.3	21.8	27.3	5.97	7.12	3.94	13.81	7.58
52	26.6	24.0	29.4	21.1	26.5	6.56	7.90	4.34	14.81	8.24
53	25.8	23.2	28.5	20.4	25.7	7.20	8.76	4.76	16.02	8.97
54	24.9	22.4	27.7	19.7	24.9	7.89	9.70	5.19	17.40	9.75
55	24.1	21.6	26.8	19.1	24.1	8.63	10.72	5.64	18.85	10.56
56	23.3	20.8	25.9	18.4	23.4	9.42	11.80	6.15	20.35	11.41
57	22.6	20.1	25.1	17.8	22.7	10.26	12.95	6.72	22.03	12.36
58	21.8	19.3	24.3	17.2	21.9	11.22	14.14	7.37	23.94	13.46
59	21.0	18.6	23.4	16.6	21.2	12.23	15.41	8.10	26.02	14.66
60	20.3	17.9	22.6	16.0	20.5	13.33	16.76	8.89	28.35	16.01
61	19.6	17.2	21.8	15.5	19.9	14.49	18.22	9.74	30.74	17.37
62	18.8	16.5	21.0	14.9	19.2	15.71	19.83	10.61	32.81	18.55
63	18.1	15.8	20.3	14.4	18.6	16.98	21.63	11.51	34.37	19.44
64	17.4	15.2	19.5	13.9	17.9	18.31	23.62	12.45	35.54	20.13
65	16.7	14.5	18.7	13.4	17.3	19.72	25.74	13.45	36.43	20.69
70	13.5	11.5	15.1	10.9	14.1	29.70	39.52	20.78	51.45	30.79
75	10.7	9.0	11.8	9.0	11.5	44.31	60.15	32.76	68.22	42.55
80	8.1	6.9	8.8	7.1	9.0	66.98	90.04	53.49	93.33	62.99
85 and over	6.1	5.2	6.5	6.0	7.4	1,000.00	1,000.00	1,000.00	1,000.00	1,000.00

Source: U.S. National Center for Health Statistics, *Vital Statistics of the United States*, annual. *Statistical Abstract of the United States*, 1987.

LARGEST GENERAL HOSPITALS IN LOUISIANA

HOSPITAL	LOCATION	NO. OF BEDS
Charity Hospital at New Orleans	New Orleans	1,500
Our Lady of the Lake Regional Medical Center	Baton Rouge	757
Louisiana State University Hospital	Baton Rouge	650
Schumpert Medical Center	Shreveport	625
Touro Infirmary	New Orleans	564
East Jefferson Hospital	Metairie	556
Southern Baptist Hospital	New Orleans	533
Ochsner Foundation Hospital	New Orleans	532
West Jefferson Medical Center	Marrero	523
Baton Rouge General Medical Center	Baton Rouge	498
Hotel Dieu Sisters Hospital	New Orleans	461
St. Francis Medical Center	Monroe	450
St. Patrick Hospital of Lake Charles	Lake Charles	416
Our Lady of Lourdes Regional Medical Center	Lafayette	397
Willis-Knighton Medical Center	Shreveport	369
Lafayette General Medical Center	Lafayette	367
Rapides General Hospital	Alexandria	349
Jo Ellen Smith Medical Center/ F. Edward Hebert Hospital	New Orleans	337
Pendleton Memorial Hospital	New Orleans	317
St. Francis Cabrini Hospital	Alexandria	304
St. Jude Medical Center	Kenner	300
Lake Charles Memorial Hospital	Lake Charles	294
Mercy Hospital	New Orleans	272
Tulane Medical Center	New Orleans	268
Terrebonne General Medical Center	Houma	235

Source: Louisiana Department of Health and Human Resources

TELEPHONE CRISIS LINES

Alexandria	318-445-4357	24 hours
Baton Rouge	504-924-3900	24 hours
Bogalusa	504-735-8500	4:30 pm – 8:00 am weekdays; 24 hours weekends & holidays
DeRidder	318-462-0609	9:00 am – 10:00 pm
Vernon Parish	239-6196	
Sabine Parish	256-5065	
Hammond-Tangipahoa	504-345-6120	4:00 pm – 12:00 midnight; other times leave message on recording machine
Houma-Terrebonne	504-872-1111	24 hours
Lafayette	318-232-4357	Counselor on line during day; answering service patches through calls other times if emergency
Lake Charles	318-439-2273	8:00 am –12:00 midnight; answering service picks up at other times and only patches through crisis calls
Monroe	318-387-5683	6:00 pm – 7:00 am
New Orleans	504-523-2673	24 hours
Shreveport	318-869-1228	8:00 pm – 12:00 midnight weekdays; 8:00 pm – 1:00 am weekends
Ville Platte	504-363-5579	24 hours

THE HISTORY OF THE CHARITY HOSPITAL SYSTEM IN LOUISIANA

1736: Jean Louis, a sailor and boatmaker, died and left $2,500 to found a hospital for the sick of the city of New Orleans. The money was used to purchase a former nuns residence and enlarge it into the Hospital of St. John. It became known as the Hospital of Charity.

1811: The Territorial Legislature and City Council took over operation of Charity Hospital. In 1813 the state government assumed full control of the hospital.

1876: Shreveport Charity Hospital opened as the second state hospital for the poor. The hospital was later renamed Confederate Memorial.

1938: Huey P. Long Memorial Hospital opened in Pineville.

1939: Charity Hospital in New Orleans moved to a new building on Tulane Avenue.

1941: E. A. Conway Memorial Hospital opened in Monroe.

1951: Washington—St. Tammany Charity Hospital opened in Bogalusa.

1955: Lallie Kemp Charity Hospital opened in Independence.

1960: Dr. Walter Olin Moss Regional Hospital opened in Lake Charles. The hospital was closed from 1969 to 1972.

1967: Earl K. Long Memorial Hospital opened in Baton Rouge.

1976: LSU took control of the Shreveport facility, which was later renamed LSU Medical Center in Shreveport.

1978: South Louisiana Medical Center opened in Houma.

1982: University Medical Center opened in Lafayette.

Source: *Times-Picayune*, New Orleans, December 2, 1986

AVERAGE WEIGHTS

Average weights arranged by height and size of frame, for ages 25 to 59, in shoes and wearing five pounds of indoor clothing for men, three pounds for women.

MEN				WOMEN			
Height	Small	Medium	Large	Height	Small	Medium	Large
5' 2"	128-134	131-141	138-150	4'10"	102-111	109-121	118-131
5' 3"	130-136	133-143	140-153	4'11"	103-113	111-123	120-134
5' 4"	132-138	135-145	142-156	5' 0"	104-115	113-126	122-137
5' 5"	134-140	137-146	144-160	5' 1"	106-118	115-129	125-140
5' 6"	136-142	139-151	146-164	5' 2"	108-121	118-132	128-143
5' 7"	138-145	142-154	149-168	5' 3"	111-124	121-135	131-147
5' 8"	140-148	145-157	152-172	5' 4"	114-127	124-138	134-151
5' 9"	142-151	148-160	155-176	5' 5"	117-130	127-141	137-155
5'10"	144-154	151-163	158-180	5' 6"	120-133	130-144	140-159
5'11"	146-157	154-166	161-184	5' 7"	123-136	133-147	143-163
6' 0"	149-160	157-170	164-188	5' 8"	126-139	136-150	146-167
6' 1"	152-164	160-174	168-192	5' 9"	129-142	139-153	149-170
6' 2"	155-168	164-178	172-197	5'10"	132-145	142-156	152-173
6' 3"	158-172	167-182	176-202	5'11"	135-148	145-159	155-176
6' 4"	162-176	171-187	181-207	6' 0"	138-151	148-162	158-179

Source: Metropolitan Life Insurance Company

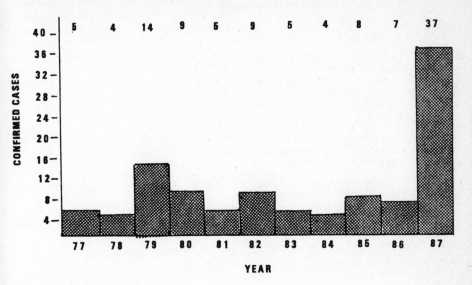

CONFIRMED CASES OF PERTUSSIS (WHOOPING COUGH), FROM JANUARY THROUGH JULY, LOUISIANA, 1977 TO 1987

LOUISIANA AIDS UPDATE

	CASES	DEATHS	PERCENT
1987 (thru 8/31/87)	110	36	33
TOTAL, ALL YEARS	500	332	66

FLUORIDE LEVELS — VOORS, ET AL

Table 1

COMMUNITIES PROTECTED BY AN ADEQUATE FLUORIDE LEVEL OF PUBLIC WATER SUPPLIES, LOUISIANA

Parish	Community	Fluoride Level (ppm)*
Allen	Kinder	2.4
Avoyelles	Bunkie	1.3
	Evergreen	4.5
	WW District 5	1.9
	Hessmer	1.0
	Mansura	1.0
	Simmesport	0.7
Bienville	Castor	1.2
	Saline	1.1
Bossier	Benton	2.6
	Plain Dealing	1.8
Calcasieu	Starks	0.8
Concordia	Vidalia	1.0
E. Carroll	Lake Providence	1.1
Evangeline	Chataignier	1.2
	Mamou	1.0
Iberville	Plaquemine	1.5
Lafourche	WW District 1	0.9†
	Lockport	1.0†
	Thibodaux	0.9†
Lasalle	Urania	1.8
Morehouse	Collinston	0.7
	Mer Rouge	0.8
Orleans	New Orleans	0.9†
Ouachita	West Monroe	0.7
Rapides	Alexandria	1.2
	Boyce	0.9
	Cheneyville	0.8
	Lecompte	0.7
Sabine	Converse	2.8
	Many	0.5‡
	Zwolle	1.1
St. Landry	Krotz Springs	2.3
	Melville	1.0
	Sunset	0.5‡
Tangipahoa	Major WW	0.7
Terrebonne	Houma	0.8†
Vernon	Anacoco	1.1
Winn	Joyce	0.9
	Sikes	1.7

----

* Source: D.C. Dial: Public Water Supplies in Louisiana. Baton Rouge: Louisiana Department of Public Works (1970).

† Mechanical fluoridation.

‡ The various wells in use differ in their water fluoride levels.

Table 2
FLUORIDE LEVEL IN PUBLIC WATER SUPPLIES OF COMMUNITIES WITH A POPULATION OF 10,000 OR MORE, LOUISIANA

Parish	Community	Fluoride Level (ppm)*
Acadia	Crowley	.1
Assumption	WW District 1	.2
Bossier	Bossier City	.1
Caddo	Shreveport	.1
Calcasieu	Lake Charles	.2
E.Baton Rouge	Baton Rouge	.2
Iberia	New Iberia	.1
Jefferson	E.Jeff.WW Dist.1	.1
	Gretna	.2
	WW District 2	.2
	Westwego	.2
Jefferson Davis	Jennings	.2
Lafayette	Lafayette	.2
Lafourche	*WW District 1‡*	.9†
	Thibodaux	.9†
Lincoln	Ruston	.4
Livingston	Gr.Livingst.W Comp.	.3
Madison	Tallulah	.2
Morehouse	Bastrop	.5
Natchitoches	Natchitoches	.2
Orleans	*New Orleans*	.9†
Ouachita	Monroe	.1
	Monroe (suburban)	.4
	West Monroe	.7
Plaquemines	Buras-Empire WW Dist.	.3
Rapides	*Alexandria*	1.2
	Pineville	.4
St. Bernard	WW District 1	.5
St. Charles	WW District 1	.2
St. John	WW District 3	.2
St. Landry	Eunice	.2
	Opelousas	.1
St. Mary	Morgan City	.2
St. Tammany	Covington	.4
	Slidell	.4
Tangipahoa	Hammond	.6
Terrebonne	*Houma*	.8†
Vernon	Leesville	.2
Washington	Bogalusa	.2
Webster	Minden	.1

----

* Source: D.C. Dial: Public Water Supplies in Louisiana. Baton Rouge: Louisiana Department of Public Works (1970).

† Mechanical fluoridation.

‡ Communities with sufficient fluoride levels are italicized.

** The population size of these communities approached 10,000 in 1975.

MARRIAGES, FINAL DIVORCES AND ANNULMENTS GRANTED
LOUISIANA, 1985

PARISH	MARRIAGES BY PARISH OF ISSUE OF LICENSE	MARRIAGES BY PARISH OF OCCURRENCE	DIVORCES BY PARISH GRANTING DECREE	ANNULMENTS BY PARISH GRANTING DECREE
TOTAL	39357	39357	17587	21
ACADIA	500	544	NR	NR
ALLEN	214	207	108 *	1 *
ASCENSION	582	539	180	-
ASSUMPTION	142	162	57 *	1 *
AVOYELLES	364	383	NR	NR
BEAUREGARD	301	282	76 *	- *
BIENVILLE	-	53	67 *	- *
BOSSIER	645	935	451	1
CADDO	2324	1978	1224	1
CALCASIEU	1653	1610	835	-
CALDWELL	126	122	61	-
CAMERON	96	116	29	-
CATAHOULA	87	92	NR	NR
CLAIBORNE	96	101	52	-
CONCORDIA	195	207	950	-
DESOTO	152	184	77 *	- *
E BATON ROUGE	3866	3676	1920	8
EAST CARROLL	59	64	23 *	- *
E FELICIANA	107	160	59	-
EVANGELINE	324	331	101 *	- *
FRANKLIN	200	197	115 *	- *
GRANT	101	178	91	-
IBERIA	629	630	256 *	1 *
IBERVILLE	248	317	NR	NR
JACKSON	151	160	68 *	- *
JEFFERSON	4386	4155	1573	-
JEFF DAVIS	297	300	129 *	- *
LAFAYETTE	1766	1588	NR	NR
LAFOURCHE	843	816	335	-
LASALLE	133	138	64	-
LINCOLN	349	294	NR	NR
LIVINGSTON	647	733	NR	NR
MADISON	41	44	NR	NR
MOREHOUSE	182	207	64	-
NATCHITOCHES	319	330	216	-
ORLEANS	4852	4879	1485	-
OUACHITA	1347	1243	679	-
PLAQUEMINES	207	267	100	-
POINTE COUPEE	161	181	50 *	- *
RAPIDES	1454	1428	748	-
RED RIVER	114	93	26 *	- *
RICHLAND	167	178	85 *	1 *
SABINE	147	164	53 *	- *
ST BERNARD	785	899	349	-
ST CHARLES	334	324	108	-
ST HELENA	104	94	36 *	1 *
ST JAMES	157	197	36	-
ST JOHN	239	246	NR	NR
ST LANDRY	719	794	291 *	1 *
ST MARTIN	323	336	130	-
ST MARY	662	652	293 *	- *
ST TAMMANY	1192	1227	NR	NR
TANGIPAHOA	815	759	2110 *	2 *
TENSAS	39	44	18	-
TERREBONNE	971	975	622	1
UNION	-	41	70 *	- *
VERMILION	447	476	147	-
VERNON	718	762	350 *	- *
WASHINGTON	370	392	224 *	1 *
WEBSTER	345	322	166	-
W BATON ROUGE	225	157	37 *	- *
WEST CARROLL	95	101	59 *	- *
W FELICIANA	80	183	34	-
WINN	156	163	99 *	1 *
UNKNOWN	7	18	1	-
OUT OF STATE	-	9	NR	NR

* SUMMARY REPORT
'NR' NO DIVORCE OR ANNULMENT DATA REPORTED BY CLERK OF COURT

Acknowledgments

State Government Agencies

Department of Agriculture
Crop and Livestock Reporting Service
Bergen A. Nelson, *State Statistician*

Office of Marketing
Harriet Waters

Department of Culture, Recreation, and Tourism
Office of Tourism

Department of Education
J. Kelly Nix, *Superintendent*

Department of Elections and Registration
Jerry M. Fowler, *Commissioner*

Office of Financial Institutions
Hunter O. Wagner, Jr., *Commissioner*

Office of the Governor
David C. Treen, *Governor*

State Planning Office
Library Resources Center
Kay W. McGinnis

Department of Health and Human Resources
Office of Health Services and Environmental Quality
Audrey P. Collins, *Statistical Supervisor*

Office of Management and Finance
Joseph Ross, *Division Director, Policy*

Department of Justice
Attorney General's Office
Kendall L. Vick

Department of Labor
Office of Employment Security
Research and Statistics Unit
Oliver S. Robinson III, *Director*

Department of Natural Resources
Office of Forestry

Department of Public Safety
Office of State Fire Marshall
Charlotte P. Vowell, *Statistician*

Public Service Commission
Edward L. Gallegos, *Chief Engineer*

Department of Revenue and Taxation
Kathleen M. Posey, *Public Information Officer*

Department of State
Jim Brown, *Secretary*

State Supreme Court
Office of the Judicial Administrator
Faye Courville

Department of Transportation and Development
Joe Rogers

Office of Aviation and Public Transportation
Kevin D. Murphy

Political Districts Section
Dot McConnell

Office of Public Works
Water Resources Section
Z. Bolourchi, *Chief*

Department of Wildlife and Fisheries
Wade Byrd, *Information Section*

University Research Agencies

Louisiana State University
Center for Wetland Resources

Division of Research
College of Business Administration

Office of State Climatology
Professor Robert A. Muller

Louisiana Tech University
Research Division
College of Administration and Business
Professor Edward J. O'Boyle

Independent and Private Agencies

Louisiana World Exposition

Mid-Continent Oil and Gas Association
Louisiana Division
William C. Bailey, Jr., *Vice-President*

Public Affairs Research Council
Emogene Pliner, *Vice-President, Research*

United States Government Agencies

Army Engineer District, New Orleans
(Corps of Engineers)
Mike Dorner

Department of Commerce
Bureau of the Census

Department of Justice
Federal Bureau of Investigation
New Orleans Office

National Oceanic and Atmospheric Administration
Hurricane Center
Dr. Harold P. Gerrish

A number of individuals, more than can be acknowledged in this limited space, also contributed to the compilation and completion of this text. Special thanks should go to Helen Kempe, the able editor of earlier editions of the *Louisiana Almanac*.

INDEX